ECONOMICS
COST AND CHOICE

J. R. CLARK
Fairleigh Dickinson University, Florham Park – Madison Campus

MICHAEL VESETH
University of Puget Sound

Harcourt Brace Jovanovich, Publishers
and its subsidiary, Academic Press

San Diego   New York   Chicago   Austin   Washington, D. C.
London   Sydney   Tokyo   Toronto

*To
Jefferson Davis Clark
(1915–1967)*

Copyright © 1987 by Harcourt Brace Jovanovich, Inc.

All rights reserved. No part of this publication may be reproduced or transmitted in any form or by any means, electronic or mechanical, including photocopy, recording, or any information storage and retrieval system, without permission in writing from the publisher.

Requests for permission to make copies of any part of the work should be mailed to: Permissions, Harcourt Brace Jovanovich, Publishers, Orlando, Florida 32887.

ISBN: 0-15-518830-5

Library of Congress Catalog Card Number: 86-70051

Printed in the United States of America

Photo Credits appear on page 834, which constitutes a continuation of the copyright page.

Preface

This textbook was written for principles of economics courses at the college level. Several special features make it particularly noteworthy:

1. CRIS CRIS stands for Cross-Reference Index System. It is a system of learning objectives that is fully integrated into this text. Each chapter begins with a series of learning objectives which are identified by name and reference number. An arrow appears in the margin of the text next to the discussion of each learning objective, indicating where important material is covered. The chapter summary, key concepts, and review questions are also keyed to these learning objectives.

The advantage of CRIS is that it enables students to read and review the text more effectively by concentrating on an easily identifiable pattern of important points and key concepts. Students can then relate these points and concepts to problems and questions in the text as well as to lectures and examinations. CRIS enables instructors to organize lectures, examinations, and assignments around the learning objectives that they believe are most important. The full use of CRIS will help students learn more material more completely while decreasing the burden on instructors.

CRIS is "transparent"; it will not impede students and instructors who do not choose to use the system. This text is the only one in the principles of economics market that offers this learning system.

The *Instructor's Manual*, the *Study Guide*, and the *Test Book* are all keyed in this noninterfering manner to CRIS. See the front inside cover and pages vii–viii for a more detailed description of CRIS.

2. Evolutionary Treatment of Macroeconomic Theory and Policy Our presentation of macroeconomics focuses on how macroeconomic events, theories, and policies have evolved over time. This approach allows students to appreciate the changes in the economy and in economic theory in an understandable, realistic context. This presentation also allows instructors the flexibility to stress the theories, events, or policies that they believe are most important.

Chapters 8 and 9 introduce the macroeconomics part of the text. Chapter 8 discusses GNP and economic growth from the Great Depression to the present day. Chapter 9 examines how the relationship between inflation and unemployment has changed in recent years. These two chapters, taken together, give the students a solid background in the history of macroeconomic events and policies. Later chapters build on this foundation and show how economic theory has evolved in response to changing economic events.

Chapters 10–12 examine how the theory of fiscal policy has changed. The discussion begins with the Keynesian theory and its policy prescriptions (Chapter 10), followed by the $AD-AS$ model of inflation and unemployment (Chapter 11), and then the demand-side and supply-side fiscal policies of today (Chapter 12). Chapters 13–15 develop monetary theory and monetary policy over these same years.

This balanced approach to macroeconomics helps students to understand the origins of the Keynesian, supply-side, monetarist, and rational expectations schools. The evolutionary treatment solves the problems that many instructors face today in teaching macroeconomics. With our approach, students learn that, as the economy changes, economics evolves with it.

3. Focus on the Real World Emphasis on the real world helps to motivate students and to provide them with a very real pay-off to their study efforts. The right example or application is often the key to helping students learn economics. We maintain a real-world focus in every chapter in the following ways:

- *Applications* Many real-world examples are used to illustrate how theories and concepts in economics work.
- *Applications boxes* Many chapters include special boxed sections that relate the theory discussed to a specific real-world problem or event.
- *Data* Real-world data are presented clearly in the many tables, graphs, and text references. Students learn how to analyze and interpret data and draw conclusions from available evidence.

4. Emphasis on the Economic Way of Thinking Economics is a way of thinking (or method of analysis) more than it is a particular body of knowledge. Sociologists, psychologists, and political scientists often examine the same content areas as economists do, but they use different methods of analysis. The economic way of thinking is what makes economics unique—and what students often have the most trouble mastering. Chapter 2 explains the economic way of thinking and the logical problems that economists attempt to avoid.

5. Clear Presentation of International Economics International economics is becoming increasingly important and is now much more likely to be included in the principles course. Chapters 28–30 present a simple and clear discussion of the theory and policy of international trade and finance. The focus here, as in the macroeconomics sections, is on the theories, recent events, and economic policies.

6. Emphasis on Both Public- and Private-Sector Choices It is important to recognize that economic choices are made in both the private and the public sectors of the economy and that participants in both sectors face economic incentives. Our book provides a balanced and complete analysis of both private and public choices. We look at the organization of each sector and then examine the successes and failures of economic actions and policies in that sector.

In addition to the features just described, the text also includes the following:
- *Key concept summaries*
- *Marginal definitions*
- *Economic issues boxes*
- *Prominent economist boxes*
- *Chapter summaries*
- *Discussion questions*
- *Suggested readings*
- *Glossary*

How to Use the CRIS System

One of the unique features of this text is the Cross-Reference Index System (CRIS). This is a comprehensive system of learning objectives designed to help students get more out of their study time and to help instructors better communicate important concepts to students.

Before we discuss what CRIS is and how it can be used, it is important to briefly state what CRIS is not. CRIS is not a watered-down, spoon-fed, pre-digested list of economic principles or facts that students are supposed to memorize. To compile such a list would work counter to our goals in teaching economics. Rather, CRIS provides a framework that students can use to more readily identify, apply, and synthesize the important concepts of economics that we want them to master.

On the inside front cover of this text are sample pages illustrating various elements of the CRIS system. Take a moment to read the brief descriptions and follow the arrow path through the simple CRIS steps.

Here is how CRIS can be used:

- **The Learning Objectives** Each chapter begins with a series of learning objectives, which are identified by name and reference number. Students learn more when they know at the start of a chapter specific points the chapter will cover. A labeled and numbered arrow appears in the margin of the text where each learning objective is discussed. The chapter summary, review questions, and key concepts are also keyed to these learning objectives.

- **Review Using CRIS** After reading each chapter, students should then read the chapter summary. If they find material there that they have not mastered, or which they are uncertain about, they can use the CRIS numbers to quickly find the problem areas and review them. Instructors can also key their class reviews to CRIS numbers, which helps students locate in the text the materials that are relevant to a particular lecture, assignment, or test.

- **Assignments Using CRIS** Each chapter's discussion questions and all of the material in the *Study Guide* are also keyed to the CRIS learning objective numbers. This helps students review all the concepts they need to answer the discussion questions. Instructors can also use the objectives as a framework for class discussion by asking how a particular concept or objective is used in dealing with each assigned problem. By using the CRIS system, students who have trouble with assignments can quickly find the relevant text sections that they need to answer each question.

- **Examinations Using CRIS** Each question in the *Test Book* for this text is keyed by number to the CRIS learning objectives. Students will be able to quickly locate the parts of the text that they need to review based on their examination errors. This should help students in an area in which many are weak: post-examination learning.

The CRIS learning objectives represent an important innovation in economics texts. Students can use CRIS to focus their study time and learn more independently. Instructors can make as much or as little use of these tools as they like, while still gaining the benefits that come with more efficient student learning.

Acknowledgments

Any work of this size benefits from the contributions of many talented people whose names do not appear of the title page. We would like to thank the following people for their help, support, and constructive criticism: Susan Loring, Bill Bayer, Steve Dowling, and Sue Miller of Academic Press and Marguerite L. Egan of Harcourt Brace Jovanovich, who supervised the completion of the text.

Many of our colleagues made contributions to the final version of this text by reviewing early drafts of each chapter. They include: Jack Adams, University of Arkansas; Loreto Alonzi, Loyola University of Chicago; John Anderson, East Michigan University; Richard Anderson, Texas A & M; Dan Barszycz, College of Du Page; Stanford Berg, University of Florida; Charles Betz, Cerritos Community College; Scott Bloom, North Texas State University; Ronald Brandolini, Valencia Community College; Elba-Collier Brown, University of Texas, El Paso; Conrad Caligaris, Northeastern University; Michael Claudon, Middlebury College; John C. Dutton, Jr., North Carolina State University; James Dyal, Indiana University of Pennsylvania; John S. Evans, University of Alabama; Rudy Fichtenbaum, Wright State; Max Fletcher, University of Idaho; Lawrence Frateschi, College of Du Page; David Gay, Brigham Young University; Fred Gottheil, University of Illinois; Douglas Greenley, Moorehead State University; Byron Grove, University of Oregon; Nicholas Grunt, Tarrant County Community College; L. Dean Hiebert, Illinois State University; Calvin Hoerneman, Delta College; Randall G. Holcombe, Auburn University; Blair Housely, West Georgia College; Bill Hunter, Marquette University; Walter Johnson, University of Missouri, Columbus; Richard Keiffer, State University of New York, Buffalo; Nicholas Kontas, Marshall University; Jules La Rocque, Lawrence University; Russell Leonard, State University of New York, Morrisville; Robert Ley, Bemidji State University; James McGowen, Jr., Belleville Area College; Robert McLean, Pasadena City College; Michael Melvin, Arizona State University; Jerry Miller, Miami University, Ohio; Joseph Prinzinger, California State University, Northridge; Terry Riddle,

Central Virginia Community College; Jeff Ryan, McHenry County College; Stephen Sacks, University of Connecticut; Tom Shepherd, Hinds Junior College; Richard Tontz, California State University, Northridge; Roger Trenary, Kansas State University; Tak Two Chen, Suffolk County Community College; Elliott Willman, New Mexico State University; Travis Wilson, De Kalb Community College; Dirk Yandell, University of San Diego; Gary Young, University of Tennessee; and William Zahka, Widener University. We thank them for their help. Any remaining errors in the text are our responsibility.

We would like to acknowledge the research assistance of Leslie Page Wolfson, Lisa Knobloch, and Glenys Hardy. Our debt is especially great to our colleagues and mentors: James D. Gwartney, Charles J. Goetz, Fredrick J. Kelly, Ernie Combs, Wade Hands, James Papke, and D. J. Weidenaar.

We would also like to thank our employers, Fairleigh Dickinson University and the University of Puget Sound, for encouraging and supporting our work.

Finally, we would like to thank our students and our families for their patience, support, and love.

Contents

Preface		v
Part 1	***An Introduction to Economics***	1
Chapter 1	**Economics: Scarcity and Choice**	3
	Scarcity, Choice, and Human Behavior	4
	The Production Possibilities Frontier	6
	Specialization, Exchange, and the PPF	12
	Markets and the Role of Price	14
	Profits, Incentives, and Entrepreneurs	15
	Middlemen and Mutually Advantageous Exchange	16
Appendix:	How to Read and Interpret Graphs	17
Chapter 2	**An Introduction to the Economic Way of Thinking**	25
	The Five Foundations of the Economic Way of Thinking	26
	The Scientific Method	30
	Positive and Normative Economics	31
	Logical Fallacies and Economic Reasoning	32
	The Role of Economists in Industry, Academe, and Government	34
Appendix:	The Economist's Toolbox — Marginal and Average Analysis	34
Chapter 3	**How Economies Are Organized**	45
	The Problem of Scarcity	46
	The Economic Goals of a Society	52
	Individual versus Social Choice: Types of Economic Organization	57
Part 2	***Markets and the Mixed Economy***	63
Chapter 4	**Demand and Supply in the Market Economy**	65
	The Concept of Demand	67
	The Determinants of Demand	69
	Changes in Quantity demand versus Changes in Demand	73
	The Concept of Supply	75
	The Determinants of Supply	77
	Changes in Quantity Supplied versus Changes in Supply	80

xii Contents

	Market Equilibrium	81
	Price Floors and Price Ceilings	89
	The Power of Price	92
Chapter 5	**Governments and Markets: The Mixed Economy**	101
	The Market and Economic Efficiency	103
	Some Necessary Conditions for Market Efficiency	105
	Government as an Economic Force	109
	Government Policies and the Market	110
	The Potential for Government Inefficiencies	119
Chapter 6	**An Overview of the Private Sector**	127
	The Relationship Between Businesses and Households	129
	Households: One Half of the Private Sector	131
	Businesses: The Other Half ot the Private Sector	136
	Concentration, Market Power, and Size	139
	Industrial Development Policy	141
Chapter 7	**An Overview of the Private Sector**	147
	The Public versus the Private Sector	148
	The Economic Functions of Government	150
	Conflicts Among Governmental Functions	153
	The Tools of Government Policy	154
	Government Resources	155
	Tax Shifting and Incidence	159
	Economic Effects of Taxes	162
	Are Taxes Fair?	163
	The Distribution of the Tax Burden	165
	Major United States Taxes	166
	The Total Tax Burden	173
	Deficits and the National Debt	174
Part 3	*Macroeconomic Goals and Problems*	181
Chapter 8	**Gross National Product and Economic Growth**	183
	A Study Guide to Macroeconomics	184
	The Circular Flow of Spending and Income	186
	National Income and Gross National Product	188
	The Financial, Government, and Foreign Sectors	189
	Measuring Gross National Product	192
	Real Gross National Product	198
	Gross National Product and the Quality of Life	200
	The Goal of Economic Growth	202
	Measuring Economic Growth	204
	Vested Interests and Economic Growth	207
	Industrial Development Policy	211
	Japan: A Textbook Case in Growth Policy	212
Appendix:	The National Income and Product Accounts	215
Chapter 9	**Inflation and Unemployment: Problems, Policies, and Perspectives**	223
	Progress Toward Macroeconomic Goals	225
	Economic Events in the 1960s	227

	The Phillip's Curve in the 1960s	228
	Economic Events in the 1970s	230
	Unemployment	237
	Inflation	244

Part 4 — Macroeconomic Theory and Policy — 257

Chapter 10 — The Keynesian Model of the Economy — 259

Classical Economic Ideas	261
The Keynesian Revolution	261
Consumption Spending	266
Investment Spending	274
Net Export Spending	278
Government Spending	279
Equilibrium Income	280
Inflationary and Recessionary Gaps	286
The Spending Multiplier	287
Simple Keynesian Theory in Perspective	293

Chapter 11 — Aggregate Demand and Aggregate Supply — 300

The Changing Economy of the 1960s and 1970s	302
The Evolution of Economic Theory	304
Determinants of Aggregate Demand	306
The Aggregate Demand Curve	309
Shifts in Aggregate Demand	309
Determinants of Aggregate Supply	310
The Aggregate Supply Curve	313
Shifts in Aggregate Supply	315
AD-AS Equilibrium	316
The 1960s: Demand—Pull Inflation	318
The 1970s: Cost—Push Inflation	319
Changing Economic Policies in the 1960s and 1970s	320
The Goal of Increasing Aggregate Supply	325
The Problem of Expectations	326
A Look Ahead	327

Chapter 12 — Fiscal Policy, Deficits, and Supply-side Economics — 332

An Introduction to Demand-side Fiscal Policy	334
The Tools of Demand-side Fiscal Policies	335
Supply-side Fiscal Policies	344
The Federal Budget Deficit	352

Part 5 — Monetary Institutions, Theory, and Policy — 367

Chapter 13 — Money and the Banking System — 369

What Is Money?	370
The Functions of Money	372
Definitions of the Money Supply	374
Problems of the Financial Sector	378
How Financial Intermediaries Work	380
How Banks Work	382
How Banks Create Money	387
Deregulation of the U.S. Financial Sector	392

xiv Contents

	Money and the Economy: Early Monetary Theory	394
	A Look Ahead	396
Chapter 14	**The Federal Reserve, Credit Markets, and Monetary Policy**	401
	The Federal Reserve System	402
	The Federal and the Banking System	408
	The Federal and the Treasury	409
	The Instruments of Monetary Policy	409
	Interest Rates and Credit Markets	416
	The Keynesian Theory of Money	427
	How Does Money Really Affect the Economy?	433
Chapter 15	**Monetarist and Rational Expectations Theories**	438
	An Overview of Monetary Theories	439
	Recent Monetary Policy	442
	The Development of Monetarist Theory	446
	Keynesian and Monetarist Comparisons	451
	The Monetarist Remedy	453
	Which Economic Theory Is Correct?	454
	The Role of Expectations in Macro Policy	456
	Macroeconomic Theories in Perspective	465
Part 6	***Microeconomics***	469
Chapter 16	**Consumer Choice: From Where Does Demand Come?**	471
	The Problem of Consumer Choice	472
	Total and Marginal Utility	473
	Deriving Demand Curves	478
	Consumer Choice in Action	481
	Price Elasticity of Demand	481
	Income Elasticity: Another Demand Measure	488
Appendix:	Indifference Curves and the Budget Constraint	489
Chapter 17	**Supply and the Costs of Production**	501
	Who Are the Producers and Why Do They Produce?	503
	The Production Function	504
	Profit-Maximizing Output	512
	Firm and Market Summary	513
	Economies and Diseconomies of Scale	518
Chapter 18	**Perfect Competition in the Marketplace**	524
	Competition as a Process	526
	Market and Firm Equilibrium	529
	Market Adjustment to Changing Demand	531
	Application: Price Ceilings	535
	Efficiency in Competition Markets	537
	A Final Word on Competition	542
Chapter 19	**Monopoly: The Case of the One-Firm Market**	547
	What Is a Monopoly?	549
	Monopoly Demand and Revenue	551
	Monopoly versus Perfect Competition	556
	Antitrust Policies	557

Contents xv

	The Debate Over Monopolies	561
Chapter 20	**Monopolistic Competition and Oligopoly**	567
	Monopolistic Competition	569
	Price and Output Decisions: Economic Theory versus Mark-up Pricing	572
	Is Product Differentiation Desirable?	577
	Oligopoly	578
	Oligopoly Behavior: The Cartel Option	583
	Implicit Collusion: Leaders and Followers	585
	Competition and Kinked Demand Curves	587
	What to Do with Oligopolies	589
Part 7	*Factor Markets and Income Distribution*	595
Chapter 21	**Resource Markets: Demand and Supply at Work**	596
	What Resource Markets Do	597
	The Derived Demand for Resources	599
	Monopoly Resource Demand	607
	Monopsony: The One-Buyer Market	609
	Resource Supply	612
	Combining Inputs: Optimal Resource Use	614
Chapter 22	**Workers, Wages, and Jobs**	619
	Labor Supply in the Economy	621
	Unions in the United States	627
	The Minimum Wage Controversy	633
	Planning for Future Labor Market Conditions	638
Chapter 23	**Profit, Interest, and Rent**	644
	Economic Profit	645
	Interest: The Price of Loans	650
	Economic Rent	658
Chapter 24	**Poverty and Income Distribution**	666
	Income Distribution in the United States	668
	Trends in U.S. Income	671
	Antipoverty Policies	676
	What Does the Future Hold?	685
Part 8	*Private versus Public Choice*	689
Chapter 25	**Externalities and Public Goods: Private Versus Public Choice**	691
	Market Successes and Market Failures	693
	Externalities	693
	Communal Goods	703
	Public Goods	704
	Private Choice versus Public Choice	705
Chapter 26	**Energy Economics**	715
	Energy Supply: Where Does Energy Come From?	717
	Energy Demand: Where Does Energy Go?	719
	Demand and Supply Interdependence	720

	Roots of the Energy Crisis	720
	A Short History of OPEC	723
	Is the Energy Crisis Over?	725
	The Consequences of Higher Energy Costs	725
	Energy Solutions: Increasing Supply	727
	Energy Solutions: Lower Energy Demand	728
	Energy Policy: Prices or Government Rules	730
	Energy versus the Environment	730

Part 9 — International Economics and Comparative Economic Systems — 735

Chapter 27 — International Trade — 737
- Why do Nations Trade? — 739
- Tariffs and Quotas — 744

Chapter 28 — International Finance — 756
- International Payments — 758
- Financing a Balance of Payments Deficit? — 758
- The Balance of Trade — 759
- Is a Payments Deficit Bad? — 761
- The IMF and the World Bank — 761
- The Mysterious Exchange Rate — 762
- Prices and Exchange Rates — 762
- The Foreign Exchange Market — 762
- The Games Exchange Rates Play — 765
- Here Is Demand, Where Is Supply? — 765
- Exchange Market Equilibrium — 766
- The Foreign Exchange Market at Work — 768
- Fixed Exchange Rates — 773

Chapter 29 — International Economic Policy — 780
- How Exchange Rates Affect the Economy — 781
- Interest Rates, Exchange Rates, and International Credit Movements — 784
- Economic Policy with Flexible Exchange Rates — 785
- Economic Policy with Fixed Exchange Rates — 788
- Domestic and International Economic Goals — 791
- The Trade Deficit: Policy Options — 793
- Lessons for Economic Policy — 795

Chapter 30 — Comparative Economic Systems — 801
- Three Choices an Economic System Must Make — 803
- Evaluating Alternative Economic Systems — 805
- Centralized or Decentralized Choice — 805
- Property Rights: Private Versus Public Ownership — 806
- The Range of Economic Systems — 807
- The Economy of the Soviet Union — 811
- Changes in the Soviet System? — 814
- Yugoslavia: The Worker-Managed Firm — 815
- The Convergence Hypothesis — 817

Glossary — 823
Index — 835

PART 1

An Introduction to Economics

CHAPTER 1

Economics: Scarcity and Choice

Having read the chapter, reviewed the chapter summary, and completed the *Study Guide* exercises, you should be able to:

CRIS

1.1 ECONOMICS DEFINED: Define economics.

1.2 MICROECONOMICS AND MACROECONOMICS: Discuss the differences and similarities between microeconomics and macroeconomics.

1.3 BASIC ECONOMIC PROBLEMS: Discuss the nature of the basic economic problems of scarcity and choice.

1.4 OPPORTUNITY COST: Define opportunity cost and be able to identify real-life examples of this concept.

1.5 PRODUCTION POSSIBILITIES FRONTIER: Define and depict in graph form the concept of a production possibilities frontier, indicating what the points lying inside and outside of the frontier tell us about total output and the use of resources.

1.6 TECHNOLOGY AND THE PPF: Graph the effect of an increased level of technology on a production possibilities frontier.

1.7 CAPITAL FORMATION: Define capital formation, discuss its effect on the future production possibilities frontier, and identify the present opportunity cost associated with it.

1.8 SPECIALIZATION AND EXCHANGE: Explain how specialization and exchange enable an economy to produce more total output.

1.9 FACTORS AFFECTING EXCHANGE: Indicate the roles that markets, prices, profits, entrepreneurs, and middlemen play in exchange and show how each concept increases the gains from specialization and exchange.

1.10 RELATIONSHIPS AND SLOPE: Discuss the differences between direct and inverse relationships, display them in graph form, and define and calculate the slope of a line.

1.1 ECONOMICS DEFINED

Economics
The social science that studies how society chooses to allocate scarce resources among its unlimited wants and desires.

Scarcity
The problem that exists when the resources available to the economy are insufficient to satisfy the unlimited human desires.

1.2 MICROECONOMICS AND MACROECONOMICS

Economic Goods
Goods that are scarce, for which our desires exceed the amount freely supplied to us by nature.

Microeconomics
The study of economic choices made by individual consumers and producers, and the markets where consumers and producers exchange goods and services.

Macroeconomics
The study of the national economy, focusing on such social problems as inflation, unemployment, and economic growth.

1.3 BASIC ECONOMIC PROBLEMS

When you first decided to take an economics course you probably had some idea or impression of the course contents. When most people think of economics, they associate it with things like the stock market, money, banking, inflation, and unemployment. While economics does relate to each of these topics in some way, it is really much more than that. **Economics** is formally defined as the social science that studies how society chooses to allocate scarce resources among its unlimited wants and desires. We are all forced to make choices, both as individuals and as a society, because we live in a world of **scarcity**. Not only are the resources that go into the production of goods and services scarce, so too are the resulting goods and services. Goods that are scarce are called **economic goods**. Because resources are scarce and goods are limited, economic actors must make choices that maximize the benefits they receive from the allocation of resources. Economics is therefore the social science that deals with human choices.

The study of economics has traditionally been divided into two perspectives: microeconomics and macroeconomics. **Microeconomics** is concerned with choices that individuals make. Thus it studies the problem of choice by looking at a single producing or consuming unit — for example, one person, one firm, one industry, or one organization — and examining the ways in which these individual units interact in markets. **Macroeconomics**, on the other hand, examines social choices (the choices of the entire society) and aggregations, or collections, of individual choices. It takes as its unit of analysis the economy as a whole, looking at such economic aggregates as the overall rate of unemployment or the rate of inflation in the economy.

Students sometimes become confused by this division of the study of economics into two parts. But it is actually quite simple. Microeconomics and macroeconomics both look at the problem of choice. Microeconomics looks at individual choices, whereas macroeconomics looks at the economic consequences of these choices for the economy as a whole. The way in which economists study the economy is similar to the way in which biologists study organisms. Sometimes they look at the ways in which single cells deal with their environment; at other times, they study the organs and structures that coordinate the actions of individual cells. A thorough understanding of an organism, such as a human being, requires the study of both microbiology and macrobiology. For the same reasons, we must study both macroeconomics and microeconomics to thoroughly understand the world in which we live.

SCARCITY, CHOICE, AND HUMAN BEHAVIOR

Scarcity exists because human wants and desires are unlimited, while the resources we use to satisfy them are finite. There are finite amounts of resources such as coal, oil, lumber, automobiles, and human labor available at any given time. The competing desires for the goods and services that these resources can produce exceeds our ability to produce them. We all experience the concept of scarce resources daily. Many people begin the day wishing they had more time to sleep and end it wishing they had more income to purchase the goods and services they desire.

While it is easy to see that we all face scarce individual or family resources, it is important to understand that the same concept applies to larger economic units, such as states and nations, as well. It may seem, for example, that a large nation like the United States has nearly infinite amounts of every natural resource. The economic fact of life, however, is that wants and desires outstrip the amount of nearly any resource you can name.

Human wants and desires are virtually infinite. People begin with the basic physiological desires for food, clothing, and shelter. Once these basic wants are satisfied, people move on to lesser wants, such as the desire for safety and security. Once these are fulfilled, people develop desires for emotional satisfaction, such as love, and group acceptance, and then move on to social wants, such as prestige and status. This process of fulfilling one set of wants and desires and then moving on to another set continues in human beings throughout their lives.

While human nature generates infinite wants, human nature and mother nature combine to limit the **resources** that are available to satisfy those wants. Economists generally identify four types of resources: land, labor, capital, and entrepreneurship. *Land*, including natural resources, exists in finite supply and is required for almost all productive activities. The amount of *labor* services available at any time depends on the size, age, skills, and preferences of the population. Labor is only made available if people are willing to forgo leisure and use their time and talents to produce goods and services. *Capital* refers to physical items used in production, such as factories, machines, and tools. The amount of capital that is available to produce goods and services is limited at any moment. *Entrepreneurship* is the willingness of individuals to take risks in the pursuit of gain by starting new businesses or introducing innovations. This human characteristic is also limited at any time. The fact of limited resources combined with the human tendency to have infinite desires guarantees that scarcity will be an economic fact of life.

Resources
Those goods and services used to satisfy wants and needs. Nearly all resources are limited in quantity.

Opportunity Costs

If scarcity is the basic economic problem, then **choice** is how human beings deal with that problem. Since there is not enough of every resource for us to have all that we want, we must choose how to allocate, or parcel out, our scarce resources among our unlimited wants and desires. We must first of all decide which of our desires will be satisfied and which will be left wanting. We must then decide how much of each of our resources to devote to each of the desires we are attempting to fulfill. Choice is the act of selecting among limited alternatives.

Choice
The process of selecting among limited alternatives. Through choice, human beings deal with the economic problem of scarcity.

Choosing one alternative over another means we have to give up something in the choice. This means that every choice has a cost. Economists refer to the value of the best foregone opportunity as the **opportunity cost** of a choice. The opportunity cost of a particular choice is the highest-valued option that has to be given up in order to choose some other alternative.

1.4 OPPORTUNITY COST

Opportunity Cost
The highest-valued alternative that must be forgone when another alternative is selected. With every choice, there is an opportunity cost.

If you could spend Saturday afternoon cutting your neighbor's lawn for $10, washing windows for $5, or getting a suntan beside your pool, the opportunity cost of your suntan would be the $10 income you could have made from mowing your neighbor's yard. Opportunity cost is not measured in money terms alone, however. The opportunity cost of attending class at 8:00 A.M., for example, is the extra hour of sleep you could have had instead or the value of the time spent with friends over early morning coffee, whichever you value most highly. If you decide to sleep an extra hour instead of attending class, an economist would say that you must value the sleep more than the benefits of attending class.

**KEY CONCEPTS
1.3, 1.4**

> Scarcity exists because our wants and desires exceed the resources available to fulfill them. The existence of scarcity requires that choices be made. Each choice has an opportunity cost. The opportunity cost is equivalent to the highest-valued opportunity that is foregone when choosing between alternatives. In effect, the opportunity cost is the value of the opportunity lost. Economic behavior is guided by opportunity cost.

Remember, in economic terms, what something costs is what you have to give up to get it. What you gain by making a choice is sometimes called the opportunity benefit of the choice. The opportunity cost of attending class may be the foregone sleep, but the opportunity benefit is the knowledge and improved grades that come from spending time in the classroom. Every choice has both an opportunity benefit and an opportunity cost. Students choose to attend classes if the opportunity benefit of so doing is greater than the corresponding opportunity cost.

Scarcity and Competition

Scarcity is an economic fact of life. Where scarcity exists, competition generally follows. When resources are scarce, individuals will compete to acquire them. We see this competition all around us. Merchants compete for shoppers' dollars. Shoppers compete with one another for the best goods at the lowest prices. We can readily see the competition among suppliers by looking at newspaper and television advertisements that compete for our attention. We can see the competition among buyers by looking at the crowds that appear at store entrances just before a big sale.

These are the most obvious examples of competition due to scarcity, but not necessarily the most important ones. College students are aware that different colleges and universities compete for their tuition dollars. Within each institution, various departments and schools compete to acquire majors. Even students themselves often compete. The number of seats available in the most popular classes is limited. Students, therefore, must compete with one another for these scarce resources. Those who are successful get the classes they want. Those who are unsuccessful must wait until the next term or take less-preferred classes.

We will discuss competition in much greater detail in future chapters of this book. For now, however, it is important to realize that scarcity is an economic fact of life. Scarcity forces choice and breeds competition.

THE PRODUCTION POSSIBILITIES FRONTIER

We have already learned that scarcity exists because wants and desires are unlimited, while the resources used to fulfill those wants and desires are limited. We have learned that scarcity means we must choose among limited alternatives. These ideas lead us to the formal definition of economics that was stated earlier: economics is the social science that studies how society chooses to allocate scarce resources among its unlimited wants and desires.

Economists commonly use graphical or mathematical tools when they analyze the choices particular units make. These tools are called **models**. A model is a simplified description of a real-world process, which, because it is

Models
Simplified descriptions of real-world processes that help us better understand the more complex real events and relationships.

1.5 PRODUCTION POSSIBILITIES FRONTIER

Production Possibilities Frontier (PPF)

A model that analyzes the various maximum combinations of total output of two goods. A PPF curve is a graphic representation of this model. At any point on the frontier (curve) all resources are used efficiently and are fully employed. A constant level of time, resources, and technology is assumed.

Technology

Know-how. The application of scientific knowledge to some useful purpose. It frequently enables us to reduce production costs per unit of output.

---

simple, allows us to better understand the complexities of the real world. Models allow us to isolate particular cause-and-effect relationships that operate in the real world but that may be difficult to perceive or understand unless simplified.

One of the most useful economic models is the **production possibilities frontier (PPF)**, which uses geometry to analyze the principles and problems involved in choosing between two products when there is a given quantity of resources from which to produce them. A production possibilities frontier shows the maximum possible combinations of two goods that can be produced with scarce resources and existing **technology**. By showing the choices that are available, the PPF helps us understand the trade-offs and opportunity costs of different choices. It can be used to analyze the choices available to the individual consumer, firm, industry, or the entire economy.

Let us use the PPF to analyze a choice problem familiar to most students. Assume that you have 10 hours of study time each week to divide or allocate between two courses, economics and calculus. Table 1-1 shows the various maximum combinations of grades you can earn in the two courses by allocating your study time in various ways. If you spend all your time studying calculus and none studying economics, you could earn an A in math, but you would fail the economics course. This is combination 1 in the table. Alternately, you could allocate all your time to economics and none to calculus. This might yield you an A in economics but an F in calculus. This is combination 5 in the table. Finally, you could choose to allocate your time so as to earn at least passing grades in both courses, such as illustrated in combinations 2, 3, or 4.

With a fixed amount of study time, if you want to earn a higher grade in one course, you must settle for a lower grade in another course. The opportunity cost of moving from combination 1 (A in calculus, F in economics) to combination 2 (B in calculus, C in economics) is the sacrifice of one letter grade in calculus. The opportunity benefit is what is gained by the choice, a two letter grade increase in your economics grade.

Production Possibilities Frontier Analysis

Information like that contained in Table 1-1 is often easier to understand when presented graphically. Figure 1-1 graphs the production possibilities frontier that Table 1-1 describes.

Figure 1-1 shows that by moving along the PPF curve from combination 1 to combination 2, you would gain two letter grades in economics (the opportunity benefit) and lose one letter grade in calculus (the opportunity cost). To state this conclusion, however, we must make several important assumptions. First, we must assume that total study time is fixed (10 hours in this case). Next, we must assume that all the study time and resources

---

TABLE 1-1   **The Trade-off between Studying Calculus and Economics**

	Possible study combinations				
	1	2	3	4	5
Calculus grade	A	B	C	D	F
Economics grade	F	C	B–	B+	A

Note. These study options are illustrated in Figure 1-1.

8 Economics: Scarcity and Choice

FIGURE 1-1   **A Student's Production Possibilities Frontier.** This production possibilities frontier (PPF) shows the maximum combinations of calculus and economics grades that can be achieved, given fixed time resources and study technology. Points such as 1 through 5, which lie on the PPF, are attainable and represent the efficient use of resources. Points such as 6, which lie on the interior of the PPF, are possible, but they represent the inefficient use of resources. Points such as 7, which lie outside the PPF, are unattainable with existing technology and resources. The PPF has a bowed shape because of the existence of diminishing marginal returns associated with devoting all study time to one subject, all else being equal.

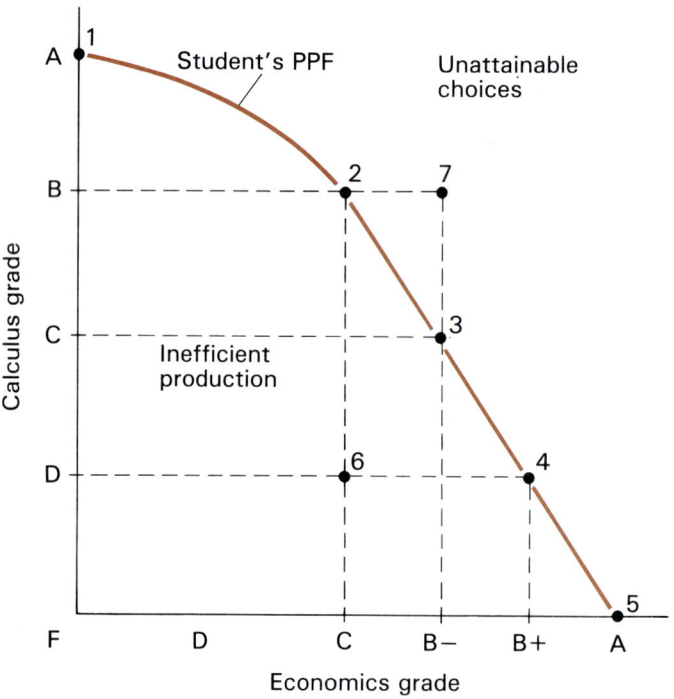

are used efficiently and not wasted. Finally, we must assume that the level of technology is constant; in other words, that some new technology (know-how) for studying does not come along that enables you to learn as much in one hour as you used to learn in two hours.

In general, production possibilities analysis requires that we assume that the time period of production and the amount of available resources are fixed, that the level of technology is held constant during analysis, and that production is carried on efficiently, so that no resources are wasted. Given these assumptions, the production possibilities frontier can provide many useful insights into the problems of scarcity and choice.

Even the simple student PPF shown in Figure 1-1 provides a great deal of economic information. All the combinations of the PPF itself represent technically efficient production. No resources are wasted in the production of combinations 1 through 5, even though they represent much different uses of time. This tells us that there are many different ways to effectively allocate resources. Resources are not always used efficiently, however. Combination 6 in Figure 1-1 shows the consequences of the inefficient allocation of resources. Suppose that you did not use all of the 10 hours available for studying. The result of this inefficiency is a combination of grades that lies beneath the PPF. These combinations are undesirable because efficient resource use produces greater total output. Wasteful combination 6 provides a D in calculus and a C in economics. The PPF tells us that by using study time more effectively you could have attained either combination 2 (a higher grade in calculus), combination 4 (a higher grade in economics), or combination 3 (a higher grade in both subjects).

The PPF helps us understand which resource uses are technically efficient and which are inefficient. The PPF also tells us that some desirable combinations are impossible. You might desire, for example, to achieve B grades in both economics and calculus. This is the combination of grades represented by 7 in Figure 1-1. While this choice is desirable, it cannot be attained given current resources and technology. In other words, it is impossible to get a B grade in both courses. This grade combination can only be attained, given this model's assumptions, if more study-time resources are made available or if some change takes place in your study technology.

The shape of the PPF curve in Figure 1-1 is also important. This PPF curve demonstrates the principle of **diminishing marginal returns.** Diminishing marginal returns refers to the fact that, after a certain point, increasing the allocation of a particular resource to production (while holding the allocation level of other resources constant) results in smaller and smaller increases in production output per unit of increase in resource use. In other words, holding everything else constant, at some point increasing the amount of a particular resource that is devoted to a particular task generates smaller increases in output. When the incremental production per unit of extra effort begins to fall, we have encountered diminishing marginal returns.

For example, by moving from combination 1 to combination 2 in Figure 1-1, you can increase your economics grade from an F to C (a gain of two letter grades), but the cost is a loss of one letter grade in calculus. This shows that the first few hours allocated to studying economics have a high grade return. However, taking more time from calculus (combination 3) adds relatively less to your economics grade. This reallocation of study time costs you one grade in calculus but does less to improve your economics grade than in the first case. As you move from combination 3 to combination 4, the trade-off becomes even more severe. The loss in your calculus grade results in a relatively small improvement in your performance in economics.

Most people are familiar with the idea of diminishing returns. The first hour studying calculus or economics frequently adds much to your knowledge. The second hour also increases your knowledge, but not as much as the first. The fifth or sixth straight hour devoted to studying one subject adds much less to your knowledge than did the first or second hour.

The frequent occurrence of diminishing marginal returns leads to what economists call the **law of increasing costs.** Because of diminishing marginal returns, the opportunity cost of an item increases as the production of that item rises, holding other factors such as resource availability and technology constant.

The effects of the law of increasing costs can be seen in Table 1-1 and Figure 1-1. The opportunity cost of further improving your grade in calculus (in terms of the foregone economics grade) rises as you devote more and more resources to studying calculus and fewer and fewer resources to studying economics. For example, by moving from point 3 to point 2 on the PPF, you can improve your calculus score by one letter grade (climbing from a C to a B) at the cost of about a half letter grade reduction in your

Diminishing Marginal Returns
The property that, as more and more resources are allocated to the production of a particular item, all else held constant, the additional output from each extra resource declines.

Law of Increasing Costs
The opportunity cost of producing an item tends to rise as more and more of it is produced, assuming that other factors such as resource availability and technology do not change.

economics score (dropping from a B− to a C). As more resources are devoted to studying calculus, however, the cost of an additional improvement in your calculus grade rises. As you move from point 2 to point 1 on the PPC, for example, your calculus score improves by one letter grade (climbing from a B to an A), but the opportunity cost is a much larger reduction in your economics grade (a drop from a C to an F). The law of increasing costs holds that the opportunity cost of any given activity rises as more and more resources are devoted to that activity.

The principle of diminishing marginal returns and the law of increasing costs appear frequently in economic analysis. When diminishing marginal returns exist, the PPF curve looks like the one shown in Figure 1-1. The PPF is not a straight line. It appears drawn in at the ends. This is because it is at the ends, when all study time is spent on either economics or calculus, for example, that the effects of diminishing returns and the law of increasing costs are most severe.

Students frequently want to know, "Which point on the PPF is the best?" They often assume that combinations like 2 or 3 are the best because they are relatively far from the origin. The fact is that no combination on the PPF is automatically the "best" in any sense. The PPF shows us the combinations we can choose among if resources are used efficiently. The answer to the question of which combination is the most desirable depends on how the individual decision maker chooses to weigh the opportunity benefits versus the opportunity costs. The "best" combination on the PPF is the one that is most preferred by the individual making the choice.

A PPF for the Entire Economy

Individuals, firms, industries, and groups all face their own production possibilities frontiers. We all experience limits to what can be produced given finite resources. Figure 1-2 shows a hypothetical PPF curve for the entire economy. This PPF curve shows the maximum possible combinations of consumer goods (such as automobiles, TV dinners, and television sets) and capital goods (such as machinery, factories, and computers) that this economy can currently produce. Given existing resources, this economy is limited to maximum combinations such as A, B, and C in Figure 1-2. These are combinations on the original PPF in the figure. As we have seen, combinations like E, which involve more consumer goods and more capital goods, are unattainable, given existing resource limits and technology. A combination such as D is attainable, but it represents an inefficient use of resources. We can use this simple model of the economy to learn about unemployment, full employment, economic growth, and the opportunity cost of growth.

Sometimes our economy experiences high levels of unemployment, such as occurred in the Great Depression of the 1930s and during the deep recession of the early 1980s. We normally think of unemployment in terms of lost paychecks and jobless workers. It is important that we also view this unemployment as an inefficient use of resources, like combination D in Figure 1-2. High unemployment is costly to the economy because it means that valuable, scarce resources are being wasted. These scarce resources are not being used to produce combinations of goods on the PPF. Solving the unemployment problem means finding ways to put these resources to work, moving the economy from combination D to A, B, C, or some other combination on the PPF.

FIGURE 1-2

Unemployment, Full Employment, and Economic Growth. This PPF for an entire economy illustrates several concepts. Point *D* is inefficient; it represents many unemployed resources. Unemployment is reduced if the economy moves to points such as *A*, *B*, or *C* on the PPF. Economic growth shifts the PPF, making a point such as *E* attainable.

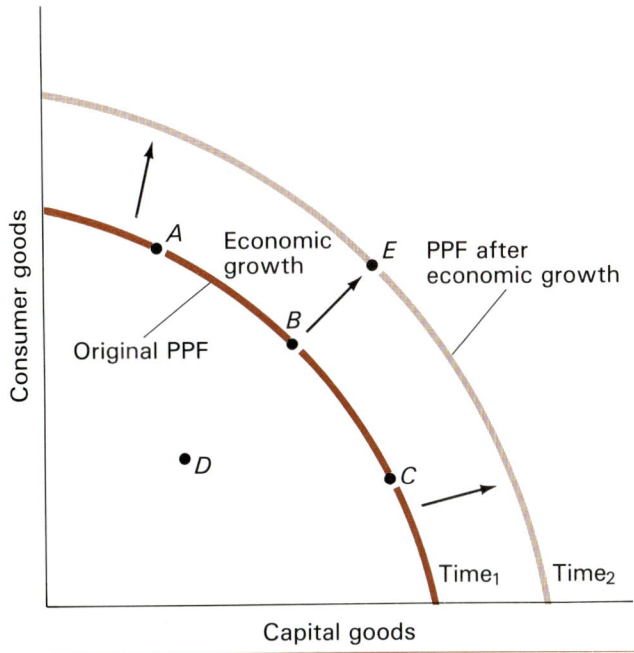

1.6 TECHNOLOGY AND THE PPF

Efficient combinations *A*, *B*, and *C* represent a fully employed economy. The economy is efficiently using all its resources at any of these combinations. A full-employment economy can produce many consumer goods and few capital goods (point *A*), or fewer consumer goods and more capital goods (points *B* or *C*). Which combination should the economy choose? Part of the answer to this question depends on whether the economy wants to experience **economic growth**. Economic growth is an increase in the economy's overall ability to produce goods and services. It is represented graphically as a shift in the economy's PPF, as shown in Figure 1-2. Economic growth means that the economy is able to produce combinations of goods and services that were previously unattainable. Combination *E*, which was unattainable initially, can be produced if the economy grows and the PPF shifts as the figure indicates.

Economic Growth
An increase in the economy's overall ability to produce goods and services.

What causes economic growth? One way in which economic growth can be brought about is through advances in technology. Technological advancement requires sacrifice, however. Improvements in technology require investment in innovation and research. Society must give up currently produced consumer goods in order to devote these resources to research and innovation. The forgone consumer goods, which satisfy our current desires but do little toward meeting future wants, are the opportunity cost of this technology-based economic growth.

1.7 CAPITAL FORMATION

A second way that economies grow is by increasing the resource base of the economy. Sometimes this can be accomplished by discovering new reserves of natural resources such as coal or oil. As in the case of technology-based economic growth, resource-based growth requires a sacrifice. These discoveries require investment in search and exploration activities. An econ-

Capital Formation
The sacrificing of present consumption in order to increase the present production of machinery, human skills, and other capital goods, which will in turn increase the ability to produce output in the future.

Human Capital
The available stock of knowledge, learning, and skills.

omy's resource base can also be increased through investment and **capital formation.** Capital formation takes place when current resources are allocated away from consumer goods and used to produce capital goods such as machines, factories, and computers that add to production both now and for years in the future. Once again, the economy must forgo current consumption to achieve the capital formation that leads to economic growth.

Capital formation is not limited to construction of new machines and factories. Much of today's capital formation takes the form of investment in **human capital.** Human capital is the stock of human knowledge and know-how that is available for production. Education is one way that the economy invests in human capital.

College students are a good example of the opportunity cost and opportunity benefit of investment in human capital. College students give up the desirable consumer goods that they could purchase if they worked at a full-time job instead of attending classes and paying tuition bills. The foregone income and consumer goods represents the opportunity costs of the education and training received. What is the opportunity benefit? A person with advanced training or education can produce more for many years to come. The student gives up current income and consumption to attend classes that lead to growth and higher income and consumption in the future. The economy, through formation of either human or physical capital, makes the same trade-off when it aims to achieve economic growth.

This brief discussion of the causes of economic growth suggests that combinations like C on the original PPF curve, with relatively few consumer goods and relatively many capital goods, are more likely to lead to economic growth than combinations like A, with more consumer goods and fewer capital goods produced. The economic growth trade-off is that the way to have more consumer goods in the future is to produce fewer consumer goods, with more capital formation, now. The high levels of consumer goods we enjoy today exist because previous generations gave up consumer goods to generate capital formation and economic growth.

SPECIALIZATION, EXCHANGE, AND THE PPF

Specialization
The process whereby an individual or group devotes more resources to the production of a single good or service, as opposed to producing many goods, then exchanges that particular item for other items that are desired.

Exchange
The process whereby individuals trade goods or services to make themselves better off. The existence of exchange make specialization possible.

Specialization occurs when a resource, such as a worker, concentrates on producing one or just a few goods or services, instead of producing a broad range of items. People are only able to specialize because they do not need to be self-sufficient in all things. A person can specialize in production of one thing, then acquire other items through exchange. **Exchange** takes place as individuals trade the goods and services that they have produced for those that others produce and sell. Specialization and exchange are important because they allow individuals to escape the confines of their individual production possibilities frontiers and, therefore, expand the production possibilities available to society.

Most exchanges that we make are voluntary. This tells us that these exchanges must be mutually advantageous, benefiting all those involved. Each side of the exchange must gain or else no voluntary exchange would be possible. We can only gain, however, if we are able to attain combinations of goods and services through exchange that we could not produce ourselves. This tells us that voluntary mutually advantageous exchange makes both traders better off by allowing them to consume combinations of items that they could not produce themselves.

Mutually advantageous exchanges are frequently based on differences in opportunity cost. Suppose, for example, that in order to type a composition for a writing class you would have to take time off from your job, thereby giving up wages equivalent to $6 worth of goods. Your roommate, however, has a different job (that pays less per hour) or is perhaps a faster typist. He or she would only have to give up $3 worth of goods in order to type the composition. It makes sense that a mutually advantageous exchange could take place in this situation. If you paid your roommate $4 or $5, for example, to take time off from work to type your paper while you worked and earned $6, you could both realize a $1 to $2 benefit (the fee minus his or her $3 opportunity cost in the case of your roommate, and your $6 wage minus the fee in your own case). Not only would the paper be typed, but each of you would be able to buy more goods than if the exchange had not taken place.

Exchange allows an individual to produce one good or service and trade that item for other desired goods. This allows a person to escape the limits of the PPF curve because it is possible to purchase an item, through exchange, for less than the opportunity cost of producing it yourself.

1.8 SPECIALIZATION AND EXCHANGE

Virtually no one in today's modern world is truly self-sufficient. We all specialize in producing one thing or another, then exchanging this item for money, which is used to purchase the other goods we desire from other "specialists" in production. A barber, for example, specializes in providing a particular service to customers. The barber exchanges specialized haircutting services for money, which is used to purchase other goods and services from other people who specialize in their production. Some people are specialists in a broad area. Farm workers, for example, must usually be able to perform many sorts of agricultural jobs. Other people are more narrowly specialized. Some financial advisors, for example, provide analysis and information about just one or two companies and their stocks. Some surgeons specialize in just one or two very technical operations.

Specialization in the real world is advantageous because firms that take advantage of specialization can produce in more efficient ways than those that do not. Adam Smith, the father of modern economics, cited the example of a pin factory in his classic work *The Wealth of Nations*[1] to demonstrate the wonder of the specialization of labor. Smith told of how simple straight pins were produced by teams of workers in the factories of his day. One workers would cut the steel wire to the proper length. Another straightened and sharpened it. A third added the pinhead. The process continued, with each worker performing a simple task precisely and quickly. Working as isolated individuals, the pin factory laborers would have produced only a few imperfect pins each day. Working together in specialized jobs, the same number of workers produced a vastly higher number of perfect pins.

Adam Smith showed that specialization can make production more efficient. We observe in today's world that many factories are organized like Smith's pin factory, with assembly lines and specialized jobs. The modern automobile factory, first perfected by Henry Ford, is an excellent example of the efficiency that is possible when specialization is employed. Specialization is a common fact of everyday life. Even grocery stores and fast food outlets find that specialization of labor increases production. Most modern college students start down the road to specialization when they select a

1. Adam Smith, *An Inquiry into the Nature and Causes of the Wealth of Nations*, New York: Modern Library, 1937.

major area of study. The efficiency gains from specialization are one force that tends to expand the amount of specialization and exchange in the world today.

How far can specialization go? One limit to the amount of specialization is the size of the market. It would make no sense to produce millions of pins, thousands of fish, or hundreds of yards of cloth in an economy with a small population or little desire for these items. We tend to observe the greatest degree of specialization in large markets, where many units of a particular item are produced and exchanged. Specialization tends to increase as markets expand and the economic units in them grow. This is why you will observe more specialization of labor in a large supermarket, for example, than in a small "mom and pop" corner grocery. In general, the degree of specialization is limited by the size of the market for any particular item.

Diminishing returns and the law of increasing costs tend to limit the potential gains from specialization. The fact of diminishing returns, discussed earlier in this chapter, means that opportunity costs increase as more and more of a single good is produced. At some point, this rising opportunity cost makes further specialization wasteful. At this point, it is actually cheaper to produce items yourself rather than producing goods for trade. A modern producer, such as an attorney, does tend to specialize in the production of a single good or service, but this concentration of effort falls well short of complete specialization. It is likely that the attorney cooks meals, does laundry, and performs household chores rather than paying others to perform these services.

Incomplete specialization is also due in part to the existence of high transaction costs (the costs of making trades). The attorney might be willing to hire someone to perform household chores, for example, but the high cost of advertising this job opening, screening applicants, and coming to terms with a suitable part-time household worker might keep this exchange from taking place.

MARKETS AND THE ROLE OF PRICE

1.9 FACTORS AFFECTING EXCHANGE

Markets
The general term for the institutions through which the exchange of goods and services takes place.

Much of the study of economics revolves around the study of **markets.** Markets are the institutions where buyers and sellers come together to exchange goods and services. Some markets are specific physical places, such as traditional farmers' markets, where farmers bring produce to find city buyers, or the stock market on Wall Street, where financial buyers and sellers congregate. However, most real-world markets are widely dispersed, so there is no single place where all buyers and sellers meet. The market for computer software, for example, encompasses all producers and potential buyers of software around the world. Even though they do not all meet in one place to make exchanges, all these buyers and sellers are participating in this market.

Markets exist because they provide an institutional structure that facilitates exchange. Markets reduce the cost of making an exchange because they bring buyers and sellers together in ways that increase the information that traders have available. Exchanges are easier and less costly to make in well-organized markets: the more organized the market, the lower the trading cost. Stock shares can be traded on the New York Stock Exchange at relatively low cost, for example, because this market effectively brings together buyers and sellers, or their representatives, in one place where buying and selling information can be quickly and cheaply exchanged. Used

1.9 FACTORS AFFECTING EXCHANGE

encyclopedias often are as valuable as stock shares, but they are less frequently traded in part because the market for these books is poorly organized. It is costly for used-encyclopedia buyers and sellers to locate each other and exchange information.

One of the functions of a market is to allow buyers and sellers to find a mutually advantageous price for their exhanges. This is important because economists think that price is a key signal to buyers and sellers. Price signals the relative scarcity of specific goods and resources. A rising price for heating oil, for example, is a signal that this item is increasingly scarce, meaning that the demand for it has risen relative to its availability. This could happen either because consumers have increased the amount of heating oil they want to purchase (because of cold winter weather, for example) or because other events have reduced the amount of heating oil that suppliers have available.

This increase in price is a useful signal. Consumers see the signal of the rising price as an indication of higher opportunity cost. When price rises, they will have to give up larger quantities of other goods to make their planned purchases of heating oil. They respond to this signal by purchasing relatively smaller quantities and by shifting their purchases to substitute items, such as fuel for woodstoves, if substitutes are available. Producers see the signal of higher price as an incentive to increase their production. Firms have a greater incentive to produce and sell heating oil, all else being equal, when prices are higher. Higher price therefore tells both buyers and sellers about scarcity and helps them make efficient choices.

A lower price for an item sends just the opposite signals to buyers and sellers. Lower price is an indication that an item is relatively less scarce. Lower price gives sellers less incentive to produce. Lower price, however, means a lower opportunity cost for buyers, who tend to purchase more at the lower price.

Price determines the relative gains to buyers and sellers. Sellers tend to reap more of the gains from exchange when the price of the good they sell is relatively high, while buyers get more of the gains when the price of the item they purchase is relatively low. Buyers and sellers thus have different interests in the direction of a change in price.

PROFITS, INCENTIVES, AND ENTREPRENEURS

1.9 FACTORS AFFECTING EXCHANGE

Prices affect profits. Producers earn high profits, all else being equal, when they receive higher prices. Profit acts as an incentive to produce. When profits are high, producers have an incentive to more completely specialize in the production of high-profit items. New firms have an incentive to enter markets where profits exist, further expanding production. The opposite set of events is triggered by low prices and profits. Low profits induce producers to switch to other markets. Firms produce less and leave the market when profits fall. Profits are the message that the market sends entrepreneurs, telling them to produce more in response to higher profits or to produce less when profits fall.

Profits are important because economists think that producers respond to the incentive, or inducement, that profits provide. Producers make choices in their own self-interest. This means that producers allocate more resources to goods in markets where profits are found. Producers allocate resources away from goods in markets where profits are not available. Prices, profits, and incentives are, therefore, of great importance in

> **1.9 FACTORS AFFECTING EXCHANGE**

Entrepreneurs
Individuals who organize resources for production, form new enterprises, or make innovations in production. Entrepreneurs accept the risk of failure in exchange for the potential of financial gain.

determining how scarce resources are allocated to the production of competing goods in market economies.

Entrepreneurs are the individuals who organize the resources needed for production. Entrepreneurs respond to profit incentives, increasing the resources available to produce goods and services in markets where profits are found and reducing the resources available in other markets. In doing this, entrepreneurs face a trade-off between risk and return. Production frequently promises a profit return, but the profit is not guaranteed. There is always the risk that the individual or firm will lose money instead. It is generally true that there are relatively low profits to be gained in businesses with lower risk and higher potential profits in areas with higher risk.

Entrepreneurs are the risk takers of economic society. They weigh the information about prices, profits, demand, and supply, and risk resources on new ventures, production, and ideas. Society has a vested interest in entrepreneurial activity because the risks entrepreneurs take benefit us all by increasing the range and quality of products available and by making existing products available at a lower cost due to improved technology or increased competition. Society gains when entrepreneurs gain, because successful new firms tend to increase income and employment.

The young men who invented the Apple computer are examples of entrepreneurs who succeeded. They risked their modest fortunes on their ability to produce a personal computer that would appeal to modern families. Their risk was a successful one, and these computer entrepreneurs are millionaires today.

Mark Twain is an example of how a failed entrepreneurial attempt can benefit society. Mark Twain ploughed the profits from his popular books into the development of a particular kind of mechanized typesetting machine. This invention was a miserable failure, costing Twain his entire fortune. Twain's loss was society's gain for two reasons. First, other inventors learned from this failure and eventually produced a workable typesetting machine. Second, some of Twain's best books were written while the threat of bankruptcy acted as an incentive for him to produce.

MIDDLEMEN AND MUTUALLY ADVANTAGEOUS EXCHANGE

> **1.9 FACTORS AFFECTING EXCHANGE**

Exchange is all the more important because it is mutually advantageous to the individuals who trade goods or services. This means that both the buyer and seller gain from the exchange. How do we know they both gain? Exchanges in a free society are voluntary. Both the buyer and seller have the option of refusing to trade. Given this option, one trades only if the trade is advantageous. Markets tend to maximize the number of mutually advantageous exchanges.

Individual buyers and sellers cannot always perform the miracle of mutually advantageous exchange on their own. As suggested earlier, high transactions, or trading, costs sometimes keep buyers and sellers from completing an otherwise mutually advantageous exchange. In many cases it is possible for **middlemen** to step in and make the market more efficient. Middlemen are individuals who specialize in bringing buyers and sellers together. Real estate agents are middlemen. Real estate agents are paid a fee by the seller of a house. In return for the fee, the agent provides potential buyers with information about the house at a low cost. The agent earns his or her fee by bringing this house to the notice of potential buyers

Middlemen
Individuals who specialize in bringing buyers and sellers together for mutually advantageous exchange.

to a greater extent than the homeowner, acting alone, could ever do. The middleman in a transaction makes many exchanges possible that might not otherwise take place. In this way, both the buyer and seller gain because of the increase in market information and decrease in trading costs that the middleman makes possible.

In a way, the existence of middlemen tells us a great deal about markets. Why do people pay middlemen, such as real estate agents, to represent them in transactions, such as home sales? The answer is that they can gain by specialization and exchange. Individuals specialize in their own particular trades. They make exchanges that are mutually advantageous. They hire middlemen, who specialize in making trades, because it is cheaper to pay the middleman than to perform the same services themselves. The middleman has an advantage in providing these services. The exchange sets price, determines profits, and sets in motion the powerful forces of incentives that allocate scarce resources to meet unlimited wants. As you can see, the basic economic problem of scarcity and choice is one that humans have learned to deal with in complex and fascinating ways.

APPENDIX: HOW TO READ AND INTERPRET GRAPHS

"A picture is worth a thousand words." There is much truth in this old Chinese saying, and sometimes it is literally true. Sometimes a photo, figure, map, or graph can say more, more precisely, than a long verbal explanation. A road map, for example, tells at a glance what you could never find out as easily or as clearly from a written explanation about distances, directions, and routes.

Economists use graphs in their analysis precisely because these pictures can say so much, so well. Mastery of the economics in this text requires that you master the simple art of reading and using graphs. This brief digression is designed to show you how to read, interpret, and use graphs. If you already feel comfortable with graphs, you need not linger here, but can return if you have trouble later in the text.

The following section explores the most basic use of graphs. If you already know how to read a graph, you can skip on to the second section.

A GRAPH IS A MAP

Most people are familiar with maps. Graphs are like maps in that they picture relationships among different things. The graphs in this appendix have grids to allow you to plot and identify points easily. The horizontal axis is labeled X, and the horizontal units measure quantities of X. The vertical axis is labeled Y, and the vertical units measure quantities of Y.

A point on a graph represents some combination of two things that are associated with one another. Suppose, for example, that X and Y represent your purchases of two grocery items, bread and beer. Suppose further that you currently purchase five units of bread (X) and four units of beer (Y) each week. This combination of purchases is presented graphically in Figure 1-3. Point A which is calculated by counting up four units on the vertical axis and over five units on the horizontal axis, indicates that you purchase

18 Economics: Scarcity and Choice

| FIGURE 1-3 | **Direct Versus Inverse Relationships.** Line segment *AB* illustrates a direct relationship. A direct relationship exists when an increase (or decrease) in the *X* variable is associated with an increase (or decrease) in the *Y* variable. In this instance, both *X* and *Y* increase as we move from *A* to *B*. Line segment *AC* illustrates an inverse relationship. An inverse relationship exists when an increase (or decrease) in the *X* variable is associated with a movement in the opposite direction of the *Y* variable. As we move from *C* to *A*, for example, *X* increases and *Y* decreases. |

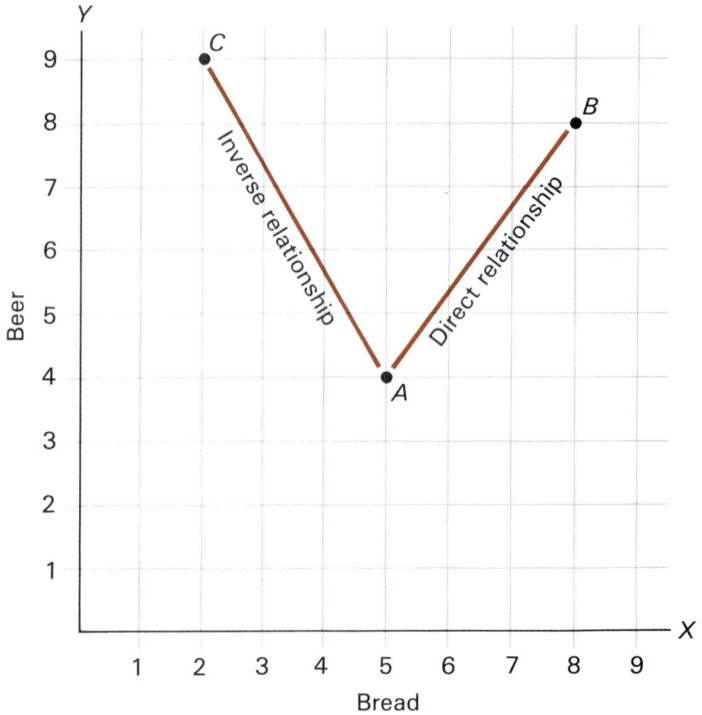

1.10 RELATIONSHIPS AND SLOPE

Direct Relationship
The relationship between two variables such that an increase (or decrease) in one implies a corresponding increase (or decrease) in the other. A direct relationship implies that the variables tend to move together in the same direction.

this combination of these two items rather than some other combination the graph shows to be possible.

Suppose, however, that something happens to alter your behavior, so that next week you purchase more bread (X) and beer (Y). Your new purchase combination is $X = 8$, $Y = 8$, which is labelled point B in Figure 1-3. The line between A and B represents a **direct relationship**. A line like AB, which slopes upward and to the right, says that variables X and Y increased at the same time. This is the sort of relationship economists would expect to see between goods that are used together, such as bacon and eggs or peanut butter and jelly. An increase in the amount of eggs purchased frequently means an increase in bacon purchases. Many economic variables display this direct relationship. The amount that families spend on consumer goods tends to rise when income rises, for example. A line showing a direct relationship also implies that the two variables decline together. This would be the case if you purchase less bacon when you buy fewer eggs.

Many economic variables are related in a different way. Suppose, for example, that your purchase of beer increases, while the amount of bread you buy falls. Your new combination of purchases would be represented by point C ($X = 2$, $Y = 9$) in Figure 1-3. If a line were drawn between A and

Inverse Relationship
The relationship between two variables such that an increase (or decrease) in one implies a decrease (or increase) in the other. An inverse relationship implies that the variables tend to move in opposite directions.

Causation
Causation exists when it can be shown that a change in one variable actually brings about a change in another. Correlation is often taken as evidence of causation, but it is not proof of causation.

Correlation
Two things are correlated when there is a systematic relationship between changes in one variable and changes in the other.

C, it would slope upward and to the left from A to C. This new line, AC, illustrates an **inverse relationship**. This is the sort of relationship we would expect to observe if X and Y are substitute goods. Substitutes are items that can be used in place of one another, such as butter and margarine or pencils and pens. Many economic variables have this inverse relationship. For example, the amount of a good purchased tends to fall when price rises and to rise when price falls. This means that the relationship between an item's price (Y) and its quantity demanded (X) would look like line AC.

In general, a direct relationship between two variables, X and Y, could exist because an increase in X causes Y to increase, or because an increase in Y causes X to increase, or because both X and Y are affected in the same way by some other force or event. The fact of the direct relationship does not tell us what causes this relationship, only that it exists. The fact that two events are correlated with one another does not mean that one caused the other. Likewise, an inverse relationship between X and Y does not tell us anything about what causes that relationship. Variable X may affect Y, Y may affect X, or both could be affected by other forces or events. Again, **correlation** between two events does not imply any **causation** between them.

Let us now look at two other basic relationships. Starting from A in Figure 1-4, suppose that Y increases but X does not. Point D ($X = 5$, $Y = 8$) would show this. When these points are connected, line AD is vertical, showing that Y is changing, but X is not. This suggests that the

FIGURE 1-4   **Relationships in which One Variable Remains Constant.** Line segment *AD* illustrates a relationship in which the *X* variable is constant, while the *Y* variable is changing. Line segment *AE* illustrates a relationship in which the *Y* variable is constant, while the *X* variable is changing.

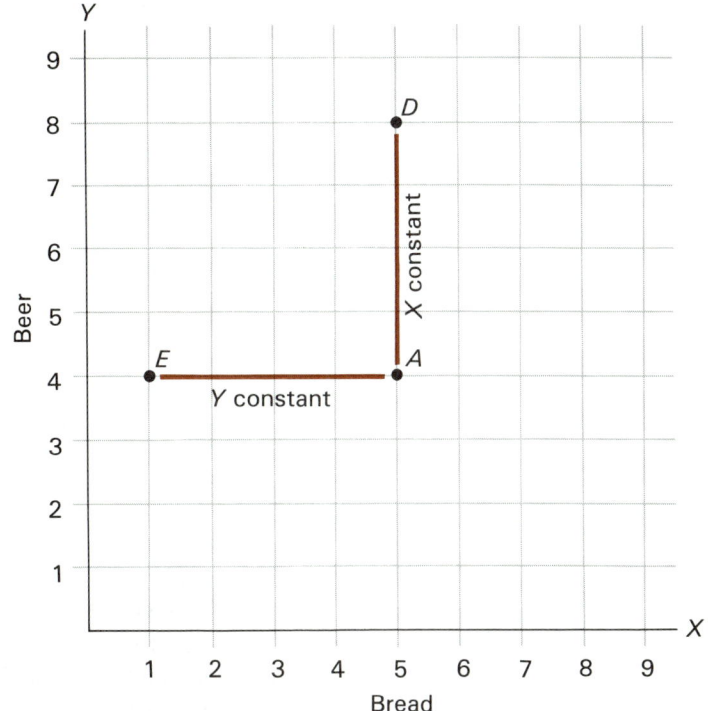

20 Economics: Scarcity and Choice

change in Y has no direct effect on X. This would happen, for example, if your purchases of bread and beer were completely unrelated, so that a decrease in the amount of bread you purchase neither increased or decreased your desired purchases of beer.

Sometimes X changes and Y does not. Starting from A, we can plot a new point E ($X = 1$, $Y = 4$) and draw a line from A to E. This horizontal line shows that Y is constant, but X is changing. This would illustrate a situation in which increased purchases of beer had no effect on the amount of bread purchased.

CALCULATING THE SLOPE OF A LINE

Slope
Mathematical measure of the relative steepness of lines or relationships. The slope is calculated as the change in the Y-axis variable divided by the change in the X-axis variable, or more simply, "the rise over the run."

Economists sometimes find it useful to measure how flat or steep a line or relationship is. The mathematical concept of **slope** is useful here. Slope is defined to be the change in the vertical axis variable divided by the change in the horizontal axis variable or, as most people remember it, the "rise" over the "run."

Let us calculate the slope of line AB in Figure 1-5. The change in the vertical axis is given by $(Y_b - Y_a)$, where the subscripts show that the values refer to starting point A and ending point B, respectively. The rise is therefore $(8 - 4) = 4$, and the run is $(X_b - X_a)$, or $(8 - 5) = 3$. The slope of line AB is therefore

$$\text{Slope} = \frac{\text{rise}}{\text{run}} = \frac{(Y_b - Y_a)}{(X_b - X_a)} = \frac{4}{3} = 1.33$$

This number means that every one-unit increase in bread (X) is accompanied by a 1.33 unit increase in beer (Y) along line AB.

Lines that are steeper have higher slope coefficients. To see this look at the line produced when point F ($X = 6$, $Y = 9$) is connected to point A. Line AF looks steeper than AB and has a higher slope coefficient. The slope of AF is given by

$$\text{Slope} = \frac{(Y_f - Y_a)}{(X_f - X_a)} = \frac{(9 - 4)}{(6 - 5)} = \frac{5}{1} = 5$$

This higher slope tells us something about the relationship between X and Y. A one-unit change in bread (X) is associated with a five-unit change in beer (Y) along line AF.

Slope also measures the steepness of lines like AC in Figure 1-3 that show inverse relationships. The only difference is that the slope coefficient is negative, telling us that the line slopes downward (minus) not upward (plus).

Line AE in Figure 1-4 has a zero slope. Line AD's slope, on the other hand, is infinite because there is no change in the run as the curve rises, making the slope a positive number divided by zero. As an exercise, calculate the numerical value of the slopes of lines AC, AD, and AE.

The graphs and other figures that you will see in the text communicate complicated ideas in an easily assimilated form. You will find that these graphical ideas are frequently used in economics and in other areas where precise communication is important.

FIGURE 1-5

Calculating the Slope of a Line. Line segment *AF* appears to be "steeper" than line segment *AB*. While both line segments illustrate direct relationships, there is some difference between them. The mathematical calculation of the slope of these lines quantifies this difference. This calculation, presented in the text, shows that line segment *AF* has a greater slope than line segment *AB*. This indicates that a given change in the *X* variable is associated with a greater change in the *Y* variable along *AF* than it is along *AB*.

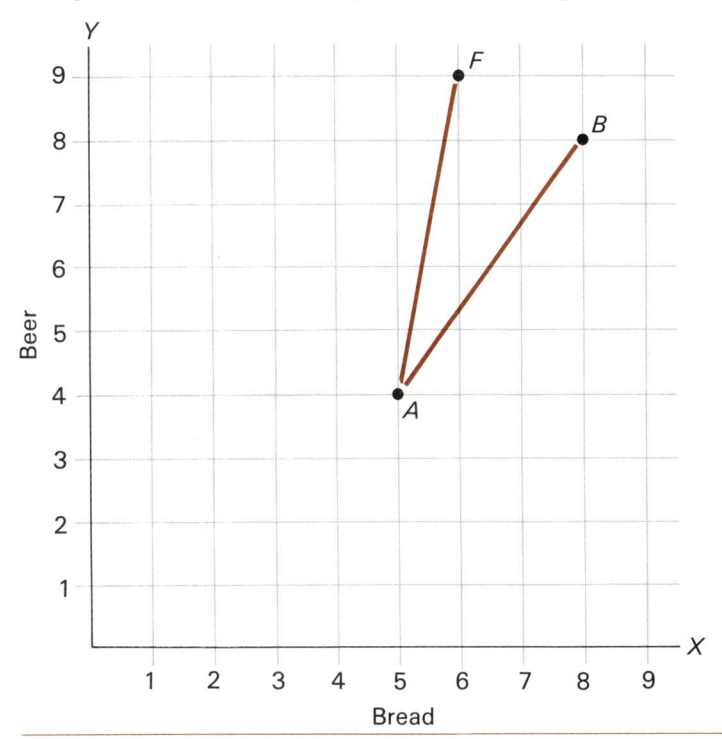

SUMMARY

1.1

1. Economics is the social science that studies the way that human beings deal with the problem of scarcity. Scarcity is the basic economic problem. It implies that the amount of resources available is not sufficient to fulfill all human desires. Resources are limited and therefore we must choose among competing uses for them.

1.2

2. Macroeconomics and microeconomics are the two major subdivisions within the science of economics. Microeconomics observes the choices and behavior of individuals as a basis for understanding economic systems. Macroeconomics looks at the aggregate consequences of these choices and studies national economic policies.

1.3

3. As people fulfill one set of desires, they create other desires. People have an unlimited capacity to create additional desires, while resources to fulfill those desires are limited. This guarantees that scarcity of limited goods and services will always exist in our society.

1.3, 1.4 ➤ 4. We deal with the problem of scarcity through choice, the selection among limited resources. Every choice has its opportunity cost. Opportunity cost is the highest-valued forgone alternative. In return for bearing an opportunity cost, we receive an opportunity benefit, the value which we receive from the alternative we choose.

1.5 ➤ 5. Economists use models to better understand the real-world problems of scarcity and choice. One particularly useful model is the production possibilities frontier. The PPF shows the maximum combinations of two items that can be produced, assuming fixed amounts of resources, such as capital, labor, and time, and fixed technology.

1.5 ➤ 6. We can interpret different production combinations in terms of the PPF. Any point located within the boundary of the PPF is obtainable, but it represents a point of production where some resources are either being used inefficiently or are not being used at all. Output can be increased by employing more resources or utilizing the existing resources more efficiently. Because of the assumptions of constant time, technology, and resources, any point lying outside the production possibilities frontier cannot be obtained.

1.6 ➤ 7. With the passage of time, production capabilities within an economy can expand. The production possibilities frontier can therefore shift outward. Any relaxation of our original assumptions (fixed time, technology, and resources) will allow such a shift to occur.

1.7 ➤ 8. Sacrificing present consumption to produce more capital goods increases an economy's ability to produce goods and services of all kinds in the future. This process is known as capital formation. It is a major factor in shifting the production possibilities frontier outward over time. This concept can be applied to both human capital (skills and knowledge) and physical goods (machinery and equipment).

1.8 ➤ 9. Specialization and exchange are fundamental concepts of economics. The process of exchange allows individuals to trade the goods and services that they produce for the other goods and services that they desire. People can specialize in the production of certain things, thereby becoming more efficient in their production, then exchange these items for other goods and services. Specialization is therefore possible only when the ability to exchange exists.

1.9 ➤ 10. Prices, profits, and entrepreneurs are all important to the markets. Prices and profits help allocate resources. Entrepreneurs take the risks that are needed to bring goods to market and to make improvements in production. Markets facilitate exchange and therefore promote the efficient use of scarce resources.

1.9 ➤ 11. Middlemen provide an important link between buyers and sellers by creating mutually beneficial markets to facilitate exchange. Middlemen provide market information to buyers and sellers at a price below what it would cost them to gather the information themselves. Middlemen are, therefore, an example of the specialization process.

1.10 ➤ 12. Graphs are useful devices that can illustrate real world concepts and help us understand them more clearly. Graphs can represent direct and inverse relationships, for example, to show how two events or variables are related. The slope of a line also measures the nature of a relationship between two things.

DISCUSSION QUESTIONS

1.3 > 1. What is the basic economic problem, and why is it that society has never been able to solve it? What role does social choice play in attempting to deal with this problem?

1.4 > 2. Assume you work for $6 an hour at your job. You have the choice of working an eight hour day, or working one half day (four hours) at your job and working the other half day as a lifeguard for $30. Suppose your preference is to take the entire day off to play golf. What is your opportunity cost? What is your opportunity benefit?

1.2 > 3. What are the two main subdivisions of economics? Explain how they differ. In what ways are they similar? Which would be used to determine how employment in the economy would react to a business recession?

1.5 > 4. If you had one week to learn how to play golf and tennis, you could spend the entire week playing golf and learn no tennis, the entire week playing tennis and learn no golf, or you could divide your time between some combination of the two.
> a. How might you display these combinations graphically?
> b. What assumptions must be made?
> c. What would happen to your tennis game if you wanted to spend more time learning golf?

1.5, 1.6 > 5. There are points of production that lie within or beyond the production possibilities frontier.
> a. Do these points represent maximum production?
> b. What do they tell you about the use of resources?
> c. How might an economy reach the point lying beyond its production possibilities frontier?

1.3, 1.4 > 6. If you choose to pursue your education and obtain a law degree instead of working now at a part-time job, what economic concept are you practicing? Does this entail an opportunity cost or benefit?

1.3, 1.8 > 7. What might be a disadvantage of specialization? Consider the field of medicine. Would you go to a doctor specializing in brain surgery for a complete medical examination? Extend this concept to our economy, and determine what other problems and benefits specialization offers.

1.4, 1.8 > 8. Your car is in need of repair. You have a full-time job, work overtime, and therefore have very little free time. You have most of the knowledge necessary to fix your car, but you would have to expend time and money to buy the parts and spend time fixing it. The local service station has offered to fix your car for $150, including parts and labor. What economic factors will affect your decision and on what basis will your decision finally be made?

1.9 > 9. In planning your vacation, you have decided to use the service of a travel agent.
> a. What role does the agent play, and what economic concept is this job an example of?
> b. Will any exchange(s) take place? How many parties will be involved?
> c. Who will benefit from the exchange(s)?

SELECTED READINGS

Blaug, Mark. *The Methodology of Economics: Or How Economists Explain.* New York: Cambridge University Press, 1980.

Buchanan, James M. "Toward an Analysis of Closed Behavioral Systems." In James Buchanan and Robert Tollison (eds.), *Theory of Public Choice.* Ann Arbor: University of Michigan Press, 1972.

Cairncross, Sir Alec. "Economics in Theory and Practice." *American Economic Review* (May 1985), pp 1–14.

Friedman, Milton. *Essays in Positive Economics.* Chicago: University of Chicago Press, 1953, chap. 1.

Heilbroner, Robert L. *The Worldly Philosophers,* 5th ed. New York: Simon & Schuster, Inc., 1980, chap. 2.

Koopmans, Tjalling C. "Economics among the Sciences." *American Economic Review,* 69 (March 1979), pp. 1–13.

Mundell, Robert A. *Man and Economics.* New York: McGraw-Hill Book Company, 1968, chap. 1.

Stigler, George J. "The Case, If Any, for Economic Literacy." In George J. Stigler, *The Intellectual and the Marketplace.* Cambridge: Harvard University Press, 1984.

CHAPTER 2

An Introduction to the Economic Way of Thinking

Having read the chapter, reviewed the chapter summary, and completed the *Study Guide* exercises, you should be able to:

CRIS

2.1 **FIVE FOUNDATIONS:** Describe the five foundations of the economic way of thinking.

2.2 **UTILITY DEFINED:** Define the economic term utility and explain why utility is subjective.

2.3 **MARGINAL DEFINED:** Define marginal and discuss how decisions are made by comparing marginal benefit and marginal cost.

2.4 **SCIENTIFIC METHOD:** List and explain the three major parts of the scientific method (i.e. induction, deduction, and verification) and be able to identify the differences between them.

2.5 **POSITIVE AND NORMATIVE ECONOMICS:** Compare and contrast positive and normative economics and be able to identify both positive and normative economic issues.

2.6 **FALLACY OF COMPOSITION:** Explain the logical problem referred to as the fallacy of composition.

2.7 **POST HOC REASONING:** Define post hoc reasoning and discuss how cause and effect relationships are related to post hoc reasoning.

2.8 **CORRELATION AND CAUSATION:** Explain the difference between correlation and causation and discuss how the distinction between the two is related to post hoc reasoning.

2.9 **SECONDARY EFFECTS:** Define secondary effects and explain why they are so important in our economy.

2.10 **ECONOMISTS:** Discuss the many different roles that economists play and the functions they serve in a modern economy.

Economist
One who observes the human choice process with the goal of analyzing, understanding, and predicting human economic behavior.

We learned in Chapter 1 that economics is concerned with how people allocate scarce resources among their unlimited wants and desires. Economics is really a study of human behavior. This chapter builds on this base by describing the methods that economists use in analyzing social choices and introducing the economic way of looking at these choices.

THE FIVE FOUNDATIONS OF THE ECONOMIC WAY OF THINKING

Economists, psychologists, and sociologists are all social scientists, but their techniques of analysis are somewhat different. They approach the analysis of a problem with different ways of thinking. Most economists would agree that there is a distinct economic way of thinking. This way of thinking is really built around five basic concepts concerning the nature of the economic world of scarcity and choice. Much of economics is simply common sense once you understand these basic concepts.

All Economic Goods Cost Someone Something

The old adage that there is no such thing as a free lunch is really true. All economic goods cost something, because in a world of scarce resources, all economic goods have an opportunity cost. Someone must give up something in order for production of a particular good or service to take place. There is no free lunch when an opportunity cost must be borne.

The satisfaction of wants and desires depends upon the use of resources. Almost no resources are so readily available from nature that we can have all we want without paying a price for them. Goods that sometimes appear to be "free" are usually not free. When you use a public park, it may be "free" to you at the time, in the sense that you do not have to pay an admission fee, but your taxes and those of other taxpayers provide the resources to build and maintain the park. On a more basic level, the park is not free because providing the park means giving up the other desirable uses of the land. If, for example, the land could have been used for apartment buildings, potential apartment residents bear a cost in that they have given up the chance to live in desirable apartments so that the land could be used as a park.

The concept that all economic goods have an opportunity cost is important because it means that no economic policy or individual action is costless. Individuals and society must weigh the benefits of any action against its opportunity cost. If, for example, someone proposes that the city library system be expanded and says that the increased services will be free to the public, you should realize that this person is wrong. If city resources are scarce, the increased library services will have an opportunity cost. People who vote for more libraries or other "free" goods should know that these items have a cost. Does the existence of this cost mean that the extra library books are undesirable? An economist would say that bigger libraries are desirable so long as the benefits are at least as great as the opportunity cost.

Human Beings Are Self-Interested and Act Accordingly

Economists believe that people act in their own self-interest. Your goal as an individual is to satisfy your wants and desires to the best of your ability

2.2 UTILITY DEFINED

Utility
Satisfaction or use value derived from a course of action or choice.

2.1 FIVE FOUNDATIONS

Incentives
The forces that influence or encourage an action or choice. Economic incentives exert a strong effect on the choice behavior of members of our society.

2.1 FIVE FOUNDATIONS

Marginal
The effects of one additional unit that is produced or consumed.

---

given the resources that you have. Economists assume that you try to get the most satisfaction from each dollar's worth of your resources. When you have to choose between two equally desirable opportunities, for example, you choose the least costly opportunity. If two opportunities have equal costs, you choose the most desirable one.

Individuals do not deliberately waste their resources. They act to maximize their satisfaction, given the resources available. In other words, they try to maximize their **utility,** given the constraint of resource limitations. Economists use the term utility to refer to the value or satisfaction that an individual derives from a choice. The utility of an expected choice or course of action is the benefit or satisfaction that it provides. Individuals have different tastes and preferences, so the utility that a choice, such as a hamburger, provides varies from person to person. Economists use utility as a concept to describe individual choices, not to compare one individual with another. The economic concept of utility will be discussed in more detail in Chapter 16.

Incentives Matter

Economists hold that **incentives** are the guideposts that individuals use in allocating scarce resources. Incentives are factors that help determine the best choice. Prices are among the most important incentives that exist. Suppose, for example, that you had to choose between two equally desirable choices, alternatives that would provide you with the same utility. Which one would you pick? If you are acting in your own self-interest, as the last point stated, you would pick the one with the lowest price. If the prices of the two goods you must choose between changed, then the incentives would also change, and so might your choice. Money prices are only one set of incentives that guide our behavior, however. Grades in school are a nonmonetary incentive. If you have only a fixed amount of time to study, you will likely spend time on the subject with the greatest potential grade gain and ignore the subject with the least potential grade loss. Grades are guideposts that help you allocate scarce time so as to maximize your utility.

The importance of incentives cannot be overstated. Incentives guide our lives everyday. Many government policies depend on incentives to work. Suppose Congress passed a $1 per gallon gasoline tax increase, for example, and gave subsidy payments to all bicycle users. This policy would provide a strong incentive to use bicycles more and automobiles less. If you had to go five blocks to the local grocery store for a loaf of bread, your choice between the use of your car and your bicycle would be affected by this incentive structure. The higher the cost of gasoline, the less likely you would be to use the car. The greater the subsidy to bicycle use, the more likely you would be to choose the bicycle. Economic incentives form a very powerful force in our lives.

Human Beings Make Decisions at the Margin

Most economic decisions concern small changes in economic behavior. **Marginal** refers to one additional unit of anything that is consumed or produced. For example, if you have consumed three beers and are considering drinking another, you are choosing at the margin. The marginal beer is the one upon which you are deciding. You are concerned with the additional item, not with those items about which you have already made choices.

2.3 MARGINAL DEFINED

Marginal analysis is important for two reasons. First, many choices really are made at the margin. Individuals frequently make decisions by deciding how to spend the next dollar, then the one after that, then the one after that, and on and on. Second, marginal analysis is important because economists can accurately model or describe how individuals make choices at the margin. The economic models of marginal choice are powerful and useful in describing real-world behavior.

Here is an example of how marginal analysis works. Suppose that we want to predict the number of workers that a moving van firm will employ. Using marginal analysis, we would ask the question, would the firm hire the first worker? Assuming that the firm's owners act in their own self-interest (they wish to maximize their income), they will compare the **marginal cost** of hiring the first worker with the potential **marginal benefit** of his or her employment. The first worker is employed if the worker's marginal contribution to profit is greater than or equal to the cost of employment. Assuming that this condition holds and the first worker is hired, then will the second worker be hired? Again the economist compares the cost to the firm of this choice with the firm's potential benefit. The process is repeated until the firm stops adding workers because the wage cost is more than the additional profits on the margin. In this way, we can analyze the employment choice and predict the employment actions of self-interested firms.

The process of marginal analysis may seem complicated, but economics uses graphical tools, which are introduced in the appendix to this chapter and used extensively in Chapters 16–19, to simplify the process. Marginal analysis has proven to be a powerful tool in analyzing the choice process.

Marginal Cost
The change in total cost that occurs when production changes by one unit; in other words, the extra cost of producing one more item.

Marginal Benefit (Utility)
The amount of satisfaction received from the production or consumption of one additional unit of a good or service.

KEY CONCEPTS 2.2, 2.3

The marginal unit is the last unit produced or consumed. Marginal utility, therefore, is the utility, or satisfaction, received from consuming the last unit. Marginal cost is the cost of producing the last unit. Marginal cost and marginal benefit guide economic decisions.

2.1 FIVE FOUNDATIONS

Information Has a Cost

When we make an economic decision, we carefully consider both the costs and benefits of that decision. When you shop for an automobile, you examine different makes and models and compare prices closely. Gathering this information takes time and effort, and at some point in your shopping it is in your self-interest to stop doing research. You have to consider whether an additional day spent looking at automobiles and gathering information about them is going to save you enough in costs to warrant your expenditure of the additional time and effort. You must make the search decision at the margin, just as we described in the previous foundation of economic thinking. Is the marginal utility of one more day of gathering information worth the marginal cost? At some point the answer to this question becomes no. It is in your self-interest to conserve time and effort as a scarce resource, just as it is to conserve money. We make economic decisions with the amount of information that we feel is worth its cost to us.

Information is scarce and costly because producing information uses up scarce and costly economic resources. Information about economic decisions is an entire industry in itself. As we noted in the last chapter, economic middlemen serve valuable market functions by providing market information to both buyers and sellers. Through specialization, middlemen are able to sell market information at a cost below that at which the buyers or sellers could produce the information for themselves.

The existence of information costs is important because it helps us understand why some individual choices are made. Suppose, for example, that we observe two automobile purchasers who set out to purchase identical cars. One buyer, a busy orthopedic surgeon, buys a car after only an afternoon of shopping. The surgeon pays a higher price than a college student on spring break, who has spent a week comparing prices all around the area. Is the surgeon irrational to pay more for the car? No, he is not. The opportunity cost of shopping is much higher for the surgeon than it is for the college student. The surgeon may give up thousands of dollars of medical fees for each day spent car shoppping; while the college student's opportunity cost will be far less. It is therefore predictable that, all else being equal, the college student will spend more time searching for the best deal and may, therefore, pay less than the surgeon. The surgeon would not be acting in his own self-interest if he spent an extra day, with an opportunity cost of $1000 in medical income, to save an extra $500 on the car.

Examples of Economic Behavior

Let's take a look at how the five basic concepts of economic analysis apply to the real world in which we live. We can understand many economic events if we apply the foundations of the economic way of thinking to the choices that individuals make.

The airfare from New York to Washington is about $60, and the trip takes approximately one hour. The Metroliner train service for the same trip costs about $25 and takes four hours. The airplane on this route is seldom occupied by unemployed or retired persons. On the other hand, the train is seldom populated by corporate presidents, wealthy travelers, or doctors and lawyers. Why do you think this is true? Is it that unemployed or retired individuals cannot afford the $60 plane fare? Not exactly. Those who use the plane spend $35 more dollars for their trip than those who take the train, but they save three hours of traveling time. A quick division of $35 by three hours will indicate why the two groups make different choices. If any travelers can earn more than $11.67 per hour during these hours, they are better off taking the plane. The opportunity cost of riding the train is three lost hours. If you are unemployed or retired, the chance to save $35 could well be worth using up three extra hours in travel. However, if you earn more than $11.67 per hour, the saving of lost wages would outweigh the extra cost of the airfare.

Here is another example of opportunity cost, incentives, and human behavior. Suppose that next Wednesday you are scheduled to take midterm exams in both calculus and economics. You will be devoting the larger part of your evenings between now and then to studying for these exams. Today your economics instructor announces that there will be a review session in economics held next Tuesday night on campus. You begin to decide whether to go to the review or spend the time studying for your calculus exam. What do you think would affect your choice of whether or not to attend the economics review? Let's assume that your instructor announces that the material in the review session will definitely be very important for the midterm exam. Does this change your choice? This information alters your incentives and increases the opportunity cost of not attending. If you are now in danger of failing economics, would this affect your choice? All these concerns would affect the opportunity cost of not attending the review session. Your behavior would most likely be based on a self-interested decision to get the most benefit from your available study time. Your human behavior would have been affected by economic considerations.

THE SCIENTIFIC METHOD

2.4 SCIENTIFIC METHOD

Scientific Method
The process of induction, deduction, and the verification of hypotheses used by economists (and all scientists) to analyze problems.

Economists are scientists and, like all other scientists, use the **scientific method** to analyze problems and construct models of economic behavior. In this way, economists can test their models and theories and improve their ability to understand and predict economic behavior. Models, as discussed in the last chapter, are simplified descriptions of real-world problems that allow us to better understand the actual events and choices. The production possibilities frontier was an economic model introduced in Chapter 1. The PPF model helps us better understand the opportunity costs that must be faced when choices are made.

There are three major parts to the scientific method as applied to understanding human behavior. The first part is the inductive approach. When economists and other scientists use **induction,** they formulate general behavior rules from real-world observations. These assumptions form the basis of the models that economists build of economic behavior. The assumptions that individuals act in their own self-interest and that they make decisions on the margin, for example, are behavior rules that economists have derived by analyzing the choices that people really do make. Using inductive reasoning, economists and other scientists reason from the particular facts to the general rules.

Induction
The part of the scientific method concerned with observing human beings and using these observations to derive hypotheses or general behavior rules.

Why do scientists attempt to build models based on inductive reasoning? Having a general rule is more useful than observing and analyzing the behavior of every living individual. It refines huge volumes of facts to workable conclusions and enables scientists to predict with relative accuracy. A model is a specific description of economic behavior based on a set of ideas and beliefs that form a general theory. Theories are systems of accepted assumptions, principles and general rules of procedure used to analyze and predict behavior. Theories cannot always perfectly predict the behavior of every individual. They are, however, powerful tools in understanding how choices are made in general. The real world is so complex and the number of variables so large that it is not feasible, even with the aid of the most advanced computer techniques, to take into account every single variable that can have an impact upon a phenomenon that economists wish to study. The task of economists is therefore largely a matter of selecting the key variables that are likely to have an impact upon the outcome. For this reason, economists acting without the use of computers may outperform computerized forecasts if they discern the key variables and those charged with programming computers do not.

Deduction
The part of the scientific method concerned with developing theories or hypotheses, then testing them against real-world facts and data.

Hypothesis
A supposition or conjecture advanced as an explanation for certain facts or events.

A second important part of the scientific method is **deduction.** While inductive reasoning moves from specific observation to general theories, deductive reasoning runs in the opposite direction. General theories come first, then they are tested to see if they accurately predict real-world behavior. Economists formulate untested rules or principles called **hypotheses.** The economist calls upon intuition, logic, or general understanding in setting a hypothesis about some economic event or individual choice. For example, based upon logic and some knowledge of individuals, he or she might guess that consumers buy more ice cream during the summer than during the winter. From this, a general hypothesis might be formed that the demand for ice cream is inversely related to the outside temperature. The economist could then test this hypothesis against real-world data by comparing figures on ice cream sales each week of the year to the temperature during that week. If real-world observations made the suggested theory seem unlikely, it would be rejected.

The third part of the scientific method involves the empirical **verification** of the general rules or hypotheses that are developed through induction or deduction, or both. This is an area in which social scientists are on softer ground than physical scientists such as chemists, physicists, or geologists. It is relatively easy to verify some hypotheses in the physical sciences. If you combine two molecules of hydrogen and one molecule of oxygen in the earth's atmosphere, you will get a molecule of water every time. The physical science hypothesis that combining the two hydrogen and one oxygen atom will yield one water molecule can be rigorously tested. Human behavior is not exactly that way. Humans are not always the same and do change behavior over time. People's behavior is affected by the forces around them at the time. It is quite difficult, then, to have as highly structured and controlled laboratory experiments on human behavior as is possible with chemical elements. In fact, many such experiments are forbidden by ethical and professional considerations.

Human behavior models, theories, and hypotheses are valuable predictive tools, but they are not capable of predicting with 100 percent accuracy. Their value rests in their ability to increase our understanding of real-world behavior and aid in the formulation of private and public policies and actions by accurately predicting behavior at a given time.

Verification
The part of scientific method concerned with comparing theories with measurements taken from the real world to determine if the theories are valid.

POSITIVE AND NORMATIVE ECONOMICS

2.5 POSITIVE AND NORMATIVE ECONOMICS

Since economics concerns itself with choice making, it is confronted with two very different types of problems. Economists are often called upon both to predict human behavior as it is and to comment on whether that behavior is in the best interest of an individual, group, or nation. That is, sometimes economists are asked to present verifiable facts concerning some issue or problem, and at other times they are asked to present judgments, or opinions, concerning those same policies. It is important that we always remember that statements concerning verifiable facts are fundamentally different from judgments or opinions based on those facts.

The science of **positive economics** is concerned with the analysis of actual human behavior and the facts that this analysis provides. Positive economics analyzes the effects of changes in economic variables on human behavior in some measurable way. As such, it deals with what is, or what actually exists and can be verified. In general, a positive statement is one that can be proven to be true or false and is not a matter of opinion or personal values. An example of a positive economic statement would be: "If the price of gasoline increases, consumers will buy less gasoline, all else being equal." One can verify whether consumers buy more or less gasoline at $1.50 per gallon as opposed to $.75 per gallon, with all other economic incentives held constant. Positive economics is factual scientific economics. It can be verified and makes no value judgments.

Positive Economics
Scientific, factual economics that deals with what actually exists and can be verified, without the use of value judgment or opinions.

Positive economic analysis cannot tell us what is best for the country or best for ourselves. We each must make these value judgments for ourselves based upon our own preferences and self-interest. Positive economics teaches us how the economy works. It does not tell us whether the way it works is "right" or "wrong." The value of positive economics lies in the understanding it makes possible. If individuals do not understand how the economy works, they may make choices that do not yield the results they expected. If you do not understand the economics advocated by a political candidate, for example, you may end up voting for someone who supports policies to which you are greatly opposed.

Normative economics, on the other hand, is concerned with ethical and value judgments. Normative economic analysis describes the economy as "it should be" from the viewpoint of the individual doing the speaking. It does not address scientifically measurable statements, but offers value judgments such as "America should increase foreign aid to underdeveloped countries." "Consumers should buy more milk and less beer." "Students should study more and play less." Your values on these issues might be different from those of the speaker. Neither viewpoint is necessarily "right" or "wrong."

> **Normative Economics**
> The type of economic analysis that describes how the economy should be, through the use of value judgments.

Positive and normative economic analyses are very different in how they approach problems. Positive analysis seeks to describe and understand the existing world. Normative analysis uses the information and data that positive economics provides to argue for or against particular policies or allocations of resources. In this sense, positive analysis provides the ammunition that normative speakers use in their arguments.

Many government choices are controversial because they make some individuals better off and harm others. Which group should government support, the gainers or the losers? A representative democracy, such as the one we live in, is designed for the purpose of making this sort of normative judgment. Positive economics can be used to define all the possible alternatives open to a country or an individual, but the choices rest with the voters and their representatives, not the economists. Positive economics can attempt to point out all the costs and benefits of any course of action. It is then the responsibility of the voters to weigh those costs and benefits and decide the course of action that is right or wrong for the country or themselves. Whenever you cast your vote in the polling booth, you have accepted the responsibility of understanding the facts concerning an economic issue and are letting your elected officials know what value system you advocate.

It is important to remember that economists who advocate a particular policy are going beyond the reach of positive economics. They address what is right or wrong given their individual value judgments. Their personal value system may be no more valid in the voting booth than is yours. In the final analysis, you and the economist are both only permitted to pull the lever once. All individuals, to exercise responsible citizenship, must address economic issues armed with positive economics and then decide upon the normative aspects of the issues themselves.

LOGICAL FALLACIES AND ECONOMIC REASONING

So far we have learned the important foundations of economic thinking and a little about how economists view social problems. It is a major goal of this text to teach students to understand how economists think. That goal, however, is far from completed as yet. Being armed with a little economic knowledge is much like being the sorcerer's apprentice of the childhood fairy tale. With just a little economic understanding, it is possible, and even easy, to make big mistakes. Even people with substantial formal training in economics sometimes fall prey to several common logical errors and confusions about human behavior. These logical errors can occur in any form of analysis and are not limited to the field of economics. Since much of economics is simply common sense and logic applied to individual behavior, we should be aware of these logical fallacies so that they do not creep into our economic analysis and render our conclusions invalid. Three important logical mistakes are the fallacy of composition, post hoc reasoning, and the failure to consider secondary effects.

The Fallacy of Composition

> **2.6 FALLACY OF COMPOSITION**

Individuals frequently make the mistake of believing that what is true for an individual or a small part of a group is also true for the entire group. A classic example of this problem involves football. If one person stands up at an exciting football game, he or she gets a better view of the field. If everyone stands up, however, only those in front get a better view. What might benefit an individual does not necessarily benefit the group. This type of error is referred to as the **fallacy of composition.**

Fallacy of Composition
The incorrect belief that what is true for the individual is also true for the entire group.

A second example of the fallacy of composition comes from the microprocessor chip industry. When one manufacturer developed an inexpensive way to make chips, there was a great opportunity for profit. Some firms earned many millions of dollars in profits in the early years of microprocessor chip production. When all producers gained the ability to produce chips inexpensively, however, supply greatly increased and the market price of chips fell. The entire group of chip producers may have even made fewer profits than before. What was good for one unit of the group was not necessarily good for the entire unit.

Suppose that the federal government were to decide to double your income tomorrow. This would certainly make you better off. If the federal government simply doubled the incomes of all citizens, would everyone be better off? The answer is no. As people began to spend their extra income, they would have to compete for the existing stock of goods and services. Prices would rise until supply and demand were in balance again; consequently, the group as a whole would not be better off than before. What was good for the individual was not necessarily good for the group.

The fallacy of composition makes it even more necessary to understand both microeconomics and macroeconomics. Individuals make decisions. Microeconomics studies these decisions taken individually. These choices can have different effects in total, however. Macroeconomics studies the aggregate effects. As you begin to apply your understanding of economics, be sure to test out your conclusions at both the individual and aggregate levels.

Post Hoc Reasoning
The principle that states that the chronological order in which events occur is related to the cause and effect of those events. It incorrectly assumes that correlation implies causation.

Post Hoc Reasoning

> **2.7 POST HOC REASONING**

Another common error in logical and economic analysis is **post hoc reasoning.** We have a tendency to believe that the cause and effect of two events have something to do with the chronological order in which they occur. This is frequently not true. Post hoc reasoning fails to consider that just because some event occurs before some other event, the first event may not be the cause of the second. People who make post hoc errors draw the wrong conclusion because they mix up cause and effect or think they see causation when there is none. An example will make the problem of post hoc reasoning clear.

Suppose that your uncle is fond of drinking straight bourbon whiskey. He believes that this libation has great medicinal powers. The next time you have a common cold, he recommends a large drink of bourbon and says that in a week or 10 days you will feel much better. You respond by taking the drink. Over the next 10 days you recover normally, and your uncle considers this proof positive that he was right about the medicinal powers of bourbon whiskey. He has fallen prey to post hoc reasoning. Just because you drank the bourbon and then got well does not imply that the bourbon caused your recuperation.

2.8 CORRELATION AND CAUSATION

Another way of stating this concept is that just because two events are correlated or associated with one another does not mean that one causes another. That is, just because two things happen at the same time does not necessarily mean that they are related to each other or that one event causes the other. A frequent debate among economists deals with whether rapid increases in money wage rates cause inflation or are caused by inflation. The cause and effect is not at all clear and therefore the application of economic theory to the problem should be made with careful consideration given to the post hoc reasoning problem.

Ignoring Secondary Effects

2.9 SECONDARY EFFECTS

Secondary Effects
Results of an initial action that are realized over time, often having the opposite effect of that action and frequently being of much greater importance.

The problem of ignoring **secondary effects** is closely related to the error of post hoc reasoning. Any cause-and-effect relationship can have both direct and secondary effects. Sometimes the secondary effects of an activity are not only opposite those original effects of an action but also much larger in magnitude. For example, the initial effects of a smallpox vaccination might be a sore arm and an ugly scab for two weeks. The long-run, or secondary, effects may well be a life-saving immunity to smallpox. A person who ignored the secondary effects in this example might argue against smallpox vaccinations because they make people slightly ill. A person who considers the secondary effects would argue in favor of these vaccinations because of their tremendous benefits. Responsible economic policy requires us to examine secondary effects.

The economic way of thinking provides useful tools that economists use to understand and predict human behavior. Economists use the scientific method to develop models and theories concerning microeconomic choices and their macroeconomic effects. This positive economic analysis provides information that is used in the normative debates that lead to government policies. The economic way of thinking is a powerful set of tools to analyze human behavior, but it is important that this thinking avoid logical errors, such as the fallacy of composition, post hoc reasoning, and the failure to consider secondary effects.

THE ROLE OF ECONOMISTS IN INDUSTRY, ACADEME, AND GOVERNMENT

2.10 ECONOMISTS

What do economists do in the real world? Economics provides those who study it with a powerful box of tools to use in analyzing, understanding, and predicting human behavior. This means that economists can be usefully employed in a variety of situations to analyze a wide variety of social and economic problems. All economic analysis has the basic goal of understanding, interpreting, and predicting human behavior, but economists use their knowledge in many different sectors of our economy in many different ways. Most economists work in private industry, the academic world, and government service. A small profession comprising only about 100,000 individuals in the United States, economists have responsibility and influence that far exceeds their relative number.

Economists in the Private Sector

Private industry economists are primarily engaged in analyzing and predicting behavior in the economy as it specifically relates to the products or services produced or used by their employers. For example, the chief economist of Exxon Corporation provides the firm's management with analyses and predictions about the domestic and world demand for petroleum and petroleum products. Economists working for a firm such as Exxon would also be responsible for analyzing domestic and world interest rates; expected changes in the exchange rates of currencies in the countries in which the firm buys and sells products; expected future wage rates; inflation rates; current and expected government tax, spending, and regulatory policies; and other important events.

Most of the economic analyses carried on in the private sector are specifically related to the goal of maximizing profits for the corporation. Consequently, most of the studies prepared by private-industry economists are the private property of the corporation and may or may not be released to the public.

Other economists are employed in the private sector by labor unions, nonprofit organizations, and a variety of other organizations. Economists are employed in the private sector because economic analyses provide information that private firms need to successfully compete in their economic environment.

Private economic research firms, such as Data Resources International, founded by the prominent economist Otto Eckstein, sell their analytical services to industry and government on a contract basis. For example, a customer might be interested in determining the expected interest rates for housing construction loans in 1990 and their accompanying impact on the demand for private residential homes. This customer would contract with D.R.I. for a complete analysis and report. Instead of having to maintain a staff of economists on their payroll at all times, clients can simply buy the specific services that they need from private research firms. Economic research firms are an example of specialization and exchange at work.

Economists in Academe

Over half of all economists in the United States are affiliated with a college or university in some way. Their duties range from teaching students a basic knowledge of how the economy works to highly specialized graduate work, training new Ph.Ds to become professional economists.

Much economic research is done in the academic setting, as well as in the private sector. Academic economists build logical, statistical, mathematical, and intuitive models of human behavior as it applies to a wide variety of economic topics.

PROMINENT ECONOMIST

Kenneth Ewart Boulding (1910–)

Born in Liverpool, England, in 1910, Kenneth Ewart Boulding attended Oxford University, graduating with first class honors. He received his M.A. degree in 1939 from the University of Chicago. He began his teaching career at the University of Edinburgh in Scotland in 1934 and later had positions with Colgate University, Fisk University, Iowa State College, McGill University, and the University of Michigan.

Professor Boulding made one of his first major contributions to economics with his now classic principles of economics text, *Economic Analysis.* As Boulding's career developed, he moved beyond the accepted bounds of economic science to include concepts from the disciplines of sociology, psychology, history, and many of the other social sciences in his analyses of social problems. Kenneth Boulding has, through effort and circumstance, developed into a "renaissance man" in the scientific world.

In recognition of his accomplishments, Kenneth Boulding was awarded the American Economic Association's John Bates Clark medal in 1949. He has held distinguished professorships at prestigious universities all over the world and continues to be a major force for change in the economics profession.

Much of the government funded research carried on in universities eventually is released to the government and the private sector as public property. This type of research is often of a more general nature than that carried on by private industry. Academic research is usually geared to broaden and expand the frontiers of economic knowledge; as such, it is not normally related to the specific products or services of an individual firm.

A good example of academic research might be a study of the expected increase in all industrial output and the reduction in unemployment in the economy if the government were to reduce taxes by 10 percent in 1990. Such a study would reach across all industries, not just a single firm. Both private industry and our government frequently contract with economists in the academic world for specific research projects.

Economists in Government

Economists are employed at just about every level of government to analyze and predict economic behavior as it applies to government policies. For example, the Environmental Protection Agency employs staff economists who analyze and predict the pollution behavior of steelmaking firms, among other things. These studies are used to help determine policies to curb pollution.

Developing effective government policy is a difficult task. At first glance, it might seem easy to pass laws forbidding steel firms from releasing ash into the atmosphere. If the restrictions are too severe, however, steel firms cannot operate profitably and must shut down, depriving the firm's owners of profit, the employees of their jobs and incomes, and the economy of the valuable steel output. These lost productions and incomes are the opportunity cost of a cleaner environment. One way that economists aid in making government policy is to analyze the situation and propose alternative policies, such as pollution taxes, pollution tax credits, mandated abatement equipment, pollution output standards, and the like. Some of these policies may reduce the opportunity cost of environmental improvements. All of these proposals, however, require a careful analysis of how both producers and consumers will react to the legislation and whether or not their expected behavior will meet the goals for which the legislation was intended.

Economists also work at the highest levels of government. The President of the United States gets advice directly from his Council of Economic Advisors. These prominent economists are charged with keeping the President advised of the current state of the economy, as well as the expected impact of federal government policies on the economy and domestic and foreign policy. In addition, many members of the President's cabinet have been economists. The Federal Reserve System, the central bank of the United States, formulates policy with the assistance of many staff economists. Every major department of the federal government employs economic expertise to analyze and predict behavior as it applies to its function.

As you can see, there are a variety of tasks assigned to the professional economists in our country. They are all responsible in some way for the basic function of analyzing, understanding, and effectively predicting economic behavior.

APPENDIX: THE ECONOMIST'S TOOLBOX —MARGINAL AND AVERAGE ANALYSIS

This chapter introduced the idea of marginal analysis and discussed how economists use the idea of behavior on the margin to describe and analyze human behavior. It is frequently the case that economic behavior on the margin is different from the overall trend in that activity. When this happens, actions on the margin are different from actions on average. This section dips into the economist's toolbox of ideas and concepts to help you understand the relationship between marginal and average measures, the differences between them, and why these differences are important.

MARGINAL VERSUS AVERAGE

Marginal analysis refers to events that involve small changes in economic activity. Average analysis refers to the overall trend in economic activity. In macroeconomics, for example, economists use these two concepts to describe the relationship between income and the amount spent on consumer goods. The **average propensity to consume (APC)** is the proportion of total income spent on consumer goods. Mathematically, the APC is defined as

Average Propensity to Consume The fraction of total income that goes for consumption spending.

$$APC = \frac{total\ spending\ on\ consumer\ goods}{total\ income}$$

If your income is $1000 and you spend $900 on consumer goods, then the average part of each dollar that is spent on consumer goods is the APC figure of 90 percent.

Marginal Propensity to Consume
The fraction of a change in income that becomes a change in consumption spending.

The **marginal propensity to consume (*MPC*)** is that fraction of any change in income that is spent on consumer goods. The *MPC* is designed to measure how consumer spending changes on the margin when income changes. It is mathematically defined as

$$MPC = \frac{\text{change in consumer spending}}{\text{change in income}}$$

The *MPC* would be 80 percent if your consumer spending increased by $80 when your income increased by $100, for example.

The *MPC* describes consumer behavior as it relates to changes in income, while the *APC* describes consumer behavior as it relates to overall spending and income. Both of these measures are useful under different circumstances. If you want to know what people do with their incomes in general, you would consult the *APC* average measure. If you want to know how people behave on the margin with respect to consumer spending, the *MPC* marginal measure tells you what you want to know. "Do Americans spend most of their income?" is a question that calls for an answer using the average measure. "Would Americans spend a large part of an increase in income caused by a tax cut?" is a question that can only be answered using the marginal measure. We will discuss how the *APC* and *MPC* are used to solve macroeconomic problems in later chapters. For the present, however, we use *APC* and *MPC* as illustrations of marginal and average concepts.

THE RELATIONSHIP BETWEEN AVERAGE AND MARGINAL VARIABLES

There are three possible relationships between average and marginal variables. The marginal variable can be greater than, equal to, or less than its average. Tables 2-1, 2-2, and 2-3 give examples of each relationship. Each table assumes a constant marginal behavior for simplicity.

In Table 2-1, for example, we have assumed that the *MPC* is 100 percent. This means that, on the margin, people spend 100 percent of any change in income. At the start, when monthly income is $1000, however, people are spending only 90 percent of their income on consumer goods, so the *APC* average is 90 percent. As monthly income rises from $1000 to $2000 to $3000 in Table 2-1, we observe that the *APC* rises because the *MPC* is greater than the *APC*. As income rises from $1000 to $2000, for example, consumption spending rises from $900 to $900 + $1000 = $1900 because the change in consumer spending is equal to 100 percent of the $1000 increase in income. The *APC* therefore rises from $900/$1000 = 90 percent at an income level of $1000 to $1900/$2000 = 95 percent at the higher income level. The rule of thumb this illustrates is that *marginal*

TABLE 2-1	The Relationship Between *MPC* and *APC* When The Marginal Variable is Greater Than Its Average

Income ($)	Consumption ($)	MPC (%)	APC (%)
1000	900	100	90
2000	1900	100	95
3000	2900	100	98

TABLE 2-2 — The Relationship Between *MPC* and *APC* When the Marginal Variable is Equal to Its Average

Income ($)	Consumption ($)	MPC (%)	APC (%)
1000	900	90	90
2000	1800	90	90
3000	2700	90	90

TABLE 2-3 — The Relationship Between *MPC* and *APC* When the Marginal Variable is Less Than Its Average

Income ($)	Consumption ($)	MPC (%)	APC (%)
1000	900	80	90
2000	1700	80	85
3000	2500	80	83

behavior pulls up average behavior if the marginal variable is greater than its average.

Table 2-2 shows a second relationship. Here we have assumed that the *MPC* marginal behavior is 90 percent, the same as the *APC* average behavior. People are spending 90 percent of their monthly income at the start, and they tend to spend 90 percent of any change in income. Table 2-2 shows that the average is constant when marginal behavior equals average behavior. People spend 90 percent of their income on consumer goods when income is $1000. When income rises to $2000, they spend 90 percent of the increase on consumer goods, so the average remains the same. The same behavior is displayed again when income rises to $3000. The rule of thumb this illustrates is that *the average is constant when marginal and average behaviors are the same.*

Table 2-3 shows what happens if marginal actions are less than the corresponding average. Here we have assumed that people spend just 80 percent of any change in income, so the *MPC* is 80 percent. At the start, when income is $1000, people are spending 90 percent of their total income on consumer goods, so the *APC* is 90 percent. When income rises by $1000, from $1000 to $2000, only $800 or 80 percent of the increase in income goes for consumption spending. The *APC* average therefore falls from 90 percent to *APC* = ($900 + $800)/$2000 = 85 percent. The *APC* average falls again as income rises from $2000 to $3000 because the *MPC* is less than the *APC*. This example illustrates the rule of thumb that *marginal behavior pulls down average behavior when the marginal variable is less than its average.*

GRAPHING THE RELATIONSHIPS

Figure 2-1 shows the way that these relationships between average and marginal spending behaviors are graphed. Note how marginal behavior pulls up average behavior when the marginal variable is higher than its average. The average is constant when marginal behavior equals average behavior.

40 An Introduction to the Economic Way of Thinking

FIGURE 2-1 **The Relationships between Marginal and Average Variables.** If marginal behavior is greater than the average, the average tends to rise toward the marginal variable. When marginal behavior is equal to average behavior, the average remains constant. When marginal behavior is less than average behavior, the average tends to fall. These graphs of the marginal and average propensities to consume illustrate these relationships.

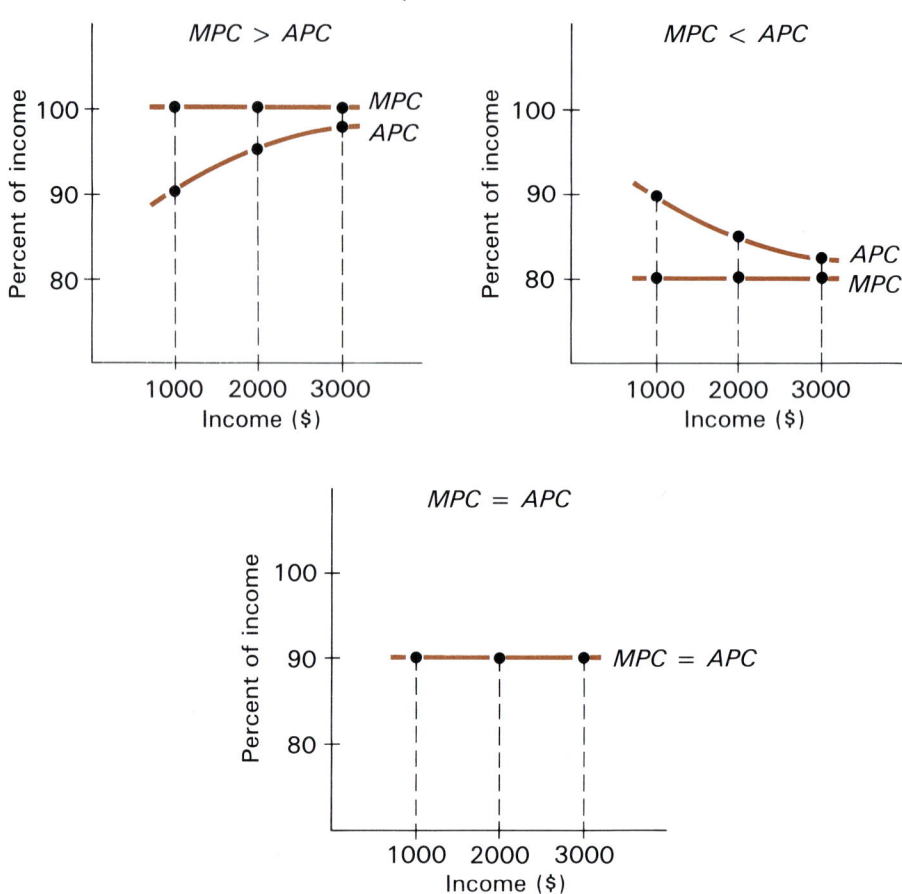

Marginal behavior pulls down average behavior when the marginal variable is less than its average. These arithmetic and graphical relationships are important and will be used in the analysis in later chapters of this text.

Figure 2-2 shows what can happen when we drop the assumption of constant marginal behavior. This figure shows curves that plot the marginal cost *(MC)* and **average total cost** *(ATC)* of producing a certain good. Cost curves such as these are frequently used in microeconomic analysis of producer behavior. The curves are more complex than the previous ones, but the relationships between marginal and average behaviors that they display are the same.

Figure 2-2 shows that, at low levels of production, the marginal cost of producing a good is less than the average total cost. As a result of this relationship, average total cost falls as output expands because low *MC* pulls down the *ATC*.

At high levels of production, on the other hand, *MC* is greater than *ATC*. The *ATC* rises as output expands because higher *MC* pulls up *ATC* as it rises.

Average Total Cost (ATC)
The total cost of producing goods or services divided by the quantity that is produced — a measure of the cost per unit of production.

FIGURE 2-2

Marginal and Average Cost Curves. This figure shows how the marginal cost (MC) and average total cost (ATC) of production are related to the level of output and to each other. Note that ATC tends to fall when $MC < ATC$, illustrating the point that the average declines when the marginal variable is less than the average variable. ATC tends to rise, as the figure shows, when $MC > ATC$. Refer back to Table 2-1 and Figure 2-1 if these concepts are not clear.

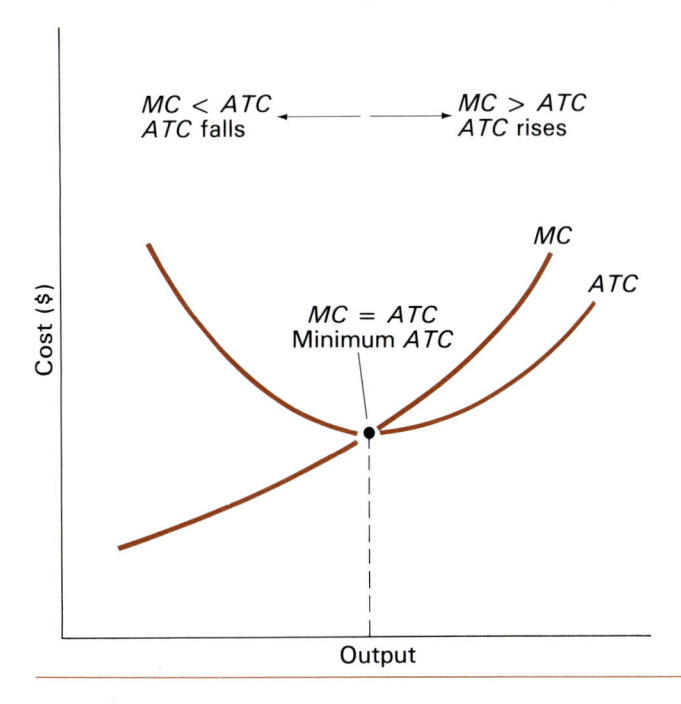

$MC < ATC$
ATC falls

$MC > ATC$
ATC rises

MC

ATC

$MC = ATC$
Minimum ATC

Cost ($)

Output

At one point ATC is equal to MC. This point represents the minimum point of the ATC curve. We can tell that this is the lowest possible ATC because $MC > ATC$ at higher levels of output, so ATC must be rising, and $MC < ATC$ at lower levels of output, so ATC must be falling. If a firm produces where $MC = ATC$, then it is producing at the lowest possible average total cost.

We will look at both cost curves and the difference between marginal and average analysis in greater depth later in this text. This brief section is not intended to convey a thorough understanding of MPC, APC, MC, or ATC. They are introduced here to illustrate the relationships between average and marginal concepts and the ways in which economists use them.

SUMMARY

2.1, 2.2, 2.3

1. Economists approach economic problems through the economic way of thinking. The economic way of thinking has five foundations.
    a. All economic goods cost someone something. Few if any resources are free. To receive some benefit, there is always a cost of some kind.
    b. Human beings are self-interested. People make choices to maximize satisfaction of wants and desires or to minimize their costs.

c. Since human beings choose in their own self-interest, incentives matter. The more utility an alternative provides, the more likely it is to be selected. Similarly, the lower the cost of an alternative, the more likely it is to be selected. Conversely, the higher the cost and the lower the use value of an alternative, the less likely it is to be selected.

d. Human beings make decisions at the margin. Most economic choices deal with small changes in economic behavior.

e. Information also has a cost. The marginal benefits and the marginal costs of gathering information must be taken into consideration.

2.4 ▶ 2. Economists analyze problems dealing with human behavior through the use of the scientific method.
a. Through induction, economists observe the behavior of individuals and formulate hypotheses or general behavior rules.
b. Through deduction, economists develop theories and then test them against real-world facts.
c. Finally, economists must verify or confirm the hypotheses or theories that they have developed through induction or deduction. The true test of a theory is its ability to accurately predict behavior.

2.5 ▶ 3. Positive economics concerns itself with what actually is and can be verified. It helps us to understand exactly how an economy works.

2.5 ▶ 4. Normative economics deals with value judgments and opinions. It attempts to state how the economy should function. A comprehensive understanding of economic issues requires a combination of positive and normative economics.

2.6 ▶ 5. A common mistake made in logical analysis is known as the fallacy of composition. This fallacy incorrectly implies that because something is good for an individual it is also good for an entire group.

2.7, 2.8 ▶ 6. Post hoc reasoning is another error made in logical analysis. It incorrectly assumes that the occurrence of an event is caused by or is in some way correlated with an event that immediately precedes it. Correlation is not the same as causation.

2.9 ▶ 7. Good economics requires that the possibility of secondary effects be taken into consideration. These effects are usually recognized over time and may have an opposite and greater long-term effect than the primary result.

2.10 ▶ 8. Economists practice their trade within private industry, academe, and government.
a. Economists employed by private industry focus their attentions on how human behavior relates to the specific goods or services produced by their industry.
b. Those working in colleges or universities teach economic theory while continuing advanced research.
c. Government economists analyze the impact of various types of government policies and legislation.

DISCUSSION QUESTIONS

2.1, 2.2, 2.3, 2.7, 2.8

1. All banks in your home town area are offering new car loans, charging 18 percent interest. Loan demand has been extremely low. The largest bank in town is contemplating reducing this rate to 16½ percent for non-customers and 16 percent for customers to increase the quantity of loans demanded. However, bank officials feel all other banks may follow suit, therefore eliminating their competitive edge. The bank hires an economic consultant to analyze this decision.
   a. According to the consultant, what would happen to the number of automobiles people wish to purchase?
   b. What would happen to the amounts of other goods and services that people wish to purchase?
   c. What would happen to the savings account balances of some depositors?
   d. Would the fact that interest rates went down before the desired quantity of automobile purchases went up be proof positive that the decline in interest rates caused the increase in car loans?

2.1, 2.2, 2.3

2. You have $20,000 to invest and absolutely no knowledge of financial markets. You would also like to purchase a new car but could wait a year to do so. Explain how you would approach the problem of deciding how much to invest, in what to invest, and when to buy a new car using the economic way of thinking. What are the opportunity costs and benefits involved in each decision?

2.4

3. By observing cars on the road year-round, you notice there are more sun roofs open in warmer weather. From this, you formulate a general rule that the use of sun roofs on cars is directly related to the weather. What component of the scientific method have you utilized in formulating this rule?

2.4

4. Why might economists not be as accurate in verifying their hypotheses as physical scientists?

2.5

5. Determine which of the following are examples of positive or normative economic statements:
   a. When banks offer higher interest rates on savings, people save more.
   b. When banks lower lending rates, people borrow more.
   c. The United States government should provide more funding for medical research.
   d. If the prices of magazines are reduced, more magazines are sold.
   e. The United States government should support the building of nuclear power plants.

2.6, 2.7, 2.8, 2.9

6. Determine if the following are true or false, and explain what economic problem they display:
   a. You have decided to leave for the beach at 6:30 A.M. so that you will not get caught in traffic. Therefore, everyone going to the beach should leave at this time.

b. If you get caught in the rain, you may catch a cold. Obviously then, if you have a cold, you must have been out in the rain.

c. You accidentally cut yourself on a rusty tin can. The pain has subsided, and you reason that a tetanus injection would hurt. You decide, therefore, that the benefits of the injection are not worth the cost in terms of pain. However, the cut later becomes infected.

SELECTED READINGS

Boulding, Kenneth E. *Economics as a Science*. New York: McGraw-Hill Book Company, 1970.

Hough, Robin R. *What Economists Do*. New York: Harper & Row, Publishers, 1972.

Keynes, J.N. *The Scope and Method of Political Economy*, 4th ed. New York: MacMillan, 1930.

Lekachman, Robert. *Economists at Bay: Why The Experts Will Never Solve Your Problems*. New York: McGraw-Hill Book Company, 1976.

Levi, Maurice. *Thinking Economically: How Economic Principles Can Contribute to Clear Thinking*. New York: Basic Books, 1985.

McCloskey, Donald N. "The Rhetoric of Economics." *Journal of Economic Literature* (June 1983), pp. 481-517.

Schultze, Charles L. "The Role and Responsibilities of the Economist in Government." *American Economic Review* (May 1982), pp. 62-66.

Tullock, Gordon. "Economic Imperialism." In James Buchanan and Robert Tollison (eds.), *Theory of Public Choice*. Ann Arbor: University of Michigan Press, 1972.

CHAPTER 3

How Economies Are Organized

Having read the chapter, reviewed the chapter summary, and completed the *Study Guide* exercises, you should be able to:

CRIS

3.1 PROBLEM OF SCARCITY: Identify the basic problem that all economic systems face.

3.2 SCARCITY VERSUS POVERTY: Explain the difference between scarcity and poverty.

3.3 FUNDAMENTAL QUESTIONS: State the three fundamental questions that all economies must answer.

3.4 MARKET ECONOMY INCENTIVES: Discuss how the price system in a market economy creates incentives for consumers and producers to make efficient choices.

3.5 PUBLIC SERVICES: Explain why public services may be free to individuals yet they are not free to the whole society.

3.6 PUBLIC SERVICE OVERUSE: Explain why consumers have a strong tendency to overuse some public services.

3.7 ECONOMIC GOALS: Define and discuss six major goals that economies generally strive to achieve.

3.8 INCOME REDISTRIBUTION: Explain the difference between an equal and an equitable redistribution of income.

3.9 ECONOMIC SYSTEMS: Define the four major categories of economic systems and discuss who answers the questions of what, how, and for whom to produce within each category of economic systems.

3.10 SYSTEM STRENGTHS AND WEAKNESSES: Discuss the strengths and weaknesses of each of the four major economic systems.

How Economies are Organized

The countries of the world differ from one another in many ways. One of the most important differences is in how the economies of different countries are organized to deal with fundamental economic problems and choices. The economy of the United States differs in many important respects from the economies of the United Kingdom, the Soviet Union, Yugoslavia, Japan, and many others. This chapter looks at both the similarities among nations and their differences. The similarities relate to the common nature of the economic problems they face. The differences occur in the ways in which they decide who makes important social and economic choices and what those choices are.

THE PROBLEM OF SCARCITY

3.1 PROBLEM OF SCARCITY

Which type of economic organization a country chooses depends upon many factors, such as the types and quantities of resources that it has, the political philosophies of its people, and the role played by government in the country. All economies, however, regardless of how they are organized, face the same basic economic problem of scarcity. They all strive to maximize the overall satisfaction of the society with the given amount of resources that they have available. This chapter discusses the basic problems that all societies face and then examines the different economic systems that have been developed to deal with these problems.

3.2 SCARCITY VERSUS POVERTY

Poverty
The lack of sufficient resources to satisfy a minimal standard of living.

There is a difference between the concepts of scarcity and **poverty.** Poverty is an absolute concept. It implies a living standard below some basic level. However, some nations are poorer than others. By this we mean that, on an absolute scale, the basic wants and desires of the population of one country may be more fulfilled than the basic wants and desires of another country. For example, malnutrition and starvation in the United States are relatively rare, while they are more commonplace in India. From this, we might conclude that there is less poverty in the United States than in India.

Scarcity, on the other hand, is a relative concept. It exists no matter how many resources are available. It is clear that scarcity exists in poorer nations where poverty rates are high. But it also exists in nations with high absolute standards of living. The human desire for resources always exceeds the finite amount available. This means that scarcity is an important common denominator of all the world's economies.

3.3 FUNDAMENTAL QUESTIONS

Because all economies must choose how best to satisfy their unlimited wants and desires with their limited resources, each must answer the three basic questions posed by scarcity: What goods and services should be produced? How should they be produced? Who should get the goods and services that are produced? These questions are frequently referred to as the "what, how, and for whom" of economics.

KEY CONCEPTS 3.3

All economies must answer the three basic economic questions of what, how, and for whom to produce.

What to Produce?

The first important economic choice or decision an economy must make is what goods and services it will produce with its limited resources. The concept of the production possibilities frontier, introduced in Chapter 1, illustrates the idea that, if an economy uses its scarce resources to produce more of one good, it cannot at the same time use those same resources to produce another good. If an economy expands the production of airplanes, ships, and nuclear missiles for its defense, for example, it must reduce production of food, clothing, housing, or any other goods that use the same resources in their production.

The question of what to produce is answered in different ways in different economies. For example, there are many more everyday consumer items such as designer clothing, candy bars, blue jeans, and automobiles manufactured and distributed in the United States than in the Soviet Union. A greater percentage of the Soviet economy's resources over the last decade has been devoted to defense-related expenditures. This difference in the types of goods produced shows that the two countries have made different "what" decisions. Relatively more scarce resources have been used to make consumer goods in the United States, while relatively more resources have been used to make defense goods in the Soviet Union. The effects of these choices are illustrated by the PPF in Figure 3-1. The PPF shows that each country has made a trade-off in choosing to produce one combination of goods over the other.

Who decides which goods and services are produced? In the U.S. economy, the question of what to produce is made primarily by consumers and producers voting in the marketplace. If a product is valued by consumers at the going market price, they will buy it. This system of dollar votes rewards successful producers with profits and sends a signal to firms to

FIGURE 3-1

What Goods and Services Are to Be Produced? The United States and the Soviet Union have chosen much different answers to the "what" question of resource use. The United States has chosen to produce relatively more consumer goods and relatively fewer defense goods. The choice by the Soviets to have more national defense has forced them to give up consumer goods they could have had instead.

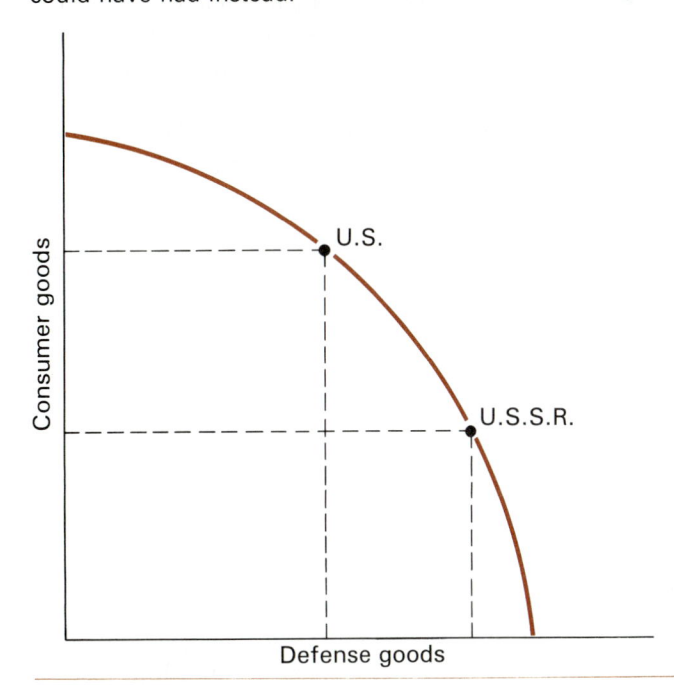

produce more of the desired good. When consumers refuse to buy a specific good or service at the going price, producers incur losses and receive a clear signal to produce less of that product. Producers respond to the signals that consumers send them, and buyers, in turn, respond to the signals that sellers give them.

Not all choices are made by individual producers and consumers, however, even in *market economies* such as the United States or Canada. A market economy is an economy in which the questions of what, how, and for whom are answered primarily through individual choices in the marketplace. Government is an important sector in all market economies. Many production choices are made directly by elected representatives, such as the amount of defense spending or the amount of resources devoted to schools and roads. Government also influences many private choices that consumers make through tax and subsidy systems that alter private incentives. Fewer "what" choices are made by individuals and more are made by government in a *command economy* such as the Soviet Union, where central planning agencies make many production decisions. The people give up the right to make many choices in the marketplace in this type of system.

How to Produce?

The second major decision that all economies must face is how to produce goods and services. People must decide what types of production processes they will use to combine their resources into finished goods and services. They must choose whether food will be produced using much capital machinery, such as combines, tractors, and seeding and fertilizing equipment, and few laborers or with many laborers using hand tools and few tractors, combines, and other capital equipment. They must decide whether a single shoe factory will use leather or plastic for the soles and heels of their shoes or whether an automobile manufacturer will use steel or fiberglass to make fenders and body parts.

3.4 MARKET ECONOMY INCENTIVES

In a market economy like the United States, the specific ways in which goods and services are produced are guided and directed by the price system, with individual producers making the choices. There is a strong incentive in market economies like the United States for producers to choose the method of production that is least costly for a given quality of good or service. For example, if either leather or plastic can be used equally well to produce shoe parts of equal quality and durability, the producer will choose whichever raw material costs the least. Consequently, if the prices of resources change over time, this will have an effect on the methods of production that are used. The producers' profits are larger if they use less costly methods of production. Since a major goal of producers is to maximize profits, they constantly strive to develop and use more efficient production methods.

The way in which an economy answers the "how" question of resource use can change as economic conditions change. In its early years, for example, the U.S. coal mining industry employed many miners and little capital equipment. Today, coal is mined with many fewer miners and much more mining machinery. This change came about primarily because the cost of labor rose much faster than the cost of machinery. As labor became relatively more costly, mine operators began to switch to the use of more machines. Whether this type of behavior was "right" or "wrong" on the part of mine producers is not a question of positive economics. The point is that as one resource becomes more expensive relative to another, producers have a strong incentive to substitute the cheaper resource for the more expensive one in their production process. Where the profit incentive system is used (for example, in the United States), it contributes to the efficiency of the economy.

Not all production decisions are made by private individuals, even in the United States. Government regulations frequently set rules that restrict individual choices. Pollution regulations, which will be discussed in more depth in Chapter 25, are an example of regulations designed to alter producer "how" choices in order to protect the public interest. It is expensive for paper mills, for example, to produce without damaging the environment. The least-cost method of producing paper would be to release noxious fumes into the air and dispose of toxic chemicals into public water supplies. In situations like this, what is best for the individual producer is not always best for society. Government regulations restrict how paper can be produced, increasing the cost of production but reducing damage to the environment. Sometimes there is a trade-off, as the PPF in Figure 3-2 shows, between production and environmental quality. Society, in making the "how" choice of resource allocation, is also choosing which combination on this PPF it most desires. More and cheaper goods? Or a cleaner, healthier environment?

Other economies, such as the Soviet Union, decide how goods and services are produced quite differently. The same central planning agency that decides what will be produced also allocates the available resources to producers. It decides which raw materials and in what quantities will be allocated to all producers in the economy. For example, the planning agency

FIGURE 3-2 **The Trade-Off Between Production and Environmental Quality.** There is frequently a trade-off between production of goods and services and environmental quality. The choice to have a cleaner environment means paying the opportunity cost of fewer goods produced.

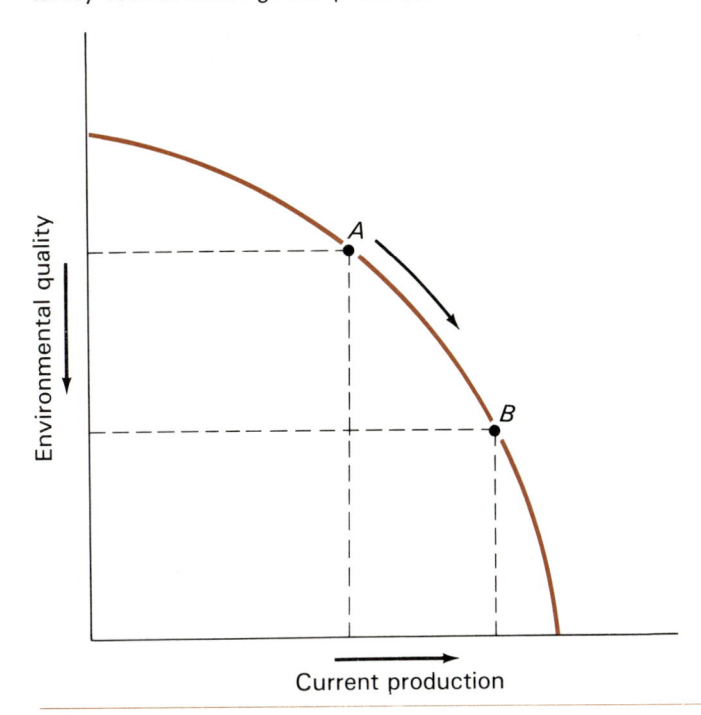

decides how much coal, iron ore, and labor a steel mill receives to produce its steel for a certain year. Since the central planning agency has this power and responsibility, the individual producer has little incentive to seek out and use the least costly resources possible.

Economists believe that planned economies tend to be less efficient in production because managers have little discretion in resource use and little incentive to seek out more effective production methods. Command economies therefore tend to produce different combinations of goods using different combinations of resources than do market economies. Sometimes, however, these short-run inefficiencies are intentional. A nation such as the Soviet Union has relatively little capital, compared to the United States. Planning, even if it is inefficient, is often designed to direct scarce capital to produce equipment and machinery that leads to high levels of economic growth. Planners must hope that the gains in future production of goods and services from economic growth are greater than the amounts of production lost due to inefficient systems of production incentives.

For Whom to Produce?

The economic question of for whom goods and services are produced has both positive and normative aspects. This is a question that deals with how the goods and services that are produced will be distributed among different individuals and groups in society. Will everyone receive an equal share of the output of the economy, or will some people get more goods and services than others? Who will decide who gets what in the economy? The positive part of economics can and does deal with these types of questions. However, the question of just how fair a specific economic system is in distributing its output is clearly a normative issue.

3.4 MARKET ECONOMY INCENTIVES

Different types of economies determine for whom goods and services are produced in different ways. In the United States economy, for example, the question of who gets what is answered primarily by consumers in conjunction with the price system, although government policies have important effects on resource allocation. Consumers have the right to spend their income in any fashion they see fit, subject to laws that restrict certain exchanges and government tax and subsidy incentives that influence other purchases. Consumers decide within these limits which goods and services they will consume based upon their income, individual preferences, and the relative prices of goods in the marketplace.

How much income consumers have has a great deal to do with what goods and services they can buy. Everyone in the United States does not have an equal income. The distribution of income is determined by both market and nonmarket actions. A farmer's income, for example, depends on many markets. Markets for labor, fertilizer, farm equipment, and loans taken together determine how much it will cost to produce a given amount of wheat. The market for wheat and, indirectly, the markets for products that use wheat, determine the price of wheat and the farmer's gross income. In general, an individual's income in a market economy is determined by what resources, such as labor or skill, a person has to sell and how highly the market values those resources.

Markets are not the only determinants of an individual's income, however. Chance has an important influence on income distribution. A wheat farmer's income often depends on the weather or some other factor that individuals cannot influence or plan for. Government policies also affect income distribution. For example, the wheat farmer pays social security taxes based upon farm income during working years. These taxes are paid to retired individuals. Social security thus reduces the income of workers and increases the incomes of those who have retired from work, thereby altering income distribution and economic incentives in important ways.

The question of income distribution in the United States will be examined in greater depth in Chapter 24. It will be shown that both income and resources are unequally distributed; although there is disagreement about how unequal the distribution is and what should be done, if anything, to alter it.

**KEY CONCEPTS
3.3, 3.4**

In a market economy, the price system coordinates the choices of individual buyers and sellers in answering the three fundamental economic questions. The prices of various goods and services help consumers choose which items to purchase and help producers decide which goods and services to make available and in what quantities. Prices therefore guide decisions concerning what to produce. The prices of various resources, such as labor, technology, and natural resources, influence the way in which firms choose how to produce goods and services. Finally, individuals earn income by selling their scarce resources, such as their labor, and using that income to purchase other scarce resources, such as food and housing. The price system influences how much income various individuals have and how many scarce resources they can purchase with it. Prices therefore influence the distribution of resources in a market economy.

**3.5
PUBLIC SERVICES**

In a market economy such as the United States, the unequal distribution of income results in an unequal distribution of resources, since the amount of goods and services that individuals can attain is, in large part, dependent on income. Government can make resource distribution more equal if it by-passes markets and distributes goods and services directly, with no monetary payment required. Many goods and services that consumers must buy in markets in the United States are provided by the government as public services in other economies. While public services, such as "free" medical care or the "free" use of public education, may be free to the individual, in the sense that the individual does not have to give up anything other than his or her time to attain these services, it is important to realize that they are not free to the whole society. As we indicated in Chapter 2, there are no free lunches in economics. When an economy provides free medical services to the population, it must use its scarce resources to do so. Those resources cannot then be used at the same time to produce other goods and services. Society bears the opportunity cost of providing public services, even if the individual does not.

**3.6
PUBLIC SERVICE OVERUSE**

People have a strong tendency to overuse goods and services that cost them the same amount no matter how much they are used. Consequently, public services are often used to such an extent that congestion results, the quality of the service declines, and scarce resources are diverted from other uses that may have higher social value. Thus, while public services have a zero price to the individual, they may have a high opportunity cost to society. For example, if medical services are provided at no out-of-pocket cost by the government, it is in the interest of individuals to visit the doctor for even minor ailments. Since no market price is paid by consumers, they use more services than they otherwise would. This requires the use of doctors, nurses, and other medical resources that could have been used for those people who are truly ill and have stronger desires for the services. If society must have more doctors, nurses, and other medical resources to counteract the shortage, it cannot at the same time have as many secretaries, nuclear physicists, or other nonmedical resources. There is an opportunity cost regardless of what system is used to decide for whom goods are produced.

Economists have long noted the possibility of a trade-off between equality and efficiency. An economy can achieve a more equal distribution of resources, for example, by providing them as free public services that can be used equally by the wealthy and the poor. This equality can reduce the individual incentive to use these scarce resources efficiently, however. In other words, there is the possibility that goods and services will be more equally divided, but that there will be fewer of them to divide because inefficiency has reduced the amounts of goods that society's scarce resources can produce.

THE ECONOMIC GOALS OF A SOCIETY

Once an economy has been organized, it attempts to direct its resources toward some specific set of economic goals. Although individual economies answer the basic economic questions differently, they all share common general goals because they share the problems of scarcity and choice. The overall goal of maximizing the satisfaction of wants and desires with the resources available can be broken into several component subgoals.

Goal 1: High Levels of Resource Employment

3.7 ECONOMIC GOALS

All economies realize that the rate at which they can produce goods and services depends directly on their level of resource use. For example, an economy with one-half of its labor force unemployed cannot produce as many goods and services as another economy of the same size with all of its labor force at work. This economic goal seems straightforward, but it is really more complex.

Policies that affect the employment of labor involve trade-offs. While in the past most economies have attempted to maximize the employment of their human resources, shifts in attitudes toward work may change this in the future. It appears that as income rises, the desire for leisure time grows stronger. Shorter work weeks, longer vacations, and earlier retirement are all ideas that interest people more with each passing year. Thus the real issue may not be maximizing employment but providing gainful employment in sufficient quantity for those who wish to work.

Maintaining high levels of resource employment also raises a concern about when to use some types of resources. Our nonrenewable energy resources will not be available in the future if we deplete them now. The question then becomes how fast should we use up these resources? There is a constant debate over whether we should maximize production and employment now to satisfy current wants and desires or perhaps produce at a slower rate leaving more resources for the future. In the case of nonrenewable energy resources, the trade-off is between present and future consump-

ECONOMIC ISSUES

The Role of Incentives: Private Priorities and Public Means

Economists believe that incentives are important. One important difference among economic systems lies, therefore, in the nature of the incentives that they provide. Some systems of incentives tend to be more efficient than others. Economists believe that market economic systems tend to be relatively efficient because both buyers and sellers are forced to be aware of the opportunity costs of their actions. Producers realize that the resources they use have valuable alternative uses. Consumers realize that the money they spend on one item could be used to purchase other items. Both sides of the market face powerful incentives to use resources wisely. These incentives are not evident when people share goods, such as the environment, or when goods and services are provided "free" by government.

Even before the birth of Christ, the Greek philosopher Aristotle noted that "What is common to many is taken least care of, for all men have greater regard for that which is their own than for what they possess in common with others."[1] This is true whether we are considering a public park in London, a factory in Gdansk, Poland, or the subway system in New York City.

Consider, for example, the incentives involved in choosing to drop litter on the ground in the park rather than dispose of it properly. If an individual chooses to litter, he or she can receive, at no personal cost, the benefit of the full use of the unspoiled park up to the time the litter is dropped. To do the "right" thing, however, the individual must expend the effort to deposit the litter in a trash receptacle. The cost of the effort is borne entirely by the individual, whlie the benefit is shared by everyone in the form of a cleaner environment. Thus people litter because the individual cost of not littering is greater than the individual benefit of properly disposing of the trash.

Once the first piece of litter is dropped, the incentives change for everyone. This unsightly litter detracts from the pleasure of others using the public service. The next individual with trash has a greater probability of choosing to litter because the individual costs and benefits have been changed by the act of the first litterer. The second individual must also spend time and energy to dispose of the trash properly. The litter that was left by the first individual has already detracted from the pleasure that the second person may get from using the park. The first person has passed a cost on to society by littering. This cost is borne by all subsequent users of the public service. Since the park is already littered, the individual benefit to subsequent users has been reduced and the individual cost of reducing the litter (picking it up) is increased with each subsequent piece of litter.

This same set of incentives and choice processes is repeated over and over in the case of almost all public services. Soil erosion of private farm land seldom goes unchecked since the owner/farmer has a personal incentive to see that the land is cared for and kept as productive as possible. This is not always the case with public lands or communal farms. History abounds with many other examples. In sixteenth-century England, cattle grazing lands were communally owned, and everyone grazed their herds there. The individual cattle owner received the benefits of each cow that grazed and became fatter because of the land, while everyone who owned the common grazing land bore the cost. As would be expected, the common grazing lands were quickly overgrazed, and not enough grass was left to seed the commons for the next year's growth. What was to the individual's benefit too quickly took precedence over what was in the public's interest. To save the grazing areas, enclosure movements were started to divide these commons into private plots. This structure changed the incentives of users. After the land was divided and enclosed, individual benefits were tied directly to individual costs. If a farmer allowed his cows to overgraze his land, his cattle had no grass the following year.

Public services are a valuable and necessary part of any economy. To truly understand the value of public services to an economy, however, one must understand both their contribution to the well-being of the society and the individual incentives that they produce.

1. Aristotle, as quoted by Will Durant in *The Life of Greece,* New York: Simon and Schuster, 1939, p. 536.

tion. Using more petroleum today simply means that there will be less available for use in the future. This trade-off creates stronger incentives for producers to search for and develop new energy sources.

Goal 2: Relatively Stable Prices

A second major goal that modern economies strive for is that of a relatively stable price level. This does not mean that prices should not change. It simply means that the economic forces within an economy that bring about large and rapid price changes affecting many goods should be moderated.

There are many reasons why price stability is important. When prices are fluctuating rapidly, investors fear that their investments might incur losses or at least smaller profits than they are willing to accept. Firms find it difficult to plan for the production of goods and services when the prices of their raw materials are constantly changing at rapid rates. For example, in the airline industry, sharp increases in the cost of fuel for airplanes may cause at least short-term losses for the airline companies. Since they have passengers who are already holding paid-for tickets, they cannot raise fares immediately. If the price of fuel changes rapidly, the airlines are hesitant to expand, open new air routes, and undertake other such activities because the risks of loss are much greater than when price changes occur at a slower pace. A relatively stable price level is conducive to a smoothly functioning and growing economy.

There are many ways in which different economies attempt to moderate large swings in the price level. In the United States, two separate types of policy are used in attempting to maintain relatively stable prices. These are monetary and fiscal policy. **Monetary policy** deals mainly with the control of the money supply in our economy by the Federal Reserve System, which is the central bank of the United States. **Fiscal policy** deals with the taxing and spending powers of government. Both monetary and fiscal policy will be discussed in much greater depth in later chapters of this text.

Goal 3: Economic Growth

Economic growth is important for at least three reasons. First, growth is necessary in order to provide employment for an expanding population. Thus, more and better jobs must be developed by industry each year. Second, since people have unlimited wants and desires, there is always a desire for more goods and services than were available in the past. Third, economic growth allows society to achieve a more equal distribution of resources with less social tension. It is easier to give the poor a bigger slice of the economic pie if the size of the pie is growing. Redistribution during periods of economic decline forces more severe trade-offs between gaining and losing groups.

Goal 4: Economic Efficiency

Economic efficiency is an important goal for the economy. An inefficient economy wastes scarce resources by using them carelessly or using them to produce goods and services that society does not desire as much as some alternatives. If the economy is efficient, scarce resources are used to make both the maximum possible amounts of goods and the particular combination of goods that is most desired.

3.7 ECONOMIC GOALS

Monetary Policy
Using various controls on the money supply of an economy to strive for a relatively stable price level and desired economic growth.

Fiscal Policy
The practice of managing government spending and taxes as a means of arriving at stable prices or other economic goals, such as growth or high levels of employment.

3.7 ECONOMIC GOALS

Economic Efficiency
The technically efficient use of scarce resources to produce those goods and services that society most prefers.

3.7 ECONOMIC GOALS

Technical Efficiency
Uses of scarce resources that produce maximum combinations of goods and services. All points on the PPF display technical efficiency. All points within the PPF are inefficient in this sense.

Figure 3-3 uses the concept of the production possibilities frontier to show that economic efficiency imposes two conditions on the ways in which resources are used. First, resources must be used with **technical efficiency**. Technical efficiency requires that resources be used without waste and in conjunction with the most productive existing technology. All of the points on the PPF in the figure exhibit technical efficiency. Points on the interior of the PPF are not technically efficient because resources are left unused or are not used as effectively as possible, such as when workers are unemployed or machines are left idle. The same resources could be used to produce the larger combinations of goods and services on the PPF.

The second requirement for economic efficiency is that resources be used to produce the most preferred combination of goods and services from among all those that display technical efficiency. All of the combinations of goods on the PPF display technical efficiency, because all the PPF points use resources effectively. However, only one combination is the one that society most prefers. This is the combination that represents economic efficiency. How can we tell which point on the PPF is "best"? This is a normative question. Market economies let consumers express their preferences for different combinations through market actions. Command economies use central planning and government decree to try to select the efficient point.

Economic efficiency is an abstract but important goal that will be further analyzed later in this text. If economic efficiency is achieved, society's scarce resources bring the greatest amount of satisfaction. If economic

FIGURE 3-3   **Technical Efficiency and Economic Efficiency.** Point A fails the test of technical efficiency because it represents an inefficient use of resources. The same resources could be used to produce the greater combination of the goods represented by the points on the PPF. All the points on the PPF display technical efficiency, but only one of them satisfies the definition of economic efficiency. The economically efficient point is the point on the PPF that society most prefers.

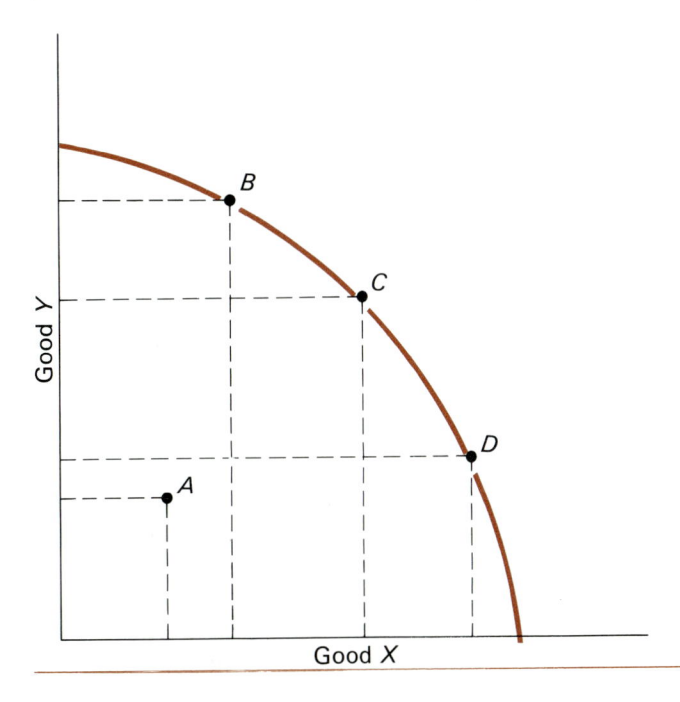

efficiency fails, however, society loses some of the benefits that its resources could provide and is therefore worse off.

Goal 5: Equitable Distribution of Income

> **3.7 ECONOMIC GOALS**
>
> **Equitable Distribution of Income**
> A distribution of income in the economy that is considered fair or just.

An **equitable distribution of income** is an important but elusive goal. It is clear that income is unequally distributed in all economies. For example, market forces result in an unequal distribution of income in the United States. Those with few marketable skills earn less than those who, for one reason or another, have more earning power. Some countries, such as the Soviet Union and China, have more equality of income, but even in these countries perfect equality of income does not exist. Some inequality of income is probably necessary in order to achieve economic efficiency. Efficiency requires effective incentives to fully employ scarce resources. But individual workers and investors have little incentive to produce if they receive the same income as others who do not work. Much of the recent increase in economic growth in China has been the result of marketlike production incentives that stimulate production but leave income less equally distributed.

> **3.8 INCOME REDISTRIBUTION**

One difficulty with the goal of an equitable distribution of income is that it depends so much on normative judgments. What distribution of income is "fair"? Some people might say that the current distribution of income is equitable, while other people might say that only a perfectly equal income allocation, where each person receives the same amount, is fair. Because this is such a normative subject, it is difficult to make many meaningful statements about what policies are required to make the distribution of income more equitable. This much we can say, however. While the current income distribution in the United States is viewed as acceptable by many, the prevailing distribution has been greatly influenced by government programs that redistribute income and resources from one group to another. These programs take many forms. For example, the tax system helps redistribute income to the extent that it taxes some groups more than others. Government programs such as social security benefits and Aid to Families with Dependent Children provide extra money to low-income groups. Government subsidy programs such as food stamps also alter income distribution. The emphasis that an economy places on the goal of an equitable distribution of income is a normative matter. It frequently involves a trade-off between equity and efficiency.

Goal 6: Environmental Quality

> **3.7 ECONOMIC GOALS**

Environmental concerns spring from the people's desire to have a clean and healthy natural environment in which to live. Forests, clean rivers and streams, and clean air to breathe are all desirable goods, but they are goods with a high opportunity cost. These are the same resources that are used by industry for raw materials, space utilization, and the discharge of polluting by-products. Industry cannot produce without the use of these resources. The trade-off is between goods and services to satisfy people's material needs and the use of resources in their natural state to satisfy people's desire for a pleasant environment.

The emphasis placed on environmental concerns in the United States has increased over the last 25 years. This has primarily occurred for two reasons. First, there is a lot of truth to the old adage that we do not realize how much we will miss something until it is gone. Clean water, vast forests, and clear air have been a part of our country since colonization. However, as we have developed into an industrial power, we have exploited our environment, little by little, to support this growth. As clean air and water, open spaces, and forests have become harder to find, we have begun to understand that these resources are economic goods rather than free goods. Like all economic goods, we must pay a price for their use and conservation. This price includes the increasing costs of the natural resources, the sacrifice of some industrial development (both in terms of alternative development and lowered production due to environmental regulations), and the medical costs associated with illnesses brought on by the deterioration of the environment. In addition, the use of pollution control equipment, the cleaning up of already polluted rivers, and the development of newer, more pollution-free production systems all have a cost. Each of these costs are borne by the members of the economy in one way or another.

A second reason for the growing emphasis on environmental concerns may well be human nature and the fact that, once one set of wants and desires is satisfied, people tend to invent additional wants and desires. As we become a more developed nation with a higher standard of living, the needs that we invent become much more sophisticated. In Colonial America, a major concern might have been producing sufficient food for everyone to stay alive. This is a basic need. It overshadowed the desire to have clean air and water, since they existed in abundance and food did not. As we grew and gained the ability to at least feed the majority of the population on a regular basis, our needs changed. As our society becomes more affluent, it creates more of a need for the aesthetic pleasures of life. The desire to enjoy the scenic beauty of a sunset or the cool pine scent of a forest probably is not very intense when one is starving to death. However, when our more basic needs are fulfilled, we appreciate and more fully enjoy the pleasures of the environment in which we live.

Regardless of the reasons, however, environmental concerns are genuine economic goals. As with all economic goals, environmental quality has an opportunity cost. Given scarce resources, higher levels of environmental quality will require that other goals be foregone. Trade-offs among the economic goals we have discussed make economic policy difficult, but they are a fact of life in our world of scarcity and choice.

INDIVIDUAL VERSUS SOCIAL CHOICE: TYPES OF ECONOMIC ORGANIZATION

Although different economies have the same general economic goals, they set about achieving them in different ways. The basic economic questions of what, how, and for whom to produce goods and services are answered in different ways in different economies. The major aspect upon which economies differ in their choice making is in who does the choosing. Individuals make most of the choices regarding what, how, and for whom in the United States economy. These decisions are made primarily in the marketplace. Many decisions are made by government, of course, but relative to economies such as the Soviet Union, governmental decision making is less important in the U.S.

3.9 ECONOMIC SYSTEMS

For simplicity, it is useful to classify economic systems into four major categories, depending on their respective degree of individual, as opposed to social, decision making. These four categories are market economies, command economies, mixed economies, and traditional economies. While we will use specific economies as examples of each category, the four categories are not exclusive of one another. If we use the United States as an example of a market economy, for example, it does not imply that it does not have any characteristics of a command or even a traditional economy. All this implies is that most of the characteristics of the U.S. economy are like those of a market economy.

The four classifications of economies are theoretical categories that have long existed. Over time, an economy may change parts of its structure and become more like another economy in order to achieve some of its economic goals. The basic organization of an economy, however, is not highly subject to change. These categories are designed to give students an overall picture of how different types of economies function; they are not designed to be accurately detailed descriptions of the economies that are used as examples. Table 3-1 presents a thumbnail sketch of each type of economic organization.

3.10 SYSTEM STRENGTHS AND WEAKNESSES

Market Economy
An economic system that answers the questions of what, how, and for whom to produce primarily through choices in the marketplace.

Command Economy
An economic system that answers the questions of what, how, and for whom to produce primarily through social choices made by a central planning agency.

3.10 SYSTEM STRENGTHS AND WEAKNESSES

Factors of Production
Inputs that are used to make outputs. Land, labor, capital, and knowledge, or "know-how," are frequently cited as the most important factors of production because they are the most important inputs used in production.

Mixed Economy
An economic system that combines the characteristics of both market and command economies. Some choices are made by individuals, while other choices are made by government.

The Market Economy

A **market economy** relies primarily on individual choice in the marketplace to decide what, how, and for whom goods and services will be produced. Most of the means of production, such as factories, machinery, land, labor, and management talent, are owned by private citizens. Those citizens are entitled to the rewards that come from the use of their resources to produce goods and services. In the market economy the government plays a relatively small economic role. In general, government provides some public services such as a legal system, roads, schools, and national defense, which are more efficiently produced by a whole society acting together in the social interest than by individuals acting in their own self-interest. Efficiency and individual freedom of choice are two of the strong points of such an economy, while inequality in the distribution of its output might be considered by some to be its most pronounced weakness.

The Command Economy

A **command economy** relies on a central planning authority to answer most of the basic economic questions. Thus it relies much more on social choice than individual choice in the operation of the economy. Most of the **factors of production** are owned or controlled by the state. The distribution of income in the economy is dictated by the central authority, usually with a major emphasis placed upon equality. While equality of income might be considered the strong point of a command economy, substantial differences in income between individuals usually exist. On the negative side, command economies do not provide as strong a set of incentives for economic efficiency as do their market-economy counterparts.

The Mixed Economy

A **mixed economy** combines elements of both market and command economies. Some mixed economies rely on market structures, with some government management of the factors of production. Other mixed economies may use central planning and government decree as their primary form of economic decision making, with only a few economic decisions being made in the marketplace.

TABLE 3-1   **How the Four Categories of Economic Organization Answer the Questions of What, How, and For Whom to Produce**

Market economy

What to Produce?	Answered primarily by consumers and producers in the marketplace through dollar votes; some public decision making
How to Produce?	Answered primarily by producers in the resource market guided by resource prices
For Whom to Produce?	Answered by consumers in the marketplace guided by prices and income
Strengths/Weaknesses	Strong incentives for efficiency in production; unequal income distribution

Command economy

What to Produce?	Answered primarily by a central planning agency
How to Produce?	Answered by a central planning agency through allocations
For Whom to Produce?	Answered by a central authority who sets wages and prices
Strengths/Weaknesses	More equal income distribution; less incentives for economic efficiency

Mixed economy

What to Produce?	Answered by public and private decision making
How to Produce?	Answered by both market and central authority decisions
For Whom to Produce?	Mixed systems of distribution
Strengths/Weaknesses	Vary depending on specific system

Traditional economy

What to Produce?	Answered based on tradition
How to Produce?	Answered based on tradition
For Whom to Produce?	Answered based on tradition
Strengths/Weaknesses	Sometimes a more equitable distribution of income; weak efficiency incentives, inability to accommodate change

In reality, since no economy conducts 100 percent of its economic affairs through markets or central planning, all economies are really mixed economies. Economists attempt to classify economies as a continuing spectrum of individual and social decision-making units. The spectrum ranges from those units that approach the ideal market economy, such as the United States, to those that approach the ideal command economy, such as the Soviet Union. The difference really comes in how many of the economic decisions of an economy are made by individuals in relation to how many of those decisions are made by government.

> **3.10 SYSTEM STRENGTHS AND WEAKNESSES**

Mixed economies combine the strengths and weaknesses of market and command economies. The efficiencies of individual choices can be combined with government policies that lead to more efficient allocation and distribution choices, for example. However, there is no guarantee that the roles assigned to government and markets in a mixed economy will always be the most efficient ones.

The Traditional Economy

Traditional Economy
An economic system that makes decisions based on established beliefs, customs, and traditions.

A **traditional economy** relies on established traditions to make many economic decisions. In countries such as India, the occupation that one may choose or the wealth that one may command is determined in large part by birthright. If your father was a goldsmith or merchant, you will probably follow in that tradition. This has a strong tendency to reduce individual freedom of choice in economic and other matters. What is to be produced and who will produce it was decided, in some cases, generations ago and is not usually subject to change.

> **3.10 SYSTEM STRENGTHS AND WEAKNESSES**

Earnings are often considered the property of an entire family in traditional economies. Everyone shares in the output of each individual. This might be considered a weak point of the system, since it does not provide strong incentives either to produce more or to save part of an individual's output. To produce more is to give everyone else more with little of the fruits of additional production going to the producer. To save more means that only a small part of that savings will be available for the use of the saver. The inability to accommodate change might also be considered by some as a weak point of traditional economies, while their stability of economic and social values might be considered a strong point.

SUMMARY

> **3.1, 3.2**

1. There are certain economic problems that all economies must face. Since resources are limited and the needs of individuals are unlimited in any economy, scarcity will always exist. Poverty, on the other hand, exists in an economy when the most basic functional needs go unfulfilled.

> **3.3**

2. There are three questions that must be answered by all producing economies:
   a. What goods and services should be produced, given the limited quantity of resources available?
   b. How should goods and services be produced from limited resources?
   c. For whom should goods and services be produced?
   The answers to these questions determine the form of economic organization a society utilizes.

> **3.4**

3. The price system coordinates individual actions in a market economy. It sends signals and influences actions that affect what is produced, how it is produced, and for whom it is produced.

3.5

4. While public services may be free to individuals, they are not free to society. Society as a whole bears the cost of all public services. It is therefore in the interest of all members of society to use public services efficiently.

3.5, 3.6

5. It is in the interest of each individual to minimize his or her contribution to the cost of providing public services. Public services contribute to the functioning of a society and provide different incentives to citizens than do private goods.

3.7, 3.8

6. The major goal within all economic systems is to obtain maximum satisfaction of wants and desires. This goal has several counterparts:
   a. Full employment of scarce resources is needed to achieve the maximum possible satisfaction of wants and desires.
   b. A stable price level is important to producers, consumers, and to those who facilitate economic growth through business investment. In the United States and elsewhere, monetary and fiscal policy are used in an effort to achieve stable prices.
   c. Economic growth is a major goal of any successful economy. As lifestyles and populations grow, economies must expand to meet the additional demands.
   d. Economies strive to become as efficient as possible. They attempt to use scarce resources to produce a maximum amount of goods and services.
   e. An equitable distribution of income is a goal of most economies.
   f. More emphasis is being placed on the environment as a major concern of economic systems in recent years. Its preservation has become one of society's primary goals.

3.9, 3.10

7. Economic systems can be divided into four major categories: the market economy, the command economy, the mixed economy, and the traditional economy. The amounts of social and individual decision making vary in each type of system and in large part define in which category an economy should be classified.

DISCUSSION QUESTIONS

3.1, 3.2

1. What is the basic economic problem all nations face? Explain the difference between scarcity and poverty.

3.3, 3.9, 3.10

2. What are the three basic economic questions that all economies must answer? Explain the differences between the following types of economies, indicating how each differs in its approach to answering these questions:
   a. market economy
   b. command economy
   c. mixed economy
   d. traditional economy

3.5, 3.6 → 3. Why is it that there is not a strong incentive for consumers to choose carefully the amount and type of public services they use? Why is it that public services are often overused?

3.7 → 4. Government has frequently devoted much effort toward stabilizing prices within the economy. What two major types of policies have been used in an attempt to produce this stabilization?

3.8, 3.9, 3.10 → 5. What are some of the features of a traditional economy that would make it an ineffective and inequitable form of economic organization for the United States?

3.4, 3.7 → 6. What government activities might you suggest to create incentives for individuals to keep New York City clean? What role could price play in providing these incentives?

SELECTED READINGS

Friedman, Milton. *Capitalism and Freedom: With a New Preface.* Chicago: University of Chicago Press, 1981.

Friedman, Milton, and Friedman, Rose. *Free to Choose: A Personal Statement.* New York: Harcourt Brace Jovanovich, 1980.

Heilbroner, Robert L. *The Worldly Philosophers*, 5th ed. New York: Simon & Schuster, 1980, Chap. 3.

Klassen, Adrian (ed.), *The Invisible Hand.* Chicago: Henry Regnery Company, 1965.

Kruger, Anne O. "Problems of Liberalization." In Arnold C. Harberger (ed.), *World Economic Growth: Case Studies of Developed and Developing Nations.* San Francisco: Institute for Contemporary Studies, 1984.

Radford, R. A. "The Economic Organization of the P.O.W. Camp." *Economica* (November 1945), pp. 189-201.

PART 2

Markets and the Mixed Economy

CHAPTER 4

Demand and Supply in the Market Economy

Having read the chapter, reviewed the chapter summary, and completed the *Study Guide* exercises, you should be able to:

CRIS

4.1 **MARKETS AND MARKET FORCES:** Define what a market is and explain what forces exist in markets.

4.2 **DEMAND:** Explain what is meant by the concept of demand.

4.3 **LAW OF DEMAND:** Explain the law of demand.

4.4 **DEMAND CURVE:** Explain what a demand curve is and indicate how it illustrates the law of demand.

4.5 **INCOME AND DEMAND:** Discuss how changes in money income affect the demand for a particular good.

4.6 **MARKET SIZE AND DEMAND:** Explain how the size of the market affects the demand for a particular good.

4.7 **SUBSTITUTES, COMPLEMENTS, AND DEMAND:** Explain how the prices of substitute goods and complement goods affect consumer choices and the corresponding demand curves.

4.8 **CONSUMERS' EXPECTATIONS AND DEMAND:** Discuss the relationship between consumers' expectations and the demand for a good.

4.9 **TASTES, PREFERENCES, AND DEMAND:** Discuss the relationship between tastes and preferences and the demand for a good.

4.10 **SHIFT VERSUS MOVEMENT:** Explain the difference between a shift in a demand curve and a movement along a demand curve.

4.11 **SUPPLY DEFINED:** Define the concept of supply.

> **4.12 LAW OF SUPPLY:** Explain the law of supply and discuss the reasons for the direct relationship between price and quantity supplied.

> **4.13 DETERMINANTS OF SUPPLY:** List and discuss the five determinants of supply.

> **4.14 SUPPLY VERSUS QUANTITY SUPPLIED:** Distinguish the difference between a change in supply and a change in quantity supplied and explain the causes and effects of each.

> **4.15 MARKET EQUILIBRIUM:** Explain what the concept of equilibrium in a market represents.

> **4.16 SURPLUS AND SHORTAGE:** Describe the situations of a surplus and a shortage in a marketplace and discuss why they might exist.

> **4.17 SHORT- VERSUS LONG-RUN EQUILIBRIUM:** Explain the difference between short-run and long-run equilibrium in the market.

> **4.18 SUPPLY AND DEMAND EFFECTS:** Explain the effects that changes in supply and demand can have on equilibrium price and quantity exchanged.

> **4.19 PRICE FLOORS AND CEILINGS:** Explain the effects of price floors and price ceilings on the market.

> **4.20 POWER OF PRICE:** Discuss the power of price to communicate, coordinate, and motivate producers and consumers.

> **4.21 ENGINE OF COMPETITION AND PROPERTY RIGHTS:** Explain what is meant by the engine of competition and property rights.

4.1 MARKETS AND MARKET FORCES

Markets
Institutions that coordinate individual choices and provide the basis for the exchange of goods and services.

As we learned in Chapter 1, when people engage in specialization and exchange, they are better able to satisfy their wants and desires. **Markets** are extremely useful mechanisms for facilitating such specialization and exchange. By coordinating the choices of literally millions of individuals through the natural forces of supply and demand, they allow buyers and sellers to make mutually advantageous exchanges. The forces of supply and demand are an outgrowth of the incentives and choices that human beings make as consumers and producers of goods and services.

Markets were originally geographic places where buyers and sellers met to exchange goods and services. Today, with our highly advanced systems of communication and transportation, we do not need a specific geographic place for a market to exist. Exchange can take place by telephone, wire, or

THE CONCEPT OF DEMAND

4.1 MARKETS AND MARKET FORCES

The market force of demand exists because people seek to have goods and services to satisfy their wants and desires. Almost all the goods and services we desire are economic in nature; they are not available in adequate quantities in nature for us to have all that we desire. Since they are scarce, we must give up something to acquire them. In a market this implies that people must pay a price for the goods and services they use to satisfy their wants and desires.

When goods and services are allocated by price through the market, each individual is limited in making purchases by his or her level of income. While income levels vary, income is always limited in some way or another. The wealthy may be able to purchase more goods than the poor, but both have finite incomes and, therefore, both must bear an opportunity cost when they purchase additional amounts of any good.

Given that we must allocate our income, we have a strong incentive to try to get the most satisfaction, or **utility**, from every dollar spent. Accordingly, we choose goods or services that yield the greatest satisfaction in relation to their price. This means that our choices change when the prices of goods change. The price of a good provides us with information concerning its opportunity cost. If a hamburger costs $1.00, for example, this means that $1.00 worth of other items must be given up in order to obtain the hamburger. If the hamburger's price rises to $1.50, this means that it now has a higher opportunity cost because a greater quantity of other goods must be given up to obtain the hamburger. The combination of purchases that maximize satisfaction before the price increase does not necessarily maximize utility after the price rises.

Utility
A measure of the satisfaction or value that an individual derives from a good or service.

4.2 DEMAND

The concept of **demand** involves the analysis of the factors that determine the amounts and kinds of goods and services that people purchase and the forces that lead them to alter their buying behavior. Demand, the analysis of buying behavior, along with supply, the analysis of factors that determine the amounts and kinds of goods and services offered for sale, determine price and quantity in the market.

What relationship do you think might exist between the price of a good or service and the quantity of it that consumers will buy? As noted earlier, an increase in the price of hamburgers increases the opportunity cost of purchasing a hamburger. More goods, and the extra utility they could provide, must be given up in order to purchase the hamburger. A utility-maximizing consumer would consider substitutes for the hamburger, such as hot dogs, which have a lower price. Even if hamburgers are preferred to hot dogs when their prices are equal, a consumer, acting on the margin, might select a hot dog over a higher-price hamburger. This action of purchasing a relatively less expensive substitute would make the consumer better off. The hot dog would provide more utility per dollar and thus be a better buy. The existence of substitutes gives consumers choices to make and is an important controlling force in the market. Individuals can alter their choices when prices change so long as substitute items are available for them to purchase.

Demand
The relationship between the price of a good and the amount of it that consumers are willing and able to purchase in a given period of time. The demand curve shows the quantity demanded per unit of time at each possible price, with all factors except price assumed constant.

4.3 LAW OF DEMAND

Law of Demand
The principle of economics that states that the quantity demanded per unit of time varies inversely with price.

4.4 DEMAND CURVE

Demand Curve
The graphic representation of the relationship between price and quantity demanded. The curve slopes downward and to the right, illustrating the law of demand.

What then do you think would happen to the quantity of a good demanded if its price increased and all other factors that affected consumer choice remained the same? The answer, for almost any good, is that the quantity demanded would fall. Consumers would begin to shift their choices to substitute goods that gave them more utility per dollar. The decision to purchase a smaller quantity of a particular good at a higher price, all else being equal, is a natural result of the desire to attain the maximum satisfaction from a finite income in a world of alternatives. This leads us to what economists call the **law of demand:** the quantity of a good demanded in a given period of time varies inversely with its price. As price increases, the quantity of a good demanded falls, and as price decreases, the quantity of a good demanded rises.

Table 4-1 presents hypothetical data regarding the demand for home computers in the United States. This table illustrates the inverse relationship between price and quantity demanded. We can convert Table 4-1 into a simple graph like the one shown in Figure 4-1 by placing the various prices on the vertical axis and the quantity demanded per unit of time on the horizontal axis, then plotting in the various price/quantity combinations listed in the table. The curve, or line, that is plotted in Figure 4-1 is called a **demand curve**. A demand curve shows the relationship between the price of a particular good and the quantity of it demanded, all factors except price held constant.

The demand curve in Figure 4-1 slopes downward and to the right. This slope, as we discussed in Chapter 1, indicates that there is an inverse relationship between price and quantity demanded per unit of time. The demand curve is a graphic representation of the information about quantity demanded and price that is contained in Table 4-1. Each point on the demand curve corresponds to a price/quantity combination in the table. If you were analyzing this information using Table 4-1, you would conclude that the quantity of a particular type of computers demanded in a given period of time increases from 100,000 to 200,000 when the price falls from $5000 to $4000. This is equivalent to saying that there is a movement along the demand curve from the combination given by point A ($5000/100,000) in Figure 4-1 to point B ($4000/200,000). Further changes in price would result in movements to other points, such as C or D, on the computer demand curve. This shows that a change in price results in a movement along the demand curve.

Demand curves of various types can be drawn. We could draw the demand curve of a particular individual, for example. This graph would show the quantity of computers demanded by the individual at each possible price. Figure 4-1 shows a market demand curve. It depicts the relationship between price and the quantity of computers demanded by all of the poten-

TABLE 4-1 **A Hypothetical Demand Curve for Computers**

Price ($)	Quantity demanded (per unit of time)	Combination
5000	100,000	A
4000	200,000	B
3000	300,000	C
2000	400,000	D
1000	500,000	E

FIGURE 4-1

A Demand Curve for Computers. The demand curve plots the quantity of computers that consumers in the market demand per unit of time at each possible price. The demand curve slopes downward, illustrating the law of demand.

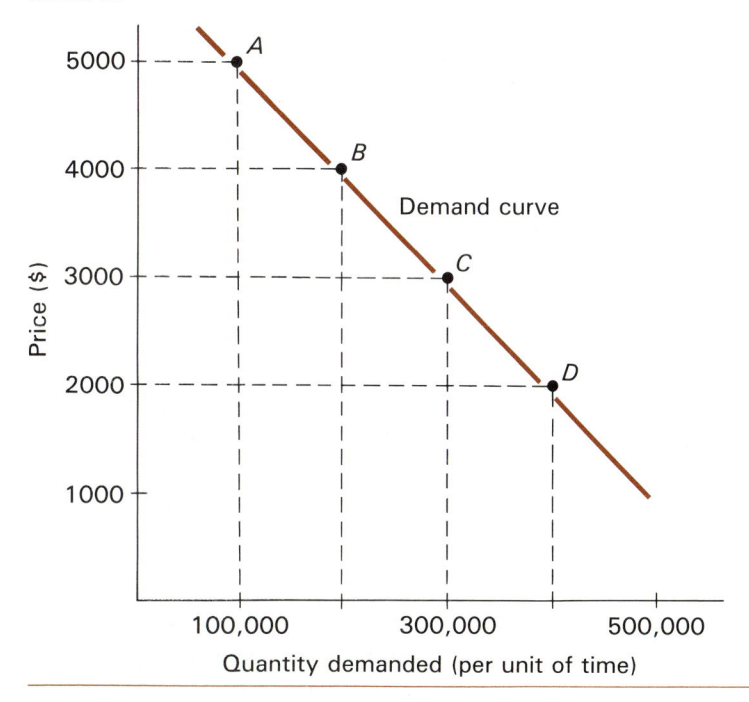

tial buyers in a particular market at a particular time. The market demand curve is found by adding up the quantities that each individual buyer would be willing and able to purchase at each price. All of the demand curves shown in this chapter are market demand curves.

KEY CONCEPTS
4.2, 4.3, 4.4

Demand is the relationship between the price of a good or service and the amount of it that consumers are willing and able to buy. The law of demand states that the price of a good is inversely related to the quantity demanded of the good. The downward sloping demand curve shows this relationship graphically.

THE DETERMINANTS OF DEMAND

Having constructed the demand relationship, it is reasonable to ask, what causes it to change? We know that demand comes from the desire of consumers to maximize the satisfaction, or utility, that they get from the goods they can purchase with their finite income. The demand for a particular product is affected by any event that might alter the utility-maximizing combination of purchases for a consumer. That is, demand is affected by any event that alters a consumer's income, his or her pattern of tastes and preferences, or the opportunity costs of various goods. Individual preferences and the utility derived from a specific good are affected by so many human characteristics that it is impossible to examine each and every one. However, there are a few things that have a particularly strong effect on

4.5 INCOME AND DEMAND

demand. The five determinants of demand discussed below are powerful forces that change demand in predictable ways. Let's examine each of these determinants in detail.

Consumers' Money Income

Suppose that everyone's money incomes were doubled. Everyone now receives twice as much income as before. What would this do to the demand for goods or services? Income would still be finite for each buyer, but the new budget constraint would allow a greater number of purchases before money ran out. We would expect individuals to purchase larger quantities of desirable goods at the current price. Looking at the demand data in Table 4-1, for example, we would expect that an increase in income would result in a larger quantity of computers purchased at each of the prices shown there. People would not be buying more computers because they were less expensive, they would be purchasing more because of a change in a factor (income) other than price. The whole demand relationship would change in this case, as Figure 4-2 illustrates.

An increase in income would cause the initial relationship between price and quantity demanded to change. The old demand curve would no longer represent the demand relationship. As the figure indicates, the demand curve would shift out and to the right if demand increased. This shift shows that a larger quantity of computers is demanded at each possible price. Economists call this shift an increase in demand.

A decrease in the incomes of potential computer buyers would cause a decrease in demand. With less income to spend, we would expect buyers to purchase fewer computers at each price. This would result in a shift in the

FIGURE 4-2 **Increase in the Demand for Computers.** When something other than a change in price occurs to make the purchase of a computer more desirable, the demand is curve shifts to the right, showing that a larger quantity of computers is demanded at each price.

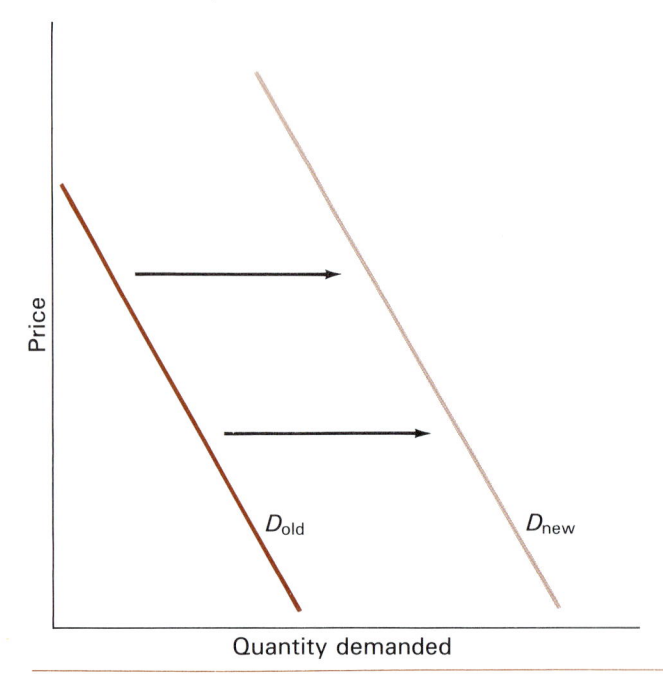

demand curve in the opposite direction from that shown in Figure 4-2. A decrease in demand would result in the demand curve shifting back and to the left. This shift in the demand curve would show that a smaller quantity of computers is demanded at each price due to the decrease in buyer incomes.

The Size of the Market

4.6 MARKET SIZE AND DEMAND

As already noted, the demand curves that we are analyzing are market demand curves. They show the combined demand intentions of all consumers in a given market. Obviously, the number of individuals in the market for a specific good or service affects its overall demand. The demand for a good in a small town, for example, tends to be less than the demand for that good in a major city.

A change in the number of consumers in a market tends to alter the demand relationship, causing the demand curve to shift. During the high-unemployment years of 1981–1982, for example, many jobless autoworkers moved away from the Detroit, Michigan, area in search of greener pastures elsewhere. The decrease in the number of consumers in the Detroit area affected the demand curves for many items. The demand curve for housing fell, for example, shifting back and to the left, because of the lower buying population.

The baby-boom generation of children born in the 1950s illustrates the way that increases in population can increase demand. The rising number of children tended to increased demands for all sorts of child-related products.

The Prices of Substitutes and Complements

Consumers choose among many different goods and services to satisfy their wants and desires. They have an incentive to ration their income among these goods and services so as to get the maximum utility per dollar expended. If an item rises in price, and its **marginal utility** remains the same, then it must provide less utility per dollar than before. Consumers therefore have an incentive to switch to other items that now provide a higher increase in satisfaction per dollar of expenditure. It makes sense, then, that the demand for one good depends on the prices of other items that are related to it. The demand for hot dogs, for example, depends on the price of hamburgers. An increase in the price of hamburgers tends to increase the demand for hot dogs. More hot dogs are purchased at each possible price because some buyers will switch from higher-priced hamburgers to hot dogs in order to increase the amount of satisfaction they get from the goods their scarce money income buys.

Marginal Utility
The change in utility that accompanies a one-unit change in the amount of a good or service consumed.

4.7 SUBSTITUTES, COMPLEMENTS, AND DEMAND

This simple explanation of why people buy different goods when price rises is important, but it does not tell us everything we need to know about the relationship between the demand for one good and the prices of others. Goods fall into three basic categories: substitutes, complements, and unrelated goods. Since unrelated goods do not affect the demand for other goods, they are of no concern at this point. Substitutes and complements are important, however.

Most people would say that it is obvious that steak, hamburger, and hot dogs are **substitute goods**. They are all meat items. What kind of relationship do we see between the prices of substitute goods and their demand curve? As was noted in the example of hamburgers and hot dogs, there tends to be a direct relationship between the demand for an item and the

Substitute Goods
Goods or services that can be used in place of each other; for example, butter and margarine.

72 Demand and Supply in the Market Economy

price of its substitute. That is, as the price of a good goes up, the demand for its substitute increases.

This relationship can be seen in Figure 4-3. As the price of butter increases, the quantity of butter demanded decreases [Figure 4-3(a)], while the demand for margarine (a butter substitute) increases at every price [Figure 4-3(b)]. Conversely, a decrease in the price of butter tends to increase the quantity of butter demanded (a movement along the butter demand curve) and reduce the demand for margarine (a shift in the margarine demand curve).

Complementary Goods
Goods or services that are used together, thereby enhancing each other's value; for example, a tape player and cassettes.

Complementary goods exhibit another type of relationship. Complements are goods that are used together, such as steak and potatoes, stereo phonographs and stereo records, or swimming suits and suntan oil. There tends to be an inverse relationship between the price of a good and the demand for its complement. If the price of a complement goes up, the demand for its complementary good goes down. For example, if the price of eggs were to suddenly increase, the demand for bacon would tend to fall. There would be a smaller quantity of eggs demanded at the higher price (a movement along the egg demand curve), so a smaller demand for bacon would result (a shift in the bacon demand curve).

Consumers' Expectations of Price and Income

4.8 CONSUMERS' EXPECTATIONS AND DEMAND

Consumers respond not only to the current price of goods, but to what they believe those prices are likely to be in the future. Expectations are therefore an important determinant of demand. If you know that the Ford Motor

FIGURE 4-3

Change in Price of Substitute Shifts Demand. The price of one good affects the demand for its substitute. (a) The price of butter rises (a movement along the butter demand curve), so people tend to substitute margarine for butter. (b) This causes an increase in the demand for margarine (a shift in the margarine demand curve).

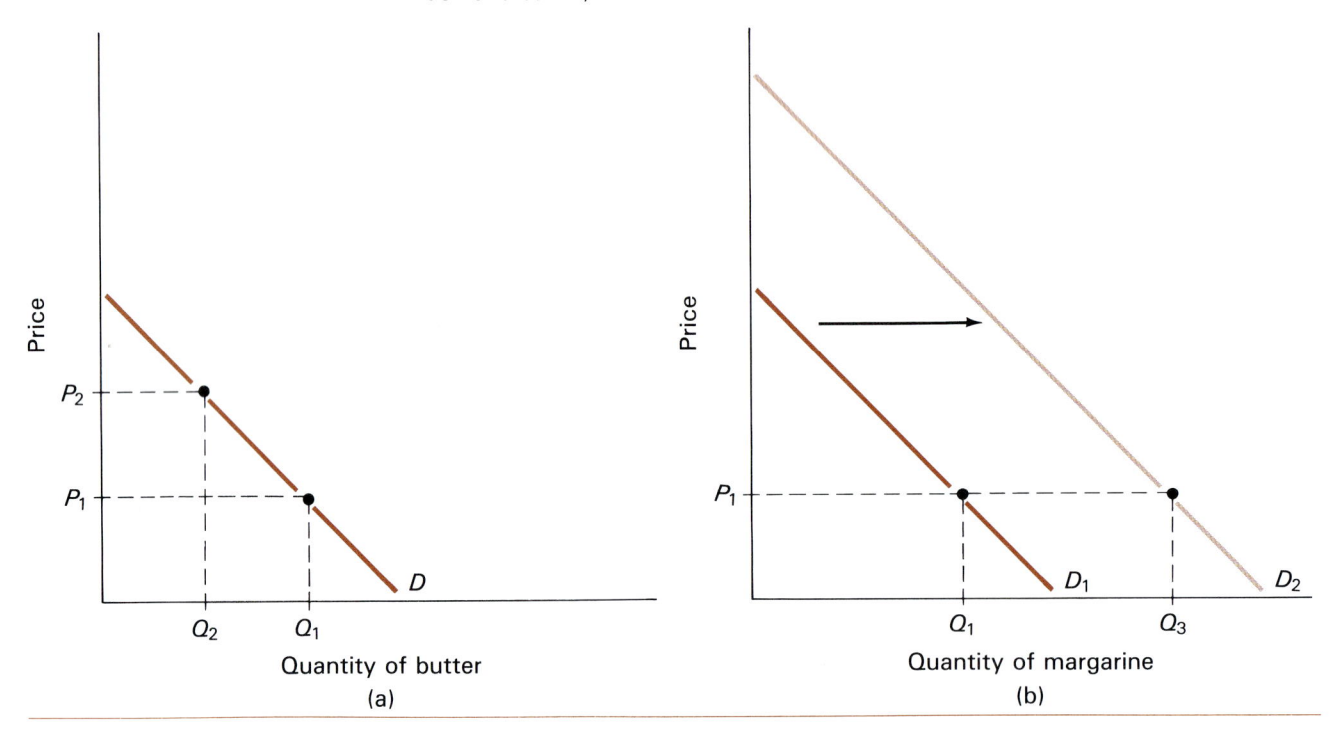

Company plans to offer large cash rebates on their cars beginning next month, you will probably keep your present car at least until then. If, on the other hand, an existing cash rebate offer will expire soon, the decision to buy a new car now might be the rational course of action. Producers also respond to this behavior in their role as buyers of resources. If the price of jet fuel is expected to rise, airlines may increase their purchases of fuel contracts at the present price. If the price is expected to fall, they will not be as willing to sign new fuel contracts at the present price. They may choose to wait and see what will happen to the market price before buying.

Consumers' expectations in regard to their own incomes also play a role in demand. If, for example, the unemployment rate is rising quickly, workers who frequently experience layoffs might reduce their present buying, or at least put off expected major purchases, until their expectations improve. If, on the other hand, consumers expect increases in their incomes in the near future, their present spending, or at least their plans for future expenditures, will frequently experience increases. Consumers act to maximize their satisfaction, both for today and the future. They can spend now or save and spend later. Expectations about price and income therefore affect both the timing of purchases and the total amounts and types of goods purchased.

Consumers' Tastes and Preferences

4.9 TASTES, PREFERENCES, AND DEMAND

The demand for a good or service can change significantly simply because the tastes and preferences of consumers change. The most obvious example of this effect is the ongoing change in clothing styles. In the 1960s, the demand for denim blue jeans was very large and growing. These pants were popular among the general population. In the late 1970s, however, styles shifted to a somewhat more dressy look on campus, a trend that even led to the development of designer blue jeans. The demand for standard blue jeans fell. This shifted the entire demand for standard denim blue jeans back, or inward, and to the left.

Tastes, along with prices and incomes, form the basis for the behavior we observe as demand. Changes in tastes and preferences can therefore shift demand curves and alter buying behavior. Advertisers spend billions of dollars each year to change tastes and cause the demand curves for their products to increase. Even politicians engage in print and media advertising, as well as personal campaigning, in an attempt to encourage an increase in demand for themselves or their point of view.

KEY CONCEPTS 4.5, 4.6, 4.7, 4.8, 4.9

The five major determinants of demand affect the entire demand relationship. These determinants are consumers' money income, the number of consumers, the price of related goods, consumers' expectations, and consumers' tastes and preferences.

CHANGES IN QUANTITY DEMANDED VERSUS CHANGES IN DEMAND

4.10 SHIFT VERSUS MOVEMENT

It is important to remember that a change in any of the five major determinants of demand will change the demand relationship and affect the location of the entire demand curve. This change in the entire demand relationship is

74 Demand and Supply in the Market Economy

Change in Quantity Demanded
A movement along the original demand curve caused by a change in price.

Change in Demand
A shift of the entire demand curve and an actual change in the demand relationship caused by a change in a determinant of demand other than the price of the item itself.

different from a change in the quantity demanded. One of the most frequently made mistakes by students in introductory economics is the failure to distinguish between a change in demand and a change in quantity demanded. The key to understanding this difference is in understanding what caused the change.

If only price changes, there has only been a **change in quantity demanded**. This results in a movement along the existing demand curve. For example, in Figure 4-4(a), we see that the price of electric power has risen from P_1 to P_2, and therefore the quantity demanded has declined from Q_1 to Q_2. There has been a movement along the original demand curve for electric power from point A to point B. None of the determinants of demand have changed, so the demand relationship and the demand curve have not changed.

Suppose, however, that one of the major determinants of demand for electric power changes. This will cause a **change in demand**. Therefore, the entire demand curve will shift. For example, if the number of consumers in the United States increases or the demand for a complementary good to electricity, such as electric appliances, increases, the demand curve for electric power will shift outward and to the right. This would mean that more electric power would be demanded at every price. This shift is illustrated in Figure 4-4(b). On the old demand curve (D_1), the quantity Q_1 is demanded at price P_1. When the demand curve shifts outward, the quantity demanded at P_1 increases to Q_2. This same thing happens at every price along D_2. At the price P_2, the quantity increases from Q_1 on D_1 to Q_3 on D_2.

Failure to understand the difference between changes in quantity demanded and changes in demand can lead to real problems in economic reasoning. For example, both the price of electric power and the quantity

FIGURE 4-4

Change in Quantity Demanded versus Change in Demand. (a) A change in price does not shift the demand curve; it only brings a movement along the demand curve. (b) A change in any nonprice determinant of demand, however, causes a shift in the demand curve, showing that a different quantity is demanded at each price.

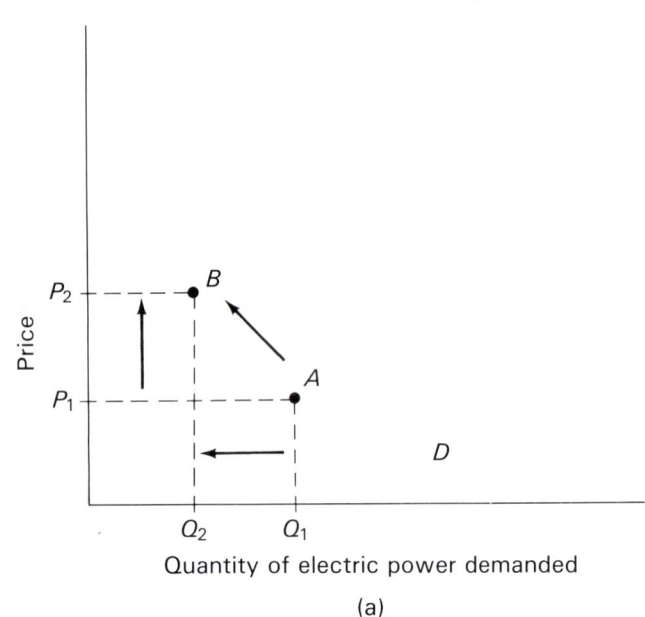

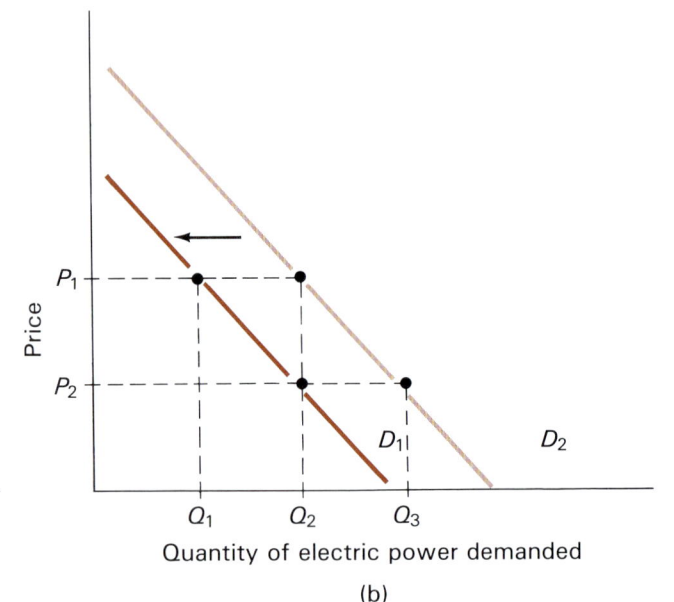

demanded is higher than it was 15 years ago. At first glance, this may seem strange. Doesn't the first law of demand say that quantity demanded varies inversely with price? Yes, but there has been a tremendous growth in the demand for electric power over the past 15 years. The demand curve for electricity has shifted far out and to the right. The law of demand still holds, but it only applies to a specific demand curve at a specific moment. If we doubled the price of electric power tomorrow, quantity demanded would fall. Just as the first law of demand tells us, consumers would move upward along their existing demand curves for electricity, reducing the quantity demanded. If, however, one of the determinants of demand changed, such as a large increase in consumers' incomes, we could expect the entire demand curve to increase. If that was the case, a new demand relationship would exist. Relative to the old demand curve, consumers would be consuming more electricity at higher prices. This is why an understanding of the differences between a change in demand and a change in quantity demanded is crucial in introductory economics.

KEY CONCEPTS 4.10

A change in any of the major determinants of demand causes a change in the entire demand relationship and a shifting of the demand curve. A change in price only causes a change in quantity demanded and therefore a movement along the existing demand curve.

THE CONCEPT OF SUPPLY

4.1 MARKETS AND MARKET FORCES

We have already learned that demand is a market force that represents the choice-making behavior of consumers in the marketplace. Supply is a market force that represents the choices that producers make. Just as consumers attempt to maximize satisfaction per dollar spent, producers work to maximize their own benefits. Both producers and consumers choose in their own self-interest in the marketplace. Producers are led to fulfill their functions of organizing and combining resources to make desired products for consumers by their desire to maximize their own self-interest.

Producers, like consumers, are guided in their pursuit of profits by the existing forces of scarcity and competition. Just as in most markets there are many consumers trying to buy the goods that are available, there are also many producers trying to produce and sell the goods consumers want most. Producers must compete among themselves not only for the consumers' dollars, but also for the resources used to make their products. This scarcity and competition forces businesses to produce their goods as efficiently as possible.

Adam Smith first wrote about this the relationship between production and producer self-interest over 200 years ago. In his book *An Inquiry into the Nature and Causes of the Wealth of Nations*, Smith said:

> It is not from the benevolence of the butcher, the brewer, or the baker that we expect our dinner, but from their regard to their self-interest. We address ourselves not to their humanity, but to their self-love, and never talk to them of necessities but of their advantages.[1]

1. Adam Smith, *An Inquiry into the Nature and Causes of the Wealth of Nations*, New York: Modern Library, 1937, p. 423.

76 Demand and Supply in the Market Economy

Since we now know that consumers demand and producers produce in self-interest, we must look more closely at the forces that guide the actions of producers. How do producers behave in their pursuit of profit maximization? Producers must decide which goods they want to produce. Consumers are willing to pay more for the goods they want most, those that give them the highest levels of utility or satisfaction. Thus, all else being equal, profits are more likely to be made with those goods consumers want most. This means that producers, acting in their own self-interest, must take into account the interests of the consumers. A producer that makes items that consumers do not desire does not stay in business for long.

4.11 SUPPLY DEFINED

Supply
The relationship between the price of a good and the quantity of it that producers are willing and able to sell. The supply curve shows the quantity supplied at each price, all factors except price assumed constant.

One important element in the production choice is the price of the items that are made and sold. **Supply** describes the relationship between the price of a good and the quantity of the good that producers are willing and able to produce and sell, all factors except price held constant. Suppose that you are a producer of pizzas. You bake these pies and sell them for $6 each, which provides a profit that is acceptable to you. Would you be more willing to produce more pies than you do now if consumers were willing to pay $8 each for the pies? Yes you would, since an increase in price would increase your potential profit from pizza production, assuming, of course, that you could produce the additional pizzas using resources that cost you less than $8 per pizza. This brief example describes the typical supply relationship: because producers respond to the profit incentive, the quantity supplied varies directly with price, increasing when price rises and decreasing when price falls.

4.12 LAW OF SUPPLY

There are really two reasons for this direct relationship between price and quantity supplied. The first, as noted above, is the profit incentive. Higher prices mean higher profits, all else being equal, and so provide businesses with an incentive to produce more. The second reason for this supply relationship has to do with the concepts of diminishing marginal returns and the law of increasing costs, which were discussed in Chapter 1. As a firm attempts to expand production in the short run, it quickly runs into diminishing marginal returns and increasing costs.

A pizza maker, for example, quickly discovers that factors such as the size of the kitchen and the pizza oven mean that employing twice as many workers and buying twice as much dough and cheese does not automatically yield twice as many pizzas per hour. The extra workers and resources do not add as much to production as the first workers did because of bottlenecks and production inefficiencies. This results in rising costs. As more pizza is produced, each additional pizza adds more to costs than did the one before it. This affects the supply relationship because pizza sellers must charge a higher price for pizza as their costs increase if they are to make similar profits.

Table 4-2 and Figure 4-5 show a hypothetical supply relationship and supply curve for computers. This supply curve slopes upward and to the

TABLE 4-2

The Supply of Computers

Price ($)	Quantity supplied (per unit of time)	Combination
5000	500,000	A
4000	400,000	B
3000	300,000	C
2000	200,000	D
1000	100,000	E

FIGURE 4-5

A Supply Curve for Computers. The supply curve shows the quantity of computers supplied per unit of time at each price. The supply curve slopes upward, illustrating the direct relationship between price and quantity supplied.

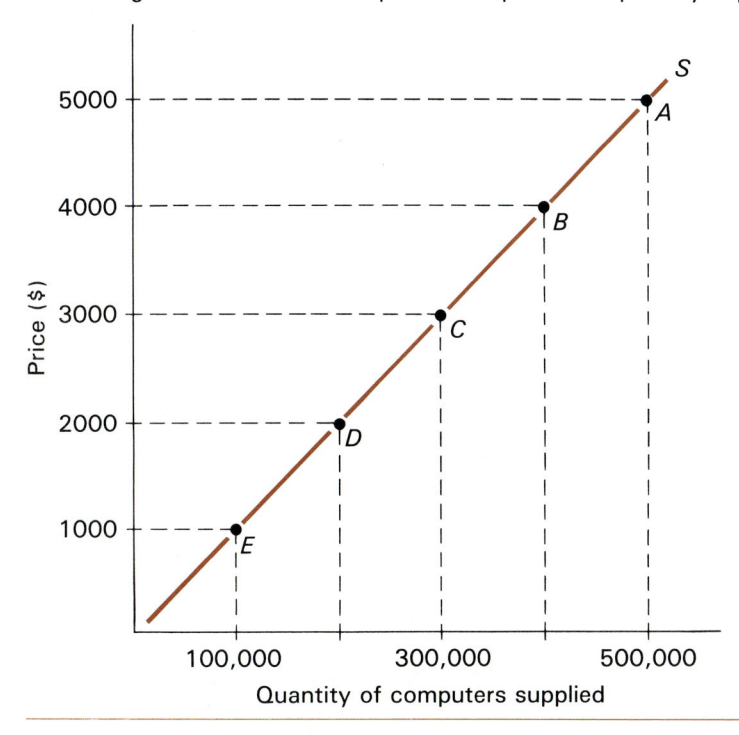

right to reflect the direct relationship between price and quantity supplied. The market force of profit incentive, on one hand, and the fact of diminishing returns and rising cost, on the other, dictate that the supply curve will be upward sloping. Producers are willing to supply more to the market at higher prices. Economists refer to this direct relationship between price and quantity supplied as the **law of supply.**

Law of Supply
The economic principle that describes the direct relationship between price and quantity supplied.

THE DETERMINANTS OF SUPPLY

4.13 DETERMINANTS OF SUPPLY

Earlier in the chapter, we learned that many factors affect consumers' decisions, but that there are five factors that are most important as determinants of demand. There are also five determinants of supply that most strongly influence the choices of producers. Just as with the determinants of demand, any change in the determinants of supply causes a change in the entire supply relationship, resulting in either an increase or a decrease in supply. The determinants of supply are the number of producers, resource costs, the level of technology, opportunity costs, and producers' price expectations.

The Number of Producers

The number and size of the firms producing a good or service affects the supply of that good. The entry of many new firms into the market increases the quantity of the item supplied at each price. An increase in the number of firms selling home computers, for example, would change the supply relationship in Table 4-2. The supply of home computers would have to shift

78 *Demand and Supply in the Market Economy*

FIGURE 4-6 **Increase and Decrease in Supply.** An increase in supply is shown in (a). Supply increases if technology improves or if resource costs fall, among other reasons. A decrease in supply is shown in (b). A smaller quantity is supplied at each price. This can occur if resource costs rise, for example.

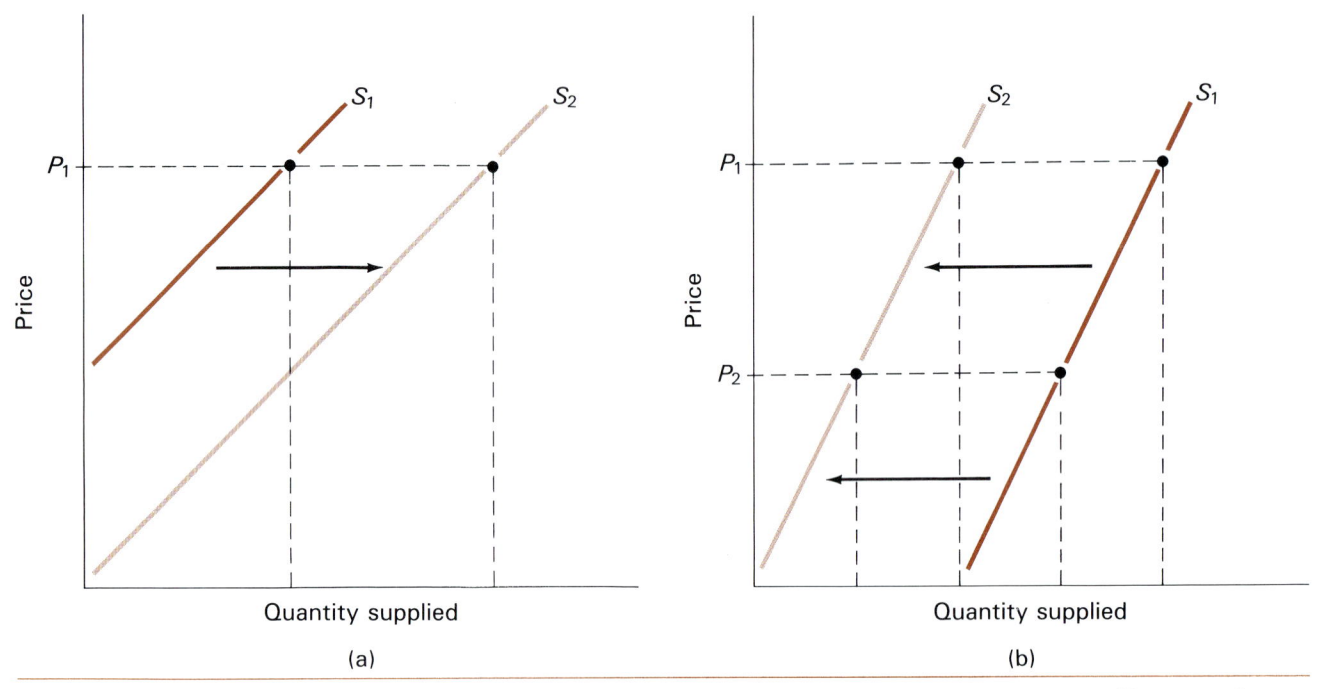

(a)

(b)

out and to the right, as does the curve in Figure 4-6 (a), to illustrate the new relationship betwen price and quantity supplied.

The failure and exit of many producers causes the supply of a good to decrease. If many firms were to leave the computer market, for example, this would cause a smaller quantity of computers to be supplied at each price. We call this change a decrease in supply. Figure 4-6 (b) illustrates a decrease in supply. The supply curve shifts back and to the left to show that a smaller quantity of the product is offered for sale at each price.

Resource Costs

The cost of producing any good or service is directly related to the cost of the resources that are used to produce it. If the cost automobile manufacturers must pay for steel goes up, their costs of production increase and their profits fall. This makes auto producers less willing to supply autos at each price. Rising costs cause a decrease in supply. This is depicted by a shift in the supply curve upward and to the left as in Figure 4-6 (b).

If, on the other hand, steel prices were to decline sharply, this would reduce production costs to auto producers and tend to increase their profits. Producers would be encouraged to supply more cars to the market at every price. This would cause the supply curve for autos to shift outward and to the right as in Figure 4-6 (a).

The Level of Technology

The technology or know-how used to produce an item has a lot to do with its production costs. The more know-how employed, in general, the more

80 Demand and Supply in the Market Economy

KEY CONCEPTS
4.13

Five major determinants of supply affect the choices of producers. They are the number of producers, the price of resources, the level of technology in the industry, the opportunity cost of producing a particular good in terms of the potential profit from selling other goods, and producers' price expectations.

Change in Quantity Supplied
A movement along a given supply curve caused by a change in price.

4.14 SUPPLY VERSUS QUANTITY SUPPLIED

Change in Supply
An actual change in the supply relationship caused by a change in one of the five major determinants of supply, which results in a shift of the supply curve.

CHANGES IN QUANTITY SUPPLIED VERSUS CHANGES IN SUPPLY

Students frequently confuse changes in quantity supplied with changes in the supply relationship itself. This difference is almost identical to its counterpart in demand. A **change in quantity supplied** is a movement along a given supply curve. It is brought about by a change in price. A **change in supply,** on the other hand, is a shift of the entire supply curve. It cannot, in the short run, be caused by a change in the price of the good. Rather, it must be caused by some change in one of the determinants of supply. When supply changes, either more or less of the good is offered for sale at every price. Figure 4-7 clearly illustrates the difference between quantity supplied and a change in supply. Remember, if only price changes there has been a change in quantity supplied. If one of the five major determinants of supply changes, the entire supply relationship has shifted.

FIGURE 4-7   **Change in Quantity Supplied versus Change in Supply.** (a) A change in price causes a movement along the supply curve. The supply curve does not change, we simply move from one price/quantity supplied combination to another. (b) A change in one of the determinants of supply, however, causes a shift in the supply curve. A different quantity is supplied at each price.

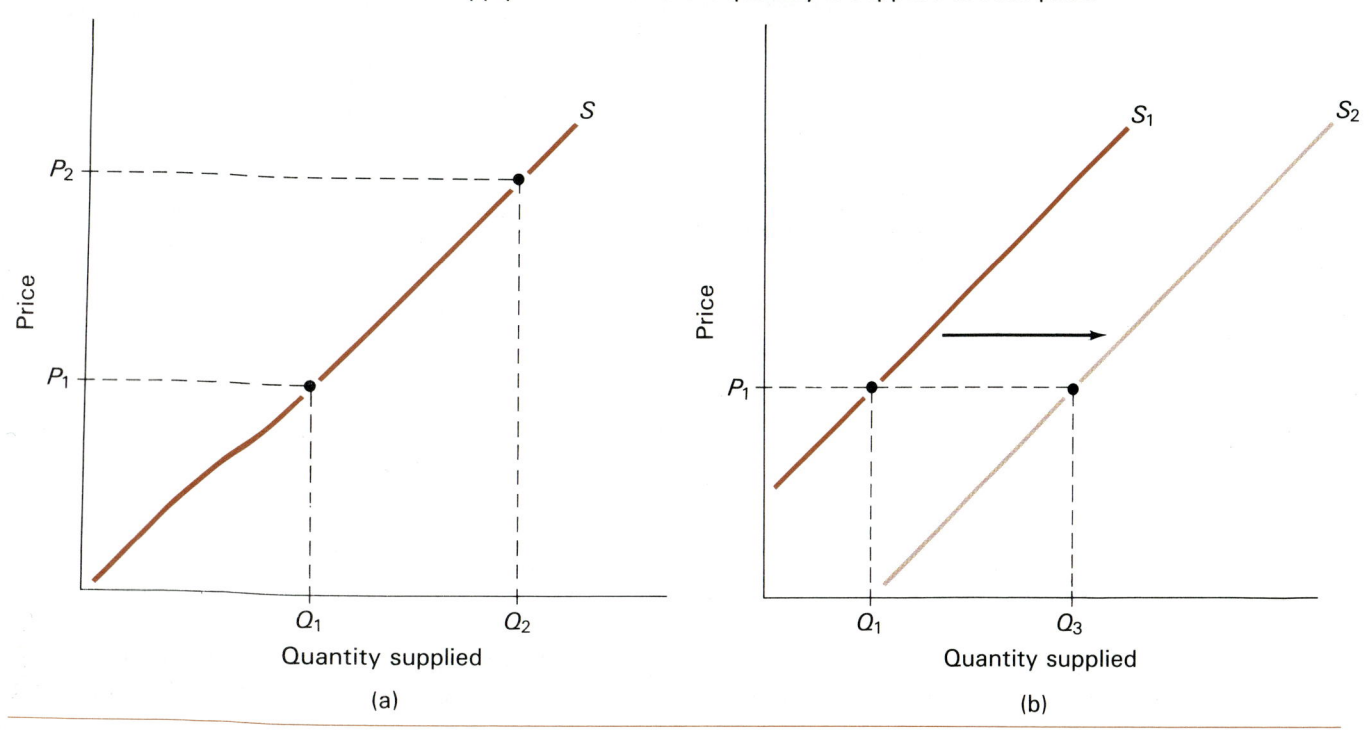

efficiently anything can be produced. Consider the development of the mass-produced microprocessor chip that is now widely used in the calculator and computer industries. When these chips were first produced, the process was slow, and expensive. As engineers developed more knowledge of how to mass-produce the chip, the cost of producing it declined sharply. This was such a major cost reduction that a hand-held calculator that cost $400 in 1970 could be bought for about $40 in 1986. From this example, it is easy to see that the development of higher levels of technology reduces costs, improves short-run profits, and increases supply.

Opportunity Costs

Most producers have the ability, over time, to produce several different types of goods. The Chrysler Corporation can produce automobiles or manufacture military tanks. A farmer can grow corn and wheat or graze cattle with just about the same basic resources. The farmer who chooses to graze cattle is giving up the potential profits from the corn and wheat that could have been produced instead. The decision to graze cattle must take these alternatives into account. In other words, the farmer must consider the opportunity cost of grazing cattle when making this choice.

How do producers decide which goods to produce? The profit potential of the different goods they can produce for sale is a key consideration. If wheat and corn both cost the farmer about $1 a bushel to produce, which will be grown? All else being equal, the farmer would choose whichever has the highest market price.

The price of one good can affect the supply of other goods. Consider, for example, what would likely happen if the United States and the Soviet Union agreed upon a new long-term grain sale. Because of the agreement, U.S. grain prices would likely remain higher than they would have without the agreement. This would cause some farmers to shift from grazing cattle or growing corn to producing wheat. The relatively higher price for wheat would tend to reduce the market supplies of corn and cattle because producers would have switched to more profitable alternative uses of their resources. On the other hand, if the government decided to place a grain embargo on the Soviet Union, wheat prices would quite likely fall and many wheat farmers might decide to plant more of their acreage in corn or soybeans or use it for cattle grazing, thereby increasing the market supplies of these items.

Producers' Price Expectations

The buying behavior of consumers is affected by their expectations regarding the future price of a product. Producers' choices are also affected by what they think is going to happen to the price of the product they produce. If, for example, a major oil company anticipated a large increase in the maximum legal price of gasoline, it would tend to hold its gasoline reserves off the market until the increase took effect. If, on the other hand, oil producers expected the government to lower the ceiling on legal gasoline prices, they might push their reserves into the market before the price decline. The supply of gasoline would shift outward and to the right. More gasoline would be supplied at every price. Producers would, in either case, respond to the incentives placed before them by their expectations of future prices.

KEY CONCEPTS 4.14   A change in price causes a change in quantity supplied. A change in any of the determinants of supply causes a change in the entire supply relationship and a shift of the supply curve.

A second major similarity between the concepts of supply and demand concerns their market curves. Just as market demand is the horizontal summation of the individual demand curves, market supply is the horizontal summation of the individual producer's supply curves. Table 4-3 and Figure 4-8 illustrate this concept.

MARKET EQUILIBRIUM

We have now had an opportunity to examine separately the mechanics of supply and demand. These forces do not, however, function separately in the marketplace. The prices goods command in the marketplace are determined by the forces of supply and demand working together. In the late 1800s and early 1900s, the distinguished economist Alfred Marshall laid much of the groundwork that constitutes our current understanding of markets. Marshall realized that neither supply nor demand independently determines value. He wrote, "We might as reasonably dispute whether it is the upper or the under blade of a pair of scissors that cuts a piece of paper,

TABLE 4-3   **Individual Firms and Market Supply**

Price	Quantity supplied Firm A	Quantity supplied Firm B	Quantity supplied Firm C	Market quantity supplied
5	25	50	70	145
4	20	40	50	110
3	15	30	40	85
2	10	20	30	60
1	5	10	20	35

FIGURE 4-8   **The Market Supply Curve Is the Sum of Individual Supply Curves.** The market supply curve is found by adding together the quantities that individual firms supply at each price. The market demand curve is similarly found through the horizontal summation of individual consumer demand curves.

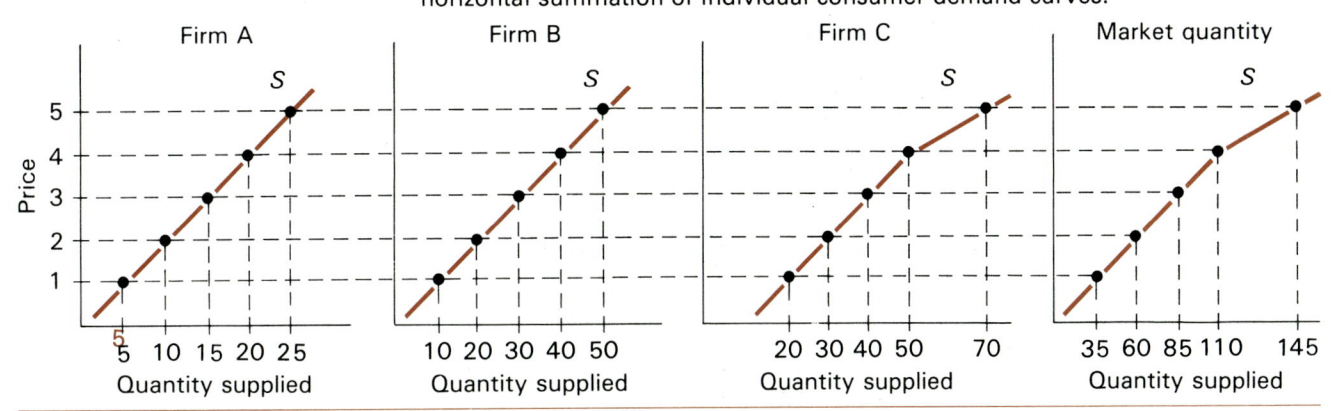

4.15 MARKET EQUILIBRIUM

as whether value is governed by utility (consumer demand) or cost of production (supply)."[2]

Table 4-4 and Figure 4-9 combine the computer demand and supply data and curves we have already developed in this chapter. Remember that supply represents the choices of producers, while demand represents the choice-making behavior of consumers. It is not difficult to see that over most

2. Alfred Marshall, *Principles of Economics*, 8th ed., New York: Macmillan, (1982) p. 348.

TABLE 4-4

Computer Demand and Supply Relationships

Price ($)	Quantity supplied (per unit of time)	Quantity demanded (per unit of time)	Market condition
5000	500,000	100,000	Surplus
4000	400,000	200,000	Surplus
3000	300,000	300,000	Equilibrium
2000	200,000	400,000	Shortage
1000	100,000	500,000	Shortage

FIGURE 4-9

Market Equilibrium Balances Forces of Demand and Supply. The computer market is in equilibrium at a price of $3000 and a quantity of 300,000. The quantity demanded equals the quantity supplied at equilibrium price. A surplus would appear if price were set at $5000 — the quantity demanded is less than the quantity supplied. The surplus would drive price down toward equilibrium. There would be a shortage at a price of $2000 because the quantity demanded would exceed the quantity supplied. The shortage would force price to rise toward equilibrium.

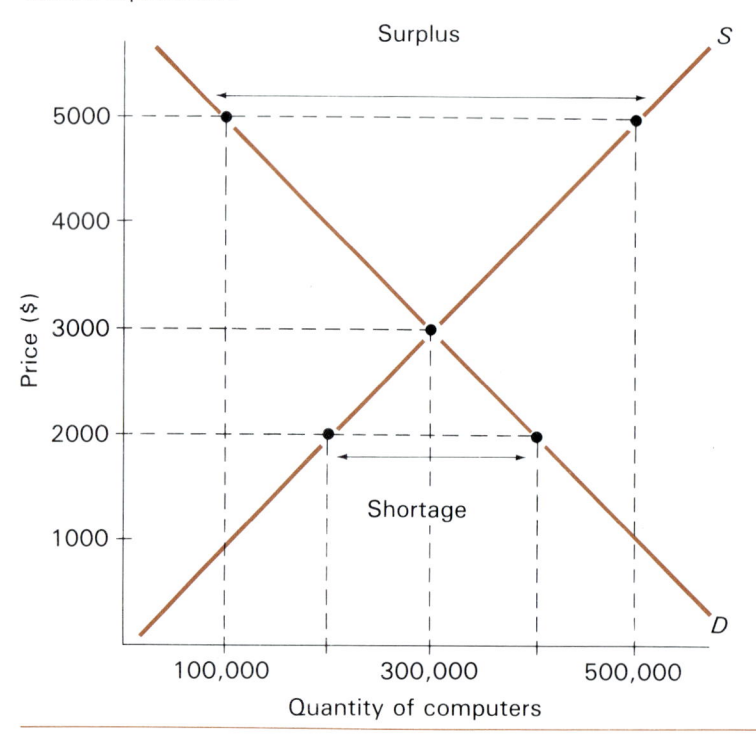

Equilibrium
Any point at which conflicting forces are in balance. In economics market equilibrium occurs at the price at which quantity supplied is equal to quantity demanded.

4.16 SURPLUS AND SHORTAGE

Surplus
A situation in which the quantity supplied exceeds the quantity demanded at the market price.

Shortage
A situation in which the quantity demanded exceeds the quantity supplied at the market price.

of the range of prices in the market, the amount of home computers that consumers are willing to buy is different from the amount that producers are willing to supply. There is, however, one price at which the desires of both producers and consumers are in harmony. This is the **equilibrium** price in the market. In scientific terms, equilibrium is a state in which conflicting forces are in balance. Equilibrium in the marketplace is the point at which the forces of supply and demand are in balance. This means that the supply and demand curves cross, or more exactly, that the quantity supplied to the market at the equilibrium price is exactly equal to the quantity demanded by consumers at that price. At the equilibrium price, the choices of producers as to how much they desire to produce and consumers as to how much they desire to buy are equal.

What about supply and demand at all the other prices in the market? To answer this we will again have to consider the incentives that guide the choices of producers and consumers. Consider, for the moment, the quantity supplied and demanded at the price of $5000. Consumers only demand 100,000 units at that price, while producers are willing and able to supply 500,000 units. A **surplus** (or excess supply) occurs at this price. Some producers will be willing to accept a lower price to get rid of the inventory of unsold computers they have produced. This lower price will cause some producers to cut back their production; others will simply not be willing to produce at all and will leave the market. On the other hand, consumers will see the lower price and increase their quantity demanded accordingly. Some consumers who were already buying computers will buy more and other consumers who had stopped using computers will re-enter the market. The surplus will be exhausted and the market will efficiently and automatically move toward the equilibrium, where the forces of supply and demand are in balance and the quantity supplied just equals the quantity demanded.

Note what happens if price is less than the equilibrium price. At a lower price, of say $2000, consumers will buy all the computers that the producers are willing to make, and then some. The quantity demanded of 400,000 units will exceed the quantity supplied of 200,000 units. A **shortage** (or excess demand) will exist. Realizing that their inventories are being depleted faster than they can replace them, producers will raise the prices of the few existing units, say to the $3000 level. Some consumers will be unwilling to pay these higher prices, thereby reducing quantity demanded to 300,000 units. Other producers will see these higher prices and be willing to increase production. Still other producers, who were unwilling to produce at all at the lower prices, will be coaxed back into the market. Quantity supplied will rise to 300,000, which is just equal to the quantity demanded by consumers. No shortage or surplus will exist.

In the above example, the market's supply-demand equilibrium is stable. By stable, we mean that once it has achieved equilibrium, the market tends to remain at equilibrium and, if the market is out of equilibrium, natural market forces will tend to move it toward equilibrium.

KEY CONCEPTS 4.15, 4.16

Supply and demand determine the price of goods in an unrestricted marketplace. Equilibrium price in the marketplace occurs at the point at which quantity supplied equals quantity demanded. A surplus exists when, at a specific price, there is an excess of quantity supplied over quantity demanded. When quantity demanded exceeds quantity supplied at a specific price, there is a shortage in the market.

4.17 SHORT- VERSUS LONG-RUN EQUILIBRIUM

Short Run
A length of time short enough so that individual producers are not able to vary production capacity.

Long Run
A length of time sufficiently long so that individual producers are able to alter production capacity to suit market conditions.

Short- and Long-Run Equilibrium

There are two separate types of adjustments that producers can make to their output that affect the concept of equilibrium. Over very short periods of time, producers can add more workers to their production line, employ the existing workers for longer hours, and in general use more of the resources directly involved in production. Some types of resources, however, are not readily available on short notice. Plant size and equipment, for example, are not things that a producer can change very quickly. It takes time for new firms to organize and enter an industry. It takes time to order and have new equipment built and installed. It takes quite a while to plan, design, build, and equip a new, larger plant to produce more. Because of these two types of adjustments, the concept of equilibrium is analyzed in two forms: long-run and short-run equilibrium.

The **short run** is defined as a time period short enough that plant capacity cannot be changed. In the short run, therefore, producers do not have enough time to adjust completely to changes in consumer demand. The **long run**, however, allows producers sufficient time to fully adjust to changes in market demand conditions, since it enables them the opportunity to expand or contract their plant size. This is very important because it tells us something about what happens to price in the marketplace over time. In the short run, an equilibrium can exist at whatever price the quantity supplied is equal to the quantity demanded. In the long run, however, that equilibrium price must at least be equal to the producer's opportunity cost of manufacturing the good. If it is not, producers will simply leave the market. Supply will then decline, driving the market price up to a point at least equal to the opportunity cost of the remaining producers.

As an example of this point, consider the situation in which there is excess supply in the marketplace. Some producers will lower their prices to dispose of excess inventory. They may sell these goods at a price below their opportunity costs. It is doubtful, however, that they will continue to make more of these goods once their inventory is depleted if market price is below producer opportunity cost. In the long run, the producer will rationally choose to produce other goods that will be profitable.

Changes in Equilibrium

Once the forces of supply and demand have reached equilibrium in the marketplace, it might appear that the equilibrium price and quantity exchanged would remain constant for long periods. This is not necessarily true. The only constant in the marketplace is the guarantee that change is always present. The behavior of consumers and producers changes in response to the circumstances they face. Therefore, the location of both the supply and demand curves will constantly be changing as the determinants of demand and supply change. This constant change implies that equilibrium price and quantity will be in a state of constant change, as well.

4.18 SUPPLY AND DEMAND EFFECTS

Let's take a look at how changes in supply and demand can change the equilibrium price and quantity exchanged. Figure 4-9 illustrated the equilibrium supply and demand conditions for computers. Figure 4-10 illustrates what happens to the equilibrium price and quantity exchanged when the supply of computers increases and demand remains constant.

Many new manufacturers may have entered the market producing computers, or the costs of resources used to produce computers may have fallen. Either of these forces would tend to increase the supply of comput-

FIGURE 4-10

Increase in Supply Creates Surplus and Lower Price. An increase in supply creates a surplus at the initial equilibrium price. Price falls in response to the surplus, and the market moves toward a new equilibrium with lower price and higher quantity.

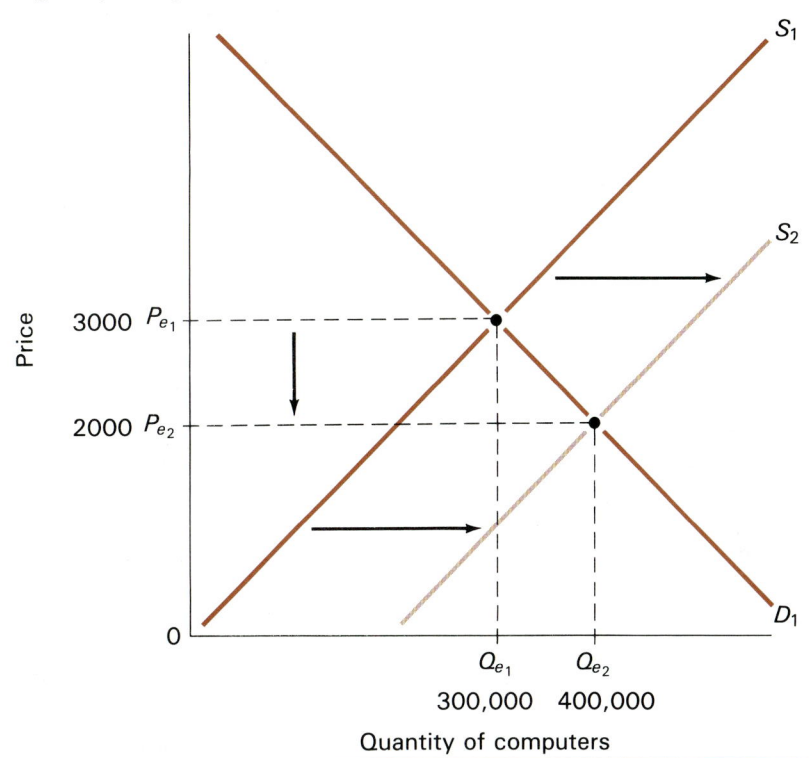

ers. The original supply and demand curves (S_1 and D_1, respectively) had reached equilibrium at the price P_e ($3000) and the quantity exchanged of Q_e (300,000). With the entry of new firms producing computers, the supply curve shifts out, as illustrated by S_2, creating a surplus of computers. Price falls in reaction to the surplus because consumers are willing to buy more computers at the lower price. As a result, the market equilibrium price falls to P_{e2} ($2000) and the equilibrium quantity exchanged increases to Q_{e2} (400,000).

We can also examine what happens to equilibrium price and quantity if one of the determinants of demand changes and the supply conditions remain constant. Figure 4-11 shows the original equilibrium in the computer market. Suppose that consumers' tastes and preferences for home computers changed, increasing the number of computers they want to purchase at each price. The demand curve would shift from D_1 to D_2, causing a shortage of computers at the initial equilibrium price. The equilibrium price would increase to P_{e2} ($4000), and since the number of exchanges would have increased, equilibrium quantity exchanged would increase to Q_{e2} (400,000 units).

When a given demand or supply curve shifts, it creates a surplus or shortage. Prices in the market change in response to the surplus or shortage, thereby causing the reactions that lead to a new market equilibrium. Sometimes, however, both demand and supply shift at the same time, making changes in price and quantity more difficult to determine. The outcome in terms of equilibrium price and quantity is determined by both

86 Demand and Supply in the Market Economy

FIGURE 4-11 **Increase in Demand Creates Shortage and Higher Price.** An increase in demand creates a shortage at the initial equilibrium price. Price rises in response to the shortage. The market moves to a new equilibrium with higher price and higher quantity.

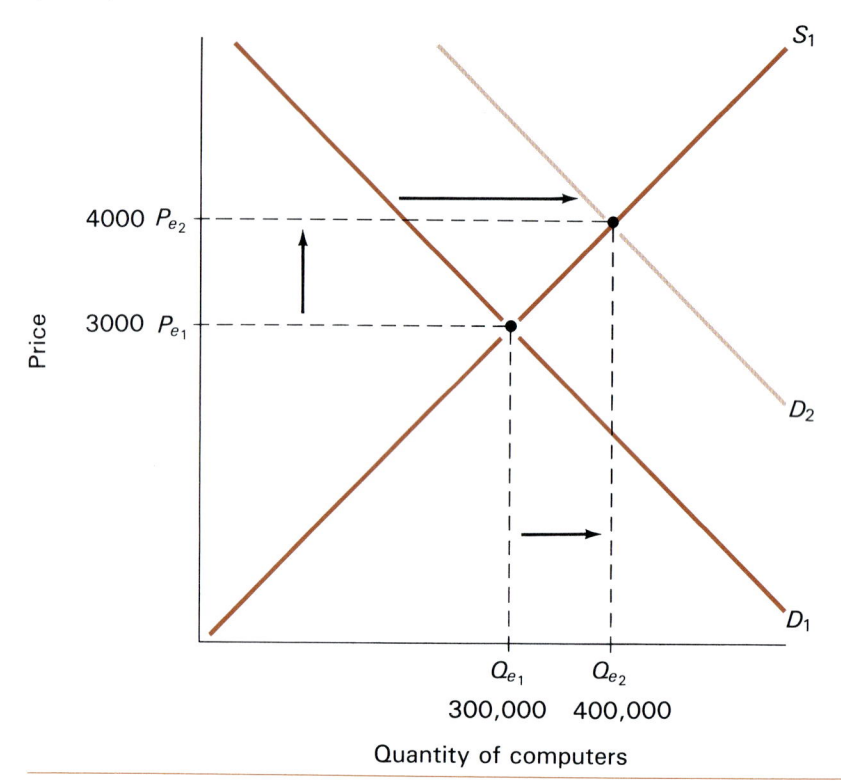

the direction and magnitude of each respective change in the supply or demand conditions. For example, Figure 4-12 illustrates equal increases in both the supply and demand for computers.

In this instance, supply has expanded from S_1 to S_2 and demand has increased from D_1 to D_2. Here we note that although the equilibrium quantity exchanged has increased from Q_{e1} (300,000 units) to Q_{e2} (400,000 units), the equilibrium price has remained constant at P_e ($3000). This is true because the increase in demand that would normally have driven the market price up was offset by the equal increase in supply, which drove price down to its previous $3000 level. Figure 4-13 illustrates what can happen to market equilibrium when supply increases and demand decreases by the same proportion. Demand has contracted from D_1 to D_2 and supply has expanded an equal amount from S_1 to S_2. Here, we see that the equilibrium price has decreased from P_{e1} ($3000) to P_{e2} ($2000), but the equilibrium quantity has remained the same.

We could conclude that price remained constant in Figure 4-12 and that quantity remained constant in Figure 4-13 because we knew that the demand and supply curves shifted by the same amounts. In general, however, we cannot draw these conclusions where both demand and supply shift at the same time. Suppose, for example, that both demand and supply increased at the same time, as in Figure 4-12, but that we do not know which shift is greater. In this case, we can conclude that the equilibrium quantity will rise, but we cannot tell whether equilibrium price will rise or fall. The increase in demand, taken by itself, tends to cause a shortage and thereby

FIGURE 4-12 **Both Demand and Supply Can Increase.** This is what happens if demand and supply both increase, as might happen if consumer incomes increased at the same time that a technological improvement took place. The equilibrium quantity increases. The price remains constant in this example, although this is not the general case. In general, it is impossible to tell in which direction price moves when supply and demand both increase.

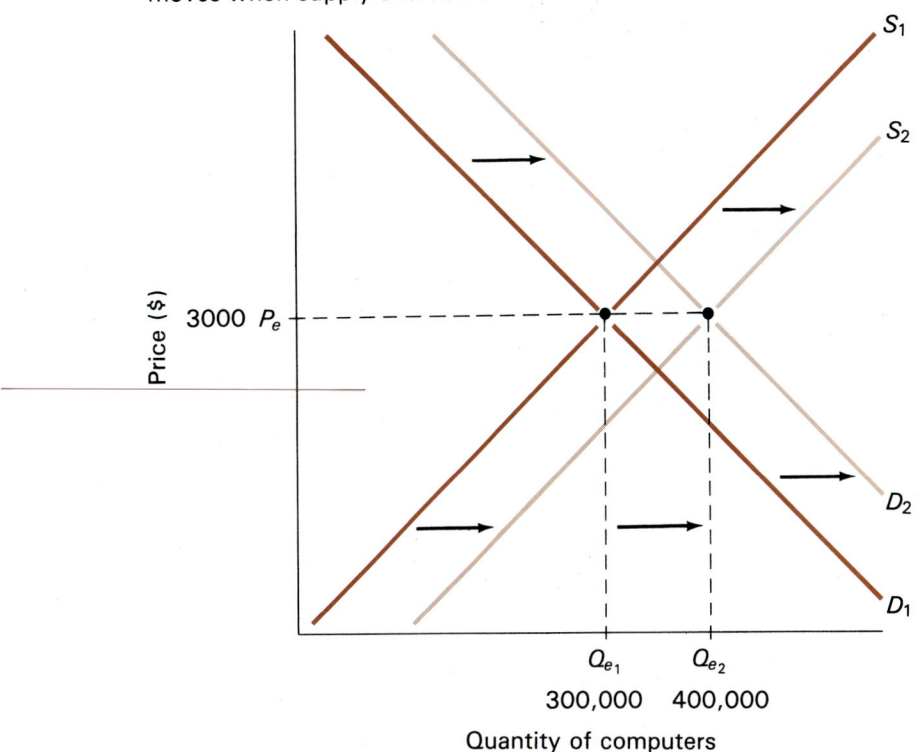

increase price. But the increase in supply, taken by itself, tends to cause a surplus and thereby lower price. The net effect in this market is that price could rise, if the increase in demand is greater, or price could fall if the increase in supply is greater.

Figure 4-13 shows a situation in which demand decreased and supply increased. We can conclude here that price will fall, but we cannot generally conclude what will happen to quantity. Quantity here is ambiguous unless we know exactly how much demand and supply change. Quantity could rise, fall, or remain the same depending on whether the decrease in demand is less, more, or equal to the increase in supply. The rule of thumb is that, in general, when both demand and supply shift it is possible to determine how one variable will change (price in Figure 4-13), but the other variable is ambiguous (quantity in Figure 4-13).

Review of Market Actions

You will be using the tools of supply and demand throughout this text, so it is a good idea to get a feel for them now. The following paragraphs describe common market changes. Read them and check them out by drawing your own demand and supply curves. Be sure you can tell what happens in each case and, more important, why it happens and what forces are at work in the market. Upward-sloping supply curves and downward-sloping demand curves are assumed throughout this section.

88 Demand and Supply in the Market Economy

FIGURE 4-13   **Increase in Supply with Decrease in Demand.** This is what happens if demand falls at the same time that supply increases. This situation might occur if consumer income fell at the same time a rising number of firms entered the market. Price falls here, and the equilibrium quantity remains the same in this example, although it is not generally possible to tell what happens to quantity when demand falls and supply rises.

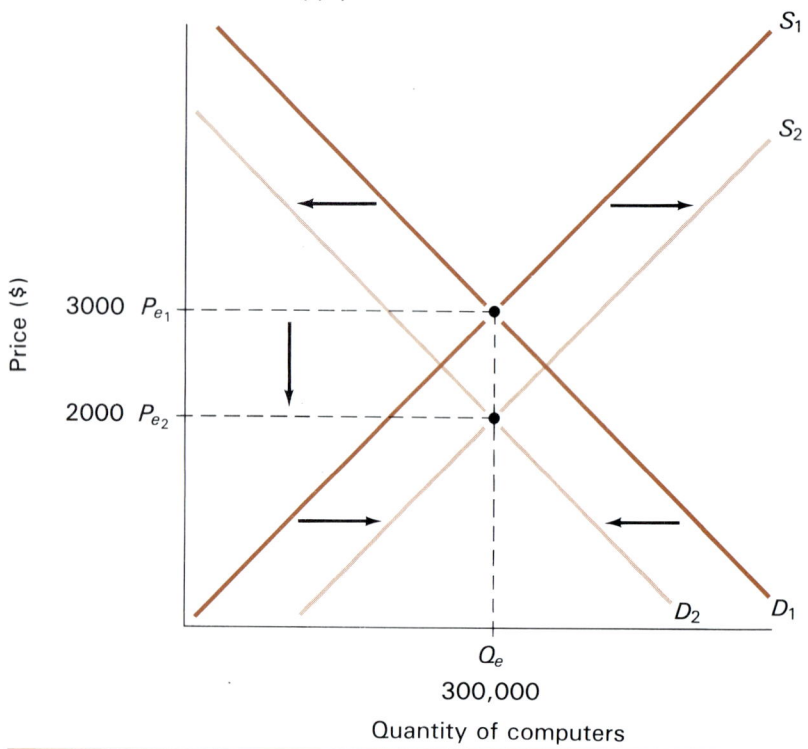

Increase in Demand   An increase in demand creates a shortage, since quantity demanded exceeds quantity supplied at the old equilibrium price. The shortage bids up price. The new equilibrium combines higher price with larger quantity.

Increase in Supply   An increase in supply brings forth a surplus of goods. Quantity supplied exceeds quantity demanded at the initial equilibrium price. Price falls in response to the shortage. The new equilibrium occurs at lower price but larger quantity.

Decrease in Demand   Falling demand brings a surplus. Producers offer more for sale than buyers desire at the initial equilibrium price. As price falls, however, quantity supplied falls, too. The new equilibrium combines lower price with lower quantity.

Decrease in Supply   Falling supply causes a shortage, which bids up price. Price rises but quantity falls.

Increase in both Demand and Supply   Quantity goes up here, but you cannot be sure about price. If supply increases more than demand, equilibrium price falls. If demand has the bigger shift, equilibrium price rises.

Decrease in both Demand and Supply This is the reverse of the last change. If both demand and supply fall, we can be sure that less is produced, but the change in price is ambiguous. The direction of the price change depends on whether demand or supply falls the most.

Increase in Demand and Decrease in Supply This is a perverse set of changes. Consumers want more, but supply falls at the same time. This combination of the forces of demand and supply gives us higher prices, but the change in quantity is ambiguous. Quantity depends on whether supply or demand shifts the most.

Decrease in Demand and Increase in Supply This is the opposite of the last entry. Price unambiguously drops, but the change in quantity cannot be determined unless the size of the supply and demand shifts is known.

PRICE FLOORS AND PRICE CEILINGS

4.19 PRICE FLOORS AND CEILINGS

The forces of supply and demand bring about an equilibrium in the marketplace. A free market brings buyers and sellers together to reach an exchange agreement. However, the price and quantity verdict of the market is not always politically popular or in the best interests of society in the long run. Sometimes government steps in with policies designed to alter the market's choice of price or quantity.

There have been times, for example, when the market price of milk has dropped so low that many milk producers were driven to the brink of bankruptcy. This happened in the U.S. dairy industry in the years just after the First World War. Through political means, the American dairy producers and the U.S. Department of Agriculture were successful in having some state laws enacted that set a legal minimum price, or **price floor,** for milk.

Price Floor
A minimum legal price in a particular market.

Milk price floors, although different in detail from those enacted after the First World War, are still with us, and they affect the market in the same basic ways as did the original price floor. The market price for milk is artificially forced above the level that the existing natural forces of supply and demand would have produced in the market. Dairy farmers make higher profits and as a result many stay in business. This, however, is a mixed blessing at best. The incentives of the marketplace have been altered, and it is only rational to expect both producer and consumer to respond to the new set of incentives. Figure 4-14 illustrates what happens.

The market for milk is originally in equilibrium at the market equilibrium price, P_{en}, of $1.00 per gallon and the equilibrium quantity, Q_{en} of 40,000 gallons per day. When the government raises the legal minimum price to P_g ($1.50 per gallon), quantity supplied in the market expands to Q_{sg} (50,000 gallons per day). Farmers respond to the new incentive of the higher price for their product by producing more milk. Consumers also respond to the new incentive of the higher price. They consume less, just as the law of demand tells us they will. Quantity demanded falls back to Q_{dg} (30,000 gallons per day). Since only price has changed, this is a change in quantity demanded, not a change in demand. The market is flooded with milk. Consumers are only buying 30,000 gallons per day and producers are producing 50,000 gallons per day at this price. We have a milk surplus.

FIGURE 4-14

A Price Floor Causes a Surplus. A price floor set above market equilibrium prevents price from falling to equilibrium. A surplus of goods accumulates.

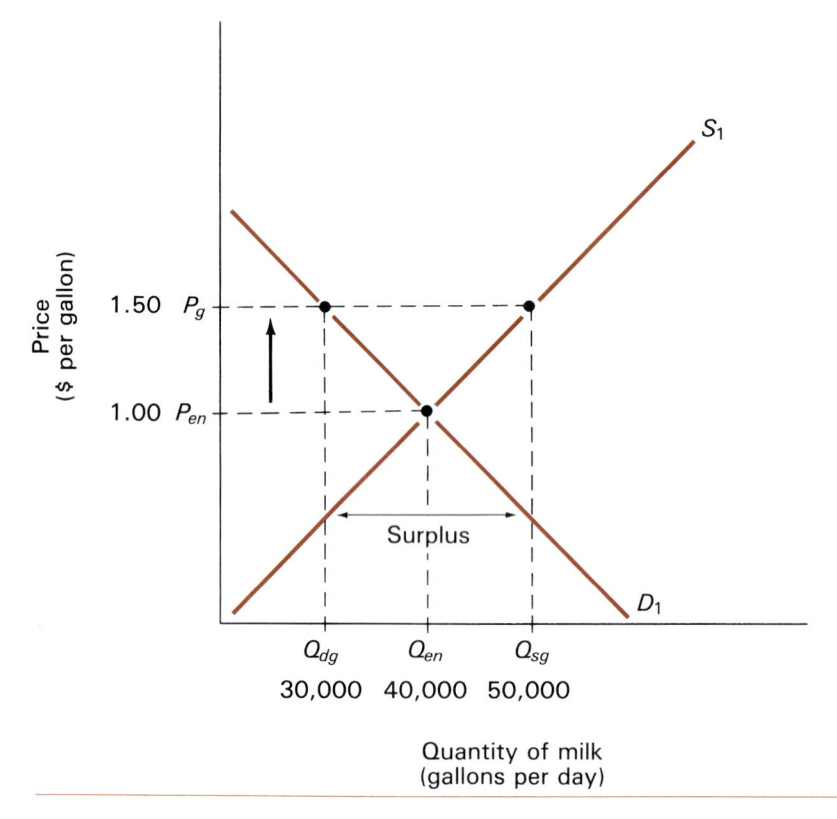

[Graph: Price ($ per gallon) vs. Quantity of milk (gallons per day). Supply curve S_1 intersects Demand curve D_1 at equilibrium $P_{en} = 1.00$, $Q_{en} = 40,000$. Price floor $P_g = 1.50$ shown above equilibrium with upward arrow. At P_g: $Q_{dg} = 30,000$ and $Q_{sg} = 50,000$, with the range between marked as "Surplus".]

The incentive structure of a market seldom can be altered without additional economic problems of one type or another being produced. In this example, we see that government policies that attempt to make consumers better off in the long run end up making them worse off in the short run. Many economists think that the true purpose of dairy price floors is simply to increase the incomes of dairy farmers.

A government determined maximum price, or **price ceiling,** can also distort the incentive structure. Figure 4-15 illustrates what happens with this type of market interference. D_1 and S_1 illustrate the market supply and demand for gasoline in the United States. The equilibrium price, P_{en}, of $1.50 per gallon and quantity, Q_{en}, of 40,000 gallons arise from these conditions. Many people must use gasoline to get to and from work as well as to meet their everyday transportation needs. The equilibrium price of $1.50 per gallon may be judged by government to be too high and be seen as placing an unfair hardship on lower-income consumers. Much of their total income would be spent on gasoline at this price. To counteract this, the government may legislate a maximum legal price of gasoline of $1.25 per gallon.

Consumers and producers both see the new price and react to the incentives before them. At the new lower price, P_g, of $1.25 per gallon, producers are willing and able to supply 20,000 gallons per day to the market. Consumers see the lower price and react by demanding 80,000 gallons per day. As a result, a shortage of 60,000 gallons per day occurs. Consumers want more gasoline than producers are supplying.

Price Ceiling
A maximum legal price in a particular market.

| FIGURE 4-15 | **A Price Ceiling Causes a Shortage.** A price ceiling set below market equilibrium prevents price from rising to equilibrium. A shortage of goods prevails, with rationing, black markets, and favoritism used to allocate the scarce items. |

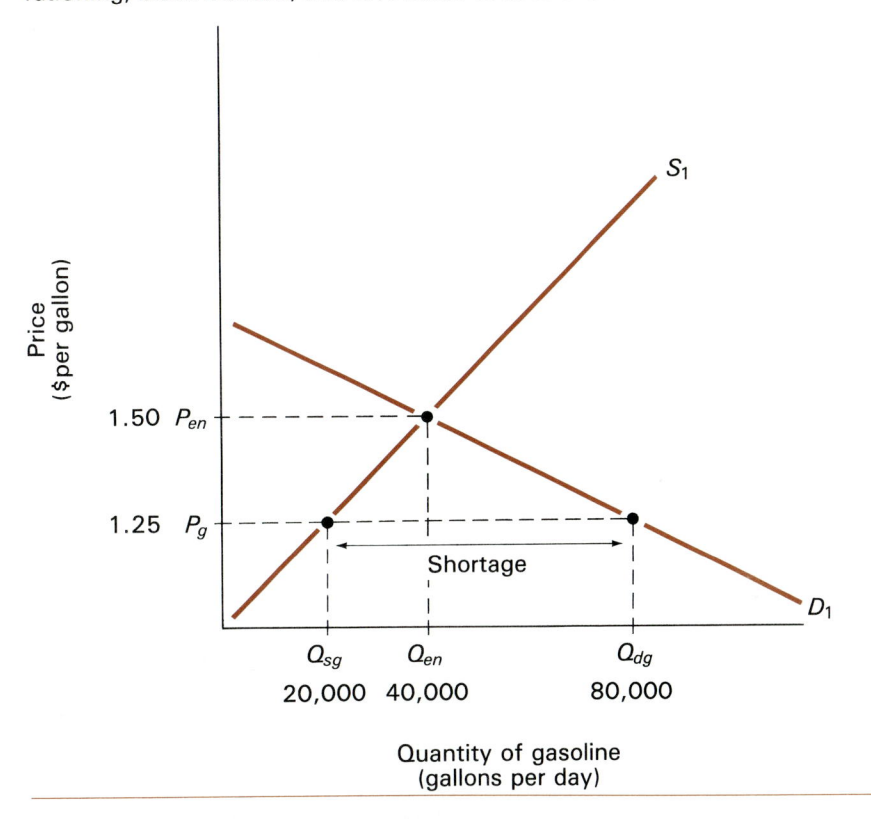

Normally, in an unrestricted market, consumers would bid the price up when faced with a shortage. Suppliers would supply a larger quantity at higher prices, and consumers would cut back the quantity demanded until an equilibrium was reached. This cannot happen here since the maximum legal price of gasoline is already fixed. The small quantity of gasoline that producers are willing and able to supply will have to be rationed among consumers by some other method. This usually takes the form of long lines at gasoline stations. A different kind of cost is passed on to the consumer. The total cost of gasoline is now $1.25 per gallon plus the opportunity cost of having to wait in line to get it. The persons who can best afford to pay the full price for the gasoline are those whose opportunity cost of waiting in line is the lowest.

Since the incentives of producers and consumers in the market have been altered by the price control, a new price system emerges. Placing a legal cap on a price in our economy is almost a sure way of producing some alternative kind of price outside the market system. Black markets and favoritism replace the market system. Gasoline that is in short supply will be sold at illegally high prices in black markets or allocated on the basis of favoritism or bribes. As already stated, it is seldom possible to alter the incentive structure in one market without producing other substantial economic effects. Markets are far from perfect allocation mechanisms, and occasionally they produce unwanted effects even when they are unrestricted. The point here is not that market restrictions are all bad or always have negative effects, but that they produce many complex problems and secon-

ECONOMIC ISSUES

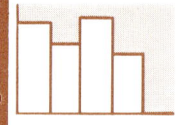

Do Rent Controls Help the Poor?

Many people favor rent controls as a way to protect low-income groups from rising housing costs. Most rent control laws take the form of price ceilings. A maximum legal price is established on existing rental housing. The price ceiling is not perfectly fixed, however, and rents can rise over time based on increased cost. In addition, newly constructed housing is often exempt, at least initially, from rent controls. The movement to establish rent controls has gained momentum in recent years, with many rent control initiatives voted into law, especially in California and the Altantic states.

The idea behind rent controls is that they allow renters to escape the impact of higher rents by keeping rents on controlled housing below the market equilibrium price. Do these laws benefit the poor, as it seems at first glance? Most economists conclude that they do not. The reason why is based on supply and demand.

An effective rent control sets the price of rental housing below the market equilibrium price. As you have seen in this chapter, such a price ceiling tends to cause a shortage. Many individuals seek rental housing because its price is relatively low, but fewer rental units are supplied because low rents give little incentive for landlords to construct or maintain rental housing. The shortage means that rental housing will be hard to find and that many consumers who want rental housing will have to look elsewhere for a place to live.

The real-world studies of rent control ordinances cited below show that rent control problems go beyond simple shortages. Rent controls set in motion a chain of events that ends up making renters, even those with low, price-controlled rents, worse off. Among the effects of price controls are lock-ins, quality changes, reduced supply, and black markets.

Lock-in Effect

Most rent-control ordinances allow landlords to raise rents when an apartment is vacated. This means that if two families, in different parts of town, leave their own rent-controlled apartments and move into the other's, each ends up paying higher rent because the landlords are allowed to increase rents to compensate for higher costs. This gives renters a strong incentive to stay in their rent controlled unit, avoiding potential rent increases, even when these units no longer fit their needs. A worker who gets a new job in a different area or town, for example, might keep the same rented house and undertake a longer commute in order to forestall rent increases. A growing family might find that they must stay in their increasingly crowded apartment, with the family tensions that usually result, because moving means giving up their "bargain" rent. In short, those who stay in rent controlled units simply to keep low rents often end up paying for their choice in other ways because they are locked in to housing that no longer fits their needs.

Quality Changes

A common problem associated with rent controls is deterioration of rental housing. Landlords who receive below-market prices have little incentive to in-

dary effects. The costs and benefits that arise from these restrictions, therefore, must be identified and carefully weighed in advance of the decision.

THE POWER OF PRICE

It is easy to overlook and underestimate the power of the economic forces that make markets work. Most people do not realize how complex a task it is to get something as simple as a pencil manufactured and into the hands of its user. Consider that the common pencil can contain graphite mined in Africa, rubber grown in South America, paint produced in Cleveland from pigments mined in Arizona, and wood grown in Oregon. The journey of

vest in renovation and maintenance. Landlords find that maintenance funds are more profitably put to other uses in markets that are not subject to price controls. Rental housing deteriorates slowly over time, becoming shoddy and less attractive to renters. Renters eventually find that lower rental costs buy them lower quality housing, making rent controls less of a bargain. A study by Mann and Veseth of voter behavior on rent controls indicates that fear of deteriorating housing quality is one reason renters vote against rent-control initiatives.[1]

Reduced Supply

Rent controls reduce the incentive to construct rental housing by reducing the potential for profit from this investment. If rent controls apply to all rental housing in a city or county, the supply of rental units tends to increase at a slower rate than would otherwise be the case, making the housing shortage even more severe. Investment funds go, instead, to other projects and to construction of new rental housing in jurisdictions that have no rent controls. If rent controls apply to existing units only, investment funds are diverted away from maintenance of existing rental units and used to construct new rental housing not subject to price ceilings. A two-tier rental housing system develops, with relatively cheap but shoddy rent-control units alongside well-maintained, but more expensive, new units not subject to price controls. Cheung even cites examples where existing units have been torn down and rebuilt, simply to allow higher legal rents, a truly inefficient use of resources made profitable by the incentives of price-control laws.[2]

Black Markets and Other Problems

How are rent-controlled housing units allocated, given the excess demand for these units? Black markets in housing sometimes develop, in which landlords demand illegal payments from renters. The renters sometimes find it cheaper to bribe landlords or building managers than to spend additional time and money searching for scarce housing units. Rent ceilings do not really keep housing costs down in these situations. Where rent-ceiling laws are enforced, scarce rental units are sometimes allocated based on influence or other political, economic, or social factors. Desirable rental units sometimes go to those with the best "connections," not to those who have the greatest need.

Rent controls are a paradox. They are intended to keep rental costs low, but they can backfire in the long run, as shortages appear, housing quality suffers, and the overall cost of living in rent-controlled units increases. Most economists agree that the social cost of rent controls exceeds whatever temporary benefits may accrue to renters. If housing costs are too high for the poor, many think that selective subsidies to low-income families, which make them better able to pay market rents, may be a better answer than rent controls that affect all renters and distort housing markets.

Additional References

Baird, C. *Rent Control: The Perennial Folly*. San Francisco: The Cato Institute, 1980

Friedman M., and Stigler, G. "Roofs or Ceilings: the Current Housing Problem." Reprinted in *Rent Control: A Popular Paradox*. Vancouver: The Fraser Institute, 1975, pp. 87–102.

Smith L., and Tomlinson, P. "Rent Control in Ontario: Roofs or Ceiling?" *American Real Estate and Urban Economics Association Journal* (Summer 1981), pp. 93–114.

1. B. Mann and M. Veseth, "Moderate Rent Controls: A Microeconomic and Public Choice Analysis." *American Real Estate and Urban Economics Association Journal*, (Fall 1983), pp. 333–343.
2. S. Cheung, "Roofs or Stars: The Stated Intents and Actual Effects of a Rents Control Ordinance." *Economic Inquiry*, (March 1975), pp. 1–21.

4.20 POWER OF PRICE

these raw materials from their origins to the pencil factory and finally into the writer's hand involve the work of literally thousands of individuals. Miners, rubber plantation workers, and laborers of all types must all do their jobs to get this simple product to market. When you think of the millions of goods and services the economy produces, it becomes clear what a complex task it is to controls all these people and circumstances.

Who manages this process in a market economy? Who keeps the miners mining enough but not too much graphite or pigments? Who guides and directs how much and what types of rubber will be produced? No one person or organization does. The forces of a market economy are really natural forces that communicate, coordinate, and motivate the actions of all the economic players. This does not imply that markets are perfect. They do sometimes fail, but the market mechanism has a tremendous power to serve the necessary functions of communicating, coordinating, and motivating the actions and reactions of producers and consumers.

Communication

The buying decisions of consumers communicate key information to producers quickly through the market mechanism. The prices at which producers are willing to supply goods and services send clear signals to consumers regarding the costs of producing goods and services and the resources used in their production. Prices guide consumers to increase or decrease their purchases. When consumers reduce their purchases of a commodity because some other substitute gives them more utility per dollar expended, this is communicated to the producers through the market price system. If prices are too low and consumers buy more than the producer is presently supplying, the price system pushes prices up communicating the scarcity of the item to the consumers and notifying the producers that more output is desired. Prices direct producers to produce more or fewer goods. Prices direct both producers and consumers in the selection of the goods and raw materials that they buy. In short, the market price is a tremendous communication link between everyone who buys and everyone who sells in the market.

Coordination

The function of coordinating the actions and reactions of all the economic players in a market is also assisted by the market price mechanism. If producers are supplying more of a commodity to the market than consumers desire, the market price falls. This serves to coordinate the desires of both producers and consumers. At the new lower price, producers will not be willing to supply as much to the market and consumers will be demanding more than they did at the old higher price. The market gropes through rounds of surpluses and shortages but always tends naturally toward an equilibrium price and quantity.

Markets also coordinate the desires of producers to produce those goods and services consumers want most. Goods that yield consumers large amounts of utility are those for which consumers are willing to pay the highest prices. Higher prices also signal more fertile grounds for entrepreneurs to seek profit opportunities. Entrepreneurs will constantly search out those opportunities that offer them the greatest potential for profit, and by doing so fulfill the strongest wants and needs of consumers.

The market is truly a dynamic mechanism, with all the economic players choosing over and over again all the time. Consumers search for and choose those goods and services that best fulfill their needs. Producers search for and produce those goods and services that prove to be most profitable for them.

Motivation

Both producers and consumers are guided in their actions by the invisible force of self-interest. As Adam Smith wrote

> Every individual is continually exerting himself to find out the most advantageous employment for whatever capital he can command. It is his own

advantage, indeed, and not that of society which he has in view. But the study of his own advantage naturally, or rather necessarily, leads him to prefer that employment which is most advantageous to society. . . . He intends only his own gain, and he is in this, as in many other cases, led by an invisible hand to promote an end which was no part of his intention. By pursuing his own interest, he frequently promotes that of the society more effectually than when he really intends to promote it.[3]

Even 200 years ago, Smith understood the motivating power of the market mechanism, and how it can harness the power of self-interest to fulfill the desires of both producers and consumers. In a market system, no central planning agency is necessary to coordinate the actions of millions of producers and consumers. The system of profits and losses acts as a reward and punishment system, rewarding the efficient producer and eventually eliminating the inefficient producer. The system of individual consumer choice permits consumers to select in their own best interest.

The motivational power of self-interest is easily seen in our human behavior. Students frequently choose to give up years of income and work very hard to acquire an education that has market value. Producers bear great capital risks to start new businesses. What forces motivate human beings to bear these costs and risks? It is the motivational power of self-interest evidenced in the marketplace. The expectation of gain in the future is one of the single strongest human drives. It motivates all the parts of the economic puzzle that come together in the marketplace.

Competition and Property Rights in the Marketplace

Although markets can and do communicate, coordinate, and motivate the various components of our economy, they do rely on two foundations for efficient operation. To fulfill these three functions well, a market must rely on the engine of competition and a system of well-defined property rights. The **engine of competition** means that there will be many producers and many consumers in the market for a particular good. The consumers' interests are protected by the fact that they may choose among many sellers and may not, therefore, be forced into exchange with any one producer if that exchange is not beneficial to them. Producers are protected by the fact that no single consumer in the marketplace has enough buying power to coerce them into exchanges that they consider nonbeneficial. When the engine of competition is not present, there is no guarantee that the interests of both consumers and producers will be simultaneously maximized.

Property rights define the acceptable and unacceptable limits of behavior in a market. If the property rights of consumers are well-defined, producers may not coerce consumers to deal with them through actions such as threats of violence or fear of reprisals. The same may be said for protecting the property rights of producers. Consumers may not use threats or other infringements on property rights to force producers to deal with them. Property rights guarantee economic security, as well. If you own a large tract of land, a producer may not build or set up a business on your premises without your permission or without compensating you for the land's use.

---

3. Adam Smith, *An Inquiry into the Nature and Causes of the Wealth of Nations*, New York: Modern Library, 1937, p. 423.

4.21 ENGINE OF COMPETITION AND PROPERTY RIGHTS

Engine of Competition
The existence of many consumers and producers in the market for a certain good or service.

Property Rights
The rights to own, occupy, or benefit from property within the economy. They define the acceptable and unacceptable limits of behavior regarding property.

ECONOMIC ISSUES

Black Markets in the Soviet Union

Markets in the United States are relatively free from government controls. In the Soviet Union, however, many government controls exist that limit the markets' ability to respond to supply and demand. Black markets frequently appear when government controls exist. A black market is an illegal market. That is, it is a market where transactions are made in illegal goods or where exchanges of legal goods take place at illegal prices. These exchanges take place, even though they are illegal, because they are mutually advantageous. Buyers and sellers both gain from the transactions, even though they may be subject to punishment if caught.

Black markets are so common in communist countries that they are almost a way of life. Hedrick Smith's account of life in modern Russia, for example, devotes an entire chapter to living *na levo,* which in Russian means "on the left" or "under the table."[1] According to Smith's description, consumers in the Soviet Union must constantly live na levo if they desire anything other than the bare minimum of consumer goods.

Prices in the black market can be much higher or much lower than "official" prices, depending on the situation. High-quality consumer goods are scarce in the Soviet Union, for example, because of government emphasis on industrial production. The official prices of desirable consumer items may be relatively low, but these goods are seldom available in government stores because the low price and low assigned production levels assure a constant shortage. (When they are available, high-quality consumer goods generally go to those at the head of the long lines that always form.) But most desirable items are seldom sold on a first-come, first-served basis. Store managers and clerks instead sell them na levo, at higher prices, to their friends and acquaintances. These black-market prices are higher than the official ones and are, indeed, higher than prices would be on a free market because the illegal sellers risk fine or imprisonment if caught. They must mark up their merchandise by an extra measure to compensate for this risk.

Sometimes high-quality goods are sold to selected customers at official prices, but *blat* is required in exchange. Blat is a Russian term for a favor or

SUMMARY

4.1
1. Markets are institutions that bring together the forces of demand and supply to facilitate mutually advantageous exchange. Supply and demand are the two natural forces present in all market situations.

4.2
2. The concept of demand encompasses the set of all factors that determine the types and quantities of goods and services that people wish to purchase at any time.

4.3
3. The law of demand states that the price of a good is inversely related to the quantity demanded of the good per unit of time. The downward-sloping demand curve shows this relationship graphically.

4.4
4. A demand curve plots the relationship between the price of a good or service and the quantity of the item that is demanded in a given period of time. It shows how the quantity demanded changes when the price of the item changes, all else held constant. The demand curve illustrates

personal debt. The idea of blat is that, "I will sell you these scarce oranges now (at the official prices), if you agree to obtain some scarce and desirable goods, such as shoes or meat, for me in the future." Blat is common currency on black markets in the Soviet Union because it does not involve extra money payments and so is technically legal.

Blat is generally less efficient than simple black-market price gouging because blat requires a coincidence of wants. That is, the use of blat in payment for scarce goods requires that both buyer and seller have specific favors that the other wants. Money is more efficient than blat because money can be exchanged for all goods, whereas a particular favor, such as getting someone good shoes that are not available in the stores, is only valuable if the person needs shoes. Unfortunately, consumer items are in such short supplies in the Soviet Union that virtually any blat favor probably has value to someone.

Prices are not always higher than the official price in black markets. There is an active black market in gasoline in the Soviet Union, for example, with prices lower than those available at official outlets. The official price of gasoline in 1982 was 40 kopecks per liter ($2.18 per gallon), but the black market price was just 12 kopecks.

Why is gasoline cheaper on the black market? The reason is that most of the black-market supply is stolen. Gasoline tank trucks can be found on many streets, with the driver selling gasoline at discount prices. The drivers carry more fuel than their records show and sell the difference on the black market as they make their rounds to fill gas station reserves. Sometimes government employees even sell the gasoline from their official cars or trucks (or even tanks!) to gain extra income.

Prices are lower on the gasoline black market because the seller steals the gasoline from the employer or the government and sells it with a near zero chance of being caught. Even at the low black market price, a gasoline seller can easily earn a relatively high income. Low prices also induce buyers to keep quiet about the source of their illegal fuel. Some Russians have probably never purchased gasoline at the high "official" price. The official price is set high to discourage waste. This scheme has backfired, however, because many Moscow motorists waste much fuel driving around looking for a black market dealer. When official gas sells for 40 kopecks and black market fuel is 12 kopecks per liter, it can be economical to waste gasoline looking for the black market rather than filling up at the official price.

Additional References

Gillette, Robert. "Black-Market Gas Pumps Never Run Dry in Russia." *Seattle Times,* January 31, 1982, p. A3.

Schmemann, Serge. "At Soviet Used-Car Lot, Whispered Deals Produce Huge Profits for Vintage Vehicles." *New York Times,* June 7, 1981, p. 3.

1. Hedrick Smith, *The Russians.* New York: New York Times Book Co., 1976.

---

the law of demand by showing that a larger quantity is demanded at lower prices.

4.5, 4.6, 4.7, 4.8, 4.9 ▶ 5. The five major determinants of demand affect the entire demand relationship. These are consumers' money income, the size of the market, the prices of substitutes and complements, consumers' expectations, and consumers' tastes and preferences.

4.10 ▶ 6. A change in any of the major determinants of demand causes a change in the entire demand relationship and a shifting of the demand curve. A change in price only causes a change in quantity demanded and therefore a movement along the existing demand curve.

4.11 ▶ 7. Supply represents the choice-making behavior of producers. Producers strive to maximize their benefits and minimize their costs. They compete with each other for limited resources as well as for consumers' dollars.

4.12 ▶ 8. There is usually a direct relationship between price and quantity supplied. This direct relationship results from the incentive effect of price changes and the law of increasing cost. This direct relationship between price and quantity supplied is termed the law of supply.

98 *Demand and Supply in the Market Economy*

4.13 ▶ 9. Five major determinants of supply affect the choices of producers. They are the number of producers, the price of resources, the level of technology in the industry, the opportunity cost of producing a particular good in terms of the potential profit from selling other goods, and producers' price expectations.

4.14 ▶ 10. A change in price causes a change in quantity supplied. A change in any of the determinants of supply cause a change in the entire supply relationship and a shift of the supply curve.

4.15 ▶ 11. Supply and demand determine the price of goods in an unrestricted marketplace. Equilibrium price in the marketplace occurs at the point at which quantity supplied equals quantity demanded.

4.16 ▶ 12. A surplus exists when quantity supplied exceeds quantity demanded at a specific price. When quantity demanded exceeds quantity supplied at a specific price, there is a shortage in the market.

4.17 ▶ 13. Market equilibrium has a different meaning in the short run than in the long run. In the long run, consumers and producers are better able to react to short-run changes in economic conditions.

4.18 ▶ 14. The market equilibrium changes whenever something happens to shift demand, supply, or both. These changing market conditions are summarized in the section titled Review of Market Actions in this chapter.

4.19 ▶ 15. Price floors and price ceilings distort the market because they prevent the market from reaching equilibrium. Price floors tend to cause persistent surpluses of items. Price ceilings tend to cause persistent shortages.

4.20 ▶ 16. Prices guide consumers and producers in choosing the goods, services, and resources that are bought. Prices and markets serve to coordinate the choices of producers to produce the goods consumers demand most in the marketplace.

4.21 ▶ 17. Competition and well-defined property rights must exist for markets to effectively communicate, coordinate, and motivate the choices of producers and consumers.

DISCUSSION QUESTIONS

4.3, 4.5, 4.7 ▶ 1. Determine what would happen to the demand for coffee in each of the following situations:
a. The Colombian Growers Association announces that the price of their coffee will increase by 30 percent effective one month from today.
b. The federal government grants a 20 percent tax reduction on federal personal income taxes.
c. The price of cream increases. You cannot drink your coffee black.
d. The prices of tea and cocoa increase to more than the price of coffee.

Discussion Questions 99

4.3, 4.4 ▶ 2. How do economists define the law of demand? Does the law relate to the demand curve? If so, how?

4.5, 4.6, 4.7, 4.8, 4.9, 4.10 ▶ 3. The demand for video cassette recorders has increased greatly in recent years, thus shifting the product's demand curve outward and to the right.
   a. What factors may have caused this shift?
   b. What are these factors called?
   c. What would cause a movement along the original demand curve for this product?

4.4 ▶ 4. How would you go about constructing a market demand curve for automobiles in the United States?

4.15 ▶ 5. Assuming that producers and consumers choose and act in their own respective self-interest, how can there ever be market equilibrium? What forces exist in a market to bring these separate interests together? (Hint: What guides producers to produce the goods consumers want most?)

4.12 ▶ 6. Explain why the supply curve slopes upward and to the right. What relationship does this represent?

4.13, 4.14 ▶ 7. Suppose the Pontiac Motor Division of General Motors has decided to supply fewer Trans-Ams to the market. Their entire supply curve will shift.
   a. What factors may have caused this?
   b. What would have happened if the supply had remained the same and the price of Trans-Ams had increased? Would the supply curve have shifted? Would the quantity supplied have changed?

4.15, 4.16 ▶ 8. Consider the following market situations:
   a. Producers supply 50,000 calculators to the marketplace. Consumers demand 50,000 calculators. Both are satisfied with the market price. What economic condition exists? Is the market price too low or too high?
   b. Producers supply 70,000 calculators to the marketplace at a price of $100. Consumers are willing and able to purchase 40,000 at this price. What economic condition exists? How can this be resolved? Is the price too low or too high?
   c. Producers supply 30,000 calculators to the marketplace at a price of $80. Consumers demand 80,000 calculators at this price. What economic condition exists? How can it be resolved? Is the price too low or too high?

4.20, 4.21 ▶ 9. Consider the following:
   a. How would your college or university bookstore communicate to consumers that the number of books they wish to purchase is more than the bookstore can get? How would the bookstore communicate to consumers that it had an excess of notebooks to sell?
   b. What would motivate you to buy notebooks from the school bookstore instead of shopping elsewhere? What would motivate the bookstore to attract you as a consumer? What role would price play in these actions?
   c. What would coordinate your desire to buy notebooks and the bookstore's desire to sell notebooks?
   d. Explain the importance of competition and well-defined property rights in the marketplace.

SELECTED READINGS

DeSerpa, Allan C. *Microeconomic Theory: Issues and Applications*. Boston: Allyn and Bacon, Inc. 1985.

Henderson, Hubert. *Supply and Demand*. Chicago: University of Chicago Press, 1958, chap. 2.

McKenzie, Richard B., and Tullock, Gordon. *Modern Political Economy*. New York: McGraw-Hill, 1978.

Schultz, Henry. *The Theory and Measurement of Demand*, Reissue. Chicago: University of Chicago Press, 1957.

Stigler, George. *The Theory of Price*, rev. ed. New York: MacMillan, 1952, chaps. 1 and 3.

CHAPTER 5

Government and Markets: The Mixed Economy

Having read the chapter, reviewed the chapter summary, and completed the *Study Guide* exercises, you should be able to:

CRIS

5.1 ECONOMIC EFFICIENCY: Explain what is meant by economic efficiency and use supply and demand curves to explain how a competitive market achieves an efficient use of resources.

5.2 EXTERNAL COSTS AND BENEFITS: Define the terms external benefit and external cost and use supply and demand curves to explain how the existence of external benefits or external costs causes a market to be inefficient.

5.3 ABSENCE OF SUPPLIER COMPETITION: Use supply and demand curves to explain how the absence of competition among suppliers leads to market inefficiency.

5.4 ABSENCE OF DEMANDER COMPETITION: Use supply and demand curves to explain how the absence of competition among demanders leads to market inefficiency.

5.5 GOVERNMENT TOOLS: List and explain the powerful tools that government can use to promote market efficiency.

5.6 MONOPOLY DEFINED: Define the term monopoly and explain how monopolies reduce market efficiency and why government antitrust laws promote market efficiency.

5.7 PROPERTY RIGHTS: Explain what is meant by the term property rights and tell how the definition and enforcement of property rights affect the incentives for individual behavior.

5.8 ELIMINATING EXTERNAL BENEFITS AND COSTS: Explain how external benefits and external costs can be eliminated or reduced by enforcing or redefining property rights.

5.9 PUBLIC GOODS: Explain what public goods are and tell why government often produces public goods.

> **5.10 ALTERING INCOME DISTRIBUTION:** Explain how and why government undertakes policies that alter the distribution of income.
>
> **5.11 GROUP DECISIONS:** Explain how and why problems of making group decisions can lead to inefficient government policies.
>
> **5.12 SPECIAL-INTEREST GROUPS:** Explain how and why the existence of special-interest groups can lead to inefficient government policies.
>
> **5.13 GROWTH INCENTIVES:** Describe the built-in incentives that promote growth in government.
>
> **5.14 COSTS, BENEFITS, AND GOVERNMENT PROGRAMS:** Explain why the existence of obvious benefits and unclear costs in government programs can lead to inefficient government policies.
>
> **5.15 SHORTSIGHTEDNESS EFFECT:** Explain the shortsightedness effect and tell how it can lead to inefficient government policies.

Mixed Economy
An economic system characterized by reliance on both private markets and government for choices involving scarce resources.

Markets are an important force in all our lives. Most of the goods and services that we buy or sell are exchanged through markets. Most of these markets perform their functions well. They effectively communicate, coordinate, and motivate producers and consumers to make efficient decisions regarding their scarce resources.

While markets are valued for their ability to facilitate mutually advantageous exchange, we must realize that markets do not always work as well as they might. The forces of competition can break down, so that markets fail to efficiently perform their tasks. Government policies can sometimes be used to correct a market failure and improve the allocation or distribution of scarce resources. Government choices are not always better than market allocations, however, so we must also be aware of potential failures in government choices. We live in an economy that combines aspects of private decision making through markets and public decision making through government. This kind of economic system is called a **mixed economy.**

To summarize, markets are an excellent way to organize economic activity, but they can sometimes benefit from appropriate government policies that correct market failures. A mixed economy combines market and government in an attempt to use resources most efficiently. In this chapter, we will examine the market with a critical eye and try to discover when markets are efficient and when market failures occur. We will briefly discuss some of the policies that government can use in dealing with these market failures. We will then step back and try to take into account the potential for failures in government choices. This will give us a greater appreciation of the role of markets and government in the economy.

This overview will help you understand the roles of the private and public sectors in modern economies. It will lay the foundation for the overviews of the private and public sectors presented in Chapters 6 and 7. Most of the specific problems and policies discussed in this chapter will be examined in greater depth in later chapters of this book.

THE MARKET AND ECONOMIC EFFICIENCY

One can look at a simple supply and demand diagram and understand the efficiency of a market. Under certain circumstances, a freely functioning market automatically achieves **economic efficiency.** That is, the forces of supply and demand automatically produce the optimal use of scarce resources.

In Chapter 4, we learned that demand is the relationship between the price of a good and the quantity that consumers demand of that good at each price. If we look at the demand curve in Figure 5-1, we can see that it also shows the maximum price consumers are willing and able to pay for each quantity demanded in the marketplace.

Figure 5-1 shows the supply and demand curves for a particular item. The demand curve in the figure can be interpreted to show either the quantity demanded at each price (the usual interpretation) or the maximum demand price for each quantity. At the quantity Q_1, for example, consumers are willing and able to pay a price of P_1 for this good. In other words, consumers value that quantity of the good such that they are willing to pay P_1 for it. Since the P_1 represents money that could be spent on other goods and services, the fact that consumers are willing to pay a maximum of P_1 for this quantity tells us that they are willing to give up P_1 worth of other goods and services to acquire it. Thus the maximum demand price of P_1 tells us how much consumers value this quantity of this item in terms of the other goods and services they could have purchased instead.

Economic Efficiency
The optimal use of scarce resources in an economy. Under certain conditions, free markets automatically achieve economic efficiency.

FIGURE 5-1

Supply, Demand, and Efficiency. The market equilibrium occurs at C. At quantity Q_1, consumers are willing to pay up to price P_1 for this good (A), and producers are willing to charge as little as P_3 for it (B). The fact that the demand curve lies above the supply curve indicates that mutually advantageous exchange can take place.

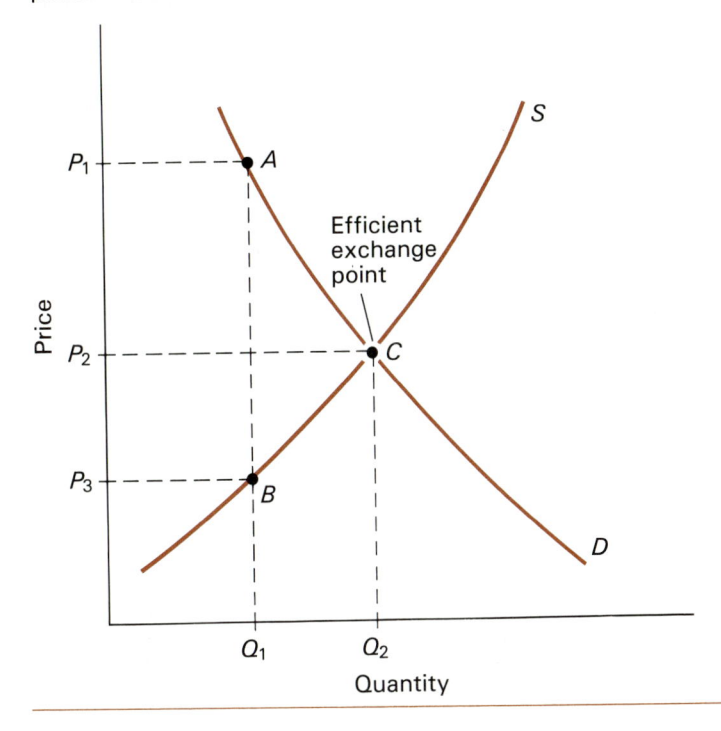

The demand curve tells us that consumers are not willing to purchase quantity Q_1 for a price higher than P_1. This suggests that P_1 is the maximum price at which consumers benefit from buying quantity Q_1. At a higher price, consumers would prefer to purchase other goods rather than buy quantity Q_1 of this item.

The supply curve also reveals something about the value of goods in this market. Remember that the supply curve shows the quantity of this item supplied at each price. In other words, producers are willing to supply the quantity Q_1 for a price of P_3. We can also interpret this supply curve another way. It tells us that producers are willing to sell the quantity Q_1 for as little as P_3. Since producers are not forced to sell their goods, this supply curve suggests that P_3 is the lowest price at which producers can experience a gain from selling quantity Q_1.

Figure 5-1 also shows that for the quantity Q_1, consumers are willing to pay a higher price than producers require in order to produce that quantity. Here is a clear case in which both producer and consumer can benefit from the production and exchange of the good. The maximum price that consumers will pay, P_1, is much above the minimum price that producers will accept, P_3. There is plenty of room here for mutually advantageous exchange. It follows, therefore, that at least Q_1 of this good will be produced.

Looking at Figure 5-1, it is easy to see that the price consumers are willing and able to pay is higher than the price that suppliers require for production for any quantity up to the equilibrium quantity of Q_2. At any quantity up to Q_2, the demand curve lies above the supply curve and, therefore, both producer and consumer can benefit from production and exchange. The incentives present in an unrestricted marketplace would eventually cause producers to produce Q_2 and consumers to buy Q_2 of the product in question.

At any quantity higher than Q_2, the price that consumers are willing and able to pay is lower than what it would require to induce producers to supply that quantity to the market. There is no potential gain for both producer and consumer, since the supply curve lies above the demand curve. The demand signal consumers send through the marketplace with their dollar votes is simply not strong enough to induce producers to respond. Since both parties cannot benefit from exchanges at any quantity above Q_2, it is reasonable to assume that only Q_2 will be produced and exchanged at a price of P_2. Any quantity less than Q_2 still leaves potential exchanges that can benefit both parties. Therefore, we can expect that, over time, producers and consumers will exploit these potential exchanges and the market will settle at the market equilibrium quantity of Q_2.

Any quantity produced in excess of Q_2 would leave the producer with products that could not be sold at a price that would meet his or her opportunity costs of production. The producer would have to dispose of the goods by lowering the price to the level indicated for that quantity on the consumers' demand curve, thereby incurring a loss. Producers would not rationally continue such loss behavior in the future. Thus quantity would decline back to Q_2, where all potential exchanges of mutual benefit to both producer and consumer had been exhausted.

5.1 ECONOMIC EFFICIENCY

This simple example demonstrates the efficiency of the market. Quantity Q_2 represents the efficient level of production in this market, given several assumptions that will be discussed later in this text. Production and exchange of quantity Q_2 is the best use of scarce resources in the market because it maximizes the number of mutually advantageous exchanges.

Since mutually advantageous exchanges make both consumers and producers better off, it follows that Q_2 maximizes the joint satisfaction of market participants. Any quantity lower than Q_2 is a poorer use of scarce resources because fewer mutually advantageous exchanges are made. Any quantity greater than Q_2 is also a poorer use of scarce resources because these exchanges are not mutually advantageous—either the buyer or the seller loses. The market, through the decentralized forces of supply and demand, achieves the efficient allocation of resources in this example.

SOME NECESSARY CONDITIONS FOR MARKET EFFICIENCY

Markets are efficient exchange mechanisms, but not in all cases. Some markets suffer from distortions that can prevent the market from efficiently maximizing the number of mutually advantageous exchanges. Several conditions are necessary for efficient exchange. When these conditions exist, the market forces of supply and demand lead to an efficient use of resources. When these conditions are not present, however, market forces fail to function efficiently. Some of the necessary conditions for market efficienctly are discussed below.

Absence of Externalities

First, for the demand and supply curves truly to represent the values producers and consumers place on a specific quantity of a good, there must be no **externalities**. Externalities exist when the full costs and benefits of a choice do not accrue to the individual making the choice.

An **external cost** exists when an individual makes a choice that imposes a side-effect burden on someone else. Air pollution is an example of an external cost. An **external benefit** exists when an individual makes a choice that provides a side-effect benefit to someone else. If someone puts money in a juke box and plays your favorite tune, for example, then you receive an external benefit.

Markets cannot be efficient when externalities are present. This means that market efficiency requires that producers not pass on any costs outside of the marketplace that are not included in the price of their goods (i.e., external costs) and that consumers not receive any benefits that are not paid for in the price of the goods they buy (i.e., external benefits). If externalities exist, then market supply and demand curves no longer accurately measure the true cost or benefit of the goods and services being exchanged. The market price is therefore no longer a true indicator of the value of the resources being used. In this situation, the market cannot effectively communicate, coordinate, or motivate producers and sellers. Examples will show that these abstract ideas are really concepts with which we are all familiar.

Suppose the supply curve in Figure 5-1 was for a steel-making firm. All the costs, including an acceptable profit to the firm, must be represented by the location of the supply curve. If the steel firm were discharging large amounts of smoke and ash into the atmosphere, the firm would be using resources without paying for them. Instead of incurring the cost of filtering the smoke and ash from their furnace and trucking it to a legal disposal facility, a polluting firm uses the atmosphere for disposal. The smoke and

---

Externalities
External costs and benefits passed on outside of the market system. For example, pollution generated by industrial production passes on a reduction in quality of life to those living in the area. This is obviously a cost to these people that is incurred outside the marketplace.

> **5.2 EXTERNAL COSTS AND BENEFITS**

External Cost
A cost borne by an individual as the result of another's choice.

External Benefit
A benefit that an individual receives for which no market payment was made.

ash would settle on the property of nearby residents, passing on to them an external cost outside of the marektplace.

The price of the steel in the market would reflect only the costs that the firm paid and not the costs that were passed on to residents who live near the steel mill. The price of steel in the market would be artificially low in the sense that the supply curve of steel would understate the true costs of producing steel. The supply curve with external costs would lie outward and to the right of a supply curve with no external cost. Such a situation is depicted in Figure 5-2(a).

The demand curve can also understate the true benefit of a good to consumers. Suppose that several houses border on a marshy area where mosquitoes breed, causing discomfort to all the residents. If the demand curve in Figure 5-1 represented the demand curve for services to drain the marsh and remove the mosquito nuisance, it would tend to understate the true value of this service to the residents of the local area. Suppose that one person pays to have the marsh drained. All the other people in the neighborhood will receive an external benefit from this action. They will receive a benefit that they did not pay for through the market. The market demand curve in Figure 5-1 would therefore not reflect the true value of the marsh clean-up because it would not reflect the value of this service to people who received the external benefits. The market demand curve would be located artificially lower and to the left of what it would have been if the external benefits had been taken into account. Figure 5-2(b) depicts the understated demand curve with an external benefit to consumers.

FIGURE 5-2

External Costs and Benefits Distort the Market. The market supply curve in (a) understates the true costs of production, leading to an external cost. The market tends to produce more than the efficient quantity when external costs exist. The market demand curve in (b) understates the true benefits available, leading to an external benefit. The market tends to produce less than the efficient quantity when external benefits exist.

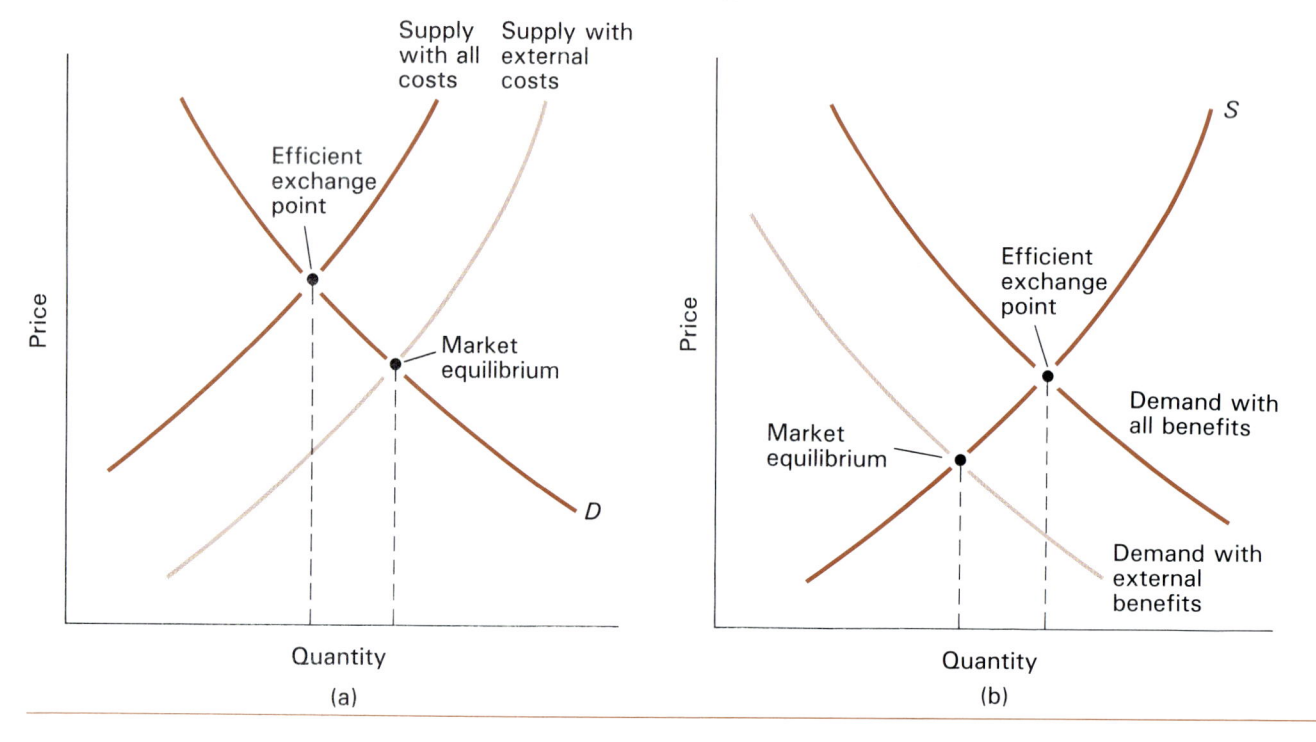

When producers pay the full costs of their production, so that there are no external costs, then their supply curve truly reflects their total costs. When consumers capture all their benefits, so that there are no external benefits, then their demand curve truly reflects their value of buying the good in question. The forces of demand and supply cannot achieve efficiency in the market so long as external costs and external benefits distort producer and consumer incentives.

Competition Among Suppliers

5.3 ABSENCE OF SUPPLIER COMPETITION

For a market to function correctly, there must be competition among both consumers and producers. In the absence of this competition on either the supply or demand side, a market cannot bring about the production of the efficient amount of goods and services desired by society. Figure 5-3 gives us a graphic view of this problem.

FIGURE 5-3

Competition Is Necessary for a Market to Be Efficient. Panel (a) shows a competitive market. The forces of supply and demand produce an efficient level of exchange. Panel (b) shows a market in which producers have colluded and restricted supply. The lower supply forces price up and reduces the number of exchanges below the efficient level. Panel (c) shows a market in which buyers have colluded to boycott a product. The boycott reduces demand, forcing price down. The number of exchanges is below the efficient level.

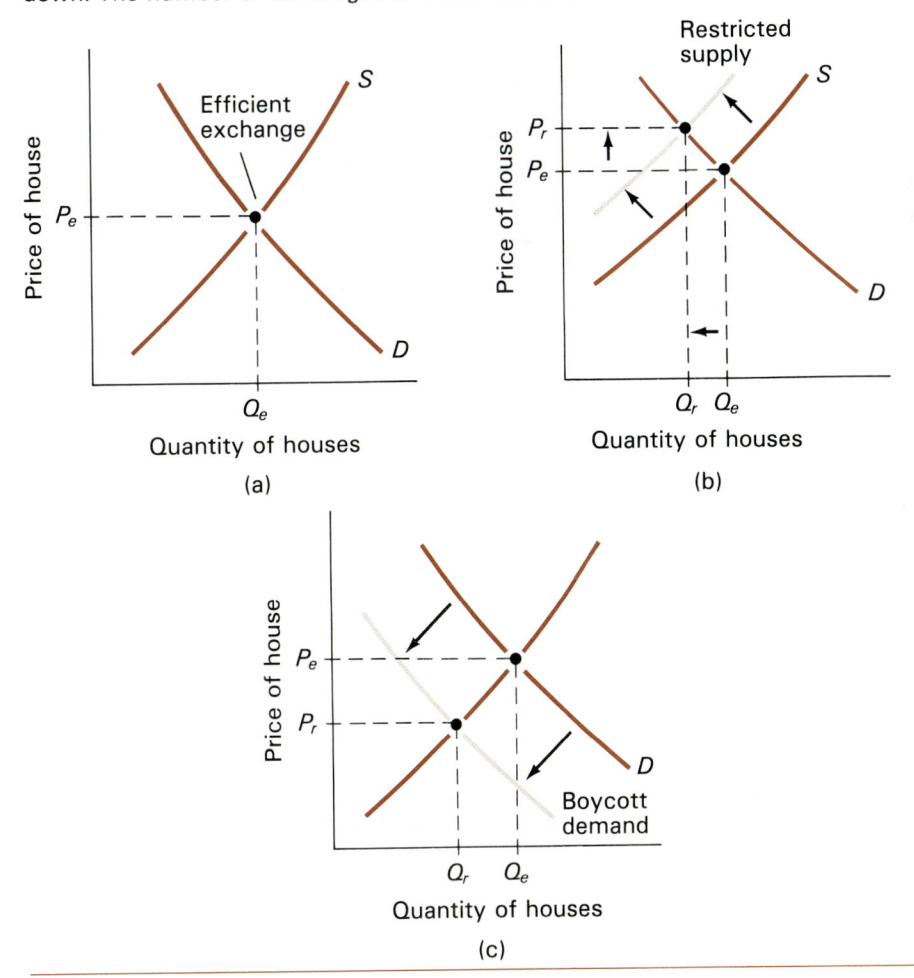

Figure 5-3(a) indicates the competitive supply and demand curves for single-family houses in the United States. Here, the market equilibrium price, P_e, and the efficient quantity, Q_e, would occur in the market. What would happen, however, if producers agreed to limit their output and force prices higher or if existing producers acted to restrict supply by erecting barriers to entry that kept new producers out of the housing construction market?

If producers were successful in limiting output by the correct amount, they might be able to increase their revenues, but at a reduction in benefit to the consumers. The supply curve would shift upward and to the left as shown in Figure 5-3(b). The price would rise to P_r (restricted price) and the quantity exchanged in the market would fall to Q_r (restricted quantity). By restricting the market in their favor, producers have eliminated some potentially advantageous exchanges, while possibly increasing their own revenues and profits.

The producers' total revenues (price per unit times quantity sold) in the competitive case would have been $P_e \times Q_e$. When the market is restricted, revenues rise to $P_r \times Q_r$. These producers would gain from restricting supply if $P_r \times Q_r$ is larger than $P_e \times Q_e$. By restricting supply, the producers may be able to increase thier revenues by selling fewer houses but at higher prices. The decline in the number of houses sold because of the increase in price can be more than offset by the profit made by charging higher prices for the houses that are actually sold.

It is not always profitable for producers to collude, however. Sometimes the decrease in quantity sold more than outweighs the increase in price to P_r. In this case, the producers sell less but also receive less total revenue ($P_r \times Q_r$ is less than $P_e \times Q_e$). Producers do not necessarily gain from restricting supply here. Whether the producers gain or not, however, the economy loses when supply is restricted because this lack of competition eliminates otherwise mutually advantageous exchanges.

Competition Among Demanders

5.4 ABSENCE OF DEMANDER COMPETITION

Consumers can also restrict the market demand to gain advantages for themselves that distort the market. In panel (c) of Figure 5-3, we note that by boycotting a particular product, such as housing, consumers can shift the demand curve downward and to the left and, therefore, lower market prices. The mechanisms of this process are much the same as when producers collude to force prices higher, but the motives are somewhat different.

An **economic boycott** is usually undertaken by consumers as a means of showing organized economic force against a single industry or producer. For example, the farm workers union mounted an effective boycott of table grapes produced in California in the 1960s. Their goal was to force grape producers to pay higher wages to the migrant workers who picked the grapes. This was an attempt to bring economic pressure on the farmers and force them to concede to the union's demands.

Economic Boycott
A consumer action in which consumers agree to restrict market demand and gain advantages for themselves (for example, lower prices) at a cost to producers.

The boycott can achieve its economic or political goals, but boycotts are inefficient in the sense that they move the market away from the efficient use of resources. Interestingly enough, an action by producers to collude and drive prices up is illegal in the United States, but the equivalent action on the part of consumers to collude, boycott a particular industry or product, and drive prices down is not illegal.

Boycotts illustrate the point that the failure of competition among demanders can cause inefficiency. The boycott restricts demand and chokes off

KEY CONCEPTS
5.1, 5.2, 5.3, 5.4

The market can efficiently allocate scarce resources under the right conditions. Demand and supply curves must correctly measure all the benefits (demand) and costs (supply) that pertain to the good or service being exchanged. Demand cannot measure all benefits when external benefits exist. Supply cannot measure all costs when external costs exist. These externalities therefore cause market failure. Competition among suppliers and among demanders is also necessary to achieve market efficiency.

GOVERNMENT AS AN ECONOMIC FORCE

Government is a powerful and necessary force in all economic systems. Most people think of government as a specific place, organization, or group of people. You might think that Congress and the President in Washington, D.C., represent the U.S. government. Government is more than this, however. The United States has almost 80,000 units of federal, state, and local government. There are over 500,000 elected government officials and millions of other people who serve government in appointive office or as civil employees in the United States. These units of government and their employees provide a broad range of goods and services to the community.

What is government? Government is really less a person or thing than it is a process. Government is the process by which society makes some allocation and distribution choices as a group rather than as individual decision makers.

5.5 GOVERNMENT TOOLS

Government defines the rules by which the economy operates. If markets are to function efficiently, a system of well-defined **property rights** and the market force of competition must be present. Government makes the laws that determine the property rights of producers and consumers. These laws both regulate private actions and contribute to the smooth functioning of markets.

Property Rights
The rights to own, occupy, or benefit from property within the economy. They define the acceptable and unacceptable limits of behavior regarding property.

Government also has the ability to levy and collect taxes as well as provide subsidies to certain individuals or groups in the economy. These two powers give government the ability to change the incentives that certain producers or consumers face. Government can strongly encourage or discourage the production or consumption of specific goods and services in the economy. By placing a heavy tax on the production of a good such as cigarettes, for example, the costs of producing cigarettes must rise, which discourages production and consumption of this product. The tax reduces the incentive to produce cigarettes.

Subsidy
A government payment to an individual or a group designed to increase their welfare or encourage certain private activities.

Government pays a **subsidy** to individuals to encourage certain activities. Students who attend state-run colleges and universities pay relatively low tuition (at least compared to tuition at private schools). The lower tuition is the result of a government subsidy. Tax dollars are used to reduce the price of higher education in an effort to encourage more people to seek out higher learning. This subsidy is paid to college students indirectly. They do not receive a direct cash payment. Instead the subsidy comes in the form of a lower price. Government also occasionally makes direct cash-payment subsi-

Direct Subsidies
Direct cash payments to producers of certain goods to encourage the production of those goods.

dies to producers of certain goods to encourage their production. These are called **direct subsidies.**

Government, through its powers to tax, subsidize, define property rights, and regulate private activities, is an important economic force in the economy. We will look more closely at all of the things that government does in the economy in Chapter 7. At this point, however, we are only concerned with how government can use its tools to correct market failures such as externalities and breakdowns in competition.

GOVERNMENT POLICIES AND THE MARKET

Many government policies are designed to facilitate the efficient operation of markets in the economy. We can divide these microeconomic policies into the major categories of maintaining competition, defining and enforcing property rights, providing public goods, and redistributing income within our economy.

Government Policies to Promote Competition

> **5.6 MONOPOLY DEFINED**

Monopoly
A market with only one supplier.

Antitrust Legislation
Laws developed to regulate competition. They prohibit activities in restraint of trade.

There have been periods in the history of the United States when businesses in a particular industry, such as sugar production, banded together to form a trust, or a **monopoly.** These monopolies would set market prices and assign specific quantities to be supplied by each member of the trust. This behavior became widespread among some industries, and the public outcry grew loud. In response, our first federal **antitrust legislation** was passed.

Today in situations in which the producers in a market might collude or agree to artificially restrict supply, our government has developed an elaborate system of laws to regulate competition. These laws are administered by the Anti-Trust Division of the U.S. Department of Justice. In general, these laws forbid activities in restraint of interstate trade. Legislation such as the Sherman Act (1890) or the Clayton Antitrust Act (1914) are designed to keep producers from making secret agreements that would set market prices or prevent free competition. There are many specific federal trade laws, and they are enforced by a large organization of federal investigators, attorneys, judges, and courts.

The teeth of the federal trade laws include the ability to place heavy fines and impose jail terms on producers. The government can force suspension of business and can seize business property when violations occur. It is important to note, however, that enforcing the trade laws is a difficult task. **Collusion** and other forms of activity in restraint of trade are difficult to detect and prosecute successfully.

Collusion
The joining together of producers to restrict supply (limit output), thereby forcing prices to increase, or consumer action to limit demand, thereby forcing prices to decrease.

Economists have mixed opinions on both the amount of and means of regulation exercised by our government. While perfect regulation of markets is a fine ideal, it is difficult to achieve. The costs of enacting and enforcing regulations are borne by taxpayers and consumers. In some instances, these costs may outweigh the benefits of regulation. Given these costs, if collusive behavior has an insufficient impact on price and quantity, the violation may not warrant enforcement activities by the Federal Trade Commission. The Commission has limited resources in terms of personnel and time and must allocate these resources to the specific cases and issues that will have the greatest impact.

While there will probably always be a continuing debate about how much and what kinds of regulation are necessary, the basic concept of government as a referee in the marketplace is reasonably well established. The function of government to balance the scales of competition is a beneficial and vital part of our economy.

Government Definition and Enforcement of Property Rights

5.7 PROPERTY RIGHTS

The second major role of government in the market is to promote efficiency by establishing the rules by which the resources of our economy, both human and nonhuman, are produced, used, and exchanged. These rules of operating the economy, and the personal incentives they provide, are the result of the government's function of defining and enforcing property rights concerning our resources. The idea of property rights is a new one for most first-time economics students. Property rights, and the way that they are defined and enforced, are a powerful economic force.

All resources are owned either by individuals, groups, or communally by the whole society. There must be some definition of who owns which resources and how the owners may use them if the use, production, and exchange of these resources is to take place efficiently. Property rights are the rules that define who owns resources and what uses owners may make of them.

You have an individual property right in your own labor and talents, for example. The system of laws in our society grants you the rights of ownership to that labor resource, as well as the right to sell that resource to others under certain conditions. Under our laws, you may not be forced into slave labor or made to sell your labor to another at a price you are unwilling to accept. This definition of your property rights was created by society acting through government. Other societies in history have defined the property right in individual labor differently. Some countries in the past have permitted slavery or indentured servitude, which are different definitions of the property rights an individual has in his or her own labor.

In the United States and most other modern nations, if you own land, you are entitled to occupy that property, build a house or other structure within legal limits on it, and sell or rent it to another at a price you are willing to accept. If you are fortunate enough to own land with oil or minerals, such as coal or aluminum, beneath it, you may use those resources within legal limits, or sell them at an acceptable price.

Property rights not only determine who owns a resource, they also determine how those resources can and cannot be used. Your ownership of land does not mean that you have unrestricted rights to use this resource. Property rights in land are not defined that way in most parts of the United States. Most local governments impose zoning laws, which regulate land use in particular areas. If your property is in a residential area, for example, local zoning laws will not permit you to build a factory on your land. Your rights to use of the land are restricted by the way that society, through government, has defined your property rights to the land.

KEY CONCEPTS 5.7

Property rights are the rights to own, use, or sell resources of almost any kind and to benefit from that ownership, use, or sale. They define what can and cannot be done with resources and who has the rights over them.

ECONOMIC ISSUES

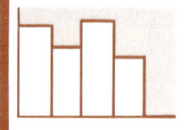

Woodstoves, Pollution, and Property Rights

Pollution can be a serious economic and social problem. People generally think of pollution in terms of large industrial firms who generate concentrated flows of pollution when they produce chemicals or metals. The pollution conflict in this case is between the large industrial polluter who gains from pollution and the many individuals who bear the external costs of the firm's actions. In recent years, however, a new type of pollution has appeared, one that takes on a much different pattern.

Millions of Americans now heat or partially heat their homes with woodstoves and fireplace inserts. The woodstove movement is a predictable response to changing economic conditions. As the cost of space heating using fuel oil, natural gas, and electricity has climbed, more and more people have substituted relatively less expensive wood heat. The initial cost of installing a woodstove or fireplace insert is relatively small, and fireplace wood is available at relatively low cost in many parts of the country. It is logical to assume that people will substitute lower-cost wood fuel for higher-cost oil and gas wherever they can. This solution to one economic problem has created another, however.

Oil and gas furnaces are relatively efficient and generate only nominal amounts of air pollution in residential areas. This is not the case with woodstoves and fireplace inserts, however. Large amounts of air pollution can exist in an area with a concentration of wood-fired stoves. Smoke from all the woodstoves can build into a smelly, uncomfortable, unhealthful fog. This has created important air pollution problems in many communities, including Missoula, Montana, and Tacoma, Washington. Woodstoves can be operated without high-pollution results, but people who burn wet wood (which is usually less costly than drier seasoned fuel) necessarily send off plumes of airborne particulates that pollute the air and cause health and aesthetic problems for others. Many of the people who suffer most from this pollution, because of respiratory ailments, are themselves woodstove users.

Why do people use woodstoves when they know that they cause undesirable air pollution and impose external costs on their neighbors? This is an example of a type of situation that economists call a *prisoners' dilemma*. A prisoners' dilemma exists when actions that are most beneficial to individuals are the opposite of those that are most beneficial to society. In this case, it is in the community's interest to restrict

Property rights have an important role in law because they determine legal liability. Your property right in your auto, for example, determines how you can use your car, but it also determines who is responsible for actions in which the car is involved. If you park your car on a hill and the brake slips, letting the car crash into another car, you are responsible for the damage. This legal liability is determined by society when it decides how property rights in autos are defined.

Enforcement of property rights is also a key feature of government. Some means must be provided to insure that property rights are respected once they are defined. A society based on law requires that rights, not force, carry the greatest weight. An economy based on exchange requires that individuals be able to retain the rights that they have purchased from others. If rights to goods that are bought and sold cannot be guaranteed, then the motivation for exchange soon breaks down. Why produce if you cannot control the fruits of your labor? Why give up resources to buy goods, if they can be taken away?

The legal system can be thought of as an institution designed to define and enforce property rights. Police and the criminal courts exist to punish those who violate others' property rights. The civil law system exists to

the use of woodstoves because the external costs are high. For each individual, however, the optimal strategy is to use the woodstove to cut heating costs. The logic is clear: as an individual, it makes sense to use your woodstove (in spite of the pollution it causes) because the extra pollution you cause is insignificant compared to the amount that already exists. As an individual, if you stop burning wood for heat (and everyone else continues to use woodstoves), the effective reduction in pollution is zero. No one individual can do very much to reduce total pollution by individual action. Therefore, because everyone has an incentive to continue to pollute so long as others do, the logical result is that everyone pollutes (which is not in their group interest), since it is not in their individual interest to stop.

When external costs (such as those produced by the woodstoves) exist, government can often step in and improve on market actions. People use woodstoves that cause air pollution because they are cheaper than other sources of heat. In theory, this pollution could be reduced in a variety of ways, such as direct regulation of woodburning, a tax on woodstoves, or a tax on firewood. Government policies could reduce woodstove pollution by forcing individuals to take the external cost into account when making private decisions.

Government antipollution actions are difficult to implement in the case of woodstoves, however, because they are so widely used in places where they are a problem. In Missoula, Montana, for example, woodstoves are a serious air-pollution danger precisely because so many people (who are also voters) own them. In a government system of majority rule, it is difficult to enact public policies that restrict the self-interest of a majority of voters. It is in the self-interest of many voters to vote against woodstove regulations, even though such regulations may make economic sense for the community as a whole. In short, woodstoves create an air pollution problem because so many people use them, but government has trouble regulating this pollution precisely because so many people cause it. This bias against public woodstove regulations therefore tends to make the pollution problem worse.

The woodstove problem is made even more difficult by the high costs of enforcing pollution regulations when the pollution is the result of many individual actions, not the actions of a few firms. Imagine how difficult it would be to police thousands of individual woodstove owners to be sure that their stoves met pollution standards and otherwise followed local rules. The high cost of enforcement might exceed any gains from lower pollution to local residents.

Woodstove pollution presents serious problems for society. History tells us that these problems should be taken seriously. Pollution in 19th-century London was largely the result of millions of individuals heating their homes with coal (industrial pollution existed, but was relatively less serious). Their combined air pollution resulted in "killer fogs" that caused the deaths of hundreds of people each year.

Additional References

Weathersby, Jeff, "Hearing May Be Kindling for Fiery Debate over Wood-Stove Pollution." *Tacoma News Tribune,* December 6, 1984.

5.8 ELIMINATING EXTERNAL BENEFITS AND COSTS

refine the definition of property rights, determine who owns the rights to particular resources, and allow individuals whose rights have been violated to extract damages from the offending party.

Property rights are also important because they affect the economic incentives we all face. Each of us has an incentive to maximize the value of our property rights. This creates a problem when property rights are not efficiently defined or effectively enforced. The market failures of external cost and external benefit, which were discussed earlier in this chapter, are caused by failure to correctly define or enforce property rights. The examples below will make this important point clearer.

Suppose that you live down the river from a chemical plant. The plant discharges waste into the river, and this causes unpleasant odors and potential health hazards in your neighborhood. The pollution imposes an external cost on you. Your property rights in your home include a general right to the natural conditions that existed when you purchased your property. Thus your property rights have been violated. When the chemical plant produces odors emanating from the river, the satisfaction or utility you get from your property has been reduced. How do you deal with this situation? You could appeal directly to the chemical firm yourself. However, this is unlikely to produce the results you desire. The firm dumps waste in the river for economic reasons. This form of waste disposal is cheaper than the alternatives. Given that there are large costs involved both in using some other form of disposal and in cleaning up the river, the corporation is not likely to change its present course of action without being compelled to do so by the authority of government.

Another way to solve this problem would be for individuals, acting on thier own, to attempt to enforce their own property rights through the legal system. You as an individual could sue the polluting firm in court for damages. The potential gain to you would be small, however, compared to the high costs of the legal process. It might be difficult, too, to prove how much you as an individual have been damaged by the pollution. Many of your neighbors could also claim damages due to the odors. The chemical firm would then be liable for high total damage claims. The firm still might pollute, however, if the cost of reducing pollution is higher than the cost of fighting the group in court. The costs involved in such a dispute escalate, and the corporation could rationally be expected to protect itself as much as possible.

It is difficult to prove these types of damages in a court of law and to attach blame to a specific firm. For example, many other chemical firms may also use the river to dump harmless waste. Your own town could well be dumping treated sewage into the river. Finding the culprit and mounting a successful prosecution frequently require the extensive resources of government. Few individuals without the assistance of government could bring about any real change in such a situation. Government antipollution regulations, which restrict the amounts and types of pollutants that individual firms can emit, are one way that government protects individual property rights. The Environmental Protection Agency's regulations are costly, but they reduce the external cost problem.

External benefits are also dealt with through the definition and enforcement of property rights. A classic example of external benefits involves the development of the Walt Disney World Amusement Park in Orlando, Florida. Whenever an attraction of this size is built, the value of commercial land surrounding it goes up. Other businesses, such as hotels and restaurants, want to acquire property located there because of the tourists who will come to the park. These other firms receive external benefits because they gain from the Walt Disney World investment without making any payment for these benefits. This can create a problem, if the inability to capture these external benefits leads the individual that produces them (Walt Disney, Inc.) to underinvest in new facilities. What incentive is there for the Walt Disney investors to expand their facilities if other local businesses will receive many of the rewards of this use of resources?

This problem need not always exist, however. Sometimes property rights can be defined such that the developer is able to "internalize" the externality. This means that the developer receives all the benefits of the resource use, so that no external benefits are produced. This gives the individual firm a greater incentive to invest resources efficiently. Knowing this economic fact, the developers of Walt Disney World bought up much more land than they needed to build the park. When the park was completed, the value of the land they had bought, but not developed, rose quickly. They sold this land to hotel and restaurant firms at high profits. The developers, by buying the land in advance, bought the right to benefit from the external benefits the park created. The higher price for the surrounding land came from the fact that the park was built. The developers of the park, through our system of property rights, were able to capture and keep the value of their positive externalities.

Government Provision for Public Goods

> ### 5.9 PUBLIC GOODS

Public Good
An item from which nonowners cannot be excluded from benefiting but whose use by nonowners does not reduce the benefits available to the owner. A lighthouse is an example of a public good.

Public goods cannot, in general, be produced efficiently in competitive markets and, therefore, must be produced by government. Public goods are items that have two important properties. First, is it impossible or very costly for the owner of a public good to exclude others from the use of the resource. Second, the fact that others use the resource does not reduce its potential benefit to the owner. A lighthouse, which warns passing ships of dangerous conditions, is an example of a public good. Suppose that one shipping firm builds a lighthouse to reduce potential losses to its ships. This lighthouse provides benefits to the firm that built it, but the firm would find it impossible or very costly to exclude other ships from also observing the warning light and gaining the benefit of increased sailing safety. This use of the resource by others, however, does not reduce the benefit that the original firm gets from the lighthouse.

The reason why private markets are inefficient in producing public goods is that every individual has an incentive to wait for others to provide the public good. Every shipping firm, for example, would want to have lighthouses available, but no individual firm would want to build them because that firm would bear all the costs while the other firms would share in the benefits. Each firm has an incentive to be a **free rider** and let others bear the cost of the public good. Relatively few public goods would be provided if private markets were left to produce them.

Free Rider
An individual who receives a benefit without making payment for it. Free riders exist when public goods or external benefits are present.

Government can solve the public goods problem because it can force those who benefit from the public good to contribute toward its production. Government can build a system of lighthouses, for example, then impose taxes on shipping firms to force them to pay for the benefits they receive. Government eliminates the free-rider problem because it can force payment, a power that private producers lack.

The value of public goods in our economy is frequently overlooked. The entire environment in which we produce and exchange goods and services is facilitated by public goods. Try to envision how goods and services could possibly be exchanged without police and fire protection, a legal system of laws and courts to settle disputes, the monetary system, and a system of national defense to protect resources from being seized by foreign powers. The fact is that exchange as we know it today would probably collapse. Public goods are keys to facilitating the functioning of a market economy. Our economy revolves around the market mechanisms but depends on public goods for that mechanism to work efficiently.

Government Redistribution of Income

Most people receive their income through markets. They receive wage income through the labor market. They receive interest income through financial markets. They earn profits and rents through markets for specific goods. Wages are the largest source of income for the economy. As we have seen, there is no guarantee that the markets in which people earn income are always efficient. Sometimes there is a potential for government to improve the efficiency of labor or other markets. When government does this, it tends to redistribute income from one group in the economy to another.

5.10 ALTERING INCOME DISTRIBUTION

Just as there is no guarantee that markets are always efficient, neither is there a guarantee that market-earned incomes will be judged as fair or desirable by society. In our market-oriented system, a person's income depends to a great extent on the value of the goods, services, and skills that one has to sell. If a person has little of value to sell, then the market may doom this person to poverty. Society may disagree with the market's harsh judgment and use government to redistribute income from those who have valuable goods, services, and skills to the poorer "have-nots" in the name of equity, compassion, or social justice. Government programs that redistribute income can therefore be thought of as policies designed to correct a failure of labor and other markets in order to produce an efficient or socially acceptable distribution of income.

Many government programs are designed to alter the distribution of income. The Social Security System, for example, imposes taxes on workers in our economy and uses the tax revenues to make payments to retired and disabled individuals, who generally have lower incomes than workers. Tax revenues are also used to redistribute income through unemployment benefits, Aid to Families with Dependent Children, and other government programs. These are examples of direct redistribution, where government taxes one individual in order to transfer income to another.

Government also indirectly redistributes income in a variety of ways. Trade restrictions, for example, alter the distribution of income around the world, although income does not necessarily flow from richer to poorer people in this case. A law that prevents imported steel from being sold in the United States imposes high costs on people who use steel products, because they must purchase higher-priced domestic steel. Steel firms and their workers in the United States benefit from this restriction in the form of higher income and profits. Figure 5-4 illustrates the impact of this trade restriction. The supply of steel falls because fewer imports are allowed. The decrease in supply causes a shortage of steel at the initial equilibrium price, forcing price higher. The new market equilibrium is achieved with a higher price and a smaller quantity of steel produced and purchased. This redistributes income in several ways. Steel purchasers pay more, reducing their effective income. Foreign steel producers receive lower income from the reduced sales in this country. Domestic steel producers receive higher income.

Trade restrictions, such as the steel example shown in Figure 5-4, illustrate the fact that government policies often have undesired side effects. The steel quota may have been intended to redistribute income from foreign steel firms to domestic steel companies and their workers. We see, however, that it also redistributes income from domestic users of steel (some of whom may have low incomes) to domestic producers of steel (many of whom have high incomes). The quota also reduces competition among steel producers, who no longer need be so concerned with foreign competitors. This lack of competition can cause market failure problems for government, as well.

Minimum wage laws are another example of indirect redistribution. A minimum wage law is essentially a special definition of a property right. A minimum wage law takes away an individual's right to sell his or her labor for less than a specified amount. Figure 5-5 illustrates the effect of a minimum wage law. The equilibrium wage rate in this market for unskilled teenaged workers is $2.50. The government-set minimum wage is shown as $3.35. This minimum wage provides higher income for some low-wage workers, but it also results in other workers, with poor skills, being unable to

FIGURE 5-4

The Impact of a Restriction on Steel Imports. Congress imposes limits on steel imports from abroad. These trade restrictions reduce the supply of steel available in this country. The price of steel rises and the quantity of steel exchanged falls below the efficient level. The higher prices redistribute income from buyers to sellers. The restriction on imports redistributes income from foreign sellers to domestic producers. The restriction on competition from abroad can cause further inefficiency.

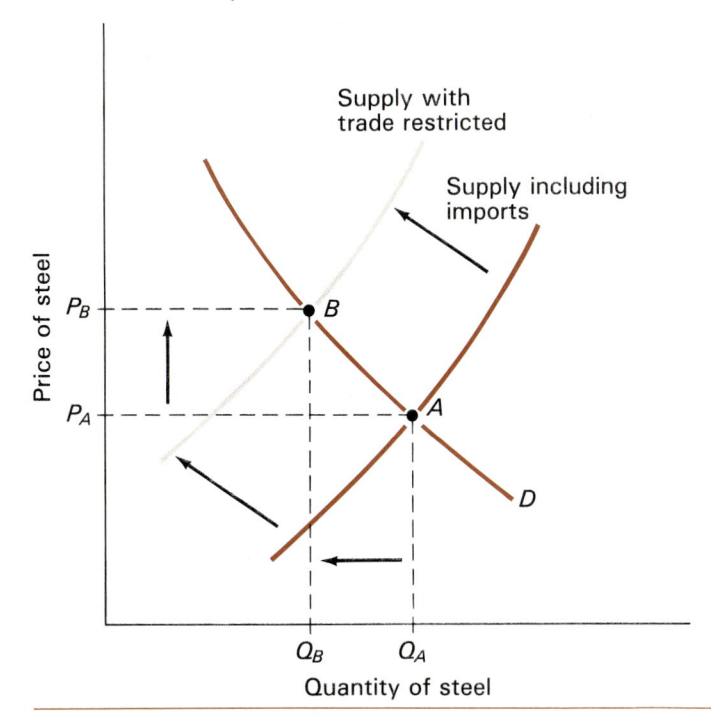

find work. High minimum wages make it uneconomic for employers to hire them. The figure shows that the quantity of labor demanded and employed falls when the minimum wage is adopted, while the quantity of labor supplied increases. Some workers who keep their jobs receive higher income, but some workers end up unemployed.

Any analysis of what government does in the United States would conclude that much of government's resources are involved in the redistribution of income from one population group to another. Even the U.S. income tax system tends to alter the relative distribution of income. Low-income groups pay relatively little tax, while higher-income groups are subject to higher tax rates. This system tends to reduce the gap between rich and poor, although the income tax is complicated and rich individuals do not always pay more taxes than do poorer individuals.

It is clear that government redistributes income, but why is government involved in this activity? Why can't individual actions be counted upon to provide effective redistribution?

Not all redistribution takes place through government. Private charities take voluntary donations from high-income households and use these funds to help low-income groups. However, private actions in this area are likely to prove insufficient, in a societal sense, for several reasons. First, charity is a public good. You gain satisfaction when you give money to the American Red Cross, for example, because you know your donation will help the needy. Others also gain from your contribution, however, and their gain

FIGURE 5-5	**The Impact of Minimum Wage Legislation.** This market for unskilled teenaged workers would be in equilibrium at a wage of $2.50 per hour. If this wage is viewed as inefficient or unjust, Congress might pass a minimum wage law setting $3.35 as the lowest legal wage rate. Fewer workers are demanded and employed at this wage rate. Workers who keep their jobs gain higher income. The figure shows, however, that some people who were employed at a wage rate of $2.50 will not be employed at $3.35. The minimum wage law redistributes income from the unemployed to those who keep their jobs as an unintended side effect.

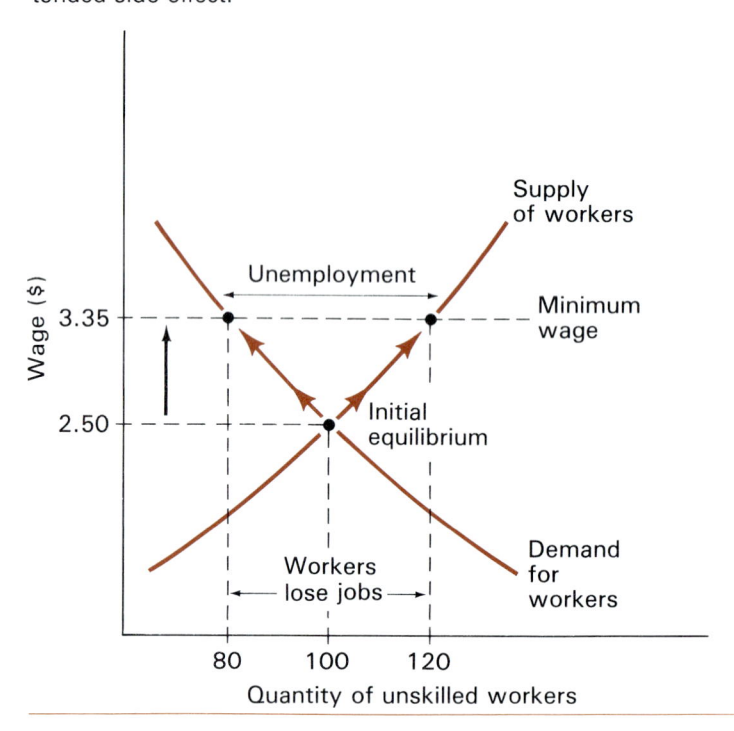

does not reduce your own satisfaction. This is the lighthouse problem discussed earlier, only with a different twist. Your neighbor might not feel a need to give to charity so long as it is known that you do. If too many people are free riders on your actions, little is done to aid the needy. Government can step in and solve this public goods problem by taxing all of us to provide for low-income groups.

Some redistribution programs might be viewed as social insurance programs. Individuals purchase private insurance, such as car insurance, in order to protect themselves from risk. Unemployment benefits and social security payments might be viewed as social insurance, provided by government, with individuals paying taxes to "purchase" the right to benefits if they suffer low income during unemployed periods or in old age. Government must use tax laws to force people to purchase this "insurance" because of the problem of adverse selection. If social insurance were left to private companies to provide, successful, high-income people, with relatively low risk, might choose not to purchase this insurance or purchase it from companies that sold policies only to them at lower rates. High-risk, low-income groups would line up to buy income insurance policies. Since the only people to buy these policies would be people who are able to pay low premiums, but who would have a high probability of collecting benefits, the income insurance companies that serve the poor would soon go out of business, leaving the poor without protection.

Government provides this social insurance through our tax and transfer system. We all pay taxes, whether we want to or not, to provide benefits to those in need. This provides a stable "social safety net" for the needy and unfortunate. This function of government is controversial, however, because it forces some individuals to involuntarily give resources to others. The involuntary nature of this transaction can lead to resentment. The tax and transfer system also affects the incentives that private markets provide. Taxes reduce the incentive to produce among workers, and government payments, which may disappear if the recipient finds work, reduce the incentive for the poor to earn incomes for themselves. In this sense, the incentives that income redistribution provides tend to make the economy less efficient than would otherwise be the case.

KEY CONCEPTS
5.6, 5.7, 5.8, 5.9, 5.10

Government policies can be used to improve market efficiency in several ways. Antitrust laws, for example, are designed to promote efficiency by maintaining competition in markets. The government can also encourage efficiency through the definition and enforcement of property rights. External costs and external benefits, for example, can be viewed as market failures due to problems in the definition and enforcement of property rights. Government also provides public goods that would not normally be produced in private markets because of the difficulty of excluding free riders and the lack of rivalry for benefits. Government also alters the distribution of income within the economy to deal with failures in labor and other markets.

THE POTENTIAL FOR GOVERNMENT INEFFICIENCIES

There are many actions that government can take to improve the ways in which private markets act. As we have just seen, government can encourage competition, efficiently define and enforce property rights, provide public goods, and redistribute income. These government activities help private markets function more efficiently. Government is not perfect, however. Government decisions are not always an improvement over private choices. There are a number of reasons why government policies can fail the test of economic efficiency. Several of these situations are discussed below.

Problems of Group Decision Making

5.11 GROUP DECISIONS

Individual decision making is relatively simple to describe. Individuals weigh opportunity costs and make choices that maximize their well-being. Group decision making is not as easy to describe. It is unlikely that all individuals in a group will have the same preferences. Some may prefer a more equal distribution of income, for example, while others may want to maintain the current distribution. One problem government faces is to find ways of discovering the preferences of individuals, then decide how to weigh the conflicting desires of different individuals. Voting is one way that group choices are made, but voting is an imperfect choice tool. The result of a public vote depends on who can cast a ballot, how those ballots are tallied, and the order in which choices are made. Government policies are sometimes inefficient because of the failure of the voting system to take into account the gains and losses that these government programs can cause.

Majority rule voting, for example, frequently leaves a large minority with a decision that they do not want. The losers in an election bear an external cost of the vote. They may suffer a loss because of the votes that others made.

No voting system is perfect, because no voting system can guarantee that both the preferences of the majority and the rights of the minority can be respected. Voting systems can also be manipulated. An individual who can control what people vote on and in what order can sometimes alter the final vote. We will look at voting problems in more detail in a later chapter.

Voting problems mean that individual market actions, even if they result in external costs or benefits, are sometimes more efficient than the government choices that voting provides. This is especially true if government choices require the use of many scarce resources.

Special-Interest Groups

One of the most powerful functions of government is to define and enforce property rights. Government sets the rules for the economic game. With this power concentrated in the hands of government, there is a natural human incentive for individuals to attempt to influence that power to their advantage or even their direct benefit. This is the basis on which the concept of special-interest groups is founded. **Special-interest groups** are organizations in our society that are united in the pursuit of common goals. Their aim is to influence government to pass legislation that is to their benefit or not to pass legislation that might harm their interests.

The economics of special-interest groups and **special-interest issues** is relatively simple. A special-interest issue is one that if voted into law by government will pass a small cost onto each individual voter and produce a large benefit for the special interest group. For example, let's assume that (hypothetically) the American Dairy Association wanted to lobby for higher minimum milk prices. Producers benefit if government raises the minimum legal price on some commodity, such as milk or other agricultural products. The size of the total benefit to producers of a five cent-per-gallon increase in minimum milk prices could literally be millions of dollars. This means that those who stand to benefit millions from such an action would be making a rational choice to invest substantial time, money, and effort to have such legislation passed. Each voter, on the other hand, will only incur a small cost (five cents each time he or she buys a gallon of milk) if the bill is passed. Most voters will not be violently opposed to the law since the individual cost to them will be small. Furthermore, the bill is likely to be presented by politicians as necessary to keep milk producers in business, or to have some other great value to the society. Accordingly, the bill is likely to pass into law. This process is repeated, however, each time a special-interest issue is brought before government.

Special-interest groups number in the thousands and are, in a political sense, highly organized. They expend substantial amounts of money and human effort to see that legislators understand and are familiar with their point of view on specific issues that affect them. Representatives of these groups are politically powerful and can influence the voting behavior of literally thousands of their groups' members. Legislators therefore tend to be heavily influenced by the wishes of special-interest groups. Since these groups are highly organized and politically powerful, it is easier for politicians to bend to their wishes than try to win votes from unorganized individuals in the economy who will only have to bear a small individual cost

---

Special-Interest Groups
Organizations that have joined together in a common special interest. Special-interest groups attempt to influence the voting behavior of legislators to the specific benefit of the group.

Special-Interest Issue
Issues that, if voted into law, provide a small cost to individual voters and a large benefit to the special-interest groups lobbying for the issues.

5.12 SPECIAL-INTEREST GROUPS

Public Sector
The part of the economy that is owned by and for the public, not by any individual. Economists frequently use the term public sector and government interchangeably.

if the special-interest legislation is passed. The political system, combined with the incentive for special-interest legislation, can result in choices that are not in the interest of a majority of voters. Some government policies that result from special-interest legislation make markets less efficient and therefore harm the market economy.

Incentives for Government Growth

Critics of government often argue that there is much duplication, slow response, meaningless work, and general inefficiency in the **public sector.** These claims may not be completely valid, since it is impossible to compare directly and exactly the public and private sectors in regard to efficiency. If the public sector is imperfect, it is also true that all private sector activities are not perfectly efficient. The most valid criticism of the public sector lies not in the actual results it may generate but in the lack of incentives for efficiency its structure produces.

It is clear that efficiency in private industry provides strong economic rewards. A firm that is managed well experiences reduced costs of production and increased profits. The owners and operators of the enterprise personally benefit from this efficiency and, therefore, have a strong incentive to pursue an increasing level of efficiency.

In the public sector, however, this incentive for profits arising from efficiency does not exist. Bureaucrats and political office holders are not able to take home the profits of an efficiently run bureau, thus there is no profit motive. Further, to operate the bureau or department more efficiently may reduce its costs of operation. This would mean that the bureau's next budget allocation from Congress might be reduced, since the bureau did not spend all its current funds. The bureau will have lost control over resources it previously had.

Bureaucratic efficiency is sometimes indirectly rewarded. If bureau chiefs or major government managers expend public funds for lavish offices or pleasant but unnecessary business trips, they personally benefit from these inefficient expenditures. They might not personally benefit from actions that increase efficiency and reduce cost.

If bureaucrats are at all interested in showing increases in efficiency to voters, they will choose to do so in those areas that are most obvious to taxpayers. They will not economize on those areas that are much more difficult to see and understand but that could generate much larger savings. For example, the Carter Administration made a highly publicized announcement that staff members were to use public transportation rather than government limousines whenever possible. This had great political appeal because it was an obvious savings that voters could identify and that was consistent with their apparent value system. Not many voters like the idea of hundreds of our elected officials riding around in limousines paid for with hard-earned tax dollars. The savings from such an action, however, were quite small compared to what might have been saved from the elimination of some large-scale but unproductive government activities. Explaining, for example, the elimination of the United States Department of Education to taxpayers would be much more complex, and some taxpayers might not agree with the decision. From this, it is easy to see that in the public sector, the existing incentives guide the bureaucrat, not to the most effective activities to pursue efficiency, but to those that improve his or her own self-interest or political image.

5.13 GROWTH INCENTIVES

The tendency for government to grow is an extension of this same set of incentives. When a government bureau is allocated a position to be filled, such as adding another secretary, clerk, or manager, this means that the bureau's work load is now divided among more workers. Each worker has less to do. As we noted previously, if any real cost savings of operating the bureau occur, the workers or managers cannot directly capture the benefits of those savings. The same incentives that guide bureaucrats to capture personal gain through plush offices or pleasant business travel also guide them to reduce their personal work load. A manager with an assistant manager and a secretary obviously can pick and choose what required work to do more than a manager who has one secretary. It is therefore in the interest of managers to try to gain more employees under them. This action reduces the personal work load of the manger and increases the amount of resources under the manager's control. Having more employees could also serve to qualify the manager for a higher-level management position in government with a higher salary.

The self-interest of bureaucrats tends to motivate them to respond to the incentives of the system. Workers in private business also face an incentive to take personal gain at their employers' expense. But the profit incentive of the employer may provide for more effective monitoring of costs in the private sector than takes place in the public sector. President Reagan is strongly in favor of reducing the size of government and he has implemented many policies designed to achieve this goal. Even so, all he has been able to do is to reduce the speed at which government expenditures have increased. This may be an indication of how powerful are the incentives for governmental growth.

Obvious Benefits and Unclear Costs

5.14 COSTS, BENEFITS, AND GOVERNMENT PROGRAMS

Another potential problem with public sector policies is that decisions tend to be based primarily on three factors: (1) the short-run benefits of a decision, (2) the ease with which voters can see those benefits, and (3) the fact that the costs of a decision occur in the future and are difficult for voters to identify.

For example, during periods of high unemployment, politicians hear a great public outcry for immediate corrective action. The politician has a strong incentive to vote for bills that will quickly increase government spending and put people to work in government and government-related jobs. The short-run benefit is that people get jobs now, and this benefit is highly visible to voters. Such behavior improves the popularity of the politician and the chances that the politician will be reelected. On the other hand, this action will also require that government acquire the funds to pay for these jobs. This means that, in the short run, either government borrowing will increase or taxes must be raised in the future to pay for the expenditure. When the employed individuals begin to spend their new incomes, this action could also, under certain circumstances, increase the rate of inflation. All these effects, however, are secondary effects. They occur in the future and are much more difficult for voters to identify than the original case of unemployment and increased government expenditures that created the jobs. When taxes must rise or inflation increases in the future, voters find it very difficult to identify the specific cause of such problems.

If a politician had realized the secondary effects in advance, and voted against the increased government spending, his or her chances of reelection would have been reduced. Even though the legislator's economic reasoning was correct, he or she would be unemployed. It is better to be a politician who wins the election and appears to the public as attempting to explain and straighten out the secondary effects later, then to lose the election and try to point out to voters that you were right. Who listens to a defeated politician?

The Shortsightedness Effect

5.15 SHORTSIGHTEDNESS EFFECT

Most political offices range in term from two to four years. The time lag between when an economic action is taken and when its full secondary effects are felt can often be longer than a term of office. Planning horizons for politicians seldom, if ever, exceed their term of office. It is irrational to be concerned heavily with decisions for which you will not be held accountable. This leads us to the shortsightedness effect of government.

The shortsightedness effect can be summed up with the following axioms: The greater the short-run benefits and the clearer and more obvious those benefits are to voters, the more likely politicians are to vote for such an issue. The more long term the costs of an economic action and the more difficult it is for voters to identify those costs, the more likely politicans are to vote for such a bill. Conversely, the further off in the future and the more difficult it is to identify the benefits of a bill, the less likely a politician is to vote for the bill. The closer the costs of an action are to the present and the more visible those costs are to voters, the more unlikely a politician is to vote for the bill. The nature of the political system therefore makes it difficult for politicians to consider the long-run economic problems of the economic systems as thoroughly as they might consider more short-term problems.

KEY CONCEPTS 5.11, 5.12, 5.13, 5.14, 5.15

Government choices are sometimes inefficient for several reasons: group choices are not always efficient because voters frequently have conflicting preferences; special-interest groups can have great influence on government choices; governments often lack private-sector incentives for efficiency; government programs often have clear benefits and hidden costs, which make it difficult to determine if a program is efficient; and voters and legislators are often shortsighted, which can lead to inefficient choices.

This chapter has examined both sides of a mixed economy. We have seen that government has an important role to play in our economy because of the existence of market failures such as monopolies and externalities. With a rising population, growing income, and increasing urbanization, it is natural to think that government might need to grow in order to deal with market failures. Markets sometimes fail, but so do governments. We have examined some of the reasons why government policies are not always perfect, such as the special-interest effect and the problem of obvious benefits and unclear costs.

SUMMARY

5.1 ▶ 1. Economic efficiency refers to an ideal allocation of scarce resources. Markets automatically achieve efficiency when demand reflects all the benefits produced, supply reflects all production costs, and there is competition among buyers and sellers. The market tends to maximize the number of mutually advantageous exchanges, thereby promoting economic efficiency.

5.2 ▶ 2. Externalities cause markets to be inefficient. An external cost exists when producers do not bear all the costs of supplying an item. Supply understates production costs and the market tends to produce more than the efficient amount in this situation. An external benefit exists when purchasers do not pay for all of the benefits they receive from the goods and services they buy. Demand understates benefits and the market tends to produce less than the efficient amount in this situation.

5.3 ▶ 3. Competition among suppliers is necessary for a market to be efficient. Without competition, producers can restrict supply and drive up price. The restricted supply causes the market to produce less than the efficient quantity.

5.4 ▶ 4. Competition among demanders is also necessary for a market to be efficient. A boycott, for example, artificially reduces the demand for an item. Less than the efficient quantity is produced.

5.5 ▶ 5. Government has many tools at its disposal that can be used to promote efficiency in the market. Among these tools are taxes, subsidies, regulations, and the power to define and enforce property rights.

5.6 ▶ 6. A market with only one seller is called a monopoly. A monopoly tends to restrict supply below the efficient level. Government antitrust policies attempt to promote market efficiency by discouraging firms from colluding and otherwise restricting supply.

5.7 ▶ 7. A major function of government as an economic force is to establish and enforce the rules by which human and nonhuman resources are produced, used, and exchanged efficiently. Property rights are the rights to own, use, or sell resources of almost any kind and to benefit from that ownership, use, or sale. They define what can and cannot be done with resources and who has the rights over them. Property rights specify the rules by which resources are exchanged, define responsibilities within an exchange, and determine individual incentives.

5.8 ▶ 8. Through our system of property rights, consumers and producers are able to identify and sometimes capture the value of positive externalities, as well as seek compensation for external costs passed on to them. Positive externalities are benefits passed on outside the market system. Negative externalities are costs passed on to third parties outside the market system.

5.9 ➤ 9. Public goods are items with the following two properties: The owner cannot exclude free riders from gaining benefits from the public good, while the benefits that others receive do not reduce the owner's own benefits. A lighthouse is an example of a public good. It is difficult to exclude nonpayers from their use once these goods are provided. Public goods are a key element in facilitating the functioning of a market economy.

5.10 ➤ 10. Government redistributes income within the economy. Direct redistribution takes place when government taxes one group in order to make payments to others. Indirect redistribution takes place when government alters prices and incomes indirectly, as through trade restrictions and minimum wage laws.

5.11 ➤ 11. Government decisions are sometimes inefficient because of the problems of making group decisions. No voting rule can guarantee that everyone will be better off. The losers in an election bear an external cost of majority-rule decision making.

5.12 ➤ 12. Special-interest groups are organizations formed within society that are united in a common, special self-interest. Their goal is to influence government to pass legislation and enforce property rights that will benefit them. A special-interest issue, if voted into law, will pass on a small cost to each individual voter and a relatively large benefit to the special-interest group. Legislators tend to be influenced by the desires of special-interest groups. It is easier for politicians to be influenced by large, organized groups than by unorganized, individual voters in our society.

5.13 ➤ 13. In government, there is no profit motive to encourage efficiency. The incentives that exist in the public sector guide bureaucrats to those activities that improve their own self-interest or political image, not to the most economically efficient course of action.

5.14 ➤ 14. Political decisions in the public sector are based primarily on three factors: (1) the decision's short-run benefits, (2) the ease with which voters can see those benefits, and (3) the fact that the costs of a decision occur in the future and are difficult for voters to identify.

5.15 ➤ 15. Most political offices range in term from two to four years. Politicians generally only make decisions thinking about their impact for the duration of their term. This creates the problem of shortsightedness in government.

DISCUSSION QUESTIONS

5.1, 5.2, 5.7, 5.8 ➤ 1. A liquor distiller is located on property overlooking a lake. To save disposal costs, waste products from the production process are dumped in the lake. This company sells its liquor for a price 10 percent lower than its competitors. Is this an efficient market? How will the understanding of well-defined property rights enter into your answer?

5.3, 5.6 ▶ 2. If Exxon owned all the gasoline stations in the United States, would the market for gasoline be efficient? Would it be legal for Exxon to completely control the entire market and price of gasoline? How would government prevent this from happening?

5.1, 5.4 ▶ 3. Suppose consumers all felt that the price for a particular brand of stereo system was too high. If consumers wanted to purchase this producer's product at a lower price, what action might they take? How will this action affect the efficient operation of the market?

5.7, 5.8 ▶ 4. Give an example of how property rights define the limits of an exchange and the responsibilities of each party to an exchange. Who enforces property rights? What could you do if you felt your property rights were being violated? Might this violation ever be to your benefit?

5.9 ▶ 5. You live near a major intersection where there presently is no traffic light. You and your neighbors feel that a traffic light is necessary at this corner. Who is best suited to provide this light? Why? Who would benefit the most from its installation? Who would bear most of the costs?

5.10 ▶ 6. What does it mean when economists say government redistributes income? Why is this so important? Why is it probably more effective for government to redistribute income than for individuals to accept that responsibility themselves?

5.12 ▶ 7. Assume the National Association of Aspirin Producers, a special-interest group, has successfully lobbied to have legislation passed so that the maximum legal price of aspirin can be raised. Producers of aspirin claim they want to raise the price of their product to cover costs of child-proof caps on their aspirin bottles. Although the caps cost 3 cents each, aspirin prices are allowed to increase 13 cents. Of what is this an example? Who bears the costs? Who receives the benefits? Are consumers likely to fight the price increase? Why or why not?

5.13 ▶ 8. Discuss the incentive of efficiency in the private versus the public sector.

SELECTED READINGS

Gwartney, James D., Stroup, Richard, and Clark, J.R. *Essentials of Economics*, 3rd ed. New York: Academic Press, 1985, chaps. 19–20.

McKenzie, Richard B., and Tullock, Gordon. *Modern Political Economy*. New York: McGraw-Hill Book Company, 1978, chaps. 21 and 22.

Phelps, Edmund S. (ed.). *Private Wants and Public Needs*, Rev. ed. New York: Norton, 1965.

President's Council of Economic Advisors, "Government and the Economy" in *Economic Report of the President*. Washington, DC GPO, 1982, pp. 27–46.

Schultze, Charles L. *The Public Use of Private Interest*. Washington, DC: The Brookings Institution, 1977.

Veseth, Michael. *Public Finance*. Reston, VA: Reston Publishing Co., 1984.

CHAPTER 6

An Overview of the Private Sector

Having read the chapter, reviewed the chapter summary, and completed the *Study Guide* exercises, you should be able to:

6.1 PRIVATE SECTOR: State who in our society owns the private sector and discuss the importance of the right of exclusion and the concept of self-interest in the private sector.

6.2 HOUSEHOLD AND BUSINESS SECTORS: Explain the relationship between the household sector and the business sector of the economy.

6.3 PRIVATE RESOURCE OWNERSHIP: Explain whether households or business own the private resources in the United States and tell how households earn income.

6.4 SOURCES AND USES OF INCOME: Explain the relationship between the sources of income and the uses of income.

6.5 SOURCES OF INCOME: Define and explain the major sources of income in the United States.

6.6 INCOME DISTRIBUTION: Cite evidence regarding the uneven distribution of income in the United States and list and explain four major factors affecting the variations in family income.

6.7 USES OF INCOME: Discuss the major uses of income for households.

6.8 TYPES OF PURCHASES: Define and contrast durable goods, nondurable goods, and services and discuss the changing pattern of consumption spending in the United States in recent years.

6.9 SAVING: Explain how saving affects future growth and development in an economy.

6.10 BUSINESS ORGANIZATION: Define the three basic types of business organization.

6.11 PROPRIETORSHIPS: List the major advantages and disadvantages of the proprietorship form of business organization.

6.12 CORPORATIONS: List the major advantages and disadvantages of the corporation form of business organization.

6.13 PARTNERSHIPS: List the major advantages and disadvantages of the partnership form of business organization.

6.14 CONCENTRATION RATIO: Explain what is meant by a concentration ratio for an industry.

6.15 CONCENTRATION AND COMPETITION: Explain why the concentration ratio is an ambiguous indicator of the degree of competition in an industry.

6.16 LARGE BUSINESSES: List and explain arguments that both support and oppose the notion that large businesses are a threat to competition.

6.17 INDUSTRIAL POLICY: List and explain the arguments that both support and oppose the notion that the United States needs a governmental industrial policy to guide business investment decisions.

6.1 PRIVATE SECTOR

Private Sector
That part of the economy that is owned by individuals and operated for their exclusive benefit.

Right of Exclusion
That right afforded to individuals, corporations, or institutions in the private sector that allows them to prohibit the public from using or benefiting from private property.

We live in a mixed economy, where some choices are made by private individuals acting in their own self-interest and other choices are made by government. This division of decision making into private and public choices makes it logical for us to divide the economy into two corresponding sectors for purposes of description and analysis. The public sector, discussed briefly in the last chapter, is that part of the economy owned communally by the public and operated for the nonexclusive benefit of the citizens. The **private sector** is owned by private individuals and is operated in the self-interest of those individuals for their private, exclusive gain. This chapter helps us better understand how the economy works by presenting an overview of the private sector. The next chapter looks at the economics of the public sector.

The private sector is characterized by the **right of exclusion.** The right of exclusion means that an individual, a private corporation, or a private institution can own property and exclude others from its use or benefit. If you own stock in a corporation, you are entitled to the exclusive private benefits of that ownership. You might enjoy a gain or suffer a loss if you sell that stock, but both the gain or loss is yours alone. Private corporations are owned by their stockholders. The goods and services corporations provide are produced in the hope of profits that primarily benefit the corporation and, therefore, its stockholders. The right of exclusion means that the owners of firms are able to exclude others from the income that their actions produce. They therefore operate these firms in their own self-interest. The concept of self-interest is the chief motivating force in the private sector.

| **KEY CONCEPT 6.1** | Only in the private sector can a private corporation, institution, or individual own property and exclude the public from its use or benefit. Self-interest is a major influence of the private sector. |

THE RELATIONSHIP BETWEEN BUSINESSES AND HOUSEHOLDS

| **6.2 HOUSEHOLD AND BUSINESS SECTORS** | The private sector is composed of two interrelated groups: *households* and *business firms*. The relationship between business and households is important because it illustrates the fundamental force that drives the economy. Figure 6-1 illustrates the **circular flow of spending and income** between households and business. |

Circular Flow of Spending and Income
A model of the relationship between spending and income for the entire economy.

It is convenient to think of the economy as two separate groups that each rely on the other for existence. Households, for example, purchase goods and services from the business sector, providing revenue and profit for the business firms. Businesses, on the other hand, employ individuals

FIGURE 6-1   **The Circular Flow of Spending and Income.** Spending by the household sector provides revenue for the business sector, which is paid as income to the household sector. Payments by households are the uses of income, while payments from business to households provide the sources of income in the figure.

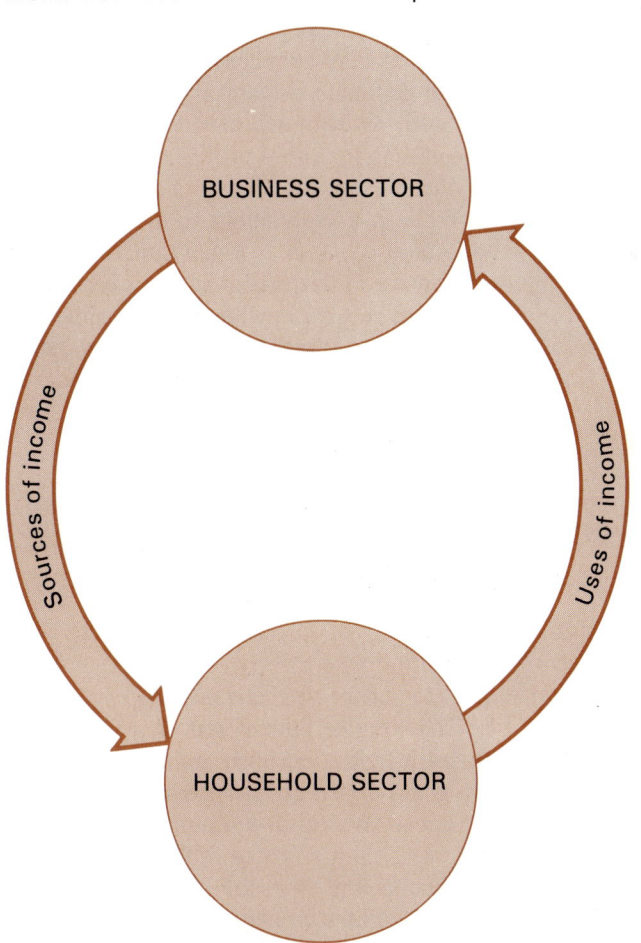

from the household sector, providing them with the income they need to purchase the goods and services that they desire. When individuals go to a store and purchase the groceries they want, for example, they create income for the people who work for the supermarket and for the owners. They also create income for the store's suppliers and for those who loaned the money to finance the store.

The circular flow diagram shown in Figure 6-1 illustrates the concept that the money that households spend on goods eventually becomes the income that households receive from the business firms they work for, lend to, invest in, or own. This concept of household spending creating household income through the business sector will be a fundamental building block of macroeconomics in coming chapters. (Note that the circular flow concept presented here is an extreme simplification of the way the economy works. This simple model ignores government, for example, which is an important force in our economy. The circular flow model will be enriched in later chapters to add more realism to its description of the economy.)

HOUSEHOLDS: ONE HALF OF THE PRIVATE SECTOR

> **6.3 PRIVATE RESOURCE OWNERSHIP**

There are over 80 million households in the United States, and the private ownership of resources is located there. All private resources are owned by individuals, and all individuals reside in a household unit. Households produce income by selling or lending their resources to businesses. You may be employed by a corporation, which means that you sell your labor resource to them. You may own corporate stocks or bonds, in which case you sell or lend your financial (capital) resources to a corporation for a payment. You may rent or even sell land that you own to a business. You may manage a business and receive profits or bear its losses. In all these cases, households produce income by selling the resources they own to business firms.

While it is convenient to divide the private sector into business and household parts, it is important for us to realize that the same people participate in both sides of the exchanges that convert spending into income. The people who spend income as part of the household group are generally the same people who, through the business sector, produce the goods and services that are purchased.

> **KEY CONCEPTS 6.2, 6.3**

All private resources in the economy are owned by individuals residing within households. Households produce income by selling these resources to business firms. Businesses and households are related by the circular flow of spending and income.

> **6.4 SOURCES AND USES OF INCOME**

The circular flow of spending and income between households and businesses provides us with an important concept because it shows us how these two parts of the economy depend on each other and provide each other with resources. We can learn more about the private sector if we look more closely at the two sides of the circular flow: the *sources of income* to households and the *uses of income* by households. Since income is not evenly distributed across households, we will also examine what factors affect distribution.

TABLE 6-1	Sources of Income, 1985		
Item		Income ($ billion)	Percent of total
Compensation of employees		2372.7	74
Proprietors' income		242.4	8
Rents		14.0	1
Corporate profits		299.0	9
Interest		287.7	9
National income		3215.6	100

Source. Economic Report of the President, 1986, Table B-23.

6.5 SOURCES OF INCOME

Wages
Compensation to households for use of their individual labor. Wages are the largest source of household income.

Proprietors' Income
As proprietors supply all four factors of production (land, labor, capital, and management skills), their income is in part a combination of wages, profits, rents, and interest.

The Sources of Income to Households

Production revolves around four categories of economic resources: land, labor, capital, and entrepreneurial skills. These resources are sold to businesses by households who receive payment for their use. For example, labor is paid wages; land use receives rent; capital is paid interest, and entrepreneurs receive the profits or losses of a business. These payments will be more thoroughly analyzed in Chapter 23. Table 6-1 shows the breakdown of the sources of income among these components for 1985. **Wages** paid as compensation to households for the use of their individual labor is the largest source of household income. The greatest portion of total income produced is paid to working men and women as opposed to those who are owners of corporate stock or other financial resources. **Proprietors' income** is really a combination of wages, profits, rents, and interest, because small individual businesses, such as lawyers and dentists, supply all four types of resources to their proprietorship. Interest income is also small relative to employee compensation.

The United States is, in an important sense, an economy built on wages and workers. Household income is directly dependent upon the quantity, quality, and types of resources that the household can supply to business. The sources of income described in Table 6-1 vary by small amounts from year to year, but the general picture that the table presents has been relatively stable over time. Wage income has remained the largest source of income in the United States for many years.

6.6 INCOME DISTRIBUTION

Median Household Income
The median of any series is the figure at the center of the distribution when all the elements of the series are ordered from lowest to highest. For example, $200 is the median number in the series $100, $200, $500. Median household income is therefore the income of the household at the center of the income distribution when household incomes are ordered from lowest to highest.

The Distribution of Income to Households

The income that households receive is not evenly distributed among them, even after government programs such as welfare payments, food stamps, and social security are taken into account. There are many ways to measure and describe the distribution of income in the United States. We will look more closely at the question of income distribution and government policies in Chapter 24. For now, Table 6-2 shows one way of looking at income distribution by presenting data for 1984 concerning the median income of different population groups.

The data presented in Table 6-2 show that median income varies considerably among households based on several factors. **Median household income** is seen to depend on sex, race, and participation in the labor force. White families enjoy a median household income well above that for black families. Female-headed families experience lower median income than those headed by males. Full-time workers, who are active participants in the

TABLE 6-2	Median Incomes of Selected Groups, 1984	
Group		Median income ($)
All families		26,433
White families		27,686
Black families		15,432
White males		16,467
White male full-time workers		24,826
White females		6,949
White female full-time workers		15,575
Black males		9,448
Black male full-time workers		16,943
Black females		6,164
Black female full-time workers		14,036

Source. Economic Report of the President, 1986, Table B-29.

working world, have higher median incomes than those with labor skills that may be less in demand by employers. These figures are for median incomes by groups, so they tell us the income of the middle individual in each group. These figures therefore mask variations in incomes within each group. Some black females, for example, earn more than some white males. Thus, it is important not to place too vigorous an interpretation on these data. Nevertheless, such large differences in median income are an indication of important inequality of income in the United States.

There are many reasons why income is unevenly distributed by the private sector. While we will examine these determinants of income distribution in more detail in Chapter 24, let us briefly discuss four factors that affect the distribution of income amoung households.

Education and Skills There are substantial differences in education, skill, motivation, and intelligence among individuals. These differences by themselves are neither good nor bad, but markets and businesses place different market values upon them. The market price for the specific resources a family might supply to businesses strongly affects family income. An individual might be a gifted poet or great philosophy teacher, but the market for these skills or education is limited. Plumbers will probably be in more demand in business and, therefore, earn more substantial incomes than philosophers. Accordingly, one household's collection of education, skills, intelligence, and talents may have a higher market value than another's, but not necessarily a higher value to society as a whole. The social value placed on these characteristics is, however, a question to be addressed in normative and not positive economics.

Mobility and Information There are substantial differences in mobility and access to market information among households. Some families are either unable or unwilling to relocate where better employment opportunities exist for their resources. When coal mining slows down in the eastern coal fields of West Virginia, it might be booming in the western coal fields of

Montana, Colorado, or Arizona. While unemployment increases in the East, jobs are available in the West. If a family of coal miners is either uninformed of this opportunity or unwilling to relocate, family income must fall, at least temporarily. The mobility of a resource and the availability of information concerning employment opportunities are key ingredients in the earning capabilities of that resource.

Wealth There are substantial differences in accumulated wealth among households. A family that has saved income and purchased income-producing financial assets such as stocks, bonds, or savings accounts has a greater earning power than one without that wealth. The income of a family is directly related to the quality and quantity of resources it can supply to businesses.

Specific Market Conditions Other factors affect the incomes of certain families. Markets do not all function without external interferences. For example, strong union contracts force up the prices paid for certain types of labor. Consequently, it is entirely possible that a union plumber could receive substantially more income than a nonunion plumber, even though the nonunion plumber worked under similar conditions, possessed the same skills, and expended a like amount of effort. This is because a union structure restricts the supply of union plumbers and raises wages above nonunion levels. These market interferences can occur on the corporate side, as well. When major employers band together in an attempt to reduce the prices they are willing to pay for labor, they are attempting to manipulate the market in their favor. They may force wages down in their area. Workers in other areas or working in other industries doing the same kind of work may earn more income. These corporations are interfering with the smooth functioning of a market. Such interferences can have substantial effects on the distribution of income.

The distribution of income in the economy affects both the total amounts and the specific types of goods and services produced. The amount of income families receive is a primary determinant of their levels of consumption and savings. The higher the level of consumption in an economy, the greater is the demand for goods and services, and the more producers are willing to produce. Consumption calls forth production and increases the demand for resources supplied by households. Saving reduces consumption and reduces demand and production. The distribution of income, therefore, has a great deal to do with how much the economy uses its resources and subsequently how much it can produce.

KEY CONCEPTS 6.5, 6.6

The quantity, quality, and types of resources that households supply to businesses determine the amount of income households receive. Variation in family incomes is due to many factors, including differences in education, skill, motivation, intelligence, mobility, access to market information, accumulated wealth, and nonmarket factors.

The Uses of Income by Households

6.7 USES OF INCOME

Households both receive income by providing resources to producers and spend income to acquire the goods and services they desire. Once income is

> **6.8 TYPES OF PURCHASES**

received, there are three basic uses for it: consumption, saving, and taxes. Table 6-3 shows the uses of income in the United States in 1985.

Personal Consumption Consumption spending is the largest single use of income in the United States, accounting for 81 percent of total spending in 1985. The level of consumption spending in an economy depends on many factors, including total income, expectations of incomes and prices, and the distribution of income. Table 6-3 divides consumption spending into three types of purchases: durable goods, nondurable goods, and services. This breakdown is useful because each of these types of expenditures is affected by different economic forces.

Durable goods are defined as items that last longer than a year. **Nondurable goods** are, therefore, items with a useful service life of less than one year. Autos, homes, and household appliances are examples of durable goods. Spending on durable goods is sensitive to current economic conditions and expectations of future conditions. Since durable goods tend to be relatively costly, consumers do not undertake these purchases lightly. In addition, durable goods that are already owned can often be made to last a little longer if the future looks uncertain for consumers. Purchases of durable items such as refrigerators and air conditioners are therefore more sensitive to economic events than are purchases of nondurable goods, such as bread and beer.

The purchase of **services** is a large and important use of income. Many of the things that consumers purchase are classified as services. These include the services of lawyers and accountants, barbers, physicians and nurses, and bankers (who supply financial services). Housing costs are also included in the service category, as are transportation services and the purchase of utilities such as electricity. Most of today's college students undertake educational programs that qualify them to supply services in the market.

Purchases of services tend to increase in an economy as income grows and the population becomes increasingly urbanized. Thus services represent a larger share of total expenditures in developed countries than they do in less-developed countries. Many services such as haircuts and laundry services, which are commonly purchased in developed countries, do not represent expenditures in less-developed countries. Households provide these services for themselves in less-developed countries rather than purchasing them from others.

Durable Goods
Goods that have a service life of greater than one year. Automobiles and boats are examples of durable goods.

Nondurable Goods
Goods with a useful service life of less than one year. Food and shampoo are examples of nondurable goods.

Services
Labor, expertise, counsel, advice, or representation provided for a fee.

| TABLE 6-3 | Uses of Income, 1985 |

Item	($ billion)	Percent of total
Personal consumption	2669.3	81
Durable goods	360.8	
Nondurable goods	912.5	
Services	1308.6	
Personal saving	129.7	4
Personal taxes	493.1	15
Household income	3294.2	100

Source, Economic Report of the President, 1986, Tables B-14, B-25.

Personal Taxes Death and taxes are, according to an old saying, the two things that are inevitable. Table 6-3 shows that personal taxes accounted for 15 percent of income allocations in 1985, although there are other ways of measuring the tax burden that give higher tax figures. In a market-oriented economy, the percentage of our personal income dollars allocated to taxes is much less than those of more socially oriented economies, such as Sweden or Denmark. This percentage has increased substantially over the last 50 years, however.

6.9 SAVING

Savings
The total accumulation of resources through past and current saving.

Saving
Income that is not spent on goods or paid in taxes in the current time period.

Dissaving
The amount by which personal spending exceeds personal income.

Capital Formation
Additions to the economy's ability to produce, such as plants, machinery, technology, and equipment.

Personal Saving Saving is the third possible use of income. Note that economists distinguish between **savings**, which is the total amount of money that has been accumulated, and **saving**, which is the additional amount accumulated in the current year. For an individual, this means that you might have total savings of $3000, of which $500 is the savings that you have added this year. In economists' terms, saving is income that is not used to pay taxes or purchase consumer goods in the current year. According to Table 6-3, households in the United States used about 4 percent of their income for saving in 1985 (note that national saving was really higher than this in 1985 because businesses are also a source of saving that is not included in this table). This figure is substantially less than the saving rate of some other developed industrial nations, such as Japan. As in all economies, some U.S. families spend more than their income. Economists refer to this type of behavior as **dissaving**.

Saving is an important economic activity because it has implications for both the present and the future. In the present, saving is an alternative to spending. Holding income fixed, more saving means less spending. Individuals who save give up the goods that these resources could have purchased now. Individuals who save reduce the total demand for goods in the present, affecting both the total amount and distribution of spending and income in the economy.

Today's saving affects the nature of the economy in the future. Saving by households and businesses provides a pool of resources that are used by households, businesses, and government to purchase goods and services. Investment spending on new factories and technological improvements is usually financed by borrowing. These investments generate new goods, new jobs, and higher incomes in the future. The amount of investment spending and **capital formation** that takes place in the future depends, therefore, on the amount of saving today. Of course, there are factors other than saving, such as the level of interest rates, profit expectations, and government tax and finance policies, that also affect investment and capital formation. Saving, along with these factors, are important influences on the economy's future economic growth.

Personal saving is important because it generates economic growth. Low saving rates retard capital formation and lead to stagnant, low-growth economies. Higher saving rates, like those associated with Japan, frequently lead to dynamic, high-growth economies. The low 4 percent rate observed in 1985 may be a harbinger of future economic problems in the United States.

KEY CONCEPT 6.9   Saving in an industrial economy affects future growth and development. Saving makes resources available to businesses to finance expansion and growth.

BUSINESSES: THE OTHER HALF OF THE PRIVATE SECTOR

Business firms bring together raw material resources and combine them to produce goods and services. Businesses either enhance the value of the resources that they use or they do not meet the test of the market. If a business cannot provide a good or service to the market at an opportunity cost less than what consumers are willing and able to pay, the business fails. Business losses and bankruptcy are the market's mechanism to cleanse itself of inefficient or unsuccessful producers. Profits and growth are the system by which businesses that pass the test of the market are rewarded. Business in the private sector operates in a dynamic environment. There are always winners and losers changing places everyday, but the process of combining resources to meet the needs of consumers goes on.

6.10 BUSINESS ORGANIZATION

The United States relies primarily on private businesses to provide goods and services. There are about 15 million business firms in the United States organized as either proprietorships, partnerships, or corporations. Table 6-4 displays the breakdown, by amount and percent of total, of the number of firms in each category and their dollar volume of sales for the year 1977 (the most recent year for which comprehensive Census of Manufacturers data are available).

While there are many more proprietorships than corporations, the corporate form of business organization accounts for most of the dollar volume of sales in the economy. The business sector is characterized by many proprietorships conducting business on a small scale and a relatively small number of corporations producing most of the goods and services. Each form of business organization fulfills a function and has specific advantages and disadvantages.

Proprietorships

6.11 PROPRIETORSHIPS

Proprietorship
A business firm that is owned by a single individual.

A **proprietorship** is a business owned by one person. The profits and losses of such a business are the personal profits or losses of its owner. In many proprietorships, the owner actually works in the business, providing entrepreneurial and personal labor services. Most businesses such as small neighborhood shops, boutiques, bakeries, and small farms are examples of proprietorships. The major advantages of such a form of business organization are that they are easy to start, not heavily regulated by government, and the proprietor has almost complete control over the business. The ease with

TABLE 6-4

The Organization of Business in the United States, 1977

	Corporation	Partnership	Proprietorship
Number of firms (thousands)	2,242	1,153	11,346
Percent of total	15.21	7.82	76.97
Dollar sales (billions)	$3,813.9	176.5	393.9
Percent of total	86.99	4.03	8.98

Source. U.S. Bureau of the Census, *Census of Manufacturers, 1977, Concentration Ratios in Manufacturing.*

which these types of businesses can be started probably accounts for the fact that there are so many of them. Although some of these firms file legal papers of incorporations so that they can make use of special tax advantages, they retain the fundamental organizational structure of unified ownership and management.

There are substantial disadvantages to this type of business, as well. First, as a single owner, one person probably has limited ability to acquire the capital needed for a business. Relative to large corporations that can sell stock to raise capital, proprietorships are highly limited in their start-up and expansion financing ability. Second, since a proprietor is only one person, it is improbable that he or she has the wide variety of business and managerial skills that several partners or a management team could bring to a business enterprise. Finally, proprietorships have both limited life and unlimited liability. When the proprietor dies, the business is usually dissolved to settle his or her financial obligations. The feature of unlimited liability means that the proprietor is personally responsible for all debts of the business. If the business fails, the personal property of the proprietor, such as his or her house, automobile, or any other assets, can be seized by the creditors of the business to pay off business debts. A high percentage of all small businesses fail within their first year. The problems of limited life, unlimited liability, and difficulty in raising business capital probably explain why corporations do so much more of the dollar volume of business in our economy.

Corporations

Corporations are the second-largest number of business firms in the economy and do most of the dollar volume of business because of their ability to produce goods and services on a very large scale. A **corporation** can raise large amounts of capital through the sale of stocks and bonds. Stocks represent ownership shares in a corporation. Existing owners sell part of the firm to others in order to raise additional resources when stock sales are made. Bonds are debt. The corporation borrows resources when it sells bonds. Through the sale of stocks and bonds, corporations can build huge manufacturing and service facilities, finance research and development, and generally pursue business interests beyond the financial reach of proprietorships or partnerships. Corporations have this tremendous capital-raising power because of two features: limited liability for loss and unlimited life.

In the eyes of the law, a corporation is a separate legal individual. It has the right to borrow money, earn profits, produce and sell goods, and perform most other legal functions that our system would permit a living person. With this identity, corporations can raise large amounts of financial capital by selling stocks or bonds. The stockholders own the corporation but are liable only for losses up to the value of the stock they own. In contrast, as already stated, a proprietor is personally liable for all debts of the business and could lose not only the investment in the business but all personal property, as well.

Corporate stock can be sold by an owner to another person without affecting the corporation. This changeover in ownership takes place all the time, but the business itself goes on as usual. This is because a corporation has an unlimited legal life. Only if the business failed, would its legal life be terminated.

6.12 CORPORATIONS

Corporation
A business firm owned by many individuals collectively. Each individual owner has a right to a share of the corporation's profits, but the individual's liability is limited to the amount of his or her initial investment.

ECONOMIC ISSUES

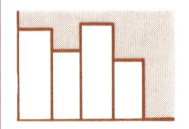

The Paradox of Corporate Accountability

Corporations control a vast amount of resources in the United States and most other nations in the free world. They determine where production takes place and how and have great influence on the jobs and incomes of millions of people. On the face of it, it seems that corporations have a great deal of power. Is this desirable? Is it dangerous? How accountable are corporations to society? Should society put so much power in the hands of large private-sector firms? As we will see shortly, this is not a question with a simple answer.

Who controls the operations of a corporation? A glance at any corporate table of organization quickly shows that the president and chairman of the board (one of whom is usually named the chief executive officer or C.E.O. of the firm) have authority for the day-to-day operations of the corporation, with broader policy authority determined by a relatively small group called the board of directors. The directors of a corporation are frequently major stockholders of the firm, distinguished citizens, or successful business people in other fields. Together, the board of directors and the C.E.O. make most of the decisions regarding the use of the corporation's resources.

It might appear that corporate power is concentrated in the hands of a narrow corporate elite. Relatively few people, with no direct accountability to the public at large, determine the actions of giant corporations. This narrow view of corporate accountability is not necessarily the case, however. Corporations are really examples of what might be called "private-sector democracy." A corporation's C.E.O. is selected by its board of directors, and the directors are themselves elected by the votes of the thousands or millions of individual stockholders. Anyone can gain a vote concerning corporate policy simply by buying a share of stock in the firm. Unlike public-sector elections, however, the one man–one vote rule does not apply. A person with 1000 shares of stock has 1000 times the voting power of a person with one share of stock.

Stock ownership in the United States is widely dispersed. Millions of Americans own stock directly and millions more own stock through their participation in mutual funds, pension plans, and life insurance policies that invest in corporate shares. This

Corporations face two major disadvantages. First, since a corporation is a separate individual from its owners in the eyes of the law, much legal preparation is required before a major corporation can be made legally viable. This involves legal filing and a continuing series of reports made to the State Corporation Commission. In the case of small businesses, the headaches of these complexities are rarely worth the advantages of the corporate form of organization.

Second, corporations are operated by teams of management specialists who serve at the pleasure of the stockholders. If the stockholders are not satisfied with the management team, they can call for a new election, but the stockholders do not directly manage the company. They have ownership, but the company's management has control. The separation of ownership and control creates a conflict of self-interest. The corporation's owners want to see corporate profits maximized because that maximizes the value of their investments. The corporation's managers may not share this goal if they are not also shareholders. The managers might prefer to seek a satisfactory level of profits, then sacrifice additional profits in order to provide valuable amenities to themselves. In simple terms, it is to the manager's interest for shareholders to sacrifice profits rather than the manager sacrificing income or working conditions.

means that millions of Americans can directly or indirectly vote on matters of corporate policy. Viewed in this way, it appears that corporations are highly accountable to the public, because millions of people can influence corporate policy by voting their shares.

Unfortunately, most corporate policies are not determined by the votes of millions of small shareholders. Small investors are usually ill-informed about corporate policies and assign their "proxy" votes to the directors. Large institutional investors, such as pension funds and insurance companies, could influence corporate policies if they wanted to, but most choose not to. Institutional investors typically have a "support or sell" philosophy concerning corporate policies. That is, they either support the decisions of the directors on important matters, or they sell their shares and invest in other firms. Sometimes uninformed small shareholders and institutional investors can account for a large percentage of the total voting shares of a corporation. When this happens, a single person or group with only 10 to 15 percent of the corporation's voting shares can gain functional control of the firm. In this situation, a small active minority can dominate a large passive majority of shareholders and determine corporate policy.

This seems to indicate that corporate power can be highly concentrated in just a few hands, reducing corporate accountability. This is not necessarily the case, however. Private corporations are heavily regulated in the United States. A corporation that is controlled by just a few people is still subject to a wide variety of federal, state, and local regulations. Corporations are also "regulated" by competitive markets. Competition from other firms limits the action of any particular corporation. Together, government regulations and market competition can limit the actions of any corporation.

How accountable are corporations to society? As this discussion has shown, the control of corporate policy can be viewed as either widely dispersed among the millions of shareholders and voters or heavily concentrated in just a few hands. This paradox cannot be easily resolved. Any social system that relies on voting for policy decisions can be viewed as either widely democratic or controlled by a narrow elite. The president of the United States, for example, is selected through a national election. This makes it seem as if the president is very accountable to the people. But most people do not vote in any election, and many who do vote are uninformed and so vote randomly or on the basis of simple images. The president needs only about half of the total vote to gain election. If only 40 percent of the population votes, a candidate needs to gain support from only about 20 percent of the total population (in other words, 51 percent of those who do vote) to win election. It can be argued, therefore, that the president is really accountable to only the 10 to 20 percent of the total population in key states whose votes really determine the election. This means that presidents, like corporations, may be accountable to relatively narrow groups.

6.13 PARTNERSHIPS

Partnership
A business firm that is owned by several individuals collectively. Each individual owner shares both the profits from the partnership and the risk of loss.

Partnerships

A **partnership** results when two or more individuals act together as business owners. They share each other's risks and rewards according to some agreement signed at the formation of the partnership, but both have unlimited liability. If the business fails, each partner is personally liable for all the debts of the business. This form of business organization has most of the advantages and disadvantages of the proprietorship but allows limited risk sharing for business owners.

Legal and accounting firms are usually partnerships. Like proprietorships, partnerships will sometimes file incorporation papers to secure certain tax advantages, such as expanded tax-deferred retirement plans, while still operating as a partnership.

CONCENTRATION, MARKET POWER, AND SIZE

As we have pointed out, corporations, while smaller in number than proprietorships, are the dominant business organization in our economy. When we think of "The American Economy," many of us think of big business. Many people believe that America is dominated by a few big businesses whose

6.14 CONCENTRATION RATIO

Concentration Ratio
The proportion of total sales in a given market accounted for by the activity of a particular number of firms. High concentration ratios indicate markets dominated by a few firms.

6.15 CONCENTRATION AND COMPETITION

philosophy is summed up by the statement "What's good for General Motors is good for the U.S.A." Are markets in the United States dominated by a few large firms? To separate fact from fiction on this issue, let's take a closer look at the facts.

Let's look at corporate concentration from the viewpoint of an economist. When a specific industry is dominated by a small number of firms, concentration is usually high. Economists use the concept of the **concentration ratio** to measure this situation. The concentration ratio is the total sales of the four, or in some cases eight, largest firms in the industry as a percentage of the total industry sales. The higher this number, the more concentrated is the market power of these firms. Table 6-5 gives examples of concentration ratios for 1977, using Census of Manufacturers data for that year.

Table 6-5 shows that some industries face high concentration ratios, while other industries have few large firms. What does this information tell us? It is easy to draw the conclusion that industries with higher concentration ratios are monopolistic and are weighted in favor of business. The popular perception is that business has an unfair advantage over consumers in markets whose concentration ratios are high. This perception is wrong for several reasons. First, a high concentration ratio shows that a few firms sell most of the goods in a market, but it does not indicate the extent of competition. It is possible for large firms to be as competitive as smaller firms. The cola market is dominated by Coca Cola and Pepsi Cola, for example. Between them, these two firms take the lion's share of this market. Yet Coke and Pepsi may behave more competitively as industrial giants than they might if they were smaller companies. Sometimes small firms lack the resources to actively compete with bigger businesses. Mergers in the beer industry since 1977, for example, have reduced the number of firms and increased the concentration ratio in this industry. But competition has probably increased among beer firms as a result of the mergers, because many small firms are now able to pool resources to more effectively

TABLE 6-5

Concentration Ratios for Selected Industries, 1977

Industry	4-firm ratio (%)	8-firm ratio (%)
Passenger cars	99+	100
Chewing gum	93	99
Home refrigerators	82	98
Aircraft engines	74	86
Sugarcane refining	63	90
Synthetic rubber	60	83
Glass containers	54	75
Motors and generators	42	55
Men's footwear	31	46
Oil field machinery	30	45
Carpets and rugs	21	35
Special tools and dies	8	10

Source. U.S. Bureau of the Census, *Census of Manufacturers, 1977, Concentration Ratios in Manufacturing.*

6.16 LARGE BUSINESSES

compete with Budweiser and Miller, the dominant firms in this industry. Big firms are not necessarily any less competitive than small firms.

Second, in some cases, markets with low concentration ratios are actually less competitive than those with high concentration ratios. This is because low-concentration markets may be composed of many firms, each of which dominates some specific geographical area. The brick and tile industry, for example, has a national concentration ratio of 12 percent, which indicates that the top four firms do not dominate the overall market (using data for 1977). This statistic is deceptive, however. On average, the top four tile and brick firms *in each local or regional market* account for 87 percent of sales in the market. Thus we can conclude that, despite its low national concentration ratio, the tile and brick industry is made up of relatively small firms that may dominate local markets but do not dominate national markets. This example illustrates the need to accurately define the relevant market when using concentration ratios to draw conclusions about competition in a market.

Finally, concentration ratios can mislead us about the nature of competition in a market because they often overlook foreign producers. Suppose, for example, that a U.S. market was 100 percent in the control of a single producer; in other words, that it was a monopoly. Would this monopoly dominate the market to an unfair advantage? This would not necessarily be the case if there was substantial pressure from foreign producers. In this instance the monopoly might be forced to give customers low prices and generous service in order to keep foreign producers out of the market. The foreign competition would not appear in the concentration ratio, but its effect would be felt just the same. The nature of competition among business firms will be discussed in more detail in Chapter 20.

INDUSTRIAL DEVELOPMENT POLICY

6.17 INDUSTRIAL POLICY

Industrial Development Policy
A set of government policies designed to encourage economic growth by controlling private investment actions.

Another issue in the business sector involves proposals for an **industrial development policy** for private-sector firms. An industrial development policy would attempt to promote rapid economic growth by controlling the pattern of business investments. Government planners would attempt to influence investment patterns, encouraging winners and discouraging losers, in order to get the greatest social benefit from scarce investment resources.

There are two reasons why some politicians and economists have called for government policies to regulate, or at least influence, investment spending. First, the U.S. economy has experienced relatively slow rates of investment and economic growth in recent decades. This low investment is partly the result of low saving rates in the United States. Proponents would attempt to encourage higher rates of capital formation in high-growth industries through government programs. Second, some private investment practices appear questionable from a societal viewpoint. Oil-producing firms in the United States, for example, were given tax incentives in the 1970s with the idea that they would invest in oil exploration to help make the United States self-sufficient in energy resources. Some of the tax-cut money paid to oil firms, however, ended up in unexpected places. Oil firms used their resources to purchase non-energy businesses, such as circuses, or to buy up one another rather than using them to explore for additional energy reserves. Mergers and takeovers increased the concentration ratio in the oil industry and made some oil investors rich, but they didn't discover a single extra gallon of oil. Oil firms made these investments because they provided a higher return to corporate shareholders than did energy exploration activities. The private self-interest of corporate owners was in conflict with the public interest in securing energy in this situation.

Proposed industrial development plans vary widely. However, they typically involve a national development bank that would route low-interest funds to specified firms and industries that are expected to generate high rates of economic growth in the future. Many of these plans are modelled on Japan's Ministry of International Trade and Industry (MITI). MITI's influence is given credit by some for Japan's rapid postwar industrial growth.

Most economists oppose plans to implement an industrial development policy in the United States. Their opposition is based on two arguments. First, economists doubt that government planners would be more effective in pinpointing high-growth industries than are private investors. They wonder how government planners could pick winners and recognize high-growth areas if the market, with its forces of profit and self-interest, cannot. Japan's MITI may have helped some industries that have since grown, but MITI has also made errors in allocating scarce resources. It is important to realize that, given scarce resources, grants to a "chosen" firm or industry mean that fewer resources will be available elsewhere in the economy. Government planners might actually choke off a valuable new industry by depriving it of capital as they attempt to expand the industries that they have identified as having higher potential.

The second argument against industrial development policies is that they would introduce politics into the investment decision. The firms and industries that would get government help might be those with the best political connections, not those with the greatest job and income growth potential. Industrial development support might end up as a life-support system for outdated but politically powerful industries.

The debate over industrial development policy is encouraging in that it focuses attention on investment and capital formation as a necessary condition for economic growth. Perhaps this debate will lead to government policies that encourage saving and investment, and so promote economic growth, but still retain the advantages of self-interest that characterize the private sector of the economy.

SUMMARY

6.1

1. The private sector is owned by individual persons and is operated for private exclusive gain. Only in the private sector can a private corporation, institution, or individual own property and exclude the public from its use or benefit. Self-interest is a major influence of the private sector.

6.2, 6.3

2. There are 80 million households in the United States. All private resources in the economy are owned by individuals living within these households. Households produce income by selling these resources to business firms. Businesses and households are related by the circular flow of spending and income.

Summary 143

6.4, 6.5, 6.7 3. The sources of household income are wages, profits, proprietors' income, interest, and rent. The uses of household income are consumption spending, saving, and taxes. The sources and uses of household income are related through the circular flow concept.

6.5 4. Analysis of the sources of income examines how household income is distributed among the four factors of production: land, labor, capital, and management skills.

6.5 5. The quantity, quality, and types of resources that households supply to businesses determine the amount of income households receive.

6.6 6. Variations in family incomes are due to many factors, including
  a. differences in education, skill, motivation, and intelligence;
  b. differences in mobility and access to market information;
  c. differences in accumulated wealth; and
  d. how nonmarket factors affect the incomes of certain families.

6.7 7. Analysis of the uses of income examines how households dispose of their income. In general, households allocate their income between taxes, consumption, and savings.

6.8 8. The goods consumers purchase can be categorized as either durables or nondurables. Durable goods have a useful life of greater than one year. Nondurable goods have a useful life of less than one year. Households also purchase services, such as housing, transportation, and professional services.

6.8 9. Consumer expenditures on durable goods decline much more than on nondurable goods when the economy is experiencing a decline in economic conditions.

6.9 10. Saving in an industrial economy affects future growth and development. Saving makes resources available to businesses to finance expansion and growth.

6.10 11. Three types of business organizations exist in our society. They are proprietorships, corporations, and partnerships.

6.11 12. Proprietorships are generally owned and managed by a sole individual who bears the responsibility of the profits or losses of the business. The main advantages of a proprietorship are:
  a. They are simple to start.
  b. The owner (proprietor) has control over the business.
  c. There is little government regulation.

6.11 13. Proprietorships are also subject to disadvantages. Among the disadvantages are:
  a. The owner has limited ability to acquire necessary capital to open the business.
  b. Because the proprietor is a single person, he or she brings limited skills and business experience to the endeavor.

c. The proprietorship has a limited life.
d. The owner is personally liable for all the debts of the business.

> **6.12**

14. Corporations are legal entities. They have the unique ability to raise substantial amounts of capital through the sale of stocks and bonds. The main advantages of the corporate form are:
    a. Stockholders have limited liability; they own the corporation but are only liable for losses up to the amount of the value of their stock.
    b. A corporation has unlimited life; only if the business itself failed, would the corporation's life end.

> **6.12**

15. The disadvantages of the corporate form of business organization include:
    a. They are legally complex to start.
    b. There is a separation of ownership and control.

> **6.12**

16. The number of proprietorships far exceeds the number of corporations in the United States. However, it is corporations that produce the most dollar sales in our economy.

> **6.13**

17. Partnerships are two or more individuals together acting as business owners. They each share in the risks and rewards of the business as designated in the partnership agreement. The main advantages of partnerships are:
    a. They are fairly simple to start.
    b. There is little government regulation.
    c. Partners share control of the business as determined in their partnership agreement.

> **6.13**

18. The principal disadvantages of partnerships include:
    a. All partners have unlimited liability.
    b. The partnership has a limited life.
    c. It is possible that the partners possess limited skills and business experience.

> **6.14**

19. Economists use the concentration ratio to measure the percentage of industry sales a number of corporations within that industry generate. This ratio is calculated by finding the total sales of the four or eight largest firms as a proportion of total sales in the market.

> **6.15**

20. Concentration ratios are not a perfect indicator of competition in a market, however. The existence of competition among large producers, local monopolies, and foreign competition all affect the interpretation of concentration ratios.

> **6.16, 6.17**

21. Two important issues with respect to businesses in the United States are:
    a. Should large businesses be more heavily regulated in an effort to promote competition?
    b. Should the government create an industrial development policy to encourage effective business growth?

DISCUSSION QUESTIONS

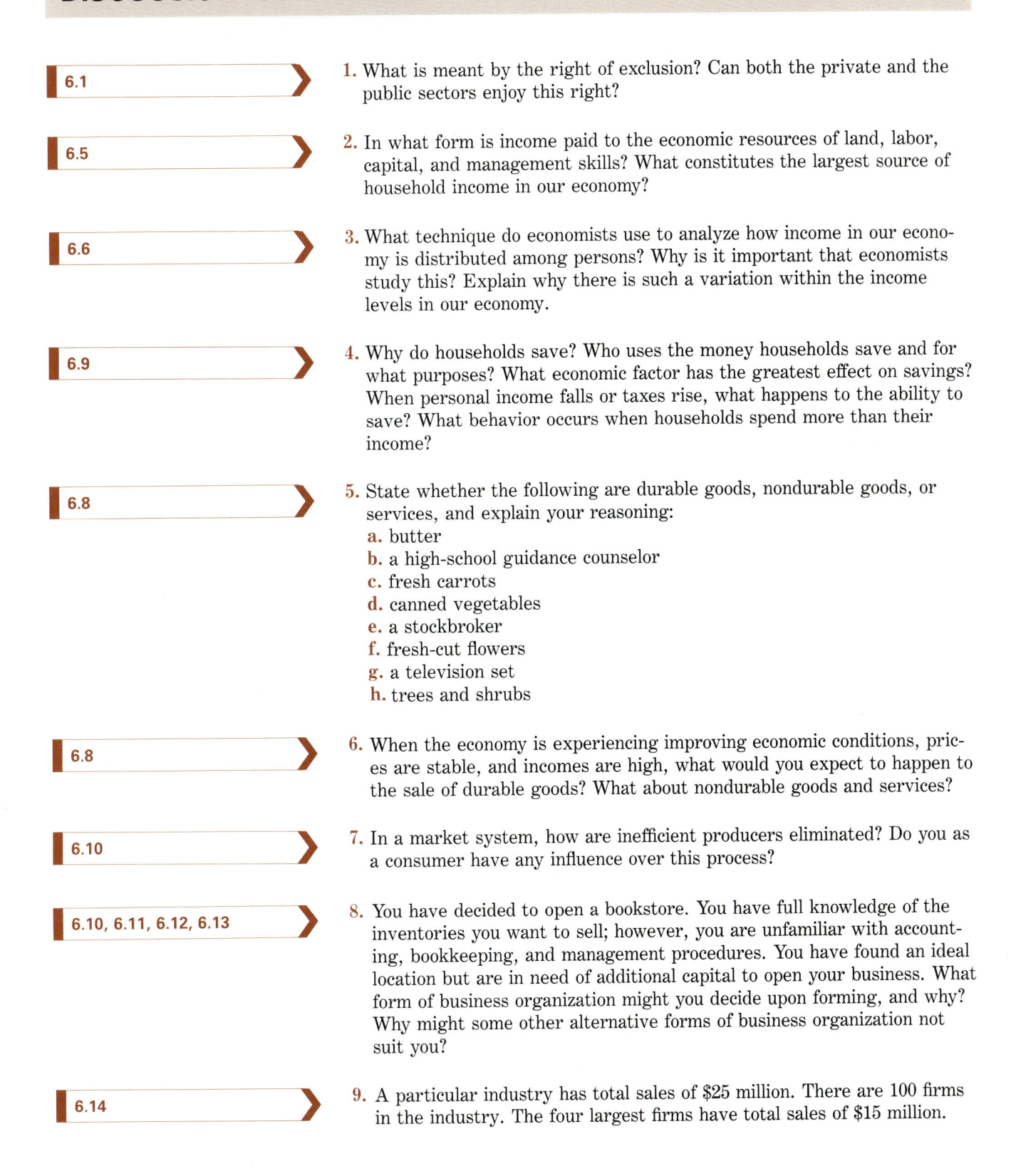

6.1 ▶ 1. What is meant by the right of exclusion? Can both the private and the public sectors enjoy this right?

6.5 ▶ 2. In what form is income paid to the economic resources of land, labor, capital, and management skills? What constitutes the largest source of household income in our economy?

6.6 ▶ 3. What technique do economists use to analyze how income in our economy is distributed among persons? Why is it important that economists study this? Explain why there is such a variation within the income levels in our economy.

6.9 ▶ 4. Why do households save? Who uses the money households save and for what purposes? What economic factor has the greatest effect on savings? When personal income falls or taxes rise, what happens to the ability to save? What behavior occurs when households spend more than their income?

6.8 ▶ 5. State whether the following are durable goods, nondurable goods, or services, and explain your reasoning:
  a. butter
  b. a high-school guidance counselor
  c. fresh carrots
  d. canned vegetables
  e. a stockbroker
  f. fresh-cut flowers
  g. a television set
  h. trees and shrubs

6.8 ▶ 6. When the economy is experiencing improving economic conditions, prices are stable, and incomes are high, what would you expect to happen to the sale of durable goods? What about nondurable goods and services?

6.10 ▶ 7. In a market system, how are inefficient producers eliminated? Do you as a consumer have any influence over this process?

6.10, 6.11, 6.12, 6.13 ▶ 8. You have decided to open a bookstore. You have full knowledge of the inventories you want to sell; however, you are unfamiliar with accounting, bookkeeping, and management procedures. You have found an ideal location but are in need of additional capital to open your business. What form of business organization might you decide upon forming, and why? Why might some other alternative forms of business organization not suit you?

6.14 ▶ 9. A particular industry has total sales of $25 million. There are 100 firms in the industry. The four largest firms have total sales of $15 million.

What is the concentration ratio of this industry? Would economists consider this industry to be highly concentrated?

> 6.16

10. What are some of the greatest assets you feel big business has brought to our economy? How may they benefit society in the future? Does big business bring any disadvantages or costs to our economy? If so, what are they?

SELECTED READINGS

Baratz, Morton S. *The American Business System in Transition*. New York: Thomas Y. Crowell Company, 1970.

Coase, Ronald H. "The Nature of the Firm." *Economica* 4 (1937), pp. 386-405.

Feldstein, Martin (ed.). *The American Economy in Transition*. Chicago: University of Chicago Press, 1980.

Friedman, Milton. "Choice, Chance and the Personal Distribution of Income." *Journal of Political Economy* 61, 4 (August 1953), pp. 277-290.

Okun, Arthur. *Equality and Efficiency: The Big Trade-Off*. Washington, D.C.: The Brookings Institution, 1975.

President's Council of Economic Advisors. "The Market for Corporate Control." In *Economic Report of the President 1985*. Washington: Government Printing Office, 1985, pp. 187-216.

Robins, P. K., Spiegelman, R.G., Weiner, S., and Bell, J. G. (eds.). *A Guaranteed Annual Income* 2 vols. New York: Academic Press, 1980.

Trebing, Harry M., (ed.). *The Corporation in the American Economy*. Chicago: Quadrangle Books, 1970.

Wilber, Charles K., and Jameson, Kenneth P. *An Inquiry into the Poverty of Economics*. South Bend, IN: University of Notre Dame Press, 1983, especially chap. 10.

CHAPTER 7

An Overview of the Public Sector

Having read the chapter, reviewed the chapter summary, and completed the *Study Guide* exercises, you should be able to:

CRIS

7.1 PUBLIC SECTOR CHOICES: Explain how choices made in the public sector are different from those made in the private sector.

7.2 PUBLIC SECTOR DIVISIONS: Discuss how the public sector is divided among different levels of government.

7.3 FUNCTIONS OF GOVERNMENT: Explain what government actions fall under the allocation, distribution, stabilization, and public-choice functions of government.

7.4 CONFLICTS AMONG FUNCTIONS: Explain and give examples of the conflicts that exist among the four functions of government.

7.5 GOVERNMENT TOOLS: List and discuss the four general tools that government uses to carry out its functions.

7.6 USES OF GOVERNMENT RESOURCES: Describe the uses of government resources and explain how resources are used differently by the federal government as compared to state and local governments.

7.7 SOURCES OF GOVERNMENT RESOURCES: Describe the main sources of government resources and explain how the federal government and state–local governments raise revenues.

7.8 TAX INCIDENCE AND SHIFTING: Explain the difference between the legal incidence and the economic incidence of a tax and discuss why tax shifting occurs.

7.9 DEMAND ELASTICITY AND TAXES: Explain how and why the elasticity of demand determines the distribution of a tax between buyers and sellers.

- **7.10 TAXES AND PRIVATE SECTOR DECISIONS:** Discuss the ways that taxes affect private sector decision makers.

- **7.11 HORIZONTAL AND VERTICAL EQUITY:** Define the concepts of horizontal and vertical equity and explain how these concepts are used to determine the fairness of a tax.

- **7.12 TAX EQUITY THEORIES:** Discuss the difference between the ability-to-pay and the benefits-received schools of tax equity.

- **7.13 CLASSIFICATION OF TAXATION:** Define the terms progressive, proportional, and regressive as they apply to taxation and explain what these terms tell us about a tax.

- **7.14 TYPES OF TAXES:** Discuss the characteristics of the major U.S. taxes: the income tax, social security tax, corporate income tax, general sales tax, and property tax.

- **7.15 SOCIAL SECURITY SYSTEM:** Discuss the problems that face the social security system and list several possible solutions.

- **7.16 TAX BURDEN:** Explain whether the total tax burden is progressive, regressive, or proportional and why.

- **7.17 DEFICITS AND THE NATIONAL DEBT:** Explain what is meant by deficits and the national debt and discuss recent trends in these two areas.

- **7.18 GOVERNMENT BORROWING:** Discuss the economic effects of government borrowing.

The last chapter examined the private sector of the U.S. economy. The private sector is important because most of the goods and services we purchase are the result of private sector activity and most of the income that households receive comes from resources sold to private sector businesses. We live in a mixed economy, however. Our economy includes both a private sector and a public, or government, sector. This chapter describes and analyzes the public sector of the U.S. economy. We will examine what government is, what it does, and how public sector actions affect the private sector's allocation and distribution of scarce resources.

THE PUBLIC VERSUS THE PRIVATE SECTOR

The last chapter told us that the private sector is made up of literally millions of separate households and firms, each making choices that affect both their individual welfare and society's allocation and distribution of

7.1 PUBLIC SECTOR CHOICES

resources. The private sector is a system of decentralized choice making, in which individuals act in their own self-interest.

The public sector differs from this description of the private sector in several important respects. First, governments exist as a mechanism for making collective, not individual, choices. Governments exist to perform the tasks that individuals acting alone cannot efficiently achieve. Therefore, government represents a system of more centralized choice than the private sector. Second, government choices are generally made by small groups of representatives or government employees, and these choices affect the thousands or millions of people who live and work within the government's jurisdiction. Finally, government choices are, at least in theory, made with the collective interest of society in mind, not the self-interest of any individual. Government is the process by which collective choices are made.

KEY CONCEPTS 7.1

Private choices are made by decentralized individuals acting in their own self-interest. Public decisions are made by centralized governmental units acting in the public interest.

7.2 PUBLIC SECTOR DIVISIONS

Government is not, as many people think, a completely centralized institution. Government in the United States is made up of three layers—federal, state and local—that encompass thousands of individual government bodies and millions of representatives and employees. Table 7-1 shows the distribution of government entities in the United States.

The federal government is the largest single public sector body in the United States, but the 50 state governments have broad powers and responsibilities that make them more important in some areas. Local governments represent a diverse group of public bodies, ranging from general purpose governments, such as county and municipal governments, that provide a variety of public services to more narrow special purpose governments, such as school districts, water and sewer districts, and Indian tribes. Each of the nearly 80,000 individual governments in the United States has the power to collect taxes, make expenditures, and pass laws or rules that affect individual behavior. In other words, the public sector of the United States is made up of nearly 80,000 individual entities, each of which can affect the allocation and distribution of scarce resources. Government in the United States is a system of **fiscal federalism**, where each level of government makes

Fiscal Federalism
The division of government tax and spending responsibilities into federal, state, and local levels of government.

TABLE 7-1 The U.S. Government System

Type of government	Number of governmental units
National government	1
State governments	50
County governments	3,042
Municipal governments	18,862
Township governments	16,882
School districts	15,174
Special districts	25,962
Total number of governmental units	79,913

Source U.S. Census of Governments, 1977, Governmental Organization, Vol.1. No.1. Washington, DC: U.S. Department of Commerce, July 1978.

autonomous spending and taxing decisions and where the actions of one government can affect those of others.

If the large number of governments listed in Table 7-1 surprises you, you may be even more amazed to learn that there are really many more governments than this. The governments listed in Table 7-1 are the ones that the federal government officially recognizes, but there are many private organizations that act like governments in certain circumstances. Governments are the mechanisms by which collective choices are made. Given this description, private organizations such as fraternities and sororities, social and professional clubs and organizations, and agencies such as the YMCA and the Red Cross are really governments in the sense that they bring individuals together to make collective choices.

Any analysis of the public sector of the United States must therefore, by necessity, be very general. It is impossible to describe or analyze the actions and effects of these thousands of separate governments. This chapter will focus on the federal government and on state and local governments combined as a group.

THE ECONOMIC FUNCTIONS OF GOVERNMENT

7.3 FUNCTIONS OF GOVERNMENT

Political Economy
The study of the economic causes and effects of political actions.

Economists have long analyzed the role of government and the impact of government actions. The original name for economics was actually **political economy,** so named because the first economists concentrated on the economic aspects of politics and government. The discipline of political economy lives on today in the economic study of political actions and public policy.

One of the first questions that political economists asked was, what role should government play in the economy? This is an important question. Previous chapters have shown that, in a variety of circumstances, the private sector, guided by the invisible hand of market competition, can make choices that efficiently produce and distribute goods and services in society's best interest. Any government action necessarily gets in the way of the invisible hand of self-interest and competition. When is this interference desirable? It is logical to suggest that government should step in only when individuals, acting in their own self-interest, cannot make efficient use of resources. The idea that sometimes government, acting for us collectively, can improve on the choices we would make as individuals leads to four general types of activities for government.

Allocation Function of Government

The first role for government is to correct market resource allocations that are not efficient. Government can sometimes do this by using taxes, subsidies, or laws to change the allocation of scarce resources in a way that makes society better off. Several examples of market failures were discussed in Chapter 5 when we first looked at the role of government in the market. In that chapter, we learned that government can promote efficiency in the market when the market failures of monopoly, externalities, and public goods exist. Let us briefly review these ideas.

Monopolies can result in an inefficient allocation of resources because monopolistic firms tend to produce less of their specific goods and charge a higher price for them than would competitive firms. Thus, government antitrust laws that regulate monopoly price and output can lead to a more efficient use of resources. Similarly, the government can improve the allocation of resources in the economy through policies that affect externalities and public goods. Firms that pollute the environment, for example, generate external costs. Government policies that regulate pollution reduce these external costs, thereby making the economy more efficient. Education is an example of a service that generates external benefits. If the government did not intervene, less than an efficient amount of education would be consumed by private individuals. Government programs that encourage education improve the way that society uses its scarce human resources. In the case of public goods, the government ensures that items such as lighthouses and national security are produced. Unless government stepped in to tax away the possiblity of free ridership, no one would pay to produce some valuable public goods.

The economic analysis of externalities and public goods will be explored in depth in Chapter 25. Most of the activities of state and local governments are designed to deal with externalities and public goods. Much of the federal government's budget goes for defense spending, which promotes the public goods of freedom and security. Many public sector activities, such as antitrust legislation, pollution controls, educational expenditures, construction of roads and bridges, and support for national defense, are undertaken as part of the allocation function of government.

Distribution Function of Government

One of the problems that people often perceive about the market economy is that it results in an unequal distribution of income and resources. The second function of government is to take collective actions that somehow improve the existing distribution of income and resources in the economy. (The inequality of this distribution and government policies that influence it will be the topic of Chapter 24.) Because people hold very different views about what the right distribution of income and resources is, this is a controversial area of government activity.

Much of the federal government's budget goes to activities designed to alter the distribution of income in society. Social security and medicare are, together, the largest single government program in the world. They will transfer an estimated $282 billion of resources from younger wage-earners to older retired individuals in **fiscal year** 1987. (A fiscal year is a 12-month period chosen to keep government accounts. Fiscal year 1987, for example, extended from October 1, 1986, to September 30, 1987.) Other programs, such as unemployment insurance and Aid to Families with Dependent Children, transfer resources from taxpayers to low-income groups.

Philosophers and politicans often suggest that the distribution function of government calls for taxing the rich to help the poor. The government programs just named seem to do this. It is important, however, to realize that this may not be the net effect of government's distributive actions. Economist Mancur Olson has pointed out that many government programs end up transferring resources from the poor to the rich. Olson notes that some low income wage-earners pay social security taxes that end up in the hands of relatively wealthy retirees. Some government actions, such as tariff and quota trade restrictions, impose a greater burden on the poor and end up helping groups in the economy that are relatively well paid. Restrictions on auto imports in the 1980s, for example, imposed a burden on all auto users in the form of higher car prices. Domestic auto producers earned

Fiscal Year
The government's accounting year. The federal fiscal year runs from October 1 to the following September 30.

higher profits because foreign competition was restricted. Some of these profits were paid as million dollar bonuses to domestic auto executives. Government actions here hurt the poor and made the rich better off. Olson suggests that, in total, government actions might actually have made the distribution of resources in the United States less equal than would have been the case without government action.

Stabilization Function of Government

The macroeconomic goals of full employment, stable prices, and economic growth are public goods in the sense that no single individual has a strong incentive to produce these events, yet they are very valuable for society as a whole. It falls to the public sector, and specifically to the federal government, to attempt to stabilize the economy in the public interest. The stabilization function of government is complex, difficult, and controversial. Much of the macroeconomics discussed in Chapters 8 through 15 of this book concerns the stabilization function of government.

Public-Choice Function of Government

One of government's most important roles is to lay out the rules by which collective decisions are made. This is important because, in many situations, the result of public votes depends on the way that those votes are tallied and the order in which votes are taken. In other words, the result of a vote often depends on how the vote is structured.

Presidential candidate Jesse Jackson stressed the importance of the public-choice function of government in the campign for the 1984 democratic nomination. Jackson said that the way public choices were made in several southern states tended to deny black voters a proportional voice in local governments.

Two voting rules were singled out as affecting black representation. The first voting rule applies to how respresentives are elected. Local government representatives can be elected at-large, where all voters choose a group of representatives, or they can be elected from individual geographic districts. Blacks receive relatively proportional representation when representatives are elected by district, because an overall minority of black voters tends to hold the majority in at least a few districts. Black representatives come from "black" districts and white representatives come from "white" districts. Elected representatives are frequently all white, however, in cities that use at-large election procedures. This happens because the overall black minority cannot outweigh the white majority in city- or county-wide ballots. Cities with 60 percent white voters and 40 percent black voters sometimes have 100 percent white elected representatives when at-large voting is used.

A second voting rule that Jackson criticized is the use of "run-off" primaries. In one case cited by Jackson, a black candidate received 45 percent of the vote in the primary election, while two white candidates received 30 percent and 25 percent each. The black candidate won the primary by getting the most votes. Because no candidate received more than 50 percent of the vote, however, the top two candidates had to enter into a run-off primary election. In this election, the black candidate still received 45 percent of the vote, but the white candidate won with 55 percent of the vote. The use of run-off primaries, according to Jackson, leads to underrepresentation of blacks in elected offices.

Jesse Jackson raised these two issues to show that how votes are taken affects who is elected and what policies are enacted into law. The public-choice function of government therefore affects the choices made to change the allocation, distribution, and stabilization functions. One can agree or disagree with Jackson's conclusion that blacks are underrepresented in government, but one cannot argue with the premise that public-choice mechanisms are important. The problems of making public choices will be discussed in greater depth in Chapter 25.

> **KEY CONCEPT 7.3**
>
> There are four types of activities that government undertakes in an effort to improve the choices that individuals make. These categories can be categorized under the four functions of government: Resource use is altered to compensate for monopolies, externalities, and public goods through the allocation function; a more desirable distribution of income and resources is achieved through the distribution function; full employment, stable prices, and economic growth are promoted through the stabilization function; the effective mechanisms for making social choices are established through the public-choice function.

CONFLICTS AMONG GOVERNMENTAL FUNCTIONS

7.4 CONFLICTS AMONG FUNCTIONS

One of the problems facing the public sector is that there are many conflicts among the four functions of government just outlined. That is, actions designed to further one role of government sometimes have undesirable consequences on other goals. Two examples will help illustrate the many conflicts among government functions that face public sector decision makers.

Sometimes the stabilization function of government conflicts with the allocation function of government. Suppose, for example, that the economy faces high inflation. One way to reduce inflationary pressures is to reduce government spending on education and national defense. Making these budget cuts might bring inflation rates down to a more acceptable level, but the cuts could also distort the allocation function of government by leaving the economy with a less than efficient level of education and national defense.

There is frequently a trade-off between allocation and distribution in public policies. Government's role under the allocation function is to use resources most efficiently. Government's role under the distribution function is to improve the distribution of income and resources. Suppose that government decided to make the distribution of income more equal by taxing workers and paying subsidies to low-income groups. This might tend to equalize after-tax income, but it would reduce production incentives around the economy. Poor people would have less incentive to use their human resources at paid jobs because they would risk the loss of their government payments. Taxpayers would have less incentive to produce because extra work would bring increased tax payments. Both taxpaying workers and subsidy recipients would face incentives to produce less, possibly resulting in less overall production. This is an inefficient use of resources, a problem that government is supposed to fight, not make worse.

These brief examples show why government policies are complex and controversial. Sometimes it is not possible to achieve one government goal without moving the economy farther from another goal. Trade-offs and

154 *An Overview of the Public Sector*

conflicts among the functions of government are a frustrating fact of life for politicians and public sector decision makers.

THE TOOLS OF GOVERNMENT POLICY

7.5 GOVERNMENT TOOLS

The public sector has several tools at its disposal with which to carry out the four functions of government just discussed. Government actions are designed to directly or indirectly alter the private sector's allocation and distribution of resources through artificial incentives.

Government Spending

Government spending is the first tool of public policy. Government can alter the way resources are allocated by purchasing different goods and services than would private buyers. Few private buyers would purchase military equipment for national defense, for example, so government spending effects this change in the way resources are used.

In addition to directly affecting the way resources are used, government spending can also indirectly affect the distribution of resources by changing relative prices and wages throughout the economy. For example, if the government decides to devote more resources to high-technology defense projects, this will tend to bid up the prices of computers and also bid up the wages of engineers. This, in turn, will affect the way that individuals in the private sector allocate resources to computers, engineering training, and their substitutes and complements.

Taxation

Nonneutral Taxes
Taxes that alter the incentives faced by the private sector.

Most people think of taxes as the way that government raises revenue to finance its spending. This is true, but it misses one of the most important aspects of modern taxation. Most taxes in the United States are **nonneutral taxes,** meaning that they tax some goods or activities more than others. The income tax, for example, often imposes a lower burden on people who donate money to charities and nonprofit organizations than on those who spend all their income on goods for themselves. The tax system thus provides an incentive for people to give more money to charities, universities, hospitals, and churches than would otherwise be the case. This is just one example of a nonneutral tax.

The U.S. tax system has many tax incentives that lead private sector actors to earn or spend income in different ways. Taxpayers who take advantage of these "loopholes" reduce their own tax bills while, at the same time, they promote some social goal, such as supporting universities and charities, that Congress has identified as being desirable. The tax system in the United States is therefore used as a tool for social policy, in addition to its traditional role as a source of government revenue. The tax system is very complex because of these tax incentive provisions.

Subsidies

Subsidy
A government payment to an individual or a group designed to increase their welfare or encourage certain private activities.

A third way that government can influence private actions is through **subsidy** payments to specific groups for specific reasons. A subsidy is a government payment to an individual or group designed to increase their welfare or induce them to take a desirable action.

Subsidies can be paid in many ways. Subsidies are frequently given, for example, by purchasing items for more than their market value. Agricultural subsidies are paid by government price support programs that guarantee farmers a set price for their goods, regardless of the market price. If there is a surplus of agricultural commodities, for example, the government frequently buys up the surplus at a support price that exceeds the market price, thereby giving farmers a subsidy. The price support subsidy increases the incomes of farmers and promotes stability in farm production. Price supports also promote surpluses of these goods, however.

Many college students receive a government subsidy in the form of work-study aid and guaranteed student loans. The federal government pays part of a work-study jobs wage bill, thus increasing the student-worker's income and employment opportunities. The federal government guarantees repayment of guaranteed student loans. This guarantee allows students to borrow at lower interest rates and at better terms. These subsidy programs make it possible for more students to attend college.

Some subsidies take the form of **transfer payments**. A transfer payment is a one-way transfer of income or resources from the government to an individual or group. Unlike the subsidies just discussed, the transfer payment recipient need not sell any good or perform any service to receive the payment. Social security, medicare, unemployment, and welfare benefits are all considered transfer payments. These transfer payments are designed to alter the distribution of income and provide some measure of social insurance against low income or high medical costs.

Transfer Payments
Payments made from government to private individuals for which no good or service is expected in return. Social security benefits and unemployment payments are examples of transfer payments.

Laws and Regulations

Government regulates many private activities through its laws, rules and regulations. Pollution regulations, highway traffic rules, and criminal and civil laws all affect the allocation and distribution of resources in the economy. Traffic rules, for example, are designed to minimize external costs imposed by dangerous drivers. Laws in many states that mandate school attendance until age 16 are designed to encourage school attendance and promote the production of external benefits. Minimum wage laws affect the distribution of income by artificially raising the wages of some unskilled workers.

KEY CONCEPT 7.5

Government uses four primary tools to perform its public sector functions. These tools are government spending, taxation, subsidies, and laws and regulations. Subsidies are used both to provide incentives and as transfer payments. Taxes both raise revenue and alter private sector incentives.

GOVERNMENT RESOURCES

One way to better understand what governments do in the United States and how they do it is to analyze the sources and uses of resources for the government sector. This way we can see what activities the resources of government support, and from where those resources come.

Uses of Government Resources

7.6 USES OF GOVERNMENT RESOURCES

Table 7-2, which summarizes the uses of government resources for calendar year 1985, shows several interesting facts about the public sector in the

TABLE 7-2   Uses of Government Revenues

Use category	Federal government 1985 ($ billion)	State–local government 1985 ($ billion)
Purchases of goods and services	353.9	460.7
(National defense)	(262.0)	—
Transfer payments	366.4	98.8
Grants to state–local government	98.9	—
Interest payments (receipts)	129.0	(31.0)
Total	983.0	517.1

Source. Economic Report of the President, 1986, Tables B-78 and B-79. Figures are for calendar years, using national income and product account definitions.

Intergovernmental Grants
Transfer payments made from one level of government to another (e.g., from the federal government to a state government).

United States. First, when total expenditures are compared, it is clear that the federal government accounts for almost two-thirds of total government resources, while the thousands of state and local governments make up the remaining one-third.

Table 7-2 also shows that state and local governments actually purchase more goods and services than does the federal government. State and local governments deliver most of the direct government services that we recieve, such as police and fire protection, education, and road and bridge services. Some of the money to finance state–local expenditures comes from the federal government in the form of **intergovernmental grants.** Most of the goods and services that the federal government purchases go toward national defense. This fact, coupled with the size of total transfer payments, makes it clear that, while the federal government performs many functions in the economy, most of its resources go for income redistribution programs and national defense. State–local governments have a relatively small role in income redistribution.

One final difference between the federal and state–local governments that Table 7-2 points out has to do with debt. Payments of interest on the national debt are a major budget item for the federal government because the federal government has borrowed trillions of dollars over the years to fight wars and to stabilize the economy. State–local governments, on the other hand, actually receive interest payments instead of paying them. Many states and localities are forbidden by state constitutions from borrowing to pay for current services. Thus states and localities have run budgetary surpluses in recent years, making them net recipients of interest payments.

We can better understand what governments do if we look more closely at the uses of governmental resources. Table 7-3 shows selected federal government outlays for fiscal year 1985. This table shows that national defense and social security are the two largest federal government expenses. However, there are many other activities and items to which the federal government devotes resources. Notice, for example, the large net interest item in Table 7-3. We will discuss the national debt later in this chapter.

Table 7-4 shows, in summary form, where state–local government resources go. Note that education, highways, and public welfare are the largest listed budgetary items. State and local governments finance the delivery of these important public services to society partly through state–

| TABLE 7-3 | Estimates of Selected Federal Government Outlays Fiscal Year 1987 |

Type of outlay	Amount ($ billions)
National defense	282.2
International affairs	18.6
General science, space, technology	9.1
Energy	4.0
National resources and environment	11.9
Agriculture	9.5
Commerce and housing credit	1.3
Transportation	25.5
Community and regional development	6.5
Education, training, social services	27.4
Health	34.9
Social security and medicare	282.4
Social security	212.2
Medicare	70.2
Income security	118.3
Veterans benefits and services	26.4
Administration of justice	6.9
General government	6.0
General purpose fiscal assistance	1.7
Net interest	147.9
Total outlays (including items not listed)	$994.0

Source. *Economic Report of the President, 1986,* Table B-74.

| TABLE 7-4 | Major State–Local Government Outlays, Fiscal Years 1983–1984 |

Outlay type	Amount ($ billions)	Percent of Total
Education	176.1	35%
Highways	39.5	8%
Public welfare	66.4	13%
All other items	222.9	44%
Total outlays	505.0	100%

Source. *Economic Report of the President, 1986,* Table B-78.

local taxes and partly through federal taxes that are paid to state–local governments as intergovernmental grants.

Taken together, Tables 7-2, 7-3, and 7-4 paint an interesting picture of government in the United States. We see that the federal government's most important functions are income redistribution (through the social security system, for example) and national defense. The state and local government system, on the other hand, delivers many of the important public services that we depend on including, most importantly, education and transportation services.

158 *An Overview of the Public Sector*

7.7 SOURCES OF GOVERNMENT RESOURCES

Excise Taxes
Taxes based on the value of goods purchased.

Sources of Government Resources

Where do governments get the resources that they use? Three revenue sources are most important: taxes, borrowing, and grants from other levels of government. Figure 7-1 shows estimated federal government receipts for fiscal year 1987. As can be seen, the personal income tax is the largest federal revenue source, followed by the social security tax, and borrowed funds. Borrowing is the third largest federal "tax" in the sense that the government acquires use of private sector resources through borrowing just as it acquires the use of private sector resources through taxes. The corporate income tax provides relatively little revenue to the federal government. The items listed as "other taxes" are mostly sales and **excise taxes** imposed on items such as liquor, auto tires, and gasoline.

State and local governments have different resource sources, as Figure 7-2 shows. Revenues for the state–local government sector come from four main sources. Three taxes, on property, sales, and incomes, account for most of the state–local governments' revenues, with federal grants accounting for most of the remaining amount. All states impose property taxes and receive federal grants. These grants are an important tool of fiscal coordination. Through grants, the federal government can help local governments pay for needed programs. The federal government also uses grants to provide incentives to state and local governments to allocate resources in ways that they might not otherwise.

Most states also impose both general sales and income taxes, although five states levy no sales tax and 10 states levy no income tax. The following states do not tax general sales: Alaska, Delaware, Montana, Oregon, and New Hampshire; and the following states do not tax most sources of income: Alaska, Connecticut, Florida, Nevada, New Hampshire, South Dakota, Tennessee, Texas, Washington, and Wyoming.

This brief overview of sources of government resources shows us which types of taxes governments use to raise revenues, but the issues of taxation

FIGURE 7-1 | **Federal Government Revenue Sources, Fiscal Year 1987** Federal government revenue comes from three main sources: personal income taxes, social insurance taxes, and borrowing.

Other taxes $59.3
Corporate income tax $86.7
Personal income tax $385.9
Social insurance tax $302.8
Borrowing $159.3

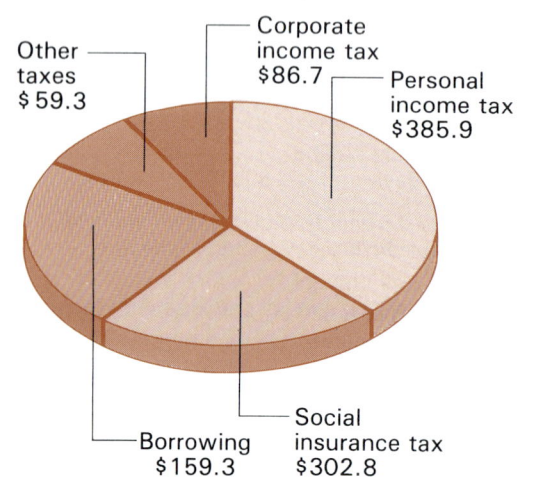

Total receipts = $994.0 ($ billions)

FIGURE 7-2

State–Local Government Revenue Sources, Fiscal Years 1983–1984 State–local government revenue come from four main sources: general sales taxes, state–local income taxes, property taxes, and grants from the federal government.

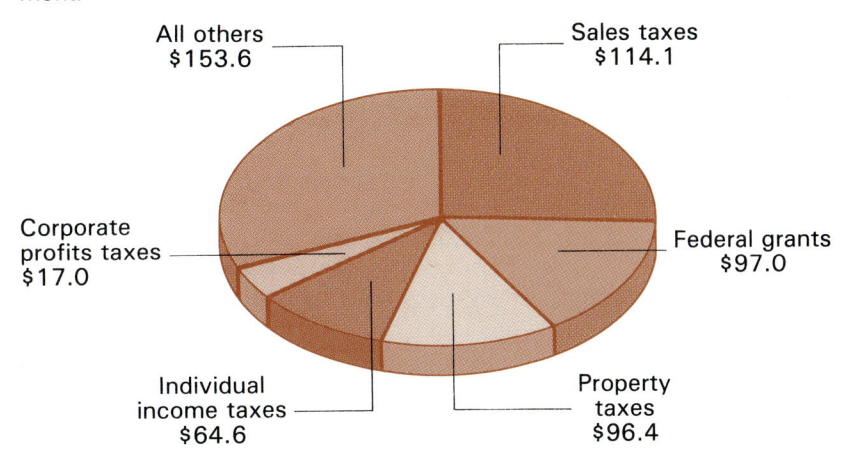

- All others $153.6
- Sales taxes $114.1
- Federal grants $97.0
- Property taxes $96.4
- Individual income taxes $64.6
- Corporate profits taxes $17.0

Total receipts = $542.7 ($ billions)

and borrowing are much deeper than this. We need to know who pays these taxes and what their economic effects are. To answer these questions, we must examine the topic of tax incidence and see how taxes can be shifted from one group to another.

TAX SHIFTING AND INCIDENCE

7.8 TAX INCIDENCE AND SHIFTING

Legal Tax Incidence
The distribution of the legal responsibility for tax payment.

Economic Tax Incidence
The distribution of the tax burden, after all economic effects have been accounted for.

Taxes seldom stay stuck. A tax imposed on one activity or good frequently ends up being borne by others. Taxes are shifted because a tax, once imposed, alters the set of incentives that the market provides. Supply and demand change when incentives are changed and taxes are shifted to new groups through the price system. This tax shifting means that **legal tax incidence** is seldom the same as the **economic tax incidence**. The legal incidence is the distribution of the tax burden as set out in law. The law determines who shall pay the tax, when, how, and in what amount. The economic incidence is the actual distribution of the tax burden after the tax-induced changes in incentives are taken into account. In simple terms, the legal incidence of a tax tells us who has the responsibility for paying it while the economic incidence tells us who really pays it in the market.

KEY CONCEPT 7.8

The legal incidence of a tax is based on who has legal responsibility for paying the tax to the government. The economic incidence of the tax is based on who actually bears the burden of the tax after all economic effects have been taken into account.

Elastic Demand
The quantity demanded changes proportionately more than the price.

Inelastic Demand
The quantity demanded changes proportionately less than the price.

7.9 DEMAND ELASTICITY AND TAXES

The extent to which legal and economic incidence differ depends on the economic conditions in the markets where taxes are imposed. We can illustrate the difference between legal and economic incidence, and see the factors that make them different, by borrowing concepts that will be discussed in greater detail in Chapter 16. Economists have developed concepts to describe how responsive demand and supply curves are to a change in price. These concepts will be used briefly here to help us understand about tax shifting.

Figure 7-3(a) shows a market with an **elastic demand.** A small change in price causes a relatively large change in the quantity of this good demanded. We frequently find elastic demands for items with many close substitutes or for goods that account for large fractions of household budgets. Figure 7-3(b) shows a market with an **inelastic demand.** A given change in price causes a relatively small change in quantity demanded along this demand curve. We frequently find inelastic demands for items that have few close substitutes or that account for a small fraction of household budgets.

Figure 7-3 uses supply and demand curves to show how the economic incidence of a tax depends on the elasticity of demand for the taxed item. Suppose that both of these markets start in equilibrium at point A, with a market price of $10. Then suppose that a $1 per item tax is imposed on each market, with legal incidence on the seller in each case. The tax imposed on the seller alters supply incentives. The tax is an additional cost item for the seller, which reduces profits. The seller responds to these incentives by offering fewer items for sale at each price or, conceptually, by offering any

FIGURE 7-3

Economic Incidence Depends on Elasticity of Demand Both markets begin at equilibrium A, with a price of $10. A $1 per-unit tax is levied on suppliers. The tax shifts the supply curve, moving the market to new equilibrium B. Most of the tax burden falls on producers in (a), where the demand curve is relatively elastic. More of the tax burden falls on consumers in (b), where demand is relatively inelastic.

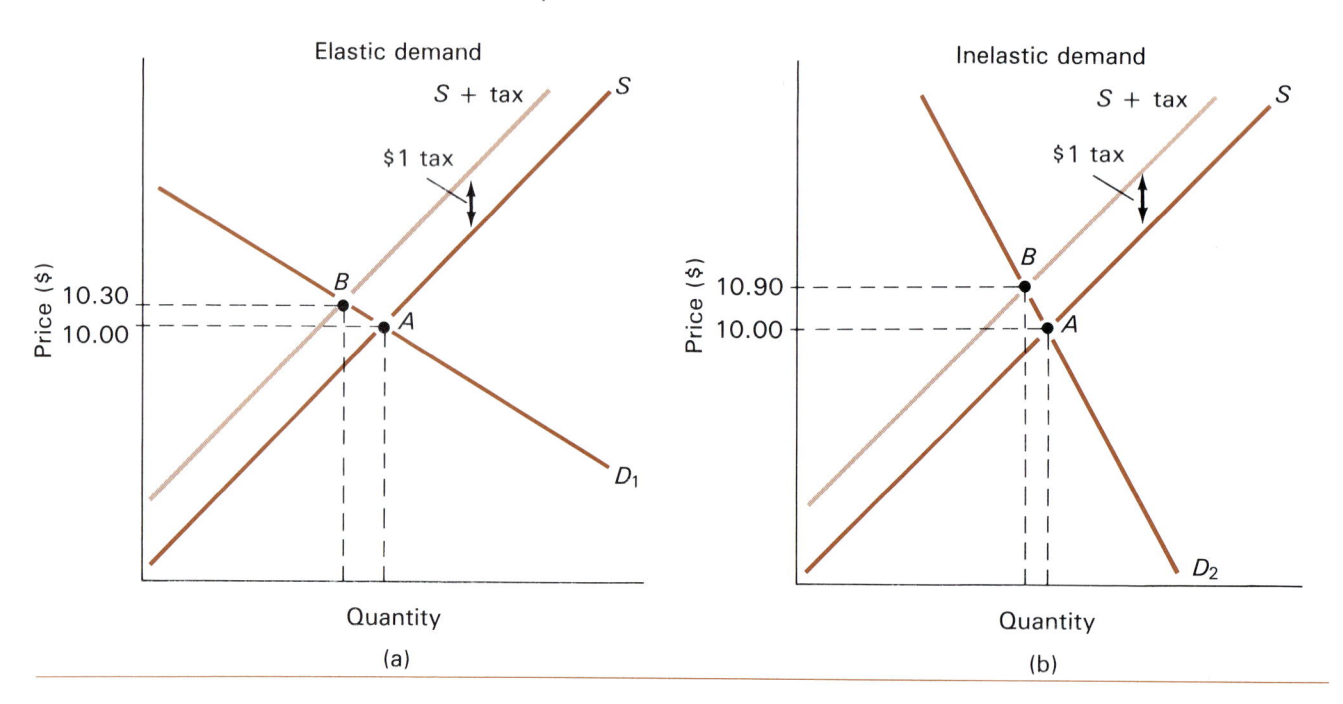

given quantity for a $1 higher price than before, this price increase being just enough to cover the extra cost of the $1 per unit tax. In short, the tax shifts the supply curves as shown in the figure, thereby reducing market supply. Both markets move from the initial equilibrium at A to the new equilibrium at B.

Who bears the burden of these taxes? The seller bears most of the tax burden in Figure 7-3(a), where the demand is assumed to be elastic. The new supply–demand equilibrium occurs at a price of $10.30, compared to the original price of $10.00. The consumer bears 30 cents of the tax burden in a higher price, but the seller bears 70 cents of the tax in the form of lower net receipts. The producer sells this item for $10.30, but pays $1.00 in tax, and so keeps just $9.30, which is 70 cents less than before the tax. The moral of the story told in Figure 7-3(a) is that, with an elastic demand, the economic incidence of the tax falls on both buyer and seller but relatively more on the seller.

The economic incidence of the tax is somewhat different when demand is inelastic. Figure 7-3(b) shows that the new market equilibrium occurs at a price of $10.90. Consumers pay 90 cents of the tax in the form of a higher price, while sellers pay 10 cents of the tax in the form of lower net receipts. The consumer and the producer share the economic incidence of a tax on an item with an inelastic demand, but the burden on the consumer is relatively greater. This means that more of the tax is shifted from seller to buyer when demand is inelastic.

Why is more of the tax shifted when demand is inelastic, as in Figure 7-3(b)? Remember the characteristics of an inelastic demand that were mentioned a few paragraphs ago. Items with inelastic demands tend to be goods with few close substitutes. Sellers can raise price in response to the tax, and there will be a relatively small decrease in quantity demanded because buyers will not be able to shift purchases to substitute items, at least in the short run. This is the opposite of what occurs in Figure 7-3(a) with the elastic demand. Elastic demands are frequently found for goods with many close substitutes. Sellers are unable to shift the tax burden to consumers in these markets because buyers can respond to higher prices by shifting purchases to other nontaxed items.

We have just seen that the economic incidence of a tax depends, in the short run, on the elasticity of demand for the taxed item. This tax burden can shift over time, however, if the supply curve changes shape. This is illustrated in Figure 7-4. Figure 7-4(a) shows the short-run effects of this tax, with price rising by 30 cents and net receipts to producers falling by 70 cents. This is the short-run equilibrium for this market. This equilibrium may change in the long run, however. The lower net receipts for firms in this market may make many of them unprofitable. Firms that lose money in the long run tend to leave this market in search of greener pastures. This changes the size and shape of the supply curve. The supply will decrease if many firms leave the market, driving up market price, as Figure 7-4(b) shows. More of the burden of this tax is shifted to consumers in the long run than in the short run.

This brief analysis has focused on the distribution of the tax burden between buyers and sellers in a particular market, but economists know that the tax burden can be shifted much farther than this. A tax on candy bars, for example, would impose burdens on candy buyers and candy sellers, following the analysis just discussed, but it would also affect other groups. A tax on candy bars would reduce the amount of candy bars sold, imposing

FIGURE 7-4

Incidence Can Change in the Long Run The short-run incidence of the tax is given in (a). Suppliers bear more of the tax in the short run, reducing their profits. This causes a reduction in supply and changes the shape of the supply curve in the long run (b). Price rises in the long run, shifting more of the tax burden on to buyers in this market.

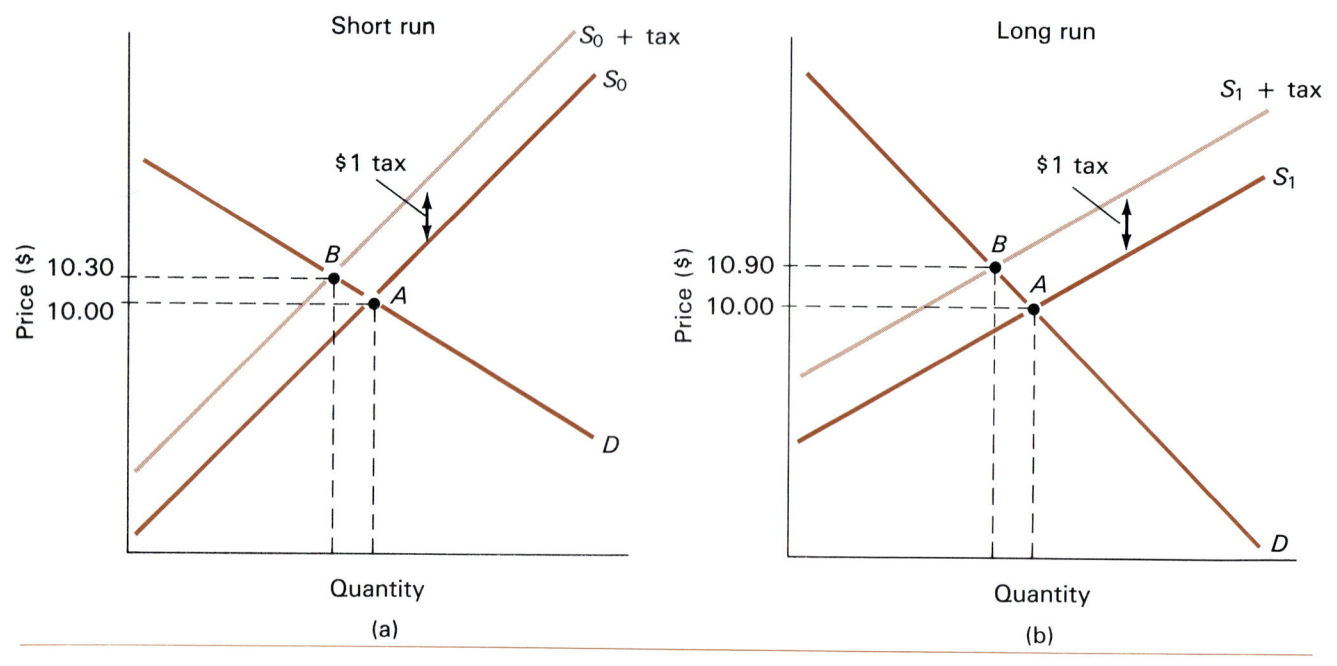

Short run — axes: Price ($) vs Quantity; curves S_0, $S_0 + \text{tax}$, D; $1 tax; points B at 10.30 and A at 10.00. (a)

Long run — axes: Price ($) vs Quantity; curves S_1, $S_1 + \text{tax}$, D; $1 tax; points B at 10.90 and A at 10.00. (b)

a burden on workers in candy factories. A decrease in candy bar sales would result in reduced demands for sugar, chocolate, nuts, and other items. Producers and workers in these markets would also bear part of the burden of the tax.

The economic incidence of a tax is often difficult to determine. Economists have disagreed for many years about who bears the burden of the corporate income tax, for example. The uncertainty about tax incidence makes imposing taxes a risky business. Politicians who vote to increase or decrease a tax often do not know who will be hurt or who will benefit because they think that the legal incidence of the tax is the same as its economic incidence. In 1985, for example, President Reagan proposed a tax-reform package that, among other things, reduced taxes on individuals and increased taxes on corporations (in terms of the legal incidence of the tax). It is unclear, however, who really bears the economic incidence of the corporation income tax. Members of Congress differed concerning this tax proposal in part depending on whether they looked at the legal incidence of the tax increase, which would fall on corporations, or the economic incidence, which could fall on consumers and workers.

Income Effect
Changes in behavior caused by reductions in purchasing power due to taxation.

Substitution Effect
Changes in spending behavior due to nonneutral taxation.

7.10 TAXES AND PRIVATE SECTOR DECISIONS

ECONOMIC EFFECTS OF TAXES

We have already mentioned that taxes alter the incentives that private individuals face. Taxes have both an **income effect** and a **substitution effect.** The income effect is that the tax reduces the income that the taxpayer has available to purchase goods and services. The substitution effect is that the tax induces the taxpayer to shift purchases from taxed items (or those that are heavily taxed) to untaxed items (or those that are less heavily taxed). The substitution effect allows individuals to avoid some of the tax burden and so shift that burden to others.

Taxes, in general, tend to affect private sector choices in five different ways. First, consumers tend to shift purchases from taxed items to untaxed ones, altering the types and quantities of goods purchased. Second, taxes tend to affect the amount of labor that households supply. Taxes reduce the amounts of goods and services that wage income will purchase. In other words, an increase in taxes has roughly the same effect as a decrease in wages, because those wages have less purchasing power after taxes. All else being equal, this tends to reduce the quantity of labor supplied to business firms.

The third economic effect of taxes is on saving. Taxes reduce income available for saving. Taxes on interest and investment income further discourage personal saving by reducing the return from these activities. This is important because saving is the source of funds that are used for capital formation and economic growth.

The fourth and fifth economic effects of taxation fall on producers. Taxes tend to reduce business output. Because taxes raise price, higher taxes tend to result in fewer goods being sold since firms produce fewer taxed goods. Taxes also affect how firms produce their goods. A tax on labor, for example, gives firms an incentive to substitute untaxed machines for taxed workers. The result is that the same items are produced with less labor, thereby causing unemployment.

With so many effects, it is frequently difficult to know what an increase or decrease in a specific tax will do to saving, labor supply, or unemployment. In addition, many taxes include specific nonneutral provisions designed to alter private behavior in specific ways. The federal income tax, for example, includes provisions designed to encourage people to give money to charities, loan money to state and local governments, purchase their homes instead of renting housing, and save for retirement. These various tax incentives add to the complexity of the tax system and force tax rates higher to compensate for the tax revenue that is lost when people take advantage of tax incentives to reduce their personal tax bills.

ARE TAXES FAIR?

Horizontal Equity
Tax fairness that is achieved when people in similar circumstances pay similar taxes.

Vertical Equity
Tax fairness that is achieved when people in different circumstances pay different taxes, and the difference in tax is appropriate to the difference in circumstances.

> 7.11 HORIZONTAL AND VERTICAL EQUITY

When Adam Smith, the father of economics, examined the problem of taxation in *The Wealth of Nations*,[1] he proposed four tests that a tax must pass in order to be acceptable. Taxes, Smith said, should be fair, economical to collect, convenient to pay, and uniform in their administration, so that taxpayers can be certain of the tax consequences of their actions. Most taxes meet the last three of these criteria, but what tax is fair? Or, more explicitly, how can we tell if a tax is fair?

Economists have developed two tests for tax equity. A fair tax should satisfy both **horizontal equity** and **vertical equity.** Horizonal equity is the idea that equals should be taxed equally. People in similar circumstances should pay similar taxes. Any tax that fails horizontal equity is arbitrary

---

1. Adam Smith, *An Inquiry into the Nature and Causes of the Wealth of Nations*, New York: Modern Library, 1937.

and unfair because it imposes different taxes on people in similar situations. Vertical equity requires that people who are in different circumstances should be taxed differently, and the difference in taxes should be appropriate to their different circumstances. A rich man and a poor man, all else being equal, should not pay the same taxes according to the vertical equity test.

> **KEY CONCEPT 7.11**
>
> The tax equity criterion of horizontal equity holds that people in similar circumstances should pay similar taxes. The tax equity criterion of vertical equity holds that people in different circumstances should pay different taxes, and that difference should be appropriate.

7.12 TAX EQUITY THEORIES

Ability-to-pay Taxation
The concept that taxes should be based on a person's ability to pay, as measured by income, wealth, or some other factor.

Benefits-received Taxation
The concept that taxes should be based on the value of the benefits that a person receives from the public sector.

These are fairly simple tests for tax fairness, but they are tests that are difficult to apply in practice because there are two different schools of thought about how we should determine when people are in similar situations and when their circumstances are different. Advocates of the **ability-to-pay taxation** hold that taxes should be levied according to a person's aiblity to pay the tax, as measured by income, wealth, or some other quality. People with the same ability-to-pay should pay the same taxes. People with greater ability-to-pay should pay more taxes. Income and sales taxes in the United States are generally based on the abilility-to-pay idea because income and consumer purchases are both generally related to an individual's income and wealth.

Advocates of **benefits-received taxation** hold that taxes should be viewed as a price that a person pays for government services. Taxes should be based on the benefits that a person receives from government services. People who receive similar benefits should pay similar taxes. People who receive more benefits should pay more taxes. The social security tax and state gasoline taxes, which are used to finance highway construction, are examples of benefits-received taxes.

> **KEY CONCEPT 7.12**
>
> Ability to pay taxation holds that taxes should be based on a person's ability to pay them, as measured by income, wealth, or some other factor. Benefits-received taxation holds that taxes should be based on the benefits that a person derives from government services.

People frequently disagree about whether a particular tax is fair because they base their evaluations on opposite schools of tax analysis. A person who thinks that ability-to-pay is the appropriate way to levy taxes might think that the gasoline tax is unfair, because it imposes different tax burdens on people with the same income if one person drives more than the other. A person who thinks that benefits-received is the appropriate basis for taxation, on the other hand, might think that the gasoline tax is fair, because people who receive the same benefits from driving on state-built highways are likely to pay about the same state gasoline taxes. We will use the ideas of horizontal and vertical equity later in the chapter to evaluate the fairness of the U.S. tax system.

THE DISTRIBUTION OF THE TAX BURDEN

7.13 CLASSIFICATION OF TAXATION

Tax Burden
The proportion of income that is used to pay a tax.

In addition to classifying taxes as fair or unfair depending on whether they meet the tests of horizontal and vertical equity, economists find it useful to further classify them depending on how the **tax burden** varies with income. The tax burden is defined to be the proportion of a person's income that goes to pay the tax. Some taxes hit high income groups the hardest, while others fall heaviest on the poor. Economists classify taxes as progressive, proportional or regressive depending on how the tax burden varies with income.

Progressive Taxes

Progressive tax
A situation in which the burden of a tax increases with the taxpayer's income.

A **progressive tax** is one that imposes higher tax burdens on families with more income. Suppose, for example, that the Johnson family's income is $20,000 per year and the Smith family earns $40,000 annually. A tax that takes $2000 (10 percent) from the Johnsons and $6000 (15 percent) from the Smiths would be progressive. The federal income tax is basically a progressive tax because the tax burden generally increases as income rises, all else being equal.

Proportional Taxes

Proportional Tax
A situation in which the burden of a tax is the same for taxpayers of all income levels.

A **proportional tax** imposes the same tax burden on all families. A proportional tax would take $2000 (10 percent) from the Johnsons and $4000 (10 percent) from the Smiths. Higher-income families pay more dollars to tax collectors but bear the same burden under this system. A flat-rate tax that is levied against all income would be an example of a proportional tax, because the same tax rate would apply to everyone.

Regressive Taxes

Regressive Tax
A situation in which the burden of a tax increases as the taxpayer's income falls.

A **regressive tax** falls heaviest on the poor. A tax that takes $2000 (10 percent) from the low-income Johnsons and $3000 (5 percent) from the upper-income Smiths is regressive. The Smiths still pay more dollars to this regressive tax, but their tax burden is lower. The general sales tax collected in most states is an example of a regressive tax. Although higher-income families tend to spend more on consumer goods than do lower-income families, lower-income families spend a larger proportion of their total income. Thus the tax burden is greater for lower-income households.

One important thing to note here is that it is incorrect to think, as many people do, that progressive and proportional taxes are the fairest, and that regressive taxes are implicitly inequitable. The fairness of a tax depends on how well it meets the tests of horizontal and vertical equity we have just discussed. The federal personal income tax is generally progressive, for example, but it contains many "loopholes" that allow some people to pay much less tax than others with the same income. The federal income tax is therefore progressive, but unfair, because it fails the test of horizontal equity.

Taxes can also be viewed as fair or as unfair depending on how they are administered (uniformly or with error or bias) and which government services they finance. The social security tax, for example, is regressive, but it is viewed as fair by many people because people who pay the tax now receive social security benefits in the future.

KEY CONCEPT 7.13

A progressive tax imposes a higher tax burden on households with higher income. A proportional tax imposes the same tax burden on all households. A regressive tax imposes a higher tax burden on households with lower incomes.

MAJOR UNITED STATES TAXES

We can now apply these ideas about taxation to an examination of the U.S. tax system. We will look at five taxes that have the most impact on the economy. These five are the federal income tax, the social security tax, the corporate income tax, general sales taxes, and property taxes.

Federal Income Tax

7.14 TYPES OF TAXES

Recent tax reform proposals by President Reagan and both houses of Congress would radically change the federal income tax. As this book goes to press, Congress is still debating the final version of the new income tax. The goal of all the tax reforms proposals of the mid-1980s has been to simplify the income tax and remove many costly tax "loopholes," thereby making the tax more efficient and increasing horizontal equity.

Prior to 1986, the income tax was extremely complex and hard to understand. Many millions of Americans ended up paying two taxes every April 15—one to the Internal Revenue Service and another to a tax-preparation service such as H&R Block. Table 7-5 suggests this complexity by showing the tax rates that applied to married couples filing joint returns in 1985. Income was taxed through a complex system of 14 tax brackets, with rates ranging from the 0 percent "zero bracket" to a top tax rate of 50 percent.

The tax brackets in Table 7-5 show the **marginal tax rates** that applied to the indicated income levels. Income taxes were calculated in the following way: the first $3670 of taxable income was not taxed, income between $3670 and $5930 was taxed at an 11 percent rate; income between $5930 and $8200

Marginal Tax Rate
The tax rate that would apply to any increase in income, not taking into account the tax burden on income already earned.

TABLE 7-5 Income Tax Rates, 1985 Rates for Married Couples Filing Joint Returns

Income Bracket	Marginal Tax Rate
$0– $3,670	0%
$3,670– $5,930	11
$5,930– $8,200	12
$8,200– $12,840	14
$12,840– $17,260	16
$17,260– $21,800	18
$21,800– $26,540	22
$26,540– $32,260	25
$32,260– $37,980	28
$37,980– $49,420	33
$49,420– $64,740	38
$64,740– $92,360	42
$92,360–$118,040	45
$118,040–$175,230	49
$175,230+	50

Average Tax Rate
The percentage of total income that is paid to taxes.

Long-Term Capital Gains
Profits made from the sale of an asset that was owned for more than six months.

was taxed at a 12 percent rate, and so on. Higher levels of income fell into higher and higher tax brackets, subject to higher and higher marginal tax rates. Any increase in income would fall into the highest tax bracket, without affecting the lower tax rates on previous income. This system of taxing income in brackets resulted in many people bearing an **average tax rate** that was well below their marginal tax rate. For example, a family with taxable income of $30,000 would pay a 25 percent tax on their last dollar of income, but would bear an average tax burden much lower than this because most of their income is taxed at less than the 25 percent marginal rate. The lower average tax rate might have made the burden of the tax bearable, but the high marginal "tax bracket" rate tended to discourage economic activity because extra income was always subject to relatively heavier taxation.

The complicated tax rate system shown in Table 7-5 is only the tip of the iceberg in terms of the complexity of the income tax prior to 1986. Income tax returns could run to many pages because of special tax incentives or loopholes contained in the tax system. Many sources of income and uses of income were subject to special tax treatment. Income from **long-term capital gains** was taxed at a much lower rate than regular income, for example. Income from state and local government bonds was not taxable at all. Expenditures on mortgage interest, charitable contributions, some medical expenses, and many other items were also subject to special tax treatment.

The complexity of the income tax system derived from attempts to make the tax system perform many tasks. The income tax was intended primarily to raise revenue, but it was also pressed into service by Congress over the years to alter the distribution of income, provide incentives to encourage capital formation and economic growth, achieve horizontal and vertical equity, encourage certain activities such as charitable giving, and help the old, poor, and weak. In the end, much income escaped taxation through the use of loopholes by the rich, the poor, and middle-income families. The shrinking tax base meant that the income tax ceased to be a very good revenue raiser, even with the relatively high tax rates shown in Table 7-5. The fact that some families took advantage of many loopholes to shelter their income while others did not meant that horizontal and vertical equity suffered.

The tax reforms of the mid-1980s aimed to improve the income tax in many ways. First, the tax became simpler. This simplification is suggested by Figure 7-6, which shows the tax rates for married couples filing joint returns as proposed by President Reagan in 1985 and the Senate Finance Committee in May, 1986. (The final form of the tax rates had not been published when this book went to press.)

Table 7-6 shows that the tax reforms simplified the income tax by reducing the number of tax brackets and by lowering the marginal tax rates. At the same time that rates were reduced and simplified, the income tax base was expanded and simplified by the elimination of many tax loopholes. Overall, Americans will now be paying lower tax rates, but they will be taxed on more of their income (with less income escaping the tax collector's reach through tax loopholes).

While the tax reform packages proposed by the president, the House, and the Senate differ in detail, they all share a basic philosophy: fewer loopholes, lower rates, and an overall simpler income tax system.

Tax reform will simplify the income tax and improve horizontal equity. Fewer loopholes means that people in similar circumstances will now be more likely to pay similar taxes. The income tax will still fail to achieve

168 An Overview of the Public Sector

TABLE 7-6

Tax Reform Proposals Tax Rates for Married Couples Filing Joint Returns

President Reagan's Proposal, 1985

Income Bracket	Marginal Tax Rate
$0– $4,000	0%
$4,000–$29,000	15
$29,000–$70,000	25
$70,000+	35

Senate Finance Committee Bill, 1986

Income Bracket	Marginal Tax Rate
$0– $5,000	0%
$5,000–$29,300	15
$29,300+	27

horizontal equity in every case, however, because even a simplified income tax will still contain enough loopholes to fill many books.

Vertical equity will not change significantly under the new tax system. The distribution of the tax burden between rich and poor will be about the same as before. That is, the overall impact of lower rates and fewer loopholes affects the rich and the poor about equally. What will change will be the differences in tax burden within each income group. Currently, people in a given tax bracket end up paying much different taxes depending on the degree to which they use tax incentives. Under the new system, with fewer loopholes, people with similar incomes are more likely to bear similar tax burdens.

The tax reform is likely to have mixed effects on saving, investment, and economic growth. On one hand, many specific tax provisions designed to encourage saving and capital formation will be lost. By itself, this would tend to discourage long run economic growth. On the other hand, lower tax rates overall could have a substantial "supply-side" effect to encourage production and investment, which could lead to more rapid growth. The actual effect will depend on which of the forces is strongest.

The income tax will always be complex and never be completely equitable. Recent tax reforms, however, will simplify the tax, reduce the inequities, and reduce the tax incentives that have in the past influenced many private economic choices.

The Social Security Tax

7.14 TYPES OF TAXES

7.15 SOCIAL SECURITY SYSTEM

The social security tax is a payroll tax. It is a tax on wage and salary income that comes right out of your paycheck, as opposed to a tax on investment or interest income, for example.

You, like many people, may have the wrong idea of how the social security tax works. You may think that the government takes social security contributions out of your paycheck and invests them in high-grade securities that are cashed-in when you retire. Nothing about this description is accurate, however. The social security "contribution" is really a tax, not an insurance or pension payment. The money that comes out of your paycheck goes to Washington, D.C., where it is almost immediately sent to retired social security beneficiaries. Your taxes pay for your parents' and grandparents' retirements. Who will contribute to your retirement social security check? Your children and others who work in the future.

The social security system is financed on a pay-as-you-go plan, which means that taxes have to be raised whenever social security transfer payments increase. The employee and employer each paid taxes of 7.05 percent of the worker's first $39,600 wage income in 1985. Economists believe that most of the employers' share of the tax is shifted to workers, who bear the burden of the tax in the form of lower wages. The tax ceiling of $39,600 rises every year and the combined tax rate of 14.1 percent increases when more money is required for social security benefits.

The social security tax is regressive for two reasons. First, the tax ceiling means that high-income people escape tax on that part of their income above the ceiling. A worker who made $39,600 and another who made $339,600 (all wage income) both paid the same social security taxes in 1985. The second reason for regressivity is that the social security tax falls on wage and salary only. Poor people who pay no income tax at all often end up with higher social security tax burdens, while people with higher incomes who earn all their income from investments or business profits pay no social security tax.

The social security program is in fiscal distress these days. Social security benefits went up rapidly in the 1970s to compensate for rising prices. High unemployment rates meant that there were fewer and fewer workers paying taxes for each retired beneficiary. Social security began to run out of money. This problem is going to get worse in the future. The post-World War II baby-boom generation is getting older. They will start retiring in a few years and the economy will be faced with tens of millions more people collecting social security checks with even fewer workers to pay taxes. When an irresistible force (the aging population) meets the undeniable fact of fewer workers, something has got to give, but what?

We could raise taxes, but social security taxes are already high. They might total 25 percent or more of income by 2010 if benefits formulas do not change. The social security tax could be expanded to include nonwage income, which would even out the tax burden somewhat, but the money still has to come from somewhere.

Another possible solution is to cut back social security benefits or to limit social security checks to only the truly needy. Social security benefits are not extravagant now, however, so reducing them could inflict real hardship on the elderly. Baby-boom workers who paid social security taxes all their working lives are not likely to support proposals that deny them retirement benefits. Another proposal would have the retirement age raised from 65 to 67 or 70 so workers would pay taxes longer and collect benefits for fewer years.

Congress enacted social security reforms in 1983 that were designed to solve the social security problems by raising taxes, delaying indexation of social security benefits, and taxing the social security benefits of high-income groups. These reforms might resolve the crisis in the retirement component of the social security system, but no change was made in the Medicare accounts, where expenses are rising much faster than taxes. Rising Medicare costs will create future deficits that exceed the revenue capacity of the social security system, even after the 1983 reforms. Social security still faces a financial crisis in the coming years. It will be up to

ECONOMIC ISSUES

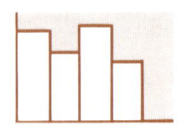

The Social Security System

The social security system is the largest single government program in the world. It collects taxes from American workers and uses these funds to provide retirement, disability, and health-care benefits to millions of recipients. In fiscal year 1985 it was estimated that social security retirement benefits would amount to over $190 billion and Medicare benefits would add nearly $70 billion more to the social security budget. This total of $260 billion is roughly equal to the size of the total federal government budget (spending on *all* items) in fiscal year 1974.

Social security was born in the depression year of 1937. The United States was among the last developed countries to enact old-age pension legislation; Bismarck's Germany introduced the first such program in the 1880s. The original U.S. social security system was of modest dimensions. Social security taxes were limited to one percent of the first $3000 of wage and salary income (employer and employee were both subject to this tax rate). The combined tax burden on the employer and employee was therefore limited to just $60 per year. These low taxes financed limited retirement benefits, with no health-care coverage. These benefits were low by today's standards.

The social security system has grown in every way since 1937. Old-age pension coverage is now nearly universal, the benefits are higher, nonpension aspects of the program, such as survivor's benefits and medicare, have been added, and social security taxes have been raised. Social security tax revenues were less than $20 billion in 1960. This represented just 18 percent of total federal tax collections. By 1985 social security taxes amounted to almost $270 billion, which is roughly one-third of the federal budget.

One of the most important aspects of the social security system is the link between tax payments and program benefits. Social security benefits are linked to taxes in two ways. Each year's total benefit bill must be raised from that year's taxes (the aggregate link), and an individual's social security tax payments helps determine that individual's future benefit levels. Social security contributions are not held in individual retirement accounts, as many people still believe, but the amount of social security taxes that a person has paid is one factor that is used to determine the amount of social security benefits he or she will receive. Computing an individual's social security benefit is no simple task. In general these variables enter into the calculations:

1. Number of years you have worked and paid social security taxes. The benefit increases, all else being equal, with years in the system.
2. Amount of wage income earned and, therefore, the amount of social security taxes paid. All else being equal, more income and taxes mean a higher monthly check.
3. Age at which you retire. There is a penalty for retiring before age 65; you cannot receive retirement benefits (except under special circumstances) before age 62 under current law.
4. Outside retirement income. Your social security

Congress and the voters to take timely actions to raise tax revenues or find ways to limit retirement benefits and medical costs without imposing unreasonable burdens on any population group.

Corporate Income Tax

In the past the corporate income tax has been a paradox. On one hand, the tax had relatively high marginal tax rates. Tax rates on corporate income ran as high as 46 percent for large corporations. On the other hand, the corporate income tax collected relatively little revenue, as the tables already presented in this chapter show. The average tax rate on corporate income was relatively low. How can a tax have high tax rates and yet collect relatively little revenue? The answer to this question is that the corporate income tax was littered with special tax incentives that allowed corporate

7.14 TYPES OF TAXES

payment is reduced by 50 cents for every dollar of wage income (above a penalty-free base) earned while retired. Investment proceeds and private pension payments aren't included in this calculation so there is no penalty for receiving them.

There are other complications. There is a minimum benefit (about $120 per month at this writing) paid to everyone eligible, regardless of other variables. To be eligible, in general, one must have worked at a job that paid social security taxes for a total of 40 calendar quarters or be married to a spouse who did.

Benefits above the monthly minimum vary directly with income, but lower-income workers end up getting relatively higher benefits per dollar of social security taxes paid. People with low lifetime wage incomes (who, therefore, paid less social security tax) receive benefits that are a higher proportion of preretirement income. An individual who has always earned high wages (who therefore paid more social security tax) receives benefits that are a smaller fraction of preretirement income. There is, therefore, a shrinking tie between taxes and benefits under current law. Increased tax contributions have no affect on payments once the maximum monthly benefit is reached.

Social security benefits hardly seem high. The $120 monthly minimum payment is meager, if it is all one has to live on. But two points should be considered before passing judgment on social security benefits. First, social security was not designed to be anyone's sole source of retirement income. Retired people are expected to have saved in years past, to collect benefits from private retirement plans, and receive financial help from family. These expectations do not repeal the reality that some retired people do, in the end, have little more than their social security check and thus live in dismal poverty. It is also important to remember that social security benefits are not taxable. This significantly increases their purchasing power. Small social security checks can replace much bigger paychecks if all the taxes, insurance, and other deductions that reduce a worker's take-home pay but do not reduce social security checks are taken into consideration. It is the replacement ratio, the proportion of taxable earnings that social security replaces, that are the best measure of the size of social security benefits.

When tax differences are taken into account, the average social security benefit is reasonably large, as measured by the replacement ratio, and has increased dramatically over the years. According to Harvard economist Martin Feldstein, for example, the average real social security benefit increased by 55 percent between 1970 and 1980. This means that the average social security check purchased 55 percent more goods and services at the end of this period than at the beginning. Suppose that a married man has earned the median U.S. income all his life and retires with his wife. This individual, under current law, receives social benefits equal to 78 percent of his peak earnings. Adjusting for taxes, the replacement ratio is really 90 percent. That is 90 percent of the peak year's disposable (after tax) income is replaced by social security benefits. When we view social security benefits this way, and remember that benefit distribution favors low-income groups, these benefits look high. This is particularly true for people with private pensions who can, it seems, retire with greater purchasing power than they had during prime working years. This rosy picture should not, however, divert our view from the poverty of some retirees who live on the minimum benefits and little else.

Additional References
Feldstein, Martin. "Slowing the Growth of Social Security," *Wall Street Journal*, September 24, 1981.
"Social Security," *Consumer Reports* (September 1981), pp. 503–510.
Veseth, Michael. *Public Finance*. Reston, VA: Reston Publishing Co., 1984, especially Chap. 13.

---

profits to escape taxation if business firms used their funds in certain ways. Many corporations took full advantage of these tax incentives and therefore paid little in taxes.

President Reagan's 1985 tax reform package changed this situation somewhat. Reagan reduced corporate tax rates to be more in line with individual tax rates. The top corporate tax bracket is now 35 percent. However, corporations now find that there are fewer and more limited tax deductions available to them, so more of their income is now subject to tax. President Reagan's plan in 1985 was to increase tax collections from corporations by making more of their profits subject to tax. At the same time, however, Reagan wanted to give corporations more incentive to expand by reducing their marginal tax rate from a maximum of 46 percent in 1985 to a maximum of 35 percent in 1986. It is too early yet to tell if Reagan's tax plan has had its desired impact on corporate incentives and tax collections.

The corporate income tax is controversial for several reasons. First, the tax falls on corporations only, not on other forms of business. This means that profits from corporations are often subject to a double-tax that profits earned by partnerships and proprietorships are not. The corporation pays taxes first. The shareholders who own the corporation also pay taxes when they receive the profits of the corporation as dividends or capital gains.

A second problem is that the corporate income tax fails the test of equity because it imposes different taxes on different corporations, depending on how able they are to take advantage of the tax incentives built into the tax system. Some corporations pay almost twice as great a tax burden as others. Treasury Secretary Donald Regan pointed out in 1984 that the corporate income tax was a de facto industrial policy for the United States because it rewarded some types of firms with low taxes and higher profits, while it discouraged other types of firms. This is a problem because some studies show that the tax system penalizes high-tech firms and other industries that many economists think will generate economic growth in the future. The tax system is probably not the best way to direct economic growth. The corporate tax system also encourages firms to finance expansion by borrowing instead of selling equity shares in themselves. This makes corporate investment very sensitive to changes in interest costs. High interest rates in the 1970s and 1980s therefore had a larger detrimental effect on corporations because of the tax system than would otherwise have been the case.

Finally, the corporate income tax is a problem because economists and policymakers are uncertain about who pays this tax. Some theories hold that consumers pay the tax in higher prices, but other theories conclude that workers bear the tax in lower wages or that all business owners end up receiving lower net profits. It is difficult to make effective tax policy when we are unsure about who pays a tax.

General Sales Tax

While the sales tax looks like it is a proportional tax, everyone does not bear the same burden. The sales tax is actually regressive, as this example illustrates. Nancy works at a print shop and earns $20,000 per year. She spends $16,000 of this total and so pays $800 sales tax (assume a 5 percent sales tax rate). Her tax burden is $800/$20,000 = 4 percent. Michael is a physician and makes $50,000 per year. He saves a relatively high fraction of his income, spending only $30,000 on consumer goods. The 5 percent tax he pays on the $30,000 spent generates $1500 in taxes, for a tax burden of $1500/$50,000 = 3 percent. They both pay the same sales tax rate, but saving is not taxed, so people who save a larger fraction of their income bear lower tax burdens. Michael and Nancy's spending habits are not unusual; sales tax burdens, in general, tend to fall heavier on the poor than on the rich.

The sales tax is less regressive in practice than this example shows, however. Food, drugs, and housing costs are tax free in most states, reducing the tax bite felt by the poor. The sales tax moves toward proportionality when these items are excluded from the tax base.

Property Tax

The property tax is a tax on the value of land and structures. Many people consider the property tax to be the least fair tax they pay because it is based on their home's value, not on their income or ability-to-pay or the benefits they receive from government. Here is how the property tax works. Your home's market value is $100,000. The property tax assessor tries to estimate market value for tax purposes. Suppose that the assessor guesses right and your property is put down at $100,000 on the tax role. Your property tax bill now depends on the local property tax rate. If the tax rate is 2 percent, for example, your annual tax bill is 2 percent of $100,000, or $2000, which works out to about $165 per month.

Who sets the 2 percent tax rate? The tax rate is determined by the relationship between total property value and local government services. Suppose, for example, that all the property in your town has a combined value of $100 million (it is probably much more than this). If the school board votes to spend $2 million of property tax revenues, then the tax rate is $2 million/$100 million, or 2 percent. The property tax rate goes up when you vote for better schools or other services funded by property tax revenues. Tax rates go down when property values rise or local government spending falls.

The property tax is controversial. High inflation in the 1970s boosted both property values and the cost of schools, police, and other local services. Taxpayers found their real incomes going down, while home values and property tax bills increased. Voters in Massachusetts, California, and other states enacted legal limits to property tax bills.

Economists do not agree on the questions of who pays the property tax and whether it is progressive, regressive, or proportional. Property ownership is more prevalent among people with higher incomes. If landowners pay the property tax, its distribution is progressive. But the economic incidence of the property tax is not so easily determined. The tax may be partially shifted to consumers or other groups. Differences in local property tax rates and errors in assessing property value make the analysis even more difficult. The prevailing view today is that the tax is progressive but that some low-income people still bear heavy tax burdens. Elderly people living on social security often pay taxes based on the high value of their homes, not the low level of their income. Most states ease this burden through special tax relief programs for the elderly poor.

The property tax is the one tax that voters can directly control at the ballot box. Voters choose to have more government services and higher taxes or lower tax rates and fewer public goods when they vote on school and park plans. Voters in California sent their legislators a message when they passed the Proposition 13 property tax limit; they did not want more government services if it meant higher taxes.

THE TOTAL TAX BURDEN

7.16 TAX BURDEN

We pay many different taxes. Income, social security, sales, and property taxes are the most important, but taxes on gasoline, liquor, tires, jewelry, corporate income, and automobiles all add to the total tax bill. Some of these taxes are progressive, but others are regressive or proportional. Joseph Pechman of the Brookings Institution studied the overall distribution of the tax burden in the United States for the period 1966–1985.[2] Pechman estimated the incidence of all federal-state-local taxes for 1985. His

---

2. Joseph A. Pechman, *Who Paid the Taxes, 1966–85*, Washington, D.C.: Brookings Institution, 1985.

conclusion about the overall distribution of taxes depends in part on assumptions about the way taxes are shifted from one group to another. Do high-income investors pay the corporate income tax, for example, or does this tax get passed on to lower-income consumers who buy corporate goods?

Pechman's study indicates that there is a relatively proportional total federal-state-local tax burden of about 25 percent of income when several different assumptions concerning tax incidence are used. Under some incidence assumptions, however, the overall tax burden could be found to be mildly progressive, with average tax burdens ranging from about 20 percent for low-income families to about 27 percent for high-income households. Certain other incidence assumptions, on the other hand, suggest a somewhat regressive total tax distribution, with average tax burdens ranging from 30 percent on the poor to 20 percent on the rich.

This distribution of the tax burden has not changed a great deal over the 20 years of the Pechman study. The overall tax burden has become somewhat less progressive, or more regressive, over time. According to Pechman, this small change in tax distribution is due to rising social security taxes, which have financed higher social security benefits for the elderly, combined with the reduced relative importance of corporate and property taxes.

The relatively small variation in tax burdens among families of different income levels indicates that the tax system does not greatly affect the overall distribution of income in the United States. If the benefits of government programs such as social security and unemployment benefits are included, government's impact on the distribution of income in the economy appears mildly progressive.

The biggest effect of the tax system on the distribution of after-tax income might not be among income classes, but within each income class. That is, the difference between the total tax burden on the poor and the total tax burden on the rich is not very great. However, individuals can take advantage of tax incentives to varying degrees in all income classes. This means that some poor people pay much higher taxes than do other poor people. And some rich people pay much lower taxes than do other rich people. The difference in the tax burden within each income class can therefore be greater than the difference among income groups.

KEY CONCEPT 7.16

The total tax burden is roughly proportional to income, at a rate of about 25 percent. The progressive income and property taxes are offset by regressive social security and sales taxes.

Deficit
The amount of government borrowing; the amount by which spending exceeds tax revenues.

7.17 DEFICITS AND THE NATIONAL DEBT

National Debt
The total amount of debt accumulated by the federal government.

DEFICITS AND THE NATIONAL DEBT

Borrowing is a major source of federal government revenue these days. Governments borrow when they spend more than they receive in tax revenue. The amount that is borrowed in a given year is called the **deficit**. The total amount of accumulated borrowing by the federal government is called the **national debt**. Data concerning deficits and the national debt are displayed in Table 7-7.

Table 7-7 shows that, while some of the national debt was caused by borrowing to finance wars, most of the national debt is the result of recent

TABLE 7-7 Trends in Federal Government Finance, Selected Fiscal Years

Year	Outlays ($ billion)	Annual deficit (surplus) ($ billion)	Accumulated federal debt ($ billion)
1929	3.1	(0.7)	16.9
1933	4.6	2.6	22.5
1939	9.1	2.8	48.2
1945	92.7	47.6	260.1
1950	42.6	3.1	256.9
1955	68.4	3.0	274.4
1960	92.2	(0.3)	290.9
1965	118.2	1.4	323.2
1970	195.6	2.8	382.6
1975	332.3	53.2	544.1
1976	371.8	73.7	631.9
1977	409.2	53.6	709.1
1978	458.7	59.7	780.4
1979	503.5	40.2	833.8
1980	590.9	73.8	914.3
1981	678.2	78.9	1003.9
1982	745.7	127.9	1147.0
1983	808.3	207.8	1381.9
1984	851.8	185.3	1576.7
1985	946.3	212.3	1827.5
*1986	979.9	202.8	2112.0
*1987	994.0	143.6	2320.6

Source. *Economic Report of the President, 1986,* Table B-73.
*Estimates

high deficits that resulted from tax cuts and increased government and defense spending in the 1970s and 1980s. The deficits accumulated during the Reagan administration set a new record for total federal government borrowing.

7.18 GOVERNMENT BORROWING

As far as Congress is concerned, borrowing is an alternative to taxation. Congress borrows when it wants to spend more money without raising taxes. It is important to understand, however, that deficit borrowing is much like a tax in its economic effects. This is true for two reasons. First, borrowing imposes a burden, just as a tax does. Government borrowing tends to drive up interest rates around the economy, as the government competes with the private sector for scarce loanable funds. This means, for example, that home and car buyers who want loans will pay more for them. Business firms that need to borrow for expansion will find borrowing costs higher, as well. These groups and the firms that they deal with end up bearing part of the burden of the deficit in higher costs, lower profits, and reduced output.

Deficit borrowing is like a tax in another respect. Taxes are a way to transfer today's scarce resources form the private sector to the public sector. Deficit borrowing also transfers today's scarce resources from the private sector to the public sector. This similarity is important. Many people think that by borrowing the government is somehow borrowing resources from the future when, in reality, resources are just transferred from one group to another today.

Crowding Out
The tendency of government deficits to raise interest rates and reduce borrowing for private investment spending.

The national debt is different from private debt in at least one important respect: it will never be repaid. Government pays off bonds that come due by issuing new bonds. In other words, government takes out new loans to pay off the old ones. The federal government can do this because it has the power to tax, which makes it an exceptionally good credit risk. However, this does not mean that the national debt is not a problem, as some people think, because "we owe it to ourselves." Deficits and the national debt are national economic problems for two reasons. First, government borrowing may result in less borrowing and investment by business firms. Government borrowing that leads to lower levels of private investment spending is often called **crowding out.** Crowding out reduces capital formation and leads to lower levels of economic growth. The second government debt problem is that interest from the accumulated national debt is now an important annual cost to government. Over the long run, taxes must be higher, or deficit borrowing even greater, in order to pay the interest on the national debt. Table 7-3 showed that interest on federal government debt amounted to over $130 billion in fiscal year 1985.

Today's debt totals are very high, but it is important to realize that previous inflation makes numerical comparisons of figures in Table 7-7 inaccurate. Adjusting for inflation, the national debt in 1983, for example, is about the same as it was in 1945. In other words, inflation wiped out most of the deficit borrowing that the federal government did between 1945 and 1983. This tells us that part of the burden of the deficit over these years fell on those households and firms who loaned money to the federal government. High inflation rates made the money they received in repayment worth less than the real value of the original loans.

High budget deficits and the growing national debt remain two of the most important economic problems in the United States. The budget deficit for fiscal year 1984 amounted to 5 percent of the gross national product. Reducing these deficits requires major reductions in spending and transfer payments, large increases in taxes, or both. While deficits impose burdens on the economy, reducing the deficits will mean a burden, as well.

The political system in the United States has found it easier to impose the burden of financing government indirectly, through deficit borrowing and inflation, than directly, through painful spending cuts and tax increases. The crowding out that accompanies deficit borrowing, however, threatens to reduce capital formation and choke off economic growth. Congress and the president must take actions eventually to bring government budgets into balance.

SUMMARY

7.1

1. Public sector choices are different from private sector choices. Private choices are made by decentralized individuals acting in their own self-interest. Public decisions are made by centralized governmental units acting in the public interest.

7.2

2. The public sector is made up of nearly 80,000 separate governmental units divided into three levels: federal, state, and local government.

7.3 → 3. Government has four functions in a modern economy.
   a. The allocation function of government is to correct for failures in private markets, such as monopolies, public goods, and externalities, that misallocate scarce resources.
   b. The distribution function of government is to take actions that result in a more desirable distribution of income and resources in the economy.
   c. The stabilization function of government is to take actions to secure full employment, stable prices, and economic growth.
   d. The public-choice function of government is to set rules for social choices that reflect the preferences and views of voters.

7.4 → 4. There are many conflicts among the functions of government. Actions designed to fight inflation, for example, might result in an undesirable change in the distribution of income or too few public goods.

7.5 → 5. Government can accomplish its goals using four tools. These tools are government spending, taxation, subsidies, and laws and regulations. Subsidies are used both to provide incentives and as transfer payments. Taxes both raise revenue and alter private sector incentives.

7.6 → 6. Budget statistics show that the federal government uses its resources for two main purposes: to supply the public good of national security and to redistribute income through social security and other programs. State and local government resources are primarily used to deal with externalities, through spending on education, highways, and related items.

7.7 → 7. The federal government's revenues are largely derived from the income tax, social security tax, and borrowing. State and local revenues are largely derived from taxes on income, sales, and property and from federal government grants.

7.8 → 8. The legal incidence of a tax is based on who has legal responsibility for paying the tax to the government. The economic incidence of the tax is based on who actually bears the burden of the tax after all economic effects have been taken into account.

7.9 → 9. The distribution of the tax burden in a specific market depends on the elasticity of demand for the taxed item. More of the burden falls on consumers when demand is inelastic, because they lack close substitute goods that can be purchased instead of the taxed item. More of the tax burden falls on sellers when the demand is elastic, on the other hand, because consumers can easily switch to nontaxed items and avoid the tax, forcing producers to bear more of the burden.

7.10 → 10. Taxes affect the private sector through the income and substitution effects that they cause. Taxes affect the choice of which goods to purchase, how much labor to supply, how much to save, how much to produce, and how that production is to take place.

7.11 → 11. The tax equity criterion of horizontal equity holds that people in similar circumstances should pay similar taxes. The tax equity criterion of vertical equity holds that people in different circumstances should pay different taxes, and that difference should be appropriate.

7.11, 7.12	12. The ability-to-pay school holds that taxes should be based on a person's ability to pay them, as measured by income, wealth, or some other factor. The benefits-received school holds that taxes should be based on the benefits that a person derives from government services. These concepts are in conflict when applied to the criteria of horizontal and vertical equity.
7.13	13. The tax burden is the proportion of income that is used to pay a tax. A progressive tax imposes a higher tax burden on households with higher incomes. A proportional tax imposes the same tax burden on all households. A regressive tax imposes a higher tax burden on households with lower incomes.
7.14	14. The federal income tax is nominally a tax on income, but the amount of tax an individual pays depends on the sources and uses of that income. Recent tax reforms have simplified the income tax, reduced tax rates, and eliminated loopholes.
7.14	15. The social security tax is regressive because it taxes wage income only and because it taxes wages up to a set ceiling. Wage income above the ceiling escapes taxation. Today's social security taxes are used to pay today's social security benefits. Future benefits will come from taxes paid in the future, not revenues collected today and invested.
7.15	16. The social security system is headed for crisis in the future because the ratio of retirees to workers is rising over time. Medicare expenses are also rising faster than tax revenues. The solution to the social security crisis will involve tax increases, benefit reductions, or some combination of these two factors.
7.14	17. The corporate income tax is a tax with high marginal rates but low tax collections. Tax revenues are low because of the tax incentives built into the tax. Corporate profits are taxed twice, once at the corporate level, then again by the personal income tax when the corporation pays dividends. The corporate income tax is a de facto industrial policy that many economists think is inefficient.
7.14	18. The general sales tax is a regressive tax because people with high incomes tend to spend and pay taxes on a smaller proportion of their income. Low-income groups often spend most of their income on taxed items, giving them a higher tax burden.
7.14	19. Most economists think that the property tax is progressive, although some low-income groups end up bearing a relatively high tax burden. The property tax is based on the value of property that an individual owns, not that person's income or benefits received.
7.16	20. The total tax burden is roughly proportional to income, at a rate of about 25 percent. The progressive income and property taxes are offset by regressive social security and sales taxes.

7.17 ▶ 21. The deficit is the amount that the federal government borrows each year because federal spending exceeds tax revenues. The national debt is the total amount of debt that the federal government has accumulated over the years. Both annual deficits and the national debt have been at record levels in recent years.

7.18 ▶ 22. Deficit borrowing is like a tax in that it transfers today's resources from the private sector to the public sector. Deficits are also like taxes in that they impose a burden on the economy. One problem with the deficit is that it tends to crowd out private investment spending that is needed for economic growth. Interest paid each year on the national debt also imposes a burden on the economy.

DISCUSSION QUESTIONS

7.3 ▶ 1. Make a list of government activities with which you are familiar. Determine whether they should be placed under the allocation, distribution, stabilization, or public-choice functions of government.

7.5 ▶ 2. Explain the difference between transfer payments and government spending. How are these two government actions different in terms of their effect on the economy?

7.8, 7.9 ▶ 3. Congress has announced that it is going to impose a tax on liquor produced in the United States. The legal incidence of this tax is on liquor producers. Explain, using supply–demand analysis, what will determine the economic incidence of this tax.

7.11, 7.12 ▶ 4. Use the concepts of horizontal and vertical equity, and the ideas of ability-to-pay and benefits-received taxation to answer the following questions:
a. The city council has proposed a tax of $5 per person, regardless of income. Is this tax fair?
b. The city council proposes to "tax" bridge users by imposing a $1 toll. Is this tax fair?
c. The city council proposes a tax of 1 percent of income to finance local schools. Is this tax fair?

7.13, 7.14 ▶ 5. Define the terms progressive, regressive, and proportional as they relate to taxes. Explain how you classify each of the following taxes: income, sales, gasoline, corporate income, social security, and property.

7.10 ▶ 6. Give an example of a tax incentive. Explain how taxes alter private sector incentives.

7.17, 7.18 ▶ 7. Explain how deficits are like taxes. Is the burden of the deficit progressive in its distribution? Explain.

SELECTED READINGS

Maxwell, James A., and Aronson, J. Richard. *Financing State and Local Governments*. Washington, DC: Brookings Institution, 1977.

Musgrave, Richard. *The Theory of Public Finance*. New York: McGraw-Hill, 1959.

Okner, Benjamin, and Pechman, Joseph A. *Who Bears the Tax Burden*. Washington, DC: Brookings Institution, 1974.

Olson, Mancur. *The Rise and Decline of Nations*. New Haven: Yale University Press, 1982.

Pechman, Joseph A. *Federal Tax Policy*, 4th ed. Washington, DC: Brookings Institution, 1983.

Pechman, Joseph A. *Who Paid the Taxes, 1966–85*. Washington, DC: Brookings Institution, 1985.

Veseth, Michael. *Public Finance*. Reston, VA: Reston Publishers, 1984.

PART 3

Macroeconomic Goals and Problems

CHAPTER 8

Gross National Product and Economic Growth

Having read the chapter, reviewed the chapter summary, and completed the *Study Guide* exercises, you should be able to:

CRIS

8.1 HOUSEHOLD AND BUSINESS SECTORS: Explain the concept of the circular flow of spending and income between the household and the business sectors.

8.2 MARKETS AND THE CIRCULAR FLOW: Explain the role of product markets and resource markets in the circular flow model.

8.3 NATIONAL INCOME: Define national income and use the circular flow model to show how national income is generated.

8.4 GROSS NATIONAL PRODUCT: Define gross national product and use the circular flow model to show how GNP is generated.

8.5 STOCK AND FLOW CONCEPTS: Explain the difference between a stock concept, such as wealth, and a flow concept, such as income.

8.6 FINANCIAL, GOVERNMENT, AND FOREIGN SECTORS: Explain how the financial, government, and foreign sectors fit into the circular flow model of the economy.

8.7 FINAL AND INTERMEDIATE GOODS: Explain the difference between final goods and intermediate goods and indicate why this difference is important in calculating GNP.

8.8 METHODS FOR CALCULATING GNP: Explain how GNP can be calculated using the income method, the expenditure method, and the concept of value-added.

8.9 REAL GROSS NATIONAL PRODUCT: Define real gross national product and explain why real GNP is a better economic indicator than GNP during inflationary periods.

- **8.10 GNP AND QUALITY OF LIFE:** Explain why GNP is not a measure of the quality of life.

- **8.11 MEASURING ECONOMIC GROWTH:** Explain how economic growth can be measured using real GNP or per capita real GNP as economic indicators.

- **8.12 PRODUCTIVITY:** Define productivity and explain how investment and technological change contribute to rising productivity and economic growth.

- **8.13 VESTED INTERESTS:** Explain Mancur Olson's theory that vested interests can cause slower economic growth.

- **8.14 INDUSTRIAL DEVELOPMENT POLICY:** Explain what is meant by an industrial development policy and list the pro and con arguments concerning the adoption of such a policy in the United States.

- **8.15 JAPAN'S ECONOMIC GROWTH:** Briefly list some of the main factors that contributed to Japan's rapid economic growth since World War II.

Macroeconomics is the study of the entire economy. It is like a complicated jigsaw puzzle. We must fit together the many pieces that make up our economy to form a picture or pattern that enables us to see the links between buyers and sellers, employers and workers, borrowers and lenders, and the private and public sectors. We must also see how our economy fits into the broader puzzle of the world of international trade and finance.

A STUDY GUIDE TO MACROECONOMICS

There are a variety of ways that we could choose to study macroeconomics. We could focus on various aspects of the economy, such as private consumers, business investment, or government programs. We could explore several different competing theories of how the economy works or even more views concerning the role that government programs and policies should play in the economy. Or we could focus on the many economic events and forces that have shaped the economy.

We will, in the next eight chapters, look at all these aspects of macroeconomics in a way that is designed to give you a sound understanding of macroeconomic theory and policy and an appreciation of the controversies and issues that surround the field of study. Our theme is the historical development of the U.S. economy, focusing on the years since the Great Depression and on the last 25 years in particular. We will see how the economy has changed and how economic theory has evolved and changed with it in an effort to better describe and analyze the economy. We will also see how economic policies have evolved and changed along with the economy and economic theory.

Here is how we will attack the study of macroeconomics. This chapter and the next provide background material that is needed to fully understand and appreciate macroeconomics, the nature of the economy, and the theory and policy material that follow. This chapter looks at how economists measure and analyze something as large as an entire economy and how economic growth takes place. The concepts of GNP and economic growth presented in this chapter are the fundamental building blocks of modern macroeconomics.

Chapter 9 provides a perspective from which to view current economic conditions, policies, and problems. We will first look at the main economic events of the 1960s through the mid-1980s, focusing on the changing relationship between inflation and unemployment during this period. The chapter includes a thorough analysis of the problems of inflation and unemployment.

The historical development of macroeconomic theory begins in Chapter 10 with an analysis of the economic theories of John Maynard Keynes, which were forged in the crucible of the Great Depression. Keynes's economic ideas were controversial but very influential. The principles of Keynesian economics are still the basis of many economic theories and policies today.

The economy and economic theory changed dramatically during the decades of the 1960s and 1970s. Keynesian economic ideas evolved into an economic model of both demand and supply in order to better understand the causes and cures of inflation. Chapter 11 looks at this aggregate demand–aggregate supply model and uses it to analyze the economic events and policies of the sixties and seventies.

One of Keynes's main conclusions was that more active government involvement in the economy was desirable. Chapter 12 looks at how government policies work and then shows how the current school of Supply-side economics, with its own view of government's role, evolved and grew in influence. We also look at one consequence of this active government role: the very large budget deficits that dominate current policy choices.

Chapter 13 begins a new unit that focuses on money and finance. Chapter 13 looks at the banking system and how banks operate and create money. The concepts of money, banks, credit, and interest allow us to expand our view of the economy and introduce new economic theories, including a simple monetarist model of the economy.

The Federal Reserve is a keystone of the economy. It regulates the banking system and makes important policy choices that have widespread effects. Chapter 14 looks at the Federal Reserve System and its economic tools. This chapter also examines the role that credit markets play in the economy and presents an outline of Keynesian monetary theory.

Chapter 15 ends our exploration of macroeconomics by discussing the monetarist school of economic theory and its recent offspring, the theory of rational expectations. These two economic theories are very influential in today's world. The policy prescriptions of monetarist and rational expectations economists are much different from those of Keynesians. We will look at how these theories differ and why.

Our complex economy is difficult to analyze, understand, and predict, which is why the field of macroeconomics is so controversial and unsettled. Economists disagree about many aspects of macroeconomic theory and policy. But many of the basic patterns can be clearly seen if we look close enough through the correct analytic lenses.

This chapter begins our study of macroeconomics by asking two basic and important questions. First we ask, "How can we best measure and

Circular Flow of Spending and Income
A model of the relationship between spending and income for the entire economy.

Aggregates
Measures of economic activity involving one or more sectors of the economy.

> **8.1 HOUSEHOLD AND BUSINESS SECTORS**

analyze economic activity involving millions of individuals?" In answering this question we will learn about gross national product, which is the fundamental building block of macroeconomics. Second, we will ask, "How does economic growth take place?" In answering this question we will learn about the role of the private and public sectors in the economy and how their interaction helps determine the economy's path through time.

THE CIRCULAR FLOW OF SPENDING AND INCOME

One simple but useful way to see how the economy's pieces fit together is introduced in Figure 8-1. This figure illustrates the basic **circular flow of spending and income** between the household and business sectors of our economy. The circular flow diagram provides a useful introduction to macroeconomics because it views economic activity in terms of **aggregates,** which

FIGURE 8-1

The Circular Flow of Spending and Income. The circular flow model shows that money flows from households to businesses to pay for goods and services, then back to households as payment for the resources that businesses use. Money flows in one direction and the goods, services, and resources that are purchased flow in the opposite direction. When this flow is measured as it passes through the product markets, the result is GNP. When the same flow is measured as it passes through the resource markets, we measure national income. A more complete picture of the circular flow is shown in Figure 8-2.

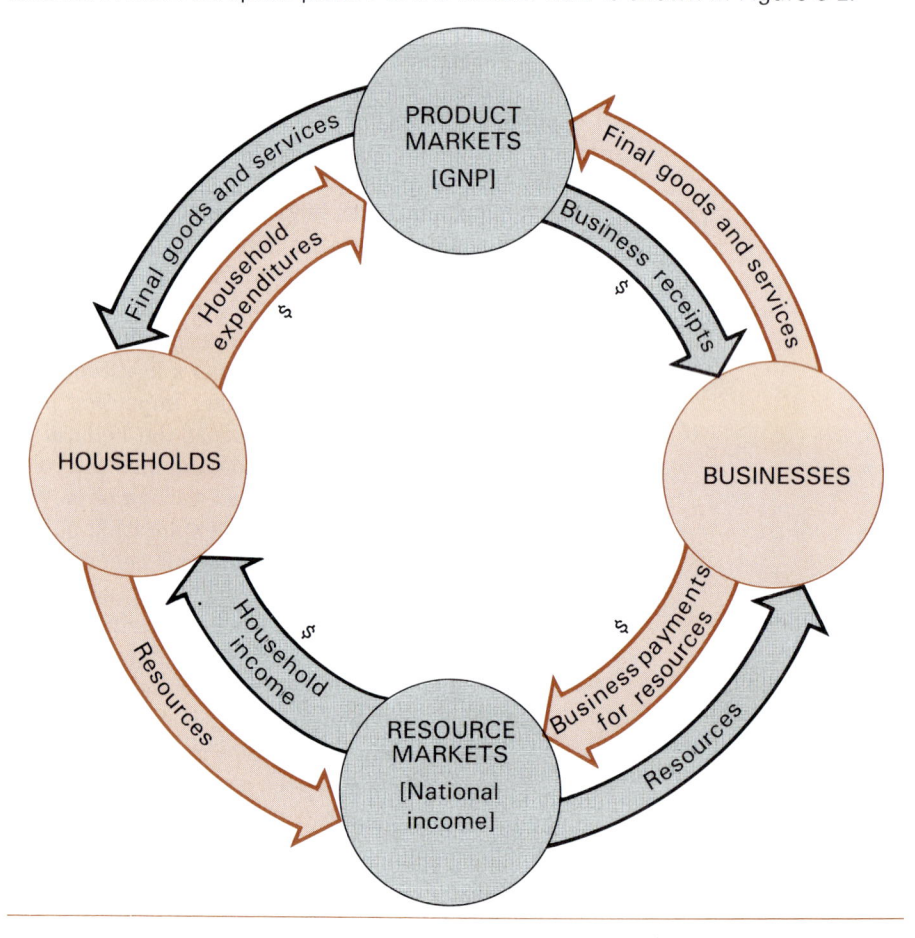

Household Sector
The part of the economy that provides resources to businesses in return for income, which is used for consumption spending, saving, and to pay taxes.

Business Sector
The part of the economy that purchases resources, organizes production, and sells goods and services.

8.2 MARKETS AND THE CIRCULAR FLOW

Product Markets
Markets where households purchase goods and services from businesses.

Resource Markets
Markets where businesses purchase labor, capital, land, and entrepreneurial skills from households.

Final Goods and Services
Those goods and services that are purchased by their ultimate users in a given period of time.

---

are economic variables that are associated with different sectors of the economy. The idea of analyzing the economy as the interaction of these aggregates, instead of focusing on purely individual behavior, is a basic difference between macroeconomics and microeconomics. Figure 8-1 presents a very simplified picture of the economy. It ignores important parts of the economy such as the government, financial, and international sectors; we will include these sectors later in the chapter. For now, this figure focuses on the basic interaction between households and business firms.

The **household sector** is a conceptual representation of that part of the economy where consumers are located. Everyone is a member of a household. Households are both consumers of goods and services and the owners of all productive resources. Economists divide productive resources into four types: land, labor, capital, and entrepreneurial ability. When resources are used by producers to make goods and services, the owners of the resources must be paid a return of some kind for their use. For example, the owner of land is paid a return called rent. Labor is paid wages, capital receives interest, and the owners of a firm receive profits or losses. These returns, or payments to productive resources, represent the income to households. The members of a household who sell their labor or talents to a business get a paycheck that provides income for them. The distribution of income among these different resources will be discussed in more detail in Chapters 21, 22, and 23.

The **business sector** is a conceptual representation of that part of the economy where firms bring together the productive resources to produce goods and services. These goods and services are sold to consumers in both the business and the household sectors. Businesses buy the productive resources from households and, therefore, pay incomes to households. Households, in return, buy the goods and services businesses produce and pay for them with the incomes they earned from businesses.

Figure 8-1 shows that the household and business sectors are linked through both the **product markets** and the **resource markets.** Product markets are where the **final goods and services** produced by business firms are sold. Resource markets are where business firms buy land, labor, capital, and entrepreneurial resources from their household owners. We can now trace out the circular flow of economic activity through the product and resource markets.

In any exchange that takes place in our economy, the seller of a good or service receives precisely the same amount that the buyer pays for that good or service. If you buy a new Ford for $10,000, you receive goods with a market value of $10,000, and Ford receives a $10,000 payment. Your expenditure of $10,000 is equal to $10,000 in income to Ford Motor Company. The $10,000 that Ford receives ultimately ends up as income to the owners of the land, labor, and capital that Ford used to make the car and to the owners of Ford Motor Company to compensate them for the risk they took in producing the car.

Businesses receive as income exactly what consumers spend to buy the goods and services they desire. In the resource markets, households receive as income exactly what businesses spend to buy the resources that they need. Business income depends on household spending in the product markets. Household income depends on business spending in the resource markets. This concept is a fundamental foundation of macroeconomics. We, as individuals, are concerned about our incomes. Figure 8-1 shows that the amount of income that people in the economy receive, as a group, depends on the amount of spending that people, as a group, undertake. In other words, the act of spending creates income through the circular flow process.

Figure 8-1 also shows that the basic circular flow between businesses and households is really made up of two types of flows. The outer circle in the figure shows the flow of real goods, services, and resources. Resources flow from households to businesses and final goods and services flow from businesses to households to complete the cycle. The inner circle in the figure shows that the flow of goods and resources is matched by an equal and opposite flow of money. As resources flow through the resource markets from households to businesses, money flows in the opposite direction from businesses to households, providing income to households. In the same way, the flow of final goods and services through the product markets from businesses to households is matched by an equal and opposite money flow from households to businesses to pay for these items.

In summary, the circular flow diagram is a useful simple picture of the economy because it shows us several relationships. First, it shows that businesses and households are interdependent and not separate and opposing forces as we sometimes tend to think. Second, the circular flow shows that spending and income are directly related because spending on final goods creates household income, which provides the means for further spending. Finally, we can see that the circular flow is really both a cycle of money and a cycle of real goods and resources.

NATIONAL INCOME AND GROSS NATIONAL PRODUCT

> **8.3 NATIONAL INCOME**

National Income
The total of all wages, interest, profits, and rents paid in the economy in a given period of time. The sum of all payments to the owners of productive resources.

> **8.4 GROSS NATIONAL PRODUCT**

Gross National Product (GNP)
The market value in current prices of all final goods and services produced in an economy in a specified period of time (usually a year).

The lower loop of Figure 8-1 shows that the productive resources of land, labor, capital, and entrepreneurship flow from households into the resource markets where they are bought by businesses. Income, in the form of wages, interest, profits, and rents, flows to households in the opposite direction. This entire lower loop of the circular flow represents **national income** in the economy. Economists define national income as the sum of all payments to the owners of productive resources, or simply the total of all wages, interest, profits, and rents paid in the economy. Table 8-1 shows that payments to employees represent the largest single source of national income. Households also receive income as proprietors of businesses, owners of rental properties, owners of corporations, and as net interest.

The upper loop of Figure 8-1 shows the flow of final goods and services through the product markets from the business sector, where they are made, into the product markets, where they are bought by households. This represents the total output, or production, of goods and services in the economy. The flow of money to pay for these goods and services is called **gross national product.** Gross national product is a measure of the value of the goods and services produced in the economy. Formally, GNP is defined as the market value, in current prices, of all final goods and services produced by an economy in a year.

KEY CONCEPTS
8.1, 8.2, 8.3, 8.4

The circular flow of spending and income shows how the household and business sectors are related. When economic activity is measured as it passes through the resource market, national income is measured. When economic activity is measured as it passes through the product markets, gross national product is measured.

| TABLE 8-1 | National Income for the United States, 1984 |

Type of income	Amount ($ billion)	Percent of total
Compensation of employees	2172.7	73
Proprietor's income	154.7	5
Rental income	62.5	2
Corporate profits	284.5	10
Net interest	285.0	10
National income	2959.4	100

Source. Economic Report of the President, 1985, Table B-21.

8.5 STOCK AND FLOW CONCEPTS

Flow Concept
A concept relating to the amount of an economic activity within a given period of time. Investment (a flow concept) adds to the economy's total amount of capital (a stock concept).

Stock Concept
A concept relating to the accumulated amount of an economic activity over time; a measure of total amount. The total accumulation of capital in the economy is a stock concept.

It is important to note here that gross national product and national income are flow concepts as opposed to stock concepts. A **flow concept** discusses the changes that occur in a unit of time. Thus, for example, the amount of water that is released by a dam per hour is a flow concept. A **stock concept** measures the total amount of something, where no change in time is considered. The amount of water behind the dam at 12:00 today would be a stock concept, for example. Another way to think of this is that a stock concept is like a still photograph, showing what exists at a given point in time, while a flow concept is like a motion picture, showing what happens over time.

GNP measures the flow of the output of goods and services per year. It is not a measure of the stock of total wealth at a given point in time. GNP is frequently explained as being analogous to a measure of the flow of water through a pipe. As a flow concept, it would not measure how much water has been pumped into and stored in a reservoir but rather how fast the water can flow through the entire system.

One of the most interesting things that Figure 8-1 shows us is that, conceptually, the value of the goods that are produced in the economy and purchased in product markets is equal to the amount of income households receive in the resource markets. Every dollar that households spend for final goods and services must necessarily be received by someone as income, in the form of either wages, interest, rent, or profit. The exact relationship between national income and gross national product is detailed in the appendix to this chapter.

Table 8-2 shows the trend in gross national product for the period 1960–1986. The gross national product of the United States was over $3.9 trillion in 1985. This means that over $3.9 trillion worth of final goods and services were produced and sold. GNP has grown from about $500 billion to more than $3900 billion in the period shown here, a dramatic increase in the value of goods produced.

Financial Sector
The part of the economy that receives saving from households and business and finances investment spending. Banks, credit unions, and insurance companies are included in the financial sector.

8.6 FINANCIAL, GOVERNMENT, AND FOREIGN SECTORS

THE FINANCIAL, GOVERNMENT, AND FOREIGN SECTORS

The circular flow diagram in Figure 8-1 ignored three important parts of the economy: the financial, government, and foreign sectors. They are included in the modified circular flow diagram pictured in Figure 8-2.

The **financial sector** takes funds from households and businesses in the form of saving. These funds are used to make loans that make possible investment spending for machinery, tools, and factories.

| TABLE 8-2 | Gross National Product of the United States, 1960–1986 |

Year	Gross national product (billions current $)
1960	515.3
1961	533.8
1962	574.6
1963	606.9
1964	649.8
1965	705.1
1966	772.0
1967	816.4
1968	892.7
1969	963.9
1970	1015.5
1971	1102.7
1972	1212.8
1973	1359.3
1974	1472.8
1975	1598.4
1976	1782.8
1977	1990.3
1978	2249.7
1979	2508.2
1980	2732.0
1981	3052.6
1982	3166.0
1983	3401.6
1984	3774.7
1985	3992.5
1986 (estimate)	4150.0

Source. *Economic Report of the President, 1985,* Table B-1.

Government Sector
The part of the economy owned by the public as a whole. The government sector includes federal, state, and local governments.

Foreign Sector
The sector of the economy that engages in trade with the residents of other countries.

The **government sector** takes funds from households and businesses in the form of taxes. Total government outlays can be divided into two groups. Government purchases goods and services in the form of *government spending* and makes *transfer payments* that add to the household sector's ability to purchase other goods and services.

The **foreign sector** affects the economy in two ways. Spending for imports (goods and services purchased from producers located in other countries) leaves the circular flow, as the figure shows, and enters the economic systems of other countries, contributing to their spending and income. Foreign purchases of our exports (goods and services sold to purchasers located in other countries), on the other hand, enter our economic system, contributing to spending and income here. The net impact of the foreign sector is measured by net exports—the total value of exports minus the total value of imports for a given period of time. In other words, net exports is the net addition to total spending resulting from the foreign sector of the economy.

The more complete circular flow diagram in Figure 8-2 provides a more realistic picture of where spending comes from (consumers, investors,

The Financial, Government, and Foreign Sectors 191

FIGURE 8-2 **The Complete Circular Flow Model.** The circular flow of spending and income from households to businesses is complicated by the existence of the financial, government, and foreign sectors. The financial sector receives saving from households and businesses and finances investment spending. The government sector receives taxes from households and businesses and provides government spending and transfer payments. The foreign sector receives payment for imported goods and provides payments for items that are exported. The upper loop of this figure shows that GNP is the sum of consumption (C), investment (I), net export (X_n), and government spending (G). The lower loop illustrates the relationship between national income and disposable income.

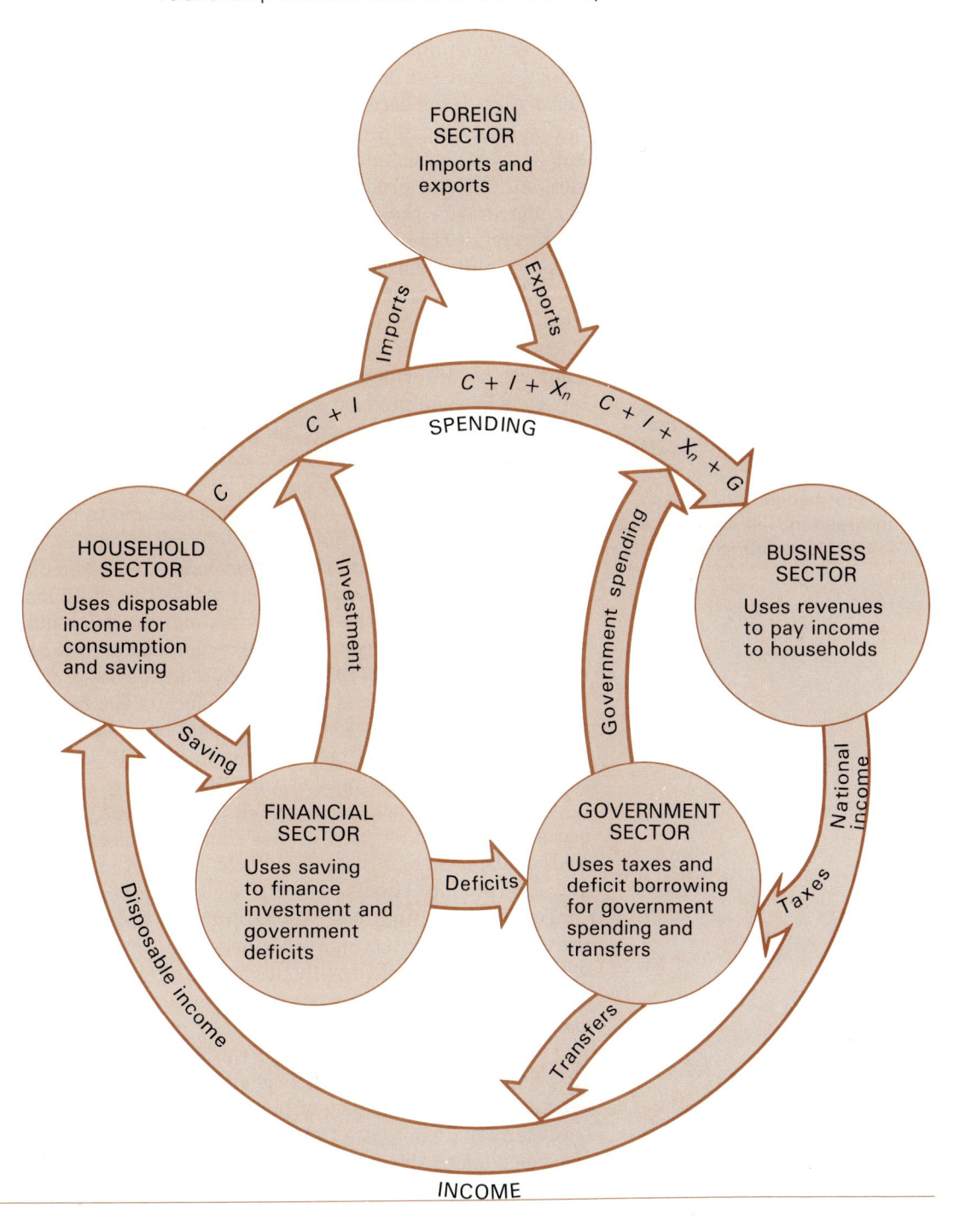

government, and net exports) and where it goes (income that makes possible consumption spending, saving, and tax payments). This circular flow diagram is a very important concept that will be used frequently in this and the next chapter.

MEASURING GROSS NATIONAL PRODUCT

The first problem economists encounter in calculating GNP is how to tally up all the various kinds of goods and services that are produced with a single measure. We might measure production by weight, or volume, or by some common unit such as dollar value. If economists used weight of output as our measure of production, a dump truck would be more valuable than a heart pacemaker because it weighs more. Services such as hair cuts could not be measured at all, even though they generate income for those who are employed in service industries. Economists have, therefore, decided to measure our national production in dollars. Dollar value is an effective common denominator for the various kinds of goods and services produced.

Second, it is important to note what kinds of goods and services are counted in the measurement of GNP and what are not. Remember that GNP is defined as the market value of all final goods and services produced. Final goods and services are those that have reached their final consumer. They are the goods and services consumers buy for their own personal use. They are not **intermediate goods and services** that people or businesses buy to help them produce some other final good or product. For example, the food you buy to eat is a final good. You are the ultimate consumer of that good. If, on the other hand, you bought bread, wine, and cheese to sell in a restaurant, that food would be an intermediate good you were using to produce the final good of a restaurant meal sold to customers. The customers are the ultimate consumers of the good or service.

GNP does not include the market value of intermediate goods because this would be double counting. That means that if intermediate goods were counted, the value of the bread, wine, and cheese would be counted once when you bought them at the supplier and again in the price charged for the restaurant meal. Gross national product in this case would not give a true measure of the goods and services produced. The bread, wine, and cheese were only produced once, but they would be counted twice if intermediate goods were included in the computation of GNP. It is for this reason that GNP only includes the market value of final goods and services.

GNP also does not include goods and services produced in an earlier accounting period, or used goods. Things like used cars or houses that are sold by one owner to the next are not included in GNP. Only new houses or new cars produced and sold in the accounting year are counted.

To be counted in gross national product, final goods and services must pass through a product market. Goods and services that are given away without cost or supplied without compensation are not included in GNP. The services of a person who stays home to clean, cook, care for children, and operate a household are not usually paid for in money. One seldom gets a paycheck for doing the laundry, washing the dishes, or chauffeuring the offspring to and from school. It is clear that these activities contribute substantially to the quality of family life, yet they are not measured in GNP because they do not pass through any monetary market. Illegal activities also come under this category. The sale of illegal drugs and other under-

---

8.7 FINAL AND INTERMEDIATE GOODS

Intermediate Goods and Services
Those goods and services that businesses purchase to aid in the production of some other (final) good. Intermediate goods are not included in GNP in order to avoid double counting production.

ECONOMIC ISSUES

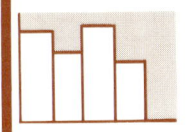

Gross Domestic Product

Gross national product is our fundamental measure of production for the U.S. economy. Many other countries, however, rely on a slightly different measure of total production called *gross domestic product (GDP)*. GDP is GNP adjusted for the existence of payments to domestic-owned resources involved in foreign production. The difference between GNP and GDP is small, but it is likely to become more important in the future.

Gross national product measures the output of resources that are owned by U.S. households. Thus, for example, if a worker from California is assigned to a temporary job in Saudi Arabia, the services that the worker produces are included in U.S. GNP. It is important to understand, however, that these services are not available for use by people in the United States. Thus GNP in this case tends to overstate the final goods and services available in the domestic economy by including the value of this foreign production by American workers.

Gross domestic product corrects for this international problem. GDP counts only the final goods and services that are produced by productive resources that are actually in the United States. GDP, then, is a better measure of the production available for use in this country.

The difference between GNP and GDP is currently relatively small for the United States. GNP in 1984 totalled $3,774.7 billion, while GDP was $3,726.7 billion. In other countries, where relatively more resources are involved in international trade, the difference is more important. Most international production statistics are therefore tabulated using GDP instead of GNP. As the foreign sector of the U.S. economy grows, we can expect that gross domestic product will come into wider use as a measure of the production available to our economy.

---

ground economy activities are also not included in GNP. It is because the production of these goods is not included in GNP measurements that GNP is not a perfect measure of the economy's total output. Starting in 1986, however, the government began to estimate the amount of economic activity that takes place in the underground ecomony, and this estimate is included in the calculation of GNP. This somewhat improves the GNP's ability to measure the level of economic activity in the U.S.

The Expenditure Method

> **8.8 METHODS FOR CALCULATING GNP**

The circular flow model in Figure 8-2 tells us that we can measure the level of economic activity using either of two approaches: the *expenditure method* that looks at product markets or the *income method* that measures economic activity by looking at resource markets. We need to understand that we can measure GNP by both methods so that we will understand that, as the circular flow diagram indicates, aggregate spending and aggregate income in the economy are identical. We can learn about how the economy fits together and how this identity comes about by looking more closely at these two ways of measuring GNP.

Expenditure Method
A method of calculating GNP by summing the dollar value of all types of expenditures. The expenditure method calculates GNP as the sum of consumption, investment, net export, and government spending.

The **expenditure method** measures the dollar value of all goods and services that are bought through the product markets. Table 8-3 shows the expenditure analysis of GNP for 1984. This method is sometimes called the upper-loop approach since it takes place in the upper loop of the circular flow diagram of Figure 8-2. The total expenditures in the upper loop can be

TABLE 8-3   Expenditure Analysis of GNP, 1984

Expenditure type		Amount ($ billion)	Percent of total
Personal consumption spending		2342.3	64
Durable goods	318.4		
Nondurables	858.3		
Services	1165.7		
Gross investment spending		637.3	17
Fixed investment	580.4		
Changes in inventories	56.8		
Government spending		748.0	20
Net foreign spending		−66.3	−2
Exports	363.7		
Imports	429.9		
Gross national product		3661.3	100

Note. Totals do not agree with Table 8-2 due to revised GNP data released in 1986.
Source. Economic Report of the President, 1985, Table B-4.

divided into four separate categories, or kinds, of expenditures, depending upon who is doing the spending. In the economy, there are four spending groups: consumers, investors, government, and foreign spenders. Together their total spending represents the market value of all goods and services produced in a given year.

$$\text{Gross national product} = \text{consumption spending} + \text{gross investment spending} + \text{government spending} + \text{net foreign spending}$$

Consumption Spending
The value of the final goods and services that households purchase. Consumption spending includes everyday items such as expenditures for food, clothing, legal services, and haircuts.

Investment Spending
The purchase of goods that increase the capacity to produce in the future. Purchases of factories, equipment, inventories, or new technology are examples of investment spending.

Consumption spending is spending by consumers on everyday consumer items. Consumers purchase some items that are relatively long lasting, such as autos and household appliances, which are classified as durable goods. Other items, such as foods, are classified as nondurables. Finally, many consumer purchases are of services, such as haircuts, banking services, education, or legal advice.

Investment spending, in economists' terms, refers to spending on new structures (both business and residential), plants, equipment, and factories that increase the economy's ability to produce goods and services in the future. Firms also invest in inventories, which are stocks of finished goods, raw materials, or intermediate goods that are accumulated in anticipation of sale or use in production. Investment, in the eyes of economists, is the purchase of some productive resource that is used to increase future output or sales. Investment spending in the GNP sense is therefore different than financial investment, which is the transfer of assets such as stocks, bonds, or savings accounts from one person to another. Many people confuse buying stocks or bonds or other financial assets with the economist's concept of investment. Remember that investment is really the creation of some new productive resource or good. When stocks or bonds are sold, people are simply transferring the ownership of existing plants or equipment from one person to another. Nothing new is created, so this is not true economic investment, thus it is not included in GNP.

Fixed Investment
Business purchases of new equipment or structures that add to the stock of capital.

Inventory Investment
The change in the value of the stock of resources that businesses have on hand for future resale or future productive use.

Gross Investment
New investment, not including any adjustment for wear and tear to existing capital.

Government Spending
Purchase of final goods and services by federal, state, and local governments.

Net Foreign Spending
The component of gross national product that results from international transactions.

Investment spending takes on two different forms. First, when businesses build new structures, buy new equipment, or construct new factories this is an addition to their stock of capital goods. This is called **fixed investment.** The second part of investment occurs when businesses either add to or reduce their inventories. They keep these inventories so that they do not have to produce at exactly the same rate that buyers want to buy their goods. When these inventories are increased, businesses are investing in future production or sales. They own the inventories just as they own their buildings or machinery, and they hold them in the hopes of selling them or using them to produce more profits in the future. This is called **inventory investment.** Total investment spending consists of spending on new plants and equipment (fixed investment) plus changes in inventory valuation (inventory investment).

Inventory investment can decline as well as increase. Sometimes consumers buy goods faster than businesses had planned and business inventories drop unexpectedly. At other times consumers may buy fewer goods than businesses expected and businesses may find their inventories at higher levels than they desire. In either case, businesses face strong incentives to adjust the rate at which they are producing goods or services in order to get back to their planned level of inventories.

The economy's capital stock of machines, tools, factories, and equipment eventually wears out. Factories and machines get old and obsolete and must eventually be replaced. So far we have been talking about new fixed investment with no allowance for wear and tear. Investment in this sense is called **gross investment.** Gross investment is a part of the calculation of gross national product. We look more closely at how allowances are made in the investment account to adjust for the wearing out of our fixed investment in the appendix to this chapter.

Government spending on purchases of final goods and services is also included in GNP. Everything from military weapons to asphalt for new roads to paper clips for holding tax returns together at the Internal Revenue Service must be bought by government. Not all government payments are included in gross national product, however, because many government programs do not purchase final goods and services but act, instead, to transfer money from one group to another. The social security program, for example, transfers income from workers to retired individuals. This is an example of a transfer payment. Transfer payments are not included in GNP because they are not the purchase of a final good or service.

Net foreign spending measures that amount of final goods and services that foreigners buy from U.S. firms minus the amount of U.S. spending on imported goods. As mentioned earlier, this figure is called net exports and is computed by subtracting the total amount of our spending on imports from the total amount of spending by foreigners in our economy:

Net exports = total export spending − total import spending

In summary then, we realize that we can account for the total output of our economy by adding up the total spending of the various groups who bought the goods and services that were produced.

$$\text{Gross national product} = \text{consumption spending} + \text{gross investment spending} + \text{government spending} + \text{net foreign spending}$$

$$\text{GNP} = C + I_{gross} + G + X_n$$

196 Gross National Product and Economic Growth

8.8 METHODS FOR CALCULATING GNP

Income Method
A method of calculating GNP by summing the value of the payments to the owners of the resources that are used in production.

The Income Method

The **income method** is the second way to calculate GNP. Table 8-4 shows the income approach to GNP. The income method calculates GNP by adding up all of the payments to productive resources that were used to produce that output. This measures the value of output as it passes through the resource markets in the lower loop of the circular flow model. The market prices of goods and services are equal to their total costs of production, including profits to the business that produces them. If we add up all the wages, interest, profits, and rents paid to produce goods and services, we get their market value. The income approach to measuring output, once it is adjusted for the existence of government and other factors not included in the simple circular flow diagram, gives us the same market value of goods and services as does the expenditure approach. Remember, when something is bought or exchanged, the seller receives exactly the same amount that the buyer spends. The seller, then, pays all the costs of producing the goods sold including his or her own profits. A dollar spent on goods or services in the marketplace produces a dollar's worth of income to the productive resources.

Table 8-4 shows that GNP is made up of income earned by workers as compensation, income that business proprietors earn, rental income, corporate profits, and net interest. The sum of these four resource payments is then adjusted in two ways to arrive at GNP.

First, we must add to national income some items that represent production but are not income. Businesses spend money on investment goods to replace or repair equipment and factories that have worn out or depreciated during the year. We do not include these expenditures in business profits in the national income account. But depreciation expenditures do represent production, so we must add them to national income as we move toward GNP. Some taxes are collected from businesses, such as customs duties and sales, excise, and property taxes. These funds are not included in national income because they are not received by any individual as income. These taxes do result in production, however, when they become part of government outlays, so they are added to national income in Table 8-4 as we move toward GNP. Finally, businesses make some transfer payments to individuals, such as pension and disability payments. These payments are not included in national income because this would count them as income twice — once to the business and again when received by the individual. These payments do result in increased purchases of final goods and services, however, so we add them to national income at this point.

Second, we must subtract two items from national income as we move toward GNP. The government pays subsidies to public enterprises such as Amtrak and the Post Office. These subsidies are included as national income because they are received by individuals, but they do not represent production. The output of government enterprises enters GNP as the value of the items produced, not as their cost. Subtracting these subsidies from national income results in the value of the output of government enterprises being correctly measured. We also subtract a "statistical error" item at this point in our calculation; this is necessary because of the problems of separately measuring such comprehensive aggregates as national income and GNP.

These adjustments to national income are necessary to prevent income or production from being counted twice or understated. With these adjustments to the figures, we can see that GNP is the sum of all income earned

FIGURE 8-4

Income calculation of GNP, 1984

Type of income	Amount ($ billions)
Compensation of employees	2172.7
Proprietor's income	154.7
Rental income	62.5
Corporate profits	284.5
Net interest	285.0
National income	2959.4
adjustments	
plus	
depreciation	402.9
indirect business taxes	304.3
business transfer payments	17.3
minus	
subsidies to government enterprises	−14.4
statistical error	−8.2
Gross national product	3661.3

Note. Totals do not agree with Table 8-2 due to revised GNP data released in 1986.
Source. Economic Report of the President, 1985, Table B-21.

in the economy. The appendix to this chapter will explore the GNP accounts in greater detail, providing more complete explanations for many of these adjustments.

The Value-Added Method

8.8 METHODS FOR CALCULATING GNP

Value Added
The increase in the value or selling price of resources that results from the production process.

There is a third way to calculate GNP that is frequently used, which is based on the concept of **value added**. The idea of value added is easy to grasp. When a potter purchases clay and creates a beautiful vase, she has taken resources with a relatively low value and made them worth more. If the clay costs $5 and the vase sells for $20, then the potter's value added is equal to the $15 difference. We can calculate the value of the final good, the vase, either by looking at its $20 price or by summing the potter's value added ($15) and the value of the resources she started with ($5). Sometimes economists find it more convenient to actually calculate GNP by adding up the values added throughout the economy.

Final goods often go through many intermediate stages in production. When this happens, we can measure the value of the final goods by taking the sum of the value added at each stage of production. The final good of bread, for example, begins as wheat, becomes flour that is made into bread at a bakery, which is eventually sold to consumers by a retail store. Table 8-5 provides a very simple hypothetical example of this process.

This example shows that we can calculate GNP as either the value of all final goods produced or as the total value added as production takes place. This tells us that GNP is created when people take resources and make them more valuable. Since GNP (and therefore total value added) also measures the economy's income, this tells us that income is also created when people take resources and make them more valuable.

TABLE 8-5

Value Added and GNP

Production stage	Input cost ($)	Output value ($)	Value added ($)
Farmer produces wheat	.00	0.10	0.10
Miller produces flour from wheat	.10	.25	.15
Baker produces bread from flour	.25	.75	.50
Retailer sells bread	.75	1.00	.25

Final good price = $1.00   Total value added = $1.00

REAL GROSS NATIONAL PRODUCT

8.9 REAL GROSS NATIONAL PRODUCT

Gross national product measures production by the value of final goods and services that the economy generates. The use of a dollar common denominator to measure production creates problems when we try to compare GNP figures for different years. The problem is that inflation can distort this comparison. Suppose, for example, that exactly the same goods were produced in two consecutive years, but that prices were twice as high in the second year than the first. GNP, because it measures the dollar value of goods produced, would be twice as high in the second year than in the first year, even though there has been no change in the amount of goods really produced. This makes GNP an ambiguous indicator of economic output during periods of inflation. **Real gross national product (real GNP)** is an improved measure of total product. Real GNP is calculated by adjusting GNP for changes in prices using a technique that will be demonstrated in the next chapter when we look at the problems of inflation and rising prices in more depth.

The figures provided in Table 8-6 show how much different the picture of the economy becomes when we measure economic activity using real GNP instead of GNP. The original gross national product figures increased every year in the period shown. Using real GNP, we can see that production fell in several of these years, indicating **recessions.** A recession is defined to be a period of two consecutive calendar quarters of falling production, as measured by real GNP, and, therefore, a period of falling income. Recessions occurred in 1970, 1974–1975, 1980 and 1982. Falling production meant rising unemployment rates during these years. Figure 8-3 plots GNP and real GNP for the years 1960-1985 so that their relative growth rates can be compared.

Two conclusions can be drawn from this figure. First, note that GNP has constantly risen during this period, often at very high rates of increase. Much of the increase in GNP in recent years, however, is due to rising prices, not rising production. The much slower growth in production is better measured by the real GNP line in the figure. The difference between GNP and real GNP in the diagram is the accumulated effect of inflation over this period.

A second fact that this figure shows is that the economy has experienced several periods of falling production, as indicated by falling real GNP. As already noted, prolonged periods of falling production and real GNP are called recessions. Periods of rising production and real GNP, on the other

Real Gross National Product (Real GNP)
Gross national product adjusted for changes in the price level. Real GNP is the best measure of the economy's total output over time.

Recessions
Periods of declining total output as measured by falling real GNP. Unemployment rates generally increase during recessions.

| TABLE 8-6 | Measures of Total Output, United States, 1960–1986 |

Year	Gross national product (billions current $)	Real gross national product (billions 1982 $)
1960	515.3	1665.3
1961	533.8	1708.7
1962	574.6	1799.4
1963	606.9	1873.3
1964	649.8	1973.3
1965	705.1	2087.6
1966	772.6	2208.3
1967	816.4	2271.4
1968	892.7	2365.6
1969	963.9	2423.3
1970	1015.5	2416.2
1971	1102.7	2484.8
1972	1212.8	2608.5
1973	1359.3	2744.1
1974	1472.8	2729.3
1975	1598.4	2695.0
1976	1782.8	2826.7
1977	1990.5	2958.6
1978	2249.7	3115.2
1979	2508.2	3192.4
1980	2732.0	3187.1
1981	3052.6	3248.8
1982	3166.0	3166.0
1983	3401.6	3277.7
1984	3774.7	3492.0
1985	3992.5	3573.5
1986 (estimate)	4112.3	3626.9

Source. *Economic Report of the President, 1986,* Tables B-1, B-2.

Expansions
Periods of rising total output as measured by rising real GNP.

hand, are called **expansions.** The expansion of the 1960s was the longest period of prosperity and rising real GNP in our recent history. The 1970s and early 1980s were characterized by several recessions. The recessionary years, when production and real GNP fell, are noted by color bars in the figure. One important goal of macroeconomics is to attempt to understand the causes of expansions and recessions and to formulate economic policies that promote stable expansion of the economy.

**KEY CONCEPTS
8.8, 8.9**

The economy's output can be measured in several different ways. The expenditure approach measures GNP as the sum of consumption, investment, net export, and government spending. The income approach measures the sum of wages, interest, rent, and profit income received by people. GNP can also be measured as the sum of the value added in the economy. GNP can be a misleading indicator of economic activity when inflation exists, however. Real GNP is a more reliable indicator of production over time because it adjusts for the distortions that inflation causes.

FIGURE 8-3

GNP and Real GNP: Two Measures of Production. Gross national product measures the dollar value of national output for each year. GNP has increased rapidly in the years since 1960. Not all of this increase in GNP is due to higher levels of output, however. GNP can also increase due to inflation, which increases the dollar value of output without necessarily increasing the quantity of goods and services produced. Real GNP is a measure of national output that adjusts for changing prices. It rises only when a larger quantity of final goods and services is produced. Real GNP has grown less rapidly than GNP in the period shown. The difference between the two lines in the figure is the accumulated impact of inflation. The color bars indicate recessions, which are periods when real GNP fell.

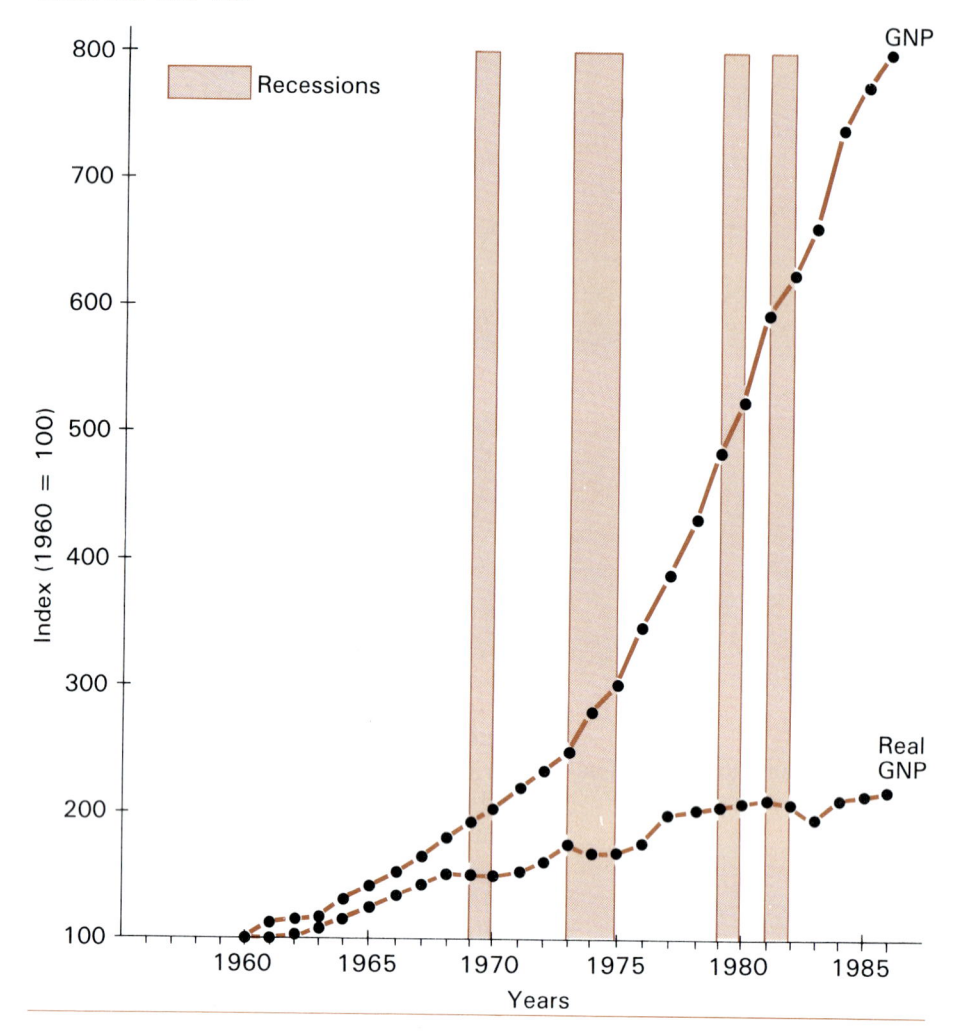

GROSS NATIONAL PRODUCT AND THE QUALITY OF LIFE

The development of the concepts of gross national product and national income accounting was a major step forward for economists in the 1940s. This breakthrough began an era in which economists could measure changes in the output, income, and employment of the economy and recommend steps to improve the economic conditions of the times. It also began a period in which government and other sectors of the economy would play a much more active role in the control and operation of the economy in which they existed. As economist Kenneth Boulding has noted,

> the Gross National Product is one of the great inventions of the twentieth century, probably almost as significant as the automobile and not quite so significant as T.V. The effect of physical inventions is obvious, but social inventions like the GNP change the world almost as much.[1]

8.10 GNP AND QUALITY OF LIFE

In spite of its great contribution to economic science, GNP is still widely misunderstood by the general population and the news media. In recent years, we have come to associate a rising GNP with a rising standard of living and quality of life. GNP is really only an indicator of short-term changes in the productive activity of an economy. It measures output in dollar terms; consequently, there are many shortcomings to this concept as a measure of the standard of living or quality of life in an economy. For example, $1000 worth of output appears identically in GNP whether it is the production of $1000 worth of heart surgery to save a person's life or a $1000 set of custom-made golf clubs to entertain that same person. Obviously the surgery contributes more to life than the golf clubs, but GNP cannot differentiate between the two. This illustrates one of several reasons why GNP cannot measure the quality of life.

GNP does not take into account changes in the quality of goods produced. Just 40 years ago, there were no hand-held calculators, wonder drugs such as tetracycline, oral contraceptives, or home computers. The television sets and many other goods that existed were of poor quality and performance compared to today's standards. GNP has no way of accounting for the contribution to the quality of life that these new and/or improved goods have made. A television set that cost $500 in 1947 has the exact same effect on GNP as a television set that costs $500 today, even though the new set may be capable of color, receive 36 channels, and answer the telephone, as well.

GNP does not consider the overall mix of output. The specific goods and services that an economy produces change over time and this affects the quality of life. During war time, the U.S. economy has produced massive amounts of airplanes, tanks, and other weapons and has given up some of the production of many consumer items, such as ladies fashions and domestic automobiles. The dollar amount of GNP has usually been higher during war time than in the periods of peace directly before and after war. This, however, does not imply that the quality of life in the economy was better during war time production. These days, many city dwellers spend money on "defensive expenditures" for such things as dead-bolt locks and window bars in order to make their homes safer. These items enter GNP with the same weight as any other expenditure, but they do not make us better off in any positive sense; they are attempts to prevent negative events. The overall mix of output can and does affect the quality of life in an economy.

Leisure is also not measured in GNP. The average work week has declined to approximately 40 hours from 50 hours in the 1920s. There is no allowance in the computation of GNP for the value of the extra leisure that today's workers enjoy. In 1982, workers in Poland went on strike and finally rioted over several work-related issues, one of which was reducing their

---

1. Kenneth Boulding, "Fun and Games with the Gross National Product — The Role of Misleading Indicators in Social Policy," in Harold W. Helfrich, Jr., ed., *The Environmental Crisis*, New Haven, CT: Yale University Press, 1970, p. 157.

work week from six to five days. Obviously, leisure time is a desired good that contributes to the quality of life, but it is not measured in GNP.

Production affects the environment and quality of life in ways that GNP cannot take into account. The production of goods and services frequently also means the production of pollutants that reduce environmental quality and, therefore, the quality of life. There is always an opportunity cost associated with the satisfaction of a set of wants and desires. The external costs that production places on society are sometimes very large, and yet they are not accounted for in the computation of GNP. This makes it impossible for GNP to measure the quality of life.

To place the concept of GNP in its proper perspective, we should realize that our modern economic policies that attempt to stabilize and improve economic conditions could not function effectively without this means of measurement. While **stabilization policies** are a long way from perfect, they have been able to eliminate the very depths of depressions such as were suffered in the late 1920s and early 1930s. We owe much of this success to national income accounting. We should, however, be mindful of its limitations, as expressed by Simon Kuznets, the Nobel Prize winner credited with the development of measuring national economic performance. As early as 1946, Kuznets stated that national income

> gauges the net positive contribution to consumers' satisfaction in the form of commodities and services: the burdens of work and discomfort are ignored . . . it is claimed that the monotony and dissatisfaction to the individual as an individual due to greater specialization and repetition of a few motions have increased, and that so has the nervous tension. . . .This aspect of economic activity . . . warns us against too easy an acceptance of the thesis that a high national income is the sole consideration in theory or the dominant motive in fact in a nation's economy.[2]

Stabilization Policies
Government policies designed to dampen swings in economic activity, reduce the impact of recessions, and moderate inflation.

THE GOAL OF ECONOMIC GROWTH

High rates of both inflation and unemployment in the 1970s and 1980s have substantially increased public interest in the topic of economic growth. Prior to that time, each new generation of consumers looked forward with some confidence to a higher standard of living than that of their parents. Increases in real income are a result of increases in real output, and the American economy has enjoyed an overall upward trend in its real output since World War II.

Economic growth is important, not only because it provides an increased standard of living, but also because it enables the economy to devote resources to new needs that develop over time without reducing the current standard of living. For example, in the last decade, the American economy has placed an increased emphasis on pollution control. More productive resources were allocated to cleaning up the environment than ever before. Without economic growth, this new use of resources would have implied a need to reduce goods and services used to satisfy other previously existing wants and needs.

2. Simon Kuznets, *National Income: A Summary of Findings*, New York: National Bureau of Economic Research, 1946, pp. 127–128.

PROMINENT ECONOMIST

Simon Kuznets (1901–1985)

Simon Kuznets, the 1971 recipient of the Nobel Memorial Prize in Economics, was largely responsible for developing the important concepts of the national income and product accounts that are discussed in this chapter. Kuznets built the framework of measurement and analysis upon which all macroeconomic theory and policy rests today.

Economists had attempted to compile measures of national economic performance for centuries, but their efforts were incomplete and often inaccurate. Kuznets pioneered the comprehensive, accurate measurement and analysis of national income and gross national product that we use today. His 1941 two-volume work, *National Income and Its Composition: 1919 to 1938*,[1] brought macroeconomics into a new modern era where quantitative measurement, analysis, and forecasting were possible. The measurements that Kuznets developed are so fundamental to economics today that most modern economists cannot imagine a world without them.

Simon Kuznets was born in Russia in 1901. He emigrated to the United States in 1921 and enrolled in Columbia University, a leading center of economic analysis. He earned his B.A., M.S., and Ph.D. degrees in economics at Columbia. Kuznets was associated with the National Bureau of Economic Research (NBER), a private association dedicated to economic analysis, for nearly all of his professional life. It was while working at the NBER in the 1930s and 1940s that he did some of his most path-breaking work.

Kuznets wore many professional hats during his lifetime. He was a noted scholar, but he was also an important teacher at the University of Pennsylvania, Johns Hopkins, and Harvard, where he retired in 1971. He received many professional honors and served as president of the American Economic Association, the American Statistical Association, and the Econometric Society.

In awarding Kuznets the Nobel Prize, the Swedish Royal Academy of Science praised his research that created an "empirically founded interpretation of economic growth, which has led to new and deeper insight into the economic and social structure and the process of development."

1. Simon Kuznets, *National Income and Its Composition: 1919 to 1938,* New York: National Bureau of Economic Research, 1941.

The goal of economic growth is widely accepted, but some people are critical of the emphasis on economic expansion. While much of economics is based upon the oversimplified concept that "more is preferred to less," some individuals and groups feel differently. Some environmental groups not only advocate more resources being devoted to pollution control but also favor activities that would clearly reduce the rate of economic growth. Legal actions have been undertaken to prevent further development of government-owned wilderness lands, to restrict or eliminate off-shore development of energy sources, and even to prohibit the sale of government lease rights to natural resources such as timber and crude oil. The economics literature of the late 1970s and 1980s contains many books and articles on the "steady state," an economy that operates at a constant level of output over time without substantial economic growth. Many people view the steady state, not economic growth, as the correct goal for the economy. The goal of economic growth is likely to remain controversial and newsworthy for many years to come.

MEASURING ECONOMIC GROWTH

Economic growth is usually measured as an increase in the real output of the economy per unit of time. Changes in real gross national product (real GNP) are therefore the basis for measurements of economic growth. For example, from 1983 to 1984, real GNP increased from $3,277.7 billion to $3,492.0 billion, a growth rate of 6.5 percent. Real GNP is used to measure economic growth even though, as is the case with GNP, it does not measure the quality of life or our standard of living. Real GNP is therefore an imperfect measure of economic growth.

Table 8-7 lists GNP, real GNP, and some other measures of economic growth in the United States from 1960 to 1985. The table shows that the U.S. economy has roughly doubled in total output since 1960, as measured by real GNP. We have also experienced several recessions during this period, as indicated by a decline in real GNP for one or more years. Recessions are identified by negative percentage changes in real GNP in the table.

One problem with real GNP as a measure of economic growth is that, while it is adjusted for inflation, it does not take into account changes in the size of the population that affect the meaning of this growth measure. A 10 percent increase in real output has a different meaning when the population is growing by 10 percent, for example, than if the population is stable. **Per capita real GNP,** which is also shown in the table, takes these population changes into account. Per capita real GNP, which is equal to real GNP divided by the size of the population, is the best measure of economic growth over long periods of time when population change is significant. This takes into consideration not only growth in economic output but also the population's growth. It is possible for real GNP to rise but per capita real GNP to fall during a period of slow economic growth. The increase in output in such a period might not keep pace with the rise in population. This is sometimes called a **growth recession** because the economy is growing, but not by enough to prevent living standards from falling. Remember, however, that GNP figures measure production only. They do not necessarily measure economic welfare.

Another problem with the use of real GNP as a measure of economic growth is that, from a theoretical standpoint, an increase in real GNP can mean one of two different things. Sometimes an increase in real GNP means that the economy's ability to produce has increased, thereby causing an outward shift in the economy's production possibilities frontier. This is economic growth as we have used the term earlier in the text. At other times, however, real GNP rises as the economy recovers from a recession that has depressed production and moved the economy to the interior of the PPF. The increase in real GNP that occurs in this year moves the economy to the border of the PPF, increasing production and income in the economy, but it may not shift the PPF outward.

Many economists and policymakers are concerned that the U.S. economy is experiencing slower economic growth in recent years than it did earlier in this century. They are concerned that much of the increase in production that takes place is recovery from recessions, which are movements back toward the PPF boundary, and not real growth that would shift the PPF boundary outward. There is, therefore, a renewed concern that government should be doing more to encourage economic growth.

8.11 MEASURING ECONOMIC GROWTH

Per Capita Real GNP
A measure of economic growth that takes into consideration both changes in output and population growth.

TABLE 8-7 — Measures of Economic Growth, 1960–1985

Year	Nominal GNP ($ billions)	Real GNP ($ billions)	Percentage change real GNP	Population (in millions)	Real GNP per capita	Percentage change in productivity
1960	515.3	1665.3	2.2	180.7	9215	1.7
1961	533.8	1708.7	2.6	183.7	9301	3.5
1962	574.6	1799.4	5.3	186.5	9646	3.6
1963	606.9	1873.3	4.1	189.2	9899	4.0
1964	649.8	1973.3	5.3	191.9	10,281	4.3
1965	705.1	2087.6	5.8	194.3	10,741	3.0
1966	772.6	2208.3	5.8	196.6	11,230	2.8
1967	816.4	2271.4	2.9	198.7	11,431	2.7
1968	892.7	2365.6	4.1	200.7	11,783	2.7
1969	963.9	2423.3	2.4	202.7	11,953	0.1
1970	1015.5	2416.2	−0.3	204.9	11,791	0.7
1971	1102.7	2484.8	2.8	207.0	12,003	3.2
1972	1212.8	2608.5	5.0	208.8	12,490	3.2
1973	1359.3	2744.1	5.2	210.4	13,041	2.0
1974	1472.8	2729.3	−0.5	211.9	12,878	−2.1
1975	1598.4	2695.0	−1.3	213.6	12,617	2.0
1976	1782.8	2826.7	4.9	215.1	13,138	2.8
1977	1990.5	2958.6	4.7	216.9	13,637	1.7
1978	2249.7	3115.2	5.3	218.7	14,243	0.8
1979	2508.2	3192.4	2.5	225.6	14,148	−1.2
1980	2732.0	3187.1	−0.2	227.7	13,996	−0.3
1981	3052.6	3248.8	1.9	229.8	14,134	1.5
1982	3166.0	3166.0	−2.5	232.0	13,646	−0.4
1983	3401.6	3277.7	3.5	234.2	13,992	2.6
1984	3774.7	3492.0	6.5	236.6	14,759	2.1
1985	3992.5	3626.9	2.3	238.8	14,962	0.3

Source. Economic Report of the President, 1986, Table B-1, B-2, B-30, B-44.

8.12 PRODUCTIVITY

Productivity
The amount of output per unit of labor input. The change in productivity is an important determinant of economic growth.

Another important measure of economic growth is the change in **productivity**. Productivity is defined as the real output produced per hour of labor. The economy tends to grow when workers are able to produce more. The increase in output per labor hour makes possible a higher standard of living for workers and others. The economy tends to stagnate and living standards deteriorate, however, when productivity falls. The last column in Table 8-7 shows how productivity has varied since 1960. Figure 8-4 provides graphic evidence of the close relationship between productivity and economic growth. There has been a very high correlation between changes in productivity and changes in real GNP in recent years.

One important question that economists have asked is, what causes rising productivity and economic growth? Most economists believe that investment is necessary to increase productivity and make the economy grow. This investment can take many forms. Some investment increases the economy's physical capacity to produce by building new factories and stores, for example. Other investments take the form of technological innovations or improvements that allow us to make more output from fewer resources. Investment in agricultural research, for example, has increased farm productivity dramatically in the last 50 years. Much of the world's economic

Gross National Product and Economic Growth

| TABLE 8-4 | **Investment, Productivity, and Economic Growth.** The nation's economic growth is measured by the annual change in real GNP. The United States has experienced relatively unstable growth, especially during the 1970s. Economic growth is highly correlated with the growth of worker productivity. This figure shows that both economic growth and productivity (measured on the left-hand scale) tend to follow the trend in investment spending (measured on the right-hand scale). Investment spending increases the capital stock, modernizes equipment, and generates technological change. Relatively large changes in investment spending are required to produce a given change in productivity and economic growth. |

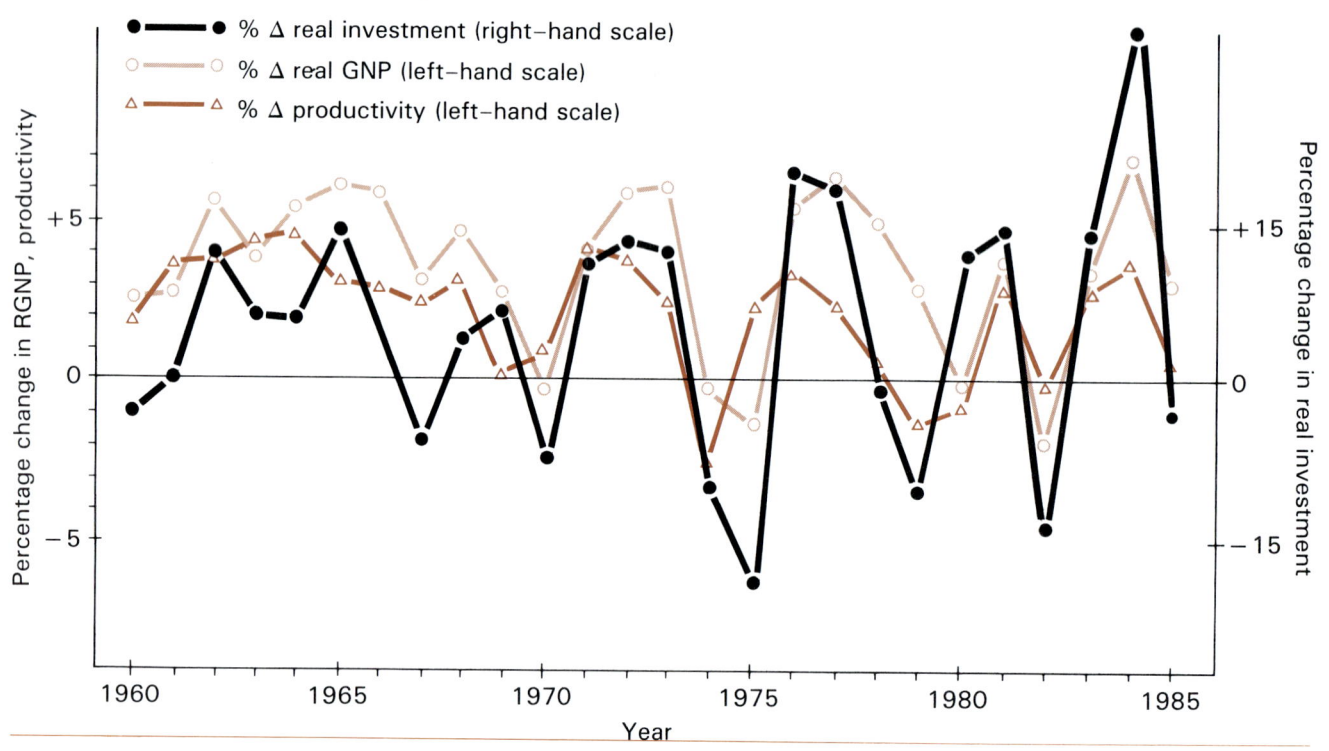

growth in the twentieth century is the result of investments, such as those in agricultural research, that improved technology. In fact, it has been estimated that about 50 percent of the economic growth of the U.S. economy since 1929 has come from technological improvements. Increases in the productive capacity with no change in technology accounted for about 15 percent of growth. Finally, some investment takes the form of investment in people, through education and training programs that make workers better able to use the tools available to them.

Investment spending is desirable because it tends to improve technology, increase productivity, and stimulate economic growth. But investment spending involves a trade-off. The resources that we invest today are not available for consumption today. We must save today in order to invest and grow in the future. The college student who has $10,000 available, for example, must decide between the purchase of a new car and investment in a college education. This trade-off applies to all investments. Saving is therefore a desirable activity because it provides resources that can be used for investment.

Depreciation
The decline in the value of productive assets, such as equipment and structures, due to their wearing out. Depreciation can be thought of as the investment necessary to offset the wearing out of capital goods. Depreciation is sometimes listed as capital consumption allowance in the GNP accounts.

Net Investment
Gross investment minus depreciation.

We noted earlier in this chapter that some investment spending each year goes to replace or repair productive goods that were produced in previous years. This is called **depreciation.** Only investment spending over and above this depreciation actually increases our ability to produce and, therefore, fosters economic growth. Economists therefore calculate the economy's **net investment,** which is gross investment minus depreciation costs. Net investment is the best measure of additions to the economy's physical productive capacity. Increases in net investment tend to promote economic growth. Net investment was actually negative during some years of the Great Depression, which indicates that the economy's ability to produce actually declined.

Figure 8-4 shows that changes in investment spending are highly correlated with changes in productivity and economic growth. Increases in productivity and growth have been closely associated with increased investment spending in the years since 1960. Decreases in investment spending, on the other hand, have been associated with falling productivity and negative economic growth. Most economists are therefore concerned that we achieve high, stable levels of investment spending in order to achieve rapid, stable economic growth. The dramatic swings in investment spending illustrated in Figure 8-4 are one reason, but far from the only reason, for the changes in productivity and economic growth shown here.

KEY CONCEPTS
8.11, 8.12

Economic growth is very important for the economy. We can measure economic growth as the increase in real GNP over time or as the increase in per capita real GNP over time. Economic growth is closely associated with increases in worker productivity. Investments in capacity and improved technology promote rising productivity and economic growth.

VESTED INTERESTS AND ECONOMIC GROWTH

8.13 VESTED INTERESTS

There are many possible explanations of why the United States has experienced relatively slow economic growth in recent decades. It is possible that inflation-caused bracket creep in the 1970s increased marginal tax rates that have reduced the incentives to work, produce, save, and invest. It is possible that ambitious government regulations have put up unintentional roadblocks to growth. It is possible that crowding-out and uncertainty about inflation and economic events have reduced investment in capital goods, education, and technology. Economist Mancur Olson, in his influential book *The Rise and Decline of Nations,*[3] presents an additional theory of slow growth. Olson notes that the slow growth problem is not unique to the United States. Most developed nations have experienced a slowing of their growth rate, yet some still grow faster than others. Table 8-8 gives comparative data about economic growth for the major developed nations.

Why do some nations grow faster than others, and why do all developed nations seem to be growing at a slower rate? Olson has reviewed many general explanations and finds that they do not explain all the cases shown

---

3. Mancur Olson, *The Rise and Decline of Nations*, New Haven, CT: Yale University Press, 1982.

ECONOMIC ISSUES

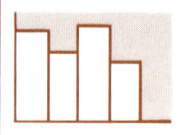

Anatomy of the Great Depression

The Great Depression of the 1930s was the most severe economic downturn to hit the United States and other world economies in recent history. Production and income fell dramatically during the Depression, putting millions of people out of work in the United States and around the world and leaving millions more with reduced standards of living. We can get something of a feel for what happened during the Great Depression by analyzing the GNP accounts for the most serious of the Depression years: 1929-1934. This analysis is presented in the accompanying table.

The U.S. economy experienced a major decrease in production and income during the years 1929 through 1934, as shown in the table. Real GNP fell by an astounding 30 percent between 1929 and 1933. This means that 30 percent fewer goods and services were being produced and that 30 percent less income was being generated in the economy. The table

GNP Accounts and the Great Depression

Item	1929	1930	1931	1932	1933	1934
Real GNP	203.6	183.5	169.3	144.2	141.5	154.3
Consumption	139.6	130.4	126.1	114.8	112.8	118.1
Durables	16.3	12.9	11.2	8.4	9.4	11.7
Non-durables	69.3	65.3	65.6	60.4	58.6	62.5
Services	54.0	51.5	49.4	45.9	46.0	49.1
Gross Investment	40.4	27.4	16.8	4.7	5.3	9.4
Fixed	36.9	28.0	19.2	10.9	9.7	12.1
Inventories	3.5	−0.6	−2.4	−6.2	−4.3	−2.7
Government	22.0	24.3	25.4	24.2	23.3	26.6
Federal	3.5	4.0	4.3	4.6	6.0	8.0
State – Local	18.5	20.2	21.1	19.6	17.3	18.6
Net exports	1.5	1.4	0.9	0.0	0.3	−1.0
Exports	11.8	10.4	8.9	7.1	7.1	7.3
Imports	10.3	9.0	7.9	6.6	7.1	7.1

Note. All figures are in billions of 1958 dollars.
Source. Economic Report of the President, 1971, Table C-2.

in Table 8-8. Olson's own theory is that special-interest groups are the most likely explanation for changes in growth rates. Olson holds that growth is inhibited when many narrow special-interest groups are able to distort the economy over a long period of time.

Here is how Olson's argument, much simplified, goes. It is always costly and difficult for groups of people to organize in their own self-interest. Some groups, such as labor unions, farmer cooperatives, and employers' associations do organize, however, when the benefits of organization are greater than the associated costs. Frequently, one of the benefits of organization is the ability, through the political system, to influence public policy in the group's favor. Organized workers in the railway industry, for example, may be able to get regulations passed that require railroads to hire more employees than are absolutely necessary for the safe and efficient operation of trains.

shows that the Depression resulted from changes in the four major expenditure categories of the GNP accounts: consumption, investment, government, and net export spending.

The table shows that consumption spending fell by about 20 percent during the early years of the Great Depression. Households purchased about 20 percent fewer final goods and services for their own use. It is not surprising that people would purchase less when their incomes fall. The table shows that the most significant spending cuts were in consumer durables such as automobiles, furniture, and household appliances. These are important sectors of the economy, providing jobs and incomes for millions of workers. Spending on consumer durables fell by almost 50 percent during the early years of the Depression. Consumer spending on nondurable goods and services also fell during these years, but by a much smaller percentage than did spending on durable items.

Investment spending also suffered a significant decrease in the Depression's early years. Investment in fixed capital and structures suffered the deepest cuts, falling by almost 75 percent in the first four years of the Depression. As we have seen, changes in investment spending are highly correlated with changes in productivity and economic growth. The huge decrease in investment spending therefore contributed to the Depression in two ways. First, falling investment spending directly resulted in falling income. If no one is purchasing factory equipment, for example, toolmakers shut down and lay off their workers. Thus falling investment spending contributes to falling household income, which leads to falling spending and income in other parts of the economy. Falling investment also contributed to the Depression because the lack of sufficient investment spending contributed to falling worker productivity and, therefore, to falling production and incomes in other sectors of the economy.

The table also shows an important shift in inventory investment. Inventory investment was positive in 1929, an indication that businesses were stocking their shelves and warehouses, anticipating rising future sales. Inventory investment became negative in the later years of the Depression, however, showing that firms were actually ordering fewer new goods than they were selling. This lack of new business orders also contributed to the economic decline.

Total government spending rose somewhat during the Depression years, as shown in the table, an indication that government spending at least partially offset falling spending in other sectors of the economy. Note two things, however. First, increases in government spending were most apparent in the federal government sector, which was much smaller than the combined state and local governments in the 1930s. Note, second, that the largest increases in federal government spending did not occur until late in the period shown here and so did relatively little to fight the depression trend in the early years of economic decline.

Net export spending also contributed to the falling real GNP of the Great Depression. The major trading countries of the world were all experiencing falling production and income in these years. Many nations adopted economic policies designed to reduce imports from abroad in an attempt to concentrate spending and income at home. The result, as the table shows, was mutually destructive. Imports fell in the United States during this period, but exports also fell and by a greater amount in the end. In spite of high trade barriers that kept many imported goods out of the economy, the U.S. net export position had worsened by 1934 to the point where we were actually exporting less than we were importing.

The Great Depression was a devastating economic event. The GNP accounts shown here help us understand what was happening to the U.S. economy during these early Depression years. In Chapter 10 we will look at one theory of why the economy changed in this way.

This regulation benefits the railway union members, but it hurts the economy by making rail transportation services more expensive than they would otherwise be. Farmers and ranchers must pay more to get their goods to market, while consumers must pay more for the final goods they buy. Less trade takes place because of the higher transportation costs. This distorts the economy, makes it less efficient, and slows economic growth. The railroad workers are hurt along with everyone else by the slower economic growth, but they are still net gainers because they receive all of the benefits of the regulations but bear only a little of the economy's slow-growth cost.

Olson suggests that, over time, special-interest groups tend to grow both in size and number in the economy. These interest groups introduce economic rigidities into the economy that make it more and more difficult to introduce new technologies and efficient economic reforms that could in-

| TABLE 8-8 | Average Annual Growth in Real Per Capita Gross Domestic Product (in percent) |

Country	1950–1960	1960–1970	1970–1980
Australia	2.0	3.7	2.4
Austria	5.7	3.9	3.8
Belgium	2.0	4.1	3.1
Canada	1.2	3.7	3.1
Denmark	2.5	3.9	2.2
Finland	3.3	4.2	2.5
France	3.5	4.6	3.0
West Germany	6.6	3.5	2.4
Ireland	1.8	3.8	2.3
Italy	4.9	4.6	2.1
Japan	6.8	9.4	3.8
Netherlands	3.3	4.1	2.3
New Zealand	1.7	2.2	—
Norway	2.7	4.0	3.9
Sweden	2.9	3.6	1.2
Switzerland	2.9	2.8	−0.1
United Kingdom	2.3	2.3	2.0
United States	1.2	3.0	2.0

Source. Mancur Olson, *The Rise and Decline of Nations,* New Haven, CT: Yale University Press, 1982, Table 1.1, p. 6. Reprinted by permission of the publisher.

crease economic growth. These rigidities include regulations, price controls, and restrictions on competition both within the economy and with other nations. Economic growth slows over time until something happens to weaken or break the rigidities that the special interests have imposed on the economy. Examples of events that can break the special interests' grip include defeat in war or a major change in technology. One reason why the United Kingdom grew so quickly in the 19th century, according to Olson, is that the industrial revolution broke up the special interests of the agricultural economy that had previously dominated. This made all sorts of changes possible that increased efficiency.

Olson cites Japan as an example of how defeat in war can lead to rapid economic growth. Many people assume that Japan's high growth rates in the 1950s and 1960s were the result of their more modern technology. It is frequently assumed that Japan's industrial base was destroyed in World War II and that they were therefore forced to invest in modern technology in the 1950s. These modern facilities, it is thought, enabled Japan to grow relative to the United States, where older technology was still in use. Olson shows that this is not a good explanation of Japan's growth. Japan's industrial base was not destroyed in World War II, yet producers in Japan replaced their existing factories with new equipment, while similar producers in the United States and other nations did not. What war defeat and the subsequent Allied occupation did, according to Olson, was break up the special interests that had previously existed in Japan, which acted as roadblocks to technological change. The sudden lack of economic rigidities made it possible for Japan to efficiently increase production and adopt new technologies.

Olson suggests that the growth of new special-interest groups in Japan, and other countries, is why growth rates have generally slowed in recent years. Countries like the United States and United Kingdom, where special interests have had the most time to grow and spread, are the most likely to experience slow growth now. The figures in Table 8-8 tend to support Olson's hypothesis.

Olson does not recommend that nations enter and lose wars in order to experience more rapid economic growth. Rather, Olson calls for reductions in barriers to international trade as a way to reduce the power of domestic special interests. Increased competition from abroad can force unions and employers groups, for example, to adopt more efficient production and pricing rules, which in turn can help the economy grow. Increased competition from the Japanese auto industry, for example, has been a factor in forcing the United Auto Workers union to grant concessions to employers that have increased production flexibility and efficiency. In other words, Olson suggests that the U.S. economy can grow if we let free trade force domestic special-interest groups to compete with foreign special interests. Olson holds that member nations of the Common Market have experienced relatively high economic growth rates because of the effect of free trade within the Common Market on internal special-interest rigidities.

Mancur Olson's theory is not the only explanation of how and why nations grow and fail to grow. No single idea can hope to explain all the variables, such as productivity, technology, and so on, that contribute to growth. Olson's analysis does, however, provide important insights into the problems of growth and the forces that sometimes stifle the growth process.

INDUSTRIAL DEVELOPMENT POLICY

These days more and more people are becoming aware of the importance of economic growth to the nation. Economists and policymakers have searched for ways to stimulate economic growth. Some people have suggested that the private sector is too interested in the status quo to be an effective engine of growth. Some proponents of pro-growth policies have suggested that government should take a more active role in promoting economic growth.

8.14 INDUSTRIAL DEVELOPMENT POLICY

Industrial Development Policy
A set of government policies designed to encourage growth, investment, and technological change in specific industries.

One controversial proposal designed to encourage economic growth is a national **industrial development policy.** An industrial development policy is a set of public policies designed to encourage rapid economic growth. Most proposals for an industrial development policy share the same basic properties. First, an industrial development bank would be set up to provide low-cost investment funds to selected industries. This bank would borrow from the credit markets through the federal government. These funds would then be re-loaned to selected firms and industries at lower interest rates than they would otherwise pay.

A second part of most industrial development plans involves granting government subsidies to certain groups that are identified as key growth-producing sectors of the economy. Growth in the high-technology sector of the economy, for example, tends to increase growth rates in other parts of the economy, as technological advances filter into the production of other goods. Subsidies might be given to encourage research or production of high-tech items.

Third, industrial development policies generally include some system for getting labor and management groups together, to get them to adopt wage and employment plans that are more likely to generate economic growth. The overall idea is that an activist public policy can increase investment, channel this investment into areas where it will generate the most growth, and induce labor and management to act together to produce efficiently.

Many politicians and some economists favor these plans for industrial development policies. They cite slow economic growth in recent years as evidence that the current system is not working to generate growth in the United States. They cite the more active government intervention in industrial policy in Japan as evidence of the potential for these policies to produce economic growth.

Plans for broad industrial development programs are opposed by many economists, however; although they may favor certain aspects of these plans, such as increased labor–management cooperation. Opponents often note that slow economic growth is partly the result of government regulations and tax policies that discourage investment and production. There are many potential drawbacks to industrial development policies. For example, there is no reason to believe that a national industrial development board will be able to accurately identify and efficiently encourage the growth industries of the future.

People who favor public policies in this area point out that Japan's regulatory agencies successfully stimulated key industries in many cases. Opponents, however, can cite other cases in which Japan's industrial policy made choices that are, in retrospect, obvious mistakes. Some growth industries were actually discouraged, while firms that subsequently declined received government assistance. It is impossible to be sure that a government loan agency will channel funds where they are the most useful. It is indeed possible that the result will be that new firms are crowded-out of the credit markets by government borrowing, thereby resulting in slower growth.

A more telling criticism of industrial development policies is that they might, following Mancur Olson's analysis, be used by special-interest groups to impose additional rigidities that further slow economic growth. An industrial development policy would be subject to political influence. Existing special-interest groups are the ones that are most able to influence political decisions. It is possible that low-interest loans and government subsidies would be used to increase the incomes of these special interests. Old industries might be protected by these subsidies, while emerging new industries are starved for capital. Labor and management might work together to erect additional trade barriers that keep out foreign competition that would benefit the economy.

It is impossible to know in advance whether the benefits of coherent public policies concerning economic growth will outweigh the costs of regulation and potential economic distortions. The issues just discussed are likely to prove critical in the future, however, as the emphasis on economic growth in the United States increases.

JAPAN: A TEXTBOOK CASE IN GROWTH POLICY

We can learn something about the factors that encourage economic growth by considering the success story of Japan. In the early 1950s the term "made in Japan" was something that consumers saw labeled on toys, Christmas ornaments, and what at the time were considered cheap, low quality goods of all types. Competition in the world market from this tiny nation about half the size of the state of Texas (143,000 square miles) was more a

8.15 JAPAN'S ECONOMIC GROWTH

source of humor than reality. In the last 30 years, however, consumers have noticed a substantial flow of Japanese manufactured goods into the world marketplace. Hardly a single household exists in the United States that does not possess at least one major Japanese product. The areas of electronics, automobiles, textiles, musical instruments, aircraft, and everyday consumer items from flatware and china to home furnishings have felt the strong competition of the Japanese economy.

How did Japan, with its relatively small population and narrow resource base, grow to produce the third largest gross national product in the world in just 30 years? The natural resources of Japan are relatively limited. Crude oil, coal, and other energy sources are very scarce in this island nation; yet the per capita gross national product of Japan is only about 20 percent less than that of the United States. The 30-year growth rate of Japanese economy has averaged over 9 percent per year, while other major industrialized countries have experienced average growth rates in the 3 percent to 4 percent range.

As previously noted, Mancur Olson's theory of special-interest groups suggests that Japan's rapid growth is the result of the breakdown in vested interests following World War II and the Allied occupation. The weakened special interests allowed efficient changes in the economy that would not have been possible otherwise. Economists have noted other important growth-producing factors in Japan, however. Other explanations for Japan's growth record revolve around public policy in the areas of personal income taxes, tax incentives on savings and investment, and the relationships between labor and management.

Taxes, Workers, and Employers

The major natural resource possessed by the Japanese economy after World War II was its labor force. Like all people, Japanese workers respond to the incentives offered them. Personal income taxes in Japan, compared to other industrialized nations such as France or Britain, are approximately 20 percent less. Average Japanese workers pay about 17 percent of their earnings in income taxes, while workers in the economies of France or Britain face between 21 percent and 24 percent of their incomes as a tax burden. This creates a strong incentive for Japanese workers to work.

The unusual characteristics of labor–management relationships in Japan also play a role. Many Japanese industrial workers, especially those who work for the largest corporations, are employed for life and have substantial job security. Also, the traditional labor–management confrontations with which the American economy is familiar are not as severe in Japan. Since they are employed by that firm for life, Japanese workers have significant personal financial incentives to see that their employer experiences long-run prosperity. Therefore, the relationship between labor and management, which is shaped by these personal financial incentives, is more one of cooperation than conflict. Public policies in the areas of income and profits taxes, as well as protective import tariffs, have contributed to the set of positive incentives that labor and management face. Due to the supportive role of public policies in these and other areas of economic concern, the Japanese economy has been characterized as one of government-assisted capitalism.

Taxes, Saving, and Investment

The savings rate in the Japanese economy is very high compared to other industrialized nations of the world. Average Japanese workers save about 20 percent of their incomes, while their American counterparts save 5 percent. The tax incentives faced by these two groups of savers can go a long way to explain this difference. Interest earned on savings in Japan is taxed at much lower rates than in the U.S. economy. For example, a high-income saver in the United States could pay up to 50 percent in taxes on each additional dollar earned in interest on savings. If there is inflation, the tax on real interest can be much higher. For example, a taxpayer in the 50 percent tax bracket might receive 10 percent interest on saving during a year with 5 percent inflation. This is only a 5 percent real-interest return. Taxes are paid on the 10 percent nominal interest rate. In this situation, the effective tax on real interest is actually 100 percent because all the real returns are taxed away. This significantly discourages saving.

The maximum marginal tax rate levied on savings interest in Japan is 25 percent. All other things being equal, Japanese savers get to keep twice as much of each dollar of interest income as do their American counterparts. Japanese regulation of financial markets, however, keeps the interest return to savers lower in Japan than in the United States. The Japanese tend to save a high proportion of their income, which is loaned at relatively low interest rates to the federal government to finance deficit spending.

Investments receive preferential treatment in Japan. When a Japanese citizen realizes a capital gain from the sale of securities, that income is not taxed at all. Japanese tax structure also offers a variety of tax credits on different types of savings. For example, a family is permitted to save toward the down payment for a home without tax liability on the principle or interest.

The tax liabilities on capital gains realized from business investments are much lower in Japan than in the United States. Given the incentive structure faced by business investors, it is not surprising that the Japanese have devoted a very large part of their gross national product over the last 25 years to investment. As noted earlier, this process of accelerated capital accumulation contributes significantly to the future growth of the economy's aggregate supply constraint.

Technology in Japan

A third major source of growth in the Japanese economy has been the adaptation of advanced western technology to their production processes. In the early 1950s, Japan became noted for producing copies of Western goods. The ability to integrate an existing technology into their older production processes has moved the Japanese economy from the position of being the copier of technology to becoming a producer of technology. For example, the concept of industrial robots (robotics) was invented in the United States. Due to rigidities in the U.S. economy, many of which are the result of special-interest forces such as labor–management concerns, the United States economy was much slower in applying this invention to widespread industrial use than the Japanese. Given their smaller population, much less narrow special-interest groups, and more cooperative labor–management relationships, the Japanese integrated robotics into widespread industrial use much faster. This reduced their production costs and increased the quality of their products in the long run.

This process made their output in fields like automobiles first more competitive and then in some cases dominant in the marketplace. As the output of the Japanese economy has grown, it has enabled them not only to adapt existing Western technology but also to develop new technology of their own. This is visible, for example, in the field of voice actuated word-processing equipment. The Japanese have developed word processors that can produce a typed copy directly from dictation. An executive can simply pick up a microphone and dictate a letter that is interpreted and then typed by the machine. No secretary is needed. While this technology has not reached the stage of mass industrial production, it is certainly further along in Japan than in Western countries. This development of technology, along with the implementation of existing Western technology, has served to expand the growth rate of the Japanese economy.

Japan, it appears, is a classical textbook case of a growth economy. Its public policy has been geared toward the development of natural resources, technology, and capital accumulation. As with all industrialized nations, the growth of Japan has not been without its costs. Air and water pollution, public health, and traditional cultural values have experienced change over the last 30 years, and will no doubt see even more change in the future. Japan's growth rate has declined in recent years, due in part to the growth of special-interest rigidities and to other influences.

APPENDIX: THE NATIONAL INCOME AND PRODUCT ACCOUNTS

8.4 GROSS NATIONAL PRODUCT

The income and product accounts provide a wealth of interesting and important information about the economy. This appendix examines the details of the GNP accounts to learn more about how the economy works. The discussion here is based on the GNP accounts for 1984 given in Table 8-9.

GROSS NATIONAL PRODUCT AND NET NATIONAL PRODUCT

Net National Product (NNP)
Gross national product adjusted for the existence of depreciation.

The first step in unravelling GNP to find its roots is the calculation of **net national product (NNP)**. Earlier in this chapter, we discussed both the output and income of the economy as if none of our resources were used up in producing them. It makes sense that the market value of something is equal to the value of the resources that went into it plus the value of the profits or losses entrepreneurs incurred in producing and selling it. The market value of a new car represents the value of the steel, rubber, paint, wiring, engineering design, entrepreneurial skill, and other resources that went into its production. There are, however, some other resources that are used up or depleted in the process of production. For example, when a factory and its machines are operated for a year, this operation places wear and tear on them. Eventually they wear out. This resource of plant and equipment depreciates with its use. Eventually this fixed investment must be replaced.

TABLE 8-9 — GNP Accounts, 1984

Item	Amount ($ billions)
Gross national product	3661.3
less: depreciation	−402.9
Net national product	3258.4
less: indirect business taxes	−304.3
less: business transfer payments	−17.3
plus: subsidies–government surplus	+14.4
less: statistical error	−8.2
National income	2959.4
less: corporate profits	−284.5
less: net interest	−285.0
plus: personal interest income	+434.8
plus: personal dividend income	+77.7
less: social insurance taxes	−305.9
plus: personal transfer payments	+399.5
plus: business transfer payments	+17.3
Personal income	3013.2
less: personal tax payments	−435.1
Disposable personal income	2578.1
less: personal consumption	−2342.3
less: interest paid to business	−77.7
less: transfers to foreigners	−1.1
Personal saving	156.9
plus: business saving	518.4
plus: state–local government saving	52.0
minus: federal government deficit	−176.4
Total saving	551.0

Note. Totals do not agree with Table 8-2 due to revised GNP data released in 1986.

Source. Economic Report of the President, 1985, Tables B-19, B-20, B-23.

As previously stated, accountants and economists call this process of the wearing out of fixed investment depreciation. If we measure the dollar value of all output in the economy, we get gross national product, but we must make sure that an allowance is made in this figure for the fixed investment that was worn out to produce it. Therefore, we subtract the depreciation figure from the investment account in gross national product to get net national product.

$$\text{GNP} = C + I_{gross} + G + X_n$$
$$\text{NNP} = C + I_{net} + G + X_n,$$

or

$$\text{Gross investment} - \text{depreciation} = \text{net investment}$$
$$\text{GNP} - \text{depreciation} = \text{NNP}$$

Net national product gives us a truer picture of the value of output that was produced. It tells us how much output we have left after the allowance for wear and tear, or depreciation, is subtracted.

8.3 NATIONAL INCOME

NATIONAL INCOME

Net national product includes some income that resources in the economy earn but that they do not receive because the government takes it. Governments have the power to tax as well as spend and can affect the circular flow. Government takes part of national income through its powers to tax. It spends its tax revenues in both the product and resource markets. Governments levy a nonincome expense item in the form of social security contributions and sales, excise, and property taxes. These **indirect business taxes** produce income for government, which is not returned directly to households in the form of income payments. These indirect business taxes are subtracted from net national product when we calculate national income because, while they are income and earned by households, they are collected from business firms and therefore not actually received by households.

Three other items that enter into the calculation of national income in Table 8-9 should be noted here. Businesses make some transfer payments to households. Businesses, in effect, collect funds from employees as pension and disability contributions and then pay these funds back to recipients. These transfer payments cannot be calculated as income for the economy because that would result in counting the funds both as income to the business and income to the household that eventually receives the funds. Business transfer payments are therefore subtracted from NNP in calculating national income in order to avoid double counting. Statistical errors also occur in calculating GNP and national income. Table 8-9 shows that these statistical errors enter as an adjustment item in the calculation of national income. Finally, we must consider government subsidies minus the current surplus of government-operated enterprises, such as government-owned railways and power stations. Subsidies are payments by the government to the producers of certain goods and services. These payments are included in national income because they are clearly income to their recipients. In order to avoid double counting, we must subtract from these subsidies the "profit" from government enterprises. This adjustment is made because the surplus revenues that the government receives from these enterprises are used to finance other government purchases or transfer payments. We would be guilty of double counting if we included these funds in national income both when the government receives them and then again when the government uses them.

Net national product less indirect business taxes, business transfer payments, statistical errors, and subsidies minus government-enterprise surplus gives us national income. National income, as noted earlier, is a good indicator of the income that is earned by the household sector of the economy.

Indirect Business Taxes
Social security contributions and other taxes that are imposed on households but collected from them indirectly through the business sector.

PERSONAL INCOME

Not all of the income counted in the national income calculation is available for the household sector to spend. Some income that is earned is not actually received by households for one reason or another. **Personal income** is calculated to estimate the income that households receive and can use to spend, save, or pay personal taxes. Several adjustments must be made in national income to arrive at personal income.

Personal Income
The income received by the household sector.

Retained Earnings
Profits from business operations that are not distributed to the owners of business. Retained earnings are used to finance future investments or other purchases.

Not all corporate and business profits are distributed to shareholders and so actually fall into the hands of households. To determine the amount of corporate income that households can spend, we must subtract corporate profits and net interest payments, then add back in the amount of personal interest, dividend, and business transfer income that individuals receive. This is a complicated way of subtracting business **retained earnings** from the accounts. Retained earnings are profits kept by businesses, which are not available to individuals. Through this process of adding and subtracting, we are left with the amount of business profits that households actually receive.

The final step in calculating personal income is to subtract social insurance taxes, which individuals cannot spend because they are deducted directly from their paychecks, and add in personal transfer payments. Government social security taxes (social insurance taxes) reduce the income of workers, while social security benefit checks (personal transfer payments) increase the disposable income of retired people. Our calculation of personal income takes both of these items into account. The result of this calculation, as Table 8-8 shows, is personal income, or the amount of income available for individual spending, saving, and the payment of personal taxes.

DISPOSABLE PERSONAL INCOME

Disposable Personal Income
The income available for households to spend or save.

Our above calculation of personal income did not account for the personal taxes, such as federal, state, and local income taxes, that we pay. These taxes represent income that we earn and receive but that cannot be spent because we pay it to the government. Taxes reduce our ability to save or to purchase goods and services. Table 8-9 subtracts personal tax payments to arrive at **disposable personal income.** Disposable income is the amount of personal income that is actually received, net of personal taxes, that we can choose to allocate to saving or to the purchase of goods and services. Economists believe that households make consumption choices based on the disposable personal income that they expect to receive, so personal disposable income is an important determinant of household spending behavior.

PERSONAL SAVING

Personal Saving
Saving by households. These resources are made available for investment spending and other uses. Total saving for the economy includes both personal saving and business retained earnings.

Table 8-9 shows how consumers allocated their personal disposable income in 1984. Of the $2578.1 billion of income available for spending, $2342.3 billion went for purchases of the goods and services that households desired. Another $77.7 billion went to pay interest to businesses for consumer loans. Transfer payments from U.S. households to residents of foreign nations amounted to $1.1 billion. This left a total of $156.9 billion in **personal saving.** Personal saving, plus the retained earnings of businesses, provide funds that can be used for investment spending to expand the economy's capacity and other activities.

TOTAL SAVING

Personal saving is a good measure of saving by households, but it tends to understate total saving in the economy. Corporations and state and local governments can also save. In fact, business saving is much larger than household saving these days. In 1984, for example, businesses added $518.4 billion to total saving on top of the $156.9 of personal saving. State and local governments saved an additional $52.0 billion in 1984, but the federal government deficit (negative saving) amounted to $176.4 billion. Total saving for the entire economy was therefore $551.0 billion. This total saving represents the amount that the economy has available for investment in new production capacity and technological improvements, among other things.

SUMMARY

8.1
1. The circular flow model shows the relationship between the household sector of the economy and the business sector. The household sector sells resources to the business sector, and the business sector sells goods and services to the household sector. Spending by the household sector therefore creates income for the business sector, income which the business sector then pays to households for their resources. This creates a circular flow between spending (by households) and income (received by households).

8.2
2. Product markets are where households purchase final goods and services from the business sector. Resource markets are where businesses purchase land, labor, capital, and entrepreneurial skill from the household sector. These two markets are the key links in the circular flow of spending and income.

8.3
3. National income is the sum of all wage, interest, profit, and rent income received in the economy in a given period of time. The lower loop of the circular flow model shows how national income is generated through resource markets.

8.4
4. Gross national product is the market value, in current prices, of all the final goods and services produced in an economy in a given period of time, usually a year. The upper loop of the circular flow model shows that GNP is generated when final goods and services are exchanged in product markets.

8.5
5. A stock concept, such as wealth, applies to the total amount of something that exists at a given moment in time. A flow concept, such as income, applies to changes that occur over a given period of time. GNP and national income are flow concepts because they describe the amount of final goods and services produced and income generated in a given period of time. GNP and national income do not measure the total amount of wealth that exists, which is a stock concept.

8.6
6. A complete circular flow model of the economy includes the financial, government, and foreign sectors, in addition to households and businesses. The financial sector receives funds from households and businesses in the form of saving and uses these resources to finance investment

spending. The government sector receives funds from households and businesses in the form of taxes and uses these resources to finance government spending. The foreign sector receives funds from households and businesses as payment for imports. It pays funds to the business sector in return for exports. The net effect of the foreign sector on the circular flow model is measured by net exports, which is the value of exports minus the value of imports.

8.7 ▶ 7. Final goods are goods and services that are purchased by their ultimate user (for a particular time period). Intermediate goods are items that are purchased by one economic agent and then resold to final users or used to make another final good that is sold during the same time period. GNP counts only the production of final goods because the same items would be counted twice if both final and intermediate goods were included in GNP. This would cause GNP to be an inaccurate measure of the value of goods and services produced.

8.8 ▶ 8. GNP can be calculated using the expenditure approach by summing the spending on final goods by households (consumption), businesses (investment), the government sector (government spending) and the foreign sector (net exports). GNP can also be calculated using the income approach by summing the wages, profits, interest, and rental incomes, then adjusting the total for the impact of depreciation, indirect business taxes, and other factors. Finally, GNP can be calculated by summing the value added by all production that takes place in the economy. Value added is defined to be the increase in the value of resources that occurs through production. This increase in value generates income and GNP.

8.9 ▶ 9. Real GNP is GNP adjusted for the impact of inflation. It is necessary to adjust GNP for rising prices during periods of inflation in order to arrive at a meaningful measure of production. GNP can rise, for example, if the amount of goods and services produced stays constant but their prices rise. This makes GNP a poor measure of production. Real GNP, on the other hand, is adjusted for price changes. Real GNP rises and falls when market production in the economy rises or falls, regardless of what happens to prices.

8.10 ▶ 10. GNP is not a measure of the quality of life. GNP measures the dollar value of goods that are produced, but it does not take into account their impact on human beings. Cigarettes enter GNP the same as anticancer drugs, for example. GNP also does not take into account changing technology or the quality of the goods themselves, only their prices and quantities. Leisure and environmental quality are ignored by the GNP calculation, although both are important to our quality of life.

8.11 ▶ 11. The percentage change in real GNP is one measure of the nation's economic growth. This shows the change in the amount of final goods and services produced, adjusted for inflation. Over longer periods of time, when population change is significant, per capita real GNP is a better measure of economic growth because it takes into account changes in both prices and population.

8.12 ▶ 12. Productivity is defined to be the real output produced per hour of labor input. Growth in productivity is a measure of economic growth because it measures our ability to produce more with a given amount of labor resources. Investment is an important determinant of productivity growth. Investment spending tends to increase the amount of capital per worker, which increases labor's ability to produce final goods and services. Technological change improves the capital that workers use in production, further increasing productivity.

8.13

13. Mancur Olson has developed a theory that predicts that interest groups, such as labor unions and manufacturers organizations, will tend to introduce structural rigidities such as price controls and work rules that reduce economic growth. Olson holds that these rigidities can be reduced, and growth promoted, through increased competition and international trade.

8.14

14. An industrial development policy would use government agencies to channel investment funds to particular sectors of the economy that are expected to generate high rates of economic growth. Those in favor of these policies hold that they would be effective because they would provide low-cost financing and government subsidies to selected industries and promote labor–management cooperation. Those who oppose industrial development policies do not believe that government planners can select growth industries any better than do private investors. They worry that these policies might merely protect old industries, not promote new ones.

8.15

15. The Japanese economy has experienced rapid economic growth during much of the post-World War II period. Many factors have contributed to high Japanese growth rates. Among these are lower taxes, a unique labor–management relationship, high rates of saving and investment, and rapid technological change in Japanese industry.

DISCUSSION QUESTIONS

8.1, 8.2, 8.6

1. The circular flow model illustrates transactions involving product and resource markets and the household, business, financial, government, and foreign sectors. Draw a complete circular flow diagram and provide real-world examples of each type of transaction or economic linkage among these markets and sectors.

8.1, 8.2, 8.3, 8.4, 8.6, 8.8

2. Most people are familiar with several basic economic documents, such as paycheck stubs, bank statements, dividend statements, and tax returns. Make a brief list of the types of information that each of these documents normally contains and explain how each item relates to the economic models and measures discussed in this chapter.

8.5

3. Explain the difference between a stock concept and a flow concept. Students normally receive two types of evaluation on their report cards: their current course grades and their overall grade-point and academic standing (including previous coursework). Which of these is a stock concept and which is a flow concept? Explain.

| 8.10 | 4. Explain why GNP is not a measure of the quality of life. List factors or information that would be included in a "quality of life" statistic. Why do you think that the government does not calculate and publish such a statistic? |

| 8.9 | 5. GNP increased in 1982, but real GNP fell. Explain how and why this can happen. Based on this, when should we be concerned about changes in GNP and when should we be more concerned about changes in real GNP? |

| 8.1, 8.2, 8.3, 8.4, 8.6, 8.8 | 6. Use the circular flow diagram to explain how GNP is calculated using the expenditure and the income approaches. |

| 8.11, 8.12 | 7. How do economists define growth? How is growth measured? What factors contribute to growth? |

| 8.13 | 8. Briefly state Mancur Olson's theory of why economic growth has declined in many industrial nations. Cite specific examples from the real world to either support or refute Olson's theory. |

| 8.14 | 9. Briefly state arguments in favor of and opposed to the institution of a national industrial development policy. What is your opinion on this issue? |

| 8.15 | 10. Discuss the factors that led to Japan's high levels of economic growth. Using Japan as a model, suggest policies that could encourage economic growth in the United States. |

SELECTED READINGS

Abraham, William L. *National Income and Economic Accounting.* Englewood Cliffs, NJ: Prentice-Hall, 1969.

Gordon, Robert Aaron. *Economic Instability and Growth: The American Record.* New York: Harper & Row, 1974.

Harberger, Arnold C. (Ed.). *World Economic Growth.* San Francisco: Institute for Contemporary Studies, 1984.

Heilbroner, Robert L. *Beyond Boom and Crash.* New York: W.W. Norton & Company, 1978.

Kuznets, Simon. *National Income and Its Composition: 1919 to 1938.* New York: National Bureau of Economic Research, 1941.

Kuznets, Simon. *National Income: A Summary of Findings.* New York: National Bureau of Economic Research, 1946.

Little, Ian M. *Economic Development: Theory, Policy, and International Relations.* New York: Basic Books, 1982.

McConnell, Campbell R. "Why is U.S. Productivity Slowing Down?" *Harvard Busines Review* (March – April 1979), pp. 36-60.

Olson, Mancur. *The Rise and Decline of Nations.* New Haven: Yale University Press, 1982.

U.S. Department of Commerce. *Survey of Current Business.* Washington, DC: U.S. Government Printing Office, monthly publication.

CHAPTER 9

Inflation and Unemployment: Problems, Policies, and Perspectives

Having read the chapter, reviewed the chapter summary, and completed the *Study Guide* exercises, you should be able to:

CRIS

9.1 MACROECONOMIC GOALS: List and describe the macroeconomic goals set out in the Employment Act of 1946 and the Humphrey–Hawkins Bill.

9.2 PROGRESS TOWARD GOALS: Discuss, in simple terms, how the economy has progressed toward its macroeconomic goals.

9.3 1960s ECONOMIC EVENTS: List and describe several important economic policies and events of the 1960s.

9.4 PHILLIPS CURVE: Draw the Phillips curve and explain what the Phillips curve relationship means and what it tells us about economic policies.

9.5 1970s ECONOMIC EVENTS: List and describe several important economic policies and events of the 1970s.

9.6 DISAPPEARANCE OF PHILLIPS CURVE: Discuss the possible reasons for the seeming disappearance of the Phillips curve relationship in the 1970s.

9.7 NATURAL UNEMPLOYMENT RATE: Explain what is meant by the natural unemployment rate and cite evidence for its existence.

9.8 1980s ECONOMIC EVENTS: List and describe several important economic policies and events of the 1980s.

9.9 MEASURING UNEMPLOYMENT: Explain how unemployment is measured and describe four problems that reduce the reliability of unemployment measures.

> **9.10 TYPES OF UNEMPLOYMENT:** Define and explain the concepts of cyclical, structural, and frictional unemployment.

> **9.11 FOUR QUESTIONS:** Discuss the four questions that we must ask in order to understand how serious the current unemployment problem is.

> **9.12 INFLATION:** Define inflation, and explain how inflation differs from deflation, disinflation, and price stability.

> **9.13 EFFECTS OF INFLATION:** List and explain the economic effects of inflation.

> **9.14 MEASURING INFLATION:** Explain how inflation is measured using a price index.

> **9.15 PRICE INDEXES:** List and describe the three most important price indexes used to measure inflation in the United States.

> **9.16 PRICE INDEX ADJUSTMENTS:** Explain how the price index can be used to adjust for inflation by converting nominal values into real values.

9.1 MACROECONOMIC GOALS

Employment Act of 1946
An act of Congress that created the President's Council of Economic Advisors and set the macroeconomic goals of price stability, full employment, and economic growth.

With the **Employment Act of 1946,** Congress set three official economic goals for the nation:

> The Congress hereby declares that it is the continuing policy and responsibility of the Federal Government to use all practicable means . . . to promote maximum employment, production, and purchasing power.[1]

The federal government's responsibility to achieve "maximum employment, production, and purchasing power" required that it attempt to achieve the goals of full employment, stable prices, and economic growth. These national economic goals are as important today as they were in 1946, but four decades of active economic policy have left the U.S. economy no closer to achieving them than it was in 1946. Inflation and unemployment remain serious economic problems today, and economic growth has been disappointing in recent decades.

Congress expanded the nation's list of economic goals with the Full Employment and Balanced Growth Act of 1978 (often called the Humphrey–Hawkins Bill). In addition to establishing new goals, this act spelled out strategies to use in achieving the old goals. The new goals this act introduced are important. They include a balanced federal government budget, which means that government spending should not exceed tax revenues, and an economy that is better able to compete on international markets. The act suggests that these goals be achieved by stimulating capital formation, such as the construction of new factories and machines,

---

1. Louis M. Hacker, *Major Documents in American Economics History*, Vol. 2. Princeton, NJ: D. Van Nostrand Co., 1961, p. 108

by promoting equal employment opportunities for all, and by reducing the federal government's presence in the economy through fewer regulations and relatively less government spending. The act also charges the president with developing a plan for attaining all of these goals.

This chapter examines the macroeconomic goals of the nation and looks at recent economic history for a better understanding of the events and policies that lie behind macroeconomic problems. The chapter concludes with a more thorough analysis of the nature and meaning of our inflation and unemployment problems and statistics.

PROGRESS TOWARD MACROECONOMIC GOALS

9.2 PROGRESS TOWARD GOALS

Figure 9-1 presents economic statistics that indicate how well the U.S. economy has done in achieving the macroeconomic goals of economic growth, full employment, stable prices, balanced government budgets, and international competitiveness set out by the Employment Act of 1946 and the Humphrey–Hawkins Bill. As is evident from the figure, these economic goals have not been fully achieved. Economic growth, as measured by the growth rate in real GNP, has had an uneven record in the years since 1960. The economy experienced relatively strong economic growth in the decade of the 1960s, but the 1970s and 1980s have been marked by several recessions that have slowed the long-run pace of economic growth.

Similarly, the U.S. economy made significant progress in reducing unemployment during the high-growth years of the 1960s. The unemployment rate fell as the economy grew. However, while unemployment has had its ups and downs in the 1970s and 1980s, the overall trend has been toward higher average levels of unemployment.

The U.S. economy has experienced at least three different periods of inflation during the years since 1960, as Figure 9-1 shows. The decade of the 1960s was a time of low but rising inflation. Inflation was much higher in the 1970s, but also less predictable. The inflation rate tended to rise and fall by relatively large amounts from year to year. Inflation in the 1980s has been low and stable in comparison to the 1970s, but it is still high when compared with the inflation rates of the 1960s.

Progress in the areas of a balanced budget and international competitiveness has also been disappointing. The economic goal of a balanced federal government budget has eluded policymakers for most of the period shown in the figure, with the problem growing larger in recent years. Gains in international competitiveness have also eluded policymakers, as is evident when the **balance of trade** is examined. The balance of trade is the dollar value of U.S. exports minus the dollar value of U.S. imports. If the United States is competitive with foreign producers, then U.S. firms should sell more than they buy from abroad, giving the economy a balance of trade surplus. Figure 9-1 shows that, by this measure, the United States has become less competitive in recent years. The U.S. trade surplus in the 1960s reversed into a deficit in the 1970s, a deficit that has grown worse and worse during the decade of the 1980s.

Balance of Trade
The value of exported goods minus the value of goods that are imported.

The economy's progress or lack of progress toward these goals is the result of the complex interplay between the economic events that have affected the nation and the economic policies that have attempted to deal with those events. The next several chapters of this book will look at these events and policies in depth, while examining the evolution of the macroeco-

226 *Inflation and Unemployment: Problems, Policies, and Perspectives*

FIGURE 9-1

Uncertain Progress Toward Macroeconomic Goals. The U.S. economy has not achieved its macroeconomic goals, as these five graphs make clear. The economy has experienced uneven economic growth in recent years. The average unemployment rate has increased. Inflation, severe in the 1970s, has decreased in the mid-1980s, but it is still higher than in the 1960s. Both the federal budget deficit and the balance of trade deficit have increased in recent years.

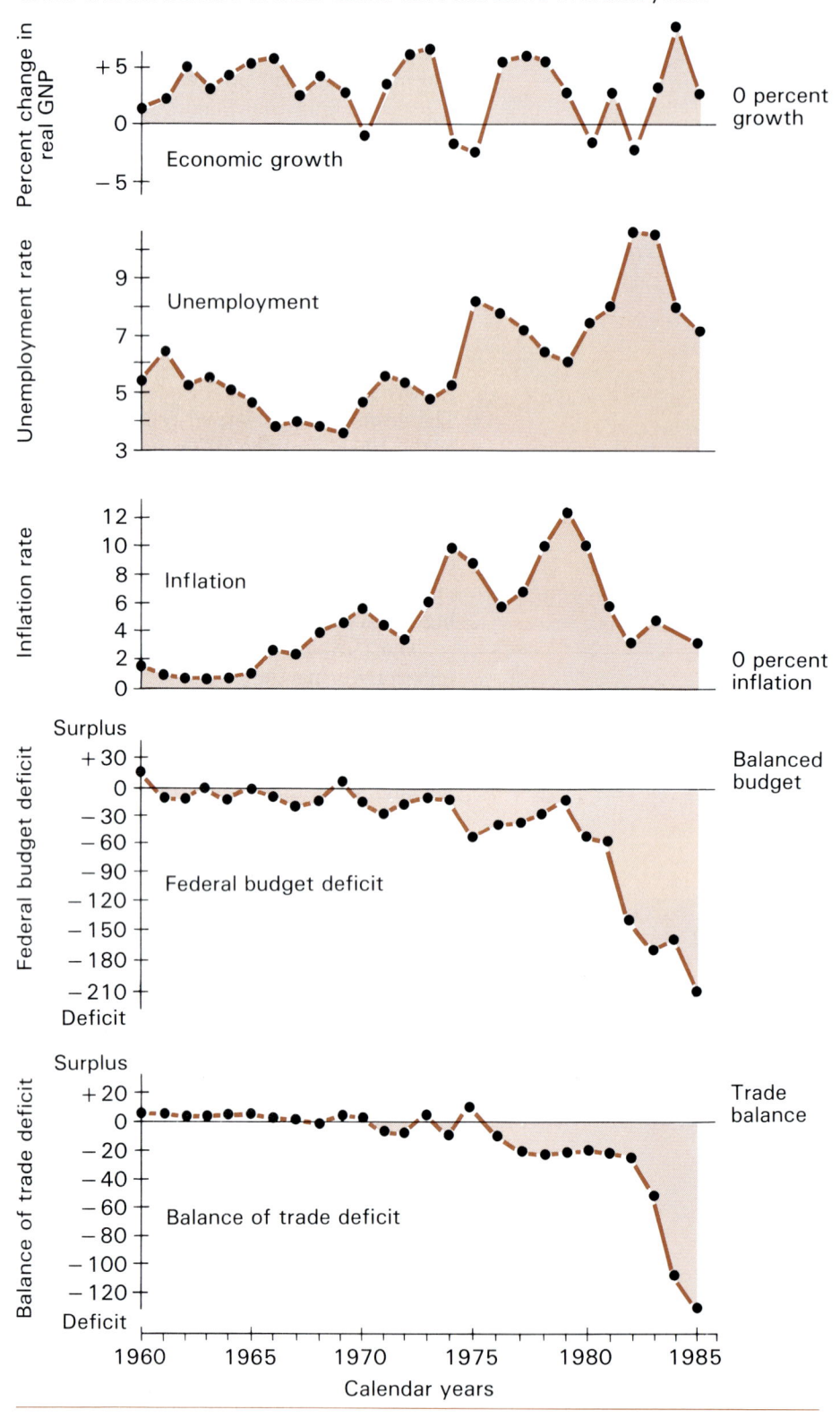

**KEY CONCEPTS
9.1, 9.2**

The macroeconomic goals of the economy are spelled out in the Employment Act of 1946 and the Humphrey–Hawkins Bill. Among the most important macroeconomic goals are economic growth, full employment, price stability, a balanced federal budget, and improved international competitiveness. The United States has not achieved these goals in recent years. Economic growth has been uneven. Unemployment is lower than in some recent years, but still relatively high. Inflation rates have been brought down in the 1980s, but they are still higher than in the 1960s. Large deficits in both the federal budget and the balance of trade indicate that the goals of a balanced government budget and international competitiveness have not been achieved.

ECONOMIC EVENTS IN THE 1960s

**9.3
1960s ECONOMIC EVENTS**

The U.S. economy entered the decade of the 1960s still recovering from a major recession. This recession had many roots, but a long and difficult strike in the steel industry was a major cause. This strike disrupted production throughout the economy's industrial sector and resulted in the loss of nearly 70 million man-days of work in 1959 alone. The ripple effects of this strike, which was not settled until early 1960, contributed to the high unemployment rates experienced early in the 1960s.

The federal government was an active force in the economy in the 1960s. The goals of full employment, economic growth, and price stability were addressed under President John F. Kennedy with three important policies. First, in 1962, the president announced "wage and price guideposts," which were suggested limits on wage and price increases. These guideposts, which were voluntary and therefore only partly effective, were designed to keep inflation down as the economy recovered from the 1959 recession.

Congress acted to stimulate economic growth in 1962 by passing a tax bill that introduced **investment tax credits.** These investment tax credits promoted capital formation by allowing firms that made new investments to receive relatively large immediate tax benefits. This effectively reduced the cost of these investments and made them significantly more profitable than before the tax credits were available.

Investment Tax Credit
A tax program that allows firms to deduct a percentage of the cost of a current investment from their current federal tax liabilities.

The most important economic policy of the Kennedy administration was the 1964 tax cut. The Kennedy tax cut (actually passed by Congress several months after Kennedy was assassinated) was designed to stimulate demand in the economy and reduce unemployment by giving consumers more disposable income. The Kennedy tax cut is recognized to be one of the most successful macroeconomic policies because consumers responded to their higher take-home pay by spending more and thereby creating more income and jobs. Unemployment fell as a result.

President Lyndon Johnson increased government spending through two programs. Johnson's Great Society social programs were aimed at the poor and the disadvantaged in the economy. At the same time, however, Johnson also increased defense spending to fight an increasingly expensive war in Southeast Asia. The double effects of spending on defense plus spending on

ECONOMIC ISSUES

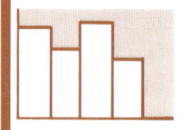

The Legacy of the Great Society

Lyndon Johnson may be remembered by many as the president who presided over an unsuccessful war in Vietnam and who let inflation get out of hand in the United States. Johnson was also responsible for implementing a set of social programs that have had a significant long-term effect on the U.S. economy. Johnson's Great Society programs were and are controversial. They have, however, changed the United States forever and have helped many millions of Americans.

Johnson became president at a time when the United States was a nation of haves and have-nots. Many households lived in comfortable prosperity, but millions of others faced hardship. Poverty and ill-health among the elderly were severe problems. Half of those aged 65 or more had no health insurance and more than one-third of the elderly had incomes below the official poverty line. Blacks and women also suffered poverty rates much above average and were often unable to secure their economic rights. Some areas of the country, such as the Appalachian region, experienced concentrated poverty and a dismal economic future.

Johnson declared war on poverty and proposed to build a Great Society with greater prosperity and equality. The results of these proposals include Medicare and Medicaid health plans for the elderly and expanded social security and veterans benefits. Government educational assistance also increased, as did spending on a variety of programs designed to help the poor and disadvantaged through cash payments, government services, or, as with food stamps and rent supplements, government assistance in meeting basic needs.

The costs of federal social programs continued to grow during the Nixon, Ford, and Carter administrations, despite selective cutbacks and economies. The increasing cost of Medicare and rising social security benefits were the largest areas of growth.

Johnson's Great Society programs have been cut back in the Reagan administration of the 1980s, as Congress and the president have sought to reduce spending to limit the growth in budget deficits. Many of the original Great Society programs are now thought to have been wasteful attempts to "throw money at problems" rather than address the real causes of those problems. In some cases, too much government interference is thought to have made the problems worse over the long run. But the Great Society programs also generated important benefits to the economy that continue to this day. Even critics of the Great Society now admit that many of these programs were necessary and beneficial. And some of the programs, such as the Voting Rights Act and policies that call for equal employment opportunity, were milestones in the struggle for greater equality in civil and economic rights and opportunities.

Phillips Curve
A graphic device that illustrates an inverse relationship or trade-off between the inflation rate and the unemployment rate.

9.4 PHILLIPS CURVE

social programs, combined with higher spending by consumers, caused the economy to begin to overheat. Inflation rates began to rise. Johnson's economic advisors recommended a temporary tax increase to reduce spending pressures that were driving prices higher. Johnson, however, balked at the idea of increasing taxes. Inflationary pressures made a tax increase unavoidable by 1967, when Johnson finally asked Congress for a special surcharge on top of regular income tax rates. The tax rise was ineffective; it came too late to halt the rise in inflation that continued throughout the decade of the 1960s.

THE PHILLIPS CURVE IN THE 1960s

Economic events in the 1960s demonstrated an important relationship between inflation and unemployment known as the **Phillips curve,** named after A.W. Phillips who first documented the relationship in 1958. The Phillips curve for the 1960s is plotted in Figure 9-2.

The Phillips curve is found by plotting the inflation rate, measured on the vertical axis, against the unemployment rate, measured on the horizontal axis. The relationship that results suggests that inflation and unemployment are inversely related. That is, it appears that higher inflation accompanies reductions in unemployment, and that lower inflation necessarily brings higher unemployment. The Phillips curve suggests that there is a predictable short-run trade-off between inflation and unemployment in a modern economy: attempts to reduce unemployment tend to cause inflation, and inflation can be fought, but only by raising the unemployment rate.

The idea of the Phillips curve relationship along with the evidence that it worked in the 1960s gave policymakers the idea that they could "fine tune" the economy. Playing inflation against unemployment does not cure both economic problems, but it might assure us of only moderate levels of each. This might be an acceptable compromise, especially if rapid economic growth is part of the bargain. Johnson's 1967 tax surcharge can be viewed as a Phillips curve policy, for example. The tax rise was intended to bring inflation down by raising the unemployment rate. Figure 9-2 shows how well this idea worked during the 1960s. The economy slowly climbed up the Phillips curve. Unemployment fell but inflation worsened during most of the decade.

Figure 9-2 shows us what the Phillips curve looks like, but it sheds no light on a more interesting question: why did this relationship exist in the

FIGURE 9-2

The 1960s Phillips Curve. The Phillips curve illustrates a trade-off between inflation and unemployment. The U.S. economy experienced a movement along the Phillips curve in the 1960s, with lower unemployment rates and rising inflation rates.

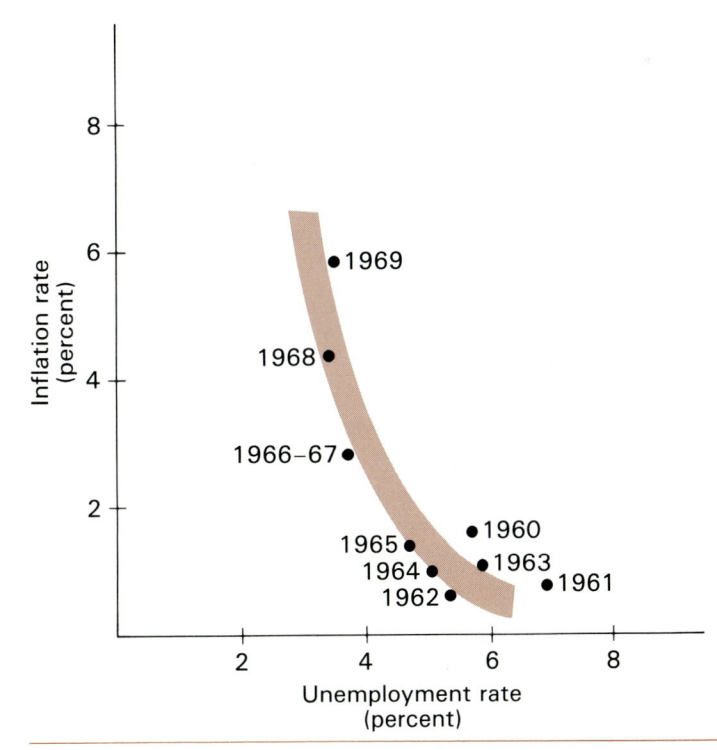

Wage-Lag Theory
A hypothesis concerning the cause of the Phillips curve that holds that inflation can temporarily reduce unemployment if wages lag behind the rise in prices.

1960s? Was there some reason for this relationship between inflation and unemployment or was it just a historical accident? There was a strong correlation between unemployment and inflation, but correlation does not prove that causation exists. What is the theory behind the Phillips curve?

Economists disagree about both the Phillips curve and the theory behind it. We will talk more about this debate in future chapters, but for now let us look at just one of several possible explanations for the Phillips curve: the **wage-lag theory.** According to this theory, higher inflation rates reduce unemployment because of a "surprise" effect. When prices go up, this theory holds, wages generally lag behind for a few months or longer until, for example, a new labor contract is negotiated. Higher selling prices and a temporarily constant wage cost generate added short-run profits for employers. These inflation-induced profits act as an incentive for businesses to expand and hire more workers. Inflation, it follows, causes more people to be hired, reducing the unemployment rate. Whether the wage-lag theory is correct or not, it is clear that the Phillips curve relationship held through the decade of the 1960s.

ECONOMIC EVENTS IN THE 1970s

**9.5
1970s ECONOMIC EVENTS**

The rising inflation of the 1960s continued in the 1970s and, indeed, inflation became the dominant economic problem of the decade. The Federal Reserve System, which regulates the economy's money and banking system, sought to reduce the inflation rate by restricting the growth of loans and debt in 1969–1970. The resulting recession reduced the inflation rate somewhat, but it did not bring it down to the very low inflation levels of the early 1960s. With inflationary pressures building and distorting the economy both at home and in international markets, President Richard Nixon took a dramatic step. On August 15, 1971, Nixon decreed a 90-day national freeze on all wages and prices, followed by a period of national wage and price controls. Nixon also imposed a temporary surcharge on all imports and lowered the dollar's international value. These international policies were designed to make the United States more competitive with its trading partners.

Nixon's wage and price controls caused inflation to moderate during 1972, as Figure 9-1 shows, but they did little to alter the public's expectations of inflation. Threfore, many of the forces that tend to cause inflation did not disappear when prices were frozen. Inflation returned in 1973, when most of the price controls were ended, at a rate of over 6 percent.

Stagflation
High or rising inflation rates accompanied by high or rising unemployment rates.

Stagflation is the combination of high unemployment and high inflation —it hit the U.S. economy with full force in 1974. Many factors contributed to the rise of stagflation. The sudden drop in the international value of the dollar made imported goods more expensive. Worldwide crop failures drove up the prices of agricultural products. Most dramatically, the Organization of Petroleum Exporting Countries (OPEC) raised the world price of crude oil and imposed an embargo on oil shipments to the United States.

Any one of these events would shake up the economy. Taken together, the result was nothing short of devastating. Prices rose and they kept rising to previously unseen heights. The Consumer Price Index jumped over 10 percent in 1974. As prices rose, consumers found that their incomes were not keeping pace with the price increases. Consumer purchasing power declined considerably, and people cut back on spending. Cars were fixed up to last one more year. Heavy coats were made to last one more winter. Purchases of durable goods like freezers and furniture were put off, too. Industry sold fewer goods because of the spending cuts, so they laid off workers. Higher unemployment rates meant that even fewer goods and services were purchased, compounding the problem. High prices caused recession, not the falling unemployment associated with the Phillips curve.

OPEC's actions in 1973–1974 not only sent prices skyrocketing, they also caused physical shortages of oil and oil-related products. Long waits in line for gasoline were only a small part of the problem. Plants and factories were forced to shut down for lack of oil used as energy source or raw material. Coal mines had to halt production because they did not have enough fuel to run mining equipment. At hospitals, some surgery was postponed or cancelled because latex tubing (made from oil products) was not available. In 1974, America learned that it was a land of shortage and scarcity, and this knowledge changed the economy.

President Gerald Ford fought inflation with his Whip Inflation Now (WIN) plan of mostly voluntary price restraints and hit back against unemployment with a 1975 tax rebate program that sent every taxpayer a $100 to $200 check. These programs were partially successful in reducing inflation and unemployment, but Jimmy Carter still nosed out Ford in the 1976 election, where economic issues played an important role.

The decade of scarcity continued under President Jimmy Carter. Carter's economic policies never seemed to get off the ground, but perhaps this was in part because the economic climate changed too much and too quickly during these years. Another oil crisis, this one triggered by Iran's seizure of American hostages, brought back the gas lines and pushed inflation rates to new heights in 1979 and 1980. The inflation rate for 1979–1980 averaged more than 13 percent.

This period also brought with it a different kind of shortage. The shortage this time was not of oil but of money. The Federal Reserve System controls the availability of money and credit in the United States. In October, 1979, the Fed put a lid on loans for the economy. The Fed's action was intended to slow down inflation by more strictly controlling the availability of money and credit in the economy. People who could not get loans to buy cars or build houses simply did not buy cars or build houses. This tight monetary policy may be credited with the subsequent decline in the inflation rate, but it might also deserve blame for the rise in unemployment that followed.

WHAT HAPPENED TO THE PHILLIPS CURVE?

9.6 DISAPPEARANCE OF PHILLIPS CURVE

The comfortable policy recommendations of the 1960s Phillips curve seemed to stop working for much of the 1970s. What happened to the Phillips curve? Figure 9-3 plots the inflation and unemployment rates for the 1970s. It is clear from the figure that the simple Phillips curve trade-off of the 1960s did not exist in the 1970s.

One theory for the disappearing Phillips curve holds that the 1970s gave us a "new" kind of inflation. The inflation of the 1960s was based on rising demand. People had higher incomes, and they used the additional money to buy more goods and services. All this spending created even more prosperity, as factories hired more workers to meet rising demand, but it also bid up prices. We call this situation **demand-pull inflation**. Rises in demand, as

Demand-Pull Inflation
Inflation caused by increases in the demand for goods and services.

232 *Inflation and Unemployment: Problems, Policies, and Perspectives*

FIGURE 9-3   **Inflation and Unemployment in the 1970s.** The relationship between inflation and unemployment in the 1970s is complex. No single Phillips curve relationship appears here. Overall, both inflation and unemployment increased during 1973–1974 and 1978–1980. It is possible to view this phenomenon as resulting from a shift from one Phillips curve for 1971–1973 to another for 1976–1979.

[Graph: Inflation rate (percent) vs. Unemployment rate (percent), showing data points for years 1970–1980]

Cost-Push Inflation
Inflation caused by rising production costs.

we saw in the earlier chapters on supply–demand analysis, tend to bid up prices and increase output at the same time. If this happened all around the economy, a Phillips curve type of relationship would appear. Rising demand based on high levels of government spending and low taxes could have been one source of the inflation of the 1960s.

The inflation of the 1970s was caused by scarcity, not prosperity, however. With oil and credit scarce, prices were pushed up, forcing consumers to cut back their purchases. Increasing production costs pushed prices up. This situation, termed **cost-push inflation,** gives us both inflation and higher unemployment, as opposed to demand-pull inflation, which tends to reduce unemployment. The idea behind cost-push inflation is that decreases in supply cause higher prices, but with reduced output and, therefore, lower employment. If supply falls all around the economy, stagflation tends to result and the Phillips curve formula breaks down.

A second explanation of the Phillips curve's seeming disappearance in the 1970s is based on the wage-lag theory discussed earlier. This theory suggests that wage increases tend to lag behind price increases, generating short-term profits that encourage business to hire more workers. This explanation of the Phillips curve only holds, however, if the inflation is unexpected so that wages do, in fact, lag behind prices. If workers and others are sophisticated about inflation and its effects, the wage-lag theory breaks down and the Phillips curve stops working. Now, for example, workers often negotiate higher and higher wage increases in anticipation of high prices at the grocery store and gas pump. Wages no longer lag so far behind prices.

FIGURE 9-4

The Natural Unemployment Rate Hypothesis. The inflation and unemployment experience of the 1970s can be interpreted as the interaction of short-run and long-run Phillips curves. For example, if the economy begins at A, attempts to reduce unemployment below the natural unemployment rate will cause inflation, a movement from A to B along the short-run Phillips curve. In the long run, however, the economy adjusts to expectations of higher inflation rates and gradually returns to the natural rate of unemployment. This causes a movement from B to C, back to the long-run Phillips curve.

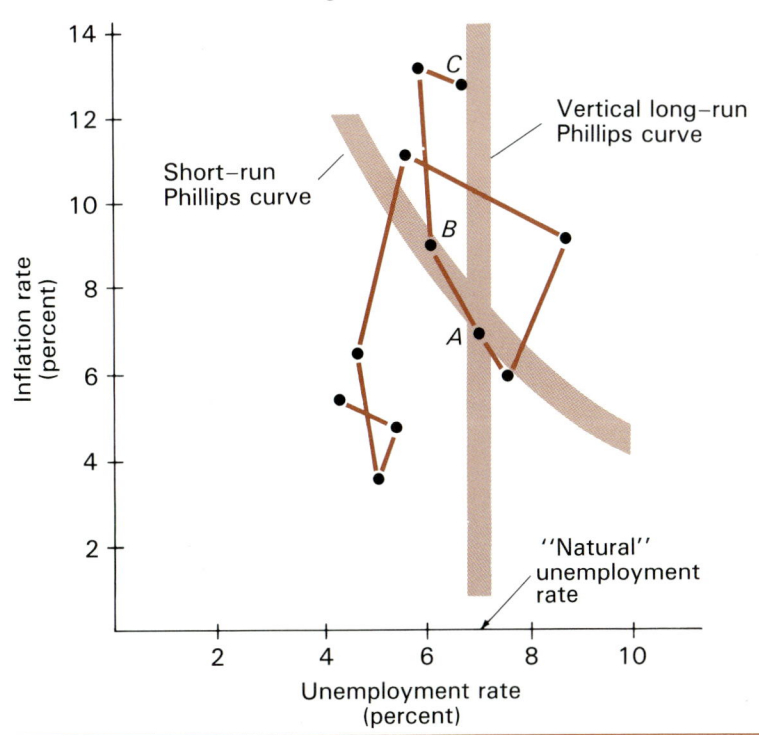

Long-Run Phillips Curve
A graphic device that illustrates the relationship between the inflation rate and the unemployment rate in the long run.

9.7 NATURAL UNEMPLOYMENT RATE

Natural Unemployment Rate
The unemployment rate that results when labor markets have found their long-run equilibrium.

Many economists believe that changes in inflationary expectations result in the vertical **long-run Phillips curve** illustrated in Figure 9-4. A vertical long-run Phillips curve means that, in the long run, the unemployment rate stays about the same, regardless of the inflation rate. In the long run, therefore, there is no systematic trade-off between inflation and unemployment.

The long-run Phillips curve is built on the idea that the economy has a **natural unemployment rate.** The natural unemployment rate is the unemployment rate that labor markets tend to move toward in the long run. This unemployment rate is "natural" only in the sense that it is the result of the forces of the demand and supply of labor. The natural unemployment rate is not necessarily the "full employment" mandated by the Employment Act of 1946. Rather, the natural rate of unemployment corresponds to the long-run equilibrium in labor markets, which may occur at full employment or may occur with relatively high unemployment levels. In general, estimates by economists of the natural unemployment rate in recent years have been higher than estimates of full employment.

It appears that the natural unemployment rate in the 1970s was around 7 percent unemployment, regardless of the inflation rate. Federal government policies attempted to reduce unemployment in the 1970s, but they only succeeded in causing a temporary decrease in joblessness by inducing unexpected inflation. Workers and employers eventually adjusted their expectations of inflation upward, and the labor markets moved back toward the long-run natural unemployment rate. Viewed in this way, the long-run result of economic policies to reduce unemployment is to cause higher inflation, with no long-run change in unemployment.

Figure 9-4 shows what happened in the 1970s according to the natural unemployment rate theory. Policies designed to use the Phillips curve to reduce unemployment caused a movement from *A* to *B* in the figure. In the long run, however, inflationary expectations adjusted and the labor markets returned to their natural unemployment rate equilibrium at *C*, but with a higher inflation rate.

Many economists today believe that the natural unemployment rate idea, with its corresponding vertical long-run Phillips curve, is valid. The data for the 1970s, shown in Figure 9-4, certainly tend to support the idea. Despite a variety of different types of economic policies, unemployment repeatedly returned to the approximately 6 to 7 percent natural unemployment rate region.

KEY CONCEPTS 9.4, 9.7

The Phillips curve illustrates a trade-off between the inflation rate and the unemployment rate. The U.S. economy displayed the Phillips curve relationship in the 1960s. Lower unemployment rates brought on higher inflation rates. This relationship changed in the 1970s. Many economists now believe that there is a vertical long-run Phillips curve at the natural unemployment rate. It may be possible to trade higher inflation for lower unemployment in the short run, through movements along the short-run Phillips curve, but this trade-off may not exist in the long run.

ECONOMIC EVENTS IN THE 1980s

9.8 1980s ECONOMIC EVENTS

The economy and economic policies again changed dramatically in the 1980s. The first change occurred in 1980, when Ronald Reagan defeated Jimmy Carter to become president. Reagan won, in part, by asking voters "Are you better off now than you were four years ago?" The Reagan landslide was an indication that voters viewed the high inflation and unemployment of the 1970s as unacceptable, and they counted on Reagan to do better.

President Reagan introduced economic policies based on **supply-side economics.** The idea of supply-side economics is to encourage economic growth for the nation by strengthening the incentives for individual economic growth. These incentives for growth and production tend to increase the supply side of the markets for output, labor, and technology, thus giving the name supply-side to these policies.

Supply-Side Economics Economic theories and policies that focus on capital formation, production incentives, and regulatory costs.

President Reagan proposed a three-year 25 percent cut in income tax rates in 1981, which Congress subsequently enacted. Reagan also sought to reduce barriers to economic growth by eliminating many government regulations on private activities.

Reagan's supply-side tax cuts resulted in very large government deficits in the early 1980s. As we will discuss in Chapter 12, these deficits were really the result of two different forces: the tax cuts and the worldwide recession of 1979–1981. High unemployment rates tend to cause budget deficits by reducing tax collections and increasing government spending needs. Reagan's tax cuts only served to make these deficits worse, at least in the short run, by further cutting tax revenues.

The economy moved out of recession in the mid-1980s, helped by at least three factors. First, Reagan's tax cuts finally succeeded in stimulating economic growth, which reduced unemployment. Second, the Federal Reserve adopted a less restrictive monetary policy, which allowed lower interest rates and greater spending in loan-sensitive sectors of the economy such as automobiles, wood products, and construction. Finally, oil prices reversed their upward trend and began to fall somewhat. The worldwide recession of the early 1980s had decreased the demand for oil and weakened the OPEC oil cartel. Lower oil prices tended to stimulate the economy just as the oil price increases in the 1970s had produced stagflation.

The economy was relatively healthy by the start of President Reagan's second term in 1985. Unemployment was below its peak, and inflation was relatively low and seemed under control. The economy was growing relatively rapidly, although economists were uncertain as to whether this high growth could continue.

Figure 9-5 presents inflation and unemployment in the 1980s. This figure shows that economic policies and events such as the supply-side tax cuts and falling oil prices served to reduce inflation by a substantial amount. Unemployment increased in 1981–1982 but moved back toward the "natural unemployment rate" by the mid-1980s.

Two economic problems appeared to be most important in the mid-1980s. First, the federal budget deficit continued to grow, despite the growing economy. Congress and the president seemed unable to do very much to

FIGURE 9-5

Inflation and Unemployment in the 1980s. Inflation and unemployment in the 1980s is consistent with the idea of short-run and long-run Phillips curves. The economy moved along a short-run Phillips curve from 1980 to 1983, with lower inflation but higher unemployment. Once expectations had adjusted to the lower inflation rate, the unemployment rate fell back to the natural unemployment rate.

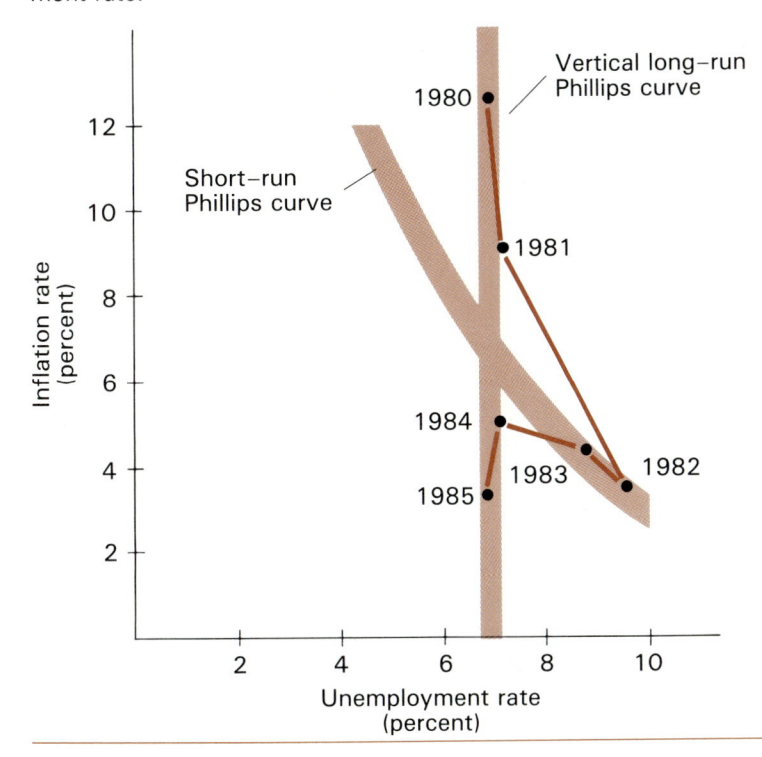

stem the rising tide of red ink. Another tide was bringing more and more imports to the United States, causing the U.S. balance of trade to swing far into the red ink of deficit. The U.S. dollar had soared to very high levels against other currencies in the mid-1980s, as the U.S. economy grew faster than the economies of other countries around the world. This strong dollar made imports relatively inexpensive and made U.S. goods hard to sell either at home or in foreign markets. Many U.S. firms found it difficult to compete with foreign producers, and some actually began to move their factories and jobs abroad.

The dual deficit problem—deficits in both the federal budget and the balance of trade—appears likely to dominate economic policy in the years to come. The problem of balancing the federal budget involves conflict between those who benefit from government spending and transfer programs on one side and those who stand to benefit from lower tax rates on the other. Congress is not well equipped to deal with such conflict, which is one reason why the deficit has grown so large in the first place.

The balance of trade deficit also involves conflict. Reducing the trade imbalance and restoring U.S. competitiveness means selling more to foreign buyers or buying fewer imported goods. Either way, this pits the United States against its trading partner nations. In 1985, for example, the Congress and the president threatened retaliatory measures against Japan unless that country agreed to open up more of its markets to U.S. goods. The Japanese economy is complex and different from ours in many important respects, however, so increasing sales to Japan is not a simple task.

UNEMPLOYMENT

We have now briefly surveyed recent economic policies and events. Upcoming chapters will look at these policies and events through the lens of economic theory, helping us to understand both how the economy has changed and how economic theories and policies have changed with it. Before moving on, however, we should pause and consider more thoroughly our two main economic problems: unemployment and inflation. In this section, we will look at the meaning of unemployment. In the next section, we will examine inflation statistics.

Measuring Unemployment

Unemployment is one of the economy's most serious problems. Economists and policymakers need to be able to measure the extent and nature of unemployment in order to be able to evaluate theories and make intelligent policy decisions to improve the employment outlook.

Unemployment is usually measured by the government's **unemployment rate.** The unemployment rate, as calculated by the federal government, is the ratio of the number of people who fit the definition of unemployed to the number of people who are in the **labor force.** The numerator of the unemployment rate is the number of **unemployed workers.** People are considered to be unemployed if they meet the following criteria: First, they must be aged 16 or over and not have earned any wage or salary income in the last month. Second, they must be actively seeking work. Finally, they must be unable to find a job in their occupation at the going wage rate. If they have not looked for work or if they have accepted pay or turned down a job in their line of work, they are not "officially" unemployed. The denominator of the unemployment statistic is the size of the labor force. The labor force is

---

Unemployment Rate
A measure of the unemployment problem. The unemployment rate is equal to the number of unemployed workers as a percentage of the labor force.

> 9.9
> MEASURING
> UNEMPLOYMENT

Labor Force
The number of people with jobs plus the number of unemployed workers.

Unemployed Workers
People who are willing and able to work and who are actively seeking employment but are unable to find work in their occupational area at the going wage rate.

equal to the number of people actively seeking to supply their labor to employers. Two groups are included in the labor force, those who are working and those who are not employed but are actively seeking work.

Table 9-1 gives unemployment statistics for the period 1960–1985. There were 8.3 million unemployed people in the United States in 1985. Another 108.8 million had jobs, so the labor force summed to 108.8 + 8.3 = 117.1 million men and women. The average unemployment rate for 1985 was equal to 8.3 million (the number unemployed) divided by 117.1 million (the labor force), which works out to a rate of 7.1 percent. No one actually goes around and counts all the unemployed people. The Labor Department estimates these figures based on a monthly telephone survey of households.

Table 9-1 tells much about the unemployment problem in the United States. First, the table shows that unemployment rates have increased, on average, since the 1960s, although joblessness has displayed cyclical ups and downs from year to year. A second interesting fact that the table makes clear is that, while unemployment has increased in the United States, the number of people who hold jobs has also risen, from 67.6 million in 1960 to over 108 million in 1985. This points out the fact that unemployment rates can be increased in two different ways. The way most people think of first is by people being laid off or fired. This is what happened in 1981–1982, according to the figures in Table 9-1. The labor force was roughly stable during 1981–1982. Layoffs caused by a recession reduced the number of people with jobs and increased the number of unemployed. The unemployment rate rose from 7.5 percent to 9.5 percent.

| TABLE 9-1 | Average Annual Unemployment Rates, 1960–1985 |

Year	Labor force (millions)	Number employed (millions)	Number unemployed (millions)	Unemployment rate (%)
1960	71.4	67.6	3.8	5.4
1961	72.3	67.6	4.7	6.5
1962	72.6	68.7	3.9	5.4
1963	73.8	69.7	4.0	5.5
1964	75.1	71.3	3.7	5.0
1965	76.4	73.0	3.3	4.4
1966	77.8	75.0	2.8	3.7
1967	79.5	76.5	2.9	3.7
1968	80.9	78.1	2.8	3.5
1969	82.9	80.1	2.8	3.4
1970	84.8	80.7	4.0	4.8
1971	86.3	81.3	5.0	5.8
1972	88.8	83.9	4.8	5.5
1973	91.2	86.8	4.6	4.8
1974	93.6	88.5	5.1	5.5
1975	95.4	87.5	7.9	8.3
1976	97.8	90.4	7.4	7.6
1977	100.6	93.6	6.9	6.9
1978	103.8	97.6	6.2	6.0
1979	109.5	100.4	6.1	5.8
1980	108.5	100.9	7.6	7.0
1981	110.3	102.0	8.2	7.5
1982	111.8	101.1	10.6	9.5
1983	113.2	102.5	10.7	9.5
1984	115.2	106.7	8.5	7.4
1985	117.1	108.8	8.3	7.1

Source. Economic Report of the President, 1986, Table B-31

A second way the unemployment rate rises is more subtle, as the figures for 1980–1981 show. The unemployment rate increased during 1980–1981, even though the number of people with jobs also increased. This is because many new workers, including many women and young people, entered the labor force during the period, increasing the number of people looking for jobs. Slow economic growth during this period meant that the number of new jobs created was less than the number of new workers that applied for work. The unemployment rate increased from 7.0 percent to 7.5 percent, even though more people had jobs.

The dilemma of the new entrants to the labor force is one reason unemployment increased during the 1970s. The workforce grew as baby-boom students entered the job market and women searched for careers outside the home. The economy of the 1970s did not grow as fast as the labor force, so many of these new entrants joined the ranks of the unemployed. Today's continued high levels of unemployment attest to the fact that economic growth has not yet caught up to the growth of the labor force.

9.9 MEASURING UNEMPLOYMENT

Unemployment and the Unemployment Rate

The unemployment rate is a convenient indicator of the unemployment problem, but it is not a perfect measurement of joblessness. There are two reasons why the unemployment rate might underestimate the unemployment problem and two reasons why it might overstate unemployment.

Underemployment For statistical purposes, people are considered employed if they have earned any wage or salary income during the past month. Part-time workers (who may be seeking full-time work) and people in low-paid temporary jobs are counted as fully employed. These people are not really unemployed (they have jobs), but some of them are not employed in a broader sense, either. We call them **underemployed workers.**

If you graduated from college with an accounting degree and spent five years pumping gas at a truck stop because no one needed an accountant, you might think that you have an unemployment problem. But the statistics would not show it. Unemployment of this sort could be a serious problem in the United States. The unemployment rate understates the problem by counting the gas-pumping accountant as employed instead of unemployed.

Underemployed Workers
Part-time workers who desire full-time jobs and workers who have jobs that do not make full use of their skills and training.

Discouraged Workers Many people who are unemployed for a long time get discouraged and stop looking for work. These people suffer the most serious unemployment problem of all. They have the wrong skills, or the right skills in the wrong place. But when they stop looking for work and give up, they reduce the unemployment rate, giving the impression that unemployment has gotten better not worse. Both the number unemployed and the labor force fall when these **discouraged workers** quit actively looking for work. The lower unemployment rate that results when discouraged workers leave the labor force should be considered bad news, but economists and politicians are more likely to view it as evidence of an improving economy. The unemployment rate does not tell us of the plight of the discouraged workers, so it tends to understate the real unemployment problem.

Discouraged Workers
People who have been unemployed so long that they have stopped looking for work and are, therefore, no longer included in the unemployment statistics.

Voluntary Unemployment The first two items on this list were reasons to believe that unemployment is a more serious problem than unemployment statistics imply. The next two items suggest that government statistics might also inadvertently inflate the real unemployment problem. One reason to believe this is that not all unemployment is involuntary, like losing a job you really want or need. Some people are voluntarily unemployed; they choose to be unemployed or to stay unemployed longer than is absolutely necessary.

Why would someone choose to be out of work? Sometimes it is a matter of tastes and preferences. People who prefer low income and leisure to higher income and work are frequently jobless. They may work just often enough to qualify for unemployment benefits or other government assistance, or they may not work at all in order to qualify for other government low-income programs. Some of these people pretend to look for work so they can continue to receive unemployment benefits, but they are really on a taxpayer-financed vacation. The government counts them as unemployed, but they are not out of work in the same sense as others.

Other people choose to remain unemployed to search for even better jobs. It takes a long time to find the "perfect" job. They might be out of work for weeks or months as they search out the best match of their talents against the available job openings. Higher unemployment in recent years is due in part to people remaining unemployed longer as they search for even better positions. The economy might benefit in the long run from higher job productivity, but it suffers in the short run from higher rates of joblessness.

People who prefer leisure or who avoid taking one job as they search for a better one are not unemployed in the same sense as others. To the extent that voluntary unemployment exists it tends to inflate the unemployment rate, overstating this economic problem.

Underground Economy
A term used to describe the "economy" in which unreported employment and unreported production and exchange of goods and services exist.

The Underground Economy There is a whole economic world that lives "off the books." The **underground economy** is a collection of illegal markets and untaxed transactions. People hide their activities from the eyes of the law because they deal in illegal goods such as drugs or because they want to avoid paying taxes on income from otherwise legal acts. This subterranean system could involve as much as $500 billion per year. The underground economy, in other words, could be big enough to employ all 1982's 10 million jobless workers at a wage of $50,000 each.

Many people who are officially counted as unemployed really have underground occupations. They work as plumbers for cash, sell firewood, deal in drugs, or engage in barter, all under the table to deceive the police or the Internal Revenue Service. They are counted as unemployed, but they are not. We cannot tell how many unemployed people are earning substantial incomes in the underground economy, but we can be sure that some of them are. The unemployment rate overestimates the number of unemployed workers because of the subterranean economy's existence. Unemployment is a difficult problem made worse because economists and politicians cannot be sure of the number of people who are truly unemployed.

KEY CONCEPT 9.9

Unemployment is measured by the unemployment rate, which is the ratio of unemployed workers to the size of the labor force. The unemployment rate is not a perfectly accurate indicator of unemployment because it cannot fully adjust for the underemployed, discouraged workers, or the existence of voluntary unemployment and the underground economy.

9.10 TYPES OF UNEMPLOYMENT

Types of Unemployment

Understanding unemployment is difficult because joblessness has many causes. The people in an unemployment line share an idled state, but they suffer it for different reasons. Economists sometimes divide unemployment into three types: cyclical, structural, and frictional unemployment.

Cyclical Unemployment We can find the cause for some unemployment in the economy's broad spending swings, the bust and boom of recession, and the good times that accompany rising and falling GNP. Consumers buy fewer new cars during a recession, so auto workers face layoffs. Jobs will not open up for these workers until the economy accelerates and spending habits resume speed. **Cyclical unemployment** is the unemployment of the Great Depression and the recessions of 1974–1975 and the early 1980s. Fighting cyclical unemployment means getting the whole economy moving. This is no simple feat, as you might guess from looking at the high peak unemployment rates shown in Table 9-1.

Cyclical Unemployment
Unemployment due to changes in the demand for the goods and services that workers produce.

Structural Unemployment
Unemployment that occurs when workers do not have the skills that are required for current job openings.

Structural Unemployment **Structural unemployment** is the problem faced by people who lack the skills needed to compete for a job in today's labor market. These people might be untrained teenagers who have few skills. Or they might be skilled workers in their 50s who find themselves replaced by computers. They have skills, but the wrong ones.

Rapid technological advancement is a good thing for the economy as a whole because it gives us better products and lower prices. Technological advances tend to increase structural unemployment in the short term, however. The government can fight cyclical unemployment by stimulating the economy using taxes or government spending or other tools discussed in this book, but there is no guarantee that increased spending alone will solve the structural unemployment problem. The ex-auto worker does not care if you buy more cars. His or her welding job has been taken by a robot.

Frictional Unemployment
Unemployment due to the inability of the labor market to match jobless workers with unfilled jobs; caused by poor information, lack of mobility, barriers to occupational entry, and discrimination.

Frictional Unemployment **Frictional unemployment** persists even among workers with needed skills during periods of prosperity. Frictional unemployment is a failure of the labor market to match up willing workers with unfilled jobs. Frictional unemployment has many causes. Some unemployment of this type is caused by lack of worker mobility. Workers who are unemployed in one city or state are often unwilling or unable to move to other areas where jobs exist. Lack of information is a second cause of frictional unemployment. Unemployed workers and available jobs frequently coexist because of the difficulty of effectively spreading information about job openings.

Discrimination against racial minorities, the young, the elderly, and women is a third cause of frictional unemployment. These groups often bear higher unemployment burdens than other population groups, in part because some employers discriminate against them in hiring decisions. Finally, barriers to occupational entry keep unemployment rates higher than they need be. Occupational licensing rules and union restrictions, for example, prevent unemployed workers from freely entering labor markets where jobs may exist. The barriers to entry have the effect of guaranteeing higher income to those who already have jobs and higher unemployment to those who cannot hurdle the barriers.

Full Employment
The level of unemployment that would occur in a growing, healthy economy.

The Goal of Full Employment

As mentioned at the beginning of the chapter, Congress has set the goal of **full employment** for the economy, but people are frequently confused about what the concept of full employment means. A zero percent unemployment rate is a practical impossibility. Some people always quit good jobs to search for better ones. Students spend time unemployed, waiting for the right job to open up. Declining industries lay off workers while other firms expand. It takes time for people and jobs to match up. Some unemployment always exists and a little unemployment is a sign of a normal, healthy economy.

The Humphrey–Hawkins Bill sets a full employment goal of 4 percent. This is the full-employment figure that economists used for their calculations in the 1960s. But most economists today would say that the economy has changed very much since the 1960s, and that it is impossible today to achieve a 4 percent unemployment rate without paying the price of extremely high inflation rates. Today full employment of the labor force would probably be achieved at an unemployment rate of approximately 5 to 6 percent. This is the unemployment rate that would result if the economy experienced rapid economic growth for several years. Six percent of the labor force would still be unemployed, even in a healthy economy, due to frictional and structural unemployment problems. It is difficult to set an exact unemployment figure for full employment, however, because the problems of underemployment, discouraged workers, voluntary unemployment, and the underground economy reduce the accuracy of unemployment statistics.

9.11 FOUR QUESTIONS

How Serious Is the Unemployment Problem?

The unemployment rate is an important indicator of joblessness, but it does not tell the whole story. Unemployment is not one problem, it is really a group of problems that we label "unemployment" for convenience. Different poeple are unemployed for different time periods and for different reasons, and no single policy or event will solve all of their unemployment problems. Consequently, the unemployment rate alone cannot provide an answer to the seriousness of the unemployment problem. To answer this important question, economists must really answer four separate questions.

How Many Are Unemployed? This is the only question for which the unemployment rate published in the newspaper is much help. The unemployment rate tells us the number of people who meet the official definition of unemployment. It is, as we have seen, a flawed measure of joblessness, but it is still a good indicator, since overall unemployment rises and falls with this statistic, even if the exact numbers are not always meaningful.

The unemployment rate for 1985 was 7.1 percent. This means that over 8.3 million people were without jobs. Eight million is a lot of people, but it might understate the degree of hardship that unemployment causes. Jobless workers have spouses and families that also suffer when paychecks stop. An unemployment rate of 7.1 percent might impose hardships of one type or another on as many as 20 million people.

Examining how many people are unemployed is the easiest way to look at the unemployment problem; consequently, it is the question most often dealt with in the press. The remaining three questions are seldom asked in the press, but they are every bit as important.

Who Are the Unemployed? Unemployment does not strike all groups evenly, as is evident from the 1985 unemployment figures presented in Table 9-2. The overall unemployment rate in 1985 was 7.1 percent, but rates for specific groups varied greatly. Adults suffered proportionately less unemployment than the population as a whole. Unemployment among females was slightly higher than unemployment among males, while blacks had unemployment rates that were more than twice those of whites. Teenage workers, just entering the labor force and searching for the "experience" that all employers seek, were hit the hardest. Teenagers as a whole endured more than 18 percent unemployment.

The vast variation in unemployment rates among these groups shows how many types of unemployment problems there are. Unemployment difficulties of adults are different from those of teenagers. The adults work in depressed industries or have obsolete skills. The young have few skills of any type and experience prejudice in the job market. Non-white unemployment is a different problem from white unemployment. Consequently, policies that try to address the problem of, say, adult white males are likely to have little effect on other groups.

How Long Have They Been Unemployed? The severity of a person's unemployment problems depends on the duration of that unemployment. Most people are unemployed for a relatively short time, less than five weeks. Workers with valuable skills move from one job to the next quickly, although poor communication and mobility problems prolong unemployment even here. Savings and unemployment compensation can often finance short job search periods. As Table 9-2 indicates, of those individuals unemployed

TABLE 9-2	Unemployment Statistics for 1985	
	Population group	Unemployment rate (%)
	All workers	7.1
	Males aged 20+	6.2
	Females aged 20+	6.6
	Teenaged males	19.5
	Teenaged females	17.6
	Whites	6.2
	Blacks	15.1
	Married men, spouses present	4.3
	Women who maintain families	10.4
	Job losers	49.8
	Job leavers	10.5
	Reentrants	27.1
	New entrants	12.5
	Duration of unemployment:	
	Less than 5 weeks	42.0
	5–14 weeks	30.1
	15–26 weeks	12.3
	27 weeks and over	15.4

Source. Economic Report of the President, 1986, Tables B-33, B-35.

in 1985, 42 percent were jobless for five weeks or less. More worrisome are the numbers of people in the next few groups. Over 30 percent of the unemployed population were jobless for between 5 and 14 weeks. These people were having more than a little trouble finding a job. Many, as the table shows, were without work for more than six months. This indicates a very serious problem. These hard-core unemployed risk becoming discouraged workers, their skills and talents lost forever because they cannot find a job.

Unemployment in a healthy economy should be mostly short term in nature. The relatively high proportion of the population that was out of work for more than a few weeks in 1985 was an indication of difficult economic times.

Why Are They Unemployed? We can gain another view of the unemployment problem by asking why people are jobless. Is their unemployment structural, frictional, or cyclical? Unemployment in a prosperous economy would include many job leavers who leave one job to look for another. This group made up 10 percent of the unemployed in 1985, however, indicating that job opportunities were limited. About half of all the jobless were job losers who lost their jobs because they had the wrong skills or were laid off because the goods they produced could not be sold. The high level of job losers indicates substantial cyclical unemployment and also suggests structural unemployment problems. Over one-third of the unemployed were stymied in attempts to enter or reenter the labor force. This is a possible indication of a stagnant economy, unable to expand to meet the needs of a growing working-age population.

Unemployment was a serious set of problems in 1985, as the figures in Table 9-2 indicate. Understanding these problems involves knowing more than numbers, however. While the basic unemployment rate provides useful information concerning the unemployment problem, asking the additional questions "who?" "why?" and "how long?" helps us better understand the nature of our current unemployment problems.

KEY CONCEPTS
9.10, 9.11

There are many aspects to the unemployment problem that are not revealed by the simple unemployment rate statistics. Unemployment can be either cyclical, structural, or frictional in nature. It can be either voluntary or involuntary. Unemployment also strikes different population groups in different ways and varies in duration.

INFLATION

9.12 INFLATION

Inflation
A substantial, sustained increase in the general level of prices.

Unemployment and inflation have both been major macroeconomic problems for most of the period since the Employment Act of 1946 was adopted. We have just seen that unemployment is a more complex problem than it is usually perceived to be. Inflation, too, is a complicated economic event.

Inflation is defined to be a substantial, sustained increase in the general level of prices. All price increases should not be called "inflation," however. Many prices rise and fall through perfectly normal movements of supply and demand. Individual price movements are not inflation. Economists reserve this label for periods when many prices rise simultaneously and possibly for related reasons. These rising prices increase the average cost, as measured

Inflation Rate
A measure of the rate of increase in the general level of prices in a given period of time.

Disinflation
A falling inflation rate; the general level of prices is rising, but the rate of increase is slowing.

Price Stability
A constant general level of prices.

9.13 EFFECTS OF INFLATION

Purchasing Power
The quantity of real goods and services that can be obtained for a given quantity of money.

Indexation
A system in which wages or other payments are automatically adjusted to reflect inflation according to changes in a price index.

Relative Prices
The price of one good compared to the prices of other goods.

---

by a *price index*, of the things we buy. The **inflation rate** is a measure of the speed at which average prices increase.

Deflation is the opposite of inflation. Deflation is a substantial, sustained decrease in the general level of prices. Deflation is historically tied to recession and depression, so the silver lining of lower prices tends to come wrapped in the dark cloud of unemployment. **Disinflation** is a period of falling inflation rates. Prices still rise during disinflationary periods, but by smaller and smaller amounts. Disinflation, and eventually **price stability**, is one goal of modern macroeconomic policy.

Economic Effects of Inflation

Inflation means that your money has less **purchasing power.** We use money like a scale or a yardstick to measure value. You can compare the cost or value of two goods by comparing their price measured in money terms. This useful yardstick suddenly shrinks when inflation hits. It takes more money to "measure" the same value. The incredible shrinking dollar is a complex set of problems. However, any list of inflation's economic effects would deal with the issues of fixed incomes, relative prices, interest rates, borrowers and lenders, savings, deadweight loss, and inflation as a self-fulfilling prophecy.

Inflation and Fixed Incomes Retired people living on fixed-dollar pensions and others who receive payments that do not vary with the price level know inflation shrinks their dollars and reduces their standard of living. The fixed amount of money buys fewer goods and services than before.

Inflation's effect on fixed incomes is important. Consider elderly pensioners who cannot pay rent or doctor bills because their fixed monthly incomes no longer stretch far enough. However, inflation's effect on fixed incomes is smaller today than in years past because many of these payments are now indexed. **Indexation** is a link to a price index. When a payment is indexed, income rises along with the inflation rate. Social security checks have been indexed for many years, reducing the burden of higher prices on retired people. Not all such payments are linked to the price index, however, so indexation has only reduced, not solved, this problem.

Inflation and Relative Prices Inflation would not be such a problem if it hit everyone and everything in the same way. Some prices skyrocket during inflationary times, but other prices stay constant or even fall. **Relative prices** are distorted by inflation. The term relative prices refers, in general, to the price of any one item compared to others. People gain or lose depending on how higher prices hit the particular goods and services they buy compared to the goods and services that they sell. Because inflation is uneven in its impact on the prices of all goods, it affects both purchasing power and the pattern of consumer purchases. Consumers buy less overall because of the dollar's shrinking purchasing power, but they tend to buy relatively more low-inflation goods and relatively less higher-inflation items. This creates winners and losers among both consumers and producers.

Inflation and Interest Rates The interest rate is an important price in the U.S. economy. Interest is the income savers receive on their nest eggs and the cost consumer and business borrowers pay for funds they spend and invest. Inflation reduces the purchasing power of interest income, so lenders demand higher payments to compensate for lower real values. Inflation,

ECONOMIC ISSUES

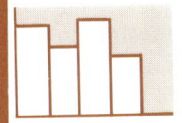

Inflation Distorts the Relative Price of Housing

Housing seems particularly susceptible to inflation's effects because housing markets are affected by inflation both directly, through the demand and supply of housing, and indirectly through the impact of inflation on mortgage loan costs. A little inflation means a lot higher housing costs. The following example shows why.

The *Wall Street Journal* reports that the price of an average new home increased from $87,000 to $100,600 in the period February, 1981, to February, 1982. This increase of about 15 percent was higher than the national inflation average during this period. It is not hard to understand why home prices rise quickly in inflationary times. Higher construction costs tend to reduce new housing supply, while the demand for housing rises at the same time. Homes were among the best inflation "hedges" during the 1970s; money invested in a house earned a higher return than cash in stocks or bonds. The forces of supply and demand therefore tend to push and pull housing prices higher during periods of rapid inflation.

People do not generally pay cash for a new house, they borrow (a mortgage loan) to make purchases as large as this. If your bank required a 20 percent down payment, this one year's inflation means that the required down payment sum increased from $17,400 to $20,120 between 1981 and 1982. One year's inflation means that you would have to have saved almost $3000 more during the year to be able to afford the new down payment.

A similar increase occurred in mortgage payments. The monthly mortgage payment is based on both the house's price and the interest rate you pay. The average mortgage interest rate in February, 1981, was 15.38 percent, so the monthly payment for an average new home would have been $892 (excluding insurance and property taxes, which might add another $100 to $400 per month to this sum). One year later the interest rate had risen to 17.33 percent. Monthly payments on the same house thus increased, boosted by higher price and higher interest rate, to the princely sum of $1162 per month.

One year's inflation between 1981–1982 raised average prices in the United States by about 10 percent, but the price of a new home (measured in monthly payments) went up by over 30 percent. As a result, young people were eligible for a home loan only if they had saved an extra $3000 during the year for the higher down payment (assuming 20 percent down). Older families, who already own homes, escaped the direct effect of higher housing prices and might have even benefited if they sold their homes at a profit. Younger people, however, found that inflation pushed home costs out of reach. This dramatic example shows how inflation, hitting some markets harder than others, distorts economic life.

Nominal Interest Rate
The interest rate, as it is commonly stated, unadjusted for inflation.

Real Interest Rate
The interest rate adjusted for the expected rate of inflation over a given period.

then, tends to drive up money or **nominal interest rates.** Figure 9-6 shows how interest rates and inflation rates have been related in recent years. Although the correlation is not perfect, the figure indicates that interest rates have tended to rise and fall with inflation rates.

The economist Irving Fisher studied interest rates and suggested that, all else being equal, an increase in the expected inflation rate brings an equal increase in interest rates. Recent experience, as Figure 9-6 shows, tends to bear out Fisher's theory. The prices of goods financed by borrowing can be doubly affected by inflation, as the housing example shows.

Inflation and Borrowers and Lenders Assume that there is no inflation. Would you be willing to lend $100 today in return for $110 a year from today? If this loan appeals to you, then you find a **real interest rate** of 10 percent acceptable. Would you make the same deal if an inflation rate of 10 percent is expected? If prices rise by 10 percent, the $110 you receive at the end of the year would have the same real value as the $100 you lent in the first place. You would make no profit to compensate you for risk and

246   Inflation and Unemployment: Problems, Policies, and Perspectives

FIGURE 9-6

Inflation and Interest Rates. Interest rates (represented by the prime interest rate) tend to rise and fall with inflation (as measured by the GNP Index). The real interest rate (the shaded area in the graph) is the difference between the nominal interest rate and the expected inflation rate. Real interest rates were low or negative in the 1970s but increased to historically high levels in the 1980s.

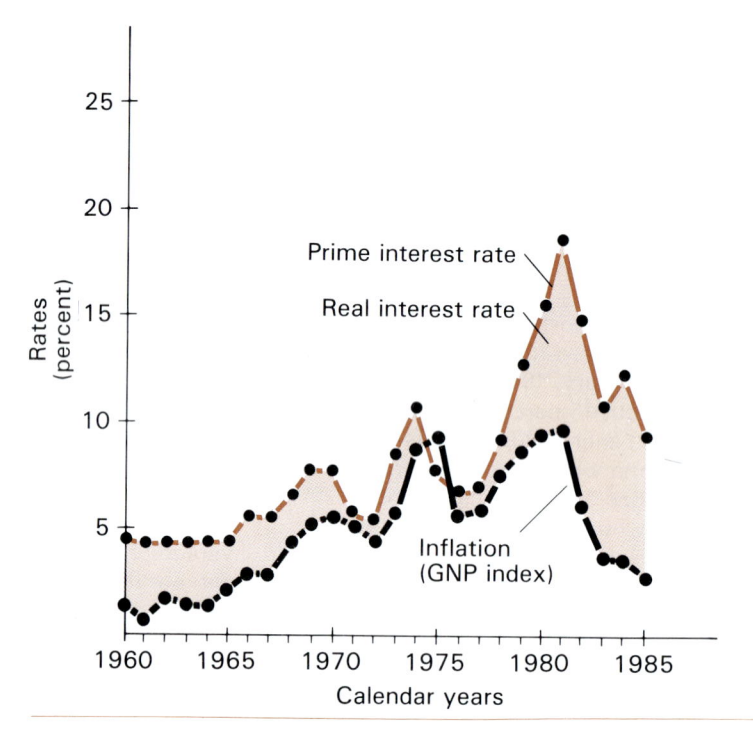

patience during the year. You would be smarter to demand an additional $10 payment to compensate for higher prices. A repayment of $120 (20 percent interest) makes sense in this situation. It would take a 20 percent nominal interest rate to provide you with a 10 percent real interest return if inflation is expected to be 10 percent.

Suppose that you and a friend strike the bargain just described. You lend your friend $100 now and your friend agrees to repay $120 in a year. Both of you expect prices to be 10 percent higher over the next year, so the repayment has three parts: the $100 principal that was borrowed, $10 to compensate you for the lost purchasing power of the $100 loan, and another $10 interest on the loan. If the inflation rate actually is 10 percent over the coming year, both of you will come out even, paying and receiving just what was expected in real terms. But inflation is seldom what we expect, so two possibilities need to be explored.

What if inflation is unexpectedly low? Your friend (the borrower) would find that the $120 loan repayment has greater real value than was expected. Borrowers lose when inflation is unexpectedly low because they give up more purchasing power than they anticipated. Lenders gain because their interest income is worth more than they guessed.

Borrowers win and lenders lose when inflation is unexpectedly high. If the actual inflation rate for the year is 30 percent, for example, the $120 your friend repays you is worth less than the $100 that was originally borrowed. Borrowers gain when inflation is unexpectedly high because they give up less real value than they bargained for. Lenders are hurt by unexpectedly high inflation because they receive lower real interest income.

Inflation was an unexpected surprise in the 1970s. Borrowers and lenders were generally amazed at how high inflation was. Borrowers gained at the lenders' expense for most of the decade. The disinflation of the early 1980s turned the tables, at least for a while. Unexpectedly low inflation put borrowers in a bind. Borrowers who figured that high inflation rates would protect them from bearing the real burden of their high mortgage payments were hit by two surprises: inflation slowed way down and a recession hit, increasing unemployment. The slower inflation meant that they had to bear unexpectedly high interest costs. The recession meant that they often lacked the income to make their mortgage payments.

Inflation and Savings Saving is important to economic growth. Savings cushion unemployment and give the economy funds needed for major spending and investment projects. Inflation discourages saving and encourages spending, to the long-run detriment of the economy.

Inflation encourages people to spend because their money might be worth less in the future. "Buy now and save before prices rise again" is the consumers' motto in high inflation times. High spending reduces the money left over for savings accounts. This spendthrift behavior might be wise, given the interest rates that many people receive on their savings. If you had put $1000 in a 5½ percent passbook savings account in 1970, it would have grown through the process of compound interest to over $1700 ten years later. But the inflation rate in the 1970s was much higher than 5½ percent. It took $2122 in 1980 to buy the goods that $1000 purchased in 1970. Thus, the $1700 savings account balance in 1980 bought fewer goods than the $1000 originally deposited in 1970 despite 10 years of interest. If you were saving for a car or house or college tuition, you would have been farther from your goal at the end of the decade than you were at the start.

Inflation's Deadweight Loss Inflation makes winners and losers, so rational people spend time trying to minimize their losses and maximize their gains. This is sensible behavior, but the time and money they spend trying to get around inflation's effects are wasted in that they do not add to the stock of goods and services available. Economists call this a **deadweight loss.**

People put a lot of effort into coping with inflation. Consumers spend time, labor, and gasoline shopping for bargains. Investors hedge their bets by buying gold and silver, investments that might protect them from higher prices but that do not build factories or harvest crops. People run back and forth between savings banks and commercial banks, trying to get the last ounce of interest on their savings before writing a check.

Inflation As a Self-Fulfilling Prophecy Inflation feeds on itself. A little inflation gives rise to more and more. Suppose, for example, that you expect inflation to be higher next year. What should you do about it? If you are smart, you will try to buy things now, before prices and interest rates rise. You will pull your money out of savings and use it while it still has high value. You will also ask for higher wages at work. All these actions make sense for you as an individual, but if everyone takes the same course only more inflation results. Higher demand couples with higher business costs to push prices up, creating the expected inflation.

Deadweight Loss
Scarce resources that are used to prevent loss or harm rather than being used to produce goods and services.

9.14 MEASURING INFLATION

Price Index
A standardized measure of the prices of certain types of goods and services.

Consumer Price Index (CPI)
A measure of inflation based on a market basket of goods and services that an average urban family would purchase.

Market Basket
A list of types and quantities of goods and services that is used to calculate a price index in order to measure inflation.

Measuring Inflation

The inflation rate, or the rate at which prices are rising, is commonly measured using a **price index,** such as the **Consumer Price Index (CPI).** It is important to accurately measure the inflation rate for several reasons. First, Congress and the president cannot make sound judgments on inflation versus unemployment issues unless they know the facts. Second, many private and public sector programs are indexed. That is, these payments are linked to a price index so that payments can be automatically adjusted for the effect of rising prices. Cost-of-living wage agreements, for example, often call for wages to be increased once a year at the same rate as the Consumer Price Index. An error in calculating the inflation rate can cause millions of workers and transfer payment recipients to be over- or under-compensated. It is also important for us, as individuals, to know how fast prices are rising so that we can take appropriate actions to protect ourselves from the effects of rising prices. Inflation can make you a winner or a loser depending on how well you anticipate price increases.

Table 9-3 lists figures for the Consumer Price Index and the inflation rate as measured by the CPI for the years 1960–1985. The Consumer Price Index numbers allow us to see how prices have changed in an absolute sense. A **market basket** of goods that cost $100 to purchase in 1967, for

TABLE 9-3

Inflation in the United States, 1960–85

Year	Consumer price index	Inflation rate (%)
1960	88.7	1.6
1961	89.6	1.0
1962	90.6	1.1
1963	91.7	1.2
1964	92.9	1.3
1965	94.5	1.7
1966	97.2	2.9
1967	100.0	2.9
1968	104.2	4.2
1969	109.8	5.4
1970	116.3	5.9
1971	121.3	4.3
1972	125.3	3.3
1973	133.1	6.2
1974	147.7	11.0
1975	161.2	9.1
1976	170.5	5.8
1977	181.5	6.5
1978	195.4	7.7
1979	217.4	11.3
1980	246.8	13.5
1981	272.4	10.4
1982	289.1	6.1
1983	298.4	3.2
1984	311.1	4.3
1985	322.2	3.6

Source. Economic Report of the President, 1986, Tables B-55, B-58.

example, cost more than $320 to buy in 1985. This tells us that inflation has dramatically changed the general level of prices between 1967 and 1985. Figures for the inflation rate tell us that we have had years when inflation has been very rapid. Prices increased by over 10 percent per year in 1974, 1979, 1980, and 1981. Inflation has been lower than this in recent years, but economists are still wary of the threat of high inflation today.

The Price Index

As noted above, inflation rates are measured using a price index. The first step in creating a price index is to pick a **base year.** Consumers are surveyed in the base year to see what types and amounts of goods they purchase. This information is used to construct a market basket of goods and services that gives heavier weight to the goods and services that are a big part of consumers' budgets and lighter weight to items infrequently purchased. The inflation rate is calculated by comparing the cost of the market basket of goods and services in the base year with the cost of buying the same market basket in another year.

For example, suppose that a base year of 1967 is selected for the price index. A study of consumer buying habits in this year will be used to produce a listing of types, qualities, and quantities, of goods that a typical consumer household might purchase. This market basket of goods is then priced in the base year, to establish a starting point, and again each subsequent year. The base year of the price index is arbitrarily set equal to an index number of 100.

The price index for a particular year is calculated by the government using the following formula:

$$\text{CPI for 1985} = \frac{\text{cost of 1967 market basket in 1985 prices}}{\text{cost of 1967 market basket in 1967 prices}} \times 100$$

The price index is what is sometimes called a pure number because it does not have any unit, such as dollars, feet, or hours, associated with it. The CPI number calculated above is only used for comparison with other CPI numbers to calculate the rate of change in prices. The price index figures in Table 9-3 can, however, be interpreted as the cost of a market basket, which makes it easier to conceptualize what the price index numbers mean. The CPI figures, for example, show that the goods that cost $100 in 1967 had a total cost of $322 in 1985.

We can use the price index numbers to calculate the rate of inflation between two years. For example, if we wanted to know what the inflation rate between 1983 and 1984 was, we would first look up the two price indexes in Table 9-3. The Consumer Price Index (CPI) for 1984 was 311.1 and the CPI for 1983 was 298.4. The inflation rate between these or any other two years is given by:

$$\text{Inflation rate} = \left(\frac{\text{CPI in later year}}{\text{CPI in earlier year}} - 1\right) \times 100$$

or

$$\text{Inflation rate} \atop \text{1983-1984} = \left(\frac{\text{CPI for 1984}}{\text{CPI for 1983}} - 1\right) \times 100 = \left(\frac{311.1}{298.4} - 1\right) \times 100 = 4.3\%$$

Base Year
A reference year used to construct a price index. The price index market basket is constructed for the base year.

Subtracting one from the ratio of the CPIs gives us the change in the price index as a decimal fraction. Multiplying by 100 converts the decimal fraction to a percentage.

The inflation index just discussed has several practical advantages. It is easy to calculate the inflation rate once the market basket is constructed. The Commerce Department employs people to check these prices monthly in every region of the country. They publish the national inflation averages as well as separate price indexes for major metropolitan areas, too. But there are important problems with measuring inflation in this way that we should be aware of.

One problem is that many people have different buying habits than the "average" market basket. Average price indexes cannot measure the true inflation rate for any individual because no one buys the average market basket.

A second problem is that buying habits change over time, but the price index market basket is not systematically updated and therefore lags behind current buying trends. People in 1984 did not really buy the same goods as were purchased in the base year of 1967 (or in 1978, which is the last time that the market basket was thoroughly updated). The price index has to hold the market basket constant so that it measures changes in price only. Since people's buying habits change over time and the price index cannot accurately adjust, the index cannot perfectly measure inflation.

The third problem with the price index is that it does not adjust for differences in the quality of goods. The prices of goods often change because their quality has increased or decreased. The price index cannot completely adjust for quality changes. If price rises but quality has improved, your purchasing power has not necessarily declined. The price index, however, will conclude that inflation has occurred, thereby reducing the dollar's value.

Official inflation measures are only general indicators of how fast prices rise. They should not be taken as precise statements of how much prices paid by any individual or group go up. The inflation index does not measure the cost of living, as many people think. A price index measures how fast the cost of a fixed market basket of goods is rising. No one really buys this fixed market basket of goods in real life, so the price index cannot tell us how fast the cost of living is changing.

9.15 PRICE INDEXES

Three Inflation Measures

Three general measures of inflation are used in the United States. Each of these indexes tells us about a different aspect of the inflation problem.

Consumer Price Index The CPI is the most widely used measure of inflation. It is designed, as its name suggests, to gauge inflation's effect on consumers. The index is calculated with the 1967 base year set equal to 100. The index has increased every year since 1967, indicating inflation in each year.

As previously mentioned, the Consumer Price Index was revised in 1978 to bring the original 1967 market basket up to date. The revision also expanded the market basket to look at a wider range of shoppers and modified the way that housing costs are measured to make the inflation measure more accurate for a broad range of uses. Housing costs are now measured using rental housing costs instead of the purchase cost of housing, which was previously employed. This change makes the CPI less sensitive to change in mortgage interest rates, which dramatically affect the cost of newly purchased housing but have relatively little effect on the cost of homes purchased in previous periods.

The CPI looks at the buying habits of urban families. If your shopping list is much different from theirs, the CPI does not accurately reflect your inflation burden.

Producer Price Index (PPI)
A measure of inflation based on a market basket of goods and services that business firms purchase.

Producer Price Index The **Producer Price Index (PPI)** is sometimes referred to by its old name, the Wholesale Price Index. The PPI measures inflation experienced by business firms. Since it looks at the average purchases of a wide range of businesses, however, it cannot really tell the inflation rate suffered by any particular firm or industry. It is nonetheless a good general indicator of price increases that firms experience.

Leading Indicator
An economic statistic that tends to foretell future changes in the economy.

The PPI is particularly useful to economists because it is a **leading indicator** of consumer prices. Changes in producer prices tend to foreshadow changes in consumer prices. Firms that bear higher costs today raise their prices in the future. If we see a 10 percent increase in the PPI in January, we can expect big increases in the CPI in February, March, or April. If you want to get an idea of where consumer prices are going in the future, keep your eye on the PPI today.

Gross National Product Implicit Price Deflator Index
A price index used to adjust GNP for inflation. All final goods and services form the market basket for the GNP Index.

GNP Implicit Price Deflator Index The **Gross National Product Implicit Price Deflator Index** is the broadest measure of inflation for the economy. The GNP Index takes as its market basket all goods and services produced in the United States. All GNP is included in the market basket for the GNP index. The GNP Index cannot tell us much about the inflation rate of any group or individual, but it does give us a good idea of how overall prices change.

KEY CONCEPTS 9.14, 9.15

Inflation is measured using a price index. A price index calculates how the cost of a set market basket of goods and services varies over time. The most widely used price indexes are the Consumer Price Index, the Producer Price Index, and the GNP Implicit Price Deflator Index. These indexes differ in that different goods and services are included in their market baskets. Price indexes are not perfect measures of inflation because their market baskets cannot reflect any one individual's purchases, nor can the market baskets accurately keep up with changing use patterns.

Calculating Real Values

9.16 PRICE INDEX ADJUSTMENTS

People who live in a world of inflation need to be able to make calculations that involve inflation rates. People frequently ask questions such as, "What was the inflation rate last year? Did our pay increase keep up with inflation?" This section provides formulas that are used to answer these questions.

The first problem is to calculate the inflation rate between two years using the CPI. We have already studied how inflation is calculated using price indexes. The inflation rate is equal to the percentage change in the CPI between the two years in question. One easy way to do this is to use the following formula:

$$\text{Inflation} = \left(\frac{\text{CPI this year}}{\text{CPI comparison year}} - 1\right) \times 100$$

Subtracting one from the ratio of the CPIs gives us the change in the price index as a decimal fraction. Multiplying by 100 converts the decimal fraction to a percentage. The inflation rate between 1978 and 1979, for example, is found by first looking up the CPI numbers in Table 9-3, then inserting the appropriate values into the formula to get

$$\text{Inflation} = \left(\frac{217.4}{195.4} - 1\right) \times 100 = 11.3 \text{ percent}$$

Another formula, which is algebraically equivalent to the previous one, can also be used to find the inflation rate. This formula is

$$\text{Inflation} = \frac{\text{CPI this year} - \text{CPI comparison year}}{\text{CPI in comparison year}} \times 100$$

Using this formula, the inflation rate between 1978 and 1979 is calculated as (217.4 − 195.4)/195.4 and then multiplied by 100 to convert this from a decimal fraction to a percentage. The answer again is that inflation was 11.3 percent in 1978–1979 as measured by the CPI. The two formulas give the same answer. You can use whichever formula you find easiest to remember or use.

Now suppose that your pay had increased from $20,000 to $25,000 during 1978. Did you beat inflation? One way to tell is to compare the increase in income to the increase in prices. Your wages went up by [($25,000/20,000) − 1] × 100, or 25 percent. Prices went up an average of 11 percent over this period, so your income increased faster than prices. Thus your real income increased.

A more exact way to look at real values is to convert everything to dollars of the same "size." Suppose, for example, that you want to compare your pay in 1978 and 1979 in dollars of the same value. You can compute this real value using the following formula:

$$\text{Value in \$1978} = \text{value in \$1979} \times \frac{\text{CPI in 1978}}{\text{CPI in 1979}}$$

Your $25,000 pay in 1979 is equivalent to

$$\$25,000 \times \left(\frac{195.4}{217.4}\right) = \$22,470 \text{ in 1978 dollars}$$

In real terms, then, your pay increased from $20,000 in 1978 to $22,470 in 1979. In other words, $2470 of the increase represented a higher purchasing power, the rest of your $5000 raise went to pay higher prices. You can use this formula to make calculations for other time periods by changing the years consistently throughout the formula. To convert a value earned or received in $year_1$ in order to compare it with a value earned or received in $year_2$, you would use the following formula:

$$\text{Value in \$year}_1 = \text{value in \$year}_2 \times \left(\frac{\text{CPI in year}_1}{\text{CPI in year}_2}\right)$$

INFLATION AND UNEMPLOYMENT IN PERSPECTIVE

This chapter has provided a brief overview of how the economy has changed in recent decades. We have also looked more closely at the economic problems of inflation and unemployment, so that we may better understand what they are and what their economic consequences are. Both inflation and unemployment impose costs on the economy, but in very different ways. Both remain important economic problems.

Our economic goals of full employment, stable prices, and economic growth have not been achieved. Why not? The next several chapters attempt to answer this question by looking at the theories of how the economy works and the policies that have been guided by these theories. We will see that changing economic events have caused macroeconomic theories to evolve and change, causing us to reevaluate policy tools. Today's inflation and unemployment problems can best be understood in the context of these changing events, theories, and policies.

SUMMARY

9.1
1. The Employment Act of 1946 set out three macroeconomic goals for the economy. These goals are generally stated as full employment, stable prices, and economic growth. The Full Employment and Balanced Budget Act of 1978, commonly called the Humphrey–Hawkins Bill, added new economic goals to this list. These include a balanced federal government budget and an improved ability to compete on international markets.

9.2
2. The U.S. economy has not met with complete success in achieving its macroeconomic goals. Economic growth has been uneven. High rates of inflation have occurred at least three times in recent years. Unemployment is still high, although it has improved since the early 1980s. The federal budget and the balance of trade deficits are both very large.

9.3
3. The U.S. economy entered the 1960s still recovering from the recession of the late 1950s. President Kennedy proposed economic policies that encouraged investment spending through tax incentives and encouraged consumer spending through tax cuts. President Johnson decided to increase spending on both domestic and military programs. His 1967 tax increase came too late to stop the rise in inflation that these spending policies produced.

9.4
4. The Phillips curve shows the inverse relationship or trade-off between inflation and unemployment. This suggests that economic policies that reduce inflation will cause higher unemployment and that economic policies that reduce unemployment tend to produce higher inflation. There are several theories that attempt to explain the Phillips curve, including the wage-lag theory. The economic events of the 1960s illustrate the Phillips curve relationship.

9.5
5. Inflation was the dominant economic event of the 1970s. President Nixon imposed a system of wage and price controls to reduce inflation in 1971. Oil prices increased in 1973–1974 due to the Arab oil embargo and again in 1979 due to the Iranian oil embargo. Higher oil prices, combined with other economic events, caused stagflation, which is a combination of high inflation and high unemployment rates. Presidents Ford and Carter attempted to deal with the stagflation of the 1970s with a variety of economic policies. The Federal Reserve adopted strict monetary policies in the late 1970s to bring down inflation.

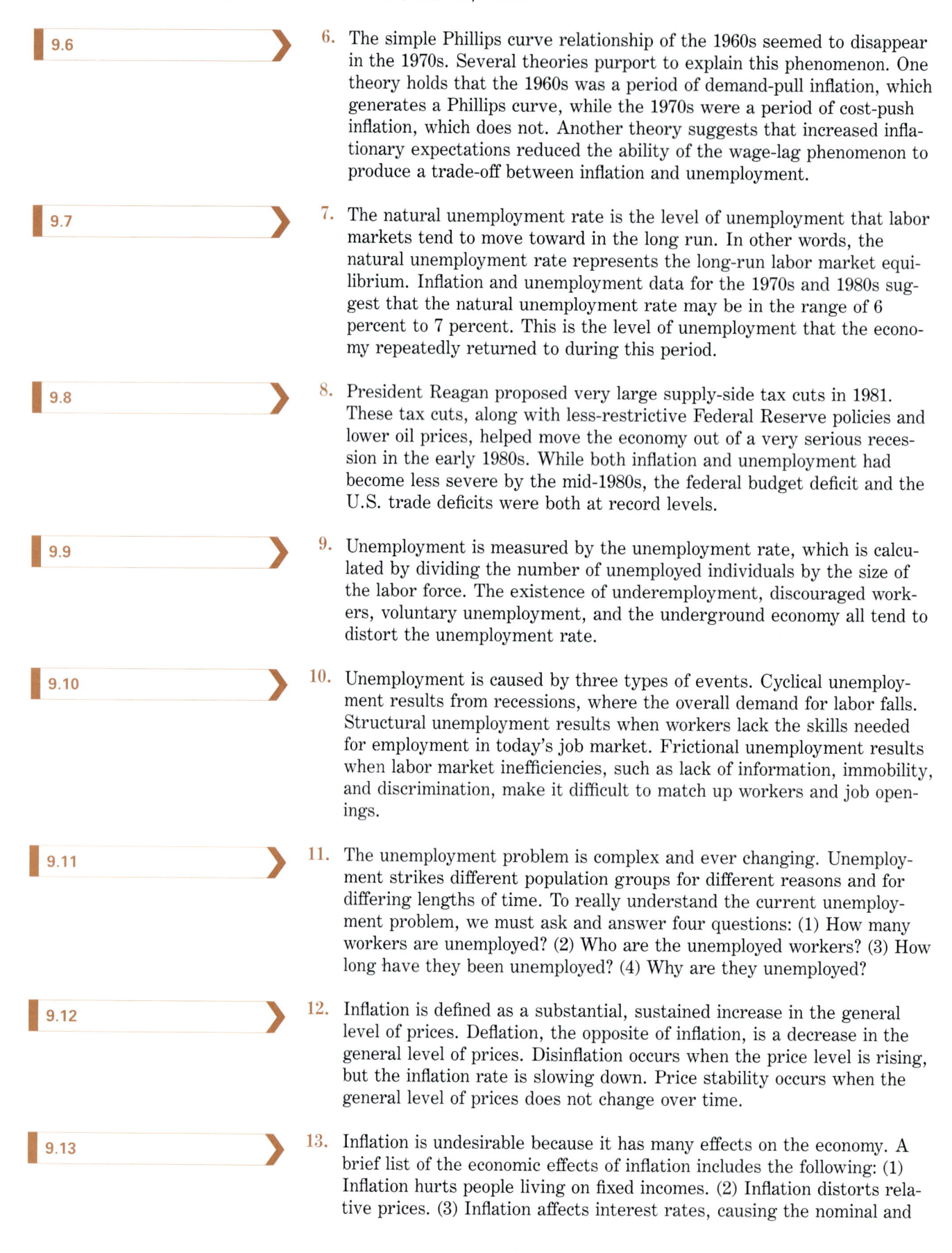

9.6 ▸ 6. The simple Phillips curve relationship of the 1960s seemed to disappear in the 1970s. Several theories purport to explain this phenomenon. One theory holds that the 1960s was a period of demand-pull inflation, which generates a Phillips curve, while the 1970s were a period of cost-push inflation, which does not. Another theory suggests that increased inflationary expectations reduced the ability of the wage-lag phenomenon to produce a trade-off between inflation and unemployment.

9.7 ▸ 7. The natural unemployment rate is the level of unemployment that labor markets tend to move toward in the long run. In other words, the natural unemployment rate represents the long-run labor market equilibrium. Inflation and unemployment data for the 1970s and 1980s suggest that the natural unemployment rate may be in the range of 6 percent to 7 percent. This is the level of unemployment that the economy repeatedly returned to during this period.

9.8 ▸ 8. President Reagan proposed very large supply-side tax cuts in 1981. These tax cuts, along with less-restrictive Federal Reserve policies and lower oil prices, helped move the economy out of a very serious recession in the early 1980s. While both inflation and unemployment had become less severe by the mid-1980s, the federal budget deficit and the U.S. trade deficits were both at record levels.

9.9 ▸ 9. Unemployment is measured by the unemployment rate, which is calculated by dividing the number of unemployed individuals by the size of the labor force. The existence of underemployment, discouraged workers, voluntary unemployment, and the underground economy all tend to distort the unemployment rate.

9.10 ▸ 10. Unemployment is caused by three types of events. Cyclical unemployment results from recessions, where the overall demand for labor falls. Structural unemployment results when workers lack the skills needed for employment in today's job market. Frictional unemployment results when labor market inefficiencies, such as lack of information, immobility, and discrimination, make it difficult to match up workers and job openings.

9.11 ▸ 11. The unemployment problem is complex and ever changing. Unemployment strikes different population groups for different reasons and for differing lengths of time. To really understand the current unemployment problem, we must ask and answer four questions: (1) How many workers are unemployed? (2) Who are the unemployed workers? (3) How long have they been unemployed? (4) Why are they unemployed?

9.12 ▸ 12. Inflation is defined as a substantial, sustained increase in the general level of prices. Deflation, the opposite of inflation, is a decrease in the general level of prices. Disinflation occurs when the price level is rising, but the inflation rate is slowing down. Price stability occurs when the general level of prices does not change over time.

9.13 ▸ 13. Inflation is undesirable because it has many effects on the economy. A brief list of the economic effects of inflation includes the following: (1) Inflation hurts people living on fixed incomes. (2) Inflation distorts relative prices. (3) Inflation affects interest rates, causing the nominal and real interest rates to differ. (4) Inflation causes borrowers and lenders to gain or lose depending on how well they have anticipated the inflation rate. (5) Inflation discourages saving and reduces the real value of accumulated savings. (6) Inflation causes a deadweight loss because people must use scarce resources in an effort to reduce inflation's negative impacts. (7) Inflation tends to be a self-fulfilling prophecy because inflation generates inflationary expectations, which, in turn, can cause inflation.

9.14 ▶ 14. Inflation is measured using a price index. The price index is calculated by choosing a market basket of goods and services for a base year. The price index then compares the cost of this fixed market basket in the base year with the cost of the same items in future years. Because price indexes must keep the market basket fixed over time, they cannot measure inflation for all groups and all periods with complete accuracy.

9.15 ▶ 15. The three most important price indexes in the United States are the Consumer Price Index (CPI), the Producer Price Index (PPI) and the GNP Implicit Price Deflator Index. Each of these indexes is useful when used correctly.

9.16 ▶ 16. Price indexes such as the CPI can be used to calculate inflation rates between years and to convert nominal values to real values so that prices and incomes can be more accurately compared over time. The text provided formulas to be used in making these calculations.

DISCUSSION QUESTIONS

9.1, 9.2 ▶ 1. List and explain our five main macroeconomic goals. Have our macroeconomic problems improved in the 1980s? Use the evidence presented in this chapter to answer the question.

9.4 ▶ 2. Draw a Phillips curve. What does the Phillips curve say about the relationship between inflation and unemployment?

9.3, 9.5, 9.8 ▶ 3. How has the relationship between inflation and unemployment changed from the 1960s to the 1980s?

9.7 ▶ 4. What is the natural unemployment rate? In what sense is it "natural"?

9.6, 9.7 ▶ 5. What is the relationship between the short-run Phillips curve and the long-run Phillips curve? Use data for the 1970s and 1980s to illustrate your answer.

9.9 ▶ 6. One news report states the number of workers with jobs has increased in the most recent month. Another news report indicates that the unemployment rate has increased. Explain how it is possible for both of these reports to be accurate.

9.10 ▶ 7. Give examples of individuals who suffer from cyclical, structural, and frictional unemployment.

8. Explain the difference between inflation, deflation, and disinflation. *(9.12)*

9. The inflation rate for next year is expected to be 4 percent. Suppose that the actual inflation rate for next year turns out to be 3 percent. Explain who would win or lose (and how) as a result of this event. *(9.13)*

10. Use the CPI data provided in this chapter to calculate the inflation rate for 1980. *(9.14, 9.16)*

11. Suppose that a person purchased a house for $50,000 in 1980 and sold it for $70,000 in 1982. Use the formulas in this chapter to calculate the real profit or loss resulting from this transaction. *(9.16)*

12. How accurate are our measures of inflation and unemployment? Explain why it is possible to argue that inflation and unemployment are either overstated or understated by official statistics. *(9.9, 9.14)*

SELECTED READINGS

Clark, Lindley. *The Secret Tax*. New York: Dow Jones Books, 1976.

Feldstein, Martin. "The Economics of the New Unemployment." *Public Interest* (Fall 1973).

Fellner, William (Ed.). *Essays in Contemporary Economic Problems: Disinflation*. Washington, DC: American Enterprise Institute, 1983.

Gordon, Robert J. "Understanding Inflation in the 1980s." *Brookings Papers on Economic Activity* 1 (1985), pp. 263–299.

Lekachman, Robert. *Inflation: The Permanent Problem of Boom and Bust*. New York: Random House, 1973.

Okun, Arthur. *Prices and Quantities*. Washington, DC: Brookings Institution, 1981.

Solow, Robert. "The Intelligent Citizen's Guide to Inflation." *Public Interest* (Winter 1975).

PART 4

Macroeconomic Theory and Policy

CHAPTER 10

The Keynesian Model of the Economy

Having read the chapter, reviewed the chapter summary, and completed the *Study Guide* exercises, you should be able to:

CRIS

10.1 CLASSICAL ECONOMISTS: Explain how the classical economists used Say's law and the concept of flexible wages and prices to conclude that a major depression would be impossible.

10.2 CIRCULAR FLOW: Draw the complete circular flow diagram and list and describe the three leakages and the three injections from the circular flow.

10.3 MACROECONOMIC EQUILIBRIUM: Explain what is meant by macroeconomic equilibrium in terms of the circular flow model and explain Keynes' view of the properties of macroeconomic equilibrium.

10.4 DETERMINANTS OF CONSUMPTION SPENDING: List and briefly discuss the major determinants of consumption spending in the economy.

10.5 CONSUMPTION FUNCTION: Draw a Keynesian consumption function and explain the relationship among total consumption, autonomous consumption, disposable income, and saving in this model.

10.6 MARGINAL AND AVERAGE PROPENSITIES: Define the following terms and explain how they are related to one another: marginal propensity to consume, marginal propensity to save, average propensity to consume, average propensity to save.

10.7 CONSUMPTION AND DISPOSABLE INCOME: Explain why the relationship between consumption and disposable income is different in the short term than in the long term.

10.8 DETERMINANTS OF INVESTMENT SPENDING: List and describe the major determinants of investment spending in the economy.

260 The Keynesian Model of the Economy

10.9 DETERMINANTS OF NET EXPORT SPENDING: List and describe the major determinants of net export spending in the economy.

10.10 DETERMINANTS OF GOVERNMENT SPENDING: Discuss the determinants of government spending in the economy.

10.11 KEYNESIAN MODEL OF EQUILIBRIUM: Draw and discuss the Keynesian model of equilibrium including consumption, investment, net export spending, and government spending.

10.12 KEYNESIAN GRAPHIC DEVICES: Draw and describe the graphic devices used in Keynesian analysis and explain the meaning of the 45-degree line.

10.13 EQUILIBRIUM INCOME: Use the Keynesian graphic model to show where equilibrium income occurs and characterize equilibrium income in terms of total spending and total income and in terms of leakages and injections.

10.14 ROLE OF INVENTORIES: Discuss the role of inventories in the adjustment to equilibrium income in the Keynesian model.

10.15 SPENDING MULTIPLIER: Discuss the concept of the spending multiplier and give its formula.

10.16 GRAPHIC MODEL OF SPENDING MULTIPLIER: Show how the spending multiplier works using the graphic Keynesian model.

10.17 PARADOX OF THRIFT: Explain what is meant by the paradox of thrift and tell why it is a paradox.

Macroeconomics did not really exist as a separate area of economic theory until the Great Depression of the 1930s focused the attention of economists and policymakers on the problems of stabilizing the entire economy. Prior to the Great Depression, many economists believed that the microeconomic forces of competition and equilibrium in individual markets would assure an equilibrium for the entire economy. The profound events of the Great Depression caused many economists to rethink their ideas concerning how the economy works.

The British economist John Maynard Keynes developed a theory that both explained how the economy could suffer a Great Depression and suggested a system of government policies that could fight economic downturns. Keynes' model of the economy was built on the idea that the total level of spending in the economy determines the total level of production and income in the economy. Keynes held that we can cause changes in income in the economy by controlling the level of total spending through the concept of the **circular flow of spending and income** that was discussed in Chapters 6 and 8.

It is important to try to appreciate the real impact of the Keynesian revolution. The theory presented in this chapter changed forever the way that we view the economy and the role of government in our private

Circular Flow of Spending and Income
A model of the relationship between spending and income for the entire economy.

economic lives. It is safe to say that our everyday lives have been changed significantly by Keynes' ideas. Keynes goes down in the history books as one of the most influential figures in the twentieth century. Like other influential thinkers, many of Keynes' ideas and proposals were and are still controversial. Not all of his prescriptions for the 1930s proved valid in the much-changed world of the 1970s and 1980s. This does not diminish Keynes' accomplishments, however. It only shows that economics must change as the economy changes, an idea that Keynes would have endorsed.

This chapter presents a simple Keynesian model of the economy and shows how this model explains changes in production and income, such as the Great Depression. We will also look at the economic policies that can be derived from this model.

CLASSICAL ECONOMIC IDEAS

> **10.1 CLASSICAL ECONOMISTS**

Classical Economists
Economists of the nineteenth and early twentieth century who did not believe that sustained recession was possible in a market economy.

Say's Law of Markets
The concept, attributed to Jean Baptiste Say, that supply creates its own demand.

Prior to the Great Depression of the 1930s, a group that has come to be known as the **classical economists** dominated economic theory. Their classical economics was based on the microeconomics of market equilibrium. They assumed that markets work to balance supply and demand; an equilibrium price provides every buyer with a willing seller and all goods offered for sale eventually find buyers. Markets that work efficiently always clear, with no persistent shortages or surpluses.

The economist Jean Baptiste Say was responsible for a simple idea that convinced many classical economists that continuing depression was impossible. **Say's law of markets** held that "supply creates its own demand." Production of $1 worth of bread by the business sector, according to the circular flow concept, necessarily creates $1 of income to the household sector. In other words, Say's law suggested that there was, in theory, just enough income to purchase all goods that are produced. Markets with flexible prices would then see that the demand and supply for specific goods fell into equilibrium. Thus the classical economics of Say's law and market equilibrium seemed to deny the possibility of a Great Depression. A general glut of goods was impossible because flexible markets would efficiently adjust, lowering prices in the face of persistent surpluses. Unemployment was believed to be either a temporary problem or the result of a voluntary choice to avoid work.

The fact that a depression did occur forced the economics profession to search for a better theory to describe how the economy works. Keynes' economic theories, developed in the early years of the Depression, proved to be the "better mousetrap" that economists needed to explain the events of this period.

THE KEYNESIAN REVOLUTION

In 1936 John Maynard Keynes published a macroeconomic theory that appeared more able to accurately describe and predict the events of that time. In this book *The General Theory of Employment, Interest, and Money*,[1] Keynes attacked the ideas of the classical economists on several fronts. He claimed that, contrary to the classical economists' contention, markets do

---

1. John Maynard Keynes, *The General Theory of Employment, Interest, and Money*, New York: Harcourt, Brace, and World, 1936.

Sticky Prices
Prices that do not fully respond to market forces, such as wages that do not fall in response to a surplus of labor.

not always adjust to equilibrium. One reason why some markets fail to clear is that they have **sticky prices** that do not quickly adjust to changes in demand and supply. If the wages of auto workers are sticky because of union contracts, for example, it is possible to have a substantial surplus of auto workers. If union contracts or other economic rigidities keep wages from falling to the market equilibrium level, high levels of involuntary unemployment can occur. Wages and prices may also be sticky because people are uncertain about the consequences of a change in price.

Keynes' most important contribution to economics was his model of the economy, which was quite controversial for its time and is still hotly debated today. In this model, Keynes chose to view the economy as being divided into sectors. He then used circular flow analysis to explain the relationship between spending and income in the economy.

10.2 CIRCULAR FLOW

Circular Flow Analysis

The circular flow diagram presented in Figure 10-1 shows the basic relationship between the household sector and the business sector. Household consumers undertake consumption spending (denoted by C in macroeconomics), which provides revenues that businesses use for production. As defined in Chapter 8, consumption spending is the value of the final goods and services that households purchase. It includes expenditures for such everyday items as food, clothing, legal services, and haircuts. Production creates income in the form of wages, rents, interest, and profits for households. Spending by households, therefore, ultimately creates income for households in the circular flow process. This means that the amount of income in the economy depends on the amount of spending that takes place.

People can do other things with their income than spend it on goods and services produced in our economy. Households can save their income or use it to buy foreign goods or pay it to the government in taxes. The three sectors that correspond to these uses of income are the financial sector, the foreign sector, and the government sector.

Injections
Economic activities that stimulate the circular flow of spending and income; investment, government, and export spending are injections.

Each of the sectors shown in Figure 10-1 is able to increase spending and income in the economy through **injections** into the circular flow. The first injection is investment spending, denoted in macroeconomics by a capital I. Investment spending is the purchase of goods—such as factories, equipment, inventories, and new technologies—that increase the capacity to produce in the future. The financial sector channels saved funds to businesses and consumers who spend them. Spending of this type is an injection into the circular flow because increased investment spending causes higher total spending and income.

Exports
Sales of goods and services to purchasers located in other countries.

The foreign sector provides an injection when **exports** are purchased. Exports are goods and services that are purchased by foreign buyers. The foreign purchaser gets the valuable good or service when exports occur, while the spending and income accrue in the United States. Exports therefore stimulate spending and income at home and are properly classified as an injection.

Government also provides an injection that directly increases total spending in the economy. Government purchases of goods and services (denoted by G in the figure) act to increase total spending on consumption (C) and investment (I). Not all government outlays are included in government spending, however. Much of government's budget takes the form of transfer payments. Transfer payments are one-way transfers of funds from

FIGURE 10-1 **Circular Flow of Spending and Income.** The circular flow of spending and income is the fundamental concept of Keynesian macroeconomics. The basic circular flow is supplemented by leakages and injections from the financial, government, and foreign sectors. The injections are investment, government, and export spending. The leakages are saving, taxes, and imports.

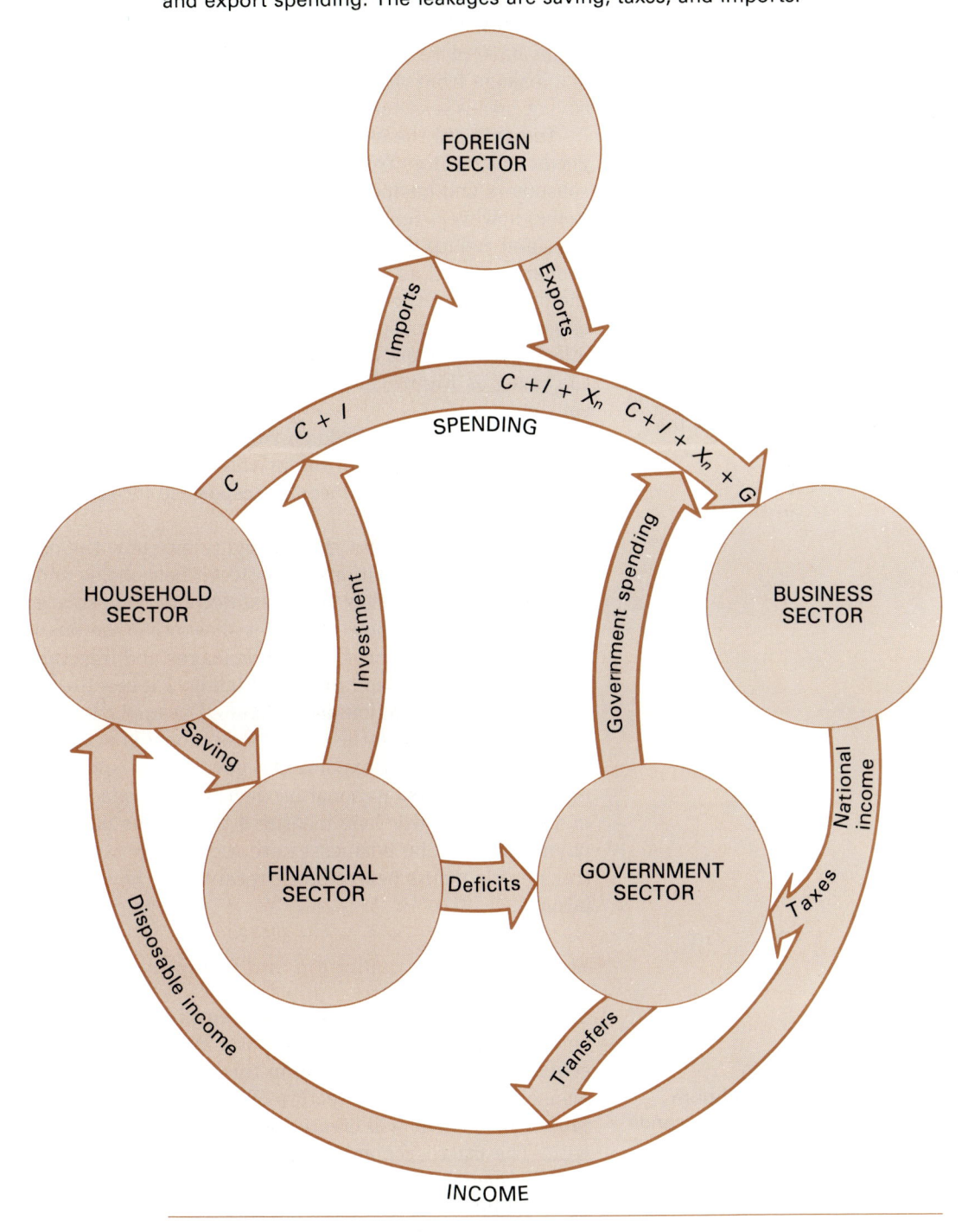

government to businesses and individuals. These transfers do not directly purchase goods and services, so they are not an injection. Rather, as the figure shows, transfer payments increase disposable income, making consumers better able to undertake consumption spending.

Leakages
Economic activities that reduce the circular flow of spending and income; saving, taxes, and imports are leakages.

Imports
Purchases of goods and services from producers located in other countries.

Net Exports
The total value of exports minus the total value of imports for a given period of time; the net addition to total spending resulting from the foreign sector of the economy.

Three **leakages** from the domestic circular flow correspond to the new sectors introduced in this figure. The first leakage is saving. Income that is not otherwise used can be sent to the financial sector and saved. Saving is important. Saving provides resources needed for investment in machines and technology that increase the economy's future ability to produce. When households save, they give up the use of some resources today so that they might have more resources in the future. In the short run, however, saving is a leakage from the circular flow. All else being equal, an increase in saving means less spending and, therefore, less income.

Imports are the second leakage from the circular flow. We import many goods and services from producers in other countries. These items benefit consumers and businesses in the United States. The purchase of these items, however, tends to stimulate spending and income in the other countries and reduce the flow of spending and income at home. Thus imports are properly viewed as a leakage from the circular flow. Note that sometimes the net effect of the foreign sector—exports minus imports, termed **net exports** (X_n)—is used in economic models instead of classifying the export injection and import leakage separately, as we have done here. The effect is the same, as Figure 10-1 shows, and the treatment is simply a matter of convenience.

Taxes are the final leakage from the circular flow. Taxes are money the government collects from the private sector to finance public sector programs. Higher taxes reduce the disposable income consumers have left to spend.

Figure 10-1 provides many insights into how the economy works. First, it shows the basic relationship between households and businesses that we have discussed in earlier chapters. Second, it illustrates the concept that spending creates income. Third, it shows that the financial, foreign, and government sectors provide both leakages and injections to the basic circular flow of spending and income. Finally, Figure 10-1 illustrates the relationship between production and income. The upper loop of the figure shows that total spending in the domestic economy is equal to the sum of consumption, investment, net export, and government spending. The upper loop measures the gross national product, or the value of all final goods produced in a year. The lower loop measures the income payments to households. The payments made by businesses are reduced by taxes but supplemented by transfer payments before being received by households as disposable income.

Macroeconomic Equilibrium and Economic Policy

10.3 MACROECONOMIC EQUILIBRIUM

Macroeconomic Equilibrium
In the Keynesian model, a condition in which total spending equals total income, or stated differently, total leakages equal total injections.

The economy is at **macroeconomic equilibrium** when the total planned amount that is spent equals the total income of the economy. This is an equilibrium because if income in this time period is $100 million and total planned spending by all sectors of the economy equals $100 million, then the $100 million spent will create the $100 million of income that we started with. The macroeconomic equilibrium occurs, in terms of the circular flow model, when total leakages (the sum of saving, imports, and taxes) equal the total injections (investment, exports, and government spending).

Keynes said that, like a competitive market, the whole economy automatically adjusts to a macroeconomic equilibrium. Spending and income, leakages and injections are all interrelated in ways that guarantee that some equilibrium is finally reached. The economy is therefore not inherently unstable.

Here is how the economy adjusts according to this simple interpretation of Keynes' theory. Suppose that income rises because of an arbitrary increase in one of the injections of government spending, exports, or investment spending. Assume, for simplicity, that Congress votes to increase spending on education and purchases computers for all public schools. The increase in injections throws the economy out of balance because leakages are temporarily less than injections. This higher spending creates higher income in the U.S. economy, but as income rises, government tax collections also rise, consumer saving increases, and people use their higher incomes to purchase more imported goods. These higher leakages balance out the increase in injections that initially pushed income higher. The economy eventually adjusts to a new equilibrium at a higher level of income, where total leakages equal injections and total spending equals total income.

Now suppose, on the other hand, that one of the injections unexpectedly decreases. Suppose that business firms are uncertain about the future and reduce their investment spending on new factories and equipment. This lowers total spending, therefore forcing a reduction in total income. Leakages and injections are temporarily out of balance. The fall in income, however, tends to reduce government tax collections, reduce household saving, and reduce expenditures on imported goods. Thus the leakages fall until they match the new lower level of injections. Equilibrium between spending and income and leakages and injections is eventually restored at a lower level of income.

While Keynes' theory suggested that macroeconomic equilibrium is stable, Keynes did not say that this equilibrium always occurs at a desirable level of income. Equilibrium, according to Keynes, occurs wherever the planned leakages and injections in the economy dictate. Equilibrium might happen at full employment, but this is not assured. Equally likely is a Great Depression equilibrium, with spending and income equal at low levels that cause very high unemployment rates.

Keynes suggested that the government could control the economy so as to avoid a depression macroeconomic equilibrium. Leakages and injections are not pure random events. Government can adjust the macroeconomic equilibrium by manipulating taxes, government spending, and transfer payments. These government actions are called **fiscal policy.** Keynes' economic theories were controversial in the 1930s and 1940s because they called for government to take an active hand in managing the economy, whereas the classical economists had proposed **laissez faire policies,** which called for little government interference in the economy.

Fiscal Policy
The practice of managing government spending and taxes as a means of arriving at stable prices or other economic goals, such as growth or high levels of unemployment.

Laissez Faire Policies
Government policies that seek a minimal level of interference with market actions.

KEY CONCEPTS 10.2, 10.3

Keynes said that the economy is stable and tends to adjust to a macroeconomic equilibrium between leakages and injections and between total spending and total income. However, this equilibrium is not necessarily desirable, and high unemployment is possible. According to Keynes, the government can use its power to influence the leakages and injections so as to guide the economy toward a full employment equilibrium.

Keynesian economic theory was an important step in the evolution of macroeconomic theory. Keynes focused his analysis on spending by consumers, investors, and government. The remainder of this chapter looks more closely at the Keynesian analysis of each of these groups' behaviors.

PROMINENT ECONOMIST

John Maynard Keynes (1883–1946)

John Maynard Keynes was born in Cambridge in 1883; this was ironically the same year as Karl Marx's death. Marx had predicted the failure of capitalism. Keynes was a strong believer in capitalism.

Keynes was educated at Eton and Cambridge. Initially, he focused on mathematics but switched later to philosophy and economics. After receiving his degree, he studied under the prominent economist Alfred Marshall in preparation for the Civil Service entrance exam. He accepted a civil service post in the India Office during the period when Britain ruled India. Keynes disliked this assignment, but while there he wrote a "Treatise on Probability" which was later the basis for his election as a lifetime Fellow to Cambridge's King's College.

Following his service in India, Keynes assisted the British Treasury in planning the financial matters of World War I. At the end of the war, Keynes was appointed representative for the British Treasury at the Versailles peace conference. He was unsuccessful in his efforts to persuade the Allies to take a more lenient attitude toward the Germans, and to protest the outcome, Keynes left the conference in 1919. Keynes began writing his controversial *Economic Consequences of the Peace* in which he predicted another war in Europe because of the harsh economic terms of the treaty.

Keynes spent the next years of his life developing economic theory. Through speculation in commodities and international currencies, he amassed great wealth for himself and King's College. In 1923, he wrote his *Tract on Monetary Reform*, which denounced the gold standard. Certainly Keynes' masterpiece was *The General Theory of Employment, Interest, and Money*, a foundation for macroeconomics for over 40 years.

Keynes advocated an expanding role for government in taxing income from wage earners and reallocating that income through increased government spending. Keynes' concept of countercyclical fiscal policy was the standard model of macroeconomics from the 1930s to the 1970s. While Keynes was certainly a revolutionary figure in economic theory, his analysis falls short of explaining modern day problems with concurrent inflation and unemployment. The rise of monetarism in the 1970s has offered a major challenge to traditional Keynesian analysis.

CONSUMPTION SPENDING

10.4 DETERMINANTS OF CONSUMPTION SPENDING

As we learned in Chapter 8, consumption spending is the largest component of total spending. The level of consumption spending is predicated on many variables. Economists believe that the level of consumption spending that a nation undertakes depends most directly on the amount of disposable income that is available. Disposable income, you will recall from Chapter 8, is basically equal to the income that households receive minus the direct taxes that they pay plus the transfer payments that they receive from government. Disposable income thus rises when direct taxes fall or when transfer payments such as social security benefits increase. Government tax and transfer programs therefore affect the level of consumption spending indirectly through their impact on disposable income.

Consumption spending also depends on the amount of wealth that households have accumulated. Wealth in the form of savings accounts, stocks and bonds, or valuable physical assets such as real estate represents an ability to spend over and above the amount of current disposable income. Consumption spending tends to be directly related to wealth. In the 1960s, for example, consumer spending increased for many reasons, one of which was the dramatic increase in stock prices during that period. People who owned stock experienced an increase in wealth as the value of their holdings increased. This higher wealth made them more willing to purchase consumer goods than they would otherwise have been. On the other hand, the stock market crash of 1929 reduced people's wealth, which led them to cut back on spending plans.

Expectations are another factor that affects the level of planned consumption spending. People who expect their disposable income to increase in the future are likely to spend more now in anticipation of this event. Thus people who expect their wages to rise or their taxes to fall or their transfer payment benefits to increase are likely to increase consumer spending. Consumption spending tends to fall, however, if households expect lower disposable income in the future.

The importance of expectations was seen in the case of President Ford's 1975 "tax rebate" tax cut. This was a one-shot tax refund of $100 to $200 paid to most households. The idea of the tax rebate was to stimulate consumer purchases, which would in turn stimulate production and reduce unemployment. Consumption spending did not rise substantially, however, even though disposable income increased. This was because consumers knew that the tax refund was a one-time-only event. They did not expect further increases in disposable income from the government, so they did not significantly alter their spending plans. This tax cut failed to significantly stimulate consumption spending because it failed to change household expectations about future taxes and income. A smaller, but permanent, tax cut might have had greater effect in this case.

Lyndon Johnson's 1966 tax increase was largely ineffective for the same reason. Johnson's tax surcharge was clearly a temporary measure. Because people did not expect a permanent change in their incomes, they did not cut back spending in the face of the tax increase, as Johnson's advisors had hoped.

The availability of credit also affects the level of consumption spending. Consumers are more likely to undertake major purchases if credit is readily available and relatively affordable. Interest rates are often as important as price when expensive items, such as real estate, are paid for with borrowed money. Higher interest rates on loans or shortages of loanable funds tend to restrict consumer purchases. In 1979–1980, for example, a variety of credit controls were instituted that tended to discourage consumer purchases of autos, homes, and other "big ticket" items.

Another factor that can affect the level of consumption spending is the demographic profile of household consumers. Consumption spending depends on the age and sex pattern of the population. Consumption spending might be expected to rise in the 1980s, for example, because the baby-boom generation that was born after World War II is now at the age when families are formed and major consumer expenditures such as homes, furniture, cars, and the like, are made. The size and composition of consumption spending is expected to change in the future, however, as the baby-boom generation ages and looks toward retirement.

Many factors affect the level of consumption spending for individuals and the entire economy. Keynes' analysis of consumption spending focused on the relationship between consumption spending and disposable income. Keynes theorized a particular type of relationship between disposable income and consumption. This relationship is discussed in more detail in the next subsection.

Keynesian Consumption and Saving

As already noted, the level of consumption spending in the economy depends on the level of disposable income. Another way of stating this relationship is by saying that consumption is a direct function of income. As income in the economy goes up, consumption spending goes up. As income in the economy declines, consumption spending also declines. We can understand this relationship between consumption and income more fully by looking at the hypothetical example displayed in Table 10-1.

Table 10-1 shows a hypothetical relationship between disposable income (Y_d), planned consumption spending (C), and planned saving (S) for an individual household. (Economists use Y to stand for income to differentiate it from I, which stands for investment spending.) The figures in the table show a direct relationship between income and consumption. We can learn a great deal about household behavior by analyzing the individual columns of Table 10-1.

Some consumption would take place even if income were zero. Consumers, as long as they are alive, have some level of consumption that is not dependent upon income. To support consumption that is greater than their income, they either consume prior savings, called dissaving, or consume other people's income, as is the case with those who receive transfer payments in our economy. Consumption that does not depend on the level of income is called **autonomous consumption**. The level of autonomous income for the economy depends on many factors, including the size of the population, the accumulated wealth of households, and their expectations concerning future income trends. The example in Table 10-1 assumes $2000 of autonomous consumption spending. This $2000 of consumption spending will exist regardless of income, at least in the short run.

The part of total consumption that does depend on level of income is called **induced consumption**. Induced consumption increases as income increases and falls as income falls. The $23,000 of total consumption spending at an income level of $30,000 in Table 10-1 is made up of autonomous spending of $2000 and induced consumption of $21,000.

The relationship between consumption spending and disposable income is called the **consumption function**. A function is a mathematical relationship between variables; in this case the variables are consumer spending and disposable income.

Saving is an important activity for individuals and society. First it is critical to understand the difference between saving and savings. Saving exists when individuals consume less than their total income. Saving is a flow concept; it represents the amount of income that is not consumed in a given period of time. Saving is equal to that part of disposable income that is not used for consumption spending. In equation form, this means that

$$Y_d = C + S$$
Disposable income = consumption plus saving

or

$$S = Y_d - C$$
Saving = disposable income minus consumption

Savings, on the other hand, is a stock concept. Savings are the accumulated amount of prior saving as measured at a particular point in time. For

---

Autonomous Consumption
The part of total consumption that does not depend on level of income.

Induced Consumption
The portion of total consumption that does depend on level of income. Induced consumption increases as income increases and decreases as income decreases.

10.5 CONSUMPTION FUNCTION

Consumption Function
A description of the way that consumption spending varies with disposable income.

TABLE 10-1 Measuring Consumption and Income

Point	1	2 Disposable income (Y_d) ($)	3 Planned consumption (C) ($)	4 Planned saving (S) ($)	5 APC (C/Y) (%)	6 APS (S/Y) (%)	7 MPC (%)	8 MPS (%)
A		0	2000	−2000	—	—	—	—
B		5000	6000	−1000	120	−20	80	20
C		10,000	10,000	0	100	0	80	20
D		15,000	14,000	+1000	93	7	80	20
E		20,000	18,000	+2000	90	10	80	20
F		25,000	22,000	+3000	88	12	80	20
G		30,000	26,000	+4000	87	13	80	20
H		35,000	30,000	+5000	86	14	80	20
I		40,000	34,000	+6000	85	15	80	20

example, last year you may have saved $100 and this year you may have saved $300. Your total savings is equal to $400, and it came about through your act of saving (spending less than your income). Changes in the flow variable saving cause changes in the stock variable savings.

Table 10-1 shows that the amount of planned saving varies with disposable income. At low levels of disposable income, such as $5000, saving is negative. This household receives disposable income of $5000 and undertakes a combination of autonomous and induced consumption spending of $6000. Thus dissaving of $1000 takes place. Saving is zero at the disposable income level of $10,000 in the table. Income and planned consumption spending are equal at this income level. Finally, positive saving exists at disposable income levels above $10,000 because planned consumption spending is less than disposable income. The amount of saving increases as income rises.

Graphing Consumption and Saving Functions

Figure 10-2 presents a pair of graphs that plot out the relationships among disposable income, consumption spending, and saving that are listed in the first four columns of Table 10-1. Figure 10-2(a) plots disposable income (on the horizontal axis) against total spending (on the vertical axis). Two lines are plotted here. The consumption spending line plots the relationship between the planned consumption and disposable income figures listed in Table 10-1. The second line in Figure 10-2(a) is a reference line, which shows all the points at which disposable income (horizontal axis) is equal to total spending (vertical axis); in other words, the points at which all income is spent. This is a 45-degree line.

One use of the 45-degree line can be seen in Figure 10-2. The 45-degree line shows all points where spending equals income. The consumption line shows how consumption spending varies with income. The consumption line and the 45-degree line intersect at point C in the figure. This corresponds to the income level at which consumption spending equals total income ($10,000). When a spending line like C intersects the 45-degree line, this tells us that total spending equals total income. For convenience, we might rename the 45-degree line the total income line. At point C, then, consumption spending is equal to total income.

270   The Keynesian Model of the Economy

FIGURE 10-2

Consumption and Saving Functions. The points on the consumption and saving functions shown here correspond to entries in Table 10-1. Consumption and saving both increase as income rises. The MPC is the slope of the consumption function. The MPS is the slope of the saving function. Saving equals zero and consumption equals income where the consumption function crosses the 45-degree equilibrium line.

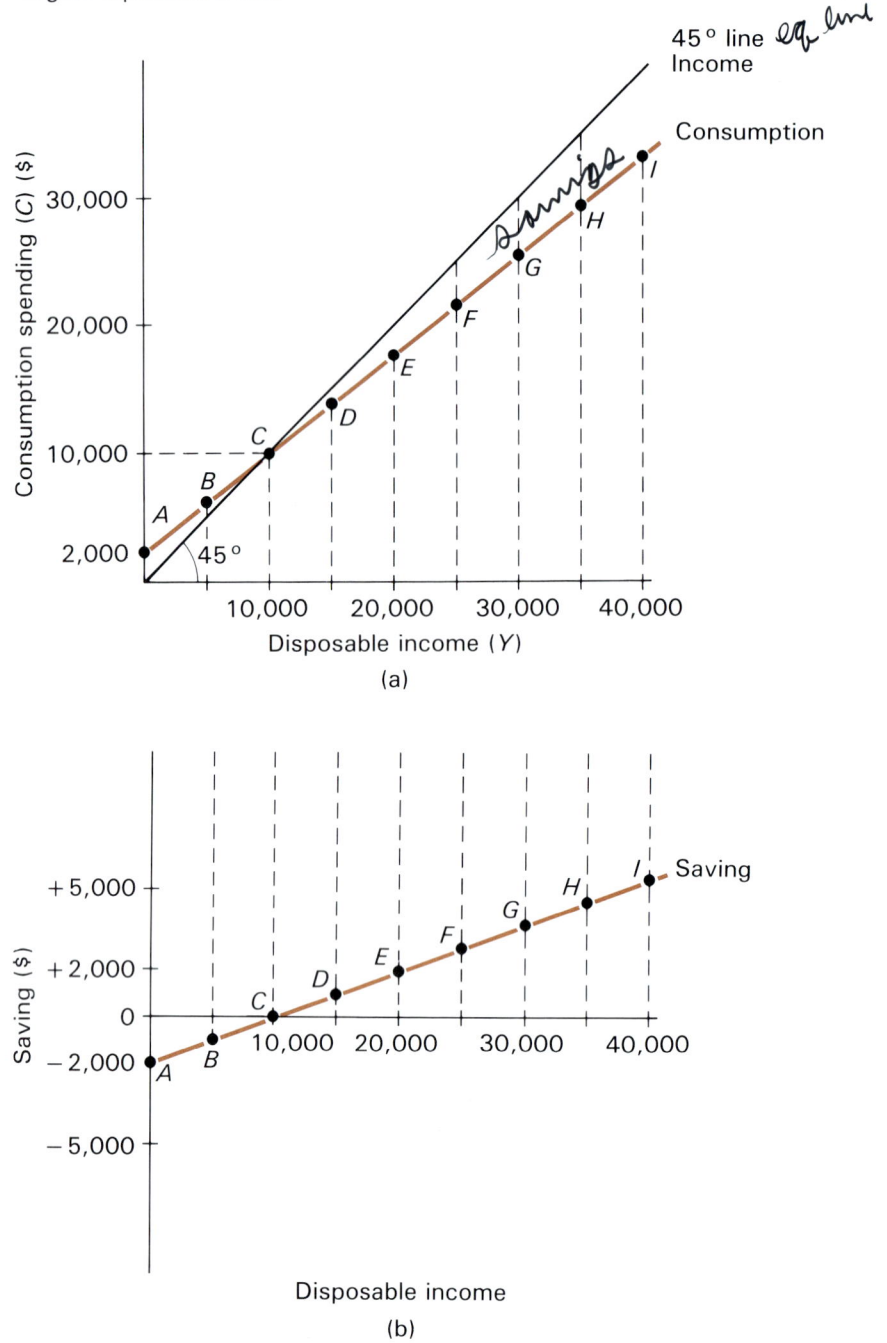

(a) Consumption spending (C) ($) plotted against Disposable income (Y), with 45° line (Income) and Consumption function passing through points A, B, C, D, E, F, G, H, I.

(b) Saving ($) plotted against Disposable income, with saving function passing through points A, B, C, D, E, F, G, H, I.

Figure 10-2(b) plots the relationship between saving and disposable income. Notice that saving is negative at low levels of income because consumption spending exceeds disposable income. Saving is zero at point C, where disposable income of $10,000 exactly equals consumption spending of

$10,000. Finally saving is positive and increasing at higher levels of income. Note that saving, as measured in Figure 10-2(b), is equal to the area between the income and consumption line in Figure 10-2(a). We can therefore measure saving either by plotting the saving function, as in Figure 10-2(b), or by measuring the difference between income and consumption spending, as in Figure 10-2(a).

APC, MPC, APS, MPS

10.6 MARGINAL AND AVERAGE PROPENSITIES

Average Propensity to Consume (APC)
The ratio of consumption to income. This ratio represents the portion of total income that consumers are consuming.

Average Propensity to Save (APS)
The ratio of saving to total income. This ratio represents the portion of total income that consumers save.

Consumption spending, as we learned in Chapters 8 and 9, is the largest component of aggregate demand. It is important, therefore, to know how consumption spending varies with income. Columns 5 and 6 of Table 10-1 provide two measures of the relationships among disposable income, consumption, and saving. The **average propensity to consume (APC)** is the ratio of the level of consumption spending to the level of disposable income. APC tells us what part of total income consumers are spending on consumption. Table 10-1 shows what happens to this ratio as income goes up. As their incomes increase, consumers spend more in total on consumption, but this spending represents a smaller percentage of their total income. The APC declines as income rises and rises as income falls. This is a relationship that makes common sense to most people.

The **average propensity to save (APS)** is the fraction of disposable income that is saved. Table 10-1 shows that the average propensity to save tends to rise as income rises. Low-income families tend to save a smaller proportion of their incomes than do higher-income groups.

The APC and APS always sum to 100 percent, as the figures in Table 10-1 show. This is true because, in the model we are using here, households can only consume or save their disposable income. It therefore follows that the percent that is consumed (APC) plus the percent that is saved (APS) must add up to 100 percent.

The APC and APS tell us how the average levels of consumption and saving depend on income. Columns 7 and 8 calculate two other important properties of consumption and saving. The **marginal propensity to consume (MPC)** is the ratio of the change in consumption to the change in income. As income rises from $10,000 to $15,000, for example, the table tells us that consumption spending rises from $10,000 to $14,000. The change in income is $5000; the change in consumption is $4000. Therefore,

Marginal Propensity to Consume (MPC)
The ratio of the change in consumption to the change in income. This ratio represents the percentage of each additional dollar earned as income that is spent on consumption.

$$MPC = \frac{\text{change in consumption}}{\text{change in income}}$$

$$MPC = \frac{\$4000}{\$5000} = .80 = 80 \text{ percent}$$

The MPC tells us what percentage of each additional dollar of income is spent on consumption. As Keynes had believed in the 1930s, as income rises in the short run, people tend to spend a smaller fraction of their total income on consumption, so they have a lower APC. But the ratio of the change in their consumption to the change in their income remains relatively constant as income changes, so the MPC is relatively constant in the short run. As income increases, consumption will also increase, but by less than the increase in income. Mathematically, the MPC is equal to the slope of the consumption line in Figure 10-2.

Marginal Propensity to Save (MPS)
The ratio between the change in saving and the change in income. This ratio represents the percentage of each additional dollar in income that is saved.

The **marginal propensity to save (MPS)** is equal to the change in saving divided by the change in income. The MPS really tells us what percentage of each additional dollar in income will be saved. As income rises from $10,000 to $15,000, for example, saving rises from zero to $1000. The *MPS* is, therefore,

$$MPS = \frac{\text{change in saving}}{\text{change in income}}$$

$$MPS = \frac{\$1000}{\$5000} = .20 = 20 \text{ percent}$$

Mathematically, the *MPS* is equal to the slope of the saving line in Figure 10-2. As Table 10-1 shows, *MPC* + *MPS* = 100 percent because the amount of a change in income that is spent on consumption plus the amount that is saved necessarily adds up to 100 percent of the change in income.

The consumption line shows the relationship between consumption spending and disposable income. If disposable income changes, we move along the consumption line to a new point on that line. For example, if income changes from $20,000 to $30,000, we would move from point *E* to point *G* on the consumption line, with consumption spending rising from $18,000 to $26,000. The consumption line can shift if some economic event, such as a change in consumer expectations, alters the amount of desired consumption spending at each income level or changes the level of autonomous consumption.

Long-Run Consumption and the Keynesian Confusion

10.7 CONSUMPTION AND DISPOSABLE INCOME

Figure 10-2 plotted a short-run planned consumption function for an individual household. Its vertical intercept was some positive number and the *APC* declined as income went up. In other words, consumers spent a smaller portion of their total income on consumption as their income increased. Keynes hypothesized this behavior in the 1930s, not necessarily for individual households, but for the economy as a whole. Not all households necessarily behave in the way that Table 10-1 describes. Some households may spend more, others may spend less. But Keynes thought that the general concepts about consumption and income that we have analyzed would hold for the economy taken as a whole.

As more sophisticated statistical techniques and the advent of the electronic computer gave economists such as Simon Kuznets the ability to test this hypothesis over long periods of time, an interesting conflict arose between theory and reality. If the relationship between consumption and income is plotted over many years, a relatively constant average propensity to consume emerges. It appears that consumers in the long run spend about the same percentage of their total income on consumption as income rises. We can see this in Figure 10-3. The long-run consumption function passes through the origin, with an *MPC* and *APC* that are the same. This long-run consumption line indicates that the *APC* tends to remain relatively constant over time as income rises. This is in conflict with Keynes' hypothesis that the *APC* falls as income rises. Does this data mean that Keynes' theory about consumer spending was wrong?

Permanent Income Hypothesis
A concept developed by Milton Friedman that states that consumers make their consumption decisions based more upon what they believe their permanent income to be than their actual income at the time consumption expenditures occur.

Much of the difference between Keynes' theory and the long-run trend in consumer spending can be explained by a concept that economists call the **permanent income hypothesis.** This theory, first developed by the Nobel Prize-winning economist Milton Friedman, contends that consumers make their consumption decisions based more upon what they believe their income

Consumption Spending 273

FIGURE 10-3   **Short- and Long-Run Consumption Functions.** Consumption has been a relatively constant fraction of income over the long run, as this figure shows. In the short run, however, consumption behavior has been different. The difference between the short- and long-run consumption functions is explained by the permanent income hypothesis.

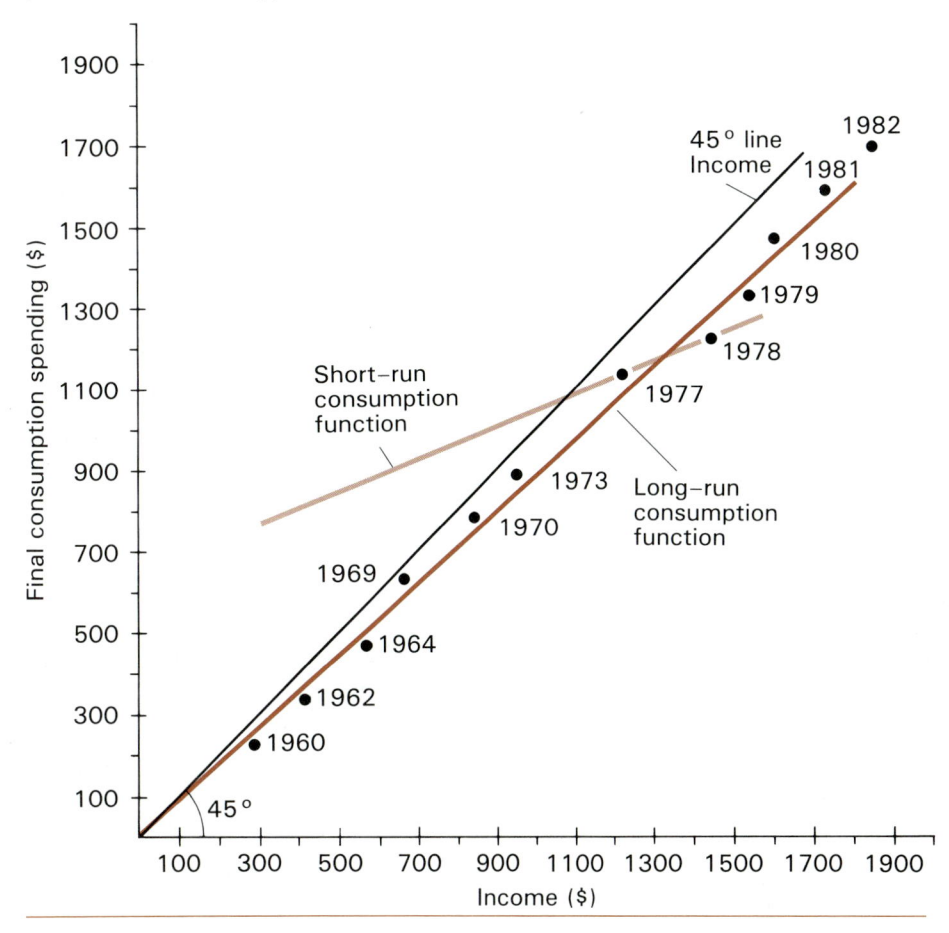

to be over some period in the future than their actual income at the time consumption expenditures occur. This means that consumption behavior can be different in the short run than the long run. For example, employees in the travel and tourism industry frequently experience large seasonal fluctuations in employment. If people in this industry earn large incomes in the summer months through overtime pay, they may not increase their consumption directly in proportion to this new higher income level. They may instead realize that their income is likely to fall during the off-season and, therefore, tend to save a much larger proportion of their income in the peak season that they would if they believed that their higher income level would persist all year long.

We can see how this concept of permanent income generates both short-run and long-run consumption functions by looking at Figure 10-3. The long-run consumption function shows that, over the long period shown here, the fraction of income spent on consumption has been relatively constant. This represents the long-run trend of how people spend their incomes. Now look at what happened in the short-run period 1977–1978. The economy was recovering from a recession in this period. The figure shows that income increased during 1977–1978, but consumption spending did not rise as much as the long-run trend would lead us to expect. Consumers had higher incomes, but they were uncertain, in the short run, that this increase in income was permanent. They therefore spent a smaller fraction of it, and saved a larger fraction of it, than would otherwise have been the case. This gives us a short-run consumption function that is consistent with Keynes' theories.

Now examine Figure 10-3 to see what happened to consumption in the next year, 1979. You can see that consumption spending increased back to its long-run trend level. This indicates that by 1979 consumers had decided that they had experienced an increase in their permanent income, and had increased consumption spending accordingly. Consumers, according to the permanent income hypothesis, base spending choices on their permanent income. Changes in short-run income generate the Keynesian consumption function we have just studied. In the long run, however, consumption spending adjusts to the permanent income level.

KEY CONCEPTS
10.4, 10.5, 10.6, 10.7

Consumption spending is a very important part of the Keynesian model of the economy. Consumption spending depends on many factors. In the short run, consumption spending varies with changes in disposable income according to the relationship described by the marginal propensity to consume. In the long run, the relationship between consumption and disposable income is described by the average propensity to consume. The *MPC* and *MPS* measure how consumption and saving respond to changes in disposable income. The *APC* and *APS* measure the relationship between total consumption and saving and total disposable income. The *MPC* is the slope of the Keynesian consumption function, which includes both autonomous and induced consumption spending.

INVESTMENT SPENDING

Capital Goods
Those goods used to increase society's ability to produce goods and services in the future, such as factories and equipment.

Investment spending is the second component of total spending. Investment spending is made up of expenditures for **capital goods,** such as new plant and equipment, and changes in inventories during a given period. Capital goods do not satisfy consumer desires by themselves. They are goods used to increase our ability to produce goods and services in the future. We cannot very well consume a manufacturing plant and get satisfaction from that consumption. We can, however, consume the output of that plant. Therefore, capital goods are not an end in themselves, but simply a means to produce an end. Net investment is how much total investment spending occurs after we make allowances for the depreciation or wearing-out of capital goods used up in producing goods and services. Net investment is therefore a measure of the net contribution made today toward the production and sale of goods in future time periods.

Investment spending is the most volatile component of total spending. Both consumption and government spending vary over the course of a decade, but the year-to-year changes tend to be relatively small. Investment spending, however, can change a great deal over relatively short periods of time. For example, during the Great Depression from 1929 to 1932 consumption spending in the U.S. economy fell from $77.2 billion to $48.6

billion. This was a relatively large decline of approximately 37 percent in consumption. Investment spending during this same period of time fell from $16.2 billion to only $1 billion. This means that investment fell 94 percent. More recently, investment spending increased by over 18 percent in the one year period 1980–1981, fell by almost as much in 1981–1982, then rose back to the 1981 level again in 1983. This shows investment's high volatility. Consumption spending, on the other hand, steadily increased at a rate of about 10 percent per year during this period.

In addition to being the most volatile component of total spending, investment spending has a great deal to do with the levels of resource use, employment, and income in the economy. If business firms are expanding plant and equipment or adding to inventories, they are increasing their demand for resources in the resource markets of the circular flow. This means a greater demand for human resources, as well. The result is higher levels of employment in the economy and greater consumer income. When investment spending is declining, the whole process is reversed. Resource demand, employment, and consumer income all begin to fall. It is, therefore, important to understand what factors make investment spending behave the way it does.

10.8 DETERMINANTS OF INVESTMENT SPENDING

Determinants of Investment Spending

What are the determinants of planned investment spending? Investment decisions are made by individual firms responding to both the conditions in their particular markets and economy-wide situations. Planned investment spending therefore depends on many factors. In terms of the entire economy, investment is heavily influenced by current sales relative to the current productive capacity of the present capital stock, expectations, and interest rates. In addition, it is influenced by the rate of return on investments, the cost of capital goods, and business taxes. We will examine each of these factors individually.

Current Sales versus Productive Capacity When the current sales of goods exceed the productive capacity of a business, this creates an incentive for owners to expand their plants. If they believe that consumers will buy more than they can produce, they are, in effect, giving up potential profits by not expanding their plant capacity. It is, therefore, rational to expect that when current sales levels in the entire economy are exceeding the productive capacity of the existing plants and equipment, overall investment spending will rise. When sales drop below productive capacity, there is not as strong an incentive to expand. Businesses either delay or cancel altogether their plans for increased investment. They may undertake investment expenditures to modernize or make their existing plants more efficient, but expansion spending would prove to be unnecessary.

Economists measure the **capacity utilization rates** for firms in the economy. When the capacity utilization rate is high, in the neighborhood of 85 percent, this suggests that firms are likely to undertake additional investment expenditures. A low capacity utilization rate of, say, 60 percent suggests that firms have plenty of excess capacity and are unlikely to undertake many additional purchases of capital goods.

Capacity Utilization Rate
Current production as a percentage of the production at the economy's maximum use of factories and equipment.

Expectations Expectations concerning the general direction the economy is moving and the demand for specific output in future periods influence the level of investment spending by businesses. Even though current sales may be below capacity, businesses may expand investment expenditures if a substantial and sustained rise in future sales is expected. If, on the other hand, worsening economic conditions appear on the horizon, businesses may believe the future demand for their product will fall and may, therefore, delay or cancel their investment plans. In summary, business optimism leads to expanded investment expenditures, while business pessimism leads to reduced investment spending.

Expectations are such a powerful influence on the level of investment spending that several professional economic forecasting organizations regularly poll top business executives to see what they believe to be the outlook for their future sales. When these expectations indicate widespread optimism, forecasters revise their investment projections upward. When there is widespread pessimism among these business executives, forecasters have a tendency to reduce their projected investment numbers.

Interest Rates Since interest rates are part of the cost of any investment undertaken by business, they are an important determinant of investment spending. If firms borrow money to build new plant and equipment, they pay interest on the money. This increases the overall cost of the investment. If businesses use their own existing funds for investment in new plant and equipment, they still bear a cost equal to the market rate of interest. Every dollar used for investment purposes is one more dollar that could be in a bank account earning interest. The foregone interest income is an opportunity cost of using these funds for investment purposes. A firm that invests either pays an interest rate to a lender or forgoes interest it could have earned on its own money by placing it in a bank account or by loaning it to another firm. The higher the market rate of interest, the more it costs the firm to invest.

All else being equal, investment spending tends to decline as market interest rates go up. Figure 10-4 illustrates the typical relationship between interest rates and the level of investment expenditures. Note that an increase in interest rates causes the amount of investment expenditures to decline along the given investment function. It does not shift the investment curve to a new level, but causes a movement along the existing investment curve, as from point B to point A.

It is important to understand that investment spending is affected by the interest rate, but investment spending also affects the interest rate. In 1984, for example, investment spending and the interest rate increased at the same time. This seemingly illogical event is easy to understand once we find out what caused the interest rate to rise. As the economy rapidly expanded in 1984, the capacity utilization rate increased. This increased the demand for investment goods, shifting the curve in Figure 10-4. As investment spending increased, firms began to borrow more in order to finance their investment plans. This increased the demand for loanable funds. This increase in the demand for loans bid up the interest rate. The result was that the interest rate increased in part because of higher levels of investment spending.

Marginal Efficiency of Investment (*MEI*)
The return on an additional dollar of investment spending. This is a measure of the profitability of additional investment spending.

The Return on Investment Firms make investment decisions by comparing the return on investment with the appropriate interest rate. Thus changes in the profitability of investment spending also affect the investment decision. Keynes measured the return on investment as the **marginal**

FIGURE 10-4

Interest Rates and Investment Spending. Investment spending tends to increase as interest rates fall, all else being equal. In this figure, this increase is seen as a movement along the curve from *A* to *B*. Changes in variables other than the interest rate that affect investment decisions can cause this curve to shift.

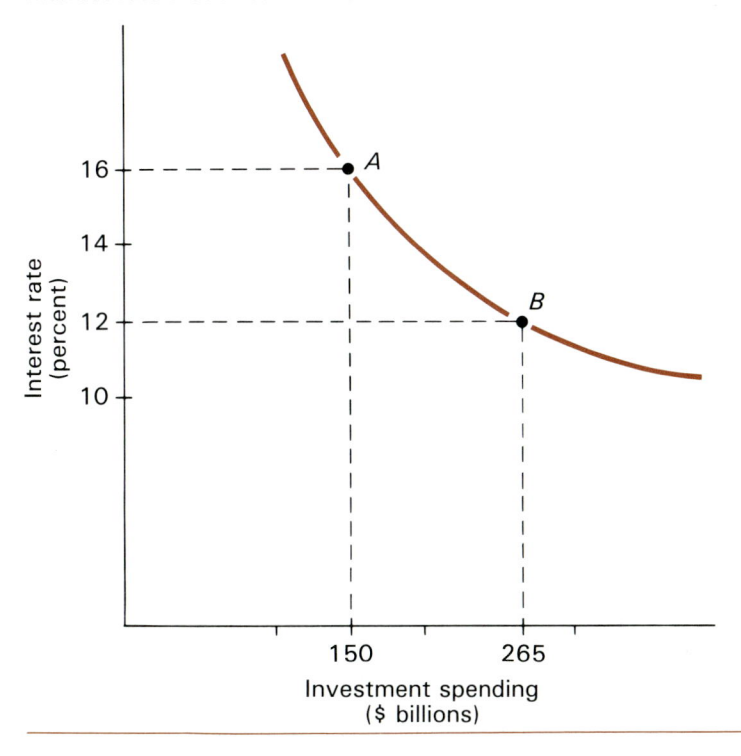

efficiency of investment (*MEI*). The *MEI* measures how an incremental investment expenditure changes the value of total output.

The investment curve in Figure 10-4 is based on the concept of the *MEI*. Firms are willing to investment $150 billion at an interest rate of 16 percent in the figure because $150 billion worth of investment projects have a marginal return, or *MEI*, of 16 percent or more. This figure also illustrates the idea that, as more and more investment takes place, the *MEI* decreases. This indicates that there is diminishing returns to investment expenditures. Changes in technology, government regulations, or other factors can cause the *MEI* to change, which would tend to shift the investment curve in Figure 10-4.

Other Factors that Affect Investment There are several other factors that can affect the level of investment expenditures in the same way as changes in the interest rates. These are factors that affect the overall cost to the firm of investing in new plant and equipment. The cost of capital goods affects investment spending. For example, if the cost of building a shoe factory or adding new heel-making equipment were to increase rapidly, and yet the price at which the firm could sell the shoes remained the same, it would become less profitable to invest. The cost of the investment relative to what it would pay in return has increased. Thus, the cost of capital goods can and does affect the level of investment expenditures. An increase in the costs of capital goods shifts the investment curve downward. Less is then invested at every rate of interest.

Taxes that government levies on business also can affect investment expenditures. Taxes reduce the real payoff to business of investing. Suppose a firm must invest $1 to earn a before tax return of 10 cents. The approximate rate of return is 10 percent. But after the corporate income tax is levied, the firm may keep only about 5 cents. This reduces the firm's approximate rate of return to about 5 percent on each dollar. Businesses would prefer the 10 percent return over the 5 percent return. Other things equal, an increase in business taxes shifts the investment function downward, meaning less is invested at each interest rate. If the government provides tax incentives for business to invest, such as investment tax credits, thereby reducing the cost of investing, we would expect the investment curve to shift upward and to the right, meaning that investment expenditures would be higher at each interest rate.

Taxes not only affect the level of investment spending, they also affect the types of investments that take place. Tax incentives built into the tax system make some types of investments more profitable, after taxes are taken into account, than other investments. In the 1980s, for example, many oil firms have found it more profitable to use their profits to purchase other oil firms, instead of investing in exploration for oil. Tax considerations are one reason why the purchase of existing firms has been seen as a more profitable "investment" than the expansion of existing firms. From the economy's point of view, of course, the purchase of one firm by another is not investment, it is just an exchange of existing assets.

NET EXPORT SPENDING

Net export spending is another component of total spending. Net export spending, as noted earlier in this chapter, is the difference between the amount that domestic sellers receive for the goods and services that they export and the amount domestic purchasers pay for the goods and services that they import from abroad. Net export spending (X_n) therefore represents the net increase (if exports are greater than imports) or decrease (if imports exceed exports) in total spending due to international trade with the rest of the world.

Many factors affect the amount of net exports. One very important determinant of net exports is the **exchange rate.** The exchange rate refers to the value of the dollar relative to the currencies of other major nations. If the dollar is high in value, this means that a given number of dollars purchases a relatively large quantity of other currencies. A weak dollar, on the other hand, means that more dollars are needed to purchase a given quantity of another currency.

The exchange rate has a major effect on the amount of net export spending. Net exports were negative in 1984, for example. Most economists believe that the very high value of the dollar on foreign exchange markets accounted for the fact that we imported more than we exported. The strong dollar made foreign goods relatively inexpensive for U.S. buyers. This encouraged U.S. firms and households to purchase many imported items. On the other hand, the high value of the dollar compared to other currencies made U.S. exports relatively expensive in other countries. U.S. exports fell as a result of the strong dollar. Exports were therefore far less than imports in 1984, making the foreign sector a net leakage.

The exchange rate is not the only factor that determines net exports. The prices of items that are traded among nations also affect this component

---

10.9 DETERMINANTS OF NET EXPORT SPENDING

Exchange Rate
The value of one currency in terms of foreign currencies.

of total spending. The rapid increases in oil prices in the 1970s, for example, reduced net export spending by increasing the cost of imports. Political factors also affect net exports. President Jimmy Carter, for example, imposed a temporary trade embargo with the Soviet Union in the late 1970s in retaliation for the USSR's invasion of Afghanistan. It became illegal to sell U.S. grain to the Soviets. This reduced the value of U.S. exports, thereby cutting net exports.

The agricultural sector has been a key export sector of the U.S. economy in recent years. Any event that significantly affects the world agricultural scene therefore tends to affect our net exports. Crop failures in the USSR, for example, tend to increase U.S. exports of grain. Successful harvests in China, on the other hand, mean reduced U.S. exports.

GOVERNMENT SPENDING

Since total spending is the sum of all planned expenditures in the economy, it must represent not only the expenditures of consumers, investors, and foreign buyers but also spending by government. Whenever government provides goods or services it must use resources. Government is a demander in the marketplace for resources alongside consumers and investors. Building an interstate highway, for example, requires physical labor, engineering services, technology, asphalt, gravel, and extensive use of capital equipment such as bulldozers and earth movers. Whenever government buys these resources it contributes to the overall amount of planned expenditures in the economy.

10.10 DETERMINANTS OF GOVERNMENT SPENDING

The government spending component of total spending has characteristics that make it different from the consumption, investment, or net export components. Government spending frequently responds to events in the economy, but it can also be used as a policy tool to alter the nature of the economy. When some part of an economic system can be controlled by forces outside of that system, economists call that part of the system an **exogenous policy variable.** Parts of overall government expenditures can be increased or decreased regardless of whether income in the economy is going up or down. Government spending can also be changed in either direction regardless of what expectations consumers or investors may have. In this way government expenditures are not only a necessary part of providing public services but also a way to either stimulate (increase) or dampen (reduce) overall spending in the economy.

Exogenous Policy Variable
A part of an economic system that can be controlled by forces outside of that specific economic system.

There has been a tremendous debate among economists as to how much government spending should be used as a control on the economy. Few economists deny that it is at times possible to use this exogenous policy variable to benefit the economy. During inflationary periods, for example, government spending can be reduced to reduce total spending and slow down the rate at which prices are advancing. When unemployment is excessive, government expenditures can be increased to increase total spending and output and therefore increase the employment of resources. When used properly, this variable has the potential to benefit the economy.

Keynes clearly saw government spending as a tool that could be used to improve economic conditions. In Keynes' view, government spending should be increased during recessions in order to stimulate the economy and move it closer to the goal of full employment. Keynes thought that government spending should be reduced during periods of too-rapid economic growth, when inflation problems could heat up. Keynes saw the government spending component of total spending as the economy's "steering wheel." With an intelligent driver at the wheel, government could steer the economy away from accidental recessions and inflations and onto the turnpike of full employment and prosperity.

EQUILIBRIUM INCOME

We will now use what we have learned about consumption, investment, net exports, and government spending to see how the equilibrium levels of total spending and income are determined. To keep our analysis as simple as possible, we assume first that there is no government sector and no foreign sector in the economy. We will then expand the model by adding in these important parts of the economy.

Consumption Spending and Equilibrium

Let us begin our analysis of equilibrium levels with consumption spending. Figure 10-2 showed the relationship between consumption spending and income. The consumption function shown in this figure was a straight line, with slope equal to the *MPC*, which showed that consumption spending increases as income rises. Figure 10-5 takes this picture of the consumption function for the economy and adds to it a fixed level of investment spending. Adding investment to consumption spending creates the $C + I$ line in the figure, which is a parallel line above the C line. The vertical distance between C and $C + I$ is equal to the amount of investment spending. The $C + I$ line shows the amount of total planned consumption and investment spending that takes place at each level of national income.

The vertical distance from the consumption function (C) to the consumption plus planned investment function ($C + I$) represents a constant level of planned investment that does not depend on the level of income in the economy. For the purposes of this chapter, planned investment is assumed to be autonomous; it does not depend on the level of income in the economy. We have added the total of consumption (which increases with income) to the constant amount of investment in the economy to get the total spending line ($C + I$) in Figure 10-5.

Equilibrium for the economy can be stated in terms of two conditions: total spending equals total income and injections equal leakages. We will examine each of these conditions separately.

Total Spending Equals Total Income The economy is in equilibrium when the income generated from production in the form of wages, interest, profits, and rents causes consumers and investors to spend an amount equal to the value of the goods produced. This translates to a dollar's worth of income bringing about a dollar's worth of expenditures on the goods and services produced. We can see this equilibrium in Figure 10-5. At an income level of $950 billion, consumers and investors combined plan to buy goods and services valued at $950 billion. In other words, producers are generating output worth $950 billion and consumers and investors plan to buy exactly that amount of goods. Total income is in balance with total spending.

Changes in the level of equilibrium income take place when the total of planned expenditures by consumers and investors turns out to be greater or less than the amount of income produced. If total spending were less than total income, as shown in Figure 10-5 at an income level of $1000 billion,

FIGURE 10-5

Macroeconomic Equilibrium. The 45-degree line in (a) shows all of the points at which macroeconomic equilibrium occurs (total spending equals total income). Total spending is made up of consumption (C line) and an autonomous level of investment spending. Equilibrium occurs where the C + I total spending line crosses the 45-degree total income line. Total spending equals income of $950 billion here. Graph(b) shows this equilibrium in terms of saving (leakage) and investment (injection). Equilibrium can be characterized as the condition where leakages equal injections (b) or total spending equals total income (a).

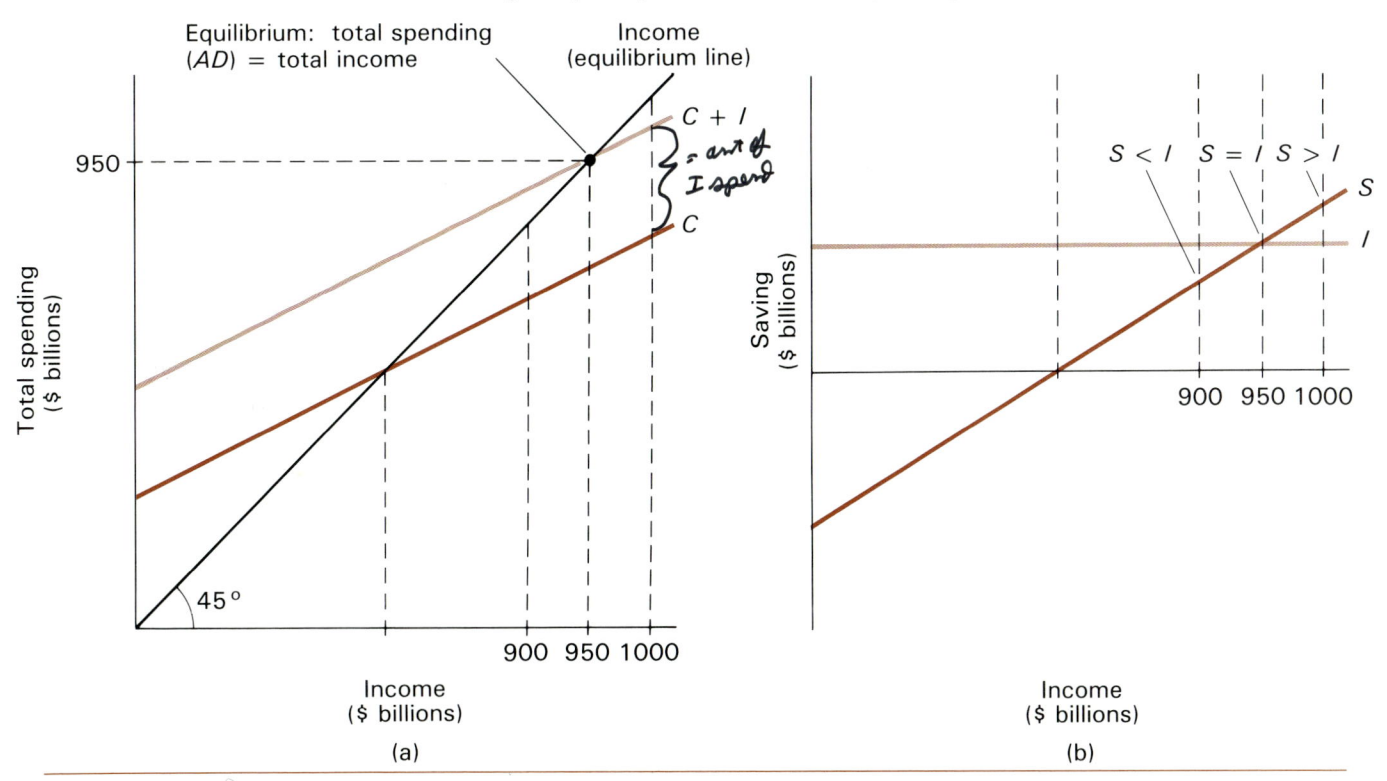

producers would have produced more goods than consumers and investors had planned to buy. These excess goods would not be bought and the inventories of producers would begin to pile up. Producers would notice that their inventories were increasing and would, therefore, plan to reduce their rate of output in the future. They would produce less so that the level of excess inventories would not continue to increase. As producers cut back on their production they will need fewer resources and thus will pay out less in income to the owners of resources. Income tends to fall toward equilibrium when total income is greater than total spending.

If total spending were greater than income, as occurs in Figure 10-5 at the income level of $900 billion, the inventories of producers would be declining. Consumers and investors would plan to buy up goods and services faster than producers were currently producing them. As inventories declined, producers would step up their future production plans to maintain their inventories. Accordingly, producers would increase their future demand for resources and pay out more in future income to the owners of resources. Income tends to rise toward equilibrium when income is less than total spending.

We can see equilibrium and the role of inventories more clearly in a tabular or numerical example of equilibrium. Table 10-2 shows a series of hypothetical data on total income, planned consumption, planned investment, planned savings, total spending ($C + I$), inventory changes, and the direction in which income is changing. We can see that at an income of $950 billion, total spending ($C + I = 950$) is equal to total income. Inventories are neither rising nor falling and there is no reason for income and employment in the economy to change. At an income level below equilibrium income, such as $900 billion, not only is total spending ($910 billion) greater than total income ($900 billion), but inventories are being depleted by $10 billion. This will cause production to increase in future periods, increasing employment and income and moving the economy toward the equilibrium income of $950 billion.

At all income levels above the equilibrium, such as $1000 billion, total income ($1000 billion) is greater than total spending ($990 billion). Inventories are rising by $10 billion and producers will, therefore, reduce their plans for future production. This will reduce income in future periods, moving the economy back toward the equilibrium level of income at $950 billion.

Injections Equal Leakages Here is another way to view macroeconomic equilibrium. The simple model that we are working with here involves just one injection into the circular flow, investment spending, and just one leakage, saving. Leakages (saving) equal injections (investment spending) at the equilibrium level of income. The common sense of this identity is that investment spending increases total spending. Saving cannot be spent on goods and services currently being produced, so it reduces spending and income.

When planned injections (i.e., planned investment expenditures) are greater than planned leakages, there are net additions to the circular flow of income. Investors are spending more and increasing the circular income flow by more than the amount being taken out of the flow by saving and taxes. Spending then increases faster than output. Inventories decline and businesses step up production, employing more resources and paying more income to resource owners. Income in the economy begins to rise.

On the other hand, when the planned leakages of saving are greater than planned injections, saving takes more income out of the circular flow than investors are putting into it. Output increases faster than spending and excess inventories begin to pile up. Producers respond by reducing their production plans, reducing their employment of resources, and therefore reduce the incomes they pay to resource owners.

The fact that equilibrium income occurs when saving equals investment can be seen in both Figure 10-5 and Table 10-2. Equilibrium income of $950 billion occurs in Table 10-2 when planned saving of $100 billion equals planned investment of $100 billion. The difference between saving and investment at other income levels shows that equilibrium does not occur here. The saving function in Figure 10-5(b) is shown along with the autonomous $100 billion level of investment spending. The equilibrium between total spending and income in Figure 10-5(a) corresponds to the equilibrium between saving and investment in Figure 10-5(b).

Investment, Inventories, and Equilibrium

The key to understanding that injections are equal to leakages at equilibrium involves a closer look at inventories and the components of total spending. Remember that planned investment is one of the components of total

| TABLE 10-2 | Equilibrium between Income and Total Spending |

	Income levels ($ billions)		
	900	950	1000
Planned consumption	810	850	890
Planned investment	100	100	100
Planned saving	90	100	110
Total spending = $C + I$	910	950	990
Unplanned inventory changes	−10	0	+10
Direction of change in income	increase	none	decrease

spending. Businesses plan to spend a certain amount on new plant and equipment (fixed investment) and either to increase, reduce, or hold constant their investment in inventories. Actual investment, however, includes all planned changes in investment plus unplanned changes. Most unplanned changes in investment come about because inventories either surpass or fall below the desired levels. At equilibrium, as Table 10-2 shows, planned investment is equal to actual investment because inventories are neither increasing nor decreasing. Inventories have no unplanned changes because the equilibrium level of income has been reached.

10.14 ROLE OF INVENTORIES

When businesses plan inventory levels, these planned levels depend on some level of expenditures that businesses believe consumers will make. If consumers save more (spend less) than had been expected, inventories will rise. Unplanned inventory investment will take place. Planned saving will be greater than planned investment. This means that some unplanned investment must exist. Businesses will reduce production in response to the unplanned inventory accumulations, and spending and income will fall toward the equilibrium level. If, on the other hand, consumers save less (spend more) than businesses expected, inventories will decline below planned levels and unplanned investment will become negative. Businesses will produce more to replenish their inventories, causing spending and income to rise toward the equilibrium level of income.

At equilibrium, unplanned investment is zero. Consumers spend and save the amounts that businesses anticipated, thus planned investment equals planned saving.

Net Exports Added to Total Spending

10.11 KEYNESIAN MODEL OF EQUILIBRIUM

The next step in building our model of the Keynesian economy is to add the foreign sector to our analysis. As noted earlier, the foreign sector provides both the injection of exports and the leakage of imports. The net effect of the foreign sector is determined by the amount of net exports, which is defined to be the value of exports minus the value of imports.

Balance of Trade Equilibrium
The condition in which the value of a nation's exports equals the value of imported goods.

Balance of Trade Surplus
The condition in which the value of a nation's exports is greater than the value of imported goods.

Figure 10-6 shows what happens when we add the foreign sector to our picture of the Keynesian model of the economy. Total spending is now seen as the sum of consumption plus investment plus net export spending ($C + I + X_n$). For convenience, we have assumed that the economy has a **balance of trade equilibrium** for the period shown in the figure. This means that there are zero net exports. The existence of positive net exports, referred to as a **balance of trade surplus,** would mean a vertical shift in the $C + I + X_n$ line in the figure, tending to increase total spending, thereby increasing the equilibrium level of income in the economy. The existence of

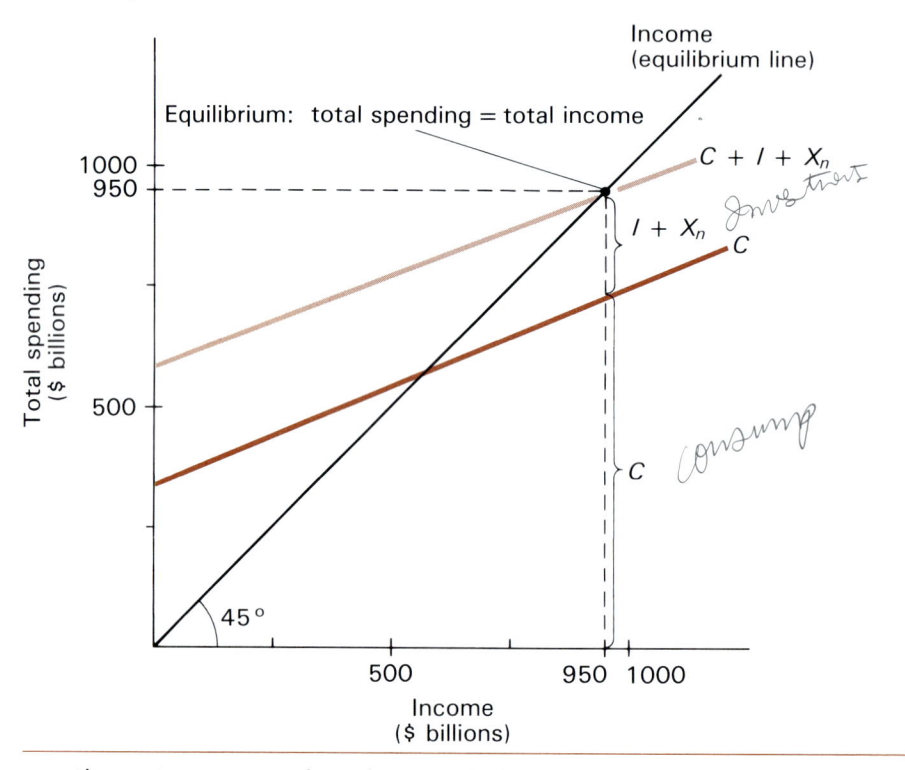

284 *The Keynesian Model of the Economy*

FIGURE 10-6   **Equilibrium with Consumption, Investment, and Net Exports.** This figure shows the equilibrium between total spending and total income when consumption, investment, and net export spending are included. A fixed amount of investment (I) and net export spending (X_n) is added to the consumption line (C). Equilibrium occurs at the point at which total spending ($C + I + X_n$) crosses the 45-degree total income line.

Balance of Trade Deficit
The condition in which the value of a nation's exports is less than the value of imported goods.

negative net exports, referred to as a **balance of trade deficit,** would cause the total spending line to shift down by the amount of the trade deficit. This would lower total spending and therefore result in a lower level of equilibrium income.

The addition of the foreign sector to our macroeconomic model does not change any of the conclusions reached in the last section regarding the nature of macroeconomic equilibrium. Equilibrium occurs where total spending equals total income, or graphically, where the $C + I + X_n$ line crosses the equilibrium income 45-degree line.

Government Spending Added to Total Spending

10.11 KEYNESIAN MODEL OF EQUILIBRIUM

As we have just seen, natural forces tend to move the economy toward equilibrium, but that equilibrium may or may not be at a level of resource use that the economy finds desirable. Adding government spending to our model gives the economy an ability to exercise some control over total spending. Government purchases of goods and services directly affect the level of total spending. In addition, government also affects spending indirectly through taxes and transfer payments that can alter the amount of disposable income available for consumption and saving.

Government spending is an injection to the circular flow of economic activity, while the taxing activities of government are a leakage from the circular flow. If government taxes away income from households or busi-

FIGURE 10-7

Government Spending Increases Equilibrium Income. An increase in government spending shifts the AD line from $C + I + X_n$ to $C + I + X_n + G$ in the figure. This causes the equilibrium level of income to rise from $950 billion to $1200 billion. Increases and decreases in government spending can cause equilibrium income to rise and fall.

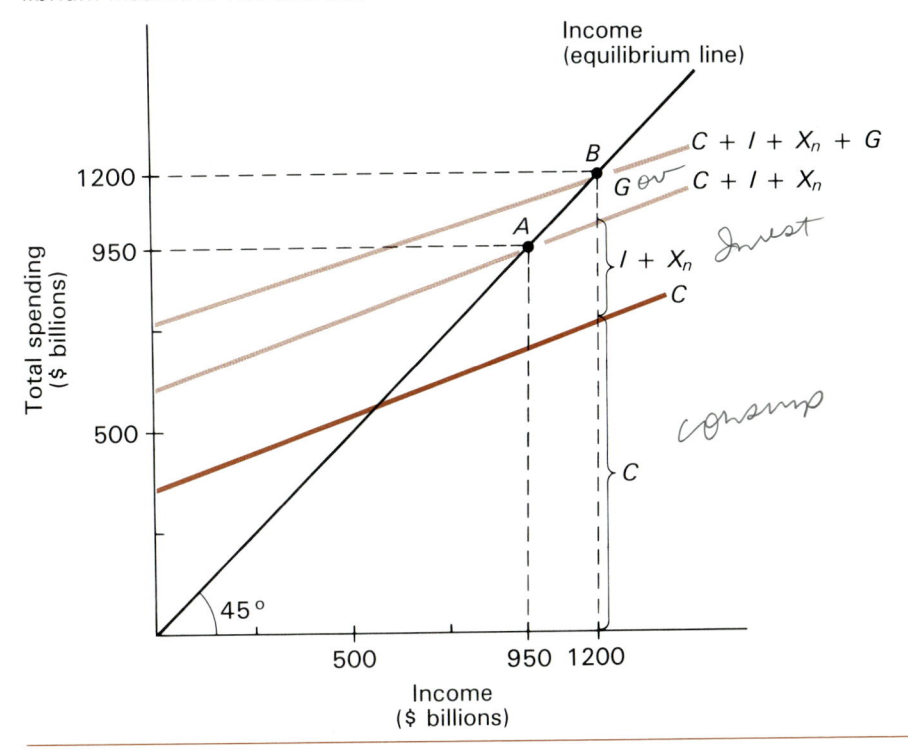

nesses, their disposable income is reduced. A reduction in disposable income causes consumption spending to fall, thereby reducing total spending and income. Government spending and taxing behavior are, therefore, an important part of total spending.

Figure 10-7 shows the economy at an equilibrium of $950 billion in income. Suppose that the full-employment level of income is $1200 billion. Government spending can help the economy move to the full-employment equilibrium. Adding government spending to that of investors, foreigners, and consumers, we get a total spending function equal to $C + I + X_n + G$. Increasing government spending stimulates output, employment, and income toward full employment. Figure 10-7 shows an autonomous $50 billion in government spending. We will assume, for graphic simplicity, that no taxes are raised to finance this government spending, so there is no change in consumption or investment as a result of the increase in government spending. The equilibrium level of income now occurs at the point at which the total spending equals $C + I + X_n + G$ function crosses the 45-degree equilibrium income line. Total spending equals total income at the equilibrium, and leakages (saving plus taxes) equal injections (investment plus net exports plus government spending.)

Increased government spending can be used to increase the equilibrium level of national income. Reductions in government spending, on the other hand, cause the economy to adjust toward a lower equilibrium income level.

The addition of government to our model alters the equilibrium conditions slightly. Equilibrium can be stated as the income level such that (1) total spending ($C + I + X_n + G$) equals total income, or (2) total injections (investment plus net exports plus government spending) equal total leakages (saving plus taxes). If we assume that the government operates with a balanced budget, so that government spending equals tax collections, which certainly has not been the case in recent years, then the previously stated equilibrium condition of saving equals investment appears.

Government spending and taxation are useful tools that can be employed to control the economy and possibly eliminate or reduce unwanted recessions and inflations. Government spending and taxing as economic tools are not, however, without their own set of problems. Government spending and taxing powers are subject to political as well as economic considerations and are often subject to problems of lags. While the correct and timely use of government spending can, at least in the short run, improve economic conditions, we must always be mindful of the fact that good economics often makes for bad politics.

KEY CONCEPTS 10.11, 10.12, 10.13

Total spending is the sum of consumption, investment, net export, and government spending. The economy is at equilibrium when total spending equals total income. Graphically, this is the point at which the total spending equals $C + I + X_n + G$ line crosses the 45-degree total income line. This equilibrium can also be characterized as the level of income at which total leakages (saving, taxes, imports) equal total injections (investment, government, export spending). Changes in total spending cause changes in the equilibrium level of income.

INFLATIONARY AND RECESSIONARY GAPS

Keynes showed that macroeconomic equilibrium does not necessarily occur at full employment. Sometimes the equilibrium level of income is less than the full-employment level of income. When this occurs, there is a **recessionary gap,** as shown in Figure 10-8(a). Here the equilibrium level of income is $950 billion, but an income level of $1000 billion would be required to generate sufficient output to reach the goal of full employment. Keynes believed that one role of government is to attempt to stimulate total spending when a recessionary gap exists, to move the economy toward full employment.

Recessionary Gap
The difference between equilibrium income and the full-employment level of income (assuming that equilibrium income is less than the full-employment level).

It is also possible for the equilibrium level of income in the economy to be higher than the full-employment level of income. This occured in the United States in 1967–1969, when income was so high that the unemployment rate dropped as low as 3.4 percent, compared to the prevailing estimate at that time that full employment meant an unemployment rate of about 4 percent. Figure 10-8(b) illustrates this situation where equilibrium income is higher than the full-employment level of income. This creates what is called an **inflationary gap.** The fact that total spending exceeds the economy's normal potential output generates inflation. Sure enough, the inflationary gap of the late 1960s led to rising inflation, as we saw in Chapter 9.

Inflationary Gap
The difference between equilibrium income and the full-employment level of income (assuming that equilibrium income is above the full-employment level).

It is also possible that the equilibrium level of income can be the same as the full-employment level of income, as illustrated by Figure 10-8(c). Keynes said that this would occur only by chance or as the result of effective government policies aimed at eliminating recessionary and inflationary gaps.

FIGURE 10-8

Recessionary and Inflationary Gaps. A recessionary gap exists when the equilibrium level of income, $950 billion in (a), is less than the full-employment level of income, $1000 billion. The recessionary gap is the $50 billion difference here. An inflationary gap exists when the equilibrium level of income, $1100 in (b), is above the full-employment level of income, $1000 billion. The inflationary gap is $100 billion here. The economy can achieve an equilibrium at the full-employment level of income, as in (c), where there is neither a recessionary nor an inflationary gap.

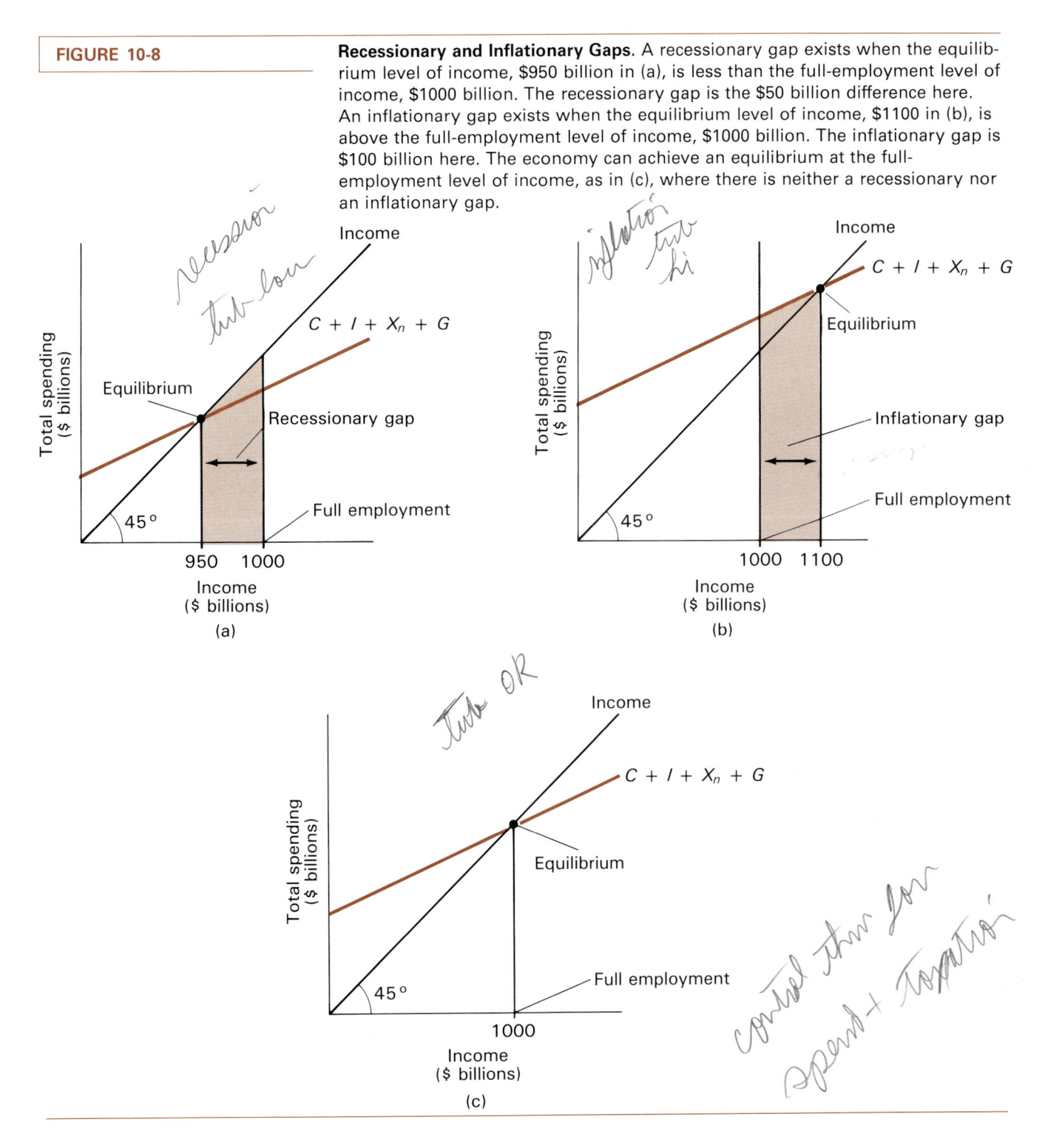

THE SPENDING MULTIPLIER

10.15 SPENDING MULTIPLIER

The analysis of government spending illustrates an interesting point about the economy. Figure 10-4 showed an economy at an equilibrium income of $950 billion. Figure 10-7 showed that equilibrium income rises by $250

Multiplier Principle
The economic principle that states that an initial independent increase or decrease in net exports, government spending, consumption, or investment will, through the responding multiplier effect, cause a larger increase or decrease in equilibrium income.

billion, from $950 to $1200 billion, when total spending rises by $50 billion due to government spending. The $50 billion increase in autonomous spending caused a $250 billion increase in equilibrium income. This illustrates what economists call the **multiplier principle.**

Let's begin our analysis of the multiplier principle with a simple example. Suppose you received $100 in income from your job as a government employee. In other words, you received $100 in income because $100 in government spending took place. You can spend this $100 or save it. You will probably spend part of the income and save the rest. Earlier in this chapter we learned that the portion of each incremental dollar in income that is consumed is called the marginal propensity to consume (MPC) and the portion that is saved is called the marginal propensity to save (MPS). Suppose that your MPC is 80 percent and you therefore spend $80 and save $20 of the $100 increase in income.

What happens to the $80 you spend? The recipient of your $80 in spending now has $80 in additional income. The recipient has the same possibilities for that $80 in additional income that you had with the $100 in income you had earned. If the recipient has the same MPC as you do, he or she will spend $64 (i.e., $80 × 80 percent = $64) and save $16 ($80 × 20 percent = $16). When the recipient of the $80 you spend then spends $64 again, that $64 will be incremental income for the next recipient. This spending and respending process continues until there is no income left to be passed on through further rounds of spending. If we look at Table 10-3, we can trace out this spending and respending process through at least eight rounds of spending.

From Table 10-3 we can see that the amount of incremental income produced at each level of spending depends on the marginal propensity to consume. Spending round 0 in the table lists the government spending that resulted in your $100 in incremental income. Your initial round of spending creates income for the recipient and that same income is spent, and respent, generating income for many other individuals. Note that at each round of spending, some part of the incremental income that each person receives is saved. It is not spent and therefore not passed on as income to another recipient somewhere further down the spending chain. The part of incre-

TABLE 10-3

How the Multiplier Works

Spending round	Incremental income ($)	Change in spending ($)	Change in saving ($)
0	—	100.00	—
1	100.00	80.00	20.00
2	80.00	64.00	16.00
3	64.00	51.00	13.00
4	51.00	40.80	10.20
5	40.80	32.64	8.16
6	32.64	26.11	6.53
7	26.11	20.80	5.22
8	20.80	16.64	4.16
All other rounds	2.65	0.68	.32
Total	500.00	500.00	100.00

mental income that is saved reduces the amount that can be passed on through spending and thus reduces the incremental income of future recipients. With each round of spending, incremental income goes down by the amount of incremental income times the marginal propensity to save. It is this saving process that limits the amount of incremental income produced through the multiplier.

A given change in autonomous consumption, investment, net exports, or government spending produces a much larger change in income in the economy, as we saw in Figure 10-7, because that initial change is multiplied through subsequent rounds of spending and respending. If we expand the idea of the multiplier over the entire economy, we realize that a given change in investment, consumption, or government spending brings about a much larger change in the equilibrium level of income. How large a change in equilibrium income that takes place depends on the size of the multiplier. The spending multiplier can be computed by the formula

$$M = \frac{1}{(1 - MPC)}$$

With an MPC of 80 percent or .80 as we used in our example, we get a multiplier of $1/(1 - .80) = 1/.20 = 5$. An initial independent increase in either consumption, investment, or government spending of $100 increases equilibrium income in the economy by $500. The point that we made about the amount of saving having an effect on the size of the multiplier becomes clearer when we recall that $MPC + MPS = 100$ percent, or 1.00. The denominator of the multiplier equation, that is $1 - MPC$ is the same thing as the MPS. Another way of looking at the spending multiplier formula is therefore

$$M = \frac{1}{MPS.}$$

How the Multiplier Works Graphically

10.16 GRAPHIC MODEL OF SPENDING MULTIPLIER

We can also show how the multiplier works its way through the economy with a graph. Assume that the economy is at an equilibrium income of $950 billion, as in our previous model. Suppose that government spending goes up by $50 billion. This will shift the total spending function upward as illustrated in Figure 10-9.

The increase in government spending initially increases income in the economy by $50 billion. This increase in income is divided into additional saving and additional spending by the initial recipients. The portion of additional income that is respent then becomes income for the recipients in the second round of spending. Recipients of the second round of spending save some of that income (20 percent) and spend some of it (80 percent). This third round of spending becomes income for the recipients who themselves save and spend according to their marginal propensities to save and consume. Equilibrium income expands with each additional round of spending. Remember, however, that a portion (20 percent) of the incremental income is saved at each round of spending. The additional spending, and therefore the additional income, gets smaller at each successive round until it drops to zero. As in our previous example, an initial increase in government spending of $50 billion caused equilibrium income to increased by $250 billion.

290　The Keynesian Model of the Economy

FIGURE 10-9　**How the Multiplier Effect Works.** Income increases from the initial equilibrium of $950 billion to the new equilibrium of $1200 billion through the multiplier effect. The figure shows the steps in increased spending and income that correspond to the spending rounds of the multiplier effect.

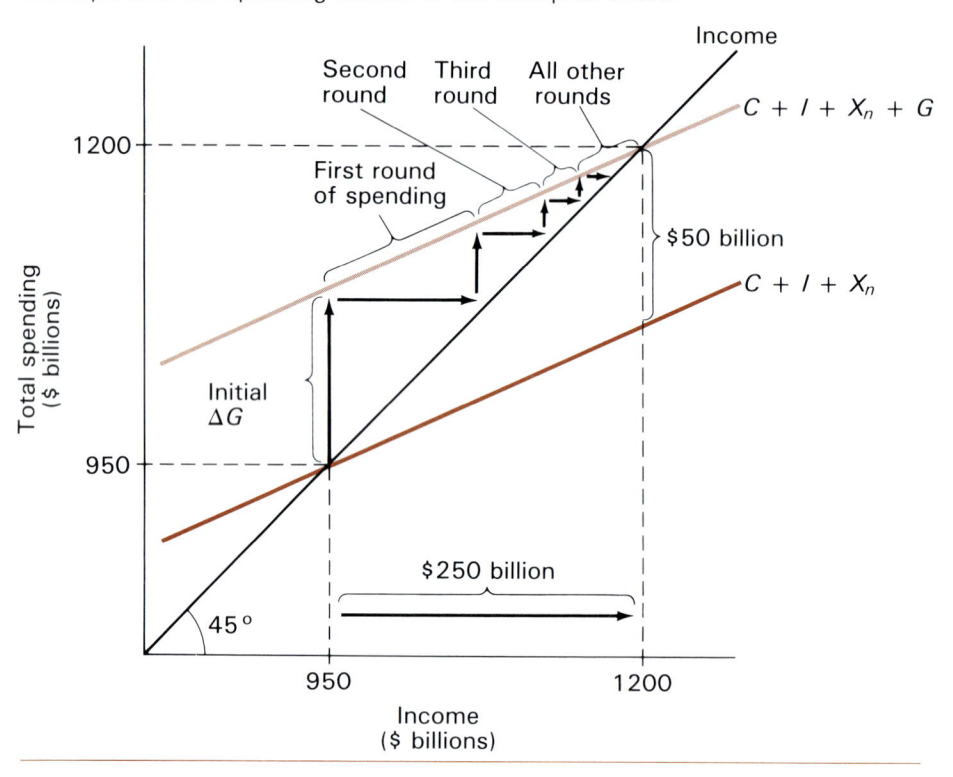

What determined how much equilibrium income would increase? The marginal propensity to consume determines the size of the change in equilibrium income. The larger the MPC, the larger the multiplier effect, since more of each additional dollar in income is passed on to future spenders.

Table 10-4 calculates the multiplier for several different MPC and corresponding MPS values. We can see that the larger the MPC, the larger the multiplier, and the larger the MPS, the smaller the multiplier. The multiplier principle works for both increases and decreases in total spending. If the economy depicted in Figure 10-9 were at an equilibrium of $1000 billion and, for example, government spending was reduced by $10 billion, the multiplier process would cause equilibrium income to fall back to $950 billion. The initial decline in spending would reduce income, which would reduce additional consumption and saving, and subsequent rounds of spending would fall as well. The amount of reduction in equilibrium income is again dictated by the MPC and the MPS.

Since many rounds of spending, respending, and saving are involved, it takes time for the multiplier to work. The process is not instantaneous. We should not expect government spending to increase today and a new level of equilibrium income to be reached tomorrow. It takes time for the full effect of the multiplier to be felt throughout the economy. There are varying estimates of how long it takes for the multiplier to work, but some significant impact can usually be felt in the first six months. As we can see from Table 10-3, the first several rounds of spending and respending have the largest effects on equilibrium income. The subsequent rounds have a declin-

| TABLE 10-4 | *MPC, MPS*, and the Multiplier |

MPC	MPS	Multiplier	Initial change in G	Change in equilibrium income
.80	.20	5	100	500
.75	.25	4	100	400
.67	.33	3	100	300
.50	.50	2	100	200
.33	.67	1.5	100	150
.25	.75	1.33	100	133

ing impact since the amount of additional income produced at each round gets smaller and smaller.

The Paradox of Thrift

10.17 PARADOX OF THRIFT

Throughout history, thrift has been considered a desirable characteristic. Economics itself is frequently associated with thrift. Saving present income for future consumption is, in general, believed to increase future consumption. This is true on an individual basis. If you save more of your income today, you can increase your future consumption. Saving is important for the economy in the long run because saved funds represent resources that are available for the investment and technological improvements that generate economic growth. When an entire economy tries to save more, however, a surprising secondary effect comes into play. If an individual saves, the person is better off. If everyone saves, however, the economy can be worse off, at least in the short run. Economists call this the **paradox of thrift.**

Paradox of Thrift
The idea that, while it may benefit individuals to save more, the economy may suffer if everyone saves more, assuming that the decrease in consumption is not matched by an increase in investment spending.

To see how the paradox of thrift works, suppose that the economy is at an equilibrium income level of $950 billion. Now suppose that, due to a change in expectations, consumers decide to spend $50 billion less and save $50 billion more. Equilibrium income depends on the amount of leakages and injections in the economy. This increase in saving means greater leakages, so the economy will adjust to a lower equilibrium level of income. As we have just seen, however, the multiplier principle means that income will fall by more than the $50 billion decrease in consumption spending. Assuming that the *MPC* is 80 percent and using the multiplier formula $M = 1/(1 - MPC) = 1/MPS$, we can calculate a multiplier of 5 for this example. This means that if consumption spending falls by $50 billion, equilibrium income will fall by 5 × $50 billion = $250 billion. Figure 10-10 illustrates this effect.

An autonomous increase in saving causes the consumption function to shift in Figure 10-10, with the consumption line shifting down by $50 billion, from C to C'. This causes the total spending line to also shift down by $50 billion, from the initial $C + I + X_n + G$ to the new $C' + I + X_n + G$. The decrease in total spending causes an unintended inventory accumulation. Total spending is temporarily less than total income at the initial equilibrium of $950 billion. The figure shows that the economy eventually adjusts to a new equilibrium, at the point at which the $C' + I + X_n + G$ line crosses the income equilibrium 45-degree line. This new equilibrium occurs at an income level of $700 billion. As predicted by the multiplier analysis, the change in income is $250 billion.

FIGURE 10-10

The Paradox of Thrift Illustrated. The economy is at initial equilibrium at point A (total spending equals total income equals $950 billion). Consumers choose to increase saving (and reduce spending) by $50 billion. This reduces consumption spending from C to C', which shifts the total spending line down, from $C + I + X_n + G$ to $C' + I + X_n + G$. Due to the multiplier principle, equilibrium income falls by much more than the initial $50 billion decrease in consumption spending. The new equilibrium occurs at point B, where income is $700 billion.

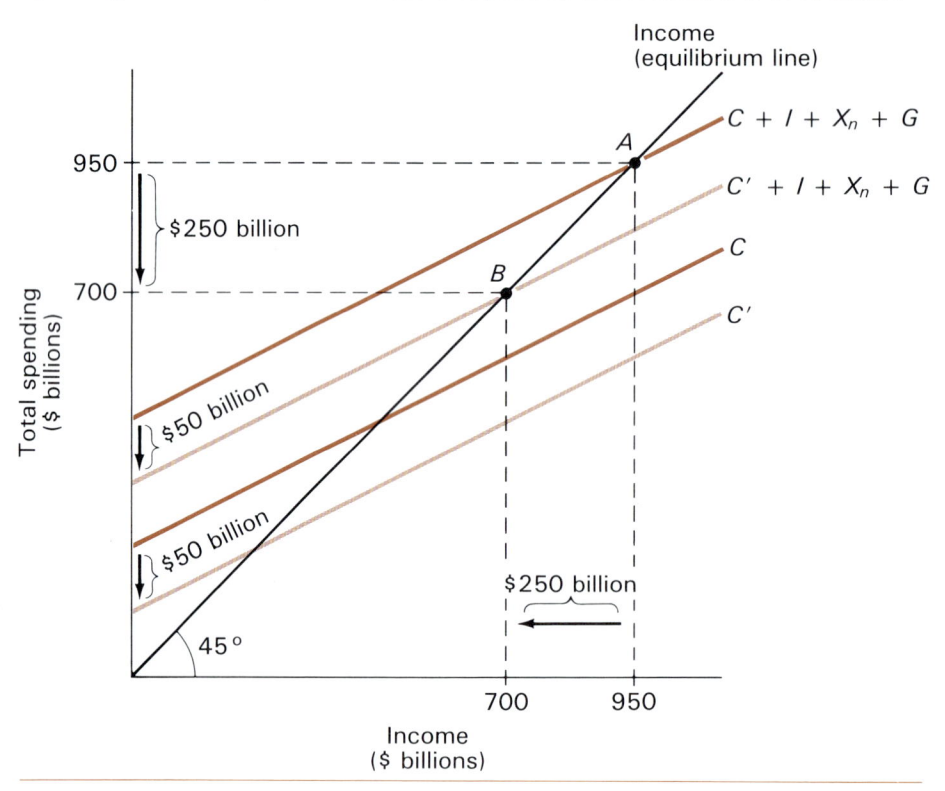

The saving of $50 billion in this example causes equilibrium income to fall from $950 billion to $700 billion. At this point saving, which will decline as income falls, again equals the investment injection. In other words, the initial increase in saving causes income to fall. Saving falls as income declines until saving again equals the investment spending injection. Assuming that investment is constant, income falls until saving returns to its original position. What makes the paradox of thrift paradoxical is the fact that income is less because of the saving, but the economy does not actually experience any additional saving because the decrease in income wipes out the initial increase in saving.

The example of the paradox of thrift is unrealistic because it assumes autonomous or fixed investment spending. In the real world, a sudden increase in saving would cause interest rates to fall, allowing investment spending to rise along with saving. There is no guarantee, however, that investment spending would rise at the same time as saving or by the same amount, so the paradox of thrift is a real possibility. Indeed, the paradox of thrift is a historical fact. People who expected bad times ahead began to save rapidly during the Great Depression. Firms expected falling income, as well, and did not increase investment spending. Income fell, making the Depression worse, exactly as we described above.

The paradox of thrift illustrates the important point that Keynes made about the economy. The economy is at equilibrium in this example, but the equilibrium is not necessarily desirable, since it is far from full employment. Government, however, has the ability to move the economy toward full employment through fiscal policy.

> **KEY CONCEPTS**
> **10.15, 10.16, 10.17**
>
> The multiplier principle explains how a given change in total spending can cause a much larger change in equilibrium income. A given change in government spending, for example, causes a chain reaction of changes in induced-consumption spending. The 45-degree line model shows how the multiplier principle works. The paradox of thrift holds that, because of the multiplier principle, a reduction in consumption spending (caused by a desire to increase saving) can bring about a much larger decrease in equilibrium income.

SIMPLE KEYNESIAN THEORY IN PERSPECTIVE

The Keynesian macroeconomic theories discussed in this chapter were revolutionary in their impact on economic theory and economic policy. Keynes saw the economy as more than just many individual supply and demand markets. He conceived of the economy as broad sectors, which acted as centers of economic activity that could be analyzed, predicted, and affected by government policy. Keynes had powerful ideas, including the concepts of equilibrium between total spending and total income, the desirability of government action to achieve full employment, and the power of the spending multiplier.

Keynesian economics was an idea whose time had come during the troubled years of the Great Depression when unemployment was the most severe economic problem. And it is important to realize that Keynesian economic theories and ideas continue to be influential today. As time went by, however, the economy began to change in many ways. High inflation became a significant problem, caused, in part, by the repeated use of Keynes' stimulative prescriptions. Economists in recent years have embroidered on the elegant cloth that Keynes created. The next chapter looks at how the economy changed in the years after the Great Depression and how economic theory changed with it.

SUMMARY

10.1

1. The classical economists' acceptance of Say's law, which held that supply creates its own demand, made them believe that a Great Depression was impossible. Say's law was thought to prevent gross unbalances in supply and demand. The classical economists also believed in flexible wages and prices, which would prevent unbalanced supply and demand in individual markets.

ECONOMIC ISSUES

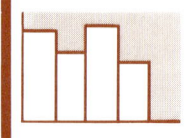

The Algebra of the Simple Keynesian Model

The simple Keynesian model of the economy that we have studied in this chapter can be easily analyzed through the use of simple algebra. In particular, use of algebraic analysis allows us to derive the spending multiplier formula discussed in the last section.

We will assume an economy where total spending consists of planned consumption spending (C), planned investment spending (I), government spending (G), and net export spending (X_n). For simplicity, we will assume that there are fixed levels of taxes (T_x) and transfer payments (T_r). Disposable Income (Y_d) is therefore equal to total income (Y) plus transfer payments (T_r) minus taxes (T_x), or

$$Y_d = Y + T_r - T_x \qquad (1)$$

Consumption Function

We can begin by writing the consumption function as an equation. We know that consumption spending (C) is made up of two parts: autonomous consumption spending (A) plus induced consumption, which depends on the MPC and disposable income ($MPC \times Y_d$). We can therefore write the following equation for planned consumption spending:

$$C = A + MPC \times Y_d \qquad (2)$$

This equation says that planned consumption will change if either autonomous consumption (A) changes or if disposable income (Y_d) changes. The MPC is assumed constant in the short run.

Equilibrium Income

Equilibrium income occurs where total income equals total spending. As noted elsewhere in this chapter, this means that equilibrium income can be written as

$$Y = C + I + X_n + G \qquad (3)$$

We can substitute the consumption function equation (2) into equilibrium income equation (3) to arrive at

$$Y = (A + MPC \times Y_d) + I + X_n + G \qquad (4)$$

Equation (1) defines disposable income, which we can now insert for Y_d in equation (4). Substituting equation (1) for Y_d in equation (4) gives us the following expanded expression for equilibrium income:

10.2 ▶ 2. The complete circular flow diagram includes five sectors: household, business, financial, government, and foreign sectors. The leakages from the circular flow are saving, taxes, and imports. The injections into the circular flow are investment, government spending, and export spending.

10.3 ▶ 3. Macroeconomic equilibrium, in terms of the circular flow model, occurs when total spending equals total income. This condition exists when the leakages from the circular flow (saving, taxes, imports) are equal to the injections into the circular flow (investment, government spending, and export spending). In Keynes' view, the economy always moves toward a macroeconomic equilibrium, but there is no guarantee that equilibrium will occur at a desirable level of national income. Keynes thought that appropriate government fiscal policy could be used to move the economy toward a desirable macroeconomic equilibrium.

10.4 ▶ 4. Consumption spending is the largest type of spending in the economy. The determinants of consumption spending include disposable income, wealth, expectations, the availability of credit, and the demographic profile of the population.

$$Y = [A + MPC \times (Y + T_r - T_x)] + I + X_n + G \quad (5)$$

Careful examination of equation (5) reveals that income (Y) appears on both sides of equation (5). If we carefully associate terms and move all terms involving Y to the left side of the equal sign, we get

$$Y \times (1 - MPC) = A + MPC \times (T_r - T_x) + I + X_n + G \quad (6)$$

If we now multiply both sides of equation (6) by 1/(1 − MPC), we get

$$Y = 1/(1 - MPC) \times [A + MPC \times (T_r - T_x) + I + X_n + G] \quad (7)$$

Equation (7) tells us that the equilibrium level of income depends on the MPC, the level of autonomous spending A, taxes (T_x) and transfer payments (T_r), and the injections of investment (I), net exports (X_n), and government spending (G). We can use equation (7) to actually calculate the equilibrium level of income. Supoose that the MPC = 80 percent = 0.8. Now suppose that A = 100, I = 200, G = 300, and $X_n = T_x = T_r = 0$ (we assume these are zero for simplicity). Insert these values into equation (7) and equilibrium income is equal to

$$Y = 1/(1 - 0.8) \times [100 + 200 + 300]$$
$$Y = 1/0.2 \times [600]$$
$$Y = 5 \times 600 = \$3000$$

The Multiplier

We can use equation (7) to derive the spending multiplier formula. We use the multiplier formula when we want to find out what change in income ($\triangle Y$) comes about when we change a level of spending, such as $\triangle A$, $\triangle I$, $\triangle X_n$, or $\triangle G$, or a change in induced consumption due to $\triangle T_x$ or $\triangle T_r$. The $\triangle$ sign denotes a "change in" the variable it is associated with. Thus $\triangle Y$ means "change in income." Let us suppose that government spending changes, but that there are no other changes in the variables in equation (7). In other words, let us suppose that there is a change in G ($\triangle G > 0$ for an increase or $\triangle G < 0$ for a decrease), but that

$$\triangle A = \triangle T_x = \triangle T_r = \triangle I = \triangle X_n = 0$$

(no change in any of these variables). This change in government spending will cause a change in Y. If we substitute $\triangle Y$ for Y and $\triangle G$ for G in equation (7) and eliminate all the variables that do not change, we see that

$$\triangle Y = 1/(1 - MPC) \times \triangle G \quad (8)$$

Remembering that MPS = (1 − MPC), we can make one last substitution and get

$$\triangle Y = 1/MPS \times \triangle G \quad (9)$$

This is the spending multiplier formula derived earlier in this chapter. Note that one can use this method to calculate the multiplier impact of changes any of the variables in equation (7) on equilibrium income.

10.5

5. Keynes theorized that consumption spending could be divided into two parts. Autonomous consumption spending is independent of the level of disposable income. The level of autonomous spending depends on many factors, such as size of the population, wealth, and expectations. Induced consumption spending, the second component of total consumption, depends on the level of disposable income in the economy. The Keynesian consumption function graphically displays these two parts of total consumption spending.

10.6

6. The marginal propensity to consume (MPC) is the fraction of a change in disposable income that becomes a change in consumption spending. The MPC is equal to the slope of the consumption function line. The marginal propensity to save (MPS) is the fraction of a change in disposable income that becomes a change in consumption spending. MPC plus MPS equals 100 percent of a change in disposable income. The average propensity to consume (APC) is the fraction of total disposable income that is used for consumption. The average propensity to save (APS) is the fraction of total disposable income that is used for saving. APC plus APS equals 100 percent of total disposable income.

10.7   7. The relationship between consumption spending and disposable income tends to be different in short- and long-term periods. In the short run, for example, households tend to treat an increase in income as a temporary change in their economic situation and expand consumption by a relatively small fraction of the change in income (this fraction is the MPC). In the long run, however, households treat this change in income as a change in their permanent income and expand consumption spending by a greater amount (spending rises to the APC level). This explains the difference between the MPC (which measures short-run behavior) and the APC (which measures more long-term trends).

10.8   8. Many factors affect the level of net investment spending in the economy. Among the most important determinants of net investment are the ratio of current sales to current productive capacity, expectations, interest rates, the marginal efficiency of investment, and taxes.

10.9   9. Many factors affect the level of net export spending. Among the most important determinants of net exports are the exchange rate, the existence of trade restrictions, and changing patterns of world trade in goods such as agricultural commodities.

10.10   10. Government spending is an exogenous policy variable. That is, the level of government spending is largely controlled by factors not internal to the economy, such as international and domestic political matters. Keynes viewed government spending as a tool to move the economy toward a desirable level of economic equilibrium.

10.11   11. In the complete Keynesian model, equilibrium income occurs at the point at which total spending equals total income. This happens at the level of income where the $C + I + X_n + G$ line crosses the 45-degree total income line.

10.12   12. The graphical Keynesian model uses the $C + I + X_n + G$ line to represent total spending. Because investment, net exports, and government spending are assumed to be exogenous (not related to the level of income) the slope of the total spending line is equal to the MPC. Total income is represented by a 45-degree line, which shows all the points at which total income (horizontal axis) is equal to total spending (vertical axis).

10.13   13. In the Keynesian model, macroeconomic equilibrium occurs when total income equals total spending ($C + I + X_n + G$). This equilibrium condition can also be stated as total injections ($I + X_n + G$) being equal to total leakages ($I + S$). In a simple model, ignoring the government and foreign sectors, the equilibrium condition becomes $I = S$.

10.14   14. The economy moves to a new equilibrium income through unplanned inventory adjustments. If current income is below equilibrium, for example, businesses experience unplanned inventory reductions, which induce them to increase production and move the economy toward the higher level of equilibrium income. If current income is below equilibrium, on the other hand, firms experience unplanned inventory accumulations. They reduce production in order to draw down these inventory levels, thereby moving the economy toward the lower level of income.

10.15 ▶ 15. An exogenous increase in spending causes equilibrium income to rise by a relatively larger amount. This is the concept of the spending multiplier. A $100 million exogenous increase in consumption spending, for example, creates $100 million in additional disposable income through the circular flow of spending and income. If the MPC equals 80 percent, then this increase in disposable income causes a further $80 million increase in spending and income, which generates additional spending increases. The total change in equilibrium income is given by the formula for the spending multiplier: change in equilibrium income = $1/(1 - MPC)$ × exogenous change in spending. The term $1/(1 - MPC) = (1/MPS)$ is called the spending multiplier.

10.16 ▶ 16. The spending multiplier can be seen using the graphic Keynesian model. The shift in total spending (vertical shift in the $C + I + X_n + G$ line) is less than the change in equilibrium income.

10.17 ▶ 17. The paradox of thrift states that, while an increase in saving is beneficial to any one individual, an increase in total saving for the whole economy can be undesirable, at least in the short run, because it results in a decrease in consumption spending, which causes a multiplier decrease in the level of equilibrium income. This is a paradox because it says that what is good for individuals can be bad for the economy.

DISCUSSION QUESTIONS

10.5 ▶ 1. Suppose you are a full-time student and you do not presently have a job. Your income, therefore, is zero. You are, however, still consuming food, clothing, shelter, and educational services. What type of consumption would this be?

10.5, 10.6 ▶ 2. You have had a bank account for three years. The balance in the account is $1500. This year, your total income will be $10,000, of which you plan on depositing $1000 into your account. Which of these figures represents saving and which represents savings? Which is a flow concept and which is a stock concept? Explain.

10.6 ▶ 3. Given the following data, define and calculate the terms listed below:

Disposable family income	Planned consumption	Planned savings
0	3,500	−3,500
4000	6,500	−2,500
8000	9,500	−1,500
12,000	12,500	−500
16,000	15,500	+500
20,000	18,500	+1,500

a. average propensity to consume
b. average propensity to save
c. marginal propensity to consume
d. marginal propensity to save

298 *The Keynesian Model of the Economy*

10.5, 10.7

4. Determine if the following would cause a movement along an existing consumption function or if the entire consumption function would shift. If a shift occurs, state the direction of the shift.
   a. Your income increases from $15,000 to $18,000.
   b. Consumers expect future prices of goods and services to rise.
   c. Consumers anticipate the unemployment level to increase and thus forsee reduced income levels in the future.
   d. Personal Disposable Family Income falls from $35,000 to $32,500.
   e. The next phase of the president's tax reduction program goes into effect next month.

10.8

5. Determine what effect each of the following would generally have on business investment.
   a. Current sales are far below the productive capacity of a business.
   b. Current sales are slightly below productive capacity, but business people expect a very large and lasting rise in future sales.
   c. Business people foresee the recession nearing its end and their outlooks indicate widespread optimism in the economy.
   d. The market rate of interest is high. The government has just announced a record high deficit and people expect this to increase rates even more.

10.13

6. What are the two major conditions that exist when the economy is in equilibrium? Interpret each of the following situations in terms of these equilibrium conditions.
   a. Total goods and services produced equal $75 million. Consumers and investors plan to buy $67 million.
   b. Consumers and investors plan to buy $80 million. Total goods and services produced equal $50 million.

10.12, 10.13, 10.14

7. If government spending equals $430 billion, taxes equal $450 billion, savings equal $600 billion, and investment equals $600 billion, is the economy in equilibrium? If not, how could equilibrium be reached?

10.15, 10.16

8. Given a marginal propensity to consume equal to .75 and an initial independent increase in investment of $15 billion, what will happen to the equilibrium level of income in the economy? What limits the amount of incremental income produced through the multiplier? Is it true that there is no time lag involved and that the effects of the multiplier are felt immediately throughout the economy?

10.17

9. Explain the different results that occur when individuals increase their saving from current income and when the economy as a whole attempts to increase savings. What do economists call this? Are the effects for the economy as a whole positive or negative? Include in your explanation the effects on resources, output, employment, and wages.

10.1, 10.3

10. Briefly summarize the differences in the way that Keynes and the classical economists viewed macroeconomic equilibrium and the economic role of government.

SELECTED READINGS

Buchanan, James M., and Wagner, Richard E. *Democracy in Deficit: The Political Legacy of Lord Keynes.* New York: Academic Press, 1977.

Dillard, Dudley. *The Economics of John Maynard Keynes.* Englewood Cliffs, NJ: Prentice-Hall, 1948.

Dornbusch, Rudiger, and Fischer, Stanley. *Macroeconomics*, 3rd ed. New York: McGraw-Hill, 1984, chaps. 3, 6, and 7.

Keynes, John Maynard. *The General Theory of Employment, Interest, and Money.* New York: Harcourt, Brace and World, 1936.

Klein, Lawrence. *The Keynesian Revolution.* New York: MacMillan, 1961.

Lekachman, Robert. *The Age of Keynes.* New York: Random House, Inc., 1966.

Peterson, Wallace C. *Income, Employment and Economic Growth*, 4th ed. New York: W.W. Norton & Company, 1978, chaps. 5–7.

Shapiro, Edward. *Macroeconomic Analysis*, 5th ed. New York: Harcourt, Brace, Jovanovich, Inc., 1982, chaps. 4 and 5.

CHAPTER 11

Aggregate Demand and Aggregate Supply

Having read the chapter, reviewed the chapter summary, and completed the *Study Guide* exercises, you should be able to:

CRIS

11.1 **INFLATION AND UNEMLOYMENT:** Use the Phillips curve to discuss how the relationship between inflation and unemployment changed during the 1960s and 1970s.

11.2 **CHANGING ECONOMIC THEORY:** Explain, in simple terms, how economic theory changed to reflect changing economic conditions in the 1960s and 1970s.

11.3 *AD–AS* **MODEL:** Draw and describe the aggregate demand (*AD*)–aggregate supply (*AS*) model of the economy and explain what variables are measured on the horizontal and vertical axes of this graphic model.

11.4 **AGGREGATE DEMAND:** List the determinants of aggregate demand and draw an *AD* curve and explain why it is downward sloping.

11.5 **SHIFTING THE *AD* CURVE:** List and describe the events that can shift the *AD* curve.

11.6 **AGGREGATE SUPPLY:** List and describe the determinants of aggregate supply.

11.7 ***AS* CURVE:** Draw an *AS* curve and describe the three portions of the *AS* curve that correspond to depression, bottleneck, and full-capacity economic situations.

11.8 **SHIFTING THE *AS* CURVE:** Discuss the factors that can cause the *AS* curve to shift in the short run and in the long run.

11.9 *AD–AS* **EQUILIBRIUM POINT:** Identify the equilibrium point in the *AD–AS* model of the economy, and explain what this point means in terms of real GNP and the price level.

11.10 DEMAND-PULL VS. COST-PUSH INFLATION: Use the *AD–AS* model to explain the difference between demand-pull inflation and cost-push inflation.

11.11 1960s AND 1970s ECONOMIC EVENTS: Use the *AD–AS* model to describe and illustrate the economic events and policies of the 1960s and 1970s.

11.12 WAGE AND PRICE CONTROLS: Use the *AD–AS* model to describe and illustrate the economic effects of wage and price controls.

11.13 INDEXATION: Explain how indexation works as an economic policy to deal with the problem of inflation.

11.14 FORD'S TAX REBATE PROGRAM: Discuss President Ford's tax rebate program and explain why it was not completely effective.

11.15 INCREASING *AS*: List several policies that could increase aggregate supply and explain the problems with each *AS* policy.

11.16 CHANGING EXPECTATIONS: Use the *AD–AS* model to explain why changing expectations are an important factor in making economic policy.

The Keynesian macroeconomic model developed in the last chapter provided a theory that helped economists understand the problem of the Great Depression. It also provided government officials with a relatively straightforward set of policy prescriptions to cure the Depression. According to the model, the level of production and income in the economy is determined by the level of total spending by consumers, investors, foreigners, and government and changes in total spending can be used to bring about needed changes in production and income.

Macroeconomic theory changed in the 1960s and 1970s as economic conditions shifted during this period. The Keynesian analysis presented in Chapter 10 made few references to the problem of inflation that has been so important in recent years. But Keynes' economic theories of the 1930s contained a blueprint for a powerful model of aggregate demand and aggregate supply, a model capable of explaining the major changes in economic events that we have experienced. In this chapter, we will first look at how economic conditions changed during the 1960s and 1970s, then we will present the model of aggregate demand and aggregate supply and analyze the macroeconomic policies that were employed during these two decades.

Keynes' theory and the policies it implies were challenged in four fundamental ways in the 1960s and 1970s. First, a competing school of macroeconomic thought called **monetarism** grew in importance during this period. Monetarism is an economic theory that holds that the growth of the nation's money supply is the fundamental factor that determines macroeconomic trends. It is an important economic theory that differs from Keynesian analysis in both its view of the way the economy works and in its prescriptions for economic policy. We cannot understand monetarism, however, until

Monetarism
An economic theory that stresses the importance of changes in the money supply on economic activities and policies.

Rational Expectations Theory
An economic theory that stresses the importance of expectations on economic activities and policies.

we learn about money and the financial sector of the economy. Our discussion of the theory is delayed, therefore, until Chapter 15.

Monetarist economics gave birth in the 1970s to the second important challenge to Keynes' theories, **rational expectations theory.** The theory of rational expectations is built on the idea that individuals and firms are fully aware of the implications of economic policies and events. They therefore undertake production and consumption decisions based on relatively accurate expectations of what is going to happen in the economy. Rational expectations differs from both Keynesian and monetarist analysis in its understanding of how the economy works and its prescriptions for economics policies. Because rational expectations theory is built on the foundations established by monetarism, we must also delay our discussion of this theory until Chapter 15.

Supply-Side Economics
An economic theory that stresses the importance of policies that try to increase aggregate supply by cutting tax rates, increasing investment, or reducing regulation.

Keynesian orthodoxy has also been challenged in the 1980s by **supply-side economics.** Supply-side economics is built on the idea that it is important for the economy to grow in its ability to produce. Supply-side economists tend to believe that Keynesians pay too much attention to the amount of total spending in the economy and not enough attention to the economy's ability to produce goods and services. They are concerned about saving, investment, productivity, and production incentives. Supply-side economics differs from Keynesian analysis, monetarism, and rational expectations in its view of how the economy works and what economic policies should be followed. We will discuss the ideas of supply-side economics in detail in the next chapter.

THE CHANGING ECONOMY OF THE 1960s AND 1970s

It is important to realize that the basic economic problems at the start of the 1960s were much like those at the start of the 1930s. The U.S. economy entered the decade of the 1960s still recovering from a major recession. Unemployment rates were high by historical standards, and the need for jobs and economic growth dominated the scene. This concern changed, however, as the 1960s progressed, as Figure 11-1 shows.

11.1 INFLATION AND UNEMPLOYMENT

Unemployment rates declined dramatically during the 1960s, but the decline in unemployment was accompanied by an increase in the inflation rate. This pattern of lower unemployment but higher inflation traces out the Phillips curve relationship in Figure 11-1. The Phillips Curve was first presented and discussed in Chapter 9. As the decade of the 1960s progressed, economists and policymakers were forced to deal with several major issues. What caused the Phillips curve? Why did inflation rise as unemployment rates fell? Economists sought policies that might cause the Phillips curve to shift in, allowing lower unemployment rates without any increase in inflation.

The rise of inflation also caused a change in the focus of economic theory and policy. Whereas Keynesian economic theory was primarily interested in what determines total spending and production, economic theory from the mid-1960s on had to focus on inflation and what economic policies could reduce it without causing unacceptably high unemployment rates.

Economists and policymakers had barely accounted for the economic events in the 1960s when a strangely different economy appeared in the 1970s. Figure 11-2 shows the inflation and unemployment rates for the 1970s. As the figure shows, inflation became an even more serious economic problem in the 1970s. The inflation rate in 1979 was over twice as high as it

FIGURE 11-1

The U.S. Economy in the 1960s. The Phillips curve relationship between inflation and unemployment prevailed in the 1960s. Demand-pull inflation brought lower unemployment rates but higher inflation rates.

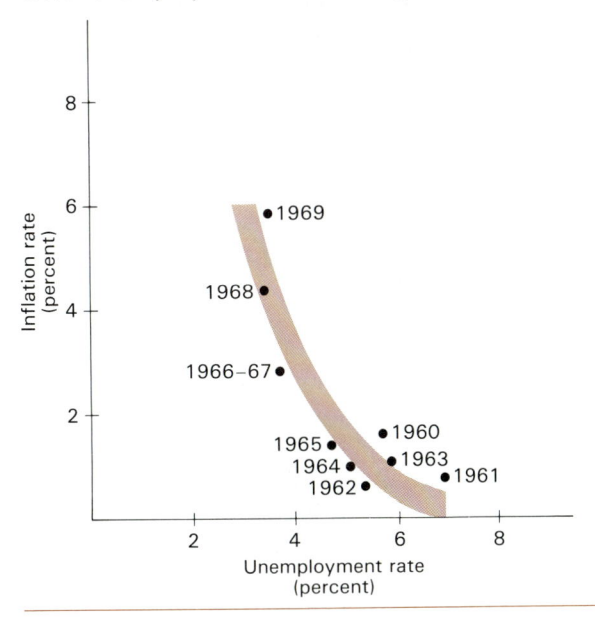

FIGURE 11-2

The U.S. Economy in the 1970s. The economic experience of the 1970s was much different from that of the 1960s. Cost-push inflation resulted in rising inflation and rising unemployment at the same time.

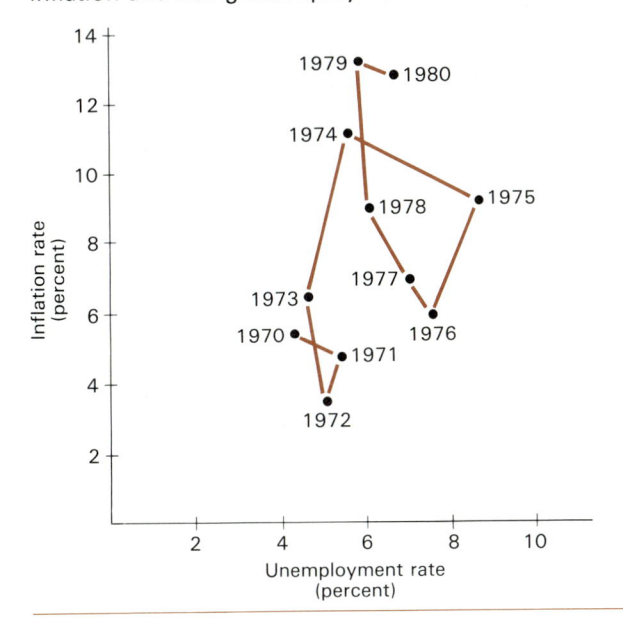

was in 1969. At the same time that inflationary problems increased, however, unemployment also worsened and the rate of economic growth slowed. Like the inflation rate, the unemployment rate in 1979 was also about twice as high as it was in 1969. In short, both of our major economic problems, inflation and unemployment, increased in the 1970s. In addition, the economy

304 *Aggregate Demand and Aggregate Supply*

was extremely unstable, as the "loops" seen in Figure 11-2 suggest when compared with the more stable Phillips curve phenomenon of the 1960s seen in Figure 11-1.

To sum up, the economy changed in several respects during the period being discussed here. In the 1960s, the problem of unemployment decreased, while the problem of inflation increased. The Phillips curve relationship was strong. Both inflation and unemployment became much worse in the 1970s, however. The economy experienced increased instability and suffered from severe economic dislocations.

THE EVOLUTION OF ECONOMIC THEORY

11.2 CHANGING ECONOMIC THEORY

The economic events of the 1960s and 1970s made economists more aware of and concerned about the problem of inflation. Clearly economic theory and policy needed to be able to deal with the high inflation rates that were observed. Yet many economists were still guided by the simple Keynesian economic model that was presented in the last chapter. This model of the economy had an important weakness. While the simple Keynesian model provides a useful framework from which to analyze the relationship between total spending and total income, it does not explicitly take into account prices. This is an important flaw. It is clear that a theory of unemployment is only a partial answer to our problems when we must also deal with inflation. We must be able to analyze and understand the causes and cures of both inflation and unemployment.

The simple Keynesian model discussed in the last chapter failed to provide a comprehensive explanation of inflation because it is, essentially, a theory of demand. In its most basic terms, this model said that we can control the economy by controlling total spending or total demand (where total spending equals consumption, investment, net export, and government spending). Figure 11-3 suggests why this theory, useful though it is in many respects, is insufficient to deal with the problem of inflation. Inflation is, after all, the phenomenon of rising prices throughout the economy. The

FIGURE 11-3

Rising Prices: The Economics of Demand and Supply. We must look at both demand and supply to understand the causes and effects of rising prices. Rising prices can be associated with rising demand, which also results in higher quantities (a). Falling supply also increases price, but it results in smaller quantities (b). Finally, rising demand can interact with falling supply causing higher prices but with an ambiguous impact on quantity (c).

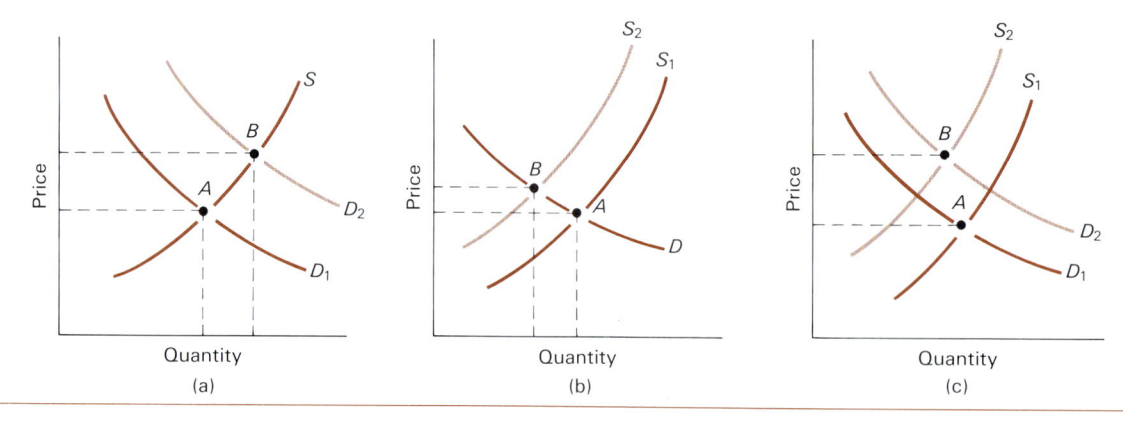

figure shows how the price of a specific item rises in the market. It is easy to see from the figure that we cannot understand what makes the price of pie rise in the market based on a theory of demand alone. Price increases are the result of the interaction of both demand and supply.

The simple microeconomic supply–demand pictured in Figure 11-3 shows that the price of specific items can rise because of demand increasing against a stationary supply curve, because of supply falling with the demand curve stationary, or because of a combination of these two effects. Price increases in the market are the result of the interaction of demand and supply.

11.3 AD–AS MODEL

The simple Keynesian macroeconomic theory presented in the last chapter did not explicitly take the concept of supply into account, so it could not really analyze price effects and inflation. However, simple Keynesian theory evolved into a more complex theory of the economy that was able to discuss both inflation and unemployment. This simple model is pictured in Figure 11-4. As we mentioned at the beginning of the chapter, this macroeconomic theory is called the model of aggregate demand and aggregate supply.

The macroeconomic model shown in Figure 11-4 bears a clear superficial resemblance to the simple supply–demand model pictured in Figure 11-3, but it is important to keep in mind that the two models are really very different. The vertical axis of the aggregate demand–aggregate supply model (AD–AS model) shows the price level, as measured by a price index such as the Consumer Price Index discussed in Chapter 9. An increase in the price level means that inflation has occurred. A decrease in the price level indicates deflation.

The horizontal axis of Figure 11-4 measures the amount of final goods that are produced and sold, as measured by real GNP. An increase in real

FIGURE 11-4

Aggregate Demand and Aggregate Supply. The aggregate demand–aggregate supply model shown here is a macroeconomic model that allows us to simultaneously analyze inflation and unemployment. AD–AS shows how the interaction of desired purchases and desired output produces an equilibrium price level (vertical axis) and real GNP (horizontal axis). Inflation results from changes in the price level. The unemployment rate is affected by changes in real GNP.

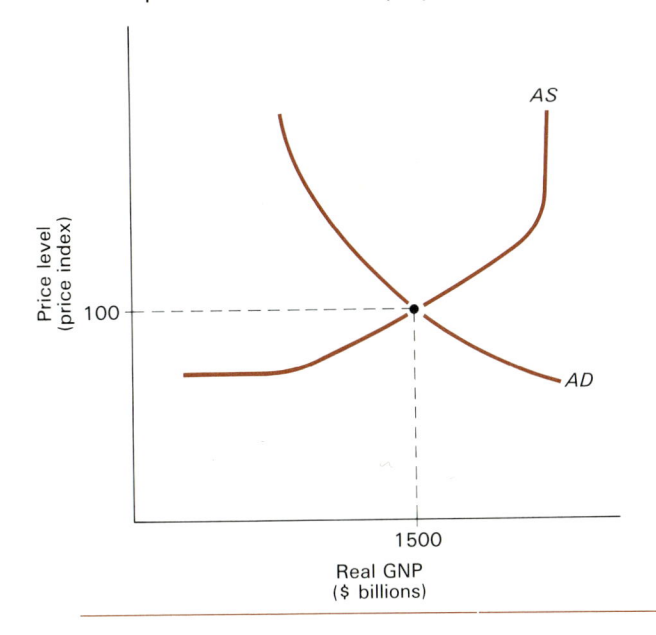

Aggregate Demand Curve
A graphic device showing the relationship between desired real purchases (for some time period) and the price level, all else held constant.

Aggregate Supply Curve
A graphic device showing the relationship between desired real output (for some time period) and the price level, all else held constant.

GNP signifies an increase in the amount of final goods and services produced and sold. This generally results in a decrease in the unemployment rate. A recession, on the other hand, is shown by a decrease in real GNP, which generally produces higher unemployment rates.

Two curves are shown in Figure 11-4. The **aggregate demand curve** (*AD*) shows the desired total amount of real goods and services demanded by consumers, investors, the foreign sector, and government at each price level. The *AD* curve is based on the concept of total spending discussed in the last chapter. Aggregate demand is therefore equal to consumption, investment, and government spending, with the effects of inflation explicitly taken into account.

The **aggregate supply curve** (*AS*) in Figure 11-4 shows the economy's desired production of real final goods. The *AS* curve plots the amount of real GNP that economic units desire to produce at each price level.

Together, *AD* and *AS* provide us with a useful model for analyzing inflation and unemployment. We will use this model to understand the economic events and economic policies of the 1960s and 1970s, but first we should look closer at the determinants of aggregate demand and aggregate supply.

KEY CONCEPTS 11.1, 11.2

The economy and economic theory changed during the 1960s and 1970s to take into account the relationship between inflation and unemployment. The Phillips curve relationship prevailed in the 1960s, but inflation and unemployment did not consistently display a Phillips curve trade-off in the 1970s. Economic theory changed its focus from Keynesian aggregate demand to an emphasis on both aggregate demand and aggregate supply.

DETERMINANTS OF AGGREGATE DEMAND

11.4 AGGREGATE DEMAND

Aggregate Demand (*AD*)
The desired total spending in the economy (measured in real GNP).

Aggregate demand (*AD*) measures the desired total spending on final goods at each price level, where the level of these purchases is measured in real terms. It is equal to the sum of desired real consumption, investment, net export, and government spending.

Aggregate demand is related to the Keynesian total spending function introduced in Chapter 10, where the determinants of consumption, investment, net exports and government spending were discussed. However, unlike the total spending function, agregate demand takes into account how changes in the price level affect the real level of total purchases. Let us briefly review the four components of aggregate demand and some of their most important determinants.

Consumption Spending

Consumption spending is the largest component of aggregate demand. As discussed in Chapter 10, consumption spending is affected by many factors. Some of the most important determinants of the level of consumption spending are disposable income, expectations, and the cost and availability of credit.

Disposable Income Consumer spending rises and falls with the level of disposable income. Disposable income is affected by, among other things, taxes and transfer payments. A direct relationship between disposable income and consumer spending makes intuitive sense. Spending by retired people increases, for example, when social security benefits grow. Conversely, spending by workers falls when social security taxes go up. Taxes and transfer payments are two important ways in which government influences consumption spending decisions through changes in disposable income.

Expectations Spending decisions are based on both current and projected future events. Expectations play a big role in the choices consumers make. People who think that their jobs are secure and pay increases are likely spend readily and buy big ticket items like cars and new homes. People who think unemployment is a possibility cut back spending in anticipation of hard times.

Inflationary expectations are important, too. People who think prices are going to jump in the future hedge by spending money now. On the other hand, people who expect stable prices spread their purchases out over a longer period. People also anticipate government acts and the consequences of those actions and then make spending choices consistent with their expectations. The power of expectations is immense.

Credit Cost and Availability Many big consumer purchases, such as autos and new homes, are commonly financed with loans. The availability and cost of credit helps determine how much consumers buy. High interest rates in the early 1980s, for example, kept consumers away from new car showrooms and real estate offices. High interest costs discouraged consumer spending.

Investment Spending

Investment spending is crucial to the economy. Spending on factories, machines, and technology adds to aggregate demand and improves the economy's ability to supply goods. Investment spending is a large and volatile component of aggregate demand. The major determinants of investment spending are interest rates, expectations, and government policies.

Interest Rates Most investments are financed using borrowed funds. Business firms weigh interest costs against expected profits from a new store or factory. Higher interest costs reduce the list of profitable investments. Thus there is usually an inverse relationship between interest rates and investment spending.

Expectations Investment choices are difficult because firms spend now (on the new machines or other investment goods), but the payoff comes months or years in the future when production finally begins. Economic events move quickly these days, so a lot can happen in a few months or years. Will consumer spending increase? Will interest rates drop further? What about government policy? A simple investment choice hinges on all these uncertain matters.

Government Policies Government policies affect investment decisions in many ways. On the local level, zoning rules can be used to either encourage or discourage investment. Similarly, the federal government frequently uses tax policy to regulate investment. For example, special tax breaks are given to encourage specific business investments.

Government Spending

Government spending is the second largest category of aggregate demand. What makes government spending go up and down? This is a complicated question because there is no one government in the United States. In addition to the federal government, the total government sector includes 50 state and over 75,000 local governments, which together have nearly as much spending clout as Congress and the president.

Government spending choices depend on many variables, including voter moods and the length of time to the next election. Among the important determinants of government spending are national emergencies, political philosophy, and automatic stabilizers.

National Emergencies   Government spending rises fastest in times of stress like war or deep recession. This follows, at least in part, Keynes' view of government as "spender of last resort" during hard times.

Political Philosophy   Ideas are important. The conservative political philosophy of Ronald Reagan held back growth in government spending just as the more liberal views of Lyndon Johnson expanded both the role of government and the size of the government budget.

Automatic Stabilizers   Many government policies automatically respond to changing economic conditions. Antipoverty programs, for example, kick in by themselves when unemployment grows and reduce spending automatically when jobless lines shorten.

Net Exports

Net exports are the smallest component of aggregate demand, but they are very important. We gain from imports by buying goods for less than it would cost us to produce them ourselves. Trade also serves as a market for U.S. goods. Many U.S. workers have jobs because of international trade. What variables influence net exports? The list includes exchange rates, barriers to trade, and politics.

Exchange Rates   Import prices and the ability of U.S. firms to compete abroad depend on the exchange rate. Imports cost more and U.S. goods sell better, for example, when the dollar falls against foreign currencies.

Barriers to Trade   Tariffs and quotas keep out foreign goods, increasing aggregate demand at home. But they also reduce export jobs if foreigners retaliate. Most economists favor free trade that increases both imports and exports.

Politics   Political actions affect international trade, too. Richard Nixon's 'ping-pong' diplomacy in the 1970s opened up China to U.S. traders. Conversely, the late Senator Henry Jackson potentionally restricted trade when he succeeded in linking U.S.–Soviet trade to human rights policies. Some types of international trade are directly tied to government action. For example, U.S. exports of military equipment, like the proposed sale of surveillance airplanes to Saudi Arabia in 1981, depend on Congressional approval.

Aggregate demand measures desired total spending, taking into account how the real level of desired purchases changes when the price level changes. It is possible to summarize *AD* by saying that it is the sum of desired total real purchases by consumers, investors, government, and the foreign sector. In other words, aggregate demand equals consumption (*C*) plus investment (*I*) plus government spending (*G*) plus net exports (X_n), or in shorthand notation,

$$AD = C + I + G + X_n$$

THE AGGREGATE DEMAND CURVE

11.4 AGGREGATE DEMAND

The *AD* curve slopes downward in Figure 11-4, showing that fewer goods and services (real GNP) are demanded as the price level rises. While the *AD* curve has the same basic downward slope as the demand curve for an individual good, it takes this shape for completely different reasons. The slope of the *AD* curve depends on how consumption, investment, net exports, and government spending react to changes in the price level. There is good reason to believe that these parts of the economy demand fewer real goods and services at higher price levels.

One reason why the *AD* curve is downward sloping has to do with the relationship between the price level and interest rates. An increase in the price level, all else held constant, tends to result in higher interest rates. As we discussed earlier, higher interest rates discourage investment spending. High interest rates also discourage consumption spending on consumer durables, since purchases of these goods are often financed by credit. Thus an increase in the price level is associated with lower real consumption and investment purchases, causing a lower level of real GNP to be demanded. The quantity of real GNP demanded is therefore lower at the higher price level because of the higher interest rates.

Lower price levels would tend to have the opposite effect on the quantity of goods demanded. Lower price levels tend to be associated with lower interest rates, which would encourage investment spending and purchases of consumer durables. The quantity of real GNP demanded would therefore rise if the price level fell.

A change in the price level can also cause a change in the real value of the assets that people hold. A rise in the price level can cause the real value of wealth to decline, for example, causing households to reduce their real level of autonomous consumption spending.

The *AD* curve is downward sloping because of the interest rate and real wealth effects just noted. The slope of the *AD* curve depends on the size of the effects such as those on investment and consumption and the magnitude of the indirect effect on consumption spending that results from these other effects.

To summarize, the *AD* curve shows how desired total consumption, investment, government, and net export spending, expressed in real terms, varies with the price level. The *AD* curve is downward sloping because, as noted above, changes in the price level tend to influence interest rates, consumption, and other factors that affect the level of investment and consumption spending.

SHIFTS IN AGGREGATE DEMAND

11.5 SHIFTING THE *AD* CURVE

A change in the price level causes a movement along the *AD* curve. The *AD* curve does shift, however, when desired total spending changes because of anything other than a change in the price level. Because *AD* is made up of desired real consumption, investment, government spending, and net export spending, the *AD* curve shifts if any of these components change for reasons other than a change in the price level. You will recall from Chapter 10, for example, that consumption spending can rise because of an increase in disposable income, an increase in wealth that causes autonomous consumption to rise, or a change in expectations that affects consumption, among other things. Aggregate demand will also rise if the determinants of investment, net exports, or government spending change to cause an increase in real purchases in these sectors of the economy.

An increase in aggregate demand would cause the *AD* curve to shift out and to the right showing that larger quantities of goods and services, as measured by real GNP, are purchased at every price level.

Aggregate demand falls whenever intended purchases contract due to something other than a change in the price level. Thus aggregate demand would fall if there were decreases in consumption, investment, government, or net export spending. Factors that would cause these spending reductions were discussed in detail in Chapter 10. A decrease in aggregate demand would cause a shift in the *AD* curve back and to the left, showing that less real GNP is demanded at each price level. Shifts in *AD*, caused by external changes in consumption, investment, net export, or government spending, are shown in Figure 11-5.

Aggregate demand describes the spending side of the economy. To understand the causes of inflation and unemployment in a modern economy, we must combine aggregate demand with the concept of aggregate supply.

**KEY CONCEPTS
11.4, 11.5**

Aggregate demand represents the relationship between the price level and changes in the real level of desired total spending. It is the sum of real consumption, investment, government spending, and net export spending. The *AD* curve shifts when something other than price level effects cause changes in desired real consumption, investment, net export, or government spending.

DETERMINANTS OF AGGREGATE SUPPLY

Aggregate Supply (*AS*)
The total intended production of goods and services in the economy (measured in real GNP).

11.6 AGGREGATE SUPPLY

Capacity
The physical ability of the economy to produce, limited by the stock of factories, machines, tools, and so on.

Aggregate supply (*AS*) describes total desired production measured by the level of real GNP. It is not the same as the supply of goods in a particular market. Rather, aggregate supply represents the entire economy's ability to generate goods and services. It therefore depends on the resources available to the entire economy and the factors that influence our desire and ability to use those resources in production.

If you think about factors that would affect the supplies of goods in many markets, you will begin to understand the factors that determine aggregate supply. Aggregate supply depends on variables that influence production choices not in just one market but in many markets throughout the economy. It hinges on problems common to most business decisions. A list of determinants of aggregate supply would include capacity and investment, technology, productivity, availability and cost of resources, expectations, and government policies.

Capacity and Investment The physical ability to produce constrains production. The economy is limited in the short run by its **capacity,** the

FIGURE 11-5 **Shifts in Aggregate Demand.** The *AD* curve increases (shift from *AD* to *AD*₁) when consumption, investment, net export, or government spending increases, all else held constant. A decrease in *AD* (shift from *AD* to *AD*₂) results from a reduction of desired purchases by consumers, investors, government, and the foreign sector.

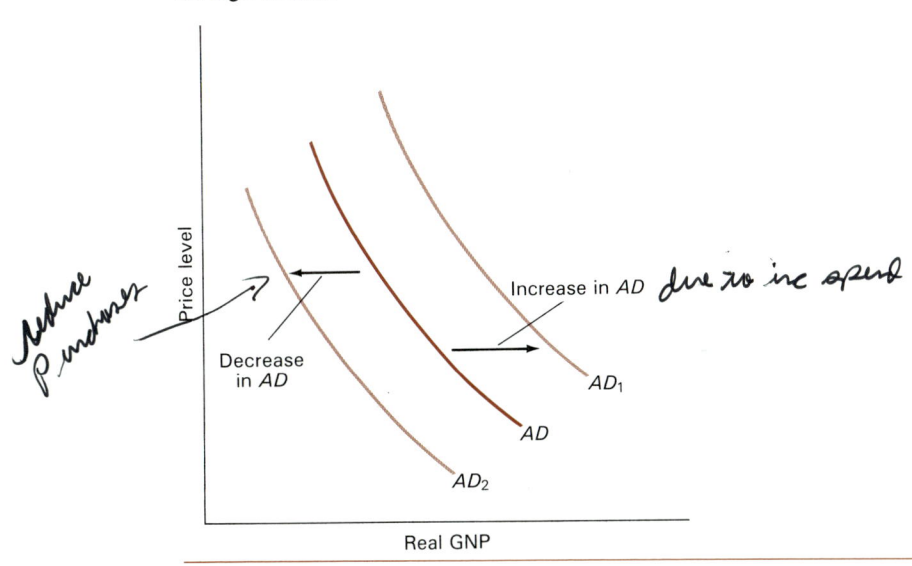

existing stock of machines, factories, trained workers, and farms. Investment spending undertaken today increases capacity in the long run. Investment replaces worn-out factories and machines and expands the economy's ability to produce. However, the consequences of investment spending take time to be felt. In the short run, investment spending adds to aggregate demand, as spending on training and tools increases total spending and income. In the long run, however, investment spending brings increased capacity and greater aggregate supply. Investment spending stimulates both aggregate demand and aggregate supply and promotes the balanced growth of the economy.

While investment spending is primarily a private sector activity, government can engage in activities that also increase the economy's capacity. Government spending on roads, port facilities, and power projects expands capacity in the same way as similar private-sector ventures.

Low investment spending in the Great Depression had a double effect on the economy. First, the low investment spending contributed to low incomes. Second, the tiny flow of new investment was not even enough to make up for depreciation, the wearing-out of existing capacity. Negative net investment meant that capacity was actually less at the end of the depression than at the start.

Technology Technological change reduces cost and increases aggregate supply. New inventions and improved processes make existing resources go farther and improve the quality of output. Technology and investment go hand-in-hand. Implementation of new technology requires business investment. The American auto industry, for example, found that it had to spend money to make money in the 1980s. High-technology automated factories, which produce cars most profitably, cost billions of dollars to construct. But technology also creates jobs in investment industries as it expands capacity.

Technology is a consequence as well as a cause of investment. Breakthroughs come only after years of research and development. Cost-cutting

Investment in Human Capital Investment in training and education aimed at increasing worker productivity.

inventions are costly to invent and expensive to put in place. The U.S. government is a big spender on research and technology. Government grants support scientific and agricultural research at many colleges and universities, for example. Breakthroughs made in these labs and in government programs like NASA have helped some U.S. producers stay competitive. However, many economists blame overall low levels of research investment for many of the problems U.S. firms face in international markets.

Productivity Labor's ability to produce determines workers' real incomes and aggregate supply. Productivity is important to economic growth. Productivity depends on many things. **Investment in human capital**, in the form of training and education, increases worker skills and therefore aggregate supply. Private firms are responsible for much of the investment in technology and capital equipment that contributes to labor productivity. Government is responsible for much of this investment in people. Public high schools, colleges, and technical schools (and similar private institutions that receive public support) all improve productivity. The skills these programs provide help both the individuals who receive the training and those who consume the lower-cost goods they produce.

Productivity has not increased as fast in the United States as it has in many other countries. Part of the U.S. productivity problem goes back to seriously low rates of investment in capacity and research. Worker productivity depends both on human skills and on technological factors. Trained workers using modern tools produce more and better output than those without the tools or training. Highly trained U.S. workers in outdated plants have little chance against more modern foreign competitors.

Availability and Cost of Resources Aggregate supply depends on the cost and supply of basic production inputs such as oil, steel, energy, labor, and natural resources. Price increases or general shortages of these goods reduce aggregate supply. Three examples show how important some items are to the economy.

Price increases and shortages of oil brought on the recessions of 1974–1975 and 1979–1980. The Arab oil embargo of 1974 and the Iranian oil cutoff of 1979, combined with price rises in each case, reduced aggregate supply and hurt the economy. Oil is so important to the economy that even small changes in its cost or availability have big effects on aggregate supply.

A shortage of a different kind brought on a recession in 1958–1959. A labor strike robbed the economy of one of its most widely used inputs, steel. Steel prices skyrocketed and factory after factory shut down for lack of raw materials.

The transportation sector is also important to the economy. A threatened train strike during President Harry Truman's administration might have brought on a recession by disrupting transportation of people and goods. Jobs disappear when no one delivers parts and raw materials. Farm produce rots, making supply irrelevant if oranges and tomatoes cannot be shipped to market. Truman threatened to call out the troops to operate railroad engines. This action prevented the economy-shattering strike.

Investments and new technology take a long time to work. They increase aggregate supply in the long run. Rising producer costs and input shortages hit in the short run, however, reducing aggregate supply and eliminating jobs in shorter time frames.

Expectations Producers, workers, and investors all base supply decisions on their view of the future. Expectations influence intended production in many ways. Firms that expect higher input prices in the future, for example, build input inventories now or produce output for inventory so that they have lower cost items to sell later. Investment and production decisions depend on projected future consumer buying and expected government policies. Action is based on anticipation, so changing expectations alter aggregate supply.

Many economists now believe that expectations concerning the price level play an important role in determining aggregate supply. The argument here is that producers base production decisions on their expectations of the price of the goods that they make and the prices of all other goods, since product, input, and capital markets are interdependent. If expectations concerning the price level change, it makes sense that producers would reevaluate their plans and change their production and investment decisions, since a change in the price level would change many prices that enter into the complex decisions that firms and consumers make.

Government Policies Government policies affect aggregate supply in ways both obvious and subtle. Government investments in power projects, highways, and in education and training have already been discussed. These activities can increase capacity in the long run and so increase aggregate supply. The government also owns many resources, such as timber and mineral deposits. Government decisions concerning the use of these inputs affect aggregate supply now and in the future.

Taxes are another variable in the supply decision. Taxes affect worker and employer incentives. High tax rates reduce the return on extra work or investment. High taxes discourage workers and firms from expanding aggregate supply. But taxes also help channel investment funds to specific purposes when tax breaks are allowed for spending in particular areas of the economy. Government tax policy is therefore an important determinant of the size and composition of aggregate supply in the short run and the rate of growth of aggregate supply in the long run.

Government regulations also affect aggregate supply. Many economists think that environmental regulations are a reason for reduced productivity in the United States. Many workers now spend their time producing cleaner air and water instead of toasters and refrigerators because of environmental regulations. This might be good for the country, but productivity falls because the better environment that results is not counted in real GNP.

THE AGGREGATE SUPPLY CURVE

11.7 AS CURVE

The aggregate supply (AS) curve maps the relationship between the desired level of real GNP produced and the price level. The AS curve takes on different shapes depending on the state of the economy. The three sections of the AS curve that correspond to these three economic situations are the depression economy, the full-capacity economy, and the bottleneck economy.

Depression Economy

Depression Economy
Aggregate supply in an economy with many unemployed resources.

A **depression economy** or an economy in a deep recession is plagued with idle resources. Such an economy has high capacity, but this potential is not realized because of deficient demand. Surplus resources, in the form of machines, factories, trucks, and workers, stand ready to answer the call to produce. Output can be expanded in the depression economy by drawing on the ranks of unemployed resources. Higher prices are not a requirement for

314   *Aggregate Demand and Aggregate Supply*

higher output in this situation. The aggregate supply curve is horizontal in a depression economy, as shown in Figure 11-6. Higher levels of real GNP are possible without rising prices because the economy is well below the point at which rising production costs become a problem. Increased demand can often be met from unused inventories accumulated before production lines shut down and workers were laid off.

Full-Capacity Economy

Full-Capacity Economy
Aggregate supply in an economy that has reached production limits determined by finite capacity.

The *AS* curve changes shape in a **full-capacity economy.** Production cannot expand further if all machines or all workers are already in use. Full capacity can coincide with full employment, but the roadblock to further production might also result from full use of machines, factories, or other nonhuman capital. The *AS* curve is vertical in a full-capacity economy. *AS* can be increased in the long run through investment, innovation, or training. In the short run, however, total output is limited. Expanded production in one part of the economy comes at the cost of reduced output elsewhere. The government can produce more planes and bombs, for example, but only by bidding workers and inputs away from other uses. Real GNP remains the same, but price levels rise as government and private firms compete for scarce resources. Any attempt to expand production brings only higher prices in the short run once capacity is reached.

Bottleneck Economy

Depressions and full capacity are exceptions, not the rule, in modern economies. Resources such as oil and skilled workers are scarce but still avail-

---

FIGURE 11-6

The Aggregate Supply Curve. The slope of the *AS* curve depends on the state of the economy. The *AS* curve is flat at low real GNP levels, then becomes upward sloping as bottlenecks appear, and finally becomes vertical when resource limits are reached. The *AS* curve is horizontal in depressions when many resources are unemployed. Higher output does not require higher price levels here. The *AS* curve is vertical when resource limits appear. Total production cannot rise in the short run even if the price level increases. Rising marginal costs and production bottlenecks bid up prices as production grows. Inflation accompanies higher real GNP in the short run.

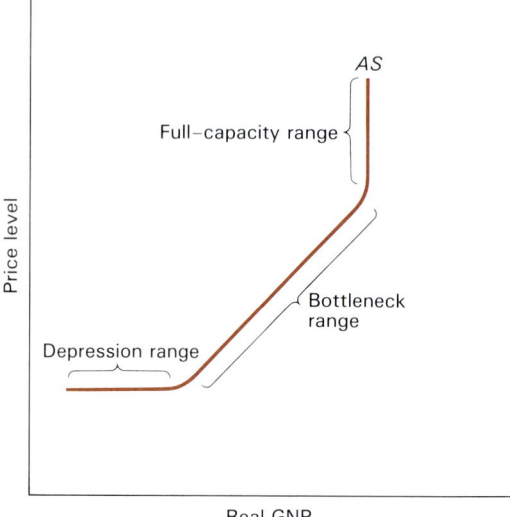

Bottleneck Economy
Aggregate supply in an economy with rising marginal costs and production bottlenecks.

able. Marginal costs rise in the short run as producers expand. This "normal" condition is described by the **bottleneck economy** portion of the *AS* curve of Figure 11-6. Real GNP grows in the short run only if the price level increases and inflation goes with expanded output.

Why does the *AS* curve slope up as this figure shows? Rising marginal costs and the incentive function of price are part of the reason. Keynes suggested that production bottlenecks are also an important determinant of aggregate supply, however. Bottlenecks are temporary tie-ups and shortages that get in the way of production. We are all familiar with traffic bottlenecks. Speed plummets when highway construction forces two lanes to merge into one. Individual drivers get in one another's way, congesting the flow of traffic. Producers do the same thing as these drivers in the bottleneck economy. Suppose, for example, that defense spending increases in a bottleneck economy. The resources needed for this expanded production will be available eventually but not immediately. In the short run, firms compete for available steel, workers, and factory space. This competition bids up price until temporary shortages (the bottlenecks) are eased. Output increases, but prices are also bid up due to the bottlenecks.

Each of these three *AS* shapes is part of a bigger *AS* curve shown in Figure 11-6. The *AS* curve is flat when real GNP is at low depression levels and then slopes up as surplus resources are used up and bottlenecks begin to appear. The *AS* curve finally finds its vertical part when capacity roadblocks appear.

SHIFTS IN AGGREGATE SUPPLY

11.8 SHIFTING THE *AS* CURVE

A change in the price level causes a movement along the existing *AS* curve. Aggregate supply shifts in the short and long run in response to the variables discussed in the last section. In other words, a change in just the price level brings a movement along the *AS* curve, from one level of real GNP to another. A change in any determinant other than the price level shifts the *AS* curve. Figure 11-7 illustrates shifts in the *AS* curve.

Aggregate supply increases when something happens to make firms want to expand production at the current price level. An increase in *AS* would cause the *AS* curve to shift out and to the right. *AS* could increase in the short run because of a decrease in the cost of a vital input such as oil, a change in government regulations that makes production less costly, or improved business expectations. *AS* could increase in the long run due to increases in capacity or productivity that are the result of prior investments in physical and human capital.

A decrease in aggregate supply would cause the *AS* curve to shift back and to the left. Examples of events that would cause falling *AS* include more costly government regulations, labor strikes or other input limitations, falling economic capacity (due to low levels of investment), or deteriorating productivity.

The *AS* curve could also shift in the short run if people in the economy change their expectations concerning some important macroeconomic variable such as the price level. Suppose, for example, that the price level for this year turns out to be higher than people and firms in the economy expected. This disequilibrium between expectations and reality could cause widespread changes in production and investment patterns. These changes would occur because firms and people would alter their current activities in response to expectations that have changed as a result of recent events. Aggregate supply could decrease, shifting back and to the left, if the price

FIGURE 11-7

Shifts in Aggregate Supply. The *AS* curve increases (shift from *AS* to *AS*₁) and decreases (shift from *AS* to *AS*₂) for many reasons. In the short run, only major changes in the cost or availability of resources is likely to produce a significant shift in *AS*. In the long run, *AS* is affected by technological progress and changes in the economy's productive capacity, among other factors.

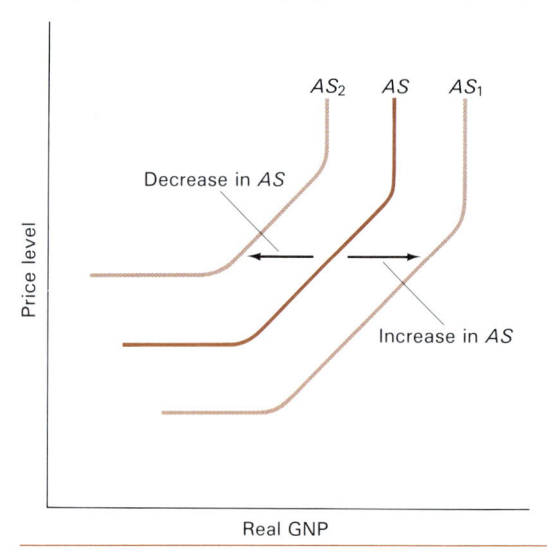

level is unexpectedly high, for example, because the unexpectedly high price level indicates higher overall business costs that reduce real profits. Firms and people might increase planned production, on the other hand, if the price level is unexpectedly low. This change in planned production due to changing expectations would shift the *AS* curve out and to the right.

KEY CONCEPTS 11.6, 11.7, 11.8

Aggregate supply represents the relationship between the price level and the real level of desired total output. *AS* is affected by many factors. Changes in the price or availability of resources can shift *AS* in the short run. Changes in capacity, technology, productivity, incentives, expectations, or government regulations can also shift *AS*, but often these shifts require more time to take place. The *AS* curve has three ranges that depend on the availability of resources in the economy: the depression, bottleneck, and full-capacity *AS* conditions.

AD–AS EQUILIBRIUM

11.9 *AD–AS* EQUILIBRIUM POINT

A macroeconomic equilibrium occurs when the quantity of goods and services that consumers, investors, foreigners, and government wish to buy at a particular price level equals the quantity firms wish to produce at that price level. Macroeconomic equilibrium takes place where the *AD* curve crosses the *AS* curve. In Figure 11-8, aggregate demand crosses aggregate supply at a price level of 100 and a real GNP of $1500 billion. Neither aggregate surplus nor aggregate shortage forces price level changes. The macroeconomic equilibrium shown in this figure is stable in the sense that the economy moves toward the equilibrium, and once there, remains in equilibrium until either *AD* or *AS* changes to upset the balance.

FIGURE 11-8

AD–AS Equilibrium. The equilibrium between aggregate demand and aggregate supply determines the economy's price level and real GNP. Changes in *AD* in relation to *AS* cause the economy to move to a new equilibrium.

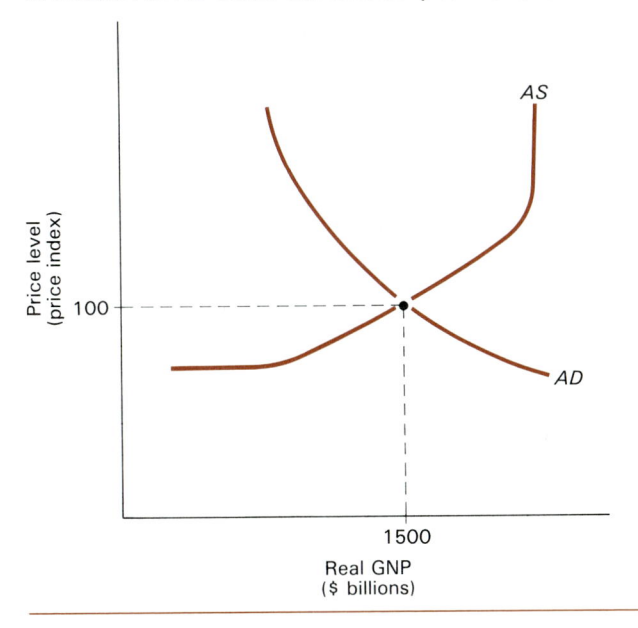

Because the *AD–AS* diagram looks so much like the supply–demand diagram developed earlier in this book, it is important to remember that they represent very different things. We will, therefore, remind the reader of these differences by briefly reviewing the meaning of the *AD–AS* diagram before using this model to analyze the economic events and policies of the 1960s and 1970s.

The first important point to remember is that the horizontal axis looks at the total production of all final goods in the economy as measured by real GNP. It does not measure the production of any one item or service. If production of apples rises and output of oranges falls, and if the changes are equal in real terms, there is no change in real GNP, although there will be changes in the individual markets for both apples and oranges.

The price level looks at the general level of prices throughout the economy using a price index. An increase in the price level means that inflation exists. This is different from the meaning of the price axis in individual supply–demand diagrams. If the price of apples rises, for example, this does not necessarily cause an increase in the price level because the prices of other goods could change to compensate. An increase in the price of apples changes only the relative price of apples. An increase in the price level represents a change in the general level of prices. If all individual prices rise at the same rate, then this increase in absolute prices does not change the relative prices of individual goods.

The macroeconomic *AD* curve is different from the microeconomic demand curve in several respects. *AD* measures total desired purchases of all final goods by consumers, investors, foreigners, and government. Higher *AD* means that more real final goods and services are demanded overall.

The *AS* curve is also different from the supply curves for individual products. The *AS* curve shows the desired level of total output at each price level, with such factors as government policies, the prices and availability of resources, technology, expectations, and government policies held fixed. The

AS curve does not shift if something happens to increase the supply of a particular product, such as apples, because this does not significantly alter the economy's capacity or incentives to produce. Instead, *AS* shifts only when major factors change, such as rising productivity or expanding production capacity, thereby increasing the overall ability to produce goods and services.

The equilibrium between *AD* and *AS* represents the price level and quantity of real GNP to which the economy moves. Once this equilibrium is reached, the economy tends to remain at the *AD–AS* equilibrium until something happens to disturb this equilibrium. Like supply–demand analysis, we can use *AD–AS* analysis to see what happens when economic events or policies cause curves to shift and the equilibrium to change. We will now use *AD–AS* analysis to illustrate and analyze the economic events and policies of the 1960s and 1970s.

THE 1960s: DEMAND-PULL INFLATION

11.10 DEMAND-PULL VS. COST-PUSH INFLATION

Figures 11-1 and 11-2 showed that there were at least two basic relationships between inflation and unemployment in the 1960s and 1970s. Sometimes there was a trade-off between inflation and unemployment, where an increase in one was accompanied by a decrease in the other. This is what occurred in the 1960s, for example, and also during 1971–1973, 1976–1979, and 1980–1982. During other periods, however, we experienced simultaneous increases in both inflation and unemployment, such as Figure 11-2 showed for 1973–1974 and 1979–1980. Simple use of the *AD–AS* model of the economy allows us to see that these different relationships have different causes, as Figure 11-9 shows.

Figure 11-9(a) shows the result of an increase in aggregate demand. Aggregate demand would increase if there were increases in any of the four components of *AD:* consumption, investment, government, or net export spending. As the figure shows, an increase in *AD* causes the economy to move to a new *AD–AS* equilibrium that has a higher price level and a higher level of real GNP. The higher price level indicates inflation. The

FIGURE 11-9

Demand-Pull and Cost-Push Inflation. Demand-pull inflation occurs when *AD* increases on a bottleneck *AS* curve. Rising *AD* pulls the economy to a new equilibrium with higher price level and real GNP, as (a) shows. Unemployment is accompanied by higher inflation when falling *AS* causes cost-push inflation, as (b) shows.

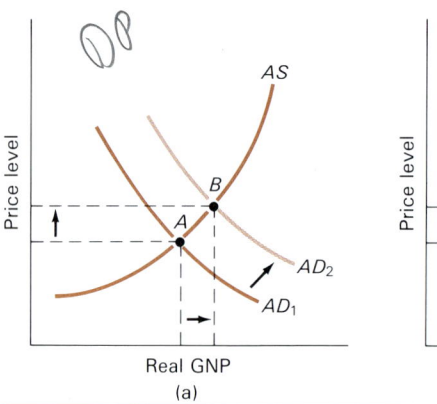

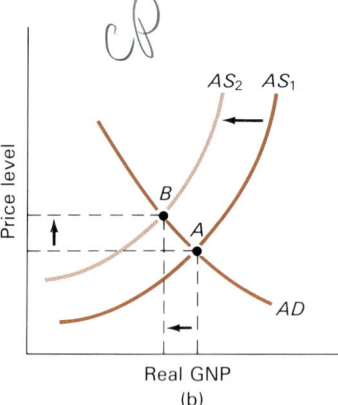

Demand-Pull Inflation
Inflation accompanied by rising real GNP caused by increases in AD.

higher level of real GNP means that more production is taking place and that more workers and other resources are being employed. Economists call this **demand-pull inflation** because the inflation here is caused by an increase in AD. Demand-pull inflation generates the trade-off between inflation and unemployment that the Phillips curve in Figure 11-9(a) indicates.

The demand-pull inflation of the 1960s was caused by rapid increases in government spending for the war in Vietnam and for the Great Society social programs. As the decade of the sixties progressed, increases in AD resulted in higher levels of real GNP, which brought with them lower unemployment rates and higher living standards for many groups. It is apparent, however, that AD grew faster than did AS during this period. The result was that the AD curve moved onto the full-capacity level, where each successive increase in AD brought higher price levels. President Johnson attempted to reverse this trend with his 1967 tax surcharge plan, but this policy was unsuccessful. Inflation still increased and firms and people in the economy began to formulate higher inflationary expectations.

THE 1970s: COST-PUSH INFLATION

> **11.10 DEMAND-PULL VS. COST-PUSH INFLATION**

Cost-Push Inflation
Inflation accompanied by falling real GNP caused by falling AS.

Figure 11-9(b) shows a different type of inflation that economists call **cost-push inflation**. The increase in the price level in this figure is caused by a decrease in aggregate supply. The important difference between cost-push and demand-pull inflation lies in how they affect real GNP. Rising production costs shift the AS curve back during cost-push inflation. Consumers are unwilling to purchase as many goods and services at the higher price level, so the economy moves along the AD curve to a new equilibrium. The price level has increased, but real GNP has decreased at the new equilibrium. Fewer goods are produced and unemployment rates are higher. Cost-push inflation generates the stagflation of the 1970s that we observed in Figure 11-2, particularly in 1973–1975 and 1979–1980.

Inflation caused by falling aggregate supply represented an important change in the economy, since cost-push inflation did not generate the familiar Phillips curve relationship of the 1960s. Inflation and unemployment both increased at the same time. There was no trade-off between these two economic goals.

Aggregate supply can fall, generating cost-push inflation, for several reasons. In the short run, falling AS is caused by increased production costs or shortages of inputs. It is no accident, for example, that the important periods of cost-push inflation in the 1970s corresponded to periods of rapidly increasing oil prices, although oil shortages and price rises were not the only cause of economic problems in these periods. The United States experienced agricultural crop failures in the early 1970s that contributed to the falling AS. The years of cost-push inflation of the 1970s also corresponded to periods when the dollar fell in value relative to other major currencies of the world. The falling dollar made imported goods and natural resources more expensive, which contributed to the higher inflation during this period.

Aggregate supply can fall in the short run for the reasons just discussed. AS can also fall in the long run if low levels of investment spending result in slow economic growth and reduced economic capacity. Many economists today are concerned that government policies may be generating insufficient investment spending now, which could have detrimental effects on AS in the long run.

KEY CONCEPT 11.10

Demand-pull inflation is caused by rising *AD* along a stable *AS* curve. Cost-push inflation is caused by falling *AS* along a stable *AD* curve. Inflation occurs in both situations, but the impact on real GNP is different. Real GNP rises under demand-pull inflation and falls under cost-push inflation.

CHANGING ECONOMIC POLICIES IN THE 1960s AND 1970s

11.11 1960s AND 1970s ECONOMIC EVENTS

The change from demand-pull inflation in the 1960s to cost-push inflation in the 1970s caused severe problems for the economy and for economic policymakers. The policy prescriptions of the 1960s did not bring the same results in the 1970s. Let us see how economic policy changed during this period as the nature of our economic problems was changing.

The Kennedy Tax Cut

As noted earlier in this chapter, the U.S. economy entered the 1960s in a major recession, with high unemployment rates and depressed living standards. President Kennedy's economic advisors, led by Walter H. Heller, the chairman of the President's Council of Economic Advisors, advised him to adopt economic policies to stimulate aggregate demand and move the economy toward full employment. To illustrate their point, they used the concept of actual GNP versus potential GNP shown in Figure 11-10. Potential GNP, sometimes also referred to as full-employment GNP or high-employment GNP, is a measure of what GNP would be in the economy if all resources were being used to capacity. Figure 11-10 shows a "GNP gap" in the early 1960s. This gap between actual and potential GNP represents an irretrievable loss of production and income. In terms of the microeconomic analysis of

FIGURE 11-10

Potential GNP and the GNP Gap of the 1960s. Potential GNP corresponds to the level of GNP consistent with full employment of the economy's resources. Problems in economic performance meant that actual GNP in the early 1960s was below this potential, giving rise to concern about policies to promote economic growth and close the GNP gap.

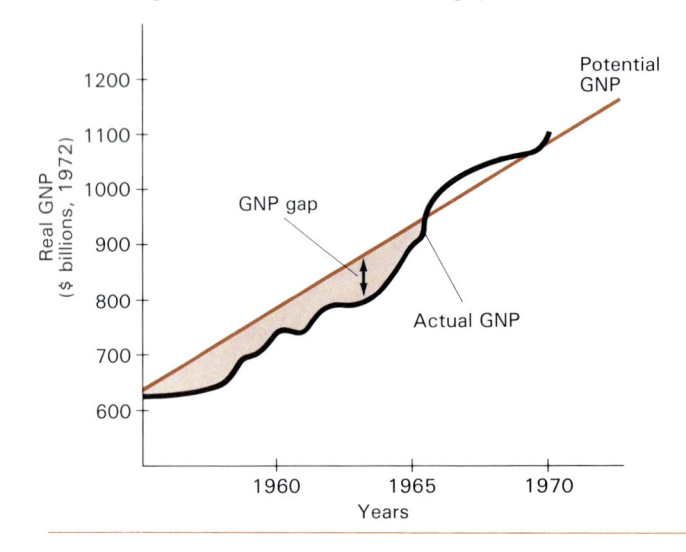

Chapter 1, the GNP gap represents an economy operating inside its production possibilities frontier.

President Kennedy's economic advisors recommended a tax cut that would stimulate consumption and investment spending. This tax cut increased AD with the results seen in Figure 11-9. Demand-pull inflation resulted. The increase in AD caused an increase in the price level, but it also increased the equilibrium level of real GNP, reducing the GNP gap and moving the economy closer to potential GNP and the goal of full employment.

The Kennedy tax cut was widely recognized as a successful application of Keynesian economic policy. Economists and policymakers began to believe that they could use the tools of government policy to "fine-tune" the economy and reduce the overall GNP gap.

Wage–Price Guidelines

The success of the Kennedy tax cut stimulated economic policymakers to search for a way to reduce the GNP gap without causing demand-pull inflation. One attempt at this desirable goal was the Wage-Price Guidelines of the 1960s.

Here is the idea behind the Wage-Price Guidelines. Demand-pull inflation results when AD grows faster than AS. During the 1960s, for example, increases in productivity were causing AS to grow slowly, by about 3.2 percent per year on average. The Kennedy tax cut stimulated AD by more than 3.2 percent, so that AD grew faster than AS and demand-pull inflation resulted. This is illustrated in Figure 11-11(a).

One way to increase real GNP without inflation is to limit the growth of AD to the rate of increase of AS. This balanced growth of AD and AS is shown in Figure 11-11(b). Real GNP grows without inflation if AD and AS both increase by the same rate. The wage-price guidelines attempted to achieve this balanced growth of AD and AS by putting pressure on unions and employers to limit wage increases to roughly the 3.2 percent average

FIGURE 11-11

The Economics of Wage-Price Guidelines. Rising wages tend to increase aggregate demand. Rising productivity tends to increase aggregate supply. If wages rise faster than productivity, as shown in (a), the result is inflation, as the economy moves from initial equilibrium A to new equilibrium B. The increase in AD overpowers the rise in AS, causing a form of demand-pull inflation. The goal of the wage-price guideline program was to limit wage increases so that AD would rise at the same rate as AS, as shown in (b). This would result in economic growth without inflation.

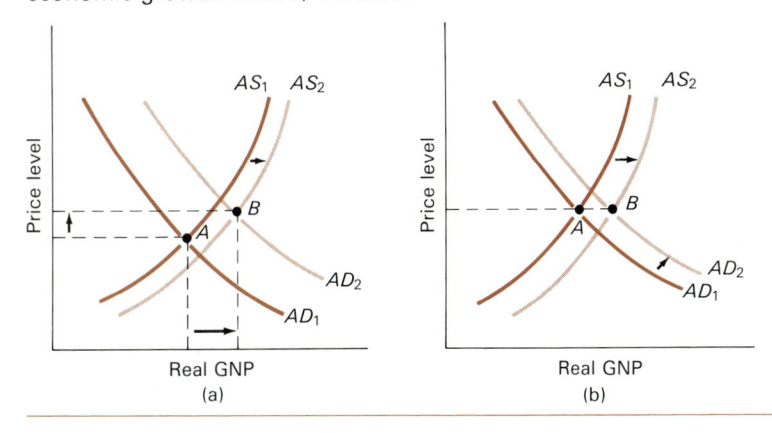

increase in productivity and aggregate supply. The idea was that this limit on wage growth would tend to limit the increase in *AD* and achieve the noninflationary growth seen in Figure 11-11(b).

The Wage-Price Guidelines were not remarkably successful. Subtle and sometimes not so subtle government pressures to limit wage and price increases did not prove sufficient to restrict aggregate demand. Remember that at this time government tax cuts and spending increases were increasing *AD* and driving inflation higher. Spending on the War on Poverty, the Great Society social programs, and the Vietnam war all increased *AD* and pulled the price level higher. Although it might be in the entire economy's interest to restrict all wage increases in order to reduce inflation, individual workers and unions saw that they would lose real income if they did not demand wage increases at least as high as the expected inflation rate. Wage increases tended to exceed the 3.2 percent guideline, and demand-pull inflation became more severe.

The Johnson Tax Surcharge

President Johnson's tax surcharge attempted to reverse the demand-pull inflation trend. When finally enacted, the Johnson tax bill imposed a temporary 10 percent increase in each household's tax liability. The goal of this proposal was to reduce aggregate demand and therefore relieve the building inflationary pressures. The tax cut proved to be too little and too late, however. Domestic spending increases and rising inflationary expectations overwhelmed the temporary tax boost, and demand-pull inflation continued.

Economic policy in the 1960s displays an interesting pattern. The most important economic problem at the start of the decade was unemployment, and economists proved able to reduce it through known Keynesian policies that stimulated aggregate demand. By the end of the decade, however, inflation was becoming the more severe problem, and mainstream economic policies were not proving remarkably successful in dealing with this problem.

Nixon's Wage and Price Controls

The growing problem of inflation in the early 1970s, combined with other economic problems of that period, induced President Richard Nixon to adopt extreme economic policies. On August 15, 1971, President Nixon announced a package of presidential orders that shook the economic world. First, President Nixon changed U.S. policy concerning the international value of the dollar. Nixon effectively broke the link between the dollar and gold and reduced the dollar's international value relative to other major currencies. Second, Nixon ordered a temporary 10 percent tax on all foreign goods, a move designed to reduce U.S. imports from abroad and stimulate spending on domestic goods. Third, and perhaps most important, Nixon announced a 90-day freeze on all wages and prices in the United States. This freeze would then be followed by a period of **wage and price controls.** Under the price control program, wages and prices could be raised only with permission of government agencies. Two special groups were formed, a Wage Board and a Price Board, to oversee the process.

President Nixon's actions were bold and unexpected. Nixon's political platforms had always called for free trade and reduced government control. It was paradoxical, therefore, for him to impose trade restrictions and tight government controls on the economy. Nixon's dramatic and uncharacteristic

Wage and Price Controls
Laws that freeze or control most wages and prices in an economy.

policies were an indication that he and some of his advisors saw the trend of economic events as alarming and dangerous.

President Nixon's price freeze expired as promised at the end of the 90-day period. The Phase I wage and price controls began in late 1971. Later, Phase II and Phase III price controls were instituted. These later price control systems were much less stringent and slowly returned wage and price determination to the market. Most price controls had disappeared by the late 1970s.

The Economics of Wage and Price Controls

11.12 WAGE AND PRICE CONTROLS

The existence of cost-push inflation in the 1970s resulted in repeated calls for wage and price controls. Cost-push inflation combines the problems of high inflation and high unemployment. Traditional Keynesian policies do not provide comfortable solutions to this problem. Government policies that try to control inflation by reducing AD through tax increases, for example, tend to further increase the unemployment problem. On the other hand, policies that attempt to control unemployment by stimulating AD tend to make high inflation rates even higher. People who are uncomfortable with these trade-offs sometimes propose the use of wage and price controls similar to those that President Nixon put in place in 1971.

Wage and price controls have different effects on the economy depending on whether the inflation is caused by demand-pull or cost-push forces. Figure 11-12 shows how wage and price controls work in both cases.

Figures 11-12(a) shows the effect of wage and price controls during a period of demand-pull inflation. An increase in AD would normally pull up the price level as real GNP increases. Wage and price controls prevent the increase in prices, but they also prevent real GNP from rising. There is no incentive for business firms to produce more if they cannot raise prices to meet their higher costs. Price controls keep the price level stable, but production cannot expand precisely because prices cannot rise. Real GNP

FIGURE 11-12 — **The Economics of Wage and Price Controls.** The demand-pull inflation shown in (a) would have moved the economy from A to B. Wage and price controls keep prices from rising but lead consumers to demand the quantity represented by point C. Real GNP stays constant and a physical shortage results. The cost-push inflation in (b) would normally result in a movement from A to B. Wage and price controls force producers to cut output to the level represented by C. Real GNP falls more than before and another physical shortage appears.

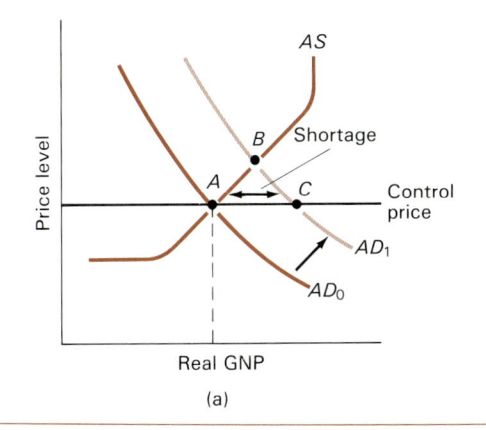

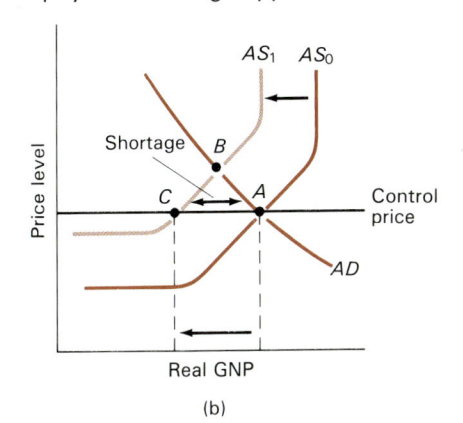

(a)   (b)

remains constant and the quantity of goods demanded increases with the rising *AD*. The result is that a physical shortage of goods appears. Inventories are drawn down and not restocked because firms cannot expand production unless the price level rises. Wage and price controls create shortages and keep real GNP from growing. The government might be forced to ration scarce commodities.

Price controls have somewhat different effects during periods of cost-push inflation, as Figure 11-12(b) shows. Falling *AS* would normally cause higher price levels and falling real GNP. The existence of wage and price controls causes the decrease in real GNP to be even more severe than would otherwise be the case. Laws keep the price level frozen, as before. Firms that cannot raise prices to meet higher costs are forced to lay off workers and cut production even more. Real GNP falls more than it otherwise would. Shortage and deep recession are the consequence of the attempt to achieve stable prices in this instance.

The *AD–AS* analysis in Figure 11-12 shows why many economists are opposed to wage and price controls. They believe that price controls impose substantial costs on the economy in terms of lost production and shortages. Often price and wage increases are not eliminated but just postponed until controls are lifted.

Proponents of wage and price controls, on the other hand, argue that controls can be effective if used properly. One cause of inflation, they state, is the existence of inflationary expectations. Wage and price controls, if they are seen as long-term policies, would tend to reduce inflationary expectations and so break the cycle of higher prices – higher wages – higher prices. In any case, proponents of price controls argue that the economic costs of controls are less than the costs of letting inflation run out of control.

Although President Nixon's price control programs covered the entire economy, control programs need not be this general. President Jimmy Carter, for example, attempted to deal with high inflation through selective **credit controls.** President Carter imposed interest rate ceilings and restricted the use of certain types of credit in order to attempt to control costs on the one hand and efficiently allocate loanable funds on the other. Carter's program, not unexpectedly, generated shortages of loans in key areas, such as mortgage loans. Carter's plan was not remarkably effective in solving the problems of the time.

Credit Controls
Government regulations that attempt to regulate the availability of credit in order to stabilize the economy.

11.13 INDEXATION

The Rise of Indexation

As inflation rates increased in the 1970s, inflationary expectations also increased. Firms and individuals who had seen price increases wipe out wage gains wanted to protect themselves from further loss of real income. They turned to indexation programs, such as automatic **cost-of-living adjustments (COLAs),** as an inflation protection.

Indexation programs, such as COLAs, tie wage or income payments to a price index. If the price index rises by 5 percent for example, the income payment automatically rises by 5 percent (or by some contractually determined percentage of the measured inflation rate). Indexation plans were widely adopted in the 1970s. Many wage agreements included COLA provisions that automatically increased wages each year by the amount of the increase in the Consumer Price Index. Many government payments, such as Social Security benefits, and private pension plans, were also indexed.

Indexation schemes do not try to hold down inflation. Their goal is to hold down inflation's damage. Indexation plans like those adopted in Brazil

Cost of Living Adjustments (COLAs)
Contractual agreements that link changes in wages and salaries to changes in a price index. COLAs are misnamed because price indexes measure inflation; they do not measure the cost of living.

and other high-inflation lands tie wages, prices, interest rates, and taxes to a price index. Prices still rise, but inflation's gains and losses are reduced because key payments in the economy automatically increase along with the price level.

Indexation reduces inflation's burden, but several problems remain. First, indexation cannot prevent high U.S. inflation from hurting U.S. producers through international trade. Firms with built-in wage increases cannot compete with sellers from low-inflation countries. Second, indexation cannot adjust all payments and prices for inflation. Different winners and losers show up depending on how price indexes change.

A third indexation failure is that it can perpetuate inflation, making it even harder to solve through other policies. Higher indexed wages unleash cost-push forces that increase prices and lengthen unemployment lines. Inflation is easier to live with, but higher unemployment rates are the painful price. In the 1980s, for example, the Italian government found that it could reduce inflation by repealing the national "scala mobile," or wage escalator system. Inflation rates fell when the indexation program ended.

The final indexation problem is technical. Which price index should be used? How should the indexation factor be calculated? These technical questions become political problems if the government adopts indexation. Labor and management, savers and borrowers, all these groups and more would lobby Congress to get an indexation scheme that favors their interests. Indexation helps reduce inflation's burden and is useful in a limited role. It is not, however, a final solution to the inflation problem.

The Ford Tax Rebates

11.14 FORD'S TAX REBATE PROGRAM

As noted earlier, cost-push inflation plagued the U.S. economy twice in the 1970s. The Arab oil embargo of 1973–1974, combined with other events of that period, generated higher inflation and unemployment rates. Stagflation created difficult problems for economists and policymakers in the Nixon and Ford Administrations. The Iranian oil embargo, combined with higher oil prices and other international problems, caused cost-push inflation in 1979–1980. This created even more difficult policy choices for President Jimmy Carter.

President Gerald Ford was determined to keep unemployment from getting out of hand. He proposed a tax rebate plan in 1975 designed to reduce the relatively high unemployment rates that prevailed at that time. Tax refunds of $100 to $200 were sent to all U.S. households over the period of a few months.

President Ford's tax rebate, like Johnson's tax surcharge of a decade earlier, was not very effective. Both of these tax programs were viewed by the economy as temporary measures. They did not dramatically affect consumption spending because they were not seen as permanent changes in income. They did not dramatically alter expectations because they were plainly seen as temporary programs. These policies illustrate the difficult problem of applying Keynesian economic theory to an increasingly complex economy.

THE GOAL OF INCREASING AGGREGATE SUPPLY

11.15 INCREASING AS

The logical way to reverse cost-push inflation is to stimulate growth in AS. Increasing aggregate supply lowers the price level and increases real GNP, fighting inflation and unemployment at the same time. This is easier said than done, however. Aggregate supply depends on many variables, such as investment, regulations, productivity, and technology.

How can government increase aggregate supply? Deregulation is one answer. Both President Carter and his successor, President Ronald Reagan, implemented a variety of programs designed to increase *AS* and spur economic growth. Carter, for example, proposed the deregulation of oil and natural gas prices. He argued that free-market prices would provide powerful incentives that would encourage energy production on the one hand and careful conservation on the other. Carter appointed economist Alfred Kahn to the Federal Aviation Administration. With Carter's support, Kahn removed many regulations on the U.S. airline industry. Greater competition resulted from deregulation and air fares initially fell, although they have increased and decreased in the years since deregulation in response to supply and demand pressures.

President Reagan increased the deregulation trend. The most notable example of deregulation under Reagan occurred in the telephone industry, where the giant firm AT&T was freed of many government regulations. In return, "Ma Bell" was split into several smaller firms. Many private companies entered the competition for telecommunications services. The Reagan administration also oversaw a dramatic deregulation of the U.S. financial system, which is still in progress today. We will discuss financial deregulation and its implications in detail in Chapters 13 and 14.

President Reagan also championed economic policies that sought to increase aggregate supply by creating greater incentives for production. Lower marginal tax rates, which give workers and entrepreneurs larger after-tax payoffs for their efforts, were a cornerstone of Reagan's supply-side economics programs. These programs will be discussed in greater detail in the next chapter.

Economic policies to encourage production and economic growth are desirable. Many mainstream economists think that the best way to encourage economic growth is to adopt long-term policies that encourage investment, innovation, and training. These programs provide most of their benefits in the future, when higher productivity and greater capacity are fully felt. Long-term, economic policies frequently encounter short-term political troubles, however. Presidents and members of Congress face election regularly, and they may not be willing to wait for the "long run" for economic success. Keynes realized that short-term policies are often required, saying that "In the long run we are all dead." In the long run, politicians can be turned out of office. Thus policymakers search for ways to increase aggregate supply in the short run. Because it may be easier to increase *AD* in the short run, many economic policies in the 1960s and 1970s focused on the demand side of the economy instead of the supply side.

THE PROBLEM OF EXPECTATIONS

11.16 CHANGING EXPECTATIONS

We have seen that the economy and economic policy changed in many ways during the 1960s. The economy's problems changed from unemployment to stagflation. The causes of these problems changed from being largely internal, such as strikes, to international in scope, such as the Arab oil embargo. Economic policies changed, with the focus slowly shifting from aggregate demand to aggregate supply. The rise in inflation was, however, perhaps the most dramatic change in the economy. With higher inflation rates came a built-in problem: higher inflationary expectations.

FIGURE 11-13 **The Problem of Inflationary Expectations.** The impact of an increase in *AD* can depend on how it affects expectations. If *AD* rises, for example, and there is no change in expectations, then the economy moves from *A* to *B* in the figure and real GNP rises. If, however, this is seen as the beginning of a period of rising inflation, *AS* may fall due to the change in expectations, moving the economy from *A* to *C*. The change in expectations prevents real GNP from growing in this situation.

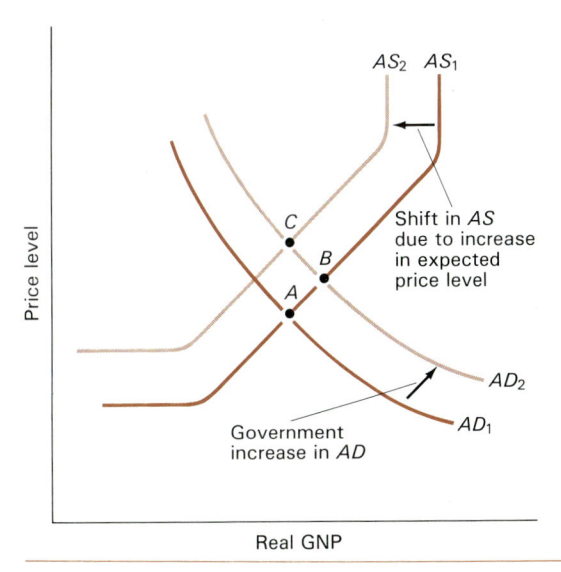

Figure 11-13 shows how the existence of inflationary expectations makes economic policy more difficult. An increase in *AD*, designed, for example, to fight unemployment, might move the economy from *A* to *B* in the figure, causing a typical Phillips curve movement. In the absence of any change in expectations, the policy has its desired effect of reducing unemployment. But expectations are not likely to remain constant in today's modern world. Firms and individuals will recognize that the increase in *AD* will generate inflation. Their expectations can change, shifting the *AS* curve as shown in the figure. As a result, the economy moves from *A* to *C*, not *A* to *B* as originally intended. Real GNP does not change in this situation; only the price level rises.

All economic policies are more difficult to successfully implement in a world of changing expectations. The rational expectations theory of economics, which will be discussed in Chapter 15, suggests that systematic economic policies, such as in the increase in *AD* in Figure 11-13, are generally ineffective when expectations are taken into account.

A LOOK AHEAD

The U.S. economy changed in many ways in the period we have discussed in this chapter. The rise of inflation and the changing relationship between inflation and unemployment were profound economic events that shaped the attitudes and behavior of a generation of consumers, producers, and policymakers. In a sense, the changes of this period were as great as those that prevailed during the Great Depression. The focus of economic theory changed too, from an emphasis on Keynesian aggregate demand to a focus on both *AD* and *AS*. Economic policies necessarily changed, as well.

The next chapter brings you up-to-date by looking more closely at how government policies work, then examining the two most important domestic economic events of the 1980s: the rise of supply-side economic policy and the coincident rise of the federal government's budget deficit.

SUMMARY

11.1 1. The relationship between inflation and unemployment changed dramatically in the 1960s and 1970s. In the 1960s, the U.S. economy displayed the Phillips curve relationship, with a distinct trade-off between inflation and unemployment. The economy experienced increases in both inflation and unemployment in the 1970s, conditions that do not fit the Phillips curve relationship.

11.2 2. Economic theory changed in several ways in the 1960s and 1970s to adjust to changes in the economy. Theory evolved from a focus on unemployment to include the analysis of inflation. Economic theory also evolved from an emphasis on the demand side of the economy to include factors affecting both demand and supply.

11.3 3. The aggregate demand–aggregate supply ($AD-AS$) model of the economy takes into account both spending and production limits. The graphic model is set within a framework that includes the price level (the vertical axis) and real GNP (the horizontal axis). The interaction of AD and AS determines the equilibrium price level and real GNP.

11.4 4. The AD curve measures the relationship between desired total real purchases (measured in terms of real GNP) and the price level. Like the Keynesian model, the AD curve is composed of four types of spending: consumption, investment, net exports, and government spending. The AD curve is downward sloping to reflect the way that changes in the price level affect the real levels of total spending. An increase in the price level, for example, tends to reduce real levels of investment and consumption spending through its impact on interest rates.

11.5 5. The aggregate demand curve shifts if any component of total spending undergoes an exogenous shift in real value. Thus the AD curve shifts due to changes in consumption, investment, net export, or government spending.

11.6 6. The aggregate supply curve measures the relationship between the level of desired total production (measured in terms of real GNP) and the price level. The determinants of AS include capacity and investment, technology, productivity, availability and cost of resources, expectations, and government policies that affect production and resource use.

11.7 7. The AS curve has three ranges with different shapes that reflect differences in economic conditions. The AS curve is flat in the depression range. This indicates excess productive capacity in the economy, so that real GNP can be expanded without inflation. The AS curve is vertical in the full-capacity range. This indicates that the economy cannot expand total output, so any attempt to increase production results in higher prices. The *AS* curve is upward sloping in the bottleneck range. In this situation, increases in total output are possible, but they cause short-term bottleneck shortages that bid up prices and cause inflation.

11.8 ▶ 8. The *AS* curve can shift in the short and long runs for different reasons. In the short run, the *AS* curve shifts due to changes in resource availability, such as major strikes and the oil embargoes of the 1970s. In the long run, the *AS* curve shifts due to changes in capacity, productivity, and technology.

11.9 ▶ 9. The *AD–AS* equilibrium occurs at the price level–real GNP combination where the *AD* curve crosses the *AS* curve. This is the state of the economy in which the level of desired total spending equals the level of desired total output. The economy tends to move toward this price level and real GNP and tends to remain there, all else being equal.

11.10 ▶ 10. Demand-pull inflation is caused by increased *AD*, with no shift in *AS*. Assuming a bottleneck *AS* curve, demand-pull inflation causes the price level to rise while real GNP also increases. This is different from cost-push inflation, which is characterized by a decrease in *AS* with no shift in the *AD* curve. Cost-push inflation causes real GNP to fall while the price level rises. Cost-push inflation therefore produces the stagflation that plagued the U.S. economy in the 1970s.

11.11 ▶ 11. The Kennedy tax cut in the early 1960s increased *AD*, moving the economy toward its potential GNP level. Kennedy's wage and price guideline program was an attempt to achieve balanced growth of *AD* and *AS* by limiting wage increases (which shift *AD*) to increases in productivity (which shift *AS*). President Johnson's tax surcharge was designed to reduce *AD* and so reduce inflation. It was less effective than planned, however, because households did not treat the tax surcharge as a change in their permanent income and so did not reduce expenditures by the desired amount.

11.12 ▶ 12. President Nixon established a system of wage and price controls in 1971 in an attempt to reduce inflationary pressures. Wage and price controls can be effective if they are successful in reducing inflationary expectations. In general, however, price controls cause shortages. The economic effects of wage and price controls are somewhat different under demand-pull and cost-push conditions.

11.13 ▶ 13. Indexation is a policy that attempts to deal with inflation by linking most wages and payments to the price index. This helps reduce the cost of inflation to the economy. Indexation does not eliminate inflation's undesirable effects, however, and can lead to increased inflationary expectations.

11.14 ▶ 14. President Ford attempted to reduce unemployment through a tax rebate program that was designed to stimulate consumption spending and therefore increase *AD*. Ford's tax rebate was not treated as a permanent increase in disposable income, however, and thus had less effect on *AD* than was intended.

330 Aggregate Demand and Aggregate Supply

11.15 ▶ 15. There are many policies that can be used to stimulate AS. Among these are deregulation, supply-side tax cuts, and policies that encourage investment and technological change. These are largely long-term policies, however, while politicians often respond to short-run pressures.

11.16 ▶ 16. Expectations have become a very important factor in macroeconomic policies. Economic policies can be successful or not depending upon whether they alter expectations concerning inflation, income, or other economic variables.

DISCUSSION QUESTIONS

11.5, 11.8 ▶ 1. Which of the following events would shift the AD curve? Which of these events would shift the AS curve in the short run? Which of these events would shift the AS curve in the long run? Briefly explain your answers for each event.
   a. an increase in transfer payments to the elderly
   b. a major decrease in price of crude oil
   c. an increase in the volume of imported goods
   d. an increase in business spending on research and development aimed at improving production technology
   e. a decrease in consumer spending due to expectations of a future recession

11.3, 11.9 ▶ 2. Draw AD–AS diagrams for each event listed in question 1. Use this graphic analysis to explain how each event would affect inflation and unemployment.

11.3, 11.4, 11.5, 11.6, 11.8, 11.9 ▶ 3. How would an increase in government spending for missile bases affect the economy in the short run (look at AD, AS, real GNP, and inflation)? In the long run? Explain.

11.3, 11.4, 11.5, 11.6, 11.8, 11.9 ▶ 4. How would an increase in investment spending affect the economy (AS, AD, real GNP, and inflation) in the short run? In the long run? Explain.

11.9 ▶ 5. Which is more inflationary in the short run, investment spending or government spending? Which is more inflationary in the long run, investment spending or government spending? Explain.

11.9 ▶ 6. The price level was roughly constant in 1954–1955, but the unemployment rate fell. Use AD–AS analysis to explain what must have occurred during this period.

11.10, 11.12 ▶ 7. What are the arguments in favor of wage and price controls? Is the argument for wage and price controls stronger when inflation is caused by cost-push forces? Explain your reasoning.

11.1, 11.10, 11.11 ▶ 8. Use AD–AS analysis to explain the economic events summarized by Figure 11.1.

11.2 ▶ **9.** Use $AD-AS$ analysis to explain the economic events summarized by Figure 11.2.

SELECTED READINGS

Bator, Francis. "The Sins of Wages," *The Economist* (March 21, 1981).

Dornbusch, Rudiger, and Fisher, Stanley. *Macroeconomics*, 3rd ed. New York: McGraw-Hill, 1984.

Hansen, Alvin. *A Guide to Keynes*. New York: McGraw-Hill, 1953.

Heller, Walter, and Schultz, Charles. "Wage and Price Controls." *Wall Street Journal* (February 27, 1980), p. 22.

Klein, Lawrence. "The Supply Side." *American Economic Review* (March 1978), pp. 1–7.

Keynes, John Maynard. *General Theory of Employment, Interest and Money*. New York: Harcourt Brace, 1936.

CHAPTER 12

Fiscal Policy, Deficits, and Supply-Side Economics

Having read the chapter, reviewed the chapter summary, and completed the *Study Guide* exercises, you should be able to:

CRIS

12.1 BUSINESS CYCLE: Describe the phases of the business cycle and discuss the role of fiscal policy in dealing with business cycles.

12.2 SPENDING MULTIPLIER: State the spending multiplier and use the multiplier concept to explain how government spending affects aggregate demand (*AD*) and the economy.

12.3 GOVERNMENT SPENDING MULTIPLIER: Explain how the multiplier effect of a change in government spending depends on the shape of the aggregate supply (*AS*) curve.

12.4 TAXATION MULTIPLIER: State the taxation multiplier and use the multiplier concept to explain how taxes affect *AD* and the economy.

12.5 TRANSFER PAYMENT MULTIPLIER: State the transfer payments multiplier and use the multiplier concept to explain how transfer payments affect *AD* and the economy.

12.6 BALANCED BUDGET MULTIPLIER: State the balanced budget multiplier and explain how equal changes in taxes and government spending affect *AD* and the economy.

12.7 AUTOMATIC STABILIZER POLICIES: Explain how automatic stabilizer fiscal policies work and discuss their advantages and disadvantages.

12.8 SUPPLY-SIDE POLICIES: List several supply-side fiscal policies and explain how they affect *AD–AS* and the economy.

12.9 TAXES AND INCENTIVES: Explain how taxes affect incentives in the economy and how lower marginal tax rates can encourage economic growth.

12.10 GOVERNMENT REGULATIONS: Discuss the problems of government regulation of the economy.

12.11 BUDGET DEFICIT: Explain what the federal government's budget deficit is and discuss how the deficit, the cyclical deficit, and the structural deficit are related and how they differ.

12.12 CROWDING-OUT EFFECT: Explain the crowding-out effect of government deficits.

12.13 SUPPLY-SIDE VIEW OF DEFICIT: Explain the supply-side view of the budget deficit's effects on the economy in the 1980s.

12.14 CROWDING-OUT CONTROVERSY: Discuss the controversy concerning whether the deficit really does cause crowding out.

12.15 BALANCING THE BUDGET: Discuss the different views concerning how to balance the budget and what role tax changes should play in deficit reduction.

12.16 BALANCED-BUDGET CONCEPTS: Discuss the concepts of the annual balanced budget, the cyclically balanced budget, and functional finance.

Fiscal Policy
The practice of managing government spending and taxes as a means of arriving at stable prices or other economic goals, such as growth or high levels of employment.

Demand-Side Fiscal Policies
Government policies designed to influence aggregate demand.

Supply-Side Fiscal Policies
Government policies designed to influence aggregate supply.

Government has been an important force in the economy ever since the Keynesian revolution of the 1930s. Government can influence the economy in many ways and there is frequent disagreement concerning which government policies should be used and when. **Fiscal policy** is the name given to government spending, taxation, and transfer payments policies that are used in attempts to achieve the three economic goals of full employment, low inflation, and economic growth.

This chapter looks at fiscal policies from three viewpoints. Many fiscal policies were developed based on our experiences in the Great Depression and in recessionary periods since. These are called **demand-side fiscal policies** because they seek to influence the economy by altering aggregate demand. Most demand-side fiscal policies are built on the ideas that Keynes developed in the 1930s.

Other fiscal policies, especially those implemented in recent years, have focused more specifically on stimulating the growth of aggregate supply. These are called **supply-side fiscal policies.** Supply-side economists and policymakers have attempted to increase aggregate supply by changing the tax system, providing investment incentives, reducing the cost of government regulation, and creating a more competitive marketplace.

In addition to this discussion of demand-side and supply-side fiscal policy, we will also examine the large budget deficits that have plagued the federal government in recent years. The reduction of these large deficits is a difficult task that continues to test the strength of both demand- and supply-side fiscal policies.

334 Fiscal Policy, Deficits, and Supply-Side Economics

AN INTRODUCTION TO DEMAND-SIDE FISCAL POLICY

> **12.1 BUSINESS CYCLE**

Business Cycles
Periods of national economic expansion that are followed by periods of declining output and income.

Countercyclical Fiscal Policy
Government spending or taxation policies that will tend to move output, employment, and income in the opposite direction than it is currently heading. These policies are used in an attempt to stabilize the economy.

Discretionary Fiscal Policy
The deliberate use of government's powers to spend and lay and collect taxes in an effort to bring about desired changes in economic conditions in an attempt to attain an optimum level of employment and income within the economy.

Expansionary Fiscal Policy
The use of increased government spending or reduced taxation in an attempt to increase aggregate demand.

Government is confronted with several problems in its attempt to maintain full employment and price stability and foster economic growth. Government policies must attempt to offset **business cycles** that occur in the economy. A business cycle is the period of time between peaks in economic activity in an economy. All economies experience expansions, peaks, contractions, and valleys in their business cycles. The typical business cycle is illustrated in Figure 12-1. The expansionary phase is characterized by increasing employment, income, and output. When the economy reaches its peak, output and income are at their maximum. During the recessionary, or contractionary phase, employment, income, and output fall. At the trough, or valley, output and income are at their minimum.

Keynes, writing in the 1930s, suggested that government could exercise **countercyclical fiscal policy** to dampen these large variations in the business cycle. Countercyclical fiscal policy attempts to reduce the size of business cycles by causing offsetting changes in aggregate demand. Government "leans into the wind" in an attempt to offset other trends in the economy. If this were done, Keynes wrote, the impact of the cycle on human suffering through unemployment would be moderated. Keynes suggested that government spending should be increased during recessionary phases to increase aggregate demand and lessen the recession. Keynes said that government spending should be reduced during recovery and peak periods to reduce aggregate demand and so lessen inflationary pressures. He also advocated tax cuts during recessions and tax increases during recovery periods because of their countercyclic effect on aggregate demand.

Today **discretionary fiscal policy** tools are widely used to bring about changes in economic conditions. Discretionary policies are actions that are taken in an attempt to achieve a particular goal. An **expansionary fiscal policy** is intended to increase aggregate demand through increases in government spending and transfer payments or through tax cuts. A **contrac-**

FIGURE 12-1

The Typical Business Cycle. A typical business cycle has four parts. The expansion continues to the peak, where the economy "turns"; the recession ends in a trough. The goal of government fiscal policies is to dampen these business cycles and promote economic growth.

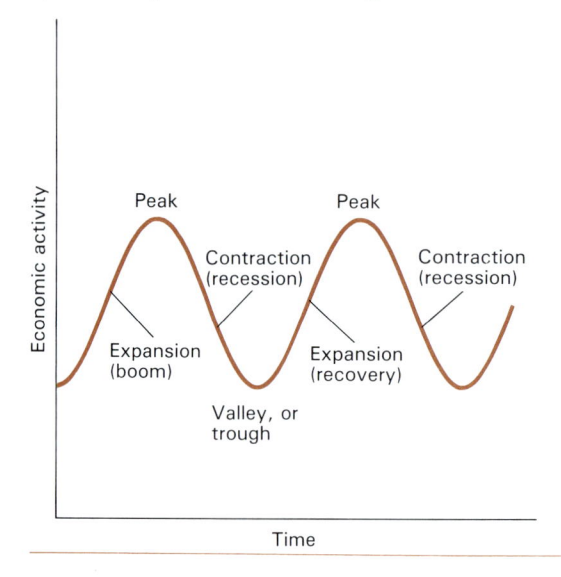

ECONOMIC ISSUES

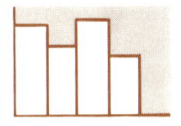

Macroeconomic Cycles

They say that history repeats itself. Many people take this saying to heart and search for recurring cycles in economic activity. The business cycle discussed in this chapter has been thoroughly studied by economists, beginning with the path-breaking work of Wesley Clair Mitchell at Columbia University early in this century and continuing through the work of his student, Arthur Burns, and the work of many economists associated with the National Bureau of Economic Research. This business cycle is not the only cyclical macroeconomic event, however.

It is possible to find macroeconomic cycles associated with many things. Sunspots, for example, run predictable, if incompletely understood, cycles. Certain types of economic activity seem to follow the same cycle as the sunspots, although a logical chain of causation is hard to imagine. Many people have noticed that there is a relationship between economic activity in the stock market and periods of domination in professional football in the United States, for example. The stock market tends to do better when teams from the old National Football League win the Super Bowl.

Perhaps the most interesting macroeconomic cycle was discovered early in this century by the Russian economist Nikolai Kondratieff. Kondratieff found a 50-year cycle of massive boom and bust in the capitalist world. Major recessions (such as those in the early 1930s and early 1980s) were followed by periods of expansion (such as in the 1950s and 1960s, and if the theory holds, in the 2000s and 2010s). Kondratieff found that wars played an important part in the change from overall recession to expanded recovery.

This 50-year cycle, called the Kondratieff long wave, is controversial. Most economists do not see why a long wave such as this should be inevitable, but there are some individuals who take the view that the long wave is sure to repeat itself.

One would think that Kondratieff would have been honored by the Soviet Union for discovering an anticapitalist cycle. In fact, Kondratieff was eventually purged because his theory, which showed capitalism going through continuing cycles, failed to agree with the Marxist dogma that capitalism was doomed to fail and be replaced by a communist regime.

Contractionary Fiscal Policy
The use of decreased government spending or increased taxes in an attempt to reduce aggregate demand.

tionary fiscal policy is intended to reduce aggregate demand by reducing government spending and transfer payments or by increasing taxes. Contractionary and expansionary fiscal policies affect both aggregate demand and aggregate supply. Keynes focused upon the effects on aggregate demand. We will look at the Keynesian demand-side view of fiscal policies first, then focus on how government policies affect aggregate supply. Future chapters will discuss the views held by non-Keynesian economists regarding fiscal policies.

THE TOOLS OF DEMAND-SIDE FISCAL POLICY

The government sector of the economy can influence aggregate demand in a variety of ways. Government can use discretionary changes in taxes, transfer payments, and government spending to alter the course of aggregate demand. Fiscal policy also uses a system of built-in automatic stabilizers that work to offset business cycles.

Government spending is the first fiscal tool we will analyze. Aggregate demand is the sum of the four spending components, consumption, investment, government, and net export spending ($AD = C + I + G + X_n$). Thus government spending can directly affect aggregate demand. An increase in government spending causes an increase in total spending, shifting the aggregate demand curve out and to the right. As we learned in Chapter

12.2 SPENDING MULTIPLIER

10, a small change in government spending can cause a relatively large increase in aggregate demand because of the spending multiplier.

Here is how the spending multiplier works. Suppose that the government purchases $100 million in new computer equipment. This $100 million represents an increase in aggregate demand because this increase in government spending represents an increase in total spending in the economy. Aggregate demand will increase by more than just this $100 million, however. The $100 million of government spending on computers becomes $100 million of income for the individuals who produced and sold the computers. These individuals will save some part of this increase in income and spend the rest. If we assume that the marginal propensity to consume (*MPC*) is 80 percent and the marginal propensity to save (*MPS*) is 20 percent, then they will spent a total of $80 million and save $20 million with their increase in income. The original $100 million of government spending causes an induced consumption expenditure of $80 million.

The chain-reaction increase in aggregate demand continues. The $80 million in additional spending results in $80 million of new income to other groups in the economy. They too will spend 80 percent of the increase in income and save 20 percent. Aggregate demand will therefore increase by $64 million, and saving will increase by $16 million. This multiplier process, which was introduced in the last chapter, continues until all of the initial $100 million of government spending has been saved.

The total increase in aggregate demand caused by the $100 million increase in government spending is equal to $100 + $80 + $64 + . . . = $500 million. The first $100 million is the original government spending. The remaining $400 million is induced consumption spending. The total of $500 million is calculated using the spending multiplier:

$$\text{Change in } AD = \frac{1}{1 - MPC} \times \text{change in spending}$$

$$\text{Change in } AD = \frac{1}{MPS} \times \text{change in spending}$$

So, in this example, with a $100 million increase in government spending and the *MPC* equal to 80 percent, or .80, and the *MPS* equal to 20 percent, or .20,

$$\text{Change in } AD = 1/.20 \times \$100 \text{ million} = \$500 \text{ million}.$$

The spending multiplier simplifies what is really a much more complex process. In the real world, people do more with their income than spend it or save it. People pay taxes, buy imports, and undertake other activities that would affect the multiplier process in subtle ways. Advanced courses in macroeconomics develop more sophisticated multipliers than the simple ones outlined here. Most estimates of real-world multipliers are rather low, in the range of 2. A $100 million change in government spending in the real world would change aggregate demand by about a total of $200 million, for example. The numbers are different in the real world, but the concepts are exactly the same as those presented here.

Multipliers and the Economy

12.3 GOVERNMENT SPENDING MULTIPLIER

The multiplier formula predicts what effect a change in government spending will have on aggregate demand. The impact of that change in aggregate demand on the economy, however, depends on which range of the aggregate

FIGURE 12-2 **Fiscal Policy Effects Depend on Aggregate Supply.** A $100 million increase in government spending causes AD to rise by $500 million, assuming the MPC is 80 percent. This causes real GNP to rise by $500 million in the depression economy (a). But real GNP does not increase in the full-capacity economy, only inflation results (b). Real GNP rises in the bottleneck economy, but by less than the $500 million multiplier total, since some of the increase in spending goes to pay for higher prices on existing goods (c).

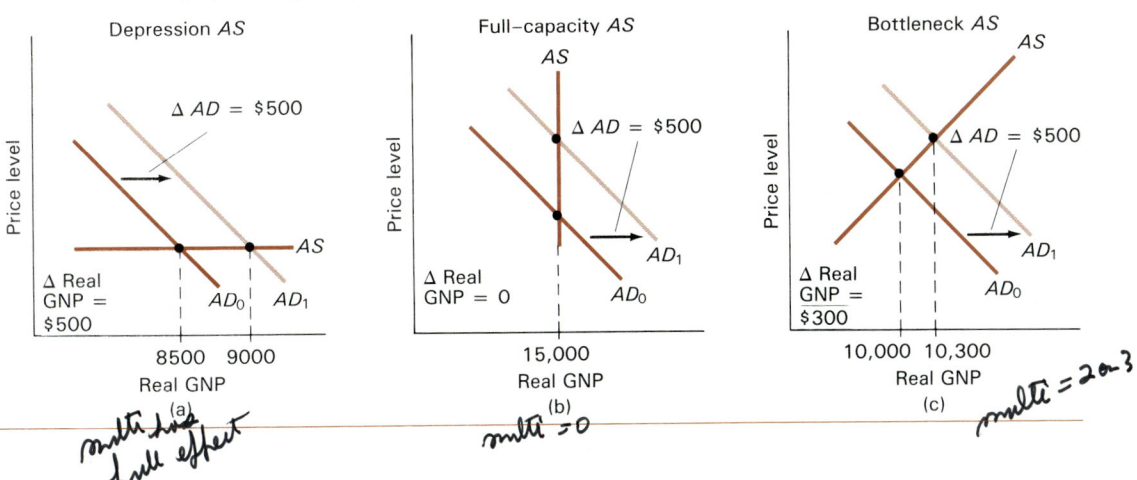

supply curve the economy is on when the fiscal policy takes effect. There are three possible results, as Figure 12-2 shows.

Figure 12-2(a) shows the impact of fiscal policy when the economy is on the horizontal depression part of the AS curve. This effect is sometimes referred to as the Keynesian multiplier effect, because Keynes often assumed a depression economy in his analysis. Here we show the result of a $100 million increase in government spending. The $100 million increase in government spending causes a $500 million total increase in AD, assuming that the MPC is 80 percent. All of this increase in spending goes to produce higher real GNP because the economy has many surplus resources. No increase in the price level takes place.

Figure 12-2(b) shows how the multiplier process works when the economy is on the vertical full-capacity range of the AS curve. This economy is fully employed. There are no surplus resources. An increase in production in one part of the economy can only occur if there is a matching decrease in production somewhere else. The composition of output can therefore change, but the total amount of real GNP produced is fixed. The $100 million increase in government spending still causes a $500 million increase in total spending in this case, but all of the increase in spending goes to pay higher prices. None of the higher spending goes to produce additional goods and services for the economy because there are no resources available to add to production, at least in the short run. High inflation occurs here, with no change in real GNP.

Figure 12-2(c) shows how the multiplier affects the economy in the bottleneck range of the AS curve. There are some unemployed resources in this upward-sloping range of the AS curve, but production bottlenecks, as described in Chapter 9, prevent them from smoothly increasing production. Temporary bottlenecks mean that higher production can take place only with higher costs and a higher price level. The $100 million increase in government spending causes a $500 million increase in AD here, as the multiplier predicts. Some of the increase in aggregate demand goes to pay

338 *Fiscal Policy, Deficits, and Supply-Side Economics*

for higher prices, and some of its goes for higher real GNP. The economy experiences demand-pull inflation, with a rising price level and lower unemployment rates.

The multiplier process describes how fiscal policies affect aggregate demand. We must know something about the state of aggregate supply in the economy, however, before we can tell for sure what the economic effects of this fiscal policy will be. In general, the multiplier impact on real GNP is less the steeper the *AS* curve, that is, the closer the economy is to its full capacity.

KEY CONCEPTS 12.2, 12.3

The spending multiplier shows how discretionary fiscal policy can be used to alter aggregate demand in response to events in the business cycle. A given change in government spending produces a relatively larger change in *AD* through the multiplier process. The impact of this change in *AD* on the economy depends on what portion of the *AS* curve the economy is facing.

12.4 TAXATION MULTIPLIER

Taxation As a Fiscal Policy Tool

The level of consumer spending depends on the level of disposable income in the economy. Disposable income depends on the level of taxation. An increase in taxes reduces disposable income, while a tax cut increases the disposable income available to consumers. If taxes are cut, consumers will spend more, thereby increasing aggregate demand. We can use the multiplier process to estimate how much aggregate demand will rise.

Suppose that the government grants a $100 million tax cut. How would this tax cut affect the economy? First, disposable income would rise by the amount of the tax reduction. Second, this increase in disposable income would induce increases in both consumption and saving. The marginal propensity to consume and the marginal propensity to save tell us how much the change in disposable income would affect the amount of consumption and savings. If the *MPC* is 80 percent and the *MPS* is 20 percent, we can predict that a $100 million tax cut will cause aggregate demand to rise by a total of $400 million, and saving will rise by a total of $100 million. Table 12-1 illustrates the taxation multiplier process.

The $100 million tax cut causes an initial increase in consumption spending of $80 million. Using the spending multiplier developed in the last

TABLE 12-1

The Taxation Multiplier Process

Round	Disposable income ($ millions)	Consumption ($ millions)	Saving ($ millions)
0 (starting point)	1000	900	100
1 (tax cut occurs)	1100 (+100)	980 (+80)	120 (+20)
2	1180 (+80)	1044 (+64)	136 (+36)
3	1244 (+64)	1093 (+51.2)	149 (+12.8)
(additional spending and income rounds)			
Total	1500 (+500)	1300 (+400)	200 (+100)

chapter, and assuming the *MPC* is 80 percent (and the *MPS* is 20 percent), we can calculate the aggregate demand will rise by a total of 1/*MPS* × $80 = $400 million.

By now, you may have noticed a difference between the effects of a change in government spending and an equivalent change in taxes. You might expect a $100 million increase in government spending to have the same effect as a $100 million decrease in taxes. This is not true, however, because government spending directly affects aggregate demand, while taxation affects consumption spending only indirectly through the effect of taxes on disposable income. Thus a $100 million increase in government spending increases aggregate demand by $500 million, but a $100 million tax cut increases aggregate demand by only a total of $400 million. The difference is that a $100 million increase in government spending directly increases *AD* by $100 million, then the multiplier process takes over. By comparison, a $100 million tax cut increases *AD* by only the $80 million of induced consumption before the multiplier process begins. This results in the lower multiplier total for the tax policy.

We can derive a special multiplier formula for tax changes. The spending multiplier is given by the formula

$$\text{Change in } AD = \frac{1}{1 - MPC} \times \text{change in spending}$$

or

$$\text{Change in } AD = \frac{\text{change in spending}}{MPS}$$

We know that, with a tax cut of $100 million, consumption spending rises by $80 million, or by the *MPC* fraction of the tax cut. Substituting

$$\text{Change in spending} = MPC \times \text{change in taxes}$$

we get the formula for the taxation multiplier

$$\text{Change in } AD = -\frac{MPC}{MPS} \times \text{change in taxes}$$

The minus sign in this taxation multiplier shows that there is an inverse relationship between the change in taxes and the change in aggregate demand. A $100 million tax cut (change in taxes = −$100 million) causes a $400 million increase in aggregate demand.

Transfer Payments and Fiscal Policy

12.5 TRANSFER PAYMENTS MULTIPLIER

Transfer payments are the third tool of discretionary fiscal policy. Transfer payments are government payments, such as social security benefits and unemployment and welfare checks, where the government does not receive any good or service in return for the payment. Transfer payments are an important aspect of the public sector, as we saw in Chapter 7. Almost half of the federal government's budget is devoted to transfer payments. Social security and medicare are the largest transfer payment programs.

Transfer payments are different in their distributional aspects than taxes or government spending. Transfer payments tend to go directly to low-income groups, for example, while government spending programs tend to directly benefit workers and producers with somewhat higher incomes. Both kinds of fiscal policy end up affecting the entire economy, however, when the indirect effects of the multiplier process are considered. The multiplier process shows that an increase in spending or disposable income in one part of the economy will indirectly increase spending and income in other parts of the economy.

Transfer payments are identical to taxes in terms of their multiplier effect on aggregate demand. A $100 million increase in transfer payments affects aggregate demand just like a $100 million tax cut. A $100 million increase in transfer payments increases disposable income by $100 million. Assuming that the *MPC* is 80 percent, this will result in $80 million of induced consumption spending. This $80 million of new spending creates $80 million of new income, which induces more consumption spending. Table 12-2 illustrates the effect of a $100 million increase in transfer payments.

The multiplier formula for a change in transfer payments is given by

$$\text{Change in } AD = \frac{MPC}{MPS} \times \text{change in transfer payments}$$

Thus a $100 million transfer payment increase with a *MPC* of 80 percent will cause *AD* to rise by

$$\text{Change in } AD = \frac{.80 \times (+\$100)}{.20} = \$400 \text{ million}$$

The difference between the taxation multiplier and the transfer payments multiplier is the absence of a minus sign in the transfer multiplier. There is no minus sign in the transfer payments multiplier because there is a direct relationship between transfer payments and aggregate demand. An increase (+ change) in transfer payments causes an increase (+ change) in aggregate demand. A reduction in taxes (− change), on the other hand, causes an increase (+ change) in aggregate demand. The minus sign in the tax multiplier formula adjusts for this inverse relationship.

Although the multiplier amounts are the same, remember that tax and transfer multipliers tend to go to different groups in the economy and, therefore, result in purchases of different types of goods and services. An increase in social security taxes, for example, directly affects workers, reducing purchases of items that younger people tend to consume. An increase in social security transfer payments, on the other hand, directly affects retired people, increasing purchases of items that older people tend to buy. Both types of payments indirectly affect other groups through the multiplier process and spending and respending.

TABLE 12-2 — **The Transfer Payment Multiplier Process**

Round	Disposable income ($ millions)	Consumption ($ millions)	Saving ($ millions)
0 (starting point)	1000	900	100
1 (transfers rise)	1100 (+100)	980 (+80)	120 (+20)
2	1180 (+80)	1044 (+64)	136 (+36)
3	1244 (+64)	1093 (+51.2)	149 (+12.8)
(additional spending and income rounds)			
Total	1500	1300 (+400)	200 (+100)

12.6 BALANCED BUDGET MULTIPLIER

Balanced Budget Multiplier
An economic principle that states that equal increases or decreases in government spending and taxation will increase or decrease equilibrium income by the amount of the original change in government spending.

Balanced Budget Multiplier

Each dollar taxed away from consumers is spent by government. It might appear that the taxing and spending behavior of government should balance itself out. It seems as though a dollar taxed away from consumers and then spent by government should have a neutral effect on equilibrium income. But equal increases or decreases in government spending and taxes do not have equal effects on the economy. In general, the **balanced budget multiplier** tells us that equal increases in government spending and taxation increase equilibrium income by the amount of the original increase in government spending. Equal reductions in government spending and taxes reduce equilibrium income by the amount of the original reduction in government spending.

To see how the balanced budget multiplier works, suppose that Congress enacts $100 million of increased government spending and finances these purchases with a $100 million tax increase. Using the multipliers developed in this chapter, and assuming the *MPC* is 80 percent, we see that the net effect of this action is to change *AD* by the amount of the change in government spending.

Change in government spending = +$100	Change in *AD* =	+$500
Change in taxes = +$100	Change in *AD* =	−$400
Net Effect: balanced budget net change in *AD* =		+$100

It is interesting to note that the net effect of the balanced budget change does not depend on the particular *MPC* that we use. That is, a $100 million increase in both taxes and government spending always causes a $100 million increase in *AD*, regardless of the *MPC*. Students who understand elementary algebra will be able to follow this simple proof. With a balanced budget change in the economy, the changes in taxes and government spending are equal, so we can assume that

$$\text{Change in taxes} = Z = \text{change in government spending}$$

where *Z* is some dollar amount. We now insert this value into the multiplier formulas:

$$\text{Net change in } AD = \text{government spending effect} + \text{tax effect}$$
$$= \left(Z \times \frac{1}{MPS}\right) + \left(Z \times \frac{-MPC}{MPS}\right)$$
$$= \left(\frac{Z}{MPS}\right) - \left(\frac{(Z \times MPC)}{MPS}\right)$$
$$= Z \times \frac{1 - MPC}{MPS}$$

If we use the fact that *MPS* is equal to $1 - MPC$, and substitute *Z* for government spending in the formula, we get

$$\text{Net change in } AD = Z \times \frac{MPS}{MPS} = Z$$

or

$$\text{Net change in } AD = \text{change in government spending}$$

The balanced budget multiplier is important. It tells us that government need not run budget deficits and borrow to influence aggregate demand. If government wants to increase aggregate demand, it can do so by increasing both government spending and taxes. This will increase the size of government, but it will also increase aggregate demand by the amount of the change in government spending. Similarly, aggregate demand will fall if both government spending and taxes are cut. A balanced reduction in the size of government, then, tends to cause a recession by reducing aggregate demand.

KEY CONCEPTS
12.4, 12.5, 12.6

Taxes and transfer payments have multiplier effects, but their multipliers are smaller than the spending multiplier. Changes in government spending have both direct and indirect induced consumption effects on *AD*. Taxes and transfers only have this induced consumption effect. Because the government spending multiplier is larger than the tax multiplier, a balanced budget change in both taxes and government spending does not leave *AD* unchanged; *AD* tends to change by the amount of the change in government spending in this situation.

12.7 AUTOMATIC STABILIZER POLICIES

Automatic Stabilizers

Automatic Stabilizers
A system of institutional structures whose purpose is to moderate the effects of changes in the equilibrium levels of income and employment.

Discretionary fiscal policy tools are employed when Congress and the president want to alter the level of aggregate demand. Other fiscal tools, however, are built into the system and work like built-in **automatic stabilizers** to dampen or moderate the effects of changes in the equilibrium levels of income and employment. The most important automatic stabilizers are the progressive income tax system and the system of unemployment transfer payments. These fiscal tools automatically work to counteract trends in the business cycle.

When the economy is experiencing declining aggregate demand, for example, the system of unemployment compensation payments automatically begins to pay benefits to the growing number of unemployed workers. As unemployment rises, the expected reduction in income and aggregate demand is limited automatically when unemployment benefits are paid. Unemployed workers have some income from unemployment benefits to offset a part of their loss of earned income. They spend this unemployment income. Aggregate demand, therefore, falls by a lesser amount than if unemployed workers had no income. In this way, the downward portion of the business cycle is slowed or reduced.

On the other hand, when the economy is expanding rapidly, fewer workers are unemployed and, therefore, fewer are receiving unemployment benefits. This helps to slow the rate at which the economy expands, reducing the movement on the upward portion of the business cycle and limiting the rate at which prices increase. We can recall that Keynes advocated this type of countercyclical fiscal policy as far as government spending and taxation were concerned. The system of unemployment compensation automatically expands when the economy is declining and contracts when the economy is expanding. It has the effect of reducing the extreme peaks as well as the extreme valleys of the business cycle, although cyclical variations in economic activity still exist.

The structure of our income tax also exercises countercyclical effects on economic activity. The income tax imposes a progressive marginal tax rate schedule on the economy. This means that as taxable income increases, the rate at which that additional income is taxed also increases. As the economy expands, employment and income increase. The progressive tax rate system means that more of the income increase goes to taxes and less goes to disposable income. Thus consumption will be less than if the tax structure were not progressive. This slows the economic expansion, reducing pressure on prices.

Progressive tax rates also act as automatic stabilizers during periods of falling income. As income falls, taxpayers find that they are in lower marginal tax brackets. This cushions the impact of falling income on disposable income. (Disposable income falls proportionately less than total income.) Although consumer spending will decline as income in the economy falls, it will not decline as much as it would if the tax system was not progressive. Part of the potential decline in consumer spending will be financed out of reduced tax collections by government. This progressive nature of our tax system, therefore, automatically acts to moderate both the peaks and valleys of our business cycle.

Unfortunately, the income tax can sometimes be a destabilizing force in the economy. In the late 1970s, for example, the economy experienced stagflation. High inflation pushed nominal incomes higher, but real incomes actually fell. The income tax was not indexed to adjust for inflation until 1985, so the higher nominal incomes of the 1970s acted to increase tax burdens, even though real income was falling. The income tax was destabilizing in this situation because it increased tax burdens, thereby discouraging spending at a time when income in the economy was falling and the stimulus of greater spending was needed.

The system of automatic stabilizers works well to dampen changes in income within the economy due to fluctuations in aggregate demand. This means that, during an inflationary period, spending and income rise by less than would otherwise be the case and that, on the recessionary side, spending and income tend to fall less than they would without automatic stabilizers. The stabilizer system absorbs some of the total impact of changes in aggregate demand on the economy.

Unfortunately, this system lends stability to income regardless of the state of the economy. Automatic stabilizers sometimes directly work against deliberate fiscal policy actions of government. Suppose, for example, that the economy is operating at an equilibrium below full employment. The effectiveness of deliberate attempts by government to increase aggregate demand and income is reduced by the system of built-in stabilizers. If government spending expands, increasing aggregate demand, our progressive tax system increases the average effective tax rate. This lessens the overall impact of a deliberate attempt by government to increase aggregate demand and reduce unemployment. A portion of the desired increase in spending is taxed away by the progressive tax system. As income and employment in the economy expand, unemployment and transfer payments are automatically reduced, absorbing part of the potential increase in aggregate demand government had attempted to produce by increasing its expenditures.

The same process takes place to reduce the effectiveness of fiscal policy in an inflationary economy. Suppose government deliberately reduces spending in an effort to reduce aggregate demand. Lower spending should reduce aggregate demand, production should fall, and resource owners should receive less income since fewer resources are employed. The system of automatic stabilizers reduces the effectiveness of this effort. As workers are laid off, unemployment compensation automatically increases, keeping the loss in income by resource owners from being as large as if there were no built-in stabilizers.

The system of built-in stabilizers involves a trade-off between automatic and discretionary fiscal policy. Automatic stabilizers tend to reduce economic fluctuations without the necessity of deliberate policy actions. But automatic stabilizers also limit the ability of discretionary fiscal policies to deal with unemployment and inflation problems.

SUPPLY-SIDE FISCAL POLICIES

Economic policy in the 1980s has been dominated by the supply-side school of fiscal policy. Supply siders tend to believe that fiscal policy has too long concentrated on increased aggregate demand as a solution to our economic problems. Figure 12-3 provides a picture of the supply-side argument.

Suppose that the economy is experiencing high unemployment, so that an increase in real GNP is desired. There are basically two ways to accomplish this result using the $AD-AS$ analysis developed in the last chapter. Figure 12-3(a) shows that an increase in AD, caused by higher government spending, lower taxes, or increased transfer payments, would increase AD and move the economy toward full employment. This causes demand-pull inflation, however, and is therefore not always in the economy's best interests. Nevertheless, Congress may still prefer to adopt this policy, in spite of the inflation, because of the political benefits that they gain from bestowing higher payments or lower taxes on their constituents.

The supply-side alternative to fighting unemployment is shown in Figure 12-3(b). An increase in aggregate supply would also move the economy

FIGURE 12-3

Demand-Side Versus Supply-Side Fiscal Policy. Fiscal policies can affect both AD and AS. Demand-side fiscal policies, as in (a), can cause demand-pull inflation. The AD curve increases, moving the economy from A to B in the figure. Real GNP rises, but the price level also increases. A successful supply-side policy, as in (b), also results in higher real GNP, but the price level can fall (or inflation can slow) as equilibrium shifts from A to C.

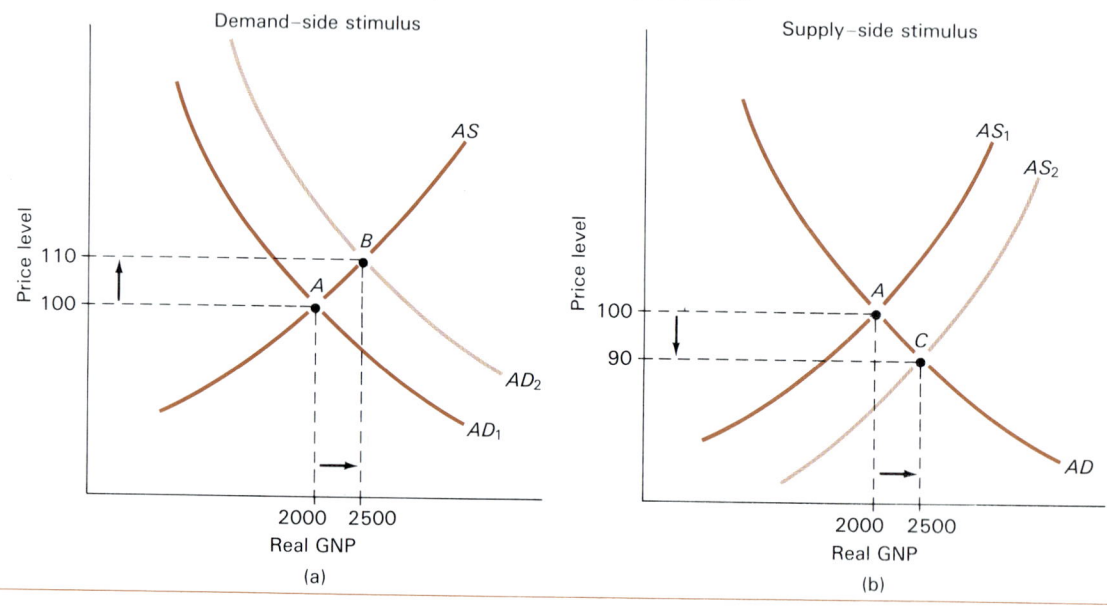

toward higher real GNP, but with a different effect on the price level. The price level, or at least the inflation rate, tends to be lower when *AS* rises than with the alternative of higher *AD*. Looking at the two figures, and noting the high inflation rates of the late 1970s, supply-side economists and policymakers have suggested that it is a mistake to continue demand-side fiscal policies when the supply-side alternative is clearly better.

12.8 SUPPLY-SIDE POLICIES

Reagan's Supply-Side Policies

President Reagan's early economic policies were clearly supply-side in their inspiration. President Reagan sought to stimulate the growth of *AS* in at least three different ways: through tax cuts, cuts in government regulations, and saving and investment incentives.

Supply-Side Tax Cuts   President Reagan proposed tax cuts that lowered the marginal tax rate for workers and investors. As discussed in Chapter 7, the marginal tax rate is the amount of an additional dollar of income that the government claims in tax revenue. The maximum marginal tax rate was lowered from 70 percent in 1980 to only 50 percent in 1984. The income tax was also indexed, so that tax burdens would not automatically rise whenever inflation caused wages and incomes to rise. These lower marginal tax rates allow workers and investors to keep more of their income and profits. This encourages them to be more productive, since they are able to keep more of the fruits of their labor and risk taking.

In 1985, President Reagan took his supply-side tax reforms one step further. He proposed a tax reform package that would reduce marginal tax rates from 50 percent to 35 percent and thus provide further incentives for production.

Supply-Side Cuts in Government Regulations   President Reagan also sought to increase aggregate supply by reducing government regulations and restrictions. The idea was to reduce business costs and increase resource availability, thereby enabling firms to increase supply.

Supply-Side Saving and Investment Incentives   President Reagan's tax cuts also provided special incentives for savers and investors designed to promote long-run increases in aggregate supply. Savers, for example, were allowed to defer tax liability of up to $2000 each year by depositing the money in **individual retirement accounts (IRAs)**. The idea was to provide a tax incentive to encourage long-term saving, although it is unclear how effective these incentives have actually been.

Individual Retirement Accounts (IRAs)
Special accounts at financial institutions that allow individuals to defer taxes on funds that are saved for retirement.

The Reagan tax cuts also included special incentives for firms to undertake investment projects. These investment incentives tend to promote capital formation, which makes possible increased aggregate supply in the long run.

The supply-side revolution of the 1980s has shifted the focus of economic policy from aggregate demand alone to the combination of aggregate demand and aggregate supply. The goal of modern economic policy, as Figure 12-4 illustrates, is to promote noninflationary economic growth by undertaking policies that increase *AS* and *AD* at the same time. This balanced growth of *AS* and *AD* tends to increase real GNP and thus reduce unemployment, but without necessarily causing the inflation problems that plagued the economy in previous years.

One important difference between demand-side and supply-side fiscal policies has to do with the time period in which the policy is designed to

346 *Fiscal Policy, Deficits, and Supply-Side Economics*

FIGURE 12-4   **Balanced Growth of *AD* and *AS*.** One goal of modern fiscal policy is to stimulate both *AD* and *AS* at the same time. When this happens, it is possible for the economy to experience rises in real GNP without inflation. In the figure, *AD* and *AS* both increase, moving the economy from initial equilibrium *A* to new equilibrium *B*. This noninflationary growth is very desirable but difficult to achieve.

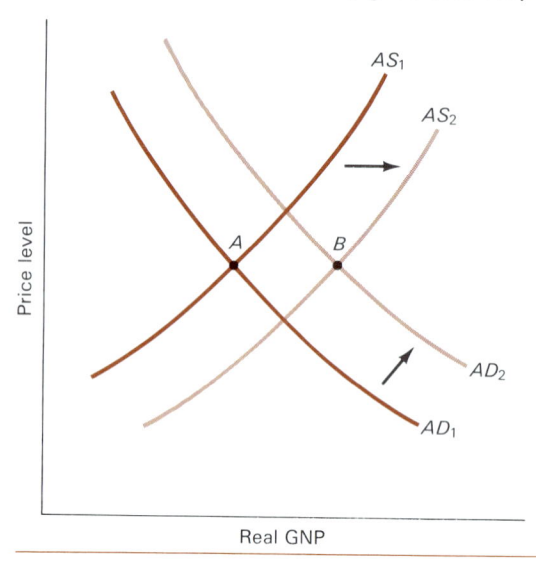

work. Many supply-side policies, because they aim at increasing *AS*, are designed to have their greatest impact in the long run. Most demand-side fiscal policies, on the other hand, are aimed at solving short-term problems.

Keynes was once challenged to defend this emphasis on short-run policy. Whenever he would mention a demand-side proposal, his questioner would interrupt "But in the long run . . ." and suggest that the eventual consequences of Keynes' policy might not be as desirable as its immediate effect. Finally, Keynes impatiently shot back, "But in the long run we are all dead!" Keynes meant that we cannot overlook today's problems completely and concentrate only on the far-distant future. People live in both the present and the future, and economic policies must deal with problems in both time frames. Fiscal policies today represent a combination of demand-side and supply-side actions.

Taxes and the Incentives for Economic Growth

12.9 TAXES AND INCENTIVES

Much of the supply-side revolution in economics has dealt with taxes. Taxes are seen as incentives or "signals" that guide private producers and consumers in making their economic choices. Recent government economic policy has focused on providing incentives for greater productivity, investment, and growth through changes in the tax system. These growth incentives were an important part of President Ronald Reagan's "supply-side economics" initiatives. In recent years liberals, such as New Jersey Senator Bill Bradley, and conservatives, such as New York Congressman Jack Kemp, have suggested that reductions in marginal tax rates can create incentives to economic growth. Let us briefly discuss how marginal tax rates affect individual decisions and economic growth.

The Incentive to Work   Let's assume that a worker earns $20 per hour. If the marginal tax rate is 50 percent, the worker would pay one half of each additional dollar earned in taxes. Therefore, if the individual were to work one additional hour, he or she would actually only receive $10 worth of benefit. Thus the worker would rationally choose not to work an additional hour if the value of the foregone opportunities was worth more than $10. If the marginal tax rate was reduced to 20 percent, however, the worker could realize $15 in benefits by working an additional hour. All other factors held constant, it is reasonable to assume that if the benefit to the worker increased, his or her willingness to provide an additional hour of labor would also increase.

In economic terms, a change in the marginal tax rates changes the trade-off between work and leisure. Current workers might be encouraged to work longer hours. For the unemployed, a reduction in marginal tax rates increases both the benefits of accepting a job offer and the opportunity cost of extending the job search. This suggests that lower tax rates might encourage greater labor supply, providing more resources to the economy. This would expand the economy's production possibilities frontier and encourage economic growth.

The Incentive to Produce
The same marginal tax rate argument can be applied to producers. A reduction in marginal tax rates increases the benefits to producers of providing more goods or services. Lower marginal tax rates increase the incentives for producers to produce. By lowering marginal tax rates, more resources are coaxed into production and the output of the economy can move toward its production possibilities frontier.

Tax Avoidance and Underground-Economy Incentives
Lowering marginal tax rates also reduces the incentive for resources to be allocated to the task of avoiding taxation, either legally or in the underground economy. This tax avoidance behavior affects workers, producers, savers, and investors. Substantial amounts of time, effort, and human talent are now spent considering ways to structure personal income so as to avoid high marginal tax rates. Many lawyers, accountants, real estate, and financial planners do nothing but provide advice on tax avoidance. (Note here that tax avoidance is a legal activity; tax evasion is not.) Those same human resources could be allocated to producing goods and services that are useful rather than to avoiding taxes. By reducing the marginal tax rates, we reduce the benefits that arise from tax avoidance. This creates incentives that channel resources to more productive uses.

The underground economy is primarily a creature created to avoid taxation. Other things constant, it is reasonable to expect that as marginal tax rates rise, the incentive to participate in the underground economy increases. As marginal tax rates fall the incentive to "go underground" decreases. By reducing marginal tax rates, it is reasonable to expect that more people will choose to work "on the books" and to produce goods and services on which taxes are paid. This reduction in tax rates could actually increase tax revenues if the reduced rate causes a larger than proportional increase in taxable activities.

Incentives to Save and Invest
The incentives faced by savers and investors also play a vital role in economic growth. Interest income on savings is taxed as regular income in our economy. As marginal tax rates rise, the after-tax return on savings is reduced. This, in turn, reduces the incentive to save. Interest income on savings is not taxed as heavily in some foreign countries, such as Japan and Switzerland. Accordingly, we see much higher savings rates in these countries. By reducing marginal tax rates, or

ECONOMIC ISSUES

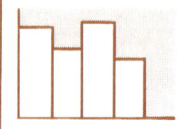

The Laffer Curve

The Laffer curve, named for its popularizer, economist Arthur Laffer, was an early totem of supply-side economists and policy makers. The Laffer curve illustrates the impact that taxes can have on production incentives and, through them, on tax collections. A hypothetical Laffer curve is shown in the accompanying figure.

The Laffer curve shows the relationship between tax rates (measured on the horizontal axis) and tax revenues (measured on the vertical axis). Here is how the Laffer curve is used. Suppose that the government wishes to raise $400 billion in taxes. The Laffer curve shows that it is possible to do this with a tax rate of 20 percent. This relatively low tax rate is able to collect this large amount of tax revenue because it encourages production and investment.

Notice what happens to the Laffer curve if tax rates are raised. The tax revenues increase as the tax rate rises, at least initially, but the higher tax rates reduce the incentives for production and investment and actually increase the incentives to enter the tax-free underground economy. The result is that at some point, such as *B* in the figure, these negative supply incentives are stronger than the effects of higher tax rates. After point *B*, an increase in tax rates actually reduces the amount of taxes collected.

There are two implicit morals to the Laffer curve. The first is that we can collect our $400 billion in tax revenues with either relatively low tax rates, such as those at point *A*, or with very much higher tax rates, such as those at point *C*. Clearly, the lower tax rates are preferred, all else being equal, because of the greater production and income they imply.

The second moral is that sometimes the government can actually increase tax revenues in the long run by cutting tax rates. Cutting tax rates could, for example, potentially move the economy from *C* to *B*, where tax revenues are maximized. Lower tax rates would be sufficient to increase production, thereby producing a larger tax base and higher eventual tax revenues.

Belief in the Laffer curve was one reason why President Reagan thought that he could cut tax rates and still balance the budget. This did not happen, of course, but economists disagree about why it did not. Supply siders argue that it is still too early to see all the effects of the lower tax rates. They argue that the incentives of lower taxes will eventually increase economic growth and balance the budget. They also note that a worldwide recession in the early 1980s left all nations with very large budget deficits that have proved difficult to remove.

even permitting interest income on savings to go untaxed, the incentive to save is increased. Saving is very important in a growing economy because it provides a pool of loanable funds (savings) for businesses to borrow and finance their expansion. Economic growth is fueled by investment and investment depends heavily upon savings.

Many economists today see lower marginal tax rates as a necessary part of any plan to encourage economic growth. As noted in Chapter 7, lower marginal tax rates do not necessarily mean that tax revenues must decline. It is possible to collect the same tax revenues with lower marginal tax rates if we impose taxes on the many sources and uses of income that are currently exempt from tax. This is the idea behind the flat tax rate proposals discussed in Chapter 7. Lower marginal tax rates are not the complete answer to economic growth problems, however. The following sections explore additional factors that affect growth.

KEY CONCEPTS
12.8, 12.9

Supply-side fiscal policies attempt to stimulate aggregate supply through tax cuts, reductions in regulation, and policies designed to increase saving and investment. Tax rate reductions are important because they provide incentives to work, produce, save and invest, and participate in the legal economy.

Other economists cast doubt on the application of the Laffer curve analysis. They note that it is impossible to know just what the economy's Laffer curve looks like; consequently, we cannot tell if we are in a situation such as C, where lowering tax rates might raise additional revenue, or in one such as A, where lower tax rates would mean reduced tax collections.

The Laffer curve certainly influenced economic thought and policy in the 1980s. It remains one of the more controversial aspects of supply-side economics.

A Hypothetical Laffer Curve. The Laffer curve is designed to show that the highest tax rates do not always bring in the most revenues. This hypothetical Laffer curve shows that the government can raise $400 billion in tax revenue with either low tax rates (A) that encourage production or with much higher tax rates (C) that discourage work and tax compliance. There is some tax rate (B) that maximizes tax revenues. Any increase in tax rates above B discourages private producers to such an extent that tax collections are actually reduced.

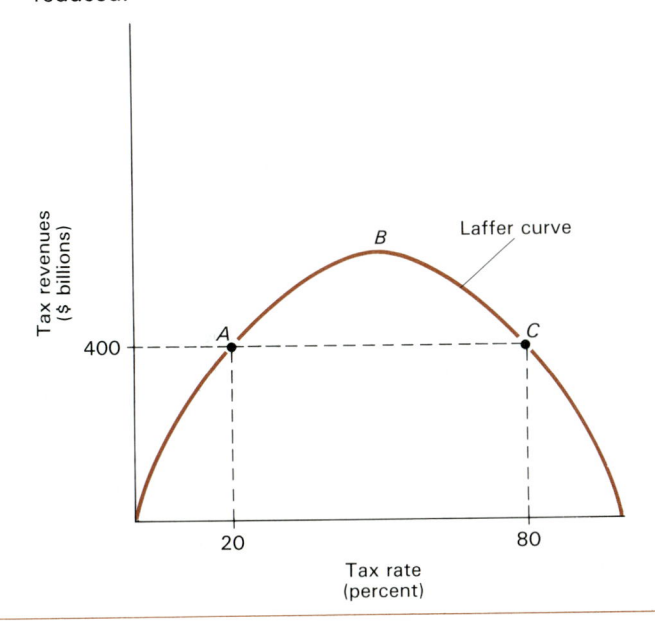

12.10 GOVERNMENT REGULATIONS

Government Regulation and Economic Growth

Taxes are not the only aspect of public policy that affects aggregate supply and economic growth. Government regulation of the private sector also influences how and where the economy grows. In Chapter 2, we introduced several cornerstones of economic thinking. You will recall that (1) scarce resources have a cost, and (2) information is a scarce and costly good. The economics of government regulation can best be understood by keeping these two ideas in mind. As our economy produces goods and services, much of this production is regulated either directly or indirectly by government.

Think for a moment about a typical day in your life. When your clock radio goes off to wake you, the radio airwaves it relies upon are regulated by government; the natural gas you use to cook your breakfast, the fiber content of your pajamas, the electricity for your lights, radio, shaver, and so on, are all produced with substantial government regulation.

The 1970s were marked by significant increases in the amount of government regulation in the economy. Many new regulatory agencies were created by government such as the Environmental Protection Agency, the Department of Energy, and the Consumer Products Safety Commission. All these agencies have been assigned the task of protecting some part of our society from undesirable economic behavior by producers. In some cases

PROMINENT ECONOMIST

Paul Samuelson (1915–   )

Paul Samuelson is arguably the most influential economist of the current generation. His work spans microeconomics and macroeconomics, popular press and scholarly journals. He has successfully instructed freshmen and forcefully pushed back the frontiers of economic theory.

As probably the best known modern Keynesian economist, Paul Samuelson believes that discretionary fiscal policy can successfully be used to reduce unemployment. He accepts the view that money exerts an influence on aggregate demand through interest rates, but he strongly criticizes the monetarists' view of the economy. Samuelson's views advocate temporary economic controls when their introduction serves a given purpose; however, he opposes permanent controls because they would probably result in black markets and long waiting lines for consumers.

Samuelson believes that, because of the possibility of government intervention into economic affairs another depression like that of the 1930s is highly unlikely. He believes that today in our democracy, government can and will "step in and turn the tide" if an economic slump were to develop.

Samuelson was the first American to win the Nobel Prize in Economics. He spent his entire academic career at the Massachusetts Institute of Technology. He has served as economic advisor to Presidents Kennedy and Johnson and wrote one of the most successful introductory economics textbooks in history. This text sold millions of copies and has shaped the thinking of both students and economists for decades. Critical of those who perceive economics to be a precise science yielding definitive answers, Samuelson teaches that economic problems are extremely complex, not allowing for generalized conclusions.

Having bridged the gap between academia and the real world, Samuelson is one of the few economists whose opinions are respected by professional economists and the general public. His writings have been successful at every level. From his highly technical "Collected Scientific Papers of Paul Samuelson," written for economists, to his popular column in *Newsweek* magazine, written for laymen, Samuelson has been an outstanding researcher, teacher, writer, and communicator.

---

these agencies have met with success in regard to their goals. For example, the Environmental Protection Agency has been instrumental in cleaning up and maintaining better water quality in some of our nation's previously polluted lakes and rivers. There are many individuals and groups who feel there is still room for significant improvement in water pollution control, but it is a fact that substantial improvements have been made. All such activity, however, does have its price.

When any price or production activity is regulated, three things are necessary. First, the regulating agency must pass and enforce the regulations. This requires personnel, time, and effort paid for with tax dollars. Second, producers in a regulated industry must not only comply with the regulations but provide proof to the government that they have done so. Time and effort are required to fill out the many forms, conduct the necessary testing, and provide whatever information is requested by the regulating agency. Third, the total cost for enforcement and compliance is ultimately paid by households. As these costs increase, producers are less willing to supply the same amount of goods to the market and, other things held constant, prices rise and the output in the economy declines.

If we multiply the cost of the time and effort devoted to regulation by both producers and regulators by the millions of products and services produced every year, we can get some idea of the overall cost of regulation. In his address to the nation on January 5, 1981, President Ronald Reagan stated that government regulations added $100 billion to the cost of goods and services bought by consumers in 1980. In addition, the government of the United States spent another $20 billion in federal paperwork, personnel, and effort to monitor and enforce those regulations.

The most important point here is that the final cost of all regulation is borne only by households because households are, ultimately, the consumers of good and the owners of all factors of production. Regulation compliance is a cost to the producer, just like labor or raw material, and that cost is reflected in the final price of the good or service when it is sold. Households pay to be protected by regulation, even when they are not aware of the regulation and may not think it necessary. On the regulating side, all such efforts are paid for by tax dollars. Who pays these taxes? Households are the ultimate taxpayers. Taxes are paid either through higher prices or through reduced income from wages, rents, and profits.

The obvious question arises: Is regulation worth the costs? The answer is sometimes yes and sometimes no. In order to make a more informed judgment on this matter, future regulators will probably examine the value of both the benefits arising from regulation and the final costs of regulation that the consumer will bear. Unfortunately, in the past, political entrepreneurs have sometimes been quick to pass laws and regulations that had benevolent intent but passed costs on to consumers that may have far outweighed the possible benefits. By reducing regulation in areas where the costs have outweighed the benefits, production costs may decline and producers may be willing to supply more goods and services in the future. One of President Reagan's first policy actions was to begin to evaluate the costs and benefits of government regulations to see if they made economic sense.

We can see how regulation can affect the economy by looking briefly at regulations that have been applied in the auto and oil industries. Consider the case of regulation of the petroleum industry. It requires tremendous capital investment to search out oil, develop it, and bring it to market to be refined into gasoline and other fuels. There are high risks in drilling for oil, and hundreds of millions of dollars can be lost before the first dollar of income is produced. In order to take these risks and spend the amounts of financial capital necessary, producers must believe that substantial profits are also possible.

At several times in the recent past, Congress has imposed, or considered imposing, price ceilings on the petroleum industry in order to keep prices artificially low and to reduce the "obscene" profits of the oil companies. While price controls do reduce profits, they often set in motion chain-reaction sets of events that have unintended consequences. If regulation imposes a price ceiling that forces the price of gasoline below the market equilibrium level, potential profits fall and producers have less incentive to explore for and develop crude oil sources. Consequently, they shift into the production of other commodities, thereby reducing future supplies of gasoline. This shift in production occurs at the same time as consumption by consumers increases. Because prices are lower, consumers have less incentive to conserve gasoline. Thus they use existing supplies of gasoline at faster rates than if the natural equilibrium market price was reached.

The long-run outcome of price ceilings on oil is over-consumption and under-production of crude oil derivatives. Sooner or later, the available supplies will have to be rationed. Either long lines will develop at gasoline stations or government will issue ration tickets for gasoline. The consumer will pay a price in terms of waiting time in line and higher taxes to pay for government efforts to regulate prices. If ration tickets are issued, even more extensive government effort and tax dollars will be expended to administer the new program.

In 1981, the Federal regulations on crude oil prices were lifted. This decontrol activity produced the effects economic theory would predict. Initially gasoline prices rose by about 5 percent. However, production increased in response to this higher price and output began to outstrip the existing demand, driving prices down below their pre-decontrol levels. In the period from 1981 to the present, oil supplies have increased even more, placing additional downward pressure on gasoline and heating oil prices.

In cases in which factors other than price are regulated, something different occurs because different private incentives are altered. Congress has repeatedly imposed regulations on the automobile industry, for example, in order to reduce auto pollution and increase environmental quality. The costs to the automobile industry of the antipollution devices and the costs to government of enforcing the regulations are passed on to consumers, who find that auto prices have risen. This can have unintended side effects that reduce the effectiveness of the original pollution regulation.

Higher auto prices, resulting from more stringent auto pollution standards, give consumers an incentive to keep their old cars longer rather than trading them in on new ones. This incentive may have defeated the intentions of the environmental regulations that were imposed in the late 1970s and early 1980s. The older cars that people kept produced more pollution than would have existed if the tighter auto emission standards had not been in place and people had purchased new cars at relatively lower prices. This was due in part to the fact that the older cars had fewer emission controls and in part to the fact that their antipollution systems tended to deteriorate over time. In short, tighter pollution regulations may have caused more auto pollution because the regulations failed to take into account how the regulations would alter consumer incentives.

These two case studies show that government regulation is a delicate process because it alters the incentives that individuals face. Regulations can at times improve the environment and the economy, but government officials need to consider the fundamental ideas of economics and the effects of altered incentives when considering new regulations. Sometimes regulations make the problem they set out to solve worse. At other times, regulations can slow economic growth, causing new problems for the economy.

THE FEDERAL BUDGET DEFICIT

12.11 BUDGET DEFICIT

Budget Surplus
A government budget whose total revenues are greater than its total outlays.

Budget Deficit
A government budget whose tax revenues are less than spending and transfer payment totals. The government must borrow the amount of the deficit.

One of the most dramatic events of the 1980s was the tremendous increase in the size of the federal government's budget deficits. It is important that we understand what these deficits are and what they mean for the economy. Like many economic ideas, deficits are more complex than they initially look.

The Keynesian conventional wisdom calls for the government to take countercyclical fiscal actions. This means that the government should run a **budget surplus** during periods of high employment and run a **budget deficit** during periods of falling income and recession. A budget surplus means that the government is taking in more in tax revenues than it is spending. Higher taxes and lower spending tend to reduce aggregate demand, all else being equal, lessening the chance for high inflation. A budget deficit means that the government is spending more than it takes in as taxes. Lower taxes

Cyclical Deficit
That part of the deficit that results from the interaction of automatic stabilizer programs and the business cycle.

Structural Deficit
That part of the deficit that results from discretionary fiscal policy actions.

and higher spending tend to increase aggregate demand, all else being equal, and move the economy out of the recession.

The system of automatic stabilizers changes the impact of fiscal policy. A portion of the actual government budget surplus or deficit is produced by deliberate fiscal policy change and a portion of it by the system of built-in stabilizers reacting to the economic business cycle. The government's budget automatically moves toward surplus in prosperous times, for example, because tax revenues increase and transfer payments fall. The budget automatically moves toward deficit during recessions, on the other hand, because tax revenues fall and transfer payment costs increase. To fully understand how government is responding to economic events, we need to determine how much of the deficit or surplus is the result of automatic reactions to business cycles, and how much is the result of deliberate changes in the structure of government spending and tax policy.

In recent years, the President's Council of Economic Advisors has divided the federal budget deficit into two parts. The actual deficit is composed of a **cyclical deficit** and a **structural deficit.** The cyclical deficit is the budget deficit that results from the actions of the automatic stabilizers described above. The structural deficit is the result of deliberate fiscal policy actions, such as legislated tax cuts and spending increases. Table 12-3 gives the breakdown of recent federal budgets in terms of cyclical and structural deficits.

The figures in Table 12-3 show how the high budget deficits of the 1980s, first discussed in Chapter 7, came to be. It is convenient to divide the data presented here into two periods: 1980–1983, when cyclical deficits were relatively high and rising, and 1983–1985, when structural deficits were relatively high and rising (both deficits were very large in 1983).

The United States had a relatively large deficit, by historical standards, in 1980. Most of this deficit was structural in nature and thus due to discretionary fiscal policy decisions. As unemployment rates increased in the early 1980s, the cyclical deficit automatically increased from $4 billion in 1980 to $95 billion in 1983. Deliberate fiscal policies did relatively little to fight this unemployment. The structural deficit fell in 1980-1981 and was less in 1982 than in 1980. Most of the government budget deficit in this period was due to the effects of automatic stabilizers.

The unemployment rate did not begin to fall, as Keynesian conventional wisdom might suggest, until the structural deficit rose. Higher structural deficits in 1983–1985 helped increase aggregate demand and reduce the unemployment rate. The higher structural deficits show that government fiscal policy was expansionary. Note that the cyclical deficit fell in 1983–1985

| TABLE 12-3 | **Cyclical and Structural Deficits, 1980–1985** |

Fiscal year	Unemployment rate (%)	Total deficit ($ billions)	Cyclical deficit ($ billions)	Structural deficit ($ billions)
1980	7.0	60	4	55
1981	7.5	58	19	39
1982	9.5	111	62	48
1983	9.5	195	95	101
1984	7.4	187	49	138
1985	7.0	208	44	163

Source. Economic Report of the President, 1984, Table 1-2 and B-29. All figures for 1984–1985 are estimates. Unemployment figures are for calendar years. Figures may not sum due to rounding.

Deficits and Crowding Out

Budget deficits and the national debt were first discussed in Chapter 7. It is important, however, that we review the economic effects of deficit spending in macroeconomic terms. The budget deficit has different effects on aggregate demand than it does on aggregate supply. These differences mean that deficits can at times cause rapid economic expansion and at other times have important contractionary effects.

12.12 CROWDING-OUT EFFECT

At first glance, it seems that a budget deficit must increase aggregate demand. Suppose, for example, that the government reduces taxes and increases spending and transfer payments. This should increase government spending directly and also increase consumption spending indirectly through increases in disposable income and the associated multiplier effects. This first glance can be misleading, however. Government must borrow resources from the private sector when it spends more and taxes less. An increase in government spending financed by borrowing may result in a decrease in private investment spending that would have been financed by loans. Economists call this the crowding-out effect.

The crowding-out effect reduces the net impact of budget deficits on aggregate demand. An increase in government spending and borrowing of $10 billion, for example, might crowd out investment spending of $5 billion. There would then be only a $5 billion net increase in spending (plus the multiplier effects of the increased spending). By comparison, there would be a $10 billion increase in spending (plus the multiplier impact) if there were no crowding out. If credit supplies in the economy are perfectly fixed, complete crowding out is possible. Here a $10 billion increase in government spending and borrowing would crowd out an equal $10 billion of investment spending. There would be a zero net impact of the deficit on aggregate demand. The budget deficit would shift spending from the private to the public sector, but it would not alter the macroeconomic equilibrium.

Thus far we have looked at how deficits can affect aggregate demand. Deficits can also affect aggregate supply indirectly through the crowding-out effect. Deficits that reduce investment spending and capital formation in the short run tend to reduce the growth of aggregate supply in the long run. Slower growth in aggregate supply means that the economy will experience higher unemployment and inflation rates than would otherwise be the case. High structural deficits in the 1980s may have reduced the unemployment rate in the United States, but many economists today are worried that this silver lining will turn out to be overwhelmed by the dark cloud of reduced capital formation and slow economic growth in the future.

Budget deficits can also cause a different sort of crowding out, one that was of much concern in the mid-1980s. If deficits cause high real interest rates, then these high interest rates tend to attract investment funds from other countries. This inflow of investment funds from abroad is desirable, on the one hand, because it reduces the impact of deficits on domestic investment spending. Funds from abroad tend to replace domestic resources that the government has borrowed to finance the deficit. Thus these capital inflows to the United States tend to reduce the crowding out of investment spending, making the crowding-out problem less severe.

The problem is not as simple as this, however. As foreigners transfer their funds to the United States, they must exchange their foreign currencies for U.S. dollars. This can have a dramatic effect on the exchange rate. Between 1979 and early 1985, for example, the international value of the dollar increased by about 50 percent compared to other major currencies. This increase in the value of the dollar made imported goods relatively inexpensive for U.S. buyers and U.S. exports relatively expensive for foreign buyers. Purchases of goods made in the United States fell as foreign and domestic buyers switched to items produced abroad. In other words, the budget deficit indirectly "crowded out" U.S. production and "crowded in" foreign imports.

There is evidence that this complex system of deficit-caused events prevailed in the mid-1980s. In 1984, for example, the federal budget deficit was approximately $200 billion. The inflow of foreign capital amounted to a net figure of about $100 billion, and the balance of trade deficit totalled about another $100 billion. This is circumstantial evidence that the deficit caused capital inflows that affected the exchange rates, encouraging imports and discouraging exports.

12.13 SUPPLY-SIDE VIEW OF DEFICIT

A Supply-Side View of the Budget Deficit

Many supply-side economists tend to view the economic effects of the budget deficit in a different light. Economist Robert Mundell is sometimes called the "godfather" of supply-side economics because of his intellectual influence on Arthur Laffer, Jack Kemp, and other supply-side figures.

In a speech before the Atlantic Economic Society in 1985, Mundell outlined the supply-side view of the effects of budget deficits on the economy. According to Mundell, President Reagan's 1981 tax cuts had the dramatic effect of increasing the profitability of investment in the United States. Business investment in the United States was suddenly much more profitable than investment abroad because firms were able to keep more of their profits, since they did not have to pay as much in taxes. This provided a tremendous incentive for investment in the United States.

Mundell views the large capital inflows noted above as the result of the increased profitability of investment in the United States. In Mundell's view, the capital inflow was caused by high after-tax profits and a healthy, expanding economy, not by the high interest rates and crowding-out that many traditional economists saw. Mundell does not see deficits as being inherently bad. He views the current deficit as acceptable if it forces Congress to reduce the size of government.

There is some evidence to support Robert Mundell's view of the deficit. The behavior of the stock market in the 1980s, for example, is consistent with Mundell's theory. If crowding out were taking place, we should expect the high interest rates and subsequent low business profits to force stock prices down. If Mundell's supply-side theory is correct, on the other hand, high business profits would have caused a stock market boom. In fact, stock prices did rise to new highs in the early 1980s, supporting the supply-side deficit theory.

12.14 CROWDING-OUT CONTROVERSY

The Debate Over Deficits and Interest Rates

Robert Mundell's supply-side theory suggests that deficits do not always crowd out investment spending. Other recent studies now call into question the notion that deficits force up interest rates. Paul Evans of the University of Houston examined periods in U.S. history when deficits were high in relation to GNP.[1] Using elaborate statistical methods, Evans tested to see if the deficits caused high interest rates and crowding out. Evans failed to find any systematic link between the large deficits and the high interest rates that would cause crowding out.

Economists have long believed that deficits force interest rates higher. They argue that deficit borrowing causes the government to compete with private borrowers for scarce loanable funds. The increase in the demand for these loans, the logic goes, can only make interest rates rise. Given Evans' research, we must now ask a different question, why don't deficits cause interest rates to rise? Evans can offer no definitive answer to this question, but he does suggest that a theory of Robert Barro's might hold the answer.

Robert Barro is a founder of the rational expectations school of economic theory, which will be analyzed in Chapter 15. Barro believes the people in the economy form accurate expectations concerning economic events and then take rational actions to deal with those events. He offers the following rational expectations theory of the deficit. Suppose that people view the deficit as causing an increase in future taxes. The government spends more than it taxes in the current time period with a deficit, but taxes will eventually be raised in order to repay the loans. The deficit may thus be viewed as a way of shifting the burden of government programs from one generation to the next.

It is possible, to use Barro's logic, that parents will not wish to impose this additional burden on their children in the form of higher future taxes. Rational individual parents would, therefore, increase their current saving in order to provide a larger future bequest to their children to help them pay these future taxes. This would allow individual parents to protect their children from the expected higher future tax burden.

Evans noted that, if parents behave the way that Barro has described, this would explain the absence of high interest rates during periods of large deficits. The increase in government borrowing would be offset by the increase in private saving. More loans would be demanded by the government, but more savings funds would be available. Interest rates would not necessarily rise and crowding out need not be a problem.

It is difficult to say if Evans and Barro are correct concerning the economic effects of the deficit. Some other studies give conflicting results and other hypotheses predict different effects. The question of the deficit and its effects is still unsettled. Economists need to devote more resources to the study of the deficit and to an analysis of its consequences.

1. Paul Evans, "Do Large Deficits Produce High Interest Rates?" *American Economic Review*, March, 1985, pp. 68–87.

KEY CONCEPTS
12.11, 12.12, 12.13, 12.14

The budget deficit represents the amount that the government must borrow to make up for spending and transfer payments in excess of tax revenues. The deficit can be divided into a cyclical deficit, which results from automatic stabilizers, and a structural deficit, which results from discretionary fiscal policies. One reason that the deficit is a problem is that it might force interest rates higher and thereby crowd out private-sector investment spending. Supply siders tend to view recent deficits as resulting from the increased profitability of investment spending, however. The deficit may not cause crowding out if saving increases in anticipation of future taxes.

12.15 BALANCING THE BUDGET

Approaches to Reducing the Deficit

An important issue concerns what policies should be used to reduce the federal budget deficit. This issue highlights the differences between demand- and supply-side economists and among different supply-side proponents. Today's budget deficits are very large. Dramatic action will be required to reduce the deficit significantly. What should be done?

Many demand-side economists have called for tax increases to reduce the deficit. They see the crowding-out effects as being very real and important and would prefer higher direct taxes to the indirect costs of crowding out, higher real interest rates, and the other deficit effects discussed earlier in this chapter.

Supply-side economists generally favor reducing the deficit through reductions in government spending and transfer payments. It is virtually impossible to balance the budget completely through spending cuts, however. Many government programs are "sacred cows," such as defense spending and social security, that cannot easily be cut, at least in the short run. The budget and the budget deficit are political animals and are therefore subject to political forces. Additional revenues will need to be raised. Two groups of supply-side economists differ concerning how this additional revenue should be raised.

One group, whom we might call "traditional" supply-side economists, favors raising taxes to reduce the deficit, providing that they can keep special incentives in the tax laws that tend to encourage saving and investment. Traditional supply siders, such as Stanford's Michael Boskin and Harvard's Martin Feldstein, view saving, investment, and capital formation as the key factors that increase aggregate supply. These traditional supply siders tend to worry about the crowding-out effects of deficits on investment spending. They would like to reduce the budget deficit to prevent investment spending from being crowded out. They would cut the deficit by raising taxes but would retain saving and investment incentives that they think are important.

A second group, whom we might call the "radical" supply siders, proposes to reduce the deficit in a different way. Congressman Jack Kemp and economists Arthur Laffer, Paul Craig Roberts, and Robert Mundell are members of this radical supply-side group. They propose implementing a flat tax, as already outlined in Chapter 7, that would close tax loop-holes, reduce special tax incentives (including those that currently encourage saving and investment), and lower marginal tax rates. They think that the production incentives provided by the lower tax rates would stimulate aggregate supply. They suggest that lower tax rates would dramatically stimulate economic growth and bring about a Laffer-curve increase in tax revenues.

The key disagreement among the traditional and radical supply siders involves which is more important to aggregate supply, saving and investment or marginal tax rates and production incentives. The traditional supply-side economists tend to favor higher tax rates to reduce the deficit, so long as saving and investment incentives are retained. Radical supply siders tend to favor lower tax rates and economic growth to reduce the deficit, even if this means giving up saving and investment incentives. It is no wonder, given the various views on this issue, that the deficit has proved so difficult to shrink. Disagreements among supply-side economists within the Reagan administration concerning the correct deficit-cutting strategy effectively paralyzed fiscal policy for some time in the mid-1980s, letting the deficit increase beyond an acceptable level.

12.15 BALANCING THE BUDGET

The Gramm–Rudman–Hollings Deficit Reduction Plan

Congress and the president found themselves unable to significantly reduce the deficit in the mid-1980s. In frustration, Congress passed the Gramm–Rudman–Hollings Act in 1985, which established a system that would automatically achieve a balanced federal budget by 1991. The Gramm–Rudman–Hollings Act was controversial. Many of the bill's supporters thought that it was a bad law and many people believe that it will ultimately be ruled as unconstitutional by the Supreme Court. Congress overwhelmingly passed it and the president signed it, in spite of these reservations, because even a poorly crafted deficit-reduction plan seemed to them to be better than the runaway budget deficits that would otherwise prevail.

The goal of the Gramm–Rudman–Hollings Act was to automatically reduce the federal deficit from over $200 billion in fiscal year 1986 to zero (a balanced budget) in fiscal 1991 by setting progressively smaller deficit ceilings for each year then forcing budget cuts to bring the deficit down to the legal maximum. Here is how the system works. A specific deficit ceiling is set for each year. The law, for example, specified a maximum deficit of $209 billion for fiscal year 1986, which ended on September 30, 1986. Congress and the President had established programs that would have resulted in a deficit of $220.5 billion for fiscal 1986, as estimated by the Congressional Budget Office and the President's Office of Management and Budget. This projected deficit was about $11.7 billion above the legal limit. Under the Gramm–Rudman–Hollings Act, $11.7 billion of budget cuts were scheduled to automatically take place, without congressional action, in order to achieve the deficit goal.

The process by which these automatic budget cuts are made is complex. Many programs, such as social security, are exempt from automatic cuts. In fact, almost two-thirds of the federal budget is protected from automatic reductions under this law. The necessary reductions are made from the remaining one-third of the budget, with half the cuts coming from defense programs and half from nondefense programs. All affected programs are reduced by the same percentage (4.3 percent in the cuts announced in January, 1986) in order to spread out the burden of deficit reduction somewhat.

In fiscal 1986, for example, Gramm–Rudman–Hollings provisions forced $5.85 billion in defense spending reductions and $5.85 billion reductions in such nondefense programs as Medicare, agricultural payments, and NASA. Congress and the president can avoid these automatic cuts if they adopt a budget that achieves the year's deficit goals. The Gramm–Rudman–Hollings automatic cuts only apply if the budget as adopted by Congress and the president has an estimated deficit that exceeds the legal limit. The deficit limit for fiscal year 1987 is set at $144 billion, and declines each year until a balanced budget is achieved in fiscal 1991.

The Gramm–Rudman–Hollings Bill was a grand compromise between Congress and President Reagan when it was enacted in 1985. On the one hand, President Reagan got something he desired: the promise of a balanced federal budget without a tax increase (there is no provision in this bill to raise taxes—all the deficit reduction comes from reduced budget outlays). President Reagan also gave up something, however, in that half of all the automatic outlay cuts will come from national defense, an area that the president was determined to strengthen. Congress, on the other hand, was able to protect certain sacred-cow programs from deficit reduction, with the necessary cuts being spread over a number of programs. Both Congress and the president have an incentive to pass laws that reduce the deficit in order to keep the additional automatic cuts as small as possible.

As noted above, automatic deficit reductions were first attempted in early 1986. At that time, there were several reasons to question how effective the Gramm–Rudman–Hollings Act would be. The first problem was the constitutional question. Many people think that the Supreme Court will not allow Congress to give up its authority, as spelled out in the Constitution, to set government spending policy. The law may be declared unconstitutional, in which case there would be no automatic deficit reductions and Congress and the president would be back to square one on the deficit issue. The second problem is technical. The law calls for budget cuts to be made based on estimates of future deficits. The budget and the economy are both very complex, however, and budget projections are often far from accurate. The difference between the estimates and the eventual reality complicates attempts to reduce the deficit automatically. A third problem is practical. The law allows individual members of Congress to appeal the automatic budget cuts, and this creates the potential for deficit reduction measures to become tied up in the courts during appeals.

In passing the Gramm–Rudman–Hollings Act, Congress in effect said that deficit reduction was its top priority and it was willing to adopt legislation to force a balanced budget in the future, even if the mechanism to achieve deficit reduction was imperfect. It remains to be seen if this system of automatic program cuts will be effective. Even if it is, however, there is still the question, which is discussed in the next subsection, of whether it is always desirable to have a balanced budget. While the huge and persistent budget deficits of the 1980s were undesirable, it is not clear that all deficits are bad.

12.16 BALANCED-BUDGET CONCEPTS

Balanced-Budget Philosophies

The effective use of fiscal policy can, and has, enabled decision makers to reduce some of the major swings in economic cycles in the last 50 years. There is, however, a continuing debate about how and when these discretionary fiscal tools should be used. We have previously taken a brief look at some of the political problems that arise from fiscal policy and the use of the federal budget as a fiscal policy tool. Here we would like to examine three of the major philosophies that have evolved regarding the need to balance the federal budget.

Annually Balanced Budget
The idea that the federal government's budget must be balanced, with tax revenues equal to total outlays, each and every year.

The Annually Balanced Budget In 1981 and again in 1983, bills were debated before the Congress of the United States that mandated that the federal government balance its revenues and expenditures each and every year. From a layman's point of view, this might seem to force the government to "live within its means" and exercise budgetary discipline. From the viewpoint of countercyclical fiscal policy, an **annually balanced budget** could be a disaster. For example, suppose the economy is experiencing declining demand, employment, and income, and therefore, declining tax revenues. The government faces a large deficit. The annually balanced budget would require a tax increase here to close the federal budgetary deficit. Unfortunately, a tax increase in a declining economy would simply reduce income, aggregate demand, and employment even further. In this case the annually balanced budget becomes a source of economic instability and contributes more to an economic problem than to its solution.

ECONOMIC ISSUES

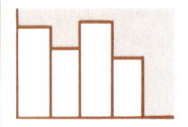

The Balanced Budget Amendment

The federal government has shouldered historically large peacetime deficits in recent years. This means that government spending has far exceeded tax collections, and government has been forced to borrow to finance the difference. Deficits of $200 billion or more were projected for some years in the 1980s. Some of the causes and consequences of these deficits were discussed in this chapter. This Economic Issue looks at one possible solution to deficit difficulties, a constitutional amendment to require an annual balanced budget.

Balanced budget constitutional amendment proposals have been around for years, but these bills must now be taken more seriously than in the past. Current high deficits have made the budget imbalance problem worse. In 1982, a balanced budget amendment for the first time gained approval of the Senate and only narrowly missed passage in the House of Representatives, an indication of growing political support for this idea. Voters around the country might someday soon be faced with deciding whether to vote for a balanced budget law.

The 1982 proposal is typical of recent balanced budget proposals. It is interesting in the way that it would regulate federal government decisions and influence fiscal policy. Federal government expenditures would be limited by the amount of revenues available, making a deficit illegal. Congress would be able to run deficits only under extraordinary circumstances; a vote of a "supermajority" of more than half of each house would be required for an unbalanced budget's passage.

A second interesting feature of the 1982 bill is that it also would limit the growth of federal tax revenues. Federal taxes would not be allowed to grow any faster than national income. This means, implicitly, that the growth in federal expenditures would also be limited by the growth in national income.

This combination of revenue and expenditure limits and supermajority voting rules means that federal government deficits would be less likely under a balanced budget rule, but the power of automatic stabilizers would also be reduced. Taxes would be less able to rise during inflationary periods, for example, and spending and transfer payments would be less able to rise during periods of high unemployment. Because automatic stabilizers would be weakened, a balanced budget amendment might reduce deficits on the one hand, while it increased instability in the economy on the other. (See the discussion in this chapter for more detail about the advantages and disadvantages of automatic stabilizers.)

Economists and politicians who are in favor of a balanced budget amendment think it is desirable for many reasons. First, they think that the detrimental economic effects of large deficits, such as crowding out, higher interest rates, and higher inflation, make annual deficits a poor policy. They also note that the political system is biased in favor of deficits, since legislators prefer to vote for spending increases but not the tax boosts needed to fund them in many cases. Even Ronald Reagan, a conservative who was

The entire concept of an annually balanced budget limits the power of government to exercise discretionary fiscal policy. While some feel that this type of restraint on government is overdue, still others feel a strong need to foster and encourage government use of discretionary fiscal tools.

Cyclically Balanced Budget
The idea that the federal government's budget must be balanced, with tax revenues equal to total outlays, over the course of the business cycle, with surpluses during years of rising income being used to make up for deficits during years of falling income.

The Cyclically Balanced Budget The **cyclically balanced budget** philosophy requires the government to balance its budget over the length of the business cycle from peak to peak. No specific time limit is prescribed for this balancing to take place. It depends on the amount of time it takes the business cycle to run its course. The budgetary surplus generated in boom periods is used to offset budgetary deficits in recessionary periods.

Like the annually balanced budget philosophy, this philosophy has intuitive appeal, but it too is accompanied by significant problems. Cyclical expansions and contractions are seldom of the same magnitude or duration. A recovery cycle from trough to peak may take more than a year and produce large surpluses. This phase may then be followed by a rather short

elected president on a balanced budget platform, found it difficult to cut government spending enough to prevent higher deficits during the first years of his administration. Perhaps a constitutional amendment could force Congress to do what it seemingly will not do voluntarily.

People who oppose a balanced budget amendment do so on several counts. First, many economists and policymakers think that such a law would be too restrictive and prevent fiscal policy from playing its important stabilization role. Recessions might be deeper and inflation rates higher, they suggest, without the offsetting force of discretionary government taxing and spending power.

Second, some observers doubt that a balanced budget amendment would have much effect on actual government borrowing. They suggest that a super-majority of Congress would simply vote for deficits each year, just as they now vote to raise the nominal national debt ceiling each term. A potential problem with the constitutional amendment, in this view, is that it might give special-interest groups even more power to get special tax and spending benefits from government. If a relatively small number of representatives can keep the rest of Congress from having an unbalanced budget by refusing to vote for it unless they are granted favors, they might be able to extract valuable concessions from the majority in return for giving up their opposition.

Other people oppose the balanced budget amendment because it does not control so-called "off-budget" borrowing. Many federal agencies engage in borrowing activities that are not included in the federal budget, and thus are not counted in the deficits. This borrowing would not be restricted by a constitutional amendment. The Federal Home Loan Bank, for example, borrows in credit markets to finance housing construction. Opponents of the balanced budget rule think that Congress might use more of these off-budget agencies to finance programs that they cannot fit within the technically "balanced" budget. Thus the balanced budget might not be balanced, in any meaningful sense, even with this constitutional amendment.

Finally, opponents of this amendment are concerned about the problem of achieving a balanced budget in the first place. Presidents Carter and Reagan were both elected with the promise to balance the federal budget within four years. Both tried, both failed, with the best of intentions. The problem is that many parts of the federal budget are entitlements, or guaranteed payments, such as social security payments, that are difficult to control. These entitlements are based on promises the Congress made in earlier years. A balanced budget amendment does little to reduce entitlement obligations, and so it might be difficult or impossible to actually meet the letter of the law and produce a constitutionally mandated balanced budget.

The arguments against a balanced budget amendment are strong, but deficits have been large in recent years and the problems these deficits lead to are serious. For these reasons, the balanced budget amendment is likely to remain an important issue in U.S. economic and political policy.

Additional References

Boskin, Michael J. and Wildavsky, Aaron, eds. *The Federal Budget: Economics and Politics.* San Francisco: Institute for Contemporary Studies, 1982.

Nordhaus, William. "How Not to Balance the Federal Budget." *New York Times,* September 5, 1982, p. D-2.

Veseth, Michael. *Introductory Macroeconomics,* second edition. New York: Academic Press, 1984, especially Chapters 10 and 11.

Veseth, Michael. *Public Finance.* Reston VA: Reston Publishing Co., 1984, especially Chapter 16.

---

and small recession. To attempt to expend all of a large surplus built up over a long and large recovery in a short recession might well propel the economy into a highly inflationary recovery. This philosophy again eliminates some of the power of discretionary fiscal policy and can contribute as much to the economic problem as to its solution.

Functional Finance
The philosophy that states government should take whatever fiscal actions are necessary to promote a noninflationary full-employment equilibrium without substantial concern for the size of deficits or surpluses.

Functional Finance The **functional finance** philosophy does not require a balanced federal budget over any period of time and places no budgetary discipline on fiscal policy at all. It requires only that the federal government take whatever fiscal actions are necessary to promote a noninflationary full-employment equilibrium. The borrowing powers of government are to be uninhibited in the pursuit of full employment and a growing economy. This philosophy, unfortunately, might well increase the inflationary bias that presently exists in our system of political economy. Legislators who would rather borrow than impose taxes on voters might continually run deficits that accumulate to amounts as large as those of the mid-1980s. On the other hand, some economists contend that the benefits of a growing full-employment economy might well outweigh any negative effects of excessive government spending.

Just which of these philosophies, if any, will become the guidepost to fiscal policy in the 1990s is unclear at this time. It is certain, however, that continuing debate and controversy will surround the use of discretionary fiscal tools as long as they are a functioning part of our economic system.

SUMMARY

12.1
1. Demand-side fiscal policy was developed in response to the existence of business cycles. In a business cycle, the economy goes through an expansionary phase, then peaks; a contractionary phase then begins, ending in a trough. Countercyclical fiscal policy is designed to reduce the severity of the peaks and troughs of the business cycle.

12.2
2. The fiscal policy tool of government spending affects aggregate demand (AD) through the spending multipier process. The government spending mutliplier is given by change in $AD = (1/1 - MPC) \times$ change in government spending or change in $AD = 1/MPS \times$ change in government spending.

12.3
3. The impact of a change in government spending on the economy depends on the nature of aggregate supply (AS) when the spending change occurs. If the economy is on the depression AS, then the full multiplier change in AD is translated into a change in real GNP. If the economy is on the full-capacity AS, however, all the multiplier increase in AD is absorbed as price changes, with no change in real GNP. Finally, if the economy in on the bottleneck AS, the multiplier change in AD is partially absorbed in changing prices and partially produces changes in real GNP.

12.4
4. The fiscal policy of taxation also produces a multiplier effect on AD, although the tax multiplier is less than the spending multiplier. This difference in multipliers occurs because taxes affect the economy indirectly, through changes in disposable income and induced consumption spending. Government spending, on the other hand, affects AD directly and then also has an indirect effect on disposable income and induced consumption. The taxation multiplier is given by:
change in $AD = (- MPC/MPS) \times$ change in taxation.

12.5
5. Transfer payments are a third tool of demand-side fiscal policy. Transfer payments affect AD indirectly because they alter disposable income and therefore cause changes in induced consumption spending. The multiplier formula for transfer payments is given by:
change in $AD = MPC/MPS \times$ change in transfer payments.

12.6
6. An equal change in both taxes and government spending does not leave AD unchanged. Because government spending has a larger multiplier impact, an equal increase in both taxes and government spending will cause AD to increase by the amount of the increase in government

spending. Thus it is said that the balanced budget multiplier is equal to one (multiplied by the change in government spending).

12.7 → 7. Automatic stabilizers are fiscal policies that, unlike discretionary fiscal policies, dampen the peaks and troughs of business cycles without explicit legislative or administrative action. Transfer payments, such as unemployment benefits, and the progressive income tax system are examples of automatic stabilizer programs. Automatic stabilizers perform useful functions, but they have some drawbacks. For example, the existence of automatic stabilizers makes it somewhat more difficult for government to alter the economy's equilibrium in response to inflation or unemployment.

12.8 → 8. Economic policy in the 1980s was dominated by the supply-side school of fiscal policy. Supply-side fiscal policies attempt to promote the growth of AS through such policies as tax cuts, deregulation, and incentives for saving and investment.

12.9 → 9. Much of supply-side economics is built on the power of taxes to alter the incentives that people face. Taxes affect the incentive to work, to produce, to pay taxes legally or to enter the underground economy, and to save and invest.

12.10 → 10. Government regulations increased significantly in the 1970s. Many of these regulations provide clear benefits to people in the economy, but they also impose costs, which are sometimes difficult to see, that people must bear. The examples of regulation of oil and auto pollution indicate that regulations are not always successful in achieving their goals.

12.11 → 11. The federal budget deficit is equal to the amount by which government spending and transfer payments exceed tax revenues. In the mid-1980s, the federal budget deficit was equal to about $200 billion, or about 5 percent of GNP. The deficit can be divided into two parts: the cyclical deficit, which results from the actions of automatic stabilizer programs, and the structural deficit, which results from discretionary fiscal policies.

12.12 → 12. Large government deficits can cause crowding out in two ways. First, deficits can drive up interest rates, which cause lower levels of investment spending. It is then possible for deficits to crowd out investment spending. Deficits can also cause an inflow of funds from abroad, which drives up the exchange value of the dollar and crowds out net export spending. Thus, deficits can crowd out spending for U.S. exports and reduce purchases of goods produced by import-competing industries.

12.13 → 13. According to the supply-side view of the deficits of the 1980s, supply-side tax cuts increased the profitability of investment in U.S. industries. This attracted investment from abroad. In this way, the deficits, which were caused by the supply-side tax cuts, actually increased investment spending instead of crowding it out. The behavior of the stock market, which rose despite the higher deficits, tends to bear out this view of the deficit's impact on investment.

12.14 → 14. There is some evidence that deficits are not always linked with higher interest rates. One theory is that people recognize that deficits represent higher future tax bills and therefore begin to save for them. The

12.15 ▶ 15. There are many views concerning how best to reduce the deficit. Demand-side economists often propose tax increases. Supply-side economists fear the disincentive effects of higher taxes and often propose cuts in government spending and transfer payments instead. Regarding taxes, traditional supply siders focus on the need for tax incentives for saving and investment, even if this means higher marginal tax rates. Radical supply siders, on the other hand, want to cut tax rates, even if this means that these tax incentives must be eliminated. The Gramm–Rudman–Hollings Act, passed in 1985, provides for automatic budget cuts if Congress and the president are unable to agree on a plan to reduce the budget deficit. The goal of Gramm–Rudman–Hollings is to achieve a balanced federal budget by fiscal year 1991.

12.16 ▶ 16. There are several theories concerning the desirability of a balanced governmental budget. One theory calls for the annually balanced budget, which means that the government could never run a deficit. A second theory calls for a cyclically balanced budget, which means that the government could run a deficit during recessions but must then experience offsetting surpluses during periods of prosperity. Finally, the theory of functional finance holds that the government should focus on stabilizing the economy first and not be tied to a balanced budget in any time frame.

DISCUSSION QUESTIONS

12.1 ▶ 1. A country is experiencing unemployment, income is falling, and output is declining. In what phase of the business cycle is this economy operating? List and describe the characteristics of all other phases of the typical business cycle.

12.2, 12.3, 12.4 ▶ 2. The federal government has just increased purchases of military hardware by $15 million. In addition, personal income taxes have been reduced by $20 million. What type of fiscal policy is being exercised? How will this affect aggregate demand? Aggregate supply? Inflation and unemployment? (Assume *MPC* is 80 percent.) Explain.

12.4 ▶ 3. What happens to disposable income when the government levies an additional $30 million tax? In turn, what will happen to consumption and savings at all levels of income? How is aggregate demand affected differently than it would have been if the government had increased spending instead? What happens to equilibrium income? (Assume *MPC* is 80 percent.)

12.2, 12.3 ▶ 4. Do equal increases or decreases in government spending always have equal effects on the economy? Explain your answer. What economic principle supports your answer?

12.4, 12.5, 12.6

5. Suppose that government spending and taxes both decrease by $10 billion. How does this affect aggregate demand? Suppose that transfer payments and taxes both decrease by $10 billion. How does this affect aggregate demand? Why are the two answers different? Do you need to know the *MPC* to answer this question? Explain.

12.7

6. Suppose aggregate demand, employment, and income are falling in the economy. Without any deliberate government intervention, what might automatically occur in the economy to help cushion these recessionary effects?

12.3

7. Assume the economy has attained macroeconomic equilibrium at a point at which resources are fully employed. If aggregate demand is increased by government spending, what will be the primary effect? If the economy was originally operating below the full-employment output, what would be the primary effect of an increase in aggregate demand?

12.7

8. Do automatic stabilizers always work effectively to absorb the effects caused by changes in aggregate demand on equilibrium income? If the equilibrium level of income is below the full-employment level of income, what would built-in stabilizers automatically do? What would happen if the effects of the stabilizers were felt at precisely the same time as the government was making deliberate attempts to reduce aggregate demand by reducing its spending?

12.8

9. Suppose that government wants to increase both aggregate demand and aggregate supply. What are examples of government policies that could achieve this goal? Explain the reasoning behind your choices.

12.11, 12.12

10. Congress has just voted to reduce tax rates. How will this affect the budget deficit? How will it affect the cyclical and structural deficits?

12.12, 12.14

11. How does an increase in the government's deficit affect the private sector of the economy?

SELECTED READINGS

Blinder, Alan S. *Fiscal Policy in Theory and Practice.* Morristown, NJ: General Learning Press, 1973.

Cagan, Phillip, ed. *Essays in Contemporary Economic Problems: The Economy in Deficit.* Washington, DC: American Enterprise Institute, 1985.

Cagan, Phillip, ed. *Essays in Contemporary Economic Problems: The Impact of the Reagan Program.* Washington, DC: American Enterprise Institute, 1986.

Economic Report of the President, 1985. Washington, DC: Council of Economic Advisors.

Pechman, Joseph, ed. *Setting National Priorities: The 1984 Budget.* Washington, DC: Brookings Institute 1984.

Pechman, Joseph, and Aaron, Henry J. *How Taxes Affect Economic Behavior.* Washington, DC: Brookings Institute, 1981.

Rivlin, Alice, ed. *Economic Choices 1984.* Washington, DC: Brookings Institution, 1984.

PART 5

Monetary Institutions, Theory, and Policy

CHAPTER 13

Money and the Banking System

Having read the chapter, reviewed the chapter summary, and completed the *Study Guide* exercises, you should be able to:

CRIS

13.1 MONEY: Define money and list the main forms of money in today's world.

13.2 FUNCTIONS OF MONEY: List and explain the functions that money performs in a modern economy.

13.3 MONEY SUPPLY: Define the *M*1 money supply and explain how and why it differs from the *M*2 and *M*3 money supply measures.

13.4 MEASURING THE MONEY SUPPLY: Explain why economists find it difficult to accurately measure the money supply.

13.5 ROLE OF FINANCIAL INTERMEDIARIES: Explain the role that financial intermediaries play in a modern economy.

13.6 MECHANICS OF FINANCIAL INTERMEDIATION: Explain how financial intermediation works.

13.7 FRACTIONAL RESERVE BANKING: Explain the principles of fractional reserve banking.

13.8 BANK ASSETS AND LIABILITIES: List the main assets and liabilities of a fractional reserve bank.

13.9 SAFETY OF DEPOSITS: Explain why deposits in a fractional reserve bank are safe under normal conditions.

13.10 MONEY CREATION: Explain how a bank can create money.

13.11 DEPOSIT EXPANSION MULTIPLIER: State the deposit expansion multiplier and explain how the banking system is able to create a relatively large amount of money from a relatively small addition to its reserves.

> **13.12 CHANGING ROLE OF FINANCIAL INSTITUTIONS:** Discuss the changing role of banks and financial intermediaries in the United States.
>
> **13.13 EQUATION OF EXCHANGE:** State the equation of exchange and define each variable in the equation.
>
> **13.14 MECHANICS OF THE EQUATION OF EXCHANGE:** Explain what the equation of exchange means, why it holds, and what it implies about the importance of money in the economy.

When we first looked at macroeconomics, we began by looking at the circular flow diagram, as pictured in Figure 13-1. This diagram is useful because it summarizes many important points about the economy. It shows, for example, that there are five basic sectors in the economy that we must understand: the household, business, government, foreign, and the financial sectors.

This chapter highlights the financial sector. The financial sector receives saving from households and businesses and uses these funds to provide loans to households, businesses, and government. It is this sector that provides the monetary fluid that circulates throughout the economy. The financial sector really binds together the other sectors of the economy using the glue of money and credit.

This chapter begins our study of money, banking, and monetary policy. We will learn what role the financial sector plays in today's world and how that role is changing. Our study of the financial sector will provide us with a better understanding of the entire economy, some new insights into economic theory, and some conflicting views about the proper course for economic policy. We begin our study of the money side of the economy by asking the question, just what is money?

WHAT IS MONEY?

13.1 MONEY

Money
Anything that is generally accepted in exchange for goods and services and in payment of debt.

When you think of the term **money,** many different thoughts come to mind. To some people, money means currency or coins. To others, money means income or wealth. Some people associate money with stocks, bonds, or precious metals such as gold or silver. It is true that money has something to do with all these individual things, but in economics money is a much broader concept. Economists define money as any item that is generally accepted in exchange for goods and services and in payment of debt.

Coins, currency, and checking accounts are money that can be spent directly. Money exists because it satisfies a human and economic need. Other financial instruments have also been invented to satisfy our needs. Credit cards, for example, are a great convenience to many people. Credit cards are not money because they are not accepted in enough different circumstances to meet the definition stated above. Credit cards are really an "instant loan" from a bank or credit card company to the cardholder making a purchase. Savings accounts and certificates of deposit are not money in the strictest sense because they cannot be spent directly. They can only be used to purchase goods and services or pay debt after they have been converted to spendable money such as cash or checking account balances.

FIGURE 13-1   **The Financial Sector in the Circular Flow Model.** The financial sector is a key part of the economy. The financial sector serves as an intermediary between surplus and deficit units. Household and business saving enters the financial sector, where it is used to finance business investments, borrowing by consumers, and deficit spending by the government.

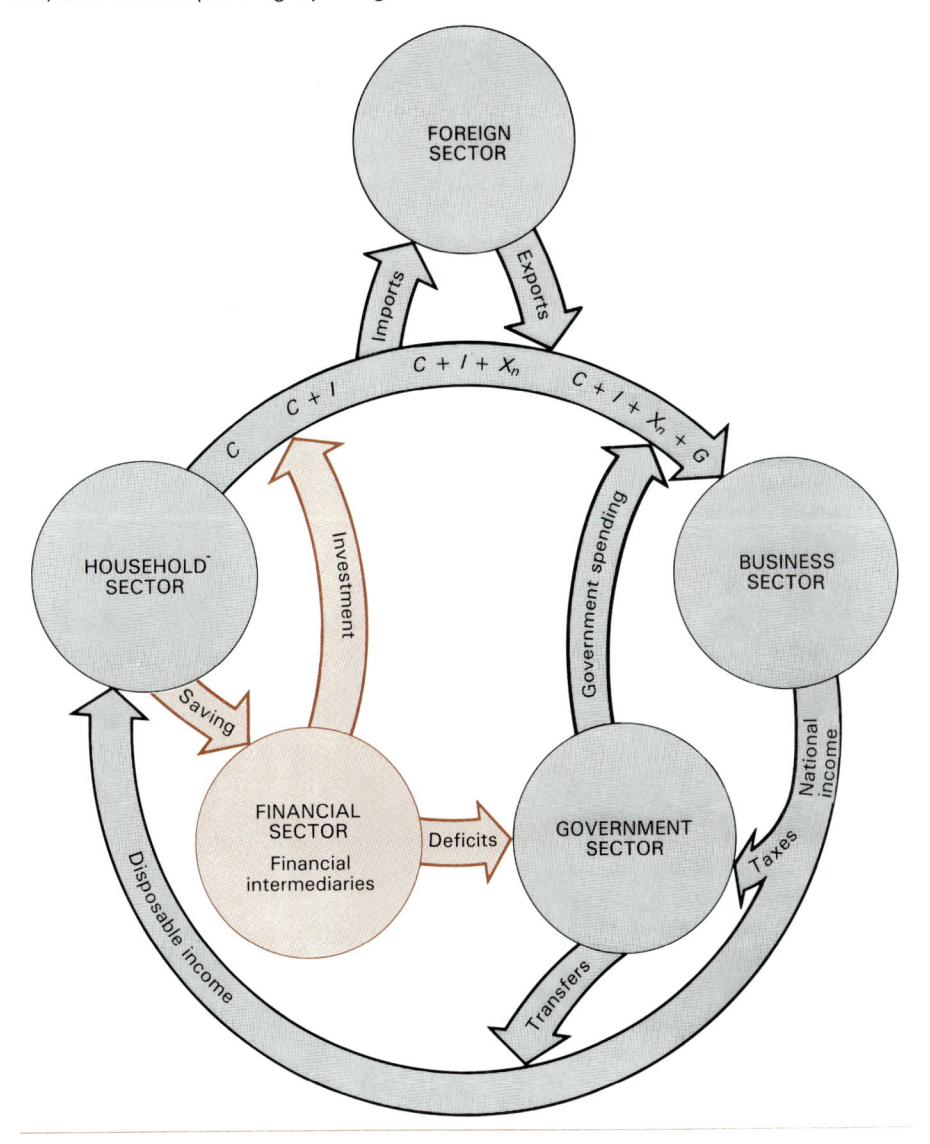

    Money is anything that is generally accepted in exchange for goods and services and in payment of debt. This means that money need not be issued by a government agency or be an item that would be recognized universally as a medium of exchange. On the Yap Island in Micronesia, for example, giant stones are used for money. These stones are so large that they have holes drilled through their center so that logs can be inserted to enable groups of men to carry them when purchases are made. The inhabitants of this U.S. protectorate in the South Pacific are civilized people, yet they choose to use large stones, as they have for years, to make important purchases and pay various debts. Thus stones that would be just rocks if they were on Long Island in New York are forms of currency on Yap Island because they satisfy the Yap Islanders' definition of money.

THE FUNCTIONS OF MONEY

13.2 FUNCTIONS OF MONEY

Many things have served as money over the course of history. Faced with such diversity, it might be difficult to understand what all of these forms of money have in common. Regardless of whether we are using stones, cattle, woodpecker scalps, or coin and currency, anything that is commonly accepted as a medium of exchange, a uniform unit of account, and a store of value is money.

Money as a Medium of Exchange

The greatest single contribution that money makes to an economy is its role as a **medium of exchange.** Money is a mutually acceptable third commodity to the parties in an exchange. It serves as a common denominator for all goods and services. For example, without money, exchange between the village butcher and the village baker would be difficult. In order for exchange to take place, the butcher must want to acquire bread and give up meat and the baker must want to acquire meat and give up bread. They must have what economists call a **coincidence of wants.** If a butcher wanted to acquire bread, he would have to find not just a baker, but a baker who wanted to accept meat in return. If the butcher wanted to acquire bread but the baker wanted fruits and vegetables, the butcher and baker could not trade. Both the butcher and baker would have to spend time and effort searching for a trading partner with whom they would have a coincidence of wants.

Money eliminates the need for a coincidence of wants. Suppose that people in the village economy pick one of their goods to serve as money. If there is money in circulation, both the butcher and the baker would be willing to accept money for their wares. The butcher could buy a loaf of bread from any baker, paying for it with money. Since the money would be mutually acceptable as a means of exchange, the baker could use the same money that he received from the butcher to buy fruits and vegetables that he wants, not just the meat that the butcher produces.

Money reduces the time and effort necessary to make an exchange. We can imagine how slow and inefficient exchange would be today without money. In a single shopping trip, for example, you may purchase 50 different food items. Without money you might have to search out many different sellers who not only had the good you desired, but also were willing to accept the goods you offered in trade. It is difficult to conceive of a contemporary economy being able to function without a form of money to speed up the process of exchange and make it more efficient. Indeed, even primitive societies typically choose some items to serve as money to facilitate exchange. The key to understanding money as a medium of exchange is that it is acceptable to the trading parties in lieu of other goods they desire. Anything that most trading partners are generally willing to accept will circulate as money.

Medium of Exchange
A mutually acceptable third commodity among the two parties in an exchange. Money, as a medium of exchange, serves as a common denominator for all goods and services.

Coincidence of Wants
The necessary condition for a barter exchange to occur, where each party to the exchange must want to acquire what the other party has to offer in exchange for what they are willing to give up. For example, a butcher who wants to acquire bread in return for meat must find and trade with a baker who wants to acquire meat in return for bread.

ECONOMIC ISSUES

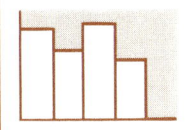

Why Do People Hold Money Balances?

One reason why fruits and vegetables are not a very convenient form of money is that they tend to spoil and lose their value over time. This makes them a poor store of value and an inconvenient medium of exchange. No one would want to hold onto banana-money for a very long period of time because of the risk that it would spoil and lose its worth. This fact is obvious to most of us when we image a world of banana-money or tomato-money, yet we all constantly hold onto paper money balances, even though these balances are constantly losing value.

Money loses value over time when inflation takes place. If you were to hold a dollar for one year in your wallet or even in a checking account, it would buy less in a year than it does now because of inflation's effects on prices. Individuals nevertheless choose to hold some of their wealth in the form of money. Why is this so? The answer is that people hold money because money provides a valuable service. Money makes exchange more convenient and less costly. Money is a highly liquid asset. Liquidity means that money may be quickly transformed into another form of wealth without high transactions costs and without losing much of its value. Some other assets or forms of wealth may not be as liquid. For example, you may hold part of your total wealth in the form of a house. The value of your house may go up or down depending on the conditions in your neighborhood, housing demand, supply, and so on. If you had to convert your home into cash, it might take a long time to sell and would probably involve brokers or real estate agent fees. Your home, therefore, is a less liquid asset than the cash in your wallet or the balance in your checking account.

Economists note that various assets have different degrees of liquidity based on how easily they can be converted into money. Money itself has perfect liquidity because it is already in a spendable form. Savings accounts are slightly less liquid because it is sometimes inconvenient to convert them to cash, such as on nights and weekends when banks are closed. Stocks, bonds, and gold and silver ingots have less liquidity than money or bank accounts, but they are still relatively liquid because organized markets exist to facilitate exchange. Gold and silver jewelry, on the other hand, are less liquid because it is more difficult and costly to buy and sell them at full value. Examples of assets that are less liquid include automobiles, houses, books, clothing, and stereo systems. Assets gain in relative value if they are more liquid because this expands their owner's options.

There are three basic reasons why individuals hold money. Individuals usually hold part of their total wealth in the form of money to meet everyday expenditures (a transactions demand), to act as a cushion against unexpected expenditures (a precautionary demand), and to maintain liquidity in the event that a profitable opportunity for trade or exchange might occur requiring quick action (a speculative demand). Money set aside in a bank account in case of future ill health would be money used as a precautionary asset, while money held in liquid form, such as in a checking account, in anticipation of buying stocks at the moment the price is right would be a speculative asset.

Uniform Unit of Accounting
Money, as a uniform unit of accounting, provides a common basis of comparison for the monetary value of goods and services.

Barter Economy
A system with no money, where goods are exchanged for other goods.

Money as a Uniform Unit of Accounting

Another vital function money serves is in providing a **uniform unit of accounting** that enables consumers and producers to effectively compare the prices of the goods and services they desire. A simple Ford Escort might cost $8,000, while a luxury Ford L.T.D. might have a basic price of $16,000. The use of money enables the consumer to quickly see that the L.T.D. costs twice as much as the Escort. In a **barter economy,** one with no money where good are traded for goods, this process of comparison would be much more difficult. An Escort could cost 100 cattle. The L.T.D. might cost 20 sheep. Here a direct comparison of the prices of the two goods would be much more difficult. This comparison would also involve the buyer's individual evaluation of the relative value of sheep and cattle. It is for this reason that we convert the market value of all goods and services to

374 *Money and the Banking System*

the common denominator of money. The gross national product is measured in dollars for this reason. It is a uniform unit of account that allows us to place relative values on all the millions of goods and services we produce.

Money as a Store of Value

Store of Value
As a store of value, money enables its holder to convert goods and services into stored-up purchasing power for the future.

The third major function of money is as a **store of value.** Money enables the holder to convert goods and services into stored-up purchasing power for the future. Suppose, for example, that you operate a tomato farm and you want to save for your children's college education. If you try to save the tomatoes you grow, within a short time period you will find yourself the proud owner of some very rotten economic goods. If you cannot capture or store up the economic value of your crop in some way, you may lose that value. Money enables you to sell your tomato crop for money, storing up its economic value and thereby reserving your purchasing power for some time in the future. If you hold money, it can in many cases store up value better than the goods or services for which it was traded.

It is hard to imagine spending even a day without using money as a medium of exchange, store of value, or unit of accounting. This is because these services of money are so very valuable to us. Yet these services are so obvious that we usually take them for granted. There is one more service that money provides that we also tend to take for granted. As explained in Chapter 1, money frees us from the burdens of a barter economy and therefore allows increased specialization and exchange. Buyers and sellers do not need to take each others' desires and preferences into account in a transaction. All goods in a market can be exchanged for money, and money can be used to buy all market goods. Money simplifies exchange and therefore increases the economy's efficiency.

KEY CONCEPTS 13.1, 13.2

Money is anything that is readily accepted in exchange for goods and services and in payment of debt. Many items have served as money over the years. Money provides a store of value, a standard unit of accounting, and a medium of exchange.

DEFINITIONS OF THE MONEY SUPPLY

13.3 MONEY SUPPLY

Money Supply
A measure of the total amount of money available in an economy in a given time period.

People do not need to hold money. They could choose, instead, to hold real assets such as autos and textbooks. If they did this, however, they would find it difficult to make many transactions. The amount of money that people choose to hold is an indication of the amount and the type of economic actions they expect to undertake. Economists measure the **money supply,** the total amount of money available in the economy, because the amount of money people hold (the money supply) is closely associated with the amount of spending they undertake (aggregate demand).

There are several different money supply definitions in use today. Each of the money supply measures attempts to gauge a different aspect of economic activity. For example, it is sometimes useful to know how much money is available for immediate spending on goods and services; but at other times, it is more useful to try to measure the availability of funds to purchase items such as investment goods and consumer durables, which are

Definitions of the Money Supply 375

TABLE 13-1

Money Supply Measures, December 1984

Item	$ billion
Currency	158.0
Demand deposits *checks*	248.3
Other checkable accounts	143.0
Travelers checks	5.2
*M*1 money supply	554.5
Money market mutual funds	168.1
Money market deposit accounts	410.0
Savings accounts	294.3
Small-denomination time deposits	897.1
Eurodollar net balances	81.5
Other short-term liquid assets	138.9
*M*2 money supply	2376.3
Large-denomination time deposits	409.7
Other liquid assets	201.3
*M*3 money supply	2987.3

Source. Economic Report of the President, 1985, Tables B-61, B-62.

[handwritten note: growth here = savings - people hedging against the future]

generally financed through loans. Economists therefore calculate several different measures of monetary aggregates, each of which provides useful information about some aspect of economic activity. These measures are presented in Table 13-1.

The *M*1 Money Supply

The first money supply measure is appropriately enough called ***M*1**. This is the measure of the money supply that most closely corresponds to the definition of money given early in this chapter, namely items that are generally accepted in exchange for goods and services and in payment of debt. The other monetary aggregates discussed below, while termed money supplies, are really attempts to measure more than money alone.

The *M*1 money definition is equal to the amount of coin, currency, **demand deposits,** travelers checks, and other checkable deposits that people hold in the economy. *M*1 is a measure of the amount of money people hold in a form that can be immediately spent. Since it concentrates on money as a medium of exchange, *M*1 is a good indicator of consumers' short-run spending plans.

Currency and coin is used for little else but to transact purchases. Demand deposits, which are checking account balances at commerical banks, are also part of this measure of the money supply. We usually hold checking account balances with the intent to write checks to pay for purchases. Today there are other types of bank accounts upon which we can write checks. **NOW accounts (negotiable orders of withdrawal)** and similar accounts in this category are really savings accounts upon which limited numbers of checks can be drawn. These accounts are all included in the *M*1 money measures, but demand deposit balances are the largest single component of the measure. Most spending in the economy takes place through checking accounts.

M1
The money supply in its narrowest form, defined as the sum of coin and currency in circulation, demand deposits in commercial banks, other checkable accounts in depository institutions, and travelers checks.

Demand Deposits
Checking accounts traditionally held only in commercial banks; today they are held at most financial institutions.

NOW Accounts (Negotiable Orders of Withdrawal)
Bank accounts upon which we can quickly and easily write checks.

M2
A broader definition of the money supply, which includes *M*1 plus savings and small time deposits (under $100,000), money market mutual funds, overnight loans from customers to commercial banks, and overnight Eurodollar deposits held by residents of the United States.

Time Deposits
Savings account balances.

Money Market Deposit Accounts (MMDA)
A type of bank account that pays interest rates that correspond to those offered by money market mutual funds.

Money Market Mutual Fund (MMMF)
A system in which the funds of many individuals are pooled and used to purchase corporate and government bonds.

Eurodollar Deposits
Dollar denominated deposits held in banks outside of the United States.

Portfolio
A collection of assets. A stock portfolio, for example, is a collection of different quantities and types of corporate stock shares.

M3
This more broadly defined category of the money supply includes *M*2 plus large-denomination (over $100,000) time deposits and long-term loans by customers to financial institutions.

The *M*2 Money Supply

The *M*2 money supply definition is an attempt to measure how able households and businesses are to purchase goods and services, using both readily spendable money (*M*1) and funds in banks accounts to which they have relatively easy access. The *M*2 money definition includes all the items in *M*1 plus **time deposits, money market deposit accounts** at banks, **money market mutual fund (MMMF)** balances, and **Eurodollar deposits.** The additional assets included in *M*2 are items that people usually hold as a store of value. These are really savings-type accounts. It is important to measure these assets because they give an indication of the long-term spending plans of consumers and because they make up much of the wealth on which people base their purchases.

Individuals frequently hold money as a store of value in the form of saving accounts, or time deposits, such as six-month savings certificates. These are funds that must be left on deposit for a specified period of time before withdrawal. In the case of the six-month certificate, a substantial interest penalty for early withdrawal is required. In the strictest sense of the law, the depository institution is not required to honor requests for withdrawal prior to the six-month maturity. Even in the case of standard passbook savings accounts, the bank usually has the legal right to, but does not enforce, the requirement of a 30-day prior notice for withdrawals.

The *M*2 money definition also includes money market deposit accounts offered by banks and money market mutual funds (MMMFs) offered by other financial institutions. These are popular accounts that are offered by a variety of financial institutions, including banks, brokerage firms, and private investment organizations. Money from thousands of individual savers is pooled and used to purchase private and public bonds. This allows the private savers to acquire fractional ownership of a diversified **portfolio** of securities and receive a high interest return, which is impossible for an individual to do with a relatively small amount of money. Many MMMFs even have arrangements with commercial banks that allow checking account-like access to the MMMF balance. Eurodollar deposits are deposits in foreign banks and other foreign financial institutions that are denominated in dollars. Years ago, these deposits existed mostly in Western Europe, but today they are held all over the world. Nevertheless, they are still referred to as Eurodollars.

The *M*3 Money Supply

*M*3 is a third and even broader definition of the money supply. It includes all of *M*2 plus large-denomination (over $100,000) time deposits and long-term loans by customers to financial institutions such as savings and loan associations and commercial banks. By including these large-denomination bank holdings, *M*3 gives a good indication of the availability of both money and loans in the economy. The additional items included in *M*3, but not in *M*2, are bank accounts that cannot readily be drawn upon by the depositor but which represent an important source of loanable funds for the banking system.

While *M*1 is a measure of money in the textbook sense of an asset that can be immediately transacted, and *M*2 measures the store of value available in the short run for all types of purchases, *M*3 is an indicator of the overall availability of money and loans in the economy. Another distinction between *M*2 and *M*3 is that *M*3 includes the part of the money supply that is widely controlled by institutions, such as insurance companies and pension funds, as opposed to individuals. As a store of value, this *M*3 compo-

TABLE 13-2

Growth Rates for Money Supply Measures, Percentage Change from Previous Year

Year	M1	M2	M3
1973	5.5	6.9	11.2
1974	4.4	5.5	8.7
1975	4.9	12.6	9.5
1976	6.6	13.7	11.9
1977	8.1	10.6	12.3
1978	8.3	8.0	11.8
1979	7.2	7.8	9.5
1980	6.6	8.9	10.3
1981	6.5	10.0	12.4
1982	8.8	8.9	9.4
1983	9.8	12.0	10.4
1984	5.8	8.4	10.9
1985	11.9	8.1	7.3

Source. *Economic Report of the President, 1986,* Table B-64.

nent behaves differently from those funds controlled primarily by individuals and small investors because it is more sensitive to changes in interest returns.

Table 13-2 shows that the three money supply measures we have discussed do not grow at the same rate. The interest-earning accounts that are included in *M*2 and *M*3 have grown faster in most years than the lower-interest spending money accounts included in *M*1. This difference in growth rates exists because economic events affect the different money supply measures in different ways. When interest rates are high, for example, people take their funds out of regular demand deposits, which generally pay no interest, and other checkable accounts, which offer relatively low interest returns, and move these funds into other types of accounts that offer a better return. This slows down the growth in *M*1 and increases the growth rate for *M*2. This is what happened in 1981, for example.

13.4 MEASURING THE MONEY SUPPLY

The money supply has become a difficult puzzle for the economics profession. Financial institutions are finding more and more types of services that they can offer to their customers. The traditional money supply measures shift in unexpected ways as consumers move their funds around to take advantage of these services. When people shift money from bank checking accounts to money market mutual funds, for example, *M*1 goes down and *M*2 goes up. But consumers are still able to spend their funds by simply writing a check. *M*1 and *M*2 have changed, but the effect on the money supply is unclear if we take a purely practical view. Thus it is hard to decide if the economy has really changed in any meaningful way. The principle difference is, perhaps, that money deposited in commerical banks is usually loaned to consumers and small businesses, while money in MMMFs is loaned to governments or large corporations. Economic forecasting has become a more difficult art and science in recent years because it is more difficult to determine whether the money supply is really increasing or decreasing or whether internal shifts are taking place within the financial sector.

Money is at once the liquid that lubricates the economy's gears and the glue that binds the various parts of the economy together. Most money, as we have seen, exists as demand, time, or other types of accounts within the

KEY CONCEPTS 13.3, 13.4

Several measures of the money supply exist. The most important money supply measures are *M*1, *M*2, and *M*3. *M*1 measures highly liquid assets, such as demand deposits, currency, and travellers checks. *M*2 includes other checkable accounts and time deposits, among other items. *M*3 includes major sources of credit availability, such as large denomination certificates of deposit. Each money measure tells us something different about the economy's ability to purchase goods and services (*M*1 and *M*2) or the availability of credit (*M*3). Deregulation of the financial sector and the creation of new asset forms such as money market mutual funds have made it more difficult to accurately measure the money supply in recent years.

PROBLEMS OF THE FINANCIAL SECTOR

13.5 ROLE OF FINANCIAL INTERMEDIARIES

Financial Intermediaries
Institutions that act as middlemen, completing credit transactions between savers and borrowers.

Surplus Units
Households, businesses, and governments that desire to consume fewer resources in the present time period than are currently available to them.

Deficit Units
Households, businesses, and governments that desire to consume more resources in the present time period than are currently available to them.

The financial sector of the economy is made up of a variety of institutions that supply different services to different groups. They have one thing in common, however; they all serve as **financial intermediaries.** Figure 13-2 illustrates the role of financial intermediaries. Financial intermediaries exist because they solve a set of problems that many groups face.

Some groups in our economy are **surplus units.** Being a surplus unit means that an individual, government, or business has more resources than it wishes to consume in the current time period. A family with high income now, for example, might desire to delay consumption until its retirement years, when it expects its income to be lower. We can think of these surplus units as savers who wish to save some money for future consumption instead of using it to finance present consumption. A family that saves $10,000 for retirement wishes to even out an otherwise uneven flow of consumption activities by spending less and saving during working years to finance greater spending during retirement years.

Other groups in the economy can be called **deficit units.** These are individuals, businesses, and governments who desire to consume more resources than they have available in the current time period. We can think of deficit units as borrowers. Borrowers want to alter their consumption of resources over time. Deficit units desire to consume more goods and services in the current time period than they have available. In return, they must be willing to reduce their consumption in later periods in order to repay the loan. A person who borrows $10,000 to buy a new car is able to consume the car's services now (rather than waiting while this amount is saved up) but must reduce consumption for several years in the future while the principal and interest on the car loan are repaid.

We discussed the benefits of mutually advantageous exchange in Chapter 1. It is clear that there is the potential for mutually advantageous exchange between surplus units and deficit units in the economy. Consider the examples used to illustrate surplus and deficit units in the above discussion. The surplus (saver) units wish to exchange current use of $10,000 in resources for greater income in the future. The deficit (borrower) units desire to increase consumption in the present by $10,000 and are willing to give up resources in the future to achieve this goal. Both groups can benefit if the saver loans money now to the borrower, who repays it with some mutually agreeable amount of interest in the future.

FIGURE 13-2

The Principles of Financial Intermediation. Surplus units are households, businesses, and governments who have more current resources than they wish to consume in the present time period. Deficit units are households, businesses, and governments who wish to consume more resources in the current time period than they have available. The financial intermediation system efficiently links together surplus and deficit units, providing higher returns, lower loan costs, and greater flexibility and liquidity.

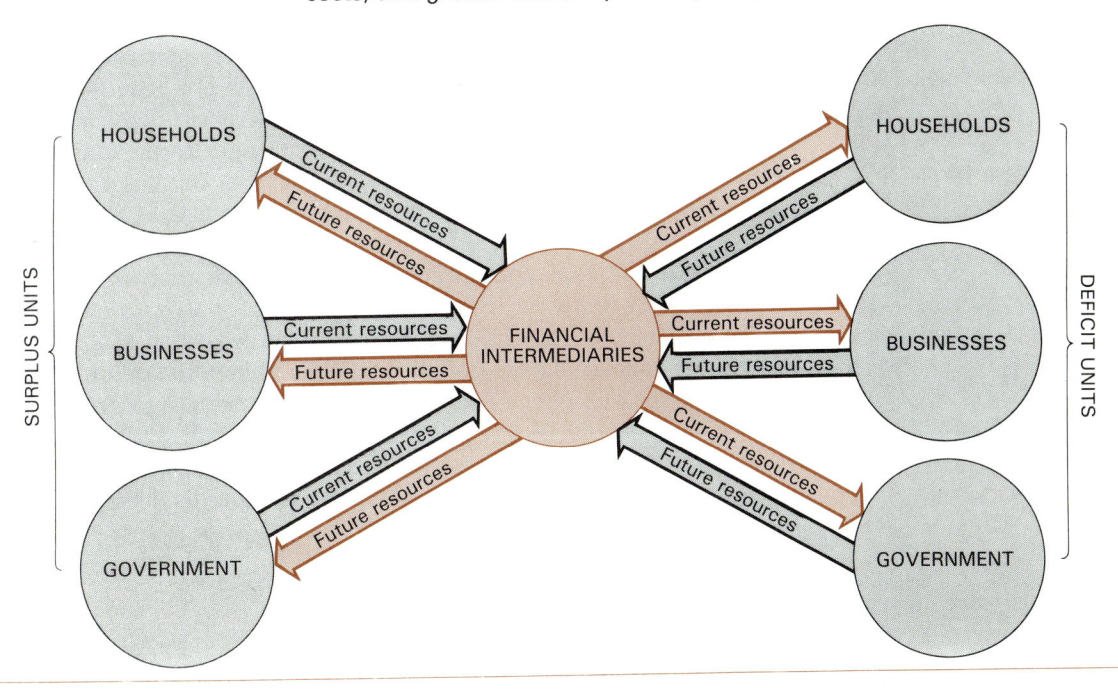

Capacity
The ability of a borrower to generate sufficient revenue (through labor or investment) to repay a loan.

Character
The tendency of a borrower to honor liabilities.

Collateral
Assets that are pledged against an obligation. Collateral becomes the property of the lender if a loan is not repaid.

Loans are exchanges between surplus (saver) units and deficit (borrower) units that make both sides of the exchange better off because both sides are able to have what they desire. Unfortunately, it is often difficult for borrowers and lenders to get together to make these mutually advantageous exchanges. Several factors tend to get in the way of these useful transactions, including information costs, risk, and preferences regarding liquidity.

Information costs can be high when it comes to making a loan transaction. First, the borrower and lender need to discover one another so that the exchange can be discussed. Then, once they come together, there is much costly data to be gathered. Bankers look at the potential borrower's "Three Cs": **capacity, character,** and **collateral.** The lender, for example, must evaluate the purpose of the loan and the economic status of the borrower to assure that the loan will be repaid. This is done to be sure that the borrower has the capacity to repay the loan. Then the lender's prior borrowing history must be checked to see if his or her borrowing "character" is sound and prior loans were repaid on schedule. Finally, the lender must also determine the value of the collateral, which are the assets that are pledged to the lender. Collateral can be seized if the loan is not repaid. All of this information is costly to gather. Sometimes the information costs can exceed the potential gains from a loan transaction. In this case, high information costs prevent an otherwise mutually advantageous exchange.

Risk is a second problem. Any loan has some risk of nonrepayment. Some types of loans are clearly riskier than others. Lenders seldom want to put all their eggs in one basket. They frequently try to reduce risk. A large lender can do this by acquiring a portfolio of loans to different types of

380 Money and the Banking System

borrowers in different types of businesses. Not all of these loans are likely to experience problems at the same time, so the overall risk on the portfolio is less than the risk on any individual loan. Small savers, however, often do not have sufficient funds to diversify their portfolio to reduce its risk. This inability, if not corrected, would tend to discourage many loans because of the high risk involved.

In order for a mutually advantageous loan to be made, borrower and lender must also have similar preferences regarding the term of the loan. That is, the period of time of the loan, such as three months or five years, must be acceptable to both groups. This can be a problem because savers often want to lend for relatively short periods of time in order to maintain high **liquidity,** while borrowers often prefer longer-term loans. This difference in term preference can reduce the number of mutually advantageous loans. Lenders want their loans to have high liquidity, so that they can be quickly and cheaply converted into other forms of assets. Borrowers, on the other hand, want to keep the terms of the loan constant so that they can effectively plan to use their resources.

Liquidity
The characteristic of an asset that enables it to be quickly and easily converted into cash without loss of value.

The problems of high information costs, undiversified risk, and differing preferences concerning the liquidity of loans reduce the potential for mutually advantageous exchange between individual surplus and deficit units. Financial intermediaries are middlemen, as discussed in Chapter 1, who specialize in services that reduce these costs and therefore increase mutually advantageous exchanges between borrowers and lenders.

HOW FINANCIAL INTERMEDIARIES WORK

13.6 MECHANICS OF FINANCIAL INTERMEDIATION

Aggregation
The principle whereby coincidence of wants is more easily attained when surplus and deficit units are brought together in large, organized groups.

Financial intermediaries increase the number of mutually advantageous exchanges between surplus units and deficit units by reducing the information costs associated with loans and by using the benefits of **aggregation** to reduce risk and term-preference difficulties and increase liquidity. It is sometimes the case that when many individuals are aggregated, or brought together in some sense, the group has different economic properties than its individual members. By aggregating savers and lenders, financial intermediaries are able to increase the number of mutually advantageous exchanges between them. Here is how one type of financial intermediary, a bank, accomplishes these goals.

High information costs, as noted earlier, reduce the benefits of loan transactions. One reason why information costs are high to individual savers is that they are unable to specialize in the skills necessary to effectively determine capacity, character, and collateral. An attorney or auto mechanic, for example, benefits most by specializing in his or her particular occupational field rather than gaining expertise in the particular skills needed to assess these loan factors. Banks, however, make so many loans that it pays them to train and employ specialists who can more easily and more accurately assess capacity, character, and collateral than could most nonspecialists. The bank can also employ large data bases and credit agencies to aid in making loan decisions. In addition, it can employ other specialists to solicit depositors and seek out borrowers, thus bringing these two groups together indirectly through the bank.

While it is obviously costly to employ these many resources in running the bank and making loans, the benefits of specialization allow the bank to reduce the information costs associated with any individual loan, thereby increasing the potential gain available to the borrower and lender. Individuals therefore deposit their funds in banks so as to gain the benefits of the lower information costs that banks produce. The bank collects a profit on the loans that it makes, but the net return that savers receive, even after this profit is taken, is still greater than it would have been without the information cost savings.

Banks pool, or aggregate, the funds of many savers. Many households and businesses deposit funds in the bank for different periods of time. The bank uses these funds to make loans. The fact that the bank operates with a pool of funds, and not just the savings of one household or firm, allows it greater flexibility, which can reduce risk, increase liquidity, and reduce problems of term preference.

An individual with just a few thousand dollars of savings would face a difficult risk decision making a loan were it not for banks and other financial intermediaries. If you loan all your money to a friend, and the friend cannot repay you, then you have lost everything. Banks reduce this risk problem by taking savings from many different people and using these funds to make many different types of loans to many different borrowers. The risk of nonpayment is therefore spread out widely, and risk is reduced. If one borrower fails to repay a loan, this has only an extremely small effect on any individual depositor of a large bank. The aggregation of savers' funds into a pool of loans in effect protects individual savers from problems caused by the failure of an individual borrower to repay. The return on this pool of loans is likely to be more stable and safer than is any individual loan with the same rate of return.

Financial intermediaries such as banks also use the process of aggregation to get around problems of differences in preferences regarding the term and liquidity of loans. Suppose, for example, that savers always want to make short-term highly liquid loans, but that borrowers always want to get long-term loans. A financial intermediary can satisfy both, within limits. The bank can make long-term loans using short-term deposits so long as new deposits by savers are adequate to pay off the people who wish to withdraw funds from the bank. If new deposits are sufficient to pay any withdrawals, then the initial deposits can be loaned for relatively long periods of time.

Travellers check companies use this principle to make funds. When you purchase $100 of travellers checks for a vacation, for example, you pay the travellers check company $100. The company uses this money to redeem the travellers checks as you spend them. In effect, you lend the company $100 now and it repays you by paying $100 to merchants that you designate. There is a period of time, however, between the moment you give the travellers check company $100 and the moment, perhaps several months later, when they pay the $100 to the merchants. In this period of time, the travellers check company has use of your funds. It is often the case that another person's travellers check purchase of $100 can be used to pay your $100 of bills. The result, if this process continues, is that the travellers check firm has virtually infinite interest-free use of your $100 plus the money of others in the same situation. The money available is called the **float**.

The float ($100 in the example above) can be counted upon to exist for a long period of time even though each travellers check transaction tends to be very short-term in nature. Travellers check companies often make long-term real-estate investments based on short-term floats. In the same way, banks can make long-term loans with short-term high-liquidity deposits so long as future deposits can be counted upon to offset future withdrawals.

Float
An asset that is temporarily owned by two individuals, as sometimes occurs in financial transactions that take place over a period of time.

Credit Unions
Nonprofit organizations that provide bank-like services to members of a particular social or occupational group. Many labor unions have formed credit unions to provide financial services to their members, for example.

Mutual Funds
Organizations that sell individual household shares in a diversified portfolio of assets.

Insurance Companies
Firms that accept current payments (insurance premiums) from clients in return for contingent claims to the future payment of specified sums (insurance claims).

Pension Funds
Organizations that use funds that workers and employers save for retirement to invest in stocks, bonds, and real assets. Pension fund assets are used to provide retirement income for participating workers.

Fractional Reserve Banking
The banking system that requires banks to keep only a portion of their total deposits in the form of cash reserves to meet the needs of their customers withdrawals. Remaining reserves may be utilized for profit-making purposes such as extending loans or purchasing securities.

> 13.7
> FRACTIONAL RESERVE
> BANKING

Banks, including savings and loans and similar organizations, are very important to the economy, but they are only one type of financial intermediary. **Credit unions, mutual funds, insurance companies, pension funds,** and other similar institutions also act as financial intermediaries, linking surplus units with deficit units. They all earn their keep by reducing information costs, diversifying risk, and providing greater liquidity.

Mutual funds, for example, take the savings of thousands of families and use them to invest in stocks or bonds. The fund's managers specialize in making these investment decisions, making them more efficient than their individual clients at this task. The mutual fund then invests in a diversified portfolio of many different stocks or bonds, rather than just one or two. This allows a higher average return with lower associated risk. Finally, the mutual fund can provide the individual investor with high liquidity while still engaging in long-term investments. The fund need not sell off its holdings, and perhaps bear an untimely loss, when an individual wants to "cash out" his or her fund shares. It is generally the case that new "deposits" into the fund can be used to pay "withdrawals" by those wishing to leave the fund.

Financial intermediaries provide services that are very important to today's economy. Without financial intermediaries we would find it much more difficult to get loans and more difficult, as well, to save for future consumption. Our economy would be a different world without the valuable services of the financial intermediaries. We can better understand how financial intermediaries work by looking at the principles of operation of what is perhaps the most important type of financial intermediary, a bank.

HOW BANKS WORK

Modern banking was invented about 500 years ago, in Renaissance Florence. Although banking has changed in many ways in the past 500 years, much has remained the same. We can learn much about how banks work today by looking at the operations of simple ancient banks.

The first banks were not really banks at all. Ancient goldsmiths often held deposits of gold for their customers. Gold was the medium of exchange with which goods and services were bought and sold. Rather than incur the risk of carrying all their gold around with them, individuals would deposit their gold with the goldsmith in return for a receipt (or certificate of deposit). Whenever someone wanted to make a purchase, the individual returned to the goldsmith and withdrew enough gold to make the exchange. When individuals sold goods or services or acquired gold in any way, they would deposit that gold with the smith. There was a constant flow of both depositors and those withdrawing gold through the goldsmith's shop daily.

The goldsmith noted something interesting and possibly to his advantage. At the end of the day, once the depositors and withdrawers had completed their business, there was always about the same amount of gold left. Deposits and withdrawals were about equal, on a daily basis, leaving the bulk of the gold that was kept on hand untouched. The smith then began to loan out a part of these excess gold balances, charging a fee, or interest rate, for its use. Goldsmiths, by making loans, became the first **fractional reserve banks.** That is, only a fraction of their deposits were actually kept on hand for the use of their depositors. The remaining funds were loaned out to provide interest income to the bank and its depositors.

FIGURE 13-3

How a Fractional Reserve Bank Works. A new deposit into a fractional reserve bank is conceptually split into two flows. Part of the deposit is held as required reserves to back up bank deposits. The reserve requirement is the fraction of the deposit that must legally be held as required reserves. The remaining excess reserves are used to make loans and certain investments, such as the purchase of government securities.

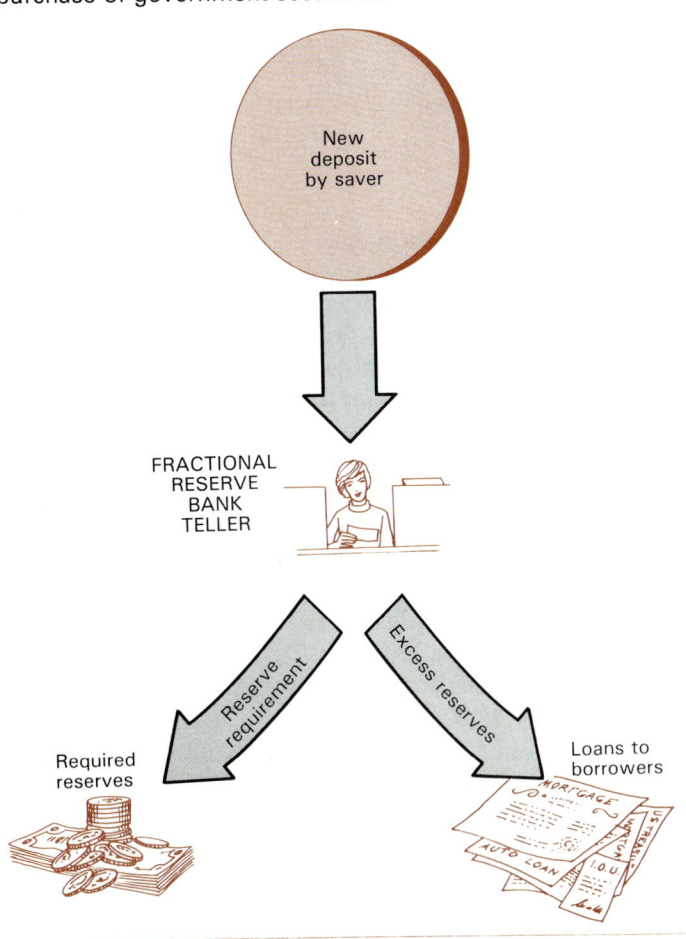

The accounts of depositors were not reduced when these loans were made. Each depositor could get his or her full account, if necessary, so long as all depositors did not withdraw everything at once. The fraction of total deposits that the goldsmith kept on hand was sufficient to meet the normal withdrawal requirements of his customers. In effect, their individual gold had not been reduced, and yet there was now more gold in circulation. The borrowers could use the gold and repay with interest.

Table 13-3 illustrates the basic principle of fractional reserve banking. Only part of an initial deposit need be held by the bank as a reserve against future withdrawals. The remainder of the funds can be used to make loans, which are ultimately spent and redeposited in the banking system.

The goldsmith who first discovered fractional reserve banking had achieved the simplest and yet the most important of commercial banking feats. He had expanded the money supply by making loans from the "unused" deposits of gold. The goldsmith had done what generations of alchemists had failed to do. The goldsmith actually created money when he made loans based on deposits.

TABLE 13-3 A Fractional Reserve Bank's Account

Assets ($ millions)		Liabilities ($ millions)	
Required reserves	100	Deposits	1000
Loans	750		
Securities	100		
Excess reserves	50		
Total assets	1000	Total liabilities	1000

Commerical Banks
Financial institutions with the primary purpose of collecting funds from depositors and loaning them out at a profit.

Bank Liabilities
Those items on the bank's balance sheet that are owed to someone else by the bank. Claims upon the bank, such as demand deposits, are the bank's liabilities.

Bank Assets
Those items that the bank itself owns. Claims the bank has upon others are the bank's assets. Banks primarily hold their assets in the form of loans, reserves, securities, buildings, and equipment.

Bank Reserves
Funds held by banks to meet the withdrawal demands of depositors. Reserves are held in the form of vault cash or deposits held at the Federal Reserve.

13.8 BANK ASSETS AND LIABILITIES

Required Reserves
The minimum amount of total reserves that a bank is required by law to hold. The reserve requirement sets the legal minimum percentage of deposits that banks must maintain as reserves.

Excess Reserves
The amount of reserves that a bank has above and beyond its legally required reserves.

As time passed, the number of depositors grew and the number of receipts for gold (certificates of deposit) the goldsmith issued also grew. The receipts assured the owners that they could withdraw their gold. Occasionally, buyers would realize that they might be able to trade the gold receipts for goods rather than have to take the time and effort to go get the gold. Buyers would sign over their gold receipts to sellers. This would order the goldsmith to pay the gold represented by the receipts to the sellers or persons who now held the gold receipts. The sellers could then take the gold receipts to the goldsmith and collect the gold. Or as an alternative, the sellers could trade the gold receipts to others for goods, and those persons could collect the gold. The gold receipts began to circulate as money, enabling buyers and sellers to transact exchanges much more quickly and efficiently. These widely circulated gold receipts were the first form of paper currency. People seldom needed to actually go to the smith to collect the gold since they could buy the goods and services they needed with the gold receipts.

People also sometimes found it convenient to pay for an item with a letter written to the goldsmith instructing him to pay a specific amount of gold to a certain payee. These letters, which might have begun "Pay to the order of . . ." were the world's first checks. Most transactions today take place with currency and checks. Modern **commercial banks** and other financial institutions owe a great debt to the ancient goldsmiths who invented the concepts of loans, currency, and checks.

The Assets and Liabilities of Modern Commercial Banks

One way to understand how modern banks work is to analyze their books. Accounting principles hold that we can understand how an organization works by looking at its assets and its liabilities.

Bank liabilities are what the bank owes to someone else. Deposits are a bank's biggest liability, because the bank owes these funds to its depositors. **Bank assets** consist of what the bank itself owns or what others owe to the bank. Loans are the most important assets of a bank because loans represent funds that borrowers owe to the bank. Banks hold their assets primarily in the form of reserves, loans, securities, and other assets like buildings and equipment.

Bank reserves are those funds the bank holds to meet the withdrawal demands of depositors. Bank reserves are divided into two categories, **required reserves** that banks must hold, by law, to meet depositor needs and **excess reserves** that banks hold over and above the legal requirement. Reserves generally are held in the form of vault cash or deposits in the

Federal Reserve Bank
A reference to one of the 12 district banks that make up the Federal Reserve System.

Central Bank
The organization in a nation that determines monetary policy, regulates the banking system, and engages in international economic relations. The Federal Reserve is the U.S. central bank.

Securities
Assets that represent payment obligations that one party owes to another. Securities pay interest and therefore produce income for their holder.

federal reserve bank, our nation's **central bank.** They earn no interest and are therefore not a source of revenue for the bank. Banks therefore face a strong incentive not to keep more of their assets in the form of reserves than is actually necessary. Other forms of assets, such as loans, do produce interest income for banks and are therefore more profitable forms in which to hold assets.

Loans are the largest asset of commercial banks. These are funds borrowers owe to the bank and upon which they pay interest. The basic business of commercial banks is to collect funds from depositors and to then loan them out at a profit. The asset of loans is offset by the liabilities of time deposits and demand deposits. The loan is what a borrower owes to the bank. Time and demand deposits are what the bank owes to its depositors.

Commercial banks also hold part of their assets as **securities.** These are payment obligations that others owe to the bank. The United States government sells U.S. securities to banks. When banks buy such securities, they are in effect making loans to the U.S. government at an interest rate. The same can be said of all the other types of securities commercial banks buy and hold. They are in reality loans (although highly secure loans) made by the banks to the issuers of the securities.

Table 13-3 shows the accounts of a simplified hypothetical bank. This bank must, by law, hold 10 percent of its total deposits as required reserves. Note that deposits are listed as a liability, which is offset by the assets of required reserves, loans, securities, and excess reserves. This bank has excess reserves of $50 million, so it has funds available to purchase securities or make $50 million of additional loans. Any new deposit into the bank would increase its liabilities (deposits) and its assets (required and excess reserves), thus making it possible for the bank to make even more loans.

13.9 SAFETY OF DEPOSITS

Why Deposits Are Safe

Commercial banks keep only a small portion of their total deposits in the form of cash reserves. The remainder of the deposits are put into other assets, such as loans and securities, from which the bank earns profits. This is what fractional reserve banking is all about. Like the goldsmiths, modern day commerical banks could not immediately repay all depositors at once if there were a "run" on the bank. This does not mean, however, that fractional reserve banking is risky or an unsound business practice. Except for periods of great uncertainty, the public has, over time, kept faith in our banking system and not withdrawn all their funds at once. Even if everyone did withdraw their funds, what would they do with them then? Money hidden in a tin can in the back yard or used to stuff a mattress does not draw interest. Any mass withdrawal is likely to be followed by mass redeposits. Accordingly, all that is necessary for a system of fractional reserve banking to work well is that the depositing public maintain faith in the system.

To help provide this faith and stability in the banking system, the federal government set up the **federal deposit insurance corporation (FDIC)** to insure the deposits of bank customers against loss. Banks do occasionally fail today, due to bad management, bad luck, or both. The Federal Reserve and the Comptroller of the Currency monitor bank stability and try to arrange for a strong bank to buy or merge with a weak bank to prevent bankruptcy. When banks do collapse, however, the FDIC pays the depositors the value of their individual deposits up to a maximum of $100,000 each

The Federal Deposit Insurance Corporation (FDIC)
The FDIC insures each deposit account in commercial banks up to $100,000. This organization was created by the federal government to generate faith and stability in commercial banks.

ECONOMIC ISSUES

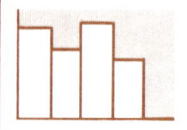

Banking Crises of the 1980s

Not everyone who reads the text section on why deposits are safe will be comforted by it. Many banks have failed or teetered on the brink of failure in the 1980s. Banks in general are safe, but individual banks can still fail, as the following case studies make clear.

Penn Square Bank of Oklahoma City

Banking has become a very competitive business in recent years. Not all banks have been able to survive this competition. The failure of the Penn Square Bank provided the first major banking crisis of the 1980s.

The Penn Square Bank boomed in the late 1970s by making energy loans. These loans went for speculative oil and gas exploration schemes. Such loans looked good in the late 1970s, when high energy costs had everyone's attention. Penn Square acted in association with many other banks, including large ones such as Continental Illinois and Seattle First National Bank, to put together many big-buck energy loans. Many of these loans were not sufficiently researched, however. The borrowers couldn't repay their loans, especially in the early 1980s when energy prices fell dramatically. Penn Square's loans were made without sufficient information and the risks were not properly diversified. The result was traumatic to Penn Square's depositors and to the national banking system.

The Penn Square Bank was declared insolvent in 1982. Bank regulators decided that Penn Square was too far gone to save and ordered the bank liquidated and its assets sold off. Many other banks found themselves in trouble because of the bad loans they had made through Penn Square. The Penn Square failure shook the banking system. Clearly banks were not as safe as they seemed. This lesson was driven home by the problems that soon appeared at the giant Chicago bank, Continental Illinois.

Continental Illinois Bank of Chicago

Continental Illinois Bank of Chicago is the largest and best known bank to suffer a crisis in the 1980s. Continental Illinois was a major lender to many businesses and to foreign governments. The bank made billions of dollars of relatively long-term loans in the 1970s and 1980s.

Continental Illinois' depositor base was somewhat narrow. Most states allow branch banking, where a single bank can have many offices around the state. This allows the bank to have a wide base of many types of depositors, including consumers, businesses, and institutions such as insurance companies and pension systems. Illinois, however, has a unit banking rule that restricts banks to a single main office. Illinois, therefore, tends to have many little banks and few large ones. Since Continental Illinois was a giant bank that did not have a wide base of depositors, it relied on a relatively small number of very large, short-term institutional depositors in order to grow. Only about 7 percent of the bank's depositors were consumers in 1984, for example, while the rest of the deposits came from large institutions.

National Credit Union Administration
An agency similar to the FDIC that provides insurance for credit union deposits.

Federal Savings and Loan Insurance Corporation
An agency similar to the FDIC that provides insurance for deposits in savings and loan banks.

($100,000 is the legal limit to FDIC protection, but the FDIC generally pays off all deposits of whatever size). Credit union and savings and loan association depositors are afforded the same kind of protection through the **National Credit Union Administration** and the **Federal Savings and Loan Insurance Corporation.**

Commercial banks are regulated by the Federal Reserve System, the federal Comptroller of the Currency, and various state level banking authorities. Fractional reserve banking is not only a valid economic concept, but it contributes significantly to the growth and stability of the economy. Banks provide a middleman service between borrowers and lenders. Savers and other depositors earn interest on their deposits and borrowers find available funds with less time and expense than if they attempted to arrange such loans from the public themselves. It is in providing such a middleman service that banks can and do expand the money supply.

Continental Illinois' problems began when a number of high-risk loans began to experience trouble. The bank had made many loans for oil-gas exploration, for example. Many of these loans were made, with little information about the borrower, through cooperative agreements with Penn Square Bank of Oklahoma City. When Penn Square went broke in 1982 because many of its borrowers could not pay, it took numerous smaller banks with it, along with $1 billion of Continental Illinois depositors' money. Other high risk loans in Latin America and elsewhere were also not paying off.

Sensing trouble, many of the bank's largest depositors began to withdraw their funds. Almost one third of the bank's $30 billion in deposits fled with the bad news. This made it impossible for the bank to remain stable. The government decided that Continental Illinois was too big to let fail, however. Many smaller banks had deposits at Continental Illinois and they might have also failed had the big Chicago bank gone under. The entire banking system would have been at risk. The FDIC was not legally required to pay off the large institutional accounts if Continental Illinois failed (FDIC insurance is limited to $100,000 per account), but a failure to do so would have shaken confidence in the banking system and perhaps caused crises elsewhere. Any policy — action or inaction — was likely to prove costly for the FDIC and the economy.

The Continental Illinois banking crisis was resolved in a unique way. As a last resort, the FDIC directly injected $4.5 billion into the bank. Technically, the aid was in the form of $1 billion in investment in the bank itself and $3.5 billion repurchase of Continental Illinois loans. The FDIC replaced several key executives at the Chicago bank and will continue to exercise considerable control of the bank over the near future.

The Continental Illinois experience teaches us several lessons about banks. Banks can work if they have the trust of their depositors. Banks must exercise sound judgment in making loans, however. Continental Illinois, Penn Square, and several other large banks in the 1980s did not monitor their loan activities closely enough. Banks also learned that they cannot ignore their depositor base in making decisions. Continental Illinois' depositors had financial savvy, and they took their money and ran when the first troubles appeared. Banks must make wise business decisions and cannot count on the public's trust in FDIC insurance to maintain faith in the banking system.

State-Insured Banks in Ohio

All banks are not insured with federal agencies such as the FDIC. Many states allow banks to insure accounts through state-run or private insurance schemes. Becuase these insurance programs are small, however, they can be undercapitalized and therefore unable to deal with a real bank failure. This situation occurred in Ohio in 1985. Several smaller, privately insured banks failed. Although they were relatively small banks, their losses were greater than the state deposit insurance fund.

When the word got out that the insurance fund was dry, people started a run on all state-insured banks because they did not want to risk leaving their deposits in "unsafe" banks. This bank panic had the predictable effect of making previously sound banks suddenly unstable. No bank, however well run and profitable, can long withstand a run of withdrawals. The governor of Ohio was forced to close the banks for a short period, much as Franklin Roosevelt had done in 1933, so that they could reopen in a less frantic atmosphere.

The 1985 Ohio bank panic shows how fragile is the trust in banks and how important that trust is to their successful operation. It also shows that deposit insurance must be real if it is to be effective. We can expect that the lessons of the panic crises of the 1980s will eventually be incorporated into more effective banking regulations and practices.

KEY CONCEPTS
13.7, 13.8, 13.9

Fractional reserve banking is based on the principle that a relatively small amount of reserves can support a much larger amount of deposits. Deposits are safe because of the existence of deposit insurance, and more important, because incoming deposits generally offset outgoing withdrawals, so that reserves are normally not called into play. The main assets of a fractional reserve bank are its required reserves, excess reserves, and its loans. The main liabilities of a fractional reserve bank are its deposits.

HOW BANKS CREATE MONEY

13.10 MONEY CREATION

Under a system of fractional reserve banking, banks lend money to borrowers from the funds they hold for their depositors. In doing this, as already noted, banks create money. That is, this process expands the supply of

TABLE 13-4

Balance Sheets for Bank A and Bank B

Assets ($ millions)	Bank A	Bank B	Liabilities ($ millions)	Bank A	Bank B
Required reserves	250	250	Demand deposits	1000	1000
Loans	750	750	Time deposits	0	0
Securities	0	0	Other deposits	0	0
Excess reserves	0	0			

money circulating in the economy. To understand how this is done we must build a simple model of the banking system and see what happens when banks make loans.

Assume that our banking system is made up of only two banks and that depositors have nowhere else to deposit their funds other than in our banking system. This may seem unrealistic, but the ideas we develop in this two-bank world can be generalized to the world in which we live. We will assume that both banks must hold 25 percent of their total deposits as required reserves. Table 13-4 presents the balance sheets of the two banks at the beginning of our example. Both banks are assumed to begin this time period with $1000 million in demand deposits (and no other liabilities); $250 million, or 25 percent, of these deposits are held as required reserves, with the remaining $750 million held as loans. The $M1$ money supply at the start of our example is $2000 million, ignoring currency and coins, half of which is held in each bank.

A bank customer has just been notified that his long lost uncle in Scotland has died and left him $100 million in U.S. currency. These funds are assumed to come from outside the U.S. banking system and not from another bank in the U.S. They therefore represent a genuine "new" injection of money. When he receives the cash, he deposits it in Bank A. The balance sheet of Bank A now looks like Table 13-5. This increases the demand deposits of Bank A by $100 million and the reserve account by $100 million. There is now $100 million more money in the U.S. economy and $100 million more reserves in the U.S. banking system. We have assumed that our banking system is required by law to keep 25 percent of its deposits as reserves so they can pay the withdrawals demanded by their customers. This means that out of the $100 million addition to the bank's reserves, they only have to keep $25 million in required reserves. The remaining $75 million is excess reserves. Since reserves sitting in the bank

TABLE 13-5

Balance Sheet for Bank A after New Deposits of $100 Million

Assets ($ millions)		Liabilities ($ millions)	
Required reserves (+25)	275	Demand deposits (+100)	1100
Loans	750	Time deposits	0
Securities	0	Other liabilities	0
Excess reserves (+75)	75		

earn no interest, there is a strong incentive for the bank to lend these excess reserves at interest.

Bob Jones, a customer of Bank A, comes in to borrow $75 million so his construction firm can build a new office building. Bank A makes the loan and its excess reserve account falls by $75 million as the funds are given to Mr. Jones, but the loans account rises by $75 million at the same time. Bank A's balance sheet now looks like Table 13-6.

Bob Jones pays his workers and suppliers the $75 million for the office building construction. We assume that the workers and suppliers all are customers of Bank B. They deposit $75 million into Bank B, which affects that bank's balance sheet. Bank B's new balance sheet is presented in Table 13-7. The bank now has total deposits of $1000 million plus $75 million for a total of $1075 million. It must add 25 percent of the new $75 million deposit, or $18.75 million, to the required reserve account. The bank then adds the remaining $56.75 million to its excess reserves.

The banking system has just created money, right before your eyes. We began this example with $1000 million in each bank, then a new deposit of $100 million entered the system. We can therefore account for $2100 million in this way. If you look at Tables 13-6 and 13-7, however, you will see that we now have a total of $1100 million (Bank A) plus $1075 million (Bank B) for a total of $2175 million of demand deposits. The banking system has created an additional $75 million of money that did not otherwise exist when Bank A made its $75 million loan. Banks create money when they make loans. This money creation process is important because economic activity, such as the $75 million office building, takes place each time a loan is made and spent.

The banking system is not finished making loans and creating money. Bank B has a strong incentive to lend its $56.25 million excess reserves to make profits. Bank B now makes a loan of $56.25 million to Samantha Ford,

TABLE 13-6   **Balance Sheet for Bank A after Lending Jones $75 Million**

Assets ($ millions)		Liabilities ($ millions)	
Required reserves	275	Demand deposits	1100
Loans (+75)	825	Time deposits	0
Securities	0	Other liabilities	0
Excess reserves (−75)	0		

TABLE 13-7   **Balance Sheet for Bank B after New Deposits of $75 Million**

Assets ($ millions)		Liabilities ($ millions)	
Required reserves (+18.75)	268.75	Demand deposits	1075
Loans	750.00	Time deposits	0
Securities	0	Other liabilities	0
Excess reserves	56.25		

TABLE 13-8

Balance Sheet for Bank A After Deposit from Ford Motor Company

Assets ($ millions)		Liabilities ($ millions)	
Required reserves (+14.06)	289.06	Demand deposits	1156.25
Loans	825.00	Time deposits	0
Securities	0	Other liabilities	0
Excess reserves	42.19		

an auto dealer, to finance the dealership's annual inventory of new cars. Samantha pays Ford Motor Company with the proceeds of the loan. Assume that Ford deposits the $56.25 million check into Bank A. The balance sheet of Bank A now looks like Table 13-8. Bank A's demand deposits have increased by $56.25 million to $1156.25 million. Their required reserves have increased by approximately $14.06 million (25 percent of the $56.25 million new deposit) to $289.06 million. Bank A can put the remaining $42.19 million into its excess reserve account, which is available for loans. In other words, Bank A now has approximately $42.19 in excess reserves that it would like to loan out.

The money supply went up again when Bank B made the loan, which was redeposited into Bank A. The total money supply is now $1156.25 million (Bank A) plus $1175 million (Bank B) for a total of $2331.25 million, of which $2000 million existed at the start, $100 million entered the system from abroad, and $331.25 million was created by banks making loans. This process of loans and deposits continues until there is no more money redeposited or loaned. Since part of each deposit is held as required reserves, the amount of each subsequent loan and redeposit falls by the amount of the required reserves on the deposit. Table 13-9 traces out the effects of our initial $100 million deposit for each subsequent round of loan making and redeposit of loan proceeds.

The Deposit Expansion Multiplier

13.11 DEPOSIT EXPANSION MULTIPLIER

We can see two important features in Table 13-9. First, the amount of new loans possible column decreases with each round. This is due to the fact that at each redeposit, required reserves had to be set aside and could not be

TABLE 13-9

Expansion of Deposits and Reserves Through Loans

	Amount deposited ($ millions)	New loans possible ($ millions)	Additional required reserves ($ millions)
1st deposit	100.00	75.00	25.00
2nd round	75.00	56.25	18.75
3rd round	56.25	42.19	14.06
4th round	42.19	31.64	10.54
5th round	31.64	23.73	7.91
6th round	23.73	17.74	5.93
All other rounds	71.19	53.41	17.81
Total	400.00	300.00	100.00

Deposit Expansion Multiplier
The principle that states that an increase in reserves in the banking system causes a greater increase in total bank deposits and therefore the money supply. The deposit expansion multiplier is the reciprocal of the reserve requirement. For example, a required reserve ratio of 25 percent would yield a deposit expansion multiplier of 1/.25, or 4.

loaned out. The second important point is that the amount deposited is not just the initial deposit. In other words, the initial deposit of $100 million increased total demand deposits in the banking system and therefore the money supply by $400 million. It did this by creating $300 million in new loans, which increased the level of economic activity in this economy.

This is a multiplier effect, much like the spending multiplier we studied in Chapter 10. Economists call this the **deposit expansion multiplier.** We can compute the deposit expansion multiplier by taking the reciprocal of the required reserve ratio.

$$\text{Potential change in money supply} = (\text{initial deposit}) \times \frac{1}{\text{reserve requirement}}$$

In our two-bank model, we assumed that the required reserve ratio was 25 percent. Our deposit expansion multiplier would therefore be 1/.25, or 4. This would mean that in a banking system with a required reserve ratio of .25, an initial deposit of $100 million would, after the loan making and redeposit process was completed, expand the money supply by four times itself, or up to the 4 × $100 = $400 million shown here.

The required reserve ratio is much like the marginal propensity to save (*MPS*) in the spending multiplier discussed in Chapter 10. The *MPS* tells us what portion of each incremental dollar in income is saved. These saved dollars cannot be passed on to be spent and respent and create the multiplier effect. The required reserve ratio tells us what portion of each incremental dollar deposited the bank is required to hold in reserve. This required reserve portion cannot then be passed on in the form of a loan to be redeposited and continue the loan making–redeposit process. Thus it is the size of the required reserve ratio that determines the size of the deposit expansion multiplier. The larger the required reserve ratio, the less of each incremental dollar of deposits can be loaned out. Therefore, the deposit expansion multiplier is smaller. From Table 13-10, it is easy to compare the various required reserve ratios and the resulting deposit expansion multipliers that they produce.

The simplified model of the deposit expansion multiplier presented here requires some qualification. In our model, we assumed that all loans were redeposited back into our banking system, dollar for dollar. In reality, not every dollar of every loan made by the banking system gets redeposited. Demand deposits can be converted into loans by banks, but part of the loans may leak into cash held by the borrower. Individuals choose to hold money for transactional, precautionary, and speculative reasons. It is entirely possible, therefore, that borrowers may choose to hold part of their loan in

| TABLE 13-10 | Impact of a $100 Million New Deposit on Money Supply and Loans |

Reserve requirement (%)	Deposit expansion multiplier	Change in money supply ($ millions)	Change in total loans ($ millions)
10	10	1000	900
20	5	500	400
25	4	400	300
33	3	300	200
50	2	200	100

cash to meet any or all of these needs. This behavior prevents the cash that is held from reentering the banking system right away and from being reloaned. This clearly reduces the size of the money multiplier.

It is also possible that banks could choose not to loan out all their excess reserves. While there is a strong incentive to loan out as much as possible since reserves do not earn interest, there are times when banks may believe that the risk of making loans to available borrowers is a more important concern. There is a trade-off between the risk a lender is willing to accept and the return on a loan. If only risky borrowers are requesting loans, the bank may feel that the market rate of interest is too low to be worth taking the risk and may choose to hold excess reserves. This keeps those funds from being loaned and redeposited and therefore reduces the potential size of the deposit expansion multiplier.

With the prevailing real-world required reserve ratios in the neighborhood of 3 to 10 percent, we might expect a deposit expansion multiplier of approximately 10. But real-world multipliers are really in the range of 2 to 3 percent. This suggests that significant leakages of cash, excess reserve holdings, and other leakages do occur in the financial system.

KEY CONCEPTS
13.10, 13.11

A bank creates money when it makes a loan. The banking system can create substantial amounts of money from a given new deposit through the deposit expansion multiplier process. A new deposit in one bank allows that bank to create money by making a loan, which allows additional deposits, loans, and money creation elsewhere in the financial system. The deposit expansion formula is given by

$$\text{Change in money supply} = \frac{1}{\text{reserve requirement}} \times \text{new deposit}$$

13.12 CHANGING ROLE OF FINANCIAL INSTITUTIONS

DEREGULATION OF THE U.S. FINANCIAL SECTOR

Financial intermediaries have long been one of the most heavily regulated sectors of the U.S. economy. The existence of a stable banking system is necessary for economic growth because reliable banks encourage saving and facilitate investment and economic expansion. The partial collapse of the U.S. banking system in the 1930s contributed to the length and depth of the Great Depression.

Congress and state legislators imposed tight regulations on the financial sector following the problems of the 1930s. These regulations sought to strengthen and stabilize the banking system by limiting competition among banks for funds. Congress imposed rules setting interest rate ceilings on bank deposits, for example. These ceilings guaranteed banks of a cheap source of funds for loan activities and limited the ability of banks to compete for deposits based on interest returns. Competition between commercial banks and thrift institutions was also limited. Commercial banks dealt largely with short-term deposits such as demand deposits and made short-term consumer and commercial or business loans. Thrift institutions, such as savings and loan associations and mutual savings banks, received time deposits and made longer-term loans, such as home mortgage loans. Thrift institutions were forbidden from offering checkable accounts that would compete with commercial bank demand deposits. Interest rate ceilings kept either thrifts or commercial banks from having a competitive edge.

Deregulation of the U.S. Financial Sector 393

The banking regulations that were appropriate for the 1930s did not meet the much different needs of the 1970s and 1980s. Relatively new financial intermediaries, such as credit unions, have become an important part of the banking scene. New financial instruments, such as money market mutual funds, gave depositors ways to earn market interest rates above the regulatory ceilings while retaining check-writing convenience. Commercial banks and thrift institutions increasingly intruded on each others' territories as competition for depositor dollars increased.

While competition heated up, the regulations that were supposed to assure a stable banking system proved incapable of dealing with the new problems. Depositors could quickly pull millions of dollars out of thrift institutions and put them into money market mutual funds when market interest returns rose above interest ceilings. This made the savings banks unstable, since they made long-term loans but were subject to short-term deposits and withdrawals. Interest rate regulations made it impossible for them to compete with these new financial instruments. Deregulation was necessary because tighter controls on banks would only have made these problems worse.

Depository Institutions Deregulation Act of 1980
A federal law that altered the regulation of depository institutions by allowing interest payments on checkable deposits, reduced the scope of interest rate ceilings, and changed the nature of bank regulation to expand the allowable activities of savings and loans, mutual savings banks, and credit unions.

Garn – St. Germain Depository Institutions Act of 1982
A federal law that widened the sources of funds for depository institutions, contributed toward the removal of interest rate ceilings, and gave regulators expanded emergency powers to deal with financially unstable depository institutions.

The **Depository Institutions Deregulation Act of 1980** was the first step in the direction of a more competitive financial marketplace. This act allowed commerical banks and thrift institutions to compete with each other and also with other financial instruments such as government bonds and money market mutual funds. The 1980 act allowed banks to offer their customers interest-earning checkable accounts and removed many of the ceilings on deposit accounts. The act also removed regulations that limited the scope of commercial bank and thrift institution loans.

Deregulation took another step forward with passage of the **Garn – St. Germain Depository Institutions Act of 1982.** This act further eliminated interest rate ceilings and allowed depository institutions to directly compete with money market mutual funds by offering their own money market deposit accounts. The 1982 act also gave the FDIC and the FSLIC expanded powers to deal with troubled banks and thrifts. Deregulation revolutionized the financial sector, providing businesses and consumers with many more financial options. Banks and thrifts now achieve stability through their ability to compete, not through ineffective artificial protective regulations. But deregulation created problems, which made the 1982 act's emergency aid provisions necessary.

The Perils of Deregulation

The deregulation of the financial sector promises many long-term benefits to the economy, but there is also the potential for many short-term problems. As noted before, some banks have failed or teetered on the brink of failure. Financial deregulation has also tended to confuse monetary policy in recent years because it is more difficult to tell what should be included in the money supply. Economists who monitor the money supply are frequently confused when new types of bank accounts are introduced, thereby making the existing data on money obsolete.

Financial deregulation has probably weakened government control of the banking system. It is now hard to tell what exactly is and is not a bank. For example, suppose that an institution offers the following services: deposit by mail, daily interest payments on deposits, monthly statements, free unlimited check writing, automatic loans up to a set maximum, and use of a Visa credit card. This sounds like the list of services that an up-to-date bank might offer. These services, and many others, do not come from a bank, however. They come from stock brokerage firms, such as Merrill Lynch, which offer integrated financial accounts for their customers, such as Merrill Lynch's Cash Management Account.

Are Merrill Lynch and other brokerage firms banks? They offer many of the same services as banks and compete with banks for funds. But they are not regulated in the same ways as banks and they do not accept deposits as banks do. Brokerage firms also have one important advantage that banks did not have in the 1980s: brokerage firms can serve customers all around the country. Banks in the mid-1980s were limited by state regulations regarding interstate banking.

The prohibition against inter-state banking will be the last of the bank regulations to go. When this occurs, borrowers and lenders will have available many new and convenient financial services. These services will be offered by new financial intermediaries that will often bear as little resemblance to the traditional savings bank as that bank bears to the ancient goldsmith who invented banking in the first place.

MONEY AND THE ECONOMY: EARLY MONETARY THEORY

We have looked so far in this chapter at money and banks. We have seen how people, as individuals, use money and how money is used by banks to make loans. These individual borrowing and lending actions have profound macroeconomic implications when they are taken together.

The earliest macroeconomic theories were based on a few relatively simple notions about money and its effect on the economy. For example, the *only* discussion of macroeconomics in American economic pioneer Richard T. Ely's 1917 text, *Outlines of Economics*, Third Edition, published by Macmillan, is found in a chapter entitled "Other Problems in Money and Banking." This discussion focuses on just one thing: the effect of changes in the money supply on the economy. To early (pre-Keynesian) economists, control of the money supply was all there was to macroeconomics.

Economists have long believed that changes in the money supply cause changes in the overall price level. One of the simplest ways to show this is through an algebraic model called the **equation of exchange.** This model represents both the first appearance of a systematic theory of macroeconomics and the earliest roots of the monetarist economic theories that we will discuss in the next two chapters.

Here is how the equation of exchange works: We know from the circular flow analysis that the dollar value of what consumers, investors, foreigners, and governments spend to buy goods and services is equal to the dollar value of what producers receive when they sell their goods and services.

$$\$ \text{ value of spending} = \$ \text{ value of production}$$

Now let us modify this identity somewhat. The value of all production is equal to the real quantity of goods produced (Q) multiplied by the price level in the economy (P). So,

$$\$ \text{ value of production} = P \times Q$$

13.13 EQUATION OF EXCHANGE

Equation of Exchange
Defined as money supply times velocity equals average price times real quantity $M \times V = P \times Q$. Total spending on goods and services is equal to the money supply times the number of times that the money supply turns over.

Velocity of Money
The term used to describe the number of times that the average dollar in the money supply is used over and over again in a year.

The dollar value of spending can be calculated as the amount of money in the money supply (M) multiplied by the **velocity of money** (V), or the average number of times each dollar is spent each year. If, for example, the money supply is $500 billion, and consumers use this money to purchase $2000 billion of goods, then it follows that each dollar has a velocity of 4 because $500 \times 4 = \$2000$. In equation form,

$$\$ \text{ value of spending} = M \times V$$

Given these ideas, we can write the Equation of Exchange as

$$M \times V = P \times Q$$
$$\$ \text{ value of spending} = \$ \text{ value of production}$$

13.14 MECHANICS OF THE EQUATION OF EXCHANGE

The equation of exchange $M \times V = P \times Q$ is a very old identity in economics. The value of final output sold by producers ($P \times Q$) must always equal what consumers paid for that output ($M \times V$). What is spent by the buyers of goods and services must be equal to what is received by the sellers.

This equation of exchange gives us a basis for analyzing the general relationship between the money supply and prices. We know from simple algebra that when the value of one side of an equation goes up, if the equal sign is to remain true, the value of the other side of the equation must increase as well. Suppose, for example, we had the following data to put into our equation of exchange:

$$\begin{aligned} \text{Money supply} &= \$5 \\ \text{Velocity} &= 10 \\ \text{Average price of goods and services} &= \$2 \\ \text{Quantity of output} &= 25 \text{ units} \end{aligned}$$

Then we know that

$$M \times V = P \times Q$$
$$\$5 \times 10 = \$50 = \$2 \times 25$$

If we increased the money supply in our economy to $10, then the equation would be

$$\$10 \times 10 \neq \$2 \times 25$$

It would then not be true that the left side of the equation was equal to the right side, and something would happen in the economy to bring the two sides of the equation back into equality. Early economists believed that both the velocity of money (V) and the quantity of output (Q) were relatively constant, at least in the short run. If this is true, then we know that the increase in M we just suggested must, by definition, bring about an equal increase in P. That is, if the money supply has doubled to $10 as in our example, and both the velocity of money (V) and quantity of output (Q) are constant, then the price level must also double. In our example, since the money supply went from $5 to $10, the price level must go from $2 to $4. In other words, a doubling of the money supply causes a doubling of prices in the economy. The new equality would be

$$M \times V = P \times Q$$
$$\$10 \times 10 = \$100 = \$4 \times 25$$

The equation of exchange and the assumption by early economists that both output and velocity are relatively constant are broad generalizations about the behavior of the economy. Modern economists understand that the way that money supply changes affect the economy is far more complicated than this. This equation of exchange example does, however, show us what would happen if the money supply were to rise suddenly and there was no change in the proportion of their income that people wanted to hold as money. There would be too many dollars chasing too few goods and services. This would force the price levels of those goods and services to rise in order to bring spending and the available output back into equality with the available money supply.

Prices did not rise during the Great Depression. The average price level fell in what economists call deflation. The equation of exchange shows how this can happen. Suppose that people, afraid of bank failures, decided to take their money out of banks. We know that this would reduce the money supply M, because banks would have fewer reserves and would therefore not be able to create or support as much money and credit. If V and Q were constant in this event, the only thing that could happen would be that the price level P would fall. This is part of what happened in the Great Depression.

We can learn more from the equation of exchange if we drop the original assumptions of our example. We are interested in economic growth without inflation. How can this occur? The equation of exchange suggests one method that has been championed by Nobel-laureate economist Milton Friedman. Suppose that V is fixed and that Q is growing by 10 percent each year. How can we keep the price level P from changing? The equation of exchange suggests that noninflationary growth can occur if the money supply M is increased at the same rate as the growth rate of the real economy Q. That is, if Q grows by 10 percent and M grows by 10 percent, P does not change. Friedman has long advocated economic policies that would steadily increase the money supply at the average growth rate of real output.

The equation of exchange is the early basis for an interesting modern school of economics called monetarism. We will look at monetarism in more depth in Chapter 15.

KEY CONCEPTS
13.13, 13.14

A simple theory of money's impact on the economy is given by the equation of exchange, $M \times V = P \times Q$. This identity suggests that, if velocity and real output are fixed in the short run, changes in the money supply directly translate into change in the price level.

A LOOK AHEAD

This chapter has looked at how the financial sector fits into the economy. We have learned about money and the money supply and about financial intermediaries. We have looked at banks and learned how banks create money. Finally, we have reviewed a simple theory of how money affects the economy. All of these useful analyses have built a strong foundation for the next step in our study of the economy. The Federal Reserve System regulates the banking sector and makes monetary policy. In Chapter 14, we will examine the Federal Reserve and see what it is, what it does, and how it works. The Federal Reserve affects both banks and the credit markets. We will look at the credit markets and see how they work and how interest rates are determined by the forces of supply and demand that operate within them. Finally, Keynesian economic theory holds that the Federal Reserve affects the economy through its impact on interest rates in the credit markets. We will review the Keynesian theory of money's influence and see how it differs from the simple equation of exchange model just presented.

SUMMARY

13.1
1. Money is anything that is generally accepted in exchange for goods and services and in payment of debt. The main forms of money today are coins, currency, and demand deposits. Demand deposits are checking account balances.

13.2
2. Money performs several functions. It is a medium of exchange that facilitates mutually advantageous exchanges of goods and services by eliminating the necessity of a coincidence of wants. It is also a uniform unit of accounting and a store of value.

13.3
3. Economists measure the money supply because changes in the money supply have important implications for the economy as a whole. The $M1$ money supply measure includes currency, demand deposits, and other highly liquid assets such as checkable accounts and travelers checks. The $M2$ money supply definition is broader than $M1$. $M2$ includes savings accounts and other less-liquid assets such as money market mutual funds. The $M3$ money supply measure is broader still. $M3$ includes such less-liquid assets as large denomination time deposits.

13.4
4. Economists find it difficult to accurately measure the money supply because of the many new financial assets that have appeared in recent years. Shifts in financial holdings of individuals from, say, demand deposits to money market mutual funds may have no real impact on economic activity, but they tend to alter the various money supply measures.

13.5
5. Financial intermediaries link deficit units with surplus units in the economy. Deficit units wish to consume more resources than they currently have available. Surplus units wish to consume fewer resources than they have currently available. Financial intermediaries facilitate the mutually advantageous exchange of credit (loaned resources) between deficit and surplus units.

13.6
6. Financial intermediation works because financial intermediaries are able to pool, or aggregate, the resources of surplus units. These firms can then specialize in making resources available to a variety of deficit units.

This process allows both surplus and deficit units higher liquidity. It also makes possible reduced risk because surplus units hold claims on a diversified portfolio of assets. Because financial intermediaries efficiently specialize as middlemen between surplus and deficit units, both parties to the credit exchange can simultaneously gain.

13.7 ▶ 7. Modern banks employ the principle of fractional reserve banking. Only a fraction of each deposit is actually held by the bank as a reserve. The remaining portion of each deposit can be used for loans, which generate profits for the bank and make possible the payment of interest to the depositors. Fractional reserve banking works because new deposits in the banking system generally offset withdrawals, so that a relatively small reserve is able to perform all the functions of a much larger total of deposits. The fractional reserve banking system works so long as it retains the trust of its depositors.

13.8 ▶ 8. Deposits are a fractional reserve bank's main liability. Deposits are funds that are owed to depositors, which is why they are listed as a liability in the accounting framework that banks use. The bank's main assets are required reserves, excess reserves, and loans. The reserve requirement determines the fraction of total deposits that banks must hold as reserves. The remaining portion of the deposits is held in the excess reserve account until some profitable use is found for it. Loans are a bank asset because they represent funds that are due the bank from its borrowing customers.

13.9 ▶ 9. Deposits in modern commercial banks are generally safe for two reasons. First, most bank deposits these days are insured by some government agency, such as the Federal Deposit Insurance Corporation (FDIC). In addition, bank deposits are generally safe because of the sound principles of fractional reserve banking. So long as people trust banks, then deposits and withdrawals balance each other and the bank can honor all of its liabilities.

13.10 ▶ 10. Banks create money by making loans. When a bank receives a new deposit, it holds part of the deposit as required reserves and typically uses the remainder to make loans. These loans represent newly created money that the borrower can spend. Thus the borrower has money while the initial depositor still has claim to the money deposited in the bank. The process of making loans in a fractional reserve banking system therefore creates money.

13.11 ▶ 11. The money creation process described above cascades through the banking system, with money created through loans by one bank becoming deposits at other banks, thereby allowing additional money creation. The deposit expansion formula gives the total amount of money that is created from a new deposit. The deposit expansion formula is
change in money supply = 1/(reserve requirement) × new deposit.

13.12 ▶ 12. The financial sector of the U.S. economy has traditionally been very highly regulated. In recent years, however, the financial sector has been deregulated to increase competition among financial intermediaries and make the financial system more flexible and responsive. This has provided many benefits to borrowers and savers, but it has also created some

13.13 ▶ 13. One model of money's influence on the economy is based on the equation of exchange. The equation of exchange is $M \times V = P \times Q$; where M is money supply, V is velocity of money, P is price level, and Q is quantity of output. The velocity of money is the average number of times each dollar of money is spent and respent in a given time period. The quantity of output is conceptually identical to real GNP.

13.14 ▶ 14. The left-hand side of the equation of exchange gives the amount of total purchases in the economy. The right-hand side equals the value of the goods and services that are produced. The equation exists because it is definitionally true that the amount that is spent ($M \times V$) must equal the value of the items purchased ($P \times Q$). The equation also suggests a relationship among the four variables. For example, if velocity and real output are constant in the short run, then an increase in money supply M necessarily implies a proportionate increase in the price level P.

DISCUSSION QUESTIONS

13.2 ▶ 1. Suppose a blacksmith is in need of leather and wishes to get rid of excess horseshoes he has produced. A toolmaker want to reduce the supply of leather he has tanned and has a need for nails. Does a coincidence of wants exist between the blacksmith and the toolmaker? Can the blacksmith acquire the needed leather? Can the toolmaker acquire the needed nails? If so, explain how. If not, then explain why not.

13.1, 13.3 ▶ 2. State the three most common definitions of the money supply. Explain the differences between them and state why there is a need to have more than one definition of the money supply.

13.8 ▶ 3. State if the following are bank assets or liabilities (as they would appear on the bank's balance sheet). Explain what characteristic makes them so.
   a. excess reserves
   b. demand deposits
   c. loans
   d. time deposits
   e. NOW accounts
   f. U.S. government securities
   g. vault cash
   h. certificates of deposit
   i. deposits held at the Federal Reserve

13.10, 13.11 ▶ 4. Suppose the reserve requirement is 20 percent. The entire commercial banking system consists of only two banks, Bank A and Bank B. A deposit of $500 from outside the banking system is made. What is the deposit expansion multiplier? Demonstrate with the use of balance sheets how the expansion process works assuming subsequent redeposits of all loan proceeds. What is the overall amount deposited? By how much is the money supply expanded? By how much have required reserves increased?

400 Money and the Banking System

13.11 → 5. What would happen to the money supply in the prior problem had commercial Bank A decided to initially loan out only 10 percent of the original $500 deposit? Would a bank ever decide to do this? Why or why not?

13.11 → 6. Explain what would happen (in concept) if you acquired a loan for $400 from Bank A in Question 5 above, but instead of redepositing the entire amount into the banking system, you chose to hold $200 as cash in your wallet.

13.13, 13.14 → 7. Given the following information, calculate the equation of exchange: money supply = $3000; average price of goods and services = $25; quantity of output = 600; velocity = 5. Suppose the money supply were increased by $2000 to a new total of $5000. Assuming that V and Q are relatively constant, what would happen to prices as a result of an increase in the money supply? What does this tell us about the general relationship between the money supply and the general price level of goods and services?

13.8, 13.11 → 8. Assume a commercial bank holds $1000 worth of federal securities. With a reserve requirement of 25 percent, what would happen to the money supply if the commercial bank decided to sell $400 worth of these securities back to the Federal Reserve?

SELECTED READINGS

Board of Governors of the Federal Reserve System. *The Federal Reserve System: Purposes and Functions*, 5th ed. Washington, D.C.: U.S. Government Printing Office, 1963. See especially chaps. 1 and 4.

Cargill, Thomas F., and Garcia, Gillian G. *Financial Reform in the 1980s*. Stanford: Hoover Institution, 1985.

Federal Reserve Bank of Chicago. "The Garn–St. Gemain Depository Institutions Act of 1982." *Economic Perspectives* (Federal Reserve Bank of Chicago, March/April 1983).

Galbraith, John Kenneth. *Money: Whence It Came, Where It Went*. Boston: Houghton Mifflin Co., 1975.

Ritter, L.S., and Silber, W. L. *Principles of Money, Banking and Financial Markets*, 3rd ed. New York: Basic Books, 1980.

Silber, William M. *Money.* New York: Basic Books, 1977.

Thompson, Lloyd B. *Money, Banking and Economic Activity*, 2nd ed. Englewood Cliffs, NJ: Prentice-Hall, 1982.

West, Robert Craig. "The Depository Institutions Deregulation Act of 1980: A Historical Perspective." *Economic Review* (Federal Reserve Bank of Kansas City, February 1982), pp. 3–13.

CHAPTER 14

The Federal Reserve, Credit Markets and Monetary Policy

Having read the chapter, reviewed the chapter summary, and completed the *Study Guide* exercises, you should be able to:

CRIS

14.1 ORIGINS OF THE FRS: Discuss the economic problems that led to the creation of the Federal Reserve System in 1913.

14.2 STRUCTURE OF THE FRS: Explain the structure of the Federal Reserve System in terms of its regional banks and operating groups.

14.3 FUNCTIONS OF THE FRS: List and explain the functions of the Federal Reserve System.

14.4 BANKS, THE TREASURY, AND THE FRS: Explain the relationships between the FRS and the banking system and between the FRS and the Treasury.

14.5 OPEN MARKET OPERATIONS: Explain what open market operations are and how the FRS uses them to regulate the supplies of money and credit.

14.6 DISCOUNT RATE: Explain what the discount rate is and how the FRS uses it to influence the availability of money and credit.

14.7 RESERVE REQUIREMENT: Explain what the reserve requirement is and how the FRS uses it to regulate the supplies of money and credit.

14.8 CREDIT DEMAND DETERMINANTS: List and explain the main determinants of the demand for credit.

14.9 CREDIT SUPPLY DETERMINANTS: List and explain the main determinants of the supply of credit.

14.10 EQUILIBRIUM INTEREST RATE: Explain how the forces of credit demand and credit supply determine the equilibrium interest rate in the credit market.

14.11 FACTORS AFFECTING INTEREST RATES: Explain how deficits, FRS policies, inflation, and business profitability affect interest rates in the credit market.

14.12 MONETARY TRANSMISSION MECHANISM: Explain how the Keynesian monetary transmission mechanism, based on the Investment Rule, links changes in interest rates and credit market conditions with corresponding changes in aggregate demand and aggregate supply.

14.13 KEYNESIAN MONETARY POLICIES: Explain how expansionary and contractionary monetary policy affects the economy in the Keynesian model.

14.14 PROBLEMS WITH MONETARY POLICY: List and explain the problems that occur in using monetary policy to stabilize the economy.

It is difficult to overstate the importance of the financial sector and the banking system in our macroeconomic system. The last chapter showed the important role that financial intermediaries play, the magical ability of banks to create money, and the key role that money played in early macroeconomic theories. This chapter adds to our understanding and appreciation of the financial sector's role and more fully develops the themes introduced in Chapter 13.

We will first examine the Federal Reserve System. Next we will examine credit markets. Many of the Federal Reserve's actions have their most direct impact in credit markets, which are financial markets where debt instruments such as bonds are exchanged. These important financial markets lie at the heart of the financial sector. We will see how they work and how they affect and are affected by economic events and policies.

Finally, we will explore a second macroeconomic theory of how money affects the economy. The last chapter presented a simple monetarist model of money's influence, which was based on the equation of exchange. This simple money model predated the Keynesian revolution in economics. Keynes proposed a different theory concerning how money affects the economy. Keynes said that changes in the money supply affect the economy through events in the credit markets. We will discuss and analyze this Keynesian view of monetary theory and its corresponding monetary policy prescriptions. This will prepare us for the next chapter, where the more recent monetarist and rational expectations macroeconomic theories are discussed.

THE FEDERAL RESERVE SYSTEM

We will first examine the Federal Reserve System. The Federal Reserve System sits atop the nation's banking system. The "Fed" is the banker's bank. The Fed is able to create money and increase bank reserves, which banks then use to create more money themselves. The Fed can therefore serve as the catalyst for the dramatic monetary chain reaction that is the

14.1 ORIGINS OF THE FRS

deposit expansion process. In this section, we will see how the Fed came to be, what it is, and how it works. We will begin our analysis of the Fed with a look at the early banking difficulties in the United States that led Congress to create the Federal Reserve System.

Origins of the Federal Reserve System

The United States banking system of the early 1800s consisted of commercial banks that were chartered by their individual state legislatures. There were no national banks as we know them today and no central bank such as the Federal Reserve System. Each state-chartered bank issued its own paper currency, accepted deposits, made loans, and performed other commercial bank functions. Some state-chartered banks issued much more currency relative to their assets than other state banks. This made the relative value of each currency different from the others. With so many different currencies in circulation, it was difficult to get a precise value of one currency compared to another.

Since banks were chartered by individual state governments, there was no national control of banking activity, no uniform national currency, and no national control over the size of the money supply. The overall money supply expanded and contracted with the various activities of the individual state banks. The unstable money supply contributed to economic instability in general. As the equation of exchange predicts, large increases and decreases in the money supply caused undesirable swings in prices and nominal income.

Congress acted in 1791 and 1816 to establish central banks to stabilize the financial sector, but each of these banks was allowed to lapse at the end of its 20-year charter. The early central banks failed because of political opposition to the degree of control that the First and Second Banks of the United States exercised over state banks. In 1863, the Currency Act established a uniform national currency, and in 1864, the National Bank Act set up a system of **national banks.** The federal office of the **Comptroller of the Currency** was established to supervise and control the activity of all banks that received their charters to operate from the federal government. These actions enabled the federal government to exercise some control over the issuing of paper money, set required reserve ratios, and therefore have more control over the size of the money supply.

These early attempts at banking regulation did not eliminate the periodic financial "panics" that severely disrupted the nation. A severe recession was brought on by such a bank panic in 1907. Output and employment fell to low levels as depositors withdrew much of their deposits from commercial banks, shrinking the money supply. Some large banks in the northeast came close to collapse. There were runs on banks. Out of fear, depositors scrambled to withdraw their funds before a bank failure. This was a serious problem, since modern banks use the fractional reserve system and therefore do not have sufficient reserves available to pay off all depositors at the same time.

The withdrawal demands of depositors became so heavy during the bank panic of 1907 that some state banks asked for and received special permission from their state governments to refuse to redeem deposits or checks for currency. In 1908 the federal government began a national study of the problem, and in 1913, Congress passed the Federal Reserve Act establishing the Federal Reserve System.

National Banks
Banks that are chartered by the federal Comptroller of the Currency. National banks must be members of the Federal Reserve System.

Comptroller of the Currency
A federal office established to control and supervise the activities of national banks.

This central banking system is of a unique design. The Federal Reserve System was intended to be the Supreme Court of banking. It was not planned as a profit-making bank but as an independent body charged with the responsibility of maintaining monetary control. To guarantee this independence, Congress gave the Federal Reserve great autonomy. The Fed is owned by the banks that are members of the system (not all banks are). Any bank with "National" in its name is a member of the Fed. Member banks elect many of the Fed's managers; but the members of the executive body, the Federal Reserve Board of Governors, are appointed by the president and confirmed by the Senate. These monetary leaders serve for long terms and Congress can neither remove them nor reduce their salary. The long terms of its leaders and the financial independence that the Fed enjoys helps insulate it from political pressures.

There are Federal Reserve district banks in 12 separate regions of the country. These district banks are owned by the commercial banks of the district that are members of the Federal Reserve System.

The Federal Reserve System was designed to be an independent agency of government. It is not subject to the direct control of the president or any other branch of government, although the Fed is sensitive to political and economic pressures. The chairman of the Federal Reserve System makes periodic reports to Congress and announces monetary targets and general policy goals.

The Fed generates its own revenues from its own investments in U.S. securities and does not have to look to Congress for budget appropriations. The relationship between the Federal Reserve System and the executive branch of government might best be described as one of partnership toward a common goal. That is, both the Federal Reserve and the president are charged with the responsibility to pursue policies that will be in the best interest of the entire economy.

Structure of the Federal Reserve System

14.2 STRUCTURE OF THE FRS

Board of Governors
Seven federal government employees appointed by the president of the United States and confirmed by the Senate who serve as the overall policymaking and controlling body of the Federal Reserve System.

Open Market Operations
The most frequently utilized instrument of monetary policy. It consists of the Fed's buying or selling existing U.S. securities to expand or contract the money supply.

Figure 14-1 shows how the Federal Reserve System is organized. The overall policymaking and controlling body of the system is the **Board of Governors,** seven individuals who are appointed by the President of the United States and confirmed by the Senate. They serve 14-year staggered terms. One appointment expires every two years. This helps to partially insulate the Board of Governors from political pressures. The governors are supposed to make their monetary policy decisions without regard to political considerations and in the best interest of the national economy.

The Board of Governors sets policy for the Federal Reserve System. This policy includes establishing required reserve ratios, conducting **open market operations** to regulate the money supply, and supervising the commercial banks and depository institutions under its control. Open market operations are Fed bond purchases and sales designed to alter bank reserves, thereby increasing or decreasing the money supply.

The Board of Governors is assisted in its function by both the **Federal Open Market Committee (FOMC)** and the **Federal Advisory Council (FAC).** The Federal Open Market Committee consists of the seven members of the Board of Governors, the president of the New York Federal Reserve District Bank, and four of the presidents of the remaining Federal Reserve district banks. This committee sets policy on the Fed's buying and selling of U.S. securities. Since open market operations are the primary tool the Fed uses to control the money supply, the committee really determines mone-

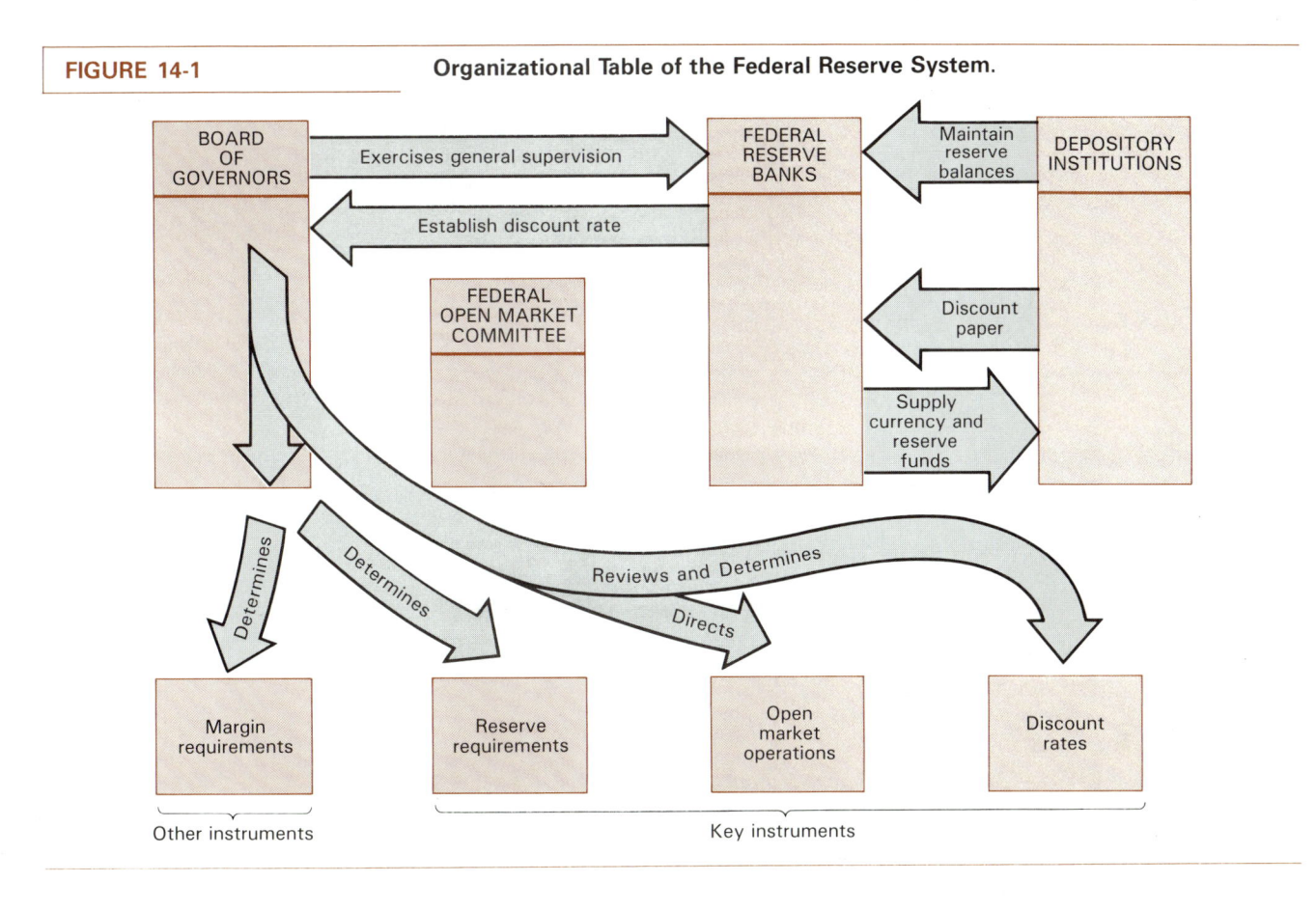

FIGURE 14-1 Organizational Table of the Federal Reserve System.

Federal Open Market Committee (FOMC)
Committee charged with the responsibility of setting Federal Reserve policy regarding open market buying and selling of U.S. securities. The members of this committee include the seven members of the Board of Governors, the president of the New York Federal Reserve District Bank, and four presidents of the remaining Federal Reserve district banks.

Federal Advisory Council (FAC)
A Federal Reserve group consisting of private bankers from the FRS districts, which meets to provide advice and exchange data regarding monetary policy and economic conditions.

tary policy for the Fed. The president of the New York District Bank holds a permanent position on the FOMC because open market operations are carried out through the Federal Reserve Bank of New York.

The Federal Advisory Council is a group of 12 prominent commercial bankers, each selected by the Federal Reserve Bank in their respective district. They meet with the Board of Governors four times a year to exchange information and views on general economic conditions and federal and commercial banking policy. This committee is the direct communication link between commercial depository institutions and the Federal Reserve System. Their function, however, is advisory only; the Fed is not bound in any formal way to respond to the views or opinions of the FAC.

The next link in the Federal Reserve System is the system of 12 Federal Reserve district banks located in Boston, New York, Philadelphia, Richmond, Atlanta, Cleveland, Chicago, St. Louis, Dallas, Minneapolis, Kansas City, and San Francisco. Figure 14-2 shows how banking responsibility for the nation is divided among the regional FRS banks. When the Federal Reserve System was first conceived, these 12 district banks were included to meet the needs for central banking in diverse regions of the country. This was an attempt not only to decentralize some of the power of the central bank but also to make it more responsive to the needs of the local communities it served. Prior to 1935, the Fed's monetary policy was dominated by the 12 presidents of the district banks. The Banking Act of 1935, however, set up the FOMC and centralized most of the authority for open market operations in the hands of the Board of Governors in Washington.

| FIGURE 14-2 | **The Federal Reserve Regional Banking System.** |

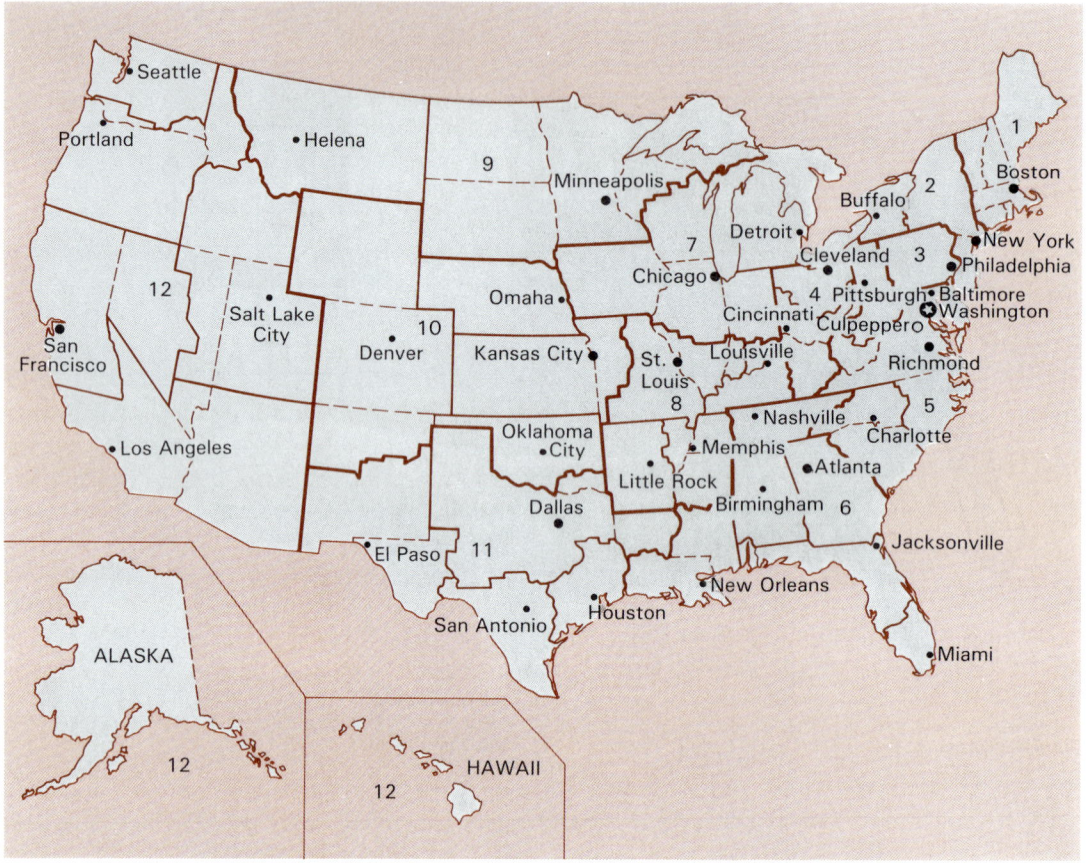

LEGEND
— Boundaries of Federal Reserve Districts
— Boundaries of Federal Reserve Branch Territories
✪ Board of Governors of the Federal Reserve System
● Federal Reserve Bank Cities
● Federal Reserve Branch Cities
○ Federal Reserve Bank Facility

14.3 FUNCTIONS OF THE FRS

The Functions of the Federal Reserve System

The 12 Federal Reserve district banks are the working arms of the Federal Reserve System. They are semipublic corporations owned by the member commercial banks of their district but regulated by the Board of Governors in Washington. They issue federal reserve notes, act as a banker's bank, provide check-clearing services, supervise member banks, and act as fiscal agents for the U.S. government.

Issue Currency The Federal Reserve banks are the only U.S. banks that issue their own currency. If you look at the paper currency in your wallet, you will see that it has the name and number of the Federal Reserve bank that issued it printed on its face. No other banks, governments, or monetary authorities in the United States have the right to issue currency. Federal Reserve currency is printed by the Treasury Department, but it is issued and controlled by the Fed. Federal Reserve currency, in terms of the Fed's balance sheet, is a liability of the Federal Reserve bank that issues it.

Discount Window
The "window" or office through which the Federal Reserve lends reserves to member banks. Loans are technically made through a process by which the FRS purchases loan assets from the bank at a discount.

Discount Rate
The interest rate that commercial banks are charged when they borrow short-term funds from their Federal Reserve district bank.

Depository Institutions Deregulation and Monetary Control Act of 1980
Legislation enacted in 1980 that gives the Federal Reserve greater control over the money supply. The Fed can now set reserve requirements for savings and loan associations, credit unions, and all other nonmembers of the Federal Reserve System. In addition to other stipulations, the act plans to have all interest rate ceilings removed from banks by 1986.

Act As Banker's Bank As a banker's bank, the Federal Reserve district bank holds the reserve deposits of commercial banks and extends loans to financial institutions. When commercial banks engage in interbank transactions, such as buying or selling securities or interbank loans with other Fed members, funds are transferred at the district bank from the account of one member bank to the account of another. There is no need to actually move money around; only bookkeeping entries are needed. This is one reason commercial banks keep portions of their reserves on deposit with the federal district bank. Also, when banks are temporarily short of funds for their required reserves, they may borrow from the Federal Reserve district bank at the **discount window.** The **discount rate** is the interest rate at which banks can borrow short-term reserves from their Federal Reserve district bank. By making these loans to financial institutions, the Fed helps the commercial banks meet their short-term liquidity needs.

Provision of Check-Clearing Services The district banks also provide a system of check clearing for commercial banks. This speeds up the process of check collections and facilitates more efficient exchange. For example, if you live in Richmond, Virginia, and send a check to your sister in Boston, she deposits that check into her commercial bank account in Boston. Her commercial bank (and all other commercial banks in the district) send all out-of-state checks to the Boston Federal District Bank for clearing. The Boston Fed then sends your check to the Richmond Fed. The Richmond Fed sends your check to your commercial bank, who deducts the amount of the check from your account. Check clearing not only enables you to send money out of your district, but speeds up the transfer, as well.

In the past, check clearing by the Fed was performed at a charge below its actual cost for members of the system. However, the **Depository Institutions Deregulation and Monetary Control Act of 1980** required the Fed to treat both member and nonmember banks equally; therefore, the cost of check clearing to member banks will rise in the future. In some major metropolitan areas like New York, private check-clearing houses are beginning to compete effectively with the Federal Reserve district banks to provide these services.

Supervision of Depository Institutions In its supervisory function, the Fed district banks audit the books of depository institutions. This is to make sure that these institutions hold the necessary required reserves and engage in sound loan-making practices. The Federal Reserve System has the authority, if necessary, to remove major officers of depository institutions from their positions if they engage in unsound banking practice. While this power is seldom exercised, it is believed to be an effective deterrent to unsound banking practice. The importance of this regulatory function lies in its ability to instill and maintain public faith in the fractional reserve banking system.

Act As Government Fiscal Agent As the government's fiscal agent, Federal Reserve district banks hold government deposits that are collected from tax revenues. They also disperse government funds when the government writes checks on those tax revenue accounts. The district banks (primarily the New York Fed) act as the agents of the U.S. Treasury when the Treasury buys or sells government bonds to finance government expenditures.

**KEY CONCEPTS
14.1, 14.2, 14.3**

The Federal Reserve was created to regulate the nation's banking system and eliminate the periodic financial crises that characterized the nineteenth century. The Federal Reserve has a unique organizational structure, with regulatory responsibility divided among regional district banks and between these banks and the central Board of Governors and FRS committees. The Federal Reserve issues currency, acts as a bankers' bank, provides check-clearing services, supervises depository institutions, and serves as the government's fiscal agent.

THE FED AND THE BANKING SYSTEM

**14.4
BANKS, THE TREASURY, AND THE FRS**

Commercial banks and other depository institutions are the largest part of our banking system. All national banks are required to be members of the Federal Reserve System. National banks are banks that are chartered by the U.S. Comptroller of the Currency rather than state banking agencies. They are called national banks even though, under law current in 1985, they cannot branch across state lines yet. National banks, such as the Seattle First National Bank, are the only banks that use the term national in their name. State banks (those chartered by their state legislatures) can join the Federal Reserve System if they desire. Today there are about 15,000 commercial banks, but only about one third of them are members of the Federal Reserve System. Of the 5000 or so members, approximately 4000 are national banks and 1000 are state banks. Member banks buy stock in their Federal Reserve district bank equal to a fixed percentage of their capital accounts and receive a 6 percent dividend on this stock.

Why aren't all banks Fed members? Reserve requirements have in the past been higher for member banks than for nonmembers. Reserves earn no interest, so membership in the Fed could increase a bank's liquidity but reduce its profitability. (There has been some discussion in recent years of having the Fed pay interest on required reserves to encourage banks to become Fed members.) Over the years, an increasing number of banks have felt that the benefits of Fed membership are less than its cost and have chosen not to join. Many existing members have relinquished their membership. Therefore the Fed's control over the money supply has declined seriously.

The Depository Institutions Deregulation and Monetary Control Act of 1980 extended the Fed's authority to many more types of depository institutions, including nonmembers of the system. The Fed, over the coming years, will phase in reserve requirements for all depository institutions including savings and loan associations, credit unions, mutual savings banks, and even commercial banks that are not members of the system. This will improve the Fed's ability to control the money supply. Nonmember financial intermediaries are now able to use the Fed's services on a fee-for-service basis, thereby expanding the Fed's role in the financial sector of the economy.

The control exercised by the Fed is, in a global sense, designed to instill and maintain public faith in our fractional reserve banking system. In addition to its control authority, the Fed sometimes acts as a lender of last resort to depository institutions in need of short-term reserves to meet their required reserve ratios. In other words, the Fed not only sets reserve requirements, but also occasionally assists banks to meet those requirements. If banks fail to keep adequate reserves on hand to meet withdrawal demands, the public might quickly lose faith and attempt to withdraw all their funds. Since the Fed tries to instill and maintain public faith in the banking system, it sometimes finds itself in the position of lending temporary reserves to tide over a troubled bank until better times. If a bank finds itself in real financial difficulty, the Fed and the FDIC or FSLIC frequently assist in arranging mergers between the ailing bank and a much stronger financial institution. In doing so, the public faith is maintained, and both the control and assistance functions of the Federal Reserve System are well served.

THE FED AND THE TREASURY

14.4 BANKS, THE TREASURY, AND THE FRS

There is an important distinction that needs to be made here between the Federal Reserve System, which is the independent central bank of the United States, and the Treasury, which is part of the executive branch of the United States government. The Fed is controlled by its Board of Governors. The Treasury is controlled by the president through the Secretary of the Treasury, whom he appoints. The Fed and the Treasury frequently work together and sometimes engage in similar activities, but they are completely separate agencies.

The Treasury can sell government bonds to finance government deficits. The Fed acts as the agent for the Treasury in selling these bonds. When the Fed sells bonds for the U.S. Treasury, however, no change in the money supply takes place. The bond sale simply takes money from people with savings and transfers it to the federal government's bank account (the savers receive federal bonds in exchange for their money). The Treasury is primarily a budgeting agency of the U.S. government and is not directly concerned with the size of the money supply. It does not issue money (except for coins). The Federal Reserve System, however, buys and sells government bonds in open market operations deliberately to expand or contract the money supply. When the Fed buys or sells bonds on its own account, this affects the reserves of the banking system and changes the money supply.

While there is cooperation between the Fed and the Treasury, they have two expressly different purposes. The Treasury finances the government through taxation and deficit borrowing. The Fed regulates the banking system and controls the money supply.

THE INSTRUMENTS OF MONETARY POLICY

With an understanding of the structure and function of the Federal Reserve System behind us, we can now take a much closer look at just how the Fed carries out its primary goal of regulating the money supply. The Fed uses three tools to expand or contract the availability of excess reserves in the banking system and, therefore, the money supply itself. These instruments are open market operations, changes in the reserve requirement, and changes in the discount rate charged by the Federal Reserve district banks. The combined activity in these three areas of general credit control constitutes the monetary policy of the Fed at any given time.

Open Market Operations

14.5 OPEN MARKET OPERATIONS

As noted earlier, open market operations, the Fed's buying and selling of government bonds on the "open market," is the most frequently used instrument of monetary control. Open market operations use bond sales and

Open Market Purchase
Purchase of securities by the Federal Reserve to increase the money supply and make credit more available.

purchases to alter the amount of reserves in the banking system and the amount of money and credit in the economy.

When the Fed wants to expand banks' reserves and the money and credit supplies, it engages in an **open market purchase.** Here the Fed buys bonds from banks or individuals in the private sector. When the Federal Reserve System buys U.S. securities from commercial banks and private investors, U.S. securities pass from their owner to the Fed. In return, the original bondholder receives a check drawn on the Federal Reserve Bank. This check is then deposited into a bank somewhere in the economy. This deposit has the same effect as we saw in Chapter 13 when a new deposit was made with money from outside the banking system. It increases the reserves of the bank that sells the security or receives the deposit from the private bond seller. The Fed credits the bank's reserves when it honors the check. This increase in reserves triggers the deposit expansion process and the money supply expands by some multiple of the initial deposit. Let's trace this process from the open market purchase of the Fed through the commercial banking system to its completion with the expansion of the money supply.

Table 14-1 illustrates the hypothetical balance sheet of the Federal Reserve district bank and commercial banks A and B before any open market action has been taken. We begin this example with a $10,000 money supply, held as demand deposits of $5000 each by Bank A and Bank B. We assume, for simplicity, that all money is held as demand deposits, not Federal Reserve notes. Assume that the reserve requirement for Bank A and Bank B is 20 percent.

The Open Market Committee of the Board of Governors now decides to expand the money supply. They implement an open market purchase by notifying the New York Federal Reserve District Bank to buy $1000 in U.S.

TABLE 14-1 **Balance Sheets Before Open Market Purchase**

Fed District Bank

Assets ($)		Liabilities ($)	
Securities	10,000	Deposit member banks	
Cash	0	Bank A	1000
(other items omitted)		Bank B	1000
		Fed Reserve notes	0

Commercial Bank A

Assets ($)		Liabilities ($)	
Required reserves	1000	Demand deposits	5000
Excess reserves	0	Time deposits	0
Loans	1000		
Securities	3000		

Commercial Bank B

Assets ($)		Liabilities ($)	
Required reserves	1000	Demand deposits	5000
Excess reserves	0	Time deposits	0
Loans	1000		
Securities	3000		

securities from commercial banks or private individuals. We will assume Bank A sells $1000 worth of its holding of U.S. securities to the New York Fed (it does not matter, in terms of the total effect, whether the Fed buys the bond from a bank or an individual). This reduces the bank's U.S. securities account on its balance sheet by $1000 to a total of $2000. In return, Bank A receives a check drawn on the Fed, or its equivalent, which shows up as an increase in Bank A's reserve deposit at the Federal Reserve district bank and as an increase in the excess reserves account of Bank A on its own balance sheet. These four entry changes are all noted in Table 14-2.

The Fed's U.S. security account has increased by $1000. Bank A's reserve account on the Fed balance sheet is also increased by $1000, which is how the Fed pays for the bond. The excess reserves account of Bank A on its own balance sheet increases by $1000, and its U.S. securities account falls by $1000. So far, no changes have taken place in Bank B.

Bank A now finds itself with $1000 in excess reserves and no change in required reserves because there is no change in demand deposit liabilities. We know from Chapter 13 that the bank faces a strong incentive to make loans on this excess reserve balance. We will assume that someone comes into Bank A and borrows $1000 to buy consumer goods. Bank A makes the loan and reduces its reserves at the Fed by $1000. The borrower makes the desired purchase, paying for it with a check drawn on Bank A. The consumer goods seller deposits the $1000 check into Bank B. We can see the new balance sheets of Banks A and B that result from these transactions in Table 14-3.

Bank B receives the $1000 deposit and puts 20 percent, or $200, in its required reserve account. The remaining $800 is held as excess reserves, available for loans or the purchase of securities. The two-bank economy now has a total money supply of $11,000, $5000 in demand deposits at Bank A

| TABLE 14-2 | **Balance Sheets Immediately After Open Market Purchase** |

Fed District Bank

Assets ($)		Liabilities ($)	
Securities	11,000	Deposit member banks	
Cash	0	Bank A	2000
(other items omitted)		Bank B	1000
		Fed Reserve notes	0

Commercial Bank A

Assets ($)		Liabilities ($)	
Required reserves	1000	Demand deposits	5000
Excess reserves	1000	Time deposits	0
Loans	1000		
Securities	2000		

Commercial Bank B

Assets ($)		Liabilities ($)	
Required reserves	1000	Demand deposits	5000
Excess reserves	0	Time deposits	0
Loans	1000		
Securities	3000		

TABLE 14-3

Balance Sheets for Banks A and B after Bank A's Loan

Assets	Bank A ($)	Bank B ($)	Liabilities	Bank A ($)	Bank B ($)
Required reserves	1000	1200	Demand deposits	5000	6000
Excess reserves	0	800	Time deposits	0	0
Loans	2000	1000			
Securities	2000	3000			

Open Market Sale
Sale of securities by the Federal Reserve to decrease the money supply and make credit less available.

and $6000 in demand deposits at Bank B. The Federal Reserve open market purchase has already increased the money supply by $1000, and the deposit expansion process has only begun. Bank B now has $800 to loan out.

As we saw in Chapter 13, this loan making and redeposit procedure will continue to expand the money supply. However, since some portion of each new redeposit must be held as excess reserves, eventually the amount of redeposit must approach zero. The deposit expansion multiplier in this case is 1/.20, or 5. The Federal Reserve's open market purchase of $1000 will result in a maximum increase in the money supply of $5000. Of this amount, $1000 was created by the Federal Reserve to pay for the bond. The remaining $4000 is created by the banking system as it makes loans.

If the Federal Reserve System decides to undertake a contractionary monetary policy, it engages in an **open market sale.** To pursue an open market sale, the FOMC would direct the New York Fed to sell some of its U.S. securities. This would be the reverse of the buying procedure. If Bank A (or one of its customers) bought $1000 worth of additional securities, this would reduce the bank's reserves. Bank A would recall existing loans or stop making new loans until it reached its required reserve ratio. Loans in the banking system and the deposit expansion multiplier would work in reverse. A $1000 sale of U.S. securities by the Fed to commercial banks or individuals would eventually reduce the money supply by up to $5000 ($1000 times the multiple deposit expansion multiplier). Remember from Chapter 13, however, that the deposit expansion multiplier in the real world is considerably less than the figures used in this example.

The Federal Reserve undertakes open market purchases and sales almost every week as it tries to regulate the supplies of money and the availability of credit in the economy. The goal of the Fed is to expand the money supply at a rate that fosters economic growth but not so fast as to stimulate inflation.

One final note on open market operations is in order. It is important not to confuse Federal Reserve open market bond sales with Treasury bond sales. The Treasury sells bonds to raise money for the federal government to spend. The money that the Treasury receives for the bonds goes into the government's bank account and is quickly spent. There is no change in the economy's money supply, only a change in ownership of it. The Fed sells bonds as a contractionary monetary policy designed to reduce the money supply. The money that the Fed receives for the bonds leaves the banking system and is no longer part of the money supply. Treasury bond sales and Federal Reserve open market sales are different in function and have very different impacts on the economy.

Open market operations are not formally announced at the time they take place, although the Fed does announce target ranges for the growth of $M1$ and $M2$, which provides the financial markets with some information about its intentions. The Fed keeps its specific open market actions secret until several weeks after they have taken place. Still, many investors are 'Fed watchers' and try to guess what the Fed has done and what its impact will be on the economy. They compare their expectations to the money supply figures that the Fed releases every Thursday afternoon.

The Discount Rate

> **14.6 DISCOUNT RATE**

Federal Reserve district banks make loans to member banks for short periods of time. Commercial banks borrow from the Fed when their reserves temporarily fall below required levels. They borrow from the Fed through the discount procedure. When commercial banks take in more deposits and their reserves rise, they repay the discount loan. The interest rate that banks are charged when they exercise this short-term borrowing privilege is called the discount rate. This discount rate represents the cost to the bank of borrowing from the Fed to maintain specified reserve levels.

Commercial banks have at least two other sources for these necessary short-term reserves. First, they can borrow through a mechanism called the **federal funds market.** This is a system in which banks with excess reserves make very short-term loans (usually less than 24 hours) to other banks who are in need of reserves. For example, if the National Bank of Boston found itself late Tuesday afternoon with $300,000 in excess reserves and no available borrowers at the moment, it could, with a phone call and a wire transaction, dump that $300,000 into the Fed Funds market for perhaps one day. At the same time, the Continental National Bank of Chicago may find that its reserves have fallen $300,000 short of the required level. Continental National Bank expects to collect a $300,000 outstanding loan on Thursday, but it is still $300,000 short on required reserves at the present time. With a phone call and a wire transaction, the Chicago bank can borrow the $300,000 it needs from the Boston bank. The interest rate the Chicago bank would have to pay on this short-term loan is called the **federal funds rate.** While the discount rate is set by the Federal Reserve System, the federal funds rate is set by the market force of supply and demand and fluctuates with banking conditions.

Federal Funds Market
The system through which some commercial banks who hold excess reserves indirectly make very short-term loans to other commercial banks in need of reserves.

Federal Funds Rate
The interest rate charged on loans made in the federal funds market.

A second way other than borrowing from the Fed that commercial banks can ensure that they always meet their required reserve ratios is to hold excess reserves, but this activity has a cost. If a commercial bank keeps a pool of excess reserves on hand as insurance in case its reserve levels fall, the bank gives up the relatively high interest income it would have earned by loaning out those excess reserves. Banks therefore hold relatively few excess reserves on average.

Commercial banks get only small portions of their loanable funds from the Federal Reserve district bank. The cost of borrowing from the Fed does, however, affect the commercial banks' decisions about borrowing from the federal funds market, as well as decisions concerning how much of their reserves they are willing to lend out any one time. Any way that a commercial bank attempts to meet its reserve requirements will have a cost. Banks either pay the discount rate at the Fed, the federal funds rate, or forego interest on holdings of excess reserves.

An increase in the discount rate is a contractionary monetary policy. As the discount rate is raised, it is more costly for the commercial banks to borrow reserves from the Fed. When banks turn to borrow from the federal funds market, this tends to drive up the federal funds rate, as well, thereby encouraging banks to hold more excess reserves (and make relatively fewer new loans) than before. As the cost of all these sources of reserves rises, the interest rate banks charge on the loans they make to customers must eventually rise. This discourages more lending by banks, and borrowers are less willing to take out loans at higher interest rates. The amount of loans, and therefore the money supply, begins to fall.

A decrease in the discount rate, on the other hand, is an expansionary monetary policy. When the Fed lowers the discount rate, this encourages banks to hold fewer excess reserves and make relatively more loans. This increases the money supply and makes credit more available in the economy.

Unlike open market operations, which are kept secret by the Federal Reserve, changes in the discount rate are openly announced and widely publicized. The Fed uses the discount rate as a way to announce its intentions. If the Fed wants the economy to know that it is adopting a more expansionary monetary policy, for example, it will announce a decrease in the discount rate and then follow up this announcement with an open market purchase to further increase bank reserves. If the Fed is adopting a more contractionary monetary policy, on the other hand, it will announce an increase in the discount rate and follow up with open market sales to reduce bank reserves.

Changes in the discount rate are powerful in part because of their **announcement effects.** Announcement effects are actions taken in anticipation of a change in economic policy. Investment behavior frequently changes, for example, in response to the announcement of a change in the discount rate. People in the private sector begin to take actions that they think will be profitable, given the announced new direction in Fed policy.

Announcement Effects
Changes in economic behavior that occur due to the Fed's announcement of plans to expand or contract the money supply.

14.7 RESERVE REQUIREMENT

The Reserve Requirement

The reserve requirement is the percentage of total demand deposits that a bank is required by law to keep on hand in the form of vault cash or deposits at the Federal Reserve Bank. Changes in this level of required reserves is one means of expanding or contracting the money supply. This means of controlling the money supply is the most powerful single tool of monetary policy. It is, however, an extremely blunt tool and is infrequently used. The impact of changes in the required reserve ratio is large because it affects both the availability of excess reserves and the size of the deposit expansion multiplier. This impact is illustrated in Table 14.4.

The banking system shown in Table 14-4 begins with $10,000 in demand deposits and a reserve requirement of 25 percent. Now suppose that the Fed reduces the reserve requirement by 5 percentage points to 20 percent. This will produce a relatively large increase in the supply of money and the availability of credit, even though there will be no net change in the banking system's reserves. Here is how the process works.

Table 14-4(a) shows the banking system before any change. The banks have $10,000 in demand deposits. Required reserves are $2500, and $7500 worth of loans have been made. Table 14-4(b) shows the initial change when the reserve requirement is reduced to 20 percent. Banks shift $500 from the required reserve account to excess reserves. These excess reserves can now be used for loans, which will be redeposited into the banking system. The deposit expansion multiplier predicts a maximum increase in the money supply of 1/.20 times new deposits, or $2500.

After the deposit expansion process has finished, as Table 14-4(c) shows, the banking system has total demand deposits of $12,500, $2500 more than before (assuming that the maximum multiplier effect takes place). The $2500 increase in the money supply exists because the change in the reserve requirement has allowed banks to make an additional $2500 worth of loans.

TABLE 14-4 Combined Balance Sheet of All Banks

(a)
With initial 25 percent reserve requirement

Assets ($)		Liabilities ($)	
Required reserves	2500	Demand deposits	10,000
Excess reserves	0	Time deposits	0
Loans	7500		

(b)
Immediately after change to 20 percent reserve requirement

Assets ($)		Liabilities ($)	
Required reserves	2000	Demand deposits	10,000
Excess reserves	500	Time deposits	0
Loans	7500		

(c)
After deposit expansion process is completed

Assets ($)		Liabilities ($)	
Required reserves	2500	Demand deposits	12,500
Excess reserves	0	Time deposits	0
Loans	10,000		

When the deposit expansion process is complete, required reserves have returned to their original $2500 level. The change in the reserve requirement has not changed the dollar amount of reserves in the banking system, it has just allowed banks to make more loans with their existing reserves. Required reserves at the beginning of this process ($2500, or 25 percent of $10,000) are the same as at the end ($2500, or 20 percent of $12,500).

A decrease in the reserve requirement is an expansionary monetary policy that increases the money supply and makes credit more available. An increase in the reserve requirement, on the other hand, is a contractionary monetary policy that tends to reduce the money supply and make loans less available. Banks must increase their required reserve accounts when the reserve requirement rises. This means that they must call in loans or make fewer new loans from excess reserves. These actions result in a relatively smaller money supply.

Changes in the reserve requirement not only change the money supply directly, they also make open market operations more or less powerful. A $1 million open market purchase, for example, expands the money supply by up to $5 million if the reserve requirement is 20 percent, but it only expands it by up to $4 million if the reserve requirement is 25 percent. The difference is due to the impact of the reserve requirement on the deposit expansion multiplier.

Since it is such a powerful tool of monetary policy, control over the required reserve ratio rests solely with the Board of Governors. The Board may consult with other committees and individuals in making its decisions on the reserve requirement, but the authority to make that decision is exclusive to the seven people who are on the Board. Reserve requirements on most bank accounts in the United States have been in the range of 3 percent to 12 percent in recent years. Time deposits have the lowest reserve requirement, while demand deposits and other checkable accounts have higher reserve requirements.

> **KEY CONCEPTS**
> **14.5, 14.6, 14.7**
>
> The three main monetary tools of the Federal Reserve are open market operations, discount rate policies, and changes in the reserve requirement. Open market operations increase or decrease bank reserves through purchases or sales of bonds. The discount rate is the interest rate that the FRS charges for loans to member banks. The discount rate serves to signal FRS intentions to the financial sector. Changes in the reserve requirement affect the number of loans banks can make with the reserves they already have.

INTEREST RATES AND CREDIT MARKETS

Federal Reserve actions influence both the amount of bank deposits (money) in the financial system and the quantity of funds available for loans (credit). The remainder of this chapter examines the financial system by looking at markets where credit transactions occur. Credit markets are institutions where loans are made, credit is exchanged, and interest rates are determined through the forces of supply and demand.

The most important reason for studying the credit market is that it sets the interest rate. Our focus here will be on the average level of interest rates throughout the economy and how they are changing. The interest rate is important because changes in the interest rate affect many important choices in the economy. Firms considering inventory or plant expansion compare potential profits to interest cost before they make a decision. Consumers decide whether to spend or save (and how much to spend or save) based on loan costs and the interest return on savings accounts. Interest is a big cost for government, too, so the interest rate affects fiscal policy. Interest rates also help determine foreign exchange rates, so international trade hangs in the balance. In short, the interest rate affects each component of aggregate demand: consumption, investment, government, and net export spending.

Who sets the interest rate? A few rates are determined by law or rule. The interest rate on conventional home mortgages, for example, is set by market forces, but it is heavily influenced by the actions of government agencies that borrow funds to be reloaned, at fixed interest rates, to home buyers and mortgage lenders. Interest rates on credit-card loans in many states are set by state law and are relatively unaffected by economic conditions. Most interest rates, however, fluctuate with the supply and demand for credit.

The Demand for Credit

Three groups dominate the demand side of the credit market: consumers, businesses, and governments. Consumers borrow to buy the goods and services they want now. For consumers, borrowing is the alternative to saving for future consumption. Consumers borrow for houses, cars, education and many other things. Investment is the primary reason for business borrowing. Businesses borrow to finance investments such as trucks and factories and to purchase inventories.

14.8 CREDIT DEMAND DETERMINANTS

Governments borrow for equally varied ends. The federal government's borrowing goes for defense spending, to solve social problems, and to pay the interest on old debt. The government also acts as a conduit for others to borrow. Federal agencies borrow funds and then relend them to small businesses, farmers, low-income home buyers, college students, and others. These people get lower interest rates because they have access to the government's low-risk, highly efficient bond market.

State and local governments borrow to build schools, bridges, and highways. Some of this money also ends up with private borrowers. Income from interest paid by states and localities is not subject to federal income tax, so these governments get lower interest rates than private borrowers. They supply funds raised this way to private firms as an inducement to build and hire workers in their area. Governments are active in credit markets, but a lot of government borrowing ends up in private hands.

There are four main determinants of the amount of credit demanded in a given time period. These are interest rates, inflation and inflationary expectations, income and income expectations, and government policies.

Real Interest Rate
The nominal interest rate adjusted for inflation. The real interest rate is calculated by subtracting the expected inflation rate from the nominal interest rate.

Nominal Interest Rate
The interest rate stated in ordinary terms, as a fraction of the amount of the loan.

Interest Rates Interest rates are the cost of a loan, so the level of desired borrowing is inversely related to the interest rate, all else being equal. Business firms borrow more, for example, at low interest rates than when interest costs are high.

The inverse relationship between interest and credit demand is complicated by two factors. The first is that government borrowing sometimes increases along with the interest rate. The national debt, as you read in Chapter 7, is continually refinanced. The interest on old debt is paid by new borrowing. High interest rates increase this expense, forcing the federal government to borrow even more to pay high interest costs. This vicious cycle keeps government borrowers busy even when rates are high.

The second factor is that borrowers often respond to **real interest rates** instead of **nominal interest rates.** The nominal interest rate is the interest rate stated in everyday terms, as a percent of the amount of the loan. The real interest rate is the interest rate adjusted for inflation. The real interest rate is calculated by subtracting the inflation rate from the nominal interest rate. Suppose for example, that the nominal interest rate rises from 10 percent to 15 percent at the same time that the expected inflation rate rises from 5 percent to 10 percent. Will people borrow less at the higher 15 percent nominal rate? Borrowing stays the same if loan seekers respond to real rates, since the real interest rate has remained at 5 percent in this example.

Inflation and Inflation Expectations Inflation is an important factor for borrowers to consider. First, higher prices mean that more money must be borrowed to buy cars and houses or pay tuition bills. This forges a direct link between inflation and credit demand. Inflation expectations are also important. Borrowers gain from unexpectedly high inflation because they can pay back loans with dollars of lower purchasing power. Put another way, an unexpectedly high inflation reduces the real interest rate that borrowers pay. People who anticipate higher inflation borrow now to lock in relatively low nominal rates and to purchase goods before prices rise. Borrowing declines when inflation is expected to slow.

Income and Income Expectations Consumers and firms borrow more when they foresee rising incomes or profits. Consumers borrow when income goes up and they can afford higher monthly car or mortgage payments. Businesses borrow to expand production and sales when they experience higher profits or when they expect higher profits in the future. Both groups borrow less when unemployment rises or when they anticipate hard times. Neither consumers nor firms want to be saddled with loan obligations during recessions.

Government Policies   Government is such an important part of the credit market that a small change in fiscal policy can cause a large change in credit demand. In 1985, for example, direct federal government borrowing amounted to 5 percent of GNP. The government was easily the largest single borrower in the U.S. credit markets that year. Credit demand changes with fiscal policies, as Congress votes for higher or lower deficits, or when government lending programs, such as Farm Home Loans, change. Credit demand also depends on state and local government borrowing policies. The Washington Public Power Supply System (a group of public utilities) borrowed over $5 billion dollars in the early 1980s to build power plants, for example.

The Supply of Credit

14.9 CREDIT SUPPLY DETERMINANTS

Credit exists because many people want to save and lend. They do this because they want to consume less than their entire income now in order to have more resources at some future date. The interest rate is the payment they receive for making their resources available to others. The four main factors that determine the amount of credit available are interest rates, inflation and inflationary expectations, saving, and federal reserve policies.

Interest Rates   Savers and lenders react to interest rates. Interest is, after all, the payment they receive. All else being equal, savers and their banks tend to make more credit available as interest rates rise. Consumers save less and banks hold more excess reserves and loan less when interest rates are falling.

Inflation and Inflation Expectations   Inflation also affects the supply side of the credit market. Unexpectedly high inflation hurts lenders, who receive lower real interest returns, while unexpectedly low inflation makes savers better off. Therefore, fewer loans are offered when inflation is high because rising prices shrink real interest returns. Lower inflation rates temporarily boost real returns, so the credit supply increases. Credit supplies tend to be inversely related to inflation rates.

Saving   Saving is the ultimate source of credit. Higher saving rates tend to increase the credit supply. What determines saving behavior? Income is one factor. Savings accounts tend to grow when income rises and fall when unemployed people withdraw funds to pay the rent. Expectations are another variable affecting saving. Americans who fear the social security system's collapse save more for their own retirement, for example; while people who anticipate social security checks when they grow old may save less than they otherwise would for retirement. Tax laws are also important. Congress set up tax-deferred Individual Retirement Accounts (IRAs) to encourage greater saving.

Federal Reserve Policies   The Federal Reserve is an important force in credit markets. The Fed uses its powerful tools to manipulate the credit supply. Open market operations, reserve requirement policies, and the dis-

Interest Rates and Credit Markets 419

count rate all affect the availability of credit. We will analyze these Fed tools in the context of the credit market.

Credit Market Equilibrium

| 14.10 EQUILIBRIUM INTEREST RATE |

The credit market is shown in Figure 14-3. This figure shows a single credit market, but there are really many markets for different types of loans, all carefully intertwined. The forces of supply and demand that we will explore in this single market show up in each of the many submarkets.

The credit demand curve (*CD*) in Figure 14-3 maps the relationship between the interest rate and the quantity of credit demanded (the dollar amount of desired loans), all factors other than the interest rate held constant. A change in the interest rate causes a movement along the *CD* curve. The *CD* curve is downward sloping to show that consumers, businesses, and many governments seek fewer borrowed funds when interest costs are high. These groups want to borrow more at low interest rates, however. There is an increase in the quantity of credit demanded as interest rates fall. The credit demand curve would shift if one of the other determinants of credit demand, such as income, inflation, or government policies, were to change.

The credit supply curve (*CS*) maps the relationship between the interest rate and the quantity of credit supplied, all else held constant. The *CS* curve is upward sloping to show that higher interest rates bring more loanable funds to the market. Banks want to make more loans when there are higher returns. Savers shift money from stocks to bank accounts when interest rates are high, further increasing the quantity of credit supplied. Conversely, lower interest rates reduce the amount of money lenders offer. A decrease in interest rates causes a reduction in the quantity of credit supplied. The credit supply curve would shift if one of the other determinants of credit supply, such as saving, inflation, or Federal Reserve policy, were to change.

| FIGURE 14-3 | **Credit Market Equilibrium.** Credit demand (*CD*) and credit supply (*CS*) reach equilibrium at a 14 percent interest rate in this example. The market forces of surplus and shortage assure that the market will move toward this equilibrium interest rate. The credit market sets the interest rates for the economy. |

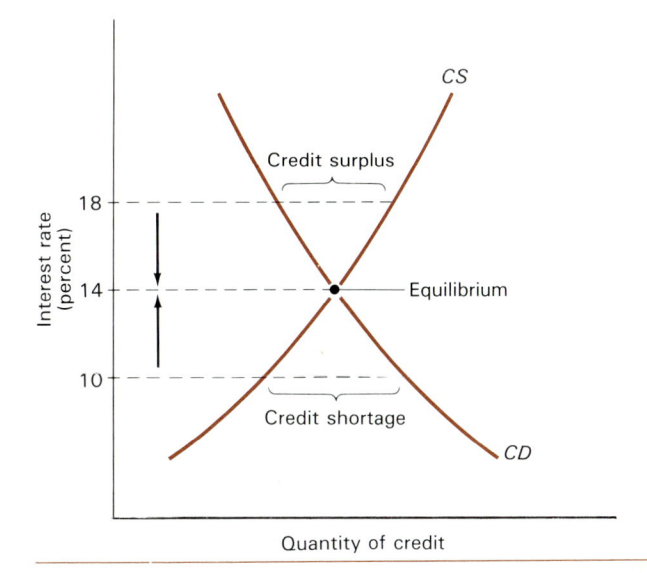

ECONOMIC ISSUES

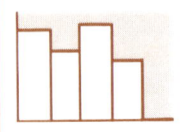

Interest Rate Ceilings

Financial institutions and credit markets are among the most heavily regulated parts of the U.S. economy. Banks in the United States are subject to audit at any time by federal agencies. Bankers must even give keys to their buildings and files to regulatory agencies so that "surprise" audits can be conducted at any time to see if all is in order. Bankers sometimes arrive at work in the morning to see federal auditors already busy in the "closed" banks.

Most bank regulations serve useful purposes. The reserve requirement regulation, for example, assures that banks have sufficient funds to meet the withdrawal needs of their depositors and allows the Federal Reserve to regulate money and credit availability. Some government regulations of financial markets are questionable, however. Two examples of controversial bank regulations are laws and rules that (1) set ceilings on the interest rates banks can pay depositors and (2) regulate the interest rates they can charge borrowers. The Federal Reserve's Regulation Q establishes deposit interest ceilings, while many state usury laws set maximum loan interest rates. Interest rate ceilings are becoming a thing of the past in many cases, however. The deregulation of the banking system started in the late 1970s has eliminated many interest rate restrictions, although many state-imposed interest rate ceilings still exist.

A case can be made for interest ceilings on both deposits and loans. Ceilings on interest paid for deposits were designed to prevent destructive competition among banks for checking and saving accounts, for example. Active competition for these accounts, many thought, might make banks less stable, since millions of dollars might be deposited or withdrawn on any given day in response to competitive interest rate offerings. Interest rate controls were designed to prevent such competition and thus give banks access to a stable pool of relatively inexpensive funds so that long-term loans could be made.

Usury laws have a long history dating back to before the time of Christ. In most states, usury laws are designed to prevent lenders from exploiting individuals who are in desperate need of funds or who have poor information about loan availability. Without these laws, some lenders might charge very high rates of interest to borrowers who cannot afford to pay them. Such loans still take place, however, even where they are illegal. In general, information about loan terms and prices is not as readily available as is information about other goods and services. Potential borrowers find it time consuming and costly to search for the best loan. Interest rate ceilings were designed, in part, to prevent lenders from taking advantage of borrower ignorance.

Both these types of laws have good intentions, but good intentions are not always enough when laws infringe on voluntary exchange. Both deposit interest ceilings and usury laws can lead to undesirable side effects that defeat their original purposes. In the 1970s, for example, high inflation rates pushed up interest rates in the United States and other countries. High market interest rates, combined with the interest rate ceilings discussed here, had several detrimental effects.

Deposit interest ceilings were designed to give banks a stable source of relatively inexpensive deposits. In the 1970s, however, many savers found they could get much higher interest returns by purchasing bonds or investing in money market mutual funds. They took their money out of low-interest bank ac-

---

The first job of any market is to find equilibrium. The credit market depicted in Figure 14-3 clears at an interest rate of 14 percent. The quantity of credit supplied at this interest rate just equals the quantity of loans demanded.

Shortage and surplus force the market to this equilibrium. Suppose, for example, that interest rates were above equilibrium, at 18 percent in the figure. Banks and savers offer many loans at this high rate, but few consumers or businesses want to borrow. The surplus of funds puts bankers in a bind. They need to make loans to pay the interest on their deposits. Interest rates must fall to bring the market into equilibrium. Lower interest rates reduce the quantity of credit supplied (a movement along the *CS* curve) but increase the quantity of loans demanded (a movement along the *CD* curve). The surplus of credit shrinks until equilibrium is found.

counts and invested it directly in the credit markets, a process called disintermediation. This disintermediation resulted in much lower reserves for banks, which had to reduce new loans and scramble for new deposits to meet their reserve requirements. Many banks ended up borrowing funds at high market interest rates to meet legal reserves. Profits fell in the banking industry as banks paid high interest for new money while receiving lower interest payments on their existing portfolio of loans.

Disintermediation caused such severe problems for the banking industry in the 1970s that most deposit interest rate ceilings are currently being eliminated. Banks still offer low-interest saving and zero-interest checking accounts, for example, but increasing numbers of deposits are going into NOW (negotiable order of withdrawal) and similar accounts that pay higher market interest rates and still allow depositors ready access to their funds.

Usury laws that limit interest rates on consumer loans produced many negative effects, too. State laws that made mortgage loans of over, say, 10 percent illegal distorted many economic decisions. First, banks in some states, with low interest ceilings, were forced to quit making loans for home purchases, since the maximum legal interest rate was less than that which the bank had to pay to attract the deposits that made these loans available. The banks' scarce reserves were diverted from consumer loans to areas with interest rates not subject to government control. Fewer consumer loans were made and more loanable funds went to commercial, industrial, and government borrowers, for example. Many banks even looked to foreign businesses and governments to make loans, since it was illegal to loan in the United States at market rates. Some of these foreign loans are now in default, adding to the financial woes of the banking system. Consumers, who were supposed to be 'protected' from high-interest loans, found they could get no loans at all. Those funds that were made available for consumer loans went to only the least-risky, most credit-worthy of borrowers. Many low-income families found themselves unable to get loans because scarce funds went to higher-income groups who were more likely to repay borrowed funds.

With few new mortgage loans being made, many adjustments were necessary in the housing market. Many people found that they could not sell their houses, even at reduced prices, because buyers could not get the needed loans to make the purchase. Many families found themselves locked into houses that no longer fit their needs. Some people even had to pass up job promotions that would have forced them to move because they could not sell their valuable homes or get loans to purchase new homes in the next city.

These examples illustrate the problem with regulations on interest rates and other important prices. Regulations are unable to adjust to changing economic conditions, such as high interest rates caused by inflation, as quickly as markets can. Interest rate ceilings in the 1970s hurt bank profits and redistributed loan funds, with many undesirable results. Adam Smith, the champion of the free market, actually favored interest rate ceilings on mortgage loans, but he understood their power. Smith thought that home mortgages were undesirable, since they diverted funds from the commercial and industrial loans he thought were more important. Smith favored mortgage interest ceilings precisely because he thought they would eliminate mortgage loans, not encourage them. Smith knew what many modern legislators have forgotten, that the power to regulate is the power to destroy.

Given the problems that interest rate ceilings can cause, it is comforting to know that the broad deregulation of the financial system that is taking place in the 1980s has set the goal of eliminating many of the interest rate ceilings discussed here.

Additional References

Peters, Helen Frame. "The Mortgage Market: A Place for Ceilings?" *Federal Reserve Bank of Philadelphia Business Review,* July-August 1977, pp. 13–21.

Veseth, Michael, *Introductory Macroeconomics,* Second Edition. Orlando, FL: Academic Press, 1984, chaps. 9 and 10.

The force of shortage works when interest rates are below equilibrium. Many people want to borrow at 10 percent interest, but banks do not have sufficient funds to satisfy all potential borrowers. Banks allocate scarce funds by lending to low-risk customers and raising interest charges. Higher interest rates make a greater quantity of credit available (movement along the *CS* curve) and reduce the number of loan applicants (movement along *CD* curve). The shortage shrinks until interest rates reach equilibrium.

Events That Cause Changes in Interest Rates

14.11 FACTORS AFFECTING INTEREST RATES

Interest rates can change for many reasons. Nominal interest rates in the United States were high and rising in the late 1970s and early 1980s, for example, but then fell dramatically in the mid-1980s. What accounts for this change in interest rates and how can we anticipate what interest rates will do in the future? In general, anything that affects credit demand or credit supply will influence the interest rate. We can understand how and why interest rates changed in the late 1970s and 1980s by looking at credit markets. The dramatic interest rate changes in this period were primarily the result of four factors: deficit borrowing, Federal Reserve policies, high profits on business investment, and high inflation.

Deficit Borrowing Federal government deficits in the $200 billion range increased credit demand in the mid-1980s. The CD curve shifted out to reflect the higher government borrowing, causing a shortage of credit at the initial equilibrium interest rate. Interest rates increased to adjust for the shortage. As interest rates increased, the quantity of credit demanded fell and the quantity of credit supplied increased until the new equilibrium was reached.

Deficit borrowing tends to increase interest rates, all else being equal. This affects consumers who borrow to purchase durable goods, businesses that borrow to finance plant and inventory investments, and governments that borrow to pay the interest on previous debt. Deficit borrowing also causes the crowding-out effect that was discussed in Chapter 7. Figure 14-4 shows the crowding-out effect graphically.

The market depicted in this figure is in initial equilibrium with $1000 billion of credit exchanged. Assume, for simplicity, that all of this credit is borrowed by private businesses for investment purposes. Now suppose that government increases the credit demand by $200 billion to finance the deficit. The figure shows that this causes interest rates to rise until the new equilibrium is reached at a quantity of $1100 billion in credit exchanged. The quantity of credit supplied has increased by $100 billion, but the government

FIGURE 14-4

Deficit Borrowing and Crowding Out. A $200 billion government deficit results in a $200 billion increase in credit demand. This shifts the credit market equilibrium from *A* to *B* in the figure. Interest rates rise and crowding out occurs because the increase in government borrowing is greater than the increase in the quantity of credit supplied at *B*. Private borrowers have only $1100 minus $200, or $900 billion, to borrow.

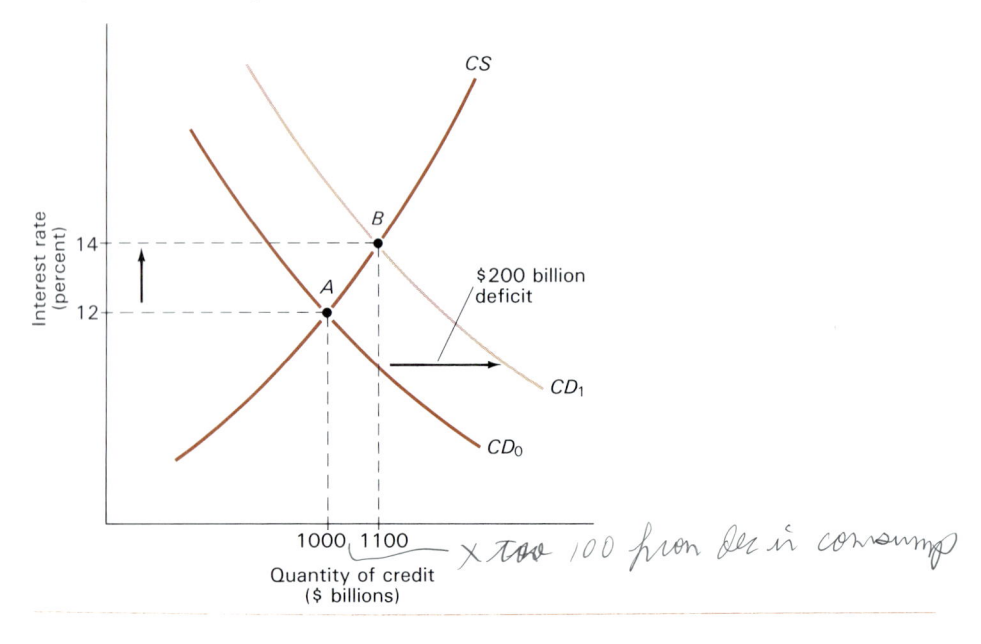

is borrowing an additional $200 billion. This means that there is now only $900 billion for private borrowing and investment, a $100 billion decrease compared to the original equilibrium. Government deficits tend to drive up interest rates and crowd out investment spending that is needed for future economic growth.

While our credit market analysis shows that deficit borrowing tends to increase interest rates, all else being equal, it is important to remember that all else is seldom really equal in the real world. Interest rates actually fell in the mid-1980s despite high deficits. This fact was earlier discussed in Chapter 12. One explanation for this phenomenon is that the falling inflation rate and the recession of the early 1980s, which reduced credit demand, offset the rising deficit in terms of their impact on interest rates.

Another explanation of why interest rates didn't rise despite the large deficit has been suggested by economist Robert Barro. Barro contends that people view the deficit as a future increase in taxes and begin to save more now in anticipation of this future tax burden. If this occurs, the increase in saving causes a shift in the CS curve, as Figure 14-5 shows. The deficit's increase in credit demand in Figure 14-5 is offset by higher saving, which causes an increase in the credit supply. The result of these two shifts is that interest rates do not necessarily rise. If the shifts in credit demand and credit supply are equal, interest rates remain the same. If the increase in credit supply exceeds the increase in credit demand, interest rates could actually fall. There is no consensus among economists concerning the magnitude of these shifts. Some, like Barro, argue that saving and credit supply shifts have been large. Many mainstream economists argue that the deficit's impact on credit demand dominates this analysis.

This analysis of the deficit tells us two things. First, the government's deficit affects the credit market, just as do the borrowing activities of other

---

FIGURE 14-5

Deficits Do Not Always Cause Crowding Out. Deficits need not cause higher interest rates and crowding out—if expectations change. Here credit demand rises due to deficit borrowing. Households regard the deficit as an increase in future taxes and therefore increase saving, which increases the credit supply in the figure. The credit market moves from equilibrium A to B, with no increase in interest rates. Economists disagree over whether expectations are as powerful as those shown here.

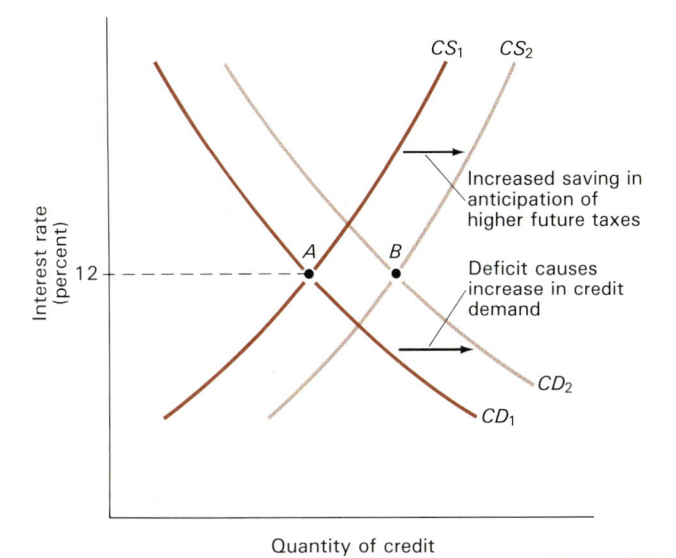

sectors of the economy. Second, government policies can affect both credit demand and credit supply, and their impact on interest rates depends on the net effect of these two forces. The high interest rates of the early 1980s could have been caused by the government's large deficits if the increase in credit demand was greater than any expected increase in credit supply.

Federal Reserve Policies Federal Reserve policies affect banks and, through them, the credit market. Contractionary monetary policies tend to reduce credit supply, shifting the *CS* curve back and to the left as Figure 14-6(a) shows. Open market sales, increases in the discount rate, and higher reserve requirements are examples of contractionary monetary policies. These policies reduce bank excess reserves, forcing them to make fewer loans. This reduces credit supply, causing a shortage of credit. Interest rates rise in response to the credit shortage.

Expansionary monetary policies, on the other hand, tend to increase credit supply and drive down interest rates. Open market purchases, reductions in the discount rate, and lower reserve requirements are examples of expansionary monetary policies. These policies tend to increase bank excess reserves, making it possible for them to make more loans. This increases the credit supply, shifting the *CS* curve out and to the right as Figure 14-6(b) shows. Interest rates fall in response to the credit surplus that results.

One reason why interest rates were relatively high in the late 1970s and early 1980s was that the Federal Reserve had adopted a tight monetary policy, which limited increases in the money supply. This tight monetary policy allowed interest rates to rise. Similarly, one reason why interest rates fell in the mid-1980s was that the Federal Reserve adopted relatively more expansionary monetary policies in this period. The credit supply grew more rapidly and interest rates fell.

FIGURE 14-6 **Monetary Policies and the Credit Market.** The contractionary monetary policy in (a) reduces the credit supply and forces interest rates higher. The expansionary monetary policy in (b) increase the credit supply and forces interest rates lower.

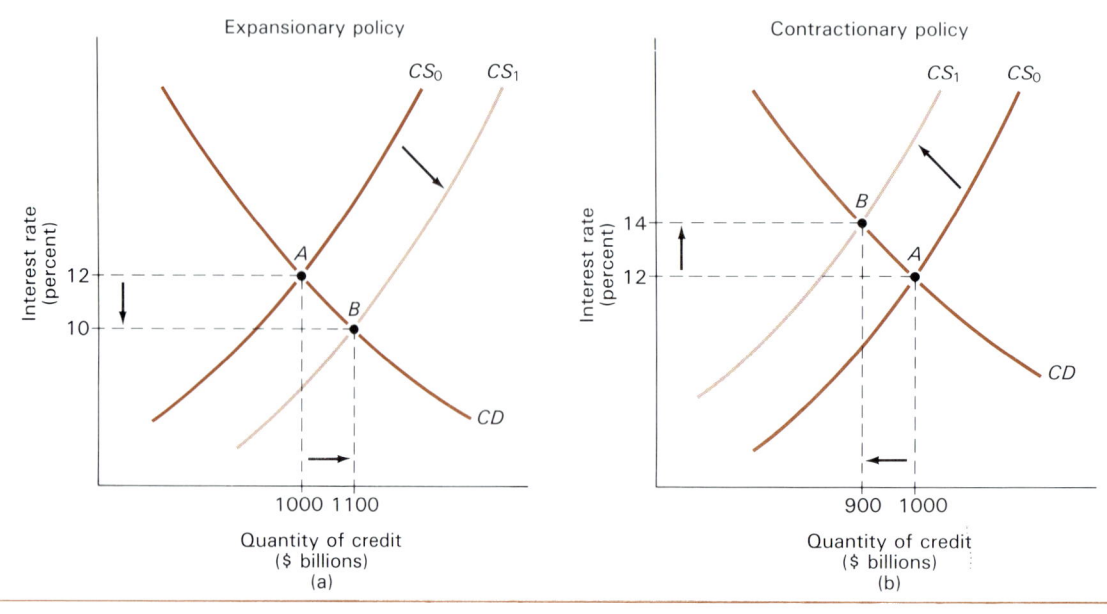

FIGURE 14-7 **The Discount Rate Since 1981.** Monetary policy has been relatively expansionary since 1981. The falling discount rate is one way the FRS announces this policy to the economy.

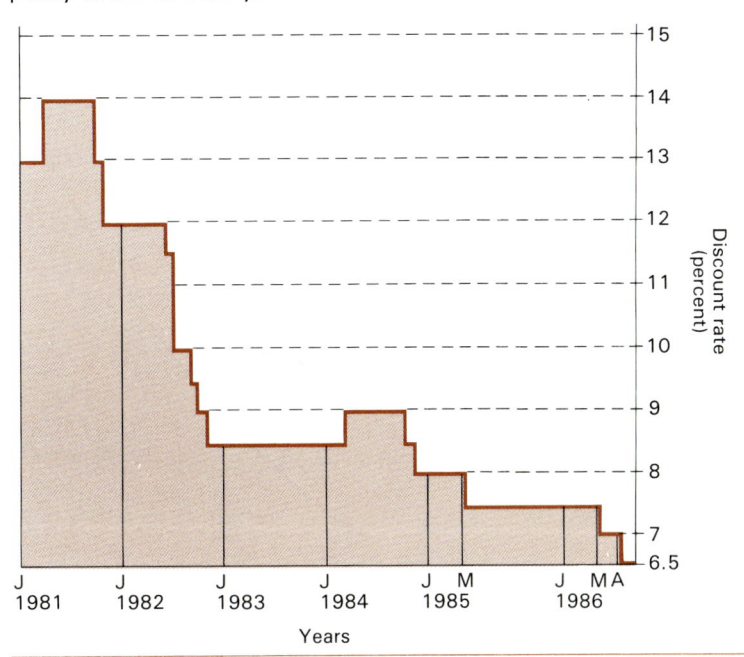

Figure 14-7 shows how the discount rate, a key signal of Federal Reserve policy, varied in the 1980s. The high discount rate in the early 1980s signals the tight money policies that prevailed then, policies that pushed interest rates up. The lower discount rate in the mid-1980s signaled the more expansionary policies that prevailed then, policies that tended to pull interest rates down. Federal Reserve policy is, then, a very important factor in determining the interest rate.

Inflation and Inflation Expectations Inflation or the expectation of higher inflation tends to drive up interest rates in the credit market. Figure 14-8 shows how expected inflation affects credit demand and supply.

Suppose that yesterday's interest rate was 16 percent. This rate was consistent with scarcity and expected inflation rates. Now suppose that this morning's announcement of a higher Producer Price Index produces higher inflationary expectations. Lender reactions are easy to predict. Higher future inflation rates shrink the real return of a 16 percent interest rate. Banks are therefore less willing to lend at 16 percent. The *CS* curve shifts back as fewer loans are offered. Borrowers react in the opposite way. Inflation reduces the real burden of repaying a loan, so it makes sense to borrow more now, buy durable goods at today's relatively low prices, and repay the loan with inflation-reduced future dollars. Credit demand rises, and the *CD* curve shifts to the right in the figure. Higher credit demand coupled with reduced credit supply serves to bid up interest rates. Thus expectations of future inflation increase interest rates today.

The existence of inflationary expectations means that Federal Reserve policies do not always work as described in the last subsection. Sometimes, for example, interest rates actually rise when the Fed undertakes an expansionary monetary policy. Here is the reason why. An open market purchase

| FIGURE 14-8 | **Inflation and Interest Rates.** Higher expected rates of inflation push interest rates higher. Both borrowers and lenders react to expectations of inflation-caused lower real interest rates. The credit supply falls, while credit demand increases. Interest rates must rise as the market equilibrium moves from A to B. The change in the quantity of credit exchanged is uncertain unless we know exactly how much CD and CS have changed. |

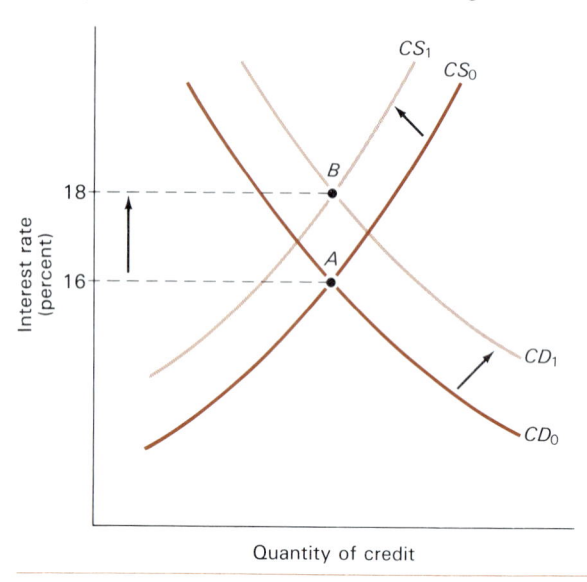

does increase bank excess reserves, thereby increasing the supplies of money and credit in the economy, as described before. This, taken by itself, would tend to lower interest rates. The problem is that some people in the economy, thinking back to the equation of exchange discussed in the last chapter, might interpret this increase in the money supply as a potential cause of inflation. They react based upon this inflationary expectation, and interest rates rise instead of fall. Federal Reserve policies are therefore sensitive to the way the actors in the economy perceive them and how inflationary expectations are altered.

Profitability of Business Investment A final factor that affected interest rates in the 1980s was the profitability of business investment. Business firms generally borrow money in order to undertake new investment activities. When investments are more profitable, firms borrow more to finance their expanded production. This increase in credit demand tends to drive up interest rates, which has the side effect of somewhat increasing investment costs and reducing business investment profitability.

One reason why interest rates were high early in the 1980s was because business investment was very profitable. President Reagan's supply-side tax cuts in 1981 increased the effective return on business investments. Firms borrowed heavily to finance expansion, pushing interest rates higher.

Interest rates fell in the mid-1980s, in part because profit rates on new investment fell. The U.S. economy slowed down in the mid-1980s, at least for a time. The high value of the dollar made U.S. goods costly to foreign buyers. This reduced the foreign sales of U.S. firms and made expanded production unprofitable. The high-flying dollar also made imported goods relatively inexpensive compared to U.S. products, which further reduced sales of domestic firms. Investment in import-competing firms was therefore less profitable than before. These and other factors reduced the profits to be earned from investment in the United States. The demand for credit for business expansion fell, and the interest rate fell with it.

We have seen that there are many factors that influence the interest rate. Interest rates first increased then fell in the 1980s. Our credit market analysis helps us understand why interest rates changed as they did. We can see that deficits, inflation, Federal Reserve policies, and the profitability of business investments all influenced the direction of interest rates in this period.

**KEY CONCEPTS
14.8, 14.9, 14.10, 14.11**

Interest rates are determined through credit markets by the forces of credit demand and credit supply. Many factors affect the demand for and supply of credit. In recent years, deficits, FRS policies, inflation, and the profitability of business investment have been important factors affecting the interest rates.

THE KEYNESIAN THEORY OF MONEY

14.12 MONETARY TRANSMISSION MECHANISM

Keynes' analysis of the economy focused mainly on aggregate demand and its determinants. Recall that the four components of aggregate demand are consumption spending, investment spending, net export spending, and government spending ($AD = C + I + X_n + G$). The Keynesian macroeconomic model is built on the idea that spending creates income. In Keynes' theory, then, changes in the money supply are only important if they cause a change in one of the four components of aggregate demand.

Monetary policy in the Keynesian analysis is important because of its effect on the credit market. Federal Reserve actions change both the supplies of money (deposits) and credit (loans) and therefore influence the interest rate. The interest rate, in turn, affects aggregate demand, primarily through its impact on investment spending. The interest rate influences investment decisions in two ways. First, the interest rate is the cost of borrowed funds. Loans finance most business investments, so net profits vary inversely with the interest rate. A fleet of new trucks that is a profitable investment at 12 percent interest would be unprofitable at a higher 15 percent borrowing cost.

The interest rate also affects investment because it is an opportunity cost. Firms that invest in machines or new factories give up the return they could have earned if the same funds had been invested in bonds or bank accounts. It does not make sense to build a new store that returns 14 percent on investment if safer government securities pay 16 percent.

The interest rate sets a lower limit on investment projects. Investors do not build factories or buy machines if they can get a better return from the bank. Business investment decisions are therefore made using the following rule:

Investment Rule
The rule that investments are made if and only if their expected rate of return is greater than or equal to the interest rate on securities of similar risk and period.

Make all investments that have an expected rate of return greater than or equal to the interest rate on securities of the same term (time frame) and risk. Reject all investments that have an expected return less than the interest return on securities of the same term and risk.

This **investment rule** makes both intuitive and business sense. If the current interest rate is 14 percent for corporate bonds of a given period and

ECONOMIC ISSUES

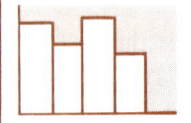

A Brief Guide to the Bond Market

The bond market is an important example of a credit market. Bond transactions are a key aspect of the financial sector of the economy. Bonds are IOUs that are sold by governments and corporations when they wish to borrow money. While most consumers and many small businesses borrow from banks and other similar institutions, governments and large corporations use the bond market. And while most individuals save at banks and similar institutions, much of our savings end up in the bond markets.

Here is an example to show how the bond market works. A firm that wishes to borrow $9000 today might sell a bond that promises to pay the buyer $10,000 in one year. The $10,000 repayment is called the *face value* of the bond. This is the amount that will be repaid when the bond comes due. The $9000 that the firm receives for the bond is called its *market value*. The difference between the $10,000 face value and the $9000 market value in this example is the bond's *discount*. The discount in this simple example is a measure of the interest that the bond will pay. The bond's buyer will lend $9000 today and in one year receive the original $9000 plus an additional $1000 of interest. The interest return on a simple bond of this sort can be calculated by dividing the discount by the market value. The interest return on this $9000 bond purchase is therefore $1000/$9000, or 11 percent.

Bonds are an important way that loans are made in our economy. Bond sellers are deficit units who seek loans. Bond buyers are surplus units that provide loanable funds. The bond market is an important institution where borrowers and lenders can come together for mutually advantageous exchange. The type of bond used in the example above is very simple: all of the interest is paid through the discount. Most bonds are slightly more complicated, having both a discount and a *coupon interest rate*. A real-world bond might have a face value of $10,000, market value of $9000, and a coupon interest rate of 3 percent. This means that the borrower agrees to pay annual interest of 3 percent of the $10,000 face value in addition to the discount. The effective interest return on this bond is the sum of the coupon interest rate and the return provided by the discount.

There are many types of bonds available. Bonds

Monetary Transmission Mechanism
The link between the credit market and aggregate demand. The relationship between interest rates and investment spending provides the monetary transmission mechanism. Monetary policy affects aggregate demand through its impact on interest rates and investment spending.

risk, then smart businesses invest only if they can beat this return. Their list of profitable investments is limited by this interest cost. The profitable investment list grows shorter when interest rates rise, other things being equal. Fewer investments pass the profit test at 18 percent interest than at lower interest costs. Lower interest costs, on the other hand, increase the number of investments businesses consider profitable. Interest rates are not the only thing that affects investment, of course. You learned in previous chapters that expectations, the health of the economy, tax policies, and the capacity utilization rate also affect the investment choice.

In Keynes' theory, investment spending is the key link between the money supply, the credit market, and GNP. The credit market determines the interest rate. The interest rate affects investment decisions. Investment spending alters aggregate demand in the short run by changing total spending. It can also affect aggregate supply in the long run by influencing technology and productive capacity.

Investment spending links money and credit with aggregate demand and supply. The investment spending link between changes in interest rates and changes in aggregate demand is called the Keynesian **monetary transmission mechanism.** In Keynes' theory, changes in the monetary system affect the economy through the credit markets, interest rates, and investment spending in a predictable chain reaction.

issued by state and local governments pay interest that is free of federal income tax liability, for example, making them popular with households in high marginal tax brackets. Some bonds pay most of their interest yearly through the coupon rate, while others pay most of their interest when the bond comes due through the discount. Bond rating services, such as Moody's and Standard and Poor's, assess the risk associated with each bond issue. The bond rating affects the demand for the bond and, therefore, its price and effective return. A bond that is viewed as a safe loan receives a high bond rating; there is a larger demand for these bonds among risk-averse individuals, so they sell for a higher market value and therefore carry a lower interest rate. Borrowers try to get high bond ratings to reduce their interest costs.

Although the face value of a bond does not change once it is issued, market forces can cause the *yield,* or effective interest return, on the bond to vary over time. Suppose, for example, that many deficit units wish to borrow and they sell bonds to do so. The laws of supply and demand dictate that an increase in supply, all else being equal, will drive down market price. The price of a simple $10,000 bond (with all interest paid through the discount) might fall from $9000 to $8000. This means that the borrower must bear a discount of $2000 and pay an effective yield of $2000/$8000, or 25 percent, to get the loan. Anyone who had purchased one of these bonds at $9000 and needs to sell it to get funds for another purpose will bear a *capital loss* because the market value of the bond has declined from $9000 to $8000. Bond prices fall when interest rates rise.

On the other hand, suppose that many savers decide to purchase bonds as a way of earning interest on their new savings. This increase in the demand for bonds, all else being equal, will drive up the market price of the bond to perhaps $9500 for a bond with a face value of $10,000. This increase in the market value of the bond means that there is now a lower discount and therefore a lower effective interest yield. The yield is now only $500/$9500, or 5.3 percent. A person who had previously purchased this bond for $9000 could sell it now for $9500 and earn a $500 *capital gain.*

To review, government and business borrowers are the suppliers of bonds to the credit markets. Lenders purchase bonds as a way to earn interest on their savings. Bonds can earn their holders a return in two ways. All bonds pay interest, either through discounts from the face value or through coupon interest payments made on a regular basis. Bonds can also increase in value, generating a capital gain, or fall in value, causing a capital loss. Bond prices vary inversely with interest rates. Higher bond prices are an indication of lower interest rates. Lower bond prices, however, mean that interest rates have increased.

The bond market is perhaps the most important part of the credit market. This brief guide to the bond market should help you understand how bonds and the bond market work.

14.13 KEYNESIAN MONETARY POLICIES

Keynesian Monetary Policy

In the Keynesian theory of money, Federal Reserve policies such as open market operations, reserve requirement movements, and discount rate changes alter interest rates, and through their impact on investment, indirectly influence aggregate demand. Let us briefly use the Keynesian analysis to describe both expansionary and contractionary monetary policy.

Expansionary Monetary Policy Suppose FRS leaders decide to stimulate aggregate demand. Expansionary policies such as open market purchases, lower reserve requirements, or a cut in the discount rate have the effects that were shown in Figure 14-6(a). Any of these actions increase the credit supply, shifting *CS* to the right. The Fed has created a surplus of credit, and all else — especially expectations — being equal, interest rates fall to relieve the market of surplus funds.

Lower interest rates lengthen the list of profitable investments. Firms implement their investment programs in response to the lower interest rates. Higher investment spending increases aggregate demand through the spending multiplier. Demand-pull inflation is the result, with higher equilibrium real GNP but more inflation. The FRS policy has reduced unemployment by increasing aggregate demand, but it has also bid up prices, assuming that the economy is on the bottleneck range of the aggregate supply curve. Aggregate supply tends to rise in the long run as investment spending adds to the economy's productive capacity. This rightward shift in AS would tend to hold inflation down in the long run by expanding AS to offset the inflationary effects of the rising AD.

We can summarize the series of events involved in expansionary monetary policy in the following chain reaction:

$$\text{FRS policy} \rightarrow \text{increase in } CS \rightarrow \text{decrease in interest rate} \rightarrow \text{increase in investment} \rightarrow \text{short-run rise in } AD + \text{long-run increase in } AS$$

Contractionary Monetary Policy Contractionary monetary policy uses open market sales, higher reserve requirements, or an increased discount rate to reduce aggregate demand. An example of a contractionary FRS policy was shown in Figure 14-6(b). An open market sale reduces the money and credit supplies. Interest rates are bid up by the shortage of credit that results. Higher interest rates force firms to reconsider investment plans. Fewer investments pass the profit test at the higher interest rate. Investment spending falls, dragging aggregate demand down with it. Real GNP falls in the short run, increasing unemployment in the economy. Aggregate supply might fall in the long run if lower investment spending drains capacity.

We can summarize the impact of contractionary monetary policies on the economy, according to the Keynesian analysis, using the following chain-reaction diagram:

$$\text{FRS policy} \rightarrow \text{decrease in } CS \rightarrow \text{increase in interest rate} \rightarrow \text{decrease in investment} \rightarrow \text{short-run fall in } AD + \text{long-run decrease in } AS$$

The results of expansionary and contractionary monetary policies using the Keynesian analysis are compared and contrasted in Table 14-5.

Monetary policy in the United States followed this Keynesian analysis for most of the period 1950–1979. The Federal Reserve System tried to establish interest rate targets. The Fed would then attempt to use its monetary tools to influence the credit market. The goal was to stabilize interest rates, which would, in turn, stabilize investment spending and aggregate demand.

Figure 14-9 illustrates how the Fed could use its monetary policy tools to target interest rates. Suppose that the Fed has established that 10 percent is a desirable interest rate, given current economic conditions and expecta-

TABLE 14-5 **Effects of Monetary Policies**

Variable	Expansionary monetary policy	Contractionary monetary policy
Credit supply	increase	decrease
Interest rate	decrease	increase
Investment spending	increase	decrease
Aggregate demand	increase	decrease
Inflation	increase	decrease
Unemployment	decrease	increase
Capacity in long run	increase	decrease

FIGURE 14-9

Using Monetary Policy to Stabilize Interest Rates. Monetary policy can be used to stabilize interest rates at some target level. Here the FRS increases credit supply in anticipation of rising business credit demand. If the monetary policy works correctly, the higher level of business credit can be supplied without an increase in the interest rate, as would occur without FRS action.

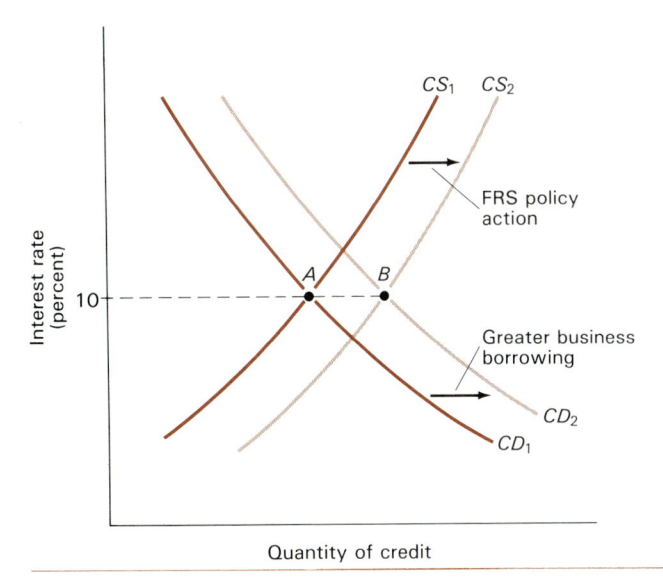

tions. In Figure 14-9 we see that the business sector has received a tax cut that increases the profits on new investments. This fiscal policy change causes business to increase borrowing to finance expansion and new technology. Credit demand rises, which would normally cause the interest rate to rise above the 10 percent target. The Federal Reserve can prevent this increase if it is able to accurately determine the increase in credit demand and can implement an offsetting increase in credit supply.

The figure shows that this monetary "fine tuning" allows the Fed to keep the interest rate at the target level despite the increase in business demand for loans. Monetary theory was for many years aimed at achieving this stability in short-run interest rates. The goal of stable, targeted interest rates was not always successfully achieved, however, because of some problems inherent to monetary policy.

Problems with Monetary Policy

14.14 PROBLEMS WITH MONETARY POLICY

Monetary policy suffers from at least three important problems that make it an uncertain policy tool.

The Variable Lag First, significant time lags exist between the time a policy is decided and the full impact of that policy is felt in the economy. It may not take very long for the FOMC to decide upon an expansion in the money supply and actually begin the process of buying U.S. securities. It takes much longer, however, for the deposit expansion process to work and then exercise an effect on the market rate of interest, investment spending, and aggregate demand.

Changes in monetary policy can take as long as 30 months to exercise their full impact. There is a **variable lag** in monetary policy. Sometimes firms are ready and waiting with investment plans, so that investment

Variable Lag
The period of time, of uncertain length, between the implementation of monetary policy and when its force is felt by the economy.

spending rapidly rises when interest rates fall. At other times, however, firms are more cautious and do not immediately begin investment projects at the first sign of lower interest costs. The uncertainty concerning the relationship between changes in interest rates and the corresponding changes in investment spending create the variable lag of up to 30 months.

A great deal can happen in an economy in 30 months. It is entirely possible that a monetary policy that was not timed correctly could exercise expansionary effects on the economy long after the economy reached full employment and was experiencing inflationary pressure. If monetary policy were, on the other hand, deliberately restrictive, its full impact might not be felt until after the expansion phase of the business cycle was over and the economy had already entered a recessionary phase. In this case, the monetary policy would have served to worsen economic conditions rather than remedy them.

The existence of the variable lag makes monetary policy risky. It is something like driving a car with a variable lag steering wheel. If you turn the wheel, the car will turn somewhere in the next 30 blocks, but it is hard to tell precisely when and where. Clearly such a car would be a hazard. Some economists believe that discretionary monetary policy is just as hazardous because of our inability to precisely predict when and where money will affect the economy.

Problems of Monetary Control The second problem is that control over financial markets and the money supply is far from precise. In our previous discussions of cash leakages and the holding of excess reserves by banks we indicated that changes in monetary policy may not have the full effect that monetary theory might predict.

There is sometimes a significant difference between theory and actual practice, and economists are not nearly as confident about precisely controlling the economy with monetary policy as they were in the 1960s. This is particularly the case today, when deregulation of the financial sector is making it more difficult to perform such basic monetary tasks as define what is really a bank or accurately measure the money supply.

While monetary policy is indeed a valuable mechanism for controlling the economy, it is not as precise a tool as a purely theoretical examination might lead us to believe. This reduces our ability to use monetary policy to fine tune the economy or target interest rates.

Problems of Expectations The third problem with using monetary policy to target interest rates and influence the economy is that expectations are very powerful in credit markets. Changes in expectations can distort otherwise simple monetary policies. Figure 14-10 illustrates the power of changing expectations.

Suppose that the Fed enacted an expansionary monetary policy with the goal of reducing interest rates and stimulating investment spending. This policy would shift the *CS* curve out, causing a surplus of credit and driving interest rates down, all else being equal. But suppose that all else is not equal. Suppose that people in the economy interpret the Fed's policy action as a likely cause of increased inflation. If this were the case, people and firms might rush to borrow more now, before the inflation comes and drives nominal interest rates higher and increases the cost of new goods. This increase in inflationary expectations would increase credit demand.

Figure 14-10 shows that, under certain conditions, an expansionary monetary policy designed to reduce interest rates can actually cause interest

FIGURE 14-10

Expectations Can Distort Monetary Policy. Monetary policy is sensitive to changes in expectations. An expansionary monetary policy increases credit supply, moving equilibrium from *A* to *B*. Interest rates fall. This assumes no change in expectations, however. If people think that the FRS action will cause higher inflation, they may increase credit demand to lock in lower real interest rates. Rising credit demand could shift the equilibrium from *B* to *C*. The result is that an expansionary monetary policy can sometimes actually increase interest rates, not lower them.

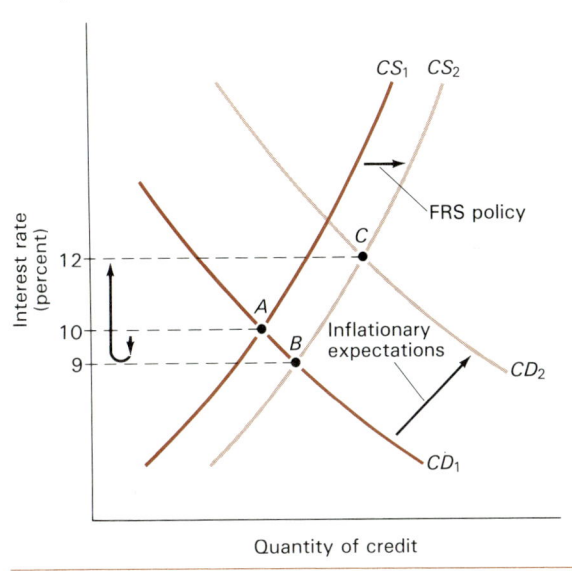

rates to rise. This can happen if the change in expectations, which affects CD, more than offsets the initial monetary policy action's impact on CS. In this case, the increase in credit demand caused by higher inflationary expectations is greater than the Fed's increase in CS. Interest rates rise instead of fall in this example.

The variable lag, errors of controlling the money supply, and the problems caused by changing expectations reduce the effectiveness of the kind of activist monetary policy practiced during the decades of the 1950s, 1960s, and 1970s. These problems with monetary policy make it difficult for the Federal Reserve to use its policy tools to stabilize interest rates and the economy.

HOW DOES MONEY REALLY AFFECT THE ECONOMY?

We have now seen two different theories of how money affects the economy. The last chapter presented a simple monetary theory based on the equation of exchange. This equation suggested that changes in the money supply directly affect the amount of total spending. In this chapter we have looked at the Keynesian theory of money. In the Keynesian model, changes in the money supply are important because they affect the credit market, interest rates, and investment spending. Money affects the economy indirectly, in this Keynesian view, through the monetary transmission mechanism.

How does money really affect the economy? Some economists still believe in the basics of the equation of exchange and its policy implications. Many other economists subscribe to the general analysis and conclusions of the

Keynesian model presented in this chapter. Many other economists, however, think that the real impact of money on the economy is best described by the modern monetarist theory or by rational expectations macroeconomic theory. We must examine these two important developments in economic theory before we can draw any firm conclusions. The next chapter looks at monetarist and rational expectations theories and reviews what economists think they know about how the economy works.

SUMMARY

14.1

1. Bank regulation has a long history in the United States. The banking system is very important, but it was subject to periodic crises and panics prior to the passage of the Federal Reserve Act in 1913. This act established the Federal Reserve System. The Federal Reserve was designed to be the Supreme Court of banking and was given substantial independence by Congress.

14.2

2. The Federal Reserve System is comprised of the Board of Governors, located in Washington, DC, which has overall responsibility for monetary policy, and 12 regional Federal Reserve banks, each of which is responsible for bank regulation within its geographical area. Two important operating groups within the Federal Reserve are the Open Market Operations Committee and the Federal Advisory Council.

14.3

3. The FRS has five main functions. It issues currency, serves as the banker's bank through transactions at its discount window, provides check-clearing services, supervises depository institutions, and acts as the government's fiscal agent in credit market transactions.

14.4

4. Membership in the Federal Reserve System imposes both costs and benefits on banks. Not all banks are members of the FRS. The FRS often acts for the U.S. Treasury, but it is important to remember that the FRS and the Treasury are distinctly different and independent institutions. The Treasury is part of the federal government, while the FRS is a semi-independent agency dealing with the overall banking system.

14.5

5. Open market operations are FRS bond market transactions designed to alter the supplies of money and credit in the economy. An open market purchase occurs when the FRS buys a bond. The FRS creates money to pay for the bond, which enters the banking system as a new deposit and an injection of bank reserves. The money and credit supplies increase through the deposit expansion process. An open market sale, on the other hand, occurs when the FRS sell a bond. This transaction reduces the amount of money and bank reserves that exist in the financial sector. An open market purchase is an example of an expansionary monetary policy, while an open market sale is an example of a contractionary monetary policy.

14.6

6. The discount rate is the interest rate that the FRS charges to member banks when they borrow reserves. The discount rate is used by the FRS

to signal its intentions to the economy. A decrease in the discount rate, for example, indicates that the FRS is adopting a more expansionary monetary stance and encourages banks to increase credit availability. An increase in the discount rate, on the other hand, indicates a more restrictive FRS policy and discourages banks from making additional loans available.

14.7 ▶ 7. The reserve requirement is the fraction of deposits that banks must hold as reserves. The FRS can use the reserve requirement to regulate the supplies of money and credit in the economy. A reduction in the reserve requirement, for example, allows banks to shift some of their required reserves to the excess reserve account, where they are available for loans. This increases the money and credit supplies through the deposit expansion process. An increase in the reserve requirement forces banks to hold more required reserves, leaving fewer excess reserves available for loans.

14.8 ▶ 8. The demand for credit depends on several factors. The main determinants of credit demand include the level of interest rates, inflation and inflation expectations, income and income expectations, and borrowing due to governmental deficits.

14.9 ▶ 9. The main determinants of the supply of credit include the level of interest rates, inflation and inflationary expectations, household and business saving, and Federal Reserve policies.

14.10 ▶ 10. The interest rate is determined by the forces of supply and demand in the credit market. The credit market tends toward an equilibrium interest rate, where the quantity of credit demanded is equal to the quantity of credit supplied. This determines a basic interest rate. The interest rate on particular credit instruments depends, in addition, on such factors as risk and time frame.

14.11 ▶ 11. Many events cause interest rates to change. For example, government deficits increase credit demand and so tend to increase interest rates, all else being equal. Higher deficits need not cause interest rates to rise, however, if saving increases credit supply at the same time that credit demand rises. FRS monetary policies also alter interest rates because they change the credit supply. Increases in the expected inflation rate also tend to increase interest rates because higher expected inflation increases credit demand while also reducing the supply of credit. Similarly, an increase in business profitability causes firms to borrow more to expand production. This increase in credit demand tends to push interest rates higher.

14.12 ▶ 12. The Keynesian monetary transmission mechanism refers to the link between monetary policy and credit markets and the aggregate demand–aggregate supply model. The investment rule holds that firms undertake investment projects so long as the risk-adjusted return on investment is at least as great as the interest rate. An increase or decrease in interest rates therefore tends to cause investment spending to change in the opposite direction. Monetary policy affects credit markets and the interest rate. Interest rates affect investment spending. Investment spending, in turn, affects the *AD–AS* model.

14.13 ▸ 13. Expansionary monetary policy in the Keynesian model has the following effects. An increase in money and credit supplies drives down interest rates and encourages increased investment spending. Higher investment spending stimulates AD in the short run and can further increase AS in the long run. A contractionary monetary policy, however, tends to reduce credit supply, increase interest rates, reduce investment spending, and contract AD in the short run.

14.14 ▸ 14. Discretionary monetary policy suffers from several problems. First, there is a variable lag between when monetary policy is undertaken and when its effects are realized. It is also difficult to accurately control the money supply in today's complex financial world. Finally, changing expectations can have undesirable or unintended impacts on monetary policy, thereby weakening its power.

DISCUSSION QUESTIONS

14.1, 14.2, 14.3 ▸ 1. Define and explain the development and the functions of the following:
   a. Comptroller of the Currency
   b. Federal Reserve System
   c. Federal Reserve District Banks
   d. Board of Governors
   e. Federal Open Market Committee

   Be sure to describe the five major services provided by the Federal Reserve district banks in your answer. Who do they serve?

14.4 ▸ 2. Who is required to be a member of the Federal Reserve System? Can banks who are not required to be members join the System? Why did many banks feel it unprofitable to be a member of the Federal System? What was done in 1980 to remedy this situation?

14.5, 14.6, 14.7 ▸ 3. What are the Fed's three principle instruments of monetary policy and how do they work?

14.5 ▸ 4. Suppose the reserve requirement is 10 percent. If the Fed, through its open market operations, purchased $2000 worth of existing U.S. securities, would it have performed contractionary or expansionary monetary policy? What would be the effect on the money supply? If the Fed instead sold $2000 worth of securities, would your answers to these questions change? If so, how?

14.5, 14.10, 14.12 ▸ 5. Explain both the short-run and long-run effects on credit and interest rates of expansionary open market operations. What other secondary effects can occur when the Fed performs open market operations?

14.6 ▸ 6. If a commercial bank's reserves temporarily fall below required levels, what means are available to the bank to replenish these reserves? Is there a charge or cost for each of these actions? If so, define what that cost is. Do these costs affect the bank's decision on where they borrow?

14.7 ▶ 7. What is the most powerful tool of monetary policy for controlling the money supply? Is this also the most frequently used method? Explain your answer.

14.12, 14.13 ▶ 8. In a step-by-step fashion, explain exactly how, in the Keynesian model, changes in the money supply are transmitted to the economy.

14.11 ▶ 9. List three events that could cause interest rates to fall. Explain how and why interest rates would fall in each case.

14.5, 14.10, 14.14 ▶ 10. Using the credit market, show the impact of an open market purchase on interest rates. Explain how the impact of an open market purchase would be different if people in the economy interpreted it as a harbinger of higher inflation in the future.

SELECTED READINGS

Friedman, Milton. *A Program for Monetary Stability.* New York: Fordham University Press, 1975.

Friedman, Milton. *Dollars and Deficits: Inflation, Monetary Policy and the Balance of Payments.* Englewood Cliffs, NJ: Prentice-Hall, 1968.

Friedman, Milton, and Heller, Walter W. *Monetary versus Fiscal Policy.* New York: W. W. Norton & Company, 1969.

Humphrey, Thomas M. "The Quantity Theory of Money: Its Historical Evolution and Policy Debates." *Economic Review* (Federal Reserve Bank of Richmond), May/June 1974, pp. 2–19.

Hutchingson, Harry D. *Money, Banking and the United States Economy,* 4th ed. Englewood Cliffs, NJ: Prentice-Hall, Inc., 1980.

Ritter, Lawrence S., and Silber, William L. *Principles of Money, Banking and Financial Markets,* 3rd ed. New York: Basic Books, Inc., Publishers 1980.

Seidman, Laurence S. "A New Approach to the Control of Inflation." *Challenge* 19 (July/August 1976), pp. 39–43.

Thomas, Lloyd B., Jr. *Money, Banking and Economic Activity.* Englewood Cliffs, NJ: Prentice-Hall, Inc., 1979, chaps. 6–9.

CHAPTER 15

Monetarist and Rational Expectations Theories

Having read the chapter, reviewed the chapter summary, and completed the *Study Guide* exercises, you should be able to:

CRIS

15.1 KEYNESIAN MODEL: Describe the Keynesian macroeconomic model in simple terms.

15.2 MONETARIST MODEL: Describe the monetarist macroeconomic model in simple terms.

15.3 RATIONAL EXPECTATIONS MODEL: Describe the rational expectations macroeconomic model in simple terms.

15.4 CURRENT MONETARY POLICY: Discuss the main events in monetary policy in recent years.

15.5 EQUATION OF EXCHANGE: Use the equation of exchange to describe the simple monetarist model of the economy.

15.6 MONETARISTS' MONEY DEMAND: Explain the determinants of the demand for money in modern monetarist theory.

15.7 KEYNESIANISM VERSUS MONETARISM: Compare and contrast the Keynesian and monetarist theories.

15.8 MONETARIST POLICIES: Explain the economic policies that monetarists favor.

15.9 VALIDITY OF KEYNESIAN AND MONETARIST POLICIES: Discuss recent evidence concerning the validity of Keynesian and monetarist economic theories.

15.10 POWER OF EXPECTATIONS: Discuss the power of expectations to shape economic events and policies.

15.11 ADAPTIVE EXPECTATIONS: Explain what is meant by adaptive expectations and how they can affect monetary policy.

> **15.12 RATIONAL EXPECTATIONS HYPOTHESIS:** Explain what is meant by the rational expectations hypothesis.

> **15.13 RATIONAL EXPECTATIONS THEORY'S INFLUENCE:** Explain how monetary and fiscal policy affect the economy according to the rational expectations theory.

When it comes to economic theory and policy, money matters. Money is an important determinant of macroeconomic performance. About this economists are generally in agreement. They disagree, however, about how much money matters, whether other types of policies also matter, and which monetary policy best promotes our macroeconomic goals. This is a lot to disagree about, but the issues are important and the economy is complex, so it is not shocking that economists should have different views on monetary theory and policy.

Since money matters, what economists think about money and monetary policy also matters. What the Federal Reserve does about money and monetary policy must, therefore, be very important. This chapter will help you understand the changing nature of the Fed's monetary policy actions in recent years in the context of the evolving view of money within the economics profession. All of this action is set, of course, on the U.S. economy's stage, which has itself changed in important ways over the years.

AN OVERVIEW OF MONETARY THEORIES

This chapter will examine three basic theories of how money affects the economy. Each theory provides a different prescription for effective monetary policy. Before looking at these theories in detail, let us briefly introduce the main identifying characteristics of each. We will discuss the new theories in more depth later in the chapter. The three main monetary theories that we will examine are Keynesian monetary theory, monetarism (both simple and modern), and the "new" monetarism that is generally called rational expectations theory. Here is a rough outline of each theory.

Keynesian Monetary Theory

> **15.1 KEYNESIAN MODEL**

We discussed Keynesian monetary theory in Chapter 14. In the Keynesian theory, monetary policy is important because of the way that it affects the credit markets. The Keynesian monetary transmission mechanism is a chain-reaction effect: monetary policy affects credit supply, which affects interest rates, which affects investment spending, which affects aggregate demand, which determines inflation and unemployment in the short run. This chain reaction can be illustrated as follows:

Changes in monetary policy → Changes in credit supply → Changes in interest rate → Changes in investment spending → Changes in aggregate demand

Keynesians believe that monetary policy can affect the economy, but that it is not the only determinant of economic activity. They believe that monetary policy and fiscal policies are imperfect substitutes, but substitutes nonetheless. Sometimes an economic problem can be best addressed using monetary policy, according to Keynesian analysis, but other times fiscal policies are preferred. Both monetary and fiscal policies can be effective because both influence the level of aggregate demand.

As discussed in the last chapter, Keynesian monetary policy tends to focus on interest rates because these rates are seen as the key determinant of investment spending and, therefore, aggregate demand. Monetary policy under a Keynesian regime would tend to try to target interest rates. That is, the Federal Reserve would attempt to manipulate the money and credit supplies so as to keep interest rates near a target level. This targeting would require that the Fed be actively involved in the credit markets. If interest rates began to rise, the Fed would have to lean against the wind, to use a popular description of Fed policy, and create money to try to bring interest rates down. If interest rates began to fall below the target level, the Fed would lean in the opposite direction and adopt contractionary monetary policies to hold interest rates in the target range.

To summarize the Keynesian view, both monetary and fiscal policies affect the economy but in different ways. Monetary policy should attempt to keep interest rates within a prescribed policy range. This requires an active Federal Reserve.

Monetarism

15.2 MONETARIST MODEL

Monetarism was a term coined in the 1960s to describe an economic theory that many viewed as an alternative to the reliance on fiscal policy, or fiscalism, that Keynesian economists sometimes advocated. We have already looked at an early monetarist theory in Chapter 13 when we explored the equation of exchange. We will review this simple model and its more elaborate modern counterparts soon, but let us first briefly sketch the monetarist creed.

Monetarists stress the importance of money as the determinant of spending behavior and nominal GNP. They tend to believe that money matters most—monetary policy is far more important than fiscal policy. Changes in the money supply directly induce changes in nominal GNP. Since real GNP is limited in the long run by factors such as resource availability, technology, and worker productivity, too rapid an expansion of the money supply can increase nominal GNP but will not necessarily increase long-run real GNP. If nominal GNP is increased due to a rise in the money supply, but real GNP is fixed, the result can only be inflation. In other words, too rapid an expansion of the money supply tends to cause inflation in the long run. This leads to the monetarist motto, "Inflation is always and everywhere a monetary phenomenon."

Monetarists believe that the interest rate is an important price in the economy—it is the result of mutually advantageous exchanges between savers and borrowers. But they do not believe that it is an important policy variable because, among other things, it can be affected by the inflation rate. It is therefore not a good indicator to use to guide monetary policy.

Monetarist believe that the Federal Reserve should attempt to target the rate of growth of the money supply instead of targeting interest rates. That is, the Federal Reserve should set goals concerning how much the money supply should increase in the future, then use the tools of monetary policy to achieve this desired rate of monetary expansion. A systematic increase in the money supply should lead to stable growth of the economy.

Constant Growth Rate Rule
Milton Friedman's proposal that the Federal Reserve should expand the money supply at a constant rate and not attempt to fine tune the economy through discretionary monetary policies.

Monetarists believe that money is so important that the Federal Reserve should not adopt activist monetary policies that might cause undesirable changes in the money supply. They favor stable monetary policies. The money supply should be allowed to grow at roughly the same rate as the real economy, in order to provide needed liquidity without causing inflation. Milton Friedman has proposed that the Fed follow a **constant growth rate rule** for monetary policy. Friedman calls for the Federal Reserve to announce that it is going to expand the money supply at a certain rate, then stick to this plan and not deviate from it in an attempt to fight short-term economic problems. Monetarists oppose the active policies that Keynesians call for, which they think tend to destabilize the economy by creating unstable monetary growth.

Let us summarize this brief and oversimplified overview of monetarist thought. Monetarists believe that money is very important and that monetary policy is more important than fiscal policy. They believe that changes in the money supply directly cause changes in nominal GNP. Monetarist are concerned that too rapid an increase in the money supply will cause inflation. They believe that monetary policy should be somewhat passive, steadily increasing the money supply at a constant rate. Monetarists do not think that it is appropriate to target interest rates, as do Keynesian economists.

15.3 RATIONAL EXPECTATIONS MODEL

Rational Expectations Theory

Money matters, but expectations also matter. We saw an example of this in the last chapter. If the Federal Reserve increases the credit supply and people interpret this as a likely cause of future inflation, then the higher credit supply does not necessarily make the interest rate fall. People might begin to demand more credit in anticipation of higher future inflation rates. The increase in credit demand and other effects of inflation could cause the interest rate to remain constant or even make it increase. This example showed us that we need to take the impact of expectations into account in economic theory and policy.

Rational expectations theory evolved from the monetarism of the 1960s. Rational expectations economists added expectational forces to the monetarist model and found that many of the theory's conclusions and prescriptions were changed. In particular, rational expectations theory suggests that systematic monetary and fiscal policies are all pretty much unable to cause any lasting change in real GNP and the unemployment rate. This is because people can take these policies into account and adjust their real behavior accordingly. Thus, for example, you might alter your expectations concerning inflation if you read that the Federal Reserve has dramatically increased the money supply. When the inflation comes, you are ready for it and can go about your business as usual. The Fed's actions may have affected the price level, but your accurate expectations have prevented this monetary policy from having any real impact.

According to rational expectations theories, the only economic policies that can have any effect on real GNP are unexpected, or "surprise," policies. Such policies are, by definition, impossible to anticipate, so people have to change their real behavior at least temporarily when they occur. In the long run, however, people change their expectations to take the new policies into account, and the result is that there is no long-lasting impact on the economy. Because surprise economic policies are ineffective in the long run and disruptive in the short run, rational expectations economists do not favor using them. Instead, these economists favor many of the systematic, nonactivist policies that monetarists advocate.

In summary, rational expectations theory suggests that private sector expectations can neutralize monetary and fiscal policies. People will understand how these policies work and undertake economic activity under an accurate set of expectations. They will attempt to insulate themselves from the impacts of economic policies, thus rendering those policies less powerful. Systematic economic policies that are fully anticipated by economic agents have little or no impact on the economy. Surprise economic policies have short-run effects, but these impacts are not long lasting. These policies are disruptive and so should not normally be employed.

Ideas can shape events. In the next section we see how ideas about money, particularly the Keynesian and monetarist theories, have shaped economic policies in recent years. We will then look more closely at the logic of these economic theories.

KEY CONCEPTS
15.1, 15.2, 15.3

In the Keynesian view, both monetary and fiscal policies affect the economy but in different ways. Monetary policy should attempt to keep interest rates within a prescribed policy range. This requires an active Federal Reserve. Monetarists believe that money is very important and that monetary policy is more important than fiscal policy because changes in the money supply directly cause changes in nominal GNP. Monetarists are concerned that too rapid an increase in the money supply will cause inflation. They believe that monetary policy should be somewhat passive, steadily increasing the money supply at a constant rate. Rational expectations theory suggests that private-sector expectations can neutralize monetary and fiscal policies. Systematic economic policies that are fully anticipated by economic agents have little or no impact on the economy. Surprise economic policies have short-run effects, but these impacts are not long lasting. These policies are disruptive and so should not normally be employed.

RECENT MONETARY POLICY

15.4 CURRENT MONETARY POLICY

Monetary policy in the years since World War II has been dominated by Keynesian thought. That is, monetary policy has focused primarily on interest rates, not the money supply itself, and monetary policy has taken an active role in managing the economy. The Federal Reserve has tended to attempt to fine tune the economy just as Keynesian fiscalists did in the 1960s. Some of the results of these Keynesian economic policies can be seen in Figure 15-1.

Keynesian monetary policy worked pretty much as advertised in the early 1960s, as Figure 15-1 shows. The Federal Reserve was able to keep interest rates nearly constant, with the prime interest rate at about 4.5 percent. To do this, however, they were forced to lean against the wind several times, which accounts for the uneven growth in the money supply for the period 1960–1966.

Monetarists would claim that the activist monetary policies of the 1960s would tend to push up the inflation rate, and with it, the interest rate. We see evidence of this in the late 1960s. Inflation accelerated, driving up the nominal interest rate. The real interest rate is approximately equal to the

FIGURE 15-1 **Money, Prices, and Interest.** Part (a) of this figure shows changes in the rate of monetary growth, while part (b) shows how these changes affected the nominal interest rate (represented by the prime rate), inflation (using the CPI), and the real interest rate (the shaded area between the two upper curves). The Keynesian monetary policy used for much of the period shown here had several effects. The relatively large variations in the money supply kept nominal interest rates stable in the 1960s but led to rising inflation rates in later years. Even so, interest rates were kept stable for relatively long periods (one to two years). This stability in nominal and real interest rates collapsed in the late 1970s.

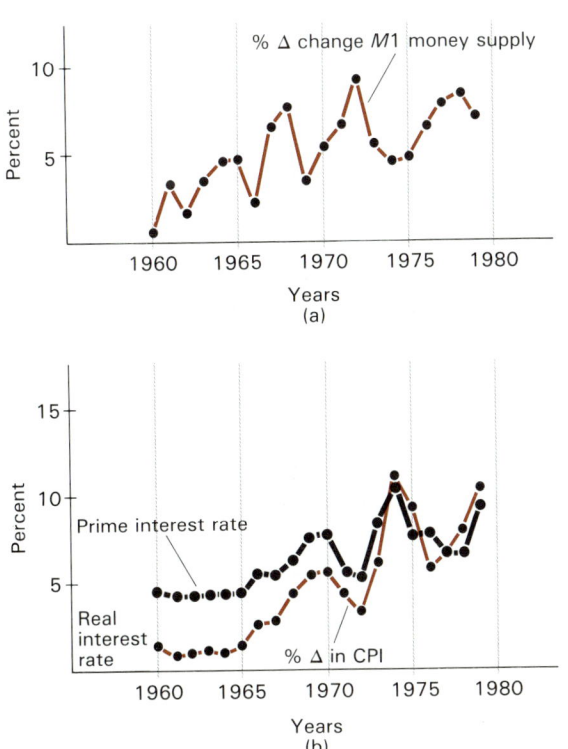

gap between the prime interest rate and the inflation rate in the figure. The Federal Reserve was able to keep the real interest rate roughly constant (and the nominal interest rate constant in the short run), but this required an even more activist monetary policy. Notice the dramatic peaks and valleys in monetary growth in the late 1960s. This shows how often the Fed had to reverse itself in order to constantly lean into a changing wind.

The decade of the 1970s was a period of many unusual economic events. The patterns of the 1960s do not consistently appear. Still, one can see traces of the impact of mostly Keynesian monetary policy in Figures 15-1. Interest rates tended to be stable for relatively long periods of a year or two before changes in inflation made them jump. The monetary policies that gave us this short-term stability seem also to be associated with the long-run inflation rate changes.

What we see in this figure is a picture of Keynesian monetary policy at work, with the Federal Reserve attempting to stabilize interest rates, at least in the short run. These policies performed pretty much the way Keynesians expected in the early 1960s. After 1965, however, we see Keynesian monetary policies that seem to display the economic effects that monetarist theory predicts. That is, the more rapid but uneven expansion of the money supply is

444 *Monetarist and Rational Expectations Theories*

associated with periods of more rapid but uneven inflation, which is what monetarist theory predicts. Changes in the inflation rate mirror changes in the money supply in their basic trend. The rise of monetarist theory and influence can thus be somewhat associated with the rise of monetarist reactions in the economy.

Monetarist economic policies have been used some in more recent years, and the results are interesting. Figure 15-2 presents data about monetary policy in the 1980s. Under chairman Paul Volcker, the Federal Reserve adopted an explicitly monetarist set of policies in October, 1979. This means that the Federal Reserve announced that it was going to attempt to control the money supply, not interest rates. It announced targets for money supply growth. Interest rates would be allowed to go where the market forces of the demand for and supply of credit took them. The Fed pledged a controlled, consistent monetary policy.

This new policy did not last long. Interest rates jumped dramatically on the Fed's announcement, which was correctly interpreted as meaning slower growth in money and credit supplies. The prime interest rate, which had been about 11.5 percent in July, 1979, and 12.5 percent in October, 1979, jumped quickly to 15.5 percent in December, 1979, and 19.5 percent in April, 1980. President Jimmy Carter saw this increase in interest rates as a great political liability in an election year. He applied political pressure to the Federal Reserve and convinced them to abandon their monetarist policies. Carter

| FIGURE 15-2 | **Monetary Policy in the 1980s.** This figure shows that Keynesian and monetarist policies have been used in the 1980s. During the two periods of monetarist Federal Reserve policy (the shaded areas in the figure), the money supply grew at relatively stable rates, but interest rates took large swings. The period of more Keynesian monetary policy in 1983–1986 showed somewhat less stability in money supply growth but more stable interest rates. The data for 1980 fits neither the monetarist nor the Keynesian mold. President Carter's credit controls distorted financial markets in 1980, leading to the unstable money supply and interest rates shown here. |

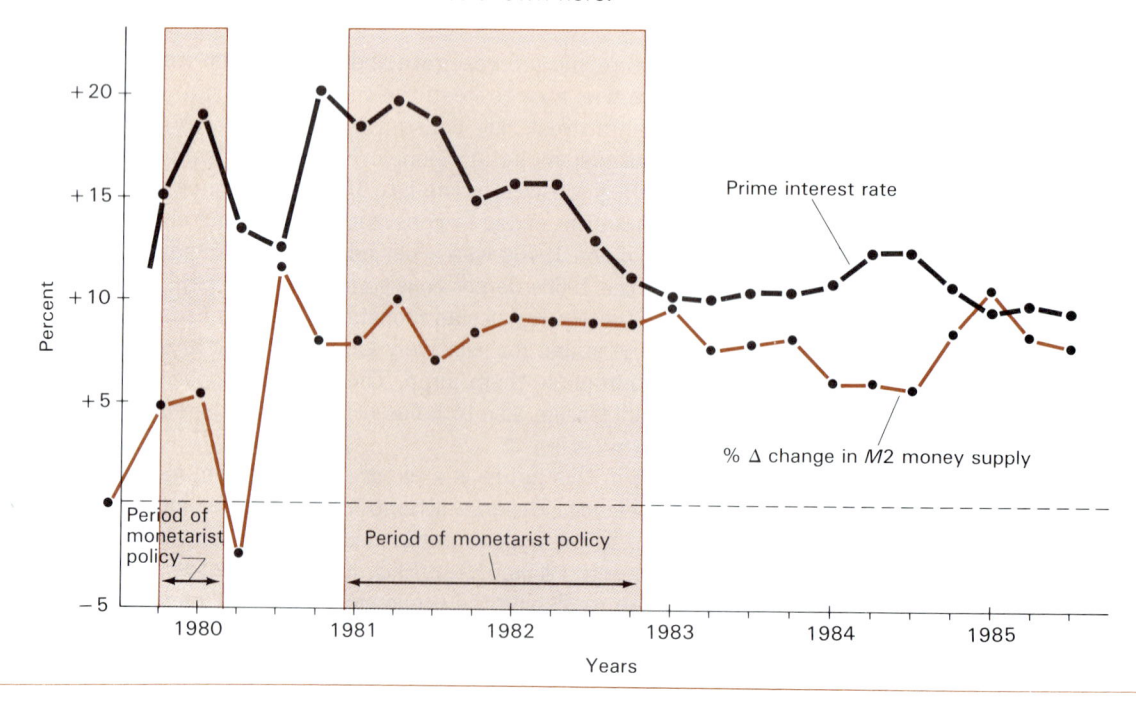

imposed a system of credit controls and interest rate ceilings in an attempt to undo what he saw as the Fed's mistakes. Carter could not shake the albatross of high interest rates, however, and Ronald Reagan defeated him in the 1980 presidential election.

President Reagan was more sympathetic to Fed chairman Volcker's monetarist ideas than was Jimmy Carter. Like Volcker, Reagan viewed high inflation as the most significant economic problem. The Fed therefore returned to its monetarist economic policies in 1981. Growth of the money supply stabilized somewhat, inflation declined, and interest rates assumed a greater variability. The economy went into a recession, with high unemployment rates.

Most economists believed that the economy would have to bear a heavy burden of higher unemployment in order to bring down inflation. The increase in the unemployment rate in the early 1980s was not as great as most economists predicted, however. This may provide partial evidence of the effects predicted by rational expectations theorists. They would predict that individuals would be able to protect themselves from the real effects of an announced, fully anticipated change in monetary policy. The existence of the recession of the early 1980s, however, tends to go against rational expectations predictions because it shows that the real economy was affected, at least in the short run, by the monetary action. On the other hand, the recession could simply indicate that people in the economy were not able to quickly adjust to the new monetary policy, even though their expectations and behavior did change. Nevertheless, the fact that unemployment did not rise as high as had been predicted suggests that some expectational forces were at work to minimize the effect of the restrictive monetary policy.

The deregulation of the financial sector, as discussed in Chapter 13, began to have major impact on the money supply measures in 1982. New types of bank accounts came into existence and financial intermediaries found themselves in new roles, facing greater competition. These rapid changes affected the money supply measures. The Federal Reserve could no longer depend on any particular money supply measure to have a consistent meaning. In this financial environment, a policy of targeting money supply growth would be like trying to hit a target placed on a moving train while sitting on a rotating merry-go-round. It was probably useless at best, and potentially dangerous, to make policy based on money supply targets while the meaning of the money supply definitions was changing each week.

It was probably wise, therefore, for the Federal Reserve to drop its formal monetarist policies in 1982. Since this period, the Fed has returned to a policy of targeting interest rates through activist, but relatively conservative, policies. Also, many economists felt that the Fed could be less restrictive because its earlier policies had reduced inflationary expectations. There is no talk of the Federal Reserve fine tuning the economy, but it is clear that the Fed does try to lean against the wind now. In May, 1985, for example, the Fed lowered the discount rate specifically in order to stimulate the economy and bring interest rates down. This is a far cry from a nonactivist monetarist policy. On the other hand, the Fed does still take money supply growth rates seriously. The Fed regularly sets and announces target growth rates for the money supply. This is completely in the spirit of the monetarist and rational expectations views. Although the Fed often missed its $M1$ targets in 1984–1985, it achieved relatively stable growth of the broader $M2$ and $M3$ monetary aggregates. This may be due to the fact that these broader money measures are less affected by changes in financial regulations than is the narrow $M1$ money supply measure.

Keynesian monetary theory and policy is not dead, but we have seen that there is much evidence that monetarist analysis is valid, and there is

KEY CONCEPTS 15.4

Monetary policy in recent years has been characterized by periods of Keynesian policy, with an emphasis on setting interest rate targets, and monetarist policy, with an emphasis on setting targets for the money supply. Deregulation of the financial sector has created some uncertainty concerning money supply measures, making strict monetarist policies more difficult to implement.

also evidence that expectations are important. We must therefore try to learn the lessons of all of these monetary theories. The remainder of this chapter goes beyond the simplified descriptions that we have been using so far. We will now look more closely at these monetary theories and the issues that surround them.

THE DEVELOPMENT OF MONETARIST THEORY

Keynesian macroeconomic theory has been very influential in the twentieth century, but it was not the first real attempt to grapple with the question of how money and other forces affect the economy. An alternative theory called monetarism predates Keynesian economics. A relatively crude early form of monetarism was briefly introduced in Chapter 13. As the economy has changed, monetarists have altered and refined their theories and revised their economic policy prescriptions. Let us review the early ideas of monetarism and see how these ideas developed into a more modern theory. Then in the next section, we will compare modern monetarist thought with the Keynesian alternative.

A Simple Monetarist Model

15.5 EQUATION OF EXCHANGE

The oldest and simplest variant of monetarism was briefly discussed in Chapter 13. This model is based on the equation of exchange. The equation of exchange starts with a fundamental macroeconomic identity that was originally presented in Chapter 8. The circular flow of spending and income for the entire economy shows that the dollar amount that households spend on goods and services equals the dollar value of the goods and services that businesses produce. The equation of exchange states this identity using four variables. We can measure the amount that households spend as being equal to the amount of money (or money supply) M multiplied by the velocity of money V, which is the average number of times households spend and respend the money supply each year. In other words,

$$\text{\$ value of total spending} = M \times V$$

The dollar value of the economy's production can also be stated in equation form. The value of total production is equal to the price level P multiplied by the level of real production Q. In other words,

$$\text{\$ value of total production} = P \times Q$$

Given these two ideas, we can state the equation of exchange as

$$\text{\$ value of total spending} = \text{\$ value of total production}$$
$$M \times V = P \times Q$$

The basic idea of the early monetarists was that the velocity of money V and, in the short run, the level of real output Q are fixed. This means that any change in the money supply directly affects the price level. In simple terms, a rapid increase in the money supply must cause inflation, an equal proportionate increase in the price level. Increases in the money supply cause inflation, according to the monetarist view, and inflation can only be caused by a level of M that is too large for a given level of V and Q. It is this train of thought that leads to the monetarist contention that, "Inflation is always and everywhere a monetary phenomenon."

The equation of exchange is a practical fact. What makes the equation of exchange a monetarist theory is the assumption that output Q and velocity V are constant. This assumption turns the equation of exchange into a theory that puts great emphasis on the money supply as a determinant of economic activity.

It is reasonable to ask how the monetarists conclude that velocity and real output are constant. Milton Friedman has defended the assumption of fixed real output with an analysis that is often called "Friedman's helicopter." What would happen, Friedman asks, if a helicopter flew over the city and dropped hundred dollar bills everywhere? Would this increase the amount of goods that people would desire to purchase? It clearly would. The dollar value of desired spending ($M \times V$) would increase because of the increased money supply. But, Friedman asks, would the money helicopter change the amount of coal in the ground, the number of apples in the markets, or the economy's capacity to produce electricity, automobiles, and other goods and services? Friedman answers no to this question. Changing the amount of money in the economy does not alter the economy's real ability to produce. Real output Q would not change, so the price P would have to rise to balance the equation of exchange.

The monetarists' assumption that velocity is fixed (or at least that it is relatively stable) is based on their analysis of consumer behavior. Monetarists believe that people have a certain demand for money that is based on how much income they have and, therefore, how much spending they wish to undertake. The amount of money that people wish to hold can be thought of as the demand for money. We can derive the monetarist demand for money from the equation of exchange. Using the equation of exchange, first solve for M in terms of the other variables. Then use the fact that the value of total production, $P \times Q$, must equal the nominal income (dollar value of income) that households receive. Using these ideas, we see that

$$M \times V = P \times Q$$
$$M = \frac{P \times Q}{V}$$
$$M = \frac{\text{nominal income}}{V}$$

Money supply = money demand

The left side of this equation is the money supply. The right side is the money demand. Monetarist theory holds that people choose to hold a fixed proportion of their nominal income as money over time. This proportion, which we will refer to here as money demand, is equal to nominal income divided by the velocity of money. That is, money demand is the amount of money needed to spend all of the nominal income, given the current velocity of money, which depends on behavioral factors, much as the Keynesian marginal propensity to consume depends on certain aspects of consumer behavior. Thus, for example, if nominal income is $100 and money tends to turn over four times each year ($V = 4$), this means that the demand for money is $100/4, or $25, because people in the economy can undertake their desired level of spending if they have $25 available. If the velocity of money is constant over some time period, then money demand is proportional to nominal income.

Simple monetarist theory looks at the economy as the interaction of money supply (largely determined by the Federal Reserve) and money demand (based on nominal income). If the money supply increases, this creates a disequilibrium between money supply and money demand. People have a larger supply of money than they care to hold, given current nominal income levels. Individuals reduce their holdings of money by purchasing real goods and services. The increased spending tends to raise nominal income in the economy, thereby increasing money demand. Nominal income continues to rise until the demand for money has increased to equal the larger supply.

A decrease in the money supply causes the opposite events to occur, in terms of the simple monetarist model. A lower money supply creates a shortage of money. People hold less money than they desire, given current levels of nominal income. They respond by holding more money and therefore purchasing fewer real goods and services. This tends to drive down income until the level of nominal income in the economy is such that money demand equals the new lower money supply.

Modern Monetarist Theory

15.6 MONETARIST MONEY DEMAND

Monetarist theory has progressed in recent years. New, more sophisticated monetarist models have appeared. The major difference in these newer models revolves around how the demand for money is defined. The early monetarists believed that the demand for money balances depended only on nominal income. More recent monetarist theory contends that money balances are only one of many forms in which individuals hold wealth. They believe that individuals build a portfolio of wealth holdings in forms such as money balances, real estate, stocks and bonds, and consumer durables such as autos, major appliances, and so on. Just how much of each of these wealth forms individuals choose to hold in their wealth portfolios depends on several variables, such as the rate of return on each wealth form, the price level, the expected inflation rate, income, and institutional forces such as the ready availability of credit. This is a more complicated, but also more realistic, view of the behavior of individuals regarding their demand for money than that of the early monetarists. Let us briefly examine how each of these factors affects the demand for money.

Income Changes in income tend to affect the demand for money balances in different ways in the short and long runs. It is not unusual to find that, as their incomes rise, individuals first hold the extra income as money balances because they are not certain whether the increase in income is permanent or temporary. They do not wish to undertake large-scale purchases until they are certain that the increase in income is permanent. This temporarily reduces the velocity of money, since consumers hold a greater fraction of total income as money and thus spend a smaller fraction of their total income than before.

Eventually, however, consumers see the increase in income as permanent and use some of the increase to purchase consumer durables such as major appliances. This reduces their demand for money, as they shift from holding money to holding real goods. Next they might purchase other items, such as real estate or stocks and bonds. These purchases further reduce the demand for money. As people make purchases and hold smaller money

ECONOMIC ISSUES

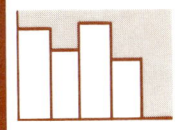

A Monetarist View of the Great Depression

While Keynesian economists have proposed many possible explanations for the Great Depression, monetarists have long believed that the Depression was the result of unwise monetary policy. Federal Reserve policies resulted in an undesirable decrease in the money supply, which led to the Depression. The accompanying table uses the equation of exchange to analyze the Depression years.

The data in the table show that the decrease in the money supply in the period 1929–1933 resulted in a rapid deflation. The GNP price index fell during this period. Real GNP also fell. This tends to support the monetarist view that these events were linked and that the rapid fall in the money supply caused the changes in the rest of the economy.

Note in the table that the velocity of money, while relatively stable in the period 1931–1934, was certainly not constant. This might seem to run against the monetarist theory, but monetarists do not think that velocity is carved in stone. We are looking at a relatively long period of time in a very unsettled period. These changes in velocity are therefore not unexpected. More modern monetarist theories have been developed to explain these velocity changes.

What we see in the table is important evidence that the Federal Reserve contributed to the Great Depression through its monetary policies. The Great Depression might not have occurred, or could have been much less severe, if the money supply had not contracted by the large percentage that we see here.

Monetarist Analysis of the Great Depression

$M \times V = P \times Q$

Year	M1	Velocity (GNP/M1)	GNP price index	Real GNP (1958 prices)
1929	26.6	3.9	50.6	203.1
1930	25.4	3.6	49.3	183.5
1931	23.8	3.2	44.8	169.3
1932	20.1	2.9	40.2	144.2
1933	19.1	2.9	39.3	141.5
1934	21.5	3.0	42.2	154.3

Source. *Economic Report of the President, 1971*, Tables C-1, C-2, C-3, and authors' calculations.

---

balances relative to their income, the velocity of money tends to return to its initial level.

What this example suggests is that, in the short run, an increase in nominal income tends to generate an equal proportionate increase in money demand, as most of the increase in nominal income is held as money. The velocity of money therefore falls in the short run as income rises. In the long run, however, the demand for money as a fraction of income returns to its previous level, as consumers hold less money and more real goods. Thus the velocity of money rises back to its initial level in the long run. This analysis helps explain why the velocity of money is constant in the long run, but could change in the short run.

Price Level Modern monetarists also believe that the amount of money balances individuals keep on hand is influenced by the price level. Suppose an individual keeps $100 per week in cash money balances to meet everyday transaction needs. If the prices of these goods and services doubled, consumers would need twice as much money to buy the same amount of goods. As the price level rises, the demand for money balances also rises.

Expected Inflation Rate Inflation reduces the purchasing power of the money balances that individuals hold. As the expected rate of inflation increases, the expected purchasing power of money balances declines. This creates an incentive for individuals to hold more of their wealth in forms that are less affected by inflation than is money. This shifting from money to other assets in the wealth portfolio reduces the demand for money. Thus the demand for money tends to fall as a fraction of nominal income, if inflation is expected to rise.

Opportunity Cost People allocate their wealth among alternate assets based on the relative returns that each offers. People who hold large money balances give up the return they could have had if they had chosen to hold stocks or bonds instead, for example. This foregone return is the opportunity cost of holding money. If the real return on real estate is rising, it is reasonable to assume that people will tend to hold more of their wealth as real estate and relatively less as money balances. The demand for money therefore depends on the return available on other assets.

Institutional Factors There are many institutional factors that affect our habits in holding money balances. We hold money balances to synchronize the difference between the moment we receive income and the longer period over which we spend our income. For example, if at the very instant we wanted to buy something we also received an income payment, there would be no need to hold cash balances. Income and expenditures would be perfectly synchronized. This is not frequently a reality, however. When we receive income we hold some money balances to help us make expenditures until we receive income again. The less frequently we receive income, the larger our pool of money balances for expenditures must be.

The availability of credit is another factor that affects the amount of money that we hold. Today, as opposed to 20 years ago, credit cards and lines of overdraft credit on checking accounts have placed readily available credit in the hands of millions of consumers. These credit balances have reduced the need for individuals to maintain large cash balances. Accordingly, the demand to hold cash balances has declined over time. This means that a smaller money supply, circulating at a higher velocity, can meet our expenditure needs. The velocity of money has, in fact, displayed a dramatic rise over the years. The velocity of money, calculated as GNP/$M1$, has risen from 3.51 in 1960 to 5.18 in 1975 to 6.35 in 1983. If consumers are holding fewer cash balances, they are holding larger portions of their wealth portfolios in other wealth forms.

Modern monetarism is still built on the idea of the equation of exchange. But modern monetarism asserts that the velocity of money and the demand for money are more complex than the simple equation of exchange suggests. The velocity of money is not constant. Velocity is affected by the list of factors just discussed. Does this make the equation of exchange useless? If velocity changes, then does the equation of exchange say anything meaningful? Martin Feldstein, former chief economic advisor to President Reagan, suggests that while velocity is not constant, it may be stable enough to make the policy of targeting the money supply effective. He makes this assessment:

> The basic criticism of any monetarist approach to policy is that the income velocity of money — i.e., the ratio of the money stock to the value of GNP at current prices — is so unstable that no purpose is served by controlling the monetary aggregates. This criticism can no longer be convincing. . . . The monetarist case for controlling the monetary aggregates never rested on their being a perfectly stable or predictable trend in velocity. What matters is that controlling the monetary aggregates is better than the alternative bases for guiding monetary policy.[1]

1. Martin Feldstein, "Monetarism: Open-Eyed Pragmatism," *The Economist*, May 18, 1985, p. 17.

**KEY CONCEPTS
15.5, 15.6**

The equation of exchange states an identity between the monetary and real sectors of the economy. This equation can be interpreted as stating a relationship between money supply and money demand that depends on the velocity of money and nominal income. Simple monetarist theory is built on this relationship between money supply and money demand. Modern monetarist theory is still based on money supply and money demand, but it recognizes that several factors besides nominal income can influence the level of money demand.

KEYNESIAN AND MONETARIST COMPARISONS

15.7 KEYNESIANISM VERSUS MONETARISM

Keynesian and monetarist theories are both influential today. They both offer insights into how the economy works and what can be done to promote stable economic growth. They do differ in several respects, however. We can learn about both schools of economic thought, and why economists frequently disagree about monetary and fiscal policies, by focusing on the main points of disagreement between monetarists and Keynesians.

Velocity and Money Demand: Income Versus Interest Rates

Comparing the Keynesian analysis in Chapter 14 with the monetarist discussion just presented, the first important difference we see concerns how the velocity and the demand for money should be treated. We have seen that monetarists view money as just that—money. People demand money based on several factors. The most important determinant of money demand is nominal income, however. People choose to hold money based on income and spending trends. This determines the speed at which money changes hands, the velocity of money.

Keynesians, on the other hand, focus on credit in their view of money. Keynesians look at how money affects the economy through its impact on the credit market. The amount of money and credit that people choose to hold, in the Keynesian view, depends on both income and interest rates, but interest rates are the important determinant of money and credit demand. Keynesians view the deposit expansion process as creating more credit and, therefore, more money. Monetarists see deposit expansion as the process of money creation; they focus more on what people do once the money is created than on what happened to create it.

All modern monetarists and Keynesians think that both income and interest rates, among other things, affect the amount of money that people wish to hold. Both income, which was listed in Chapter 14 as a determinant of credit demand, and interest rates, which are an opportunity cost of holding money balances, affect money demand. Keynesians and monetarists disagree, however, about the relative importance of income versus interest rates and other factors in determining the amount of money and credit people wish to hold and about the velocity with which money circulates.

Monetary Transmission Mechanism

Another difference between the Keynesian and monetarist models concerns the mechanism by which monetary policy is transmitted to the economy. In the Keynesian model, an increase in the money supply causes an increase in the credit supply. This tends to reduce interest rates, which stimulates higher investment spending, thereby increasing aggregate demand.

Monetary policy in Keynesian theory is transmitted to the economy through the interest rate/investment spending mechanism.

The monetarist money transmission mechanism is more direct. An increase in the money supply creates a surplus of money. The money supply is temporarily greater than the money demand, which is determined by income and other factors. People reduce their surplus holdings of money by exchanging money for goods, services, real estate, stocks, bonds, and other assets. The increase in the money supply directly produces an increase in aggregate demand, whether or not interest rates change.

The Importance of Fiscal Policy

Monetarists and Keynesians differ in their opinions about the need for and the effectiveness of using fiscal policy to control the economy. Monetarists contend that the economy contains built-in, or natural, forces that can move it toward and help it maintain a relatively stable macro equilibrium approximating full employment.

Monetarists believe that fiscal policy simply crowds out private spending and has, therefore, little or no net impact on aggregate demand. An increase in government spending requires either higher taxes, which crowds out private consumer behavior, or deficit borrowing, which crowds out private investment spending. The crowding-out effect offsets the government spending, making it impotent to change aggregate demand. In the monetarist view, fiscal policy can, at best, briefly increase total spending through a rise in velocity if government spends money faster than the crowded-out private sector would.

Monetarists believe that fiscal policies are often used by political entrepreneurs who exploit their political interests to get elected and to promote special-interest legislation. Monetarists also think that the shortsightedness effect results in short-run fiscal policies that are not in the economy's long-run interests.

Keynesians contend that, while the economy automatically adjusts to an equilibrium, there is no guarantee that equilibrium occurs at full employment. Keynesians therefore advocate a strong, active role for government spending and taxation to reach and maintain full-employment equilibrium income.

Keynesians point out that fiscal policy is not necessarily impotent, as the monetarists contend, and that it generally can affect aggregate demand. Multiplier analysis shows that government spending financed by higher taxes does, in fact, increase total spending because government spending has a larger multiplier effect than does taxation. This was the balanced budget multiplier concept discussed in Chapter 12. Government spending financed by deficit borrowing can also stimulate aggregate demand, according to the Keynesians, so long as crowding out is not complete. If the government borrows and spends $200 billion, for example, but private borrowing and investment spending falls by only $100 billion, there would still be a net $100 billion increase in aggregate demand, which would then grow through the multiplier effect.

Finally, in monetarist terms, Keynesians believe that fiscal policy can influence the level of economic activity by changing the velocity of money. Deficit spending, for example, might drive up interest rates, which, according to modern monetarist analysis, could yield a higher velocity of money and therefore have the same general effect as an increase in the money supply. Keynesian Nobel Prize recipient James Tobin has noted that "the

TABLE 15-1 Comparison of Monetarist and Keynesian Theory

Point of comparison	Keynesian	Early monetarists	Modern monetarists
MONEY DEMAND	Depends on the interest rate, the cost of holding money, and income.	Depends on nominal income; the greater the income, the greater the demand for money balances.	Depends on price level, return on all wealth forms, expected rate of inflation, and institutional factors, in addition to income.
TRANSMISSION MECHANISM	Increases in money supply reduce interest rates, which increases investment, increasing aggregate demand.	Increases in money supply cause direct increases in consumption spending, which increases aggregate demand.	Increases in money supply cause direct increases in both consumption and investment spending, which increases aggregate demand.
IMPORTANCE OF FISCAL POLICY	Necessary and effective in pursuing desired levels of aggregate demand.	Unnecessary and ineffective in pursuing desired levels of aggregate demand.	Unnecessary and ineffective in pursuing desired levels of aggregate demand because of crowding out and short-sightedness effect.
IMPORTANCE OF MONETARY POLICY	Less powerful than fiscal policy.	Very important, but tends to cause inflation.	Very important; money is the primary determinant of nominal GNP.

patent success of fiscal stimulus in promoting recovery in the United States in 1983–84 reinforces the Keynesian side of this old debate."[2]

The Importance of Monetary Policy

Monetarists think that monetary policy can affect the economy, but they think that it is likely to be inflationary. They are therefore cautious about the active use of monetary policy to influence the economy. As noted above, they do not think that fiscal policy can have much positive effect on the economy, either. Monetarists therefore tend to favor laissez faire economic policies, which leave the private sector pretty much alone to generate production and income without government interference.

Keynesians think that monetary policy can be effective in a recession if it can reduce interest rates and increase investment spending, although they view monetary policy as a less direct and probably less powerful alternative to fiscal policy. Keynesians tend to favor activist economic policies, designed to move the economy toward the goal of full employment.

It is certain that the debate between monetarists and Keynesians is far from over. The primary differences between the Keynesian and monetarist positions are summarized in Table 15-1.

THE MONETARIST REMEDY

15.8 MONETARIST POLICIES

According to monetarists, discretionary fiscal policy is more a part of the economic problem than the solution.

2. James Tobin, "Monetarism: An Ebbing Tide," *The Economist*, April 27, 1985, p. 23.

Contrary to the many Keynesian claims of a fine-tuned management of the economy by a delicate touch on the tiller, monetarists argued that nobody knows enough about the dynamics of economic events to be able to soften hard times or cool off overheating.[3]

If the monetarists find discretionary fiscal policy problematic, what solution do they offer instead? Monetarists would neutralize the power of government to exercise discretionary policy and then use monetary policy to expand the money supply at a fixed rate that approaches the average growth rate of the economy. Milton Friedman, the best known monetarist, has stated that

> if we cannot achieve our objective by giving wide discretion to independent experts, how else can we establish a monetary system that is stable, free from irresponsible government tinkering, and incapable of being used as a source of power to threaten economic and political freedom? My choice . . . would be a legislative rule. . . . I would specify that the reserve system should see to it that the total stock of money rises month by month . . . at an annual rate of X percent, where X is some number between 3 and 5.[4]

A fixed rate of money growth would, in the eyes of the monetarists, reduce future uncertainties. Decision makers could enter into contractual agreements with less fear of large monetary changes in the future. A steady monetary growth would exercise automatic dampening effects on cyclical fluctuations in the economy. The constant increase in the money supply, according to the monetarists, would tend to even out economic cycles, reducing the severity of both inflationary booms and recessionary declines.

According to monetarist Sir Alan Walters, sound monetary policy has three goals: (1) to maintain liquidity in the very short run; (2) to avoid inducing fluctuations in the short to medium run; and (3) to control inflation in the long run. Thus monetary authorities, in Walters' view, should be willing to take the day-to-day actions necessary to assure that the economy has ready access to the money that it needs to keep the financial system running soundly. This means perhaps creating money to ward off a bank run, for example.

In the short run, the Fed should avoid inducing fluctuations by keeping the average growth rate of money constant. This prevents problems caused by uneven money growth or interest rate targeting. In the long run, inflation is controlled by keeping the money supply from growing too rapidly. Walters contends that, in the past 10 years, countries such as Japan, which have followed the policies he outlines, have had a much smoother ride. That is, they have experienced fewer financial crises, lower inflation, and less severe fluctuations in real GNP.

WHICH ECONOMIC THEORY IS CORRECT?

15.9 VALIDITY OF KEYNESIAN AND MONETARIST POLICIES

Which economic theory is correct? Both monetarists and Keynesians can cite evidence to support their theories. Figure 15-3, for example, provides data that seem, at first glance, to support the monetarist view. Figure 15-1

---

3. Alan Walters, "Monetarism: The Right Stuff," *The Economist*, May 4, 1985, p. 32.

4. Milton Friedman, "Should There Be an Independent Monetary Authority?" in Leland B. Yeager, ed., *In Search of a Monetary Constitution*, Cambridge, MA: Harvard University Press, 1962.

| FIGURE 15-3 | **The Relationship between Money and GNP.** There has been a strong overall relationship between the money supply and GNP in the years since 1960. This does not necessarily mean that changes in the money supply cause changes in GNP, however. |

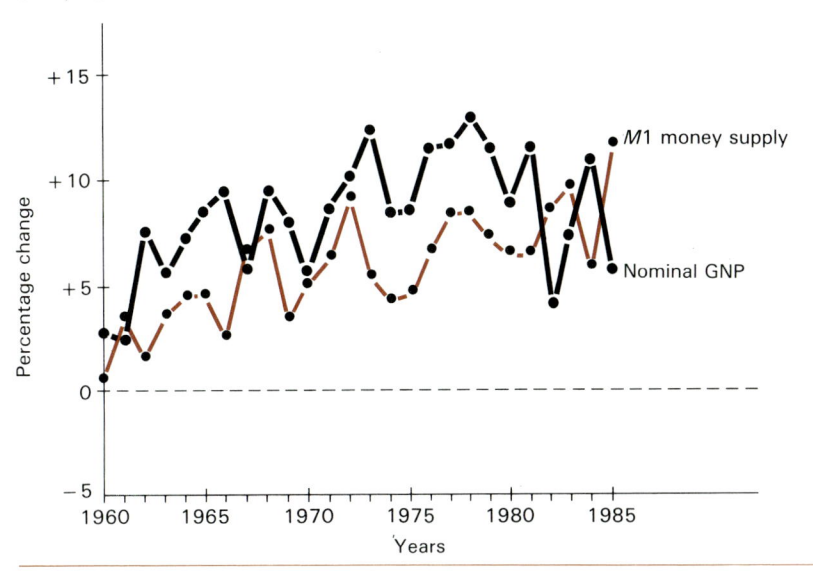

shows the relationship between the money supply and GNP in the United States in the years since 1960. GNP and the money supply, as shown here, rise and fall in the same general trend. This would seem to support the monetarist idea that changes in the money supply cause the changes we observe in GNP.

It is an error, however, to simply conclude from Figure 15-3 that monetarism is the correct theory. First, we know from Chapter 2 that correlation is not causation. That is, the fact that the money supply and GNP move together over time does not necessarily mean that the money supply causes the observed changes in GNP. Changes in GNP might cause the movements in the money supply, or it could be that both variables are influenced by some third factor. In addition, it is possible that changes in the money supply are causing these changes in GNP, but that the money supply changes are the result of the credit market, interest rates, and investment spending (the Keynesian view) not a direct relationship between money and spending (the monetarist view).

It is impossible in the real world to actually prove that an economic theory is valid because so many factors affect the economy besides the money supply and fiscal policy. Milton Friedman makes a strong case for monetarism in his and Anna Jacobsen Schwartz's book *A Monetary History of the United States*,[5] but Keynesian theorists can also cite studies that show the power of their analysis. In short, the evidence does not allow us to completely accept either theory, nor can we eliminate either of them as being obviously wrong.

An unbiased observer of this debate would have to conclude that both monetarist and Keynesian theories provide important insights into how the economy works. Each theory has influenced the other, to the benefit of both. Milton Friedman has said that "we are all Keynesians now" referring to the

---

5. Milton Friedman and Anna Jacobsen Schwartz, *A Monetary History of the United States*, Cambridge, MA: Harvard University Press, 1963.

PROMINENT ECONOMIST

Milton Friedman (1912–   )

Milton Friedman, Nobel laureate (1976) and professor emeritus at the University of Chicago, is one of the most influential economists of this century. His reputation is based primarily on his opposition to government intervention in the economy through discretionary monetary policy. He has always doubted that government can successfully control the economy and has suggested that changing the supply of money serves only to further destabilize the economy.

One of Friedman's most outstanding contributions to economics is his book *A Monetary History of the United States (1867–1960)*, coauthored by Anna J. Schwartz in 1963. It includes evaluations of major economic changes in the United States for almost a century. Friedman and Schwartz contend that these major fluctuations were caused by monetary mismanagement. Friedman recommends that government should not intervene because its use of monetary and fiscal policy leads to even greater economic problems in the long run. Friedman has been a staunch defender of the free-market economy because he believes that government action often has the reverse effects of those that were intended.

For 28 years (1948 to 1976), Friedman served as professor of economics at the University of Chicago. He has also served on the staff of the National Bureau of Economic Research since 1948. Upon his retirement from the University of Chicago, Friedman began research at Stanford's Hoover Institution. He is well known for his columns in *Newsweek* and has had a substantial impact upon current economic policy. He supports the money-supply rule, which states that the economy's supply of money should be expanded in proportion to the rate of economic growth.

Friedman's writings have also had a substantial impact on laymen in our economy. He authored a best-selling book that was also developed into a multipart television series entitled "Free to Choose." In both the book and the television series, Friedman educated a generation of laymen in the merits of a free-market economy and a reduction in government regulation and economic intervention. Always a controversial figure, Milton Friedman has certainly changed some of the thinking of economists, bureaucrats, and laymen in the last half of the twentieth century.

---

influence of Keynesian analysis on economists of all stripes. Keynesians also acknowledge the influence of monetarist thinkers. Indeed, the permanent income hypothesis that we discussed in Chapter 10 as an explanation of the Keynesian consumption function was developed in the 1950s by monetarist Milton Friedman.

Both monetarists and Keynesians in the 1980s are busy perfecting and expanding their models to take into account recent developments in the economy. Some of the most important new ideas concern the effect of expectations on the economy, which is the topic of the remainder of this chapter.

THE ROLE OF EXPECTATIONS IN MACRO POLICY

15.10 POWER OF EXPECTATIONS

We act and react in a world of expectations. Our actions today are heavily influenced by what we believe the situation may be tomorrow. Suppose, for example, that we believe that housing prices will rise in the future. This affects our behavior now. We are more likely to buy a new house today if we think that housing prices will rise in the future. Conversely, we are more likely to put off the housing purchase if we expect housing prices to fall in the future.

The power of expectations to influence our actions means that announcement effects can be important. The Federal Reserve's announcement of a higher discount rate, for example, can cause people to purchase new houses and cars immediately in order to avoid the higher interest rates they might expect in the future as a result of this Federal Reserve policy. As people learn more about how the economy functions, this learning process influences both their expectations for the future and their behavior today. We realize that economic theory is a simplified description of human behavior, and as human behavior changes over time, so must economic theory.

We can better understand economic events and theories if we take the power of changing expectations into account. In Chapter 9, for example, we discussed the Phillips curve. The Phillips curve, discovered by A. W. Phillips, shows a trade-off between the inflation rate and the unemployment rate. The Phillips curve, as shown in Figure 15-4, accurately described economic conditions in the 1960s in the United States, but events in other years do not appear to fit the original Phillips curve mold. As Figure 15-4 indicates, it is possible to plot out a series of Phillips curves for the 1970s and 1980s. This makes it appear that the Phillips curve has shifted several times in recent years. But what made the Phillips curve shift?

One explanation for the shift we see in the Phillips curve could be that borrowers, lenders, employers, and workers were more sophisticated in the 1970s than they were in the 1960s. It could be that these groups ignored the rising inflation of the 1960s in making their decisions. If they did not

FIGURE 15-4

Shifting Phillips Curves, 1960–1985. Data on inflation and unemployment for 1960–1985 seem to show a series of shifts in the Phillips curve over this period. Each outward shift resulted in higher inflation and higher unemployment.

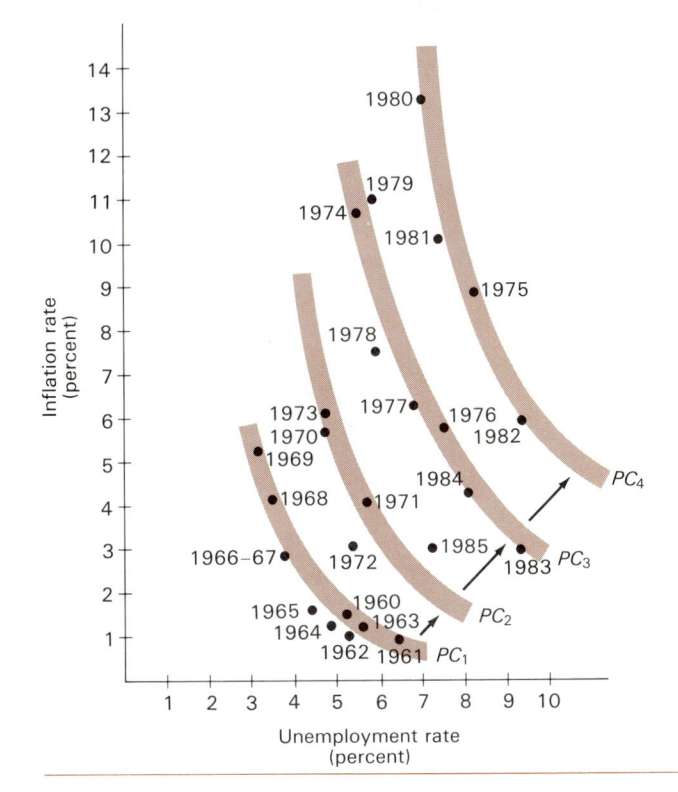

take inflation into account in making decisions, then workers and lenders were worse off. Workers saw the unexpected inflation reduce their real wages, giving them less purchasing power than they bargained for. Lenders saw unexpected inflation reduce the real interest rate, shrinking the purchasing power of the loan repayments they received. Unexpected inflation tends to benefit employers and borrowers. Employers saw unexpected inflation reduce the real cost of labor at the same time that output prices increased. Unexpected inflation can, therefore, artificially increase profits. Borrowers became better off because unexpected inflation reduced the real value of the loan repayments they made.

Now let us suppose that these groups all learned from the experience of the 1960s and began to expect inflation in making their economic decisions. This change in expectations could shift the Phillips curve out and up, increasing both inflation and unemployment.

If inflation is expected, for example, borrowers will want to borrow more in order to buy goods now, before prices go up, and to get loans at the relatively low current real interest rates. Lenders, on the other hand, will be less willing to make loans if they expect inflation in the future. The impact of these inflationary expectations was discussed in Chapter 14, where we saw that expectations of higher inflation tend to drive up the interest rate. Higher interest rates mean higher costs for business investment in plant and inventory purchases. Firms must charge higher prices to sell today's goods at a profit when interest costs rise. And they tend to invest less in job-creating new factories due to higher interest costs. These forces tend to produce higher inflation and higher unemployment, which is what a shift in the Phillips curve indicates.

Workers and employers also act differently when they expect inflation. Workers will demand wage increases in expectation of higher prices. These wage increases will cause layoffs in some industries, increasing unemployment. Employers, at the same time, may mark up their prices in anticipation of general cost increases. This tends to increase inflation. The combination of these actions causes both higher inflation and higher unemployment rates, which is what the shift in the Phillips curve shows.

Changing expectations are not the complete explanation of the Phillips curve shifts we observe in Figure 15-4. Economists are still uncertain about both what causes the basic Phillips curve relationship and what makes it shift. We can see, however, that changes in inflationary expectations would alter the economic behavior of workers and employers, borrowers and lenders. The combined effects of these reactions to expectations of higher inflation could, in fact, cause both higher inflation and higher unemployment, shifting the Phillips curve.

Adaptive Expectations

It is unrealistic to believe that people do not take expected future events into account when making economic decisions. It is also unrealistic to believe that expectations, no matter how intelligently devised, are always correct. Economists themselves have not been very accurate in predicting rates of inflation or unemployment, so it is unlikely that other people are any more accurate. It is more likely that noneconomists formulate expectations for the future based on past experience.

The **adaptive expectations hypothesis** contends that the primary determinant of future expectations is the actual experiences of the decision maker in the recent past. For example, decision makers base their expecta-

Adaptive Expectations Hypothesis
The economic theory that contends that the primary determinants of future expectations are the actual recent past experiences of decision makers.

15.11 ADAPTIVE EXPECTATIONS

tions about future inflation rates on past and present inflation rates. When workers negotiate a contract for next year, they might consider that two years ago the inflation rate was 10 percent and this year it is 13 percent. They might, therefore, feel that the rate of inflation is rising above the 13 percent range. If the actual rate of inflation this year turned out to be 10 percent, they would revise their expectations downward next year. In any case, this means that there is a substantial lag in the formulation of expectations. Expectations will not be revised downward until after actual experience shows downward movement. Alternatively, expectations will not be revised upward until after actual experience shows upward movement.

This adaptive expectations hypothesis can go a long way to explain why the Phillips curve shifts out over time. Consider Figure 15-5 where the economy is operating at point 1 on the lowest Phillips curve shown. Unemployment is at 6 percent, the long-run, or natural, rate of unemployment, and inflation is running at 8 percent. The natural rate of unemployment is the measured rate of unemployment that would prevail in the economy in long-run equilibrium, where there is no cyclical unemployment. Now suppose that the Federal Reserve expands the money supply so rapidly that inflation rises above its expected 8 percent level. Employees, workers, borrowers, and lenders expect 8 percent inflation, but actual inflation rises to 10 percent. Employers' real costs of labor fall as nominal wages are held constant and the prices they receive expand by 10 percent. This tends to artificially increase firm profits, giving business an incentive to expand production. Employers demand more labor and output increases. The economy moves to point 2 in Figure 15-5, with 10 percent inflation but only 4 percent unemployment.

FIGURE 15-5

The Adaptive Expectations Hypothesis. The adaptive expectations hypothesis holds that people slowly adjust their inflationary expectations based on past experience. An unexpected inflation can temporarily move the economy from 1 to 2, but the unemployment rate returns to 3 once expectations catch up. Another inflation moves the economy to 4, but unemployment returns to 5 when inflationary expectations adapt to the higher price level. An attempt to slow inflation moves the economy to 6 briefly, with higher unemployment, but adaptive expectations move the economy back to 3 in the long run.

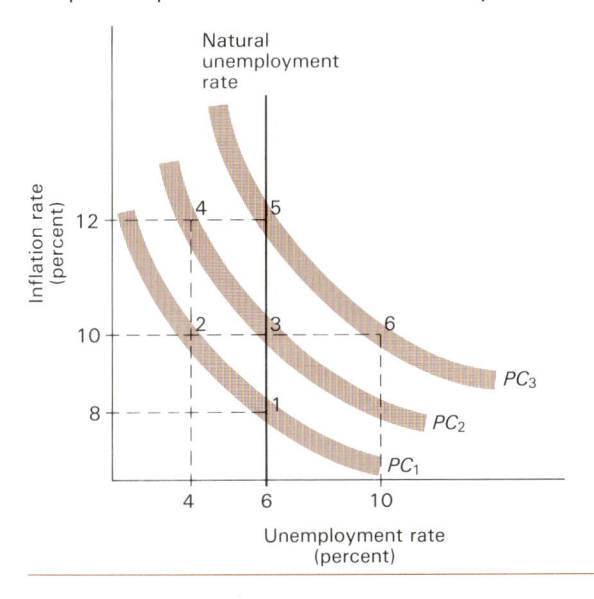

The movement along the Phillips curve just described does not last forever, however. Workers soon realize that the expected rate of inflation was below the actual rate and revise their wage demands upward as they negotiate their next contract. Real wages and prices fall back into equilibrium. The price of labor rises, and employers reduce the quantity of labor they demand. Unemployment rises again, moving back to its long-run natural rate. The economy slips back to point 3 in the figure, on a new Phillips curve. The economy still has 10 percent inflation, and unemployment has returned to the 6 percent natural unemployment rate level. Expansionary monetary policy is applied again and the short-run effect is to move to point 4. Unemployment falls back to approximately 4 percent as workers suffer wage illusion. The rate of inflation rises to 12 percent, and workers adjust their wage demands upward. The economy falls back to point 5, with 12 percent inflation and the same natural rate of unemployment of 6 percent.

This same adaptive-expectations result occurs when actions are taken to reduce inflation by increasing the unemployment rate. A contraction in the money supply produces lower cash balances than people want to hold, thus individuals will reduce their spending. Employers will reduce output and lay off workers. There will, however, be a time lag between the moment spending is reduced and the resultant reduction in the inflation rate. The economy might well move to point 6, with a very high unemployment rate of 10 percent. The expected rate of inflation might still be 10 percent. Workers will search for jobs with real wages that represent a 12 percent inflation rate. That is, workers will continue to demand wages that producers cannot or will not pay. Job search time will increase and unemployment will rise. Actual prices will, as a secondary effect, begin to fall. This experience will then affect the inflation rates that workers expect. Once unemployed workers are out of work long enough to see prices fall, they will adjust their unexpected rate of inflation downward. Job search time will fall as employees demand lower real wage increases. Employment may then return to its natural level, and the economy will move back to point 3, with 10 percent inflation and 6 percent unemployment.

The combination of the Phillips curve and the theory of adaptive expectations suggests that economic policy can affect unemployment in the short run only. In the long run, expectations adjust to the economic policies, and unemployment returns to the long-run equilibrium rate. Figure 15-6 plots the inflation and unemployment rates for the 1970s and 1980s. The pattern of inflation and unemployment in this period generally supports the adaptive expectations hypothesis. Unemployment has repeatedly returned to the 6-to-7 percent level that many economists now associate with the natural unemployment rate.

Rational Expectations Theory

The adaptive expectations hypothesis holds that decision makers base their future expectations exclusively on past events. For example, if the inflation rate has been rising rapidly for the past year, decision makers expect that rate to continue to rise rapidly in the foreseeable future. Adaptive expectations theory does not take into account the effect current monetary policy might have on future economic events. Even though the rate of inflation may have been increasing rapidly over a given period, monetary policy changes today could reduce the inflation rate in the future or make inflation higher.

FIGURE 15-6

The Natural Unemployment Rate and Adaptive Expectations. Data on the inflation and unemployment rate for 1960–1985 generally support the adaptive expectations and natural unemployment rate hypothesis that was shown in Figure 14-3. The same pattern of short-term Phillips curve-like data, with long-run movements back to a fixed unemployment rate, appears here.

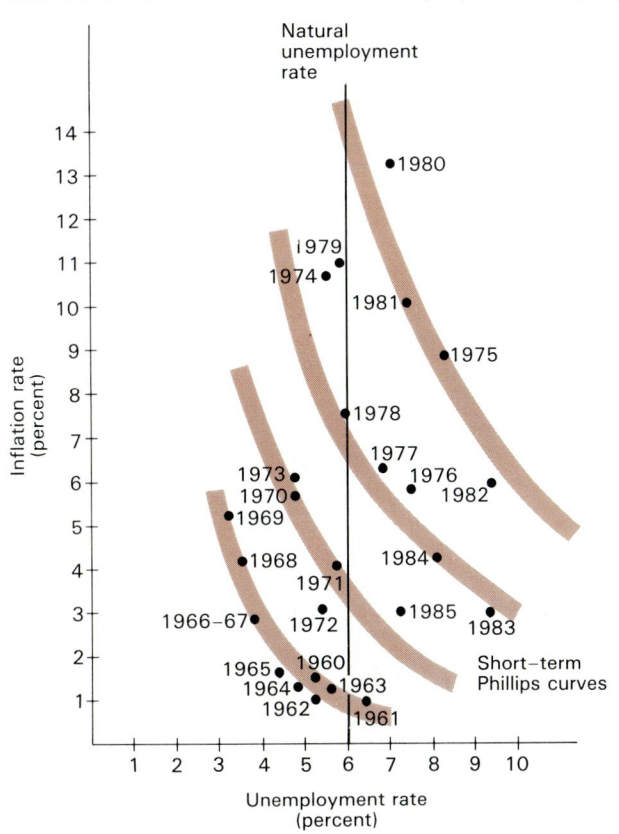

15.12 RATIONAL EXPECTATIONS HYPOTHESIS

Rational Expectations Hypothesis
The economic theory that contends that people will consider all the relevant information available to them in formulating their future economic expectations including past trends and current actions.

The **rational expectations hypothesis** suggests that people consider all the relevant information available to them in formulating expectations about the economic future, including both past trends and present actions. Unlike the adaptive expectations theory, rational expectations implies that people not only learn from past experience but combine that learning with present events to anticipate changes in future economic conditions. Chapter 14 touched on this concept briefly in the discussion of the announcement effects of monetary policy. The announcement of changes in monetary policy, such as discount rate changes, has a significant effect on the rational expectations of decision makers. Rational expectations theory implies that any change in macroeconomic policy quickly adjusts the expectations of decision makers. This means that discretionary macro policy will be ineffective in changing output, employment, and real income. In other words, the rational expectations theory holds that people react to changes in economic policy so fast that the policy has no real effect on the economy. Consequently, monetary and fiscal policies are both powerless to produce changes in the economy. An example will make this idea clearer.

Suppose that an expansionary monetary policy is announced. This policy is designed to stimulate aggregate demand in the short run, thereby reducing unemployment. If the rational expectations theory holds, economic

ECONOMIC ISSUES

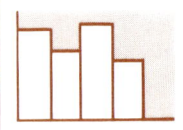

Rational Expectations in the Classroom

Expectations are abstract; you cannot see them. Thus many students have trouble seeing how powerful expectations can be and how the ideas of rational expectations theory work. This brief example is offered to help make these concepts clear.

Suppose that a university's English Department has established policies for its literature classes. The rules are as follows: (1) All exams will follow the essay format. (2) Students must achieve a 90 percent average on exams to qualify for an A grade. (3) Instructors should attempt to give approximately 20 percent of their students A grades. While it is unlikely that formal rules like these are often really used, we all know that norms and expectations develop in college classes and elsewhere. We can therefore treat these rules as formal requirements or as informal guidelines and see how they work.

Given the literature class grading rules described above, we can imagine that literature professors and students will seek out a classroom grade "equilibrium." Professors will tend to write exams that enable about 20 percent of their students to receive A grades. Students will respond to these standards and study accordingly. Those students who need A grades to get into law school, for example, will tend to work hard enough to get at least a 90 percent average. The interaction of the students, the professors, and the rules will eventually achieve some equilibrium where the class grade results end up pretty much as everyone expects.

Now suppose that at the start of a new semester the English Department announces a change in its rules for the coming term. The new rules are as follows: (1) All exams will follow the essay format. (2) Students must achieve a 95 percent average on exams to qualify for an A grade. (3) Instructors should attempt to give approximately 20 percent of their students A grades. Notice that the new rules set a higher percentage standard for the A grade.

What do you think will happen to the classroom equilibrium as a result of this systematic policy change? Will students need to study more? Will more learning take place? This is not necessarily the result of this policy, although it may be its intent. A very likely result is that professors will lower their grading standards or write less difficult exams in an attempt to give 20 percent of their students A grades. Students, realizing this, will not increase their study burden. The literature classes can easily adjust to the new rules. The exam averages will rise (this is sometimes called grade inflation), but there will be no real change in the number of A grades or the amount of learning that takes place. In other words, there will be no real change in the classroom equilibrium, only a nominal change in the exam scores themselves. It might take students and professors a little time to

decision makers will immediately recognize that the long-run outcome of this policy will be an increase in the inflation rate. They will immediately revise their inflationary expectations upward and choose accordingly. Workers will build in higher expected rates of inflation into their future wage demands. Lenders will demand higher interest rates today in the expectation of higher inflation rates tomorrow. Producers who contract to supply goods in the future will build in higher expected inflation rates into their future contract prices today.

Remember that the goal of the expansionary monetary policy was to stimulate aggregate demand. As a group, decision makers have already incorporated the long-term effect of the monetary expansion into their actions today. Prices, wages, and interest rates begin to rise immediately and aggregate demand might not increase in the short run as the expansionary policy intended. The lower interest rates that an increase in the money supply normally generates, for example, could be offset by the higher interest rates that an increase in inflationary expectations causes. The overall result could be no change in interest rates, and therefore, no change in investment spending. The goal of the monetary expansion has been

learn how this new system works, but we can expect them to settle into this new grade equilibrium eventually.

This example illustrates the rational expectations idea that systematic changes in a policy might have nominal effects (the grade inflation above) but no real impact. If you think of the Federal Reserve as setting the rules of the game, and think of everyone in the economy as the students and professors, then you capture the flavor of rational expectations theory. A fully anticipated change in the monetary rules has no effect on the economy if individuals alter their expectations and behavior in appropriate ways.

Now let us examine what would happen if the English Department enacted a "surprise" policy change. Suppose that the new rules listed above were adopted just before final exams, with the understanding that they would apply to both current and future literature classes. In the short run, students and professors would find that their expectations and the real world no longer matched. Students who had achieved an average of 91 percent on previous exams might find that it is now mathematically impossible for them to reach the new 95 percent average score that is necessary for an A grade no matter how well they do on the final exam. Other students might find that they need to study harder and score higher than before in order to achieve the expected grade. The professor might find that it is impossible to write a meaningful exam that would produce the desired percentage of A grades.

We can see that this surprise change in the grading policy does produce real results, unlike the systematic change discussed above. Students might temporarily be forced to study harder and learn more for the final exam in order to earn their expected grade. Professors might find themselves forced to give lower overall grades, reducing the class gradepoint average. In other words, this surprise policy might actually affect the classroom equilibrium in meaningful ways. Students might learn more but receive lower grades.

Would this change in grade averages and study habits be long lasting? This does not seem likely. By the next semester, we would expect to find that students and professors have adjusted their expectations to the new rules. No permanent change in study habits, A grades, or learning would occur. Only the exam averages would be affected in the long run.

If, once again, you think of the Federal Reserve as setting the rules of the game and everyone else as students and professors, you can understand why rational expectations theorists think that surprise monetary policies can have some impact on the economy but that the effect will only be temporary. Expectations and rational behavior eventually adjust to the new set of rules.

This example asks you to draw on your intuition to see how expectations and policies interact. It illustrates the idea that we all undertake activities in our own self-interest based on expectations. According to the rational expectations theory, systematic policies have little effect because we are able to adjust our expectations to them. Surprise policy changes have disruptive short-term effects but are of little use in the long run.

Rational expectations theory, as illustrated by this example, is built on the classical microeconomic idea that individuals act in their own self-interest, given the system they face and the information they have about how that system works. Rational expectations theory is often called the "new classical economics" because, like the pre-Keynesian classical economics discussed in Chapter 10, it is built on the microeconomic foundation of individual self-interest.

neutralized by the speedy adjustments in the expectations of decision makers.

Economists who advocate the rational expectations hypothesis believe that discretionary monetary policy is detrimental to the stability of the economy. The only way that monetary policy could really increase aggregate demand would be if the actual size of the expansion were greater than the public expected it to be. In other words, discretionary macro policy only works if decision makers can be fooled as to its real magnitude. If decision makers are fooled, their inflationary expectations are less than the actual rate and short-run expansion takes place. The adjusted behavior of decision makers does not negate the effects of the expansionary policy. To paraphrase Abraham Lincoln, the Federal Reserve must fool all of the people all of the time to make its monetary policy work if the rational expectations theory holds.

Realizing that decision makers can adjust their expectations quickly, rational expectations theorists contend that the only macro policy that benefits the economy is one that is gradual and continuous. Discretionary macro policy should not be used to stimulate or contract the economy. Rational expectations economists advocate the use of a policy such as Milton Friedman's 3 percent money growth rule, where monetary policy is not used at the discretion of the Fed. Instead, the money supply expands at some constant rate, keeping expectations on a constant gradual growth pattern, as well. This, they believe, eliminates many of the destabilizing effects of the discretionary macro policy that the economy has experienced over the past 20 years.

The theory of rational expectations credits decision makers with the ability to learn from the past and incorporate both past learning and current events into their future expectations. This appears to be a more realistic view of human decision-making ability, but rational expectations theory is not without its critics. Some economists contend that the current functioning of an economy is much too complex to be widely understood by the average decision maker. They believe that the adaptive expectations hypothesis, which relies more on past events, is more representative of the analytical ability of the average citizen. Just which theory of expectations is correct is still subject to debate.

It is reasonable to expect, however, that the economic understanding possessed by the average citizen is rising over time. The fact that college and university students read and become familiar with such theories is itself evidence of movement toward greater economic understanding.

The Influence of Rational Expectations Theory

15.13 RATIONAL EXPECTATIONS THEORY'S INFLUENCE

Rational expectations theory has had a major influence on economic theory, but so far, a smaller effect on economic policy. More and more economists are now convinced that rational expectations theory is the "new" classical economic theory. This view is not universally held, however.

Rational expectations theory has served to reinforce the call for stable, predictable monetary policy. As noted earlier in this chapter, inflation in the early 1980s slowed more quickly than most economists had predicted and with smaller increases in the unemployment rate. The contractionary monetary policy of this period was not as neutral as rational expectations theories might predict, but the recession was not as severe as monetarist or Keynesian theories predicted, either. The existence of powerful expectational forces is one explanation for these observations. This experience probably indicates that expectations are very important in monetary policy, but that they are not as powerful as the rational expectations model predicts.

Rational expectations has influenced monetary theory and policy. Thus, far, however, its biggest policy impact has probably been on the fiscal side. Many of President Reagan's supply-side economic policies can be interpreted as having a rational expectations bent. For example, the 1981 tax cut package can be seen as the kind of fiscal policy that would appeal to rational expectations economists. The tax cut was widely announced, systematic, and tended to reduce the presence of government in the economy. President Reagan's tax reform proposals are also rational expectations policies in this light.

Perhaps rational expectations theories have had their most important impact on fiscal policy in the 1980s in the debate over the budget deficit. As discussed in Chapter 12, the traditional view is that deficits are undesirable because they cause higher interest rates and crowd out investment spending. Robert Barro, a rational expectations theorist, has proposed that people adjust their expectations to the deficit and save more today in anticipation of higher taxes in the future. Barro thinks that this keeps the deficit from having the undesirable effects that economists commonly suggest. In other words, deficits have no effect on the economy if they are fully anticipated. President Reagan has seemingly adopted Barro's rational expectations view of the deficit, and recent studies have tended to support this view.

MACROECONOMIC THEORIES IN PERSPECTIVE

This chapter concludes our survey of macroeconomic theory. Macroeconomics was born in the Great Depression and has evolved through periods of high unemployment, business cycles, rising inflation, stagflation, and disinflation. As the economy has changed, economic theory has also changed. Keynesian theory competes with the ideas of monetarists, supply siders, and rational expectations theorists. Various people and groups now recommend demand-side and supply-side fiscal policies, while others champion either activist or systematic monetary policies. It is sometimes easy to get lost in the competition of theories, policies, and goals.

We can clear up some of this confusion by remembering that economics is a social science that looks at how people behave when faced with choices. The economy has changed over the years because the choices that people face have changed and the institutions that shape those choices have also changed. The growth of government transfer-payment programs such as social security, the rise of inflation, and the deregulation of the financial sector are just three examples of changes in the economy that have altered the choices that people face and therefore have altered the way that people and the economy behave.

Economic theory is an attempt to describe and understand how people behave. As we learn more about human behavior and as the economy has evolved, our economic theories have changed. Because it is not always easy to understand how people behave and what shapes their behavior, we often get competing theories of economic behavior, such as the Keynesian and monetarist monetary theories.

Finally, economic policies are based on the nature of current economic problems, our theoretical understanding of how the economy works, and our values and goals concerning what type of economy we desire. Because they have different values or goals, people often disagree about what economic policies are appropriate or desirable at any given time.

In a world of economic problems, it is not always comforting to find that economists cannot agree about theories or policies. But what seems like a confusion of macroeconomic ideas is really the natural consequence of the study of complex human economic behavior and the attempts of policymakers with different goals and values to apply this knowledge to reduce the economic problems that people face.

SUMMARY

15.1

1. Keynesian monetary theory is built on the link between interest rates and investment spending. Monetary policy affects the credit supply directly, which causes interest rates to change, which eventually alters

investment spending and aggregate demand (*AD*). The link between monetary policy and *AD – AS* is thus indirect, working through the credit markets. Monetary policy should attempt to achieve target interest rates in the Keynesian view. Fiscal policy can also alter *AD – AS* through the multiplier analysis discussed in Chapter 12.

15.2 ➤ 2. Monetarists believe that money occupies a more central place in macroeconomics than most Keynesians think it does. They believe that changes in the money supply directly cause changes in *AD*. Monetarists do not think that the interest rate – investment spending link is as important as most Keynesians believe it is. Consequently, they believe that the Federal Reserve should attempt to achieve target rates of monetary growth rather than target interest rates. Because fiscal policy has no direct effect on the money supply, monetarists do not think that fiscal policy is a very powerful policy tool.

15.3 ➤ 3. Economists of the rational expectations school do not think that either monetary or fiscal policy is generally effective. According to rational expectations theories, the power of actions based on accurate expectations often prevents a discretionary monetary or fiscal policy from having very much effect. Consequently, systematic economic policies, which can be fully anticipated, have no real impact on the economy. Only "surprise" economic policies can cause changes in the real economy, and these changes are only temporary.

15.4 ➤ 4. Keynesian monetary policies were dominant during most of the 1960s and 1970s. These policies managed to stabilize interest rates in the short run but allowed inflation rates to rise in the long run. The FRS shifted to a monetarist policy of setting target rates for monetary growth in 1979. This policy was short lived because President Carter reacted by imposing a system of credit controls on the economy. The FRS returned to a policy of targeting money supply growth in 1981 – 1982, which contributed to the substantial decline in inflation rates during this period. With financial deregulation distorting the standard money supply definitions, the FRS returned to a less-restrictive discretionary money policy after 1982.

15.5 ➤ 5. The equation of exchange describes a simple monetarist model of the economy. The equation of exchange states that $M \times V = P \times Q$, where M is the money supply, V is the velocity of money, P is the price level, and Q is the level of real output. If we assume that the velocity of money and the level of real output are relatively constant, then changes in the money supply directly translate into changes in the price level. Inflation is, therefore, "always a monetary phenomenon." The equation of exchange can also be manipulated to show that:
money supply = $M = (P \times Q)/V$ = (nominal income)/V = money demand.
Thus monetarists view economic activity as the result of the interaction of money supply and money demand, where money demand depends on nominal income and the institutionally determined velocity of money.

15.6 ➤ 6. Modern monetarist theory is still based on the idea of money supply and money demand, but it has developed more sophisticated models of the determinants of money demand. In the modern monetarist theory, money demand depends on many factors, including income, the price level, the expected inflation rate, opportunity cost, and institutional factors such as the structure of the financial system.

15.7 ▶ 7. Monetarist and Keynesian economic theories differ in their views concerning how money affects the economy. Keynesians view interest rates as the most important determinant of the amount of money and credit people wish to hold. Monetarists view the level of income as having greater impact. Keynesians think that monetary policy affects the economy through the interest rate–investment spending linkage. Monetarists think that changes in the money supply directly cause changes in aggregate demand. Finally, Keynesians think that monetary and fiscal policy can both be effective demand-management policies. Monetarists, on the other hand, view fiscal policy as impotent and think that only monetary policy can have a substantive impact.

15.8 ▶ 8. Monetarists do not favor discretionary policies. They believe that a laissez faire fiscal policy should be pursued and that monetary policy should be aimed at expanding the money supply at a constant rate equal to the growth rate of the economy in real terms. This "policy of rules" is designed to accommodate economic growth without stimulating inflation.

15.9 ▶ 9. Both monetarist and Keynesian theories provide important insights into the way that money affects the economy. Economic events in recent years have often supported the monetarist view of monetary policy, although fiscal policies have also been important.

15.10 ▶ 10. Expectations are very important to economic policy. It is possible, for example, that changes in inflationary expectations cause the Phillips curve to shift. It is clear, in any case, that changes in expectations can alter the economic behavior of many workers, employers, borrowers, and lenders.

15.11 ▶ 11. The idea that historical events shape expectations of the future is called the adaptive expectations hypothesis. The adaptive expectations hypothesis helps explain why many economists believe in the natural rate of unemployment. Unexpected changes in economic policy can cause temporary movements away from the natural unemployment rate. When expectations eventually adapt, however, the economy returns to the natural unemployment level.

15.12 ▶ 12. The rational expectations hypothesis holds that people take into account all available information when formulating expectations and making economic choices. Expectations therefore adapt instantaneously to changing economic conditions and events.

15.13 ▶ 13. If the rational expectations hypothesis holds, then systematic monetary and fiscal policies have no effect on the economy in real terms because individuals are able to fully anticipate them. Unexpected economic policies can cause short-term changes in the real economy only until expectations catch up with them. Rational expectations economists favor moderate, systematic economic policies that do not disrupt the economy by unsuccessfully trying to solve short-term economic problems.

DISCUSSION QUESTIONS

15.5
1. Explain how the equation of exchange is derived from the circular flow model of the economy. How do the monetarists defend their assumption that V and Q are fixed in the short run?

15.2, 15.5, 15.6
2. What is the major difference between the early monetarists and the modern monetarists? Which group stresses the importance of the determinants of money demand? What are these determinants? Explain each of them and their relationship to the demand for money balances.

15.2, 15.8, 15.9
3. Monetarists criticize governments' discretionary macro policy as a part of our economic problems. What is their logic in declaring that fiscal policy is impotent? What do they offer as a solution?

15.10
4. The economic decisions faced by workers, employers, lenders, and borrowers are frequently based upon expectations. What are some of these expectations and how might they affect the decisions of workers, employers, lenders, and borrowers?

15.10, 15.11
5. Suppose workers and employers expect inflation to be 7 percent this year. In their bargaining efforts, workers agree to a 9 percent wage increase. However, during the year inflation reaches 12 percent. Who experiences gains and losses in this situation? What economic term can be used to describe this situation?

15.11, 15.12
6. Compare and contrast the adaptive expectations hypothesis and the rational expectations hypothesis. Consider the following:
   a. Interest rates for the last two years were 10 percent and 12 percent, respectively.
   b. Unemployment last year was 10 percent.
   c. The Fed announces substantial decreases in the money supply today.
   d. The government announces a 3 percent tax reduction to go into effect in July.
   e. Inflation five years ago was 8 percent.
   Which of the above would be taken into consideration by adaptive and rational expectations theories?

SELECTED READINGS

Blinder, Alan S. *Economic Policy and the Great Stagflation*. New York: Academic Press, 1979.

Forman, Leonard. "Rational Expectations and the Real World." *Challenge*, November/December, 1980.

Friedman, Milton. "A Memorandum to the Fed." *Wall Street Journal*, January 30, 1981, p. 18.

Friedman, Milton, and Schwartz, Anna Jacobsen. *A Monetary History of the United States*. Cambridge, MA: Harvard University Press, 1968.

McCallum, Bennett. "The Significance of Rational Expectations Theory." *Challenge*, January/February, 1980, pp. 37–43.

Modigliani, Franco. "The Monetarist Controversy or Should We Forsake Stabilization Policies?" *American Economic Review*, March, 1977, pp. 1–19.

Sargent, Thomas J. *Rational Expectations and Inflation*. New York: Harper and Row, 1986.

Sijhen, J. J. *Rational Expectations and Monetary Policy*. North Holland: Sitjoff and Noordhaff, 1980.

Tobin, James. "Inflation and Unemployment." *American Economic Review* 62 (March, 1972), pp. 1–18.

Willes, Mark H. "'Rational Expectations' As a Counter-revolution." *The Public Interest*, Special Issue, 1980, pp. 81–96.

Part 6

Microeconomics

CHAPTER 16

Consumer Choice: From Where Does Demand Come?

Having read the chapter, reviewed the chapter summary, and completed the *Study Guide* exercises, you should be able to:

CRIS

16.1 PROBLEM OF CHOICE: Explain the basic problem of the consumer and tell why consumer choices are necessary.

16.2 UTILITY AND MARGINAL UTILITY: Define utility and marginal utility and explain how economists use these concepts to model consumer choice behavior.

16.3 DIMINISHING MARGINAL UTILITY: Explain what is meant by diminishing marginal utility and tell why we assume that marginal utility declines.

16.4 CONSUMER CHOICES: Explain how consumers make choices among different goods with different prices and tell how marginal utility enters the consumer choice.

16.5 MAXIMIZING UTILITY: Describe the choice process by which consumers maximize utility and explain what is true about the marginal utility per dollar of each good consumed when utility is maximized and why this condition holds.

16.6 CONSUMER DEMAND: Explain how consumer choice changes when the price of a good rises or falls and tell why demand curves slope downward.

16.7 SUBSTITUTION AND INCOME EFFECTS: Define the substitution and income effects and explain when and how they alter consumer choices.

16.8 PRICE ELASTICITY OF DEMAND: Define price elasticity of demand, give the elasticity formula, and describe what is meant by elastic and inelastic demand, both in general terms and using the elasticity formula.

16.9 ELASTICITY AND TOTAL REVENUE: Explain the relationship between elasticity of demand and the effect of changing price on total revenue and tell why this relationship holds.

16.10 DETERMINANTS OF ELASTICITY: List the factors that determine price elasticity for a given product and explain how each affects elasticity.

16.11 INCOME ELASTICITY: Define income elasticity, give the income elasticity formula, and explain what is meant by income elastic and income inelastic demand, both in general terms and using the elasticity formula.

16.12 USES OF ELASTICITY: Give examples of how price and income elasticity are used in the real world.

16.13 INDIFFERENCE CURVES AND BUDGET LINES: Derive the demand curve for a good from a set of indifference curves and budget lines and graphically illustrate both the income and substitution effects.

Macroeconomics and microeconomics are inseparably intertwined. Previous chapters of this text presented a picture of the macroeconomy. They explained such topics as how inflation and unemployment are caused, what their economic effects are, and how monetary and fiscal policy deal with these problems. The approach we have taken is clearly macro, but the tools we have used are partly micro—supply and demand analysis is often the best way to see how government policies affect the economy. Micro and macro are economic Siamese twins. They are different yet they are the same. In this chapter, we will look behind supply and demand curves to see the foundations of economic analysis. We will find out from where demand curves come, what determines their shape, and what makes demand change.

THE PROBLEM OF CONSUMER CHOICE

Government and investment spending are important, as we saw in earlier chapters, but consumer spending is the biggest component of GNP, accounting for nearly two-thirds of total spending. We have already examined the determinants of aggregate consumer spending, such as income, the marginal propensity to consume, taxes, transfer payments, and the like. Consumer spending however, is really an individual activity. Individual consumers choose which goods they purchase and how much they spend. In this chapter we will examine how they make these choices.

16.1 PROBLEM OF CHOICE

Opportunity Cost
The highest-valued alternative that must be foregone when another alternative is selected. With every choice, there is an opportunity cost.

The basic problems of the consumer (and of society, too) is scarcity and choice. Consumers live in a world of scarce resources. Time, money, and assets are all finite. But wants and desires are limitless. The consumers' dilemma is how best to use scarce resources to satisfy their endless desires.

The fact that resources are finite means that every choice has an **opportunity cost**. Each time you choose to spend time or money in one way, you forego all the other alternatives you might have had instead. The true cost of any choice is not just the time or money you have spent, but its opportunity cost, the value of the best alternative given up. Consumers go about making the subtle choices economists observe as demand curves by comparing the utility or satisfaction they receive from a given choice with the opportunity cost of that choice.

TOTAL AND MARGINAL UTILITY

> **16.2 UTILITY AND MARGINAL UTILITY**

Utility
A measure of the satisfaction or value that an individual derives from a good or service.

Consumers generally try to use their scarce resources in a way that maximizes their satisfaction. In economic terms, they maximize **utility.** Utility is an all-purpose abstract measure of individual well-being or satisfaction. While utility itself is subjective in nature and cannot be measured in an exact fashion, we can learn a great deal about how human beings behave by approximating a measure of utility and applying that approximation to develop a theory. Consumer choice behavior can be analyzed by supposing that utility can be measured and then analyzing the actions that lead to its maximization. The idea of applying an abstract means of measurement to satisfaction or well-being ends up giving us important insights into real-world consumer behavior.

Suppose we could put a "utility meter" on a consumer like you and measure the way your well-being changes when you consume different bundles of goods. What sorts of readings might we observe? Table 16-1 and Figure 16-1 show how utility might change as you consume more and more of a single item (slices of pizza, in this example) in a given time period (the lunch hour). This utility meter would measure the satisfaction or use value (utility) you get from consuming different goods. For example, if you consume a slice of pizza and your utility meter reading goes up from its previous reading of zero to a new rating of 40, we would say that eating the first slice of pizza gives you 40 additional units (referred to as utils) of satisfaction.

Total Utility
The total satisfaction (total utils) derived from consuming a combination of goods.

Marginal Utility
The change in utility that accompanies a one-unit change in the amount of a good or service consumed, with preferences and the quantities of other goods held constant.

The reading on the utility meter indicates **total utility.** Total utility is the total amount of satisfaction or well-being you receive from all the goods and services you eventually consume (including the pizza). The change in the reading on the total utility meter that comes from consuming one more unit of a good or service indicates the **marginal utility** you receive from that additional good or service as you consume it. Marginal utility is the change in total utility attributed to the consumption of one additional unit of a good or service with preferences and the quantities of other goods consumed held

TABLE 16-1	**Total and Marginal Utility from Pizza**		
	Slices of pizza (per lunch)	**Total utility**	**Marginal utility**
	0	0	—
	1	40	40
	2	70	30
	3	90	20
	4	105	15
	5	115	10
	6	123	8
	7	128	5
	8	130	2
	9	130	0
	10	130	0

474 Consumer Choice: From Where Does Demand Come?

FIGURE 16-1 **Total and Marginal Utility Curves.** (a) Total utility from pizza rises as more is consumed, all else being equal. (b) But extra pizza slices fall in marginal utility. These curves are derived from the information in Table 16-1.

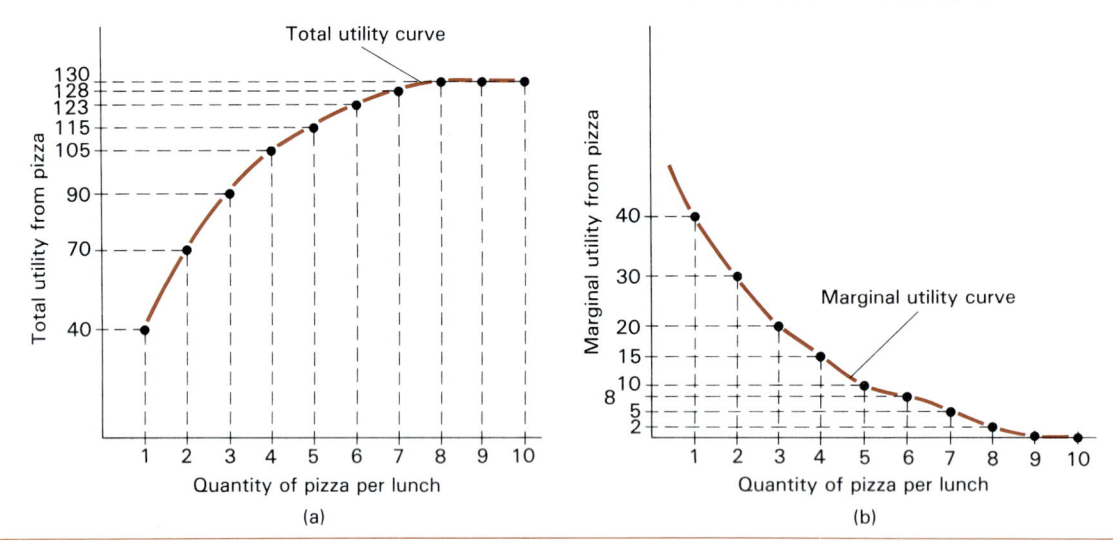

constant. Both total and marginal utility are subjective concepts, however, and vary from person to person. You may like pizza more than your roommate does and therefore get more utility from consuming it. Since utility is based upon personal preferences, it must be subjective.

The total utility you derive from consuming pizza is directly related not only to your preferences but also to the amount you eat. All else being equal, the more pizza you consume, the better off you are.

Do you gain equal satisfaction from each slice of pizza you consume in a single lunch hour? The answer is no, and we can observe this relationship between pizza eating and utility in Table 16-1 and Figure 16-1. The first slice of pizza increases total utility by 40 utils (it has a marginal utility of 40 utils). The second pizza slice is desirable, too, but not such a treat as the first. Total utility rises from 40 to 70 utils when the second slice is consumed. This means the second slice added 70 minus 40, or 30, utils to satisfaction. Therefore, the second slice has a marginal utility of 30 utils.

16.3 DIMINISHING MARGINAL UTILITY

By looking at the table and figure, we can see what happens as more and more pizza is consumed in a fixed time period. We observe here the principle of **diminishing marginal utility.** Marginal utility declines as the quantity of an item consumed per time period increases. At some point, additional consumption of a single good, all else being equal, runs into diminishing returns. The extra utility of the next unit is less than the utility provided by the one that came before.

Diminishing Marginal Utility
The property that marginal utility declines as the quantity consumed per time period increases.

The idea of diminishing marginal utility makes good common sense. Chances are you get more satisfaction from the first slice of pizza than from the sixth, and consumption behavior reflects this. One indication of diminishing marginal utility is the common tendency to consume a variety of goods, not just one or two. If marginal utility were constant or rising, we would expect to observe people buying large quantities of their "favorite" goods, to the exclusion of other items. Instead we see people buying a little each of a long list of goods, thereby avoiding the low marginal utility that consumption of large quantities of one or two goods brings.

KEY CONCEPT 16.3

Diminishing marginal utility refers to the fact that as you consume more of a commodity, the increment to total utility gained from each additional unit declines.

16.4 CONSUMER CHOICES

The Choice Process

Since consumers wish to maximize total utility from the scarce resources they command, it seems only natural that you would want to know how much pizza and other goods and services to buy. If money were unlimited and no other goods were available, you would buy pizza until you no longer received any satisfaction from it, that is, until the marginal utility of pizza dropped to zero. However, because money is finite and there are many items from which to choose, you select from these different items so that your scarce money buys as many utils as possible. Table 16-2 indicates this type of choice behavior.

We can assume for the moment that you are having lunch at a local establishment that features SMOG pizza (sausage, mushroom, onions, and green pepper) and a variety of video games. Pizza sells for 50 cents per slice and the video game tokens also cost 50 cents each. Table 16-2 shows the marginal utility you might derive from various quantities of pizza and video games. You have $5 to spend during lunch and must decide what to buy.

We can break this simple choice problem into several steps. Out of the $5 budget how should you spend the first 50 cents? The tables shows that 50 cents spent on the first slice of pizza yields 40 utils, while playing a video game the first time only yields 16 utils. The rational choice would be the first pizza slice rather than the first video game play, since the utility rating of the pizza is higher.

How should the second 50 cents be spent? You can buy either a second slide of pizza (a marginal utility of 30 utils) or the first video game (a marginal utility of 16 utils). The marginal utility of the second slice of pizza is still higher than the first video game, therefore pizza would be the logical choice (check the table to see why). You spend the third 50 cent income increment on pizza, too, for the same reason (again check the table to see why).

TABLE 16-2 Marginal Utility from Pizza and Video Games

Quantity	Marginal utility Pizza	Video Games
1	40	15
2	30	13
3	20	10
4	15	8
5	10	7
6	8	5
7	5	3
8	2	2
9	0	2
10	0	1

We can extend this same choice process to the fourth 50 cent coin. The choice now would be between the fourth slice of pizza (a marginal utility of 10 utils) or the first video game (a marginal utility of 16 utils). In this case, you would play the video game because the marginal utility of pizza has fallen below the marginal utility of blasting video invaders.

This choice process can be extended throughout all of the remainder of the $5 budget. If we take a minute to work through the table, comparing marginal utility for each succeeding 50 cent income unit, we will find that, using the marginal utility method, you will end up buying six slices of pizza and four turns at the video game. That combination will exhaust the $5 budget and maximize utility. It is impossible to redistribute the $5 between these two goods and get a higher level of total utility.

Maximizing Utility

16.5 MAXIMIZING UTILITY

The choice process we have examined is a key principle of microeconomics and revolves around the concept of marginal or incremental choice. Individuals make choices by weighing alternatives at the margin and choosing the best way to use the next unit of a scarce resource. The scarce resource here is money and the consumer weighs the marginal utilities of different goods in making a choice.

Consumer choice is a delicate process but one that everyone goes through every day. Think for a moment about walking up to a coin-operated candy machine. What goes through your head as you fish around for the right change? You subconsciously weigh marginal utilities, asking yourself which you want more right now, the Snickers or the Almond Joy? Or would you rather wait, save your appetite and money, and buy something else later? In making these choices you behave just as in the marginal utility example above.

When we worked through the last example of spending money on pizza and video games based on highest marginal utility, you may have noticed something interesting. In the process of maximizing utility, funds were spent so that the marginal utility of the last slice of pizza and the final video game play were the same! The last 50 cents spent on pizza had the same marginal utility as the last 50 cents spent on video games. This is not an accident, even though the numbers might not work out perfectly in every example. If the marginal utility per dollar ($MU/\$$) spent on pizza is equal to the marginal utility per dollar ($MU/\$$) spent on video games, then it is impossible to increase total utility by spending 50 cents less on pizza and 50 cents more on video games (or any other redistribution of spending totals).

Why is the $MU/\$$(pizza) = $MU/\$$(video games) = $MU/\$$(any other goods you might buy) a necessary condition for utility maximization? To understand this more fully let's try another example. Suppose that you have your budget all worked out and find that the $MU/\$$ of pizza is much higher than the $MU/\$$ of the last video game (this would happen, using the figures of Table 16-2, if you purchased four slices of pizza and six video game plays). If that were the case, it means that you could reallocate your funds (spend less on games and more on food) and get a utility bonus. The utility gained from the extra pizza would be more than the utils lost from fewer video game plays. You would thus benefit by redistributing your expenditures until the two $MU/\$$ are equal and utility is again maximized.

A utility-maximizing consumer ends up getting the same marginal utility per dollar from each good, not because he or she tries, but because that is

PROMINENT ECONOMIST

John Kenneth Galbraith (1908–   )

John Kenneth Galbraith was born in Ontario, Canada, in 1908 and graduated from Toronto University in the field of agriculture. He was a research fellow at Cambridge University (England) and his academic years were spent at Harvard as Paul M. Warburg Professor of Economics until his retirement in 1975. Galbraith's years in public service served to mold his economic views. From 1941 to 1943, Galbraith was responsible for wartime price controls at the U.S. Office of Price Administration. This experience taught him an understanding of the corporate basis for setting prices.

In Professor Galbraith's opinion, large corporations "create" wants and needs for consumers through their advertising efforts rather than fulfill wants and needs as indicated by accepted economic theory. For this reason, Galbraith has strongly advocated an expansion in the amount of government intervention in the marketplace. He is a supporter of government price controls and large social programs aimed at redistributing income from the wealthy to the poor. In support of his position on corporate advertising, Galbraith has said "The fact that wants can be synthesized by advertising, catalyzed by salesmanship and shaped by discreet manipulation of the persuaders shows that they are not very urgent."[1]

From 1943 to 1948, Galbraith served as an editor of *Fortune* magazine. At the close of World War II, he was appointed Director of the Office of Economic Security Policy in the State Department. Under the Kennedy Administration in 1961, Galbraith was sent to India as a U.S. Ambassador. There he began studying the problems of developing countries, and his findings were published in *Ambassador's Journal* in 1969. In 1971, Galbraith was elected to the office of President of the American Economic Association.

Each of Galbraith's publications is unique in that it addresses the layperson. However, because of this focus, there is an absence of emphasis on statistics and empirical research in his work. This lack of established scientific method has frequently brought criticism from his fellow economists, who have branded his writings as caustic, controversial, and unconventional. Nevertheless, critics admit that Galbraith has always conveyed his message with clarity.

1. John Kenneth Galbraith, *The Affluent Society,* Boston: Houghton Mifflin, 1958, p. 123.

---

the result of maximizing total utility with a fixed budget total. This phenomenon is referred to as the utility maximization rule and can be stated algebraically as

$$\frac{MU_a}{P_a} = \frac{MU_b}{P_b} = \frac{MU_c}{P_c} = \ldots = \frac{MU_n}{P_n}$$

where MU is the marginal utility of a good or service and P is its price.

KEY CONCEPT 16.5   The utility maximization rule states that $MU_a/P_a = MU_b/P_b = MU_c/P_c = \ldots = MU_n/P_n$.

What Utils Are and Are Not

Economists use the ideas of utility, marginal utility, and the mythical util measure to better understand consumer choices. These tools are powerful

Ordinal Measure
A measure that allows qualitative comparison only. Temperature is an ordinal measurement, since 32 degrees is warmer than 16 degrees but not twice as warm.

Cardinal Measure
A measure that allows qualitative and quantitative comparisons. Length measures (such as feet, inches, and yards) are cardinal, for example, since two yards is twice as long as one yard.

> **16.6 CONSUMER DEMAND**

Law of Demand
The principle of economics that states that the quantity demanded per unit of time varies inversely with price, all else being equal.

but easy to misunderstand or misuse. Before we go on, therefore, it's important to get two facts about utils and marginal utility theory straight.

First, no one would imply people run around with a utility-meter attached to their heads, checking the util numbers before buying another slice of pizza or some other good. We cannot really measure satisfaction using utils or anything else, but that does not make marginal utility theory less powerful. We observe people behaving, in buying goods and making other consumer choices, exactly as they would if they were making marginal utility choices using the utility-meter process described here. Marginal utility theory is a model that helps us describe and better understand the real world, even though the real world is much different. That is the real value of any theory. For example, U.S. astronauts learn how to pilot the space shuttle and other vehicles by working with computer programs that are, in the end, just a bunch of zeros and ones recorded on a silicone chip. The reality and the model are different, but the insights from one transfer directly to the other. That's what we're doing here.

Second, you should realize that utility is measured arbitrarily. Utils are an **ordinal measure** of satisfaction. Ordinal measures allow qualitative measures but not quantitative ones. Temperature is an example of an ordinal measure, since it is accurate to say that 32 degrees is warmer than 16 degrees but inaccurate to say that it is twice as warm. Any utility scale that preserves the ordering of first to last choice works just as well when measuring ordinal utility. Utils are not a **cardinal measure,** however. A cardinal measure allows both qualitative and quantitative comparisons. Length measures (such as feet and inches) are cardinal, since two feet is twice as long as one foot.

In Table 16-1, for example, we see that the first slice of pizza yields 40 utils, while the third slice adds just 20 utils. This only means that the first slice gives more satisfaction than the third slice (the conclusion we derive from an ordinal measure); it does not mean that the first slice is twice as good as the third slice (the conclusion that a cardinal measuring system would give).

DERIVING DEMAND CURVES

The **law of demand** holds that, all else being equal, the quantity of a particular good demanded varies inversely with its price. This law is the reason the demand curves we've drawn in this text have sloped downward. Common sense tells us that the law of demand is true, but we can see why by using marginal utility theory to derive an individual consumer's demand curve.

Consider once again our pizza example. We have already determined that you would demand six slices of pizza at lunch if pizza sold for 50 cents per slice, video games cost 50 cents per play, and income was $5. (Preferences, income, and the prices of other goods are the "all else" we hold constant in this example.) This combination can be plotted as point A on the individual demand curve in Figure 16-2, showing that six slices of pizza is the quantity demanded at a unit price of 50 cents.

A demand curve shows how the quantity demanded changes when the only thing that varies is a product's price. What would happen to your demand for pizza if its price were to change to $1 per slice, all else constant? The law of demand says the quantity demanded should be less at

FIGURE 16-2

Demand Curves for Pizza. (a) The quantity of pizza demanded per lunch changes from six (point *A*) to three (point *B*) when price rises from $.50 to $1 (see the text for the reasoning behind this). (b) When income falls, the quantity demanded at $.50 changes from six (*A*) to five (*C*), shifting the demand curve.

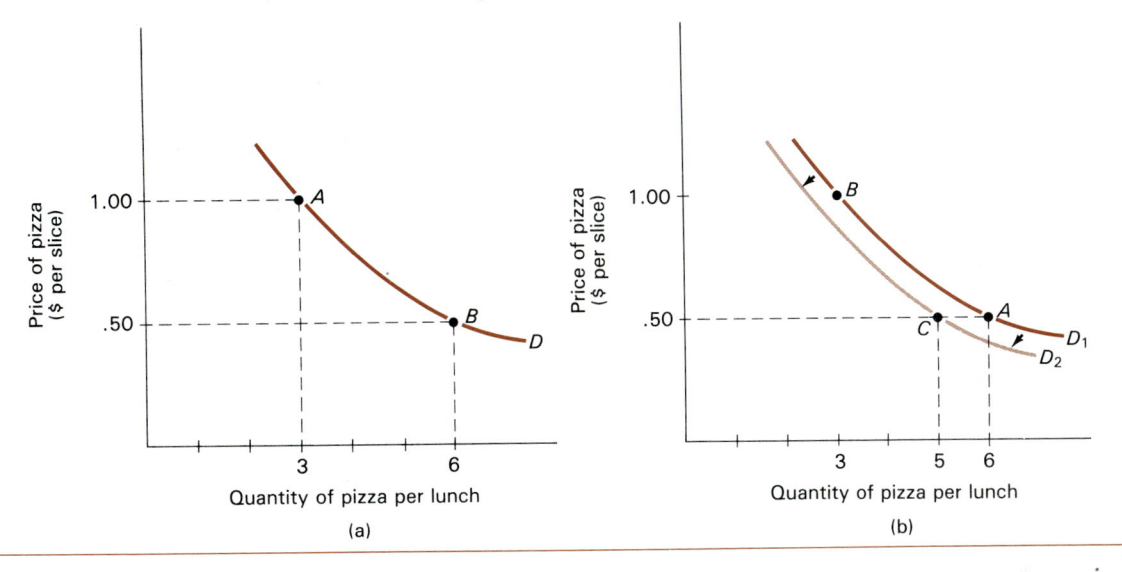

the higher price, and the figure shows that this is so. Why? Let's go back to Table 16-2 to find out.

How would you spend the $5 lunch budget if pizza cost a $1 per slice and video games were 50 cents per play? The first thing to note is that the opportunity cost of a slice of pizza has changed. Before, with both goods selling for 50 cents, eating an extra slice of pizza meant giving up just one video game play. Now, however, pizza's higher price means each extra slice forces you to give up twice as many games. This rising opportunity cost changes your choice.

The first $1 spent on pizza yields 40 utils, but the same dollar could buy the first two video game plays, which have a combined utility of 28 utils (see Table 16-2 for marginal utility information). The first dollar goes to pizza, since it yields more satisfaction than the two video games. The second dollar buys pizza, too. The second slice of pizza yields 30 utils, more than the 28 utils of the first dollar spent on video games. Buying pizza with the third $1 adds 20 utils, which is less than the 28 utils the first two video games provide, thus you choose the games. The fourth dollar buys a third slice of pizza (with a marginal utility of 20 for pizza and a marginal utility of 10 plus 8, or 18, for the third and fourth video game plays). The fifth dollar is spent on video games (with a marginal utility of 15 for the fourth pizza slice and a marginal utility of 10 plus 8, or 18, for the third and fourth video game plays). Your final choice then is to spend the $5 on three pizza slices at $1 each and four video game plays at 50 cents apiece. This utility-maximizing combination fulfills the equal marginal utility per dollar rule. The last dollar spent on pizza adds 15 utils, the same as the last dollar spent on video games.

If we plot the new quantity demanded (three slices) at the new price ($1), we get point *B* on the demand curve in Figure 16-2. We can perform the same exercise at other prices and derive something like the individual demand curve shown in the figure.

Why Do Demand Curves Slope Downward?

So far we have seen that the demand curve does, in fact, slope downward, but we have not yet figured out why it does so. We do not know what makes quantity demanded vary inversely with price. One reason is because consumers make choices so that the marginal utility per dollar of each good is equalized. Remember that marginal utility falls as more of one good is consumed. This means that if prices, preferences, and income remain the same, a utility-maximizing consumer buys more of a particular item only if its price falls enough so that its own marginal utility per dollar becomes equal to that which is available from other goods. If the price of the good rises, on the other hand, it makes sense to switch purchases to other goods that yield more utility per dollar.

Another way to explain downward-sloping demand curves is to focus on the way changing one good's price alters purchasing power and relative prices. A **relative price** is the price of one good compared to that of another. How does an increase in the price of pizza, for example, affect consumers? Since pizza costs more, every slice they buy leaves them with less money to spend on remaining slices and on other goods. The **income effect** of a price movement is the change in buying behavior that results from changes in purchasing power.

Pizza price increases alter the trade-off between pizza and other desirable items. The **substitution effect** of a price movement is the change in buying behavior that results from a change in the relative prices of goods. It comes from the tendency to substitute relatively cheaper goods for those that increase in relative price. The combination of the income effect (fewer goods can be bought at higher prices with a fixed money income) and the substitution effect (cheaper goods are substituted for higher-priced ones because they yield more marginal utility per dollar) enforces the law of demand.

The same ideas work when price falls. People buy more pizza (and often more of other goods) when the per-slice price drops because their dollar budgets stretch farther at the lower price (the income effect) and because lower-priced pizza purchases provide more marginal utility per dollar than alternative goods (the substitution effect).

Changing Tastes and Preferences

Tastes and preferences are demand curve shifters. Tastes, and the marginal utility numbers that represent them, change with age, social trends, income, experience, and time. Changing preferences affect demand curves, shifting them so that different quantities are purchased at each price.

We can examine the way changing tastes affect demand by using a simple example. Suppose you meet a group of people who are really interested in video games. They like to play and compete for the highest score. Buying video game plays is now more enjoyable to you. How could this change in behavior be illustrated using marginal utility theory? The extra satisfaction that you get from video games now would increase the utility of each game and probably boost the marginal utility, as well.

Suppose that the marginal utility figures for video games in Table 16-2 double (the first play provides 30 utils, the second 26 utils, and so on). How many video games and pizza slices would you now buy, assuming both still cost 50 cents? By working this problem out, it is easy to see how changing tastes for video games shift the pizza demand curve of Figure 16-2.

16.7 SUBSTITUTION AND INCOME EFFECTS

Relative Price
The price of one good compared to the prices of other goods.

Income Effect
The change in buying behavior that results from a change in purchasing power, relative prices held constant.

Substitution Effect
The change in buying behavior that results from a change in relative price, purchasing power held constant.

CONSUMER CHOICE IN ACTION

The theory of consumer behavior helps us understand how individual buyers and sellers behave. Three examples show consumer choice theory at work.

Have you ever wondered how stores decide which goods to put on sale at reduced prices? Often the choice is based on a rough calculation of income and substitution effects. A store manager who lowers price thinks you'll buy more of the sale items than you otherwise might (and less of substitute goods, too). But lower price has an important income effect. Lowering the price of one good frees up income for other items, often those sold at higher regular prices. Retailers hope you'll spread your savings around the store and end up generating more profit than if all prices had stayed high. Loss leaders, that is, items sold below cost, are often used to get you into the store to buy other goods at regular prices.

The old adage that time is money is also illustrated in consumer behavior. Have you ever gone to a store, found the item you wanted, but put it back and left without making a purchase because the check-out line was too long? The item may have been worth the money but not the time spent waiting to pay for it. Time and money both generate utility, so smart buyers watch how they spend both of these scarce, valuable resources. Convenience stores have sprung up across the country to take advantage of the time/money trade-off. These stores often charge higher prices but promise shorter lines. In today's world, many people maximize utility by spending more money to save some time.

Price Discrimination
The practice of selling identical goods to different buyers for different prices.

Utility theory also helps us understand what economists call **price discrimination**. Price discrimination is the practice of selling identical goods to different buyers for different prices. Movie admissions, haircuts, airline tickets, and a variety of other items (mostly services, since they are more difficult to resell) are subject to multiple pricing based on age, sex, or as with airline tickets, length of stay or other restrictions.

Why do firms sell similar items to different buyers for different prices? One reason is that some buyers have different preferences. They derive different marginal utility from goods than do other buyers. For example, business travellers are willing to pay more for airline tickets than are people who are on vacation because they may need to attend important meetings in several cities in a brief period of time. Price discrimination lets the airlines charge various travellers according to their willingness to pay through the use of length-of-stay restrictions that keep the business traveller from buying a tourist's cheaper ticket.

Income differences are important to buyer behavior, too. Children and retired people often have less spending money than the age groups in between. Childrens' rates and senior-citizen discounts lower the prices these groups pay at the barber, theater, or sporting events, for example. Producers give these age groups a price break because they might not buy at all otherwise.

PRICE ELASTICITY OF DEMAND

16.8 PRICE ELASTICITY OF DEMAND

All demand curves are not alike. Butter and margarine might taste alike to you, but their demand curves are likely to have different characteristics. How quantity demanded reacts to price movements and how demand shifts when income changes are two very important considerations for economists

Price Elasticity of Demand
A measure of the responsiveness of demand to changing price.

Coefficient of Elasticity
A measure of price elasticity; a ratio that compares the percentage change in quantity demanded with the percentage change in price.

Elastic Demand
Demand in which the quantity demanded changes proportionately more than price (the elasticity coefficient is greater than one).

Inelastic Demand
Demand in which the quantity demanded changes proportionately less than price (the elasticity coefficient is less than one).

(who study markets), business firms (who sell in those markets), and governments (who tax markets). Economists study the relationship between change in price or income and the resultant spending changes using elasticity measures.

Price elasticity of demand (or just elasticity of demand) measures the relationship between changes in the price of a good and changes in the quantity of it demanded. The **elasticity coefficient** η (the Greek letter eta) is a ratio, comparing the percentage change in quantity demanded with the percentage change in price. The general formula for price elasticity is

$$\eta = \frac{\text{percentage change in quantity demanded}}{\text{percentage change in price}}$$

If the demand for a product is relatively responsive to a change in price, then the percentage change in quantity demanded should be greater than the proportionate change in price (when price drops by 10 percent, people buy 20 percent more, for example). We call this an **elastic demand.** Elastic demand yields an elasticity coefficient that is greater than one (ignoring the sign on the coefficient). Changing price has a relatively large effect on the sale of goods with elastic demand.

The demand for other products is not as relatively responsive. A 10 percent change in price might result in only 5 percent more sales, for example, yielding an elasticity coefficient of less than one. This is an **inelastic demand.** Changing price has little relative effect on consumer purchases.

KEY CONCEPT 16.8

The price elasticity formula is η = (percentage change in quantity demanded)/(percentage change in price).

Calculating Elasticity

Elasticity is a powerful tool, thus it is important to be able to calculate and use elasticity measures. Figure 16-3 gives two examples to help you get the hang of elasticity problems.

Panel (a) of the figure shows a demand curve for pizza. The elasticity coefficient helps us find out if this demand curve is relatively responsive to changes in price. It tells us if the quantity demanded changes much in comparison to a given price change.

The percentage change in quantity demanded is calculated by taking the difference in quantity between A and B (7 − 3 = 4) and dividing by the average quantity along this arc (this method is called arc elasticity). The average quantity is (7 + 3)/2 = 5. The percentage change in quantity is thus 4/5, or 0.8 (80 percent). In general, you can calculate the percentage change in quantity between A and B with the following formula:

$$\text{Percentage change in quantity demanded} = \frac{Q_A - Q_B}{(Q_A + Q_B)/2}$$

where Q_A is the quantity demanded at A and Q_B is the quantity demanded at B.

We now want to compare this change with the change in price. We calculate the percentage change in price using the same method. The formula is:

$$\text{Percentage change in price} = \frac{P_A - P_B}{(P_A + P_B)/2}$$

where P_A is the price at A and P_B is the price at B.

FIGURE 16-3

Elastic and Inelastic Demand Curves. The demand curve in panel (a) is elastic over the range between A and B: the elasticity coefficient is greater than 1 ($Q_A = 7$, $Q_B = 3$, $P_A = 1.0$, $P_B = 2.0$). The demand curve in panel (b) is inelastic over this range ($Q_A = 5$, $Q_B = 4$, $P_A = 1.0$, $P_B = 2.0$). See the text for elasticity calculation.

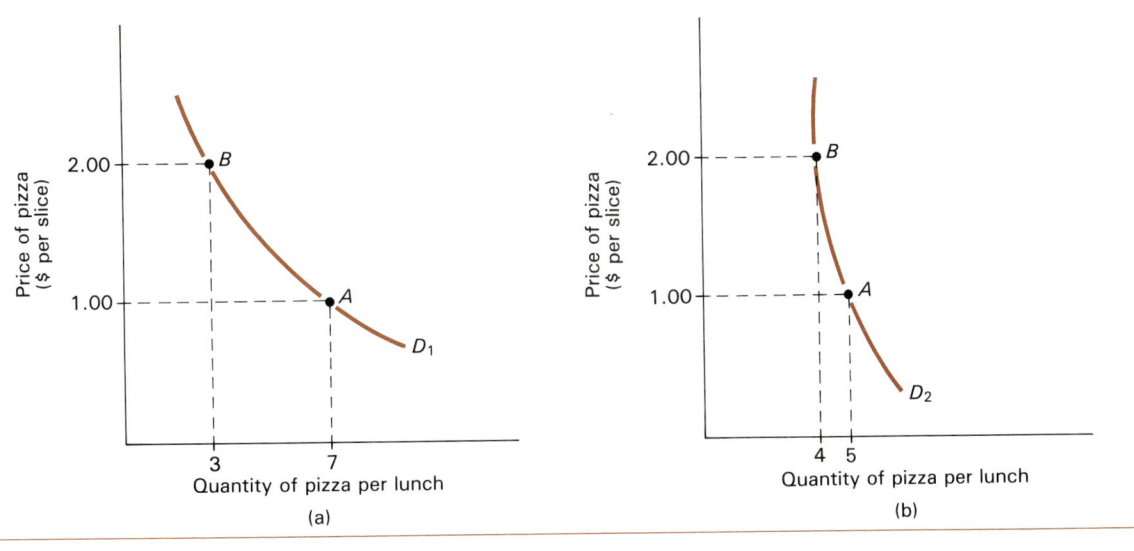

The change in price is $1 minus $2 = −$1, thereby making the average price ($1 + $2)/2 = 3/2, or 1.5. Thus the percentage change in price is −1/1.5 = −2/3, or −0.666 (−66.6 percent).

The elasticity coefficient is the absolute value of the ratio of these two percentage changes (an absolute value takes just the positive value of any number, positive or negative, so the absolute values of +1 and −1 are both +1, for example). The complete elasticity formula is:

$$\eta = \frac{Q_A - Q_B / [(Q_A + Q_B)/2]}{P_A - P_B / [(P_A + P_B)/2]} = \frac{(Q_A - Q_B)(P_A + P_B)}{(P_A - P_B)(Q_A + Q_B)}$$

Note here that the elasticity formula is quite different from the slope of the demand curve. Performing this calculation shows that the demand curve between these two points is elastic, since it has an elasticity coefficient of 1.2, which is greater than one.

An elasticity coefficient of 1.2 tells us that, on average, over the arc between points A and B on the curve, a 10 percent change in price brings a 1.2 × 10 percent, or 12 percent, change in the quantity demanded. In other words, the quantity demanded changes 1.2 times the change in price. The quantity demanded changes relatively more than price on this elastic demand curve.

Panel (b) in Figure 16-3 shows a demand curve with different characteristics. The same change in price, from A to B on the curve, brings a much smaller change in quantity demanded. Use the formula above to calculate the coefficient of elasticity for this demand curve. You'll find this demand is inelastic, with an elasticity coefficient of just 1/3, or 0.33.

An elasticity coefficient of .33 tells us that between points A and B on the demand curve the quantity demanded changes only a third as much as the price. A 10 percent price cut would increase consumer purchases by only about 3.33 percent. Thus it would not provide much benefit to a retailer to put this good, with its inelastic demand, on sale.

16.9 ELASTICITY AND TOTAL REVENUE

Elasticity and Total Revenue

The elasticity coefficient gives a precise picture of the relationship between price and quantity demanded. Sometimes, however, all we need to know is whether the demand for a good is elastic (η greater than one) or inelastic (η less than one). The total revenue test works well in this case.

What happens to the total amount spent on a good (price multiplied by quantity) when its price changes? If demand is elastic, there is an inverse relationship between the change in price and the change in total revenue. Total revenue rises when price falls, and buyers spend less, in total, when price goes up. The demand curve in Figure 16-3(a) illustrates this relationship. If price rises from $1 to $2, many people switch to other goods. Total expenditure falls from $7 at point A (seven pizza slices sold at $1 each) to $6 at point B (three slices sold at $2). Rising price brings lower total revenue.

The demand curve in Figure 16-3(b) has an inelastic demand. There is a direct relationship between price and total revenue here. Total revenue increases when price goes up and decreases when price falls. This is because the quantity sold changes relatively little; consequently, the price change has a big effect. Total revenue rises from $5 (five units sold at $1 each) to $8 (four units sold at $2 each) when price increases from $1 to $2 in the figure.

Consumers and producers are interested in elasticity measures because they have a stake in the expenditure total. Suppose, for example, that bad weather destroys part of the pineapple crop. Falling supply forces the price of pineapples to increase. This situation affects buyers and sellers in different ways depending on the elasticity of demand. If the demand for pineapples is inelastic, the higher price increases total income to pineapple producers, while the buying public spends more dollars for less fruit. The story changes if pineapple demand is elastic, however. A higher price now means a comparatively large decrease in the quantity demanded. Many consumers won't pay the higher price and will buy other goods instead. Total income falls for pineapple producers because buyers are spending less in total on this item.

The demand for many agricultural goods is inelastic, leading to a peculiar boom-and-bust cycle. If the weather is good and the crop successful, big supplies force down price. Falling price, with inelastic demand, means lower income to farmers, who paradoxically suffer financially from their successful harvest (as a group, that is; some individuals may gain). Suppose, however, that hail destroys the crop, bringing down market supply and pushing up price. With inelastic demand, higher price means greater total dollar sales, and farmers benefit from the higher revenues.

Elasticity and the Demand Curve

Demand curves take on different shapes, depending on their elasticity characteristics. Figure 16-4 shows five demand curves along with their elasticity coefficients.

A perfectly inelastic demand is one in which the quantity demanded is fixed [Figure 16-4(a)]. It does not change regardless of price (at least within some price range). A type of good that might have a demand like this is one that has few substitutes, such as the demand for whole human blood in hospitals. Since quantity demanded is fixed, total revenue rises whenever price does and falls when price declines.

The relatively inelastic demand curve shown in Figure 16-4(b) is relatively steep, showing that quantity demanded responds little to changes in

FIGURE 16-4

Five Different Demand Elasticities. These five demand curves have very different price elasticity properties. While differing slopes are an indication of elasticity divisions, be sure to remember that slope changes with the definition of price and quantity units. You can only be sure about elasticity through calculation.

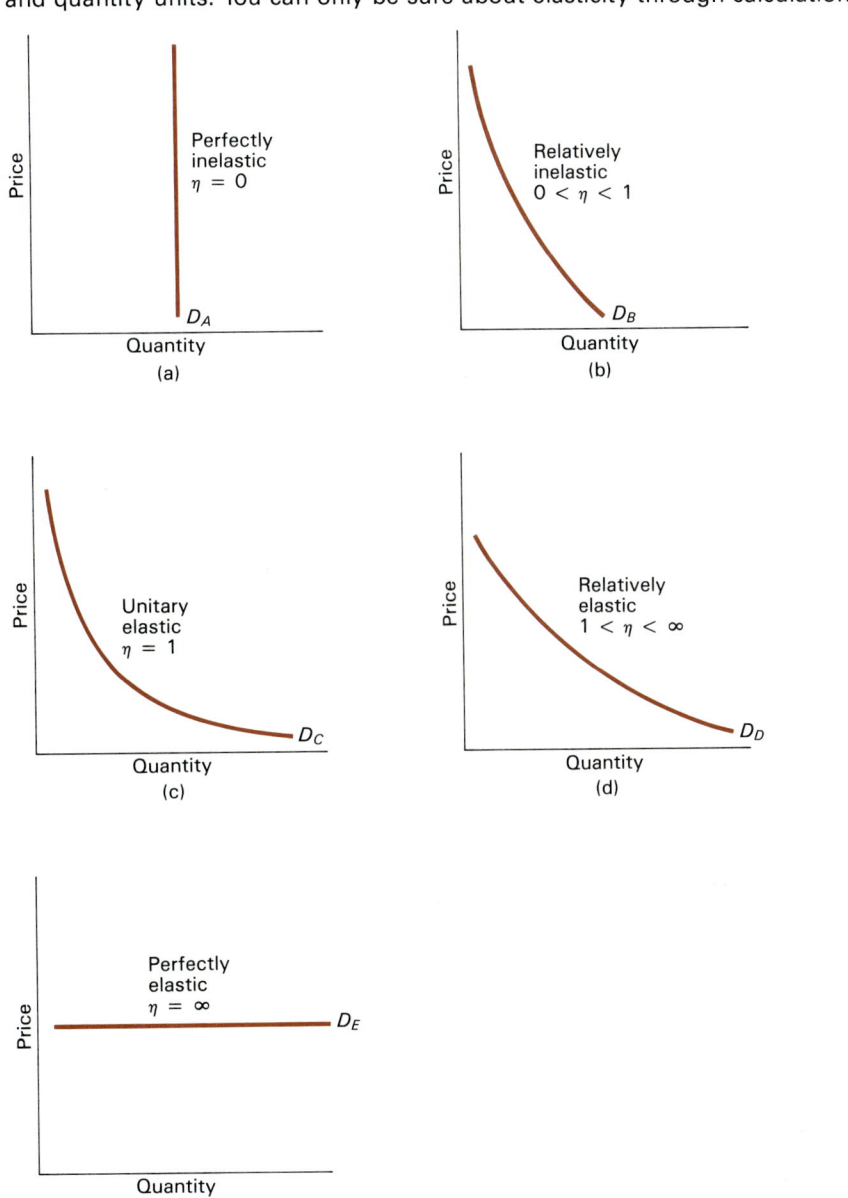

(a) Perfectly inelastic, $\eta = 0$, D_A

(b) Relatively inelastic, $0 < \eta < 1$, D_B

(c) Unitary elastic, $\eta = 1$, D_C

(d) Relatively elastic, $1 < \eta < \infty$, D_D

(e) Perfectly elastic, $\eta = \infty$, D_E

---

price. Total revenue and price move in the same direction with inelastic demand.

When the elasticity coefficient is exactly equal to one it is a sign of **unitary price elasticity.** This type of demand curve, depicted in Figure 16-4(c), is a rectangular hyperbola of the form price × quantity demanded = constant. The interesting thing about unitary elasticity is that total revenue is always the same, regardless of price. A 10 percent increase in price brings about a 10 percent decrease in quantity demanded. The two forces of price and quantity exactly offset each other, leaving total revenue

Unitary Price Elasticity
Demand in which there is an equal proportionate change in price and quantity demanded (the elasticity coefficient is equal to one).

constant. Food is one type of item that has a unit elasticity. People tend to spend a relatively constant fraction of their income on food; consequently, increase in food prices is temporarily met with an equal decrease in the quantity demanded.

We have already discussed the properties of the relatively elastic demand curve shown in Figure 16-4(d). A given change in price brings a greater percentage quantity response for goods with elastic demand. Total revenue and price vary inversely in this case. Lower prices bring in greater total revenues for goods with elastic demand.

The graph in Figure 16-4(e) shows a perfectly elastic demand curve. It is a horizontal line. This demand curve says that there is only one price at which this good is purchased. If price goes up, quantity demanded falls to zero. Economic theory suggests that this is what the demand curve for an individual seller's output looks like in a competitive market. If there are thousands of competing apple buyers and sellers, for example, any single firm can sell all it wants at the going market price, but it can't sell anything at a higher price, since the buyers will go elsewhere. Look closely at this demand curve; you'll see it again in the next chapter.

One note of caution is in order here. It is generally not acceptable to think about demand curves of different elasticity like those in Figure 16-4, in terms of their slopes (steep, flat, vertical, horizontal, and so on). Slope is not the same as elasticity, because the slope of a demand curve depends on the units we use to measure price and quantity.

Slope deceives. The elastic demand curve of Figure 16-3(a), for example, would be steep and look falsely inelastic if quantity were measured in dozens or hundreds rather than single units. And the inelastic demand curve of Figure 16-3(b) would appear flat and falsely elastic if we measured price in hundreds of dollars or quantity in tenths of a unit. Like mushrooms and toadstools, elasticity and slope are related, but they're not the same. In fact, in the strict sense of economic theory, almost all demand curves have an elastic, inelastic, and unitary elastic region. We can see this concept illustrated in Figure 16-5. Along the demand curve from points A to B, demand is inelastic; therefore, increases in price will bring increases in total revenue, as we see in panel (b). At point B in panel (b), demand is unit elastic and total revenue is at its maximum. Between points B and C, however, demand is elastic; therefore, increases in price will bring reductions in total revenue.

The Determinants of Elasticity

16.10 DETERMINANTS OF ELASTICITY

What determines whether the demand for a good is elastic or inelastic? The question really goes back to the preferences of the individuals who buy the good. Their incomes and their attitudes toward other goods and services contribute to demand elasticity. Among the characteristics that affect an individual good's elasticity of demand are the ease of substitution, budget shares, and time frames.

Ease of Substitution All else being equal, the greater the number of substitutes a good has and the greater the degree of its substitutability, the more elastic is its demand. All unleaded gasoline is pretty much the same, for example. If there is another gas station across the street, it is easy to substitute one firm's product for that of its competitor. The demand for a single station's gas is highly elastic because of the ease of substitution. If

FIGURE 16-5

Elasticity and Total Revenue. Almost all demand curves have an elastic, unitary elastic and inelastic region. From points *A* to *B* demand is inelastic, and increases in price increase total revenue. From points *B* to *C* demand becomes elastic, and price increases reduce total revenue.

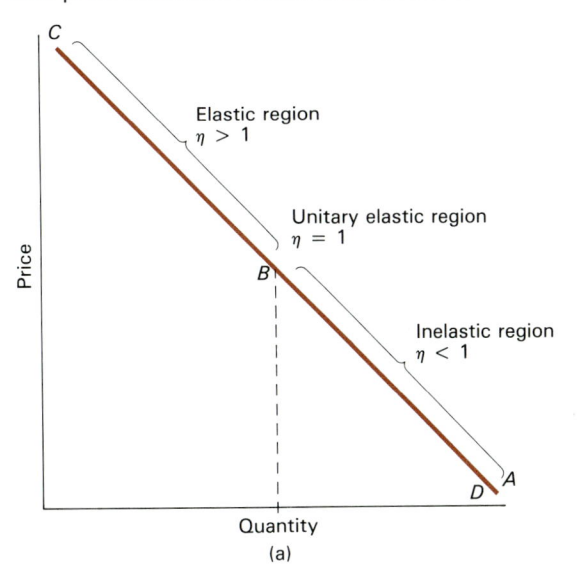

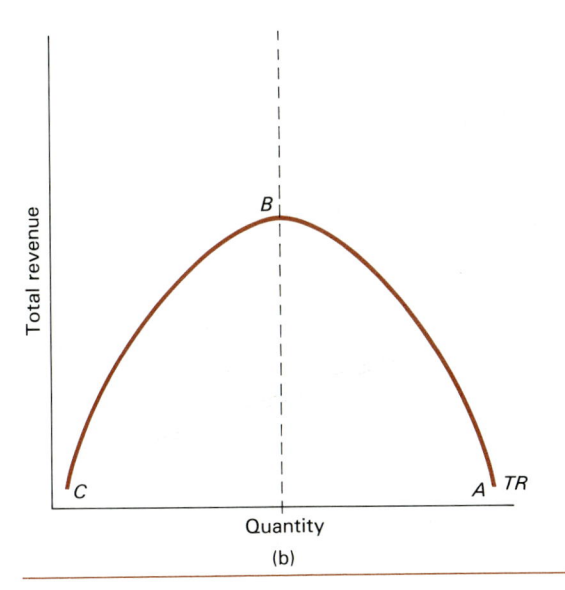

(a)

Elastic region $\eta > 1$

Unitary elastic region $\eta = 1$

Inelastic region $\eta < 1$

(b)

there is only one gas pump in town, however, it is not as easy to substitute another firm, thus the demand for this firm's product is apt to be more inelastic.

Budget Share If total spending on a particular good by an individual buyer is insignificant, then demand is less responsive to price (in other words, the income effect is low). No one spends much money on salt, for example, because a pound of salt is inexpensive and lasts a long time. It's a pretty trivial part of one's budget. The demand for salt is inelastic because of this and because there aren't many good substitutes. If an item eats up a big slice of a consumer's pay, however, the individual is nearly forced to buy less when price rises. Demand tends to be more elastic for goods that fit this description.

Time Frame Demand elasticity depends on the time frame we allow for adjustment and measurement. Two examples illustrate the time factor. The demand for home heating oil is inelastic in the short run, especially if the short run is a frigid winter. People who heat with oil must buy a certain amount to keep their houses warm. The quantity demanded falls when price rises, as people turn back their thermostats, but not by that much. Demand is more responsive in the long run, however. People insulate their houses or switch to gas or electric heat. The long-run response to price is greater than it is in the short run.

The demand for warm coats in cold climates is also apt to be relatively inelastic in the short run. Everyone needs a warm coat when snow falls and the thermometer plunges. But people buy coats in the long run. If price rises today, most folks can easily make their old coats last a little longer. Demand might be more elastic in this longer time frame. Table 16-3 illustrates the price elasticity of demand for several goods and services in both the short run and the long run.

INCOME ELASTICITY: ANOTHER DEMAND MEASURE

> **16.11**
> **INCOME ELASTICITY**

Income Elasticity
A measure of the responsiveness of demand to changing income.

Income elasticity measures the response of demand to a change in income with all else, including price, held constant. Income elasticity measures how far demand curves shift when income changes. The formula for income elasticity is

$$\text{Income elasticity} = \frac{\text{percentage change in quantity demanded}}{\text{percentage change in income}}$$

Some items take a constant share of income; the amount purchased rises and falls with monthly pay. A 10 percent increase in income, for example, might bring a 10 percent increase in the amount of soda pop purchased. This would yield an income elasticity of one. This equal proportionate change in income and quantity demanded is referred to as **unitary income elasticity.**

Unitary Income Elasticity
Demand in which there is an equal proportionate change in income and quantity demanded.

Some goods respond more dramatically to changes in income. A 10 percent increase in income might yield a 20 percent increase in the number

TABLE 16-3

Price Elasticity of Demand in the Short Run and the Long Run

Commodity	Price elasticity Short run	Long run
Electricity	−0.13	−1.89
Water	—	−0.14
Movies	—	−3.69
Gasoline	−0.15	−0.78

Note. These figures were taken from H.S. Houthakker and L. D. Taylor, *Consumer Demand in the United States: Analysis and Projections,* Cambridge, MA: Harvard University Press, 1970, and J. L. Sweeney, "The Demand for Gasoline: A Vintage Model," monograph, Department of Engineering Economics, Stanford University.

Appendix 489

Income Elastic Demand
Demand in which the quantity demanded changes proportionately more than income.

Income Inelastic Demand
Demand in which the quantity demanded changes proportionately less than income.

Inferior Good
A good for which demand varies inversely with income.

of restaurant meals purchased, for example. This would yield an income elasticity of 2.0. When income elasticity is greater than one, it is referred to as **income elastic demand.**

Basic necessity items tend to be income inelastic. A 10 percent increase in income probably doesn't have much of an effect on the amount of toilet tissue you buy, for example. The income elasticity is less than one in this case, showing that demand changes proportionately less than income. This is referred to as **income inelastic demand.**

Finally, some items are **inferior goods.** An increase in income leads to a decrease in purchases of these items, but sales go up when income falls. Beans and cheaper cuts of meat or perhaps canned Spam might qualify as inferior goods, for example. People switch to steak when their incomes are rising but buy more beans and franks when income begins to fall.

> **KEY CONCEPT 16.11**
>
> The income elasticity formula is income elasticity = (percentage change in quantity demanded)/(percentage change in income)

16.12 USES OF ELASTICITY

Using Income Elasticity

Income elasticity is a theoretical tool with many practical applications. Department store managers, for example, might use the income elasticity concept to guide their buying choices for the Christmas season. If they expected income in their towns to rise by approximately 10 percent over the year, they would also anticipate an increase of about 10 percent in the sale of goods with unit income elasticity. Thus they would be justified in ordering fewer items with income inelastic demand and fewer inferior goods, since higher income would mean fewer sales of inferior goods. If, on the other hand, the managers thought income was going to fall over the year, they would be justified in ordering more inferior goods and cutting back on purchases of income elastic items.

In a very broad sense, this concept of income elasticity could be applied to the stock market. Firms that sell mostly income elastic items tend to exaggerate the business cycle. Their revenues increase faster than income in good times and fall more than income in recession years. Firms that market income inelastic goods are more stable. Their sales rise and fall with the economy, but by smaller amounts. Finally, companies that sell inferior goods might move opposite to general economic conditions, with sales increasing when national income falls and decreasing when prosperity returns.

APPENDIX: INDIFFERENCE CURVES AND THE BUDGET CONSTRAINT

16.13 INDIFFERENCE CURVES AND BUDGET LINES

Consumer choice is the problem of picking the best bundle of goods and services from all available combinations, given fixed preference, income, and price limits. This kind of choice problem lends itself to analysis using the graphic devices of indifference curves and budget lines. Budget lines and indifference curves are the analytical tools that help us understand and more accurately predict how consumers choose the most preferred bundle of goods and services.

Consumer Choice: From Where Does Demand Come?

THE BUDGET LINE

Budget Line
A graph showing the combinations of two goods that can be purchased by spending a given amount of money.

A **budget line** is a function that shows all the combinations of two goods a person can buy, given income and market prices. Figure 16-6(a) shows the budget line for a student with $5 to spend on food and fun each week. The two goods shown here are slices of pizza (measured on the horizontal axis) and video game plays (measured on the vertical axis). Assume that pizza sells for $.50 per slice and video games cost $.50, too.

Budget line AB shows all the combinations of these two goods that $5 might buy. If the student spends all of the $5 on pizza, 10 slices of pizza and no video game plays (point B on the line) can be purchased. An alternative would be to spend all income on video games. This would buy 10 video game plays and no pizza, the combination represented by point A on the line. Chances are the student will choose neither extreme, choosing instead some intermediate point such as a combination like five slices of pizza (at a cost of $2.50) and five video game plays (at a cost of $2.50). Each point on the budget line is a combination of pizza and video game plays that adds up to the $5 total.

The slope of the budget line shows the price trade-off between the two goods. Every time the student gives up one slice of pizza (at a cost of $.50) enough money is made available to buy one video game play (at a cost of $.50). The slope of budget line AB is −1/1, reflecting this trade-off (slope equals rise/run).

BUDGET LINE MECHANICS

Several events change the amount of goods and services the consumer can buy. The budget line moves to show changes in purchasing power when

FIGURE 16-6

Budget Lines. (a) Budget line AB shows all combinations of pizza and video games that can be purchased with $5 if pizza costs $.50 per slice and video games cost $.50 per play. (b) The budget line shifts in to CD if income falls to $2.50. The budget line's slope does not change unless prices change, as when pizza's price rises to $1 on the AC budget line.

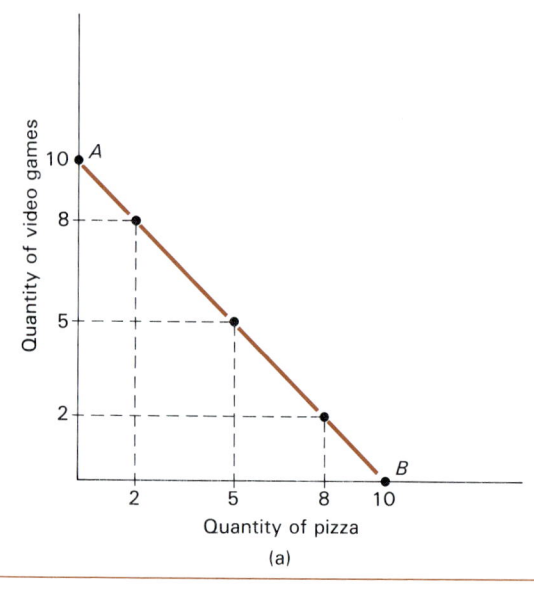

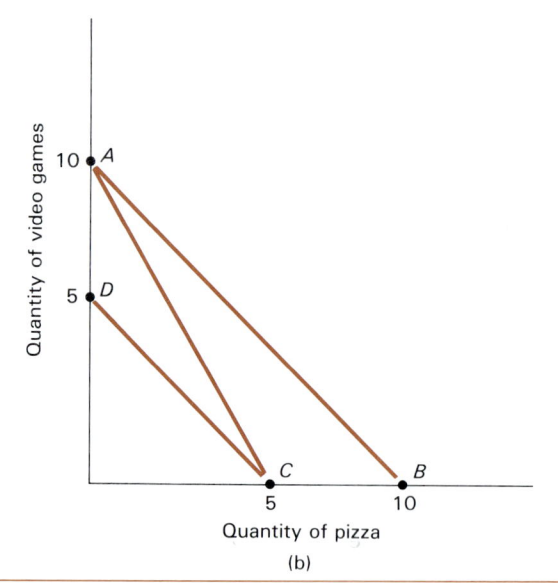

either income or prices change. Figure 16-6(b) illustrates these budget changes.

Suppose the student's income falls from $5.00 to $2.50 per week. This change reduces purchasing power by 50 percent, but it doesn't directly alter market prices or the trade-off between pizza and video games. Reduced income is shown by a parallel shift in the budget line from *AB* to *CD* in Figure 16-6(b). Now the student chooses between five slices of pizza (at a cost of $2.50) or five video game plays (at a cost of $2.50) or any intermediate combination on line *CD*. The relative prices of pizza and video games haven't changed, so the slope of the new budget line *CD* is the same as the old budget line *AB*.

Something different happens when income stays the same but price changes. Let's go back to the original budget line *AB* and assume that the price of pizza rises from $.50 per slice to $1 (the price of video games remains at $.50 each). The $5 spent on pizza now buys $5/$1 = 5 slices, as represented by point *C* in the figure. (There's no change in the maximum number of plays that can be bought.) The new budget line is given by line *AC* in Figure 16-6(b). The budget line has a new slope to reflect the new trade-off between pizza and video games. The student now gives up two video games (−2) for each extra pizza slice (+1), thus the budget line's slope is −2/1. The line is closer to the origin to show that higher prices have reduced the student's real income. The student now chooses from among smaller quantities of pizza and games.

INDIFFERENCE CURVES

We can also graph the way a person ranks different groups of goods. To do so, however, we need to illustrate the student's preferences so we can see how economic events affect individual choices. Indifference curves are a convenient way to accomplish this. An **indifference curve** is a graph that shows all combinations of two goods that give an individual the same level of total utility, or satisfaction. The individual is indifferent between combinations on a particular indifference curve. Figure 16-7(a) presents an indifference curve of the various combinations of pizza and video games that would yield the level of satisfaction for our hypothetical student.

Indifference Curve
A graph showing all the combinations of two goods that yield the same total utility.

The indifference curve shown here is labelled U_{50} to indicate that all these pairs of goods yield a total utility level of 50 utils. Given the initial combination at point *X* of six pizza slices and four video game plays per week, for example, the student would be no better or worse off if the consumption bundle were switched to *Y* (more games but much less pizza) or *Z* (fewer games but much more pizza). The indifference curve is constant so long as individual preferences stay the same; it changes only if something happens to alter individual tastes.

Why does this indifference curve have the bowed U-shape? The answer is that the shape of the indifference curve is based on diminishing marginal utility. This is true because the slope of the indifference curve indicates the rate at which an individual can substitute one good for another and still have the same level of total utility. For this reason, economists call the slope of the indifference curve the **marginal rate of substitution.** For example, in Figure 16-7(a), to move from point *Y* with nine games and three slices to point *X* with four games and six slices means that the student consumes three additional slices but must give up five video games. In other

Marginal Rate of Substitution
The ratio at which two goods substitute for each other to yield a constant level of utility to the consumer; the slope of the indifference curve.

FIGURE 16-7

Indifference Curves. (a) The U_{50} indifference curve shows that combinations X, Y, and Z all yield utility level 50—the individual is indifferent among these choices. (b) Other indifference curves indicate inferior and preferred combinations. Any point on the U_{50} indifference curve is preferred to any combination on the U_{30} curve but is inferior to any combination on the U_{90} curve.

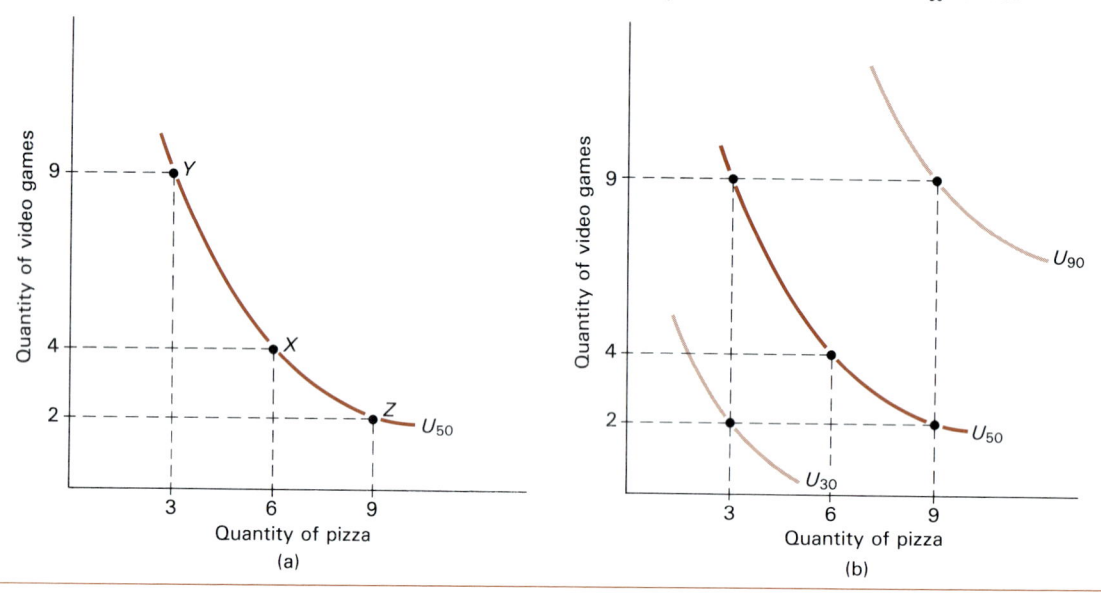

words, over the arc from point Y to point X, video games can be substituted for pizza slices at a ratio of 5 to 3 with the student maintaining the same level of total utility. The marginal rate of substitution is therefore 5 to 3. Each slice gives the student the same satisfaction as 1.66 (that is 5/3) video games. This is the same thing as saying that one slice substitutes for 1.66 video games. Note what happens here, however, when the student moves from point X (four games and six slices) to point Z (two games and nine slices). The student gives up two games and gains three slices while keeping the same level of total utility. Here games and slices have substituted for each other at a ratio of 2/3. Obviously, the marginal rate of substitution has changed. Each pizza slice now yields the student as much satisfaction as .67 of a video game. We can see that as the student consumes more pizza and less video games the marginal utility of pizza falls and the marginal utility of video games rises. This means that as more pizza is consumed, it takes larger and larger numbers of slices to replace the utility lost by consuming fewer video games.

The marginal utility of pizza declines as you consume more and more of it. For example, it takes progressively larger quantities of pizza to replace the lost utility of a foregone video game. In other words, the marginal rate of substitution changes because of diminishing marginal utility. It takes a lot more pizza to make our student indifferent to the first few video game plays. This changing trade-off (changing marginal rate of substitution) yields the indifference curve's shape.

FAMILIES OF INDIFFERENCE CURVES

If an indifference curve shows equally good combinations, how do we tell which ones are better and which are worse? Figure 16-7(b) show how these differences are derived from indifference curves.

Every person has a family of indifference curves, with one curve for each possible level of utility, or satisfaction. Indifference curve U_{30} in the figure contains smaller quantities of both of the two goods. It shows combinations of goods that our hypothetical student considers equally good but inferior to those on the U_{50} indifference map. All combinations on the U_{90} indifference curve have larger quantities of games and pizza than corresponding points on either U_{30} or U_{50}. The U_{90} combinations are therefore preferred to those on the lower indifference curves.

Figure 16-7(b) shows three indifference curves, but there are actually many more between these. Indifference curves are densely packed. Some indifference curve passes through each possible combination of housing and food. (Indifference curves never cross, however, since it is impossible for the same combination to be both indifferent and preferred to another.) A rule of thumb for working with indifference curves is that an individual is indifferent between points on the same indifference curve but prefers goods on higher curves (curves farther from the origin) to those on lower curves.

INDIVIDUAL CHOICE

Individuals choose to be on the highest indifference curve available, given budget limits. Figure 16-8 shows a budget choice for our hypothetical student.

Which point on budget line AB is best? Combination Y is available but is a poor choice, since it is on the U_{40} indifference curve. Preferred combinations on higher indifference curves are available. Combination W is preferred because it is on the much higher U_{60} indifference curve, but it is not a feasible choice since it is not on the AB budget line. Our student cannot purchase W, given current income and market prices. The best available

FIGURE 16-8

Individual Choices. Combination X is the preferred choice in this figure. No combination on the budget line AB yields higher utility (is on a higher indifference curve). Choice W is preferred to X, but it cannot be attained at the prices and income of this example. Combinations like Y are affordable, but are not selected, since they yield lower utility — Y is on a lower indifference curve. The consumer's utility optimum occurs at combination X where the budget line and the indifference curve are tangent.

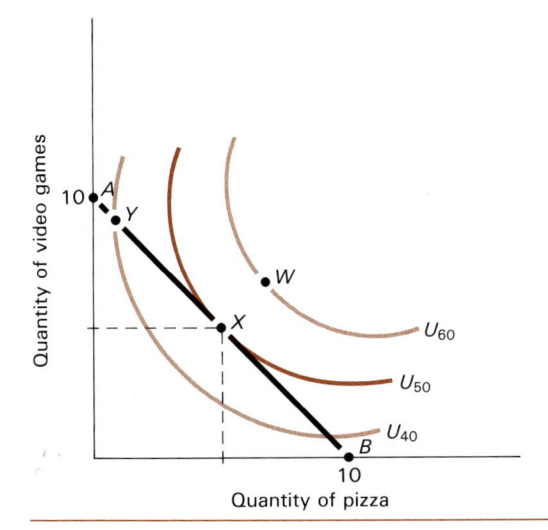

choice is the X combination of pizza and video games in the figure. This is the point where the U_{50} indifference curve is tangent to the AB budget line. No higher indifference curve can be attained. Any other point on the budget line (such as Y) means a movement to a lower, inferior indifference curve.

A rule of thumb for choice analysis is that individuals, trying to be as well-off as possible, choose the budget line combination that puts them on the highest possible indifference curve—the point where the budget line is tangent to an indifference curve. At this point, the slope of the budget line (the ratio of the prices of the two goods) is equal to the slope of the indifference curve (the ratio of the marginal utilities of the two goods). Since $MU_X/MU_Y = P_X/P_Y$ (the slope of indifference curve equals the slope of budget line), it follows that $MU_X/P_X = MU_Y/P_Y$. This is the same condition for utility maximization that was presented earlier in this chapter. The marginal utility per dollar is equal for all goods at the consumer optimum.

Individual choices are affected by three factors: preferences, which determine indifference curves, and income and prices, which set the budget line. Changes in any of these three variables alter individual choice.

DERIVING A DEMAND CURVE

As just stated, consumer choices are delicate. They vary with prices, income, and preferences. Figure 16-9 shows how the quantity of pizza demanded changes when the price of pizza rises from $.50 to $1 per slice. The altered consumer choice gives rise to the individual demand curve shown in the figure.

Rising pizza price doesn't alter the maximum number of video games that $5 buys, but it does reduce the maximum possible pizza purchase by half. The budget line shifts from AB to AC in the figure. Our student must now choose the combination that yields the highest total utility from among the combinations on the more restrictive AC budget line. The highest

FIGURE 16-9

Demand Curves Derived. The consumer optimum changes from X to Z in panel (a), as the price of pizza rises from $.50 (on the AB budget line) to $1 per slice (on the AC budget line). The change in consumer choice is plotted on the individual's demand curve in panel (b).

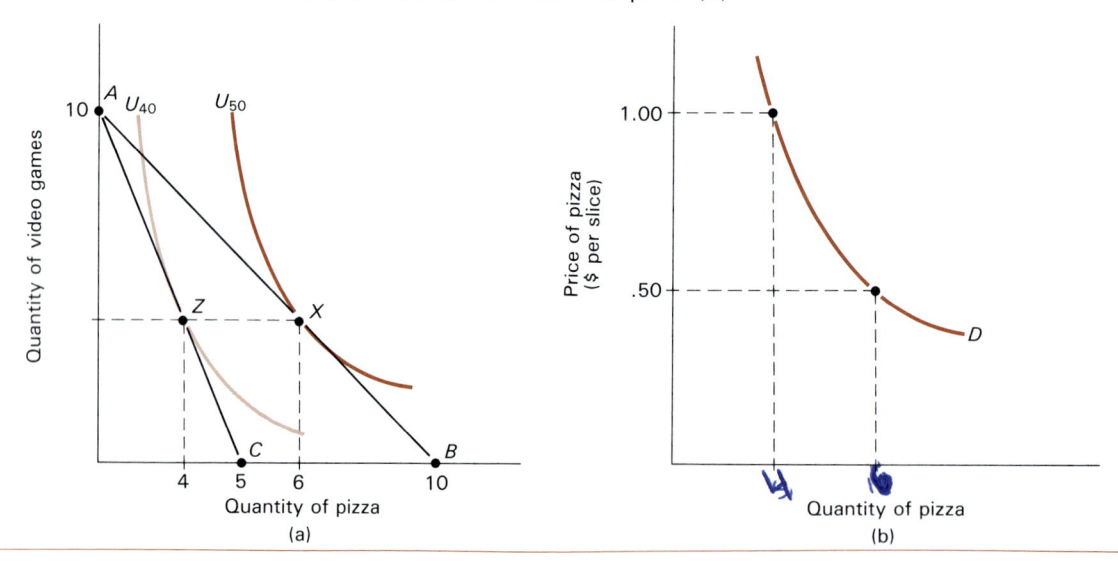

indifference curve that is now available is U_{40}, which by definition provides less total utility than the initial U_{50} indifference curve. This is an indication that higher prices make this buyer worse off.

As the price of pizza goes up, the quantity demanded of pizza falls. Just four slices of pizza are bought by the utility maximizing student at this price. This fact is reflected in this figure's demand curve. Demand curves are derived by using indifference curves and budget lines, noting changes in consumer choice when the price of one good is varied. As an exercise, see what happens when pizza's price is further increased to $2. (To do this, shift the budget line, then find the quantity of pizza that corresponds to the highest indifference curve.) Plot this new point on the demand curve.

INCOME AND SUBSTITUTION EFFECTS

We can use indifference curve analysis to graphically display the income and substitution effects discussed earlier in this chapter. Figure 16-10 illustrates the effects of an increase in income. Let's assume that someone has put pizza on sale for $.25 per slice, shifting the student's budget line from AB to AC in the figure. Pizza is cheaper now, so we could expect our student to buy more pizza and fewer video game plays. But pizza's lower price also increases overall purchasing power. There is now more money available to buy other goods besides pizza. Thus there may be an income effect as well as a substitution effect.

One way to measure income and substitution effects is shown in Figure 16-10. Let's divide the movement from X (the initial choice) to Z (the new choice) into two parts. First, let's allow prices to change (causing the slope of the budget line to change) but reduce income so that the student stays on

FIGURE 16-10

Substitution and Income Effects. The price of pizza falls from $.50 to $.25 in this figure, shifting the budget line from AB to AC and changing the consumer optimum from X to Z. Economists divide the total change (X to Z) into two parts. The substitution effect (X to Y) is the buying change that takes place if prices change but income is reduced so that the consumer remains on the original U_{50} indifference curve. Budget line FG in the figure has the same prices as AC but lower income. The income effect (Y to Z) is the change that occurs when income is increased to the new AC budget line.

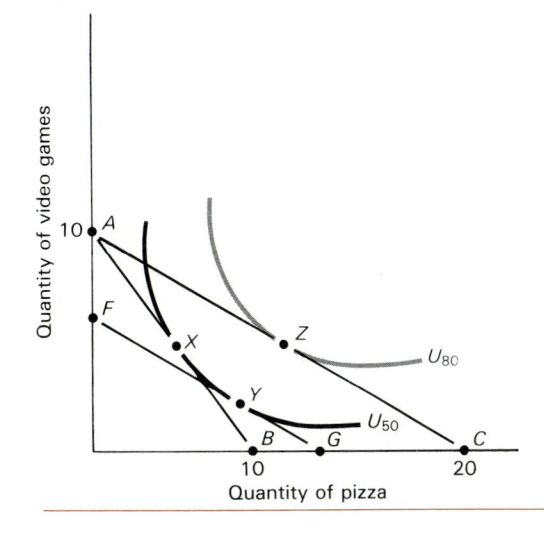

the original indifference curve. This requires a budget line like *FG* in the figure. The consumer choice, given this budget limit, is *Y*. The movement from *X* to *Y* (more pizza, fewer video game plays) is the substitution effect. It is the effect of changing prices with all increases in purchasing power removed.

Now let's give our student enough income to move to the new budget line *AC*. This shifts the budget line from *FG* to *AC* and changes consumer choice from *Y* to *Z*. This movement shows a small increase in pizza consumption and a large increase in video game purchases. The movement from *Y* to *Z* is the income effect. As an exercise, plot the income and substitution effects of raising the price of pizza from $.50 to $1.

APPLYING INDIFFERENCE CURVE AND BUDGET LINE ANALYSIS

Indifference curve and budget line analysis can be used to work through the changes in income discussed earlier in this chapter. It would be beneficial practice for you to attempt to figure out the shape of an indifference curve that tends to produce an inelastic versus an elastic demand curve. It might also be valuable to try to imagine what shape of indifference curve yields an inferior good whose purchase declines as income rises. In analyzing these questions you'll begin to understand the power of indifference curve analysis.

SUMMARY

16.1
1. The problem of consumer choice is to allocate scarce time and money resources to satisfy infinite wants and desires. The fact of scarcity means that consumers must consider the opportunity cost of their choices.

16.2
2. Economists assume that individuals act to maximize total utility. Utility is a measure of satisfaction or well-being.

16.2, 16.3, 16.4, 16.6
3. Marginal utility is the change in total utility that occurs when an additional good or service is consumed. The assumption of diminishing marginal utility makes sense because use of marginal utility analysis leads to conclusions about consumer behavior, such as a preference for variety in consumption and the law of demand, that are consistent with our observations of real-world actions.

16.4
4. Consumers decide how best to spend scarce income by comparing the marginal utility per dollar of alternative goods. Goods with high marginal utility are selected first. Those with lower marginal utility are purchased only if income allows.

16.5
5. Utility is maximized when all income is spent and each incremental choice has taken the good with the highest marginal utility per dollar. At equilibrium, the marginal utility per dollar is equal for all choices.

16.5
6. Utils are a convenient way to analyze consumer choice, and this analysis yields verifiable predictions. Utils are assumed to be an ordinal measure,

not a cardinal one, and therefore cannot be compared for different individuals.

7. **16.6** — The law of demand states that, all else being equal, the quantity of a particular good demanded varies inversely with its price. The law of demand is based on diminishing marginal utility.

8. **16.6** — A change in price alters the $MU/\$$ a consumer choice yields. Changes in buying behavior move the consumer toward a new utility maximum.

9. **16.7** — The substitution effect refers to the fact that a change in relative prices moves consumers to buy more of the relatively cheaper good and less of the relatively more expensive substitutes.

10. **16.7** — The income effect refers to the fact that a change in price alters purchasing power, affecting the consumer's ability to buy all goods.

11. **16.7** — A change in the price of one good brings both income and substitution effects. The substitution effect of a price increase tends toward larger purchases of the relatively cheaper item.

12. **16.7** — The income effect of a price increase tends toward smaller purchases of all goods. The net effect on demand depends on the relative size of income and substitution effects.

13. **16.7** — Changing tastes and preferences alter the $MU/\$$ of goods and so alter consumer choices. Changing consumer choices result in demand curve shifts.

14. **16.7** — Stores take advantage of income and substitution effects when they put certain items on sale. Purchases of complements and other items in general compensate for the lower price of the sale item.

15. **16.7** — Price discrimination is practiced because different consumers assign different utility to goods and so are willing to pay different prices.

16. **16.7** — Time is allocated the same way as income. Consumers weigh the marginal utility of various activities in choosing how to spend their time.

17. **16.8** — Price elasticity measures the percentage change in quantity demanded that accompanies a given percentage change in price. The elasticity coefficient η is the absolute value of the percentage change in quantity demanded — $(Q_A - Q_B)/[(Q_A + Q_B)/2]$ — divided by the percentage change in price — $(P_A - P_B)/[(P_A + P_B)/2]$. Demand is elastic if the coefficient is greater than one, inelastic if it is less than one, and unitary elastic if the coefficient equals one.

18. **16.9** — Elasticity and the change in total revenue that accompanies a price change are related. Total revenue and price are inversely related for elastic demand but rise and fall together with inelastic demand.

19. **16.10** — Demand curves can have five possible elasticity characteristics, ranging from perfectly elastic (horizontal) to perfectly inelastic (vertical). The slope of a demand curve does not necessarily indicate its elasticity, since

different measurement units of price and quantity change slope but don't affect elasticity. Almost all demand curves have an elastic, inelastic, and unitary elastic region.

16.10 ➤ 20. Ease of substitution affects elasticity. Elasticity increases with the ability to substitute other goods. Demand tends to be more inelastic for items that take a small share of the household's budget. Elasticity often increases with budget share.

16.10 ➤ 21. Luxury goods tend to have more elastic demands than do necessities, which tend to have more inelastic demands. Time frame also affects elasticity. In general, demand is more elastic in the long run, but elasticity may vary over the long run for some goods depending on the individual good and its uses.

16.11 ➤ 22. Income elasticity measures the percentage change in quantity demanded that accompanies a given percentage change in income. The demand for a good is either income elastic (the elasticity coefficient is greater than one) or inelastic (the coefficient is less than one).

16.11 ➤ 23. Inferior goods have a negative income effect. An increase in income results in less quantity demanded.

16.12 ➤ 24. Income elasticity can be used to predict demand shifts as income rises or falls.

16.13 ➤ 25. Budget lines plot all combinations of two goods that can be purchased with given income at fixed prices. An increase in income shifts the budget line but does not alter its slope. Changing prices rotate the budget line, changing its slope.

16.13 ➤ 26. Indifference curves show all combinations of two goods that provide the same total utility. Consumers are indifferent between combinations on a given indifference curve but prefer combinations on higher indifference curves over those on lower indifference curves. Diminishing marginal utility results in a changing marginal rate of substitution, thereby giving indifference curves their distinctive U-shape.

16.13 ➤ 27. Consumers choose the budget line combination that puts them on the highest possible indifference curve. This combination occurs at the point where the indifference curve and budget line are tangent. At this point, the slope of the budget line (P_X/P_Y) equals the slope of the indifference curve (MU_X/MU_Y), so $MU_X/P_X = MU_Y/P_Y$.

16.13 ➤ 28. Demand curves are derived by plotting the new consumer choices as the price of one good is varied.

16.13 ➤ 29. The substitution effect is found by noting how buying behavior changes when the consumer is constrained to the original indifference curve. The income effect is found when the consumer moves from this point to the new indifference curve (see text figures).

DISCUSSION QUESTIONS

16.2, 16.5, 16.11

1. The following table shows the total utility an individual derives from consuming movies and bacon cheeseburgers (in units per week). Use this table to answer the following questions.

	Total utility	
Quantity	Movie admissions (per week)	Bacon cheeseburgers (per week)
0	0	0
1	100	40
2	160	70
3	190	90
4	215	105
5	235	115
6	245	120

   a. Derive a marginal utility table for movies and hamburgers from the information supplied in the above table. Does this example display diminishing marginal utility? Explain.

   b. Suppose this consumer has $10 per week to allocate between these two goods. Movies cost $2 per admission and bacon cheeseburgers are priced at $2 each. What is the utility maximizing choice? Explain how you arrived at your answer.

   c. Suppose that spendable income rises to $16, while prices remain at $2 each for the two items. How does the quantity demanded of each good change? Explain how you arrived at your answer.

   d. Suppose income remains at $10, but the price of a movie rises to $4, while hamburgers remain at $2, with no change in quality of either good. How does the quantity of each good demanded change? Explain how you arrived at your answer.

16.8, 16.9

2. Use the demand information from Question 1 to calculate the coefficient of elasticity of movie demand. Is demand elastic or inelastic? Does the total revenue test give the same conclusion? Explain.

16.8, 16.10

3. Can you tell anything about the price elasticity of demand for bacon cheeseburgers from your answers to Question 1? Why or why not?

16.11

4. Use the information from Question 1 to calculate the income elasticity of demand for movie admissions and bacon cheeseburgers. Are either of these items inferior goods? Explain.

16.2, 16.3

5. A line from a Gilbert and Sullivan operetta goes, "If you have nothing else to wear / But cloth of gold and silkens rare / For cloth of gold you cease to care. / Up goes the price of shoddy." Use marginal utility theory to describe the economic behavior behind this rhyme.

16.5, 16.6, 16.8, 16.10

6. You observe the price of a particular good rising, with no change in the quantity demanded. Use the tools of this chapter to suggest at least four different explanations for this observation.

SELECTED READINGS

Alchain, Armen A. "The Meaning of Utility Measurement." Reprinted in Breit, William, and Hochman, Harold M. (Eds.), *Readings in Microeconomics*, 2nd ed. New York: Holt, Rinehart and Winston, 1971.

Galbraith, John Kenneth. *The Affluent Society*. Boston: Houghton Mifflin, 1958.

Hicks, John R. "Value and Capital." Reprinted in Needy, Charles W. (Ed.), *Classics of Economics*. Oak Park IL: Moore Publishing Company, Inc., 1980.

Mansfield, Edwin. *Microeconomics: Theory and Applications*, 5th ed. New York: W. W. Norton, 1985, chap. 3.

Stigler, George. "The Development of Utility Theory." *Journal of Political Economy* (August – October, 1950), pp. 307 – 327, 373 – 396.

Tesler, L. G. "Some Aspects of the Economics of Advertising." *Journal of Business* (April, 1968), pp. 166–173.

Veblen, Thorstein: "Conspicuous Consumption." Reprinted in Needy, Charles W. (Ed.), *Classics of Economics*. Oak Park, IL: Moore Publishing Company, Inc., 1980.

CHAPTER 17

Supply and the Costs of Production

Having read the chapter, reviewed the chapter summary, and completed the *Study Guide* exercises, you should be able to:

CRIS

17.1 TYPES OF FIRMS: Explain the differences among sole proprietorships, partnerships, and corporations and tell how they differ in liability and reward characteristics.

17.2 GOAL OF FIRM: Explain the goal of the firm and determine whether profit maximization is the only possible goal.

17.3 PRODUCTION FUNCTION: Define the production function and explain the difference between inputs and outputs.

17.4 FIXED AND VARIABLE INPUTS: Define fixed inputs and variable inputs and explain how and why they differ.

17.5 SHORT RUN AND LONG RUN: Explain the difference between short run and long run in economics and tell how production choices are different in the two time frames.

17.6 TOTAL AND MARGINAL PRODUCT: Define total product and marginal product and explain why economists assume diminishing marginal product.

17.7 EXPLICIT AND IMPLICIT COSTS: Define explicit cost and implicit cost, give examples of each, and explain why profit is counted as a cost by economists.

17.8 ACCOUNTING AND ECONOMIC PROFITS: Explain the difference between accounting profits and economic profits and tell which gives a better picture of the success of the firm and why.

17.9 FIXED AND VARIABLE COSTS: Define fixed cost and variable cost, explain which costs are fixed and which are variable in the short run, giving examples of each, and describe why costs are not fixed in the long run.

	17.10	**FIXED COST CURVE:** Draw a fixed cost curve and explain its shape.
	17.11	**VARIABLE COST CURVE:** Draw a variable cost curve and explain its shape.
	17.12	**TOTAL COST CURVE:** Draw a total cost curve and explain its shape and the relationship between fixed, variable, and total costs.
	17.13	**MARGINAL COST:** Define marginal cost, draw a *MC* curve, and explain how marginal cost is derived from total cost information.
	17.14	**AVERAGE TOTAL COST:** Define average total cost, draw an *ATC* curve and explain how it is derived. Then discuss the relationship among price, *ATC*, and economic profit and between *MC* and *ATC*.
	17.15	**ENTRY AND EXIT:** Define entry and exit and explain how they are related to economic profit.
	17.16	**AVERAGE VARIABLE COST:** Define average variable cost, draw an *AVC* curve and explain how it is derived, then discuss the relationship among price, *AVC*, and the shut-down point and between *MC* and *AVC*.
	17.17	**AVERAGE FIXED COST:** Define average fixed cost, draw an *AFC* curve, and explain how it is derived.
	17.18	**PROFIT-MAXIMIZING OUTPUT:** Explain and show the profit-maximizing level of output for a firm with constant marginal revenue.
	17.19	**FIRM AND INDUSTRY SUPPLY CURVES:** Derive firm and industry supply curves and show how they are related.
	17.20	**COST CURVES AND SUPPLY CHANGES:** Explain and show how cost curves, individual firm supply, and market supply change in the following situations: change in one firm's variable costs, change in many firms' variable costs, change in short-run fixed costs, change in long-run fixed costs, or change in demand.
	17.21	**SUPPLY CHOICES:** Describe how supply choices change in the long run and explain what the long-run *ATC* is and how it is related to short-run *ATC*.
	17.22	**RETURNS TO SCALE:** Define constant returns to scale, increasing returns to scale, and decreasing returns to scale and tell how they relate to the shape of the long-run *ATC* curve.

In past chapters, supply and demand curves were used to illustrate how markets function through the choices of consumers and producers. This chapter examines in much greater depth the problem of producer choice and the supply curves those choices generate.

Supply curves, like their demand-side partners, are aggregations. They summarize the individual acts of many separate economic players. Supply curves don't shift by themselves; they do so only if enough individual producers alter output choices. The supplies of corn, natural gas, and other items are most affected by two fundamental factors: (1) the costs of production and (2) the nature of competition among suppliers. This chapter focuses on production costs, while the next two chapters explore the nature of competition among suppliers and the role of government in improving the efficiency of markets.

WHO ARE THE PRODUCERS AND WHY DO THEY PRODUCE?

17.1 TYPES OF FIRMS

Sole Proprietorship
A business firm that is owned by a single individual who receives all the firm's profits and is liable for all the firm's debts.

Partnership
A business firm that is owned by several individuals collectively. Each individual owner shares both the profits from the partnership and the risk of loss.

Corporation
A business firm owned by many individuals collectively. Each individual owner has a right to a share of the corporation's profits, but the individual's liability is limited to the amount of his or her initial investment.

Everyone is a producer in the sense that we all produce valuable goods and services, whether they are sold in markets or supplied for our own use. When people band together to produce more complex goods, or make them more efficiently, the result is a firm.

Firms come in many shapes and sizes, the most basic being a **sole proprietorship.** This is a business owned by a single individual who receives all of the rewards from the business and bears full liability for all of the losses. Examples of sole proprietorships include many dental and law offices, barber shops, and "family" grocery stores. While individually owned, these firms often employ others. The key characteristic is not size but sole ownership. There are over 11 million proprietorships in the United States, comprising about 77 percent of the individual business in the economy. These firms tend to be small, however, and account for only about 9 percent of the total dollar volume of sales reported by all business firms.

A **partnership** is more complex. Partners share ownership of the business and, therefore, split the profits and share liability for business debts according to some preset formula. Many small firms, and some relatively large ones, are partnerships. There are about 1.1 million partnerships in the United States, accounting for about 4 percent of the total dollar volume of sales in the economy.

A **corporation** is the most complicated form of business. Many corporations are owned by hundreds or thousands of individual stockholders, each of whom has claim to a set proportion of the firm's profit but limited liability for the corporation's debt. Ownership and management of corporate firms are generally separate. Shareholders elect a board of directors, which hires and fires top management.

Most firms in the United States are partnerships or sole proprietorships, but these firms tend to be small. Most of the goods and services in our economy are supplied by a relatively small number of large corporate firms. There are about 2.2 million corporations in the United States, comprising about 15 percent of the total number of business firms. These corporations account for over 87 percent of the total dollar volume of sales in the economy. Corporate ownership is widely dispersed throughout the population, with many people unknowingly owning corporate stock through pooled insurance and pension fund assets.

17.2 GOAL OF FIRM

Profit
The difference between total revenue and total cost (see Economic Profit).

In economics, it is generally assumed that **profit** is the producer's main motivation. Businesses are successful to the extent that they generate profits, which reward the firm's owners for risk taking, entrepreneurial skill, and management expertise. Firms that earn profits survive and grow. Those that lose money eventually disappear from the business scene. This is the Darwinian side of economics.

Profit maximization is not the only goal that guides producer decisions, however. Sometimes firm ownership and day-to-day management are much different (as in some large corporations). Managers sometimes aim for an "acceptable" level of profit, sacrificing higher earnings for the firm's owners in exchange for job amenities for themselves. Other firms try to maximize sales revenues or market shares, rather than profit. Selling more goods does not always mean more profit if production costs are greater than selling price. Finally, some firms sacrifice short-term profits to finance charitable and cultural activities, which often improve the long-term business and social environment.

There are as many firm motives as there are business managers. All firms, however, are constrained by the reality of profit and loss. The analyses in this chapter assume that firms aim to maximize profits.

THE PRODUCTION FUNCTION

17.3 PRODUCTION FUNCTION

Input
Resources used in production.

Output
The goods and services that result from production.

Production Function
The relationship between the various inputs to a production process and the maximum output that can be produced per unit of time.

Fixed Input
Input whose use does not change with the level of output in the short run.

Short Run (in production)
A time frame sufficiently brief that firms must treat some costs as fixed.

17.4 FIXED AND VARIABLE INPUTS

Long Run (in production)
A time frame sufficiently long to make all inputs and costs variable.

Production is the act of combining **inputs** to make **outputs**. The **production function** is a description of the process by which inputs are combined to produce the goods and services that firms make and sell. The production function expresses the relationship between various combinations of inputs and the maximum possible output attainable for each combination of those inputs. Production functions are, in some cases, quite complex. For example, textbooks like the one you are reading are relatively common goods. The production of books require inputs such as paper, ink, cloth, thread, and glue for production. This brief input list doesn't really reveal the textbook production function, however. This textbook was written and edited on microcomputers, electronically typeset on a minicomputer, and printed on a high-tech press. The pages were cut and assembled using one set of machines, bound on another, then distributed to college bookstores through an elaborate transportation system. Many workers and machines all across the country were part of this book's production function. Most other goods you buy and use have similarly complex production functions.

The recipe by which inputs are combined to make outputs is complex, varies from good to good, and is often different in competing firms that make the same good. Nevertheless, the production functions of items as dissimilar as textbooks and auto mufflers have important properties in common. From these similarities we can develop a general theory of producer behavior that can help us understand supplier decisions even in complex firms.

Some production ingredients can be classified as **fixed inputs.** These are production inputs whose use does not vary in the **short run,** regardless of the amount of output produced. The short run is a period of time of such duration that at least one of the inputs in the production process is fixed. The printing presses and binding machines used to produced this book are fixed inputs, for example. The number of these inputs used stays the same, in the short run, no matter how many books are made. In the **long run,** however, these machines, and the size and location of the production facilities, are variable. Over a longer period of time, newer, larger presses and

17.5 SHORT RUN AND LONG RUN

Variable Input
Inputs whose use varies with output in the short run.

17.6 TOTAL AND MARGINAL PRODUCT

Total Product
The total quantity of goods produced.

Marginal Product
The change in total product when one input is added, all other inputs held constant.

binding machines can be bought and installed or a larger plant can be built, if necessary. In the long run, all inputs can be varied, and therefore, all costs are variable costs.

Other types of inputs are **variable inputs.** Variable inputs are resources whose use depends on the amount of output produced in the short run. The amount of ink used by a publisher, for example, varies directly with the number of books printed. It takes more ink to print more books. The use of individual inputs is also variable in another sense. Different inputs may be substituted for one another depending on cost, availability, or other factors. A publisher might substitute a more expensive kind of paper that absorbs less ink, in return for using less ink in the printing process. This substitution choice will, however, depend on the current prices of the two different kinds of paper and the price of ink.

One last important point should be made here about fixed and variable costs. Fixed costs are those costs that are not changeable over the planning period, while variable costs can change over the period. Therefore, the longer the period under consideration, the greater the proportion of total costs that are variable.

Figure 17-1 shows two common production function properties. What happens if we increase the use of one variable input (labor, for example), while holding all other inputs, fixed and variable alike, constant? More inputs lead to more outputs giving the rising **total product** curve the figure shows. But is each additional worker as effective as the previous one? What happens to labor's **marginal product** — the amount of extra output each additional worker adds to production, all other inputs held constant — as production expands?

Increasing just one variable input, with all others held constant, will eventually incur diminishing returns. Workers are first assigned to the firm's most productive jobs. As the work force expands, these positions are soon filled. Additional workers are assigned to jobs, such as feeding materials to machines, checking inventory, or filling in for others during rest

FIGURE 17-1

Total and Marginal Product Curves. Total product increases as more labor input is mixed with fixed amounts of other resources (a), but labor's marginal product falls as diminishing returns set in (b).

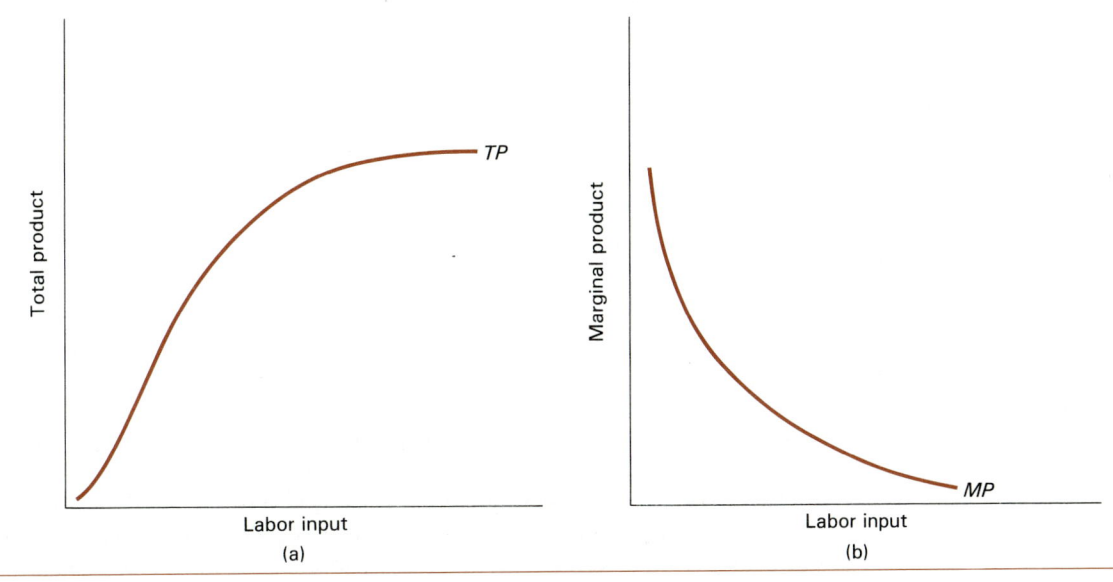

breaks, that add less to output. At some point, the marginal product of any single input falls. Falling marginal product means that, in the short run, doubling the number of workers on the production line does not double the amount of goods produced. The extra workers added to the production process at this point have lower marginal product, so their use eventually pushes up production costs.

The concept of diminishing marginal product is very important because it means that business firms cannot simply crank up production lines and produce as much as possible. Doubling the payroll does not necessarily double output, and there is much more to production than just a single input. Therefore, firms must base business choices on a close analysis of all production costs.

Types of Costs

What types of costs do businesses consider when they decide how much to produce at today's price? Economists find it useful to divide production costs in two ways: explicit versus implicit costs and fixed versus variable costs.

> **Explicit Costs**
> Out-of-pocket costs paid by a firm (accounting costs).

> **17.7 EXPLICIT AND IMPLICIT COSTS**

> **Implicit Costs**
> The opportunity costs of business operation.

Explicit versus Implicit Costs When people are asked to give examples of production costs, they tend to focus on such things as out-of-pocket payments to workers, suppliers, and managers. These types of items are what economists classify as **explicit costs.** Explicit costs are the bills and payments that accountants deal with in figuring profit and loss. But explicit costs are not the only costs a firm bears. Business owners also bear **implicit costs.** Firm owners who invest in their business give up the return these funds could have earned in the best alternative use. Owners who invest their own time and talents in production give up the income they could have earned working elsewhere.

You should recognize these implicit costs as the opportunity costs of the time, talent, and money that business owners invest in their firms. These opportunity costs are not included in the explicit costs that accountants calculate, but economists include them, along with explicit costs, in their calculations. Giving up the chance to earn an extra $100 elsewhere is, to the economist, just as real a cost as paying out $100 for inputs.

> **Accounting Profit**
> Profit equal to the total revenue minus the sum of all explicit costs.

> **Economic Profit**
> Profit in which both explicit and implicit costs are considered; economic profit is different from accounting profit.

Since economists and accountants use different measures of cost, they get different profit results. **Accounting profit** is the difference between total revenue and the explicit costs of production. **Economic profit** is the difference between total revenue and total cost, where total cost includes both implicit and explicit costs.

> **17.8 ACCOUNTING AND ECONOMIC PROFITS**

The definitional difference between accounting profit and economic profit is important. Suppose a pastry chef receives $20 for a fancy cake that took three hours of his work and for which he spent $5 for ingredients. The accounting profit is $15. But this accounting profit masks an economic reality. The chef could have earned $7 per hour working for a local cafe. The real cost of the cake is $5 for ingredients plus $21 in lost wages. There's no economic profit here because the cake, which was considered profitable when measured by accountants, actually generated a $6 economic loss when measured by economists.

> **Fixed Cost**
> The cost of fixed inputs; cost that does not vary with the level of output in the short run.

> **Variable Cost**
> The cost of variable inputs; cost that depends on and changes with the level of output in the short run.

Fixed versus Variable Costs Fixed and variable inputs generate fixed and variable costs. **Fixed costs** are the costs associated with fixed production inputs. **Variable costs** are the costs associated with variable inputs. These costs are of both explicit and implicit varieties. The chef's fixed costs in the last example include both the explicit rental cost of his shop, which he must

> **17.9 FIXED AND VARIABLE COSTS**

pay regardless of output, and also some implicit costs such as forgone interest return on the money he has invested in ovens, kitchen tools, and other equipment. Variable costs include both the explicit costs of variable inputs such as butter, flour and sugar, which vary in use with the chef's production, and also the implicit variable cost of forgone wages. The more cakes the chef makes, the more time he spends, and therefore, the more outside income he gives up.

Why do economists treat fixed and variable costs differently when they are both costs of the firm? One reason is that fixed costs are just that, fixed (in the short run), so producers can do nothing but pay them. In the short run, therefore, they are not important to the production choice. The firm cannot reduce fixed costs by producing fewer goods nor can it increase fixed costs by producing more. A profit-maximizing firm treats fixed costs as a given, in the short run, and concentrates on the relationship between variable costs and sales revenues, which are both affected by output choices. In the short run, fixed costs are not considered in the production decision. In the long run, however, the firm has sufficient time to change its level of fixed costs so, in effect, all costs are variable. In the long run, then, the firm considers both fixed and variable costs in making output decisions.

A Guide to Cost Curves

The production decisions facing the firm can be understood more easily by examining its costs. We can see those costs more clearly by plotting cost curves. Table 17-1 and Figure 17-2 provide examples of how costs vary with output.

Table 17-1 shows cost information for Wood Crafters, a sole proprietorship in the Pacific Northwest. The firm manufactures and assembles oak desks. Wood Crafters is a small firm, but its cost curves exhibit the common properties that economists can identify for almost all producers, big and small. By examing the cost table and the corresponding cost curves, we can see how cost is calculated and measured. The eight columns in Table 17-1 correspond to the eight factors that enter into the calculations of cost: output, fixed cost, variable cost, total cost, marginal cost, average total cost, average variable cost, and average fixed cost.

Output The first column of Table 17-1 shows output, the quantity produced. We are interested in the way that cost varies with output. The purpose of analyzing costs is to find the level of output that maximizes profits. Output in this example is measured in desk units produced per week.

17.10 FIXED COST CURVE

Fixed Cost Wood Crafters bears fixed costs of $300 per week. The same $300 cost is paid whether output is 10 desks or none at all (fixed cost is a constant, or horizontal, line in Figure 17-2). The fixed cost includes both explicit costs, such as the shop's rent, and implicit costs, such as the shop owner's foregone return on investment in power tools, for example. These costs are fixed in the short run only. In the long run, the firm can alter where it produces, how it produces, and the size of the plant.

17.11 VARIABLE COST CURVE

Variable Cost Variable costs rise in Table 17-1 from zero, when nothing is produced, to $800, when output equals 10 desks per week. There is a direct relationship between output and variable cost, as both the table and figure illustrate. Increased production requires more variable inputs, such as wood, sandpaper, varnish, labor, and power. This causes variable costs to

508 Supply and the Costs of Production

TABLE 17-1				Cost Schedule for Wood Crafters			
(1)	(2)	(3)	(4)	(5)	(6)	(7)	(8)
Quantity (per week)	Fixed cost ($)	Variable cost ($)	Total cost ($) (2) + (3)	Marginal cost ($)	Average total cost ($) (4) ÷ (1)	Average variable cost ($) (3) ÷ (1)	Average fixed cost ($) (2) ÷ (1)
0	300	0	300	—	—	—	—
1	300	50	350	50	350	50	300
2	300	80	380	30	190	40	150
3	300	90	390	10	130	30	100
4	300	120	420	30	105	30	75
5	300	170	470	50	94	34	60
6	300	240	540	70	90	40	50
7	300	330	630	90	90	47.14	42.85
8	300	460	760	130	95	57.50	37.60
9	300	600	900	140	100	66.07	33.33
10	300	800	1100	200	110	80	30

FIGURE 17-2   **Cost Curves for Wood Crafters.** (a) Total cost rises as output goes up. Constant fixed costs are supplemented by rising variable expenses. (b) Marginal cost first falls, then rises.

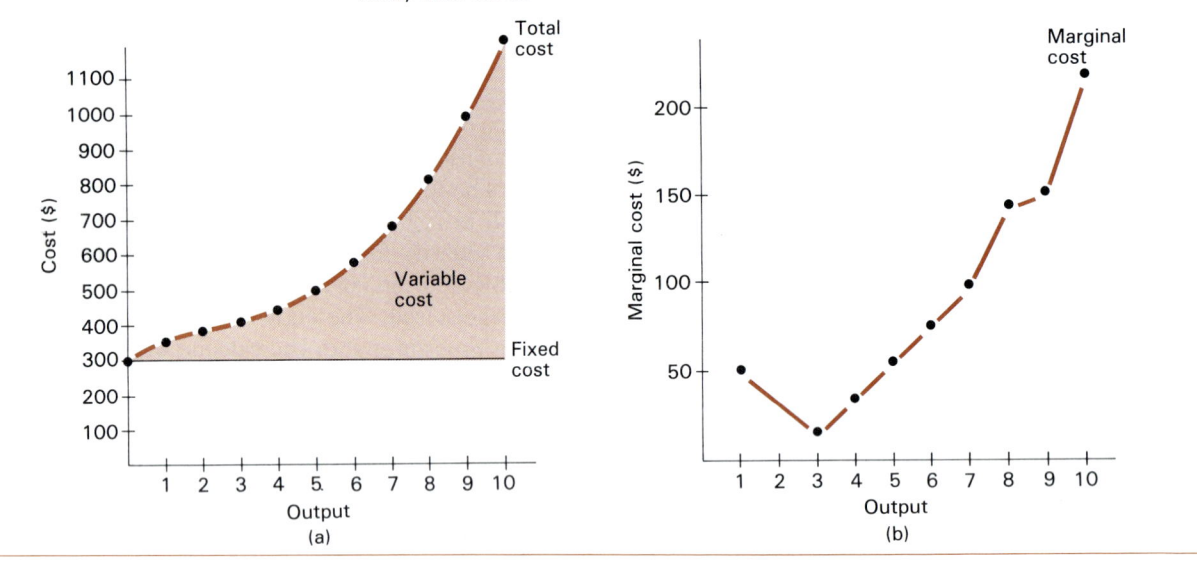

rise. Variable costs include both explicit costs, such as the cost of nails and screws, and implicit costs, such as foregone outside income.

17.12 TOTAL COST CURVE

Total Cost   Total cost is the sum of fixed and variable costs. Notice how the composition of total cost changes in Figure 17-2 (a) as output increases. Most costs are fixed when output totals are small, but variable costs dominate at high production levels. Total cost includes all costs, both fixed and variable, explicit and implicit.

Marginal Cost (MC)
The change in total cost (or variable cost) that occurs when output changes by one unit.

17.13 MARGINAL COST

Marginal Cost   Marginal cost (*MC*), shown in the fifth column of Table 17-1 and the lower graph of Figure 17-2 (b), is the key to producer choice in the short run. Marginal cost measures how much total cost changes when output is increased or decreased by one unit; in other words, it tells how much the next (or last) item adds to cost.

Marginal cost is determined by calculating the change in total cost when output changes by one unit. In Table 17-1, for example, total cost is $300 if nothing is produced and rises to $350 when output is one desk. The marginal cost of the first desk is therefore $50 because that is the extra cost of the first desk. (Note the paradox: the first desk actually costs $350 to produce (total cost equals $300), but you would only save $50 by not making it, since the $300 fixed costs would still be there! The $50 marginal cost is a subtle but important measure of the cost of production).

Total cost rises again to $380 when output increases to two units. The marginal cost of the second desk is $30 ($380 minus $350). It would be valuable practice for you to check the remaining marginal cost figures in the table to make sure that you understand how the figures were calculated. Since fixed cost does not change with output, it is just as easy to figure marginal cost by calculating the change in variable cost when output rises by one unit. By checking the table it is easy to see that this rule holds.

The shape of the marginal cost curves shown in Figure 17-2 (b) is typical of marginal cost curves in the real world. Marginal costs initially fall when output expands, because the firm takes advantage of production line efficiencies. Firm owners find they can make three desks per week in only a little more time than it takes to make two, for example, because many of the cutting and finishing tasks can be combined. The third desk's marginal cost is therefore low.

Marginal costs do not, however, keep falling forever. Remember that, in the short run, some inputs are fixed. Diminishing marginal returns eventually appear as more and more variable inputs are combined with a set quantity of fixed inputs. For example, there is a limit to the amount of wood that one table saw can efficiently saw in a week. At some point, any attempt to put more wood through the saw causes such things as wasteful mistakes and machine breakdowns that drive up production costs. Marginal costs begin to rise as output increases past this point and become very high when output nears the plant's maximum capacity as determined by the quantity of fixed inputs.

17.14 AVERAGE TOTAL COST

Average Total Cost (ATC)
Total cost divided by the level of output.

Average Total Cost Average total cost (*ATC*) is found by dividing total cost by the number of items produced. The first desk generates total cost of $350 and thus its *ATC* is $350. Total cost rises to $380 when the second desk is built, but *ATC* falls to $380/2, or $180. Check through the *ATC* figures in Table 17-1 to see how they are calculated.

Figure 17-3 shows the *ATC* curve. Average total cost initially falls for two reasons. First, as output expands, the $300 per week fixed costs are divided over a larger number of desks, bringing down average costs. Second, the first items produced have low marginal costs, which helps bring down average costs. The second desk has a marginal cost of just $30, for example. This low marginal cost helps bring down average cost from $350 for the first unit to $180 for the second. Average total cost rises eventually, when higher marginal costs pull up production costs despite falling fixed costs per unit.

Here's a useful mathematical property that was presented in Chapter 2. Average total cost falls when *MC* is less than *ATC* and rises when *MC* is greater than *ATC* [*MC* cuts *ATC* from below (*MC* = *ATC*) at the *ATC* minimum].

510 *Supply and the Costs of Production*

FIGURE 17-3

Marginal and Average Costs. U-shaped *ATC* and *AVC* curves intersect *MC* at their minima. The *AFC* curve constantly falls as fixed expenses are spread over larger output totals.

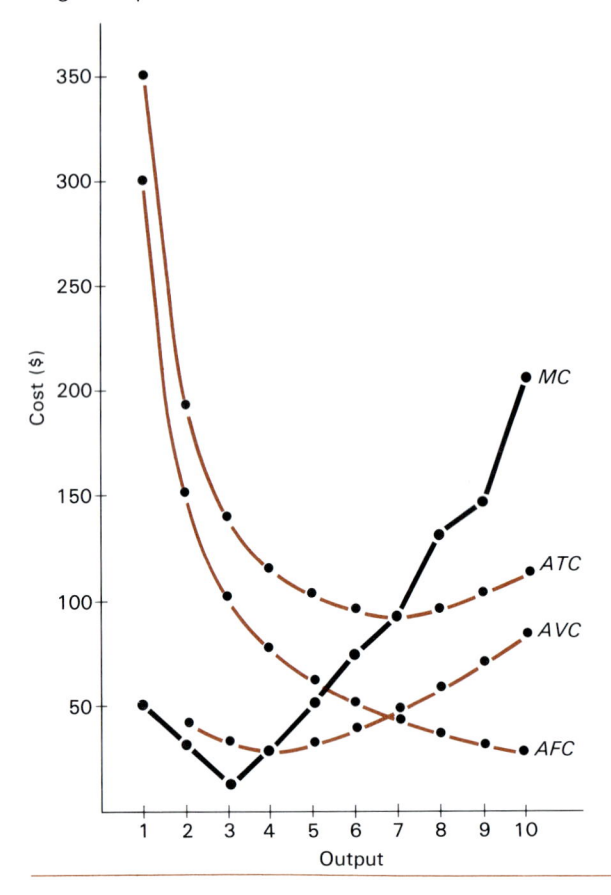

Why does this relationship between *MC* and *ATC* hold? An example makes the relationship between average and marginal quantities clear. Suppose your current exam average in this class is 75 percent. What happens to your grade average if your future exam grades are less than the average (say, your next grade is only 60 percent)? The lower marginal exam pulls down the average. This is the same thing that low marginal cost does to average cost. Conversely, if you get 95 percent on your next two exams, and you have a past average of 75 percent, the higher marginal scores pull up your lower average. That is what high marginal costs do: they pull up lower average total costs. What happens to your 75 percent average if the next exam grade is 75 percent, too? Nothing, and that is what happens to *ATC* when output goes from six to seven, where *MC* equals *ATC* in the table.

One reason that calculating *ATC* is helpful is that it makes it easy to check for the existence of economic profits. Table 17-1 shows, for example, that average total cost is $90 at an output level of seven desks per week. Whether or not this level of production yields a profit depends on the price Wood Crafters gets for their desks. There are three possibilities—the price can be equal to, greater than, or less than *ATC*.

Suppose the desks sell for their average total cost (price equals the *ATC* of $90). This is the firm's **break-even point,** the point where economic profits are zero. Total revenues exactly equal total cost. It might seem

Break-even Point
The production level at which the firm earns zero economic profit; the level of output at which price equals *ATC*.

Normal Profit
The profit available in the best alternative use of the firm's resources; normal profit takes into account the implicit costs of production.

17.15 ENTRY AND EXIT

Entry
New firms come into the industry, generally because they are attracted by economic profits.

Exit
Old firms leave the industry, generally because they are in pursuit of economic profits in other industries.

17.16 AVERAGE VARIABLE COST

Average Variable Cost (AVC)
Variable cost divided by the level of output.

Shut-down Point
The production level at which total revenues just equal variable costs, below this point the most profitable output level is zero in the short run; the level of output at which price equal AVC.

strange that a business would even bother to produce if it just breaks even. Recall, however, that total cost, as measured by economists, includes opportunity cost. Breaking even, in this sense, means that the firm's owners receive as high a return on time and money as could be earned in the best alternative opportunity. The firm earns a **normal profit,** an accounting profit equal to that available in alternative industries, when it breaks even with price equal to ATC.

The second possibility is that price is greater than ATC. Suppose, for example, that desks sell for $92, while ATC is equal to $90. Each desk would bring in a $2 economic profit in this case. A price above average total cost signals the existence of economic profit, that is, a profit greater than can be earned in an alternate business. If these profits persist in the long run, we might expect to observe **entry** into this industry. Other firms in other industries who might presently be earning zero economic profits would enter the woodcrafting business and set up shop in hopes of also earning positive economic profits.

The third possibility is that price is less than ATC. If price is $88 and ATC is $90, then each desk produced earns a $2 negative economic profit. This is a signal that better returns are to be had in other lines of business. The firm might **exit** from this industry if these losses persist over time and try to enter some other industry where it believes economic profits can be made.

Average Variable Cost   Average variable cost (AVC) is calculated by dividing total variable cost by output. Production of six desks, for example, requires total variable cost expense of $240, so average variable cost is $240/6, or $40. Figure 17-3 shows an average variable cost curve.

Average variable cost is useful in making some important production choices. Suppose the firm is currently producing four desks per week (AVC equal $30, ATC equals $105). If desks sell for $105 (or more), the firm earns a normal profit (or more). If desk prices are between $30 (AVC) and $105 (ATC), then the firm loses money but at least takes in enough revenue to meet its variable cost bills. Production continues, at least in the short run, despite the loss, since the firm loses less money by producing a little than by shutting down while still paying fixed costs.

A price below $30 hits the **shut-down point,** however. If price is less than AVC, then the firm is not taking in enough revenue to cover variable costs, not to mention fixed costs. Each unit that the firm produces in this instance costs more in variable costs than the price for which the unit can be sold. Not only does the firm lose its fixed costs but also the difference between price and average variable cost on each unit it sells. The more units the firm produces, the more money it loses. The firm cuts its loss by shutting down production. If the firm shuts down, fixed expenses must still be paid, but no loss on operating expense is borne since there are no variable costs when output is zero.

Examine the shape of the AVC curve. It has the same relationship to marginal costs as the ATC curve just discussed: marginal cost pulls down AVC when MC is less than AVC; it cuts the AVC curve from below at its minimum, where MC equals AVC; and it pulls up AVC when MC exceeds AVC. Both AVC and ATC curves have a characteristic U-shape.

| **KEY CONCEPT 17.16** | Marginal cost intersects average variable cost and average total cost at their minimum point. |

512 Supply and the Costs of Production

> **17.17 AVERAGE FIXED COST**

Average Fixed Cost (AFC)
Fixed cost divided by the level of output.

Average Fixed Cost The difference between the average total and average variable cost curves is made up of **average fixed costs (AFC)**. An AFC curve is shown in Figure 17-3. The average fixed cost curve continually declines, approaching the output axis but never getting there. Average fixed cost falls as output increases because a constant fixed cost total is divided among larger and larger quantities of production. Falling AFC pulls down the ATC curve initially, while rising MC eventually pushes it back up. The shape of the ATC curve depends on the relationship between falling AFC and rising MC as output expands.

PROFIT-MAXIMIZING OUTPUT

We can use cost curves to see how firms decide how much to produce at each price. Suppose that oak desks currently sell in local stores for $130 each. For now we will take this price as fixed. Wood Crafters cannot charge more than $130 if it expects to see any customers, and it has no reason to charge less. The firm can sell as many desks as it wants at $130. The next major decision for Wood Crafters, then, is to determine what level of production maximizes profits, given their costs and the $130 price. Figure 17-4 shows the producer's choice.

Marginal Revenue (MR)
The change in total revenue or receipts when the quantity sold changes by one unit.

Figure 17-4 shows the types of the marginal and average cost curves we have been working with, and one useful addition. A straight line is drawn at price equals $130. This line indicates a constant **marginal revenue (MR)** of $130. Marginal revenue is the amount by which the firm's total revenues change when sales are increased by one unit. Each desk sold brings in the same extra revenue ($130) as the one before it. We now have both cost and

> **17.18 PROFIT-MAXIMIZING OUTPUT**

FIGURE 17-4

Profit-Maximizing Output Choice. Wood Crafters maximizes profit by producing at point A, where marginal revenue (price) equals marginal cost. Profit (price minus ATC multiplied by the quantity sold) is measured by the shaded rectangle in the figure. Point B, where price equals ATC, is the break-even point. The firm earns zero economic profit at this price–quantity combination. Point C, where price equals AVC, is the shut-down point; the firm is best off ceasing production when price falls below this point, since neither fixed nor variable expenses are met.

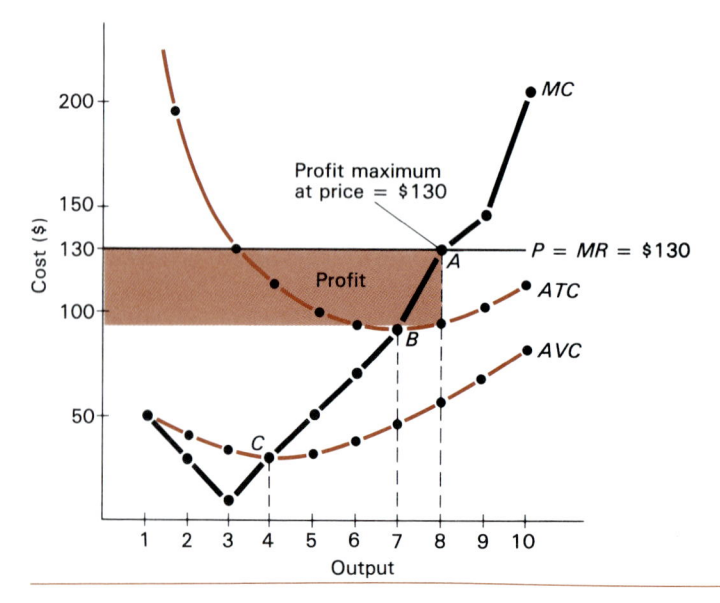

revenue information to determine how Wood Crafters will alter its output in an attempt to maximize its profits.

The easiest way to find the profit-maximizing output is to compare marginal revenue (MR) with marginal cost (MC) in the figure. If the firm produces the first desk, it has a marginal cost of just $50, yet it brings in $130 additional revenue, thereby generating a profit. The second desk adds just $20 to cost, yet it yields MR of $130. Thus it, too, is profitable. If we compare MC in the figure with the constant price of $130, we will find that the first seven desks produced per week all bring in more additional sales dollars than they add to cost.

Consider the eighth desk, however. Its marginal cost is $130, equal to the selling price. Should the firm produce this desk? Yes. A desk that costs $130 to produce and sells for $130 earns zero economic profit. But, because economists include foregone alternative profits as a production cost, zero economic profit means an accounting profit equal to that available in the best alternative use of the firm's resources. The firm makes as good a profit by 'breaking even' on the eighth desk as it would on any alternative use of its time and tools.

The ninth desk's marginal cost is $150; therefore, the firm would lose money selling it for $130. A business maximizes profit by setting output at the level at which marginal cost equals marginal revenue (price). This rule yields the highest profit total because each item produced adds more to revenue than it adds to cost. In this way, unprofitable items with marginal costs that are greater than their marginal revenues, like the ninth desk above, are avoided.

We can see the profit in the figure if we look closely. Per-unit profit is given by the difference between price (the MR curve in the figure) and average total cost (the ATC curve). Average total cost is $95 at the eight-desk output level, so average profit is $130 minus $95, or $35 per desk. If we multiply this unit profit by the quantity produced (eight desks), we get the area of the shaded rectangle in the figure, which corresponds to an economic profit of $35 times 8, or $280 per week.

KEY CONCEPT 17.18

The profit-maximization rule states that a firm maximizes profit by setting output at the level at which marginal revenue equals marginal cost.

FIRM AND MARKET SUPPLY

17.19 FIRM AND INDUSTRY SUPPLY CURVES

We have just learned something about the supply of oak desks: one firm (Wood Crafters) is willing to supply eight desks per week at a price of $130 per desk. That is a point on an individual firm's supply curve. The market has its own supply curve, and as we learned in Chapter 4, the supply curve of the entire market is the horizontal summation of the individual firms' supply curves. As we have just seen in this chapter, supply is based on marginal cost.

An individual firm produces where price equals marginal cost because that level of output maximizes profits. The firm's marginal cost curve is also its supply curve because it shows the relationship between price and the profit-maximizing quantity supplied. Figure 17-5 shows this relationship. The marginal cost of the sixth desk is $60, so six desks are offered for sale if price is $60. The quantity supplied rises to seven desks if price goes up to $70; the seventh desk's marginal cost is $70, so it cannot be profitably sold

514 Supply and the Costs of Production

FIGURE 17-5

Marginal Cost Determines Supply for Firm. The firm's short-run supply curve is determined by its marginal cost curve. The firm's marginal cost curve (a) and its supply curve (b) are the same at prices above the shut-down point.

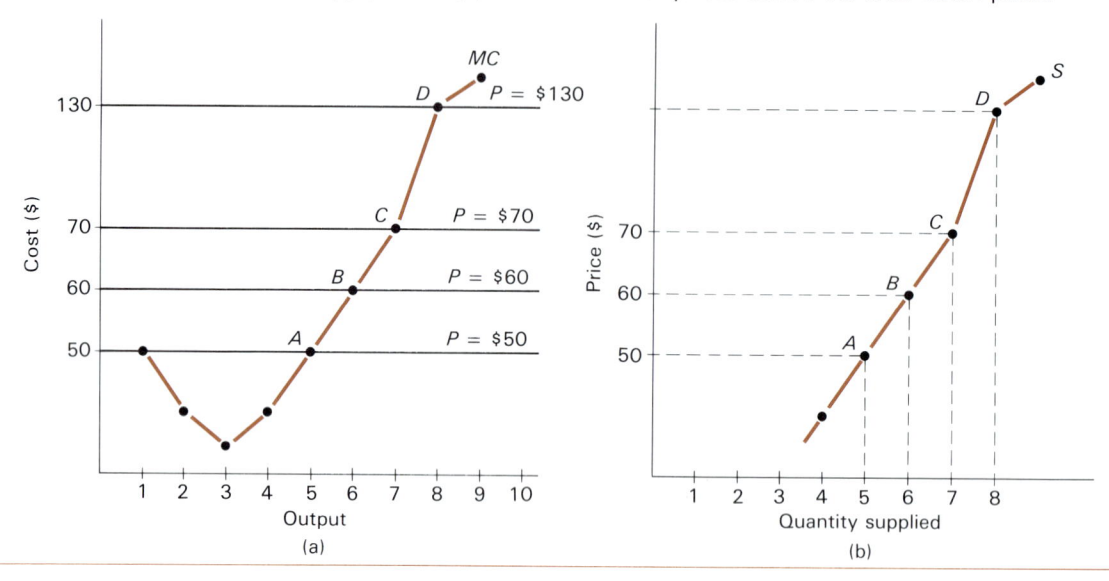

for any lower price. For the same reason, quantity supplied falls when price falls.

An individual firm's marginal cost curve is its supply curve, with one exception. If price falls below the shut-down point where MC crosses AVC (see Figure 17-4), the profit-maximizing price is less than the average variable cost, so a profit-maximizing firm would not earn enough revenue to pay its variable cost bills, much less cover fixed costs. The firm in this instance maximizes profit (or minimizes loss) by stopping the production line, and at least temporarily, halting production. The quantity supplied at a price like $25 in this example is zero.

KEY CONCEPT 17.19

The supply curve of the individual firm is equal to its marginal cost curve above average variable cost.

17.20 COST CURVES AND SUPPLY CHANGES

Market supply curves are built by summing the actions of individual firms, just as were the market demand curves we discussed in the last chapter. Figure 17-6 shows how to calculate market supply curves from the supplies of individual producers. The quantity produced by each firm at a given price is totaled to find market supply.

Shifting Supply curves

Several events make supply curves shift, changing the price/quantity relationship, under different circumstances. The events include changes in variable costs, changes in fixed costs, and changes in demand.

Change in Variable Costs: Single Firm If a single firm's variable costs change, thereby altering marginal costs, the result is a change in that firm's supply curve. The firm's supply schedule increases by shifting out to the

FIGURE 17-6

Firm and Market Supply Curves. Market supply curves are found by summing the quantities supplied by individual firms at each price.

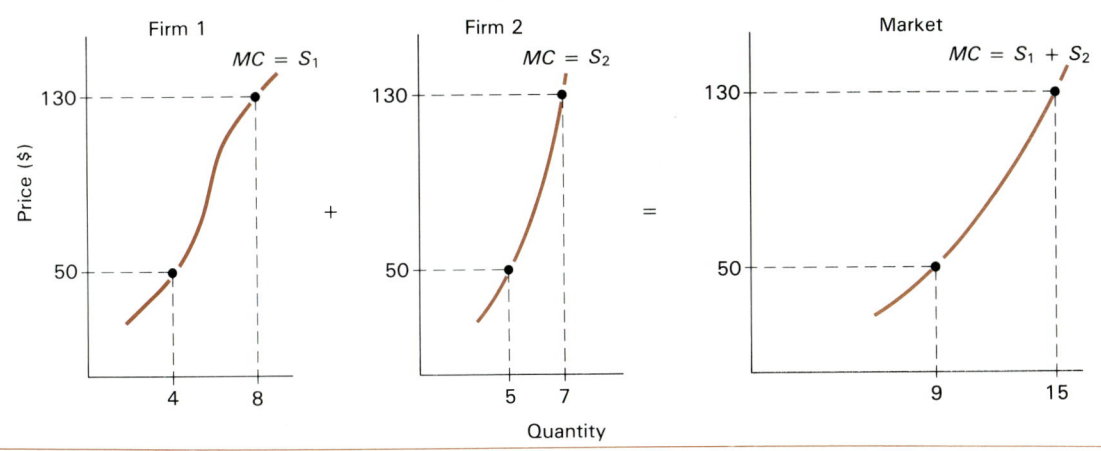

Change in Variable Costs: Many Firms Suppose, on the other hand, that many firms experience lowered marginal costs, such as would happen if the cost of a widely used input fell. For example, if the United Mine Workers Union accepted a reduced wage rate, it would reduce labor costs to all firms producing coal with union labor. This affects the supplies of many individual firms that use coal as an input either directly or to generate electric power and so changes market supply, as well. If marginal costs decline, market supply increases, forcing down price as equilibrium quantity rises.

What events lead to changing marginal costs, and therefore, shifting supply curves? Supply curves shift when the price of a variable input, like labor or raw materials, changes. Government policies can shift private-sector supply curves, too. Certain types of taxes and regulations affect the production costs of many firms. New technology also affects supply. Both fixed and variable costs are often changed when new machines (increases in fixed investment costs) replace less efficient workers (cutting variable costs).

Change in Fixed Costs: Short Run If fixed costs change in the short run, such as when warehouse rental costs or fixed interest expenses change, output does not change. Short-run output decisions are based on marginal cost and price, not on fixed costs. Any change in fixed costs affects the firm's profits in the short run (profits rise if fixed costs fall, for example). But that is no reason to alter production levels, because a change in fixed costs does not alter the profit-maximizing output level, the point at which MR equals MC.

If output of eight desks per week at a price of $130 each maximizes Wood Crafters' profits when fixed costs are $300 per week, then it is also the profit peak if fixed costs are $375 or $250. A change in fixed costs alters profits, but not production, in the short run, since marginal cost curves depend on variable, not fixed charges.

ECONOMIC ISSUES

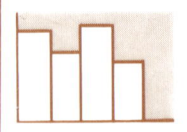

The Corporate Income Tax

In this chapter, we discussed the many costs that businesses bear, but we failed to mention one important cost that some businesses pay, the corporate income tax. The corporate income tax is controversial. Economists and policymakers these days are debating the size, role, and very existence of the corporate income tax. This Economic Issue analyzes this key business cost.

We looked briefly at the corporate income tax in an earlier chapter. The corporate income tax is a tax on corporate profits. These profits are subject to a progressive tax rate structure, with a maximum tax rate of 46 percent, (See Chapter 7 for more information about public-sector tax rates.) One of the reasons that the corporate income tax is controversial is that it is based upon a calculation of profit that is different from the way that either accountants or economists calculate profit. Accountants figure profit by subtracting explicit costs from total revenues. Economists calculate economic profit by subtracting both explicit and implicit costs from total revenues. The corporate tax laws, however, introduce new definitions of cost into the profit equation. Corporations can reduce taxable profits by taking advantage of loopholes in the tax laws. Economists give the name tax expenditures to tax rules that reduce taxable profit, and therefore decrease taxes, when individuals or firms conduct business in a specific way. Firms that invest in new factories, for example, can receive accelerated depreciation and tax credit advantages. Counter to accepted accounting practices, tax laws allow the cost of some long-lasting goods to be expensed, or depreciated, completely in the current year, rather than being spread out over the working lifetime of the item.

The corporate income tax statutes are full of tax expenditures that allow some firms to reduce taxable profits by producing or investing in particular ways. Are these tax expenditures desirable? The answer to this question depends on how you view the economic effects of tax expenditures. Tax expenditures reduce the tax base of the corporate income tax. With a smaller tax base, higher tax rates are needed to collect the same amount of revenue that would have been taken in without these tax laws. Tax expenditures mean higher tax rates, and therefore, higher taxes for businesses who cannot or do not take advantage of these loopholes. Tax expenditures tend to distort the way corporations used scarce resources. Corporations no longer maximize economic profits, which provides many advantages to the consumer. Now they maximize taxable profits, which can be much different. Scarce resources are diverted to different uses because of the way tax laws make corporations figure profit.

On the other hand, however, many corporate tax expenditures are designed to provide incentives for private firms to use their resources for socially desirable activities. Investment spending, for example, is an area that receives many tax expenditures. Firms are encouraged to invest in new plant, equipment, and technology. They might not invest as heavily without the tax expenditure's incentives. Investment is a requirement for economic growth, so the incentives that tax expenditures provide may enhance the long-run expansion of the economy.

It is an odd tax that can be opposed by both conservative Ronald Reagan and liberal Lester Thurow. However, both liberal and conservative econ-

Change in Fixed Costs: Long Run Changes in fixed costs are absorbed by the firm in the short run, but they can affect supply in the long run. Supply changes in two ways in the long run. First, in the long run, individual competitive firms change fixed inputs and pick new production processes so they can minimize profit. If fixed costs rise, for example, firms might, in the long run, choose a production technique that uses fewer fixed inputs and more variable ones — if such a decision reduces total cost at the desired output level. Many automated production lines in the real world illustrate this process. These adjustments affect market supply.

New firms enter and old firms exit an industry depending on the existence of positive economic profit (which lead to entry) or negative economic profit (which lead to exit). Changing fixed costs, which alter profit in the short run, lead to entry (which increases supply) or exit (which decreases supply) in the long run.

omists and politicians find fault with the corporate income tax on grounds of fairness or equity. The conservative argument against the tax is that it puts an extra tax on corporations that does not apply to partnerships and sole proprietorships. The profits from these forms of business are taxed by the individual income tax when they are paid to the business owners. Corporate profits, on the other hand, are subject to a double tax. Corporate profits are taxed first at the corporate level and again when they are paid out as dividends to corporate shareholders, since the shareholders must pay personal income taxes on the dividends they receive.

How big a difference does this make? Suppose that both a corporate firm and a partnership earn $100 profits. Assume all profits are paid out to business owners. If the partnership owners are in a 50 percent individual tax bracket, they keep $50 of the profits for their own use. If the corporation is in the 46 percent corporate income tax bracket and the shareholders are in the 50 percent individual income tax bracket, however, shareholders keep just $27 of the $100 profit after taxes. The corporation pays 46 percent of its profits to the tax, leaving $54 to be distributed as dividends. The shareholders pay 50 percent of these dividends as personal income taxes, leaving just a $27 after-tax profit. The argument is that this double taxation is unfair because it treats corporate and noncorporate profits differently. Some economists argue that it is inefficient, as well, because the double tax discourages investment in corporate firms.

Liberals find fault with the corporate income tax on other fairness grounds. They suggest that the corporate tax lets some high-income individuals escape taxation. A physician or lawyer might incorporate his or her business for tax purposes, for example. The owners draw a nominal salary from the corporation, keeping individual taxable income low. Most of the firm's profits are retained by the corporation and taxed at the corporation tax rate only. How does this benefit the doctor or lawyer? First, the corporation may be able to purchase tax deductible amenities, such as fancy cars, and treat them as business costs for tax purposes. The business owner in effect receives part of his or her salary in tax-deductible amenities. The second way the doctor or lawyer benefits is because small corporate firms, those with relatively small profits, are not subject to the high tax rates that apply to bigger firms like General Motors or IBM. The owner of a law firm might find it advantageous to incorporate so that firm-retained profits are taxed at a 20 percent corporate income tax rate, rather than at the 50 percent individual income tax rate that might apply if the firm were a partnership, for example.

Many people have called for the reform or removal of the corporate income tax because it distorts resource allocation, imposes unfair double taxation, and allows some individuals and firms to escape taxes they might otherwise have to pay. The corporate tax has declined so much in revenue importance in recent years that a *New York Times* headline made reference to the "quiet repeal" of the tax.[1] Special interest effects, however, are likely to keep the corporate tax on the books in the years ahead. Special interests can sometimes influence Congress to grant them favorable tax treatment that gives them an advantage over other firms, thereby increasing tax rates or reducing tax revenues that the government collects. The corporate tax today is more notable for its tax expenditures, the taxes it does not collect, and their economic effects than for the revenues it generates.

Additional References

Pechman, Joseph A. *Federal Tax Policy,* 3rd ed. Washington, DC: The Brookings Institution, 1977.

Thurow, Lester C. "Abolish the Corporate Income Tax," *Wall Street Journal,* July 6, 1977, p. 12.

Veseth, Michael. *Public Finance.* Reston, VA: Reston Publishing Co., 1984, especially chap. 14.

1. Arenson, Karen W. "The Quiet Repeal of the Corporate Income Tax." *New York Times,* August 2, 1981.

17.21 SUPPLY CHOICES

Change in Demand When demand curves shift, bidding up or driving down market price, the supply curve itself does not change. Changing demand alters price, causing firms to adjust output to the new price = MC output level, but that does not shift supply. A change in demand brings a new price and a movement along the existing supply curve, but supply does not shift unless costs change as described above.

Supply in the Long Run

Producer choice in the short run means picking the profit-maximizing output level, the quantity at which price and marginal costs are equal. Long-run production decisions are more complex. The long-run problem is to choose the optimal plant size, that is, the level of fixed input investment that maximizes profit by minimizing cost. Figure 17-7 shows the long-run producer choice.

FIGURE 17-7

Long-Run *ATC*. Producers pick the plant size that minimizes *ATC* for the planned output level in the long run. If Q_B is the planned long-run production, then the optimal plant size corresponds to the ATC_2 cost curve, since this fixed input expenditure has the lowest *ATC*. Long-run *ATC* curves show how planned costs vary with output in the long run.

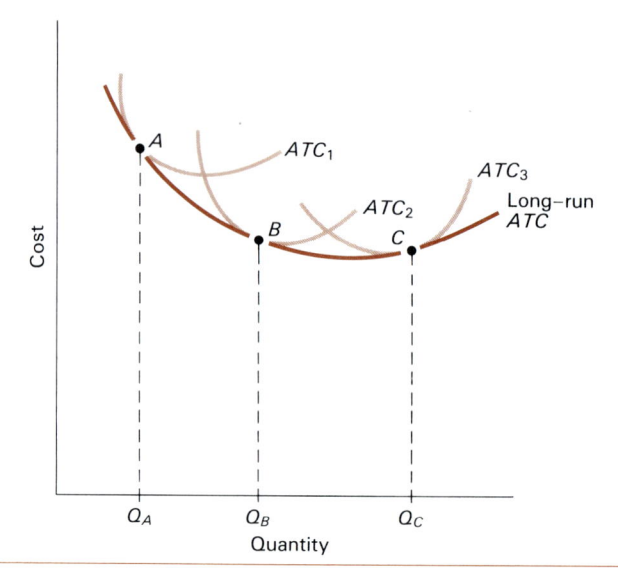

Long-Run *ATC*
The curve connecting segments of the short-run *ATC* curve that illustrates different plant sizes.

Economies of Scale
Factors that reduce average cost as production expands in the long run.

Diseconomies of Scale
Factors that increase average cost as production expands in the long run.

How big should the new plant be? Each of the *ATC* curves in Figure 17-7 corresponds to a different plant size. If the firm's output in the long run is quantity Q_B in the figure, then the plant size corresponding to ATC_2 is appropriate. This fixed input investment minimizes *ATC* and so maximizes profit. Profit in this case is the difference between *ATC* and price at this output level. But this plant size is inefficient if long-run output is higher (Q_C in the figure) or lower (Q_A in the figure). Different plant sizes maximize profits given different long-run supplies.

The long-run *ATC* curve in the figure connects segments of the various short-run *ATC* curves. **Long-run *ATC*** shows how cost and planned output vary for an individual firm in the long run. In the short run, the firm operates wherever price equals marginal cost, given current plant and other fixed inputs. In the long run, however, businesses adjust fixed inputs to place themselves on the long-run *ATC* curve, where *ATC* is minimized and profits maximized.

KEY CONCEPT 17.21

In the long run, firms attempt to adjust fixed inputs to produce at the minimum point on their long-run average total cost curve.

ECONOMIES AND DISECONOMIES OF SCALE

17.22 RETURNS TO SCALE

What do long-run *ATC* curves look like? The answer depends on how business expansion is affected by **economies of scale** and **diseconomies of scale**. Businesses, as they expand, can take advantage of longer production runs, use more efficient large-scale technology, and gain from increasing specialization by workers and managers. They sometimes get better input prices, too, because they order in bulk. These economies of scale tend to reduce production costs, lowering long-run costs.

But expansion isn't always cheaper. Sometimes expanding firms bid up input prices, especially if needed resources are scarce. Bigger production lines are not always more efficient, either. Managerial efficiency can decline in a big, bureaucratic organization. Some big firms lose the entrepreneurial spark and ability to control costs that made them efficient when they were of smaller size.

The shape of the long-run ATC curve depends on which force is greater, the cost-lowering influence of economies of scale or the cost-boosting influence of diseconomy. Three possibilities are shown in Figure 17-8.

Increasing Returns to Scale
Falling long-run *ATC* over the relevant output range.

Increasing returns to scale occur when the long-run ATC is downward sloping. Rising long-run output leads to lower average costs because economies of scale dominate. Bigger firms are more efficient. In general, when a firm faces increasing returns to scale, if it doubles the amount of all the inputs that it uses the firm will produce more than double its output. Markets where increasing returns to scale exist tend to be dominated by relatively few large, efficient producers. There are increasing returns to scale in the computer chip industry, for example. This market is now dominated by a few huge firms that bring costs down by mass producing silicone chips. Smaller firms would not be competitive due to their higher costs.

Constant Returns to Scale
Constant long-run *ATC* over the relevant output range.

Constant returns to scale exist when the forces of economy and diseconomy of scale balance. If the firm doubles the amount of all the inputs it uses, output will double as well. Larger firms have no particular advantage in this situation. Markets experiencing constant returns to scale are often characterized by many firms of roughly equal size.

Decreasing Returns to Scale
Rising long-run *ATC* over the relevant output range.

Decreasing returns to scale exist when diseconomies dominate. Average costs rise, in the long run, as production increases. The advantages of larger plant size are offset by the problems of coordinating a bigger staff, managing larger inventories, and dealing with a wider distribution network. If a firm facing decreasing returns to scale doubles its inputs, it can expect output to expand less than proportionately.

Business firms can sometimes change the shape of their long-run ATC through effective management that reduces diseconomies of scale. A big

FIGURE 17-8   **Returns to Scale and Long-Run *ATC*.** The shape of the long-run *ATC* curve depends on the existence of production economies and diseconomies of scale. (a) A falling long-run *ATC* shows increasing returns to scale, which reduce costs as output expands. (b) Constant returns to scale bring a flat long-run *ATC* curve. (c) *ATC* rises in the long run when decreasing returns to scale are present.

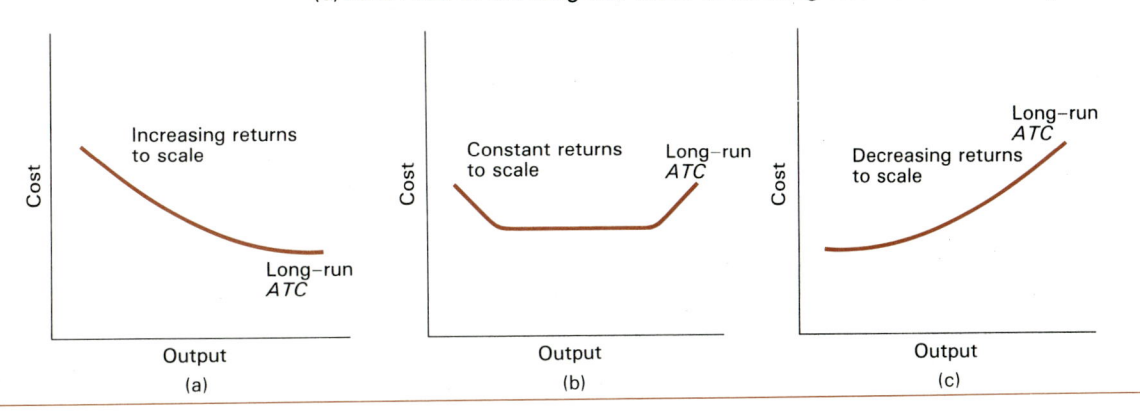

firm, for example, can break itself into smaller divisions, allowing closer monitoring of production techniques and greater cost control.

Economies and diseconomies of scale are important determinants of firm size, but they are not the only ones. The degree of competition in a market also makes a difference. The next two chapters explore the opposite ends of the competitive spectrum—from perfect competition to pure monopoly, with a look at the many shades in between. This analysis puts cost curves to work to see how markets link producers and consumers.

SUMMARY

17.1
1. Sole proprietorships are firms with a single owner who has full claim on profits and full liability for losses. Partnerships are firms that are owned by a group of individuals, each responsible for the debts of the firm and each with a claim on firm profits. Corporations are firms that are owned by many individuals, each with a claim to potential profits but with only limited liability for losses.

17.2
2. There are many possible business objectives, but the theory of supply and costs generally assumes that firms seek to maximize profits.

17.3, 17.4, 17.5
3. The production function describes the way inputs are combined to produce outputs. Some inputs are fixed in the short run. They do not vary with the level of production. Other inputs are variable. Their use rises and falls with output. All inputs are variable in the long run.

17.6
4. Total product rises as more inputs are employed, but diminishing marginal product is commonly encountered. Here, rising incremental use of a given input (all else held constant) adds progressively less to total product.

17.7
5. Explicit costs are out-of-pocket payments the firm must meet. Implicit costs are the opportunity costs the firm's owner bears. The most important implicit cost is foregone profit. Profit is a real cost to the firm.

17.8
6. Accounting profit looks at revenues minus explicit costs; thus it gives an incomplete picture of the status of the firm. Economic profit looks at revenues minus both explicit and implicit costs (like foregone profit); therefore, it is the best measure of a firm's success or failure.

17.9
7. Fixed costs are the cost of fixed inputs. These costs do not vary with output in the short run. Variable costs are the costs of variable outputs. Variable costs depend on the level of production.

17.10, 17.11, 17.12
8. Fixed costs are graphed as straight lines since fixed costs are the same regardless of production level. Variable costs rise as production increases. Total costs are the sums of fixed and variable costs.

17.13
9. Marginal cost is the change in total cost when output changes by one unit; it measures the cost of producing the next (or the last) unit.

Marginal cost falls initially as output expands, but it eventually rises. Diminishing marginal product forces up marginal costs.

17.14 ▶ 10. Average total cost equals total cost divided by the quantity produced. The firm earns positive, negative, or zero economic profits depending on whether price is greater than, less than, or equal to *ATC*. *ATC* falls when *MC* is less than *ATC* because low marginal costs pull down average cost. *ATC* rises when *MC* is greater than *ATC* because high marginal costs push up average cost. The *MC* curve crosses *ATC* at the *ATC* minimum.

17.15 ▶ 11. New firms enter an industry, in the long run, in response to positive economic profit. These profits are profits in excess of those available elsewhere. Firms exit an industry when economic profits are negative, because greater returns are available in other businesses.

17.16 ▶ 12. Average variable cost equals variable cost divided by quantity produced. The firm is able to meet its variable costs so long as price is greater than or equal to *AVC*. The firm is better off shutting down when price is less than *AVC*.

17.17 ▶ 13. Average fixed cost equals fixed cost divided by quantity produced. *AFC* falls as output increases because fixed costs are divided over larger and larger quantities.

17.18 ▶ 14. Marginal revenue is the additional revenue generated by the sale of the next (or last) unit of production. Assuming constant marginal revenue, the firm maximizes profit by producing at the output level at which marginal revenue equals marginal cost. This level of output maximizes profit (or minimizes loss).

17.19 ▶ 15. The firm's marginal cost curve is its supply curve, since it shows the *MR* equals *MC* profit-maximizing quantity for each price. The market supply curve is found by summing the quantities that individual profit-maximizing firms wish to produce at each price.

17.20 ▶ 16. A change in a single firm's variable costs shifts its marginal cost curve and so alters the profit-maximizing output at the going price. A change in just one firm's output does not alter market supply, however. A change in variable (and therefore marginal) cost for many firms alters both individual output choice and shifts the market supply curve. Price changes in the market.

17.20 ▶ 17. A change in fixed costs does not change producer decisions in the short run, since fixed costs do not enter into the *MR* equals *MC* profit calculus. A change in fixed costs in the long run, however, causes market entry if falling fixed costs yield positive economic profits or market exit if rising fixed costs cause negative economic profit.

17.20 ▶ 18. Changes in demand affect market price but do not shift cost curves. Firms move along their existing individual cost curves to the new profit-maximizing equilibrium.

17.21 ▶ 19. Fixed inputs can be varied in the long run as the firm adjusts to changes in price and quantity. Firms adjust fixed inputs to minimize *ATC* at the

522 Supply and the Costs of Production

intended output level, since this maximizes profits. The long-run *ATC* curve shows how quantity and *ATC* vary for the firm in the long run as fixed inputs are adjusted.

> 17.22

20. Increasing returns to scale exist when the long-run *ATC* curve is downward sloping. Average costs fall in the long run as plant size is expanded. Constant returns to scale generate a flat long-run *ATC* curve. Average costs remain the same as plant size increases. Decreasing returns to scale generate an upward-sloping *ATC* curve. Bigger plants are not as efficient as smaller ones, as their higher average costs indicate.

DISCUSSION QUESTIONS

> 17.9, 17.13, 17.14, 17.16, 17.17

1. The following table shows cost figures for a hypothetical firm, with many of the entries left blank. Use what you've learned about cost in this chapter to calculate the various cost measures and fill in the blanks. Be prepared to explain how you arrived at your answers.

Quantity	Fixed cost ($)	Variable cost ($)	Total cost ($)	MC ($)	ATC ($)	AVC ($)	AFC ($)
0	100	0	100				
1	100	20	120	20	120	20	100
2	100	30	130	10	65	15	50
3	100	35	135	5	45	11.67	33.3
4	100	44	144	9	36	11	25
5	100	60	160	16	32	12	20
6	100	80	180	20	30	13.3	16.67
7	100	105	205	25	29.29	15	14.29
8	100	140	240	35	30	17.50	12.5
9	100	190	290	50	32.22	21.11	11.11
10	100	270	370	80	37	27	10

> 17.10, 17.11, 17.12

2. Plot the cost curves from the completed table in Question 1. What properties would you expect each curve to display? Do the curves you've plotted display these characteristics? Explain.

> 17.18

3. Suppose that market price is $25 for the output of the firm in Question 1. What is the profit-maximizing output? Does the firm earn an economic profit? If so, how much? Should the firm produce at all? Explain.

> 17.14, 17.16

4. State, in your own words, the relationship between the marginal cost curve and the *ATC* and *AVC* curves. Explain why this relationship holds.

> 17.10, 17.13, 17.14, 17.16

5. Draw the *MC*, *ATC* and *AVC* curves for a typical firm. What happens to each curve if:
   a. fixed costs increase
   b. marginal costs increase
   c. both fixed and marginal costs increase

17.21

6. How do producer choices differ between the short run and the long run? (Hint: What variables does the firm control in the short run? The long run?) Explain.

17.14, 17.21, 17.22

7. The following table presents the long-run average total cost data for three firms at various levels of output. Graph the long-run average total cost curves for each firm over the range of output given. State whether each firm is encountering increasing, constant, or decreasing returns to scale over that portion of its long-run average total cost curve for which you have data.

Output (in units)	FIRM 1 ATC ($)	FIRM 2 ATC ($)	FIRM 3 ATC ($)
10,000	2.00	2.00	2.00
20,000	1.75	2.00	2.25
30,000	1.50	2.00	2.50
40,000	1.25	2.00	2.75
50,000	1.00	2.00	3.00
60,000	.75	2.00	3.25

SELECTED READINGS

Alchain, Armen A. "Costs and Outputs." Reprinted in Breit, William, and Hochman, Harold M. (Eds.), *Readings in Microeconomics*, 2nd ed. New York: Holt, Rinehart, and Winston, 1971.

Buchanan, James M. *Cost and Choice*. Chicago: Markham, 1968.

Knight, Frank H. *Risk, Uncertainty, and Profit*. Boston: Houghton Mifflin, 1921.

Stigler, George J. "The Division of Labor Is Limited by the Extent of the Market." Reprinted in Breit, William, and Hochman, Harold M. (Eds.), *Readings in Microeconomics*, 2nd ed. New York: Holt, Rinehart, and Winston, 1971.

Stigler, George J. "The Economics of Scale." *Journal of Law and Economics* (October, 1958): pp. 54–71.

CHAPTER 18

Perfect Competition in the Marketplace

Having read the chapter, reviewed the chapter summary, and completed the *Study Guide* exercises, you should be able to:

CRIS

18.1 PERFECT COMPETITION: Define perfect competition and explain how economists use the model of perfect competition to increase understanding of real-world markets.

18.2 ASSUMPTIONS OF PERFECT COMPETITION: List and explain the six assumptions of perfect competition and explain why each is important to the functioning of a competitive market.

18.3 PRICE TAKERS: Explain what a price taker is and why competitive producers and consumers are assumed to be price takers.

18.4 ATOMISTIC COMPETITION: Explain what atomistic competition is and how it is related to perfect competition.

18.5 IDENTICAL PRODUCTS: Explain how the assumption of identical products assures that there is just one price in each market.

18.6 PERFECTLY COMPETITIVE COSTS: Draw *MR, MC,* and *ATC* curves for an individual firm in a perfectly competitive market, show the profit-maximizing level of output and explain why profits are maximized there, then discuss the relationship between market demand and the demand or marginal revenue curve perceived by individual suppliers.

18.7 ECONOMIC PROFIT: Explain why economic profits may be either positive, negative, or zero for individual firms in the short run and explain the long-run consequences of each short-run profit level.

18.8 ADJUSTMENTS TO DEMAND: Explain how both individual firms and market supply adjust to an increase in demand in the very short-run, short-run, and long-run time frames and draw figures to illustrate these adjustments.

18.9 ADJUSTMENTS AND SUPPLY: Discuss the impact of entry, exit, and plant-size adjustments on supply in the long run and analyze the determinants of the shape of the long-run supply curve.

18.10 ELASTICITY OF SUPPLY: Define elasticity of supply, explain the difference between elastic and inelastic supply curves, and discuss the determinants of supply elasticity in the very short-run, short-run, and long-run time frames.

18.11 ELASTICITY AND TIME FRAME: Explain why supply tends to be more elastic as the time frame considered lengthens.

18.12 PRICE-CEILING EFFECTS: Explain how a price ceiling affects a perfectly competitive market in the very short-run, short-run, and long-run time frames.

18.13 ECONOMIC EFFICIENCY: Define economic efficiency and explain, using supply and demand curves, how perfectly competitive markets automatically achieve it.

18.14 THE INVISIBLE HAND: Explain what is meant by the invisible hand of the marketplace, explain what goal it achieves, and name the economist who first discussed it.

18.15 MARKET FAILURES: List and define market failures that violate the assumptions of perfect competition.

Markets are the set of institutions where the many buyers and sellers you read about in previous chapters come together to set price and decide how society's scarce resources are allocated. Markets help determine how much scarce land, labor, and capital goes to make corn and how much is used to produce computer discs, for example. Markets are where that most important economic activity takes place: exchange.

In a mutually advantageous exchange, consumers trade their money for goods and sellers trade their goods for money (which buys other goods). Buyers and sellers make a 'fair' exchange, for example, trading $50 cash for goods worth $50, and both buyer and seller gain. We know they both gain because exchange is voluntary. They would not complete a transaction if it didn't benefit them.

Exchange makes both trading parties better off, and a significant portion of production and consumption activities are centered around competitive markets where these exchange transactions are efficiently completed. This chapter presents a simple economic model of a competitive market and uses that model to explore the interrelationship between the entire market and the individual firm. We will see how firms and markets adjust, and we will explore the important characteristics of competition. We will also identify and analyze some of the factors that can cause markets to function with less efficiency than the economic ideal.

COMPETITION AS A PROCESS

It is important to realize the role played by the process of competition in the economy because it is an extremely beneficial force. Competition in the marketplace benefits both the producer and the consumer. The fact that firms must compete with each other for the consumers' dollars means that each producer must attempt to provide better quality goods at a lower price to attract the consumer. It also means that firms must attempt to provide substitutes that offer the consumer a wider range of choices in the marketplace and that no single producer in the market can restrict supply and force consumers to pay artificially higher prices. If one firm fails to offer high quality goods and lower prices or to provide substitute choices to the consumer, another firm will.

On the demand side of the market, the buying power of consumers is diverse. Each consumer must compete with all the other consumers for scarce goods and services. Demand-side competition prevents a single consumer from restricting demand and forcing the producer to sell at an artificially low price. If one consumer refuses to buy, this does not necessarily mean that all others will follow suit. This helps the market to function more efficiently to bring buyers and sellers together and increase the possibility of mutually beneficial exchange.

Perfect Competition

Before we begin the explanation of the perfectly competitive model, a word about terminology is in order. The terms competition and perfect competition are frequently used interchangeably in economics. However, it is necessary to make a distinction between them at this point in the text. Competition, as we use the term here, implies the process of competition or rivalry between sellers or buyers. The term perfect competition refers to the perfectly competitive model market structure presented in this chapter.

Each market is different. The markets for bath soap and fluorescent lights both depend on supply and demand forces, but they are quite different in other ways. Producers make different goods using different inputs, and they face different costs. Buyers are different, as well. They make purchases in different quantities for different reasons with different income and price elasticities.

> **18.1 PERFECT COMPETITION**
>
> **Perfect Competition**
> The model of an ideal market; a market characterized by many buyers and sellers trading identical products under conditions of perfect information, free entry and exit, and zero transactions costs.
>
> **18.2 ASSUMPTIONS OF PERFECT COMPETITION**

In a world of confusing differences, there is an advantage to simplification. By stripping markets to their basics and searching the bare bones for shared properties, economists can more easily come to understand the market process. This is what economists have done with the economic model of **perfect competition**. Perfect competition describes a simple, standardized market for a particular type of good. Economists analyze the perfectly competitive market to see more clearly the powerful forces that are at work in all competitive markets, even those that do not fit the ideal mold. The model of perfect competition helps us understand the underlying forces that operate in the seemingly dissimilar markets in the real world.

Perfect competition models an ideal competitive market, one where pure competition sets the pace. It includes those market properties that promote active competition among buyers and sellers and encourage free exchange of goods and services. The model of perfect competition is built upon the assumptions of many buyers, many sellers, identical products, free entry and exit, perfect information, and zero transaction costs.

> **18.3 PRICE TAKERS**
>
> **Price Takers**
> Individual buyers and sellers who behave as if they cannot alter market price through buying or selling.

> **18.4 ATOMISTIC COMPETITION**
>
> **Atomistic Competition**
> Competitive markets in which individual buyers and sellers are too small to affect prices.

Many Buyers There are thousands of individual buyers in a perfectly competitive market. Each individual demand is so small, compared to the larger market demand, that it has no effect on price. Buyers are therefore **price takers**. Market demand and price do not change if one or two buyers change their minds. Demand curves only respond to broader forces. The market, not individual buyers, sets price in perfect competition.

Many Sellers As we discussed in the last chapter, there are many independent producers, each supplying goods based on costs and price. Each seller is relatively tiny (like an atom) compared to bigger market forces, so the name **atomistic competition** is sometimes used to describe this situation. The market is so large relative to the individual seller than a change in the amount an individual seller is willing to supply to the market has no effect on market price. Therefore, no individual firm can impose price. Sellers are price takers, too. The market, not individual producers, sets price.

> **18.5 IDENTICAL PRODUCTS**

Identical Products A key assumption of perfect competition is that all goods produced in a given market are identical. Goods of different quality or with different characteristics are sold in different markets. This assumption is important because it means that price, not quality or advertised image, is what counts. Consumers make purchasing choices among goods based on their relative prices. Producers who try to charge more than market price attract no buyers. Price is the key variable for both buyers and sellers.

Free Entry and Exit Firms are free to enter markets when positive economic profit attracts them and free to leave or exit if negative economic profits persist. Free entry and exit is an important stimulus to competition. No individual seller can expect to earn economic profits for long if other firms are free to enter the industry and compete for the customers' dollars.

Perfect Information Buyers and sellers are assumed to be knowledgeable about the markets and goods involved. Price is common knowledge. There are no technological secrets that give one firm an advantage over others. Perfect information also means that all buyers and sellers in a given market trade at the same price. No secret discounts or illicit markups are possible.

Zero Transactions Costs The process of buying and selling is itself costless. Firms and consumers agree on price without negotiation expense or costly lawsuits to determine who has the right to sell what. This assumption assures that all mutually advantageous transactions take place and that demand and supply curves accurately reflect buyer benefit and seller cost.

Let's see how this ideal market works. The lessons learned transfer easily to real-world markets that do not meet all six perfect competition criteria. Industries that fail one or more of the perfect competition tests often demonstrate a sufficient degree of competitiveness to bring their actions and reactions into a close approximation of this competitive model. The model of perfect competition yields analyses and conclusions that contribute a great deal toward describing an imperfect real world.

The Firm in a Perfectly Competitive Market

Individual firms in a perfectly competitive market take price as given. It is a piece of information that they cannot change and therefore is one to which

528 *Perfect Competition in the Marketplace*

FIGURE 18-1 **Market and Typical Competitive Firm.** (a) Market supply and demand, made up of thousands of individual buyers and sellers, set price. (b) A typical price-taking firm maximizes profit by setting output where marginal cost equals marginal revenue (market price). This market is in long-run equilibrium, where price equals ATC and zero economic profits prevail.

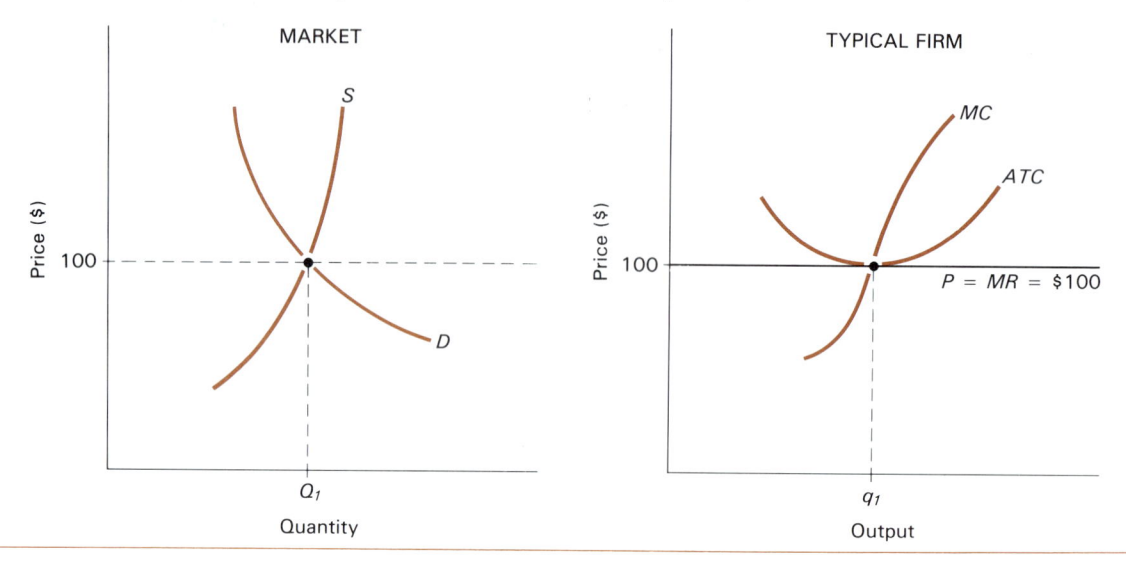

18.6 PERFECTLY COMPETITIVE CURVES

Average Revenue (AR)
Total revenue divided by the units sold; the per-unit revenue received by the firm.

they must adjust. Figure 18-1 shows the perceived relationship between the market and the firm.

Price is set in the market by the broad forces of market supply and market demand. Thousands of sellers and thousands of buyers, acting independently, determine equilibrium price. If price is above equilibrium, the surplus of goods drives down price. A price below equilibrium brings shortage and forces up price. Quantity supplied equals quantity demanded at equilibrium. Both buyers and sellers exchange desired amounts.

Since single firms lack the power to decrease market supply, no individual firm can force up the price of its goods by offering to sell less. Conversely, an individual firm cannot drive down price by flooding the market and attempting to cause a surplus. The individual firm's increased output is insignificant in the vastly larger market supply.

Even if an individual firm's production decisions cannot alter price, the firm must still attempt to determine what output will maximize its profits. Figure 18-1 illustrates how individual firms in a perfectly competitive market determine their profit-maximizing output. Individual firms are price takers. They behave as if they face a horizontal, perfectly elastic demand curve. They behave as if they can sell any quantity they can produce at the going market price. As far as individual firms are concerned, market price is constant regardless of quantity sold. This implies that **average revenue** (**AR**), total revenue divided by units sold, is the equal-to price, since all units are sold at the same price. (This is easy to see with some simple algebra. Let P stand for price and Q stand for quantity. If $TR = PQ$ and $AR = TR/Q$, then $AR = P$ if all units are sold at the same price.)

Table 18-1 shows how the individual firm's marginal revenue and average revenue curves are derived. If the firm's management assumes the firm can sell any quantity of desks for a per-unit price of $100 (the market equilibrium price in Figure 18-1), then the firm's total revenues are given by the second column of the table (total revenue equals price times quantity sold).

TABLE 18-1

Marginal and Average Revenues for an Individual Firm

(1) Quantity sold by individual firm	(2) Market price ($)	(3) Total revenue (1) × (2) ($)	Marginal revenue ($)	Average revenue (3) ÷ (1) ($)
1	100	100	100	100
2	100	200	100	100
3	100	300	100	100
4	100	400	100	100
5	100	500	100	100
6	100	600	100	100
7	100	700	100	100
8	100	800	100	100
9	100	900	100	100
10	100	1000		100

Since price does not vary with the individual firm's production level, average revenue and marginal revenue are both constant and equal to price. This relationship gives the horizontal MR curve for the individual firm (not for the market) shown in Figure 18-1. It would be beneficial practice for you to work through the math in Table 18-1 to see from where average and marginal revenue curves are derived.

Individual firms behave as if they can sell as much output as they can produce at the going price, which, in fact, they can. Producer choice in the short run, therefore, follows the outline sketched in the last chapter. Firms maximize profit by setting output at the level at which marginal revenue (price) equals marginal cost (see Figure 18-1). The amounts produced by individual firms at different prices add up to the market supply curve used in earlier chapters.

KEY CONCEPT 18.6

The profit maximization rule for perfect competitors states that firms produce at the output level at which marginal revenue equals marginal cost.

MARKET AND FIRM EQUILIBRIUM

Equilibrium of the Firm
The output level at which the firm maximizes profit; the point where marginal revenue equals marginal cost.

Figure 18-1 shows a market and a typical firm in equilibrium. The equilibrium price is $100 and no shortage or surplus exists that would tend to cause a change in price. The typical firm has found the profit-maximizing **equilibrium of the firm,** producing where marginal revenue (price or average revenue) equals marginal cost.

Equilibrium and Profit

18.7 ECONOMIC PROFIT

At equilibrium the typical firm has three short-run possibilities in regard to profit. These are illustrated in Figure 18-2. The first possibility, shown in both Figure 18-1 and 18-2, is a zero-profit equilibrium. The profit-maximizing output corresponds to the quantity at which price equals ATC, total revenue equals total costs, and economic profits are zero.

FIGURE 18-2

Firm Equilibrium in the Short Run. Individual firms earn (a) zero, (b) positive, or (c) negative economic profits in the short run, depending on the relationship between price and ATC. Long-run adjustments tend to drive out profits.

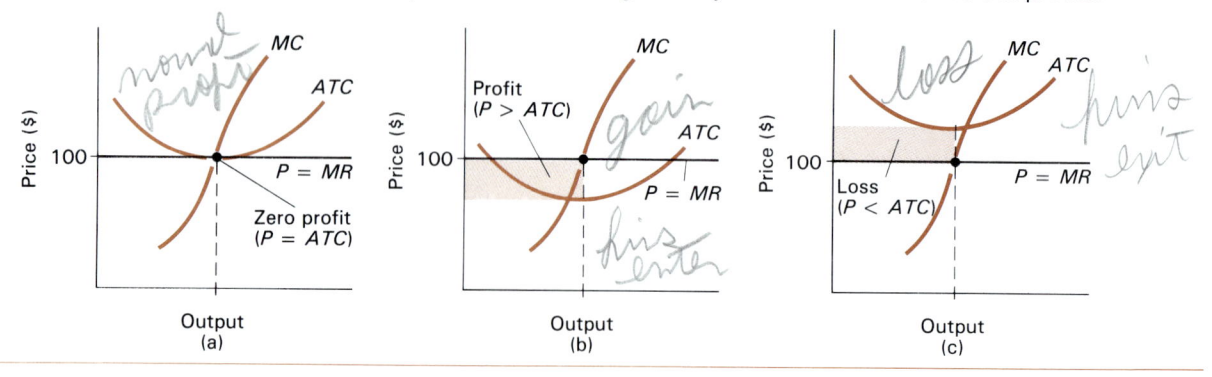

Why would a firm produce without profits? One important point raised in the last chapter is that economic costs include normal profit. A firm, like the one in Figure 18-2(a), that earns zero economic profit is receiving as high a return as that available elsewhere in the economy. There is no reason to exit from the industry because no better alternative exists elsewhere, but there is also no reason for other firms to enter the market either.

Positive economic profit, illustrated in Figure 18-2(b), is the second possibility. Price exceeds ATC at the firm equilibrium in this instance. The shaded area measures the short-run economic profits. Short-run economic profits, if they persist, attract other firms to the industry in the long run. Entry into the industry eventually increases market supply and drives price back down toward the zero-profit level.

Short-run equilibrium with a loss, or negative economic profit in the vocabulary of economics, is the third possibility as illustrated in Figure 18-2(c). This firm maximizes profits, like the others, at the output level at which price equals marginal cost. But this price is less than the average total cost of production. This market price is not high enough to cover production costs. The total loss is measured by the shaded rectangle of the figure. While this firm might earn an accounting profit in instances where revenues are more than out-of-pocket costs, it clearly makes a negative economic profit. Negative economic profit means the firm earns less than the owner would receive on a similar investment in another industry.

To understand why a firm would continue to produce while earning an economic loss, it is necessary to recall the logic of the last chapter. Fixed costs must be paid whether the firm produces or not, so they are irrelevant to short-run decision making. The firm minimizes its loss by producing at the level at which price equals marginal cost, so long as revenues at least cover variable costs. If revenues do not cover the variable costs of production, the firm loses less by shutting down.

The firm that incurs short-run losses cannot, however, last in the long run. These firms will eventually exit from the industry. When firms exit a market there is a decrease in supply in the long run, which produces a supply–demand shortage and eventually a higher market price. Losses tend to disappear for the remaining firms as price rises.

Firms earn positive, negative, or zero economic profit at equilibrium in the short run, depending on whether price is above, below, or equal to average total cost. In the long run, however, entry and exit tend to drive away profit and loss, leaving the long run equilibrium shown in Figure 18-1. The long-run equilibrium is characterized by supply–demand equilibrium in

PROMINENT ECONOMIST

Friedrich-August vonHayek (1899–   )

Friedrich-August vonHayek was born in Vienna in 1899. After graduating from the University of Vienna at age 22, he entered the Austrian Civil Service for six years, then served for four years as the Director of the Austrian Institute for Economic Research. In 1931, he accepted the Tooke Chair of Economic Science at London University, becoming a British citizen six years later. In 1950, he moved to the United States, where he found a position with the University of Chicago in the social and moral sciences. This academic climate was to prove to be ideal for his developing philosophies.

All of Hayek's early publications were focused on the problems of economic stability. His theories were greatly influenced by the high inflation of the 1920s. Some of these early publications were *Prices and Production* (1931), *Monetary Theory and the Trade Cycle* (1926, 1933), and *Monetary Nationalism and International Instability* (1937). Two of his best-known works were *Profits, Interest and Investment* (1939) and *The Pure Theory of Capital* (1941). In these, he focused his attention on resources allocated to producing capital goods and the demand for the consumer goods that are produced by capital goods.

While at the University of Chicago, Hayek directed his attentions to the importance of individual freedom in such works as *The Political Ideal of the Rule of Law* (1955) and *Law, Legislation and Liberty* (1973, 1976, 1979; 3 volumes). Hayek suggested that economic freedom must be maintained in order to guarantee individual freedom. Consequently, he opposed socialism. Hayek suggested that government should only use its power to provide services that the market is unable to provide and to provide a framework for the market. It is this aspect of his career for which Hayek has become most recognized.

In 1974, Hayek was awarded the Nobel Prize for Economics. With his diverse background and dedication to his work, Hayek has contributed significantly to the field of economics.

the market (hence, no pressure on price), with the typical firm earning zero economic profit.

Two Important Functions of Profit

Profit is an important economic signal. First, profit tells entrepreneurs which markets to enter. Positive economic profits attract new firms. Profit also indicates which markets to leave, since negative economic profits force firms to exit. Firms use the profit signal as a guide to their production and investment choices.

Profit also serves to separate successful, efficient firms who remain in business from less efficient ones who, because of high costs, fail and exit. Profit, not government regulations or other artificial devices, determines the allocation of scarce resources among competing ends in the competitive market.

MARKET ADJUSTMENT TO CHANGING DEMAND

Market equilibrium is not only important, it is dynamic in nature. Supply and demand curves frequently shift, sending the market in search of a new equilibrium. The following example, illustrated in Figure 18-3, explains how the market and its constituent firms adjust to changing conditions.

FIGURE 18-3

Adjustment to Increased Demand. Demand increases from D_0 to D_1. Price alone changes in the very short run. Firms adjust output to the higher price in the short run, moving market equilibrium from A to B and typical firm equilibrium from X to Y. Entry increases supply in the long run, moving market equilibrium to C and firm equilibrium to X, assuming no long-run cost changes. The long-run supply curve S_{lr} shows how price varies with quantity supplied in the long run.

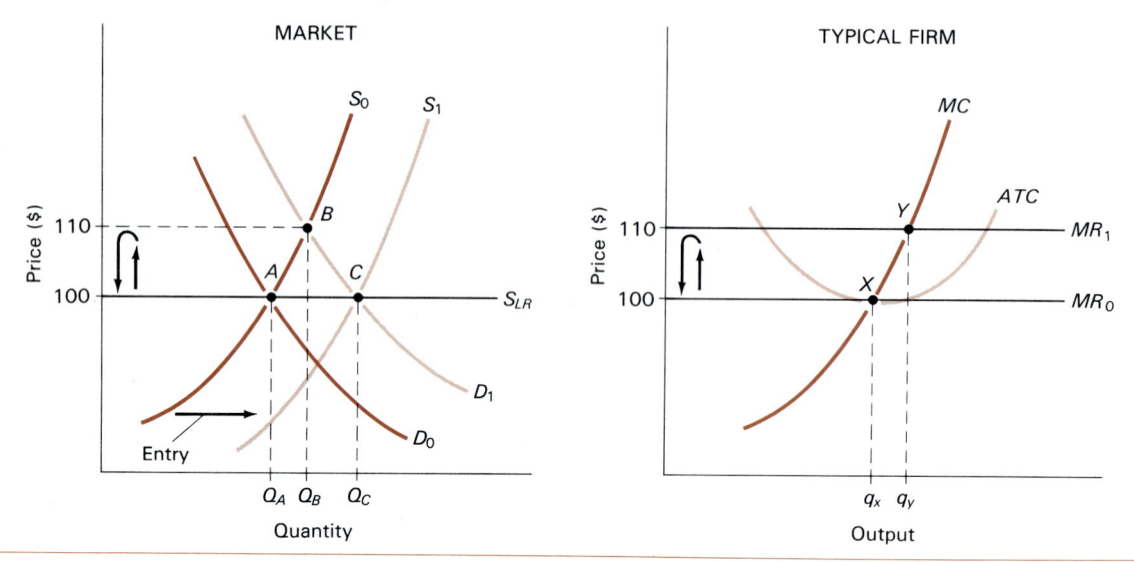

The perfectly competitive market for desks is shown in Figure 18-3. There are thousands of producers, each making identical goods, and thousands of buyers, each searching for the lowest price. No barriers to entry or exit exist. All traders have complete information of market conditions. There are no transaction costs to keep buyers and sellers from making mutually advantageous exchanges.

The market has found equilibrium at point A in the figure, where equilibrium price is $100 per desk. The typical firm shown here is in long-run equilibrium. It maximizes profits at point X, where marginal cost equals marginal revenue (price) of $100. The average total cost is $100 at this output level, so zero economic profits are earned. This means that the desk-producing profits are equal to opportunity cost. The owner of the typical firm has no incentive to exit from the industry because no better profits are possible elsewhere. There is also no positive economic profit incentive for others to enter the market. This is the starting point for our analysis.

Let's assume that a profound event is about to to disturb the desk market. Millions of consumers are about to buy personal computers to play games, keep accounts, and process words. Each computer needs a place to rest — a desk. The demand for desks thus shifts from D_0 to D_1 in the figure. As a result, market equilibrium shifts from point A to point B, equilibrium price rises from $100 to $110 per desk, and equilibrium quantity increases from Q_A to Q_B.

Very Short Run
A time period so short that firms are unable to change output.

18.8 ADJUSTMENTS TO DEMAND

Short-Run Adjustments

The typical firm responds to changing demand differently depending upon the time frame within which it must complete the adjustment. In the **very short run** the firm's hands are tied. It takes a little time to arrange for increased output. For example, the firm must have time to buy more raw materials and hire more labor. Price, not quantity, adjusts in the very short run. The typical firm continues to produce at X (quantity q_x) in the figure and earns positive economic profits from higher price in this brief time span.

The output level (q_x) that maximized profit at the old price of $100 per desk does not do so at the new, higher equilibrium price of $110. The firm adjusts production in the short run to maximize profits, given the new market conditions. Profits peak at the output level where marginal cost equals marginal revenue (price) of $110. ($q_y$). The firm's short-run adjustment is to move along its marginal cost curve, producing a greater quantity at the higher market price. Short-run equilibrium occurs when the market finds supply–demand equilibrium (at point B) and individual firms again maximize profits, given the market price (at point Y).

Long-Run Adjustments

18.8 ADJUSTMENTS TO DEMAND

Firms adjust to new market conditions in two ways in the long run. First, firms enter into or exit from industries in the long run, buying or selling fixed inputs, depending on whether economic profit or loss prevails. Second, firms adjust their use of fixed inputs, altering plant size and changing technology, depending on their long-run output plans. Both of these adjustments influence long-run market supply.

18.9 ADJUSTMENTS AND SUPPLY

Figure 18-3 shows one long-run supply adjustment possibility. The figure here assumes that cost conditions are unchanged in the long run, so the only adjustment is through entry and exit. This assumption makes the diagram easier to follow and gives the flavor of long-run adjustment. Adjustment in the real world would be more complex, with entry and exit taking place alongside shifting marginal and average cost curves as existing firms adjust plant size to higher output totals.

The typical firm's short-run equilibrium at point Y shows an economic profit. Price ($110) exceeds average total cost. New firms enter the industry in the long run to gain a piece of these profits. Entry shifts the supply curve from S_0 to S_1 in the figure. The new market equilibrium is at C, at the old price of $100 per desk. Entry brings down price in the long run, and individual firms adjust output to the new price. The typical firm produces at X in the long run.

In the long run, price adjusts differently than output to changes in demand. Price does not necessarily go back to its original value in the long run, as shown in Figure 18-3. Long-run price adjustments produce the long-run supply curve, S_{lr} in Figure 18-3, which links the long-run equilibriums. The shape of the long-run supply curve depends on the degree of entry or exit and the way costs change when output and plant size rise or fall in the long run. There are three possibilities. Firms can have constant, increasing, or decreasing returns to scale.

The long-run supply curve is flat in an industry with constant returns to scale. Price may rise in the short run, in response to rising demand, but it returns to its old level in the long run. Constant returns to scale means constant long-run costs.

Industries with increasing returns to scale (decreasing costs) tend to have downward-sloping long-run supply curves. Higher quantity in these industries comes with lower cost in the long run. Price may rise in the short run, if demand increases, but long-run adjustments increase supply enough to provide lower costs and prices.

Firms with decreasing returns to scale (increasing costs) tend to have upward-sloping long-run supply curves. Higher output comes with higher

534 Perfect Competition in the Marketplace

price, even in the long run, in these industries. These different long-run supply curves were illustrated in Chapter 17.

Elasticity of Supply

So far in this chapter we have seen that changes in market price bring about changes in the quantity that firms are willing to supply to the market. An important consideration, however, is how much quantity supplied changes in response to a price change. In effect, it would be quite valuable to know how sensitive quantity supplied is to changes in market price. The concept of **elasticity of supply** enables us to measure this price sensitivity. Supply elasticity is the percentage change in quantity supplied divided by the percentage change in price. Elasticity of supply is just like the demand elasticity concepts presented in Chapter 16 with "quantity supplied" substituted for "quantity demanded."

Time frame is the most powerful determinant of supply elasticity. Supply responses differ in important ways depending upon whether very short-run, short-run, or long-run time frames are being considered. In addition, other factors determine supply response within each time frame. Figure 18-4 shows supply curves of differing elasticity.

Very Short Run The very short run is a time frame so short that firms cannot adjust production in response to changing market conditions. Supply is fixed in the very short run, giving the perfectly inelastic supply curve shown in Figure 18-4(a). Quantity supplied cannot vary in the very short run, so price alone responds to changing demand.

How long is the very short run? The answer is that this time frame varies from industry to industry. Some firms with large inventories of standardized goods can respond smoothly to market events. These firms can increase quantity supplied without much difficulty, so their supply curves do not display the completely inelastic shape shown in Figure 18-4(a). Other firms find the very short run to be much longer. Firms that are operating at full capacity or that build special-order goods cannot quickly gear up to meet sudden increases in demand. They can only raise price and fill their order books in the very short run. They slowly put together the resources to expand output in the future.

Short Run The short run is the time period in which firms adjust to changing prices by moving along their marginal cost curves, finding the new output level where *MR* equals *MC*. The short-run supply curve takes the shape of the firms' combined marginal cost curves for a given market. Supply may be relatively inelastic, as in Figure 18-4(b), or more elastic, as in Figure 18-4(c). Supply elasticity depends in this instance on how marginal costs vary with output. If incremental costs rise slowly with output, supply will tend to be elastic. If costs rise quickly, supply will be more inelastic. What determines which case prevails? Short-run supply elasticity depends on production technology and how close firms are to their maximum capacity. Supply tends to be more inelastic when capacity limits are reached in the short run.

Long Run Many factors affect supply curves in the long run. Supply curves may be inelastic, elastic, perfectly elastic, as shown in Figure 18-4(d), or even downward sloping if economies of scale are present. Supply elasticity depends on the interplay of returns to scale, entry and exit, and the way that input costs change as whole industries expand or contract. In

---

18.10 ELASTICITY OF SUPPLY

Elasticity of Supply
A measure of supply response to changing prices; the percentage change in quantity supplied divided by the percentage change in price.

18.11 ELASTICITY AND TIME FRAME

FIGURE 18-4

Elasticity of Supply. Supply is perfectly inelastic in the very short run, as (a) shows. Supply can be either inelastic (b) or relatively elastic (c) in the short run. Long-run supply curves can take on many shapes, like the perfectly elastic supply curve in (d). Figure (e) shows how the supply curve rotates over time, becoming more elastic as the time frame lengthens.

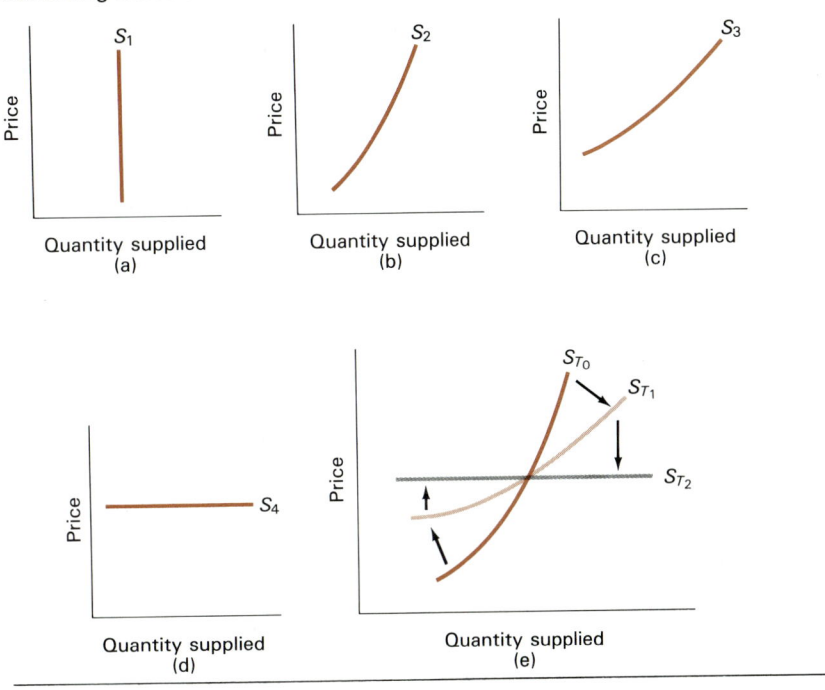

general, supply curves tend to be more elastic in the long run than in the short run because the long run allows firms to adjust plant size to changing market conditions. This allows a greater quantity response to a given change in price. In the short run, when price rises, for example, firms can only move along existing marginal cost curves by more fully using existing capacity. In the long run, however, firms can build bigger plants, thereby producing even more goods at the same price. Bigger quantity response makes for a more elastic supply curve. Figure 18-4(e) illustrates the way supply curves change shape over time, becoming more elastic in the long run.

APPLICATION: PRICE CEILINGS

18.12 PRICE-CEILING EFFECTS

When government imposes regulations such as price ceilings, both firms and markets must adjust. This introduces a new element to the market model we have developed. Figure 18-5 and the following example illustrate this point.

For purpose of analysis, suppose Congress is concerned that the high price of gasoline is placing an unfair burden on lower-income citizens and is considering a law that puts a ceiling price of $.80 on each gallon. The consequences of this regulation are illustrated in Figure 18-5. The gasoline market is in long-run equilibrium at a price of $1. Market equilibrium is at point A, and typical firms earn zero economic profit at point X. Once a ceiling price of $.80 is imposed, the quantity demanded rises from A to C, a movement along the demand curve, while the quantity supplied falls from A

FIGURE 18-5

Price Ceiling in Short and Long Run. The $.80 price ceiling moves this market away from long-run equilibrium. The lower price increases quantity demanded from A to C, while moving quantity supplied in the short run from A to B. The typical firm sets output at X before the ceiling and at Y after it. Negative economic profits in the short run produce exit in the long run. This shifts the supply curve and produces an even smaller quantity supplied, D.

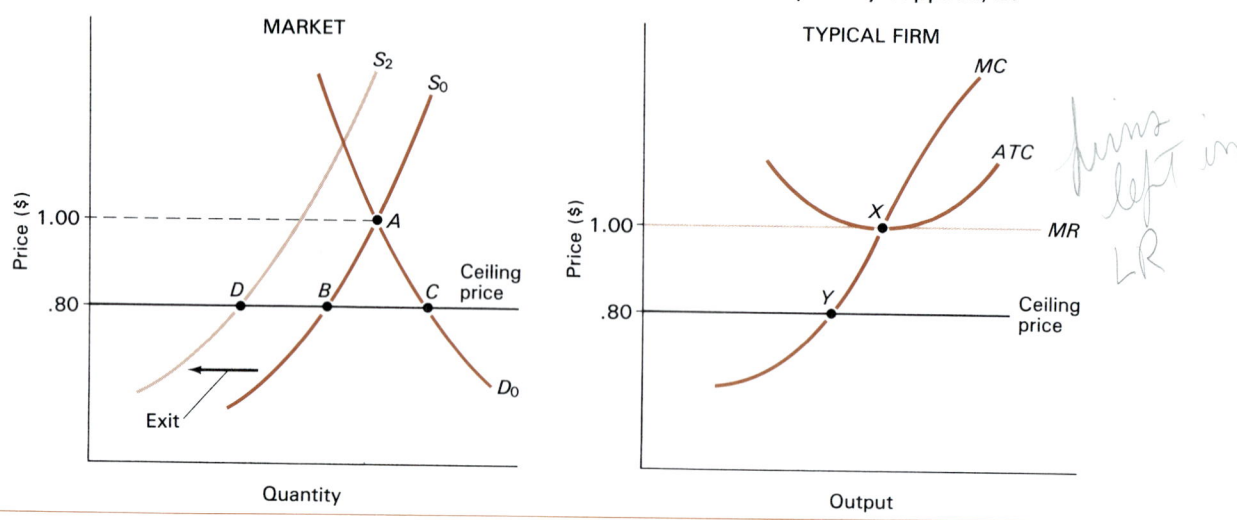

to B, a movement along the supply curve. The price ceiling creates a shortage of gasoline at the $.80 maximum price.

The firm adjusts to the ceiling in several ways. In the very short run, as noted before, output is fixed and only price changes. The typical firm continues to produce at X and suffers drastically reduced profits. In the short run, when output decisions are made, firms move to the new profit-maximizing point Y, where marginal cost equals marginal revenue (price) of $.80. The market moves along its supply curve from A to B as individual firms move along their marginal cost curves from X to Y.

The long-run adjustment is more complex. The typical firm shown in Figure 18-5 earns a negative economic profit at the $.80 price. It maximizes profits by losing money because price is less than ATC. The firm shuts down if the $.80 price is less than AVC. Firms live with these losses in the short run, but they adjust in the long run. If costs cannot be altered, the main adjustment is exit. Firms leave the industry, seeking higher profits elsewhere, shifting supply in the long run to S_2 in the figure. This long-run adjustment makes the shortage even bigger at the $.80 ceiling price. Firms supply D, while consumers demand the much larger A.

If all firms' cost curves looked like the typical firm in the figure, and they could not be altered in the long run, then this market would be doomed. No firm can earn a normal profit at the $.80 ceiling price. All firms exit, and the gasoline industry has been regulated out of business.

The long-run effects of regulation on markets depend on the long-run costs of the firm. Firms that exit from the gasoline industry are forced to sell off their fixed inputs, and by producing less, they reduce demand for variable inputs. These actions lower resource costs to the firms that remain in the industry. If costs fall enough, a new long-run equilibrium may be established at the ceiling price, with the firms that remain in the industry breaking even at $.80 because of lower costs. A shortage still exists, but production continues.

Black Market
The buying and selling of illegal goods or the buying and selling of goods for illegal prices.

A **black market** is another possibility. A black market is the name given to illegal transactions at prices that violate price regulations. Firms need more than the $.80 ceiling price to break even, and some consumers are willing to pay more than the legal price. The large shortage of gasoline at the ceiling price suggests the possibility of illegal trades at illegally high prices. A dual market in gasoline may appear. Some gasoline is sold at the ceiling price, but most business goes to the underground black market where prices are higher, but supplies are greater, too. Black markets are common when government price ceilings create shortages. They are also common in economies such as the Soviet Union, where there are many government controls.

Long-run plant changes are a third option. Firms might alter plant size in the long run, adjusting to the lower price, and thus find long-run equilibrium. Quality change is also possible. Firms incurring losses might reduce costs by changing the quality of the goods they sell. In economic terms, this would actually amount to producing a different good. The new gasoline might be of lower octane or contain more contaminants, but it could be supplied in the long run at $.80. Better gasoline might be available at a higher price on the black market.

EFFICIENCY IN COMPETITIVE MARKETS

> **18.13 ECONOMIC EFFICIENCY**

> **18.14 THE INVISIBLE HAND**

Economic Efficiency
The allocation of resources among various uses that maximizes the value of the goods produced. Under certain conditions, free markets automatically achieve economic efficiency.

Invisible Hand
Adam Smith's name for the beneficial forces of competitive markets.

One reason economists are so interested in perfect competition is the relationship between perfect competition and **economic efficiency**. An economy in which every market meets the perfect competition criteria achieves economic efficiency automatically, without government intervention in market acts.

Adam Smith noted the market's advantages in his famous *Wealth of Nations*. Smith stressed the paradox of the market: self-interested buyers and sellers, with no thought of any social benefit, inadvertently produce efficiently, as if guided by an **invisible hand**. The invisible hand of exchange in perfectly competitive markets assures the best use of society's scarce resources.

In the broadest sense, economic efficiency means the allocation of resources shown in Figure 18-6. This figure shows a production possibilities frontier (PPF) for a simple economy that uses its finite resources to produce two goods, guns and butter. As noted in earlier chapters, the PPF shows an economy's production constraint. The PPF shows all combinations of the two goods that are possible given current technology and finite resources. Gun-butter combinations like X are possible, but they are inefficient in a technical sense. Better use of scarce goods makes possible larger quantities of both goods, such as the combination represented by point Z on the PPF border. Even larger quantities might be preferred, such as combination Y in the figure, but Y is unattainable, given current resources and technology. Society must choose among the combinations on its PPF.

KEY CONCEPT 18.14

Economic efficiency requires that resources be allocated to their highest valued alternative. Highly competitive markets tend to allocate resources in this fashion and are therefore more economically efficient than other markets.

538 Perfect Competition in the Marketplace

FIGURE 18-6

PPF and Economic Efficiency. The production possibilities frontier shows all combinations of two goods that the economy can produce with given scarce resources and existing technology. (a) Combination X shows a wasteful use of resources, Y is an unattainable combination, and Z is on the PPF boundary. Economic efficiency requires that resources be used effectively (economy on the PPF) and that the most desired combination of goods be produced. (b) Combination A is wasteful, and B is unattainable. Only combination C is an efficient allocation of resources.

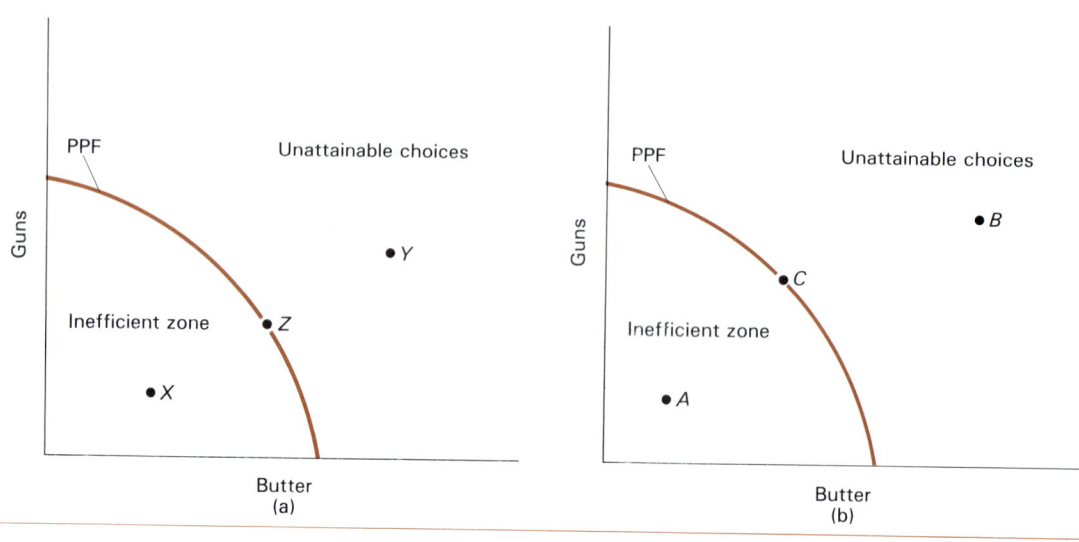

18.13 ECONOMIC EFFICIENCY

Diminishing Returns and the Shape of the PPF

In the preceding chapter, we analyzed the concept of diminishing returns. The production possibilities frontier is convex to the origin (bowed outward) because diminishing returns exist. For example, as we shift more of the economy's resources toward the production of guns and away from the production of butter, it takes larger and larger sacrifices of forgone butter production to produce additional units of guns. This implies an increasing opportunity cost of producing either good and illustrates how relative prices change. A price is a partial measure of what we have to give up to get a certain good. The figure shows that, as we produce more guns, we must sacrifice larger amounts of butter. The relative price of guns increases and the relative price of butter falls.

Consumers make their buying decisions based on the marginal utility and price of a good. As relative prices increase, we expect consumers to reduce their quantity demanded of a good. This is how the society is guided through the competitive market mechanism to its optimum point on the PPF. If a market is perfectly competitive, all possible mutually beneficial exchanges will take place and the society will end up at a point such as C on its PPF. The specific point on the PPF (specific combination of guns and butter) an economy chooses is directed by the changing relative prices of the goods it is producing.

Economic Efficiency and the PPF

18.13 ECONOMIC EFFICIENCY

Economic efficiency means that resources are used to produce that highest-valued combination of goods, the one that society prefers above all other possible combinations. Combination C in the figure is the efficient point. Combination A, on the other hand, is a wasteful use of resources and combination B is unattainable.

Perfectly competitive markets force firms to operate efficiently on the PPF, and through market prices, they guide firms to society's most preferred point. All this is done cheaply through decentralized choices made by individual buyers and sellers. No government regulation can improve on the perfectly competitive economy's choice.

Figure 18-7 gives a simple view of how perfect competition accomplishes this result. The demand curve in a perfectly competitive market reflects what people are willing to pay for goods and, therefore, the value of the alternative goods consumers are willing to give up. The supply curve in a perfectly competitive market is the industry's marginal cost curve. It explicitly measures what goods cost to produce and implicitly measures the value of the alternative goods that could have been produced using the same resources.

The total area between supply and demand curves represents society's gain from production. Society gains because the goods produced yield highly valued benefits (as the demand curve shows) that outweigh the production costs (opportunity cost is given by the supply curve).

Figure 18-7 breaks the total gain into two parts. Consumers gain because they can buy goods for less than the demand curve says they would be willing to pay for them. Producers gain because they sell goods for more than the supply curve says they would be willing to accept for them. The combined gains add up to the economy's benefit.

The exchange illustrated in Figure 18-7 is efficient because any change in the market reduces the economy's gain. If an economy produces less than the market equilibrium, some of the gain is lost. If the economy produces more than the market equilibrium, the goods produced cost more to make than they benefit consumers. The market's invisible hand leads to the efficient quantity.

FIGURE 18-7

Efficient Markets Maximize Social Gain. Efficient markets maximize social gain. The consumers' gain shown here results because buyers pay less than the demand curve says they are willing to pay. The producers gain because they receive a price greater than the cost of production. Social gain is the sum of the gains to consumers and producers.

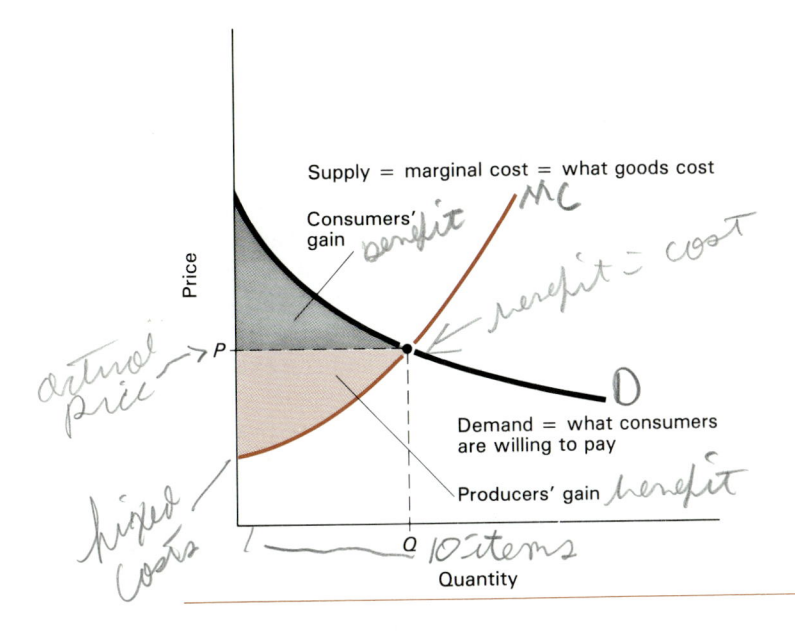

ECONOMIC ISSUES

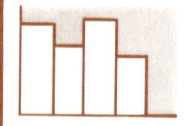

Dairy Price Supports and Marketing Orders

On the face of it, the U.S. dairy industry appears to meet most of the assumptions of perfect competition. Production of milk and other dairy products is characterized by many small firms producing virtually identical products. There are over 216,000 dairy farmers in the United States; yet competition in this important market fails. Why? Competition is prevented by government regulations that use price supports and marketing orders to keep prices higher than would be the case in the absence of these government controls. This Economic Issue looks at price supports and marketing orders to see how they distort competition in the marketplace.

Government regulation of the dairy industry began after the First World War. Farmers in this period engaged in cutthroat competition for lucrative drinking milk contracts. (Higher prices are normally paid for milk sold as drinking milk than for milk used to produce other dairy products, such as ice cream and cheese, for example.) At one point, competition for these profitable contracts became so fierce that the cost differential between drinking milk and other milk disappeared. Competition for drinking milk contracts forced down the price of drinking milk, reducing dairy farmer incomes.

This chapter has described the many effects competition has on price, profit, and cost in the short run and the long run. These effects did not happen in the dairy industry, however. Dairy farmers organized to use political power to reduce competition and keep prices and profits high. They formed cooperatives to reduce what they viewed as destructive competition. Under co-op agreements, members were paid the same price for their milk, regardless of whether it was used for drinking or processing. Consequently, there was no incentive to compete for sales of high-priced drinking milk, which would have driven down the price. Through their actions, the co-ops were able to

---

Competitive markets are very good at allocating resources; however, we still frequently see government setting price ceilings, price floors, or engaging in other market interferences for two specific reasons. First, perfect competition leads to efficiency, but it doesn't always yield a distribution of income and wealth that everyone finds equitable or desirable. Markets, left on their own, might make a few individuals rich and many poor. Equality and efficiency are often a trade-off. Sometimes government attempts to correct unsatisfactory or inequitable (but efficient) market results. The second rationale for government action is that real-world markets don't always exhibit perfect competition or even a level of competition that enables them to approach efficiency.

Market Failures

18.15 MARKET FAILURES

Real-world markets seldom meet all the conditions for perfect competition. Imperfect information and high transactions costs, in particular, distort the market's invisible hand. Markets for many goods are characterized by serious violations of other perfect competition assumptions. Among the factors that distort perfect competition are the market situations of monopoly, oligopoly, and monopsony and the existence of externalities, public goods, and government policies.

Monopoly Perfect competition requires thousands of price-taking producers, but this atomistic competition does not always prevail in the real world. Barriers to entry, such as patents, trade secrets, and government restrictions, create **monopoly** markets, markets in which just one firm offers a particular good for sale. Monopoly firms maximize profits by producing

Monopoly
A market with only one supplier.

restrict supply, reduce competition, and increase the prices of their goods.

The dairy industry carried the co-op agreements a step further by instituting a market order. A marketing order is a price-control system adopted by vote of the dairy industry and administered, starting in 1935, by the U.S. Department of Agriculture. It accomplishes by law what dairy co-ops sought to do by voluntary, but possibly illegal, action. In essence, a marketing order is a price control. The government "orders" a fixed price for milk in each of 49 regions. This price is based on prices in Minnesota and Wisconsin where milk co-ops are particularly strong and milk prices, according to *Consumer Reports,* are particularly high. All farmers receive the order price for their milk, reducing any incentive for them to compete on the basis of price for sales.

The marketing-order program has one side effect that students of supply and demand can quickly guess. High government-set prices lead to a surplus when the quantity of milk produced exceeds the quantity consumers want to buy at that price. Surplus is frequently the case in the dairy industry. Congress acted in 1949 to remedy this problem by instituting a system of price supports. The government agrees to purchase surplus dairy products at fixed prices. These prices have been high enough in recent years to induce substantial oversupply by dairy farmers, with resulting heavy purchases by government buyers. Marketing orders combined with price supports have kept dairy prices high in the United States and have resulted in substantial accumulated surpluses of butter, cheese, and powdered milk. Similar programs have had similar results in many European countries.

Dairy marketing orders and price supports are examples of the special-interest effect of political decision making. These government programs benefit specific groups by imposing higher costs on millions of consumers. They also distort the beneficial effects of perfect competition. Households buy less milk than they would at lower market-set prices, and dairy farmers use valuable resources that would be allocated to the production of other goods by an uncontrolled market. With price supports and marketing orders, many American refrigerators are empty of milk, while warehouses stand full of dairy products.

Additional References

"Milk: Could It Cost Less?" *Consumer Reports Magazine,* June, 1982, p. 18.

Dunphy, Stephen H. "Next Week's Rise in Dairy Price Support Expected to Further Fuel Inflation." *Seattle Times,* September 25, 1980, p. 27.

---

fewer goods and charging a higher price than would a competitive industry with the same costs. Monopolies distort economic efficiency. The next chapter presents the monopoly market situation and examines government's role in regulating these firms.

Oligopoly
A market with just a few sellers, each of whom can influence price.

Oligopoly Oligopoly is another market situation in which perfect economic efficiency might not prevail. Oligopoly markets are dominated by just a few large businesses. These firms might be fiercely competitive, forcing down price to marginal cost, or they might behave more as a joint monopoly, cooperating to keep prices high. They might also settle on some mutually profitable equilibrium, neither maximizing group profit nor achieving an efficient competitive market. Many important markets in the United States, such as those for automobiles and steel, for example, can be classified as oligopolies. Chapter 20 discusses the economics of oligopoly in depth.

Monopsony
A market with a single buyer.

Monopsony Competition breaks down among buyers in some markets. The quintessential case is a **monopsony,** a market in which there is just one buyer. Monopsony demanders buy less than a corresponding competitive market might, but they also pay less. Like monopoly, monopsony pushes the economy's allocation of resources away from the efficient ideal. Chapter 21 explores the consequences of monopsony in resource markets.

Externalities
External costs and benefits passed on outside of the market system.

Externalities **Externalities** exist when individuals do not bear the full cost or receive the full benefit of their decisions. Externalities distort supply and demand, leading the market's invisible hand to an inefficient outcome. Pollution is an important example of an externality. Producers who pollute do not bear all the costs of their production choices, so their output decisions are not always in the best interest of society. We will look at externalities and government's role in correcting for external costs in Chapter 25.

Public Goods
Items from which nonowners cannot be excluded from benefiting but whose use by nonowners does not reduce the benefits available to the owner. A lighthouse is an example of a public good.

Public Goods Competition is based on rivalry. If one consumer buys and eats a specific apple, that means another consumer cannot buy and eat that exact same apple. In effect, consumers rival for the apple. But rivalry fails in markets for **public goods.** If government builds a lighthouse to guide its military ships away from danger, privately owned merchant ships also get the benefits, but they do so without paying the cost. The merchant ships' use of the lighthouse benefits them without reducing the lighthouse's value to the government ships. The market demand for lighthouses and other public goods doesn't reflect their true benefit, since each individual is encouraged to hold back and let others buy. Public goods, and government's role in their provision, are discussed in Chapter 25.

Government Policies Government policies can distort competitive markets just as the market failures mentioned above can. Government does many things that influence demand, supply, and price. Government collects taxes, pays subsidies, sets price ceilings and price floors, levies tariffs and sets quotas on international trade, and buys and sells goods. Government policies can be aimed at market failures in an attempt to restore efficiency, but they can also be aimed at competitive markets themselves, reducing social gains. In an attempt to improve equity, government policies may reduce economic efficiency. Since the overall net effect on the well-being of society is difficult to define and measure there will probably be a continuing conflict between these two goals for the foreseeable future.

A FINAL WORD ON COMPETITION

As we have discussed above, competition can break down in many ways. Realizing that human beings are self-interested, it would be unrealistic to believe that they do not attempt to overcome the economic discipline forced upon them by market competition. They attempt to exploit the areas of market failure when they can. It is natural that producers attempt, where possible, to collude or at least cooperate to gain an advantage in the marketplace. Consumers, too, face a strong incentive to avoid competition from other consumers where possible. As consumers we all want producers to compete fully since we gain the benefits of that competition. We do not, however, wish to compete fully with other consumers for the goods and services we desire. For example, if you find a new home you are interested in buying at a real bargain price, you do not tell all your neighbors and friends about its availability since they too might wish to compete with you and subsequently drive the price upward. Producers use advertising, price, market information, style, location, service, and any other available means to attempt to gain at least a temporary advantage in the marketplace.

The whole function of profits is influenced by the competitive process. As George Guilder, the contemporary supply-side oriented author, states: "In the real world competition means the competitive pursuit of transitory positions of monopoly."[1] Most producers wish to develop and exploit a temporary monopoly position in a marketplace and hold onto that position until other producers catch up and eliminate the temporary monopoly profits

1. George Guilder, *Wealth and Poverty,* New York: Basic Books, 1981, p. 136.

SUMMARY

18.1
1. Each market is different, but we can learn about the powerful common forces of market action by analyzing a model of perfect, or pure competition. Even markets that do not display pure competition are subject to many of the forces discussed in this chapter.

18.2, 18.3
2. The first assumption of perfect competition is that there are many buyers, no one of whom is able to influence price. Buyers are therefore price takers.

18.2, 18.4
3. A second assumption of perfect competition is that there are many sellers, each of whom is as small compared to the market as atoms are to real-world structures (hence the name atomistic competition). Because individual sellers cannot influence price, they, too, are considered price takers.

18.2, 18.5
4. A third assumption of perfect competition is that products are assumed to be identical so price, not quality or advertising, determines which goods are purchased.

18.2
5. A fourth assumption of perfect competition is that free entry and exit are assumed to exist. New firms enter an industry in response to positive economic profits. Firms that earn negative economic profits eventually exit.

18.2
6. Perfect information means that all buyers and seller have identical, complete information about market events. This fifth assumption of perfect competition leads to uniform pricing.

18.2
7. The sixth assumption of perfect competition is that zero transaction costs assure that all mutually advantageous exchanges are completed.

18.6
8. Competitive firms are price takers. The prices they receive are a given, so they behave as if each faces a perfectly elastic (horizontal) marginal revenue curve. Average revenue equals price equals marginal revenue from the firm's view.

18.6
9. Competitive firms set production at the quantity that maximizes profit. This occurs at the output level at which marginal cost equals marginal revenue or price, since they are the same thing.

18.7
10. A competitive firm may earn positive, negative, or zero economic profits in the short run, depending on the profit-maximizing output level and the relationship between price and *ATC*.

18.8 ▶ 11. The market adjusts in several ways, over several time periods, to a change in demand. In the very short run, firms cannot alter output, so price is the only variable. An increase in demand results in higher prices for the existing output level in this time frame.

18.8 ▶ 12. Market adjustment takes the form of both price and output movements in the short run. Output can vary in response to changing demand in the short run. Firms choose the new profit-maximizing output level (where *MC* equals new price). This increase in an individual firm's output is a movement along the market supply curve.

18.8, 18.9 ▶ 13. Higher prices increase economic profit in the short run. Entry (and plant-size adjustments) increase supply in the long run.

18.9 ▶ 14. Firms enter or exit an industry in the long run in response to positive or negative economic profits.

18.9 ▶ 15. The long-run supply curve plots the relationship between price and quantity supplied in the long run, when adjustments such as entry and plant-size changes have taken place.

18.9 ▶ 16. The shape of the long-run supply curve depends on whether the industry experiences constant, increasing, or decreasing returns to scale.

18.10 ▶ 17. Elasticity of supply measures the way supply curves respond to changes in price. Supply curves tend to be perfectly inelastic in the very short run, since output is assumed not to vary in this time frame. Supply curves may be elastic or inelastic in the short run, depending on how marginal cost varies with output.

18.11 ▶ 18. Supply curves tend to be more elastic in the long run, as entry, exit, and plant-size adjustments increase the quantity supplied at a given market price.

18.12 ▶ 19. A price ceiling has different economic effects depending on the time frame under consideration. In the very short run, price falls and production changes little. In the short run, a price ceiling results in less production by each firm and a movement along the industry supply curve. A shortage results, with potential gains for black market traders who sell at prices above the ceiling level. In the long run, short-run losses lead to exit, making the shortage even worse.

18.13 ▶ 20. Perfectly competitive markets display the property of economic efficiency. Efficiency means that scarce resources are put to their most valuable use.

18.13 ▶ 21. Demand curves in competitive markets reveal the benefits that purchasers get from various goods. Supply curves reveal the true cost of production.

18.13 ▶ 22. Producing less than the efficient amount means foregoing goods with a greater value than cost. Producing more than the efficient level means goods cost more than their value to buyers.

18.14

23. Adam Smith's concept of the invisible hand indicates that the incentives provided by the marketplace lead decision makers toward economic efficiency. By pursuing their own self-interests, the efficient level of output is attained in a free market.

18.15

24. Real-world markets often fail to meet the assumptions of perfect competition. Perfect competition is affected by the existence of monopolies, oligopolies, monopsonies, externalities, public goods, and government policies. Monopoly exists when just one firm supplies goods and can therefore set price. Oligopoly is a market in which a few sellers act together to control supply. Monopsony is a market in which there is just one buyer. Monopsonists, like monopolists, are not price takers. Externalities and public goods are market failures, too. Economic agents cannot capture all the costs or benefits of their actions, nor can they exclude others from gaining benefits, when these conditions and goods exist. Government policies, like the price controls discussed in this chapter, also lead the market away from efficiency.

DISCUSSION QUESTIONS

18.7, 18.8, 18.9, 18.10, 18.11

1. Draw a market and typical firm in long-run equilibrium. Explain how a market and a firm would adjust in the very short run, short run, and long run to each of the following events:
   a. decrease in demand;
   b. increase in fixed costs;
   c. increase in marginal costs.

18.11, 18.12

2. What determines the shape of a market's long-run supply curve? When will it be flat? Upward-sloping? Downward-sloping? Explain. (Hint: What forces affect the firm in the long run?)

18.13, 18.14

3. Explain economic efficiency in your own words. Why do competitive markets automatically achieve efficiency? How does the invisible hand work?

18.13, 18.14

4. Suppose that you are the head of a command economy. Your task is to allocate resources to achieve economic efficiency without the use of markets. You assign resources to different industries, then set the prices at which consumers can buy goods. What information would you need before making resource assignments? Make a complete list. Why is the market's invisible hand able to achieve efficiency without any individual collecting all this information? Explain.

18.12

5. What is your opinion of price ceilings? Be prepared to state and defend your answer.

18.10, 18.11

6. Use the ideas developed in this chapter to discuss the probable very short-run, short-run and long-run supply elasticities of the following products: orange juice, personal computers, apartment units, and vintage wine.

SELECTED READINGS

Hayek, F. A. "The Meaning of Competition." In *Individualism and Economic Order.* Chicago: University of Chicago Press, 1948. pp. 134–170.

Robinson, Joan. "What Is Perfect Competition?" Reprinted in Breit, William, and Hochman, M. (Eds.), *Readings in Microeconomics,* 2nd ed. New York: Holt, Rinehart, and Winston, 1968, pp. 197–206.

Smith, Vernon. "An Experimental Study of Competitive Market Behavior." *Journal of Political Economy* (April, 1962), pp. 111–137.

Stigler, George J. "Perfect Competition Historically Contemplated." *Journal of Political Economy* (February, 1957), pp. 1–17.

Veseth, Michael. *Public Finance.* Reston, VA: Reston Publishing Company, 1983, chap. 2.

CHAPTER 19

Monopoly: The Case of the One-Firm Market

Having read the chapter, reviewed the chapter summary, and completed the *Study Guide* exercises, you should be able to:

CRIS

19.1 MONOPOLY: Define monopoly, list and explain the four assumptions that economists make about monopoly markets, and explain why each assumption is necessary for a monopoly to exist.

19.2 BARRIERS TO ENTRY: Define barriers to entry and explain how each of the following items is used as an entry barrier: government regulations, high fixed costs, economies of scale, trade secrets, and control of critical resources.

19.3 MONOPOLY DEMAND AND REVENUE: Describe how a monopoly firm's view of its demand curve differs from that of a perfectly competitive firm and explain how marginal revenue is calculated and how the marginal revenue curve of a monopolist differs from that of a perfect competitor.

19.4 PROFIT-MAXIMIZING RULE: State the profit-maximizing rule used by monopolists in setting their output and price and explain the roles that demand, marginal revenue, and marginal cost play in the monopoly production choice.

19.5 MONOPOLY PRICE: Explain how the monopoly firm sets price once it has selected the profit-maximizing output level and indicate whether the price is equal to, greater than, or less than (a) marginal cost and (b) marginal revenue, then explain why.

19.6 PRICE DISCRIMINATION: Define price discrimination and explain how a monopoly can use price discrimination to increase revenue and profit.

19.7 PRICE DISCRIMINATION CONDITIONS: List and describe the three conditions necessary for successful price discrimination and explain why each condition is required.

19.8 MONOPOLY VS. PERFECT COMPETITION: Discuss the relationship between monopoly and perfect competition, concentrating on whether monopoly firms produce more or less than would perfectly competitive firms with the same costs and whether they charge the same, higher, or lower prices, then explain why economists think that monopolies tend to be inefficient.

19.9 FIGHTING INEFFICIENCY: List several government policies aimed at discouraging monopolies or reducing monopoly welfare losses.

19.10 MONOPOLY PRICE REGULATIONS: Describe how different monopoly price regulations work and explain why a policy that assures a monopoly a fair return is not necessarily an efficient policy.

19.11 ANTITRUST LEGISLATION: Discuss the limits to antitrust legislation and explain why monopoly firms can sometimes be more efficient than perfectly competitive industries.

19.12 STATIC AND DYNAMIC EFFICIENCY: Explain the difference between static and dynamic efficiency and discuss why Schumpeter thought that monopolies encourage dynamic efficiency.

19.13 GOVERNMENT REGULATIONS: Discuss Posner's idea that government regulation leads to monopoly and explain the different ways in which government regulations can create monopoly power.

In Chapter 18 we examined the model of perfect competition as one form of market structure. In perfect competition there are thousands of relatively small, seemingly identical firms producing seemingly identical products, with price as the sole determinant of consumer behavior. In this chapter we will look at the case of a single producer, or monopoly firm, in an attempt to compare and contrast the two polar cases of market structure. We will then consider the market structures of monopolistic competition and oligopoly as hybrid combinations of perfect competition and monopoly in Chapter 20. In this way we will explore the effects of different types of competitive behavior on the market.

Real monopolies, especially unregulated ones, are hard to find. Most firms face at least some competition. The fact that there are only a small number of pure monopolies in the real world does not make the analysis of monopoly behavior a purely academic exercise, however. Many firms are able to behave like monopolies, within certain limits. The college bookstore is not a real monopoly, for example. There are many other places that sell books and school supplies. But if you need a particular book used only in a single class, or if you need an examination blue book five minutes before class, there are not many substitutes for the college bookstore. This gives the bookstore manager the ability to behave like a monopoly in certain situations.

Understanding how monopolies work is important in establishing a basis for comparison with other market structures. For example, a knowledge of monopolies and perfectly competitive firms will make it easier to understand the next chapter's examination of the oligopoly firms and the quasi-competitive monopolistic competitors that dominate most consumer-goods markets. The study of monopoly firms also forces us to look at the problems of government regulation and to better understand the trade-offs between equity and efficiency and between efficiency and innovation that are part and parcel of government's "visible hand" in the market.

WHAT IS A MONOPOLY?

Many people grow up thinking that monopoly is, at least in part, a game manufactured by Parker Brothers that models the real estate market in Atlantic City, New Jersey. This notion is not far wrong. The goal of the Parker Brothers game is to get a monopoly by owning all of the firms in a certain market, such as Park Place and Boardwalk or all four railroads. More interesting, however, is the Parker Brothers monopoly itself. Parker Brothers is the monopoly supplier of this game. It is the only firm allowed to sell this diversion, and until a recent court decision altered the rules, the firm was even able to prevent others from selling similar items.

Assumptions of Monopoly Markets

19.1 MONOPOLY

The key aspect of the monopoly market is the single seller. Buyers compete for scarce goods, but the sole seller sets supply. Price and quantity are fixed at the level that maximizes the sellers' profits, given their production costs and the consumers' buying characteristics. The four most important properties of the monopoly model discussed in this chapter are the single seller, the single product, the absence of close substitutes, and the existence of barriers to entry.

Single Seller In a true monopoly market, there is just one firm selling the product. The next chapter looks at situations in which a few large firms dominate the market or where several firms conspire to behave like a monopoly.

Single Product The monopoly firm makes just one item. This simplifies the analysis of costs and revenues.

No Close Substitutes There are no close substitutes for the good the monopolist sells. This is an important assumption. You can be the only producer of a good and yet have no monopoly power if there are many substitutes for your good. Harcourt Brace Jovanovich, Inc., is the monopoly producer of this textbook, for example. Copyright laws forbid others from selling this book or from using portions of it in their books. Yet there are many other economics books on the market, some of which might be easily substituted for this one. What is the result? Harcourt Brace Jovanovich has a technical monopoly, but it behaves more like a competitive firm. A true monopoly is the only producer of a good with no close substitutes.

Barriers to Entry Monopolies sometimes earn higher profits than do otherwise identical competitive firms. All else being equal, the greater profit potential should attract other firms to the market, increasing competition and destroying the monopoly. The key to the monopolist's continued existence is therefore a barrier to entry, which keeps other firms from entering the market.

19.2 BARRIERS TO ENTRY

Types of Barriers to Entry

As already stated, barriers to entry are obstacles that serve to keep other firms from entering a market and competing with the existing firm. These barriers can be both obvious and subtle, but they most frequently take one of the five following forms: government regulations, high fixed costs, economies of scale, trade secrets, and control of critical resources.

Government Regulations Government rules, laws, and regulations act as entry barriers in many ways. Patents and copyrights are clear examples. Government gives patent and copyright holders the power to exclude competitors for a fixed period of time. This encourages authors, composers, artists, and inventors to produce new works that benefit the whole economy. Government also creates monopolies and monopoly power through its regulatory agencies. Licensing rules limit entry into such industries and professions as medicine, law, teaching, hairstyling, and taxi services, among others. Rules and regulations make it costly and difficult to enter these markets, giving firms already there some measure of monopoly power.

High Fixed Costs Firms make a profit by selling goods at a high enough price to cover both their fixed and variable costs. Fixed costs are the costs of fixed inputs, such as plant and machinery. Variable costs are the costs of variable inputs, such as labor and raw materials. Fixed costs that are very high discourage firms from entering the market and increasing competition, since the chance of making a profit is small. A firm that is labeled a **natural monopoly** is usually one that fits this pattern of high fixed costs and low variable costs.

Natural Monopoly
A market in which a single supplier has lower costs than do many smaller, competitive firms.

The fixed costs of supplying electricity, natural gas, water, sewer, and telephone services are very high. It takes large-scale plants and equipment to produce these goods and services efficiently. This requires large amounts of capital. These fixed costs are so high that the monopoly firm already in business has a substantial advantage. No potential competitor is likely to invest in all the fixed costs necessary to enter this market. In this instance, a natural monopoly can sometimes be more efficient than several competitive firms would be. Fewer scarce resources are invested in fixed set-up costs, freeing resources to be used elsewhere in the economy.

High fixed costs can also be a different sort of barrier. Many consumer items, such as soap flakes and cigarettes, carry famous brand names. Consumers buy these goods because of name familiarity and image more than price. Any new competitor must bear the high advertising costs needed to create a new brand. These high initial costs also serve to keep competitors out of the market.

Economies of Scale Economies of scale also give existing firms an advantage that keeps out new firms. If economies of scale exist, big firms with high output and long production runs have lower costs than smaller, new firms. This lets the larger firms set lower prices, and still earn a profit. The ability of larger firms to set prices below the levels possible by smaller firms who might wish to enter the industry is a sure barrier to entry.

Trade Secrets Some firms gain a monopoly by keeping certain aspects of their business secret so that others can't use this information to produce competing products. Many of IBM's products, for example, contain chips or operating systems that have secret designs and operations. Firms that want to compete with IBM by making plug-compatible gear, for example, must break the secret code by reverse engineering, a costly and time-consuming process that discourages entry. IBM can maintain its monopoly power in certain markets by keeping close watch on its trade secrets and by constantly innovating. Firms that break the old codes find their advantage short lived if a new, more powerful secret system is on the way.

Control of Critical Resources Some firms use monopoly control of a scarce resource to keep out competitors. This is clearly a direct entry barrier. The classic example of this type of barrier involved the Aluminum Company of America (ALCOA) before World War II. Alcoa, at that time, owned the vast majority of the world's available bauxite deposits. Bauxite is a key ingredient in the making of aluminum, and firms that might have wished to enter the aluminum manufacturing industry could not do so because they could not get the bauxite they needed. Another example involves cattle ranching on the Western frontier of the United States. While vast range lands were opened by the government to many cattle producers, the limited plots with access to open water were quickly claimed by the largest producers. For over a decade, large cattle producers were effective in controlling entry into the beef-producing industry by restricting access to open water.

MONOPOLY DEMAND AND REVENUE

19.3 MONOPOLY DEMAND AND REVENUE

Monopoly price and output are different from the perfect competition model we studied in the last chapter. Unlike perfectly competitive firms, monopoly firms are not price takers. Monopolies can set any price they want, but they live with the knowledge that quantity demanded varies inversely with price. If price is too high, less is sold. In order to sell more output, monopolists must lower price on all the units they sell.

Monopolies are price seekers. Therefore, they determine their best price/output combination by searching out the most profitable demand curve combination. Table 19-1 and Figure 19-1 show how monopoly production decisions are made.

TABLE 19-1

Demand versus Marginal Revenue for a Monopoly

Price ($)	Quantity demanded	Total revenue ($)	Marginal revenue ($)
200	0	0	—
190	1	190	190
180	2	360	170
170	3	510	150
160	4	640	130
150	5	750	110
140	6	840	90
130	7	910	70
120	8	960	50
110	9	990	30
100	10	1000	10

FIGURE 19-1

Demand and Marginal Revenue Curves. Marginal revenue is less than price for monopoly firms. See Table 19-1 for derivation of these curves.

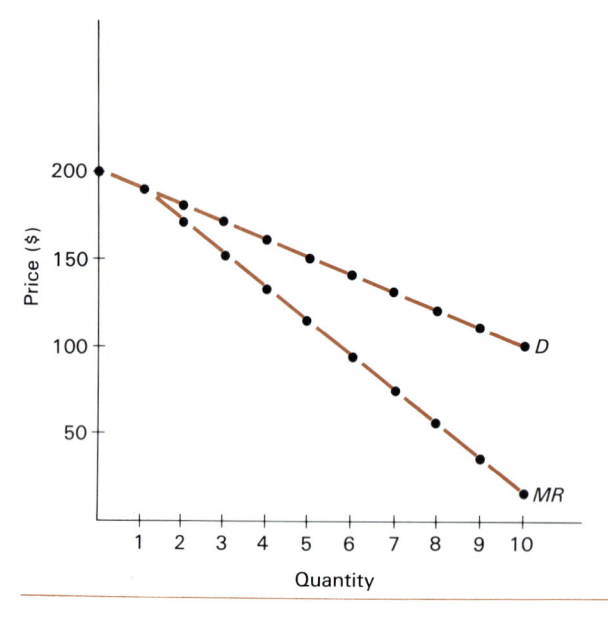

Table 19-1 shows the demand schedule for this monopoly market. Quantity varies inversely with price, as expected. Quantity sold falls when price rises, and lower prices increase sales volume. The monopoly firm, unlike its competitive cousin, cannot assume a perfectly elastic demand (the ability to sell unlimited quantities at the market price). Marginal revenue is constant for competitive firms but falling for the monopolist.

Table 19-1 derives the monopolist's marginal revenue (MR) curve. When the monopoly firm seeks to sell more, it faces the market demand curve. The only way the firm can sell more is to lower price from $150 to $140 on every unit sold. This is both good news and bad news to the monopoly firm. The good news is that there is a greater quantity demanded at the reduced price. The quantity sold goes from five to six units at the lower price, and the increased quantity sold boosts total revenue. The bad news is lower price. There is less per-unit revenue coming in on the original five unit quantity because of the lower price. The monopoly firm sells more units, but it takes in less revenue on each unit.

The fact that a monopoly firm must lower price on all units sold in order to sell more units results in the difference between price and marginal revenue we observe in the figure. The sixth unit sells for a price of $140, but it adds just $90 in marginal revenue to the total revenue. Total revenue for five units is $750 (5 times $150). Cutting price and increasing the quantity sold boosts total revenue to $840 (6 times $140). Total revenue rises by just the marginal revenue of $90 ($840 minus $750), not by the demand curve price of $140.

Marginal revenue is less than the selling price for the monopoly firm. Marginal revenue is greater than zero, as in this example, so long as the demand curve remains elastic. Price and total revenue move in the same direction here. Marginal revenue is negative on the inelastic part of a demand curve, however. Lowering the unit price reduces total revenue when demand is inelastic, while raising the unit price increases total revenue.

Monopoly Demand and Revenue 553

Monopoly Price and Quantity Decisions

> **19.4 PROFIT-MAXIMIZING RULE**

A monopoly firm uses the marginal revenue curve to determine the profit-maximizing output level, then uses the demand curve to pick the corresponding price. Figure 19-2(a) shows how this decision is made.

The monopoly firm sets output at the level at which MR equals MC (point A in the figure) for the same reason competitive firms follow this rule. The last item produced brings in additional revenue equal to the extra cost. It is unprofitable to sell more than this quantity, since output beyond this point has a higher marginal cost than marginal revenue. The MC equals MR intersection determines the quantity produced, Q_M.

> **19.5 MONOPOLY PRICE**

The demand curve determines price. Monopoly firms use the demand curve to find the highest price buyers will pay for quantity Q_M. This price (point B on the demand curve in the figure) corresponds to price P_M. The monopoly firm may or may not earn economic profits at this price/quantity combination, depending on the relationship between monopoly price P_M and ATC.

It is easy to visualize a situation in which the monopoly firm might incur economic losses. In Figure 19-2(a), the ATC curve is above the monopoly firm's demand curve. Here average total costs would exceed price at every level of output, and it would not be possible for the firm to make a profit. A real-world example of this is provided by the case of West Virginia Intermountain Cable Television Corporation. In almost all geographic areas there

FIGURE 19-2

Monopoly Misconceptions. Monopolies do not always earn economic profits, as (a) shows. This monopoly sets output at A and price at B to maximize profits. But price is still below ATC at C, because of high fixed costs. Monopolies do not operate on the inelastic portion of their demand curve, as (b) shows, since inelastic demand means negative marginal revenue. No matter how you draw this picture, the MR equals MC rule means that the monopoly sets price and quantity on the elastic part of the demand curve.

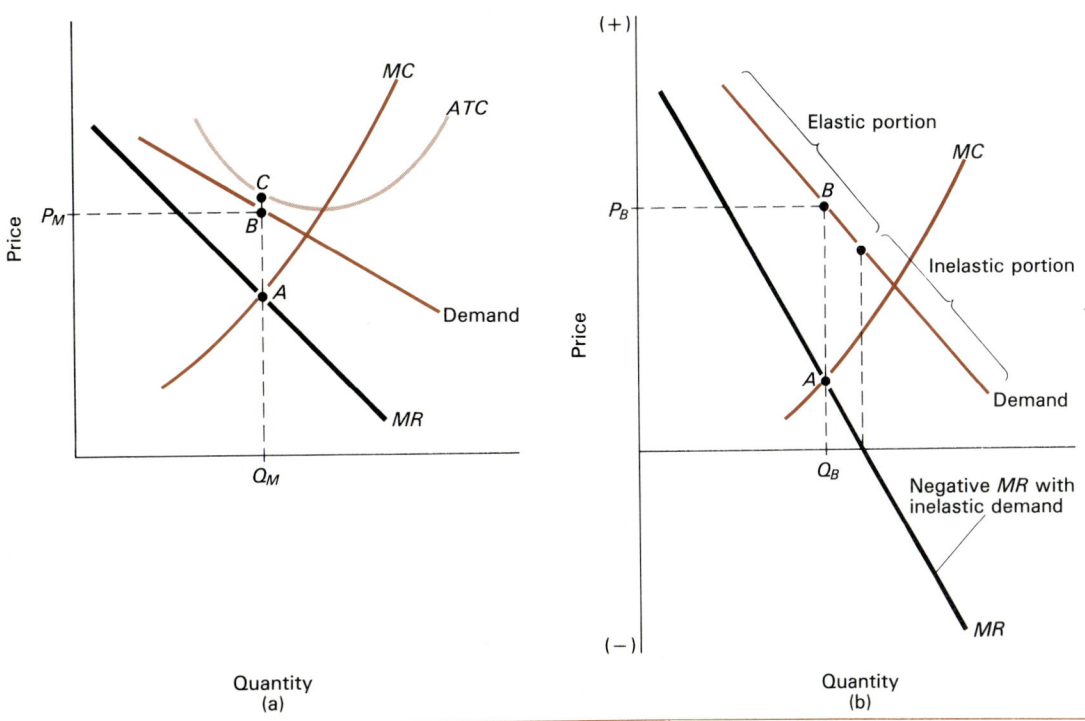

is only one franchise for providing cable television service. West Virginia was no exception when Intermountain Cable Corporation bought its franchise in 1978 and began construction of its cable system. Unfortunately, stringing cable through highly mountainous terrain to small towns where only a few people could afford to buy the service raised Intermountain's average total costs above the level of revenues they could collect from subscribers. The monopoly failed. Monopoly is no guarantee of economic profit, but monopoly firms are more likely to earn profits than would competitive firms in the same industry.

> **KEY CONCEPTS 19.4, 19.5**
>
> The profit-maximization rule for monopolists states that monopoly firms produce at the output level at which marginal revenue equals marginal cost and charge the price indicated on the demand curve for that amount of output.

What does the monopoly firm's supply curve look like? Monopolies don't have a supply curve in the usual sense. Monopolies offer only a single price/quantity combination for sale, the one that maximizes their profits. Their supply point is price/quantity combination B in the Figure 19-2(a).

It is true that monopoly prices exceed marginal cost. Monopoly firms charge higher prices than would be charged by competitive firms with the same costs. There are, however, several misconceptions held by people in regard to monopolies which should be clarified here. For example, people often assume that all monopolies earn a profit. Monopolies are more likely to earn profit than similar competitive firms, but no profit is guaranteed! But as we have already noted, Figure 19-2(a) shows a profit-maximizing, but money-losing, monopoly. High average costs can exceed even monopoly prices, bringing loss, not profit. Many monopoly firms, like metropolitan bus systems, for example, earn negative profits, even when they follow the *MR* equals *MC* rule.

Some people also mistakenly assume that monopolies are more likely to exist in markets in which demand is inelastic, where the monopoly firms can exploit consumers by raising prices. This idea is easily disproved, as Figure 19-2(b) shows. Marginal revenue is negative when demand is inelastic. Cutting price to increase quantity sold lowers total revenue (a negative marginal revenue) when demand is inelastic. How can a monopoly set a positive marginal cost equal to a negative marginal revenue? It is impossible, as the figure shows. A monopoly facing an inelastic demand raises price and reduces quantity sold until the firm enters the elastic part of the demand curve. At this point, *MR* is positive and the *MR* equals *MC* rule holds. Profit-maximizing monopolies always operate on the elastic portion of the demand curve.

Finally, monopolies don't charge customers the highest possible price, as many people think. Monopolies charge the profit-maximizing price, which is often less that the maximum price many buyers would pay. The highest possible price would mean few sales and little profit. Monopolies set price at the level that maximizes profits, at the price that corresponds to the *MR* equals *MC* quantity.

Price Discrimination

19.6 PRICE DISCRIMINATION

Monopolies can gain greater profits if they engage in price discrimination. Price discrimination exists when a firm charges different customers different prices for the same goods. Price discriminating monopolies divide customers according to demand characteristics. They charge a higher price to those who are willing or able to pay more. Figure 19-3 shows how monopoly price discrimination works.

The hotel monopoly shown in Figure 19-3 is very much like the Holiday Inn being the only motel in an isolated town. It acts like a monopoly because it has no competitors and no close substitutes. This hotel serves two types of customers. Some are travelling salespeople who must spend the night at the hotel in order to visit all of their customers (Market A in the figure). Others are tourists who have the option of driving 50 miles to the next town (Market B in the figure).

How does the hotel set rates? It could charge both groups the same monopoly profit-maximizing price, but price discrimination would allow the hotel to raise more total revenue while selling the same quantity. The hotel management first finds the profit-maximizing quantity, the output level at which marginal cost equals marginal revenue for both types of hotel customers. In this case, MR_T equals MC at a price level of $20. Thus the management sets price at the level at which MR and MC equal $20 in each submarket. This leads to a higher $100-per-night room rate for salespeople, who have a more inelastic demand curve, and a lower $50-per-night rate for tourists, who have a more elastic demand curve. This dual pricing system raises more revenue at the same cost than simply charging both groups the monopoly price of $60 per night.

Price discrimination is not uncommon in today's world. Hairstyling prices, theatre and airplane tickets, and telephone rates are all varied, one way or another, so that different classes of customers pay different rates. Discounts for children and senior citizens are a common form of price discrimination. These groups often have less to spend than others. Discounts let stores and theatres sell more to these groups, while still charging other customers a higher price.

19.7 PRICE DISCRIMINATION CONDITIONS

Price discrimination is profitable, but it isn't possible in every market. Three conditions are necessary for successful price discrimination: different demand curves, the ability to charge different prices, and a way to prevent product resale.

FIGURE 19-3

Monopoly Price Discrimination. Demand curves A and B represent two types of hotel customers, with different demand characteristics and different marginal revenue curves. The price-discriminating monopoly firm first adds the two curves together to find the point at which MR_T equals MC. This marginal cost is then used to divide the total quantity and set price for each class of customer. Total revenues rise from $1800 ($60 times 30) with the single monopoly price to $2000 ($100 times 10 plus $50 times 20) with price discrimination.

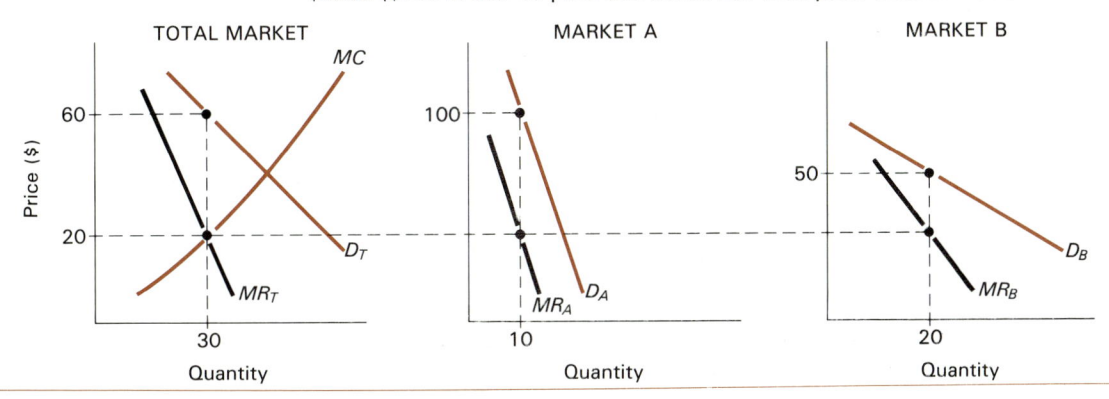

Different Demand Curves Different customers must have demand curves with different characteristics and it must be possible to segregate buyers according to their demand types if price discrimination is to be employed. For example, the demand for bus rides by commuters who must get to work is more price inelastic than the demand for bus rides by retired senior citizens.

Variable Pricing To engage in price discrimination, the monopoly firm must find a way to charge one group more than another. Secret discounts and store coupons are two ways to vary price. Customer restrictions, such as age or sex limits, are another. Senior discounts and ladies nights are effective price discrimination techniques, for example, because some buyers (such as men at a baseball game) are willing to pay full price even though others (such as women) pay a lower price. In addition, men and women often attend events as couples, so reducing the price for women also tends to increase the number of men who purchase full-price tickets.

Prevention of Resale Price-discriminating firms must also be able to prevent low-price buyers from reselling products to those who are charged a higher price. Price discrimination falls apart when resale takes place. This explains why movie theaters use price discrimination for admission, giving students a discount, for example, but not for popcorn sales. The ticket sellers can prevent resale of a student ticket, but the theater could not prevent a student from buying popcorn at a discount price, then reselling it to others who don't qualify for lower price.

MONOPOLY VERSUS PERFECT COMPETITION

> 19.8
> MONOPOLY VS. PERFECT COMPETITION

The output decisions of monopoly firms are significantly different from the decentralized decisions of many firms in a perfectly competitive market. Over two hundred years ago Adam Smith noted that

> The Monopolist, by keeping the market understocked, by never fully supplying the effectual demand, sell their commodities much above the natural price, and raise their emoluments, whether they consist of wages or profit greatly above their natural rates.[1]

Many economists would contend that the monopolist's choices lead to inefficiency. Monopoly firms misallocate scarce resources by charging higher prices and producing less output than would similar competitive firms. Figure 19-4 illustrates this comparison.

Suppose that a monopoly firm has the same costs as do firms in a perfectly competitive industry producing the same good. Under this assumption, the *MC* curve in Figure 19-4 corresponds to the competitive industry's supply curve. The competitive market equilibrium is given by point *C*, where market demand intersects the *MC* supply curve. If this market were perfectly competitive, it would achieve economic efficiency at price P_C and quantity Q_C.

How does monopoly compare with perfect competition? By setting output at the level at which *MC* equals *MR*, rather than at *MC* equals price, the monopoly firm produces less than would a competitive industry. In addition to producing less (Q_M versus Q_C in the figure), the monopoly firm

---

1. Adam Smith, *An Inquiry into the Nature and Causes of the Wealth of Nations* (1776 Cannan's Edition), Chicago: University of Chicago Press, 1976, p. 69.

FIGURE 19-4

Producer Choice: A Competitive Firm versus a Monopoly. A competitive firm takes market price and produces at X in panel (a). As panel (b) shows, the monopolist compares marginal cost and marginal revenue, producing at A, where MC equals MR, and setting price at B. A competitive industry with the same costs would produce at C, where MC (supply) equals demand, with lower price and larger quantity. A fixed price at P_C makes marginal revenue constant; the monopoly behaves like a competitive firm.

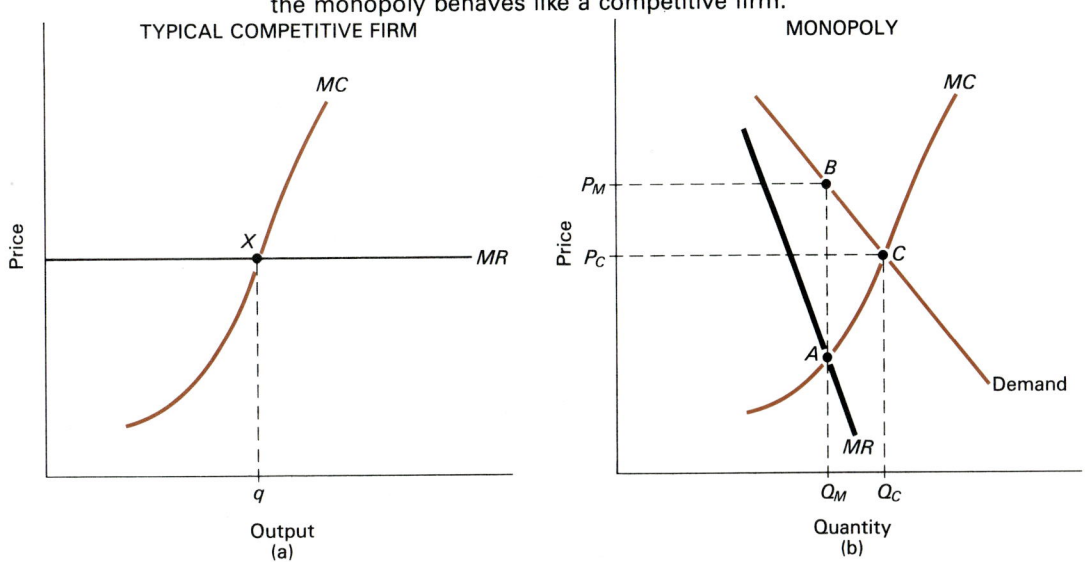

charges a higher price (P_M compared to P_C) than would perfectly competitive firms. If perfect competition achieves economic efficiency, as we proposed in the last chapter, then this monopoly is inefficient. Too few resources go to the production of the monopolist's good and too many resources end up in other, less valuable uses.

A monopoly firm that is inefficient also distorts the distribution of income within the economy. Higher monopoly prices and profits move money from buyers to monopoly producers. The distribution of income is shifted away from the consumers, who pay higher prices, in favor of the owners of the monopoly firm.

KEY CONCEPT 19.8

Monopolists supply less quantity to the market and charge higher prices than would a perfect competitor with the same cost structure. Monopoly is therefore inefficient in the economic sense.

ANTITRUST POLICIES

19.9 FIGHTING INEFFICIENCY

Antitrust Laws
Laws designed to prevent businesses from engaging in activities that reduce competition, set price, or in other ways restrain trade.

So far we have seen that monopolies can redistribute wealth toward themselves if they make economic profits by reducing quantity and charging higher prices than those that would be charged by a competitive firm. They also, in many cases, reduce the efficiency of markets. In such cases it is sometimes possible to produce gains in economic efficiency through the use of government intervention in the marketplace. If the assumptions we laid out in Figure 19-4 hold, then there is a definite failure of the marketplace to attain ideal economic efficiency and **antitrust laws** may be able to move the

558 *Monopoly: The Case of the One Firm Market*

Sherman Antitrust Act
The 1890 federal law making most monopoly practices illegal.

Clayton Antitrust Act
The 1914 federal law outlawing such monopoly pricing practices as price discrimination.

economy toward efficiency by changing the way the market in Figure 19-4 works. Several options are available to government policymakers.

Federal laws approach some monopoly situations directly by making practices that lead to monopolies illegal. The **Sherman Antitrust Act** (1890) and the **Clayton Antitrust Act** (1914) are the basis of many lawsuits that have forced single sellers to behave more like competitive firms. Antitrust suits have broken big monopoly firms, such as the old Standard Oil Trust, into many smaller, more competitive firms, such as Exxon, Chevron, and others. Suits brought under antitrust legislation have also ended collusive agreements among "competitors" to set monopoly prices. Other antitrust policies have removed the entry barriers that made monopolies possible in the first place.

Price regulations are another way to make monopolists more efficient. Suppose Congress imposes a control price of P_C on the monopoly in Figure 19-4. The monopoly firm can charge no other price than P_C. The monopoly is now a price taker, since it cannot alter price by manipulating production. The monopolist reacts by setting MR equals MC at P_C just as a competitive firm would. Thus the monopoly maximizes profit at the same combination (price P_C and output Q_C) as a perfectly competitive industry might.

Taxes and subsidies are a third potential antitrust policy. Congress can tax away some of the monopolist's economic profits, giving these funds to buyers. Demand for the monopoly good increases, and monopoly output moves toward the efficient level when this policy is followed.

Monopoly Price Regulations

19.10 MONOPOLY PRICE REGULATIONS

Government price regulations that are designed to increase economic efficiency sometimes encounter uncomfortable trade-offs, as Figure 19-5 makes

FIGURE 19-5

Monopoly Price Regulation. Which price should regulators set for this monopoly? Price P_A is the monopoly profit-maximizing price. Price P_B moves the monopolist to the perfectly competitive output, but the monopoly earns negative economic profits since $P_B < ATC$. Price P_C allows the firm to earn a normal profit, but fewer goods are produced than would be under perfect competition.

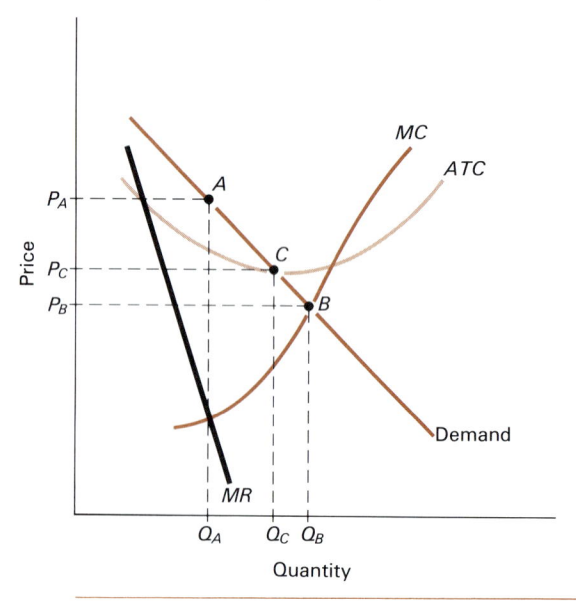

clear. Left to its own, this monopoly would set price at P_A. It sets price at the demand point that corresponds to the MC equals MR quantity. The monopoly earns economic profit, since P_A is higher than ATC at this output level (see the figure).

Government regulations designed to achieve economic efficiency would set price at P_B to force the monopolist to produce at B. This is the short-run equilibrium that would prevail in a competitive market. This efficiency-promoting price regulation suffers an important flaw, however. The monopoly might go out of business in the long run. The P_B price is less than ATC, so this monopoly will make negative economic profits unless it receives a government subsidy or is allowed to practice price discrimination to generate more revenue.

What is the middle ground between inefficient monopoly profits and a price regulation that drives a useful firm out of business? One solution is to allow monopolies to charge prices that reflect a "fair" return, or normal profit. Many public utility firms fall under such regulations, which lead to prices like P_C in the figure. Price equals average total cost in this instance, so the firm earns zero economic profit. Zero economic profit means that profits just equal those available elsewhere, the fair return the regulators intend.

What is the trade-off in regulating a fair rate of return that sets price equal to ATC? The price that is "fair" and generates the normal profits necessary to keep the monopoly in business is not efficient. Fewer goods are produced than if perfect competition prevailed. Government regulators must carefully weigh the benefits of regulation against its costs and against the risk of regulating the firm out of the market.

Monopoly regulations also risk waste. If public officials set monopoly prices at the break-even point, monopoly managers have little to lose and much to gain by padding cost figures. There is a strong incentive for the monopoly to invest in plush offices, fancy company cars, expensive worker lunchrooms, and big donations to local charities. The regulated monopoly finds these purchases relatively costless to themselves, because the regulatory agency simply boosts prices to cover the added costs and assure a "fair" return. The price that regulated firms are permitted to charge is often based on what are called cost plus rules. Rates are set to generate enough revenues to cover costs plus a fixed percentage return. Cost-increasing expenditures, like plush offices, increase the cost on which regulated prices are based. A regulated monopoly can increase profits through creative waste, since added expenditures generate higher costs, which in turn allow higher legal prices and provide higher total profits.

19.11 ANTITRUST LEGISLATION

Limits to Antitrust Legislation

It is reasonably clear that government intervention in markets can in some cases produce economic gains. The most important issue here, however, is how far should antitrust policy go in regulating monopoly price and production activity? Cost is the first restriction on government enforcement activities. It is expensive to investigate and prosecute monopoly offenders. Sometimes the benefits of antitrust actions are not worth the costs. The Justice Department's antitrust suit against IBM lasted from 1969 to the early 1980s, costing millions of dollars in lawyers' fees, court costs, lost profits, and staff salaries. The suit was eventually dropped because it simply made no cost/benefit sense to carry it on further.

A second limit to antitrust policy is based on the possibility of productivity differences between monopoly and competitive firms. The efficiency analysis of Figure 19-4 assumed that both firm types have the same costs. This is not necessarily so. Monopolies might be bigger, thereby allowing them to use more efficient large-scale technology and longer, cost-saving production runs. One big monopoly firm might be able to supply goods at a lower cost than many smaller, less effective competitive producers.

Cable television is an example of a natural monopoly. It is more efficient to have one firm wire a city for cable and provide diversified services than to have many competing firms do so, with each bearing the high fixed costs of poles, cables, and transmission facilities. Electricity, telephone, and water services are all most efficiently supplied by monopolies for similar reasons.

Natural monopolies are a trade-off. Production by a monopoly is more efficient than production under perfect competition, but monopoly pricing and production choices are still inefficient. Many natural monopolies, such as utilities and telephone companies, are allowed to retain monopoly status because of their economies of scale but are regulated to reduce the inefficiencies that monopoly pricing produces.

Government encourages some monopolies because they foster innovations that benefit society more than the costs imposed by their inefficiency harm society. Some monopolists keep competitors out of their markets by constantly improving their products and funding research that leads to new products. Patent and copyright laws give inventors and authors a temporary monopoly over new goods. The monopoly-pricing loss is small compared to the potential knowledge gain.

George Stigler, a Nobel Prize-winning economist from the University of Chicago, suggests another limit to government regulation. Stigler claims that government does less to break up monopolies than it does to create them. Government passes laws that restrict entry into industries, keep cheaper foreign goods out of the market, or otherwise give individual firms the power to set price. If old laws are the cause of the monopoly power, as Stigler suggests, is there any reason to believe that new laws that regulate monopolies will be much different? The possibility that monopoly regulations make the monopoly problem worse are an important limit to antitrust policy.

Quality is a final limit to government regulations. Government policies that successfully regulate prices and quantities may fail to keep quality constant. City rules that regulate taxi fares, for example, sometimes result in run-down cabs and poor taxi service. Shoddy, inferior goods may result from "efficient" rules and laws.

Monopoly regulation is delicate. Federal policy in recent years has moved to encourage greater competition and lower entry barriers rather than imposing direct government regulation of monopoly firms, but these regulations have had mixed results. For example, airline fares fell in the late 1970s when price regulations were lifted. But many airlines were at or near bankruptcy by 1982. Service in some areas had deteriorated as unregulated firms abandoned marginal markets. Local telephone rates went up, not down, when the Justice Department opened the telephone market to competition. These attempts at deregulation to encourage competition are not as yet obviously successful, at least in the short run. The long-run consequences will no doubt conform to economic theory, but they may indeed be in the quite distant future.

THE DEBATE OVER MONOPOLIES

Two of the most controversial public policy issues debated today question how serious the monopoly problem is and whether or not government antitrust activities should increase. These issues, like all other economic issues, must be weighed out in regard to both their costs and benefits. While we have discussed the costs side of these issues, the benefits have not as yet been developed in detail.

Static versus Dynamic Efficiency

> **19.12 STATIC AND DYNAMIC EFFICIENCY**

Static Efficiency
The most efficient use of current resources, without regard for economic growth.

Dynamic Efficiency
The use of resources that leads to high rates of economic growth in the future.

Economist Joseph Schumpeter viewed monopoly profits as the price of progress. Monopolies might misallocate resources today, reducing **static efficiency,** but they encourage economic growth and lead to **dynamic efficiency** according to Schumpeter. Static efficiency refers to the most productive use of today's resources, ignoring future consequences. Dynamic efficiency refers to a use of resources that generates rapid economic growth, making productive use of resources over time.

Schumpeter thought that big firms use innovation to keep one step ahead of potential competitors. The innovation and research and development investment that monopolies use as an entry barrier end up benefiting the whole economy over time.

If Schumpeter's hypothesis is correct, then monopolies are a trade-off. We observe static inefficiency now but dynamic efficiency, with higher income and productivity, later. Antitrust policies might be undesirable here. They might increase production and lower prices in the short run but reduce the potential for economic growth in the long run. Schumpeter's proposition is hard to prove or disprove. In support of Schumpeter's argument, the fastest growing firms do seem to be those who innovate the most, but we do not have conclusive evidence that most innovations are the product of the biggest, most monopolistic firms. In effect, the most that we can say on the innovation benefits of monopoly is that the jury is still out.

The Importance of Antitrust Policies

> **19.13 GOVERNMENT REGULATIONS**

Many economists have tried to measure the welfare loss from monopoly. In this instance, welfare loss refers to the value of lost production and misallocated resources. University of Chicago economist Arnold C. Harberger examined the monopoly problems in the 1950s. His study of manufacturing industries led to a surprisingly low estimate of welfare loss. He estimated monopoly losses at less than 1/10 of 1 percent of gross national product, which is just about enough to buy every family in America a good steak dinner, but no more. Even this small fraction of GNP is big in dollar terms, but does it justify an active antitrust policy? One interpretation of Harberger's analysis is that antitrust policy is more of a problem of income distribution than economic efficiency. Monopolies, according to this view, are more important for the way their higher prices and profits change the distribution of income by shifting income from consumers to the owners of monopoly firms than for the inefficient way they allocate scarce resources.

University of Chicago law professor Richard Posner reworked Harberger's monopoly analysis in the 1970s. His new estimates found a larger welfare loss (6/10 of 1 percent of GNP) in mining and manufacturing sectors of the economy. Posner faulted Harberger for restricting his research to manufacturing firms. He suggests bigger welfare losses are found in government-regulated industries such as oil, airlines, motor carriers, dairy products, eyeglasses, and physicians' services. Licenses and government permits serve as entry barriers in these markets, while price controls reduce competition. Overall, regulation drives up prices and makes monopoly profits possible.

Posner estimates the loss in the regulated sector of the economy to be around 1.7 percent of GNP. This, by itself, is a substantial problem; however, if we add this to the estimated loss in other areas of the economy, the monopoly problem takes on the appearance of a major public-policy issue. The most surprising facet of the monopoly problem is that it is a problem that government has largely created itself through anti-competition regulation.

19.13 GOVERNMENT REGULATIONS

Special Interests and Monopoly Regulation

Regulated industries often appear to be the ones that are the most monopolistic. In observing this reality, economist George Stigler suggests that most regulations such as pollution taxes or trust-busting lawsuits, are not imposed on unwilling firms. Stigler thinks that firms seek regulation to keep competitors out and push up profits. Firms use regulation as another tool to increase profits.

There are several ways in which regulation can be used to increase private profits. Government sometimes provides a source of subsidy payments and a way to control entry through licenses, permits, and other restrictions. Firms use the public sector to set high prices, as with agricultural support prices, and to affect the prices of substitutes, complements, and inputs. Stigler says that any firm or industry that can will seek out regulation. The desired regulations tend to keep other firms out of the market, keep prices high, or pay subsidies to firms or buyers. Other desired regulations might make substitute goods more costly, make complementary goods cheaper, or reduce the cost of inputs. In considering all these possibilities, Stigler notes that it is not surprising to find that regulated firms earn monopoly profits.

The dairy industry is an example of a successful regulated monopoly. Government regulations boost dairy profits in several ways. Price supports on milk keep the price far above the market equilibrium. The government buys up the surplus and stores it as butter and cheese. By 1980, the government had warehouses full of surplus butter and cheese around the country. Eventually the government simply gave away some of the surplus to poor people in an effort to reduce storage costs.

For years, the dairy industry used government regulations to give butter an edge over the substitute good, margarine. It was once even illegal to sell margarine in some states with powerful dairy lobbies. In other states, margarine had to be uncolored, so as to look more like lard than butter, or be labeled oleomargarine, a less desirable name for marketing purposes. Restaurants were discouraged from using margarine by rules that forced them to notify customers that they were not being served butter. All these regulations were designed to keep demand for butter high by discouraging the sale and use of margarine.

The Political Economy of Monopoly Regulation

How do firms go about getting profitable regulations? Some industries claim they and their workers need protection from foreign competition or from destructive domestic competition. They claim that such competition would drive down price and bankrupt existing firms, hurting consumers in the long run. Other regulations are the result of political contributions or favors.

Sometimes the only voice that Congress hears is the voice of special interest. This is an example of the special-interest effect discussed in Chapter 5. Individual consumers have too little to gain or lose to make their voices heard on some issues. Special-interest groups, on the other hand, have a powerful incentive to promote regulations that increase their profits. The result is that Congress listens for the "voice of the people" and hears only the very well-organized and funded shouts of special interest. As a result, legislators enact regulations that provide large, concentrated benefits to the industry being regulated and pass small individual costs onto every consumer buying the special-interest group's products.

If Stigler's view is correct, that special-interest groups are encouraged by the political system to seek beneficial regulation, then there must be some form of public policy that best deals with the issue. **Deregulation** has been proposed by economists as one solution. If regulations create monopoly power, fewer regulations might improve efficiency. The problem here is to avoid throwing out the baby with the bathwater. Not all industry regulations are inefficient. Even deregulation might not work if interest groups are as powerful as Stigler suggests. The major task is to define which regulations offer benefits that outweigh their costs. Given the complexity of determining the costs and benefits of legislation, it may indeed be more efficient to attempt a reform of our political system first.

Deregulation
The policy of reducing or eliminating government regulations that affect private individuals and firms.

SUMMARY

19.1

1. A monopoly is a single-seller market. One firm sets price and quantity, subject to market demand limitations. There are few unregulated pure monopolies in the real world, but many firms are able to exercise monopoly power to a limited extent. The monopoly firm discussed in this chapter is assumed to be the sole producer in a market and to sell a single product that has no close substitutes.

19.2

2. Monopolies can only exist over time if there are barriers to entry that keep other firms from entering the market and increasing competition. Government regulations are one source of entry barriers. Patents, copyrights, licenses, and other government regulations restrict entry into selected markets. High fixed costs can act as an entry barrier, too. Natural monopolies, like electric and sewer utilities, for example, are monopoly firms. High fixed costs make it difficult for other firms to enter the market and earn profits. Economies of scale also serve as entry barriers when existing firms, with high output, have lower marginal costs than smaller, new entrants. Trade secrets are another type of entry barrier. New firms must break trade secret barriers to produce goods that compete with existing firms' products. Trade secrets are a common entry barrier in high-technology markets.

19.3, 19.4

3. The monopolist is a price seeker not a price taker. Monopolists seek out the price-quantity point on the demand curve that maximizes profits.

Monopolists maximize profits by comparing marginal cost with marginal revenue. Marginal revenue is not constant for the monopoly firm. Marginal revenue is less than the selling price. The MR curve lies below the demand curve. The monopoly must cut price on all units it sells in order to increase quantity demanded, so the additional revenue is less than the price of the extra goods sold.

19.4 → 4. The profit-maximizing output for the monopolist is found by expanding production until MR equals MC. The last item produced adds as much to revenue as it does to cost. Production beyond this point would result in MC being greater than MR and thus would earn negative profit.

19.5 → 5. Once monopoly output level Q_M is set, the monopoly price is set by finding the corresponding price on the demand curve. P_M is the market clearing price, given Q_M units produced.

19.5 → 6. Price is higher than marginal cost for the profit-maximizing monopoly, but that doesn't mean that all monopolies earn high profits. A monopoly can even lose money if ATC is greater than P_M at the profit-maximizing (loss-minimizing) point. Monopolies also operate on the elastic portion of the demand curve. Marginal revenue is negative, making it impossible for MR to equal MC, when demand is inelastic.

19.6 → 7. Monopoly firms can increase revenue (and profit) by selling their goods to different buyers at different prices—a practice called price discrimination. In the example in the text, the monopoly firm picked total output levels by setting MC equal to MR_T, the marginal revenue curve for the total market. Prices and quantities in individual markets were then set using MC equals MR_A equals MR_B to divide output among the markets.

19.7 → 8. Monopoly firms can engage in price discrimination if their buyers have different demand characteristics, if it is possible to charge different prices to different buyers, and if the firm can prevent resale.

19.8 → 9. Monopoly firms differ from perfectly competitive firms in several respects. Monopoly firms face downward-sloping demand and MR curves. Perfectly competitive firms act as if they face perfectly elastic (horizontal) MR curves. Monopolies produce smaller quantities and charge higher prices than would perfectly competitive industries with the same cost curves facing the same demand curve. Given these assumptions, monopoly producers are inefficient. Too few scarce resources are used to produce monopoly goods.

19.9 → 10. Antitrust legislation tries to restore efficiency to monopoly markets by regulating monopolists or preventing their formation in the first place. The Sherman Antitrust Act and the Clayton Antitrust Act forbid certain monopoly practices such as collusion and some artificial barriers to entry. Price regulations are another common way to regulate monopoly firms. Government regulations that set price in monopoly markets indirectly affect how much is produced. Taxes and subsidies are also sometimes used to regulate monopolies.

> **19.10**

11. The monopoly profit-maximizing price and quantity is often inefficient. If government sets price at the efficient (perfect competition) level, however, the monopoly firm may lose money and eventually exit the industry. This destroys a valuable industry and makes its goods unavailable to consumers. A price set to equal *ATC* assures the continued existence of the firm by giving it a normal profit—a profit equal to the fair return available elsewhere in the economy. This price regulation still leads to higher prices and lower quantity than those that might exist under perfect competition.

> **19.11**

12. Antitrust legislation has several limits. Cost is one limit. Government lawsuits and regulations are costly. The cost of regulation sometimes exceeds the social gain. Furthermore, some large monopoly firms may have lower production costs than would many small perfectly competitive sellers. A monopoly might be more efficient than competitive firms would be in this instance. Similarly, monopoly firms that use innovation as an entry barrier are a mixed blessing. They may charge higher prices than competitive firms, but their new products and improved technology are an important social benefit. Excessive regulation might destroy this valuable resource. Finally, some economists think that government regulations do more to create monopolies than to restrict them.

> **19.12**

13. Schumpeter argued that monopoly profits are the price society pays for innovation. Monopolies may misallocate resources in the present, resulting in static inefficiency, but their innovations generate economic growth and dynamic efficiency in the long run. Schumpeter's hypothesis, however, is difficult to prove. It is hard to tell if society is a net beneficiary of monopoly actions.

> **19.13**

14. Harberger measured the welfare loss to monopolies in the 1950s and found it to be low. Monopolies are not a major cause of inefficiency, he suggested. Posner, after reestimating the welfare loss, concluded that monopoly does reduce economic welfare, but that monopoly power is most concentrated in exactly those markets that government regulates. Government regulations are seen to be a major cause of inefficiency. Stigler suggests that special-interest groups use government regulation to gain monopoly profits. Firms seek price controls and entry-limiting government regulations that increase profit.

DISCUSSION QUESTIONS

> **19.3, 19.4, 19.5, 19.8**

1. Draw marginal cost, marginal revenue, and demand curves for a monopolist. Show the profit-maximizing price and quantity. How would the monopolist respond to a tax that raises marginal cost? How does this response compare with a competitive firm's reaction? Explain.

> **19.3, 19.8**

2. Explain why the marginal revenue curve lies below the demand curve for a monopolist. What is the relationship between marginal revenue and demand for an individual firm in a perfectly competitive market? What about for a perfectly competitive industry? Explain.

19.5, 19.8 ▶ 3. "A monopolist never sets price and quantity on the inelastic portion of the demand curve." Is this statement true or false? Explain your reasoning.

19.2 ▶ 4. Explain why barriers to entry are necessary to the existence of monopolies.

19.3, 19.4, 19.5, 19.10 ▶ 5. Draw the demand, marginal revenue, marginal cost, and average total cost curves of a monopolist that earns negative economic profits while producing at the level at which MR equals MC. What happens to the size of the loss if the monopolist increases or decreases production? Explain.

19.10 ▶ 6. What price should regulators impose on monopolists? List different pricing theories that regulators could follow. List the advantages and disadvantages of each pricing technique.

19.11 ▶ 7. List the advantages and disadvantages of antitrust regulations. Explain the reasoning behind your answer.

SELECTED READINGS

Bork, Robert H. *The Anti-trust Paradox*. New York: Basic Books, 1978.

Harberger, Arnold C. "Monopoly and Resource Allocation." *American Economic Review* (Spring, 1954), p. 267.

Machlup, Fritz. *The Political Economy of Monopoly*. Baltimore: Johns Hopkins University Press, 1952.

Posner, Richard A. *The Economic Analysis of Law*. Boston: Little Brown, 1972.

Posner, Richard A. "The Social Cost of Monopoly and Regulation." *Journal of Political Economy* (May, 1975), p. 969.

Schumpeter, Joseph. *Capitalism, Socialism, and Democracy*. New York: Harper and Brothers, 1942.

Stigler, George J. "The Economic Theory of Regulation." *The Bell Journal of Economics and Management Science* (Spring, 1971), pp. 3–21.

Stigler, George J. "The Economists and the Problem of Monopoly." *American Economic Review* (December, 1982), p. 1.

CHAPTER 20

Monopolistic Competition and Oligopoly

Having read the chapter, reviewed the chapter summary, and completed the *Study Guide* exercises, you should be able to:

CRIS

20.1 MONOPOLISTIC COMPETITION: Define monopolistic competition and list and explain its three important characteristics.

20.2 FIRM'S DEMAND CURVE: Explain how an individual firm's demand curve in monopolistic competition differs from that faced by firms in either perfect competition or pure monopoly.

20.3 DETERMINING DEMAND CURVES: Discuss the economic variables that determine the size and shape of an individual firm's demand curve under monopolistic competition.

20.4 DEMAND, MR, MC, AND ATC: Draw demand, *MR*, *MC,* and *ATC* curves for a monopolistic competitor, explain how the firm chooses price and quantity, and show whether the firm earns positive, negative, or zero economic profit.

20.5 ADVERTISING AS PRODUCT DIFFERENTIATION: Discuss the role of advertising in monopolistic competition and tell how it affects demand, cost, and profit.

20.6 LONG-RUN EQUILIBRIUM: Draw the long-run equilibrium of a monopolistic competitor and explain why zero economic profits prevail and why the firm experiences excess capacity in the long run.

20.7 DESIRABILITY OF DIFFERENTIATION: Explain whether product differentiation is desirable or undesirable, giving arguments for both sides of this question.

20.8 OLIGOPOLY: Define oligopoly and compare and contrast oligopoly with perfect competition, monopoly, monopolistic competition, listing the similarities and differences.

568 *Monopolistic Competition and Oligopoly*

- **20.9 CHARACTERISTICS OF OLIGOPOLIES:** List the three main characteristics of oligopoly markets and explain why each is important and how each affects the behavior of individual firms.

- **20.10 CONCENTRATION RATIOS:** Explain what is meant by a concentration ratio and indicate whether concentration ratios are high or low in oligopoly markets and why.

- **20.11 CAUSES OF OLIGOPOLY:** List two economic causes of oligopoly and explain why each cause tends to reduce the number of firms in a given market, then explain the difference between horizontal and vertical mergers.

- **20.12 CARTELS:** Define a cartel and explain why profit-seeking firms form cartels, then describe the three problems that industry members must solve before they can form a successful cartel.

- **20.13 CARTEL SUCCESS:** List and explain four important factors that contribute to cartel success and tell how each secret to success is a solution to the three problems discussed in the previous objective.

- **20.14 PRICE LEADERSHIP:** Explain what is meant by price leadership and discuss why firms would follow a price leader instead of setting their own prices.

- **20.15 KINKED DEMAND CURVE:** Draw a kinked demand curve and its corresponding *MR* curve, indicate why the slope of the demand curve is different above and below the kink, and explain the shape of the *MR* curve.

- **20.16 KINKED DEMAND AND PRICE:** Explain how the existence of a kinked demand curve would reduce price flexibility, even among otherwise competitive oligopoly firms, and cite problems of the kinked demand curve theory in explaining oligopoly behavior.

- **20.17 REGULATING OLIGOPOLIES:** List and discuss the pros and cons of regulating oligopoly firms and discuss whether bigness equals badness.

The vast majority of products that are advertised on television and in newspapers, purchased in the supermarkets and department stores, and found in the home do not fit exactly the description of the perfectly competitive market. For example, some goods consumers purchase may not necessarily be identical to those from competing suppliers. Some goods may have individual differences or advertised properties that make similar products far from the same. Consumers might not always buy the lowest priced goods, since quality and prestige differences enter into their choices. There may be thousands of firms producing a given product or just one, a monopoly, selling one of the goods consumers normally purchase. Some consumer markets are dominated by just a few big manufacturers. In other words, consumers buy many items in markets that fit neither the description of monopoly nor that of perfect competition presented in the last two chapters.

In the last two chapters, the market models of perfect competition, where thousands of firms compete to sell identical products, and monopoly, where one firm dominates supply, were developed. These market models are important because they show how supply decisions are made and how competitive forces work. Many real-world markets, however, do not look much like pure competition, but they are not monopolies, either. They fall somewhere in between. This chapter looks at this in-between world of imperfect competition.

Real-world markets differ in all sorts of ways. Economists find that many imperfect markets are characterized by monopolistic competition or oligopoly. The remainder of this chapter explains what these terms mean, how these markets work, and what effects monopolistic competition and oligopoly have on the prices buyers pay and the quantities they purchase.

MONOPOLISTIC COMPETITION

20.1 MONOPOLISTIC COMPETITION

Monopolistic Competition
Competitive markets characterized by product differentiation; each firm has a limited monopoly over its particular good.

Monopolistic competition describes a market in which many firms compete selling similar goods. While sellers offer similar items, such as different types of cola drinks, these goods are not identical in consumers' eyes. Through advertising, for example, the Bayer aspirin company has created a perceived difference between its product and other aspirin products. Advertising of the brand name Bayer aspirin in comparison to other generic aspirins stresses the differences between what are essentially very similar products. While Bayer aspirin may have the same chemical formula as other aspirins, the strength of its brand loyalty created through advertising makes it unique in some sense. These unique differences give the monopolistic competitor its own submarket, which gives it some monopoly power.

Characteristics of Monopolistic Competition

20.1 MONOPOLISTIC COMPETITION

Markets that display monopolistic competition tend to share three major characteristics: many relatively small firms, free entry and exit, and product differentiation.

Many Relatively Small Firms Many sellers compete in these markets and no single firm is big enough to dominate. In this respect, these markets are similar to the competitive markets we studied in Chapter 18. The existence of many sellers provides the short-run rivalry that the name monopolistic competition suggests.

Free Entry and Exit Old firms can leave markets like these if losses persist. New firms can enter if economic profits lure them in. Free entry and exit assure competition in the long run. Existing firms cannot be complacent if potential new competitors abound.

Product Differentiation Product differentiation is the key to monopolistic competition. The goods sold in these markets are not identical, as they are under perfect competition. Firms in markets characterized by monopolistic competition sell products that, although they are similar in overall form or function, differ in actual or perceived ways from one another. Since consumers think of similar products as different, it is convenient to think of these not as single markets (the market for aspirin, for example), but as sets of related markets (the market for Bayer aspirin, the market for Saint Joseph's aspirin) that consumers treat as substitutes. Individual sellers have monopolies over their particular goods, although they are not true monopolies. Buyers have access to goods of other producers that are close, if not perfect, substitutes.

Differences in products can be actual variations in function or performance or simply perceived variations. Advertising, imagery, and promotion are sometimes as important as production cost for monopolistic competitive firms. Managers may spend thousands or millions of dollars on product design, packaging, advertising, and celebrity endorsements to create an important difference advantage over the competitor's goods. The logic of product differentiation is easy to guess. If you think Izod Lacoste "alligator" sports shirts are somehow better than similar Sears products, you may be willing to pay more for them.

A clever advertiser can turn a sow's ear into a silk purse, if a silk purse sells better. All cigarettes are pretty much the same, for example, yet they are promoted to appeal to different groups of buyers. Marlboro cigarettes were once thought of as an inferior women's brand, with modest sales. A big ad campaign featuring he-man cowboys opened up a new market, making the same Marlboro cigarettes the best-selling brand in the world.

Location is an additional means of differentiating a product in the market. For example, many hotels operate several different restaurants or food outlets within their building. They might have a coffee shop, a bar, a formal dinner restaurant and so on. All of these outlets serve food and beverages produced in the same central kitchen, but coffee served in the coffee shop is frequently priced lower than coffee served in the bar or formal dining room. The coffee itself is identical, but the location in which it is served differentiates the product and therefore the price is different.

Many markets for consumer goods in the United States can be characterized by the product differentiation noted here. Clothing, furniture, jewelry, and fast food industries, among others, meet the conditions for monopolistic competition.

Demand Curves in Monopolistic Competition

20.2 FIRM'S DEMAND CURVE

Product differentiation makes demand curves faced by individual firms different from those in either monopoly or perfectly competitive markets. Figure 20-1 shows the way we described demand curves in earlier chapters. As shown in Figure 20-1(a), the market demand curve is downward sloping in a perfectly competitive market, but individual firms behave as if they faced a horizontal or perfectly elastic demand curve. Perfectly competitive firms take market price as constant. They assume they can sell any amount of their output at the going market equilibrium price.

In a monopoly market, the single seller's output is equal to market supply. Market demand, not some fraction of it, is the monopoly's concern. These price-searching firms know they face downward-sloping demand curves. Because they sell more if they reduce price, they make price and output calculations based on marginal revenue and marginal cost curves, as shown in Figure 20-1(b).

Individual firms are neither real monopolies nor complete competitors under monopolistic competition. The overall demand for aspirin, for example, is divided among several product-differentiating firms, as Figure 20-2 indicates. Each firm has some influence over the price it will charge. The

FIGURE 20-1

Firms in Perfect Competition and Monopoly. These graphs show how individual firms viewed demand in previous chapters. (a) The market demand is downward sloping in perfect competition, but individual firms behave as if they face perfectly elastic demand. (b) Monopoly firms use market demand and marginal revenue to make price–quantity decisions.

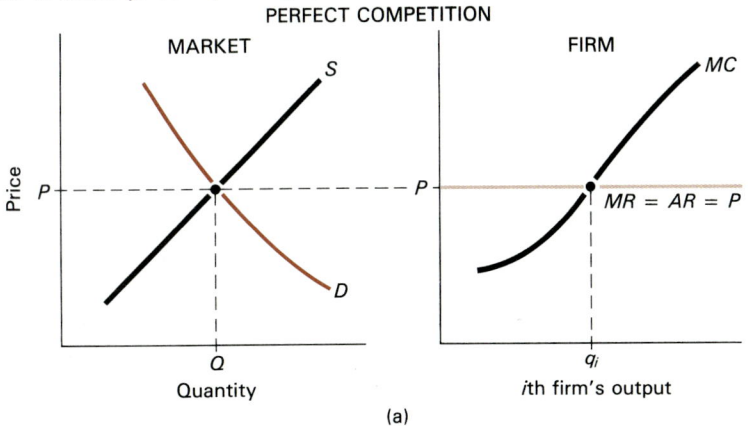

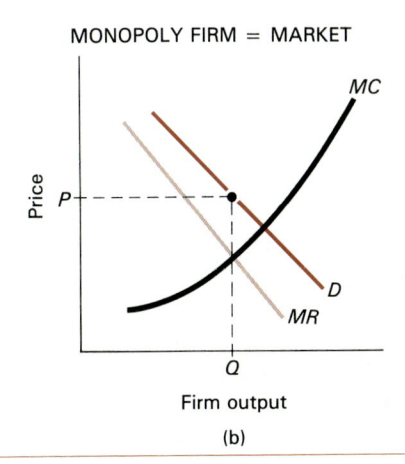

demand curves for aspirin X and aspirin Y shown here are pieces of the bigger market demand curve for aspirin.

Firm X in the figure has established a dependable old firm image. People associate this aspirin with dependability and high quality. The result of effective advertising is that the demand for aspirin X is less elastic than demands for other aspirin. Many consumers think aspirin X is sufficiently different from other aspirins to continue to buy it even if its price rises while the prices of other aspirins stay the same.

Firm Y in the figure has been less successful in carving out a niche in the market. Product differentiation is not complete here, so consumers see other aspirins as closer substitutes. This affects Firm Y's demand curve, as the figure shows. Its slice of market demand is more elastic than Firm X's, which means that when Firm Y raises price, it experiences a larger drop in sales.

20.3 DETERMINING DEMAND CURVES

What determines the size and elasticity of an individual firm's demand curve? The nature of the overall market demand is part of the answer. If the demand for bathing suits is price inelastic, for example, this affects the pricing options available for all the product-differentiating firms in this

572 *Monopolistic Competition and Oligopoly*

FIGURE 20-2

Firms in Monopolistic Competition. Each monopolistic competitor has a monopoly over its own differentiated product. Both firms set output at A, where MC equals the MR for their product, then set price at B, the corresponding point on their demand curve. Differences in demand account for interfirm price differentials here. Each firm's demand is a segment of market demand for these products. The degree of product differentiation determines the shape of the individual firm's demand.

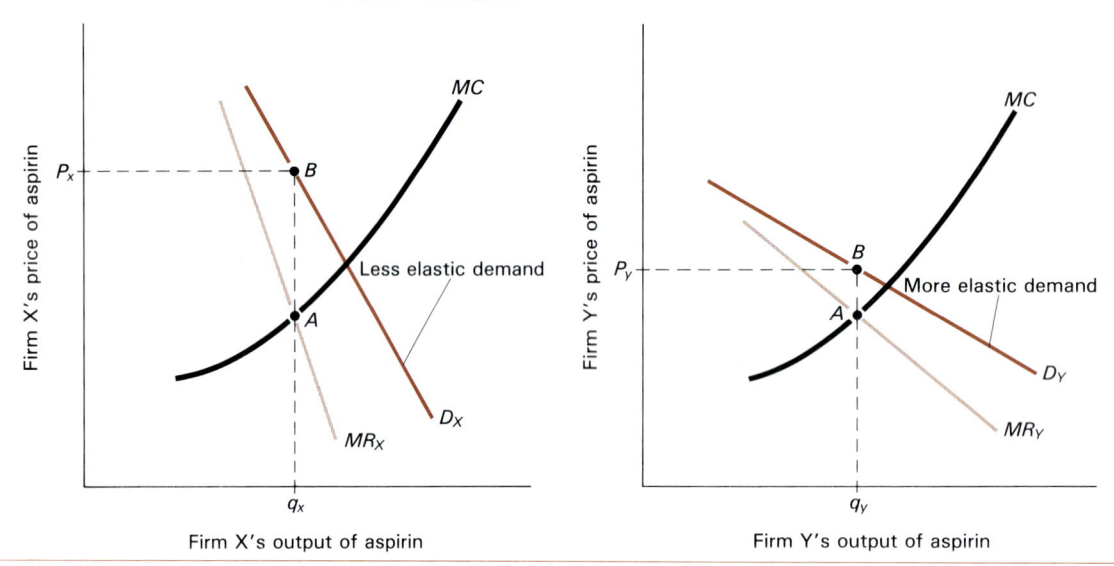

market. Each seller's demand curve therefore depends, in part, on the market demand curve.

The degree of product differentiation and brand loyalty is a second factor. Firms that can successfully establish their product in buyers' minds can expect less price-sensitive sales than businesses whose goods are seen as being much like the rest.

Finally, the degree and nature of competition among firms affects demand for the items. Suppose aspirin X goes on sale at a lower price. How much does quantity demanded increase? In markets where goods are close, but not perfect, substitutes, elasticity of demand depends on how the other makers of aspirin react. Competitors must decide whether they will also cut price or perhaps add more advertising or start some type of promotional contest to attract buyers. Individual firms make price and output choices based on how they perceive their own product's demand and marginal revenue curves, taking into account likely competitor reactions to changing price.

PRICE AND OUTPUT DECISIONS: ECONOMIC THEORY VERSUS MARK-UP PRICING

20.4 DEMAND, MR, MC, AND ATC

Firms engaged in monopolistic competition set price and output following the same rules as all producers. They equate marginal revenue and marginal cost. Monopolistic competitors produce at the output level at which marginal cost equals their submarket's marginal revenue curve, point A in Figures 20-1 and 20-2. They then set price at the point on the demand curve, point B in the figures, that corresponds to this output. All firms search for this profit-maximizing price–quantity combination, but differences in individual demand curves mean different price and quantity results for different firms. The maker of famous aspirin X gets a higher price for its goods than does the maker of "ordinary" aspirin Y.

> **KEY CONCEPT 20.4**
>
> Monopolistic competitors, like all producers, maximize profits by producing at the output level at which marginal revenue equals marginal cost and charging the price indicated on their demand curve for that amount of output.

Mark-up Pricing
A pricing rule that sets price by adding a fixed percentage to cost.

Some students are skeptical of economic theories that propose that firms use marginal revenue, marginal cost, and demand curves to set price. Students who have worked in stores know that managers generally use a rule of thumb to set prices. **Mark-up pricing** is one such rule. Prices are determined by taking cost and adding on a percentage markup. Different percentage markups are used for different goods.

Mark-up pricing is completely consistent with economic theory if the mark-up formulas retailers use take into account elasticity of demand, as they generally do. Items with low elasticity of demand, like aspirin X in Figure 20-2, get a high markup. Marginal cost, point A in the figure, is "marked up" by 50 percent to get the profit-maximizing price. Other goods with more elastic demand curves, like aspirin Y, get a lower percentage markup. The difference between marginal cost, A, and price, B, is less.

You can go to the store and test this markup pricing theory. Most retail stores use codes to print cost information on price stickers. Some stores use the CHARLESTON code, for example, where C is the code for 1, H is the code for 2, and so on. Figure out the store's code and you can determine each item's cost and markup. See if the markups you discover are consistent with elasticity of demand for different goods.

Pricing rules of thumb generally take elasticity of demand into account, with high markups for goods with few substitutes and inelastic demand and lower markups for goods with more elastic demand curves. Managers who know no economics, but use markup methods, are often the unknowing practitioners of the textbook pricing theories described here.

Profits in the Short Run

Having your own piece of the market is no guarantee of economic profit in the short run, as Figure 20-3 shows. Some firms, like Firm X in the figure, succeed. They are able to set price above average total cost and so earn the economic profits represented by the shaded area in the figure. Firm Y is not so lucky, however. Even profit-maximizing price P_y is less than average total cost. Firm Y earns the economic loss shown here.

Economic profits in the short run depend on two important variables that firms can influence. The first is cost. Firms can cut costs by finding more efficient production techniques, motivating managers and workers to increase output, or by cutting expenditures on advertising and promotion. Profits may eventually appear if costs fall enough.

20.5 ADVERTISING AS PRODUCT DIFFERENTIATION

The other option is to try to alter the product's demand by taking market shares from other similar products. If Firm Y can get the consumer's attention by making them aware of undiscovered advantages or new and improved attributes, it can make the demand for its product both larger and less elastic. This lower elasticity makes higher markups possible. The gain in Y's demand probably comes at a loss for X. Sometimes overall demand increases when one firm's promotion works, benefiting its competitors, too.

574   *Monopolistic Competition and Oligopoly*

FIGURE 20-3   **Short-Run Winners and Losers.** Not all monopolistic competitors earn high profits in the short run. Firm X's demand is bigger and less elastic than Firm Y's, so X earns positive economic profits, while Y earns a loss. Advertising and quality differences are among the tools competing firms use to draw demand from others and reduce price elasticity.

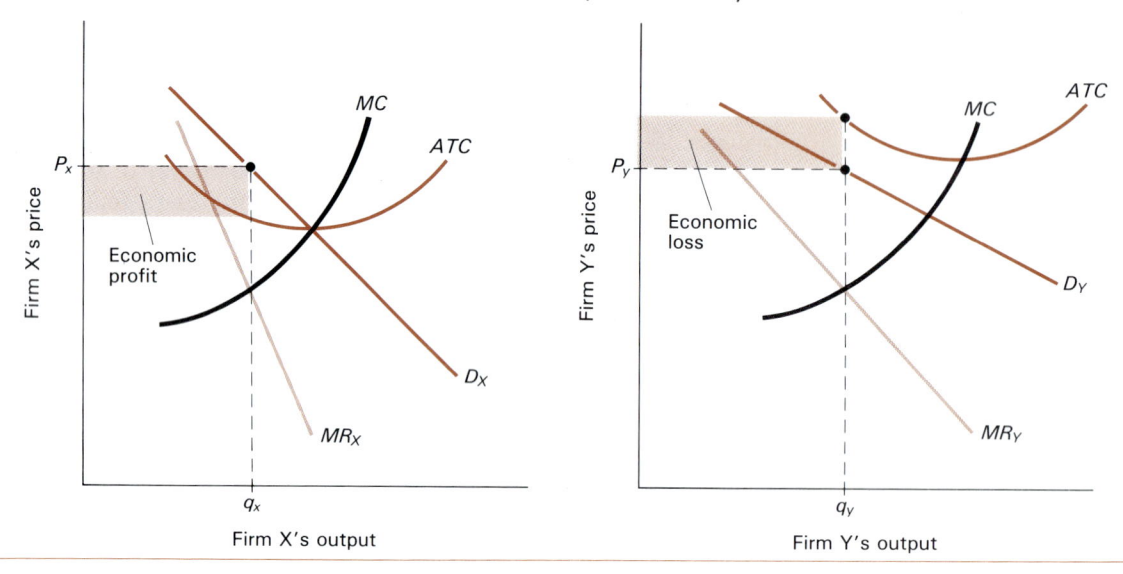

The makers of Seven-Up soda have been particularly successful at product differentiation. Seven-Up was once primarily a mixer (a soda used in mixed drinks). This is a market with limited demand. Seven-Up's producers decided to enter the bigger soft drink market as a differentiated product. The "Un-cola" ad campaign of the 1970s convinced people that, because Seven-Up isn't a cola, it is somehow radical and unconventional. Millions of people, wanting to be just as different as their friends, bought up the same old Seven-Up for the new reason. Seven-Up struck again in the 1980s with an ad blitz based on its lack of caffeine. Seven-Up never had caffeine, but few people cared until the new ads made them want a caffeine-free drink. Sales soared.

Using advertising, packaging, celebrity endorsements, and other gimmicks to increase demand does not necessarily guarantee profits, however. Product differentiation is expensive, and advertising and promotion costs increase along with demand. Bigger losses, not profits, may result from an increase in advertising expenditures. Sometimes advertising even backfires. Schlitz beer released "macho" ads in the mid-1970s, showing grizzled beer guzzlers who resorted to violence when told their favorite brew was not available. These ads seemed to terrify beer drinkers who did not view themselves as a part of the macho group. Demand declined and Schlitz sales went down the drain.

It is also important to note that, while advertising can measurably affect the market image and demand curve for a given product, it also serves a very beneficial function for consumers. In addition to the persuasive function of advertising it also serves to inform consumers of available products and offers comparisons of features and prices between these products. In a world in which consumers must gather information to make purchase decisions, this information is frequently distributed through advertising at a lower cost to consumers than if they had to gather the necessary information themselves. While the prices of goods must, of course, reflect the costs borne by producers to advertise the product, this information is usually distributed to consumers in a cost-efficient manner. Advertising is, in many cases, the most effective means of reducing information and transactions costs to the consumer. Many economists contend that the mere existence of advertising implies that producers have some control over their demand. Therefore, advertising is particularly pertinent in markets with monopolisticly competitive producers, oligopolies, and monopolies.

Monopolistic Competition in the Long Run

Free entry and exit assures the zero-profit long-run equilibrium shown in Figure 20-4. The entry of new firms or the exit of old ones alters the typical firm's market share, shifting the demand and MR curves, until price finally equals ATC, as shown in the figure.

Here is how the long-run equilibrium comes about. Suppose that there are too many firms in this industry, given product demand. If many businesses have losses in the short run, some exit the industry. Each of the remaining firms inherits a bigger slice of the total demand, since the industry demand is divided among the smaller number of firms. This means that each of the remaining firms faces a larger demand than before. When the exit of failing firms ends, and market shares stabilize, the typical surviving firms earn zero economic profit. Remember, however, that zero economic profit means firms are earning a return as high as that available in other businesses.

The existence of positive economic profits, on the other hand, brings entry. New firms enter the industry to get these high returns. Entry of new firms draws customers away from businesses already in the market. Demand shifts away from old firms as new ones take their customers.

20.6 LONG-RUN EQUILIBRIUM

FIGURE 20-4

The Long Run: Zero Profits and Excess Capacity. Entry by new firms, which reduces demand for goods sold by firms already in the market, forces economic profits to zero in the long run, as shown here. The typical firm prices at A, where MR equals MC, then sells at B, the corresponding demand point. Price equals ATC at this point, however, so zero economic profits prevail. The optimal plant size (lowest ATC) is at C. These firms don't make the best use of their production capacity, but they would earn negative profits if they did.

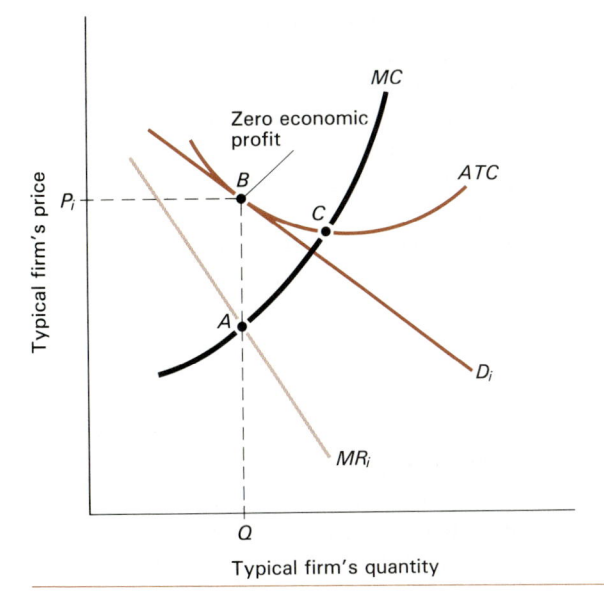

ECONOMIC ISSUES

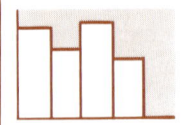

Advertising

Advertising has an important impact on consumer preferences and demand. Many firms use promotion and advertising expenditures to change consumer buying habits. Readers of this book are all familiar with modern advertising. Television and radio programs are peppered with paid promotions. Newspapers and magazines are also full of commercial messages. Billboards and sponsored events are all around us. Advertising is everywhere. Is advertising desirable? Economists see two sides to today's multi-billion dollar national advertising budget. This Economic Issue looks at advertising and its many roles in a modern economy.

Advertising's most important function is to improve the flow of information. Information about goods and services, prices, and qualities is costly and scarce. To see this, suppose you needed to know the answer to this question, "What is the best deal on running shoes in the local area?" This is not an unusual question. It is the kind of problem that consumers seek to solve every day. Finding the answer to this question, however, requires a wealth of information that most consumers would have great difficulty in assembling if there were no advertising. To find out where the best deal on running shoes is, one must first know what different brands of running shoes are available. Then one must discover something about the relative merits of different shoes. Finally, one must find out the price of these shoes at different stores and locations.

This is a lot of information to gather and most people would not go to all the trouble to find out all these things about every purchase they make. The cost of finding the information they seek might well outweigh any savings to be gained on making a more informed choice. They could gain greater utility if information were cheaper and they did not have to spend as much time and money to acquire market information.

Advertising is useful because it reduces the cost of searching for the best deal. Producers and retailers spend money to make information about their products known to the public. Anyone interested in running shoes, for example, will find many advertisements on television, radio, newspapers, and in sports magazines telling them about the differences in running shoes and announcing sale prices. It may still be difficult to get the very best deal on each purchase, but advertising increases consumer information and so leads buyers to get higher utility from their scarce income. They can make choices that save money or use money to buy goods that generate higher levels of satisfaction.

Advertising is valuable for the information it

Previously profitable firms that experience falling demand move toward the zero profit point shown here.

Long-run equilibrium brings zero economic profits in both perfect competition and monopolistic competition. Lack of entry lets profit persist in the long run for monopolies. This does not mean that perfect competition and monopolistic competition end up at the same place in the long run. There are two important differences in the long-run equilibrium conditions between perfect competition and monopolistic competition.

Long-run equilibrium for a competitive market has two important properties: (1) price equals marginal cost, and (2) firms produce at the minimum point on their *ATC* curves. (Review Chapter 18 if you've forgotten these facts.) Prices that equal marginal cost are important because they send out efficient price signals. These prices tell the economy the value of the resources used up in production. Minimizing *ATC* means that plant capacity is most efficiently used. Any other output level would cost more to produce.

Figure 20-4 can also be used to show how monopolistic and perfect competition differ in the long run. Price exceeds marginal cost at monopolistic competition's long-run equilibrium, sending a false price signal to the economy. Individual buyers give up more for these goods when they buy

makes available, but it is not a free lunch. Advertising is expensive. Advertisements add to the cost of production and sales, so consumers end up paying for the information they get in higher prices, whether they want it or not. People who buy Chrysler cars, for example, must realize that the cost of their automobiles includes both the expense of building them and the cost of television ads during Sunday football games. One minute's advertising on a top-rated television show can cost over $150,000. A one-minute ad costs $1 million during the football Super Bowl. That is a high price to pay for the information made available. Consumers might be better off if the producers of some products stopped advertising and cut price instead. This is particularly the case in markets for goods that are uniformly priced or where quality differences are slight. Consumers could subscribe to information services, such as *Consumer Reports* magazine, to get the information they need at a lower cost than with today's expensive advertising system. Even under the present system, consumers can buy unadvertised or "low ad" goods such as generic brands if they wish to avoid or reduce their information costs.

Advertising is also criticized because many ads do not really inform so much as they try to manipulate. They attempt to create a need where none exists and to distort consumer preferences. They try to get consumers to buy different goods or pay higher prices from them. One firm, for example, introduced "doggie juice," a beef-flavored liquid beverage for dogs. The product was an initial success, not because dogs were tired of water, but because a successful ad campaign made dog owners want to try this new item. No one forced buyers to purchase this new good, so we must conclude that they did so because buying doggie juice increased their utility. Yet many people question whether ads that promote these goods increase social welfare in any meaningful way.

Successful advertising campaigns are one way that firms can gain the power to raise price. Producers and retailers that gain a brand name that is recognized as standing for quality, for example, can charge higher prices than can other sellers for the same goods. Consumer magazines conclude that most color televisions are about the same. Most are very good. Yet Sony televisions sometimes sell for hundreds of dollars more than competing brands. The solid reputation for quality and innovation that Sony has established through advertising is one reason for this price differential.

Advertising informs, but it also manipulates. Are the benefits of promotional campaigns worth the cost in higher price and purchases of unwanted or unneeded goods? Individual buyers must weigh these choices.

Additional References

Birnbaum, Jeffrey H. "Location, Volume, Marketing Make Prices Vary Widely in New York City." *Wall Street Journal*, December 3, 1981, p. 1.

Buchanan, Norman S. "Advertising Expenditures: A Suggested Treatment." *Journal of Political Economy* (August, 1942).

Creisman, Richard. "Is Exec Barking up the Wrong Tree with Dog Juice? Buyers Say No." *Advertising Age* (January 11, 1982), p. 1.

Leibenstein, Harvey. "Bandwagon, Snob, and Veblen Effects in the Theory of Consumers' Demand." *Quarterly Journal of Economics* (May, 1950), pp. 44–49.

---

them than society gives up in resource cost to produce them. This results in inefficient economic decisions.

Plant capacity is inefficiently used in the long run, too. Long-run equilibrium occurs far from the optimal plant size at which ATC is minimized. This means that firms end up with excess capacity that keeps price high. Resources are again inefficiently used. Since monopolistic competitors want to maximize profits, it would seem reasonable to ask why they don't cut price and increase production in the long run to take advantage of lower average costs. A look at the figure shows why. Average total cost falls when output expands, but price would have to fall even more to sell the extra goods. A firm producing at optimal point C would earn an economic loss and might not live to see the long-run results.

IS PRODUCT DIFFERENTIATION DESIRABLE?

20.7 DESIRABILITY OF DIFFERENTIATION

The desirability of product differentiation and the monopolistic competition it causes is a topic of debate among economists. Some economists argue that product differentiation is undesirable because it misallocates resources in three ways. First, they contend that resources are, at least in part, misallocated in advertising and promotion. Ads that give consumers the information they need to make intelligent choices are not inefficient. As previously mentioned in this chapter, informative advertising reduces information costs to the consumer and makes for more efficient exchange between consumer and producer. However, advertising gimmicks that try to create previously nonexistent needs, or that deceive to gain attention, are hard to justify. The resources that go into these ads are misallocated because they could be put to more productive uses.

Second, some economists contend that product differentiation is inefficient because it sometimes tricks consumers into buying goods they do not want or need. Almost everyone at some time in their life has seen an ad and made a hasty decision to buy something, only later to throw it away or have it sit unused on a shelf. The resources wasted in this type of buying are a measure of the inefficiency that false ads cause.

Finally, most economists would agree that product differentiation and monopolistic competition bring about the inefficient pricing (price that is greater than marginal cost) and excess capacity problems illustrated in Figure 20-4.

There is, however, a positive side to the issue of product differentiation. It is easy to see that variety and freedom of choice are positive benefits for consumers. Product differentiation gives buyers a greater variety of goods from which to choose than is afforded by the identical goods produced in perfect competition. Economists who believe individuals are the best judges of their own welfare have a hard time arguing with the results of product differentiation. Students who pay $20 extra for jeans with a famous person's name across the back may indeed be better off in their own view. These students may value the brand name on the jeans more than the $20 additional price. The decision is, after all, a voluntary purchase.

In some other cases, differentiation takes the form of innovation and improvement. Differences that really make goods better or cheaper are not inefficient. The innovation that takes place in markets like these may be worth the cost of a few distorted price signals.

OLIGOPOLY

20.8 OLIGOPOLY

Oligopoly
A market with relatively few interdependent producers; in such a market, actions taken by one firm affect output decisions by the others.

Oligopoly exists when a market is dominated by a relatively small number of large firms. Interdependence is the key characterististic of oligopoly. The decisions of firm managers in an oligopolistic market is highly dependent upon how they think their rival producers will respond to their decisions. For example, Exxon's marketing decisions affect the options available to Mobil, Shell, and others. Oligopoly is in some ways like three people in a canoe. If any of them moves, all must make adjustments.

20.9 CHARACTERISTICS OF OLIGOPOLIES

Characteristics of Oligopolies

Oligopolistic markets tend to share three major characteristics: there are a few large firms in the market, the firms are interdependent, and there are barriers to entry.

Few Large Firms The oligopolistic market is dominated by a small number of firms, each capturing a relatively large share of total demand. Not all firms need be large, however; small firms may coexist with the dominant big ones. Economists sometimes use concentration ratios as an indicator of

Concentration Ratio
The percentage of total market sales that is taken by the largest few firms.

20.10 CONCENTRATION RATIOS

oligopoly's existence. The **concentration ratio** is the percentage of total market sales made by the 4, 8, or even 20 largest firms in an industry. When the concentration ratio is high, there are a few large firms dominating the industry. As we can see from Table 20-1, a few big firms have the lion's share of the market in such U.S. industries as automobiles, aluminum, cereals, gasoline, tires, and soap products. Concentration ratios can also be used to measure the percentage of total market assets, employees, or even value added to production attributable to the 4, 8, or 20 largest firms.

Concentration ratios are an approximate measure of the degree of competition in a given industry, but this measure does have several important flaws. First, concentration ratios tend to overestimate the degree of competition in industries that are highly localized in nature. For example, some industries are composed of many different producers, each of whom is perhaps the sole producer in a given geographic area. If we were to measure the total annual sales accounted for by the 20 largest dairy producers in the United States, for example, this would indeed be a low concentration ratio. Probably less than 20 percent of national sales could be accounted for by these firms. If however, we were to look at dairy sales in a suburban or rural region, quite frequently we would find one or two producers supplying the entire local market. If we relied on concentration ratios alone to indicate the degree of competition in the dairy industry, we would be misled. While on a national scale the industry might appear quite competitive, on the local level, where we all buy the goods, the industry is not so competitive.

Another problem with the concentration ratio concept is that it tends to understate the degree of competitiveness present in industries with strong foreign competition. The U.S. auto industry, for example, has a very high concentration ratio, since there are really only four major domestic producers. Competition from Japan, Germany, and France are not included in the auto industry concentration ratio, yet it is clear to consumers and producers alike that these countries offer substantial competition in that industry. If we were to rely on the concentration ratio alone, we would believe that the auto industry was not very competitive, when in fact, it is quite competitive at the showroom level where consumers buy the product.

Another shortcoming of the concentration ratio as a measure of competition is that it tacitly overlooks the existence of substitutes that are not a direct part of the industry. For example, the automobile industry might

TABLE 20-1 — **Concentration Ratios in Manufacturing, 1977**

Industry	Number of firms	Concentration ratios Top 4 firms	Top 20 firms
Motor vehicles and auto bodies	254	.93	.99
Aluminum	12	.96	1.00
Cereal	32	.89	1.00
Soap and detergents	554	.59	.82
Tires and tubes	121	.70	.97
Petroleum refining	192	.30	.81
Newspapers	7821	.19	.45
Soft drinks	1758	.15	.36

Source: *Concentration Ratios in Manufacturing,* 1977, Table 7, U.S. Department of Commerce.

appear to be highly concentrated with very few producers. Autos, however, compete for the consumer's dollar with all other forms of transportation, such as buses, airlines, motorcycles, and even bicycles and walking. While the big three American auto makers might at first appear to have little competition in their industry, they are indeed subject to the engine of competition. A similar example of the failure of concentration ratios to take into account the existence of substitutes is provided by Alcoa Aluminum. In the 1940s, Alcoa Aluminum was prosecuted by the U.S. government as a monopoly. They were, at that time, the only U.S. producer of aluminum, but they argued that they competed with the scrap aluminum industry, as well as the glass, steel, and even paper producers in the container industry. The problem with concentration ratios is that they must draw artificial distinctions between competitors.

Before leaving the concept of concentration ratios, something should be said about the long-run trend of this measure of competitiveness. Unfortunately, there appears to be widespread belief among the lay population that American industry has, over the last few decades, become increasingly more concentrated and less competitive. If this is the case, such a trend has not been detected in the study of concentration ratios. Many people are surprised to learn that, according to a study by P.W. McCracken and T.G. Moore, since the turn of the century the overall degree of concentration in American industry has not increased markedly.[1] While we read front page headlines in the media about the current megamergers of firms like DuPont and Conoco, at least so far these changes have not exerted noticeable effects on the overall competitiveness of American industry. While this new wave of mergers may change the future degree of competition, for now, its impact has not been very large.

Interdependence Big firms in oligopoly markets are so interdependent that it is impossible to draw an individual firm's demand curve without specifying assumptions about the actions of other firms. While the overall demand for automobiles may be easy to estimate, what happens to the quantity demanded of Ford Mustangs when their price is increased is much more difficult to model. The response to the Mustang price increase depends on what sorts of price and nonprice strategies other big car makers adopt. Ford might sell many fewer cars, or the same number, or maybe even more, depending on how GM, Chrysler, Toyota, and others react.

This tremendous interdependence is why **administered prices** exist in oligopoly markets. While in the final analysis, prices are still determined in the marketplace, no simple MR equals MC rule can be applied to the complicated actions and reactions that are possible in markets in which oligopolies prevail. Modeling the pricing and output behavior of oligopolists is much more complex, since it depends in large part on how rival producers will respond to each others' changes in price.

Administered Prices
Prices that are set by management and not completely determined by demand and cost factors.

Barriers to Entry Competition in the long run is reduced by overt or subtle barriers to entry that make it difficult, and in some cases almost impossible, for new firms to enter the industry despite the existence of positive economic profits. High start-up costs are a common entry barrier in oligopoly markets. Potential new firms must risk large sums to build factories or establish a new product brand. For example, to just begin manufacturing automobiles on a competitive scale with GM or Ford would take

PROMINENT ECONOMIST

Joan Robinson (1903–1983)

Joan Robinson was instrumental in developing the modern theory of monopolistic competition. In her book, *The Economics of Imperfect Competition,* Robinson redefined the market demand curve to account for interdependence among firms. She used differences among products to define an industry, much like Alfred Marshall had done before her. She viewed each individual firm as a monopolist facing a downward-sloping demand curve. This represented a curve affected by the behavior of other "monopolists" in the industry. She also neglected consideration of product differentiation and quality competition within an industry as Chamberlin had done.

Professor Robinson, however, contributed more to economics than her theory of monopolistic competition. She was one of the major economists who worked with Keynes during the development of his General Theory. She was in agreement with Keynes' view that the market economy is inherently unstable. She recognized that markets suffer from more than instability and have internal problems such as income inequality, pollution, manipulation of demand, and business concentration.

Professor Robinson was educated at Girton College, Cambridge, and was Professor Emerita of Economics at Cambridge University. Robinson continued in the Cambridge tradition of dissent from the traditional orthodoxy. In her delivery of the Richard T. Ely lecture to the American Economic Association in 1971, she argued that the economics profession faces a major crisis. She felt that, to date, economists had not developed a meaningful theory of "what employment should be for." This concerns "the allocation of resources between products, but is also bound up with the distribution of products between people." She believed that the relative earnings of people depend on union influence and bargaining powers, as well as market conditions.

Recently, Professor Robinson had became an outspoken critic of the capitalist system. Her work in economics was expansive, covering topics such as capital theory, international trade, growth theory, comparative systems, and Marxian economics.

---

hundreds of millions of dollars in capital. If new firms wanted to enter the market, the existing firms would be able to cut price for a period to make entry for these new firms difficult. This is done often enough to discourage entry into the industry.

20.11 CAUSES OF OLIGOPOLY

What Causes Oligopoly?

While economists have been successful at identifying several broad characteristics common to many oligopolies, no completely unified theory of oligopoly behavior has, as yet, emerged. We have observed that oligopolies exist in some industries and not in others. Of even more significance, however, would be an understanding of the economic conditions that lead to oligopoly. Oligopolies, in many industries, are the result of economies of scale and interfirm mergers.

Economies of Scale Economies of scale give bigger firms a competitive advantage over smaller competitors. Average total costs fall as output expands when economies of scale are present, at least up to a point. Big high-output firms, therefore, have lower average costs than smaller ones, so they can earn profits while charging lower prices than their smaller competitors. The smaller firms are driven from the market unless they increase output or use nonprice tactics, such as advertising and product differentiation, to make up for higher average costs.

Economies of scale move some markets toward oligopoly even when entry is open. Three or four big firms, operating at the optimal (lowest average total cost) plant size, can fill up a market, producing enough to meet the available demand. Oligopoly is a natural outcome of competition in markets like these.

The automobile industry is an example of a natural oligopoly. A modern robot-equipped auto production line minimizes cost by producing at least 250,000 units of the same (or similar) model per year. A full-line auto manufacturer sells from four to six model lines. It does not take many efficient assembly lines or auto manufacturers to satisfy the United States' annual 8 to 10 million unit auto demand at this rate. A few efficient producers are all this market can hold.

Mergers A **merger** takes place when one firm acquires another, so that two old firms now share one management and ownership. Mergers take two forms: vertical mergers and horizontal mergers. Sometimes one firm tries to reduce cost and gain efficiency by integrating the whole production and sales process under one corporate roof. This is a **vertical merger.** A computer manufacturer, for example, might acquire other firms that produce electronic chips and keyboards, while also merging with a retail sales outlet. The resulting firm might be more efficient than competitors if the merger reduces the firm's transactions or information costs of doing business. By having its own chip and keyboard suppliers and its own retail outlets, the new firm may save time and resources in not having to search out and bid on components and sales agreements.

A **horizontal merger,** a merger that joins two or more previously competing firms, is common in oligopoly markets. In the early 1980s, many large firms merged or bought out smaller competitors, such as was the case in the DuPont–Tenneco deal. In this process, smaller firms unite under one management and are thus better able to defend themselves from bigger competitors. Such mergers sometimes increase competition in an oligopoly market, even though fewer firms are left to compete. Big firms can, however, grow bigger through horizontal merger by acquiring the next-largest company. Horizontal merger, carried to the limit, leaves just one monopoly firm. The Justice Department monitors horizontal-merger activity in the United States and tries to halt mergers that reduce competition. U.S. history has noted two periods in which horizontal mergers were very frequent and gave birth to many of today's industrial giants. From the late 1800s to about 1904 and then again from 1916 to 1929, horizontal mergers provided the basis for what we know today as General Electric, General Mills, United States Steel, Standard Oil, and others. These mergers led to concentrations in manufacturing, metals, tin cans, and other large industries.

In more recent years, the beer industry has experienced increased merger activity. There were once hundreds of small breweries in the United States. The concentration ratio has recently increased, however, as the two biggest brands, Budweiser and Miller, have increased market share. Smaller firms have been merged in often bloody takeover battles. Economies of scale are the reason for these mergers. National brands need to have big-capacity regional plants to produce at the least cost and highest profit, but the optimal brewery plant size produces more beer than smaller firms can sell. Mergers that result in one big brewery producing the many merged brands make these firms competitive with the giants. G. Heilman Brewing

Merger
An action in which one firm acquires ownership of another or several firms join under single management.

Vertical Merger
A merger in which one firm produces inputs used by another (e.g., beer maker merges with a bottle producer).

Horizontal Merger
A merger between two previously competing firms.

is now a major national brewer, for example, even though it does not have a big-name national beer brand. Each regional G. Heilman brewery uses its large capacity to produce nearly a dozen brands of beer. Each of these brands was once made by an independent firm with its own brewery and relatively small sales. Merger and large-capacity production facilities saved these brands from beer oblivion by bringing down cost to the point where the small brands can compete with Budweiser and Miller.

OLIGOPOLY BEHAVIOR: THE CARTEL OPTION

20.12 CARTELS

Having identified the characteristics of an oligopolistic market, the next important step is to determine how oligopolists behave. Do they compete fiercely, cutting price and boosting quality as they fight for a bigger market share, or do they hold back, limiting production and forcing prices higher? Do they compete, conspire, or collude? Oligopoly behavior varies considerably from industry to industry, so there is little that can be said that applies to all cases. Oligopolies might behave like competitive firms, but the small number of firms in oligopoly markets also makes **collusion** possible. Collusion takes place when firms enter into secret agreements to set price or otherwise restrict competition.

Oligopoly firms can gain by becoming a **cartel,** entering into profitable agreements to limit output, fix price, and split profits. Such cartels are illegal in the United States, but legal and relatively common in other countries. Through the cartel, many firms can behave like one and gain monopoly profits. Figure 20-5 shows the logic behind this move.

If the firms in this industry behave as competitors, they might end up at a short-run equilibrium like point A in the figure. Price P_A and total output Q_A are at the competitive levels, but P_A equals ATC, so zero economic profits prevail.

Collusion
A secret agreement to engage in illegal activity.

Cartel
Firms that organize by formal agreement to reduce total output, increase price, and gain higher profits.

FIGURE 20-5

Cartel Profits. A perfectly competitive industry with these demand and cost curves would find long-run equilibrium at A, where price equals marginal cost and zero economic profits prevail. Firms can gain the higher profits of monopoly pricing if they form a cartel, set production quotas, and move to B in the figure.

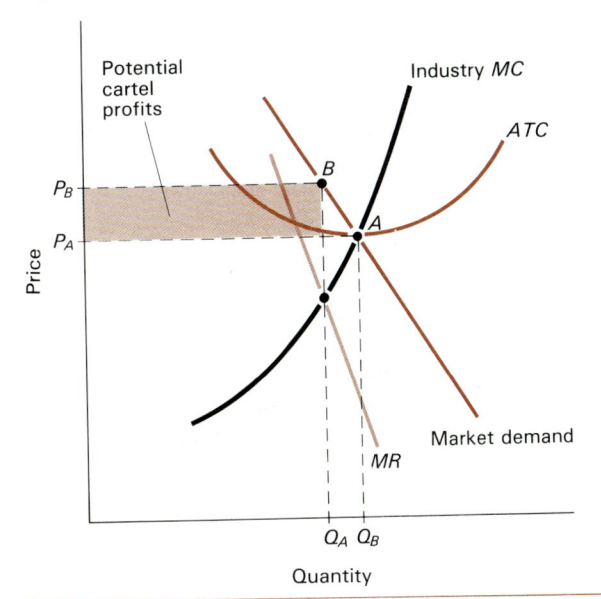

Suppose, however, that the managers of these firms meet and pool their information about demand and cost. They might jointly agree to reduce total production to Q_B in the figure (the output level at which MR equals MC) and set price at the corresponding demand curve level P_B. The result of collusion is that economic profits for the group rise from zero at A to the substantial shaded area in the figure at point B. The group gains higher profits from its price–quantity conspiracy.

Colluding firms agree on a single price and divide the market by assigning output quotas that represent maximum production levels for each firm. Cartels result in higher prices and lower quantities, as the figure shows, and distort the efficient allocation of resources.

How to Start a Cartel

Cartels are quite profitable, but we know that many firms choose not to form cartels. One reason is that interfirm price-fixing agreements are against the law. The threat of legal punishment deters some profit-hungry firms. The reality of cartel economics stops others. Cartels are, by their nature, unstable. The mutual desire for greater profits that makes producers join a cartel and other price-fixing agreements also sets the stage for the group's eventual destruction. A successful cartel needs to be able to control the supply of substitutes, assign production quotas, and detect and punish cheating.

Control Supply of Substitutes No cartel works well if buyers can avoid high prices by purchasing noncartel substitutes. A successful cartel must bring together enough producers to constitute a big share of the market, then get them to agree on a common price. This can be difficult, especially if different firms have different cost curves. A price that generates profits for a firm that has efficient new plants might mean losses for others in the industry. Cartels are also doomed to failure if the biggest firms in an industry refuse to take part, or if there exists significant noncartel competition from abroad.

Another important reason why some firms choose not to join a cartel is that noncartel firms can gain from the cartel's actions without being a member. Suppose that there are five firms in your market and the other four form a cartel. You hold out and refuse to enter the cartel. The other four firms reduce output and force price higher, which benefits them through higher profits. This action also benefits you, the nonmember, too. You can increase price and profit along with the others, but you are not forced to limit output to an assigned quota, as would be the case if you were a cartel member. You can take full advantage of higher prices and increase production and profit even more. Many potential cartels never form because each big firm waits for its competitors to move first.

Assign Production Quotas Even if all or most firms in a market agree in principle to cartel formation, members still must find a way to divide production and profit among themselves. Unanimous agreement on a cartel scheme can be hard to reach since a higher production quota for Firm A means other firms get a smaller cut. Cartel members are better as a group if they reduce output, but they must decide which firm should cut production the most. The cartel must decide which firm gets the biggest slice of the profit pie. There is no guarantee that a mutually agreeable division can be found.

Detect and Punish Cheating The paradox of the cartel is that, while all gain by restricting output, each individual cartel member has a vested interest in cheating on the agreement by producing more than the assigned output quota. The cheating firm gains because it gets added revenue from profitable secret sales. The rest of the cartel members lose, however, since the increase in total output inevitably drives down price.

The incentive to cheat and produce more makes cartels unstable. First one, then another firm cheats. If the gains from illegal production are high, if cheating is hard to detect, and if cheaters are difficult to punish, the cartel usually disintegrates. The cartel decomposes into a set of separate, competing firms once again.

Secrets of Cartel Success

> **20.13 CARTEL SUCCESS**

Cartels start the game with three strikes against them. Hold-out firms, the problems of dividing output, and the probability of cheating all work against cartel formation and stability. Cartels are most likely to organize and prosper when these four basic conditions exist: few firms, few buyers, identical products, and stable demand.

Few Firms A small number of producers in a market makes the problem of gaining mutual agreement concerning production quotas and prices easier than if there are tens or hundreds of parties to an agreement. A smaller numbers of firms does not guarantee an acceptable cartel agreement, but it does reduce the costs of bargaining and the difficulty of detecting cheaters.

Few Buyers It is easier to monitor the sales of individual firms if there are relatively few buyers of the cartel's product. Having a small number of buyers reduces the cost of monitoring for cheating.

Identical Products Cartels are more likely to be found where different firms sell homogeneous products. If each firm's product is different, an individual firm can cheat and undercut the cartel's price by offering higher quality than others at the same price. Quality-based cheating can destroy a cartel as quickly as would price cuts.

Stable Demand Cartels fare better in markets with stable demand, where monopoly price and quantity decisions are infrequently made. Constant alteration of prices and production quotas strains cartel agreements in markets with unstable demand.

The most famous cartel is OPEC (the Organization of Petroleum Exporting Countries). We will look at OPEC in detail when we explore energy markets in Chapter 26.

IMPLICIT COLLUSION: LEADERS AND FOLLOWERS

Cartels are just one way that firms set price in oligopoly markets. Collusive agreements need not be formal. Sometimes firms adopt standard pricing rules of thumb that limit competition, as when every firm marks up cost by a standard 50 percent. No illegal price fixing is involved, but fixed prices show up anyway.

Price Leadership
A situation in which one firm sets prices that are adopted by competing producers.

> **20.14 PRICE LEADERSHIP**

Price leadership is another practice that limits competition among oligopoly firms. One firm, often the biggest or lowest-cost producer, assumes a

PROMINENT ECONOMIST

George J. Stigler (1911–   )

George J. Stigler graduated from the University of Washington in 1931. He is a past president of the American Economic Association and is best known for his strong defense of competitive markets. The Royal Swedish Academy of Sciences declared that his "studies of industrial structures, functioning of markets and the causes and effects of public regulation" have opened significant areas for further economic research. For this contribution, he received the 1982 Nobel Prize in Economics.

During his professorship at the University of Chicago, he was a strong critic of government intervention, which was presumed to be fueled by special-interest groups. He believed that the strong competitive forces of the industrial economy need only a moderate amount of antitrust action to preserve an acceptable level of competition. Stigler's research in the area of antitrust action, specifically the Sherman Act and recent antimerger legislation, has clearly highlighted the benefits of preserving competitive markets and reducing business collusion. He has recommended a reduction in the discretionary power of regulatory agencies such as the SEC, ICC, and CAB and has been especially concerned that such agencies will become captives of the industries they are regulating.

During his presidential address to the Mont Pelerin Society, a market-oriented group of economists, Stigler said the following: "We are presented with two kinds of policies: those which greatly benefit the few and slightly injure the many and those that benefit slightly the many and injure the few greatly. Hence, for almost every individual policy proposal of a socialist variety, there will be a cohesive, well-financed, articulate special interest group to support it, and a large, poorly informed majority that, if it is

---

Predatory Pricing
The act of one firm cutting price to drive competing firms from the market.

leadership role, announcing the prices of its products. Other firms follow suit, setting prices consistent with those of the leader. No overt collusion takes place in this instance. There is no formal price agreement among the firms. Individual producers are free to undercut the leader. Smaller firms, however, are unwilling to break with the leader of the pack, especially if the announced prices are profitable, and entry barriers prevent new firms from taking away customers.

Price leaders in industries with economies of scale are sometimes able to enforce their leadership when others fail to follow their lead. Big, low-cost firms can use **predatory pricing** to make smaller firms toe the line. Big firms with economies of scale can set price lower than smaller competitors and still make a profit. The small firm stands to lose money in the short run and might go out of business or be taken over by the big firm in the long run. Small firms, aware of this possibility, choose to follow the leader rather than enter into costly battles.

Price leadership gets around antitrust laws that prevent cartels if no one can prove that managers actually agreed to hold the leader's price. "Competitive firms have identical prices," an oligopolist might argue, "so similar price is no proof of collusion." The recording of a single phone call between the price-setting executives of two firms, however, was enough to bring antitrust charges in 1983.

Another problem with price leadership is that leaders and followers often have different goals. Leader firms are likely to set the price that maximizes their own profits, not those of the industry or the followers. Big

informed correctly, will be weakly opposed and often will be simply unaware of the proposal."

A substantial portion of Stigler's work has been devoted to the scientific study of economic and political institutions. He has researched the relationship between the profit rate in a particular industry and the degree to which the industry output is concentrated in a few large firms (*Capital and Rates of Return in Manufacturing Industries,* Princeton: Princeton University Press, 1963). Stigler's study confirmed that there was a statistically significant correlation between profit ratios and industrial concentration. At first he believed the correlation was because concentrated industry output meant that an industry could avoid profit-lowering competition. Later, he offered another opinion regarding the correlation because of a change in the interpretation of the evidence.

In a second study, Stigler worked with J.K. Kindahl to analyze price stability. After examining purchase invoices of buyers of industrial products, the two concluded that there was considerable price flexibility. This finding was in opposition to the widely accepted notion that an important sector of the economy set prices by management decision, insulating those prices from normal competitive pressures.

A third area of importance has been Stigler's analysis of the economies of information. Price theory suggests that competition among sellers, with the factor of buyer self-interest, will not tolerate different prices for the same goods sold in the same market. In his analysis, Stigler recognized that this does not always hold true, and he set forth a model based on the cost of searching for price information. He felt that price theory ignores the cost of acquiring price information and this accounts for a customer in the marketplace being offered the same goods at different prices. Buyers will obtain only as much price information as they think they need. If faulty information is obtained, it will encourage price rigidity and misallocation of resources.

Stigler's formal education in economics took place at the University of Chicago during the Depression. In 1939, he was an assistant professor at Iowa State College and later the University of Minnesota. After a brief stay at Brown, he went to Columbia. While there (1947 to 1958), he published *The Theory of Price* and several monographs for the National Bureau of Economic Research. In addition, he coauthored "Roofs or Ceilings, Foundation for Economic Education" with Milton Friedman. They proposed that rent controls distort rental markets, resulting in shortages of apartments. The benefits sought are short-lived. In the long term, property values decline and the tax base is eroded. Ultimately, the national income is reduced.

While Stigler has made contributions to economic thought, oligopoly theory, utility regulation, and production and cost theory, his goal has been to understand the world rather than change it. Stigler, along with J.M. Buchanan and Gordon Tullock, has been responsible for challenging economic theory as an empirical study of democracy.

---

firms with low costs might slowly lead the followers to their demise, setting prices that drive smaller competitors out of business.

COMPETITION AND KINKED DEMAND CURVES

> **20.15 KINKED DEMAND CURVE**

Kinked Demand Curve
The demand curve in which competitors will match a price decrease but will not match a price increase. The curve is therefore elastic above the market price and inelastic below the market price.

Some oligopolies stick to current prices, keeping price fixed, even when production costs change. One reason for this is the existence of implicit collusion. Follower firms hold price until they see how the leader acts. Collusion or price leadership is not the only reason for sticky prices, however. Another explanation, using **kinked demand curves,** shows that even competitive firms can have inflexible prices. The kinked demand model is shown in Figure 20-6.

The firm demand curve shown in Figure 20-6 has a kink at the current price of P_A. The kink means that the price–quantity relationship above point A is different than the relationship below it. This kinked demand occurs in oligopoly markets when competitive firms match any price cut but temporarily maintain their prices when another firm raises its rates. To understand this behavior, put yourself in the place of an oligopolist. If one of your few competitors were to raise its price from P_A to P_B in the figure, you know that its share of the market (its quantity demanded) would decline a great deal (to Q_B) and more consumers would buy from you. Your revenues would go up. You would not raise price unless you had to due to cost increases or some other compelling reason. If, on the other hand, one of

588 *Monopolistic Competition and Oligopoly*

FIGURE 20-6

The Kinked Demand Curve. In a market with few competitors and readily available price information, if a single competitor raises price from P_A to P_B, the quantity demanded would decline from Q_A to Q_B. This would be a very large decrease, since other firms would not follow the price increase. If, however, that same firm lowered price from P_A to P_C, other competitors would also lower price and the single firm's quantity demanded would only increase from Q_A to Q_C.

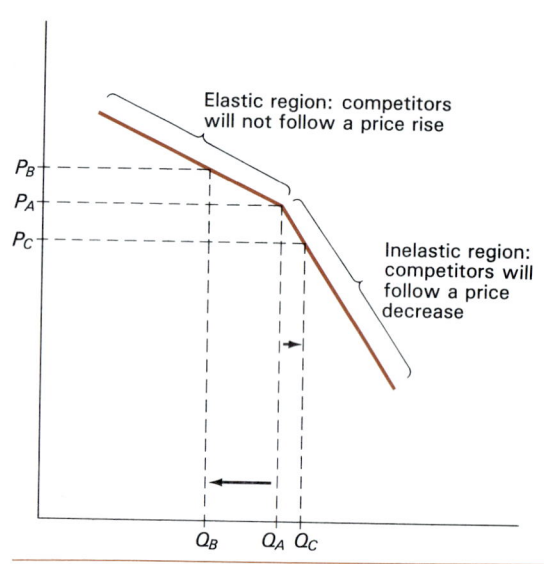

your few competitors were to lower its price from P_A to P_C, you know that its share of the market would increase. Fewer consumers would buy from you since your price would be higher than your competitor's. To protect your share of the market, you would be forced to lower your price to P_C to match your competitor. Since you and all the competitors would lower price, the quantity demanded of each firm would only increase slightly (to Q_C). From this, it is easy to see that oligopolists in a market will follow a price decrease but not a price increase.

KEY CONCEPT 20.15   Oligopolists may face kinked demand curves because their competitors will follow price decreases but will not follow price increases.

The result of the competitive behavior just described is that the demand curve is relatively flat and elastic at prices higher than the current one. Any single firm that raises price experiences a large loss in market share, as customers buy from others who hold their prices fixed. In other words, the quantity demanded of a single firm's product will be very responsive to a price increase. The demand curve is steeper and more inelastic at prices below P_A. If this firm cuts price, it will not pick up many new customers, since its price cut is matched by other competitors. Thus relatively large price cuts below P_A do not increase an individual firm's sales by much.

Price changes are risky when competitors behave as just described. A firm that earns profits at the current price thinks twice about either cutting or boosting its charges when it thinks that competitors will match its price cuts but not match price increases. The argument that firms in this position tend to stick to current prices is made even stronger if the firm calculates its marginal revenue curve.

The kink in the demand curve is a mathematical discontinuity and marginal revenue is undefined at this point. You can calculate MR for either the more elastic demand segment above Q_A or the less elastic one below it, but no MR exists at Q_A itself. The MR curve in Figure 20.7 has two segments and an undefined region to illustrate this problem.

The consequence of kinked demand and uncertain MR is that the marginal cost curve can shift a considerable distance, as the figure shows, and not alter the MR equals MC profit-maximizing output. Costs change, but the most profitable price–quantity combination stays the same. This explains the observed inflexibility of some oligopoly prices.

The kinked-demand curve theory suggests that many price rigidities in oligopoly markets are not due to overt or implicit price-fixing by colluding firms. Price movements in this instance are restricted by uncertainty. Oligopolies cannot find MR and are uncertain about the wisdom of increasing price alone or leading a potentially self-destructive charge of all producers to a lower price level.

WHAT TO DO WITH OLIGOPOLIES

20.17 REGULATING OLIGOPOLIES

Current regulatory policies toward oligopolies show how uncertain lawmakers are about the oligopoly problem. Economists have no general theory of oligopoly behavior. These firms may compete, form cartels, set leader–follower prices, or follow other rules and strategies not mentioned here. Each market has different characteristics in regard to economies of scale, product differentiation, pattern of firm size, and so on, that influence the nature and degree of the resulting competition.

FIGURE 20-7

Kinked Demand and Oligopoly Pricing. How does this oligopoly behave when marginal cost rises, as shown here? The firm continues to produce at Q_A and set price at P_A if it faces a demand curve with a kink at the current price–quantity point A. Marginal revenue is undefined here, so a change in MC doesn't alter the profit-maximizing combination. See the text for an explanation of the "kink."

1. "Competition and Market Concentration in the American Economy." Subcommittee on Antitrust and Monopoly. U.S. Senate, March 29, 1973.

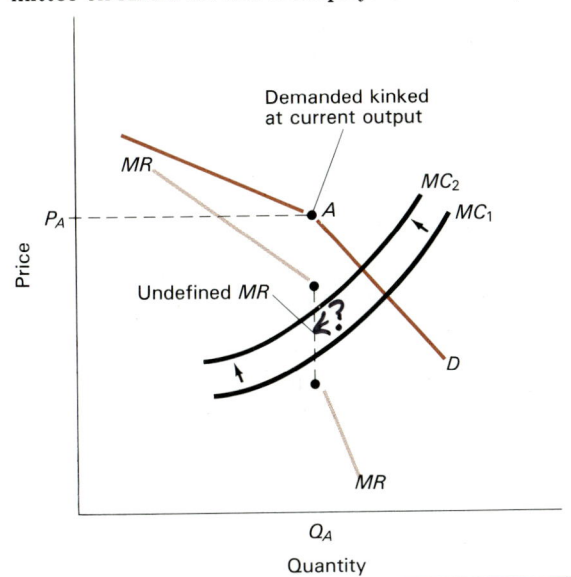

Cartels and horizontal mergers that give firms monopoly power are undesirable because they raise price and misallocate scarce resources. Many regulatory policies and laws are designed to discourage these activities. Some horizontal mergers increase competition, however, by giving smaller firms the clout to take on their bigger competitors. The difficulty, for example, in identifying the difference between a merger of two computer firms that increases competition and one that reduces it clouds public policy on oligopoly.

Lawmakers are also aware that bigness isn't necessarily badness, especially if economies of scale are present in production. Big firms with huge plants are often more efficient than many small, competitive producers. Regulations that discourage bigness to protect consumers from price-increasing monopoly might result in higher prices in the long run, since scale economies are foregone.

Finally, some people argue that large firms, like oligopolies, are the most innovative and do the most to advance technology. This argument, as noted in the last chapter, is hard to prove or disprove.

Today, public policy toward oligopolies remains uncertain. Unless we know for sure how firms in a particular industry behave, it is hard to tell whether the benefits of increased regulation are worth the many costs.

SUMMARY

20.1
1. Monopolistic competition describes a market in which many firms compete, selling similar but not identical products. Each firm has a limited monopoly over its particular product. Monopolistic competition is characterized by many relatively small firms, free entry and exit, and product differentiation. Product differentiation can refer to real differences in quality or function or perceived differences created by advertising and promotion.

20.2
2. Monopolistic competitors face neither the perfectly elastic demand curves of perfect competition nor the market demand curves of monopoly. Each firm's demand curve is a part of the industry demand.

20.3
3. The size and shape of an individual firm's demand curves depend on the nature of the demand for the industry's product and the degree of product differentiation.

20.4
4. Individual firms set price and quantity following the *MR* equals *MC* rule of monopoly. Firm output is targeted for the level at which *MR* equals *MC*, and the demand curve is then used to determine the corresponding price.

20.4
5. The markup between marginal cost and price in monopolistic competition depends on the elasticity of demand for the item in question. The more elastic demand is, the lower the markup. Markups are higher with less elastic demand. Real-world firms that use markup pricing formulas, where different goods are marked up by different percentages, often arrive at the *MR* equals *MC* rule of economic theory.

6. Monopolistic competition does not guarantee profits in the short run. Firms can earn zero, negative, or positive economic profits, depending on the relationship between price and *ATC* at the profit-maximizing output.

7. One way to increase profits in the short run is to cut cost by using fewer or cheaper resources. If, however, these cost-saving measures affect the quality or the public perception of the item, quantity demanded may fall a great deal and profits may actually decline. Another way to increase profit is to increase advertising, in hopes of increasing demand. This does not necessarily guarantee profit, however, since advertising costs rise along with potential sales. Informative advertising can contribute to economic efficiency by lowering information costs to the consumer. Persuasive advertising, on the other hand, can sometimes contribute to economic inefficiency by inducing consumers to buy goods for which they have no genuine need.

8. Free entry guarantees zero economic profits in the long run for monopolistic competition. New firms enter and loss-making old firms exit until profit falls to zero. Entry and exit in monopolistic competition alter the way in which industry demand is divided among individual firms. Entry, for example, results in smaller demand for each existing firm, while exiting firms boost the demand curves of those who stay behind.

9. Monopolistic competition results in excess capacity in the long run. The long-run zero-profit equilibrium output falls below the minimum point of the *ATC*, where both costs and profits are lower.

10. Product differentiation has both costs and benefits. Product differentiation may be inefficient, since monopolistic competition results in prices greater than marginal cost, sending false price signals to the economy. Product differentiation may also involve the misallocation of resources to advertising that may not really inform. Two advantages of product differentiation are that it increases the choices available to consumers and encourages innovation and quality improvement.

11. Oligopoly is competition among the few. It is a market in which a few large firms dominate supply. The three basic characteristics of oligopoly markets are (1) that they are made of up a few large firms, (2) that they are interdependent, and (3) that there are barriers to entry. Oligopoly firms are interdependent because decisions made by one supplier alter the price and quantity choices of the rest. Barriers to entry keep new firms out of oligopoly markets. Entry barriers can be formal, as with legal restrictions, or informal, like high start-up costs and the threat of predatory pricing.

12. Oligopoly markets have high concentration ratios. While many firms may compete in these markets, a few big suppliers control a high percentage of all sales. Administered prices exist when the economic forces of cost and demand are not the only determinants of price. Strategic behavior helps set prices for oligopolies.

Many oligopolies are the result of economies of scale. A few large firms,
13. producing at low *ATC* using the optimal plant size, can supply all buyers. The number of firms in these oligopolies is determined by the

optimal plant size and the size of the market. Mergers also reduce the number of competitors. Vertical mergers bring all production under one roof, making firms more efficient. Horizontal mergers bring together firms that once competed. Concentration ratios rise and the number of firms falls as horizontal mergers take place.

20.12

14. Oligopoly firms can increase profits if they collude by adopting price-fixing agreements like cartels. A cartel sets price and quantity using the same procedure as do monopolies. The group produces at the output level at which *MC* equals *MR*, then sets price at the corresponding point on the product demand curve. Potential cartels must solve three problems. They must first control the supply of substitute goods. If they do not, buyers will flock to noncartel sellers. Second, cartels must assign production quotas. Cartels earn monopoly profit by reducing output and increasing price. The lower total production is divided among cartel members using a quota system. Finally, cartels must detect and punish cheaters. Individual firms must be prevented from exceeding their production quotas. Cartel members tend to cheat because the cheater gets the gain of higher sales, while all cartel members share the burden of lower price. Cheating is contagious. Cartels are unstable because member after member tries to increase profit through "illegal" extra production until the cartel finally falls apart.

20.13

15. Cartels are more likely to succeed if there are few firms in an industry. Quota agreements and production monitoring are more easily accomplished with only a few firms with which to deal. Cartels are more likely to succeed if they sell to a few competitive buyers. This makes policing of cheaters easier. Cartels that sell a homogeneous product are more likely to succeed because price reductions through quality differences are more difficult. Cartels are more likely to succeed in markets with stable demand, where prices and production quotas are infrequently changed.

20.14

16. Cartels are just one way that firms set prices in oligopoly markets. Some markets display leaders and followers. Leader firms are often the biggest or lowest-cost producers. They announce prices that other firms follow. Price leadership reduces competition. Big firms can force followers to go along with their prices by the threat of predatory pricing.

20.15, 20.16

17. One explanation of inflexible prices in oligopoly markets is the existence of kinked demand curves for individual producers. These demand curves have different slope and elasticity above and below the current price–quantity combination. The kink occurs if an individual firm assumes that its competitors will match any price reduction but not immediately match any price increase. These strategic assumptions imply that any price change is risky. The result is inflexible prices. The marginal revenue curve is undefined at the kink quantity. Marginal cost changes over this undefined range do not alter the profit-maximizing price–quantity relationship.

20.17

18. Oligopoly markets have both positive and negative aspects from a public policy perspective. These markets are less competitive and may set higher monopoly prices, but large firms and high concentration ratios are not always undesirable, especially when they bring economies of scale, lower prices, and product innovation.

DISCUSSION QUESTIONS

20.1, 20.8, 20.9
1. What are the most important differences between markets characterized by monopolistic competition and oligopolies? What are the consequences of these differences in the short run? In the long run? Explain.

20.4
2. Draw a figure showing the *MC*, *ATC*, *MR*, and demand curves of a monopolistic competitor earning positive economic profits. Show the firm's profit-maximizing price and quantity. Explain how price, quantity, and profits are affected under the following circumstances:
   a. an increase in market demand.
   b. new firms entering the industry.
   c. an increase in variable costs (shifts *MC* curve).
   d. an increase in fixed costs.

20.6
3. Draw the long-run equilibrium for monopolistic competition. Explain why this equilibrium has excess capacity. Why don't firms cut price and increase production to the optimal (lowest *ATC*) plant size?

20.12, 20.13
4. "Greed creates cartels and greed drives them apart." Explain why this statement is true. Discuss the conditions necessary for cartel formation and stability.

   Price leadership is observed in many oligopoly markets. Why should competing firms follow the leader's pricing moves? Discuss the advantages and disadvantages of being a price follower.

   Draw a figure showing the kinked demand curve model of oligopoly price setting. Why does the kink exist? How does the kink alter the shape of the *MR* curve? Why does this *MR* curve make prices insensitive to changes in *MC*? Explain.

   Should the government forbid horizontal mergers in markets with few producers? State your opinion and defend your answer.

SELECTED READINGS

Adelman, M.A. "Two Faces of Economic Concentration." *Public Interest* (Fall, 1970), pp. 117–126.

Brozen, Yale (Ed.) *The Competitive Economy.* (Morristown, NJ: General Learning Press, 1975.

Chamberlin, Edward H. *The Theory of Monopolistic Competition.* Cambridge, MA: Harvard University Press, 1933.

Demsetz, Harold. "The Nature of Equilibrium in Monopolistic Competition." Reprinted in Breit, William, and Hochman, Harold M. (Eds.), *Readings in Microeconomics*, 2nd ed. New York: Holt, Rinehart and Winston, 1971, pp. 253–261.

Dewey, Donald. *The Theory of Imperfect Competition.* New York: Columbia University Press, 1969.

Fellner, William. *Competition among the Few: Oligopoly and Similar Market Structures.* New York: Kompf, 1949.

Kessel, Reuben A. "Price Discrimination in Medicine." Reprinted in Breit, William, and Hochman, Harold M. (Eds.), *Readings in Microeconomics*, 2nd ed. New York: Holt, Rinehart and Winston, 1971, pp. 370–398.

Robinson, Joan. *The Economics of Imperfect Competition*, 1933 reprint edition. New York: St. Martins Press, 1969.

Scherer, F.M. *Industrial Market Structure and Economic Performance*, 2nd ed. Chicago: Rand McNally, 1980.

PART 7

Factor Markets and Income Distribution

CHAPTER 21

Resource Markets: Demand and Supply at Work

Having read the chapter, reviewed the chapter summary, and completed the *Study Guide* exercises, you should be able to:

CRIS

21.1 RESOURCE MARKETS: Explain why resource markets are important to the economy and discuss how they affect income distribution, resource allocation, and how production takes place.

21.2 PRICE AND RESOURCE ALLOCATION: Explain how price determines how scarce resources are used and what it tells us about a resource's value.

21.3 DERIVED DEMAND: Explain why the demand for resources is called a derived demand and indicate on what resource demand depends.

21.4 *TPP* AND *MPP*: Explain how total physical product and marginal physical product are calculated and describe the relationship between *TPP* and *MPP*.

21.5 *VMP*: Explain why an individual firm's demand for an input is equal to that input's value marginal product and tell how *VMP* is calculated and why a profit-maximizing competitive firm hires an input up to the amount at which input price equals *VMP*.

21.6 OUTPUT, PRICE, PRODUCTIVITY, AND DEMAND: Explain how changes in output, price and productivity affect the demand for inputs.

21.7 DEMAND ADJUSTMENTS: Discuss how individual firms and resource markets adjust to a change in the demand for an input.

21.8 ELASTICITY OF DEMAND: List five factors that determine the elasticity of demand for an input and explain how each one affects elasticity, then discuss the conditions that lead to elastic and inelastic demand.

21.9 MONOPOLY AND *MRP*: Define marginal revenue product and explain why a monopoly uses *MRP* instead of *VMP* to make input choices, then indicate whether monopoly firms use more or less resources than do competitive firms.

21.10 MONOPSONY AND *MRC*: Define monopsony and discuss the conditions that make monopsony possible, define marginal resource cost and explain why a monopsony uses *MRC* instead of price in making hiring decisions, then discuss whether monopsony markets use more or less resources than do competitive markets and whether they pay higher or lower resource prices.

21.11 MONOPOLISTIC MONOPSONY: Draw the appropriate figure for a monopolistic monopsonist, then explain how this firm would make its input decision and how this choice would differ from the choices made by a monopoly, a monopsony, and a competitive firm.

21.12 RESOURCE SUPPLIES: List four factors that influence resource supplies in general and explain how each affects the amount of resources offered at each price.

21.13 PROFIT AND INPUT USE: Explain how managers use profit as a guide to trial-and-error decisions on input use.

21.14 OPTIMAL RESOURCE USE RULE: Explain why a profit-maximizing firm combines resources so that $MPP_X/P_X = MPP_Y/P_Y$ for inputs X and Y.

Some of the most important forces that affect our lives every day depend on the economics of resource markets. Resource markets determine, in part, how goods are produced, how scarce natural and human resources are used, and how income is distributed. To put all this in personal terms, resource markets help decide how much you get paid, whey types of jobs are open to you, whether you are employed or out-of-work, and the cost of the goods and services you buy. This chapter looks at general principles that govern resource markets. The fundamental facts of supply and demand affect the way all resources are priced and used.

WHAT RESOURCE MARKETS DO

21.1 RESOURCE MARKETS

Resource markets are markets where land, labor, capital, and natural resources are exchanged according to the principles of supply and demand. It is convenient to think of them as input markets, since all these resources are inputs used to produce the outputs that business, government, and consumers buy. Resource markets do the things that all markets do. They connect buyers with sellers, set quantity, and determine price. Because resources are the essence of economic life, however, resource markets really do more. The interaction of supply and demand in resource markets helps answer three important questions, who gets what, where resources go, and how goods are made.

Income Distribution: Who Gets What

Look at your family's slice of the nation's income and you'll see how important resource markets are. Wages are the biggest single source of income in the United States, and most wages are determined through labor markets. Whether the people in your family earn high salaries or relatively low wages, work overtime or part-time, are unemployed or are not in the job market at all is, in part, a result of labor market events.

Your family may also earn income from investments, such as interest on savings, dividends on stock shares, or profits from business ownership. The resource involved here is capital. Your saved funds earn that interest because they finance machines, factories, and computers used in production. The market for capital resources helps determine this share of your income.

Farmers, miners, and lumberjacks all know how important resource markets are to their economic well-being. Their incomes depend on the value of the natural resources they produce. A shift in the market price of the resource they produce can mean large changes in income for the individuals involved in these markets. For example, if the market price of wheat (a resource used in the making of bread) falls, the income of wheat farmers also falls.

Resource markets are not the only determinants of family income in the United States. Government policies, such as taxes and transfer payments, and laws that set wages and prices in some markets also influence income distribution. Resource markets, however, create the geography of income peaks and valleys that the government policy seeks to level.

Resource Allocation: Where Things Go

Professional sports is a prime example of how resources are allocated through resource markets. Baseball fans hope their favorite team can become a winner and go to the World Series. One way to make your team stronger is to bid for talented ball players on the free-agent market. Teams bid for the services of players who are not bound by contracts to other teams.

21.2 PRICE AND RESOURCE ALLOCATION

Price is the factor that determines which teams get the best players. Price allocates scarce human resources such as strike-out pitchers and hard-hitting center fielders. If a player is an all-star, for example, his price rises until only one team is left in the bidding. The team that offers to pay the most, because it stands to gain the most from this player's efforts, wins the bidding process. Here price has decided where scarce resources go.

The baseball players' market is not large. Only a few thousand people earn their living playing professional baseball, but it illustrates what resource markets do in the rest of the economy. The forces of supply and demand set price. Price determines which firms and industries use a valuable input and which do not. Resources go where they are the most productive or useful. They go to the firms that can make the best use of them because these firms outbid the rest to get the resources they need.

The electronics industry shows how changing prices alter resource allocation. When computer chips were expensive because they were costly to produce, they went only to their most valuable uses, calculators and computers that were used in science and industry. Fast, accurate calculations were valuable to these users, so they bid computer chips away from less productive uses. Over time, however, computer chip technology changed, increasing supply. Now low-cost chips are everywhere. You can find them in inexpensive digital watches, home telephones, and video games. Lower price makes possible these popular, but less productive, uses.

Shifts in resource prices sometimes result in new inventions. As leather's price increased in the 1950s, for example, producers found it too costly to employ leather in many of its traditional uses. The solution was naugahide (artificial leather). Cheaper naugahide was used in places where only the general look and feel of leather were important, while real leather was allocated to those places where the unique qualities of leather itself were required.

Input Choices: How Goods Are Made

Finally, resource markets help decide how the goods you buy are produced. Producers can make goods using different "recipes" or technologies. They can use different combinations of capital, labor, and natural resources to produce the same goods. When one resource rises in price, a signal that it is more valuable elsewhere, other inputs are substituted for it. Changing price alters the way goods are made. Firms try to find the least-cost combination of inputs for each possible level of output.

Because the cost of labor has risen compared to the cost of capital, many items in the United States are produced by means of **capital-intensive production,** a form of production that uses more machines per worker. Cars that were once largely hand-made are now welded and painted by clever machines that do more for less cost than their human predecessors. As workers become expensive, they are no longer allocated to low-productivity jobs. In some banks, for example, customers who want to perform routine banking transactions, such as making deposits and cashing checks, are told to see the computer down the hall, a cash machine. Only customers with more complex transactions see a human teller. Oddly, many bank customers say they prefer the machine.

Resource markets even determine how nations wage war. The U.S. Department of Defense has developed a capital-intensive, high-technology war machine. Relatively few soldiers are required to run the tanks, airplanes, missiles, and rocket launchers that would be used in war. China's army is different in ways that reflect resource costs in that country. Capital is scarce and expensive in China. The Chinese army, like the rest of the country, conserves capital and uses **labor-intensive production.**

THE DERIVED DEMAND FOR RESOURCES

The forces of supply and demand set resource prices and, therefore, determine income distribution, resource allocation, and production decisions. People supply resources because it is profitable to do so. Others buy them to use in production because this is also profitable. The motives of self-interest guide resource allocation and production. The analysis of producer choice in the last four chapters has helped us understand how resource supply decisions are made. Let us now focus on what determines the demand for resources.

Resource demand is a **derived demand.** Firms hire workers, buy machines, and purchase other inputs because of the demand for the goods and

---

Capital-Intensive Production
A production process that uses relatively more capital than labor to produce goods.

Labor-Intensive Production
A production process that uses relatively more labor than capital to produce goods.

Derived Demand
Demand for one product or resource that depends and is based on the demand for another product or resource.

> 21.3
> DERIVED DEMAND

Marginal Productivity Theory
The theory that resources are paid according to their marginal products.

21.4 TPP AND MPP

Total Physical Product (TPP)
Total production, measured in the number of items produced in a given time period.

services they produce. The demand for the workers, machines, and steel used to make automobiles, for example, is derived from the demand for the cars themselves. Lower demand for cars would mean lower demand for the inputs used to make them.

Resource demand, however, is more complicated than this simple derivation. Firms hire workers and buy other inputs based on a careful weighing of each input's cost and its ability to produce. Economists model these choices using the tool of **marginal productivity theory.**

Marginal Physical Product

Let us look at the simplest of all resource choices. How does a single price-taking firm decide how much labor to use, all other factors held constant? The example we will use is a firm called Strawberry Fields Forever, Inc., which harvests and sells fresh strawberries. The firm leases strawberry fields that have already been planted, so rent on the fields is a fixed cost. It hires workers in a competitive labor market. It can hire as many workers as it needs for $5 per hour, and since all workers have identical skills and talents, there is no quality difference among potential employees. The firm sells output in a competitive strawberry market. It can sell all its production for $.50 per pound. The manager of this firm has an important job. He or she must find the profit-maximizing number of workers to hire, given these parameters.

How does management decide how many workers to put to work? Should they hire just a few workers, since each worker's labor costs $5 per hour? Or should they hire many workers, so that the firm can sell many pounds of berries? The firm's manager cannot decide how many workers to hire without knowing something about labor's ability to produce.

How does the **total physical product (TPP)** of labor change when the number of workers employed increases, holding the amount of other resources used in production (land, machinery, and so on) constant? Total physical product is the firm's total output, measured in number of items produced in a given time period. Chances are that the relationship between a resource and its TPP is something like that given by Table 21-1 and graphed in Figure 21-1. Increasing the number of workers in the berry fields increases total harvest and TPP rises. Diminishing returns set in

TABLE 21-1 How Many Workers Should Be Hired?

Number of workers	Total physical product (pounds of strawberries)	Marginal physical product (pounds of strawberries)	Price of output (price per pound)	Value marginal product ($)
0	0	—	—	—
1	20	20	.50	10.00
2	38	18	.50	9.00
3	53	15	.50	7.50
4	65	12	.50	6.00
5	75	10	.50	5.00
6	83	8	.50	4.00
7	89	6	.50	3.00
8	94	5	.50	2.50
9	98	4	.50	2.00
10	100	2	.50	1.00

FIGURE 21-1

Total and Marginal Physical Product. Total physical product increases at a decreasing rate, as more workers are added to fixed amounts of other resources. The falling marginal physical product curve results.

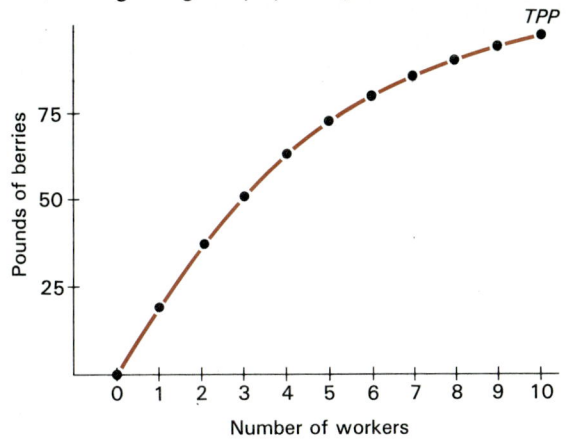

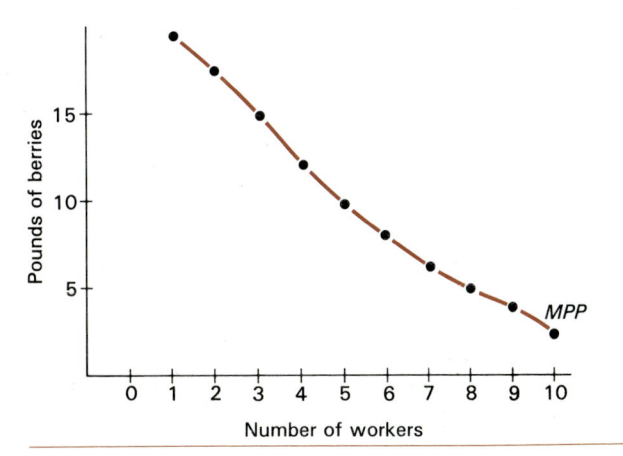

Marginal Physical Product (MPP) The change in total production that occurs when the amount of a single input is changed by one unit, holding all else fixed.

quickly, however. Doubling the number of pickers from 5 to 10 does not double the amount of berries produced.

Another way of stating this relationship is that the **marginal physical product (MPP)** of labor declines as more of it is added to production, other inputs held fixed. Marginal physical product is the change in total output when the amount of a single input (labor in this example) is changed, all other inputs held constant. For example, adding a second worker increases hourly total production from 20 to 38 pounds of berries. The second worker's MPP is therefore 18 pounds (thirty-eight minus twenty) of berries. The first several pickers have high MPP because they work in uncongested fields. There are plenty of berry containers, lots of unpicked plants, and adequate space for them to work efficiently. As more and more labor is added to the fields, however, MPP declines. The sixth worker, who must sometimes halt work and wait while extra containers are brought to the field, adds just eight pounds per hour to production. The congested fields reduce the worker's MPP.

Diminishing marginal physical product sets a limit to the number of workers, machines, or other resources a firm employs, holding other resources fixed. At some point, the cost of an extra input is greater than the value of its production.

Productivity
The amount produced per input used, or more generally, the ability to produce efficiently.

It is also important to note that increasing the amount of available of what was previously the fixed resource increases the **productivity** of the variable resource. For example, the marginal productivity of labor might be declining as the fields become more congested, nevertheless, an increase in the number of berry fields available to be picked will increase the productivity of labor. Alternatively, if there are many fields available to be picked, an increase in the number of laborers will increase the productivity of the berry fields.

Resource Demand: Value Marginal Product

> **21.5 VMP**

Value Marginal Product (VMP)
The extra revenue an additional input produces for a competitive firm, other inputs held fixed (MPP multiplied by selling price).

Having calculated the *MPP* per hour for the firm's workers, the manager now has enough information to determine the optimum size of the work force. Since strawberries sell for $.50 per pound, Table 21-1 can be used to calculate the workers' **value marginal product (VMP)**. Value marginal product is the value in dollars and cents of the goods each additional worker adds to production. It is calculated by multiplying the *MPP* of labor in the table, expressed in pounds of strawberries, by the price of those strawberries, $.50 per pound in this example. The *VMP* result is the dollar value of additional resources, as measured by the extra revenue they generate for employers. Check Table 21-1 to be sure you see how *VMP* is calculated.

KEY CONCEPT 21.5

VMP = *MPP* × output price.

Figure 21-2 shows the *MPP* curve for Strawberry Fields Forever and the corresponding *VMP* curve when berries sell for $.50. You can use these curves, and the information in Table 21-1, to decide how many workers the firm should hire.

Is the first workers profitable to employ? The first worker's *VMP* is $10, while his or her wage is $5. It makes sense for the firm to pay $5 to hire someone who adds $10 to revenues. Since *VMP* is greater than the wage, this is a profitable worker. The *VMP* of the second worker is $9, compared to the same $5 wage. Therefore, the firm's manager would be smart to hire this worker too.

The third and fourth workers are also profitable at the $5 wage rate (check the table and figure to see why). The fifth workers' *VMP* is $5, which is equal to the wage rate. The firm, by hiring this worker, expands production without reducing profit. Workers 6 through 10, however, should not be hired because their wages exceed their *VMP*. They add more to wage costs than their production adds to revenue. Only a foolish manager would hire more than five workers in this example. The berry firm's profit-maximizing labor demand is at point *A* in Figure 21-2, with five workers hired at the $5 wage rate.

Profit-maximizing firms continue to hire a resource until its *VMP* equals its price. This holds for labor, capital, or any other input, given these assumptions. Competitive firms follow the $VMP_X = P_X$ rule when deciding how much of resource *X* to purchase at wage or price P_X.

KEY CONCEPT 21.5

The resource allocation rule states that $VMP_X = P_X$.

FIGURE 21-2

Value Marginal Product Is Resource Demand. Firms use *MPP* to calculate *VMP*. Value marginal product is the firm's input demand curve. Rising output price shifts *VMP*, increasing the number of workers demanded from *A* to *B* in the figure.

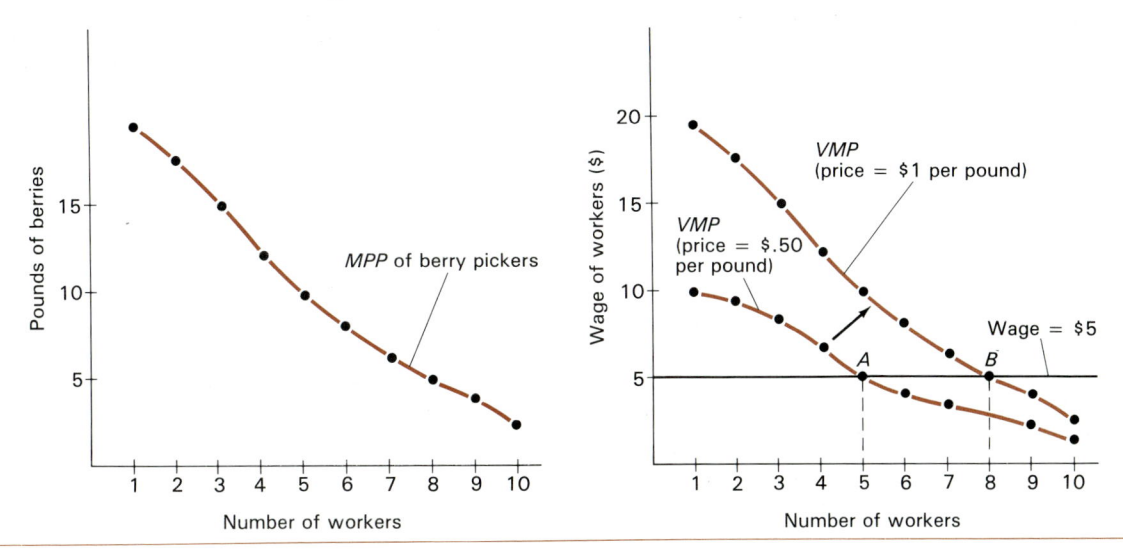

21.6 OUTPUT, PRICE, PRODUCTIVITY, AND DEMAND

When a firm uses only one variable input, then its *VMP* curve for a given resource is also its resource demand curve, since it shows how much of that input the firm demands at each price. Market demand curves for the variable input of firms of this type are the sum of the *VMP* or demand curves of the individual firms.

Changes in Resource Demand

What makes resource demand change, causing shortages, surpluses, and price movements that make the news? There are two important demand shifters that affect resource markets: the price of the output and changes in productivity.

Price of Output The demand for resources is a derived demand. The demand for berry pickers necessarily depends on the demand for berries. Suppose that the demand for strawberries has suddenly jumped in the local area, and the price of strawberries has increased from $.50 to $1 per pound. This price increase doesn't affect the *MPP* of berry pickers. They become neither more nor less productive. But the *VMP* does increase because each extra bucket of berries is worth twice as much now. If you compute *VMP* of the berry workers using a $1 price, you will get the *VMP* (price = $1 per pound) curve shown in Figure 21-2.

The second picker still increases production by 18 pounds of berries per hour (*MPP* equals 18 pounds), but this worker's value marginal product rises from $9 at the old price of $.50 per pound to $18 at the new $1 price. The sixth worker, who was not hired before, is now profitably employed, since his or her *MPP* of 8 pounds is worth $8, far more than the $5 wage rate. The manager of this firm should now expand the work force until *VMP* of labor equals the price of labor. This condition is met at point *B* in the figure, with eight workers in the field.

The demand for resources rises and falls with the price of the goods they produce. Higher selling prices boost VMP and the demand for resources. Lower selling prices mean fewer resources employed.

Changes in Productivity Changes in productivity are a second reason for shifts in resource demand curves. Suppose, for example, that workers learn a new way of berry picking that doubles their hourly output. Workers who pick more berries have a higher MPP and hence greater VMP. A profit-maximizing manager would hire more of these more talented employees, given sufficient demand for berries. Their ability to produce more output more than justifies the extra wages paid.

Many things affect productivity. Changes in technology, improved skills, and government regulations all affect a resource's marginal physical product. Workers in the United States produce more today than in earlier times because they are better trained and they have more and better machines with which to work. The increase in technology and an input mix of more capital per worker are reasons for higher labor productivity. As stated earlier, the actual mix of inputs can affect productivity a great deal. It is entirely possible that an increase in the amount of capital used in a productive process would increase the productivity of labor and an increase in the amount of labor available would increase the productivity of capital.

Demand Adjustments Between Market and Firm

21.7 DEMAND ADJUSTMENTS

What happens to a resource's price when output prices or productivity change? The answer depends on how many firms are affected. We have assumed that employers are price takers, purchasing resources in competitive markets. This means that individual employers are small compared to the market and cannot directly affect market price. Resource prices do not move if final product price or changes in productivity alter demand for only a few firms. These changes are too small to alter market price. If many producers are affected, however, market demand shifts and complex adjustments take place.

Suppose that rising berry prices increase VMP and boost the demand for pickers throughout the strawberry industry. How does the market for berry workers change? How do individual berry producers react? Figure 21-3 shows what happens.

Higher strawberry prices increase the demand for berry pickers from VMP_0 to VMP_1 in Figure 21-3. Individual firms increase their work forces from A to B in the figure. Since many firms now seek more labor, the market demand for berry workers increases from D_0 to D_1. There is a shortage of workers at the $5 wage rate, since the quantity of workers demanded (point Y) is less than the quantity supplied (point X). Shortage forces up the wage rate paid to $6 in this example.

Firms must adjust to higher wages. They cannot profitably employ as many workers at $6 per hour as they could at $5. The VMP equals price rule moves the firm to point C in the figure. It hires more workers than in the beginning but less than it would have if wages had not risen. The market moves to equilibrium at C as firms lay off these previously profitable employees.

Elasticity of Resource Demand

21.8 ELASTICITY OF DEMAND

The elasticity of demand for a resource determines many important issues, such as whether a wage increase will bring big layoffs or whether firms will

FIGURE 21-3   **Adjustments between Firm and Resource Market.** An increase in *VMP* makes it profitable to hire more workers, moving the firm from *A* to *B*. Increased hiring, if experienced by many firms, shifts the market demand curve, raising wages from $5 to $6. The firm reduces the quantity of labor demanded to *C* when wages increase.

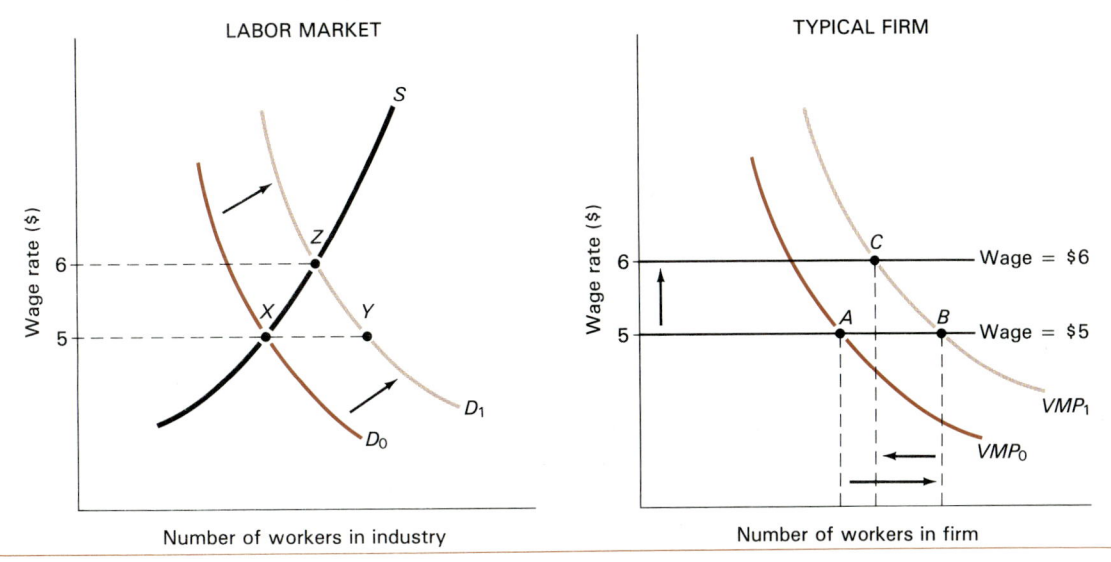

use more computers as the price of computers falls. The key issue here is, however, what determines the elasticity of resource demand?

Producers are affected in many ways by changing input prices, so there is no simple answer to what determines the elasticity of resource demand. There are, however, several major variables that influence the ways in which firms adjust to changing input prices and therefore affect the elasticity of resource demand. We will discuss each of these briefly.

Shape of MPP Curve   How quickly does *MPP* fall as more and more labor, for example, is added to production? The shape of the *MPP* curve is an important determinant of an input's elasticity of demand. Suppose, for example, that the *MPP* curve is steep, like the one in Figure 21-4(a). An increase in resource price brings little change in the quantity demanded here. Laying off a few workers might free enough machines to bring the *VMP* of the remaining workers to a profitable level.

Compare this with the flatter *MPP* curve in Figure 21-4(b). The same increase in price brings higher unemployment in this instance. There is less difference in *MPP* here. Employment must fall much further before *MPP* rises to meet the new higher wage. The shape of the *MPP* curve is determined by production technology. Marginal physical product falls quickly when inputs are used in fixed proportions. The *MPP* of a second typist is low if there is only one typewriter, for example. Conversely, *MPP* is flatter when the relationship among inputs is more flexible.

Ease of Substitution   Ease of substitution among inputs is a second determinant of elasticity. We calculate *MPP* curves by varying the use of one input while holding the others constant. In the real world, however, managers are free to substitute one resource for another. Here's how substitutability shapes resource demand.

FIGURE 21-4

Elasticity of Resource Demand. A steep *MPP* curve leads to a steep *VMP* and inelastic labor demand in (a). The flatter *VMP* in (b) means a more elastic labor demand. The slope of the *MPP* is one of several determinants of elasticity of input demand.

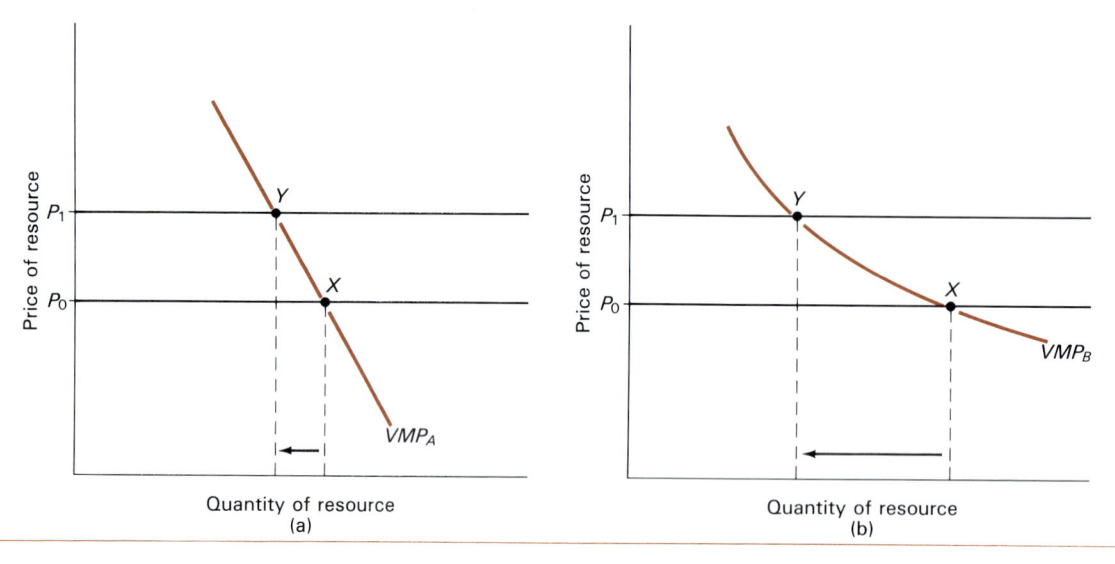

Suppose that it is easy to substitute capital for labor in grocery stores. If the price of labor rises relative to capital, store managers fire some workers and install computerized check-out stands. The few remaining clerks, equipped with high-technology price-scanners, produce as much as did more workers and fewer machines. The demand for labor is more elastic here, because higher price brings a big cut in the number of clerks demanded.

Sometimes it is not easy to substitute one resource for another, so resource demand is more inelastic. The production function for a haircut is pretty much fixed, for example. One barber, one customer, and a pair of scissors is the most efficient resource mix. If barbers' wages rise, the barbershop manager cannot very well substitute capital for labor by reducing the number of barbers and giving each remaining barber two scissors. There are many production processes that involve fixed combinations of inputs, where input substitution is difficult or impossible. If the price of tires rises, for example, Ford Motor Company would probably find it difficult to reduce its use of tire inputs from four to three tires per new car. This fixed proportions production process leads to more inelastic input demand.

Time Frame Demand for a resource can be either elastic or inelastic depending on the time frame of the discussion. In the short run, for example, the demand for diesel fuel is relatively inelastic. Firms with trucks, buses, or furnaces that use this input have little choice but to buy it in the short run when price rises. Their investment in fixed inputs that use diesel fuel restricts their ability to buy and use less when price increases.

The story is different in the long run, however. Firms can change fixed inputs in the long run, altering plant size and technology to minimize average costs. If another fuel is cheaper, or if new trucks or furnaces are available that use less fuel, firms can switch to the cheaper alternative. This reduces the amount of diesel fuel they purchase. In the long run, then, the demand for inputs like diesel fuel is more elastic than in the short run.

Elasticity of Product Demand Higher input costs eventually translate into higher output prices as firms adjust production to maximize profits. Fewer goods are sold at these higher prices, however, so fewer resources are used. This chain reaction links the elasticity of resource demand to the elasticity of demand for the goods resources produce.

Inelastic demand for output leads to more inelastic input demand, all else being equal. If, for example, the demand for college education is inelastic, then the demand for college professors will also be relatively inelastic. The strength of the faculty wage negotiations will depend upon how sensitive students are to increases in the prices they must pay for education. If tuition is increased and students purchase almost as much education as before, the demand for faculty services will be inelastic. If however, students are very sensitive to tuition costs, and buy many fewer course units when tuition costs rise, the demand for faculty services is elastic as well. An elastic demand for college classes means that there is an elastic demand for professors.

Share of Total Cost Finally, elasticity of demand depends on how much money the firm spends on a particular resource compared to other inputs. Suppose, for example, that wages rise at a capital-intensive tire factory. Higher labor costs do not greatly affect total cost and profit, so the firm can absorb higher costs without big production cutbacks. Labor demand might be relatively inelastic in this instance, all else being equal, with little reaction to changing wages.

The story is different when capital costs rise in a capital-intensive firm. Here an increase in capital costs means a big increase in total cost. The firm might have to cut production signficantly and sell off part of its capital base to make up for the higher costs. Input demand for capital is more elastic here than in the previous example.

All five of these elasticity determinants are important. They often combine in complex ways. What happens to the demand for fast-food workers when their wages rise? Will hamburger firms hire many more teenagers if they offer to work for lower pay? Fast-food businesses are labor intensive, but they have difficulty substituting capital for labor in the short run. What does the *MPP* curve for fast-food workers look like? Is the demand for Big Macs elastic or inelastic? We can determine how wage changes affect fast-food workers only when we have considered all these factors.

MONOPOLY RESOURCE DEMAND

Thus far we have looked at the resource demands of firms that both buy inputs and sell their outputs in competitive markets. This analysis is useful because it lets us see the cost versus productivity concerns that all managers weigh in making production decisions. Remember, though, that real-world markets do not always fit the perfectly competitive mold. Does a monopoly firm demand productive resources in the same way?

21.9 MONOPOLY AND *MRP*

Monopolies are like competitive firms in that they compare an input's cost with the value of its added production in deciding how many workers or machines to use. The actual calculations are different, however. Monopolies tend to use fewer resources than would similar competitive firms. Table 21-2 and Figure 21-5 show the monopoly picture.

The monopoly firm described in Table 21-2 buys labor services in competitive markets. It can hire as many workers as it desires at the market wage of $5 per hour because the firm is a price taker in input markets. The

TABLE 21-2

Monopoly and Marginal Revenue Product

Number of workers	Marginal physical product (pounds of strawberries)	Marginal revenue of strawberries ($)	Marginal revenue product ($)
1	20	.80	16.00
2	18	.60	10.80
3	15	.33	5.00
4	12	.25	3.00
5	10	.15	1.50
6	8	.10	.80
7	6	.05	.30
8	5	−.05	−.25
9	4	−.10	−.40
10	2	−.25	−.50

FIGURE 21-5

MRP Is Monopoly Resource Demand. A monopoly hires inputs at B, where MRP equals wage or price. A competitive firm, using price instead of MR in its calculations, employs resources at A, where VMP equals price.

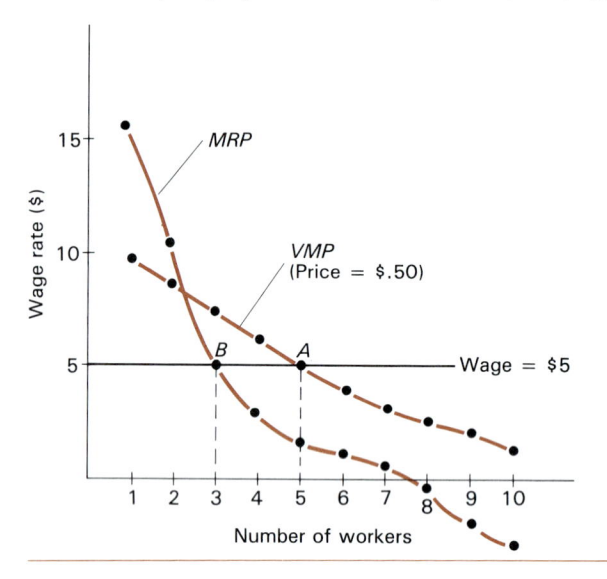

Marginal Revenue Product (MRP)
The extra revenue an additional input produces for a monopoly, other inputs held fixed (MPP multiplied by MR).

firm has a monopoly on its output market. It is the only berry seller in the region. Like the competitive firms discussed before, the manager of the berry monopoly first calculates the marginal physical product (MPP) of its work force. A competitive firm would then multiply MPP by the constant output price to arrive at a VMP, which represents the firm's labor (resource) demand curve.

Life is more complex for the monopoly manager. Price depends on the amount produced, since the monopoly is the only seller. More workers and higher production mean lower price. Marginal revenue, not price, therefore, guides monopoly decisions. The monopolist uses information about labor's MPP and the marginal revenue of the berries produced to arrive at each additional worker's value to the firm. This is the monopoly's measure of **marginal revenue product (MRP)**.

Table 21-2 shows how *MRP* is calculated. The first worker picks 20 pounds of berries per hour. These berries have a marginal revenue of $.80 per pound. Total revenue rises by $.80 for each pound of berries sold, so the worker's efforts add revenue equal to an *MRP* of 20 lbs. times $.80 cents, or $16. The second worker adds 18 pounds per hour to production, but this extra output means a lower monopoly selling price. The marginal revenue of the second worker's production is just $.60 per pound, giving an *MRP* of $.60 times 18, $10.80. The second worker's efforts add $10.80 per hour to monopoly revenues. (Review Chapter 19 if you've forgotten why marginal revenue declines as output rises.) Use Table 21-2 to calculate the *MRP* for the remaining workers.

Marginal revenue product (*MRP*) and value marginal product (*VMP*) measure the same thing. Both measure the dollar amount of revenue an extra resource unit adds. The term *VMP* is used when firms sell in competitive resource markets where an individual firm's price does not vary with its output and resource demand. Remember, in competitive markets, price equals marginal revenue so the competitor's *MRP* is equal to the firm's *VMP*. Marginal revenue product is used for monopolies, where marginal revenue is different from price and higher levels of production mean lower selling price. In monopolies, *MRP* and *VMP* measures are quite different.

Table 21-2 holds a riddle. Why do workers 8 through 10 in the table have negative *MRP*, meaning that their employment reduces firm revenues, when they have positive *MPP*? They produce positive amounts of goods. How can it be that workers make more goods, but their employers have less to show for it? The answer to this paradox is that the monopolist enters the inelastic portion of the berry demand curve at these relatively high production levels. The monopolist takes in less total revenue, causing negative marginal revenue, when it cuts price to sell more on an inelastic demand curve. The negative *MRP* we see here is the consequence of inelastic demand. Thus these "productive" workers will not be hired.

The number of workers the monopoly will hire is illustrated in Figure 21-5, which compares the monopoly with a similar competitive firm. The competitive firm hires resources until *VMP* equals price. This firm therefore maximizes profits at point *A*. Five berry pickers are employed by the competitive firm at the $5 wage rate. The monopoly uses fewer labor resources and produces less output. The monopolist hires resources until their incremental cost (price) equals the extra revenue they produce (*MRP*). Marginal revenue product equals price at point *B* in the figure. The monopolist hires just three workers in this example.

This analysis shows another side of the monopoly problem. You learned in Chapter 19 that monopolies tend to produce fewer goods and charge higher prices than would similar competitive firms. Now we see that this inefficiency is contagious. It is spread to the resource markets, where monopolies employ fewer workers, machines, and other inputs than would competitive firms.

MONOPSONY: THE ONE-BUYER MARKET

> **21.10 MONOPSONY AND *MRC***

All our analysis so far has assumed perfectly competitive resource markets, where many buyers and sellers meet to exchange homogeneous input resources. These assumptions do not always hold in the real world. For example, many resources are not homogeneous. All coal or natural gas may be about the same, but workers certainly are not. Furthermore, the capital

610 *Resource Markets: Demand and Supply at Work*

Monopsony
A market with a single buyer; a monopoly purchaser of a resource.

machines produced by various manufacturers are differentiated products too. It is often the differences among workers or tools that are most important. Models of monopolistic competition and oligopoly, not perfect competition, are more appropriate in resource markets where quality differences prevail.

You can get a better understanding of these imperfect resource markets by looking at the extreme case of **monopsony**. Monopsony describes markets in which there is just one buyer. There is no competition on the demand side of the market.

Monopsonies exist is some resource markets. College baseball and basketball players cannot sell their labor to the highest professional team bidder, for example. They are drafted by a single team and must play for that team or not at all. Many company towns, where one firm dominates the labor market by employing much of the population, fit the monopsony model. The federal government is the monopsony purchaser of some goods, such as B-1 bombers and Trident submarines. Finally, resources with highly specialized uses frequently have only one or just a few potential purchasers, who might exercise monopsony power.

Monopsonies use fewer resources and pay a lower price for them than would buyers in a similar competitive market. Table 21-3 and Figure 21-6 tell the monopsony story. This berry firm is a monopsonist because it is the only employer of berry workers in the region. It sells its production on competitive national berry markets, however, so it is an output price taker. The firm's manager has already calculated worker *VMP* (see the figure). How many workers should be hired, given the labor supply curve in the figure? The employment decision is made by comparing *VMP* with **marginal resource cost** (*MRC*). Table 21-3 shows how *MRC* is calculated.

Marginal Resource Cost (*MRC*)
The increase in total resource cost when one more input is employed.

The labor-supply curve shows the number of berry pickers who are willing to work at each wage rate. It shows that one worker can be hired for $1.50 per hour. The *MRC* of the first worker is equal to this wage. What happens if the firm wants to hire two workers? The supply curve says that wages must rise to $2.25 per worker to attract the second employee from competing jobs or desirable leisure activities. Adding the second worker increases labor cost by more than $2.25 per hour, because both employees must be paid the same $2.25 wage. We assume the firm cannot price discriminate in paying employees. The result is that hiring the second worker raises the hourly payroll from $1.50 for one worker to a total of

TABLE 21-3 — **Monopsony and Marginal Resource Cost**

Number of workers	Wage rate ($)	Total resource cost ($)	Marginal resource cost ($)
0	0	0	0
1	1.50	1.50	1.50
2	2.25	4.50	3.00
3	4.00	12.00	7.50
4	5.00	20.00	8.00
5	6.00	30.00	10.00
6	7.00	42.00	12.00
7	8.00	56.00	14.00
8	9.00	72.00	16.00
9	12.00	108.00	36.00
10	15.00	15.00	42.00

FIGURE 21-6

Monopsony Labor Demand. A monopsony hires three workers, because this is the quantity at which *MRC* equals *VMP*. The monopsony pays workers at *C* the $4 necessary to attract three workers to this market.

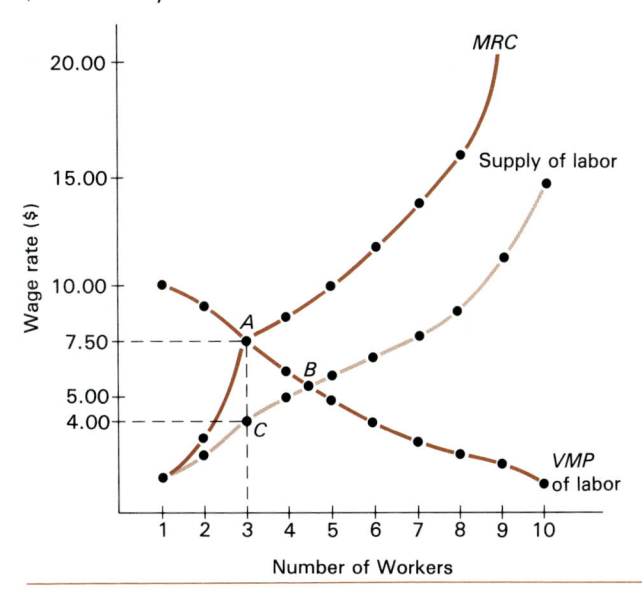

$2.25 times 2, $4.50, for two. The second worker, who is paid $2.25, has an *MRC* of $3.

This scene is repeated as the third worker is hired. The labor-supply curve says that wages must rise to $4 to attract a third picker to this job, boosting the hourly payroll to $12. This is an increase of $7.50 per hour. The third worker's *MRC* is therefore $7.50. Work through Table 21-3 to see how the *MRC* is calculated for other workers.

The monopsonist's *MRC* curve in Figure 21-6 is above the corresponding supply curve for the same reason that a monopolist's *MR* curve lies below demand. You learned about this in Chapter 19. When a monopsonist hires an extra worker or other resource, input prices must rise to attract the input from its best alternate use. This increases total resource cost far more than the cost of the extra input itself.

The monopsonist decides how many resources to employ by comparing the extra cost against extra revenue, just like the other firms discussed in this chapter. The monopsonist hires workers and other resources until the additional cost (*MRC*) equals the extra revenue produced (*VMP*). This corresponds to point *A* in this figure. A competitive resource market would end up at *B*, where the quantity of labor demanded (*VMP*) equals the quantity of labor supplied.

The wage rate the monopsonist pays is tricky, so look at the figure carefully. This monopsonist hires three workers because that's the quantity at which *MRC* equals $7.50, which in turn equals *VMP*. The last worker hired adds as much to cost as to revenue. But there is no need to pay the worker this high $7.50 *VMP*. The supply curve says this worker can be lured from other work for just $4 per hour (point *C* in the figure), and that is what he or she is paid. This wage is less than the worker's value marginal product. It is also less than the price that would prevail in a competitive labor market.

Workers in company towns sometimes suspect that the town's sole employer isn't giving them a fair shake. They are right if the employer acts like a monopsony and the workers' idea of being fair means that the

ECONOMIC ISSUE

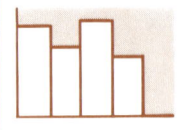

Automation and Unemployment

American industry is becoming increasingly computerized. Robots and computers are doing more and more of the tasks that were once performed by human workers. Many people view this trend with alarm. They are convinced that computers will replace human beings in large numbers, leading to a new era of high technology-based unemployment. In general, economists are less concerned about this trend than others. Why? This Economic Issue looks at the way economists view technological change and its likely effect on income and employment.

Every labor-saving technological change has been condemned by someone. Farm equipment, such as plows, tractors, and harvesters, each replaced many individual workers. Each textile factory of the industrial revolution replaced hundreds of individual spinners and weavers working by hand or with primitive equipment. Even big efficient supermarkets operate with less labor than would an equivalent number of smaller mom and pop neighborhood stores. In short, history is filled with innovations that put people out of work. In spite of this, however, more people work today than in any era of the past. Today's workers have higher real incomes, meaning they can buy more goods and services, than in other years. Few of today's workers would trade places with their counterparts in previous generations.

Why have technological improvements, such as automated assembly lines, actually benefited workers in the long run? Economists cite several reasons. First, new technologies are adopted because they produce goods at lower cost or produce better quality goods. Price reductions and quality improvements benefit workers because workers are also consumers and are better off when they are able to buy more and better goods.

Second, lower price and better quality tend to increase the amount of goods consumers want to buy. This stimulates production and, indirectly, encourages firms to hire more workers. Higher output effects often offset the tendency of machines to replace workers.

Henry Ford's innovative auto assembly line illustrates the importance of output effects. Prior to Ford's first plant, autos were virtually handmade and very expensive. Many man-hours went into each car. Ford's factory replaced many workers with machines, so fewer workers were needed for each car. Did this

---

monopsonist employer should pay a competitive wage. Figure 21-6 shows that a monopsony hires fewer workers and pays them lower wages than would a competitive resource market.

RESOURCE SUPPLY

21.12 RESOURCE SUPPLIES

So far we have concentrated on resource demand, but a complete understanding of these markets requires an examination of what determines resource supply. We have less to say about resource supply in this chapter because it is harder to generalize about so many different human and natural resources. Each scarce resource is different in its physical properties, the way it is produced, and the factors that govern its scarcity, thus resource supplies should be analyzed individually. The concept of resource supply is so important and somewhat unique that the entire next chapter is devoted to its analysis. A few generalities are possible, however. Resource supplies are limited by many factors, among them production costs, resource limits, technology, and market competition.

Production Costs Many natural resources are expensive to harvest or extract. Fixed and variable costs determine how much is made available at a given price. This sometimes leads to perverse results. When oil prices shot

result in unemployment in the auto industry? On the contrary, more auto workers found jobs because consumers purchased many more of the less expensive cars. Each car required fewer workers, but so many more cars were produced that more jobs at higher wages were the result. Many technological advances have followed this pattern. An initial reduction in the number of workers needed, the substitution effect of capital for labor, is followed by an increase in employment because of the increased output effect.

A final reason that labor-saving technology does not necessarily result in mass unemployment is that capital and labor are complements not just substitutes. More and better machines increase the productivity of workers, boosting their value marginal product. More productive workers can earn higher wages in a competitive labor market. Auto workers today, for example, earn high wages as much because computer technology makes them more productive as because they are skilled in particular tasks.

Automation and technological advances are not to be feared or opposed because, as history shows, the substitution effect of capital replacing labor is often dominated by an output effect of higher production levels that require more of both resources. Technology does not benefit everyone, however. Some workers are hurt by automation, particularly those who are unable to adapt to changing technology or who have specific skills and cannot find work in other areas when machines take their jobs. These groups, and their unions and employers, sometimes form a special-interest group that tries to prevent or delay technological change. Economists understand why these special interests want to preserve existing production technologies. They temporarily preserve current job and income patterns. These activities, however, are socially undesirable on two counts. First, attempts to halt technological change keep prices unnecessarily high and reduce the output effects that benefit other workers. Consumers and workers in other fields lose when unions and others slow automation. Second, attempts to slow automation are only temporary and can be ultimately destructive to the groups they are intended to benefit. If U.S. unions keep their employers from adopting labor-saving technology, for example, this gives foreign firms that use more efficient techniques a big advantage. The U.S. industry can be eliminated by cheaper and better goods from more efficient foreign producers. High unemployment in the early 1980s in U.S. auto and steel industries can be blamed, at least in part, on the failure to change to more efficient production techniques in earlier years.

Additional References

Eckaus, Richard S. "The Factor Proportions Problem in Underdeveloped Areas." *American Economic Review* (August, 1955), pp. 319–338.

Greenberger, Robert S. "Resisting a Trend, Machinists Union Continues to Oppose Concessions." *Wall Street Journal*, September 2, 1983, p. 3.

Miller, Roger Leroy. *Intermediate Microeconomics.* New York: McGraw-Hill, 1978.

---

up in the United States in 1973–1974, for example, many firms thought it wise to switch to cheaper coal-fired furnaces. Two important things happened. First, the increase in the demand for coal that occurred when oil-consuming industries switched to its use drove up the price of coal. Second, oil is a big input cost in the transportation of coal once it is mined. Higher transportation costs altered coal supply, leading to higher prices for both coal and oil. This interdependence is common among resource supplies.

Resource Limits Some natural resources face short-term or long-term physical limitations that affect supply. The supply of natural gas is limited in the short run by the number of producing wells and their capacity. It takes years to bring a new oil field into production, so short-run supply limits prevail. More binding supply limits exist in the long run, as nature's bounty runs out.

Technology Improved technology makes more resources available, thereby increasing supply. Many oil wells that were given up as dead in days past have been revitalized with technology's help. New techniques, such as injecting old wells with steam to force out oil dregs, get more oil out of dry holes. New production methods are often expensive, so they are used only when high price makes them worthwhile.

Market Competition Finally, input supplies depend on the nature of competition among resource producers. Lower prices and larger quantities are likely, for example, if many firms compete to produce resources, as opposed to there being a monopoly resource seller. Compare for example, oil's high price and limited production during the years in which OPEC had a highly functioning cartel. Once the British developed the North Sea oil fields, the United States completed the Alaskan oil pipeline, and other competitors entered the active world oil market, crude became more available. As a result, its price increase has slowed and actually declined in some cases. The difference between more competitive oil markets and the monopoly-like OPEC cartel are one reason for this dramatic difference in the relative supplies of this resources.

COMBINING INPUTS: OPTIMAL RESOURCE USE

The problem of deciding how much labor to hire, as we have seen, is a difficult one. A firm's manager must know all about *MPP*, *MRP*, *VMP*, and the like. This is a lot to know for what probably seems like a relatively simple business decision.

> **21.13 PROFIT AND INPUT USE**

Real-world firms practice all of the economic theory you have learned here, and yet they may not even know it. A manager does not have to know all the terminology of marginal revenue product or marginal resource costs to know when the firm is making more profits and when it is making less. Firms can learn through trial and error, so long as they keep an eye on the profit gauge of success. Managers often arrive at the profit-maximizing resource use by trial and error. Low profits are sometimes a sign that too many inputs are being used, so managers cut back on resource demands. At other times, however, profit rises when more workers are hired and more output is produced. Profit-seeking firms vary resource use and let profit be their guide to efficient input decisions. Profits peak when they have found the right number of workers or machines.

Production decisions are trickier when more than one resource is being used, as is almost always the case. Managers usually find the profit-maximizing combination of capital, labor, and natural resources through trial and error combinations. It is both interesting and beneficial, however, to know the theory behind their eventual choice. A complete understanding of the economic theory involved would eliminate much of the trial and error process and enable managers to make more valid decisions more quickly.

> **21.14 OPTIMAL RESOURCE USE RULE**

Suppose our hypothetical berry firm needs two kinds of workers in its berry fields. It needs pickers who are paid $5 per hour and bosses who are paid $8 per hour to supervise workers in the field. It needs both kinds of labor, and each is productive. How does one decide how many of each to hire? Trial and error profit maximization would arrive at a combination of pickers and bosses that satisfies the condition $MPP_X/P_X = MPP_Y/P_Y$. This is referred to as the optimal resource use rule. The *X*s and *Y*s identify the marginal physical products and prices of the two types of inputs used. It helps to think of MPP_X/P_X as the *MPP* produced per dollar spent on resource *X*.

KEY CONCEPT 21.14   The optimal resource use rule states that profit-maximizing firms employ inputs *X* and *Y* to the point where $MPP_X/P_X = MPP_Y/P_Y$.

Why does the optimal resource use rule hold? Let X stand for pickers and Y stand for bosses in this example. Suppose for a moment that MPP_X/P_X (pickers) is bigger than MPP_Y/P_Y (bosses). An extra dollar spent on hiring more pickers might increase output by 5 pounds of fruit, for example. An extra dollar paid to hire more supervisors adds just 3 pounds to total production. What should the firm do? The answer seems clear. The firm should hire more high MPP/P pickers and fire some relatively low MPP/P bosses. It will get more total product for the same cost by using more pickers and fewer supervisors. The extra berries the firm gains (5 pounds per dollar spent) by hiring pickers exceeds the berries it loses (3 pounds per dollar spent) when it reduces the supervisors' hours.

The firm has reached the profit maximum for a given total payroll when $MPP_X/P_X = MPP_Y/P_Y$. It is impossible, given this equality, to increase total product without spending more on workers. In a more complex production process, with many inputs, the profit-maximizing and cost-minimizing rule is $MPP_X/P_X = MPP_Y/P_Y = MPP_Z/P_Z$ for as many inputs as are used in production. If an employer were already cost minimizing and the relative price of, say, input X fell, then we could expect that the employer would use more of X and less of the other resources. Alternatively, if the relative price of X were to rise, all else being equal, we could expect the employer to use less of X and more of its input substitutes.

The MPP/P rule tells both employers and their employees an interesting fact. A profit-maximizing employer pays some employees more than others only when there is a corresponding difference in their productivity. Firms that pay higher wages to inputs with the same MPP will find themselves beaten in the profit race by competitors who make more efficient production choices.

The two remaining chapters in this unit discuss labor and capital markets in more depth, then the first chapter of the next unit looks at the income distribution that these markets produce.

SUMMARY

21.1

1. Resource markets are markets in which land, labor, capital, and natural resources are exchanged. These might just as well be called input markets because resources are used as inputs to production. Resource markets partly determine the distribution of income. Income is generated when resources are used to produce and sell goods and services. The return on different resources affects who gets what.

21.2

2. Resources are allocated by price. Price sees that scarce resources go to their best use. Markets that set prices thus decide where scarce resources go. Price also determines how different resources are combined in production. Production might be labor intensive under one set of resource prices and capital intensive under another set of resource prices.

21.3

3. The demand for an input is called a derived demand because it is derived from the demand for the final good or service that the input is used to produce. For example, the demand for steel workers is derived

21.4 ▶ 4. Economists use marginal productivity theory to describe resource demand. Total physical product (*TPP*) rises as more of one input is added to production, all other inputs held fixed. Marginal physical product (*MPP*) declines as more of one input is added, all others held fixed. Additional inputs go to less productive jobs, which run into bottlenecks caused by relative shortages of other productive inputs.

21.5 ▶ 5. A competitive firm's demand for labor, capital, or other resources is determined by that input's value marginal product (*VMP*). Value marginal product is found by multiplying *MPP* by the selling price of the good or service produced. Value marginal product equals *MPP* times output price. The *VMP* represents the extra revenue that the next or last resource unit generates for the firm. Firms decide how much of an input to use by comparing *VMP* (revenue) with the resource's price (cost). A profit-maximizing competitive firm hires an input at the point where VMP_X equals P_X. The *VMP* curve is thus the firm's resource demand curve.

21.6 ▶ 6. Input demand depends on many things. Changes in the output prices directly alter resource demand because they change *VMP*. Holding *MPP* constant, *VMP* rises with the price of output, increasing input demand. Value marginal profit falls when output price falls. Input demand also depends on productivity. Value marginal product rises when a resource becomes more productive, assuming no change in output price. This is because productivity boosts *MPP*. Lower productivity forces resource demand down.

21.7 ▶ 7. An increase in output price or productivity has little or no effect on the resource market and prices if just one or a few firms are affected. A general increase in *VMP* means firms demand larger input quantities. Market demand increases for these resources, forcing up price. Firms adjust to the higher price by finding the new *VMP* equals *P* point, with a smaller quantity demanded. Firm and market eventually find equilibrium.

21.8 ▶ 8. The shape of the *MPP* curve is one determinant of the elasticity of an input's demand. Steep *MPP*, where productivity declines swiftly as more inputs are added, leads to relatively inelastic input demand. A flatter *MPP*, where productivity changes are less severe, means relatively elastic input demand. Elasticity is also affected by the ease with which different inputs can be substituted for one another. Inputs that can be easily replaced by other resources tend to have more elastic demand. Time frame also determines elasticity. Many resources that have a relatively inelastic demand in the short run can be replaced with substitutes in the long run. Elasticity of input demand is also influenced by the elasticity of product demand. An increase in input prices has less effect on input use if the demand for the output is inelastic, for example. Finally, resources that account for much of a firm's total cost tend to have a more elastic demand than those that are smaller budget items.

21.9 ▶ 9. Monopolies tend to demand lesser quantities of the inputs they use than do competitive firms. Monopoly input demand is given by a resource's marginal revenue product—*MPP* multiplied by the marginal revenue of the goods produced. Monopolies maximize profit by producing where marginal input cost (wage or price) equals marginal input gain (*MRP*).

10. A monopsony is a market with just one buyer. Monopsony buyers tend to demand smaller quantities of resources and pay them a lower price or wage, compared with competitive resource markets. A monopsony calculates the marginal resource cost in making input decisions. Marginal resource cost is the change in total resource cost that occurs when extra inputs are employed. A monopsony maximizes profits by demanding the quantity of an input that results in its cost (*MRC*) being equal to the value of the goods produced (*VMP*). The price or wage the input receives is determined by the supply curve. Price is less than *VMP* in this instance.

11. Resource supplies depend on many factors. Each resource market has different characteristics. Production cost, natural resource limits, technology, and the degree of competition among suppliers, however, affect the supply of all resources.

12. Many firms decide how many inputs to use by trial and error. Profits fall when they move away from the optimal use, and peak when the theoretical optimum is attained.

13. The profit-maximizing combination of inputs occurs when $MPP_X/P_X = MPP_Y/P_Y = MPP_Z/P_Z$, where X, Y, and Z are inputs used in production. The output per dollar spent on inputs is equal, so there is no way to alter production to get more output for the same input. If MPP_X/P_X is greater than MPP_Y/P_Y, however, the firm can get more output for the same cost by using less Y and more X.

DISCUSSION QUESTIONS

1. The accompanying table shows information about the number of workers, total product per day, and output price for a hypothetical perfectly competitive firm. Use the information given there to
   a. calculate each worker's *MPP*;
   b. calculate each worker's *VMP*;
   c. determine the profit-maximizing number of workers to employ, given that the wage rate is $60 per day.

Number of workers	TPP (per day)	MPP	Price ($)	VMP ($)
1	50		4	
2	90		4	
3	120		4	
4	150		4	
5	165		4	
6	175		4	
7	180		4	

21.5 ▶ 2. Plot the *VMP* curve from Question 1 and show how the profit-maximizing number of workers is determined graphically.

21.4, 21.9 ▶ 3. The accompanying table shows information about the number of workers, total product per day, and marginal revenue for a hypothetical monopoly. Use the information given there to
   a. calculate each worker's *MPP*;
   b. calculate each worker's *MRP*;
   c. determine the profit-maximizing number of workers for this monopoly, given that the wage rate is $60 per day.

Number of workers	TPP (per day)	MPP	MR ($)	MRP ($)
1	50		5.00	
2	90		3.00	
3	120		2.00	
4	150		1.50	
5	165		.50	
6	175		−1.00	
7	180		−2.00	

21.4, 21.5, 21.9 ▶ 4. Plot the *MRP* curve in Question 3 and compare it with the *VMP* curve in Question 2. Explain why these two curves are different even though the corresponding *MPP* curves are the same.

21.10, 21.11 ▶ 5. A monopsonist hires a worker with a *VMP* of $7.50 and only pays the worker a $5 wage. Explain why this sends an inefficient price signal to resource markets. (Hint: What does the monopsonist wage tell other markets about the opportunity cost of labor?)

21.2, 21.3 ▶ 6. Are the wages set by competitive resource markets fair? Just? Defend your answer to this question.

SELECTED READINGS

Eckhaus, Richard S. "The Factor Proportions Problem in Underdeveloped Areas." Reprinted in Breit, William, and Hochman, Harold M. (Eds.), *Readings in Microeconomics*, 2nd ed. New York: Holt, Rinehart and Winston, 1971. pp. 319–338.

Leftwich, Richard H. *The Price System and Resource Allocation*, 7th ed. Hinsdale, IL: Dryden Press, 1979.

Russell, R.R. "On the Demand Curve for a Factor of Production." *American Economic Review* (September, 1964); pp. 726–733.

Terborgh, George. *The Automation Hysteria*. New York: Norton, 1966.

Wicksteed, Phillip H. "The Scope and Method of Political Economy in the Light of the 'Marginal' Theory of Value and Distribution." Reprinted in Needy, Charles W. (Ed.), *Classics of Economics*. Oak Park, IL: Moore Publishing Company, Inc., 1980. pp. 321–333.

CHAPTER 22

Workers, Wages, and Jobs

Having read the chapter, reviewed the chapter summary, and completed the *Study Guide* exercises, you should be able to:

CRIS

22.1 IRON LAW OF WAGES: Explain the iron law of wages and tell why Thomas Malthus and Karl Marx thought this law applied, then discuss whether the law applies today.

22.2 SUBSTITUTION AND INCOME EFFECTS: Explain substitution and income effects in regard to the supply curve of labor.

22.3 DETERMINANTS OF LABOR SUPPLY: List and discuss several factors that determine the location of the supply curve of labor.

22.4 WAGE DIFFERENTIALS: Explain why workers in different countries and different occupations receive different wages, then list and discuss four market factors that determine wage differentials.

22.5 LABOR MARKET IMPERFECTIONS: List four labor market imperfections that create wage differentials that are not justified by differences in labor demand and supply alone and explain how each imperfection causes wages to be higher for some than for others.

22.6 DISCRIMINATION: Explain why discrimination hurts both the workers who are discriminated against and the employers who do the discriminating.

22.7 HUMAN CAPITAL: Define human capital, tell how it differs from physical capital, and explain why employers tend to underinvest in human capital relative to other inputs from which they can capture the full benefit of their investment.

22.8 LABOR UNION ACTS: Explain the major contents of the Sherman Antitrust Act, the Norris–Laguardia Act, the Wagner Act, the Taft–Hartley Act, and the Landrum–Griffin Act as they apply to the key powers of and controls placed on labor unions since 1890.

22.9 UNIONS AND WAGES: List three ways that unions help to increase the wages of their members, and use labor demand and supply curves to explain how each method works.

- **22.10 UNION MONOPOLY:** Draw a graph showing how a union monopoly would set wage and union membership and explain why the union's wage is higher than wages in competitive markets.

- **22.11 EMPLOYERS' ASSOCIATION MONOPSONY:** Explain how an employers' association monopsony would set wages and determine the quantity of labor demanded, then draw a graph showing how wage rates and the size of work force are determined.

- **22.12 LABOR STRIKES:** Explain why a strike is possible when a monopoly union negotiates wages with a monopsonist employers' association.

- **22.13 STRONG UNION CHARACTERISTICS:** List four characteristics of a strong union and explain how each characteristic affects the union's ability to raise wages.

- **22.14 MINIMUM WAGE LAWS:** Define minimum wage laws and describe how they affect labor markets.

- **22.15 MINIMUM WAGES AND COMPETITIVE MARKETS:** Explain why economists think minimum wages cause higher unemployment in competitive labor markets, then draw a graph of a competitive labor market and show how minimum wages affect supply, demand, wages, quantity demanded, and quantity supplied.

- **22.16 MINIMUM WAGES AND MONOPSONY:** Explain how minimum wages increase both wages and employment in monopsony labor markets and discuss why evidence favors the view that the minimum wages cause unemployment.

- **22.17 CAREER PLANNING:** Explain how predictions of changes in product and labor demand and supply, geographic and occupational mobility, and pecuniary versus nonpecuniary costs and benefits affect plans for future careers.

22.1 IRON LAW OF WAGES

Iron Law of Wages
Theory held by Malthus and Marx, among others, that wages fall to subsistence levels in the long run.

One reason economics used to be called the dismal science is that economists used to believe in the **iron law of wages.** This law, developed during the years of the Industrial Revolution, held that wages for the mass of workers would never vary from the subsistence level for very long. Workers, in the long run, would be paid just enough to exist and reproduce, but no more. Social observers found evidence of the iron law in the low wages and poor living conditions of many industrial workers during the Industrial Revolution.

British clergyman–economist Thomas Malthus (1766–1834) believed that population growth trends were the iron forces that made wages tend toward subsistence. Death rates were high for people of all ages during this period. These high death rates reduced the labor supply, which, in turn, resulted in higher wages. High wages temporarily provided better living conditions, thereby enabling more people to survive and reproduce. Consequently, the labor supply was increased and wages fell. Because of lower wages, living conditions declined and fewer people survived to reproduce. The resulting decrease in the labor supply started the cycle again. Thus Malthus saw subsistence as the dismal equilibrium of the working population.

Karl Marx (1818–1883) thought subsistence wages were the result of capitalism's inevitable exploitation of the working class. According to Marx, capitalist business practices create a "reserve army of the unemployed," which guarantees low wages. So long as unemployment persists, there will always be jobless workers willing to take jobs away from others by offering to work for a little less. This hopeless job competition lines the pockets of employers, Marx thought, while wages fall to subsistence levels.

Economic conditions are significantly better today. Current wages are well above the subsistence minimum in the United States. Though poverty and unemployment are important problems, government programs keep them from causing the calamities earlier thinkers predicted.

As we learned in Chapter 8, labor is the factor of production that receives the largest single share of national income. This is not by accident, since labor clearly is the most important factor of production from the viewpoints of both the consumer and the producer. Wages earned through the sale of individual labor represent the largest and most frequent source of household income in our economy. In this chapter, we will examine the theory behind the supply of labor. We will find out how much labor workers are willing to supply to the economy and why. We will also find out why some individual workers earn so much more than others, as well as what institutional forces serve to alter the market outcome of wage decisions by workers and producers.

LABOR SUPPLY IN THE ECONOMY

The labor supply function for the entire economy is based upon some rather simple applications of the laws of supply and demand that we discussed in Chapter 16. First, there is a relative scarcity of labor, since for all of us, there are only 24 hours in a day and working is only one of many things we want to do. Hours must be devoted to sleep, eating, transportation to and from work, recreation, and so on. This means that one hour devoted to work cannot at the same time be devoted to other things we need and enjoy. For the purpose of analysis, we will put all those other things we want to do with our time under a single category that we will call leisure. With only labor and this other composite category of leisure available, whenever we demand leisure for one hour, we must reduce the supply of labor by one hour. In other words, the cost to us of one hour of labor is foregoing one hour of leisure. Alternatively, we "buy" our leisure time with the foregone wages we surrender by not working. This labor–leisure tradeoff can produce a supply curve for labor. The supply of labor can be visualized as a positive function of the wage rate, as it is in Figure 22-1. Note, however, that as wages rise, beyond some point the labor supply curve becomes vertical and the number of hours workers are willing to supply does not continue to increase.

22.2 SUBSTITUTION AND INCOME EFFECTS

As wages rise, workers experience both a substitution effect and an income effect. In the case of the substitution effect, as wages rise, workers substitute work for leisure because the "cost" of their leisure has gone up. In effect, each hour of leisure costs the workers the foregone wage rate they would have earned if they had worked that hour. Therefore, as the wage rate increases, workers supply larger quantities of labor to the

622 *Workers, Wages, and Jobs*

FIGURE 22-1

The Supply Curve of Labor. In general, the supply curve of labor is a positive function of the wage rate. As wages rise from W_1 to W_2 the substitution effect dominates as workers substitute work for leisure since each additional hour of leisure "costs" them more in forgone wages. Beyond W_2, as wages rise the income effect dominates since workers demand more leisure (a normal good) with their increased income from higher wages.

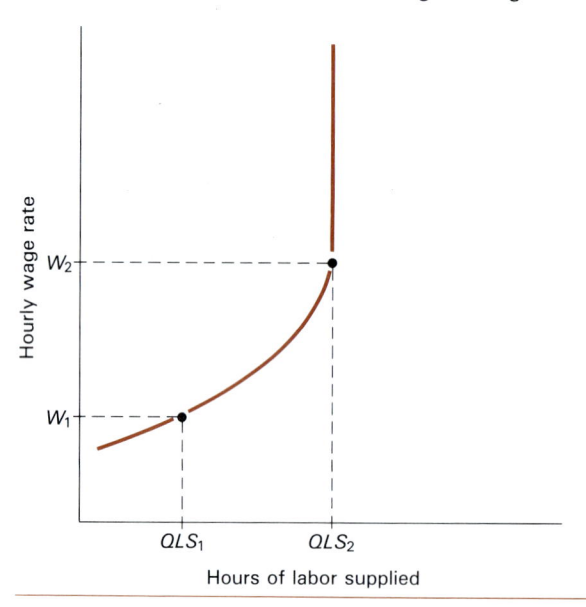

market. The region of the labor supply curve in Figure 22-1 from wage rate W_1 to W_2 illustrates where the substitution effect dominates the income effect and quantity supplied increases with the wage rate. In the case of the income effect, as wages rise, workers now have more income and therefore demand more of all normal goods. Since leisure is a normal good, we would expect workers to demand more of it and therefore supply less labor. In the portion of the labor supply curve above the W_2 wage rate the income effect dominates the substitution effect and the amount of labor supplied does not increase further as wages increase. Beyond some income level, workers will choose to consume more leisure rather than to work more.

It is also important to remember from Chapter 16 that if only the wage changes we move along a given supply curve. If some factor other than wages changes, such as an increase in the working age population, we will observe a relocation of the entire supply curve. In the following section, we will examine some of the factors that determine the location of the supply curve of labor. Finally, you should remember that the wage rate that affects decision makers is the real wage rate not the nominal wage rate. While all wages may rise over time due to inflation, workers base their willingness to supply labor upon increases in their purchasing power. Throughout this chapter, the analysis will revolve around changes in the real wage rate.

What Determines Labor Supply?

22.3 DETERMINANTS OF LABOR SUPPLY

It is first important to separate the supply of labor in a particular market from the supply of labor in general. Factors that influence the supply of labor in the market for college professors are not the same things that determine the supply of labor for firefighters. All sorts of variables enter individual labor market decisions. You are familiar with many characteristics of different labor markets. You might make a list of the many factors that you are considering as you make career decisions. All these differences make each labor market unique.

Some economic and social factors affect all labor markets. A list of the general determinants of labor supply includes population, traditions and social customs, government policies, and institutional forces.

Population Population limits the supply of human resources in an economy. This limit is not as restrictive as it might seem. Increased productivity enables fewer workers to produce more goods, making scarce human inputs go further. When labor demand exceeds population limits, a nation can import **guest workers** from high population countries, as several European countries have done. They might purchase labor-intensive goods from other lands, as the United States has done. Labor is imported indirectly through the imported goods that foreign labor produces. In addition, people may enter the work force from the previously nonworking population. The large influx of women into the work force in the 1970s and 1980s is a clear example of how this population limitation can become less restrictive.

Guest Workers
Foreign workers who are allowed to participate in a nation's labor market in order to relieve a labor shortage.

Traditions and Social Customs Traditions and social customs help determine what fraction of the population enters the labor force. In the Middle East, for example, tradition holds that women should stay in the home. The labor force in Islamic countries is, therefore, largely limited to the male population. Western lands now encourage women to work, increasing the supply of human resources, but small children are forbidden to take jobs as they do in other cultures. American students tend to spend more years in school than do students in other lands. This reduces supply in quantity terms, but perhaps increases labor quality. Religious beliefs limit the types of and times that work can be performed in most cultures.

Government Policies Government policies alter the labor–leisure choice in many ways. Taxes are the most obvious influence, since they reduce take-home pay and cut the effective wage rate. Transfer payment programs, like social security in the United States, are another important influence on labor supply. Social security payments, which can begin as early as age 62, discourage older workers from continuing on the job. The U.S. labor supply is diminished by the smaller number of older workers in the work force.

Institutional Forces Labor unions and various other organizations that control working contracts also have major effects on the supply of labor. For example, when the United Auto Workers struck against General Motors in 1984, for all practical purposes, the supply of auto assemblers to General Motors was zero. Unions, guilds, professional organizations, and other groups that have the power to contract for wages and working conditions or bargain collectively in almost any fashion have at least some ability to change the supply of labor by limiting membership, acquiring jurisdiction over available work, and influencing labor legislation. We will take a much closer look at unions in later sections of this chapter.

Why All Workers Are Not Paid Equally

22.4 WAGE DIFFERENTIALS

One important characteristic of wages in the United States is that they vary considerably from job to job and from industry to industry. Figure 22-2

624 *Workers, Wages, and Jobs*

FIGURE 22-2   **Median Salaries for Selected Occupations, 1980.** *Source:* U.S. Department of Labor, Bureau of Labor Statistics.

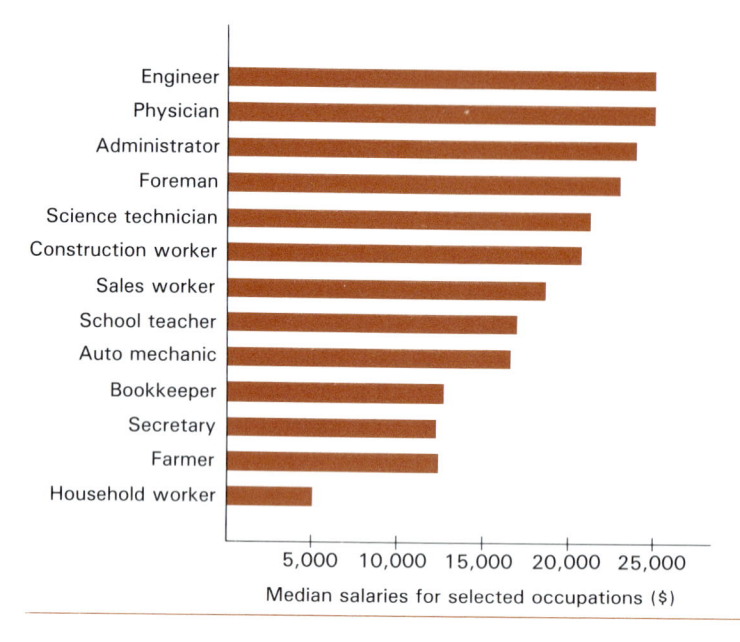

Occupation	
Engineer	~25,000
Physician	~25,000
Administrator	~24,000
Foreman	~23,000
Science technician	~21,000
Construction worker	~20,500
Sales worker	~19,000
School teacher	~17,000
Auto mechanic	~16,500
Bookkeeper	~13,000
Secretary	~12,500
Farmer	~12,500
Household worker	~5,000

Median salaries for selected occupations ($)

shows median U.S. salaries of workers in selected occupations in the early 1980s. The large variation in pay among different occupations is often matched by equally big variations within each job classification.

Why does payday mean plenty to some and poverty to others? What accounts for wage differentials? Do unions drive up wages? Are minimum wage laws a useful way to help low income workers? How can you plan for the future, to avoid low income and unemployment? This chapter looks for answers to these and other questions.

Workers in some regions and industries are paid more than those in other areas. Some of these wage differentials are the consequence of competitive labor markets. The forces of labor supply and labor demand, as discussed in the last chapter, cause wage differentials. Workers get more, all else being equal, when they have higher value marginal product or when labor supply restrictions force up wages. Among the variables that account for many wage differentials are capital and technology, labor quality, demand for output, and risk and worker preference.

Capital and Technology   Capital and technology determine, to a great extent, how much workers can produce. In years past, we might have talked only about how skilled or highly motivated the workers were. Today worker productivity depends at least as much on how well-equipped their factory is and how modern the production technology. Capital investment and high-tech facilities make each worker's effort count for more goods and services produced. Auto workers today earn higher incomes than those in the 1950s. One reason for their higher wages is that auto factories are more capital intensive. With more machines at their command, workers can produce more cars and generate more revenue for the firm than in years past. Wages are high in the United States and other developed countries in part because workers in these lands combine their talents with machines and computers that increase productivity.

Labor Quality   Machines are not everything. Labor quality depends on motivation, generalized and specialized skills, judgment, and problem-solving abilities. College students count on better wages for higher-quality labor. Students bet tuition dollars that their education will pay off in higher paychecks and improved living conditions. They bet correctly, by the way. Undergraduate educational investments pay a good money return in higher lifetime earnings and an even better, though abstract, return in bettered quality of life.

Demand for Output   Consider the plight of buggy-whip makers in the days of the first horseless carriages. Both jobs and wages for these workers declined as demand shifted from buggies to Buicks. When hand-held calculators took over the market, workers in firms that manufactured slide rules were laid off. These types of situations are repeated many times over every year, as new products arrive and demand shifts away from old ones. The people who make and sell high demand goods benefit from higher pay and greater job opportunity. Falling demand for the goods a worker produces indirectly brings falling demand for that worker as well.

Risk and Worker Preference   Some jobs entail physical risk, while other occupations are dirty or involve low-status work. People who prefer not to risk their lives or who prefer not to get dirty or work at night, for example, do not compete for these kinds of jobs. This reduces labor supply and raises wages. The supply of labor is high, on the other hand, for jobs with little risk and high social status, keeping these wages lower. These factors help explain why riggers, who work high in skyscraper skeletons, get paid more than bank clerks, and why garbage collectors often earn more than school teachers.

These four supply–demand variables explain many wage differentials, but they do not account for some of the differences we observe in the real world. Wages would tend toward equality if we had perfectly competitive labor markets, since workers in low-wage jobs would search for higher-paying jobs in other industries and occupations for which they were qualified. These movements would drive up low wages and pull down higher ones. Some wage differences would still exist, but not the great variations we observe today. In the following section we will examine why large pay differences persist.

Labor Market Imperfections

22.5 LABOR MARKET IMPERFECTIONS

Labor supply and demand in the real world do not always obey the rigid rules of perfect competition. Labor markets are not perfectly competitive, they function in ways that keep unemployed workers from finding jobs, keep low-wage workers from moving up to higher pay, and allow employees who do the same work to be paid different wages. Wages and productivity are not always directly related when labor markets are not perfectly competitive. Among the market imperfections that explain, in part, why such large wage differentials exist are lack of mobility, information imperfections, artificial restrictions, discrimination, and investment in human capital.

Lack of Mobility   Mobility is a valuable asset. Workers who can move from job to job, state to state, or industry to industry can take advantage of wage differentials and get higher pay. If housing construction is booming in the Sun Belt, but a bust in the Frost belt, mobile carpenters in the North can make higher wages by moving South. Those who lack mobility cannot directly gain from wage differentials. The cost of mobility is clearly a transactions cost. It is a cost of bringing buyer (employer) and seller (potential employee) together. Someone in some way must pay the cost of getting the employee and employer together. Americans now move around more than in earlier days, but lack of mobility is still a major cause of unemployment. Pockets of high unemployment coexist with patches of labor shortage. The wage differentials that accompany them would not long exist if workers were more willing and able to move where the jobs are.

Information Imperfections Mobility problems are compounded by information imperfections. Information is costly in the labor market just like any other market. The labor market is not efficient in getting data about wages and job openings from employers to workers. Newspaper classified ads, state employment offices, and private employment agencies all spread labor market information. Information costs are also an example of a transactions cost. For employer and employee to meet, they must know of each others' needs. To bring about the transaction of hiring labor, information costs must be paid by someone. Many job openings are not advertised and employment agencies handle only a small number of local jobs. Information about wages is always hard to find. An important job information system is the 'old boy' network. Word-of-mouth sometimes fills jobs as well as do sophisticated computer job banks.

Artificial Restrictions Artificial market restrictions account for many wage differentials. Unions restrict labor supply in some markets, for example, driving up wages. Occupational licensing rules restrict the supplies in such occupations as barbers and lawyers. Current restrictions on the number of medical school slots available limit the supply of doctors in the future. Wage rules, like minimum wage laws, alter paychecks in other ways. The minimum wage law increases the wage paid to some unskilled workers because paying less violates federal law. Demand, supply, and wage rates are directly or indirectly controlled in many labor markets, forcing wages away from their free market rates.

22.6 DISCRIMINATION

Discrimination Women and blacks make lower wages, on average, and have higher unemployment rates than do white male workers. Old and young workers earn lower average wages than do middle-aged ones. Some of the wage gap is probably due to differences in education, experience, mobility, and the type of work performed. These factors cannot explain all the differences, however. Discrimination distorts labor markets, adversely affecting minorities, women, the young, and the old. Some employers discriminate in filling job vacancies and making promotions, and some unions discriminate in making membership decisions.

Economists who have analyzed labor market discrimination conclude that it hurts both those who suffer discrimination and those who practice it. People who are discriminated against are losers. They experience reduced income and job security. Employers who practice discrimination lose money because they pass up the chance to hire skilled workers who happen to be the "wrong" sex, age, or color. They hire only those who fit the "right" mold. The discriminating employer loses a chance to use many valuable inputs because of personal prejudice.

No competitive business can ignore the value of scarce resources such as skilled or talented blacks and women and still earn profits as high as those businesses who make full use of these workers' talents. Profits are not everything, however. Employers may knowingly sacrifice money profits to gain psychic benefits from discrimination. This is an economic problem because the worker who is discriminated against bears part of the cost of the employer's decision.

> **22.7 HUMAN CAPITAL**

Investment in Human Capital Production takes two types of capital: physical capital, like machines, and human capital, workers' education and skills. Workers with greater stocks of human capital are generally more productive and tend to earn higher wages. Wages stay low in some jobs, however, because some employers are unwilling or unable to invest in human capital as they would in physical capital. What is the difference between investment in physical and human capital? A bank can buy a new computer and the machine's productivity "belongs" to the firm. The bank is relatively sure of getting its money's worth out of this investment because it owns the machine. The bank can capture the value of its investment. Suppose, however, the bank invests in human capital by training tellers to be loan officers or computer programmers, for example. Worker productivity rises, but the bank has no guarantee of profit from this latter investment because the human capital "belongs" to the trained worker, who can quit and move to a higher-paying job at some other firm.

Employers are not eager to invest in many types of human capital because workers are mobile and the employer finds it difficult to capture the value of his or her investment. Workers can take the firm's investment with them. Businesses are more likely to invest in very specialized training that cannot be easily applied in other jobs. Workers can, of course, invest in their own human capital, such as in college educations, but they are sometimes hindered in their efforts to do so. This is so primarily because their human capital cannot serve as readily as security for the investment as can physical capital like machines or buildings. Government student loan programs are one attempt to overcome these difficulties.

UNIONS IN THE UNITED STATES

Unions are one reason for U.S. wage differentials. Unions are an important aspect of U.S. labor markets. Less than 25 percent of all U.S. workers belong to labor unions, but these organizations are concentrated in key industries, including auto and steel production, mining and manufacturing, construction, retail trades, transportation, and state–local governments.

> **22.8 LABOR UNION ACTS**

The History of Unions in the United States

There have been labor unions in the United States for nearly 200 years, but their history can be divided into three distinct eras.

The Anti-Union Era From the late 1700s until the early 1930s both employers and the legal system of the United States were clearly opposed to union activity. During this anti-union era, pro-union activists were viewed as a threat to the established rights of management to determine wages and working conditions. The Sherman Antitrust Act of 1890 was designed to

Strike
A situation in which organized labor withholds its services in order to gain concessions from an employer.

Boycotts
Organized attempts to influence labor negotiations by refusing to purchase a firm's products.

Lockouts
An antistrike tactic; employers close their doors rather than paying higher wages or negotiating with unions.

Blacklist
Lists of "undesirable" workers, frequently those with pro-union sympathies. Blacklisted workers are often unable to find work.

Yellow-Dog Contracts
Contracts in which workers pledge not to join or support a union. Some employers once made workers sign these agreements as a condition of employment.

Norris–Laguardia Act
Labor legislation that, among other things, outlawed the yellow dog contract.

Wagner Act
Labor legislation that, among other things, officially recognized labor's right to organize and bargain collectively.

Taft–Hartley Act
Labor legislation that, among other things, gave the president of the United States the power to force unions back to work for a 90-day period when the nation's safety or welfare was endangered by a strike.

Landrum–Griffin Act
Labor legislation that primarily required regularly scheduled elections of union officers and prohibited certain persons from holding office. It also made certain illegal acts involving unions federal crimes.

keep businesses from colluding to restrain trade and to prevent monopolies. The act was also interpreted by the courts to include union activity and was frequently used to forbid the formation of unions.

Early guilds and unions brought together skilled craftsmen to gain higher wages and better working conditions. Union growth was limited in the early days by active employer opposition and unfavorable court decisions. Unions used **strikes,** where workers walked off their jobs, and **boycotts,** where they refused to buy goods made by nonunion firms, to try to win their points. Employers had their own weapons to fight union organizers. Frequently, employers could obtain injunctions (court orders) prohibiting union activities such as strikes. They also used **lock-outs,** where workers were denied work and wages, to break the union. **Blacklists** were another anti-union tool.

Blacklists were lists, circulated among employers, of union sympathizers. Inclusion on a blacklist often made it difficult to be hired. **Yellow-dog contracts** forced workers to promise not to join a union as a condition of employment. Employers used strikebreakers and even tried to "negotiate" with picketing union members through acts of violence in the early days of the labor movement.

The Pro-Union Era

Congress enacted several pro-union laws in the 1930s. In this pro-union era, the new rules gave unions more equal legal footing with employers and set down rules to control management opposition. In 1932, the **Norris–LaGuardia Act** was passed. This act made yellow-dog contracts nonbinding on workers and made it much more difficult for employers to get court injunctions against certain union activities. In 1935, the **Wagner Act** gave wide-sweeping equal powers to labor. It recognized the right of labor to both organize and bargain collectively with employers and outlawed many established anti-union practices by management. Management could no longer blacklist employees or discriminate in any way against them in regard to union activity or interfere with labor's rights to organize. The act established the National Labor Relations Board to oversee union–management relations and investigate and punish unfair labor practices. Unions grew quickly in both membership and power from 1935 to the late 1940s.

The Era of Regulated Unions

The scales of justice tipped again in 1947 with the **Taft–Hartley Act.** This act was designed to place significant controls on the growing strength of unions. Specifically, it established certain unfair labor practices on the part of unions and regulated their internal operating procedures. The act also established more clearly defined rules of the collective bargaining process and gave the president of the United States the right to force unions back to work under certain conditions when the nation's safety or welfare was endangered. Again in 1959, Congress chose to regulate union activity with the **Landrum–Griffin Act.** This act requires regularly scheduled elections of union officers throgh secret ballot, prohibits convicted felons and Communists from holding union office and controls loans of union funds to union officers. Under the act, embezzling union funds is made a federal offense and the rights of union members to nominate candidates and vote in union elections is guaranteed.

Union growth has slowed in recent years, with actual decreases in union membership in the 1980s. This decline in the growth rate has been due to several factors. Industrial growth in the United States is slowly shifting away from traditional union territories. Heavily unionized industries in the

Northeast have suffered decline in recent years, hurt by recession, cheaper foreign imports, and changing public attitudes toward unions. Meanwhile, economic growth has been concentrated in the South, where union influence is not as strong. Higher wages in union industries have put many of these firms at a competitive disadvantage, compared with nonunion and foreign producers. Finally, the output of the entire economy has been moving away from the manufacturing of goods (industries where unions have been very strong) to the production of services (industries that have not had strong union participation).

Recession hurts union growth because unions must concentrate on holding existing jobs and wage agreements rather than on expanding membership. Union membership has increased, however, in the public sector, where more school teachers and municipal employees now have Teamsters or AFL-CIO union cards.

Today's unions play many roles. Collective bargaining enables union members to get pay, working condition, and health insurance benefits that might not otherwise be possible. Union retirement systems allow workers to accrue pension assets even when they change jobs. With company pensions they might lose their retirement check by moving to another firm. Unions negotiate for working conditions, safety rules, promotion structures, job security, disciplinary safeguards, and vacation time. The union's most important job is to negotiate wage rates. Most members value their union for its ability to get them higher pay.

How Do Unions Raise Wages?

22.9 UNIONS AND WAGES

Real-world unions use a variety of direct and indirect policies to alter labor demand and supply and push wage rates higher, as Figure 22-3 shows. Unions can increase their members' wages in three ways: by affecting the labor supply, the labor demand, and the cost and availability of substitute inputs.

FIGURE 22-3

Unions Raise Wages Using Demand and Supply. Unions can increase the wages of their members by (a) increasing demand (through labor-intensive safety regulations, for example) or (b) restricting labor supply.

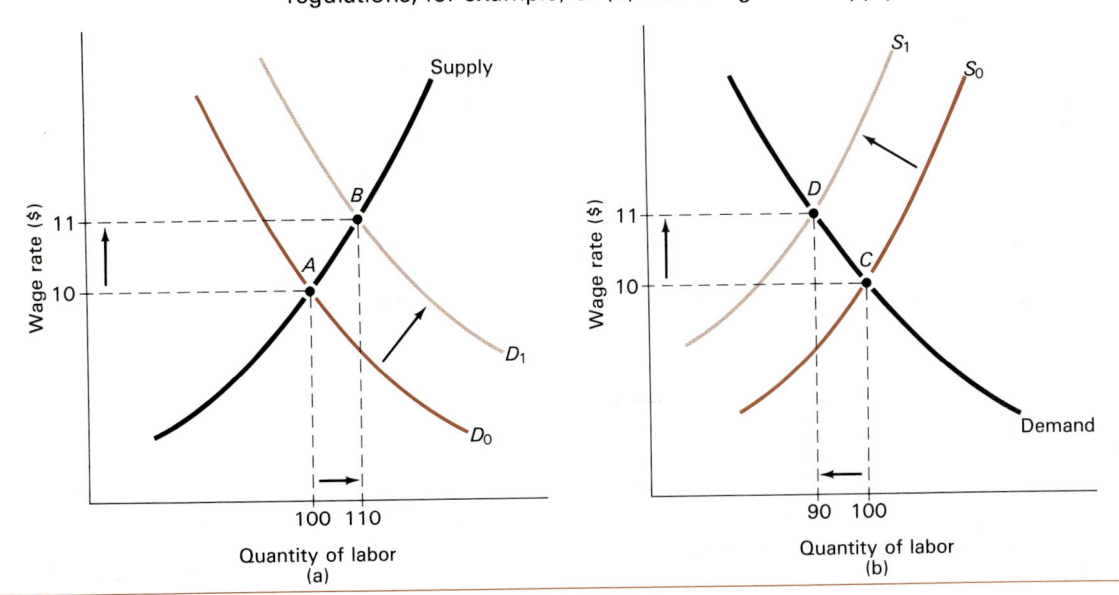

Union Shop
A firm where all employees must belong to a union.

Restrict Supply   One way that unions gain pay increases is by reducing labor supply. Some supply restrictions are direct.

A **union shop**, for example, forces all employees to be union members. Those workers who do not want to pay union dues, or who cannot meet other unions requirements, cannot be hired, even if they are willing to work for less than union wages. Some unions, especially in construction trades, run supply-limiting apprenticeship programs. Workers must pass through a union training program before they are eligible for a job. By restricting the number of apprenticeship openings, the union limits competition for scarce jobs and keeps union wages higher. The total number of jobs available falls as wages rise.

Sometimes unions use the political system to restrict supply. Special-interest legislation accomplishes the union's goal of restricting supply. Workers in many occupations must pass government licensing exams to qualify for work. Barbers, pharmacists, and morticians are licensed by the state, for example. Unions in these occupations have a vested interest in keeping these tests difficult, so that competition from new entrants will not drive down market wages.

Increase Demand   Unions increase wage rates when they are able to increase labor demand. Increasing labor demand forces wage rates higher, while increasing the number of union workers hired. (See Fig. 22-3). Work agreements and safety rules that lock employers into labor-intensive technology are two demand-increasing actions.

Airline pilots in the past few years have lobbied against "unsafe" changes on jet flightdecks, for example. New Boeing 757 airplanes can be flown by two pilots, while older planes needed three workers up front. This change means a big difference in the number of pilots demanded by airlines. The unions have lobbied the government to force airlines to use three pilots for safety reasons, even though the cockpit is designed for just two. Railroads have long been accused of feather-bedding practices that put many workers on each train in the name of increased safety. Union agreements sometimes require railroads to have a fireman on duty in every engine, even those that have no fire for the fireman to tend.

Some unions try to increase demand for the products that they produce by calling for boycotts of nonunion goods. Television commercials ask consumers to "look for the union label" on clothing, for example. Implicit to this jingle is the message to refuse nonunion goods. If the commercials work, demand for union workers increases, boosting wages and employment in these unions.

Unions can also affect labor demand indirectly. Every local government in the United States has, for example, a building code, a list of rules for new construction. Union leaders are frequent members of the committees that set these standards, in part because they are knowledgeable about building techniques and in part because they have a vested interest in construction choices. It is no surprise, then, that small armies of union carpenters, plumbers, and electricians are sometimes needed to bring a building "up to code."

Control of Substitutes   Finally, some unions increase employment and wages by controlling the use and price of substitute labor supplies. Union leaders frequently call for higher minimum wages and more generous social welfare programs. Their attitudes are probably grounded in an honest concern for the poor, but these policies also indirectly keep union wages high. Minimum-wage workers are imperfect substitutes for union workers in some jobs. Keeping the minimum wage high gives skilled union workers an advantage over less-skilled but cheaper workers. Similarly, social welfare progams help the poor, but they also provide work disincentives that keep these individuals out of labor markets. Both minimum wages and social welfare programs, because they reduce labor supply, tend to increase union wages.

Unions expand membership and increase job security by negotiating agreements that restrict each worker to just a few possible jobs. Employers often cannot hire "utility" workers, workers who do a little bit of everything. Instead they must hire specialized workers from different unions for each production task. Symphony orchestra players, members of the musicians' union, for example, cannot set up their chairs and music stands or move them from one place on stage to another. That is a job for members of the stagehands' union. Both musicians and stagehands must be employed for each concert, increasing total union employment, but driving up ticket prices.

Economic Models of Union Behavior

Unions want higher wages for their members. But they must decide what wage to demand. This is a complex decision because bigger paychecks generally bring layoffs, other things being equal, as firms adjust to higher labor costs. Economists who have studied labor markets suggest that the optimal union wage demand depends on many factors such as the elasticity of labor demand or the characteristics of supply. How easily employers can substitute other factors, such as capital and nonunion workers, for union labor also has an effect on wage demands. Union wage demands also depend on the nature of competition in the labor market. Figure 22-4 shows one model of union behavior: a monopoly.

22.10 UNION MONOPOLY

All workers are union members under a union-shop agreement, so the union is effectively the monopoly supplier of labor. The union can use monopoly price-setting tools to increase its members' share of employer profits. Figure 22-4(a) shows a labor market where supply-demand equilibrium occurs at point A, with wage rate of $10 per hour. The monopoly union calculates a marginal revenue curve. This curve shows how much total labor income rises when an extra worker is added. The union then treats the labor supply curve as a marginal cost curve. The profit-maximizing union sets its membership limit at B and wages at the corresponding demand curve point C. As a result, a monopoly union demands a wage rate of $12. This maximizes the income gain for the Q_u workers who have jobs at this rate. The catch is that fewer workers have jobs than under the competitive system.

22.11 EMPLOYERS' ASSOCIATION MONOPSONY

Strikes and labor–management disagreements are common in some industries. One reason is that employers are not blind to the threat that monopoly unions pose to their profits. Competing firms sometimes come together to bargain with monopoly unions, forming employers' associations that sometimes act like the monopsonists you read about in the last chapter. Labor-market disruptions are possible when monopoly labor meets monopsony management. Figure 22-4(b) shows what happens here. The monopoly union in this picture tries to maximize worker welfare by setting employment at A, where MR crosses the supply curve, then demanding the $12 wage given by point B on the supply curve. The monopsony management has other ideas, however. Management maximizes profits from labor by

FIGURE 22-4

Union Monopoly and Union versus Employers Association. A competitive labor market finds equilibrium at A in panel (a). The monopoly union chooses to use Q_u workers and demand higher $12 wages. The union uses its monopoly power to increase labor gains. Negotiations break down when monopoly union meets monopsony employers in panel (b). Monopoly wants B, while monopsony wants A. A strike may follow if neither side is willing to sacrifice income or profits to the other.

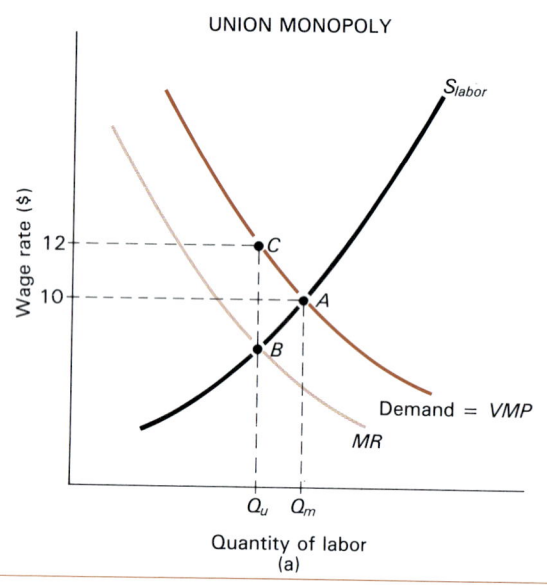

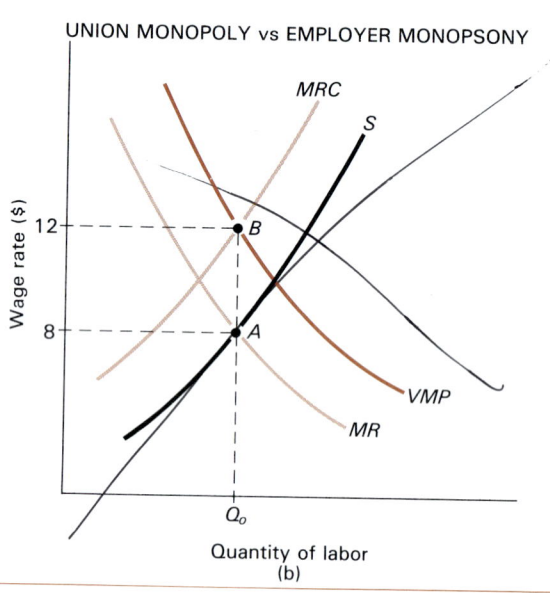

UNION MONOPOLY
(a)

UNION MONOPOLY vs EMPLOYER MONOPSONY
(b)

22.12 LABOR STRIKES

hiring workers at B, where MRP equals VMP. The last worker adds just as much to revenue as to cost here. Management then sets wages at the corresponding labor supply point A, with an $8 wage rate.

The exact wage rate that workers in this labor market get is impossible to tell, since the union maximizes worker gain at $12, while the employers maximize profit with a $8 wage. A union contract might end up with wage rates anywhere from $8 to $12. Alternatively, negotiations might break down and a strike might be called, making both sides worse off.

Figure 22-4(b) shows both labor and management agreeing on the same Q_o quantity of labor, but disagreeing on the wage to be paid. This is a special case, drawn to make the figure easier to read. In general, monopoly union and monopsony management disagree about both the wage and the quantity of labor.

What Makes a Union Strong?

22.13 STRONG UNION CHARACTERISTICS

Some unions are successful, while others fail. Some industries are heavily unionized, while other labor markets have no union members. Unions succeed if they are able to raise wages without putting employers out of business or causing their members to be laid off. Union success is, therefore, tied to inelastic labor demand curves. If labor demand is inelastic, higher wages bring little change in employment. If labor demand is more elastic, however, wage hikes lead to greater layoffs. Following this logic, there are some conditions that lead to successful unions, among them inelastic product demand, a high percentage of unionized firms, an inability of firms to substitute capital for labor, and wages that are a low fraction of total costs.

Inelastic Product Demand If demand for the product is elastic, wage-based price increases produce large cuts in the quantity of goods and, eventually, labor demanded. If the goods that union workers make have an inelastic demand, however, higher costs and prices make less difference to output and employment.

Unionization of Most Firms Unions have a better shot at success if they can organize most firms in a particular market or industry. It is risky to demand higher wages if only a few firms are unionized. Lower-cost non-union firms might capture most of the market, leaving union members and the firms they work for out in the cold.

Inability to Substitute Firms that can easily substitute capital for labor are not ripe targets for union organizers. Higher wages in this instance might harm as many workers as they help. Unions have better success in industries where other resources cannot be easily substituted for labor. The quantity of labor demanded is less sensitive to changes in its price under these circumstances.

Wages as Low Fraction of Total Cost Unions have a better chance when wages are a small fraction of the firm's total cost. Rising wage costs have smaller price effects in these industries, especially if the elasticity of substitution between union labor and other inputs is relatively low. Unions have less power when wages are a big part of production costs. Firms know that a relatively small change in wage rates leads to big cost, price, and profit movements.

THE MINIMUM WAGE CONTROVERSY

22.14 MINIMUM WAGE LAWS

Minimum Wage Law
A federal law that sets wage floors in many labor markets.

The U.S. government regulates labor markets in many ways, setting health and safety rules and restricting union and anti-union practices. One of the most controversial labor market policies is the federal **minimum wage law.** The minimum wage applies in many markets for unskilled labor, although agricultural firms and some other employers are exempt from minimum wage regulations. The minimum wage in 1985 was $3.35 an hour. A wide variety of industrial and commercial employers had to pay their workers at least this minimum hourly rate.

The rationale for the minimum wage is not difficult to guess. Wages in some labor markets are very low, so low that a person working a 40-hour week might still be unable pay rent and buy food. The minimum wage was designed, theoretically, to assure all workers some minimum standard of living. Its intent was to established a wage floor beneath which no employed worker could sink. However, there has been a great deal of controversy over whether minimum wage legislation has been successful in putting a safety net under low-income living standards.

The minimum wage is controversial because experts disagree over the economic effects of wage floors. Some argue that minimum wages cause unemployment. Others say that minimum wages increase employment opportunities for unskilled workers! To understand more fully how such divergent arguments can be made, we will look closely at each side of the minimum wage debate.

ECONOMIC ISSUES

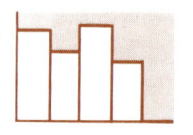

Lowering the Minimum Wage for Teenagers

Unemployment among teenagers is a serious economic problem. Teenagers have higher unemployment rates than many other groups. Unemployment rates for teens in general have averaged around 20 percent in recent years, and unemployment among black workers under 20 has been close to 50 percent at times.

Teenage unemployment is a serious problem because young workers need to get and hold jobs to gain the experience and training that can lead to higher incomes and better jobs in the future. Young people who fail to get work as teenagers, and who do not finish high school or go on for more education, face an uncertain future. Their inability to find and hold work when young adversely affects their ability to find and hold jobs as adults. Unemployment is complicated, so it is dangerous to generalize about it, but one thing is clear: The lack of jobs for young workers is one factor that contributes to the long-run unemployment problems of some groups.

What causes high teenage unemployment rates? The economic theory presented in this and the last chapter suggests that unemployment is the result of a combination of low value marginal product and high wage rates. Teenaged workers are relatively unskilled and, therefore, cannot add high levels of incremental production, at least at the start. Federal and state minimum wage laws set wage rates above the market equilibrium level and indirectly cause unemployment for this group.

How can teenage unemployment be reduced? One way out of this dilemma is for teenaged workers to gain better educational and job skills. If teenagers were more productive, they might be better able to find and hold jobs, even at today's minimum wages. In the short run, however, it is unlikely that this problem can be solved through better education and training, especially since much of the needed training normally takes place on-the-job. Another solution is to reduce the minimum wage that teenaged workers are subject to.

Congress has considered lower minimum wages for teenagers several times in recent years but has yet to enact this measure. The idea behind the lower

22.15 MINIMUM WAGES AND COMPETITIVE MARKETS

The Case Against Minimum Wages

Economists and policymakers who oppose minimum wage laws generally feel that minimum wages are a bad trade-off. They raise wage rates for some, but put others out of work. Their conclusions are derived from analysis of minimum wages in competitive labor markets, like the one shown in Figure 22-5(a).

The equilibrium wage rate in the competitive labor market shown in Figure 22-5(a) would be just $2.50 per hour, or $100 for a 40-hour week. This wage is low, but it has the advantage of being the equilibrium price. All 100 workers who seek jobs at $2.50 per hour find them. Low wages are based on low productivity, low final good prices, and the other factors.

What happens when Congress establishes a minimum wage of $3.50 in the labor market shown in Figure 22-5(a)? The minimum wage acts as a price floor. It is illegal to pay workers less than this amount. The minimum wage has two undesirable effects. First, the higher wage causes more people to seek employment in this labor market. Teenagers may leave school to look for work, for example, increasing the quantity of labor supplies from the 100 at point A in the figure to the 110 at point B, corresponding to the minimum wage rate.

While more people look for work, fewer jobs are available. Profit-maximizing employers cut payrolls as wage rates rise because fewer workers have value marginal product greater than or equal to the higher wage. The quantity of labor demanded and hired falls from 100 at the $2.50 wage to just 85 at the $3.50 wage, point C in the figure. The minimum wage

wage is to reduce the cost of employing young workers, so that businesses will have an incentive to hire more young people. Proponents of this measure suggest that these workers, once on the job, will gain income, training, and experience that will help them move from low-paying minimum wage jobs to other occupations. They see a lower minimum wage for teenagers as a good way to get young people started on a working career.

Many people oppose lower minimum wages for teenagers. The opposition argues that such a wage is unfair and would have no long-term benefits to workers, only to employers who could hire workers for less. The lower wage would be unfair to teenagers because they would receive less income then older minimum wage workers for equal work. It would also be unfair to older workers, since they would risk being replaced by cheaper, younger employees. When teenaged workers were old enough to qualify for the higher adult minimum wage, opponents claim that the workers would probably be laid off, replaced themselves by teenagers, just as they replaced adults before them. This argument implicitly assumes that teenaged workers will not move into better jobs or gain productivity and skills through on-the-job training. This assumes that many or most minimum wage jobs are dead-end jobs, with little hope of advancement or training.

A lower teenaged minimum wage is controversial because it would create winners and losers. Most of the teenaged college students who read this book, for example, are probably opposed to such a law because they would stand to lose from this enactment. A lower minimum wage might reduce their income from summer and part-time work. College students are better educated and trained than many of their high-school cohorts who did not go on to receive advanced training or who dropped out of school to find work. These workers, who experience high unemployment rates, are the potential winners.

Should the minimum wage for teenagers be reduced? This remains a controversial question. Whether the gain to unemployed young people is worth lower incomes for those who already have a job is a normative question. Economists can point out the positive costs and benefits of this proposal, but politicians and policymakers must make the normative decision to keep or revise minimum wage laws.

Additional References

Abowd, John M., and Killingsworth, Mark K. "The Minimum Wage Law's Winners and Losers." *Wall Street Journal,* September 10, 1981, p. 26.

Fourcans, Andre. "The Minimum Wage and Unemployment: A French View." *Wall Street Journal,* November 8, 1981, p. 12.

Ris, Cindy. "First Step on Job Ladder Can Be Tough, Many High School Graduates Discover." *Wall Street Journal,* July 2, 1980, p. 3.

Veseth, Michael. *Introductory Macroeconomics,* 2nd ed. Orlando, FL: Academic Press, 1984, especially chap. 3.

FIGURE 22-5

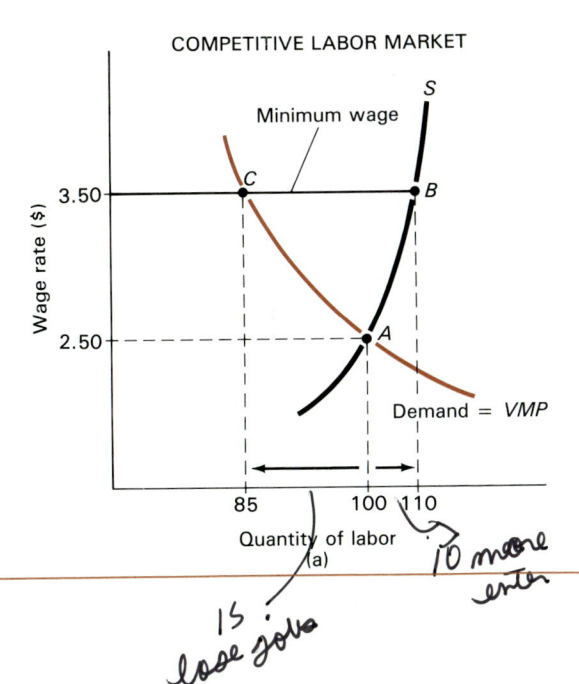

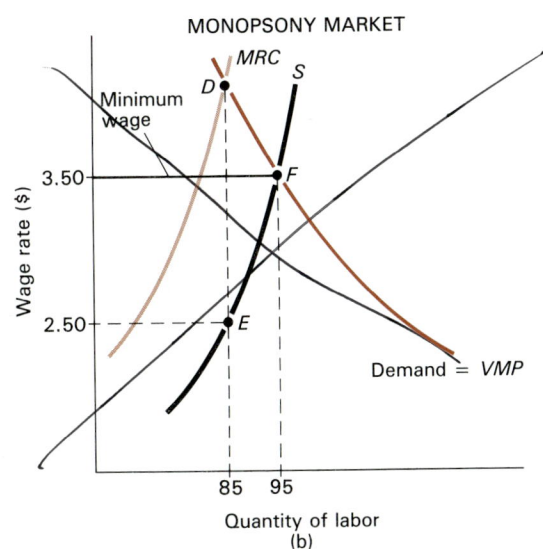

results in more people competing for fewer jobs. Unemployment among unskilled workers goes from zero in this example, 100 workers equals 100 jobs, to much higher levels — 110 workers seek 85 jobs as a result of the minimum wage.

> **KEY CONCEPT 22.15** A minimum wage law increases the level of unemployment for all workers whose VMP is lower than the legal minimum wage.

Minimum wages, in this competitive labor market view, are desirable only if the wage gains to the 85 workers who keep their jobs are considered to be higher than the costs to employers and others. On the negative side, employers pay more for labor inputs, and some workers experience income losses because they lose their jobs when wages increase. Other people lose because they are enticed into the labor market by the higher minimum wage but cannot find work. Finally, consumers lose if the higher minimum wage raises costs and prices. Policymakers must weigh the two sides of this trade-off and decide whether gains to some are worth the loss to others. The outcome of such a decision is, of course, a normative question.

Some economists believe that one partial solution to the unemployment problems of unskilled workers is to abolish minimum wage laws. Proponents of this view feel that when competitive market forces set wage rates, the employment of unskilled workers increases. Wages would fall but new employment opportunities would arise, creating jobs for the hard-core unemployed of our economy. Workers who take low-wage jobs would acquire skills and talents that would let them eventually move up into higher paying jobs. The lower wages would compensate employers for the training they supply. Many unskilled workers would find that low wages in the short term lead to higher wages later, as valuable skills were acquired. Under the present system, many unskilled people get no chance to acquire job skills, since minimum wages keep them unemployed.

Minimum Wages in Monopsony Markets

22.16 MINIMUM WAGES AND MONOPSONY

The reply to anti-minimum wage forces takes two forms. Some proponents of minimum wage laws think that wage floors are justified even if they cause unemployment. Those who are unemployed, they say, can take advantage of welfare and unemployment benefits and may be eligible for retraining programs. Those who work at least earn a living wage. That is better, they think, than having millions of workers laboring at subsistence wages. People who take the normative view that the losses to those who are unemployed are worth the gains to those who have jobs are in favor of minimum wage laws.

A second argument in favor of minimum wages is more subtle. Some economists attack the assumption that markets for unskilled labor are competitive. They argue that these workers are poorly informed about wages, working conditions, and job opportunities. No unions exist to protect these workers and negotiate fair pay. Employers, on the other hand, are thought to be better organized and more powerful. Employers in these labor markets may have some power to set wages. They are able to behave as monopsonists, as Figure 22-5(b) shows.

If employers act as monopsonists, they demand the quantity of labor at which value marginal product (VMP) equals marginal resource cost (MRC).

This corresponds to point *D* in the figure. This point as discussed in the last chapter, maximizes employer profit because the revenue added by the last worker (*VMP*) just equals the extra cost of hiring that worker (*MRC*). The monopsonist then offers the lowest wage necessary to attract this many workers, the $2.50 wage at point *E* in the figure. Monopsony employers not only hire fewer workers than would competitive firms, but they also pay them lower wages.

Something unexpected happens when a minimum wage is imposed in monopsony markets like the one shown in Figure 22-5(b). The wage floor both boosts wages and increases the number of jobs. Here is the logic behind this statement. The minimum wage floor means that employers no longer face upward-sloping labor supply and *MRC* curves. If the minimum wage is $3.50, for example, the first worker must be paid $3.50 even if the worker is willing to work for less. The second worker must be paid $3.50, and so on. Marginal resource cost is equal to the $3.50 minimum wage rate over a wide employment range.

When faced with a minimum wage law, a profit-maximizing monopsony behaves in a more competitive manner. Profits still peak when employers follow the rule of setting *MRC* equal to *VMP*. With *MRC* now constant at $3.50, the new profit-maximizing point is at *F* in the figure. The firm hires workers until the *VMP* of the last worker is just equal to the $3.50 minimum wage. The monopsony firm hires more workers with a $3.50 minimum wage regulation than it would have at the $2.50 monopsony wage in this example. Minimum wages are desirable, in this view, because they take away employers' monopsony power and force them to behave more like competitive firms.

Who Is Right about the Minimum Wage?

A very important issue in the minimum wage debate concerns whether this type of legislation causes or cures unemployment. There are two ways to approach this question. One method is to examine the assumptions behind each argument. First we must know whether the markets for unskilled workers are competitive or whether they lean toward monopsony power. The evidence here is on the side of competition, though no one argues that all the conditions of perfect competition are met in the markets for unskilled workers. A few large firms, like McDonalds and Kentucky Fried Chicken, for example, are big employers in these labor markets, but they do not lack for competition. Thousands of smaller firms also hire minimum wage workers. Organized monopsony is impossible.

A second way to investigate this mystery is to look for evidence of the wage and unemployment changes that each model predicts. We have trouble here because, unlike physical scientists, social scientists cannot run "control" economies and compare them with economies that have adopted new policies. Existing evidence is strongly on the anti-minimum wage side. Unemployment rates among unskilled workers are high in the United States. Teenaged workers suffered a 23.7 percent unemployment rate in 1982, for example, and black teenage unemployment was 44 percent. These high jobless rates for unskilled workers come closer to competitive labor market predictions than those made by the monopsony model.

The minimum wage law is controversial because some people think wage floors help the poor and others think they hurt them. It is impossible to absolutely prove the point either way. It is fair to say, however, that most economists believe that minimum wages cause unemployment, and most economists would prefer market-determined wage rates.

PLANNING FOR FUTURE LABOR MARKET CONDITIONS

22.17 CAREER PLANNING

This book is read mostly by college students, many of whom are still trying to figure out what to do with their lives. You have seen that labor markets, with their many controls and imperfections, make wages and salaries high in some kinds of occupations and low in others. There is constant demand for some workers, while other, equally skilled, people are unable to find a job. How can you plan for the future in this uncertain world?

Wages and jobs are tough to predict. Most past guesses about how markets will change far in the future have turned out to be wrong. There are a few techniques, however, that have been proved through the years. If you want a good job with high pay, you should make informed choices, remain mobile, and consider nonpecuniary payoffs.

Making Informed Choices

When planning for a career, you should ask yourself several questions. What jobs will be in demand in the future? Where will the highest salaries be found? One way to prepare for the future is to try to predict changes in labor and product demand and supply and be ready for them. Which major should you choose? There are two training strategies here. One is to gain specific training in an occupation you think will be in high demand. A correct guess brings you much income, but a wrong guess makes you poorer. Your specific training makes it more difficult to move among job markets if the demand for your specific talent falls. The other strategy is to spend more time on basic skills like writing, thinking, and problem solving. These skills prepare you for many jobs, not all of which are likely to disappear at once. Specific training has higher return, but it is risky. A broader liberal education gives a lower average return but with less risk. These conclusions are based on averages, of course, and do not necessarily apply to the actions and outcomes of specific individuals.

Where will jobs be in the future? A Department of Labor study identifies the following areas of job growth and decline between now and the 1990s. Occupations with high-growth potential include engineers, scientists, health workers and administrators, technicians, computer specialists, social scientists (including economists), accountants, architects, and secretaries. The government predicts declining markets for the following occupations: teachers, stenographers, keypunch operators, telegraph workers, printers, bakers, and farmers. This is an incomplete list. Interested readers should consult the U.S. Labor Department's publication, *Occupational Outlook Quarterly*, for a more complete discussion.

Remaining Mobile

Mobility is a valuable attribute in a world of changing labor markets. Workers who are mobile can move quickly from low-wage jobs and labor markets to high-wage ones, taking advantage of changing demand and supply condition. Mobility takes two forms: geographic mobility and occupational mobility. People who are willing and able to move to where there are more job openings or higher salaries are less likely to be unemployed than are those who stick to a particular city or region. People who are willing and able to try new jobs are less likely to suffer long spells of unemployment than are those who are unwilling to change. Both kinds of mobility are important in many occupations.

Engineers, for example, are often asked to move from region to region as job needs shift. Those who move with the job have lower unemployment and higher average income than do those who do not. On average, most engineers change job speciality at least once during their careers, going from mechanical engineering jobs to electrical engineering tasks, for example. Those who can make such changes gain from their mobility.

Considering Nonpecuniary Payoffs

Money is not everything in life, and you make a mistake if you aim for the best-paying job without considering your tastes and preferences about life and work. Each job generates two sorts of payoffs: money rewards that you can spend, and psychic rewards that you receive directly from the work you do. Any job is a package of wages, working conditions, and other attributes. People who are planning careers should consider both money and psychic costs and rewards. In other words, you should pick the suit that fits you best, not just the one with the deepest pockets.

SUMMARY

22.1

1. Marx, Malthus, and other economists once believed in the iron law of wages. According to the law, wages inevitably find equilibrium at the subsistence level. Malthus thought population cycles brought subsistence wages. Higher wages led to population growth, which bid down wages and caused starvation. Subsistence was equilibrium in Malthus' world. Marx thought that capitalist employers used the "reserve army of the unemployed" to bid wages to subsistence levels. Wages today are well above subsistence, although poverty is still a problem.

22.2

2. The supply of labor is subject to both income and substitution effects. In the substitution effect, workers substitute labor for leisure as wages rise, since their "cost" of leisure increases with the forgone wage rate. The income effect occurs when, as wages rise thereby increasing income, workers choose to demand more leisure (a normal good).

22.3

3. Different factors affect the supply of workers in individual markets. Some things influence all labor markets. Population, for example, is one limit to total labor supply. Traditions and social customs, such as whether women are allowed to work outside of the home, and religious practices that restrict labor also affect the size of the labor force, as do government policies, such as taxes and transfer payments, and institutional forces like unions.

22.4

4. Differences in wage levels are caused by a variety of market and nonmarket factors. Capital and technology differences account for some wage differentials. High capital quality and quantity and modern technology increase worker productivity, making higher wages possible. Labor quality also affects wages. Workers with high-quality human capital can produce more, boosting labor demand and wage rates. Wage rates differ, as well, becuase of variations in the demand for output. Workers are paid more in markets where output is scarce and prices

high. Finally, risk and worker preference affect wages through their influence on labor supply. Few workers want to take high risk jobs, as a result, the labor supply is smaller, thereby making wages higher than they would otherwise be for these occupations.

22.5 ▶ 5. Lack of mobility is a labor market imperfection that allows wage differences to exist over time. Workers who cannot or will not move from low-wage to high-wage regions must live with lower pay. Wages would be more equal in a perfectly mobile society. Information imperfections also lead to wage differences. Workers have trouble finding out about alternative jobs and wages, so even mobile workers cannot always move to close wage gaps. Artificial restrictions, such as union rules, occupational licensing requirements, and minimum wage laws, also alter wage rates. Some wage differences, such as those between men and women, or blacks and whites, are partly the result of discrimination.

22.6 ▶ 6. Discrimination hurts both those who are discriminated against and those who discriminate in hiring. Workers who suffer discrimination earn lower wages and have fewer job opportunities. Employers who practice discrimination earn lower profits because they fail to use labor resources most effectively.

22.7 ▶ 7. Employers are sometimes less willing to invest in human capital than they are to invest in physical capital because in human capital the employer cannot capture the value of his or her investment. Workers can quit and take their training with them. Lower levels of human capital investment keep more workers in lower-paying jobs than would otherwise be the case. Workers do not invest as readily in human capital because their "capital" cannot as easily serve as security for the investment as could physical capital like buildings or machines.

22.8 ▶ 8. Unions have existed in the United States for almost 200 years. Unions have grown most rapidly in the past 50 years. Union growth has slackened in the past few years, however. Recession and industrial movement to nonunion sunbelt states have hurt union growth. The biggest recent union gains have come from public sector union movements.

22.8 ▶ 9. The Sherman Antitrust Act of 1890 was designed to prohibit business from colluding to restrain trade. This act was also applied by the courts in the early days of unionism to restrain union activity. The Norris–LaGuardia Act of 1932 made yellow-dog contracts nonbinding on workers and made it more difficult for employers to obtain court injunctions against certain union activities such as strikes. The Wagner Act of 1935 (Labor's Magna Charta) guaranteed labor both the right to organize and to bargain collectively. It outlawed employer discrimination against workers for union membership or activity, prohibited company unions, and set up the National Labor Relations Board to oversee labor–management relations. The Taft–Hartley Act of 1947 defined and outlawed unfair labor practices, regulated the internal management practices of labor unions, placed greater controls on the collective bargaining process, and granted the president of the United States the power to force unions back to work under certain conditions when the nation's safety or welfare was endangered. The Landrum–Griffin Act of 1959 placed even greater controls on the operation of unions. It required regularly scheduled elections of union officers by secret ballot, controlled the loan of union funds to union officers, and guaranteed the rights of union members to nominate candidates and vote in union elections.

22.9 10. Unions can restrict supply to push up wages. Labor supply falls if workers must pay union dues or participate in union apprenticeship programs before accepting work. Unions can also push wages higher by increasing labor demand. Safety rules that require many workers on the job increase labor demand, for example. In addition, unions can increase wages by increasing the cost of substitute labor supplies. Higher minimum wages reduce competition from unskilled labor, for example.

22.10 11. Unions sometimes act like a labor monopoly, applying the rules of monopoly pricing to wage negotiations. One strategy is for the union to set membership limits at the point at which labor supply equals the workers' marginal revenue. This strategy leads to higher wages and a smaller labor force than with competitive markets.

22.11 12. One labor model shows a union monopoly confronted by a monopsonistic employers' association. Union monopoly models call for high wages, but the employers' association monopsony maximizes profits with much lower wages. Strikes and other labor strife are possible here, except in the public sector where strikes are often illegal.

22.13 13. Unions are strong if they can raise wages without big layoffs. An inelastic labor demand curve is needed to make these goals possible. The following conditions promote union strength: inelastic product demand, the inability of employers to substitute capital for labor, the unionization of most firms in an industry, and wage costs that are a small fraction of total production costs.

22.14 14. Minimum wage laws are government rules that put a floor under the wage rates that can be paid in many labor markets. The minimum wage rate was $3.35 in 1985.

22.15 15. Minimum wages are controversial. Some economists think minimum wages cause high unemployment. Others think minimum wages help the poor. The case against minimum wages is based on the belief that markets for unskilled labor are competitive. A minimum wage set above equilibrium increases the quantity of labor supplied, but reduces the quantity of labor demanded, thereby causing unemployment. Minimum wages also create winners and losers. Those who keep their jobs get higher wages. Those who lose their jobs get neither wage income nor a chance at the on-the-job training and experience needed to succeed and earn higher pay.

22.16 16. The case for minimum wages is built on the belief that competition breaks down in markets for unskilled labor. Employers may act as monopsonists, hiring fewer workers at lower wages than would be the case in competitive markets. Minimum wage laws both increase wages and make more jobs available in monopsony markets, because the government-set wage takes away the monopsonist's power to set wages. Monopsonists therefore behave more like competitive firms. Which side is right about minimum wages? The assumption of monopsonistic employers is hard to defend, given the thousands of firms that compete for unskilled labor. A few large firms may have some market power, however. High unemployment rates among unskilled workers (44 percent for black teenagers in 1982) support the competitive labor market view of minimum wages. Most economists think minimum wages cause unemployment.

> 22.17

17. How should one pick a future career so as to gain high income and avoid unemployment? Planning with an eye toward future changes in product and labor supply and demand is important. The text gave examples of labor markets that are predicted to grow and shrink in the coming decade. One must also choose between specific training, with high return and high risk, or broad education, with lower average return but lower risk. In addition, mobility is an important determinant of individual income. Individuals who are willing and able to move to new occupations or different geographic regions are likely to have higher average incomes than those who are not so mobile. Finally, jobs generate both pecuniary (money) and nonpecuniary (nonmoney or psychic) costs and benefits. People planning future careers should consider both money and other job attributes in their choices.

DISCUSSION QUESTIONS

> 22.4, 22.5, 22.6, 22.7

1. Use the tools developed in this chapter to explain why
   a. secretaries earn more than farmers;
   b. union workers earn more than nonunion workers;
   c. truck drivers earn more than college professors;
   d. men earn more than women;
   e. workers in northern and western states earn more than those in southern states.

> 22.1

2. Explain why the iron law of wages no longer applies in the United States. Give reasons why wages have not fallen to the subsistence level.

> 22.9, 22.13

3. Union and nonunion employers compete in many product markets. How do union wage-increasing tactics affect nonunion workers and firms? Explain using labor market models.

> 22.4, 22.5, 22.9

4. Unions are frequently found in manufacturing industries but are less common in agricultural firms. Use the tools of this chapter to explain these differences.

> 22.14, 22.15, 22.16

5. Are minimum wage laws good economic policy, or should minimum wage laws be repealed? List arguments on both sides of this issue, then state your own opinion.

> 22.15, 22.16

6. Congress recently considered legislation that would set a lower minimum wage for teenaged workers than for unskilled adults. Should this policy be adopted? Give arguments on both sides of the issue, then state your own opinion.

SELECTED READINGS

Feldstein, Martin. "The Economics of the New Unemployment." *Public Interest* (Fall, 1973), p. 86.

Okun, Arthur. *Prices and Quantities*. Washington, DC: Brookings Institution, 1981.

Rees, Albert. *The Economics of Work and Pay*. New York: Harper & Row, 1973.

Rees, Albert. "The Effects of Unions on Resource Allocation." Reprinted in Breit, William, and Hochman, Harold M. (Eds.), *Readings in Microeconomics*, 2nd ed. New York: Holt, Rinehart and Winston, 1971, pp. 444.

Reynolds, Lloyd G. *Labor Economics and Labor Relations*, 6th ed. Englewood Cliffs, NJ: Prentice-Hall, 1974.

Rottenberg, Simon. "The Baseball Players' Labor Market." *Journal of Political Economy*, 64 (June, 1956): pp. 242–258.

CHAPTER 23

Profit, Interest, and Rent

Having read the chapter, reviewed the chapter summary, and completed the *Study Guide* exercises, you should be able to:

CRIS

23.1 ECONOMIC VS BUSINESS PROFIT: Explain the difference between economic profit and business profit and tell why economic profit is a more meaningful description of business gains.

23.2 SOURCES OF PROFITS: Explain from where profits come, and list five basic reasons for economic profit, indicating how each works and whether it leads to profit in both the short and long run.

23.3 GOVERNMENT REGULATIONS AND PROFIT: Explain why government regulations are a source of economic profit.

23.4 ECONOMIC FUNCTIONS OF PROFITS: Discuss the economic functions of profits and list five things that profits do in a modern economy, explaining profit's role as incentive in each.

23.5 MONOPOLY PROFITS: Discuss the two sides of monopoly profits, indicating how are they bad and how are they good.

23.6 INTEREST AND PAYMENT VALUES: Explain how the interest rate links together the present and future values of payments.

23.7 INTEREST RATE AS PRICE SIGNAL: Explain the information that the interest rate communicates to borrowers and lenders and tell why the interest rate is an important price signal.

23.8 INTEREST RATE DETERMINANTS: List and discuss five important determinants of interest rates.

23.9 INFLATION PREMIUM: Explain why an inflation premium is attached to interest rates and indicate whether interest rates in the real world tend to rise and fall with inflation.

23.10 PRIME INTEREST RATE: Discuss what the prime interest rate is and indicate why it is important.

23.11 CREDIT MARKETS: Explain how interest rates are set by credit markets and indicate who the credit suppliers and credit demanders are.

Economic Profit 645

- **23.12 RATIONING CREDIT:** Explain how the interest rate rations credit between savers and borrowers and discuss how this rationing improves economic efficiency.

- **23.13 ECONOMIC RENT:** Define economic rent and explain how it differs from property rental and economic profit.

- **23.14 ECONOMIC RENT AS A SURPLUS:** Explain why economic rent is a surplus—a payment that has no incentive effect.

- **23.15 SINGLE-TAX MOVEMENT:** Discuss Henry George's single-tax movement and tell why George thought a tax on land's rent would be fairer and more efficient than other taxes.

- **23.16 RENT-SEEKING BEHAVIOR:** Explain what is meant by rent-seeking behavior and discuss whether it promotes economic growth or leads to inefficiency.

Profit, interest, and rent are the capitalist side of free market economies. They are payments that exist because resources are privately owned. Property rights are held by profit-seeking individuals and firms, not by the people or the state. Socialist governments view profits and the like with suspicion, wondering if they are earned wages or unearned surplus. You can decide for yourself as we explore a little of capitalism's roots.

Profit, interest, and rent are the economic returns paid to three important production resources: entrepreneurs, capital, and fixed inputs, those inputs with fixed total quantity. Profit, interest, and rent are important for at least three reasons. First, each economic return provides an incentive. Scarce resources are allocated in new ways when the promise of return is offered. Profit, interest, and rent thus help determine how society's resources are allocated among competing uses. They help decide whether scarce credit goes to build houses or factories, for example.

Second, profit, interest, and rent affect the distribution of income among population groups. These economic returns reward some groups more than others. Not everyone benefits equally from profit, interest, and rent, however. This fact contributes to the income inequality discussed in Chapter 24.

Finally, profit, interest, and rent send important price signals to the economy. They tell buyers and sellers and producers and consumers about the value of different activities. These price and profit signals are necessary to efficient economic decisions.

ECONOMIC PROFIT

23.1 ECONOMIC VS BUSINESS PROFIT

You read in Chapter 17 about the difference between the way economists calculate profit and the business or accounting definition. As you recall, business, or accounting, profits are equal to the difference between a firm's total revenue and its total explicit costs. Explicit costs are all the money expenses the firm bears, such as wages for labor, payments for raw materials, tax payments, interest on loans, and so forth. To calculate accounting profit, you subtract explicit costs (money the firm pays out to individuals and other firms) from total revenue (money the firm takes in); the difference is the accounting profit.

The calculation of profit is sufficient for the uses accountants make of it and it is required to be calculated in this manner by the U.S. tax code. Economists, however, attempt to measure something quite different in their calculation of profit. They change the profit definition in one important way. Accounting profit includes explicit costs, but it does not consider implicit costs. If you start your own business, you put time, talent, and effort into the enterprise. You probably risk money, too. Your resources are valuable and could have earned a return in another business. Therefore, these resources have an implicit cost: their opportunity cost.

Accountants do not consider opportunity cost because it never shows up on the firm's books. Opportunity costs are indeed difficult to measure, and no one ever sends a bill to a firm that reads "please pay opportunity cost of $1000." These costs are real enough, however.

Suppose you set up a consulting firm. You write custom software for small business computer operations. Your firm sells services worth $5000 per month, pays explicit costs of $4000, and you earn a $1000 profit, as measured by accountants. But remember, your skills as a programmer and entrepreneur also have value. You could have earned $2000 per month working for another firm. Given this opportunity cost, your consulting firm is not making money, it is losing $1000 per month because you are earning $1000 less than the best alternative return on the time and money you have invested.

The difference between accounting and economic profit may be clearer now. Accounting profit says the software firm earns $1000 profit, but economic profit, because it includes both explicit and implicit costs, calculates a $1000 loss. Economic profit is more accurate in the eyes of economists because, as in the firm just described, if economic loss continues, a firm will surely go out of business.

A firm earns a positive economic profit when its accounting profits exceed those available in the best alternative opportunity. A firm earns zero economic profit when its accounting profit is just equal to the best alternative return. Negative economic profit, as in the software example, means the firm earns less accounting profit than its resources could attract elsewhere. All references to profit in the remainder of this chapter refer to economic profit, not accounting profit.

> **KEY CONCEPT 23.1**
>
> Accounting profit equals total revenue minus explicit costs.
> Economic profit equals total revenue minus both explicit and implicit costs.

23.2 SOURCES OF PROFITS

From Where do Profits Come?

Profits could not exist in a completely static, perfectly competitive economy. Imagine a world with free markets and unchanging income, tastes, prices, costs, and technology. Many buyers and sellers compete for identical products in a closed environment. This is a world of zero profit. Firms enter or exit industries until all potential for economic profit disappears, and once this equilibrium is reached, nothing ever disturbs it. The lack of change in markets, prices, and costs means a stable zero-profit equilibrium.

Does this sound much like the world you live in? If not, then the differences between this world and yours explain why profit and loss exists. Look back over the zero-profit world of the last paragraph. Profits exist in the real world because the real world is quite different from our previous example. Some of the important differences that make profits possible are changing demand, changing costs, changing technology, monopoly, government regulations, and the factors of risk, uncertainty, and entrepreneurship.

Changing Demand Demand is not static in the real world. Income, tastes, and population are always changing. These demand movements create profit and loss in the short run. Firms in markets with increasing demand see the prices they receive increase. When price rises above *ATC*, economic profits appear. Review Chapter 17 if you have forgotten the relationship between price, *ATC*, and profit. Sometimes, as during periods of rapid economic growth, the demands for most goods increase at the same time, raising price and creating profits in many industries. But changing demand has another side, too. Increasing demand for calculators, for example, can mean falling demand for slide rules. Price and profit fall in industries with shrinking markets.

Changing Costs Profit can appear and disappear even when demand is stable. Profits change if production costs shift as, for example, if input prices change. Firms with falling costs, all else being equal, are "rewarded" with positive profit. Firms that experience rising costs see profits shrink, at least for a time.

Changing Technology Production costs depend on the prices of inputs and the technology that combines inputs to make outputs. Innovation and changing technology are a source of profit in two ways. First, more efficient technology reduces cost and therefore increases the chance of profit. The automobile firm that installs robots in its assembly line is an example. It earns positive profits if its lower costs, combined with constant market price, generate a higher return than other firms receive. The early innovator gets the reward of low cost and greater chance of profit. Innovation also brings profit when new or better goods are created. The innovating firm gets a shot at monopoly profits until other firms catch up. Profit is not guaranteed, however. The bankruptcy courts are filled with unprofitable innovators.

Monopoly Economic profits also exist, in the short and long runs, when barriers to entry prevent competition and create monopolies or monopoly price-setting power. This link with monopoly is probably one reason profit has a bad name in many countries. While profit often goes to firms, like those described above, who satisfy rising demand, produce more efficiently, or innovate and improve technology, it can also go to monopoly firms that set higher prices and produce smaller quantities compared with corresponding perfectly competitive markets. Profit in the short run, however, is not proof of monopoly, even though many people who complain about obscene business profits often attempt to link the two. Competitive firms can earn profits, and monopoly firms sometimes earn losses.

> **23.3 GOVERNMENT REGULATIONS AND PROFIT**

Government Regulations Government regulations, such as price controls and occupational licensing restrictions, also produce profits. Regulations increase profits by setting price higher than would otherwise be the case or by creating barriers to entry that let existing firms charge higher prices without competition from new entrants. This source of profit will be discussed in more detail later in this chapter.

Risk, Uncertainty, and Entrepreneurship All of the preceding five factors we have discussed are subject to change. In a dynamic economy, cost, regulations, demand, technology, and even monopoly power in a marketplace can sometimes change swiftly, turning a profitable opportunity into a loss. Profits come from the entrepreneur's ability to anticipate such change and react accordingly. Those who correctly anticipate changes, exploit opportunities that are not highly recognized, act swiftly and correctly in the face of innovation, and take calculated risks feared by others generate profits. Those who fail in such efforts generate losses. Profit is the incentive that induces entrepreneurs to undertake risk, anticipate and choose carefully in the face of uncertainty, and therefore, improve the value of the resources they use. If there were no risk, uncertainty, or change, there would be no use for entrepreneurs and no profits. As early as 1921, the prominent economist Frank Knight contended that risk taking and uncertainty were the real sources of economic profit. Many types of risks can be insured against, such as the death of a key corporate manager or the loss of an arm by a famous baseball pitcher. However, uncertainty about business conditions like declining demand or rising costs cannot be insured against. Accordingly, economic profits are necessary incentives for entrepreneurs to face uncertainty and take uncovered business risks.[1]

What Do Profits Do?

23.4 ECONOMIC FUNCTIONS OF PROFITS

Profits play several key roles in a modern economy. Some profits are accidental. They go to stores that were lucky enough to be selling umbrellas the day the monsoon hit town. Even these random profits have a purpose, however. Profits are both a reward and an incentive. Some of the economic functions of profits include rewarding efficiency, compensating for risk, encouraging competition, encouraging innovation, and promoting monopoly.

Reward Efficiency Bigger profits go to the most efficient firms in any industry. Given today's selling price, the most efficient firms produce at the lowest cost and therefore earn the highest profit. This encourages firms to be efficient, which is both good for them because they earn profits, good for consumers because lower costs eventually become lower prices, and good for society. Efficient producers do not waste resources, so society extracts more goods and services from its finite resource base.

Compensate for Risk Firms that innovate or enter new markets take risks. No entrepreneur is likely to risk time and money on a new wrinkle if no individual gain is possible. The potential for profit encourages innovation. Profit rewards risk takers who succeed. A growing economy needs risk-taking entrepreneurs who build the engines of growth and change.

Encourage Competition New firms enter markets and old firms leave them using profit as their guide. If positive profits prevail in the video game industry, for example, these high returns attract investors, entrepreneurs, and workers from other areas of the economy. Profit is the signal that sends resources to where they are needed or desired the most. Entry increases

---

1. Frank H. Knight, *Risk, Uncertainty and Profits*, New York: Harper Torchbooks, 1957.

competition, bidding down prices and forcing firms to produce at peak efficiency.

Encourage Innovation Firms that innovate by making new and better products and finding more efficient ways of making old ones are rewarded with profit. The innovator has a temporary monopoly over the new good or process. This encourages individuals and firms to seek better techniques and produce new products. Innovation and technological change are important because they expand the choices available to consumers and promote economic growth.

23.5 MONOPOLY PROFITS

Promote Monopoly Here we see the profit paradox. Profits both encourage competition and provide an incentive to destroy it. Profits encourage competition and efficiency in some markets, but they also encourage firms to devise plans to earn monopoly profit by creating entry barriers. Many big computer firms, for example, keep key details of their operating systems as **trade secrets** so that competitors cannot sell compatible products. These firms go to great lengths to protect their secrets, spending large sums on security measures. The high costs of trade secrets are worth it to the firm since it receives the benefit of monopoly profit. Society, however, loses twice. Trade secrets reduce competition and lead to inefficient monopoly price and quantity decisions. Further, the resources that are used to protect trade secrets, like those used to create other artificial barriers to entry, are wasted. They could be better used elsewhere in the economy to produce items that consumers really want.

Trade Secrets
Processes or products kept hidden by a firm to prevent competition and assure a return on its research and development investment.

Why doesn't the government outlaw trade secrets? Some economists argue that the high cost of trade secrets is worth it to society, too. Firms would not invest in research and development if they did not have the incentive of temporary monopoly profits. Some monopoly profit may be the price of innovation.

Are Profits Good or Bad?

All profits are not created equal, as you have probably concluded from this discussion. Profits have two faces in a modern economy. It is a mistake to curse them because they are not always an obedient servant of efficiency.

The sunny side of profit is its role as a competitive carrot, spurring firms to cut costs, take risks, and innovate. Profit makes sure that no competitive firm can long rest on its laurels, not with new firms entering the market to try to grab the brass profit ring.

The dark side of profit is its tendency to create monopoly. Monopoly firms earn profits by restricting their output to inefficiently low levels. They sell less and charge higher prices than would more efficient competitive firms. Economists are divided, as you read in Chapter 19, about the severity of the monopoly problem and the distortions that monopoly profits cause. The influential Austrian–American economist Joseph Schumpeter (1883–1950) argued that monopolies are more innovative than other firms that cannot risk new products and techniques in their highly competitive markets. Schumpeter thought that monopoly profits were a good trade-off when innovation and economic growth were added to the bargain. If Schumpeter was correct, then the dark cloud of monopoly profit has a silver lining. While monopoly pricing leads to inefficient use of today's resources, monopoly innovation improves technology and expands the economy's production

PROMINENT ECONOMIST

Joseph Schumpeter (1883–1950)

Austrian-born Joseph Schumpeter began his professional career as a lawyer but later became a professor of economics. From 1919 to 1920 he was employed as the Austrian Minister of Finance and later taught economics at several European universities. After two visiting professorships at Harvard in 1927 and 1930, he emigrated to the United States and accepted a professorship at Harvard.

Schumpeter was respected for his scholarly achievements, but he was also well-known as a free thinker among economists. He flatly rejected the view that pure competition was the proper standard for judging the economic efficiency of markets. During his career, mathematical economics was gathering great momentum, but he had no use for analysis that reduced economic decision making to sets of mathematical equations. During the period in which Keynesian doctrine was most popular, Schumpeter was boldly non-Keynesian.

In 1949 Schumpeter was elected president of the American Economic Association. He is probably best recognized among economists for his view on entrepreneurship and the future of capitalism. It was his belief that the continued improvement in the economic well-being of the majority of the population was a direct result of creative and innovative responses by business entrepreneurs. It was during the early stages of the development of capitalism that there was an ideal environment for the innovator. Entrepreneurs willing to take risks in the pursuit of an innovative idea provided a flow of improved products at a reduced cost. Profits were the rewards for those who successfully instituted these ideas, and losses served to eliminate those who failed. It was these forces that Schumpeter said would generate widespread prosperity.

Although he admired the dynamic capitalist system, Schumpeter predicted that it would generate the seeds of its own destruction. He feared that the success of capitalism would eventually "undermine the social institutions which protect it."[1] The large technologically efficient organizations would dampen innovative zeal and the risk-taking entrepreneur would be replaced by a committee. Compromise and organizational survival would replace innovation and creativity as the primary objectives in business decision making. Also, the affluence produced by a capitalist system would generate the wealth necessary to support a substantial intellectual class, which would probably lack an understanding of and an appreciation for the capitalist system. This affluence would breed a generation of business leaders incapable of defending the system against its intellectual critics, who would lead the masses toward socialism.

1. Joseph A. Schumpeter, *Capitalism, Socialism and Democracy,* New York: Harper Torchbooks, 1950, p. 67.

possibilities frontier, making more goods and services available in the future.

INTEREST: THE PRICE OF LOANS

Money's services are exchanged when money is borrowed and lent. Money exchanged in this way is called a loan. The interest rate is the price of the loan, the cost of borrowing, and the payment for lending.

Why is there an interest rate? Why should you have to pay to use someone else's money if you pay it back? This is a more important question than you probably think. Plato thought that interest payments were unethical. He did not think that money should gain in value through exchange. People earn money, he concluded, money cannot earn money. Moslems also

Usury Laws
State laws that limit legal interest rates.

think interest payments immoral. Banks do not pay interest in Islam, and Moslems in the United States face a moral dilemma with every bank statement. **Usury laws** in the United States make it illegal to charge interest rates above some legal maximum. These laws are remnants of long-held prejudices against borrowing and lending.

The mistake people make in condemning interest is that they do not understand the link between money and resources. Money is nothing by itself. It takes on value only because it can be used to command resources. People who lend money are really transferring the use of their resources to borrowers for some period of time. If the resources and the goods and services they produce have value, then the lenders are due a payment to compensate for their opportunity cost. The opportunity cost here is the return that these resources could have produced if they had not been lent. Borrowers are willing to pay interest because of the gain they achieve by having command over these resources now, not later.

23.6 INTEREST AND PAYMENT VALUES

The Interest Rate As a Link between Present and Future Values

Present Value
The current value of a payment due at some future date.

We realize that borrowers are willing to pay something for the right to command resources now as opposed to some time in the future. If we value a resource today more than that same resource tomorrow, then obviously receiving that resource earlier has value for us. In effect we have a time value for resources. The exact relationship of that time value can be clarified by understanding the concept of **present value.** If we placed $100 in a savings account paying 5 percent interest, then at the end of one year we would receive $105. In other words, $100 today has the same value as $105 one year from now if the interest rate is 5 percent.

The interest rate is another way of stating the price of impatience. It is the price we pay to gain immediate control over resources. Stated from the lender's viewpoint, it is the minimum he or she is willing to accept in order to surrender present command over resources until some future date. The interest rate is the connecting factor between present and future values. The present value of the amount (A), paid (t) years from now at an interest rate of (r) is equal to

$$\text{Present value} = \frac{A}{(1 + r)^t}$$

For example, our $105 paid one year from now at 5 percent interest is equal to $105/1.05 = $100. In other words, $100 today is worth $105 one year in the future. We can use the same calculation in reverse to determine future value. The future value of the amount A, paid t years in the future at an interest rate of 5 percent is equal to:

$$\begin{aligned}\text{Future value} &= \text{present value } (1 + r)^t \\ &= \$100(1.05) \\ &= \$105\end{aligned}$$

From the above two paragraphs, we can see that future value is nothing more than compounding interest and present value is just discounting the compound future value. As a borrower, in order to gain the immediate use of $100 worth of resources that are one year in the future, we are willing to pay $5 extra in addition to the $100 lent. As a lender, we would be willing to sacrifice for one year the use of $100 worth of resources that we have now in return for a 5 percent payment in addition to the return of our original $100 lent.

KEY CONCEPT 23.6

Present value = future value/$(1 + r)^t$
Future value = present value$(1 + r)^t$

The concepts of present and future value can be extended to any number of time periods in the future by simply increasing the value of t in the equations above. For example, the future value of the original $100 deposit paid two years from now at a 5 percent interest rate would be

$$\begin{aligned} \text{Future value} &= 100(1 + .05)^2 \\ &= 100(1.1025) \\ &= \$110.25 \end{aligned}$$

We can see that over the two year time period the $100 deposit grows to $110.25 at the 5 percent interest rate. Stated in present value terms, $100 today at a 5 percent interest rate has the same value as $110.25 paid two years from now. The present value of $110.25 two years in the future at 5 percent is $100.

$$\begin{aligned} \text{Present value} &= \$110.25/(1 + .05)^2 \\ &= \$110.25/(1.1025) \\ &= \$100 \end{aligned}$$

To get a better idea of what present values look like at different interest rates and different time periods in the future, see Table 23-1. To find the present value of one dollar a given number of years in the future simply come down the year column to the appropriate year and read across to the interest rate at which the dollar is to be discounted. For example, the present value of $1, fifteen years from now at 6 percent interest is .417, or 41.7 cents. As a borrower, you would be willing to pay $1 fifteen years from now at 6 percent interest in return for the use of 41.7 cents today. If you were a lender, you would be willing to loan 41.7 cents today at 6 percent interest in return for the payment of $1 fifteen years from now.

Interest Rates as Key Signals in the Economy

23.7 INTEREST RATE AS PRICE SIGNAL

The interest rate is an important price. The interest rate tells borrowers how much value lenders put on the resources they command. It tells borrowers how much lenders must be paid to part temporarily with their

TABLE 23-1

Present Value of One Dollar at Various Interest Rates and Maturities

Year	Interest rate (percent)		
	4	6	10
1	.962	.943	.909
2	.925	.890	.826
3	.890	.839	.751
4	.855	.792	.683
5	.823	.747	.620
10	.676	.558	.385
15	.555	.417	.239

resources. The interest rate signals lenders, in turn, how productive the resources are when put to the borrower's use. The interest rate (price) borrowers are willing to pay for loans signals the profit potential of their investment plans.

Interest rates are agreed upon when money resources are exchanged. A mutually advantageous interest rate serves two purposes. It pays lenders at least as much as they could receive in the best alternative use of their funds and it charges borrowers no more than the return they gain from their current use of scarce resources. This exchange promotes economic efficiency by moving resources from lower-value to higher-value uses. This is an important task.

23.8 INTEREST RATE DETERMINANTS

What Determines the Interest Rate?

Interest rates differ according to the nature of the loan. Such factors as who is making the loan, for what purpose, for how long, or in what economic climate, helps explain why interest rates differ. The five interest rate determinants discussed below — time preference, risk premium, administrative costs, inflation premium, and supply and demand for loanable funds — explain why interest rates exist, why some loans carry higher interest costs than others, and why interest rates for all types of loans rise and fall.

Time Preference   The fundamental reason for interest rates is that lending is costly. Lending has an opportunity cost. Which would you rather have, $1000 today and the command of the resources these funds could purchase, or the promise of $1000 in the future? Most people prefer today's payment to tomorrow's promise. Time has value in economics, and resources held today are worth more than those promised for the future. Lenders must be paid to give up their preferred choice. They must be paid to compensate them for giving up the use of their resources in the present.

Interest rates tend to rise as the loan's term lengthens. Longer term means that lenders are giving up command of their resources for a longer time and are probably taking greater risk. Long-term loans, therefore, tend to carry higher interest rates than equivalent short-term ones.

Risk Premium   Loans are risky propositions. There is always a chance that the lender will not be repaid and must resort to costly legal means to gain his or her due. A **risk premium** is automatically included in each loan as a kind of insurance policy against default. The added interest on repaid loans compensates the lender for loans that are not paid back.

The risk premium helps explain why some loans have higher interest costs than others. A credit-card loan carries a high interest rate, for example, because there is a high probability of default. The typical credit-card loan is not secured by **collateral.** What can the bank do if you do not pay your credit-card bill? They cannot come and repossess your house or car. They can sue you, but this is costly and unlikely to generate cash quickly. The high risk of nonpayment translates into high risk premium interest rates.

Home mortgage loans have a lower interest rate. This is true because most banks require large down payments for these loans, so people who are poor credit risks often cannot get a loan. If you do not pay your mortgage, the bank repossesses the house and probably sells it for more than the amount of the loan. There is small chance of the bank taking a loss on a home loan, even when the lender defaults. The lower risk is reflected in lower interest costs.

Risk Premium
The portion of the interest rate that compensates lenders for the risk that they will not be repaid.

Collateral
Assets pledged against a loan; if the loan is not repaid, the lender may seize the collateral.

ECONOMIC ISSUES

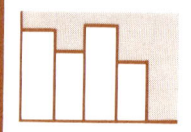

Interest and Usury

Wages, profits, and interest account for the income that individuals receive. Of these three income sources, interest represents something of a historical paradox. Most people in the Western world today accept interest payments and income as the necessary consequences of mutually advantageous exchanges involving credit. State usury laws make payment of very high interest rates a criminal offense under some circumstances, but interest itself is perfectly legal, in general. It is therefore interesting to note that the payment of any interest at all was once considered both illegal and sinfully immoral in Western cultures. And interest is still a sin in some parts of the world.

Early philosophers, from Aristotle on, condemned interest, which they equated with immoral usury, on the logical grounds that interest is a payment that is not earned. Joseph Schumpeter summarizes the view of Thomas of Aquinas this way:

> Interest is a price paid for the use of money; but, viewed from the standpoint of the individual holder, money is consumed in the act of being used; therefore, like wine, it has no use that could be separated from its substance as has, for example, a house; therefore charging for its use is charging for something that does not exist, which is illegitimate (usurious).[1]

Credit, interest, and banking go hand-in-glove. Banking as we understand it today was invented in 14th-century Florence. Medieval banking was made difficult, however, because of Church law that outlawed any interest payment. Loans were to be repaid as made. Any required repayment over and above the amount of the original loan was usury. Usurers risked censure by Church authorities, which doomed them to Hell. However, as de Roover has noted, "theological opinion did not necessarily agree with the views commonly held by practical men ignorant of casuistic subtleties."[2]

Medieval bankers desired to retain the good will of the Church for a variety of reasons, not the least because Church authorities were some of their best

---

1. Joseph A. Schumpeter, *History of Economic Analysis*, New York: Oxford University Press, 1954, p. 94.
2. Raymond de Roover, *The Rise and Decline of The Medici Bank, 1397–1494*, Cambridge: Harvard University Press, 1963, p. 10.

Loans on new or used cars fall somewhere between these two extremes. A car provides collateral for the loan, but risk remains. Cars, unlike houses, can be simply driven away, making repossession difficult or impossible. The higher interest rate for car loans reflects higher risk.

The reputation and economic status of borrowers contributes to the risk premium. The risk premium is nil when IBM goes to the bank. Repayment is nearly certain. Poor people are often considered such a bad credit risk that they cannot get loans at any price through legal lenders. They are forced to go to illegal loan sharks who demand astronomical interest payments for even modest, short-term loans.

Risk premiums also depend on the prospective use of the funds. A firm that wants to build a McDonalds hamburger store across from a college campus probably pays a lower risk premium than another investor who wants the money to invest in riskier enterprises.

The government helps set interest rates through its influence on the risk premium. Some loans are guaranteed by the government. If the lender does not pay, the federal government will. This shrinks the risk premium to zero and accounts for the lower interest rate on some student and mortgage loans.

Administrative Costs The cost of setting up, processing and administering a loan also adds to the interest rate. Costly loans bear a higher **adminis-**

Administrative Cost Premium
The portion of the interest rate that compensates lenders for costs of administering the loan.

customers. But banking cannot be profitable without interest payments. The Florentine bankers therefore found ways around the interest prohibition. Interest was sometimes paid in the form of "voluntary" gifts or as compensation for imagined damages. In many cases loans were disguised as other types of transactions to hide the interest payments. Illicit loans were made in foreign currencies, for example, with repayment due in the domestic coin. Artificial exchange rates between the currencies, specified in the contract, allowed for the legal payment of what was effectively interest. In this way a foreign exchange transaction was used to disguise a credit exchange.

Church authorities were divided concerning the status of interest paid by governments to private lenders in Florence. Some theologians thought that government-paid interest was not usury, while others held all interest to be immoral. Florentine government in the Renaissance was therefore financed through deficits that were or were not usury, depending on which Church order was consulted.

The question of the morality of paying interest may seem merely curious to Western readers, but it is of more practical concern to Muslims even today. The Koran, which forms the basis of Muslim law and religion, outlaws all interest payments. Muslim nations, such as Pakistan, Saudi Arabia, and Egypt, therefore face the difficult problem of squaring the practical requirements of modern finance with the moral requirements of ancient law. Egypt allows interest rates as a basic financing mechanism and concentrates law enforcement on moneylenders in local villages who charge as much as 3 to 5 percent per month to poor borrowers. In this respect, Egypt has adopted a Western view of interest, despite the Koran's prohibition of interest payments.

Pakistan has attempted to bring its economic policies into line with traditional Koran teachings. Interest is being gradually eliminated in the Pakistan economy. Borrowing and lending are being replaced with direct investment. Pakistani savers "invest" with government agencies, which in turn "invest" in private enterprises. Savers receive a return on investment if the enterprises turn out to be profitable. Savers thus receive profits, which are morally acceptable, instead of immoral interest. Interest-free (but potentially profit-paying) "equity-participation" accounts were initially successful in the early 1980s, but the jury is still out concerning their long-run viability.

The moral controversy concerning interest and usury serve to remind us that we live in a complex world, where there is more than practical economic matters to consider. Mutually advantageous exchanges can be discouraged or forbidden because of moral or philosophical concerns.

Additional References

de Roover, Raymond. *The Rise and Decline of the Medici Bank,* 1397–1494. Cambridge: Harvard University Press, 1963.

Pine, Art. "Pakistan Bends Economy to the Koran." *Wall Street Journal,* September 9, 1981, p. 1.

Siddiqi, S.A. *Public Finance in Islam.* Lahore, Pakistan: Sh. Muhammad Ashraf, 1979.

Schumpeter, Joseph A. *History of Economic Analysis.* New York: Oxford University Press, 1954.

---

trative cost premium** as part of the interest rate. Home loans have substantial front-end costs, for example, but these are spread out over a 10- to 20-year term of the loan. A low interest premium covers these costs. Credit-card loans, on the other hand, require costly monthly collection and billing. These higher costs are reflected in a higher interest fee.

Administrative cost and risk premiums explain why some loans are subject to higher interest rates than others. These two factors don't explain why the interest rate on a given loan might increase or decrease in the coming months. For the answer to why interest rates change we need to look to the last two determinants.

23.9 INFLATION PREMIUM

Inflation Premium
The portion of the interest rate that compensates lenders for expected inflation, which reduces the purchasing power of repaid funds.

Inflation Premium In earlier chapters, we discussed both nominal and real variables like income and interest rates. Remember that real interest rates are the nominal, or market, rate of interest minus the rate of inflation. For example, if the market rate of interest is 10 percent and the rate of inflation is 5 percent, then the lender is earning a 5 percent real interest rate (10 percent minus 5 percent equals 5 percent). Inflation rates get built into the interest rate. Borrowers and lenders react to the expected inflation rate over the period of the loan. The **inflation premium** is a practical necessity. Higher prices reduce the real value of the loan repayment. Banks and other lenders must raise nominal interest rates to maintain constant real returns. The inflation premium has been a powerful force in setting interest rates in

Prime Interest Rate
The interest rate that large banks charge their best customers; the interest rate on short-term low risk loans.

recent years. For the remainder of this chapter, the supply and demand for loans will be discussed relative to the real, rather than the nominal, interest rate. Figure 23-1 shows how the **prime interest rate** has varied with the inflation rate between 1970 and 1985. The message this figure tells is clear. Interest rates and inflation rates rise and fall together.

This relationship between inflation and interest rates is one reason businesses fear unanticipated inflation so much. Inflation bids up interest costs and makes inventories and investments more expensive than businesses had anticipated. Higher interest rates also discourage consumer purchases. The U.S. auto industry found itself impaled on the double-edged sword of rising inflation and higher interest rates in the early 1980s. High inflation-induced interest rates not only made modernization and down-sizing of new car models expensive, they also discouraged consumers from buying the new products because of the high price of car loans. Auto manufacturers lost millions of dollars.

Politicians and business people were puzzled in 1982 when the inflation rate dropped substantially but the interest rate did not. What, they thought, can possibly be keeping interest rates so high? Figure 23-1 certainly suggests that lower inflation and reduced interest rates should go together. These politicians and business people overlooked two important issues. First, the inflation premium depends on the expected future inflation rate, not the current one. Lenders who do not expect inflation to stay low are not likely to make low interest loans. The second issue is that inflation, while important, is not the only factor changing interest rates.

Supply and Demand for Loanable Funds If everyone wants to buy a specific good or service but no one wants to sell, scarcity forces up the price. The same thing happens to the interest rate if many people want to borrow but few people are willing to lend at the going interest rate. Scarcity forces interest rates up during tight money times and bids them down when easy money prevails.

FIGURE 23-1

Interest Rate Trends. Interest rates tend to rise and fall with inflation rates, as this graph shows. The prime interest rate moved in roughly the same direction as the inflation rate in the period shown here. The real interest rate is the difference between the nominal rate and the inflation rate.

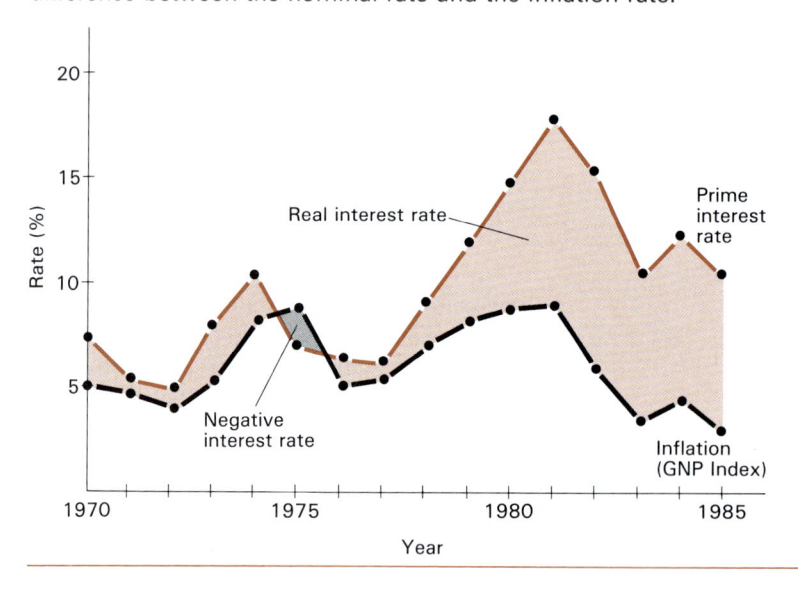

Scarcity kept interest rates high in 1982 despite lower inflation premiums. The Federal Reserve restrained credit growth while the federal government borrowed tens of billions of dollars to finance the deficit. So much additional borrowing made loans scarce and kept nominal interest rates high while real interest rates hit record levels.

The interest rate you pay on a loan is the combination of all five of these determinants. Your interest rate depends on time preference, which is treated as a constant, cost and risk premiums, which vary with the loan and the borrower, an inflation premium, which depends on expected inflation rates, and the supply and demand of loanable funds. Government policies affect this interest rate in two ways. Government guarantees and usury limits make some rates lower than they would otherwise be. Increased government borrowing, on the other hand, tends to make money scarcer and drives up interest rates.

The Prime Interest Rate

23.10 PRIME INTEREST RATE

The prime rate is the interest rate that banks charge their most creditworthy customers for short-term, low-cost loans. You can think of the prime as a bank's announced miniumum interest rate. In fact, however, many banks actually make loans at below-prime interest rates to certain borrowers. Interest rates on many loans are directly tied to the prime interest rate. A local store, for example, might be able to borrow for inventory investment at prime plus 3 percent.

Prime rate loans have little risk or cost associated with them. The prime rate therefore reflects the important inflation and scarcity premiums that affect other loans. An increase in the prime rate means that expected inflation rates have increased or money is tighter. If these trends continue, rising prime rates lead to higher interest rates for cars, houses, and consumer loans, too. Lower prime interest rates eventually translate into lower interest costs on other loans, except where government controls prevent interest rate movements.

The prime rate has an interesting history. It was invented during the Great Depression when interest rates were low and dropping. Government securities earned just 1/2 percent interest in 1933. Deflation was part of the reason why interest rates were so low. Falling prices brought down interest rates with them. It is hard to make money borrowing and lending with interest rates of 1 percent or less. The banking industry invented the prime rate as an interest rate floor. They used the prime rate to hold the line on falling interest charges. These days the prime rate is not so much a floor as a flag. It signals bank intentions and tells the economy which way financial winds are blowing.

Who Sets Interest Rates?

23.11 CREDIT MARKETS

Interest rates are set by the market forces of supply and demand. Lenders supply loans and borrowers demand them. Bond markets are the biggest credit markets. **Bonds** are nothing more than I.O.U.'s. They are a promise to pay a set amount on a specific date in the future. When you buy a bond, you lend money in return for the promise of repayment of a larger sum in the future.

Bonds
Promises-to-pay issued by firms and governments.

Savers are the source of the credit supply. Individuals, government, and businesses with available funds offer to lend them to others, depending on the interest rate. Little credit is supplied when interest rates are low.

Potential lenders can more profitably use the resources themselves. As interest rates rise, however, the interest return gradually exceeds the opportunity cost of lent funds. Lenders find they can earn more by lending money than by using it themselves.

Governments, businesses, and individuals are also the demanders of loans. Many people lend, by saving money for their children's college expenses, for example, and borrow to purchase a house at the same time. The quantity of loans demanded varies inversely with the interest rate. At an interest rate of 6 percent, for example, investors only borrows if they can use borrowed resources to earn at least a 6 percent return. Less loans are demanded as interest rates rise, because fewer borrowers can achieve returns that exceed the higher interest cost.

Supply and demand changes explain many of the interest rate movements seen in Figure 23-1. The federal government became a big borrower in the late 1970s and early 1980s, for example, with annual deficits of between $100 and $200 billion each year. The high loan demand made loans scarce and boosted interest rates as the figure shows.

How Interest Rates Ration Loanable Funds

23.12 RATIONING CREDIT

The interest rate rations loans, seeing that resources go to their most productive uses. Suppose, for example, that the interest rate is 10 percent on short-term loans. Businesses and individuals who can achieve a return of 10 percent or more, whether in money from investment loans or in satisfaction from consumer loans, gain the use of scarce credit. They get the funds available at this interest rate. The interest rate eliminates potential borrowers who have less valuable uses for these resources.

Interest rates also ration credit on the supply side of the credit market. At a 10 percent interest rate, only funds with opportunity costs of less than 10 percent are lent. Individuals who could have earned 8 percent if they kept their money for the time period make the loan at a 10 percent interest rate assuming that risk and cost factors are equal. Another person who could earn 12 percent on funds does not make a loan, however, because the opportunity cost exceeds the interest rate.

The interest rate sees that money and resources go where they are the most productive. Credit goes from lender to borrower if the borrower's use is more valuable than the lender's. Credit stays with the lender, however, if the lender's best alternative use of the resources generates a higher return than the borrower's planned use.

ECONOMIC RENT

23.13 ECONOMIC RENT

Economic Rent
Payment to a resource above that required to induce its supply.

Rent, in common parlance, means the price paid for rental housing. Economists use this term in an entirely different way. While you pay rent to your landlord, your landlord may or may not receive **economic rent.** Economic rent is the payment that a resource receives over and above the amount required to induce its supply to a given use. In simple terms, if your landlord is willing to rent a two-bedroom apartment for $250 per month, but the scarcity of rental housing allows a $300 per month rent, then the $50 difference between actual payment ($300) and the amount required to induce supply ($250) is economic rent. Economic rent is linked to scarcity. If a resource is scarce or fixed in total supply, some surplus payment or economic rent is possible.

Land and Economic Rent

Land, a fixed resource, often earns economic rent, making the confusion between rental payments and economic rent natural. All references to rent in the rest of this chapter refer to economic rent. Figure 23-2 shows land rents.

Imagine that land in a rural region is fixed in total supply, giving the vertical land supply curve of Figure 23-2(a). Since land cannot be produced, an increase in its price can do nothing to increase its quantity supplied. Assume, as well, that this land has only one possible use, cattle grazing. If the land is not used for this purpose, it lies fallow, with no economic return. The opportunity cost of grazing cattle is zero since nothing is given up when cattle graze on the land.

The demand for this grazing land is shown in Figure 23-2(a). The demand curve is derived from the land's value marginal product when mixed with grazing cattle. The land's rental price, if market forces operate, is the P_1 equilibrium shown in the figure. The return earned by land in this example is pure economic rent. Since it has zero opportunity cost, the land would be supplied for any positive payment. Despite this, the land earns a high fee. All that fee is economic rent.

Economic Rent as a Surplus

23.14 ECONOMIC RENT AS A SURPLUS

Economists say that economic rent is a surplus, or unearned, payment. The payment increases the income and wealth of landowners, but it does nothing to change resource allocation. Rent therefore serves a lesser incentive function than other resource payments. While rent does serve as an efficiency incentive for users of an input, it does not have the same effect upon suppliers. Rent indicates the scarcity value of an input and encourages users and potential users to allocate the resource to its best use. Rent does not, however, encourage suppliers to supply either more or less of the resource

FIGURE 23-2   **Land and Economic Rent.** The fixed supply of land in (a) has no alternative use. All payments to this resource are rent. Rent is a surplus, as (b) shows. Changes in demand alter the economic rent that landowners receive, but the changes have no incentive effect because they don't alter the amount of this resource supplied.

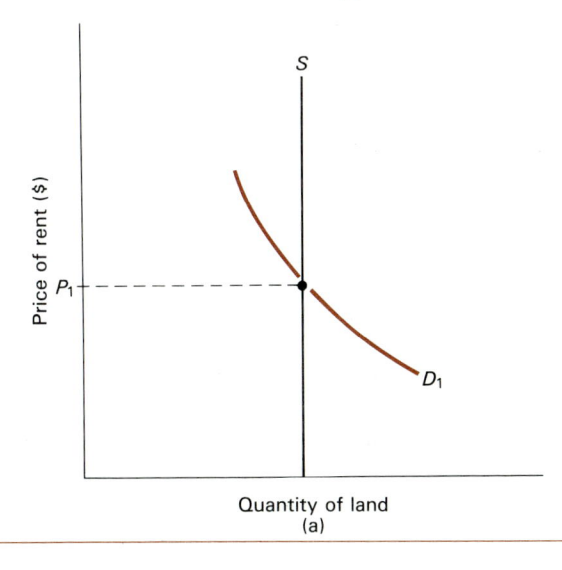

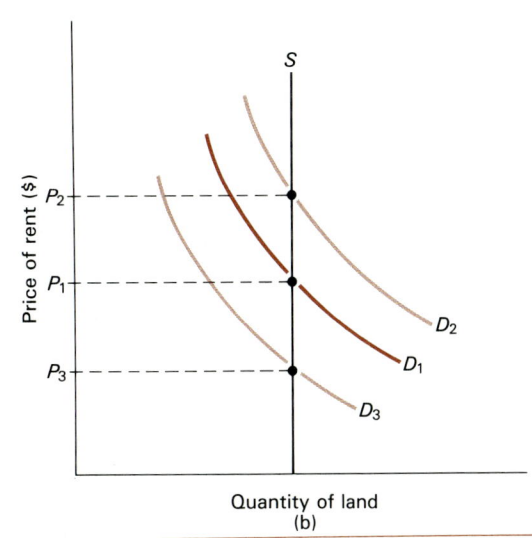

to the market, since by definition, rent is a payment beyond what it would take to induce the resource to be supplied. In this sense, high rents just transfer income from one population group to another. To see this point, look at Figure 23-2(b).

Suppose that the demand for grazing land with no other possible use increases because the demand for beef has increased. Increased demand for grazing land shifts the demand curve in the figure from D_1 to D_2. This increases the payment to landowners from P_1 to P_2. Notice, however, that the amount of grazing land available does not increase, since land is a fixed resource and no more can be produced. Higher demand simply produces higher rent but does not change the way resources are allocated to grazing land versus other possible uses. Higher rents transfer income from beef buyers to grazing-land owners without inducing greater production of land, the scarce resource.

Now suppose that the demand for grazing land falls because, for example, consumers find that beef-eating promotes heart disease. Demand for grazing land falls from D_1 to D_3 in the figure, with price cut from P_2 to P_3. Lower demand reduces the rents that landowners earn, but it does not alter resource allocation the way price changes do in markets with more normal supply curves. No change in the quantity of grazing land supplied is apparent here.

Because economic rents are surplus payments, they can rise or fall without altering resource allocation. To return to the apartment example of the previous section, if your landlord is willing to supply your apartment for $250, but receives $300 now ($50 economic rent), the supply choice remains the same even if the price falls to $275. The lower price reduces the economic rent the landlord receives, but it does not change his or her decision to lease the apartment.

Henry George: The Single-Tax Movement

23.15 SINGLE-TAX MOVEMENT

Henry George, an influential 19th century philosopher and social activist, saw in economic rent both the cause of modern economic problems and their potential cure. His volume *Progress and Poverty* (1876) called for a single tax on land's rent to replace all other tax levies.

George thought that land rent causes poverty. His logic, much simplified, goes as follows: Land is a fixed resource and cannot be increased in total supply. High land fees just transfer income from poorer consumers to richer landowners. According to George, landowners do not earn this income. Land value increases because of increased economic activity, new roads, parks, and schools, and related factors. All these variables are outside the landowner's control, and many of them are financed by tax dollars. George questioned the justice and efficiency of, for example, the poor being taxed to build a new school that, because it raises property values, makes their home rental fees higher. In this case, the poor lose while their landlords earn greater rent.

The solution to this problem, according to George, is a tax on economic rent. Such a tax would be fair, George said, because landlords who benefit financially from government services would be the ones who paid the tax. The single tax would also be efficient because it would collect fees without changing the way resources are allocated. A tax on land's rent would reduce the landlord's income without changing the amount of land supplied, since by definition, rent is income over and above that needed to induce supply. Single-tax collections would not distort markets the way other taxes do.

Henry George was successful in influencing discussion and thought, even if his tax reforms have not been widely adopted. His disciples still proclaim the single-tax message. Discussion in recent years has focused on a variation of the single tax called site-value taxation. Some economists propose replacing the current property tax, which taxes both land and structures, with a single tax on land's site-value alone. Site-value taxation differs in many ways from George's single tax on rent, but it is the rent tax's modern descendent.

Economic Rents in Other Markets

Land rent is a notable example of economic rent, but it is far from the only one. Economic rent exists whenever any resource receives payment above that which is required to induce its supply. Rents are unlikely in competitive markets without entry restrictions. If landlords are willing to supply apartments for $250 per month, for example, then a $300 per month apartment price earns economic profit and economic rent for current landlords. This induces entry into the apartment market by others, who seek high profit and rent returns. Entry, as discussed earlier in this text, increases supply and drives down price. If no entry barriers exist, apartment prices eventually fall to the $250 per month level necessary to induce their supply.

Economic rent can only exist in the long run if natural or artificial barriers keep competitors from entering the market and lowering price. Monopolies, then, can earn economic rent in the long run. Monopoly profits, if they exceed the return required to induce supply, are protected by the entry barriers discussed in Chapter 19. These rents may not induce entry into the monopoly market, protected as it is by entry barriers, but they do induce entry into the monopoly business, through rent-seeking behavior.

Rent-Seeking Behavior

> **23.16 RENT-SEEKING BEHAVIOR**

Since economic rent can be earned when an individual or firm has control of a resource with limited supply and restricted entry, it is natural for entrepreneurs to search for opportunities to gain these advantages. Rent-seeking behavior describes activities designed to acquire the ability to earn economic rent. There is one very important distinction to be made here between profit seekers and rent seekers. Profit seekers enter markets open to everyone in pursuit of profit. Rent seekers pursue profits by seeking protection from competition. Rent earners simply collect rents on resources for which entry is restricted.

Some rent-seeking behavior takes a productive form. Firms invest in innovations and improved technology, for example. They hope to profit from the valuable patent rights to such improvements because patent rights restrict entry and yield their owners the chance to earn rent. These activities promote dynamic efficiency by expanding the economy's technology base and increasing productivity.

Other forms of rent-seeking behavior are inefficient, from society's view. Another way to gain rent is to use the political system to keep competitors out. Tariff and quota trade barriers let domestic firms charge higher prices by limiting competition from foreign firms. Price controls and licensing restrictions imposed by government restrict entry and often generate potential rents. New York City's policy of limiting taxi competition is a classic example of economic rent. The number of taxi medallions, which show the holder's right to compete in the cab market, are strictly limited. Cab medallions that originally sold for just a few dollars are now being sold by their owners for upwards of $100,000. Those who bought the original medallions and sell them now for $100,000 are rent earners. They are simply collecting economic rent on a resource for which entry into the market is restricted. Those who buy the medallions now for $100,000 are really buying the right to sell taxi service, but they will earn no rent because the $100,000 payment in effect is the present discounted value of future rents they might earn. Such is the symbolic power of a taxi's medallion to extract rent.

Economic rents can also exist when imperfect mobility or information and high transactions costs limit market choices. Lawyers and physicians may earn economic rent, for example, because consumers find it difficult and costly to shop around for legal and medical services. Once you are one firm's client or patient, the firm has some ability to extract rents from you. Fees can be high enough to earn rent before it pays you to spend the time and money it takes to find another supplier of these services.

Some organizations intentionally limit supply in the hope of earning economic rent. Collector plates and artists' prints are often issued in limited numbers to increase their price and value. Seats on the New York Stock Exchange are also limited, an unnecessary restriction given the increasingly computerized nature of financial transactions. Stock exchange seats sell for over $100,000 because of their potential to earn rent. The $100,000 price represents the present discounted value of the future rents the owner might earn.

SUMMARY

23.1

1. Business profit is calculated as the difference between total revenues and total explicit cost. Economic profit also considers implicit costs such as the business owner's opportunity cost. Normal profit is included as a cost of the firm when calculating economic profit. A firm that earns accounting profits equal to those available elsewhere has zero economic profit. Positive economic profit signals profits above those available elsewhere in the economy. Economic profit is a better signal of business performance than is accounting profit, since firms that earn positive accounting profits but negative economic profits soon exit from the industry.

23.2

2. Changing demand both creates and destroys economic profits. Firms in rising-demand markets see prices rise and profits appear. These profits disappear in the long run in competitive markets. Changing costs also create profits. Falling costs create profits in the short run, as *ATC* falls below price. These profits disappear in the long run in competitive markets. Changing technology is another reason for profits. Firms that improve technology and produce at lower cost than other firms earn profits, at least in the short run. Monopoly power also creates profits. Firms that restrict entry can earn economic profits in both the short and long runs.

23.3

3. Government regulations create economic profits by limiting entry in some markets and setting price and quantity controls in others.

23.4 ▶ 4. Profits reward efficiency. Firms with lower costs than their competitors have a better chance to earn profits. Profits compensate for risk. Entrepreneurs risk time, effort, and money in businesses. Profit is the incentive that makes this risk acceptable. Profits also encourage competition. The existence of positive profits brings new firms into competitive markets, forcing down price and increasing market supply. Profits encourage innovation, since innovative firms gain temporary monopoly status and can earn higher profits than firms who fail to improve technology. Finally, profits encourage monopoly. Because of monopoly's profit-earning power, firms have an incentive to gain monopoly status by inventing new products or establishing other entry barriers.

23.5 ▶ 5. Profits encourage competition, efficiency, and innovation, but on the negative side, they also encourage monopoly. On the positive side, Joseph Schumpeter said that monopolies hold their market power by being innovative. If monopoly equals innovation, then even monopoly profits have a silver lining.

23.6, 23.7 ▶ 6. Interest rates are the price of loans. They are the price paid when money's services are exchanged over time. A loan has value and a price because it represents command over resources. A person who lends today is really giving up command over resources to the borrower for a period of time. If lending the resources has value, then the value must be paid for through the interest rate.

23.8 ▶ 7. Time preference is one interest rate determinant. Time preference derives from the common desire to consume earlier rather than later. The borrower must compensate the lender for postponing consumption. A risk premium adds to the interest rate. The risk premium compensates the lender for the risk that lent funds will not be repaid. The interest premium is low on loans with sound collateral and high on less certain loans. An administrative cost premium is also part of the interest rate, varying from low to high depending on the proportionate cost of processing the loan. The supply and demand of loanable funds is also an interest rate determinant. The interest rate is low when loanable funds are plentiful, but high when loanable funds are tight.

23.8, 23.9 ▶ 8. Inflation reduces the value of loan repayments, so more dollars must be repaid to compensate for each dollar's shrunken value. This inflation premium is part of the interest rate. The inflation premium equals the expected inflation rate during the loan's term.

23.10 ▶ 9. The prime interest rate is the interest rate that banks charge their best customers. Prime rate loans are short-term, low-risk credit transfers. The prime interest rate reflects changes in inflation and scarcity premiums for loans.

23.11 ▶ 10. Interest rates are set on credit markets, like bond markets, where credit is supplied and demanded. Individuals, business, and government savers supply credit, generally through financial intermediaries like banks. Individuals, businesses, and governments demand credit, too. The equilibrium interest rate is that rate at which credit supply equals credit demand. High federal borrowing in the late 1970s and early 1980s was one factor that pushed the equilibrium interest rate high.

23.12 ▶ 11. Interest rates ration funds between borrowers and lenders. Lenders give up use of their funds if the interest return exceeds their best alternative use of resources. Borrowers undertake loans if the return on their use of resources exceeds the interest cost of them. At equilibrium, the credit market transfers resources from lenders with low-valued uses to borrowers with higher-valued uses. This tends to increase economic efficiency.

23.13 ▶ 12. Economic rent exists when a resource receives payment above the price necessary to induce its supply. Economic rent is different from the usual definition of rent — the payment for rental property. Confusion over the difference between economic rent and the usual definition of rent is heightened by the fact that land sometimes earns economic rent. Land that is fixed in supply often earns economic rent. If the land has no alternative use, any payment it receives is economic rent, since it would be supplied even at zero price.

23.14 ▶ 13. Economic rent is a surplus since it serves no incentive function. An increase or decrease in rent does not change the amount of a resource supplied to the market. If a landlord is willing to rent apartments for $250, but currently receives $300 ($50 economic rent), then a price reduction to $275 per month does not alter the number of apartments offered for rent. The new price is still above the price needed to induce supply. Only the rent surplus has changed.

23.15 ▶ 14. Nineteenth-century social activitist Henry George called for a single tax on land's rent. George held that this tax could replace all others, improving equity and efficiency. George viewed rents as unjust because they result from public sector activities, not the efforts of landowners. A tax on rent would be efficient because it would collect revenues without altering supply. Site-value taxation is the current offshoot of the single-tax movement.

23.16 ▶ 15. Individuals often undertake behavior that puts them in a position to collect economic rent. These activities are called rent-seeking behavior. Some rent-seeking behavior is efficient as when firms try to invent new and better products to gain temporary profits. Other rent-seeking behavior is inefficient, as when firms seek government controls and entry barriers that keep competition out and waste resources.

DISCUSSION QUESTIONS

23.2, 23.4, 23.5 ▶ 1. Are economic profits a desirable or undesirable feature of a modern economy? Explain the role of profits.

23.2 ▶ 2. Under what conditions, in the short run, can a firm earn economic profits? When are economic profits possible in the long run? Explain.

23.1, 23.13, 23.14 ▶ 3. Explain how economic profits differ from economic rents.

[23.7, 23.8, 23.9, 23.10, 23.11, 23.12]

4. Suppose that the federal government has run a budgetary deficit and enters the credit market to finance excess spending. The increase in demand for credit raises interest rates. Explain how this event affects borrowers and lenders. How does the higher interest rate affect the distribution of funds between borrowers and lenders? Explain.

[23.7, 23.8, 23.9, 23.10, 23.11, 23.12]

5. Listed below are several loans that often carry different interest rates. List the variables that determine interest rates in general and explain how they affect the interest rate on each of these loans:
   a. home mortgage loan
   b. student tuition loan
   c. vacation loan
   d. loan at a pawn shop
   e. credit-card loan.

[23.7, 23.8, 23.9, 23.10, 23.11, 23.12]

6. Economists have observed an inverse relationship between interest rates and the amount of business investment. Use the ideas developed in this chapter to explain this relationship.

[23.13, 23.14, 23.15]

7. Use supply and demand curves to show the result of a tax on land rent. Explain how each of the following factors is affected: supply, demand, price, quantity, and rent.

[23.4, 23.16]

8. The first part of this chapter said that profits were desirable because they encourage competition. The last section of the chapter implies that economic rents are often undesirable because they encourage some types of competitive rent-seeking behavior. Are these views consistent? Explain each type of competition, then compare the profit-seeking and rent-seeking behavior.

SELECTED READINGS

Brofenbrenner, Martin. "A Reformulation of Naive Profit Theory." Reprinted in Breit, William, and Hochman, Harold M. (Eds.), *Readings in Microeconomics*, 2nd ed. New York: Holt, Rinehart and Winston, 1971, pp. 411.

Dewey, Donald J. "The Geometry of Capital and Interest: A Suggested Simplification." Reprinted in Breit, William, and Hochman, Harold M. (eds.), *Readings in Microeconomics*, 2nd ed. New York: Holt, Rinehart and Winston, 1971, pp. 423.

Schumpeter, Joseph. *History of Economic Analysis*. New York: Columbia University Press, 1953.

Wicksell, Knut. "The Influence of the Rate of Interest on Prices." Reprinted in Needy, Charles W. (ed.), *Classics of Economics*. Oak Park IL: Moore Publishing Company, Inc., 1980, pp. 67.

Wicksteed, Phillip H. "The Diagrammatic Exposition of the Law of Rent and Its Implications." Reprinted in Needy, Charles W. (ed.), *Classics of Economics*. Oak Park IL: Moore Publishing Company, Inc., 1980, pp. 107.

CHAPTER 24

Poverty and Income Distribution

Having read the chapter, reviewed the chapter summary, and completed the *Study Guide* exercises, you should be able to:

CRIS

24.1 **INCOME DISTRIBUTION:** Describe the income distribution in the United States and explain how it is possible to conclude that income is either evenly or unequally distributed.

24.2 **LORENZ CURVE:** Draw a Lorenz curve and explain why a straight-line Lorenz curve shows an equal distribution of income, then draw a Lorenz curve that represents current income distribution in the United States and explain why this curve shows income inequality.

24.3 **RESOURCE DISTRIBUTION:** Explain why resources are more evenly distributed in the United States than is income and draw a Lorenz curve for income 'adjusted' to include in-kind benefits.

24.4 **1970–1980 INCOME TRENDS:** Describe the trend in income in the United States over the period 1970–1980 and explain how money income can grow while real incomes remained roughly constant.

24.5 **POVERTY GROUPS:** List the four groups with the highest poverty rates in the United States and explain why each group is likely to be poor.

24.6 **CAUSES OF POVERTY:** List the three major causes of poverty in the United States and explain how each leads to low income.

24.7 **ANTIPOVERTY TOOLS:** List five important antipoverty tools that government uses and give an example of each policy type.

24.8 **REDISTRIBUTIONAL POLICIES:** List three different general redistributional policies available to government and explain how the policies are similar and how they are different.

24.9 ABSOLUTE AND RELATIVE POVERTY: Explain the difference between absolute poverty and relative poverty and discuss how it is possible to reduce one type of poverty while making the other worse.

24.10 LEAKY-BUCKET PROBLEM: Explain what is meant by the leaky-bucket problem and discuss how it limits government transfer programs.

24.11 CASH AND IN-KIND TRANSFERS: Explain the difference between cash and in-kind transfers and give arguments for and against each.

24.12 FEDERAL TRANSFER PROGRAMS: List several major federal transfer programs and indicate whether each uses cash or in-kind transfers.

24.13 ANTIPOVERTY PROGRAM CRITICISMS: List and explain four important criticisms of current antipoverty programs.

24.14 NEGATIVE INCOME TAX: Explain how a negative income tax would work and discuss the advantages and disadvantages of the tax compared to today's transfer payment system.

24.15 LIMITS TO INCOME REDISTRIBUTION: Discuss the limits of government's ability to redistribute income.

24.16 FUTURE INCOME REDISTRIBUTION: Discuss two views of income distribution in the future and give arguments that future incomes will be either more or less equal than today.

Poverty
The condition of inadequate earnings; lacking earnings that are sufficient to purchase some minimum living standard.

Ernest Hemingway once wrote, "The very rich are different from you and me. . . . Yes, they have more money."[1] He was right. The rich *do* have more money, or as an economist would say, they command more resources, since that is what money represents. However, the poor are different in more ways than just money. When we look at the problem of **poverty** in the United States, it is the many other differences between high and low income families that strike us.

Economists today define poverty much as Mark Twain might have. Poverty is inadequate earnings. Poverty is characterized by an income level incapable of sustaining a minimum standard of living. Poverty and scarcity are related, but they are different. Scarcity is an inevitable fact of economic life so long as wants are infinite and resources finite. Poverty, however, is not necessarily inevitable. There is no logical reason why the economic pie cannot be divided so that all households have some minimum living standard.

1. Ernest Hemingway, "The Snows of Kilimanjaro."

The level of income that corresponds to that minimum living standard varies depending on who is setting the poverty standard and how it is being set. Still, most people agree that the distribution of income in the United States and other countries is remarkably unequal and that poverty is an important economic and social problem, regardless of the technical measures used to set its scale.

The question of income distribution is important in market economies. People "vote" for goods and services in markets by means of dollars rather than ballots. The poor have considerably less market clout than those with more income.

This chapter looks at the distributional consequences of the prevailing pattern of wages, profits, interest, and rents. It considers whether this income distribution is desirable and looks at who the poor are and why they are poor. It then examines government policies that have been developed to reduce poverty and considers how effective these policies have been. Finally, the chapter looks at whether the income distribution in the United States has become more or less equal over time.

INCOME DISTRIBUTION IN THE UNITED STATES

24.1 INCOME DISTRIBUTION

Income distribution in the United States can be made to look either soothingly even or shockingly unequal, as American economist Arthur Okun has said. The soothing view, according to Okun, is that affluent families with incomes exceeding $50,000 took in only about 2 percent of disposable income in the early 1970s. Adjusting for inflation, the numbers are about the same today. The shocking part is that the same statistics, cited in Okun's book, *Equality and Efficiency: The Big Trade-off?*,[2] tell us that the 1 percent of families with the highest incomes shared as much after-tax income as the bottom 20 percent of the population. Okun notes that some people can feed their pets better than others can feed their children.

Income in market economies depends on what you have to sell and how much others are willing to pay for it. Most of what people sell is their labor. About 75 percent of national income comes from wages, salaries, and other worker compensation. Wages are different for different jobs for the many reasons noted in earlier chapters. Remember that we discussed differences in labor supply, labor demand, productivity, investment patterns, risk, and the degree of labor market competition.

24.2 LORENZ CURVE

Economists use a graphic device called a **Lorenz curve** to illustrate how unequally income is distributed. A Lorenz curve, like the one shown in Figure 24-1, plots the total percent of income on the vertical axis and measures that against the total percent of families or households on the horizontal axis.

Lorenz Curve
A graphic technique used to illustrate the degree of equality or inequality of income distribution.

A perfectly straight, diagonal Lorenz curve line, like that shown in Figure 24-1, indicates perfect equality in income distribution. The bottom 20 percent of the population has 20 percent of total income, the next 20 percent of the population has 20 percent of total income, too, and so on up to the top 20 percent of the population, which also has 20 percent of the total income. All groups share income equally. The straight-line Lorenz curve represents an unattainable ideal. No society on earth has ever had a perfectly equal distribution of money income. Even socialist countries, such as the People's

---

2. Arthur Okun, *Equality and Efficiency: The Big Trade-off?* Washington, DC: Brookings Institution, 1975.

FIGURE 24-1 **Lorenz Curve for the United States, 1980.** The Lorenz curve shows the degree of income inequality. A diagonal line indicates perfect equality of income distribution—this line would apply if everyone had exactly the same income. Income in the United States is far from equal, as the deeply bowed Lorenz curve of this figure shows. Source. Bureau of the Census, *Money Income of Households, Families, and Persons in the United States: 1980.*

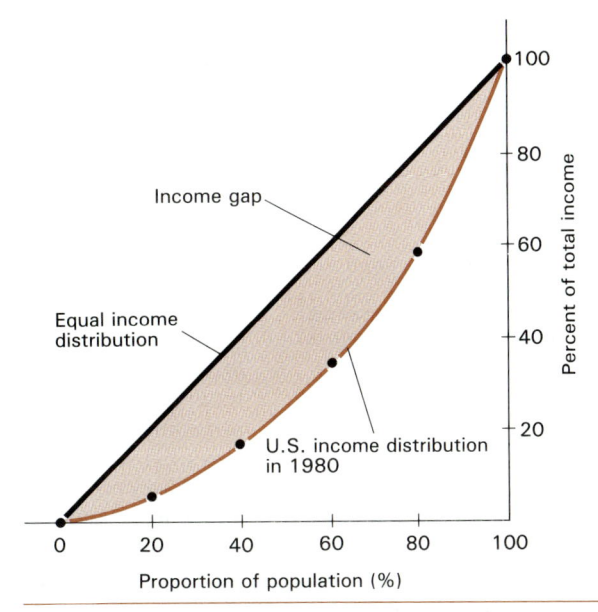

Republic of China and the Soviet Union, which have government-fixed wages, end up paying some people more than others. These governments use unequal wages to reward achievement, compensate for risk and hardship, or encourage higher output.

The bowed curve in Figure 24-1 gives the actual distribution of money incomes in the United States for 1980. Families with incomes in the lowest 40 percent of the population received just 16.7 percent of total income. Families in the top fifth of the income distribution, on the other hand, received almost 42 percent of the total. Median family income for 1980 was $23,974. The income gap between the top and bottom is sizable. Families in the top group had a median income of $34,534, while those in the bottom group received just a $10,286 median income. The median is the middle number in an ordered series. A few families received millions. Many lived on almost nothing. This is, indeed, an unequal distribution of income.

This view of income inequality in the United States may be shocking, but we must step back and examine these statistics before drawing bold conclusions. It is exceedingly difficult to measure the way resources are distributed among families. The figures presented here are instructive, but they look at only part of the picture. Several other factors should be considered.

Income measurements, like those employed in Figure 24-1, do not take into account differences in wealth. An elderly couple with low income, but a valuable stock portfolio, may not really be as poor as a young family just starting out who has an equal income but no savings. Most people view the two cases as different, since the family with accumulated wealth can draw on it to increase income when needed. The other family, however, has human capital—youth and vigor—that the elderly couple may lack. Comparing the two (or comparing these two against other families) in income statistics is bound to be misleading.

PROMINENT ECONOMIST

Lester Carl Thurow (1938–)

Lester Carl Thurow was born in Livingston, Montana. He received his formal education at Williams College (B.A.), Oxford (M.A.), and Harvard University (M.A. and Ph.D.).

After completing his graduate work, Thurow became an assistant professor of economics at Harvard University and later professor at Massachusetts Institute of Technology. He served as a staff economist for the President's Council of Economic Advisors in 1964–1965 and was also a consultant to many government agencies and private corporations.

Perhaps best known for his column in *Newsweek Magazine,* Thurow has written widely on such topics as taxation, income redistribution, monetary policy, political economy, and poverty and discrimination. Politically, Thurow might be considered a liberal since his writings frequently advocate an expanded role for government and greater income redistribution. While, like most economists, he does not imply that government is the perfect redistribution mechanism in the economy, he does feel that it may be the lesser of two evils when one must choose between the market structure and government regulation. Thurow has certainly accomplished a great deal in the economics profession in a short period of time.

24.3 RESOURCE DISTRIBUTION

In-Kind Benefits
Benefits supplied as goods or services (such as medical care) instead of cash.

The second problem is that income is not the only way people acquire resources, and these resources are not necessarily distributed as unequally as is money income. Many families receive substantial **in-kind benefits.** The elderly receive health care, for example, through the Medicare and Medicaid programs. Others receive valuable educational benefits. These programs, and others like food stamps, make low-income groups better off by giving them goods rather than money. Figure 24-2 shows how the income distribu-

FIGURE 24-2   **Distribution of Income and Resources.** Money income is just one measure of the distribution of resources. When income is adjusted to include in-kind payments like medical care and education, the distribution is more equal than for money alone (the adjusted-income Lorenz curve is closer to the diagonal line than is the money income distribution).

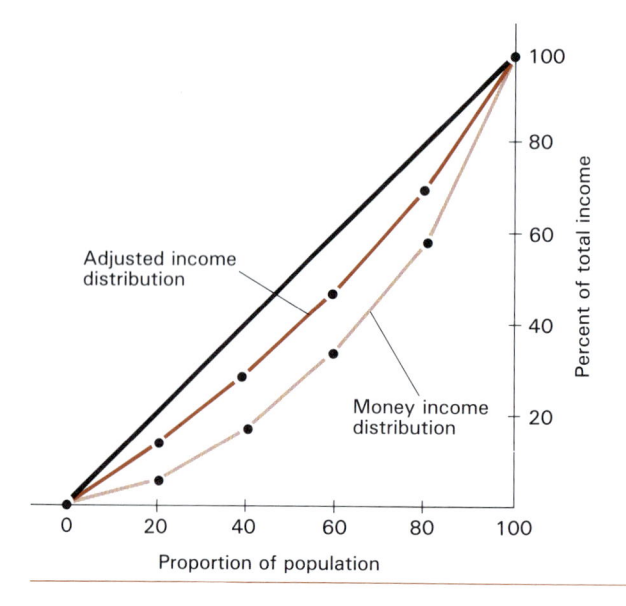

tion changes when income is adjusted to include both cash and in-kind payments. Adjusted income, including some in-kind payments, is not allocated evenly to all, but its distribution is much less unequal than money income.

The problem is further complicated by the fact that the adjusted-income Lorenz curve in Figure 24-2 includes estimates of some government in-kind payments, such as medical care and education, but cannot include the many in-kind benefits received by all groups. It is hard to say what the true distribution of resources in the United States looks like. Even economists and statisticians argue about the exact dispersion and the best way to measure it. What we can say about the distribution of resources in the United States is very general in nature. We can say that there is an unequal distribution, by any measure, biased toward high-income groups. We can say that there is poverty, and we can say that some families have little income and receive few in-kind transfers. Beyond this, it is hard to be more specific and still paint an accurate picture of the economy. Reducing the incidence of poverty in the United States is, however, an important social goal.

KEY CONCEPTS 24.2, 24.3

The Lorenz curve for the United States is bowed toward the origin, an indication of unequal income distribution. When income is adjusted to include in-kind transfers, however, less inequality is observed.

TRENDS IN U.S. INCOME

24.4 1970–1980 INCOME TREND

Family incomes have either grown by leaps and bounds or remained depressingly constant in recent years, depending on how you look at income data. Figure 24-3 shows the two views.

FIGURE 24-3

Income Trends, 1970–1980. Money income grew rapidly during 1970–1980, but most of this gain was wiped out by inflation. Real income (as measured by median income) was about the same at the end of the decade as at the beginning.

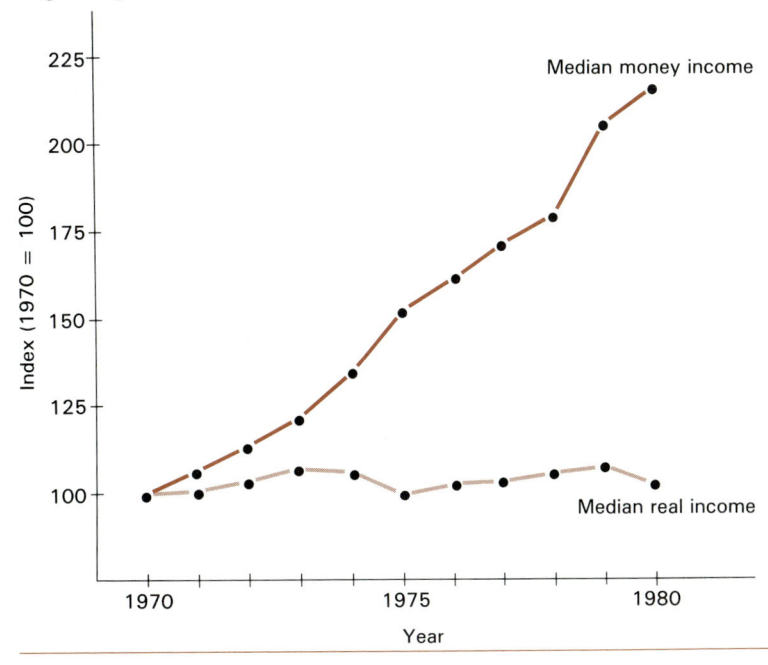

The median money income of families in the United States has surged to high levels in recent years. Median income more than doubled in the decade of the 1970s, from $11,106 in 1970 to $23,974 in 1980. Such high income growth, one might expect, would do much to reduce poverty. Yet money income distribution remained much the same over this period. This is true because much of the increase in median income, as the figure shows, was just an illusion. High dollar amounts were offset by equally high prices. When median income figures are adjusted for inflation, the trend in real income is seen to be relatively constant. The seemingly high 1980 median income purchased about the same quantities of goods and services as did the fewer, but more valuable, dollars of 1970.

The income picture changes if we take a longer view. The 1950s and 1960s were a period of both rising income and a declining income gap, as measured by the post-transfer distribution of resources. Real incomes grew over much of this period. The distribution of income, adjusted to include in-kind transfers, moved away from inequality.

Income stagnated in the 1970s and early 1980s because the economy of this period combined rapid inflation with high unemployment rates. Price shocks, such as high oil prices, combined with high interest rates, fluctuations in the exchange rate, and agricultural problems combined to keep real income and the income distribution from achieving a substantial change.

24.5 POVERTY GROUPS

Who Are the Poor?

Poverty, like income, is not evenly distributed. The official poverty line for a family of four was approximately $10,500 in 1984. Families receiving less cash than this are counted as officially poor. Eleven percent of the population, that is one family in nine, fit this definition in the high-growth year of 1984, which had about 7.4 percent unemployment. This is about the same proportion as suffered poverty in 1967, before many of President Lyndon Johnson's Greaty Society social welfare programs were instituted.

Poverty, as defined by the numbers economists analyze, strikes all social and ethnic groups to some extent. Four groups are most likely to be counted among the poor, however: blacks, women, the young, and the aged. Table 24-1 shows poverty's uneven distribution in 1982.

Blacks Blacks make up about one third of all poor families in the United States, and over 35 percent of all black families in 1982 were below the poverty line. This is an indication of how concentrated poverty is among blacks. By comparison, about 30 percent of Hispanic families had cash receipts below the poverty line, but only 12 percent of white families were poor, as defined here.

Table 24-1 shows black poverty in several ways. First, among workers with full-time jobs (the first five rows on the table), blacks have consistently lower median income than whites. White males aged 25–34, for example, have a median income of $18,106. The median income for black males in the same age group is $13,784. This is an indication of how much lower blacks' wages are, given that both groups have full-time jobs. Table 24-1 also shows that female black workers have lower earnings than their white counterparts.

Now look at the median income figures for all individuals, both workers and those without full-time work (the last four rows in the table). The black–white income difference is even wider here. White males aged 35–44 have a median income of $20,581, for example, compared to $12,642 for black males of the same age.

| TABLE 24-1 | Median Incomes, Selected Groups, 1980. |

	Incomes ($)

Group	Aged 15-19	Aged 20-24	Aged 25-34	Aged 35-44	Aged 45-54	Aged 55-64	Aged 65-69	Aged 70+
Full-time workers								
All persons	7,255	10,773	15,654	18,496	18,082	17,476	15,647	14,963
White males	7,746	12,275	18,106	22,209	23,021	21,559	20,179	18,212
Black males	*	10,233	13,784	15,824	14,706	14,042	*	*
White females	6,759	9,456	12,299	12,518	12,209	12,174	12,925	11,937
Black females	*	9,160	11,423	11,259	11,445	10,224	*	*
All individuals								
White males	1,842	8,244	16,099	20,581	20,775	16,761	9,334	6,831
Black males	1,526	5,808	11,008	12,642	11,478	8,252	5,279	4,084
All males	1,801	7,923	15,580	20,037	19,974	15,914	8,953	6,545
All females	1,673	5,286	6,973	6,465	6,403	4,926	4,379	4,168

Source: Bureau of the Census, *Money Incomes of Households, Families, and Persons in the United States:* 1980.
Note: Insufficient data.

Blacks suffer higher poverty rates than other groups for a variety of reasons, including discrimination. Some of these reasons are discussed in more detail in the next subsection. Many black workers have poor education and training and, therefore, have low value marginal product on the job. Low productivity means that these individuals are likely to find work in low-paying minimum wage jobs and are likely to be unemployed more often than other groups with higher productivity.

Women More than 45 percent of all poor families were headed by women in 1982. Female workers earn, on average, considerably less than male workers, especially in middle age, as can be seen in Table 24-1. In the case of full-time workers, white males aged 35–44 have a median income of $22,209, while white females earn a median of just $12,518. The median income gap between black women workers and black male workers is somewhat narrower but still sizable: $11,259 versus $15,824. Furthermore, median income remains roughly constant for women as they grow older, while income grows for men. This indicates that many women have dead-end jobs, where opportunities for advancement and higher pay are limited.

The figures for all women, both workers and nonworkers, tell the same story. Median income for all males aged 35–44 is about three times that for all women of the same age.

Women suffer poverty for some of the same reasons given for blacks; that is, poorer education and training. In addition, some women tend to have less stable employment patterns than white males. Women move in and out of the labor force more often than other groups, a pattern that reduces productivity and therefore affects their wage levels and employment opportunities.

The Young Young people, both black and white, have lower wages and lower incomes than older groups. Almost 22 percent of young people in the United States lived below the poverty line of cash income in 1982. The median income for full-time workers aged 25–34 is $15,654, for example, while full-time workers aged 15–19 and 20–24 earn just $7,255 and $10,773, respectively. Median income figures for young people, including both workers and nonworkers, show an even bigger income gap. Median income for all males aged 25–34 is $15,580, while median income for males aged 15–19 and 20–25 is just $1801 and $7923, respectively. Young people are more likely to experience poverty than older individuals.

Most young people aged 15–19 are full-time students. Those who are not students make up most of the work force in this age group and therefore by definition have left school at an early age and have very little education to offer an employer. This fact means they have lower value marginal product than other workers. Low value marginal product means a low demand for this class of labor, with high unemployment and low wages the result. The young also have less experience than other workers in many respects. They are even less experienced in the important skills of job search, making their low income more difficult to remedy.

The Old The elderly are the fourth group to experience a high incidence of poverty in the United States. About 15 percent of the elderly had cash income below the poverty level in 1982, this despite the nearly universal receipt of Social Security payments among this group. Table 24-1 shows that elderly workers earn only a little less than younger workers but that few of the old work. The median income for white males, the highest income group, is just $6831 per year. Elderly women and blacks earn less. These median income figures do not, however, include the value of Medicare and other in-kind benefits the elderly receive, and therefore they tend to overstate income differences.

Many elderly workers suffer from poorer health and more lost work time than other groups in the economy. This fact contributes to low value marginal product. In addition, many elderly workers have retired from full-time jobs and work at part-time jobs that have lower wages and are less stable than other occupations.

What Are the Causes of Poverty?

24.6 CAUSES OF POVERTY

The incidence of poverty is high for blacks, women, youthful, and elderly workers. Economists who have studied the poverty problem point to three basic reasons for low income among these groups: unemployment, inadequate education, and discrimination.

Unemployment If wages are the economy's biggest income source, then the inability to find and keep a full-time job is an important reason for low income. Unemployment rates in the late 1970s and early 1980s were high by historical standards. All population groups experienced higher joblessness than in boom years. Even so, unemployment affects some groups more than others. Figure 24-4 gives selected unemployment rates for 1982.

The unemployment rate for all workers was 9.7 percent in 1982, but the pattern of unemployment was far from even. White males had a lower unemployment rate, at 7.8 percent, than black males, who experienced 16.2 percent unemployment. Teenagers, and in particular black teenagers, experienced very high levels of unemployment. Teenaged black males, as the figure shows, suffered a 44 percent unemployment rate. White females had a 7.3 percent unemployment rate in 1982, lower than the rate for either black or white males. This is an unexpected statistic, since unemployment rates for women have generally been higher than those for men. Remember, though, that women also earn less than men, so this low unemployment rate is an indication that employers substituted lower-paid females for higher-wage males during the 1982 recession year. As well, more women now head households than in past years. The population group called heads of households has a history of relatively low unemployment rates.

FIGURE 24-4   **Selected Unemployment Rates, 1982.** Source. *Economic Report of the President, 1983.*

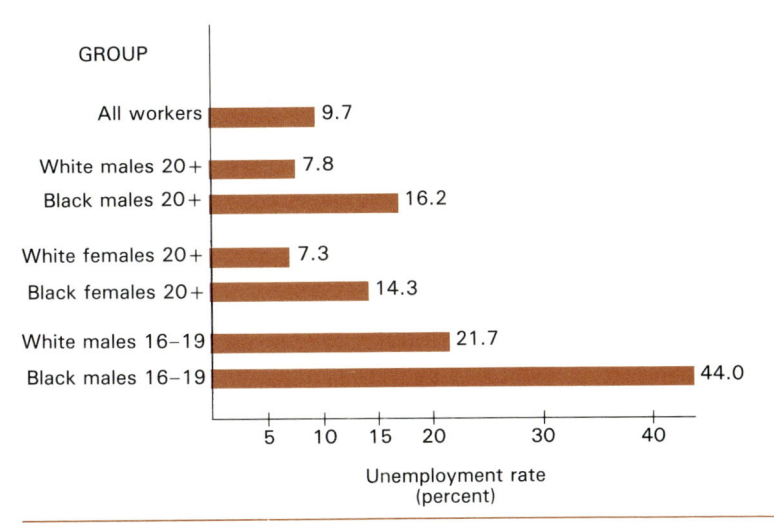

Group	Unemployment rate (percent)
All workers	9.7
White males 20+	7.8
Black males 20+	16.2
White females 20+	7.3
Black females 20+	14.3
White males 16–19	21.7
Black males 16–19	44.0

Inadequate Education   Inadequate education is a related cause of poverty. Often the poor cannot find or keep jobs because they have poor educations and inadequate general work skills. Many poor people cannot even read well enough to fill out job application forms. Low-paid unskilled labor and hard-core unemployment are all that many illiterate or poorly educated people can expect from the job market.

Inadequate education can make poverty hereditary. The children of poor parents may be forced to leave school at an early age to find work so that they can contribute to family income. The poor education that brought poverty to the parents is passed down by force of circumstances to their children.

The system of financing public schools in the United States sometimes adds to the poor's problem of inadequate education. Most public schools are financed with local property tax revenues. If individuals in a neighborhood have high income and valuable property, it is easier to raise enough tax revenue to pay for quality education. If individuals in a neighborhood are poor, however, educational quality is likely to suffer.

It is an unfortunate Catch-22. Individuals in a neighborhood are poor because they have poor educations. Because they are poor, however, they cannot raise enough taxes to pay for better schools. So their children stay poor. Federal, state, and local governments are trying to eliminate income-related differences in the quality of education through busing programs that move low-income students to schools in more affluent areas and college financial aid programs targeted at low-income students. Big gaps, however, still exist in many places between education in rich and poor districts.

Discrimination   Discrimination adds to the poverty problem. Groups that suffer prejudice bear higher poverty rates. Laws in the United States ban discrimination in most labor markets, reducing this problem, but discrimination is a difficult nut to crack.

Overt discrimination is unprofitable for both employee and employer. The employer who is prejudiced makes a choice and pays a cost. He or she often ends up hiring workers of the "right" color, race, or age who may be less productive than the young, old, black, or female workers who are turned away. Employers who hire the best workers produce more at a lower cost than those who practice discrimination. If markets were perfectly competitive, discriminators would soon be driven out of business by more efficient nonprejudiced competitors. Market imperfections in the real world reduce the discrimination penalty and make government policies necessary.

While overt discrimination is a problem, discrimination can take more subtle forms that are even more difficult to deal with. An engineering firm might have a policy of hiring only college graduates, for example, regardless of their sex or color. But few women or blacks are on the payroll. The firm does not set out to discriminate, but its hiring rules, combined with biases in the educational system noted above, mean that few qualified minority job applicants exist. Discrimination is the result, but not the intent, here.

Other forms of discrimination get so deeply embedded into the hiring system that they are difficult to change. A personnel manager often develops a mental profile of a successful employee, one who works hard, gets along with fellow workers, has a good attendance record, and who stays with the firm long enough to make up for training expenses and low initial productivity. Individual job applicants who do not fit the group mold, because they are too young, too old, or black, or female, are not hired based on their own merits. They bear the burden of previous workers' good and bad habits that have nothing to do with their own habits. This kind of job discrimination is really the most serious and the most difficult to change.

ANTIPOVERTY POLICIES

It is possible for society to change the distribution of income, raising poor people's living standard and leveling income differences. Income distribution can change for many reasons. Private charity, for example, often redistributes income and goods from one population group to another. Government redistribution programs, however, are larger and more important in the United States.

Governmental Antipoverty Tools

> **24.7 ANTIPOVERTY TOOLS**

Government policies change the distribution of income in five basic ways: through taxes, government spending, transfer payments, laws, and investment.

Taxes Taxes reduce the disposable incomes of some groups more than others, tilting the income balance. The progressive income tax in the United States takes little or nothing from low-income groups but imposes progressively higher marginal tax rates on upper-income families. The top marginal tax rate is 28 percent. The highest marginal tax rate was 70 percent before the 1981 tax cuts and has been as high as 90 percent.

A progressive tax system makes the distribution of after-tax disposable income more equal than the before-tax income pattern. Low-income families pay little or no income tax in the United States, so they retain most of their income and can spend it for consumption. Middle- and upper-income groups, on the other hand, pay much of their income to the government to satisfy income tax liability. The progressive tax helps close part of the resource gap between the rich and poor, except where high-income families can take advantage of tax loopholes to avoid tax payments.

Government Spending Government spending is a powerful force in the economy, accounting for about 20 percent of total spending in the United States. Government purchases of items as diverse as books, tanks, and typewriter ribbons affect the output of goods and the demand for resources in all sorts of ways.

Government spending alters patterns of production and income. Many government spending programs have built-in anti-poverty devices that require government suppliers to pay market wages and give some of their business to minority-owned firms. Many of these programs also impose penalties if the suppliers discriminate in hiring. These restrictions give most government expenditures an antipoverty aspect.

Transfer Payments Cash and in-kind transfers directly alter resource distribution. Social Security payments, unemployment benefits, and welfare checks all go to groups with incidences of high poverty.

The U.S. system of progressive income taxation combined with high levels of transfer payments serves to redistribute income. Taxes come mostly from middle- and upper-income households and go to pay subsidies to mostly low-income households. The result, in theory at least, is an income distribution that is much less unequal than if no such tax/transfer system existed. In general, the tax-transfer system is like Robin Hood, taking from the "rich" and giving to the "poor." This pattern does not always hold for individuals, however. Some high-income households escape taxation, because of loopholes in the tax laws, and some low-income groups fail to qualify for transfer payment programs, because of gaps in the social safety net.

Laws Laws and regulations, such as tariffs and minimum wage regulations, change relative prices and wages. This, in turn, alters the income distribution. Minimum wage laws, for example, increase the paychecks of some low-income groups, even though others are made jobless by higher wages. Antidiscrimination laws make discrimination more difficult for employers and union officials, indirectly increasing the incomes of blacks and other groups. Tariffs that, for example, make imported tomatoes more expensive, indirectly increase employment and income for unskilled U.S. farm workers.

Investment Finally, government investment in human capital through education and physical capital such as machines and highways alters market return and distributive shares. Government training programs help the poor acquire marketable skills. Government-financed research helps U.S. industry progress, indirectly creating new job opportunities. Both types of investment result in higher productivity and higher value marginal product, which, all else being equal, means higher wages and more jobs for U.S. workers.

24.8 REDISTRIBUTIONAL POLICIES

Fighting Poverty: Which Way Is Best?

We have just discussed five basic government policies to deal with the issue of poverty. There are, of course, many variations and combinations of these policies that are possible, but this complicated mix of antipoverty programs really boils down to a few fundamental choices. Fighting poverty generally means choosing among three alternative social policies: economic growth, direct redistribution, and indirect redistribution.

24.9 ABSOLUTE AND RELATIVE POVERTY

Absolute Poverty
Poverty defined as a physical standard of living.

Relative Poverty
Poverty defined as the gap between income groups.

Economic Growth   Economic growth alters the distribution of income and wealth indirectly. Economic growth increases the economy's ability to produce all goods and services. It shifts out the production possibilities frontier, making both rich and poor better off.

Whether or not this will improve the distribution of income depends on your point of view. Economic growth reduces **absolute poverty** because it tends to improve the standard of living for all groups in the economy. This is what happened in the United States during the 1960s. Economic growth does not necessarily reduce **relative poverty,** however. The gap between the rich and the poor can increase along with economic growth. While both groups are better off, the rich can gain more than the poor, resulting in the poor having a smaller proportional wedge of a larger total pie.

One potential problem with economic growth as a policy tool is that it depends on the benefits of government policy flowing from high- to low-income groups. Economic growth is often encouraged by promoting saving, investment, and innovation. This means giving production incentives to upper-income groups. The rich get helped first, and as the economy grows, the poor also benefit.

A second problem is political. Politicians who want to help the poor often balk at plans that give initial benefits to the rich and then count on market actions to redistribute benefits to other groups. Politicians, as Charles Schultze, economics chief in the Carter administration, has noted, view the market as an untrustworthy black box. They would rather take matters in their own hands than risk the market's methods. They especially distrust market-based policies that claim to provide eventual gains to the poor by initially benefiting the rich.

In contrast, most economists feel that economic growth is an effective antipoverty tool so they favor progrowth policies. They note that the biggest gains in the war against poverty have come during periods of rapid income growth. Attempts to redistribute income in a static economy have been less successful. Taxes and transfers that aim to shift income from one group to another have provided disincentives to production and growth. Policies that aim to stimulate growth may increase income inequality in the short run, but they tend to raise overall living standards in the long run.

Economic growth, even when it works and has political support, is not a complete answer to distributive problems. Researchers report that a sizable number of the poorest households are unlikely to benefit from increased economic activity. They need more direct help.

Direct Redistribution   Direct redistribution is the second alternative. Government takes from one group and gives to another. The Social Security system, for example, collects payroll taxes from today's workers, who gain the right to future payments, and provides direct payments to retired households.

Direct transfers alter the relative distribution of income, closing the gap between the rich and the poor. These transfers, however, suffer from an important risk that Arthur Okun calls the **leaky-bucket problem.** Government alters the total amount of goods available when it carries resources from one group to another. Government's bucket, however, has holes that reduce both the amount being transferred and the size of the pie.

Okun cites four leakages. Administrative costs create the first hole. Income transfers are not free. Government hires people, buys computers, prints forms and, generally, spends large sums to move money from A to B.

24.10 LEAKY-BUCKET PROBLEM

Leaky-Bucket Problem
The problem that government transfer payment programs use up resources as they transfer them among income groups, thereby reducing the size of the net transfer.

Even though administrative expenses are small compared to today's large transfer payment total, they still eat into the pie as it is redivided. Work effort is the second leakage. Higher tax rates, combined with more generous government assistance to those with low incomes, reduce the pay-off for hard work, effort, and skill. If there isn't much difference between the winners and the losers in a race, there is not much incentive to work hard to come in first. Lower work effort reduces productivity and shrinks total output. Greater income equality under these circumstances comes at the price of inefficiency and slower economic growth.

Saving and investment leakages also appear. Taxes to finance payments to the poor reduce the return on saving and investment and therefore discourage these activities. With higher tax rates on income and less return on investment, individuals have less incentive to save. The existence of government low-income and retirement programs gives individuals less need to save for the future or for emergencies. The incentive is to consume resources today, not forgo consumption for future needs. The consequences of this trend have been discussed in earlier chapters. Less saving means less capital accumulation. The economy's stock of machines and factories is lower than it might be under a different tax/transfer system. This leads to lower worker productivity, lower growth rates, and perhaps, higher inflation and longer unemployment lines in coming years.

Finally, Okun lists socioeconomic leakages. The tax/transfer system affects people's attitudes in ways that discourage risk, innovation, and self-reliance. This robs society of valued resources and, again, reduces efficiency in the short run and economic growth in the long run.

Indirect Redistribution Many government policies alter the distribution of resources indirectly. Education and training programs, for example, do not put cash directly in poor people's pockets. They do, however, increase the individuals' chances of earning higher wages. Minimum-wage laws increase the income of some workers by forcing firms to pay higher wage rates. Other low-income people are hurt, however, because higher wages reduce overall labor demand. Tariffs and quotas alter the distribution of purchases in favor of goods made in the United States, boosting the income of workers in domestic import-competing industries. The trade-off is that retaliatory trade restrictions imposed by other countries reduce the income of workers in export industries. Price ceilings on necessities like food, housing, and fuel help the poor stretch their limited money incomes to buy more goods and services. These ceilings, at the same time, reduce producer incentives to make these items available.

An advantage of indirect subsidies is that they seldom require public funds. No tax/transfer payment is involved. Government passes a law or regulation and indirect actions redistribute income. This does not mean that these programs are a free lunch. The cost of indirect redistribution is not borne by government, but the costs are real. Minimum wage laws increase business costs and prices, reduce profits, and restrict employment opportunities. Tariffs increase import prices and distort economic efficiency. Price ceilings hold down seller incomes and create shortages.

One risk in using indirect transfer policies is that more even income distribution comes at the cost of slower economic growth, or even declining total incomes. Programs that distort resource use and reduce the incentive to produce and grow are risky. They might result in a more equal division of a smaller economic pie, making no one better off.

24.11 CASH AND IN-KIND TRANSFERS

Cash Versus In-Kind Transfers

Resources can be transferred from one group to another as cash, to be spent as the recipients like, or as specific goods and services. Both types of transfers are used in the United States. The elderly receive money social security checks, for example, but Medicare benefits buy medical services only. Which type of transfer is best is an issue of debate between economists and politicians.

Many economists prefer cash transfers for two reasons. First, cash gifts are likely to have fewer holes in their buckets. The administrative costs of cash transfers are often less than for in-kind grants, while the other leaks are no greater. Second, cash payments are favored because they are more responsive to the preferences of individual recipients. In-kind payments provide the goods and services that politicians think the poor want or need. With cash payments, the poor decide for themselves how to spend the money. Government sometimes puts parks and swimming pools in poor neighborhoods in an effort to improve the quality of life, raise property values, and provide recreation otherwise unavailable. The poor might rather have the money to spend on fuel bills. If individuals are the best judges of their own needs, then cash payments are a cheaper way to achieve a given increase in living standards.

While cash transfers are less costly and allow recipients to choose the goods they receive, arguments can also be made in favor of in-kind payments. Voters are sometimes willing to support in-kind gifts when they oppose alternative cash payments. This may be because the givers' preferences are important to the transfer. Taxpayers sometimes distrust the decisions of poorer recipients and prefer to give them specific goods rather than counting on them to buy what is best. Elderly pensioners might save cash for their children instead of buying needed health care, for example.

Sometimes in-kind gifts have lower cost to the government than cash payments. The federal government gave cheese and butter to poor families in 1982. The families were not given cash because the government was already committed to purchase the cheese and butter items under agricultural price-support agreements. Giving dairy products to the poor resulted in small additional expense and saved the government the cost of storing surplus cheese. Some of these items ended up in the hands of the nonpoor, however. Corruption and inefficiency are another leak in the transfer bucket.

Federal Government Transfer Payment Programs

24.12 FEDERAL TRANSFER PROGRAMS

The process of redistributing resources in the United States is complex, since federal, state and local governments are all part of the system. Taxing, spending, transfer payment, and regulation activities all alter the way economic resources are divided among population groups. Direct transfer programs are the federal government's biggest job, as measured by budget outlay. Transfer payments accounted for over 40 percent of all federal expenditures in fiscal year 1981. This is almost 60 percent of nondefense spending.

About two-thirds of federal government transfers are cash payments. Social Security and Supplemental Security Income programs pay cash to elderly individuals. Supplemental Security Income is an income-tested program. It goes only to low-income elderly. Unemployment insurance payments are made to individuals who have lost their jobs. Workers' Compensation benefits go to individuals injured on the job. Aid to Families with

Dependent Children (AFDC) goes to low-income households with children, mostly single-parent families in which the mother is the head of household.

In-kind transfers account for about one-third of federal transfer payments. Medicare, Medicaid, and Food Stamps are the largest items. Medicare and Medicaid provide medical services for elderly and low-income people, respectively. The Food Stamp program supplies low-cost food to low-income people.

Researchers disagree about how well these programs, plus their private sector and state–local government counterparts, have done in improving the distribution of income. Some studies conclude that government transfer programs have significantly narrowed the income gap in the United States. The poor have gained in both absolute and relative terms according to these studies.

Other studies draw different conclusions. Some studies show that the growth in transfer payments over the last 20 years has resulted in little change in income distribution. They conclude that when income distribution is measured before government programs are taken into account, the distribution has become more uneven in recent years. The rich have gotten richer and the poor have gotten poorer. Government programs have filled the gaps at the same rate that the differences have grown. On net, they conclude, there has been remarkably little change in income distribution in the past few decades.

We can conclude from these studies that government transfer programs do tend to even out the income distribution, but the resulting division of national income is still unequal. It is not clear, however, whether growing transfer payments over the past 30 years have really had much impact on income distribution.

24.13 ANTIPOVERTY PROGRAM CRITICISMS

Criticisms of Current Antipoverty Programs

How well the current system of antipoverty programs does its job is also a controversial subject. Specific transfer programs have their opponents and proponents. Contradictory studies make it hard to tell how effective the transfer system has been. Despite disagreement about specific programs and proposals, many observers see four important weaknesses in the current system. These four criticisms are cost, negative work incentives, complexity, and fraud.

Cost The current system is too expensive compared to its achievements, according to prominent economist Mordecai Kurz. The hole in the bucket is too big. Billions of dollars spent on antipoverty programs have done precious little to help the poorest groups or narrow income gaps.

Negative Work Incentives Negative work incentives perpetuate poverty. The current system fails to reward those who work to increase income. They often find that income from a low-paying, full-time job is little more than they would receive without work. This is especially true because gaining private employment often means losing public payments. People on welfare in some states, for example, find that they must remain completely unemployed, since taking even a part-time job to supplement income would mean losing all their transfer income, food-supplement, health care, and rent subsidy benefits. They face an either–or system: either accept government payments or live on their own earnings. There is no incentive to work

ECONOMIC ISSUES

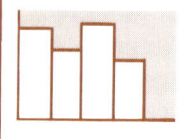

The Catholic Bishops' 1984 Draft Letter on the Economy

The U.S. economy is a powerful growth machine that creates jobs, income, wealth, and an enviable standard of living for millions of workers, investors, and business owners. The fruits of the capitalist economy are not evenly divided, however. Some people look at the economy and see its wealth, while others look at the same system and focus on its inequality. Is this wealth acceptable if it brings with it inequality? Is greater equality desirable if it comes at the cost of more government control and less growth? These are important social questions that have been asked for centuries. At least one important social group has recently concluded that the unequal distribution that exists in the United States is morally wrong.

In November of 1984, a committee of Roman Catholic bishops released a draft of a pastoral letter concerning economic policy in the United States. The jist of this much-publicized letter was that current economic policies have proved inadequate in dealing with the problems of poverty and the unequal distribution of income. The letter cited persistent hunger, homelessness, and racial discrimination as evidence of failed economic policies.

Archbishop Rembert G. Weakland, chairman of the committee that issued the report, said "We find it a disgrace that 35 million Americans live below the poverty level and millions more hover just above it. We are appalled at the sad sight of extreme poverty elsewhere on this globe."

The bishops' letter said that, "We believe that the level of inequality in income and wealth in our society and even more inequality on the world scale must be judged as morally unacceptable." The letter concluded that "In our judgement, the distribution of income and wealth in the United States is so inequitable that it violates this minimum standard of distributive justice." As evidence to support this view, the bishops cited statistics that showed that, in 1982, the

---

Negative Income Tax
A proposal to substitute a system that pays cash transfers (through the income tax system) for the current transfer payment system.

24.14 NEGATIVE INCOME TAX

for those whose prospective working income is less than the value of the government payments they currently receive.

Complexity   The variety of cash and in-kind programs is very complex and not well coordinated. This confuses recipients and makes it hard for government to help the truly needy.

Fraud   The combination of programs leads to fraud that can increase cost, reduce the amount of money available for legitimate recipients, and erode public support.

There are several alternatives to the present program. Welfare reform has been a high priority item for years. Reforms, however, are sometimes seen as an excuse to cut benefits; thus political maneuvering slows progress and cuts support for programs aimed at the truly needy. Some economists and politicians suggest replacing the present conglomeration of transfer payments with a single cash transfer plan, a negative income tax.

The Negative Income Tax

Proponents of a **negative income tax** think this plan would give the poor what they really need, money, at a lower administrative cost with less disincentive to work. The current system taxes family income above a threshold level. Income of poor people bears no tax. They can receive a small tax credit. The transfer payment system operates separate from the income tax.

richest 20 percent of the population received more income than the bottom 70 percent.

The 120-page report, titled the "Pastoral Letter on Catholic Social Teaching and the U.S. Economy," noted several areas where economic policies could be altered to equalize the distribution of income:

- The report said that government policies should be changed to encourage labor unions, which the bishops said could prevent worker intimidation and reduce unfair labor practices.
- Business, labor, and government should work together to bring down unemployment rates. Economic programs should be aimed at hard-core unemployment and the problems of the working poor.
- Government programs should be used to create jobs to bring down the national unemployment rate to the 3 to 4 percent range. Public service jobs programs could create employment for disadvantaged groups by building much needed bridges, roads, and low-cost housing.
- These government jobs programs could be financed through cuts in defense spending. The arms race, the bishops' letter said, diverts valuable resources from the more important task of meeting human needs.
- The U.S. tax system should be altered to discourage consumption and promote saving.
- U.S. foreign policy should shift away from military ends and move to reduce poverty and hunger abroad. The United States should increase support for international agencies that provide development assistance to poor third world nations.
- The U.S. welfare system, which the bishops described as "woefully inadequate," should be thoroughly reformed.

The purpose of the pastoral letter was to provide "moral guidance" and to add the bishops' voices to the public debate concerning economic policy. The report was issued by a five member committee of the National Conference of Catholic Bishops.

The bishops' report on the economy was greeted with support among some groups and opposition from others. A lay commission of prominent Catholics published its own document in response to the bishops' proposals. The lay commission's report stressed capitalism's great ability to create income and wealth. Taken together, the two reports showed that questions concerning the distribution of income are important and controversial. The trade-off between the efficiency of the free market and the potential of greater equality through government intervention poses questions that will always fuel intense debate.

Additional References

"Capitalism and the Bishops" (editorial). *Wall Street Journal,* November 13, 1984, p. 26.

Briggs, Kenneth A. "Catholic Bishops Ask Vast Changes in Economy of U.S." *New York Times,* November 12, 1984, p. 1.

A negative income tax would collect tax from people with income above a break-even level and pay a subsidy to people with lower income. Families with no earned income at all would be guaranteed a maximum payment, which would be phased out as incomes rose. Figure 24-5 shows how a hypothetical negative income tax might work.

A family with no wage income, for example, might receive a maximum $10,000 tax-free payment through the income tax system. As income rises, the size of the negative tax payment would fall. The transfer payment might disappear entirely at $15,000, the break-even point. Families with income above $15,000 would not receive a subsidy, they would pay taxes.

The negative income tax would even out income differences and probably cost less to administer than the current hodgepodge of transfer programs. Work incentives are a prominent feature of this alternative transfer payment system, but the net gain from work is still reduced by lost negative tax payments. An individual who goes from zero to $15,000 in wage income in this example really gains only $5,000, since the individual would have received $10,000 without working.

The negative income tax concept has not been adopted for several reasons. Current income tax credits for low-income workers are a small step toward the negative tax, but replacing the entire welfare system with negative taxes remains a remote possibility. Some people object to the high tax rates they think would be needed to fund such a program. Others prefer in-kind grants over cash payments because the in-kind grants assure a minimum standard of living for the poor. Transfer recipients have a vested interest in the stability of the programs that provide them with benefits.

FIGURE 24-5

The Negative Income Tax. This figure shows how a negative income tax might work. The axes show before-tax and after-tax income. The 45-degree line shows how income would be distributed if no taxes or transfers existed. The negative income tax pays a subsidy to low income groups (a $10,000 payment to a family with zero earned income in this figure). The subsidy declines as earned income rises and finally turns into a tax for households with income above $15,000.

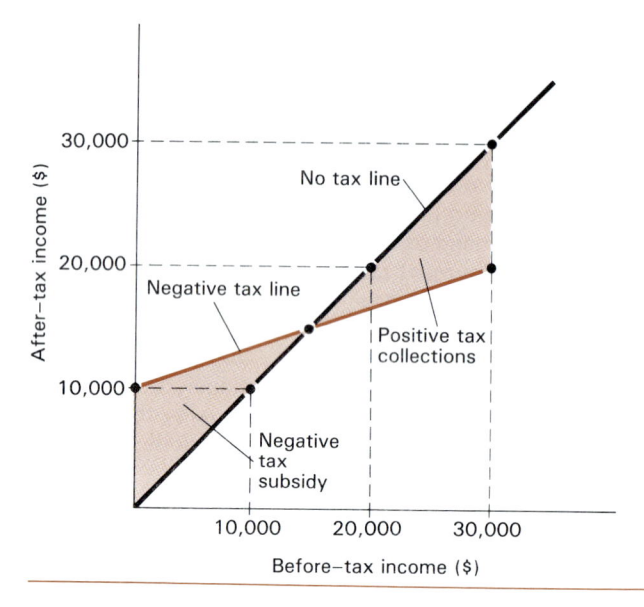

They risk being made worse off with an unknown alternative. They fear, as well, that transfer payments might be cut more easily if they were part of the broader income tax system. Thousands of government workers have a vested interest in continuing the programs that employ them, too.

Negative income taxes would help solve the present system's four problems, but current programs have advantages and institutional momentum that keep the negative tax merely a proposal for now.

Limits to Antipoverty Programs

24.15 LIMITS TO INCOME REDISTRIBUTION

There are significant limits as to how far current antipoverty programs can go in improving distribution. We may have reached a point of diminishing returns in our redistributive efforts. The income tax system, designed to take more from the rich than from the poor, is distorted by loopholes and exclusions. It has become less progressive over the years, reducing its redistributive effect.

Programs that try to reduce low income sometimes encourage it. High social security payments, which fight poverty among the elderly, induce people to retire earlier. They trade away higher incomes for the increased leisure of retirement. They may be better off, but the measured income distribution becomes more uneven. High unemployment benefits are a similar disincentive to work. Much of the transfer payment system ends up shifting income back and forth among middle-income groups, doing little to alter the overall balance.

Finally, some observers think that there is no broad public support for programs that really alter income distribution. Political parties, they point out, do not seem committed to helping the poor if high taxes are the price to be paid.

WHAT DOES THE FUTURE HOLD?

24.16 FUTURE INCOME REDISTRIBUTION

Two distinctly different views dominate current discussions in regard to how poverty and unequal income distribution will change in the future of our economy. The optimistic view of the future is that the stagnation of the 1970s was an anomaly and thus won't be repeated. High rates of economic growth, fueled by high-tech industries, will increase the standard of living of all groups and cut the income gap between the rich and the poor. A trend toward prosperity and equality is seen in this view.

But other people see the advancement of high-tech computerized production as a threat to a more equal income distribution. Computerization means fewer jobs and the end of the industrial paycheck that brought higher living standards in the post-World War II era. Robots and computerized machines will replace assembly-line workers, for example, putting people out of high paying jobs in auto and steel factories. The new jobs that are created by advances in technology will not fit these low-technology workers. They will be forced to accept lower wages or live with unemployment.

High-tech advances will create a dual economy, according to some futurists. A well-trained elite will earn high pay for providing knowledge-based services, such as computer programs and financial services. The bulk of the work force, according to these pessimists, will be stuck in low-income jobs, building or operating computers, for example, or supplying services like waiting tables or clerking. The gap between well-educated rich and less-skilled poor will grow bigger. Worse, there will be little opportunity for low-pay workers to advance to higher-paying jobs.

How will the future turn out? Economist Kenneth Boulding gives what is probably the best answer to questions about the future. He notes that the most common characteristic of the future is that it is not what we expected. We are surprised by the future when it arrives. The best way to prepare for the future, according to Boulding, is to get ready to be surprised.

SUMMARY

24.1
1. Income inequality in the United States is either great or small, depending on how you look at it. Only a few families receive very high incomes, but these high-income few control as many resources as many significantly poorer households.

24.2
2. The Lorenz curve illustrates income inequality. A straight-line Lorenz curve shows a uniform distribution of income. All groups have the same income.

24.2, 24.3
3. The U.S. Lorenz curve is bowed toward the origin, which is an indication of unequal income distribution. When income is adjusted to include in-kind transfers, however, less inequality is observed.

24.4
4. Money income in the United States grew during the period of the 1970s. Median family income increased from $11,106 in 1970, to $23,924 in 1980. But the distribution of income was little changed. Real income

(income adjusted for inflation) was relatively constant during this period. Real median incomes were about the same in 1970 and 1980. Both of these 1970s trends were different from the 1950s and 1960s, when both real and money income increased and income differences narrowed.

24.5

5. Four groups have the highest incidence of poverty. Blacks comprise the first group. They experience lower wages, higher unemployment, and lower incomes than whites of the same age and sex. Poor incomes and inadequate education, and discrimination are reasons for black poverty. Women comprise the second group with a high incidence of poverty. Women often receive low wages and end up in dead-end jobs with little chance for advancement. On average, women tend to have less job training and less stable employment patterns than men. The young have higher poverty rates, too. High unemployment and poor skills are two reasons for low incomes in this group. The young lack job skills that could increase their value marginal product. They also lack experience in finding jobs. The elderly comprise the last group with high poverty rates. Fewer older people work. Their incomes are low compared to other groups. When they do work, the elderly are more likely to take part-time work, with lower wages and less job security than full-time occupations.

24.6

6. Unemployment, inadequate education, and discrimination are three causes of poverty. Unemployment is concentrated among young and black workers. Adult women had lower unemployment rates than adult men in 1982, but they also received lower wages. Inadequate education dooms many to unemployment. Illiterate or poorly educated workers have little chance for good jobs or high wages. Poor parents sometimes need the help of their children's labor to pay bills. Their children may quit school to work, passing poor education and poverty on to the next generation. Discrimination against blacks, women, the young, and the old reduces their wages and increases their unemployment rates. Discrimination takes many forms, making it difficult to fight.

24.7

7. Five government policies alter income distribution and fight poverty. These policies are taxes, government spending, transfer payments, laws and regulations, and investment in people, machines, and knowledge.

24.8, 24.9, 24.10

8. There are three general redistributional policies available to the government: economic growth, direct redistribution, and indirect redistribution. Economic growth expands total income in the economy, reducing absolute poverty, but possibly increasing relative poverty. Economic growth is distrusted by politicians who balk at providing direct benefits to high income groups so that the poor may indirectly benefit. Direct redistribution fights poverty through transfer payments like social security. The leaky-bucket problem limits these policies. Government consumes resources when it transfers money or goods from the rich to the poor. At some point, the leak makes further transfers unwise. Indirect redistribution uses price controls, tariffs, and regulations to alter income distribution. Equality may gain, but misplaced incentives sometimes mean that efficiency and economic growth suffer.

24.11

9. Cash benefits have two advantages. They are cheaper to make (in other words, there is a smaller leak in the bucket), and they let the recipients choose what they need most. In-kind transfers allow the giver to decide

24.12 ▶ 10. About two-thirds of the federal government's transfer payment programs involve cash benefits. Social Security, Supplemental Security Income, unemployment benefits, workers' compensation, and Aid to Families with Dependent Children are the biggest cash programs. About one-third of the federal government's transfer payment programs involve in-kind transfers. Medicare, Medicaid, and Food Stamps are the biggest in-kind programs.

what the poor receive. Some in-kind gifts, like cheese and butter transfers in 1982, are cheaper than cash transfers because they use up surplus goods.

24.13 ▶ 11. Studies disagree about the redistributive impact of these programs. Some studies show that they tend to equalize income distribution, others indicate that transfers just make up for an otherwise widening income gap. Current transfer programs are criticized because they cost too much for the effect they have on the poor. They also weaken work incentives. Current programs are also seen as being too complex and uncoordinated. Fraud adds to expenses and weakens public support for transfer programs.

24.14 ▶ 12. The negative income tax has been proposed as a way to replace the current system of transfer payments with a unified program. It would work through the income tax system. Low-income families would get an income tax "refund" in place of current transfer programs. Everyone would be guaranteed some minimum income through the tax system. The negative tax would disappear as income rises, eventually turning into a positive tax on families with incomes above the break-even level.

24.15 ▶ 13. Antipoverty programs are limited by incentives, diminishing returns, and public support. Many transfer programs do not really change income distribution, they just transfer income back and forth among middle-class families.

24.16 ▶ 14. One view of the future is that income will grow and become more equal as high technology generates rapid economic growth. The trends of the 1960s will replace the stagflation of the 1970s. An opposing view is that high technology will kill off traditional industrial jobs, eliminating the middle class. Remaining workers will be either highly trained, high income managers and thinkers or lower-paid service and production workers.

DISCUSSION QUESTIONS

24.2 ▶ 1. Is the perfectly equal distribution of income given by the straight-line Lorenz curve of Figure 24-1 desirable? Explain how production incentives would be affected by perfect income equality.

24.3 ▶ 2. Explain why resources are more evenly distributed than income in the United States. What is the difference between the two?

24.5, 24.6 ▶ 3. This chapter lists four groups who experience high incidence of poverty and three causes of poverty. Describe how each poor group is affected by each poverty cause.

24.7, 24.8, 24.10 ▶ 4. Explain the difference between direct transfers, indirect transfers, and economic growth as antipoverty devices. Which is the best way to reduce income inequality? Defend your choice.

24.11 ▶ 5. Are cash payments or in-kind payments the best way to help the poor? Explain.

24.14 ▶ 6. Should the negative income tax be substituted for today's complicated transfer payment system? Who would gain? Who would lose?

24.9, 24.15 ▶ 7. Is there a trade-off between income equality on one hand and efficiency and economic growth on the other? Explain the reasoning behind your answer.

SELECTED READINGS

Anderson, Martin. *Welfare: The Political Economy of Welfare Reform in the United States*. Stanford, CA: The Hoover Institution, 1978.

Campbell, Colin D. (ed.), *Income Redistribution*. Washington, DC: American Enterprise Institute, 1977.

Clark, John Bates. "The Distribution of Wealth." Reprinted in Needy, Charles W. (ed.), *Classics of Economics*. Oak Park IL: Moore Publishing Company, Inc., 1980, p. 167.

Kurz, Mordecai. "Negative Income Taxation." Reprinted in Boskin, Michael (ed.), *Federal Tax Reform: Myths and Realities*. San Francisco: Center for the Study of Contemporary Problems, 1982, Chapter 11.

Okun, Arthur. *Equality and Efficiency: The Big Trade-off*. Washington, DC: Brookings Institution, 1975.

Thurow, Lester C. *Poverty and Discrimination*. Washington DC: Brookings Institution, 1969.

Veseth, Michael. *Public Finance*. Reston VA: Reston Publishing Co., 1983.

PART 8

Private Sector Economics: Private versus Public Choice

CHAPTER 25

Externalities and Public Goods: Private versus Public Choice

Having read the chapter, reviewed the chapter summary, and completed the *Study Guide* exercises, you should be able to:

CRIS

25.1 **MARKET FAILURES:** List examples of market failures, situations in which private markets fail to efficiently produce goods and services.

25.2 **EXTERNALITIES:** Define externality and give examples of external costs and external benefits, explaining why each is an externality.

25.3 **EXTERNAL COSTS:** Explain why external costs such as pollution lead markets to produce too many of the items that generate external cost, then use supply–demand curves to illustrate this market failure.

25.4 **PRIVATE VS. SOCIAL COSTS:** Explain the difference between private cost and social cost and tell why this difference is important.

25.5 **EXTERNAL COSTS POLICIES:** List four policies that government can use to deal with external costs like pollution and list the advantages and disadvantages for each policy.

25.6 **EXTERNAL BENEFITS:** Explain why private markets produce too few of goods that provide external benefits, then use supply–demand curves to illustrate this market failure.

25.7 **PRIVATE VS. SOCIAL BENEFITS:** Explain the difference between private benefits and social benefits and tell why this difference is important.

25.8 **EXTERNAL BENEFITS POLICIES:** List several government policies to deal with external benefit problems and explain how each policy works.

25.9 HIGH TRANSACTIONS COSTS: Explain how high transactions costs cause externalities.

25.10 RIVALRY AND EXCLUSION: Explain the difference between rivalry and exclusion and tell why private goods are said to be goods where both exclusion and rivalry exist.

25.11 COMMUNAL GOODS: Explain what is meant by a communal good, using the ideas of rivalry and exclusion, and list several communal goods.

25.12 COMMUNAL GOODS POLICIES: Explain what happens to communal goods without government intervention and tell which government policies are useful in solving communal goods problems.

25.13 PUBLIC GOODS: Explain what is meant by a public good, using the ideas of rivalry and exclusion, and tell why free-riders are a problem for public goods.

25.14 PRIVATE MARKETS AND PUBLIC GOODS: Explain why private markets are poorly equipped to deal with public goods.

25.15 VOTER PREFERENCES: Explain why majority rule voting is not always an accurate reflection of voter preferences and discuss the problems of intensity of preferences and voting cycles.

25.16 AGENDA: Explain what is meant by an agenda and discuss how the power to set the agenda influences public choice.

25.17 DISTRIBUTION OF GAINS AND LOSSES: Explain how a law's distribution of gains and losses among voters affects its likelihood of passage.

25.18 DISTRICT LINES AND CHOICE: Explain how district lines influence public choices.

25.19 VOTE TRADING AND LOGROLLING: Explain how vote trading and logrolling work and how they affect representative voting systems.

25.20 PUBLIC CHOICE SHORTCOMINGS: Explain why public choices made through elections are often as imperfect as private choices made through markets.

Markets are like people, good at some things and not so good at other things. Like people, markets benefit from help in those situations in which their abilities fail. Government, society's collective arm, is sometimes called upon to assist the market mechanism. This chapter examines the long arm of the law and evaluates government's performance in this microeconomic role.

MARKET SUCCESSES AND MARKET FAILURES

25.1 MARKET FAILURES

We have already seen examples of market failures in previous chapters. For all their many advantages, markets do not always make socially desirable decisions. Sometimes monopolies, oligopolies, and cartels arise, for example, distorting resource use. Sometimes the income distribution the market dictates is uneven, with many poor people and only a few rich ones. Earlier chapters examined the role of government in correcting these market failures.

Markets are often the best way to make economic choices. Markets allocate and distribute scarce resources efficiently and at low cost — at least they do so when the assumptions of perfect competition hold. These assumptions, first stated in Chapter 18, include the conditions that many buyers and many sellers compete for identical resources. Monopoly and monopsony, therefore, prevent the market mechanism from functioning as efficiently as it could. We also assume that buyers get full benefit of their purchases and sellers bear full cost of their production decisions. This means that there are no **externalities** or **public goods**.

Externalities
Externalities are the costs or benefits that decision makers impose on others not party to their decisions. Externalities are also sometimes referred to as spillover effects or neighborhood effects.

Public Goods
Items, usually services, where neither rivalry nor exclusion prevail; for example: lighthouses and national defense.

Public Choice
Choices made by society through government.

Markets break down when externalities and public goods appear. The market's invisible hand makes mistakes. It allocates too many resources to the production of some goods and too little elsewhere. Government can sometimes improve the economy's efficiency, moving us closer to the most preferred point on the production possibilites frontier, through wise economic policies.

Government policies, however, do not always make economic sense. Just as markets sometimes fail to make efficient private choices, government sometimes fails to make efficient **public choices.** Then we have a real dilemma: we must choose between imperfect markets or imperfect government. We will explore this problem later in the chapter. To start, however, we will look at the economic problem of externalities and the policies government uses to deal with this market failure.

EXTERNALITIES

25.2 EXTERNALITIES

Externalities exist whenever decision makers fail to bear all of the costs or reap all of the benefits of their actions. Externalities are costs or benefits that accrue to individuals who were not party to the decisions that produced the externalities. Some costs or benefits spill over onto others in their economic neighborhood. Externalities are, therefore, sometimes called spillover effects or neighborhood effects.

External Costs
Costs of a choice not borne by the decision makers, but imposed on others.

External Benefits
Benefits from a choice not received by the decision makers, but received by others.

You live in a world of **external costs** and **external benefits.** Suppose your roommate decides to smoke big black cigars and play Rolling Stones records at full blast through the night before final exams. Your roommate makes the decision and bears some of the costs of this choice in terms of poorer health, reduced hearing sensitivity, lost sleep, and poorer grades. You, however, bear some of the costs, the external costs, because you are negatively affected by another's choice. You also suffer sleeplessness and reduced ability to study.

Sometimes you benefit from another's actions, thereby gaining external benefits. A friend plays the piano, for example, and frequently plays Bach and Brubeck on your dorm's piano. The pianist plays because she enjoys it. She receives benefits from this allocation of time resources. Others who appreciate this music in the building also gain even though they are not

694 Externalities and Public Goods: Private versus Public Choice

party to the decision to play or not to play. They gain external benefits from the pianist's decision to practice in a public area.

The idea of external cost and external benefit is not difficult to grasp, but the consequences of externalities are important and frequently more far-reaching than they appear. Some of government's most important policies are designed to regulate externalities. Government gets involved in external costs and benefits because there are externalities of far greater consequence in our economy than the examples we have considered so far. In the remainder of this chapter, we will take a closer look at external costs and external benefits, the market failures they produce, and the government policies that try to correct these market failures.

Pollution and External Costs

Pollution of air, water, and land is today's most controversial example of external costs. Newspapers are filled with examples of foul, smoggy air, undrinkable water, and toxic-waste dumps that make whole areas deadly neighborhoods. Imperfect market incentives frequently encourage firms to engage in these socially undesirable activities. Figure 25-1 shows the pollution problem.

Producers in competitive markets make decisions based on the **private costs** of producing goods. Private costs are the costs that are borne directly by firms, such as payroll costs and payments for raw materials. Firms try to minimize their private costs when they produce. When externalities are present, private costs differ from **social costs**, the total costs to society. Private costs plus external costs equals social costs. This creates the market failure shown in Figure 25-1(a). A polluting firm lowers its private costs by polluting and passing on the costs of proper disposal of industrial waste to others, thereby increasing social cost. Figure 25-1 shows the market for

> **25.3 EXTERNAL COSTS**
>
> **Private Costs**
> The costs borne by the individual making an economic choice.
>
> **25.4 PRIVATE VS. SOCIAL COSTS**
>
> **Social Costs**
> The costs of a choice to society; the sum of private and external costs.

FIGURE 25-1

The External Costs of Pollution. (a) External costs lead this market to produce at A, where social costs exceed the amount buyers are willing to pay. The efficient quantity is at C. A Pigovian tax places a per unit tax on the producer equal to the amount of external costs produced. This shifts the producer's supply curve back to the point where it is equal to the social cost curve.

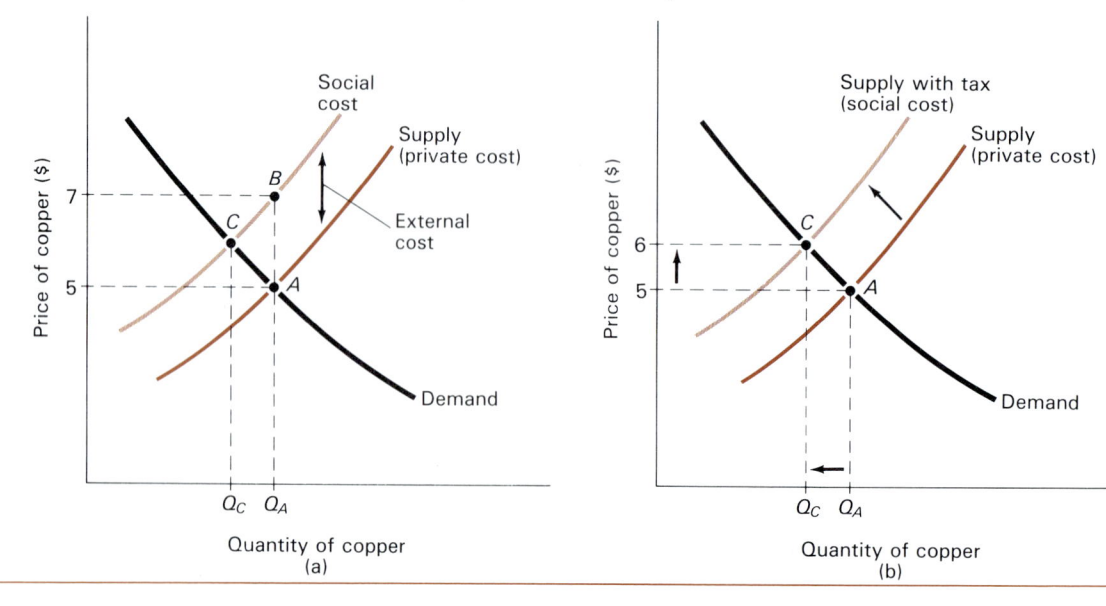

copper, a vital commodity in a modern economy. While vital, producing copper imposes external costs on those who live near the smelters. They live with soot, smoke, and cancer-causing chemical emissions. The private costs the copper firms and their customers bear are less than the total costs to society of smelting copper.

The copper market produces too much copper when external costs are taken into account. The market, ignoring external costs because buyers and sellers are not liable for them, produces at point A in the figure. This is an inefficient output level for society. Buyers are willing to pay $5 for the last unit of copper produced (see the demand curve), and producers are willing to sell it, since their private marginal cost is just $5. Society, however, bears a total cost of $7 for the last unit of copper, $5 in the private costs of producing it and $2 more in the external costs of reduced environmental quality and higher rates of cancer death.

It is easy to see that the firm uses resources with a social cost of $7 to produce goods valued at just $5 in the marketplace. This obviously wastes resources, yet it is what happens in a market when external costs are present. The copper market would be efficient if production were reduced to point C, where the cost to society of the last unit of copper produced is just equal to the price buyers are willing to pay.

The external costs of pollution are a serious economic and social problem. Health experts estimate that thousands of hours of worker time are lost each year because of the external effects of cigarette smoking alone. Add to this the pollution produced by cars, factories, and stores, and you have an important health problem. Production, income, and satisfaction all suffer from the external cost burden.

Pollution is an important example of external costs, but it is not the only one. Many private actions generate high social costs and require government regulation. Drunken drivers impose a higher risk of death and disfigurement on other drivers, for example. This external cost is significant, especially at night, when law enforcement officers say a higher percentage of drivers are drunk. Thousands die each year from this external cost.

KEY CONCEPTS
25.3, 25.4

Goods that generate external costs tend to be overproduced in private markets because their private costs are less than their social costs, thus the producer of the goods reaps a net gain. Goods that generate external benefits tend to be underproduced because their private benefits are less than their social benefits. The producer cannot capture all of the gain of his or her efforts.

25.5
EXTERNAL COSTS POLICIES

External Costs and Government Policy

Deciding which government policies should be used to reduce an external cost problem is a key economic issue today. Sometimes no government policy is best, especially when external costs are small or highly concentrated, as with your record-playing roommate. It is probably best for society to let the two of you find a solution to this limited problem. The cost of the social resources it would take to settle the problem in the courts, for example, would likely exceed the potential benefits gained.

At other times, as with air and water pollution, external cost problems are severe enough to require collective action through government. A range of policy options is available here, each with distinct advantages and disadvantages. Among the government actions that can be used to reduce or

ECONOMIC ISSUES

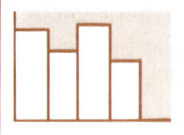

Public Choices about Pollution

This chapter presented the economic theory of externalities and pollution. Some government policies are desirable when pollution exists, but which ones? And how should public choices regarding pollution controls be made? This Economic Issue looks at an example of the difficulties involved in answering these questions.

A Tacoma, Washington, copper smelter has been singled out by the Environmental Protection Agency as an important polluter. The smelter is said to emit cancer-causing effluent, imposing a serious health risk on residents of the local area. It may be dangerous to breathe air or eat crops grown within a certain radius of the Tacoma smelter. Estimates of the degree of danger vary considerably, however.

It would be an easy solution to shut down the smelter, were it not for the economic importance of this employer in the local area. Many jobs in this locality depend on the smelter's continued operation.

The first question public policy must answer is, how do we weigh potential loss of life, estimated by the EPA at one additional cancer death per year, against the lost income, jobs, and economic welfare that come with closing this polluting employer? It appears that any attempt to significantly reduce smelter pollution would raise costs so much as to make the smelter's operation unprofitable.

If this question isn't difficult enough, policymakers must then decide who is to make this choice. This is a nontrivial matter, since different groups are likely to make different choices. Government administrators usually make regulatory choices, but the EPA introduced a new idea in its Tacoma regulation. Federal regulators decided to leave the decision about smelter regulation up to local groups. The people most directly affected by the pollution would be allowed to decide between jobs on the one hand and cleaner environment and fewer cancer deaths on the other.

---

control external costs are direct regulation, output taxes, effluent taxes, and marketable pollution rights.

Direct Regulation   Direct regulation is the first external cost solution. The government can step in and set specific limits to the actions private producers can take, and it can back up its regulations with threat of fine or imprisonment. Drunken driving is forbidden in the United States, for example, and those convicted of this offense generally pay a fine and spend at least a day in jail. Drunk driving persists, however, an indication that direct regulation does not always work.

The Environmental Protection Agency (EPA) uses direct regulation to control air and water pollution at thousands of separate industrial sites. The EPA sets emission limits for a variety of pollutants and monitors pollution levels at each factory. This policy has the advantage of directly limiting pollution levels, thereby reducing external costs. There are also several disadvantages. First, direct regulation is costly and likely to be inefficient. It is expensive to set pollution standards and monitor results in thousands of individual plants and factories. It is hard to tell if the benefits of reduced pollution are worth the extra expense to government and industry. It is also likely to be inefficient, since EPA regulators, who cannot know all the details of each firm's production process, cannot always tailor regulations to individual cases. In some cases, it might be possible to have both less pollution and higher profits if different pollution standards or procedures were employed.

Second, direct regulations sometimes alter the firm's incentives in undesirable ways. A business subject to direct controls can satisfy the letter of the law by either reducing pollution or finding a way around the EPA

Is it best to let voters decide important issues like this? There is a firm belief in democracy and majority rule in the United States, but economists have shown that voting is not always the best way to make collective choices. Nobel prize-winning economist Kenneth Arrow has shown that voting systems have an inherent inconsistency. As the voting cycle discussion in this chapter illustrates, no voting rule can always be counted on to reflect the preferences of the voting population.

James Buchanan and Gordon Tullock have carried the analysis of voting behavior in a different direction. Buchanan and Tullock have shown that public choices are likely to reflect the preferences of special interests to a great extent. Voting is a voluntary activity that requires much information. Special interests can exploit the rational ignorance of some voters and the indifference of others to obtain concessions from the majority. Voting minorities are sometimes able to gain benefits for themselves and impose costs on the majority through clever use of voting rules.

Having studied public choices using the same tools used to analyze private choices, economists have concluded that there is no guarantee that a public vote on smelter pollution, or other externalities policies, would be any more efficient than arbitrary government regulation. Local voters might be persuaded by vocal environmental activists, for example, and vote for tight pollution controls. Or the special interests of industry and labor groups might sway the final vote. The public choice depends on more than just social value and social cost, as we have discussed in this chapter. It depends, as well, on the distribution of the perceived costs and benefits of pollution controls within the voting population and the size and composition of the group that casts the ballots. Public choices like these are not any more insulated from failure than are the private choices that lead to the pollution problem in the first place.

Additional References

Arrow, Kenneth J. *Social Choice and Individual Values,* 2nd ed.) New Haven: Yale University Press, 1963.

Buchanan, James, and Tullock, Gordon. *The Calculus of Consent.* Ann Arbor: University of Michigan Press, 1971.

Gillie, John. "Stronger Controls on Smelter Favored by Most in TNT Poll," *Tacoma News Tribune,* July 24, 1983, p. 1.

Mueller, Dennis C. *Public Choice.* New York: Cambridge University Press, 1980.

Weathersby, Jeff. "EPA Asks: Is Smelter Worth Risk?" *Tacoma News Tribune,* July 13, 1983, p. 7.

---

regulations. A firm might, for example, hire a meteorologist to monitor weather conditions to determine when it is possible to pollute more without setting off EPA pollution alarms. This might result in just as much pollution as before regulations were imposed, but now it comes when the wind and rains are right and the effluents are blown over or around monitoring instruments. In this instance, scarce resources are invested in getting around the rules, not in reducing pollution or reducing production costs.

Direct regulations sometimes inadvertently increase pollution levels. Existing plants and factories are often allowed higher pollution levels than new ones under grandfather clauses in pollution laws. Pollution standards on new factories are set high to make up for high-pollution older plants. The result of these rules is that some corporations find it too expensive to build the highly regulated new factories, so they keep using the inefficient old ones. Since old factories pollute more than new ones, tight pollution controls reduce economic growth while they increase pollution.

Some economists think the EPA's direct regulation of automobile pollution in the 1970s actually increased car-caused smog. The expensive antipollution devices required on new cars pushed up their prices. Many buyers kept older, high-pollution cars on the road longer to save money. Air quality went down, not up, because the cleaner new cars sat on dealer lots rather than being on the highways as replacements for old high-pollution cars. Looser, but less expensive, auto emission controls might have resulted in less pollution by encouraging more people to buy new autos and trade in high-pollution ones.

Finally, direct regulations flow from the government, a political animal, so special-interest effects are possible. Sometimes regulated firms can influence their regulators, with inefficiently large amounts of pollutants as the result. An issue in the early 1980s was whether the EPA was in heavy industry's pocket. If it was, then direct regulation let too many external costs loose in the economy.

Output Taxes
Welfare economist A.C. Pigou suggested output taxes as a pollution solution earlier in this century. Figure 25-1(b) illustrates a Pigovian pollution tax.

Pigou reasoned that the problem with pollution and similar problems is that private costs do not reflect all costs to society, so one way to solve the problem is to raise private costs. The easiest way private costs can be increased to reflect social costs is through taxation. Government can impose a per-unit tax on producers' output, with the tax set equal to the amount of external costs produced. A perfect pollution tax, as the figure shows, shifts the supply curve back until it merges with the social cost curve. The tax makes the private firm behave as if it is bearing all the costs of production, and the market moves to the efficient point C in the figure. The tax makes production decisions that are based on private costs reflect social costs.

Pigou's simple theory has several practical flaws. First, it imposes the same tax on high-pollution and low-pollution firms. Businesses that invest in antipollution equipment pay the same taxes on the goods they produce as those who continue to pollute. Second, it is difficult to accurately value external costs, so there is no guarantee that scientists or political regulators can accurately set the tax. The tax might be too heavy or too light, with problems in each case. Finally, pollution still exists under this plan. Pollution is reduced, but only because output has fallen. We are left with an "optimal" level of production and pollution, where the benefits of pollution-producing goods exceed the cost of further reducing emissions. This is an outcome that leaves many still suffering external costs.

Effluent Taxes
Taxes based on the amount of pollution a firm produces.

Effluent Taxes
Effluent taxes have been suggested by economist Charles Schultze and others as a better way to solve the pollution puzzle. Under an effluent tax system, the government would tax the amount of pollutants each factory produced, much as a sales tax taxes the amount of goods you buy, not the goods themselves as with Pigou's tax. A copper smelter would be taxed on the amount of arsenic it releases, not on the amount of copper it makes. High-pollution firms could keep releasing pollutants into the air and water, but they would have to pay the price. Each pound of effluent would be subject to tax.

Effluent taxes count on the engine of competition to reduce pollution costs. High-pollution firms would have higher costs and lower profits than their low-pollution competitors. Any firm that reduces pollution would pay less tax, and potentially, earn higher profits. Competition for profits would lead firms to reduce pollution to the efficient level. What would the government do under an effluent tax scheme? The EPA's role would be to set tax rates, monitor effluent production, and collect tax revenues. The government would get richer while the environment got cleaner.

The concept of effluent taxation also has some distinct disadvantages. Some of the problems discussed above for other policies would still exist. High-polluting firms might try to get around regulations or pollution-monitoring devices. They might also influence the EPA to set the effluent tax rates too low. A more serious problem is that Congress is not likely to adopt such a scheme in the first place. Legislators mistrust what Schultze calls the magic of the market. They prefer direct regulations that they can see to policies that count on the invisible hand of incentive and competition to reduce pollution, even when the direct regulations do not work as well.

PROMINENT ECONOMIST

Kenneth Arrow (1921–   )

Kenneth Arrow received his undergraduate education at the College of the City of New York (now known as City College of the City University of New York) and his graduate degree at Columbia University in 1940. Since then, he has been with the University of Chicago as an assistant professor and at Stanford University until 1953, when he was appointed professor of economics and statistics. From 1968 to 1979, Arrow was at Harvard University as professor of economics.

In 1972, Kenneth Arrow and J.R. Hicks were awarded the Nobel Prize in Economics for their research in the areas of welfare theory and general economic equilibrium theory. Arrow is well known for his publications in linear programming and capital theory. In one of his most influential books, *Social Choice and Individual Values,* Arrow demonstrated how preferences of individuals are related to collective decision making. Here Arrow related the "paradox of voting" to the concept of economic efficiency.

Arrow strongly supports decontrol of oil prices because he feels that it will decrease the power of OPEC and reduce the trade imbalance caused by hefty oil imports. Arrow practices what he preaches. When he moved to his current professorship in 1979 at Stanford, he selected a home within walking distance to the campus and insulated it to the fullest.

Kenneth Arrow's understanding of the shortcomings of the social choice process and support of free markets has placed him among America's leading voices in the economics profession.

Legislative bodies sometimes also suffer from shortsightedness, a point we have discussed in earlier chapters. Due to the shortsightedness effect, they prefer regulatory benefits that they can see today, even if they have higher costs in the long run.

Marketable Pollution Rights A final proposal calls for the government to define property rights in pollutants and let the market allocate them. The EPA might, for example, issue 100,000 certificates, each of which gives the owner the right to dump one pound of arsenic into the air. The EPA would then auction these rights to the highest bidder.

This radical plan has several advantages. First, the total amount of pollution is limited by the EPA's issue of certificates. This reduces total pollution as effectively as direct regulation. Second, firms who pollute now bear the costs of their acts, since they must purchase pollution rights. High-pollution firms must buy more rights than their low-pollution competitors. Profit-maximizing managers would find ways to reduce pollutants, since such investments would give them a competitive advantage. Finally, firms that produce goods so valuable that the pollution side effect is justified could continue in operation. Total pollution would be reduced under this plan, while the rights to pollution would go where they generate the highest social value.

The pollution-rights scheme also has its problems. For example, enforcing the new property rights in pollution could be costly. The EPA would have to monitor all polluters to see that they do not exceed their effluent budget. The decision to print a given quantity of certificates is a political one. It is hard to tell whether the EPA would issue the efficient number of certificates, or if industry would influence it to grant too many licenses to pollute. The special-interest effects that we discussed earlier could be very important here. With literally millions of dollars in increased costs at stake, the regulated industries would have strong incentives to devote substantial resources to influencing the decisions of the regulators. Campaign contributions and active political support would tend to flow from the regulated industries toward candidates who assist the polluters and away from candidates who favor more stringent pollution control.

Government's role in regulating pollution and other external costs is limited in several ways. Government policies are costly: they divert resources from alternative uses. The gains from regulation must be weighed against their social costs. Regulations that improve on market choices in theory might be undesirable in the real world if the size of the external costs is small and the cost of implementing the policy high or if political considerations make effective regulation unlikely.

Education and External Benefits

> **25.6 EXTERNAL BENEFITS**
>
> **Private Benefits**
> The benefits received by the individual making an economic choice.

Education is an example of an activity that generates important external benefits. Both the student and society in general benefit when a person acquires education or training. The person who pays for the education benefits because education increases individual earnings and otherwise improves quality of life. These are the **private benefits** of this action. Society in general also benefits from having educated citizens. The society receives external benefits because educated people produce better goods, invent new technologies, and do other cost-reducing and quality-increasing things. The **social benefits** of education are far greater than its private benefits. Private benefits plus external benefits equals social benefits.

> **25.7 PRIVATE VS. SOCIAL BENEFITS**
>
> **Social Benefits**
> The benefits of a choice to society; the sum of private and external benefits.

The difference between social and private benefits that occurs when external benefits exist means that the market fails to produce the ideal quantity of the good in question, as Figure 25-2(a) shows. The demand curve for education reflects the private benefits that educational consumers receive. The market, using demand equals private benefits as its guide, finds equilibrium at A, where market supply equals market demand. The market, however, ignores the external costs. The last unit of education in the figure is worth $5000 to society, but it costs just $3000 to produce. Society would gain from the production of even more education than this market-clearing amount.

Society is best off at point C in the figure, where more education is produced. This is the point that the market would select if demand reflected both private and external benefits. This is the optimal equilibrium that would result if the social benefit curve were market demand. The market underproduces education, compared with this efficient amount. In general, external benefits lead to market failure because market demand, and therefore market quantity, is too low, given higher social benefits.

External Benefits and Government Policy

> **25.8 EXTERNAL BENEFITS POLICIES**

The best government policy to deal with external benefits is sometimes no policy at all. When external benefits are low and government policy costs are high the situation may best be left as it is. If individuals receive most of the benefits of their actions, and the cost of government interference is high, the costs may not be worth the additional benefits to be gained. Some externalities, like your piano-playing friend in this chapter's first example, are best enjoyed and left on their own.

FIGURE 25-2 **Education and External Benefits.** (a) External benefits lead this market to produce at A, where social benefits exceed the cost of supplying more education. Society benefits by expanding production to C. (b) A Pigovian subsidy effect provides a subsidy payment to purchasers of education just equal to the external benefit that education provides. This merges the demand and social benefit curves.

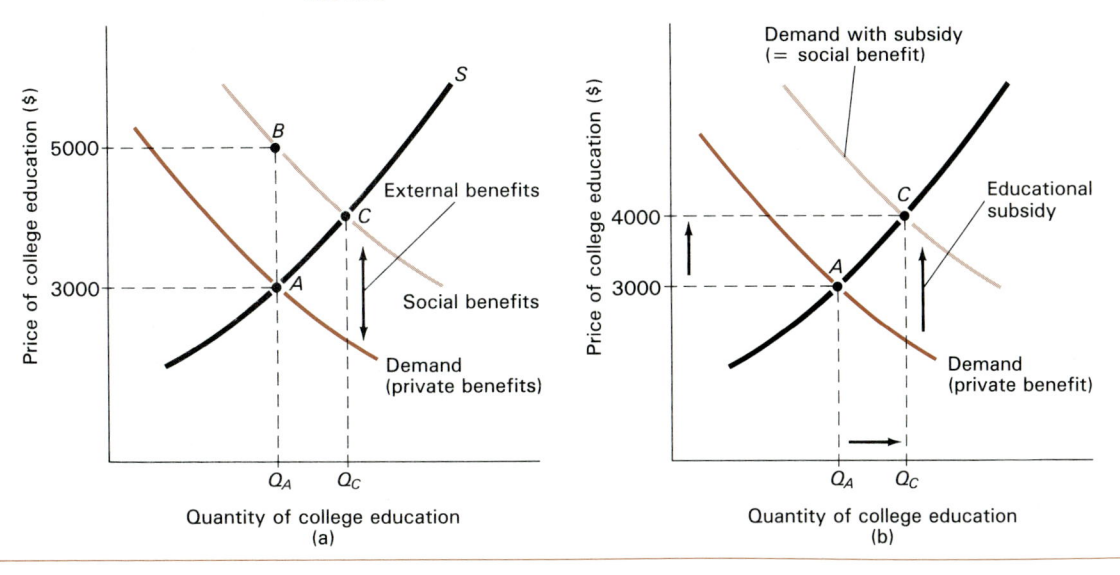

Other externalities do require government help, however. Much less education might be produced and consumed, with detrimental effects, if government let educational markets alone. That is why education, along with national defense and income maintenance, are among the big three government spending areas.

If the market provides too little education, how should government encourage greater production? A short list of policies would include subsidies, free provision, and forced consumption.

Subsidies A.C. Pigou suggests a system of subsidies for external benefits to match his suggested taxes for external costs. Figure 25-2(b) shows how a Pigovian subsidy works. The government provides a subsidy to people who purchase education, lowering the effective price of these services and increasing demand. A perfect subsidy, one just equal to the size of the external benefits, increases demand until it merges with the social benefit curve in the figure. Private demand, given the subsidy's help, now reflects social benefits and the market produces the efficient amount of educational services.

Subsidies are a frequently used external benefit tool. Almost all college students benefit from government subsidies that reduce tuition costs and increase the number of students in college classrooms. Students in public colleges and universities see the biggest subsidy in low tuition rates. Tuition and fees do not generate enough revenue to cover college costs. Government subsidies make up the difference. Students at private colleges pay higher tuition, but they get subsidies in other ways. Work-study and federal grant programs help them afford tuition bills. Federal laws that encourage charitable donations to private schools also reduce tuition costs. All these subsidies end up shifting the demand for college education out and to the right.

Figure 25-2(b) shows one side effect of these subsidies. Higher demand means higher price, all else being equal. Students who do not receive a subsidy pay higher tuition bills than they otherwise would. Students who do receive subsidy payments at private schools pay higher initial tuition costs, but they pay a lower effective price after the subsidy's effect is taken into account.

Free Provision Free is the ultimate subsidy. The consumer pays no out-of-pocket cost for goods that are free to individuals. The goods are not free to society, however, because they have opportunity costs. High school educations are free to individuals in the United States. This substantial subsidy suggests that the external benefits of education are large. Free education implicitly suggests that far too little education would be consumed at any positive price. Too many shortsighted students would drop out of high school if tuition were charged, robbing themselves of private benefits and robbing society of external benefits.

Mandatory Consumption Sometimes even free is not a low enough price, especially if consumers do not see the long-run private benefits they derive from short-run costs. Primary and secondary schooling is not only free in most U.S. states, it is required. The legal mandate to attend school for a minimum time corrects for market problems that shortsightedness and external benefits create.

Other Goods with External Benefits

Education is the most important item that supplies external benefits, if we measure importance by the size of federal, state, and local government expenditures, but it is not the only one. Highways, parks, theaters, urban development, open-space preservation, and many other public projects generate external benefits as well. Take highways as an important example. The U.S. Interstate Highway System is a wonder of the world. It efficiently connects cities and markets across the country. You can get on Interstate 90 in Boston, for example, and not hit a stop light until you reach Seattle.

The drivers and truckers who use this highway system receive private benefits from it. Driving time, cost, danger, and wear-and-tear are all reduced by the efficient highway system. A person who never sets a wheel on an interstate highway also gains external benefits. The highways system expands markets, drives down price, and opens up choices that would otherwise be unthinkable. No wonder federal, state, and local governments spend so much on highways and education. The social benefits of these goods are very large.

From Where Do Externalities Come?

25.9 HIGH TRANSACTIONS COSTS

Externalities are not a disease so much as a symptom. Externalities result from high transactions costs that keep buyer and seller from efficiently exchanging property rights. You can see the role of transactions costs in creating externalities if you imagine a world in which there are no transactions and no enforcement costs. Property rights are costlessly enforced and exchanged. When, for example, a steel factory begins polluting the environment, the local residents quickly enforce their rights to clean air. In this case, it is against the law for someone to take away their property—clean air, pristine environment, and good health—without compensation. The courts act quickly and the polluting firm has a choice. The firm must immediately compensate local residents or stop polluting.

The important thing about this example is that there are no external costs here. If the firm stops polluting, it does not impose external costs. If the firm pays affected local citizens for their property rights, no externalities are produced either, since the residents have voluntarily exchanged rights for cash. Markets handle all transactions efficiently.

The real world, however, does not solve externality problems this way. High transactions costs get in the way. It is costly for government to enforce property rights. It is difficult to bring suits in the courts, to prove damages, and to settle claims. The costs are so high that few individuals find it in their self-interest to go to these ends. The result is that externalities continue and government action is required.

If high transactions costs create externalities, is it not possible that lower transactions costs would reduce these problems? Some economists believe that government should limit its actions in some areas to those of an enforcer. Enforce property rights, open the courts to inexpensive lawsuits, and get out of the way, they say. In many cases, private activities, with lower transaction costs, would let groups work out externalities problems at lower cost themselves.

COMMUNAL GOODS

25.10 RIVALRY AND EXCLUSION

Rivalry
The condition where use of a good by one person reduces the amount available for consumption by others.

25.11 COMMUNAL GOODS

Exclusion
The condition where individuals can exclude others from benefiting from a good or service.

Communal Good
Goods where exclusion does not exist but rivalry does; for example, highways and fisheries.

25.12 COMMUNAL GOODS POLICIES

Markets are at their best when they exchange private goods. Private goods are items that display the characteristics of **rivalry** and **exclusion.** Exclusion is the ability of individuals to exclude others from gaining benefits from property rights that they own. Rivalry is the condition that one person's use of a good or service diminishes the amount available for consumption by others. A banana is an example of a private good, given these definitions. If you own a banana, you can use it and you can exclude others from using it. If you eat the banana, there is one less banana left in the world for others to consume. Both rivalry and exclusion prevail here. Most items we buy and sell are private goods.

A few items are **communal goods;** rivalry for their use exists, but exclusion does not. A public beach is a good example of a communal good. No one can be excluded from using the beach because it is owned by the state or municipality. Beach space is scarce, however, so rivalry prevails. If one person put up his or her beach umbrella, there is that much less space left for others to use. Public beaches and public parks are two examples of communal goods we have all experienced. Previous chapters introduced you to the idea of communal goods by discussing the problem of cattle grazing on the commons in English villages. Perhaps more important, however, are communal resources such as timber stands, wilderness areas, clean air and water, and fisheries.

Communal goods require government regulation because of the peculiar incentives that common ownership presents. Take a river salmon fishery as an example. All fishermen have equal right to cast a line in search of salmon. There are, however, biological limits to the number of salmon that should be caught in any year. The fishery loses value if too few salmon get past the fishermen to spawning areas because future salmon runs are reduced. There is a point at which further fishing reduces the fishery's value.

Individual fishermen do not have any incentive to stop fishing at the right time. While fishermen as a group lose if fishing is continued, individual fishermen have a strong incentive to continue to cast their lines. This is true because an individual fisherman gets all the gain of the extra fish caught, but does not bear the full cost of this action. The cost, the long-run decline in fish runs, is shared with all others who catch salmon. It is a simple calculation. An individual gets all the gain, but pays little of the cost, so he or she keeps fishing. Without government regulation, common resources such as fisheries, grazing lands, timber stands, and the like are soon overused and their value declines.

Anyone who drives a car is familiar with this communal goods problem. Highways are a excellent example of a communal good, since everyone has access to these roads, but each car rivals the others for space. Many roads are overused, bogged down in commuter tie-ups every day. It is the same story here as the salmon fishery above. Each individual driver's decision to use the road is efficient for him or her, but the combination of all these choices taken together is an inefficient traffic jam.

Government regulation of communal goods takes many forms. Many areas try to solve traffic problems by encouraging mass transit use by providing special bus and car-pool lanes on congested roads, for example. The federal government owns much of the undeveloped communal land in the United States and leases it, at a controlled rate, to private users, preventing overuse. The government's policies toward communal goods were controversial during the Reagan administration. Conservationists claimed that land and mineral resources were being overused, with detrimental long-run consequences. The administration countered that its policies were wise in both the short and long runs and that previous policies had inefficiently locked up valuable resources. This debate points out the problems of deciding the "optimal" use of communal resources when market prices fail to accurately value scarce resources.

Government regulations sometimes are not enough to deal with some communal goods problems. The oceans of the world have no respect for national borders. They wash all shores. This makes purely national communal goods policies ineffective. It does little good for the United States to regulate its fishery industry, for example, if foreign vessels overharvest seafood just off our shores. The international Law of the Sea conference tries to set rules that balance national needs with communal resource limits, but compromising these two interests has proven to be a difficult task.

KEY CONCEPTS 25.12

Individuals tend to overuse communal goods because each individual gets the gain from his or her actions, but shares the cost of reduced resource availability with all others.

PUBLIC GOODS

25.13 PUBLIC GOODS

Public goods are items that display neither exclusion nor rivalry. Peace and freedom, or their complement, national defense, is the best example of a pure public good. If the government protects some people from foreign invasion, for example, it cannot fail to protect the rest. People who do not "pay" for national defense cannot be excluded. If a hostile force invades New Jersey, peace and freedom are lost for all. If invasion is prevented, all gain. At the same time, however, one person's gain from peace and freedom does not diminish the benefits that others receive. There is no rivalry. Your personal safety does not reduce the amount of safety left for others to share.

Public goods are wonderful things, but they are wonderful things that markets fail to provide in adequate quantities. Each individual has the incentive to be a free rider, as you learned in an earlier chapter, and let others pay for public goods. This is a smart strategy for an individual because free riders pay nothing but share the gain equally with everyone else. It is a poor strategy, however, for society. If everyone decides to be a free rider, no individual has any incentive to produce the public good and valuable benefits are lost.

Here is an example of the public goods problem that will hit boaters close to home. A lighthouse is a public good. A lighthouse warns sailors of danger. Consumers of this service are not rivals, and exclusion is a practical impossibility. All boaters can see the lighthouse whether or not they have paid for it, and those who have paid cannot exclude those who have not paid from using its services. Once the lighthouse is built, people who did not contribute to its construction get a free ride. The problem for society and government is, who builds the light house?

24.14 PRIVATE MARKETS AND PUBLIC GOODS

Government is the public goods answer. Government, acting for society, builds lighthouses, provides national defense, and provides or regulates other public goods. Government gets around the free-rider problem because it has a power that markets lack. Government can force payment from free riders through the tax system.

Government does a better job of producing public goods than would markets, but government intervention is no guarantee that the efficient amount of public goods are produced. At what point are the benefits of additional expenditures on weapons systems no longer worth the other goods and services forgone? This is an extremely difficult question to answer, given the subtle and uncertain way peace and freedom are produced in today's world. Rational people can easily disagree about guns versus butter choices.

KEY CONCEPTS 25.13, 25.14

Markets undersupply public goods because individuals have the incentive to be free riders, to let others buy, then gain costless benefits. Too little of the public good is produced and purchased without government help.

PRIVATE CHOICE VERSUS PUBLIC CHOICE

Private choices, through markets, are imperfect when externalities, communal goods, and public goods exist. This is also true when monopoly, monopsony, or income distribution problems arise, as noted in earlier chapters. Government has the potential to improve on market choices in each case; the correct government policy can, in theory, offset inefficient market incentives. Is public choice in the real world efficient? Is there any guarantee that public choices are any better than inefficient private ones?

The remainder of this chapter outlines how public choices are made and explains some of the problems that crop up when people make choices using votes instead of dollars. The conclusion of this discussion is a limited case for government intervention. Public choices surely can improve on market failures in theory. Public choices, however, suffer from many of the same imperfections as private choices. In general, there is no guarantee that

PROMINENT ECONOMIST

James Buchanan (1919–   )

James Buchanan is most frequently recognized for his approach to the analysis of the public sector. Before his work became popular, most economists were content to concentrate on the workings of the marketplace, its shortcomings, and what government action could do to correct deficiencies. Political scientists and economists perceived the public sector as a type of superindividual, a creature making decisions in the public interest. Buchanan changed this view. He pioneered the academic movement that some have called the "public choice revolution."

Buchanan's view of government is that it is an outgrowth of individual behavior. He considers individuals to be the ultimate choice makers, shaping and molding group action as well as private affairs. Through his use of the basic tools of economics, he has developed theories that explain how the political process works. Buchanan uses the approach of scientific politics.

In their ground-breaking book, *The Calculus of Consent,* Buchanan and Gordon Tullock develop an economic theory of constitutions. They analyze political behavior under alternative decision rules. They also develop theories of behavior involving special interest, logrolling, and other activities often occurring through the public sector.

In his more recent book, *The Limits of Liberty,* Buchanan applies his individualistic perspective to explain the creation of property rights, law, and government. He closely examines some of the economic problems of the 1970s that might have arisen from public-sector action.

Buchanan, who won the 1986 Nobel Prize for Economics, has written widely on such topics as externalities, public finance, and public goods. He received his doctoral degree from the University of Chicago and taught at Florida State, the University of Virginia, and UCLA. He is currently the general director of the Center for the Study of Public Choice at Virginia Polytechnic Institute. His teachings have shaped the thinking of economists and graduate students for over two decades now, and many of his graduate students have gone on to become famous economists themselves.

public choices are efficient. Case-by-case analysis is needed to determine when government policies work.

25.15 VOTER PREFERENCES

Direct Voting

The basic voting problem is how to weigh the preferences of dissimilar individuals in arriving at a public choice. If voters disagree, as they nearly always do, how do we decide which side wins? This is a question that markets for private goods answer in an elegant way. If you like rock music and your friend likes classical music, the market gives each of you what you want. You pay for the items you desire, and you get them. Your friend is not affected. Your friend pays for the music he or she prefers and gets it. You are not affected. Each of you pays for and get only those things that you prefer.

This happy marriage between preferences and outcomes is impossible with public goods, however. If your friend wants high spending on national defense and you want a nuclear freeze and less defense spending, you cannot both have what you want at the same time. Society has to choose between your desires. Dictators make social choices in some lands, but voting is the way public choices are made in democracies.

Majority-rule voting is the most-used public choice tool. This mechanism weighs individual preferences and picks the option favored by 51 percent or more of the voters. This is a simple, inexpensive, and decisive way to make public choices. Majority-rule voting, however, is not a perfect public choice tool. For one thing, it fails to account for the intensity with which preferences are held. If 51 percent of the population is only marginally in favor of the president's policies, for example, while 49 percent are deeply opposed to them, the president wins because more people vote for him than against him. The depth of preferences counts less than the number of people who hold them under majority rule.

Voting Cycles

Majority rule votes have another flaw. The person who sets the voting **agenda**, the order of voting on related issues, often determines which issues win and which lose. Figure 25-3 presents an example that makes this problem clear.

Here is a simple public choice problem. Figure 25-3 shows a three-person society. The three individuals are called Bruce, Ernie, and Doug. They need to make a budget choice. They must decide how many resources go to a public good, such as defense, and how many to private goods, such as food and housing. Their options are shown as points on their economy's production possibilities frontier. The efficient combination is the one society most prefers and therefore the one, we hope, that wins when they vote.

The three voters' preferences for these combinations are shown in the accompanying table. Bruce prefers budget combination *A*, with many public goods and fewer private ones. His second choice is combination *B*, and his third choice is point *C*. He votes rationally, picking *A* over *B*, for example, *B* over *C*, and *A* over *C*. Ernie has different preferences; he picks *B* over *C*, *C* over *A*, and *B* over *A* (see the figure). Doug's preferences are different still. His voting order is *C*, *A*, *B*.

Which of the three options the majority favors depends on what order they vote on the budget choices. Suppose, for example, that Bruce sets the agenda and requires that the vote be taken between *B* and *C* first, with the winner tested against proposal *A*. Note carefully what happens here. Bruce and Ernie both favor *B* over *C*, so it wins the first vote, and Bruce and

> **25.16 AGENDA**
>
> **Agenda**
> The order in which issues are considered and votes taken.

FIGURE 25-3 **Majority-Rule Voting Problems.** Which point on the production possibilities frontier do these three voters prefer? The majority-rule choice depends on the order in which alternatives are considered.

Voter	First choice budget	Second choice budget	Third choice budget
Bruce	A	B	C
Ernie	B	C	A
Doug	C	A	B

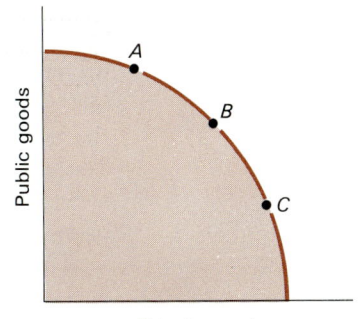

Doug both vote for *A* over *B*, so *A* wins the election. The result is that *A* is the majority-rule winner.

This conclusion changes, however, if we put Ernie in charge of the agenda, holding voter preferences constant. Ernie's agenda is to put *A* and *C* in the first election, with the winner tested against *B* (his first choice). Look at the table to see how this election comes out. Ernie and Doug both vote for *C* over *A* (*C* wins), but Bruce and Ernie both vote for *B* over *C* in the run-off. The result is that Ernie's choice *B* is the majority-rule winner.

Doug can swing the election result in his favor if he sets the agenda. Doug chooses to put *A* versus *B* in the primary election, and the winner against *C* in the run-off. The result is that *A* wins the first election (see the figure), but Doug's first choice *C* wins in the final.

Which choice is society's first choice (the efficient point — *A* or *B*)? Which choice is the people's choice? These voting cycles show that the public's preferences are not always the only thing that determines how an election comes out. Majority-rule votes work best when just two choices are available, which puts much power in the hands of the people who set the voting agenda. They can influence the vote in their favor, distorting government policies along the way. The theory of voting cycles was developed by Kenneth Arrow, the subject of one of this chapter's Prominent Economist features.

Distribution of Costs and Benefits

> **25.17 DISTRIBUTION OF GAINS AND LOSSES**

Public policies generate costs and benefits. Some groups stand to benefit greatly from the goods and services the government provides, while others stand to pay much of their costs. Rational voters choose to vote for policies that provide them with benefits that are at least as great as their individual costs. This leads to two public choice problems, however.

The first problem is that voters may be shortsighted; they may underestimate the benefits that government provides and so vote against needed public services. Many government services, such as police protection, are invisible. People are seldom aware of them when they work, they only see them when they fail. It is easy for people to undervalue these benefits and, implicitly, overvalue the tax dollars they pay as they cast ballots for issues and candidates. The invisibility of public goods may lead voters to choose too few government programs.

On the other hand, the uneven distribution of government's costs and benefits sometimes leads to special-interest legislation that overextends government's hand. This special-interest effect was discussed in earlier chapters. Many government policies, such as subsidies and tariff taxes on imports, have concentrated benefits and widely dispersed costs. Suppose, for example, that a tariff on imported pickup trucks is before Congress today. This bill provides high benefits to a relatively small number of domestic auto producers and their workers. Wages, jobs, and profits rise in the U.S. pickup truck industry if the tariff passes. The costs are even greater than the benefits, but they are spread over the whole population more evenly. The millions of people who buy imported trucks or who purchase goods and services from firms that use them stand to lose. Each of these individuals bears a small loss, however, compared to the intense gain on the other side.

The outcome of the vote on imported truck tariffs will be heavily influenced by the special-interest effect. Chances are the pro-tariff group will work hard to lobby Congress in favor of the tariff. Their high potential gains make it profitable for this special-interest group to spend millions to convince voters and their representatives of the need for tariffs. The people who stand to bear the burden of the tariff in the form of higher prices have little incentive to make their voices heard, however. The small individual benefit from defeating the tariff is less than the cost of fighting it. As a group, truck buyers would benefit from keeping tariffs off the products they buy. As individuals, however, they have no incentive to fight special interests. So bills that favor concentrated interests and impose burdens on widely dispersed groups tend to pass, even when they are not in the public interest.

District Lines and Voting

25.18 DISTRICT LINES AND CHOICE

Most public choices are made through representatives who are elected to represent the interests of their constituents. Sometimes representative voting works fine, but often it breaks down because of the way geographic lines are drawn for district elections.

Suppose you are electing representatives to a state convention to choose a new tax system. Fifty-five percent of the state's voters, those in rural areas, favor lower taxes, but 45 percent, those living in cities, want higher taxes. If the choice is made by a statewide general election, chances are that the low-tax group will win, since this view is held by a majority of voters. Suppose that district lines are carefully drawn, a process sometimes called gerrymandering, to combine city and rural districts in devious ways. One-third of the districts, for example, might be all rural and sure to vote for lower taxes. The remaining districts, however, might combine large city areas with smaller sections of rural land. Each of these districts has a 52 percent majority in favor of higher taxes.

The outcome of this election it determined by how the district maps are drawn. The few all-rural districts elect low-tax delegates, but the rest of the districts have a narrow high-tax majority, so they are likely to elect high-tax delegates. A large majority of the elected representatives might well favor higher taxes, while a majority of voters favor lower taxes. The district lines, not voter desires, determine the public choice in this example. Given this fact it is not surprising that republicans and democrats scramble every 10 years to redraw district lines in their favor.

The district line problem can be important. The U.S. president is elected not by popular ballot, but through a system of electoral votes, where each state is a district that must cast all of its ballots for one candidate or another. The division of voters in this way means that the candidate picked by the majority of voters need not win the presidential election. The popular winner, however, has also received the majority of electoral votes in all recent elections. If you were to leave the total number of votes for each candidate constant, for example, and change the way a few thousand votes were divided among the states, you could change the course of U.S. history. Nixon could have defeated Kennedy in 1960 if votes had been distributed differently among the states so that the electoral vote would have swung in his favor. By the same logic, Humphrey could have defeated Nixon in 1968 and Ford could have won against Carter in 1976 without changing the vote totals, only their interstate distribution need have changed.

Representative Voting Problems

25.19 VOTE TRADING AND LOGROLLING

Representative voting is not perfect even when district lines are wisely drawn. Representatives engage in vote trading and logrolling to gain extra votes for bills that benefit their districts, even when they are not in the best interest of the state or nation as a whole. Vote trading is easy to explain. One representative votes for another's questionable bill if the other representative will return the favor. That way both representatives get their bills and can show off at election time. Logrolling is just vote trading carried to an extreme. A group of representatives agrees to vote for a package of bills, each of which benefits a member's district.

The problem with vote trading and logrolling is that these practices sometimes generate inefficient public choices. Representatives who vote for three bills that are bad for their districts to get one "good" one through might get reelected. They might even be benefiting their districts, if the gains from the favorable bill exceed the costs of the three others. It is likely that society pays a higher price, however. The resources that go to these public uses might have been better used elsewhere in the economy.

Public versus Private Choice

> **25.20 PUBLIC CHOICE SHORTCOMINGS**

This discussion has concentrated on the problems of public choice to make a point. Government policies that, in theory, improve on the market are not always the ones that, in practice, are adopted by government officials. This does not mean that government is evil, a breeding ground of conspiracy and special interest. It means that public choices are not automatically efficient or better than private ones.

The moral of this story is that the case for government action is limited, even when monopoly, monopsony, externality, communal and public goods, and income distribution problems exist. Through the decade of the 1960s, public opinion in the United States appeared to shift toward the belief that government was a vehicle to right most of the wrongs of the economy. Many members of society began to feel that government was some sort of super individual more capable of dealing with social problems than were mere individuals. Many tasks were assigned to government that were simply beyond its ability to achieve. One of the most sobering realities to emerge from the study of public choice in the last 20 years has been the fact that government is in many cases a limited vehicle for social change. One of the most powerful messages of public choice economics has been the severely limited ability of government to act as a vehicle for registering preferences and enhancing the general welfare. Due to the rational-ignorance effect and the shortsightedness effect discussed in Chapter 5, as well as the shortcomings of public choice discussed in this chapter, we must continue to ask if the benefits of government action are worth their costs. We must also ask whether public choices are really better than self-interested private ones. These are the practical questions that economists, voters, and policymakers must ask when considering collective action in the future.

SUMMARY

> **25.1**

1. Markets are successful in the efficient allocation and distribution of resources when the assumptions of perfect competition prevail. Markets are inexpensive systems of exchange. However, previous chapters showed how markets fail when monopoly, oligopoly, monopsony, and unequal income distributions exist. Markets also fail to achieve efficiency when externalities, communal goods, or public goods exist.

25.2 ▶ 2. Externalities exist whenever decision makers fail to bear all of the costs or reap all of the benefits of their choices. Externalities are sometimes called spill-overs or neighborhood effects. External benefits exist when one person's actions provide benefits to individuals not party to the benefit-producing choice. Education is an example of an activity that generates external benefits.

25.2, 25.3 ▶ 3. External costs exist when one person's actions impose costs on individuals not party to the cost-producing choice. Pollution is an example of an activity that generates external costs.

25.4 ▶ 4. External costs lead to market failure because supply curves reflect private costs, which are less than the social costs of production. Private costs plus external costs equal social costs. Because supply does not reflect all production costs, markets for goods with external costs produce too much; that is, they produce more output than the efficient quantity.

25.5 ▶ 5. Direct regulation is one solution to the external cost problem. The EPA can force firms to limit effluent emissions, for example. Direct regulation is costly, however, and gives firms the incentive to get around pollution rules, not solve pollution problems. Sometimes direct regulations even increase pollution levels. Output taxes have been suggested by economist A.C. Pigou as a potential solution. Pigou would tax the output of polluting firms until their private costs, including taxes, equal the social costs. This plan would work in theory, but it might fail in practice because of problems involved in setting the correct tax rate. High-pollution and low-pollution firms would bear the same tax, giving firms little incentive to clean up their acts. Effluent taxes are another possible solution. Firms would be taxed based on the quantity of pollutants they emit. Low-pollution firms would have lower costs and possibly higher profits than would high-pollution firms. Competition would drive away pollution. Effluent tax rates might not be efficiently set, however. Furthermore, legislators distrust markets and competition as methods to solve pollution woes. Marketable pollution rights are a final possible solution. The EPA would issue pollution certificates, which polluting firms would purchase. Firms would have an incentive to pollute less in order to reduce the cost of purchased pollution rights. Pollution would take place only where its benefits exceeded its costs.

25.6, 25.7 ▶ 6. Education provides external benefits, meaning that private benefits—the market demand curve—are less than social benefits. Private benefits plus external benefits equals social benefits. Market demand that reflects only private benefits is too little when external benefits exist. The market provides less than the efficient amount of goods such as education.

25.8 ▶ 7. Subsidies, suggested by Pigou, are one way to solve external benefit problems. Subsidies reduce effective price, increase market demand, and move the market toward the efficient amount. College students receive a variety of subsidies on this basis. Free provision of goods with external benefits is one solution that is effective in the case of goods that consumers would demand too few of at any positive price. High school is provided "free" in most areas, for example. These goods are free in the sense that no price is charged; they are not free to society, however.

Mandatory consumption is a final policy. Primary and secondary schooling in the United States is not only free, laws require that students must attend. Without mandatory attendance laws, students would acquire too little education, robbing society of private and social benefits.

> 25.9

8. Externalities are the result of high transactions costs that keep individuals from exchanging and enforcing property rights. One solution to some externality problems is to lower transactions costs to encourage greater exchange of external cost and benefit rights.

> 25.10, 25.11

9. Communal goods are goods for which rivalry exists, but exclusion does not. Individuals cannot be excluded from a communal good, but each user leaves less for others to consume.

> 25.12

10. Individuals tend to overuse communal goods in the absence of government controls. Each individual receives the gain from his or her actions, but shares the cost of reduced resource availability with all others. Overuse soon occurs. Parks, beaches, highways, and fisheries are examples of communal goods.

> 25.13

11. Public goods are items, usually services, for which neither exclusion nor rivalry prevails. All people have access to public goods, but one person's consumption does not reduce the amount available for others. The services provided by national defense and lighthouses are two examples of public goods.

> 25.13, 25.14

12. Markets undersupply public goods because individuals have the incentive to be free riders, to let others buy, then gain costless benefits. Too little of the public good is produced and purchased without government help.

> 25.14

13. How much of a public good is enough? This is a difficult question to answer and one reason why public goods policies are controversial.

> 25.15

14. Private choices, made through markets, are imperfect when externalities, public goods, and communal goods exist. Are public choices, made by government through voting schemes, any better? In general, there is no guarantee that public choices are perfect either. Voting involves the problem of bringing together differing private preferences into one public policy. Majority-rule voting is the most-used public choice mechanism. One problem with majority-rule voting is that it does not take into account intensity of preferences, only the number of people who cast ballots for each issue.

> 25.16

15. Public choice through voting is different than private choices made through markets in a fundamental way. All must live with the public choice. Each individual chooses for himself or herself in market activities. Majority-rule voting is uncertain when there are more than two choices. Voting can cycle from one winner to another, depending on the order in which votes are taken. The person who sets the agenda, who decides the order of voting, influences the outcome of many votes.

> 25.17

16. Voters who weigh individual costs and benefits in casting ballots tend to underallocate resources to public services that provide invisible benefits, such as police protection. Special-interest groups, who receive concen-

trated benefits from laws, are more likely to make their preferences known than are the majority of people, who have little to gain or lose from a particular bill. The distribution of costs and benefits determines which groups make their views known.

25.18 > 17. The division of voters into districts also affects voting outcomes. The same voters, divided in different ways, can elect different "majority rule" representatives. The presidential elections of 1960, 1968, and 1976, for example, could all have had different winners under a different set of state district lines.

25.19 > 18. Representatives often engage in vote trading and logrolling to get laws that favor their districts through the legislature. Representatives agree to vote on one another's bills to form rolling majorities. Each traded vote may make sense for the individual representative and his or her district, but the grand total of bills passed is not necessarily efficient.

25.20 > 19. Public choice has many problems. There is no guarantee that public choices are perfect or even better than private choices in every case. Policymakers must ask whether private or public choices are best, and whether government gains are worth government's cost for each program considered.

DISCUSSION QUESTIONS

25.2, 25.6, 25.8 > 1. Many people give money, goods, and services to charities. These charitable contributions are encouraged by the government through subsidies built into the tax system. Use the tools of this chapter to explain why the government should be involved in charitable contributions.

25.2, 25.3, 25.5 > 2. Cigarette smoking generates external costs. What government policies are appropriate to deal with this problem? Why has government not stepped in to regulate cigarette smoking in all public places? Explain.

25.10, 25.11, 25.12 > 3. Most local governments in the United States use zoning laws to keep different land uses apart. Some areas of town can only be used for single-family houses, for example, while others can only be used for commercial properties. Use the tools and ideas of this chapter to explain why zoning is an appropriate government concern.

25.5 > 4. A college produces education, but the college's heating plant pollutes the air. What government policy best regulates this situation? Explain.

25.15, 25.16 > 5. List the advantages and disadvantages of majority rule voting. Is it a good way to make group choices? What other ways of making collective choices can you think of? Are they better or worse than majority rule? Explain.

25.15, 25.16, 25.17, 25.18, 25.20 > 6. Does the system of public choice in the United States produce too much government or too little? Explain.

SELECTED READINGS

Buchanan, James M. *The Demand and Supply of Public Goods*. Chicago: Rand McNally, 1969.

Coase, Ronald. "The Problem of Social Cost." Reprinted in Breit, William, and Hochman, Harold M. (eds.), *Readings in Microeconomics*, 2nd ed. New York: Holt, Rinehart and Winston, 1971, p. 484.

Hardin, Garrett. "The Tragedy of the Commons." *Science*, January 1968, pp. 86-89.

Kneese, Allen V., and Schultze, Charles. *Pollution, Prices, and Public Policy*. Washington, DC: Brookings Institution, 1975.

Samuelson, Paul A. "The Pure Theory of Public Goods." *Review of Economics and Statistics*, November 1954, pp. 387-389.

Schultze, Charles. *The Public Use of Private Interest*. Washington DC: Brookings Institution, 1976.

Veseth, Michael. *Public Finance*. Reston VA: Reston Publishing Company, 1983, chaps. 3 and 6.

CHAPTER 26

Energy Economics

Having read the chapter, reviewed the chapter summary, and completed the *Study Guide* exercises, you should be able to:

CRIS

26.1 ENERGY: Explain why energy is important to the economy, and list ways in which energy is used as a consumption and production good.

26.2 ENERGY SUPPLIES: List the three main energy supplies in the economy, and explain how these energy sources are similar.

26.3 ENERGY SUPPLY IN SHORT RUN: Explain why the supply of energy is inelastic in the short run, and discuss the role of capital equipment in energy production.

26.4 FINITE ENERGY RESOURCES: Explain how finite energy resources force a trade-off between present and future energy use, and discuss the factors producers must consider in deciding when to use a finite natural resource.

26.5 COMMUNAL ENERGY RESOURCES: Explain why producers are likely to deplete a communal energy resource too quickly.

26.6 ENERGY USES: List the three main uses of energy in the economy, and explain why energy is often inefficiently used.

26.7 ENERGY DEMAND IN SHORT RUN: Explain why the demand for energy is inelastic in the short run, and discuss the role of capital equipment in energy consumption.

26.8 ENERGY PRICE INCREASE: Explain why an increase in the price of one energy source (for example, oil) leads to higher prices of other energy sources (coal and natural gas.)

26.9 RISING ENERGY PRICES: List the four factors that helped produce the problem of rising energy prices, and explain how these factors affected energy demand and supply.

26.10 ENERGY PRICE CONTROLS: Explain why energy price controls result in increased dependence on foreign supplies of energy.

26.11 ENVIRONMENTAL REGULATIONS: Explain how environmental regulations add to the energy crisis.

26.12 OPEC: Explain what OPEC is and how it acts like a cartel, list and analyze the economic factors that led to OPEC's monopoly power, and then discuss the role of U.S. economic policies in OPEC's growth.

26.13 OIL IMPORT QUOTAS: Explain why quotas to limit oil imports in the short run resulted in greater reliance on oil imports in the long run.

26.14 ECONOMIC FORCES AGAINST OPEC: List and discuss the economic forces that have reduced OPEC's ability to raise price in the 1980s.

26.15 HIGHER ENERGY COSTS: List and discuss five important consequences of higher energy costs and explain who wins and who loses when energy prices rise.

26.16 INCREASING ENERGY SUPPLY: List and discuss three ways of increasing energy supply, and explain why each method of increasing supply means higher energy costs.

26.17 REDUCING ENERGY DEMAND: List and discuss four ways of reducing energy demand, and give the advantages and disadvantages of each.

26.18 ENERGY CONSERVATION POLICY: Explain why higher prices are a better energy conservation policy in the long run than in the short run.

26.19 HIGHER ENERGY VS. ENVIRONMENTAL QUALITY: Discuss the trade-off between higher energy supplies and environmental quality, and then discuss the problem of whether energy or environmental concerns should have priority.

26.1 ENERGY

Energy is the engine that drives the economy. Think of all the ways we use energy and how dependent we are on it. Take the book you are now reading as an example. Energy is a vital input in the process that results in your reading this book. It took energy to cut the trees, make the paper, produce the ink, set the type, print the pages, bind them together, and get the book to your local bookstore. You are probably reading indoors, using electric lamps to light this page, which is another use of energy. The authors composed these words on micro-computers, and stored the manuscript on magnetic diskettes, which is an energy-intensive way of writing.

Books are impossible without many energy inputs. Now think of how much energy goes into the other goods and services you use every day. Energy is the key to the production and consumption of most of the goods and services we desire. If there is no free lunch, as economists say, then there is no energy-free lunch, either.

Energy is costly, a fact that is somewhat hidden by the oil price cuts that began in 1986. We must give up large amounts of other goods and services to have higher energy supplies. This chapter examines the causes and consequences of high energy costs, and tries to analyze the energy problem through the eyes of economists. To do this, we look first at the economist's most powerful tools: energy supply and energy demand.

ENERGY SUPPLY: WHERE DOES ENERGY COME FROM?

People get energy from the most unlikely places. Many Americans heat their homes with wood stoves, thus burning trees to keep their dens cozy. Families in other countries burn cow dung for the same reason and with the same result. Wind farms in California and Oregon use huge windmills to generate power. Geothermal springs provide power in Iceland and in parts of Idaho. Solar power is also of growing importance. Raisin growers have always used the sun's energy to dry their fruit. Now homeowners are using the sun to heat water and keep inside temperatures high. Farmers in some areas get energy from agriculture waste, converting manure into energy-rich methane gas.

> **26.2 ENERGY SUPPLIES**

Energy is all around us in nature, but many energy forms are hard to use. Energy in the United States means primarily three commodities: oil, natural gas, and coal. We get almost half the energy we use from oil, much of which is imported. About half the remaining energy comes from natural gas, with energy from coal accounting for almost 20 percent of total energy supply. Hydroelectric and nuclear power are important in some parts of the country, but they supply little energy compared to oil, natural gas, and coal. Falling water produces about 4 percent of the economy's power, and nuclear power produces about 3 percent of the total.

> **26.3 ENERGY SUPPLY IN SHORT RUN**

Oil, natural gas, and coal are much different in their physical properties, but they share many important similarities. First, supplies of each are relatively inelastic in the short run. Huge investments in exploration, extraction machinery, and processing equipment are needed to make the energy in these commodities available. Energy is the most capital-intensive industry; it takes time to put new capital in place to expand production. In the short run, then, the maximum amount of energy available from a given source is not very responsive to changes in price. Higher energy prices give producers an incentive to increase quantity supplied, but greater output must wait for long-run changes.

Finite Resources: Allocating Energy Over Time

> **26.4 FINITE ENERGY RESOURCES**

A second important similarity among oil, natural gas, and coal is that they come from prehistoric deposits of plant life, and are changed into an accessible energy form by centuries of geologic pressures. Coal is obtained in the same way as diamonds; that is, by putting carbon-based matter under pressure for centuries. This means that oil, natural gas, and coal are **finite resources** in total supply. More new trees can eventually replace the ones burning in the fireplace, but it is impossible to reproduce coal or oil in the same way. Finite oil, gas, and coal supplies mean that the economy faces the difficult choices illustrated by Figure 26-1.

Finite Resources
Resources for which there is a limited supply and which are virtually impossible to reproduce in the future.

Figure 26-1 shows the production possibilities frontier for a finite natural resource such as coal. The economy begins at point A, where much of the coal resource remains undiscovered or unused. Once all coal is located,

718 Energy Economics

FIGURE 26-1   **Finite Natural Resource Choices.** Starting at *A*, with resources inefficiently used, in which direction should the economy go? If finite resources are saved for the future (*B*), less is available for today's needs. But using more now (*C*) bodes ill for the future.

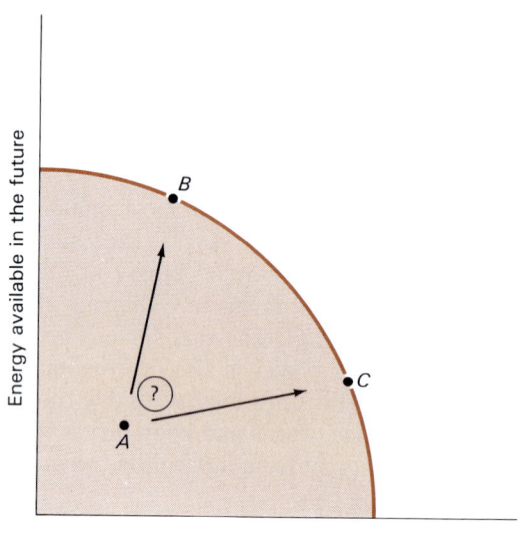

[Graph: quarter-circle production possibilities frontier with axes "Energy available in the future" (vertical) and "Energy available in the present" (horizontal). Point A inside with "?", point B on frontier upper-left, point C on frontier lower-right.]

however, the economy must make a choice: either to use most of the coal supply now, moving to a point like *C* on the production possibilities frontier, or to use less now and save more for the future, a point like *B* on the frontier.

This is an extremely difficult problem to resolve. On the demand side, there are many uses for coal in the present. Producing more coal-based energy could increase consumption and help build capital goods that generate economic growth. Producing now looks like a good idea. More current production, however, means less left over for future generations. They will have fewer raw materials with which to satisfy wants and desires at least as great as today's.

Supply adds to the problem. Production of coal, like that of other goods, displays diminishing marginal returns. As more coal is produced, marginal costs rise, so increasing quantities of other goods and services must be given up to get the extra coal (or oil or natural gas) needed. Producing more now therefore means higher costs and prices now and even higher costs and prices in the future. High production costs push prices up now, while diminished future supplies means higher prices later. This is especially true for society, since more expensive energy sources, like solar and nuclear power, must be used when demand exceeds the quantity of cheaper energy supplies available.

Picking the right allocation of a finite natural resource between the present and the future means weighing the value of using the resource today against the likely value of using it in the future, with rising marginal costs as added complication. Many finite natural resources in the United States are owned or produced by private firms. They decide how much to produce now versus how much to "save" in the earth for future generations by comparing the profits from current production with the probable price and cost of producing in later years. This is difficult because it is impossible to know for sure what future input costs or output prices will be. And this production is sometimes inefficient. Prices and costs in the real world do not always reflect opportunity costs, so private choices do not always achieve the social goal of the "optimal" long-run use of a finite natural resource.

The problem becomes still more difficult if more than one private producer has the right to extract coal or oil or another resource from the same field. Suppose that both you and a competitor have tapped the same underground oil pool. While you both might agree that it makes sense to slowly pump petroleum from the common pool, saving much of it for future production at higher future prices, each of you knows that every gallon the other firm gets is one less left for you.

26.5 COMMUNAL ENERGY RESOURCES

This is the problem of the communal resource discussed in Chapter 25. While society is best served by production a little at a time over the years, the two oil firms are more likely to pump the well dry quickly. Each produces more than is most profitable in the long run to keep the competition from getting it first in the short run. Society suffers in the long run as oil supplies run out and costs and prices soar. Government help is sometimes needed to keep communal supplies of finite natural resources from being too quickly used. The problem of how best to use finite natural resources over time in the real world remains among the most important problems in economics.

ENERGY DEMAND: WHERE DOES ENERGY GO?

26.6 ENERGY USES

Energy demand in the United States has three important parts: industrial use, residential-commercial use, and transportation. Industrial production and residential-commercial demand use almost ¾ of total energy supplies. Energy is a raw material in industry—it generates heat, makes welds, and fuels the productive processes that make steel, minerals, chemicals, electronics, and more. Energy is a source of lighting and environmental control for residential and commercial uses. We use power to see and to keep warm in the winter and cool in the summer. The remaining ¼ of total energy goes to transportation—powering cars, trucks, railroads, and airplanes.

Energy use is relatively inefficient. Lighting fixtures, furnaces, and mechanical engines extract relatively little of the energy in the resources they use. Much of the valuable energy does not get used. It just dissipates into the atmosphere as waste heat.

26.7 ENERGY DEMAND IN SHORT RUN

Energy uses, like energy supplies, require substantial capital investments. Look at your personal energy demand to see that this is true. Expensive wiring of your house and your city is required before you can use electricity. Then you must purchase costly electrical appliances, such as stoves, freezers, and television sets, to tap power potential. Furnaces and air conditioners are also expensive, and your investment in automobiles is high. With energy demand so tied to a fixed set of capital goods, users find it difficult to alter their energy use significantly in the short run, even when prices rise. Energy demand tends to be inelastic in the short run because industrial, commercial, and residential users are tied to fixed furnaces, auto designs, and production processes in the short run. Demand is more elastic in the long run, however, because consumers can switch to more energy efficient capital goods, such as high-mileage cars or heat pump furnaces.

DEMAND AND SUPPLY INTERDEPENDENCE

26.8 ENERGY PRICE INCREASE

Supply Interdependence
A change in the price of an energy source which creates a change in the price of some other energy source.

Both energy demand and supply are affected by the usual economic determinants: price, production cost, prices of substitutes and complements, and others you have already learned about in other chapters. The energy puzzle gets more complex, however, because energy demands and supplies are interrelated in complex ways. An example of **supply interdependence** is when the price of one energy source rises, for example oil in the 1970s, the prices of all other energy sources must also rise. The reasons for this are quite complex; however, here is a brief sketch of the process.

When oil prices rise, consumers try to switch over to other, less expensive energy sources, like natural gas and coal. Many cannot do this in the short run, however, because of the cost of investing in new equipment to use coal instead of oil. Others cannot do it at all because of government regulations. Coal is, after all, more likely to produce air pollution than oil. Still others cannot switch because of individual production processes. Some chemicals made from oil cannot easily be produced from coal or gas, for example. When those buyers who are able to do so switch from oil to coal or gas the demand for oil substitutes rises and, given inelastic short-run supplies of these resources, prices must rise, too. Higher oil prices push up coal and natural gas prices.

The story does not end here. Industries, stores, transportation firms, and residential consumers must all make investments in new capital goods to convert from oil to coal and gas. They buy new machines, furnaces, and production lines. The result is that the demand for capital goods, which require much energy in their production, also rises. It takes energy to make new capital goods, and to save energy. Demand for energy rises, thus pushing prices even higher.

Finally, one form of energy is often used as an input in the production of other forms. Coal mines, for example, use electricity produced from coal, oil, and gasoline-fueled machines and transportation to produce their goods and get them to market. When the price of oil goes up, the cost of producing coal also rises, further boosting its price. When oil shortages prevailed during the 1973–74 embargo, coal mines ran out of petroleum-based fuels and had to shut down briefly. No oil meant no coal. The prices of both energy sources increased even further.

The moral of this story is that, with the demands and supplies of major energy sources so inter-connected, changes in the price of one energy source quickly translate into higher prices for them all.

ROOTS OF THE ENERGY CRISIS

26.9 RISING ENERGY PRICES

Why did energy prices rise so high in the 1970s, leaving energy shortages and a future of even higher costs? This is a complicated issue, with many angles and aspects. No simple answer can capture all the problems and events that contribute to today's energy picture. Any survey of this problem, however, must focus on four factors that contributed to the high energy demand and lower energy supplies that constitute the energy crisis: economic growth, price controls, environmental regulations, energy and oil shocks.

Economic Growth High rates of economic growth and urbanization in the 1950s and 1960s, in the United States and around the world, increased the demand for energy products of all kinds. Economic growth is energy-intensive as more goods are produced and distributed to more consumers along increasingly complicated transportation links.

Households in the United States, that benefited from economic growth, invested their gains in goods and services that used much energy. They bought many private automobiles, which used more energy than public transportation such as buses and trains. They built roads and highways that also required a big energy investment. They bought single-family homes that often used more energy than multi-family apartment buildings. They took longer automobile trips, which burned more fuel. They bought more imported goods, with a corresponding increase in energy used in transportation. Economic growth is a desirable social goal, but the growth that took place in the 1950s and 1960s also boosted energy demand.

26.10 ENERGY PRICE CONTROLS

Energy Price Controls Energy prices stayed low in the 1950s and 1960s. Oil prices, for example, fell in real terms during this period. The phenomenon occurred despite rising energy demand because many energy prices were set by the government, not by the market. Price ceilings on oil and interstate sales of natural gas, for example, kept these prices below market equilibrium rates. Figure 26-2 shows the consequences of these price controls.

The equilibrium price of oil in this figure is at *A*, but the government-set ceiling price is below this equilibrium price. The low ceiling price has two effects in the short run. Producers limit energy production to point *B* on the supply curve at this price, since higher output is unprofitable. Much of the finite resource is best left in the ground and saved for the future. The quantity of energy demanded is at *C*. The shortage of oil—the difference between high quantity demanded and lower quantity supplied—is met by imports from foreign suppliers, often at prices above the domestic ceiling price.

FIGURE 26-2

Energy Price Controls. Point *A* is the market equilibrium. Energy price controls push prices below equilibrium. Producers supply quantity *B* while consumers demand amount *C*. The difference between *B* and *C* must be imported from abroad.

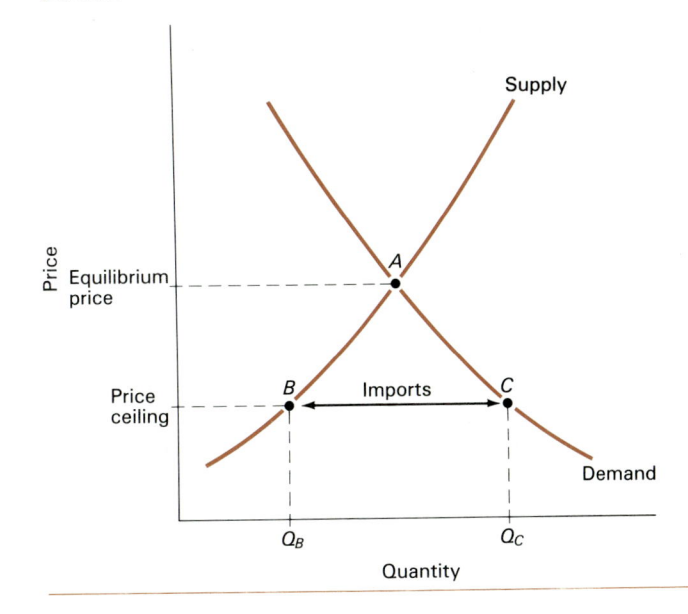

The domestic shortage, and the need to import to fill the gap, grows even larger in the long run. Low energy prices discourage exploration for and production of new energy sources on the supply side. Demand for energy grows, however, because it pays to substitute cheap energy for more expensive resources in production and heating. The energy shortage, and the need to import from abroad, gets bigger in the long run.

> **KEY CONCEPT 26.10** Price Controls which hold energy prices below their natural equilibrium levels tend to increase consumption and reduce production of energy thereby aggravating an energy shortage.

26.11 ENVIRONMENTAL REGULATIONS

Environmental Regulations Environmental regulations during this period affected energy demand and supply in a variety of ways. Firms that had to reduce pollution switched from cheap high-sulphur coal to more expensive substitutes. Firms had to invest in new plants and equipment to reduce pollution, but these machines were energy-intensive themselves, adding to demand. Environmental rules made it harder to search for and exploit new energy sources. Auto pollution laws forced manufacturers to sacrifice high mileage for low emissions, which further increased energy demand.

26.12 OPEC

Oil Shocks
Large increases in the price of oil which greatly affect the oil-using economies of the world because of the short term inelastic demand for the product.

Oil Shocks A group of oil exporting nations, lead by Venezuela and Saudi Arabia, formed the Organization of Petroleum Exporting Countries (OPEC) in 1960. OPEC today does not include all oil exporters. Mexico is a non-member, for example. Still, OPEC controls much of the world's crude oil supply. OPEC's influence increased during the 1960s, as the governments of mid-east oil countries slowly gained control over oil production within their borders.

OPEC's power became clear in 1973. A war between Israel and Egypt prompted the Arab members of OPEC to embargo sales to Israel's supporters, the United States, in particular. Imported oil still came to this country, but short-term shortages appeared and oil prices increased dramatically. Gasoline prices doubled overnight, from 30 cents to 60 cents per gallon, as crude oil prices jumped from about $2 per barrel to about $12 per barrel.

OPEC used its near-monopoly power to set international oil prices again and again in the 1970s. Oil costs rose from $12 per barrel in 1973–74 to over $35 per barrel in the early 1980s. Gasoline prices in the United States peaked at over $1.50 per gallon during this period. Oil prices softened during the recession years of the early 1980s, however, as falling world production led to falling energy demand.

A second oil supply shock hit the United States in 1979–80. A revolution swept the Shah of Iran from the throne and replaced him with anti-American leaders. Iranian protestors kidnapped American diplomats and held them hostage for more than a year. The U.S. government responded to the hostage crisis by freezing millions of dollars of Iranian funds in the United States. Iran, the second largest oil exporter after Saudi Arabia, implemented an embargo of oil sales to America. Lines at gas stations lengthened for the second time in the decade, and oil prices pushed higher.

A SHORT HISTORY OF OPEC

In the 1950s, oil from Middle East fields was controlled by big international oil firms, who paid host governments a relatively low royalty, based on the low prices that were current at that time. Oil-producing countries did not get rich from their oil production during this period. OPEC was formed in 1960 to try to reverse this situation. The Organization of Petroleum Exporting Countries is an example of a cartel, as discussed in Chapter 20. OPEC is an attempt by major oil-producing nations to increase economic profits by exercising monopoly power. OPEC members restrict output to get higher profit-maximizing prices.

26.13 OIL IMPORT QUOTAS

OPEC did not gain economic power immediately. Economists think that unwise economic policies in the United States gave OPEC its eventual advantage. U.S. oil producers, afraid of cheap imports from the Middle East and elsewhere, lobbied for oil import quotas in the 1960s. Oil imports fell temporarily, but higher U.S. production drained the most easily obtainable oil supplies here, leaving lower supplies for future years. Oil reserves were low by the 1970s, and additional supplies had high marginal cost. Oil imports increased as the combination of falling domestic supply, price controls, and rising demand created an increasing production shortfall. The United States, once an oil exporter itself, imported nearly half its oil by the early 1970s.

Supply-demand conditions were ripe for OPEC price increases by the 1970s and other market changes had paved the way, too. OPEC governments gained control of oil reserves from the international oil companies by nationalizing the oil fields and production facilities within their borders. These governments could now regulate production levels directly. They controlled prices through a system of production taxes that were passed along to oil buyers as higher prices. Most of the price of a barrel of oil now consists of taxes collected by the producing country.

With greater control of supply and large and inelastic (in the short term) demand, OPEC was in an ideal position to follow cartel strategy. In 1973 OPEC raised price, cut production, and earned higher profits. Oil prices increased by 600 percent initially. Higher OPEC oil prices were announced at least once a year during the 1970s. Oil that cost $2 per barrel at the start of the decade cost over $30 by its end. Given oil's importance to the economy, and the relationship between oil prices and the cost of other energy resources, these were revolutionary price increases. World-wide inflation took off and world-wide unemployment lines lengthened. A net transfer of income from the world's rich and poor nations to OPEC members took place.

In the United States and other importing countries, governments tried to reduce imports with production incentives and conservation programs. Demand and supply were both inelastic in the short run, however, so these programs had little effect on oil prices or import levels.

26.14 ECONOMIC FORCES AGAINST OPEC

OPEC in the 1980s

OPEC still influences world oil prices, but its power has declined in the 1980s. OPEC's short-run profits provided the world economy with incentives that mean lower oil revenues in the long run.

Oil demand and supply in non-OPEC countries is inelastic in the short run, but more elastic in the long run. Producers and consumers in the

United States and other developed nations have adjusted to higher oil prices in the years since the first OPEC price increases. Gas-stingy cars, better building insulation, and more energy-efficient production techniques have all reduced energy demand. North Sea and Alaskan oil discoveries, among others, have reduced dependence on OPEC supplies. Market conditions no longer allow OPEC to set its own price.

Non-OPEC oil producers, such as Great Britain and Mexico, are more important today. Raising price is not nearly as good a strategy for OPEC now. Higher prices will now benefit other groups as much as OPEC. These outside producers stand ready to sell for less if OPEC raises price too high. OPEC's power falls as it comes to control a smaller proportion of the world's oil reserves.

World-wide recession has cut oil demand at the same time that OPEC's control of supply has decreased. Closed factories do not need oil or oil-based chemicals, for example. Unemployed workers do not drive as much or take long oil-consuming vacations. Lower world income and lower world oil demand mean lower prices. OPEC even cut prices in the early 1980s, to preserve its market.

Finally, OPEC members realize that their oil wealth is not unlimited. Oil exporting countries must carefully make today's production and pricing decisions with an eye toward the future, since finite oil reserves must be made to produce income far into the future. High production and lower prices now mean less left to sell in future years. High prices and lower output today, however, give buyers incentives to shift away from oil consumption, reducing demand and price in the future. OPEC's leaders, and oil producers everywhere, must take both present and future demand and supply forces into account in plotting their course. Already the oil world is changing for them. OPEC, once a net recipient of petrodollars, now borrows on world credit markets. OPEC's spending on economic development programs exceeds current oil revenues.

These many forces came to a head in 1986, with the result being a dramatic fall in the prices of oil, petroleum products, and related goods. Oil prices fell from about $25 per barrel to less than $15 in a matter of weeks in early 1986. This price collapse was due in part to a collapse — at least temporarily — in OPEC's output limitations.

Saudi Arabia is the largest OPEC oil producer. As world oil demand fell and non-OPEC supplies increased (from Mexico and the North Sea holdings of Great Britain and Norway in particular), Saudi Arabia found itself the "swing producer" in OPEC, varying its own output to offset production swings by other nations. The Saudis were forced to cut back their production dramatically to hold prices up in the face of falling demand and rising non-cartel supply. Essentially, Saudi Arabia was bearing all the burden of keeping oil prices up while other OPEC countries and non-OPEC producers such as Mexico and Great Britain reaped the benefits of the Saudi sacrifice.

Finally, in 1986, the Saudis decided the burden of maintaining oil prices was too great. Saudi Arabia began to increase production dramatically to regain its share of the world market. The Saudis could do this profitably because their oil has relatively low marginal cost compared to North Sea and Mexican petroleum sources. The sudden increase in oil supply drove down oil prices. This was good news for oil-consuming countries such as the United States. Inflation rates and interest rates fell. Oil-producing nations such as Mexico and Great Britain found that production revenues were lower, creating budget problems for them.

IS THE ENERGY CRISIS OVER?

Do today's lower oil prices mean that the energy crisis is over? No. There are several reasons to be concerned about energy costs. First, the decrease in oil prices may not be permanent. Future OPEC or Saudi actions could force oil prices back up in coming years, although most experts do not forsee prices rising to their early-1980s' peak of $36 per barrel.

Second, it is important to remember that oil is just one source of energy, albeit a very important one. Increasing oil supplies and lower oil prices may reduce the demand for more expensive energy sources such as nuclear power in the short run, but rising energy costs in the long run are a fact of life that cannot be ignored. The marginal cost of increased energy production is relatively high, and OPEC price cuts can only postpone, not prevent, eventual higher energy costs.

Finally, lower energy prices today may serve to increase energy consumption in the future, which could make oil-consuming nations even more vulnerable to energy cartels in the future. Indeed, many experts think that the 1986 Saudi price cuts were intended to force out non-OPEC producers and encourage consuming nations to go on an energy binge, increasing long-run demand. Today's lower oil prices may therefore contain the seeds of future dramatic price increases.

The moral of this story is that lower short-term oil prices do not mean that there is no energy problem. We must still be concerned about long-run trends in energy production and consumption. With this in mind, let us explore the policies that can be used to deal with the potential long-run problems of high opportunity-cost energy.

THE CONSEQUENCES OF HIGHER ENERGY COSTS

> **26.15 HIGHER ENERGY COSTS**

The higher energy costs of the 1970s and early 1980s had a variety of economic effects that we may experience again in the future. Rising costs cause substitution effects, alter output prices, reduce economic growth, and redistribute income. Let's examine each economic effect briefly.

Energy Substitution Effects
The move away from items or processes that use large amounts of energy to those that use smaller amounts of energy.

Substitution Effects Higher energy costs alter incentives for producers and consumers. Both groups are driven to substitute items that use little energy for those that are more energy-intensive. These **energy substitution effects** bring many changes.

The big, heavy, powerful, low-mileage American cars of the 1950s have been largely replaced by smaller, lighter, more gas-efficient models. This substitution has meant higher sales of imported Japanese cars and higher unemployment in the U.S. auto industry. Japanese cars were thought to be more fuel efficient and of higher quality than American products. The prices of big cars fell and little-car prices increased when people who could afford to switched to smaller models. Many low-income families found the only cars they could afford to buy were big used Buicks and Cadillacs, which consumed large quantities of high priced premium fuel, adding to the families' poverty woes.

Substitution effects alter jobs and lifestyles. More people substitute public transportation for a car, use insulation to bring down high oil bills, and live closer to work to avoid high commuting costs.

ECONOMIC ISSUES

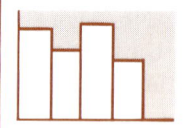

THE ECONOMIC EFFECTS OF LOWER OIL PRICES IN 1986

The lower oil prices of 1986 had effects like those just described, but in the opposite direction. Lower oil prices cause substitution and output effects, for example. Sales of larger and more powerful cars increased as gasoline prices fell. Oil-fired furnaces began to replace the now-more-costly coal facilities in some areas. Lower fuel prices stimulated production of many items. Inflation fell in the United States, and economic growth was encouraged, at least temporarily. Income was redistributed as well, away from those in the oil production industries and toward those who purchased oil and oil products.

One lesson that we learned in 1986 was that falling oil prices could be as troublesome as rising prices, but in different ways. Several states, such as Texas, Oklahoma, and Alaska, depend on oil revenues to finance public services. As oil prices fell, these states found their budgets out of balance and they were forced to severely cut back in important areas such as education. Oil consumers sometimes found their tax bills increased to make up for falling oil revenues.

Falling oil prices also had some negative indirect effects that became apparent in 1986. Many U.S. banks had made loans to oil-producing countries who were less able to repay their debts after oil price declines. Some U.S. banks therefore found themselves weakened because lower oil prices made prior loans less secure.

Finally, some countries found that they were at least temporarily worse off as oil prices fell due to the policies that they had previously enacted to deal with rising oil costs. Brazil, for example, had been a major oil-import nation in the 1970s and suffered large losses when oil prices declined. Brazil adopted policies designed to reduce oil imports, largely by producing alcohol from plant matter. This "gasahol" was costly, but it made sense to use it so long as oil prices were above $25 per barrel. As oil prices fell in 1986, however, Brazil's huge investment in gasahol production facilities no longer made economic sense. Brazil found itself saddled with large debts (from loans used to build the gasahol facilities) and high production costs. Ironically, lower oil prices in 1986 made Brazil worse off in the short run, just as higher energy costs a decade before had also made the country worse off.

Output Effects When input costs rise, the firm's profit-maximizing output tends to fall. Higher costs mean lower profits and, all else being equal, less output, too. Firms cut back production to keep profits from falling as higher costs make previous production levels unprofitable. Higher energy prices are one reason for the higher unemployment levels of the 1970s and 1980s. Employment increased, however, when OPEC reduced prices in the face of world-wide recession in the early 1980s.

Price Effects Lower supply means higher prices. When price rises in many markets, the consequence is inflation. At least a portion of the high inflation rates of the 1970s can be attributed to energy-related cost increases. While other economic factors played major roles in this inflationary period, energy price increases were certainly a contributing factor. Less output and higher prices mean that workers have less real income. This was an economic fact of life in the 1970s that may continue to be important in the 1980s.

Economic Growth Higher energy prices reduce the chances for economic growth in a variety of ways. Capital goods, such as machines and factories, generate economic growth. These goods increase in relative price when energy prices go up because they are energy-intensive to produce. Higher energy prices therefore mean more costly capital and less investment for the future. Households that suffer from falling real income are less likely to save and invest for future needs when today's living standard is declining. This reduces the pool of funds available to finance capital expenditures. People, governments, and nations borrow more to pay today's energy bills, further diminishing credit available for investment. Government is also an energy consumer that can become involved in the **crowding-out effect:** higher energy costs "crowd out" investments in education and research that fuel economic growth. All these actions add up to less investment in the future because of the higher energy costs of living today.

Crowding-Out Effect
A situation where investments in growth for the future are curtailed or crowded out because of current high energy costs.

Redistribution of Income Higher energy prices both reduce the size of the economic pie and cut its slices in different ways. High energy costs alter the distribution of income in many ways. The most apparent redistribution during the 1970s was the net transfer of billions of dollars from the industrial countries to OPEC member states. Other transfers also took place. Some private energy suppliers received increased income. Exxon, a major oil company, is frequently named as the most profitable company in the world.

With the energy prices high, activities that produce more power have high value marginal product and so earn high returns. Many construction workers collected thousands of dollars each month for their work on the Alaska Pipeline, for example. Their efforts were worth high wages because they helped bring to market highly-valued Alaskan oil.

If some get richer in a shrinking world, others must get poorer. Workers in energy-intensive auto and steel factories in the North lost out. They experienced high unemployment. Gas station employees were also laid off. The economic effects of higher energy prices rippled through the economy, shifting prices and incomes and altering wages and interest rates. No one escapes the magnetic pull of higher energy costs.

ENERGY SOLUTIONS: INCREASING SUPPLY

26.16 INCREASING ENERGY SUPPLY

The long-run problem of rising energy costs can be approached using basic economic analysis. Simple supply and demand analysis suggests three possible solutions: increase supply, reduce demand, or impose a price ceiling below the equilibrium price. We have already seen that the price ceiling is not a long-run solution. Figure 26-2 shows that price controls encourage demand, discourage supply, increase imports, and make energy problems even worse in the future. Assuming price controls are not the answer to today's problems, we can still take several steps to increase energy supplies including new energy sources, new technology, and subsidized production of energy.

New Energy Sources The supply of energy is inelastic in the short run. It is impossible suddenly to double a nation's production of oil or coal, for example. Solutions to higher energy prices must, therefore, come in the long run. One way to increase energy supplies is to find new sources of oil, natural gas, and coal. Firms now explore areas where energy resources are known to hide, but where high production costs had made extraction unprofitable before.

Energy may be plentiful in the world in an absolute sense, but only highly concentrated forms of energy, such as oil and coal, are profitable to produce and use when energy prices are low. As price rises, more expensive energy sources become efficient. Nuclear power is expensive, for example, but it becomes competitive when rising oil prices make electricity generated in other ways more costly. New energy sources can increase the amount of energy supplied, but not without a corresponding increase in price.

New Technology New technologies can increase the supply of energy from existing sources. **Dry wells** can now be made to produce oil again, but at a cost. Steam is injected into oil wells to force heavy residual oils to the surface. This expensive process is only worthwhile if oil earns a high enough price.

Some energy is free. Wind, sun, and surf are nature's gifts. These energy sources have always existed, but it will take advanced technology to make these resources useful at a cost we can afford.

Subsidized Production A third solution is to subsidize production of energy. This would increase energy supply while reducing the prices consumers pay. President Carter proposed subsidies for production of energy from oil shale. The logic of this policy is to subsidize costs in early stages of production and hope that economies of scale will eventually bring prices down. Subsidies in the short run would make possible larger long-run energy supplies at lower cost. The short-run story, however, is the same as in the first two cases: more energy means greater cost through higher prices for new energy sources through new technology, or through higher taxes, to pay subsidy bills.

The message is that, while many energy supplies are finite in total supply, energy is still abundant if price rises high enough to make production profitable. If it takes higher price to increase energy supplies, perhaps the solution to the high energy prices lies in reducing demand.

ENERGY SOLUTIONS: LOWER ENERGY DEMAND

Dry Wells
The injection of steam into oil wells to force heavy residual oils to the surface.

26.17 REDUCING ENERGY DEMAND

Any major change in energy demand must take place over time. The economy's ability to reduce energy consumption in the short run is severely limited. Higher prices, laws and regulations, subsidies and rationing are four policies that reduce the amount of energy demanded, and are discussed below.

Higher Prices The paradox is that one way to reduce energy's price in the long run is to increase its price in the short run. Since energy-use decisions involve high capital use, higher prices today induce producers and consumers to adopt energy-saving ways in the long run. If high oil prices cause a factory to install an energy-saving boiler now, for example, the firm will keep the new equipment — keeping demand low — even if oil prices fall in later years. High prices now reduce demand and price in the long run.

Some prices can be raised right now to reflect today's high energy costs. Electric rates, for example, are set by public regulatory agencies in most areas. These regulated prices are often set with an eye toward fairness and the problems of the poor. There is, however, less concern about what price message consumers and producers are sent. Electricity that costs 10 cents to produce on the margin is sometimes sold for half as much. There is little incentive to adopt energy-saving technology here. Utility prices that reflect energy's high marginal costs would go a long way toward encouraging conservation and reducing the quantity of energy demanded.

Proponents of free market solutions to high energy demand suggest that energy markets be deregulated. They want to let prices rise to market levels. Some even propose that additional taxes be imposed on energy to further increase price and encourage conservation. Some economists want to put high taxes on gasoline and imported oil to reduce OPEC's ability to raise price, a different but related goal.

KEY CONCEPT 26.18 — Higher energy prices in the short run tend to reduce energy demand in the long run by giving producers and consumers the incentive to purchase energy-saving capital goods.

Laws and Regulations Government regulates many private activities. Many of these regulations in turn affect energy use. Building codes in most areas set the rules by which construction takes place. Building codes that mandate deep insulation, storm windows, and fuel-efficient heating devices force consumers to save energy. These rules, however, cut both ways. They also make new construction more expensive, so fewer energy-efficient new homes are sold, and some potential buyers continue to live in energy-wasting older homes.

Federal laws now require American auto manufacturers to meet minimum fuel-efficiency requirements, another example of energy regulations at work. Auto makers must pay a fine if the average fuel consumption of their cars, weighted by sales, exceeds the federal limit. Detroit's cars now get higher mileage than they did a few years ago, but it is not clear whether this is because of the force of regulations or consumer demand for gas-stretching cars. In any case, auto firms found it more profitable to pay fines in 1983 than to cut back sales of big cars, when falling gasoline prices made demand for larger models surge.

Subsidies
Grants of public money which are designed to induce consumers and producers to convert to energy-saving equipment.

Subsidies Subsidies are a third way to reduce energy demand. The government can encourage producers and consumers to reduce energy demand by paying part of the cost of investment in new equipment. Some of these subsidies are paid directly to consumers. Homeowners in Washington and Oregon, for example, found that a federal agency would pay half the cost, or more, of insulating their house in 1982. Free water-heater wraps were distributed as an incentive to reduce energy waste.

The tax system provides another way to pay energy subsidies. Firms get a tax break on new investment, encouraging them to update technology and save energy. Homeowners get a tax credit when they insulate their houses or buy certain other energy-related goods.

Subsidies are another example of the pay now-save later problem. Subsidies that induce producers and consumers to convert to energy-saving equipment reduce energy demand in the long run. That, all else being equal, means lower prices. Of course, someone must pay for subsidies in the short run, so higher costs today are not avoided. The difference is in who bears the higher short-run costs: energy users or taxpayers.

Rationing A final way to reduce energy demand is to use government controls to ration energy supplies. Gasoline and other items were rationed during World War II and the Korean War. Some states rationed gasoline during the oil embargoes of the 1980s through even-odd day gas sales. The federal government even prepared gas coupons, in case rationing became necessary in the gas-short days of the 1970s. Rationing is seen as an emergency action, not one likely to be adopted during normal times. Rationing is expensive, inefficient, and prone to illegal sales through black markets. Governments through the centuries have found it difficult to ration goods with coupons as efficiently as markets ration goods with price.

Some government price controls indirectly ration energy, however. Price controls on interstate sales of natural gas, for example, encouraged Texas producers to sell their gas within the state at prices above the federal ceiling. This left a smaller amount of natural gas for consumers in other states who were forced to buy from Canadian suppliers at higher prices. The price ceiling indirectly allocated scarce U.S. supplies to consumers in states that produced this product, leaving less for consumers in other states.

ENERGY POLICY: PRICES OR GOVERNMENT RULES?

26.18 ENERGY CONSERVATION POLICY

An important issue in energy policy is whether producers and consumers are best motivated by higher prices or by government regulations and subsidies. Many people favor government controls because they discount price effects. They say, for example, that they will keep their thermostats set at 75 degrees, no matter how much oil costs, because they want to be warm in the winter. Rules, regulations, and subsidies are the only way to change energy use in the United States, they suggest. Economists disagree with this view because they think that rational people are more likely to react to the incentive of high energy costs than to government gimmicks.

One reason for the difference of opinion is probably that the two groups are looking at different time periods. Higher prices have little effect on energy use in the short run because of the large expenditures necessary to alter energy use. Long-run changes are more likely, however. Government energy programs can have greater short-run effects than higher prices, but may be less effective in the long run. The choice between prices and regulations is, perhaps, a choice between the incentives of **decentralized markets** and **centralized control,** and between short-run and long-run effectiveness.

Decentralized Markets
Markets which are not controlled by a centralized regulatory authority.

Centralized Control
Control which is concentrated in the hands of a single authority.

ENERGY VERSUS THE ENVIRONMENT

"O Mother won't you take us down to
Mullenberg County? Down by the Green
River where we used to play?
"I'm sorry my darling but you're too
late in asking. Mr. Peabody's coal trains
have hauled it away."

26.19 HIGHER ENERGY VS. ENVIRONMENTAL QUALITY

This traditional song of the Appalachians illustrates an uncomfortable trade-off of our high-energy days. More and cheaper energy often comes at the cost of reduced environmental quality. High sulphur coal is less expensive than other types that pollute less. If industry uses more of the cheaper coal it will release more ash into the atmosphere. It is also cheaper to strip mine coal than to extract it in ways that does less damage to the environment. Which process we use will greatly affect the environment we enjoy. There is much coal and oil on federal land, in national forests, and in national parks. Should we disturb the shrinking wilderness to get more oil?

If off-shore oil is discovered, are oil spills that kill sea life, pollute beaches, and destroy valuable shellfish beds worth the price?

The trade-off between energy and economic growth on the one hand and environmental quality on the other is a fundamental tension of modern life. Government has traditionally stepped in on the side of wilderness, clean air, and environmental quality. Economists can make a case for this bias in government policy, since the environment is a communal good supplying external benefits. Too much pollution, too little park land, and insufficient environmental quality would probably result from unregulated markets. Society should preserve its inheritance, at least up to a point.

The problem is finding the point where an extra megawatt of electricity has greater long-run value to society than an extra moose or acre of wilderness, and weighing dirty air against jobs and income. As energy prices continue to rise and environmental quality deteriorates, the critical point on the production possibilities frontier between energy and environment will shift. Which way we will go and whether we will make the right choices will be influenced by both economic and political forces.

Having read this discussion, you should now realize that the energy crisis is more than long gas lines and more, even, than high energy costs. The energy crisis is really a set of fundamental economic trade-offs: economy versus environment, fairness versus efficiency, private incentives versus government control, and present versus future costs and benefits. Each of these choices is difficult in itself, and energy problems ask us to weigh them all at once. Policymakers, as they make energy choices, must take all these factors into consideration.

SUMMARY

26.1
1. Energy is the engine that drives the economy. Energy is used as a raw material in production, in the transportation and distribution of finished and intermediate goods, and for space-heating.

26.2
2. Energy comes from many sources but the most important energy sources are oil (about 47 percent of total energy supply), natural gas (27 percent), and coal (19 percent). Hydroelectric and nuclear power supply a total of 7 percent of total energy.

26.3
3. Energy supply is inelastic in the short run because large capital investments are required for energy use. These investments cannot easily be changed in the short run.

26.4
4. Energy supply decisions are complicated because of the trade-off over time that applies to finite natural resources such as oil, coal, and natural gas. More production now means less output in the future. Producers must weigh present and future costs and prices in deciding how much to produce and when to produce it. These are difficult and uncertain choices.

26.5
5. Some resources are used up too quickly because they are communal goods. Two producers who have tapped the same oil pool are each induced to produce too quickly to prevent the other from getting potential profits.

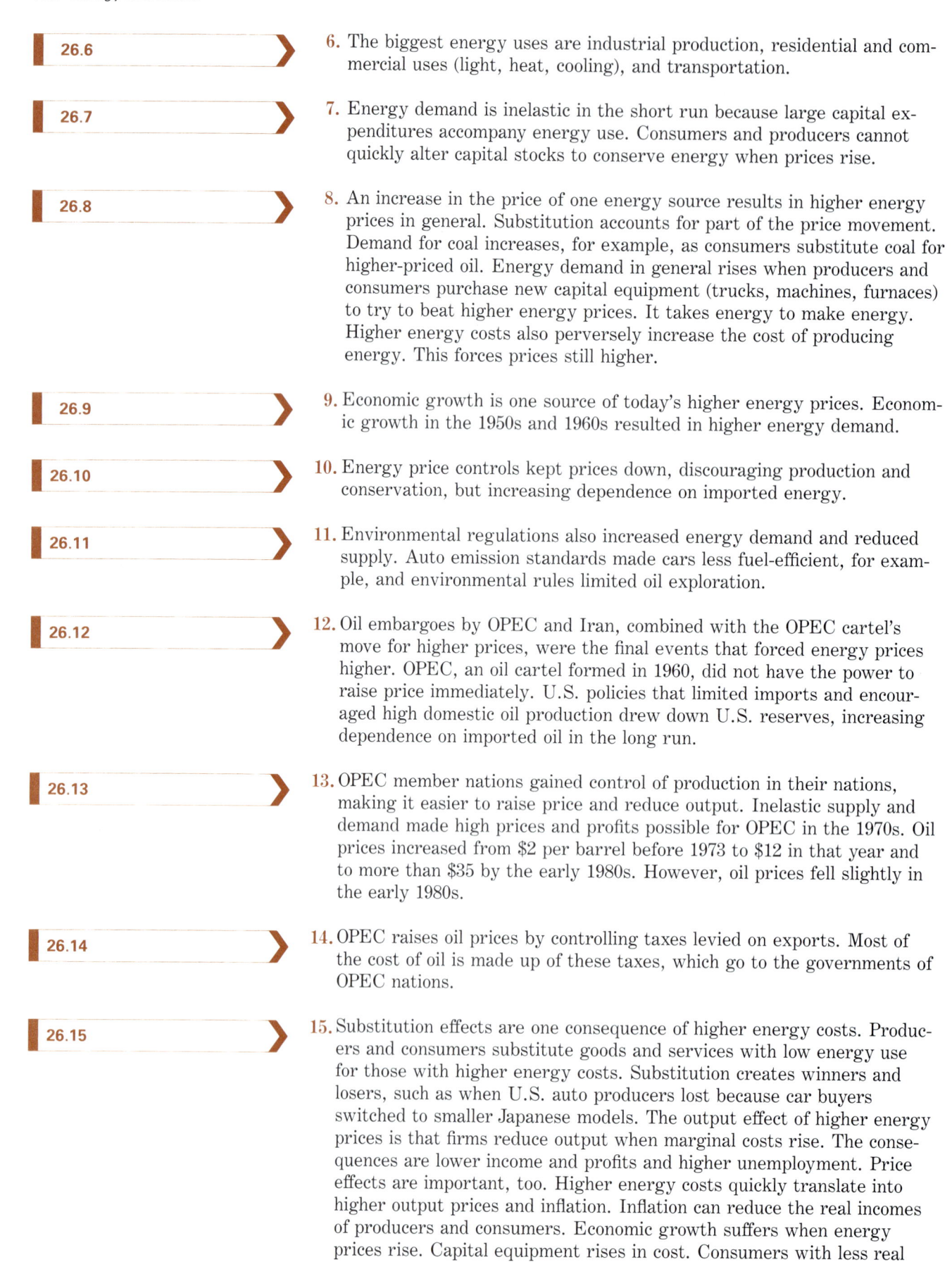

6. The biggest energy uses are industrial production, residential and commercial uses (light, heat, cooling), and transportation.

7. Energy demand is inelastic in the short run because large capital expenditures accompany energy use. Consumers and producers cannot quickly alter capital stocks to conserve energy when prices rise.

8. An increase in the price of one energy source results in higher energy prices in general. Substitution accounts for part of the price movement. Demand for coal increases, for example, as consumers substitute coal for higher-priced oil. Energy demand in general rises when producers and consumers purchase new capital equipment (trucks, machines, furnaces) to try to beat higher energy prices. It takes energy to make energy. Higher energy costs also perversely increase the cost of producing energy. This forces prices still higher.

9. Economic growth is one source of today's higher energy prices. Economic growth in the 1950s and 1960s resulted in higher energy demand.

10. Energy price controls kept prices down, discouraging production and conservation, but increasing dependence on imported energy.

11. Environmental regulations also increased energy demand and reduced supply. Auto emission standards made cars less fuel-efficient, for example, and environmental rules limited oil exploration.

12. Oil embargoes by OPEC and Iran, combined with the OPEC cartel's move for higher prices, were the final events that forced energy prices higher. OPEC, an oil cartel formed in 1960, did not have the power to raise price immediately. U.S. policies that limited imports and encouraged high domestic oil production drew down U.S. reserves, increasing dependence on imported oil in the long run.

13. OPEC member nations gained control of production in their nations, making it easier to raise price and reduce output. Inelastic supply and demand made high prices and profits possible for OPEC in the 1970s. Oil prices increased from $2 per barrel before 1973 to $12 in that year and to more than $35 by the early 1980s. However, oil prices fell slightly in the early 1980s.

14. OPEC raises oil prices by controlling taxes levied on exports. Most of the cost of oil is made up of these taxes, which go to the governments of OPEC nations.

15. Substitution effects are one consequence of higher energy costs. Producers and consumers substitute goods and services with low energy use for those with higher energy costs. Substitution creates winners and losers, such as when U.S. auto producers lost because car buyers switched to smaller Japanese models. The output effect of higher energy prices is that firms reduce output when marginal costs rise. The consequences are lower income and profits and higher unemployment. Price effects are important, too. Higher energy costs quickly translate into higher output prices and inflation. Inflation can reduce the real incomes of producers and consumers. Economic growth suffers when energy prices rise. Capital equipment rises in cost. Consumers with less real

income save less and borrow more. Fewer funds remain to finance the investment that leads to economic growth. Income redistribution results from higher energy prices. Income flows from oil consumers to oil producers. Changes in relative prices also create other winners and losers.

26.16 ▶ 16. New energy sources are one way to increase supply and keep energy prices from rising faster. Higher energy supplies, however, are only available at high cost. New technologies, such as solar panels and shale oil, are also possible. They are, however, also expensive, pushing energy prices and costs still higher. Subsidies can keep the costs of new energy sources and technologies down, but tax costs rise.

26.17 ▶ 17. Higher energy prices in the short run tend to reduce energy demand in the long run by giving producers and consumers the incentive to purchase energy-saving capital goods. Some economists propose special taxes that raise energy prices in the short run to hold demand down in the long run. Laws and regulations, such as building codes and auto fuel economy standards, are another way to lower energy demand in some areas. Subsidies to encourage conservation also reduce demand. Producers and consumers get subsidies through the tax system, for example, encouraging them to make energy-saving investments. Rationing is a final way to limit demand, but it is only likely in case of national emergency. Rationing is expensive, inefficient, and prone to illegal black-market sales.

26.18 ▶ 18. Some economists say that individuals are unresponsive to price changes, so government regulations are necessary. Others argue that prices are the best way to change energy consumption behavior. Higher prices are a more effective long-run tool, but do little to increase supply or reduce demand in the short run. Temporary government policies are more powerful in the short run, but are not always long-lasting.

26.19 ▶ 19. A trade-off between energy consumption and environmental quality exists in the short run. Economists and policymakers have trouble deciding the point where energy problems should make way for environmental concerns.

DISCUSSION QUESTIONS

26.2, 26.3, 26.4 ▶ 1. Here's a simple problem to show the difficulties of deciding when to produce a finite natural resource. You own a coal mine with just three tons of coal in it. The cost of producing coal is $10 per ton for the first ton, $11 for the second, $12 for the third. You can sell the coal for $12 this year, or wait and sell it for $14 next year. Profits you receive today can be invested either in equipment that reduces the cost of producing coal next year by $1 per ton or in government bonds that pay a 25 percent return. How much coal should you produce this year? (Hint: calculate profits under each of the three different possible allocations.) How much next year? What should you do with coal revenues? Explain how you arrived at your answers.

26.10	2. Why do energy price controls lead to energy shortages (or imports) in the short run? In the long run? Are price controls good or bad? Explain.
26.5	3. Oil and natural gas reserves are a communal good. What effect does this fact have on the need for government regulations to control oil and natural gas production? Explain.
26.15, 26.16, 26.18, 26.19	4. Today people use wood stoves instead of oil heat. Explain how this substitution affects the markets for wood, wood stoves, and oil. What are the likely environmental trade-offs of increased wood use? Is the increased use of wood stoves a good idea from society's point of view? Explain.
26.4, 26.7, 26.8, 26.14, 26.15, 26.18	5. Should the federal government impose a 50 cent per gallon tax on gasoline? State arguments both in favor of and against this proposal. What are the likely economic effects of such a plan? Who would gain and who would lose in both short and long runs? Explain.

SELECTED READINGS

Carson, Robert B. *Microeconomic Issues Today: Alternative Approaches*, 3rd ed. New York: St. Martin's Press, 1983. See Issue 3: "Energy Economics: What Ever Happened to the Energy Crisis?"

Gwartney, James D. and Stroup, Richard. *Economics: Private and Public Choice*, 3rd ed. New York: Academic Press, 1982, chapter 28.

Landsberg, Hans H. "Energy" in Pechman, Joseph A. (ed.), *Setting National Priorities: Agenda for the 1980s*. Washington, D.C.: Brookings Institution, 1980.

Roberts, Marc J. and Stewart, Richard B. "Energy and the Environment" in Owen, Henry and Schultze, Charles L. (eds.), *Setting National Priorities: The Next Ten Years*. Washington, D.C.: Brookings Institution, 1976.

Sweeney, James L. "The Response of Energy Demand to Higher Prices: What Have We Learned?" *American Economic Review* (May 1984), pp. 31–37.

Williams, Stephen F. "Running Out: The Problem of Exhaustible Resources" *Journal of Legal Studies* (January 1978), pp. 165–99.

PART 9

International Economics and Comparative Economic Systems

CHAPTER 27

International Trade

Having read the chapter, reviewed the chapter summary, and completed the *Study Guide* exercises, you should be able to:

CRIS

27.1 OPEN AND CLOSED ECONOMIES: Explain the difference between an open economy and a closed economy.

27.2 TRADE: Expain why necessity is not the only reason for trade among nations, and explain trade based on comparative advantage.

27.3 COMPARATIVE ADVANTAGE: Define comparative advantage, and explain the role of opportunity cost in determining the direction of trade.

27.4 ABSOLUTE ADVANTAGE: Define absolute advantage, and explain the role of absolute advantage in determining the direction of trade.

27.5 DIRECTION OF TRADE: Given data about two nations producing two goods, determine absolute and comparative advantage, and predict the direction of trade.

27.6 PRODUCTION AND TRADE POSSIBILITIES CURVES: Show trade and the gains from trade using production possibilities curves and trade possibilities curves.

27.7 TERMS OF TRADE: Define the terms of trade, give an example of mutually advantageous terms of trade and explain how the terms of trade affect the distribution of the gains from trade.

27.8 ECONOMIC EFFECTS OF TRADE: List and analyze the economic effects of trade on production and consumption.

27.9 WINNERS & LOSERS IN INTERNATIONAL TRADE: List and analyze the winners and losers from international trade.

27.10 TARIFFS AND QUOTAS: Explain what tariffs and quotas are and how they affect the prices and quantities of imported goods, and illustrate tariffs and quotas using import supply and demand curves.

- **27.11 TARIFF BURDEN:** Define the consumer burden and the producer burden of a tariff, and discuss the relationship between the distribution of the tariff burden and the elasticity of demand for imported goods.

- **27.12 DISTRIBUTION OF TARIFF BURDEN:** Illustrate the distribution of the tariff burden using supply and demand curves.

- **27.13 TARIFFS PRO AND CON:** List and evaluate the arguments in favor of tariffs and the arguments against tariffs and other trade restrictions.

- **27.14 DISTRIBUTION OF TARIFF GAINS AND LOSSES:** Explain how the distribution of tariff gains and losses affects the political decision to impose trade restrictions.

- **27.15 VOLUNTARY EXPORT AGREEMENTS:** Discuss the pros and cons of voluntary export agreements, and explain how they are similar to and different from quotas.

- **27.16 CUSTOMS UNION:** Define a customs union, and explain its advantages.

- **27.17 FUTURE OF U.S. TRADE:** Discuss the future of U.S. international trade.

27.1 OPEN AND CLOSED ECONOMIES

Open Economy
An economy that trades with other countries.

The United States is an **open economy**, an economy that interacts with other nations in many ways. Goods and services are exchanged across national borders. Mutually advantageous international trade increases production, makes higher production possible, and lowers prices, shifting out the economy's production possibilities frontier. Every international trade action has an equal and opposite financial reaction. Goods go from A to B, so money payments must go from B to A. This everyday event becomes more interesting when A and B have different currencies. Now two prices are important, the price of the good and the price of the currency, the exchange rate.

National economies affect one another because their goods markets, credit markets, and exchange markets are all related. This means that events in the U.S. affect the lives of foreign consumers, producers, and investors, and foreign policies affect us. The nations of the world are like so many toy boats in a bathtub: political and economic waves in other countries rock you, and your actions send ripples that are felt on faraway foreign shores.

Closed Economy
An economy with no interaction with other countries.

The economic models discussed so far in this text have described a **closed economy.** The United States is such a dominant economic force that the traditional focus on closed economy economics is understandable. Other countries do not take this parochial view, however. If you were taking this course in England or Japan, your study would have started here. International economic events often overshadow purely domestic matters in other countries.

This chapter sets the stage by looking at international trade and its economic effects. International economic interdependence is rooted in international trade. The obvious first question is . . .

WHY DO NATIONS TRADE?

27.2 TRADE

To the layman, the obvious reason why nations trade is to acquire goods that they cannot produce themselves. There are, however, several more important and interesting reasons for trade known to economists. For example, look around your home and make a list of imported goods you buy or use. You might discover imports of light bulbs, automobiles, clothing, textiles, televisions, radios and other electronic gear, typewriters, agricultural goods, and many more items around the house. U.S. consumers bought over $261 billion in imports in 1981. Foreigners bought over $233 billion of our goods that year.

The goods on your list are probably not things that cannot be made in the United States. Most imported goods could be produced here and many of them are. Technology permits us to produce almost any import or a reasonable substitute, if we so desire. International trade, in most cases, is not based on necessity. Why then, do nations trade? The answer is because of the Law of Comparative Advantage, which we discussed in Chapter 1 of this text. We will explain the Law of Comparative Advantage again here in more detail and apply it to analyze the costs and benefits of international trade.

The Law of Comparative Advantage

27.3 COMPARATIVE ADVANTAGE

This old question was posed by the 19th century English economist David Ricardo. Ricardo observed a peculiar pattern of trade between Great Britain and Portugal. Great Britain exported cloth and imported wine from the Portuguese. Ricardo wondered why this particular pattern of trade had developed.

Necessity was not the answer to Ricardo's puzzle. He found that both countries were able to produce both goods with the same technology. Tastes were not the answer either. The exporting Portuguese seemed to like the wine even better than the importing British. It was technically possible for Britain to export wine and import cloth from Portugal. Ricardo decided to find out why this did not happen.

Ricardo felt that perhaps there was some difference in productivity that determined the trade patterns. He began his study by defining a basic resource unit composed of fixed amounts of labor, capital, and natural resources, and he studied productivity in each country. Ricardo found that his resource bundle, set to work in British mills, could produce 4 yards of cloth. Used in British vineyards, the same resources yielded 6 bottles of wine. The story was different in Portugal. A bundle of resources used in Portuguese mills made 5 yards of cloth. The output was 15 bottles of wine for each resource bundle used to make wine in Portugal.

TABLE 27.1

	EACH RESOURCE BUNDLE PRODUCES		
Country	Cloth (yards)		Wine (bottles)
Great Britain	4	or	6
Portugal	5	or	15

27.4 ABSOLUTE ADVANTAGE

Absolute Advantage
The ability to produce a good or service with fewer resources than other nations.

27.5 DIRECTION OF TRADE

Comparative Advantage
The ability to produce a good or service at lower opportunity cost.

Law of Comparative Advantage
Theory that international trade and production specialization is based on differences in opportunity cost.

This was quite a paradox. A bundle of resources employed in Portugal would make more wine than in Britain, the expected result, and more cloth, too. Ricardo said that Portugal had an **absolute advantage** in producing both wine and cloth.

If Portuguese firms are more productive than British producers—getting more output per unit of input—it seems strange that they should even bother to trade. Ricardo wondered why a highly efficient country would buy goods from a less efficient neighbor. Why did Portugal buy cloth from Britain?

The cloth-wine trade did not make sense. Portugal, with unlimited resources, would be better off making both goods itself and buying neither from the British. Ricardo found his answer by incorporating the fundamental economic fact of scarcity into his analysis. Neither Portugal nor Britain had unlimited resources. Land, labor, and capital are scarce. Labor used to make cloth must be taken away from wine production. More cloth means less wine. In economic terms, the forgone wine is the opportunity cost of producing cloth.

Ricardo decided that international trade was based on differences in opportunity costs. Opportunity costs measure what a nation gives up in production. Let's apply the idea of opportunity cost to the cloth-wine example. Table 27-2 displays this concept.

Britain can use a bundle of resources to make either 4 yards of cloth or 6 bottles of wine. What does a yard of cloth cost? Every extra yard of cloth means giving up 6/4 = 1½ bottles of wine. What does a bottle of wine cost? Britain gives up 4/6 = ⅔ yard of cloth for every bottle of wine it makes. Compute the math yourself to be sure you see where these numbers come from.

Portugal has different costs. The Portuguese choose between 5 yards of cloth and 15 bottles of wine each time they allocate a resource unit. If they make cloth, each yard costs them 15/5 = 3 bottles of wine that could have been produced instead. When they make wine, however, they give up just 5/15 = ⅓ yard of cloth.

We must consider here who has the **comparative advantage** in producing cloth. A yard of cloth costs 3 bottles of wine in Portugal, but just 1½ bottles in Great Britain. Britain is the cheaper producer, based on opportunity cost. Ricardo said that Britain should specialize in its comparative advantage and export the relatively cheap cloth to those with higher comparative costs.

Now we should consider who has the comparative advantage in wine. A bottle of wine costs ⅔ yards of cloth in Britain, but only ⅓ yard in Portugal. The **law of comparative advantage** says the Portuguese should specialize in wine and export it. Each country sells the good in which it has a comparative advantage and buys the relatively cheaper import.

TABLE 27.2

	OPPORTUNITY COSTS	
Product	**Great Britain**	**Portugal**
1 bottle wine	⅔ yard cloth	⅓ yard cloth
1 yard cloth	1½ bottles wine	3 bottles wine

KEY CONCEPTS
27.2, 27.3

Mutually beneficial trade is based upon the Law of Comparative Advantage. Any two parties can both gain from trade if they have different opportunity costs for producing a given good.

Gains From Trade

The most significant point to arise from Ricardo's study was that both nations gain from this pattern of trade. We can see this more clearly through a simple example. Suppose that the two countries agree on a **terms of trade** of 1 yard of cloth exchanged for 2 bottles of wine. One bottle of wine trades for ½ yard of cloth. Is trade mutually advantageous?

Great Britain produces cloth at a cost of 1½ bottles of wine. Would they be willing to sell the cloth at this price? Yes. The cloth, with opportunity cost = 1½ bottles, earns a profit when sold for 2 bottles of wine. Would Britain want to buy wine at this price? Yes again. Why produce wine that costs ⅔ yard of cloth if you can buy it for the equivalent of ½ yard at this terms of trade?

Great Britain gains from trade at these prices. They sell cloth for more than its opportunity cost and buy Portuguese wine for less than it would cost to produce it themselves. Another important question which arises is, if Britain gains, must Portugal lose?

Portugal also gains from trade. The Portuguese are happy to sell wine for ½ yard of cloth; it only costs them ⅓ yard of cloth in opportunity cost to produce it. They are pleased to buy the cloth for 2 bottles of wine, too. They would have to give up 3 bottles of wine to produce a yard of cloth themselves. Each nation sells at a profit and buys for less than the cost of home production. Both countries gain from international trade. The potential for gain is shown in Figure 27-1.

Each country has 100 resource bundles to use in production of wine or cloth. Britain can have either 400 yards of cloth, if they completely specialize in textiles, or 600 bottles of wine if they completely specialize in wine production or any combination of the two given by the simple **production possibilities frontier** (PPF) in the figure. The PPF shows the nation's production limits. Britain chooses a combination on the PPF such as point *A* where they produce 300 yards of cloth and 150 bottles of wine.

The British escape the bounds of their PPF through international trade. They specialize in cloth, their comparative advantage, and trade each yard of cloth for 2 bottles of wine. With trade they can have any point on the **trade possibilities curve** (TPC) in the figure. They could, for example, specialize in cloth, producing 400 yards of cloth and no wine, and then trade 80 yards of fabric for 160 bottles of wine. This swap puts them at a point such as *B* in the figure. They have 160 bottles of wine and still keep 400 − 80 = 320 yards of cloth. They consume more of both goods than if they produced them at home. Point *B* gives more wine and more cloth. Trade is advantageous to the British.

The same idea applies to Portugal. The Portuguese choose between 500 yards of cloth — if they completely specialize in textile production — or 1500 bottles of wine, if they completely specialize in this good. Or Portugal could produce any other combination given by a point on their PPF, given 100 resource units and the productivity of this example. Without trade, they are limited by the PPF, they consume a point such as *C* in the figure, with 1300

27.7
TERMS OF TRADE

Terms of Trade
The ratio of two goods in international trade.

Production Possibilities Frontier
A curve showing the maximum amounts of two goods a national can produce with scarce resources.

27.6
PRODUCTION AND TRADE POSSIBILITIES CURVES

Trade Possibilities Curve
A graph showing combinations a nation can trade for with given terms of trade.

FIGURE 27-1

Gains from Trade. Production possibilities curves (PPCs) show what each nation can produce and consume without international trade. Great Britain and Portugal are limited to points like A and C. The trade possibilities curves (TPCs) show the combinations of wine and cloth they can trade for at the exchange rate 1 cloth = 2 wine.

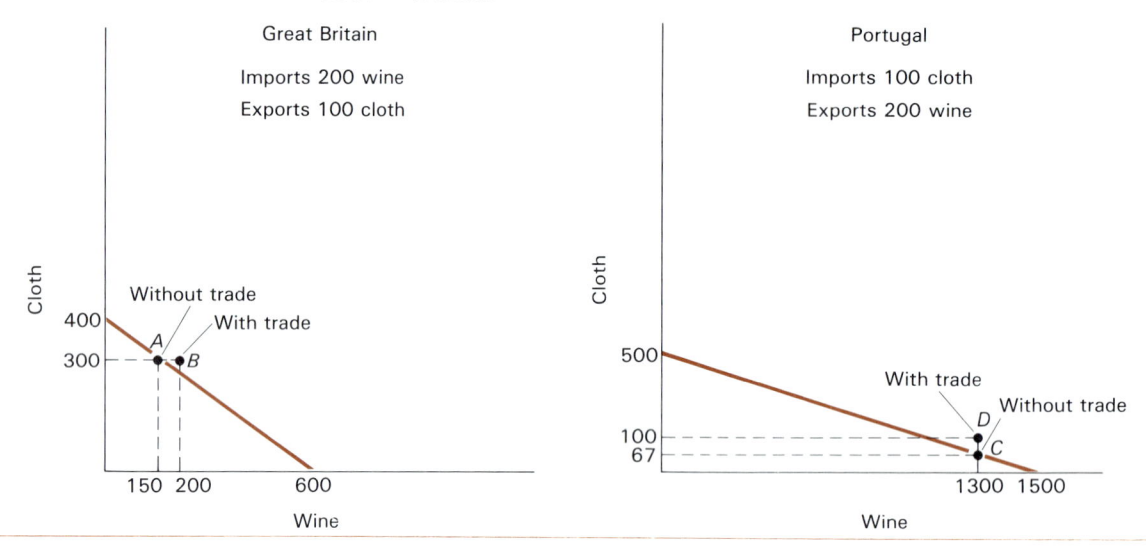

bottles of wine and 67 yards of cloth. Now suppose they specialize in wine, their comparative advantage, and produce 1500 bottles of it, then trade wine for cloth at the going terms of trade. Now they can have any point on their TPC, such as point D. The Portuguese use all their resources to produce 1500 bottles of wine, (complete specialization) and trade 160 of them to the British for 80 yards of cloth. They now have the 80 yards of cloth and the remaining 1500 − 160 = 1340 bottles of wine. They have more cloth than before trade and more wine too.

Comparative Advantage In The Real World

The theory of comparative advantage not only made sense to Ricardo but works very well today. You need not look far to see comparative advantage at work. The United States buys oil from the OPEC nations and sells them agricultural goods, among other things. Comparative advantage explains this pattern of trade.

The United States has the technical ability to meet its own oil needs and yet we buy costly oil from the OPEC cartel. We do this because U.S. oil production has an opportunity cost. Thousands of workers and machines would have to be diverted from production of other goods and put to work finding and producing oil. We could increase domestic oil production, but the extra oil would cost us much more than OPEC's price. The fact is that we gain from the present trade with OPEC.

OPEC gains as well. OPEC could, in fact, meet its own food needs but it would be expensive to make the deserts fertile. Resources would need to be pulled away from oil production and other competing uses. OPEC could grow its own food, but they would have to give up much more than they do with international trade.

The Law of Comparative Advantage really works and its happy result is greater production and lower costs. We all have a stake in exchange.

27.8 ECONOMIC EFFECTS OF TRADE

Economic Effects Of Trade

We have shown that it is possible for both countries to consume more with trade than they could without trade. Where did the additional goods and services come from? Table 27-3 shows the puzzle.

Total cloth output was 367 yards before trade and 1450 bottles of wine were produced. Both totals grow after trade. Where did the extra come from? No more resources are available. Both countries still have just 100 resource units, the same as before. Technology has not changed. The productivity of each resource has remained constant. What has changed however, is that each nation has specialized in its area of comparative advantage. Less wine is given up when cloth is produced in Britain. Less cloth is forgone when Portugal specializes in the wine. The number of resources has not changed, but specialization, which is impossible without trade, means resources go where they are the most productive. Total output rises, so more can be consumed and both nations gain.

The key to understanding the gains from specialization and trade is to carefully examine the "Without Trade" portion of Table 27-3. It would admittedly be possible for Britain to produce nothing but cloth and Portugal to produce nothing but wine. If the two countries did so, the total amount of wine and cloth available to consumers in the two countries would be the same as listed in the "With Trade" section of Table 27-3. However, this would also mean "without trade." British consumers would have no wine and Portugese consumers would have no cloth—both of which are desirable goods. But if either of the two nations tried to produce some of the good in which it did not have a comparative advantage (wine in Britain or cloth in Portugal) output of the other good would decrease by a relatively large amount, since each would be faced with a fairly high opportunity cost in attempting to produce the other good (wine in Britain and cloth in Portugal). It is this fact—the high opportunity cost of producing wine in Britain or cloth in Portugal—that makes autarky, or an attempt to be totally self-sufficient in all goods, an inefficient policy compared to the benefits gained from specialization and trade.

International trade affects the economy in many ways. Trade allows countries and firms to specialize. This specialization allows firms to schedule longer, more efficient production runs and to employ large-scale production techniques that further reduce opportunity costs. Everyone gains because one country produces a good at low cost instead of many small, costly factories dividing output.

27.9 WINNERS & LOSERS IN INTERNATIONAL TRADE

International trade creates winners and losers. British wine drinkers gain in this example. Inexpensive imported wine costs less than expensive domestic goods. The Portuguese wine producers gain, too. They sell more

TABLE 27-3

Production Gains from Trade. The same resources produce both more wine and more cloth when specialization and exchange take place.

		Without Trade			With Trade	
Country	Point	Wine	Cloth	Point	Wine	Cloth
Great Britain	A	150	300	B	0	400
Portugal	C	1300	67	D	1500	0
TOTAL		1450	367		1500	400

wine and gain more profit with trade than without. Portuguese cloth buyers and British cloth producers likewise gain from lower prices and higher sales, respectively.

Trade makes losers, too, and the losers often call for trade restrictions to keep imports out. For example, import-competitors stand to lose in the wine/cloth trade. British wine makers and Portuguese cloth manufacturers are both threatened by cheaper imports. Some consumers lose from the opening of trade, too. The price of cloth in Britain rises, for example, when Portuguese buyers bid prices up by increasing overall demand for these goods. Wine drinkers in Portugal pay a little more, too, because British oenophiles (wine snobs) add to demand for their favorite vintages. International trade tends to equalize relative wages and prices across national borders.

International trade increases production, the result of specialization, and makes higher consumption levels possible. Nations gain from trade because they can escape the bounds of their PPC curves, but individuals gain and lose as trade changes wages and prices and redistributes income within each country.

TARIFFS AND QUOTAS

27.10 TARIFFS AND QUOTAS

Tariff
A tax on imported goods.

Quota
A physical limitation on the quantity of imports.

Free trade benefits the majority of consumers and producers, but hurts important import-competing industries and worker groups in each nation. Firms and unions threatened by import competition lobby for trade restrictions like **tariffs** and **quotas.**

A tariff is a tax on imported goods. Tariffs were once an important source of government revenue. Their main function these days is to discourage international trade. Here is how a tariff works.

The market for imported scotch whiskey is shown in Figure 27-2. The free trade price is $10 per bottle. A $2 per bottle tariff reduces import

FIGURE 27-2

The Effects of a Tariff. A $2.00 tariff decreases supply. Firms supply less because their net receipts are reduced by the tariff. The import tax drives price up from $10 to $11 in the figure. The quantity of imports falls.

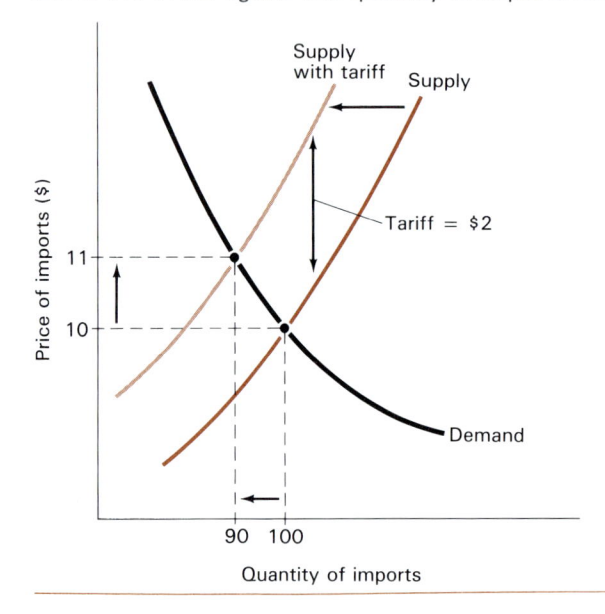

supply. Firms who pay the tariff supply less because of their lower net price or increase price. They would need to charge a $12 price to take in a net $10 after the tariff. The tariff produces a $2 vertical shift in the supply curve shown here.

Falling supply bids up price and reduces the quantity imported. Price rises to $11 per bottle. Some consumers quit buying the import at the higher price, while others switch to domestic substitutes. Profits, output, and employment all rise in these import-competing industries.

A quota is a more direct way to keep imports out. Congress votes to limit imports to a specific physical quantity and sometimes sells the right to import these scarce goods. There is a big scotch shortage at the old $10 price in Figure 27-3. The 50-bottle quota limit leaves many scotch drinkers dry. Price rises until quantity demanded falls to equal the quota limit of 50. The price goes from $10 to $18 in this figure.

Economists dislike tariffs and quotas. Both disrupt international trade. They raise import prices, discourage specialization, and disrupt the mutually advantageous system of comparative advantage. Both trade restrictions are bad, but quotas are the evil of two lessers. The market still works, after a fact, with tariffs. Consumers who want more imports can get them, if they pay tariff-inflated prices. The market fails completely, however, when quotas are imposed. An increase in demand by thirsty scotch drinkers in Figure 27-3 would bring only higher price and monopoly profits to those permitted to import the quota amount. Imports of extra goods to meet higher demand are illegal.

KEY CONCEPT 27.10

Both tariffs and quotas reduce import quantities, and raise import prices reducing the potential gains from specialization and trade. They shield domestic industry from international competition and reduce economic efficiency.

FIGURE 27-3

The Effects of a Quota. A quota puts a lid of 50 on the number of goods imported in this market. The shortage disappears when price rises to $18 per bottle, a price high enough to adjust the quantity demanded to the limited supply.

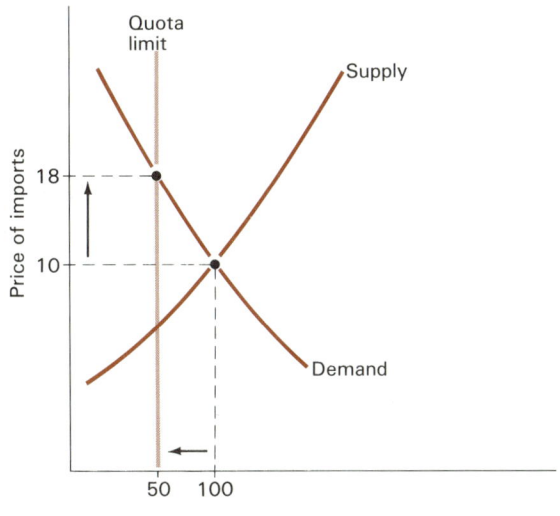

27.11 TARIFF BURDEN

Consumer Burden
The part of a tariff paid by consumers as higher price.

Producer Burden
The part of a tariff paid by sellers in lower net price.

27.12 DISTRIBUTION OF TARIFF BURDEN

Who Pays The Tariff?

It may be surprising to discover who actually bears the burden of trade restrictions. The tariff is levied against foreign producers, but they do not really pay all of it. Look back at Figure 27-2. A $2 tariff was put on imported whisky here, but the price only went up by $1. The **consumer burden** of this tariff was the $1 higher price, plus the value of the lost imports. Who paid the other half of the tariff? The **producer burden** falls on sellers as lower net price and reduced sales. Foreign producers receive $11 for the scotch, but pay a $2 tax. They keep just $9, one dollar less than before. The lost net revenue, and the value of lost sales, is the producer burden.

The tariff's burden is not always split exactly in half as Figure 27-2 shows. The distribution of the tariff depends in part on the nature of import demand. Figures 27-4 and 27-5 tell the story.

Some imports face an inelastic demand curve like the one shown in Figure 27-4. Suppose that auto buyers view imported cars as significantly different from domestic models. Since the two are not close substitutes, buyers do not switch from imports to domestic cars when the tariff is imposed. They buy almost as many Toyotas as before when price rises. Import demand is relatively unresponsive to price changes, giving the steep demand curve of this figure.

Let's consider carefully who pays the tariff here. A $1000 per car tariff reduces import supply and forces price up. The price here rises by $900 to $8900 per car. Buyers pay most of the tariff in the form of higher import prices. The producer burden is comparatively light. In general, a more inelastic import demand means a greater consumer tariff burden.

Producers bear the brunt of the tariff when import demand is elastic as Figure 27-5 shows. Buyers in this market think that imports and U.S.-built cars are much the same. They switch from one to the other depending on

FIGURE 27-4

Tariff with Inelastic Demand. Demand is unresponsive to price changes here. Most of the $1000 tariff on new cars is passed on to consumers. Producers pay $100 of the tariff in lower net revenue, and consumers pay the rest.

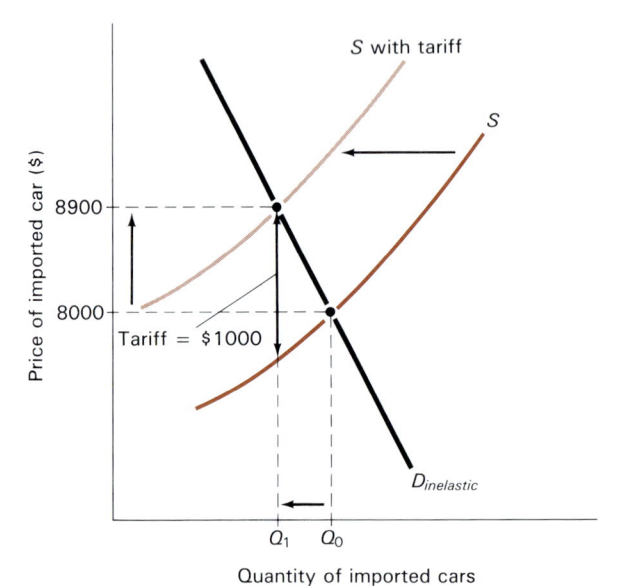

FIGURE 27-5

Tariff with Elastic Demand. Producers pay more of the tariff when demand is responsive to price changes. Price rises by $200 in this market when the $1000 tariff is imposed. The rest of the tariff falls on foreign producers. Compare with Figure 27-4. Note price and quantity differences.

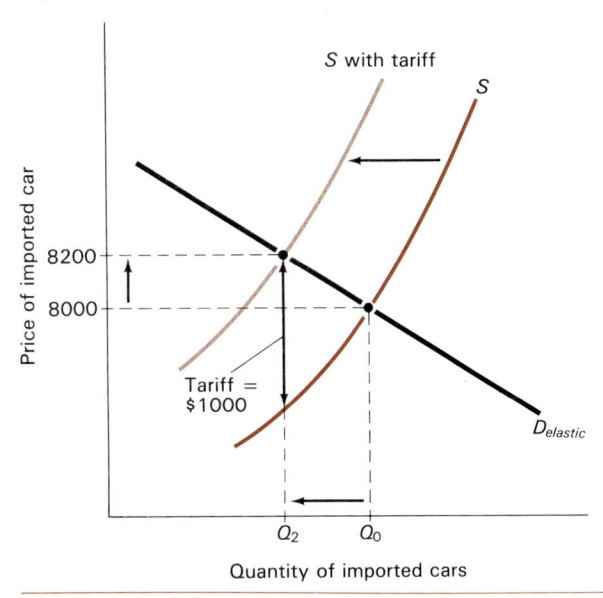

price. The flatter demand curve shows that quantity demanded is highly responsive to changing price.

Note what happens when the tariff is imposed here. Importers again reduce supply when faced with higher tariff costs. Falling supply creates a shortage and bids price higher, but not very much higher. Buyers switch to domestic substitutes when import prices go up. Sellers limit price increases or lose their market. The consumer burden is just $200, much less than in the inelastic demand case. Sellers must receive $8200 but pay the $1000 tax, so their net price is $7200, or $800 less than before the tariff. They pay most of the burden here.

Tariffs on goods with elastic demands collect relatively little revenue, but successfully protect domestic industries by discouraging imports. Look at the reduced quantities in the two figures. Tariffs on goods with inelastic demands do little to reduce imports, but bid up price and collect substantial revenue for the government. Perhaps the British taxed colonial tea imports to collect taxes paid mostly by colonial consumers. The Boston Tea Party that resulted shows how controversial tariffs can be.

Arguments For Tariffs

27.13 TARIFFS PRO AND CON

Most imported goods face some tariff or quota barrier. If tax revenue is not the main reason for trade barriers, why do they exist? Several arguments that have been advanced in favor of these trade restrictions are discussed below.

Protection   Many trade barriers exist simply to protect jobs and profits in U.S. industries. Tariffs and quotas divert demand from cheaper imports to domestic production. Protective tariffs are enacted to save U.S. jobs from "unfair" foreign competition. Foreign firms are often said to have an unfair advantage because wages or other costs are lower for them. Economists

ECONOMIC ISSUES

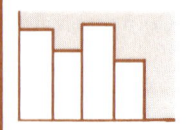

Trade Barriers

Trade restrictions are a recurring theme in economic discussions. International trade is often welcomed during periods of prosperity when unions and businesses see international trade as the opportunity for increased sales in growing foreign markets. Trade takes on a different color during recessions, however, when firms scramble against foreign competitors in shrinking markets. Calls for protectionist policies, like tariff and quota trade barriers, are often heard at times like these. Trade barriers are proposed to protect domestic jobs and income from foreign competition.

Few things in international economics are as simple as they seem, however. Trade restrictions are a complicated package of actions and reactions. Most economists think that most trade restrictions are unjustified and detrimental to the economy's overall economic health. Economists suggest that trade restrictions are a classic example of a special-interest effect, where a relatively small number of gainers (who seek the higher incomes that trade restrictions create for them) impose costs on a much larger group. Since these gains are highly concentrated, while the higher costs are dispersed over large population groups, the political system tends to respond favorably to special interest tariff and quota proposals.

What are the economic disadvantages of tariffs and quotas? You know, from reading this chapter, that a tariff on imported autos, for example, raises the price that buyers must pay and reduces the quantity imported. Thus, the tariff reduces the foreign competition that domestic auto producers face, assuming that buyers switch from foreign to domestic products, which is not always the case. Domestic auto firms, their workers and owners, tend to gain from the protection that tariffs afford. U.S. residents who buy imported cars tend to lose because they must pay higher prices for fewer goods. These are important economic effects, but the impact of trade restrictions does not end here.

Many U.S. workers are employed in processing, selling, and servicing imported goods. A tariff or quota on imported cars, for example, threatens the jobs of over 140,000 people who work in the over 7000 imported car dealerships in the United States. Many more workers are employed in transporting, assembling, and preparing foreign autos, and making

recognize that the unfair advantage is usually just comparative advantage at work. Opportunity costs are less in other lands, so their goods can be imported for less. Protective tariffs that disrupt free trade destroy comparative advantage.

Infant Industries A better argument for tariffs and quotas is that they provide protection for infant industries. Sometimes a country meets all the requirements for a new industry. Demand is there, the technology is available, capital and labor are ready, too. Start-up costs, however, are high in many industries. Cheaper foreign imports keep domestic producers from starting factories that could, eventually, grow to compete in world markets.

A temporary tariff is sometimes justified to protect infant industries. The tariff protects the young industry while it grows and expands production to meet domestic needs. Consumers pay higher prices in the short run, but additional jobs are created in the new industry. Tariffs come off in the long run and prices fall back to world levels. Trade restrictions of this kind can be powerful. Japan protected its auto industry after the Second World War. Japanese firms grew to meet their domestic market and then expanded to sell to the rest of the world. Japan might not have such a potent auto industry today if the initial quotas had not been imposed.

The problem with infant industry tariffs is that they often outlive their purpose. Tariffs designed to protect weak infants often hang around to keep mature firms fat.

and selling accessories for these goods. A tariff does not always increase U.S. employment; sometimes trade restrictions merely rearrange unemployment, creating jobs in Detroit, for example, but putting people out of work elsewhere.

A basic rule of international trade is that nations that want to export must also import. One danger of trade restrictions that reduce imports is that they may unintentionally reduce exports, too, putting workers in exporting industries out of work. The link between imports and exports is established in two ways. First, the money U.S. consumers pay for imports of Japanese cars creates income in Japan. This income is spent, in part, on products that the United States exports. If we import less, foreign buyers have less money with which to purchase our goods.

The second link between imports and exports is political. It is not uncommon for a nation to retaliate when tariffs are imposed on its products. A tariff on Japanese cars can lead to a counter-tariff on U.S. agricultural goods, for example. Tariff wars can escalate until trade is virtually eliminated. This is what happened in the depression years of the 1930s when the Smoot-Hawley tariffs in the United States brought on similar high tariffs in other countries. Trade, and the gains from trade, came to a halt, and the depression deepened as a result of retaliatory tariffs.

Tariffs and quotas can damage the U.S. economy in other ways, too. Many goods that the United States exports use imported inputs. A tariff-induced increase in production costs makes U.S. firms less able to compete with foreign firms, hurting employment and income in America.

Sometimes tariff effects are even more complex. When U.S. auto makers called for limits of imports of Japanese cars in the early 1980s, for example, the *Wall Street Journal* pointed out that lower imports of inexpensive cars meant bigger imports of expensive oil. If auto buyers were forced to switch from gas-thrifty Toyotas and Hondas to thirstier Chevys and Fords, higher oil imports would be required to supply the extra fuel that bigger American cars would use. Reduced imports of one good can sometimes lead to higher imports of another.

Finally, economists think that the costs of most tariffs to all groups in society far outweigh the gains they provide to special interest groups. However, economists have been touting free trade since Adam Smith's days, and tariff and quota trade barriers continue to exist.

Additional References

Baldwin, Robert E., "The Political Economy of Postwar United States Trade Policy," *The Bulletin,* New York: New York University, Graduate School of Business Administration, Center for the Study of Financial Institutions, (1974-76).

Finley, Murray H., "Foreign Trade and U.S. Employment," in *The Impact of International Trade and Employment,* Dewald, William G., Ed. Washington, DC: U.S. Department of Labor, 1978.

Lindert, Peter H. and Kindleberger, Charles P., *International Economics,* 7th ed. Homewood, IL: Richard D. Irwin, Co., 1982.

Simison, Robert L., "Car Wars: Protectionism Battle Over Imports of Autos May Head for Congress," *Wall Street Journal,* February 15, 1980.

Competition Problems Some tariffs are imposed to deal with anticompetitive import practices. Sometimes foreign sellers dump goods on international markets for a lower price than they charge in their home countries. They do this to drive other producers from the market or to get rid of excess production abroad while keeping higher prices at home. Tariffs to limit this practice are sometimes justified. U.S. steel producers call for tariffs against foreign imports today, citing dumping as their reason.

Some foreign producers receive subsidies from their governments. These side payments make imports cheaper than unsubsidized domestic goods. Governments "export" unemployment through subsidies that increase domestic production and exports, but put foreign competitors out of work. Tariffs to discourage this practice are also sometimes called for.

Trade barriers are also useful if the seller is a monopoly, able to extract high price for imports. Many economists have called for a tariff on OPEC oil imports. Oil producers would bear much of the tax, they argue, and lower U.S. sales would remove some of OPEC's monopoly power.

Some experts favor tariffs for strategic reasons. The threat of tariffs, they claim, is a weapon. Tariffs, quotas, and other trade limitations help the United States meet its foreign policy goals, and force other countries to keep their markets open to U.S. exports.

National Defense Trade barriers are sometimes required for national security reasons. Here is an outlandish example of the national defense reasoning. Suppose Greenland has a comparative advantage in auto production. Cheap Greenland cars flood our markets and finally put the U.S. car industry out of business. The United States specializes in making other goods and trades them to Greenland for cars. This pattern of trade is good for us all, so long as trade lines remain open. Now suppose that the United States and Greenland go to war. We would need a healthy auto industry to make jeeps and tanks and other military vehicles, but none would exist because of trade's effects. We would be at a comparative disadvantage in this war.

The national defense argument suggests that trade barriers be erected around industries vital to national defense so that they would be ready in case of war. Many countries keep otherwise uneconomic airline, aerospace, and shipping firms in business for defense reasons. National defense tariffs are a trade-off. Consumers pay higher prices and lose the benefits of comparative advantage in time of peace. They gain an important advantage in wartime, however.

KEY CONCEPT 27.10 Tariffs have been justified on the grounds of national defense, imperfect international competition, and protection for infant industries.

Arguments Against Tariffs

The arguments against tariffs have already been stated. Free trade increases production by allowing greater specialization and makes nations as a whole better off. Resources go to their best use. Most tariffs actually protect the public from the production and consumption benefits of comparative advantage. Gains to the many, however, frequently make way to the special interests of the few when politics is involved, as noted earlier in the text. Is a particular tariff really justified by competition problems, national defense, or infant industry concerns? This question is often difficult to answer.

Perhaps the most convincing argument against trade restrictions is that tariffs beget tariffs and quotas beget quotas. Today's U.S. tariff against Japanese goods results in tomorrow's Japanese tariff against items made here. Both countries suffer from higher prices and falling employment. Nations that try to make themselves better off by restricting imports risk starting a trade war that makes all worse off.

The Political Economy of Tariffs

27.14 DISTRIBUTION OF TARIFF GAINS AND LOSSES

Economists tell us that tariffs and other trade restrictions make the importing nation worse off by raising prices and forcing an inefficient use of scarce resources. Why does Congress pass tariff laws if they are detrimental to U.S. consumers?

Part of the answer to this question lies in the distribution of the gains and losses from tariffs and similar trade barriers. It involves the special interest effect discussed in the first part of this text. Suppose a tariff is imposed against imported shoes. This tariff forces a relatively small increase in the price of shoes across the country. Shoe buyers are worse off, but the loss is widely dispersed. No one spends enough money on shoes to make it worthwhile to organize an Association of Shoe Buyers to lobby Congress against the new tax. Individual shoe buyers lose just a little from the shoe tariff, so they have little incentive to make their loss known to elected representatives.

Compare this with the position of shoe producers and shoe workers. They stand to gain or lose heavily from a tariff that keeps foreign shoes out and protects U.S. shoe jobs and profits. They have a strong incentive to organize and lobby Congress in favor of trade restrictions. Congressional representatives hear from those—such as shoe producers—with concentrated gains, but never hear the voices of those—such as shoe consumers—whose loss is large in total, but spread over large numbers of individuals. This stacks the deck in favor of special interest bills, such as protective tariffs.

Congress does not hear from the majority on issues like tariffs. Individual shoe buyers pay too small a cost to make anti-tariff action economical. The total loss to all individuals is high, however. Special interests stand to gain enough to make organization and political lobbying profitable. Congress responds to the voice of the people, but the only voices it hears are those of pro-tariff special interests.

Protectionism And Voluntary Export Agreements

27.15 VOLUNTARY EXPORT AGREEMENTS

The case for free trade is convincing in theory, but it does not put bread on the table if you have been laid off because people are buying cheaper foreign goods instead of the ones your firm makes. Calls to "Buy American" and save domestic jobs are always heard, but the cry is louder in recessionary periods like the early 1980s.

Voluntary export restrictions are an interesting response to recent tariff and quota threats. Japanese auto producers, faced with possible U.S. trade restrictions in the early 1980s, voluntarily agreed to limit their exports to the United States for a period of time. The effect was the same as a quota, but voluntarily imposed by the foreign producers themselves.

Why would Japan agree to limit exports to the United States? One reason is that the voluntary quota imposed by the Japanese might be less restrictive now and easier to remove later than any tariff or quota barriers imposed by Congress. Another reason is that Japanese producers get the benefits of higher prices when import supplies are restricted. Compare this to a tariff where the foreign supplier sells less and also receives a lower net price. Toyota and Nissan executives might prefer free trade, but if limits are to be imposed, they would rather have higher net prices with voluntary export restrictions than lower net prices with a tariff.

Some U.S. groups are calling for domestic content regulations. Under these regulations, certain items, such as autos, would have to have a set fraction of their product, for example 50 percent, produced in the United States before they could be sold here. Domestic content rules have applied for years in many less developed countries. Foreign producers would be forced to shift at least some production to this country, creating jobs here, in spite of higher U.S. costs and allegedly lower U.S. quality. Volkswagen and Honda opened factories in the United States in the last few years in part, no doubt, in anticipation of domestic content legislation.

Voluntary export limits show how seriously the protectionist movement is taken by foreign producers. Do these agreements benefit countries, like the United States, that gain protection from them? Some American groups gain in the short run, but the economy as a whole suffers because the efficiencies of comparative advantage are foregone. Domestic producers might lose in the long run for a different reason. Lower exports mean that

Customs Unions

> **27.16**
> **CUSTOMS UNION**

Customs Union
Groups of nations having free trade among themselves and unified tariff barriers with other countries.

European Economic Community (EEC)
A customs union including major European nations; also called Common Market.

Customs unions like the **European Economic Community** (EEC), often called the Common Market, are a successful compromise between protection and free trade. Members of a customs union agree to drop all trade barriers among themselves and to adopt a unified system of external trade barriers. Trade between France, Germany, and Britain, for example, takes place as if they were all part of one country. The separate states in this country can be thought of as a big customs union. Most trade barriers are forbidden between the states.

Free trade among members of the customs union generates the benefits of comparative advantage. Import prices drop and export employment rises. Productivity increases, too. A customs union creates trade among its members, but also destroys some trade with non-member countries. Great Britain had to impose new tariffs against Canadian and Australian goods when it entered the EEC, for example, but found French trade restrictions eliminated. Trade is created within the common market, but reduced with outside trading partners.

The EEC has been largely successful, but some problems remain. Formal trade barriers among member nations have been dropped, but more subtle barriers remain. Arbitrary quality and safety standards still prevent free trade. A system of internal subsidies has replaced tariff barriers in some industries. The EEC finds itself in the peculiar position of granting subsidies to French farmers to protect them from Italian competition, then giving subsidies to the Italians, too, to protect them from the French. After more than 25 years, the EEC still has a few bugs to work out, but the benefits of even limited free trade probably outweigh the costs of this alliance.

THE FUTURE OF U.S. TRADE

> **27.17**
> **FUTURE OF U.S. TRADE**

What is the future of U.S. trade? Some economists think that U.S. industries will export more and import more, too. Many of today's fastest growing industries are in high-tech areas such as electronics, computers, and genetic engineering, for example. Innovative U.S. products, invented and produced here, are important exports.

The United States has a comparative advantage in inventing and perfecting new technological wonders, but production often shifts abroad where costs are lower, once the product is sufficiently standardized. The wizards at Atari perfected the video game, for example, and found a tremendous market in the United States. However, it only made sense to keep their factories here so long as new innovations and improvements were being made frequently. Atari production moved to factories in places like Taiwan and Hong Kong, once new product problems were solved.

Will other high-tech industries follow the trend of invention, innovation, and standardization in the United States, then switch to mass-production abroad? If they do, then Americans will come to depend even more on international trade. The profits from yesterday's imported standardized products will finance the high-tech innovation that yields tomorrow's exports.

SUMMARY

27.1 1. International economics is important because we live in an open economy that trades and interacts with other nations. A closed economy is one without money or goods connections to other lands.

27.2 2. Relatively little international trade is based on absolute necessity. Most goods we import could be produced here.

27.3 3. Ricardo analyzed international trade to determine why countries import goods they could produce themselves. Ricardo noted that some nations have an absolute advantage in goods that they import. A country has an absolute advantage in producing a good if it can produce a larger quantity with given resources than other nations.

27.4 4. Ricardo decided that, since resources are scarce, trade is based on differing opportunity costs. The law of comparative advantage is based on opportunity cost differentials.

27.5 5. A nation has a comparative advantage in producing wheat if it gives up fewer other goods and hence has lower opportunity cost than other nations when producing wheat.

27.7 6. The terms of trade is the ratio at which two goods are exchanged. Mutually advantageous trade takes place when two nations exchange goods at a terms of trade that lies between the opportunity costs of production of the two goods.

27.6 7. Opportunity costs and trade-offs can be visualized using production possibilities curves. Gains from trade can be visualized using the trade possibilities curve, which plots the combinations of two goods that a nation can achieve with trade at a given terms of trade. The law of comparative advantage holds in the real world. The U.S. gains by trading with OPEC since we can buy oil for less than it would cost us, in terms of other forgone goods, to produce it ourselves. OPEC gains because these nations can buy our goods for less than their OPEC opportunity cost.

27.8 8. International trade increases total production. Nations are able to produce and consume greater combinations of goods through trade, compared with those possible without trade. The consumption gains from trade are made possible by production gains. Trade increases production by encouraging efficient specialization in goods in which a nation holds a comparative advantage.

27.9 9. Trade creates winners and losers. Consumers can buy imports for less than they would in the absence of trade. Workers and firms in exporting industries gain, too. Trade reduces employment and profits in import-competing industries, however, and tends to bid up the price of goods sold abroad.

27.10 ▸ 10. A tariff is a tax on imported goods. A quota is a physical limit on the quantity of a good that can be legally imported. Both tariffs and quotas reduce import quantities and raise import prices.

27.11 ▸ 11. The consumer burden of a tariff is the higher price and lower quantity passed on to consumers when the tariff/tax is imposed. The producer burden takes the form of lower net price, selling price minus tariff, and smaller sales quantity that the tariff forces.

27.12 ▸ 12. Elasticity of demand is one determinant of the distribution of the tariff burden. The consumer burden increases when the demand for the tariffed good is more inelastic. The consumer burden falls and the producer burden grows when demand is more elastic.

27.13 ▸ 13. Protection is one argument for tariffs. Tariffs protect jobs and profits in domestic industries by discouraging imports and encouraging consumption of home-produced goods. The infant industry argument for a tariff holds that trade restrictions can be desirable if they shelter a growing new industry so that it can eventually compete on international markets. Tariffs can also be justified as a response to international competitive imperfections such as dumping and monopolies. The national defense argument maintains that tariffs are sometimes necessary to reduce reliance on foreign producers for vital commodities. The arguments against tariffs stress the advantages of specialization and the production and consumption gains from trade.

27.14 ▸ 14. Legislatures sometimes vote for policies, such as tariffs, that make voters worse off because of special interest effects. The costs of a tariff are widely dispersed. Consumers each pay slightly higher prices and thus have little incentive to take action to oppose individual trade restrictions. The firms and workers who are protected by tariffs get a highly concentrated gain. They have a large incentive to organize and express their preferences. This leads to pressure groups that stack the deck in favor of trade restrictions.

27.15 ▸ 15. Voluntary export agreements allow a nation to impose a quota against its own exports. These agreements sometimes reduce pressures for tariffs and quotas in importing countries. Export limitations allow exporting nations to set less restrictive limits and more easily increase trade once protectionism threats have abated. Domestic content laws are another trade restriction that attempts to create jobs at home by requiring goods to be at least partially produced in the home country.

27.16 ▸ 16. A customs union is a set of countries that adopts uniform trade restriction for non-members, and sets free trade among members. The European Economic Community (EEC), often called the Common Market, is an example of a customs union.

27.17 ▸ 17. What is the future of U.S. trade? The United States may become more dependent on international trade if recent trends prove long-lived. U.S. firms these days seem to have a comparative advantage in innovation and technology, but not in mass production. Goods may be invented and perfected in the U.S. and initially exported, but production may shift abroad, thus making the U.S. an importer, once the product is standardized.

DISCUSSION QUESTIONS

27.10

1. Suppose that cheap shoe imports from Brazil and other newly developed countries have flooded U.S. markets and caused unemployment in the domestic shoe industry. A tariff on these inexpensive imports has been proposed to bring their cost up to that of comparable U.S. products. Explain who would gain from such an action, who would lose, and why. Make your explanations as complete as possible.

27.4, 27.5, 27.6, 27.7, 27.10

2. The United States currently imports oil from Saudi Arabia. Trade takes place according to the laws of comparative advantage. Congress is considering a tariff on imported oil. Can this tariff:
   a. reduce oil imports?
   b. end oil imports?
   c. reverse trade, so that we sell oil to Saudi Arabia?
   Explain your reasoning in each case.

27.3, 27.4

3. Wade and Marti are thinking about swapping services. If Wade works one hour he can type 2 pages of a report or clean and gap 4 spark plugs. Marti, working one hour, can type 3 pages or clean and gap 8 spark plugs. Who has the absolute advantage in typing? According to the theory of comparative advantage, who should do the typing? Give an example of an exchange rate that would prove mutually advantageous. Explain your reasoning for each question.

27.10, 27.11 27.12

4. Who would bear the burden of a tariff on foreign car imports, U.S. consumers or foreign producers? Defend your answer.

27.10, 27.11

5. Should tariffs or quotas be used to restrict auto imports? List the arguments on both sides of this issue and then state your own position.

SELECTED READINGS

Baldwin, Robert E. "The Political Economy of Postwar United States Trade" reprinted in Baldwin, Robert E. and Richardson, J. David, (Eds.), *International Trade and Finance Readings* 2nd ed. Boston: Little, Brown, 1981.

"Car Wars: Protectionism Battle Over Imports of Autos May Head for Congress," *Wall Street Journal*, February 15, 1980. Stages are illustrated in "The Saudis Build a Pittsburgh," by Douglas Martin (*New York Times*, January 31, 1982).

Finley, Murray H. "Foreign Trade and United States Employment" reprinted in Baldwin, Robert E. and Richardson, J. David. (Eds.), *International Trade and Finance Readings* 2nd ed. Boston: Little, Brown, 1981.

Ricardo, David. "On Foreign Trade" reprinted in Needy, Charles W. (Ed.), *Classics of Economics*, Oak Park IL: Moore Publishing Company, 1980.

Ricardo, David. *Principles of Political Economy and Taxation*, London, 1817 (reprints are available).

Vernon, Raymond "International Investment and International Trade in the Product Cycle" reprinted in Baldwin, Robert E. and Richardson, J. David (Eds.), *International Trade and Finance Readings* 2nd ed. Boston: Little, Brown, 1981.

CHAPTER 28

International Finance

Having read the chapter, reviewed the chapter summary, and completed the *Study Guide* exercises, you should be able to:

CRIS

28.1 BALANCE OF PAYMENTS: Define the balance of payments, list the four major payment types, and explain what balance of payments surplus and deficit mean.

28.2 BALANCE OF PAYMENTS DEFICIT: List several options for financing a balance of payments deficit and explain how each would work.

28.3 U.S. BALANCE OF PAYMENTS: Discuss the recent U.S. balance of payments experience.

28.4 BALANCE OF TRADE: Define the balance of trade and explain how it differs from the balance of payments.

28.5 U.S. BALANCE OF TRADE: Analyze the recent U.S. balance of trade experience.

28.6 INTERNATIONAL PAYMENTS DEFICIT: Discuss the consequences of international payments deficits, and explain whether deficits are "bad" or "good."

28.7 THE IMF AND THE WORLD BANK: Define the IMF and the World Bank, explain their functions, and how their international roles differ.

28.8 EXCHANGE RATES: Explain what an exchange rate is and what a change in the exchange rate means.

28.9 EXCHANGE RATES AND PRICES: Explain the relationship between the exchange rate and the price of foreign imports.

28.10 FOREIGN CURRENCY: List several reasons for people to purchase foreign currencies. Explain why the demand for a foreign currency is said to be a "derived demand."

28.11 CURRENCY APPRECIATION AND DEPRECIATION: Explain what currency appreciation and depreciation signify, and explain how one currency's appreciation and another's depreciation are related.

28.12 DERIVED DEMAND FOR FOREIGN CURRENCY: Explain how the demand curve for francs is derived from the U.S. demand for French goods, and explain how the demand for the dollar is derived from the French demand for U.S. goods.

28.13 DERIVED DEMAND FOR THE DOLLAR: Explain how the demand for the dollar creates the demand for the franc.

28.14 EXCHANGE MARKET EQUILIBRIUM: Draw demand and supply curves for the franc and the dollar and explain how the foreign exchange market adjusts to the equilibrium exchange rate.

28.15 CURRENCY VALUE: Explain what it means for a currency to be overvalued or undervalued, and explain what foreign exchange arbitrage dealers do to help exchange rates move toward equilibrium.

28.16 THE EFFECT OF TARIFFS ON CURRENCY VALUES: Explain how a tariff on coffee affects the demand and supply for the cruzeiro and discuss how the resulting exchange rate creates winners and losers in the U.S. and in Brazil.

28.17 RAPID ECONOMIC GROWTH AND EXCHANGE RATES: Explain the relationship between rapid economic growth and a nation's exchange rate, and discuss why high-growth nations often see their currencies depreciate.

28.18 INFLATION AND EXCHANGE RATES: Explain the relationship between inflation and the exchange rate, and discuss whether high-inflation countries normally see their currency appreciate or depreciate.

28.19 INTERNATIONAL EXCHANGE RATES: Discuss how international interest rate differentials affect exchange rates, and explain why high U.S. interest rates caused dollar appreciation in the early 1980s.

28.20 OFFICIAL INTERVENTION AND DIRTY FLOAT: Define official intervention and managed exchanged rates, and explain why a nation would want to intervene in foreign exchange markets.

28.21 EXCHANGE RATES AND THE BALANCE OF PAYMENTS: Discuss the relationship between the exchange rate and the balance of payments, and explain whether a deficit country normally experiences currency appreciation or depreciation.

28.22 FIXED EXCHANGE RATES: Explain how fixed exchange rates operate and who acts to see that the exchange rates are fixed.

758   International Finance

The nations of the world are a lot like individual people and businesses. Nations have personality characteristics, attitudes, or tendencies. Nations make friends, have fights, compete with one another, and cooperate on political, economic, and social programs.

Nations, like people and firms, engage in financial dealings. International finance is a complicated set of debits and credits, made more difficult by the existence of scores of different world currencies. These currencies make international transactions more colorful. American tourists, for example, have fun spending millions of lira or thousands of yen for a single purchase. Currencies make exchange riskier, however, because currency values fluctuate hourly, altering prices, payments, and financial returns.

This chapter explains how the foreign exchange, international payments, and exchange rates work and how they affect you.

INTERNATIONAL PAYMENTS

Accountants keep track of money that comes into a firm's coffers as payment for goods sold or return on investment, and money that leaves to pay for inputs or as payment on debt. The firm's books show its financial health. No company can long exist if outflows persistently exceed inflows.

Economists keep similar records for the nation as a whole. The **balance of payments** accounts look at all international payments and the **balance of trade** keeps track of money involved in international trade.

The balance of payments is the broadest measure of international financial health. Money enters the United States for four reasons: 1) as payment for exports, 2) as gifts or transfer payments from abroad, 3) as investment by foreigners—as when the Japanese Sony company builds factories in the United States, and 4) as profits and interest payments from U.S. investments abroad. Money flows out of the country for four similar reasons: 1) as imports, 2) as transfers—such as foreign aid to less developed countries, 3) as investments by U.S. firms in foreign lands, and 4) as profit and interest payments to foreign investors.

Some countries take in more funds than they pay out. Their inflows of money exceed outflows. These countries are said to have a **balance of payments surplus.** Other economies pay out more than they receive in these four categories. They experience a **balance of payments deficit.** The United States has been in the latter group in recent years. High payments for oil and interest payments to foreign lenders, among other things, have kept money flowing out of the nation.

FINANCING A BALANCE OF PAYMENTS DEFICIT

To understand what a Balance of Payments deficit means, consider what happens if you personally spend and pay out more than you earn or receive from others. How could you finance this deficit?

You could pay the deficit difference by drawing down your savings or checking account. You can do this once or twice, assuming you have money in the bank, but this is not a permanent solution because your bank account eventually dries up. A second option is to borrow. Others—people with a surplus—might lend you money to pay the difference. This strategy, like dissaving, does not work forever because you cannot expect to continually borrow to pay the rent.

**28.1
BALANCE OF PAYMENTS**

Balance of Payments
The record of a nation's international payments; total money inflows minus total money outflows.

Balance of Trade
The value of exports minus the value of imports.

Balance of Payments Surplus
A condition where total money inflows exceed total money outflows for a nation.

Balance of Payments Deficit
A condition where total money outflows exceed total money inflows for a nation.

**28.2
BALANCE OF PAYMENTS DEFICIT**

A third solution is to sell off some assets, such as furniture, a car, stocks, or bonds. You can finance the deficit this way while your assets hold out. Eventually, however, you must do something to address the cause of the deficit. You must find a way to take in more money, by taking a second job, for example, or pay out less.

A nation is somewhat like an individual in its balance of payments. Deficit countries, like the United States, must eventually make up the difference between money coming in and money going out. The United States pays its bills in several ways, one of which has been to sell gold from Fort Knox. As the gold supplies fall, borrowing becomes more important. Central banks in many nations agreed to hold dollars as IOUs against U.S. debts. Interest rates rose in this country—in part to attract inflows of investment funds from abroad. These are temporary solutions to the balance of payments problem, however. The long-term key lies in making U.S. goods attractive to foreign buyers and U.S. markets profitable for foreign and U.S. investors.

> **28.3 U.S. BALANCE OF PAYMENTS**

KEY CONCEPTS 28.1, 28.2

A balance of payments surplus means a nation receives more money inflows as payment for exports, transfer receipts, investments, and interest and profit payments than it pays out for exports, transfers abroad, investment abroad, and foreign interest and profit payments. A balance of payments deficit means that total outflows exceed total money inflows during a given time period.

THE BALANCE OF TRADE

> **28.4 BALANCE OF TRADE**

The balance of trade is another indicator of international economic transactions. The balance of trade looks at just one piece of the puzzle, international trade. The balance of trade compares exports and imports of merchandise and is important because it paints a picture of the competitive health of producers in different countries. The balance of trade looks at trade in goods and services, ignoring investments, transfers, profits, and so on.

> **28.5 U.S. BALANCE OF TRADE**

The United States had a history of balance of trade surplus in the 1950s and 1960s, as Figure 28-1 shows. Exports of agricultural products and manufactured goods exceeded imports of raw materials and other goods in this period. However, surplus turned to substantial deficit in the 1970s. There were several reasons for this change: 1) increase in imported oil; 2) change in exchange rates; 3) product life-cycle theory; and 4) high interest rates and low investment spending.

First, surplus turned to deficit because of oil. Billions of extra dollars leave the country each year to pay for high-priced petroleum imports. This is bad for the balance of trade, but good in a larger economic sense. Trade following comparative advantage makes both trading partners better off.

Second, some U.S. imports, such as autos and television sets, are goods that we once exported. This trade reversal has come about in part because of changes in exchange rates. Changes in the dollar's international value in recent years have made foreign imports cheaper and raised U.S. prices abroad. Price changes caused by fluctuations in exchange rates discouraged exports and contributed to balance of trade deficits. We will discuss exchange rates in more detail later in this chapter.

760 International Finance

FIGURE 28-1

U.S. Balance of Trade. U.S. merchandise exports exceeded imports during the 1960s, giving a balance of trade surplus during most of these years. Substantial deficits have been the rule in recent years, however.

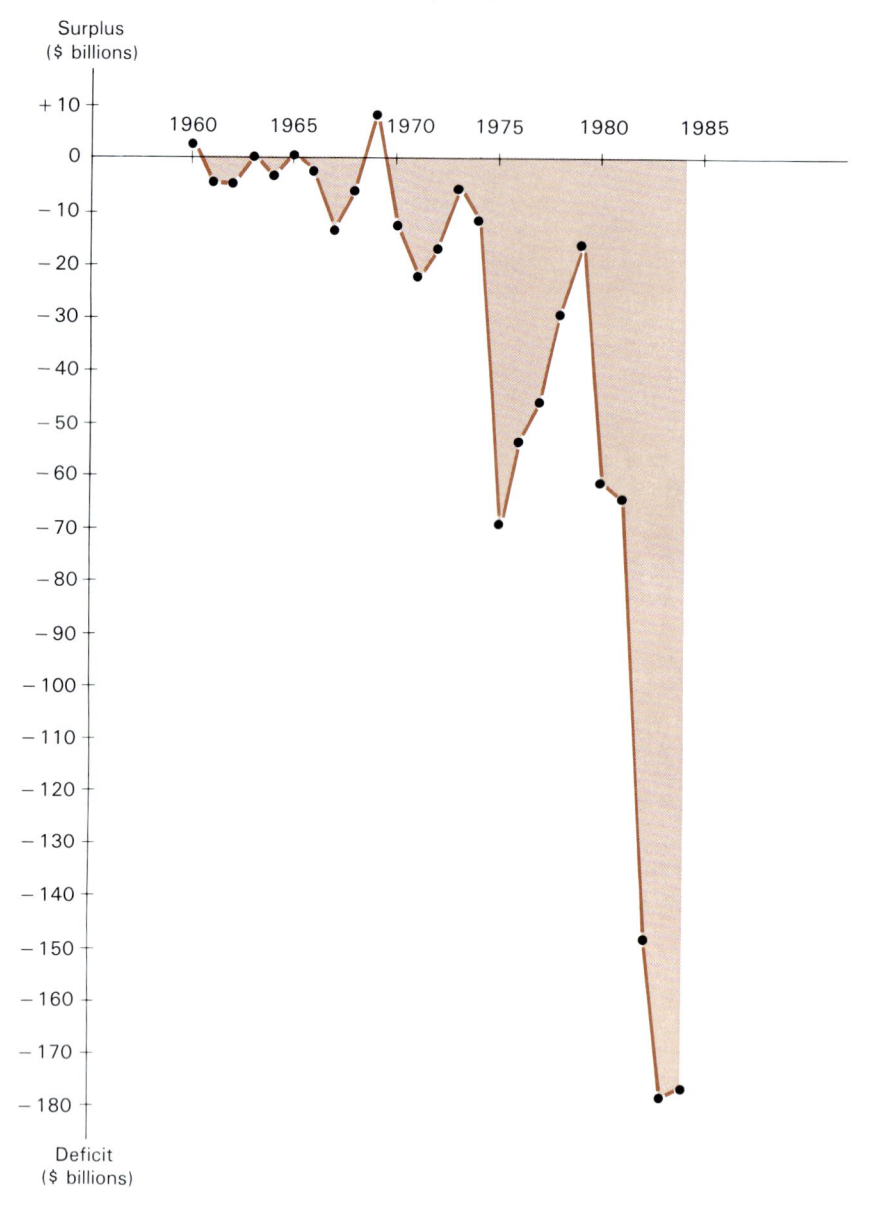

Source: *Economic Report of the President,* 1983.

Third, another part of the puzzle is the product life-cycle theory. The United States has a comparative advantage in innovation and the free communication needed to bring new products to market. New products initially exported by U.S. firms eventually become standardized and production then shifts to lower-cost factories in other countries. U.S. consumers now import goods that once were produced at home.

Fourth, high interest rates and low investment spending in the United States have discouraged innovation and reduced U.S. exports of new high-technology goods.

KEY CONCEPT 28.4

The balance of trade is equal to the value of exports minus the value of imported goods. The United States once had balance of trade surpluses because agricultural and manufactured exports exceeded the value of imported goods. We have experienced very large balance of trade deficits in recent years, however, as oil imports increased and exchange rate changes reduced import prices and raised the cost of U.S. goods to foreign buyers.

IS A PAYMENTS DEFICIT BAD?

International payments deficits are a cause for national concern because of their long-run consequences. A nation that runs a deficit one year and a surplus the next has no need to worry. Debits and credits cancel out in the long run. Countries with continuing deficits, however, must eventually deal with the financial imbalance. A persistent deficit is a symptom of deep economic problems at home. Deficits force a nation to consider whether there has been a shift in its comparative advantage or whether their domestic industries are out of touch with the market. Perhaps home-technology has become obsolete or investment funds are fleeing abroad. Nations sometimes find it less painful to run deficits and, say, borrow the difference, than to solve these nagging economic problems.

A balance of trade deficit means that we spend more on imports than others spend on our exports. Viewed another way, however, it means that we are trading a few of our export goods for many more imported foreign goods. In this light, a balance of trade deficit in dollars is a surplus, measured in real goods and services.

Which is more important, the money or the goods? Adam Smith answered this question in 18th Century England. In Smith's day a group called the **mercantilists** dominated economic policy. They said that the goal of international trade should be to amass a fortune; that is, to have a surplus of money and gold. Smith's answer, in his book *Wealth of Nations*, was that the wealth of a nation is not in its money, but in the real things that its people have. Smith did not favor balance of trade surplus if it meant giving up needed goods and services to get unproductive gold.

Mercantilists
18th century merchants and economists who favored trade restrictions to protect gold accumulations.

International Monetary Fund (IMF)
The central bankers' central bank; international organization that makes loans to nations to finance balance of payments deficits.

> 28.7
> THE IMF AND THE WORLD BANK

THE IMF AND THE WORLD BANK

Nations are not on their own in dealing with international financial problems. Two international organizations stand ready to help. The **International Monetary Fund (IMF)** is the bankers' central bank. It helps regulate international finance much as the Federal Reserve minds domestic financial markets in the United States. The IMF's most important function is to finance temporary balance of payments deficits, while promoting policies that correct the payments imbalance.

IMF loans go to deficit countries, but come with strings attached. The recipient nation must agree to enact policies such as tax increases, exchange rate adjustment, or monetary policy changes, for example, that move the country back towards international payments equilibrium.

The **World Bank** makes loans, too, but its aim is to help less-developed countries advance. The World Bank acts as a financial intermediary,

World Bank
International organization that makes loans to less developed countries to encourage economic development (also known as the International Bank for Reconstruction and Development).

borrowing in world credit markets and lending—at relatively low interest rates—to finance economic development projects such as railways, rural electrification and water projects, and agricultural improvements, in poorer countries. World Bank loans are not designed to solve balance of payments troubles; their goal is to improve living standards around the world.

THE MYSTERIOUS EXCHANGE RATE

> **28.8 EXCHANGE RATES**

Most Americans are happily oblivious of exchange rates. They feel a certain pride when they hear that the dollar is stronger, and an uncertain shame when its value drops, but they do not know why. Ignorance, however, is not bliss where exchange rates are concerned.

In other countries, the average person is a foreign-exchange wiz because a small exchange-rate change makes a big difference in prices, real income, and buying habits. The exchange rate is important to Americans because it affects the prices they pay, their jobs, their incomes, and national economic policy.

Currency is the yardstick we use to measure value. We in the United States use the dollar to compare the cost and value of different items. Foreign currencies perform the same functions in their home countries. It is as if each country has adopted a separate measure of length, weight, or volume. All these different units are equally able to measure a given distance, but it is tough to find your way in a foreign land without a conversion table to help you find a way to go back and forth between the different measures.

PRICES AND EXCHANGE RATES

> **28.9 EXCHANGE RATES AND PRICES**

The exchange rate converts value measures from one currency to another, an important function. Suppose you are visiting France and you find an attractive sweater that would cost $20 at home. The Paris price is FFr150 (150 French francs). Is this a good buy? If the exchange rate is FFr1 = $.10 ($1 = FFr10) the answer is yes. The FFr150 sweater costs the equivalent of $15.00. Buy it in Paris. What if the exchange rate is FFr1 = $.20 ($1 = FFr5)? The sweater now costs $30.00 measured in U.S. currency. The sweater at home is a better buy.

French buyers of U.S. goods live in a mirror-image exchange-rate world. A French exchange student is pricing a U.S. camera that sells for $50. A similar model sells for FFr400 at home. Should she buy it? At the FFr10 = $1 (10 cents per franc) exchange rate it is a bad deal. The camera costs the equivalent of FFr500, so she should buy it at home. The camera only costs FFr250 if the exchange rate is FFr5 = $1 (20 cents per franc). The U.S. camera is the better buy at this currency rate.

You have just learned the first use of the exchange rate. It helps determine the cost of imported goods. An exchange rate change means new prices for buyers figuring in another currency. The sweater is priced at FFr150 and the camera costs $50 in either case, but they are a bargain or a bad deal depending on the exchange rate.

THE FOREIGN EXCHANGE MARKET

Foreign Exchange
Foreign currencies; people purchase foreign exchange because they want to purchase foreign goods.

No individual or organization sets the exchange rate in most countries. That job falls to the **foreign exchange** market. The exchange rate is the price at which foreign currencies are bought and sold.

28.10 FOREIGN CURRENCY

Derived Demand
A demand for one good based on demand for its complement.

28.11 CURRENCY APPRECIATION AND DEPRECIATION

Depreciate
To decrease in the relative value of a currency.

It may seem surprising that there is a market for foreign currencies. Why would someone want to buy money from other countries? People buy foreign currencies because they want to buy foreign goods. Sellers in France or Japan demand to be paid in their home currency. If you want to import their goods, you must first buy the necessary foreign currency. The demand for foreign exchange is a **derived demand.** The demand for foreign exchange depends on the demand for foreign goods. Let's see where the foreign exchange market comes from.

Demand for Francs

Assume that you have just entered the import-export business. You have decided to finance your college education by importing a particularly revolting brand of French wine. This wine sells for FFr20 on the Paris export market. You are pretty sure you can sell it at home, but price is important. How much should you buy? The answer depends on the demand for the wine at home, shown in Figure 28-2, and the exchange rate.

Suppose the exchange rate is FFr1 = $.20 today. How much does the wine cost? A FFr20 bottle of this wine costs $4.00 at this exchange rate. This is a high price for bad wine, so not many bottles will be sold. This is point A on the wine demand curve in the figure. At this exchange rate, you want to buy only a few bottles of wine. Since you do not want much wine, you do not need to buy many francs for your import purchases. There is a small quantity of francs demanded. This is point A on the franc demand curve in Figure 28-2.

What happens if the exchange rate changes? Suppose the franc **depreciates** the next day, falling from FFr1 = $.20 to FFr1 = $.10. The franc is cheaper, so the FFr20 bottle of wine is cheaper, too. The wine costs just $2.00 now. You can sell more wine at $2.00. This is point B on the wine

---

FIGURE 28-2

The Derived Demand for Francs. The demand for the franc is derived from the demand for French imports. French goods become cheaper for U.S. buyers when the franc depreciates. U.S. buyers want more imported goods, so more francs are also demanded. French goods cost more when the franc appreciates. Fewer French goods and less French currency are demanded. Points A, B, and C on the wine demand curve correspond to A, B, and C on the franc demand.

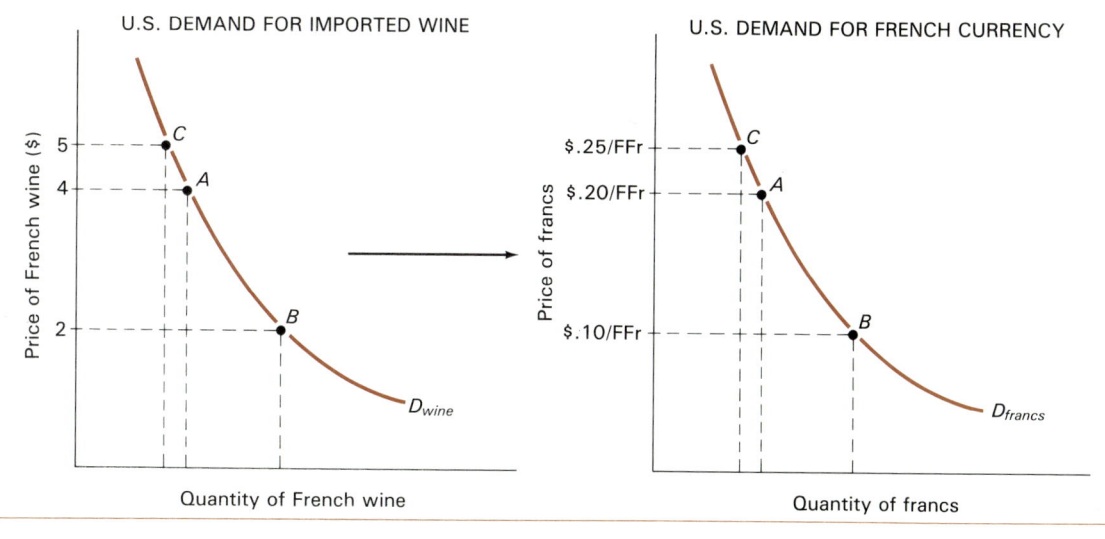

Appreciate
To increase in the relative value of a currency.

demand curve. You buy more wine and therefore need to buy more francs to pay the bill. This is point *B* on the franc demand curve.

What happens if the franc **appreciates** to FFr1 = $.25? The franc costs more dollars, so the French wine also costs U.S. buyers more money. The wine costs $5.00 per bottle at this exchange rate. There is not much demand for expensive bad wine, so little of the wine is imported and there is only a small quantity of francs demanded at this exchange rate. The small quantity of wine demanded at point *C* means a small currency demand at point *C* in the figure. The demand for the franc derives from the U.S. demand for French imports.

Demand for the Dollar

> 28.12
> DERIVED DEMAND FOR FOREIGN CURRENCY

This is only one side of the foreign exchange market. To see the other we must imagine the other side of foreign exchange transactions. For example, the French are busy in the foreign exchange market. Some French students are paying their tuition bills by importing American blue jeans. They need to buy dollars to pay for the jeans imports. The number of dollars they need depends on how many jeans they want to import. This depends, too, on the exchange rate. Figure 28-3 tells the story.

The exchange rate today is 20 cents per franc (FFr5 per dollar, in Parisian terms). Are the jeans a good deal? $20 jeans cost FFr100 at this price. This is point *A* on the jeans demand curve. Many French buyers will pay this price. The amount of dollars demanded here depends on the number of jeans purchased at this price.

What happens if the dollar depreciates? If the dollar drops from FFr5 to FFr4, so that it takes fewer francs to buy a dollar, the U.S. jeans are also cheaper. The jeans now cost just FFr80, a better deal for French buyers. More jeans are demanded at point *B* on the jeans demand curve, so the quantity of dollars demanded also rises. This is point *B* on the dollar demand curve.

Fewer dollars are demanded when our currency appreciates. If the dollar rises to FFr10 (10 cents per franc) it takes FFr200 to buy the $20 jeans.

FIGURE 28-3

The Derived Demand for Dollars. Dollar demand comes from the demand for U.S. goods. U.S. exports are less expensive when the dollar depreciates. More dollars are demanded to buy more U.S. goods when the dollar's value is low.

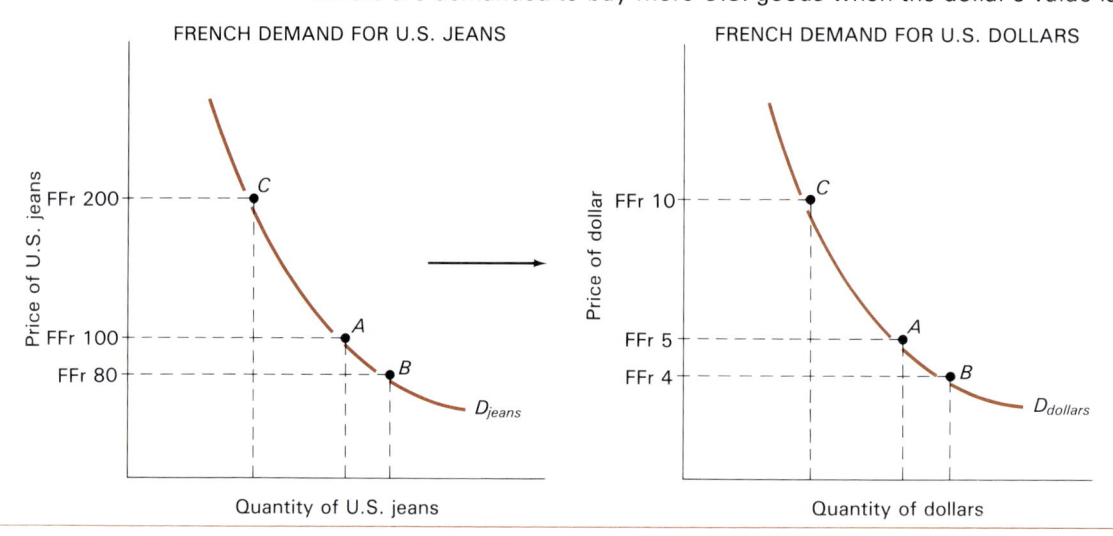

Only a few pairs are sold at jeans demand point C, so only a few dollars are demanded to make the deal. This corresponds to dollar demand point C.

THE GAMES EXCHANGE RATES PLAY

This example illustrates the subtle ways exchange rates affect economic activity. Look back at the two examples just given. What happened when the exchange rate changed from FFr1 = \$.20 to FFr1 = \$.10? The U.S. student said that the franc depreciated; that is, it became cheaper. His French wine was also cheaper. U.S. buyers find that French goods are cheaper. French wine makers gain, while U.S. wine makers worry about cheaper imports taking their market.

The French students saw this exchange rate shift differently. They said that the change from 20 cents to 10 cents per franc made the dollar appreciate. It took more francs to buy a dollar after the change. U.S. imports cost more in France. French import buyers suffered along with U.S. export firms, but French firms that compete with imports were happy to see foreign prices rise.

Exchange rate movements make some people winners and others losers. If the dollar appreciates, as in this example, U.S. firms sell fewer goods abroad, but foreign producers sell more here. Unemployment grows in the United States. American buyers find cheaper imports when the dollar appreciates, so inflationary pressures subside.

A falling dollar brings the opposite result. U.S. exporters sell more abroad because cheaper dollars mean cheaper prices in foreign markets. Unemployment falls in the U.S. when the dollar depreciates. Prices go up, however. Imports cost more, boosting the price level, when the dollar loses value against foreign currencies.

KEY CONCEPT 28.10 The demand for a country's currency is derived from the demand for its goods. As the price of a country's currency appreciates, the price of its goods to foreign buyers rises, reducing the demand for its goods. As the price of a country's currency falls, the demand for its goods increases.

HERE IS DEMAND, WHERE IS SUPPLY?

So far, we have seen what the exchange rate is, what it does, and we have found the demand for foreign currencies. A market cannot, however, live with just demand. We need supply curves, but so far they are nowhere to be seen. Who supplies French francs and U.S. dollars?

The supply curves have been here all along, we just have to look for them, as Figure 28-4 shows. The people in the U.S. supply dollars to the market. Why do they sell their dollars? They sell them when they trade them for francs.

We Americans see ourselves as franc demanders. We want to buy the French currency to buy French goods. The French look at our behavior from a different point of view. They see our acts as offering dollars for sale in exchange for their francs. We see ourselves demanding francs, but they see us as the suppliers of dollars. Both views are correct because they are simply two sides of the same market transaction.

766 International Finance

FIGURE 28-4

Exchanging Dollars and Francs. U.S. import buyers provide the supply of dollars on foreign exchange markets. High demand for the franc at an exchange rate of 10 cents per franc (point C on the FFr demand) means that many dollars are made available at the equivalent FFr10 per dollar exchange price (point C on the $ supply).

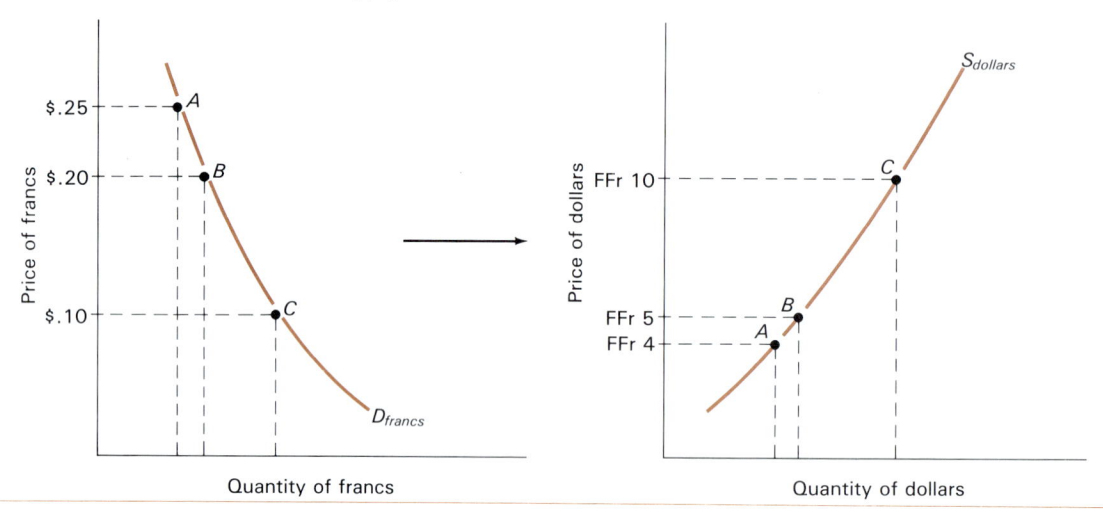

Americans want to buy many francs when the exchange rate is 10 cents per franc, at point C on the FFr demand curve in Fig. 28-4. View this from the other side of the Atlantic. The French see Americans offering to sell many dollars in exchange for francs at the equivalent price of FFr10 per dollar. This is point C on the dollar supply curve. The large quantity of francs demanded translates into many dollars offered for sale on the foreign exchange market.

When the franc appreciates fewer francs are demanded. For example, at 20 cents per franc fewer are demanded, so fewer dollars are offered in exchange at the equivalent rate of FFr5 per dollar. This corresponds to point B on both curves. The lower demand for francs at this exchange rate translates as fewer dollars supplied.

28.13 DERIVED DEMAND FOR THE DOLLAR

U.S. groups who want to buy foreign currencies supply dollars to the foreign exchange market. Who supplies francs? French importers who demand U.S. dollars. The supply of francs is derived from the demand for dollars as Figure 28-5 shows. Points A, B, and C here correspond to dollar demand and the corresponding franc supply at different exchange rates.

EXCHANGE MARKET EQUILIBRIUM

28.14 EXCHANGE MARKET EQUILIBRIUM

Supply and demand get together in the foreign exchange market where dollars and francs or any other pair of currencies are exchanged. There are two ways to view this market, as supply and demand for francs, or as a market for dollars. Both views give the same answers, you just pick one currency as price and the other as quantity. You can look at the market correctly either way. Figure 28-6 shows the exchange market equilibrium.

This market is in equilibrium at an exchange rate of 20 cents per franc (U.S. view) or FFr5 per dollar (French perspective). If the exchange rate drifts away from equilibrium for some reason, the forces of shortage and surplus force it back to its market-clearing level.

FIGURE 28-5 **Demanding Dollars Means Supplying Francs.** French buyers who demand dollars provide the international franc supply. Only a few dollars are demanded at FFr10 per dollar, so only a small quantity of francs is offered for sale at the equivalent 10 cents per franc exchange rate.

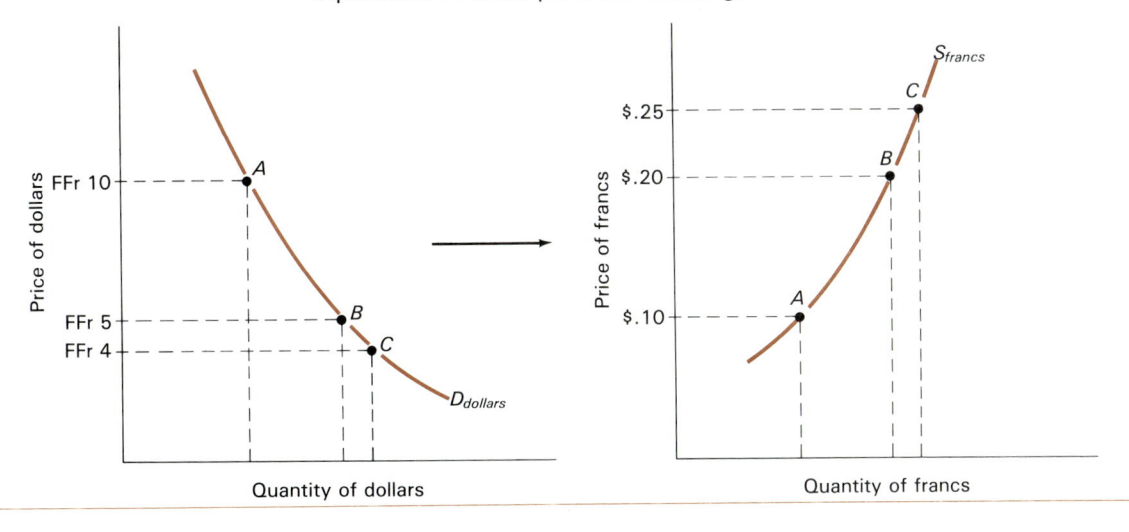

FIGURE 28-6 **Exchange Market Equilibrium.** The foreign exchange market finds equilibrium at FFr5 = $1 (20 cents per franc). Surplus and shortage act here, as in any market, to assure equilibrium.

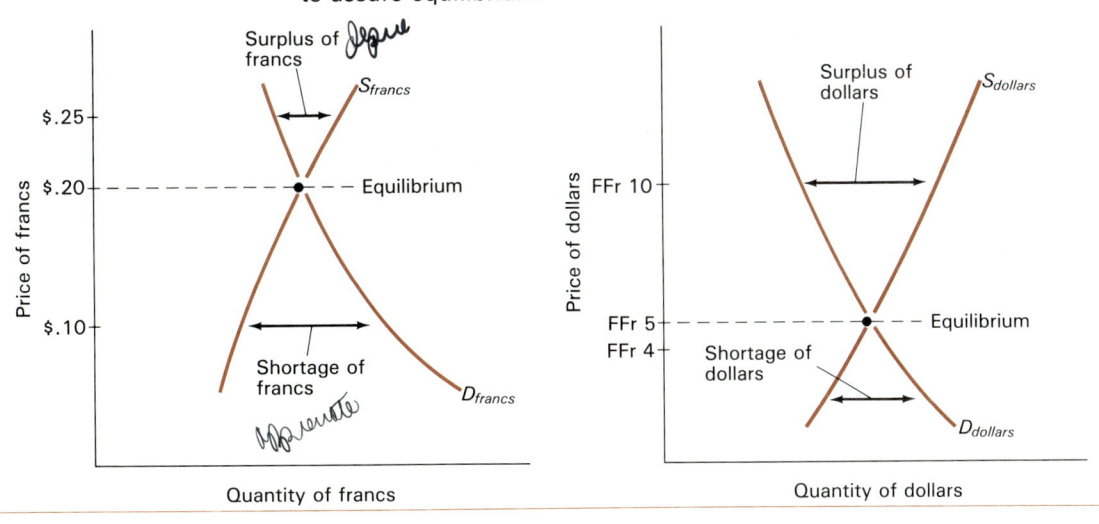

28.15 CURRENCY VALUE

Over-valued
An exchange rate below market equilibrium.

Under-valued
An exchange rate above market equilibrium.

Suppose the exchange rate moves from 20 to 25 cents per franc, as in Figure 28-6. At this price, the franc is **over-valued**. There is a surplus of francs and a corresponding shortage of dollars at this exchange rate. Frustrated French import buyers bid the dollar up, and the franc depreciates until the equilibrium is finally restored.

The franc is **under-valued** at an exchange rate like 10 cents per franc in the figure. There is a shortage of francs, and a corresponding surplus of dollars, at this exchange rate. U.S. buyers bid up the franc's price. The franc appreciates and the dollar falls until equilibrium is reached again and quantity demanded equals quantity supplied.

768 International Finance

Arbitrage
Riskless speculation; buying currencies on one foreign exchange market to sell at a profit elsewhere.

Who makes sure that the market finds equilibrium? Foreign exchange **arbitrage** dealers make it their business to find and destroy disequilibria. Suppose, for example that the franc is selling for 19 cents in New York and 21 cents in Paris. Arbitragers quickly spot the difference and buy up cheap francs in New York, selling them for the higher price in Paris. Multiply that small profit by the millions of francs that they buy and sell, and you can see how profitable this work can be. Arbitrage brings the two markets to equilibrium. Increased arbitrage demand for francs bids the price from 19 to 20 cents in New York. Increased arbitrage supply in Paris drives that price down from 21 to 20 cents. International equilibrium is restored and the arbitragers collect the profit.

THE FOREIGN EXCHANGE MARKET AT WORK

Exchange rates change whenever the supply and/or the demand for foreign currencies shift. The following are some examples of important exchange rate determinants. The figures used in these illustrations show just one side of each foreign exchange market; however, the same outcome will occur, if you look at exchange from the other side of the market.

> 28.16
> THE EFFECT OF TARIFFS
> ON CURRENCY VALUES

Tariff on Coffee   Tariffs and quotas reduce imports, but they have an unexpected side effect when exchange rates get involved. Suppose that the United States imposes a big tariff on a major import like coffee, perhaps in an attempt to weaken a coffee cartel or monopoly. Coffee prices go up in the United States and Americans buy less coffee. The economic effects of such an action do not end here.

Less coffee is demanded after the tariff, so U.S. coffee importers do not need to acquire as many Brazilian cruzeiros for their import purchases. The demand for cruzeiros falls, as Figure 28-7 shows, and the cruzeiro depreciates agains the dollar. The dollar appreciates against the cruzeiro.

FIGURE 28-7

Tariffs and the Exchange Rate. This tariff on Brazilian imports reduces the demand for the cruzeiro. The Brazilian currency depreciates, with the unintended effects discussed in the text.

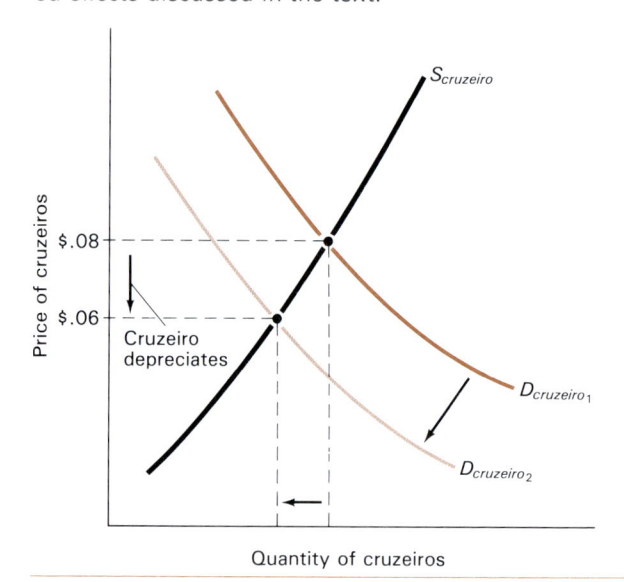

These exchange rate effects mean several things. First, the tariff is not as effective as first thought. The tariff made coffee prices rise in the United States, but the falling cruzeiro means that all Brazilian imports including coffee fall in price. Coffee prices still go up, but not as much as before.

Second, coffee is not the only product affected. All Brazilian imports cheapen when the cruzeiro depreciates. U.S. firms that compete with Brazilian imports face strong competition against cheaper imports. U.S. firms that sell to Brazil are also hurt. Appreciation of the dollar means that their goods cost more to Brazilian consumers, who buy less of them. U.S. exports to Brazil decline.

The tariff was meant to reduce coffee imports. The exchange rate side-effects are that more non-coffee goods are imported from Brazil, but fewer U.S. goods are sold there. Unemployment rates rise in the United States as we buy more from Brazil and sell them less.

28.17 ECONOMIC GROWTH AND EXCHANGE RATES

Economic Growth The exchange rate is tied to economic growth in a subtle way. The U.S. economy grew more rapidly than other nations in the late 1970s. How did the strength of the U.S. economy affect the exchange rate? The strong economy meant a weak dollar and the dollar fell.

When economic growth occurs people have higher incomes. They spend much of the increased income, and some of this spending goes for added purchases of imports, as Figure 28-8 shows. U.S. consumers bought more Italian shoes, cars, wine, and electronic gadgets. This helped Italian industry, but disrupted exchange markets. Increased U.S. buying flooded exchange markets with dollars. The increase in the supply of the dollar bid down the dollar's value against the lira. The dollar depreciated and the lira appreciated.

Rapidly growing countries often experience depreciation of their currency. Oddly enough, this helps them grow even more. The falling dollar made U.S. goods cheaper in Italy and increased the price of Italian goods in America. U.S. firms exported more due to depreciation, while the rising lira

FIGURE 28-8 **Economic Growth and the Exchange Rate.** Economic growth in the United States increases demand for Italian imports. The dollar depreciates against the lira.

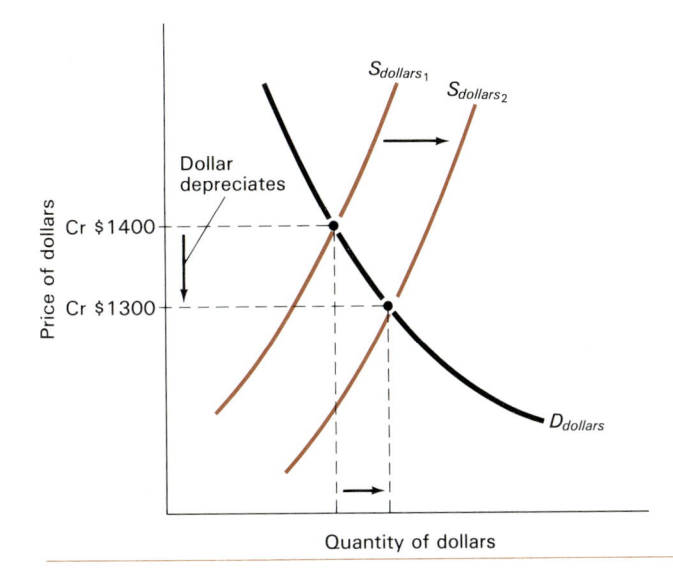

28.18 INFLATION AND EXCHANGE RATES

encouraged some buyers to switch from, say, Italian soave to Californian chardonnay wine.

Inflation and the Exchange Rate The exchange rate responds quickly to international inflation rate differences. British inflation rates were as much as double U.S. inflation rates in the 1970s. High inflation rates push a country's currency down. For example, imagine that you have the choice of buying a $100 U.S. radio or a similar British model that sells for £40. If the exchange rate is $2.50 per pound, you are probably indifferent between the two goods. They both cost 100 U.S. dollars. Now suppose that prices are stable in the U.S., but that the British have 25 percent inflation. The U.S. radio still sells for $100 one year later, but the British model now costs £50, 25 percent more. Which one are you going to buy now?

Falling demand for high-inflation British goods makes the demand for their currency fall as Figure 28-9 shows. At the same time, buyers in England start to import more goods from low-inflation U.S. firms. The supply of pounds rises as their demand for U.S. goods increases. The result is a smaller demand for pounds coupled with an increasing supply causing the pound to depreciate. The exchange market moves from initial equilibrium at *A* to a new balance at *B*, as shown in Figure 28-9. The high-inflation pound falls in value while the lower-inflation dollar appreciates.

Exchange rates partially protect countries like Britain from their high inflation woes. Inflation makes home prices rise, but the falling pound keeps the price of British goods abroad roughly the same. Exchange rates that adjust like this keep high inflation rates from killing export sales. Depreciation also means that low-inflation U.S. goods cost more abroad. The dollar is more expensive, so U.S. goods sell for higher prices in other countries. The exchange rate also protects the British market from cheaper items from low-inflation countries.

FIGURE 28-9

Inflation and the Exchange Rate. Depreciation is the lot of high inflation countries. The demand for the pound falls as British prices rise. British buyers demand more imports, increasing the supply of the currency. The pound depreciates as equilibrium moves from *A* to *B*. The exchange rate change partially offsets inflation's international effects.

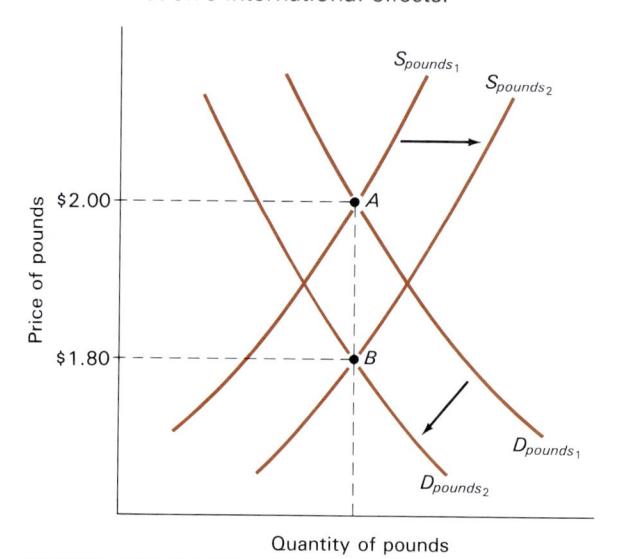

28.19 INTERNATIONAL EXCHANGE RATES

Interest Rate Differences People do not buy foreign currencies for import purposes alone. Banks, insurance companies, and large corporations invest their funds in the credit markets of many countries. If interest rates rise in West Germany, for example, big firms jump to take advantage of the higher return. They buy German bonds or make deposits in German banks. There is a catch, however. They must exchange dollars for deutsche marks to make German investments before they can get the higher foreign interest return.

Interest rate differences are an important part of the foreign exchange market. High U.S. interest rates are one reason for the dollar's appreciation in the early 1980s.

Real interest rates reached record levels in the United States in the early 1980s. Many foreign investors could not pass up the higher return available in America. Mexican investors pulled pesos out of their financial institutions and used them to buy dollars to put in American money market funds. The supply of pesos rose on the foreign exchange market and the Mexican currency fell in value against the dollar. The peso's depreciation meant that U.S. goods cost more in Mexico, but Mexican goods were cheaper in the United States. See Figure 28-10.

To find out whether this international credit flow was good for Mexico, we must weigh the trade-off. Credit flowed out of Mexico, making loans harder to get and driving up that country's interest rate. U.S. imports cost more in Mexico, so the exchange rate change added to inflation. However, there is a silver lining. Mexican exports to the United States rose because the dollar price of these goods fell along with the peso.

Intervention
Government or central bank foreign-exchange transactions intended to alter the exchange rate.

28.20 OFFICIAL INTERVENTION AND DIRTY FLOAT

Official Intervention Sometimes the Federal Reserve (usually referred to as the Fed) and foreign central banks **intervene** in foreign exchange markets. They buy or sell foreign currencies to artificially alter exchange rates. Rather than let the exchange rates of their currency float (be determined by market forces), they "prop up" currencies to end or limit depreciation. This

FIGURE 28-10

Interest Rates and Exchange Rates. High U.S. interest rates attract funds from Mexico. Increasing peso supplies drive down the exchange rate. The high-interest dollar appreciates while low interest rates force Mexico's currency to fall in value.

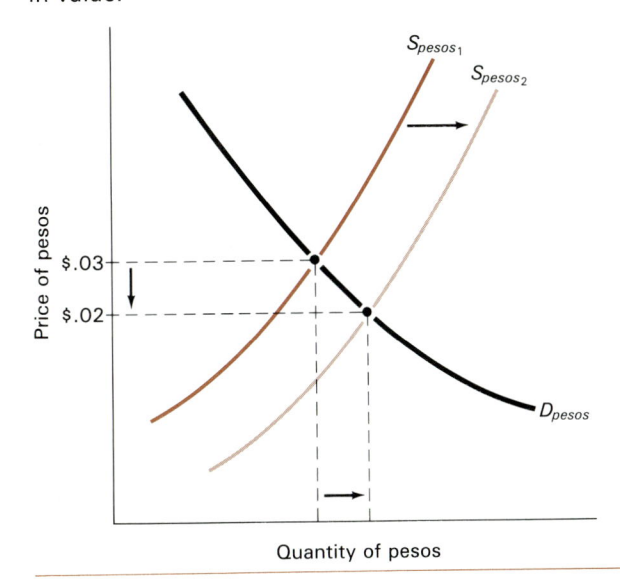

Dirty Float
Limited intervention by the central bank or government to prevent exchange rates from floating freely with supply and demand.

is sometimes referred to as a system of managed exchange rates or **dirty float.**

Why would the Fed intervene to force the dollar's value higher? Pride could be the reason, but it is hard to imagine conservative Fed bankers pushing exchange rates around for ego gratification. Anti-inflation policy is a better reason for official intervention. Dollar appreciation lowers import prices and so reduces inflation. Falling exports and rising imports lower aggregate demand in the United States, taking more pressure off inflation. Defending the dollar is another of the Fed's economic weapons.

Another reason for U.S. intervention is that billions of dollars have flowed out of the U.S. economy over the years. Many of these dollars have ended up in the vaults of foreign central banks where they are held as official reserves. Central bankers trust that their dollars have value, so they do not rush to exchange them for gold or their own currency.

If the dollar starts sliding against other currencies there is a risk that foreign countries will start an international bank "run" on the Fed. If all these countries try to sell their dollar reserves at once, the dollar depreciates dramatically, and there are adverse economic effects around the world. Part of the Fed's intervention concern is to keep the dollar strong enough to warrant international faith. So the Fed buys up excess dollars using its reserves of foreign currencies or loans from other central banks to keep the dollar strong.

The United States is not the only country that intervenes in foreign exchange rates. Most major countries intervene from time to time. This sometimes creates international economic conflict. The Fed might want to keep the dollar from falling in value. Other central banks sometimes try to make the dollar cheaper in order to reduce the cost of imports from the United States, for example.

OPEC (the Organization of Petroleum Exporting Countries) demands payment for its oil in dollars, not francs, pounds, Saudi riyals, or some other currency. If the British, French, or Japanese want to buy oil, they first have to buy dollars. This makes the value of the dollar an important economic statistic. If the dollar appreciates against the yen, for example, Japanese buyers also find oil prices rising. Higher oil payments reduce aggregate demand and boost production costs, cutting Japanese aggregate supply. Stagflation follows this shift of *AD* and *AS*.

What happens when the United States intervenes to increase the dollar's value and other governments step in to make it depreciate? The conflicting policies distort foreign exchange markets and send exchange rates shooting off in unexpected directions. A financial conflict erupts, and no country's policy is particularly effective.

28.21 EXCHANGE RATES AND BALANCE OF PAYMENTS

Balance of Payments Problems Market exchange rates are part of the solution to a country's balance of payments woes. The exchange rate, assuming no official intervention, automatically changes to reduce balance of payments problems. Figure 28-11 shows how this system works.

The United States has a balance of payments deficit with West Germany. This deficit is a sign that more dollars are leaving the country, exchanged for deutsche marks than DMs are entering and being exchanged for dollars. The market interpretation of this condition is simple. A balance of payments deficit means there is a surplus of dollars — more leaving the United States than entering — and a shortage of deutsche marks — more demanded than supplied. The deficit might have resulted from a rising demand for German goods, like the shift shown in Fig. 28-11.

FIGURE 28-11

Balance of Payments Adjustment. An increase in demand for German goods caused this U.S. balance of payments deficit. The DM appreciates and the dollar falls in value, automatically shifting trade patterns and adjusting for the payments problem.

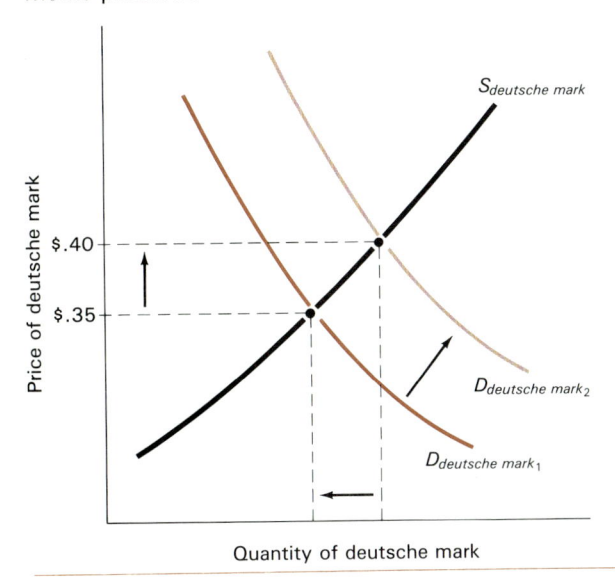

The market reaction to this imbalance is that the surplus dollar depreciates and the DM in short supply rises in value. This exchange rate adjustment helps bring the balance of payments back into equilibrium. The falling dollar encourages U.S. exports, so more money comes into America, and discourages the import flow of money to other lands. The result is that the U.S. payments deficit shrinks and Germany's surplus also grows smaller.

Automatic exchange-rate movements cannot solve all balance of payments problems, especially when official intervention keeps exchange rates from finding their own level. Flexible exchange rates keep surplus and deficit from getting out of hand.

FIXED EXCHANGE RATES

28.22 FIXED EXCHANGE RATES

Flexible Exchange Rates
Exchange rates that are set by supply and demand.

Fixed Exchange Rates
Exchange rates that are set by central banks.

Flexible exchange rates, where currency values are set by market forces, have only been around since about 1973. **Fixed exchange rates** prevailed in the world for most of the post–World War II period. Many small countries still fix their exchange rates against a major currency and members of the European Economic Community adopted a plan to fix exchange rates, within limits, for EEC currencies, while letting currency rates with non-EEC nations float on the market.

In a fixed exchange system, central banks agree on an official exchange rate, which is something like an exchange rate price control. When market forces start to push exchange rates away from the official rates, central bankers actively intervene, buying and selling currency, to make the official price stick.

Fixed exchange rates put an extra burden on countries with balance of payments deficits. A U.S. payments deficit, as explained earlier, pushes the dollar down when flexible exchange rates apply (see Figure 28-11). This cannot be allowed to happen under a fixed-rate regime. The Fed would be

ECONOMIC ISSUES

Flexible Versus Fixed Exchange Rates

There is nothing so basic to international trade and finance as the system of exchange rates that underlies it. Individuals, firms, and nations that wish to exchange goods or make investments across national borders must exchange currency in today's world. What system works best to make these transactions? This is a question that has been the subject of renewed debate in recent years. Many economists have called for a return to the fixed exchange rate system to reduce the chances of renewed inflation. Other economists think that the current system of flexible exchange rates works best. This is not a liberal–conservative issue, there are economists and policymakers from both left and right on both sides of this question.

The recent history of exchange rates is revealing. The world operated under a system of fixed exchange rates between 1946 and 1973. John Maynard Keynes was the principal architect of the Bretton Woods agreement that served as the foundation for this exchange rate regime. Exchange rates were set by central banks, such as the Fed, during the period. Exchange rates were not entirely fixed, however, since nations with prolonged balance of payments deficits sometimes devalued their currency, to realign the fixed exchange rates at a new level.

Flexible exchange rates have been the general rule since 1973. Major trading nations found it impossible to maintain fixed exchange rates in the turbulent, rising inflation world of the early 1970s. A flexible exchange rate plan was adopted at the Smithsonian conference to help nations better adjust to changing internal and external economic balance. Most exchange rates are set by the market forces of supply and demand. However, exchange markets are not completely free of controls. Major nations have, at different times, intervened in exchange markets to artificially alter currency values. They have sometimes operated under a system of dirty float or managed exchange rates. The United States intervened in 1983, for example, selling dollars to drive down their value because the strong dollar was thought to be hurting U.S. export industries and raising import costs for foreign buyers.

Some nations have even reverted to a fixed exchange-rate system. Member nations of the European Economic Community, for example, have adopted a system that provides fixed exchange rates within the EEC, although exchange rates between the EEC and other countries are subject to market changes.

Are the two exchange rate systems equally good? Many economists think that flexible exchange rates tend to promote inflation. They point out that the average inflation rate during the years of fixed exchange rates (1946–73) was much lower than during the years of flexible exchange rates (1973–present). Why should flexible exchange rates have an inflationary bias? The argument is that fixed exchange rates automatically control money supply growth. If the Fed increases the money supply rapidly, for example, U.S. interest rates fall and the dollar depreciates. The Fed, under flexible exchange rate rules, lets the dollar fall. High money-supply growth and the falling dollar both tend to cause inflation in the United States.

If exchange rates are fixed, however, the Fed must intervene on the exchange market to prevent a change in the dollar's value. The Fed buys dollars on foreign exchange markets, boosting the dollar's value

Special Drawing Rights (SDRs)
International central bank reserve; sometimes called paper gold because SDRs can be used like gold for central bank transactions.

Devaluation
Lowering a currency's fixed exchange rate.

forced to step in and defend the dollar by buying up the surplus greenbacks with reserves of foreign currency, gold, or by using its **special drawing rights.** Special drawing rights are international central bank reserves, sometimes called paper gold because they are used, like gold, to settle central bank transactions. The International Monetary Fund regulates SDR accounts and transactions much as the Fed regulates internal banking in the United States.

The Fed has no problem propping up the dollar if the deficit is short lived. A persistent deficit, however, means a continuing drain on U.S. reserves. Nations with long-term deficits are eventually forced to **devalue** their currency; that is, to change its official value to an exchange rate closer to the market clearing price. The United States devalued the dollar several times in the early 1970s in the face of persistent balance of payments problems.

and, as a side-effect, reducing the U.S. money supply. The Fed's initial attempt to increase money supply is limited by its responsibility to keep the exchange rate fixed. Economists, many of them monetarists, who subscribe to this argument suggest that the high inflation of the 1970s was not caused by the oil crisis or other external problems. They suspect that flexible exchange rates allowed high levels of monetary expansion, which caused rapid price inflation.

A change to fixed exchange rates, according to proponents of this view, would have the additional advantage of encouraging international trade by increasing stability and reducing risk. Flexible exchange rates change from day to day, making pricing and planning decisions difficult. Firms are unwilling to enter into otherwise advantageous long-term trade and finance agreements because exchange rate changes can quickly wipe out expected profits. A movement to fixed exchange rates, by reducing the uncertainty associated with international transactions, could encourage greater trade, benefiting all parties.

The proponents of flexible exchange rates do not deny that flexible rates have some disadvantages, but they suggest that the benefits are worth these costs. The principal benefit is that exchange rates move efficiently to equate supply and demand. Exchange rates move daily, but these movements are relatively small and are a response to important economic events. Daily central bank intervention would be needed under fixed exchange rates to keep currency rates constant. A nation that could not continually support its currency would be forced some day to devalue by a large amount. Small daily currency movements may be less disruptive to trade than larger but less frequent currency changes.

Proponents of flexible exchange rates suggest, further, that international traders and investors can avoid the risk of unexpected currency movements by taking advantage of the forward exchange market. The forward market exchanges currencies for delivery in the future at fixed prices agreed upon today. Individuals who will pay or receive future payments in a foreign currency can buy or sell on the forward currency market and thereby protect themselves from flexible exchange currency risk.

Many economists who favor flexible exchange rates do so because flexible exchange rates are thought to cushion an economy from external shocks, like oil price increases, that would more severely disrupt a fixed exchange-rate world. For example, if oil prices rise under fixed exchange rates, the United States might have to severely contract its money supply to prevent the dollar from falling. The result might be a severe recession. Under flexible exchange rates, however, the exchange rates change, so the internal economy does not need to contract so severely in the face of an external shock. The money supply can be increased in the United States, to partly counteract the contractionary effects of higher oil costs. Proponents of flexible exchange rates think the ability of flexible rates to cushion the economy from external shocks is important enough to outweigh any advantages the fixed-rate system might have.

Which is better, flexible or fixed exchange rates? As you can see from reading this section, there are sound arguments on both sides of this issue. The choice of an exchange rate regime boils down to a choice between potentially lower inflation rates (fixed exchange rates) and an economy potentially more secure from external shocks (flexible exchange rates). No exchange rate system is ever truly flexible or fixed, however. Governments intervene in nominally flexible systems, and market forces affect the level of fixed exchange rates, too.

Additional References

Lindbert, Peter H. and Kindleberger, Charles P., *International Economics,* 7th ed., Homewood, IL: Richard D. Irwin, 1982.

Artus, Jacques R., and Young, John H., "Fixed and Flexible Exchange Rates: A Renewal of the Debate," International Monetary Fund Staff Papers, December 1979.

The major question in international finance today is, are fixed exchange rates a good idea or are market determined currency values a better system? This questions is discussed in more detail in this chapter's Economic Issues section.

SUMMARY

28.1

1. The balance of payments is the broadest measure of a nation's international financial health. The balance of payments measures money inflows

and outflows resulting from trade, transfer payments, investment, and interest and profit return on investment. A balance of payments surplus means a nation receives more money inflows as payment for exports, transfer receipts, investments, and interest and profit payments than it pays out for exports, transfers abroad, investment abroad, and foreign interest and profit payments.

28.2

2. A balance of payments deficit means that total outflows exceed total money inflows during a given time period.

28.3

3. Nations can finance a balance of payments deficit in the short run by borrowing or selling assets such as gold reserves. In the long run, a balance of payments deficit requires some lasting adjustment to earn more foreign income or reduce payments abroad.

28.4

4. The balance of trade is equal to the value of exports minus the value of imported goods. The United States once had balance of trade surpluses because agricultural and manufactured exports exceeded the value of imported goods.

28.5

5. The United States has experienced very large balance of trade deficits in recent years, however, as oil imports increased, and exchange rate changes reduced import prices and raised the cost of U.S. goods for foreign buyers. The Product Life Cycle Theory is one explanation for the U.S. trade deficit. America has a comparative advantage in innovation and marketing, but standardized goods are eventually produced in low-cost foreign factories.

28.6

6. Deficits are bad because they suggest an international financial disequilibrium. Some internal or external adjustment is required to set things right. Adam Smith noted that deficits, measured in money, are not always bad. A trade deficit means a goods surplus.

28.7

7. The International Monetary Fund is the central bankers' central bank. It makes loans to nations with balance of payments deficits on the condition that they enact deficit-reducing economic policies. The World Bank makes economic development loans to less developed countries.

28.8

8. Exchange rates are mysterious because most people misunderstand them. Currencies are a medium of exchange and measure of value. Exchange rates allow conversion from one currency measurement base to another.

28.9

9. Exchange rates are important. Changing exchange rates alters relative prices, and so affects buyers, sellers, and other economic participants. The price of foreign goods varies directly with the value of the home country currency. A French good that costs FFr150 in Paris is inexpensive in the United States, just $15, if the exchange rate is FFr1 = 10 cents. It is expensive, however, if the franc is expensive. The price is $30 if the franc's price rises to 20 cents. The price of U.S. goods in France and other foreign countries varies in the same way.

Summary 777

28.10 ▸ 10. The foreign exchange market is the market where foreign currencies are exchanged for one another. The demand for foreign exchange is called a derived demand because people want to buy currency so they can use it to buy foreign goods, for example.

28.11 ▸ 11. The demand for francs is derived from the demand for French goods. As the franc's price rises, meaning that the franc appreciates, French goods become more expensive to U.S. buyers; therefore, fewer French goods and French currency are demanded. French goods fall in price to U.S. buyers as the franc depreciates, so more French goods and French currency are demanded. French buyers and other foreign buyers need to purchase the dollar so they can buy U.S. goods. As the dollar appreciates, it takes more French currency to buy both the dollar and U.S. goods. However, the franc price of U.S. goods falls when the dollar depreciates. Because the exchange rate compares two currencies against one another, appreciation of one currency—the dollar, for example—necessarily implies the depreciation of the other.

28.12 ▸ 12. U.S. goods are more expensive abroad when the dollar appreciates, so French consumers buy less of them. U.S. exports and French imports fall. The franc depreciates when the dollar appreciates, however, making French goods cheaper in the United States. French exports and U.S. imports rise. French exporters, French import-competing firms, and U.S. import consumers tend to gain when the dollar appreciates, but U.S. exporters, U.S. import competing firms, and French consumers who buy U.S. goods lose.

28.13 ▸ 13. U.S. importers demand francs but, in this act, they supply dollars to the foreign exchange market. The demand for francs creates the supply of dollars. The demand for dollars creates the supply of francs.

28.14, 28.15 ▸ 14. Exchange markets seek equilibrium, just as other supply-demand markets do. A surplus of dollars occurs when the dollar is overvalued, priced above the market equilibrium price. The dollar depreciates. The dollar tends to rise when it is undervalued. Foreign exchange arbitrage dealers help assure equilibrium by buying and selling off equilibrium.

28.16 ▸ 15. A tariff on coffee reduces the demand for the cruzeiro (Brazil's currency). The dollar appreciates against the cruzeiro, accidentally reducing the price of Brazilian goods in the United States and reducing U.S. exports to Brazil.

28.17 ▸ 16. Countries that experience rapid economic growth normally purchase more foreign goods, thereby increasing the demand for foreign currencies. The home currency depreciates.

28.18 ▸ 17. High inflation countries frequently suffer currency depreciation, which offsets the disadvantage of higher prices.

28.19 ▸ 18. Interest rate differentials are an important determinant of modern exchange rates. Capital flows to high-interest rate countries. Foreign investors must purchase dollars to invest in U.S. credit markets, thus

19. Official intervention occurs when a country's central bank or government buys or sells currency to alter the exchange rate. Intervention has been important in recent years because most international oil payments are made in dollars; thus, countries try to increase the value of their currency against the dollar.

20. Exchange rates tend to automatically adjust for balance of payments deficits. Deficit nations normally experience currency depreciation, which tends to reduce imports and encourage exports, thus reducing the payments deficit.

21. Exchange rates do not always rise and fall with market forces. Fixed exchange rates are set by central banks, which intervene to keep the exchange rates fixed by buying and selling foreign exchange. Exchange rates were fixed during the period 1946–73. The European Economic Community today uses a system of relatively fixed exchange rates.

DISCUSSION QUESTIONS

1. Many Japanese car firms are considering moving production from Japan to the United States to escape U.S. trade barriers. How will this change imports and affect the demand for the yen? the supply of the yen? the exchange rate between the dollar and the yen? Explain.

2. Who gains and loses from the exchange rate change in Question 1? Make your list as complete as possible. How would car firms that stay in Japan be affected? Explain.

3. Your firm has agreed to pay a Japanese supplier 100 million yen at the end of the month. You have just learned that the inflation rate in Japan is increasing. The U.S. inflation rate is stable. Should you buy the yen now, or wait until the end of the month to make your foreign exchange transaction? Explain your reasoning.

4. Income is growing in West Germany while France is suffering a recession. How does this affect a flexible exchange rate between the two countries? How does your answer change if the exchange rate is fixed? What official actions are required? Do these actions increase or decrease the income gap between the two nations? Explain.

5. Are fixed exchange rates better than flexible rates? List the advantages and disadvantages of each system. Which do you think is best? Defend your choice.

SELECTED READINGS

Artus, Jacques R. and Young, John H., "Fixed and Flexible Exchange Rates: A Renewal of the Debate" reprinted in Baldwin, Robert E., and Richardson, J. David, *International Trade and Finance Readings*, 2nd ed., Boston: Little, Brown and Company, 1981.

Lindert, Peter H. and Kindleberger, Charles, *International Economics*, New York: Richard D. Irwin, 1982.

Martin, Douglas, "The Saudis Build a Pittsburgh," *New York Times*, January 31, 1982.

Meier, Gerald M. *Problems of a World Monetary Order*, Cambridge: Oxford University Press, 1982.

Solfe, Sidney E. and Burke, James L., *The Great Wheel: The World Monetary System*, New York: McGraw Hill, 1975.

Whitman, Marina von Neumann, "International Interdependence and the U.S. Economy," reprinted in Baldwin, Robert E., and Richardson, J. David, *International Trade and Finance Readings*, 2nd ed., Boston: Little, Brown and Company, 1981.

CHAPTER 29

International Economic Policy

Having read the chapter, reviewed the chapter summary, and completed the *Study Guide* exercises, you should be able to:

CRIS

29.1 EXCHANGE RATES AND PRICES: Explain how changes in the exchange rate affect the prices of imports, exports, import-competing goods, and items that are produced with imported input.

29.2 EXCHANGE RATES AND INCOME DISTRIBUTION: Explain how changes in the exchange rate affect the distribution of income.

29.3 EXCHANGE RATES AND AGGREGATE DEMAND: Explain how changes in the exchange rate affect aggregate demand.

29.4 EXCHANGE RATES AND AGGREGATE SUPPLY: Explain how changes in the exchange rate affect aggregate supply.

29.5 EXCHANGE RATES, INFLATION AND UNEMPLOYMENT: Use *AD–AS* analysis to explain how changes in the exchange rate affect inflation and unemployment.

29.6 EXCHANGE RATES, CREDIT MARKET CONDITIONS: Discuss the relationship between changes in a country's credit market conditions and changes in its exchange rate.

29.7 FLEXIBLE EXCHANGE RATES, MONETARY POLICY: Explain how monetary policy affects the economy under a system of flexible exchange rates.

29.8 FLEXIBLE EXCHANGE RATES, FISCAL POLICY: Explain how fiscal policy affects the economy under a system of flexible exchange rates.

29.9 FIXED EXCHANGE RATES, MONETARY POLICY: Explain how monetary policy affects the economy under a system of fixed exchange rates.

29.10 FIXED EXCHANGE RATES, FISCAL POLICY: Explain how fiscal policy affects the economy under a system of fixed exchange rates.

- **29.11 ECONOMIC GOALS:** Discuss the relationship between the domestic and the international economic goals of the United States.

- **29.12 ECONOMIC POLICY OPTIONS:** Discuss the domestic and international impact of trade restrictions, voluntary export agreements, exchange rate intervention, and classical medicine.

- **29.13 ECONOMIC GOALS FOR GROWTH:** Discuss the relationship between economic growth and the other domestic and international economic goals of the economy.

One of the clearest lessons of recent history is that it is a mistake to ignore the international aspects of any major economic policy or problem. In the past, economics was often discussed in the United States as if the rest of the world did not exist. In the 1970s and 1980s, however, it has become clear that we must take into account international cause and effect. The oil embargoes of the 1970s made us painfully aware that events in other nations could have real and significant effects at home. The large trade imbalances that the United States has experienced in the 1980s have demonstrated that foreign competition and international financial developments must be reckoned with.

We have looked at international trade and international finance in Chapters 26 and 27. This discussion has focused on many of the microeconomic aspects of international economic interactions. Macroeconomics also has an international side. Monetary and fiscal policies cause important changes in exchange rates and trade patterns. These international effects are too large and important for us to ignore. This chapter combines the basic macroeconomic ideas discussed in Chapters 8 through 15 of this book with the international economic principles presented in Chapters 26 and 27.

Our first goal in this chapter is to understand how macroeconomic policies work in a modern open economy. We will examine the impacts of monetary and fiscal policies with an emphasis on how they affect exchange rates and international trade. We will then look at how domestic economic policies affect the international goals of the economy. Finally, we will explore the difficult trade-offs that the economy faces as it attempts to reduce its large balance of trade deficit.

HOW EXCHANGE RATES AFFECT THE ECONOMY

Our analysis of international economic policies begins with the exchange rate. As we saw in Chapter 27, the exchange rate is a key linkage between economic systems. Almost all international transactions necessarily involve a foreign exchange transaction. We can therefore learn a great deal about how economic systems are connected by focusing on the exchange rate. Changes in the exchange rates affect international trade patterns which, in turn, alter prices, the distribution of income, aggregate demand and aggregate supply, and inflation and unemployment. We will review each of these exchange rate effects and then proceed to our analysis of international macroeconomic policies.

29.1 EXCHANGE RATES AND PRICES

Trade and Prices

Let us review what we learned in Chapter 27. What does a rising dollar (dollar appreciates against other currencies) do to prices in the United States? A rising dollar means that the dollar buys more foreign currency, and therefore more foreign goods. When the dollar appreciates, import prices fall — after a brief lag — while declining prices work their way to consumer markets. Cheaper imports tend to force down the prices for U.S.-made substitutes, as domestic firms respond to the foreign competition.

Many U.S. firms use foreign-produced inputs such as raw materials and intermediate goods. The rising dollar is good for these firms because it lowers their production costs. Lower production costs tend to increase the supply of items that use foreign inputs, which results in lower prices for these goods, all else being equal.

A strong dollar also tends to lower the price that U.S. buyers pay for U.S. export goods. To see why this is true, let us look at an example of a good that the United States usually exports: wheat. What happens to the price U.S. buyers pay for wheat when the dollar appreciates? U.S. wheat costs more yen when the dollar appreciates. Foreign buyers switch to less costly grains and buy wheat from other exporting countries. Many countries will produce more grain themselves rather than purchase higher-cost U.S. wheat exports. The falling foreign demand for U.S. wheat will tend to bid down the price of wheat, all else being equal. American buyers benefit from the reduced export demand because they pay fewer dollars for wheat.

An appreciating dollar forces U.S. prices down. Imports cost less, import-competing firms lower prices to hold on to their customers, items that use imported inputs experience lower costs, and exported goods are cheaper to U.S. buyers. The dramatic appreciation of the U.S. dollar in 1979–1985 had all the effects just discussed. Inflation rates in the United States fell because of the exchange rate's impact on the prices of imports, import-competing goods, and exports.

A depreciation of the dollar would tend to have the opposite effect on prices. Prices tend to rise in the United States when the dollar depreciates. As the dollar depreciates, imports become more expensive, U.S. import-competing producers are able to raise prices, costs and prices rise for American items that use imported inputs, and the domestic price of U.S. export goods such as wheat also rise. The logic of these price increases runs parallel to the analysis of dollar appreciation.

29.2 EXCHANGE RATES AND INCOME DISTRIBUTION

Distribution of Income

The price changes just discussed alter the distribution of income in trading countries. A rising dollar, for example, shifts income away from workers in import-competing and export-based industries. In the 1980s, for example, the rising dollar tended to reduce the relative incomes of workers and businesses and industries, such as agriculture, which depend on exports, and steel and automobiles, which compete with imported goods. The rising dollar tends to increase income in jobs that use cheaper imports as an intermediate good. Firms that import and process foreign steel or agricultural goods increase their share of domestic markets.

Dollar depreciation has the opposite consequences. Imports cost more, so incomes rise for workers in import-competing firms. Income also rises in export industries. Export sales jump when the dollar slumps, increasing income for workers and firms in these industries.

29.3 EXCHANGE RATES AND AGGREGATE DEMAND

Aggregate Demand

Dollar appreciation reduces aggregate demand (*AD*) because the net export component of *AD* falls. The rising dollar increases imports (a leakage) and reduces exports (an injection). The decrease in net exports has a multiplier effect on aggregate demand. As we saw in Chapter 11, falling *AD* tends to lower real GNP, but the price level or the inflation rate also falls.

A falling dollar, on the other hand, tends to result in demand-pull inflation. Imports decline and exports increase when the dollar depreciates. This causes an increase in the net export component of *AD*, which results in a multiplier increase in aggregate demand. Rising *AD* increases both real GNP and the price level, all else being equal.

29.4 EXCHANGE RATES AND AGGREGATE SUPPLY

Aggregate Supply

Exchange rate changes also affect aggregate supply for the economy. Changing input prices are the most important effect here. The dollar's appreciation tends to reduce production costs and increase aggregate supply by lowering the cost of foreign-made production goods, such as steel and minerals, and by reducing the demand for U.S. inputs in industries that face stiffer foreign competition. The falling dollar, on the other hand, makes imported inputs and intermediate goods more expensive. Production costs rise and aggregate supply falls when the dollar depreciates.

29.5 EXCHANGE RATES, INFLATION AND UNEMPLOYMENT

Inflation and Unemployment

Because exchange rate changes affect aggregate demand and aggregate supply, they must also affect inflation and unemployment in the economy. The *AD-AS* effects of changes in the exchange rate are summarized in Figure 29-1. When the dollar appreciates, *AD* tends to fall due to lower net

FIGURE 29-1

Exchange Rates and the Economy. Aggregate demand falls when dollar appreciation discourages net exports. Cheaper imported goods reduce production costs, increasing *AS*. The economy moves from initial equilibrium *A* to new equilibrium *B* in the first figure. *AD* rises when the dollar depreciates, but *AS* falls if higher import prices boost production costs. The economy moves from *A* to *B* in the second figure.

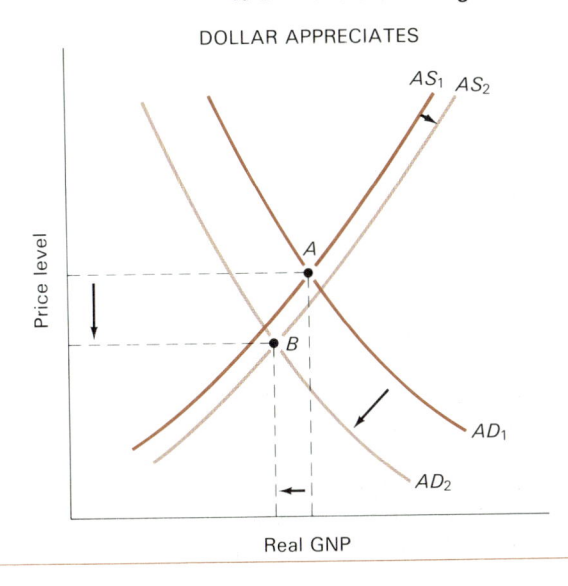

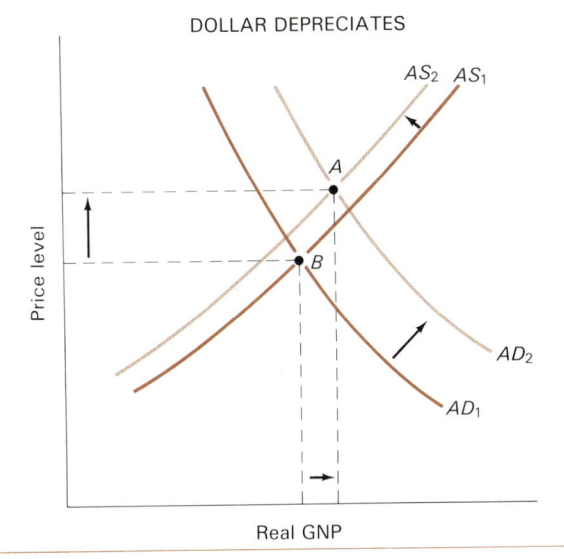

exports, but AS tends to rise due to lower import costs. The appreciating dollar is deflationary, but its unemployment effect depends on whether AD or AS shifts the most. The AD effect often dominates in the short run, as Figure 29-1 illustrates, and real GNP falls. This is what happened in the United States in the early 1980s. As the dollar appreciated dramatically, the U.S. inflation rate fell, but so did real GNP, pushing the economy into a serious recession with very high unemployment rates.

Dollar depreciation means inflation, as the figure shows. When the dollar depreciates, the result is that AD rises, fueled by rising exports and reduced imports, but AS falls because imported inputs cost more. Inflation increases as a result of these exchange-rate induced changes in AD and AS. The AD shift is often greater in the short run, as Figure 29-1 indicates, so a falling dollar often boosts real GNP and lowers unemployment.

This discussion has focused on exchange rates and international trade. It is important to remember, however, that exchange rates do not shift by themselves. Exchange rates are determined by the foreign exchange markets discussed in Chapter 28. Exchange rates therefore change only when events cause changes in the demand for or supply of foreign currencies.

INTEREST RATES, EXCHANGE RATES, AND INTERNATIONAL CREDIT MOVEMENTS

29.6 EXCHANGE RATES, CREDIT MARKET CONDITIONS

Interest rates and the credit market activities that produce them have been key determinants of short-run exchange-rate movements in recent years. Many factors, including income differentials and changing patterns of comparative advantage, alter exchange rates over long periods, but interest rates, inflation, and official intervention are the principle causes of short-term change. For example, in the early 1980s, high real U.S. interest rates, caused by large U.S. budget deficits and the relatively high profitability of investment in the United States, caused the dollar to appreciate, which in turn caused falling net exports and the large balance of trade deficit shown here.

Figure 29-2 shows how the U.S. tax cuts and budget deficit, which affected the U.S. credit market, caused the dollar to appreciate on international foreign exchange markets. Huge federal deficits increased credit demand in the early 1980s. President Reagan's supply-side tax cuts also increased the profitability of business investment in the U.S., increasing credit demand for this purpose. The credit demand (CD) curve in Figure 29-2 therefore shifted out and to the right. This would normally cause interest rates in the U.S. to rise to very high levels. Interest rates did not rise as expected, however, because of the international effects. Foreign leaders shifted funds to the United States. This had two effects on the markets shown in Figure 29-2. First, the increased availability of foreign credit funds increased the U.S. supply of loanable funds, shifting the credit supply (CS) curve in the figure. The rise in U.S. interest rates was relatively modest because much of the rising credit demand was accommodated by an increase in credit supply from abroad.

This international credit movement had anothr impact, however. Foreign leaders had to sell their own currencies and purchase dollars in order to lend to U.S. firms and the U.S. Treasury. The credit flow into the United States therefore caused an increase in the demand for the dollar that caused a significant appreciation of the dollar. This dollar appreciation, as discussed earlier, affected trade patterns, income distribution, AD, and AS.

FIGURE 29-2

International Credit Flows. The rising deficit increases credit demand (CD), which tends to drive up interest rates. The U.S. credit market moves from A to B in the first figure. Higher U.S. interest rates attract credit from abroad. This inflow of credit increases U.S. credit supply (CS), so the credit market ends up at equilibrium B. The inflow of credit also increases the demand for the dollar on foreign exchange markets. The equilibrium moves from X to Y, with the dollar appreciating in the process.

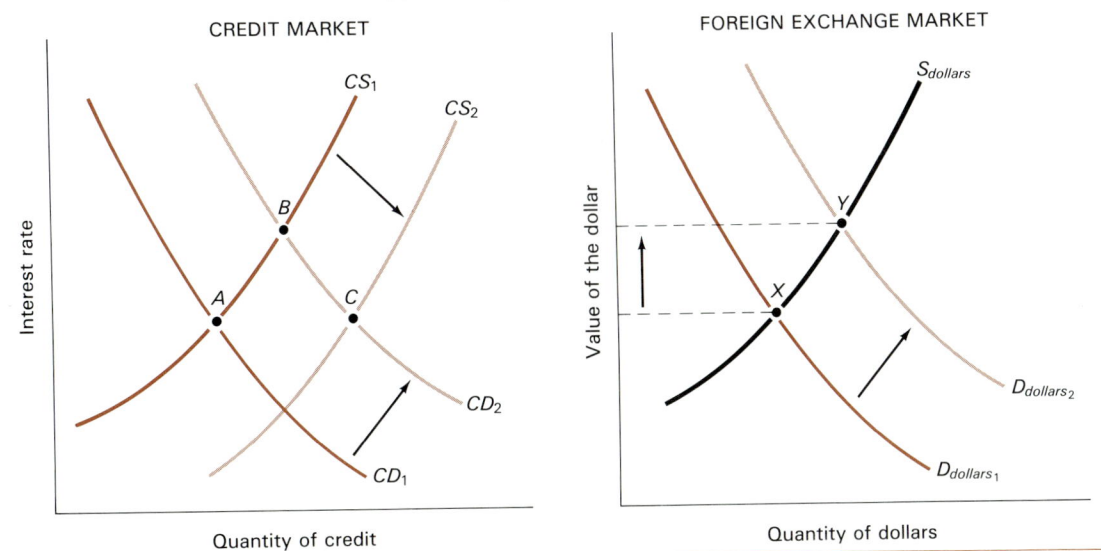

This example shows that changes in credit markets in one country can have international effects that are important. Monetary and fiscal policies will, therefore, have international implications that must be considered.

ECONOMIC POLICY WITH FLEXIBLE EXCHANGE RATES

Chapters 8-15 of this book focused on the closed-economy effects of monetary and fiscal policy. A complete view of economic policy needs to also consider the impact of changes in the exchange rate, trade patterns, and international credit flows. Let us see how economic policy works in an open economy. To keep our analysis fairly simple, let us suppose that the economy is experiencing relatively high unemployment rates, such as those that prevailed in the United States in the early 1980s. Let us examine how expansionary monetary and fiscal policies aimed at stimulating the economy would work in this situation. (Note: some students may wish to briefly review the earlier macroeconomic chapters, particularly Chapters 11, 12, and 14, before or after reading this section.)

Monetary Policy with Flexible Exchange Rates

> 29.7 FLEXIBLE EXCHANGE RATES, MONETARY POLICY

The Federal Reserve can use monetary policy to attempt to stimulate the economy and reduce unemployment. Expansionary Federal Reserve policies bring both national and international effects for the U.S. economy. The dual impacts are illustrated in Table 29-1, which shows how domestic and international cause-and-effect relationships are tied together. The domestic or closed economy results of monetary policy are well known. Using Keynesian analysis for simplicity, an open market purchase or other expansionary

786 International Economic Policy

TABLE 29-1	Expansionary Monetary Policy with Flexible Exchange Rates Policy: FRS Undertakes Open Market Purchase
Domestic Effects	**International Effects**

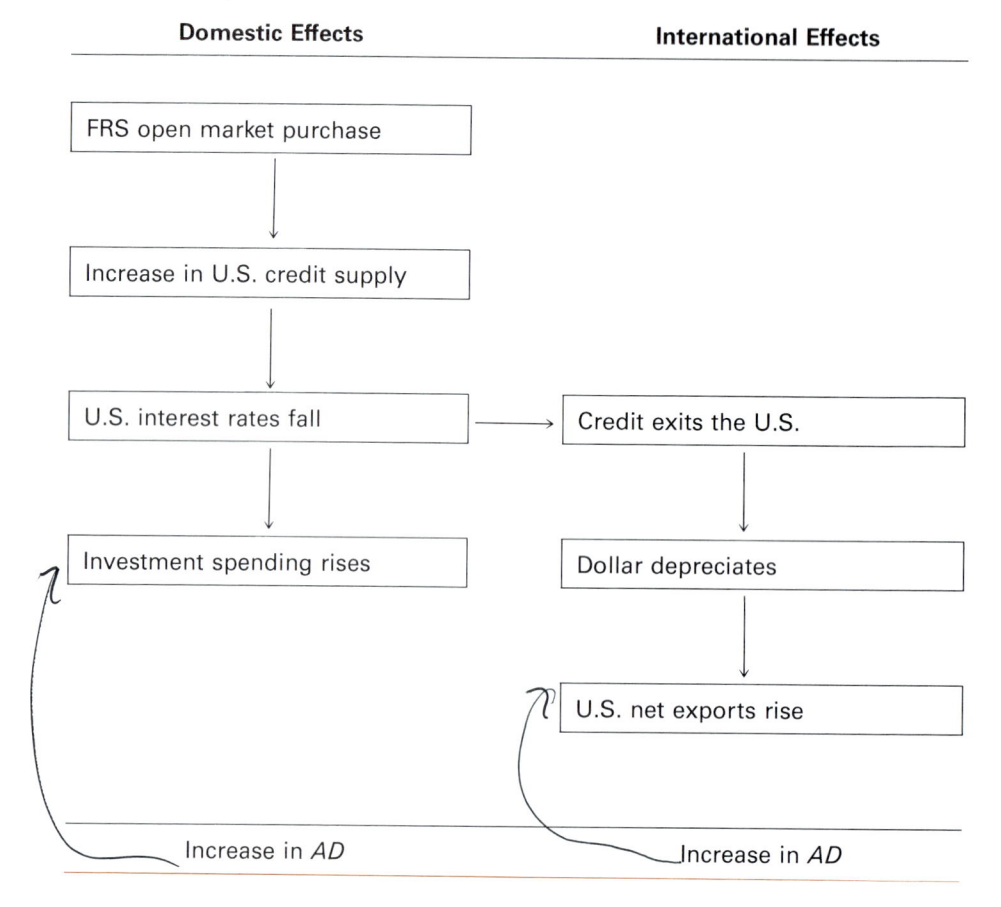

```
         FRS open market purchase
                   │
                   ▼
        Increase in U.S. credit supply
                   │
                   ▼
          U.S. interest rates fall ──────────▶ Credit exits the U.S.
                   │                                    │
                   ▼                                    ▼
         Investment spending rises              Dollar depreciates
                                                        │
                                                        ▼
                                               U.S. net exports rise

              Increase in AD                      Increase in AD
```

action increases money and credit supplies in the United States. This tends, all else being equal, to bid down interest rates and encourage greater investment spending. Increased investment spending boosts aggregate demand in the short run and tends to increase aggregate supply in the long run by increasing capacity and improving technology. Ignoring the international effects, then, expansionary monetary policy tends to cause demand-pull inflation in the short run due to the rise in AD.

Do international events alter these conclusions? Let us focus on the exchange rate for a moment. Expansionary monetary policy causes the dollar to depreciate. Lower interest rates in the United States cause credit to exit. International investors seek higher returns elsewhere. They sell dollars and buy foreign currencies so that they can lend their credit abroad. The credit exit keeps U.S. interest rates from falling as far as they otherwise would, and forces dollar depreciation.

The dollar's depreciation makes this FRS policy at once more expansionary and more inflationary. Credit leaving the United States pushes the dollar's value down. This makes imports more costly and makes U.S. exports more attractive abroad. Increased exports and reduced imports further boost aggregate demand. Aggregate supply falls due to higher import costs, however.

Table 29-1 shows that monetary policy still works, even when the international effects are included. In fact, monetary policy is now more effective than in a closed economy because it has a dual impact on the economy. This monetary policy expands both the domestic investment sector and it also tends to expand the net export sector of the domestic economy.

Fiscal Policy with Flexible Exchange Rates

29.8 FLEXIBLE EXCHANGE RATES, FISCAL POLICY

Table 29-2 summarizes the way that fiscal policy works in an open economy. Here we assume that a tax cut has resulted in a large deficit. Table 29-2 shows that the tax cut stimulates the domestic economy through the spending multiplier process. The resulting deficit, however, must be financed in the credit markets. All else being equal, the increase in credit demand to finance the deficit causes U.S. interest rates to rise. Higher U.S. interest rates in turn attract credit from foreign countries. This inflow of credit keeps U.S. interest rates from rising as severely as would otherwise be the case. The domestic effects of this policy are therefore to increase AD at home and to stimulate the economy.

The inflow of foreign credit also affects the exchange rate, as the table shows. Foreign lenders must purchase dollars in order to lend their funds in the United States. This tends to bid up the international value of the dollar. The dollar's appreciation makes U.S. export goods more expensive to foreign buyers and reduces the cost of imports from abroad to U.S. consumers and businesses. The United States therefore tends to export less and import

---

TABLE 29-2 | **Expansionary Fiscal Policy with Flexible Exchange Rates Policy: Tax Cut that Increases Deficit**

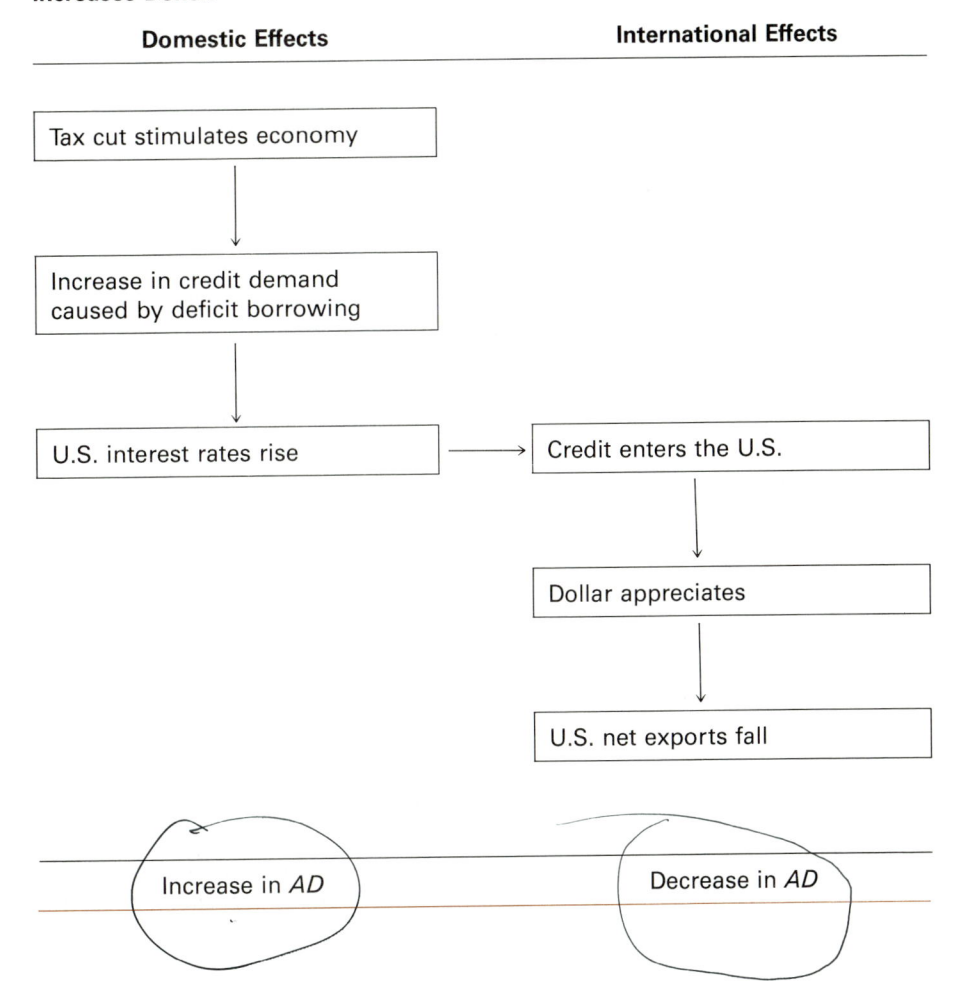

Domestic Effects / **International Effects**

Tax cut stimulates economy
↓
Increase in credit demand caused by deficit borrowing
↓
U.S. interest rates rise → Credit enters the U.S.
↓
Dollar appreciates
↓
U.S. net exports fall

Increase in AD / Decrease in AD

more. Net exports fall in America, which causes a multiplier decrease in aggregate demand.

As Table 29-2 suggests, fiscal policy tends to be relatively ineffective in a world of flexible exchange rates because the international effects tend to offset the domestic effects. The deficit may stimulate domestic spending on the one hand, but it also tends to reduce net export spending due to the exchange rate effects. Overall, the impact on the economy will be relatively small, at least compared with the same policies in a closed economy.

What are the implications of this analysis? Monetary policy is the most important tool for economic policy in these days of flexible exchange rates. Monetary policy gains strength from international effects while fiscal policy is diluted by exchange-rate changes. This suggests that we should rely more on monetary policy to influence AD, but we still cannot ignore fiscal policy. While fiscal policy is less powerful in changing AD, it still has an important impact on interest and exchange rates.

ECONOMIC POLICY WITH FIXED EXCHANGE RATES

Economic policy prescriptions depend on the prevailing exchange rate regime. Exchange rates were fixed between 1946–73 and many countries use some variant of a fixed exchange-rate system today. The nations of the European Economic Community, for example, attempt to keep their exchange rates relatively fixed among themselves. Many less developed countries also attempt to keep their currencies at a constant exchange rate relative to a major trading nation such as the United States or Japan.

Fixed exchange rates were discussed in Chapter 28. Under a system of fixed exchange rates, the central bank (the Federal Reserve System in the United States) must intervene whenever the exchange rate deviates from its official value. If the dollar begins to appreciate, for example, the FRS must sell dollars in order to bring the dollar's value back down to its official rate. If the dollar begins to fall or depreciate, however, the FRS must buy up dollars on the exchange markets in order to keep the exchange rate constant.

In a system of fixed exchange rates, then, the Federal Reserve plays two roles. It is, first, in charge of U.S. monetary policy. But it is also required to keep the exchange rate fixed. This additional responsibility changes the way that economic policies work. We can see this if we briefly examine the way that expansionary monetary and fiscal policies would work under a system of fixed exchange rates.

Monetary Policy with Fixed Exchange Rates

29.9
FIXED EXCHANGE RATES, MONETARY POLICY

Table 29-3 presents a schematic diagram that simplifies the analysis of monetary policy under fixed exchange rates. An open market purchase increases the U.S. supplies of money and credit and tends to drive interest rates down, all else being equal. Looking at the international effects, however, we see that all else is not equal. Lower U.S. interest rates cause profit-seeking individuals to pull their funds out of U.S. banks and financial intermediaries and lend the funds abroad, looking for higher returns there. Thus the interest rate does not fall as much as we might guess if we had ignored the international side of this policy.

As people take their funds abroad, they sell dollars and purchase foreign currencies. This would cause the dollar to depreciate under a system of

Economic Policy with Fixed Exchange Rates 789

TABLE 29-3   **Expansionary Monetary Policy with Fixed Exchange Rates Policy: FRS Undertakes Open Market Purchase**

Domestic Effects	International Effects	FRS Action

```
Open market pur-
chase
     │
     ▼
Interest rates fall ────────▶ Credit exits U.S.
                                     │
                                     ▼
                              Dollar depreciates ────▶ FRS pur-
                                     ▲                  chases
                                     │                  dollars to
                              Dollar returns to origi-  keep ex-
Credit supply falls           nal value        ◀──────  change
     │                                                  rate con-
     ▼                                                  stant
Interest rates return
to original level
```

| Little or no change | Little or no change | |

flexible exchange rates. Recall, however, that we are looking at a fixed exchange-rate system here. The Fed must move to keep the exchange rate constant. It must buy up the surplus of dollars on the foreign exchange markets in order to keep the dollar from depreciating. Consider what this means. The Fed has injected more money into the U.S. financial system with its open market purchase, but then the system of fixed exchange rates forces it to buy back those same dollars in order to stabilize the exchange rate.

As Table 29-3 indicates, monetary policy is not very effective under a system of fixed exchange rates. Anything that the Fed does to stimulate the domestic economy it will likely have to un-do to keep the exchange rate fixed. Monetary policy, which we saw to be very powerful with flexible exchange rates, is much less effective under a system of fixed exchange rates. This perhaps explains why the Fed adopted a relatively passive policy aimed at keeping interest rates and exchange rates stable during most of the fixed exchange-rate era. The Fed has been more active in making economic policy in the flexible exchange-rate years since 1973.

Fiscal Policy with Fixed Exchange Rates

29.10 FIXED EXCHANGE RATES, FISCAL POLICY

While fixed exchange rates weaken monetary policy, they tend to strengthen the power of fiscal policy. Table 29-4 presents a schematic analysis of an expansionary fiscal policy under a system of fixed exchange rates.

790   International Economic Policy

| TABLE 29-4 | Expansionary Fiscal Policy with Fixed Exchange Rates Policy: Increase in Government Spending Causes Deficit |

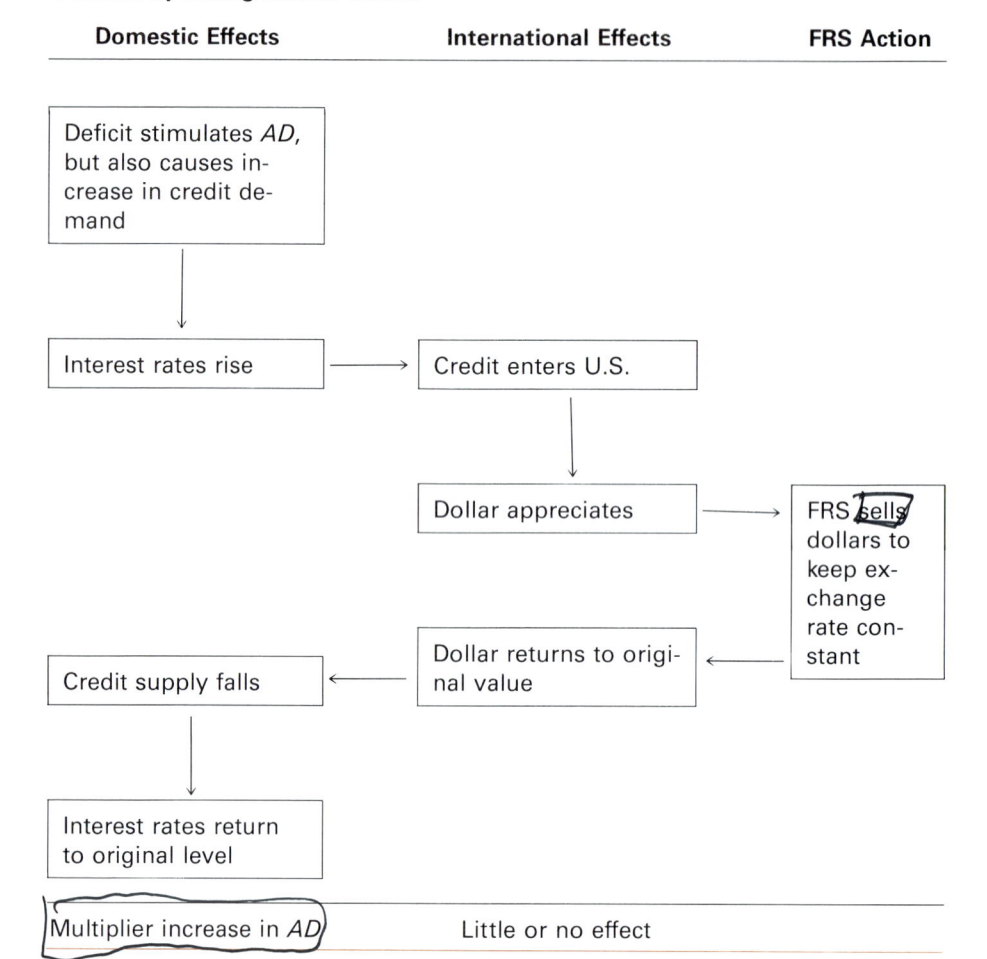

Domestic Effects	International Effects	FRS Action
Deficit stimulates *AD*, but also causes increase in credit demand		
↓		
Interest rates rise →	Credit enters U.S.	
	↓	
	Dollar appreciates →	FRS sells dollars to keep exchange rate constant
Credit supply falls ←	Dollar returns to original value ←	
↓		
Interest rates return to original level		
Multiplier increase in *AD*	Little or no effect	

Suppose that Congress increases government spending, creating a deficit, in an attempt to reduce unemployment. This causes *AD* to rise through the multiplier process; but the deficit represents an increase in credit demand that tends to bid up interest rates. As interest rates rise, foreign leaders shift funds to the United States from other countries in order to gain the higher return in the U.S. This inflow of credit from abroad keeps U.S. interest rates from rising as much as they might otherwise increase.

Under a system of flexible exchange rates, this credit inflow would cause the dollar to appreciate for reasons discussed earlier in this chapter. Under a system of fixed exchange rates, however, the Fed must take actions that keep the dollar from rising in value. They must increase the supply of dollars on the foreign exchange markets to keep the exchange rate fixed. As the Fed does this, it has two impacts—as Table 29-4 indicates. First, the exchange rate stays fixed. But, second, the increased supply of dollars represents an increase in the U.S. money and credit supplies. Interest rates stay stable, despite the deficit, so that the fiscal policy enjoys its full multiplier effect on aggregate demand.

While monetary policy is relatively ineffective under fixed exchange rates, fiscal policy is much more effective. The responsibility of keeping exchange rates fixed forces the Federal Reserve to adopt policies that support the expansionary fiscal policy by also expanding the money and credit supplies at the same time.

Why was macroeconomic policy so depressingly unsuccessful in the 1970s? Part of the blame can be laid on failure to adjust to changing exchange-rate regimes. Fiscal policies dominated the economic scene in the 1950s and 1960s because monetary actions were constrained by fixed exchange rates. Exchange rates became flexible in the early 1970s, however, and the balance of power in economic policy changed. The prescriptions of fiscal policies that worked so well in the 1960s were almost useless in the flexible exchange-rate environment of the 1970s. Battling inflation and unemployment with taxes and transfer payments made little sense under flexible exchange rates.

While fiscal policy actions continued, monetary policy changed. Monetary policy was suddenly free of the fixed exchange rate constraint. Fiscal policies were ineffective, so monetary authorities tried to make up the difference, fighting stagflation with rapid monetary expansion. Many economists blame the high inflation rates of the 1970s on an over-rapid expansion of the money supply that followed the change to the flexible exchange-rate system.

DOMESTIC AND INTERNATIONAL ECONOMIC GOALS

29.11 ECONOMIC GOALS

We have just seen that domestic macroeconomic policies can have international effects that make them stronger in some cases and weaker in others. Under a system of flexible exchange rates, for example, monetary policy is relatively effective while fiscal policy is less powerful. International economic effects can therefore influence our choices concerning domestic economic policies.

In Chapter 9 we discussed the economy's macroeconomic goals. We saw that price stability, full employment, economic growth, a balanced federal budget, and a balance of trade equilibrium are all goals for the economy. Figure 29-3 shows how the United States has fared in attempting to achieve all these goals. Note, in particular, the recent trend in the balance of trade. While inflation has been reduced and unemployment has declined somewhat, the United States has suffered a rapid deterioration in its ability to compete with foreign producers—as evidenced by the balance of trade deficit. This deficit tell us that we are importing far more goods and services than we are exporting, which is an indication that domestic producers are suffering from foreign competition. As has been noted earlier, the rapid appreciation of the dollar in the early 1980s is a major reason for this undesirable international trade balance.

Attempts to solve our domestic economic problems affect our progress toward our international economic goals. We must therefore keep the interrelationship between domestic and international economic goals and policies firmly in mind. For example, under a system of flexible exchange rates, an expansionary monetary policy increases *AD* at home, but it also causes the dollar to depreciate, which stimulates net exports and therefore helps reduce the balance of trade deficit. This policy can thus reduce unemployment at home and also improve our ability to compete on international markets, so long as the money supply growth does not trigger inflation, which could hurt the U.S. trade position. An expansionary fiscal policy, on the other hand, is relatively ineffective in changing *AD* at home and has the undesirable side effect of causing the dollar to appreciate, which reduces net

792 *International Economic Policy*

FIGURE 29-3

Domestic and International Economic Goals. The United States has not achieved all of its macroeconomic goals. Economic growth has been uneven. Unemployment, while high, has fallen from its peak in the early 1980s. Inflation has also declined. The federal budget deficit and the balance of trade deficit have both increased, however. Domestic and international economic goals are interrelated.

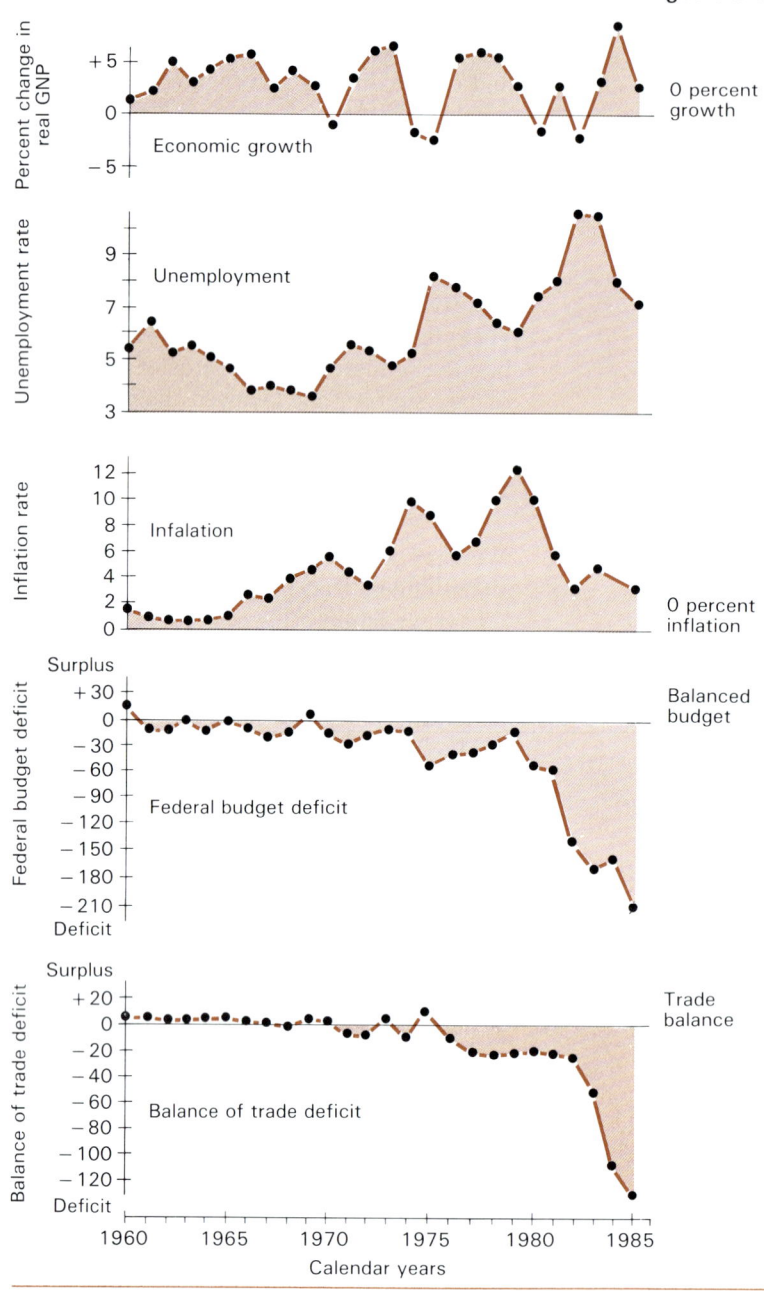

exports and makes the balance of trade deficit worse. We need to keep both the domestic and international effects of these policies in mind when we examine our policy options.

Figure 29-3 suggests that fiscal policy dominated economic events in 1980-85, with budget deficits forcing the dollar higher and causing increasing balance of trade problems. Conservative monetary policies in the early

1980s aimed at reducing inflation in the U.S., also contributed to the dollar's rise, as noted in Chapter 28.

These international trade problems cannot be ignored because they are linked very directly to our domestic economic goals. As we import more and export less, this has a direct impact on the characteristics of employment and unemployment in our home economy. In 1984-85, for example, the influx of imports tended to cause unemployment in the manufacturing sector of the U.S. economy. Economic growth in the United States was concentrated in the service industry, where competition form abroad is less intense (in fact, America is a major exporter of financial, insurance, and other services) while the economy actually lost jobs in its industrial core. Thus the balance of trade problems in this period pushed the U.S. economy toward a larger service sector and a smaller manufacturing sector.

THE TRADE DEFICIT: POLICY OPTIONS

29.12 ECONOMIC POLICY OPTIONS

Policymakers in the United States face a difficult task in the late 1980s. They must attempt to reduce the balance of trade deficit without making other economic problems worse. That is, they must attempt to stimulate exports and/or reduce imports, but without increasing the federal budget deficit, reducing economic growth, increasing unemployment, or re-igniting inflation. This is a very difficult problem. With so many economic goals, it is difficult to avoid uncomfortable trade-offs. Let us examine some policies that have been suggested to reduce the balance of trade deficit and examine the trade-offs that each policy requires. The international economic policy menu includes tariff and quota trade restrictions, the negotiation of voluntary export agreements with other countries, exchange rate intervention, and the so-called "classical medicine."

Tariff and Quota Trade Restrictions

As the trade deficit increased in 1984-85 and industrial employment in the United States fell, Congress began to consider protectionist legislation. Tariffs and quotas, which were discussed in Chapter 27, were proposed. These trade barriers were aimed at reducing imports from abroad and, as well, at forcing other nations to increase their purchases of U.S. export items. The threat of these trade restrictions did have some effect. The Japanese government, for example, introduced policies and programs that were designed to encourage purchases of U.S. goods, although the total effect of these policies on the trade deficit is likely to be relatively small. Japanese auto companies have begun investing in U.S. assembly plants, which create some jobs for U.S. auto workers. These Japanese factories are at least partly designed to reduce the impact of future U.S. trade restrictions on sales of Japanese autos in this country.

Although trade restrictions would seem to be a good solution to the problem of high imports from abroad, most economists consider them a poor solution to the problem of the trade deficit. High tariff and quota trade barriers do tend to reduce imports, but they also tend to reduce exports. This is true for two reasons. First, our trading partners sometimes retaliate when we impose trade restrictions. Our tariffs on imported steel may be matched by their tariffs on U.S. agricultural exports. Neither side really gains here. The second reason is that foreign countries need to sell to us in

794   International Economic Policy

order to earn income to pay for imports from the United States. If we stop buying their goods, they cannot pay for U.S. exports.

Trade restrictions also tend to slow economic growth. U.S. firms that are protected from foreign competition have little incentive to invest in more efficient production technology. Trade restrictions can also increase the cost of inputs imported from abroad, which increases production costs.

Tariff and quota trade restrictions, then, may do little overall to reduce the trade deficit. They tend to cause inflation and slow economic growth, which can increase unemployment over time. Although they are often politically popular, these trade restrictions are usually poor economic policy.

Voluntary Export Agreements

Voluntary Export Agreements
Quota agreements that are negotiated between exporting and importing countries. These agreements are substitutes for trade restrictions imposed without negotiation by importing countries.

There is more than one way to limit imports. **Voluntary export agreements** represent a second policy option for reducing the trade deficit. Under a voluntary export agreement, foreign countries "voluntarily" agree to limit their exports to the United States. These agreements are often voluntary in name only, because exporting countries often agree to limit exports only because they fear that the we might impose more severe restrictions if no agreement is reached. Voluntary export agreements are therefore perhaps better viewed as trade restrictions that are negotiated rather than imposed. Voluntary export agreements limited foreign competition in the automobile and textile industries, among others, in the 1980s.

Because voluntary export agreements have much in common with tariffs and quotas, in terms of their economic effects, economists tend to oppose them for the same reasons that they oppose other trade restrictions. The voluntary restrictions, however, have one additional disadvantage in that they can create international **cartels** that reduce competition once the export limits are lifted.

Cartels
Organizations of producers that attempt to increase profits by restricting supply in a market.

Japan agreed to a voluntary export limit on autos in the early 1980s, for example, which required that the government set export limits for each auto manufacturer. Each of these firms exported only its most profitable cars to the United States and earned higher profits because the voluntary export limit not only reduced Japanese competition for American car manufacturers, it also reduced the degree to which Japanese automakers competed with each other in the U.S. market. The formal voluntary export agreement covering automobiles expired in March 1985, but the Japanese continued to restrict auto imports to America, in part because they found these limits, which reduced competition, to be profitable for Japanese car firms.

Exchange Rate Intervention

Another option to reduce the trade deficit is for the Federal Reserve to go directly to the exchange markets and intervene to depreciate the dollar. The FRS would sell dollars on foreign exchange markets. The falling dollar would make U.S. products more competitive abroad, increase exports, and increase the cost of imported goods to U.S. buyers. If the trade deficit is the result of an over-valued dollar, the intervention to depreciate the dollar, as discussed in Chapter 28, seems to be a reasonable policy option.

Exchange market intervention has several flaws. The FRS can only alter the exchange rate if other central banks cooperate and stay out of currency markets themselves. U.S. reserves are limited, so intervention cannot be sustained for long periods. Thus the FRS may not be able to cause the dollar to fall for a long enough period for the U.S. economy to gain back the industrial jobs that have been lost.

Exchange intervention is risky because it may result in higher inflation at home. This is possible for two reasons. First, the FRS would need to increase the supply of dollars to drive the dollar's exchange value down. This increase in the U.S. money supply would tend to stimulate AD at home and possibly unleash demand-pull inflation. Inflation is also likely to be triggered by the higher costs of imported goods that occurs when the dollar depreciates.

Exchange intervention to depreciate the dollar, therefore, risks reigniting inflation and may not result in a long-lasting change in either the exchange rate or the trade balance. For these reasons, the FRS has refrained so far from adopting this policy option.

The Classical Medicine

Classical Medicine
Policies that attempt to reduce trade deficits by causing recessions that reduce domestic income.

The traditional cure for the balance of trade deficit is called the **classical medicine.** The classical medicine is to force a recession in order to reduce imports. This policy requires that domestic macroeconomic goals be sacrificed so that international goals can be achieved.

The classical medicine policy is designed to improve the trade balance in two ways. First, imports are reduced by the direct effects of a government-induced recession. Unemployed workers buy fewer imported cars and spend less money on foreign clothes, food, and travel. Falling domestic incomes therefore reduce spending on imports. Second, exports are encouraged by the indirect effects of the recession. A recession at home tends to allow domestic firms to cut prices and reduce production costs (by cutting wages, for example). These changes tend to make U.S. goods more competitive abroad, so exports rise. The combination of lower imports and increased exports improves the balance of trade deficit.

Classical medicine can be an effective way to reduce the trade deficit, especially when it is combined with exchange intervention to reduce the value of the domestic currency. It is, however, an extremely painful policy. The burden of eliminating the trade deficit is borne directly by the individuals in the economy who experience increased unemployment and declining standards of living, at least in the short run.

LESSONS FOR ECONOMIC POLICY

We have seen that economic policy is plagued by trade-offs. Policies that aim to cure domestic economic ills frequently have undesirable international side effects. But policies, such as classical medicine, that try to solve international problems often have unacceptable domestic effects on inflation or unemployment. Sometimes the solution to our economic problems appears hopeless.

29.13 ECONOMIC GOALS FOR GROWTH

It is important to remember that all our economic goals are related. Trade-offs among individual economic goals are sometimes unavoidable. But sometimes achieving one goal makes it easier to gain the others. Economic growth, one of the economic goals discussed in Chapters 8 and 9, is the key to all our other problems. Economic growth reduces unemployment by creating jobs for the growing population. Economic growth reduces inflation by expanding aggregate supply to balance the rise in aggregate demand. Economic growth reduces the size of the government's expenditures on

ECONOMIC ISSUES

The Latin American Debt Crisis

The United States' international economic problems are small compared with those of some less developed countries. In the early 1980s, for example, the plight of several Latin American nations came to national attention. The Latin American debt crisis illustrates the interdependent nature of the international economy and the difficult trade-offs that nations face in dealing with international economic problems.

Growth is the key to solving many economic problems. This is especially true of very poor nations, such as those in Central and South America. Growth requires resources, however. In the 1970s, many Latin American nations borrowed money from developed countries with the intention of investing in their own economies to promote economic growth. Table 29-5 shows that some of these countries accumulated huge international debts. Chile, for example, had an international debt equal to almost 90 percent of its yearly gross national product.

Events in the late 1970s and early 1980s intensified the debt crisis. Oil prices increased, interest rates increased, and the price of many Latin American primary product exports fell. These countries found that they were paying out more for oil and interest, but earning less for their exports. They were unable to pay back their debts to banks and international institutions in the developed countries. The specter of a default by the less developed countries appeared, which could have led to a financial collapse or panic in the United States.

The financial problems of the Latin American nations were solved by the interaction of two forces. First, the International Monetary Fund, discussed briefly in Chapter 28, provided additional loans to some of these nations, although under rather severe conditions. Borrowing nations were forced to devalue their currencies, to make their exports more attractive, and to adopt "classical medicine" economic policies. Citizens in Argentina, Brazil, Mexico, and the Dominican Republic found their standards of living reduced virtually over night. There were riots in some places and people died. International debt quickly became more than an abstract concept.

The U.S. trade deficit was the second force at work to reduce the Latin American debt crisis. The strong dollar made Latin American exports of manufactured goods, raw materials, and agricultural products inexpensive for U.S. buyers. Increased sales to the United States allowed less developed countries to earn the revenue they needed to pay their international debts. This illustrates the subtle interdependence of international trade and payments problems. The U.S. found that it must import from Latin America in order to gain repayment of loans to these countries. But this results in a trade deficit, which creates economic problems at home. If the trade deficit is reduced by cutting imports, however, then the less developed countries would be unable to repay their debts, which could cause financial problems in the United States.

The Latin American Debt crisis was less severe by 1985 than it was earlier in the 1980s, but it remained an important international economic problem. Less developed countries faced the difficult trade-off between paying their debts (and thereby qualifying for future loans) and preserving the living standards of their citizens. The lending nations faced the trade-off between trade deficits and problems in their financial sectors.

TABLE 29-5

Latin American Debt Crisis, 1984
(Selected Countries)

Nation	Foreign Debt ($ billion)	Debt as Percent of GNP
Argentina	$45.3	70.6%
Brazil	93.1	41.1
Chile	18.6	89.1
Mexico	89.8	60.5
Peru	12.5	79.5

automatic stabilizer programs, thus reducing the budget deficit. Finally, economic growth tends to improve domestic technology and productivity, which makes the United States more competitive on world markets and thus reduces the trade deficit.

If economic growth is the key for solving our macroeconomic problems, then how do we promote economic growth? There is no magic formula for growth, but history does provide some lessons that are useful.

Professor Arnold C. Harberger has studied economic growth around the world and has formulated some general rules based on the experience of nations that achieved economic growth and those that did not. (Arnold C. Harberger, ed. *World Economic Growth: Cases of Developed and Developing Nations*, San Francisco: Institute for Contemporary Studies, 1984.) Harberger recommends that nations promote economic growth by engaging in international trade with the minimum possible number of trade restrictions. Free trade encourages competition, efficiency, and dynamic change in the economy. Harberger recommends that domestic wage and price controls be avoided because they tend to distort resource allocation. He further recommends that government budgets be kept under control and large budget deficits, such as those in the United States, be avoided.

Harberger's view is a conservative one. He basically calls for limited government involvement in the economy and stresses private action and free competition as the sources of growth. Not all economists agree with this view. Many economists believe that government policies provide direction for the economy that promotes economic growth. They also see government as a force to encourage saving, investment, and technological progress, all of which are needed for economic growth.

Economic policy is always controversial. We are often forced to choose between competing economic goals. Even when we identify one goal — economic growth — as the key to the rest, we are still likely to disagree about the best way to achieve that goal.

SUMMARY

29.1 1. Changes in the exchange rate affect many prices in the economy. When the dollar appreciates, import prices fall directly because fewer dollars are needed to purchase foreign goods. Competition from cheaper imports tends to drive down the prices of U.S. import-competing products. The stronger dollar makes U.S. export goods harder to sell abroad, which tends to drive down their prices at home. Items that use imported inputs experience lower production costs when the dollar rises, which tends to reduce their prices as well. Prices of these items tend to rise when the dollar depreciates.

29.2 2. Changes in the exchange rate alter the distribution of income in the economy. Workers and firms in exporting and import-competing industries experience a relative decline in their incomes.

29.3 3. Changes in the exchange rate alter the level of net exports in the economy, which affects aggregate demand. *AD* rises when the dollar depreciates because net exports are stimulated. *AD* falls when the dollar appreciates because the stronger dollar tends to increase imports and reduce exports.

29.4 ▶ 4. Changes in the exchange rate also affect aggregate supply (*AS*) through changes in the cost of imported inputs. *AS* rises somewhat when the dollar appreciates because imported inputs fall in price. *AS* falls somewhat when the dollar depreciates because production goods from abroad cost more to the U.S. firms that use them.

29.5 ▶ 5. Changes in the exchange rate affect inflation and unemployment in the economy. When the dollar appreciates, *AD* falls and *AS* rises somewhat. Real GNP tends to fall, creating unemployment, while the inflation rate is reduced. The U.S. economy experienced this event in the early 1980s. However, real GNP tends to rise, reducing unemployment, and inflation increases when the dollar depreciates.

29.6 ▶ 6. Changes in the credit market affect interest rates, which are a determinant of the exchange rate. Higher U.S. interest rates, for example, encourage credit to enter the United States to gain the higher return. This has two effects: the credit inflow tends to reduce U.S. interest rates somewhat; and the credit inflow represents an increasing demand for the dollar, which causes the dollar to rise in value.

29.7 ▶ 7. Monetary policy is relatively effective under a system of flexible exchange rates. An increase in the money and credit supply tends to reduce interest rates, which causes credit to exit the country. As credit leaves the country, the dollar depreciates, which encourages exports and discourages imports. *AD* rises because both investment spending and net export spending rise.

29.8 ▶ 8. Fiscal policy is relatively less effective under a system of flexible exchange rates. An increase in the deficit, designed to stimulate *AD*, tends to raise interest rates, which causes an inflow of credit from abroad. While this credit inflow reduces the crowding-out effect, it also increases the demand for the dollar, so the dollar appreciates. This dollar appreciation reduces net export spending, which tends to offset the expansionary impact of the original fiscal policy.

29.9 ▶ 9. Monetary policy tends to be relatively less effective under a system of fixed exchange rates. An increase in the money supply tends to drive down interest rates, which would normally cause the dollar to depreciate. The FRS must purchase the excess dollars on the foreign exchange market in order to preserve the fixed exchange rate relationship. Thus the FRS must reduce the money supply, which it had initially increased. The FRS is relatively unable to affect the money supply under flexible exchange rates.

29.10 ▶ 10. Fiscal policy tends to be relatively more effective under a system of fixed exchange rates. Deficit spending increases *AD* directly, but tends to cause the dollar to appreciate. The FRS must increase the money supply in order to maintain the fixed exchange-rate relationship. This allows the initial fiscal policy to have its full multiplier impact on the economy.

29.11 ▶ 11. Our domestic and international economic goals are closely interrelated. For example, the rising international trade deficit has had an important impact on unemployment in the United States. Likewise, any attempt to achieve domestic economic goals will affect exchange rates, which will affect the trade balance.

29.12 ▶ 12. There are several international economic policies that could be used to attempt to reduce the trade deficit, but all of the policies have some undesirable side effects. Among the options that are available are tariff and quota trade restrictions, the negotiation of voluntary export agreements, exchange rate intervention designed to reduce the dollar's foreign exchange value, and the "classical medicine" of domestic recession to reduce imports and encourage exports.

29.13 ▶ 13. Economic growth is the key to both domestic and international economic goals. Economic growth tends to reduce unemployment, moderate inflation, reduce the budget deficit, and make the economy more competitive on international markets. Slow economic growth can make all these problems worse. Economists disagree concerning the best way to stimulate economic growth.

DISCUSSION QUESTIONS

29.1, 29.2, 29.3, 29.4, 29.5 ▶ 1. Suppose that you are a stock market analyst. You have read a prediction that the dollar will depreciate by 20 percent in the next two years. Use this information to make a list of the economic effects of the depreciation on the U.S. economy.

29.1, 29.2, 29.3, 29.4, 29.5 ▶ 2. Based on the list you prepared for question 1, make a second list of investment advice that you would give to your clients. Which U.S. firms and industries will likely experience higher income and profits? Which will tend to decline? Explain the reasoning behind your advice.

29.7, 29.8 ▶ 3. Compare and contrast the effectiveness of contractionary monetary and fiscal policy under flexible exchange rates. Which policy is more effective? Explain.

29.9, 29.10 ▶ 4. Compare and contrast the effectiveness of contractionary monetary and fiscal policy under fixed exchange rates. Which policy works best? Explain.

29.1, 29.4, 29.5, 29.7 ▶ 5. The Japanese central bank is considering a contractionary monetary policy. Explain how this would affect the U.S. economy under a system of flexible exchange rates. Is this good news for the U.S.? Explain the reasoning behind your answer.

29.6, 29.7, 29.8 ▶ 6. The FRS began a contractionary monetary policy in 1979. At the same time, Congress increased spending, financing the deficit by borrowing from the public. How would this combination of policies affect a closed economy? How would it affect an open economy with flexible exchange rates? What is the difference, if any, between your two answers? Explain.

29.5, 29.7, 29.8

7. You are a member of the President's Council of Economic Advisors. The economy is experiencing high inflation, rising unemployment, a falling dollar and a substantial balance of trade deficit. The president just called — he wants a plan to reverse these problems on his desk in the morning. What would you recommend? Sketch your plan and explain why you chose this policy.

SELECTED READINGS

Adams, John (ed.) *The Contemporary International Economy*, New York: St. Martin's Press, 1985.

Caves, Richard E. and Jones, Ronald W., *World Trade and Payments: An Introduction* (4th edition), Boston: Little, Brown, 1985.

Cline, William R. (ed.) *Trade Policy in the 1980s*, Cambridge: MIT Press, 1983.

Dornbusch, Rudiger, *Open Economy Macroeconomics*, New York: Basic Books, 1980.

Dornbusch, Rudiger and Frenkel, Jacob A. (eds.) *International Economic Policy: Theory and Evidence*, Baltimore: Johns Hopkins Press, 1979.

Harberger, Arnold C. (ed.) *World Economic Growth: Case Studies of Developed and Developing Nations*, San Francisco: Institute for Contemporary Studies, 1984.

Williamson, John, *The Open Economy and the World Economy*, New York: Basic Books, 1983.

CHAPTER 30

Comparative Economic Systems

Having read the chapter, reviewed the chapter summary, and completed the *Study Guide* exercises, you should be able to:

CRIS

30.1 ECONOMIC SYSTEM: Explain what is meant by an economic system; identify the economic system in the United States; and explain what institutions are included in the economic system.

30.2 ECONOMIC SYSTEM CHOICES: List the three basic problems an economic system must solve; give examples of each problem; and explain why each choice must be made.

30.3 ECONOMIC SYSTEM CRITERIA: List three criteria for evaluating an economic system; explain why they are important; and explain the difference between static and dynamic efficiency.

30.4 CENTRALIZED AND DECENTRALIZED CHOICE: Explain the difference between centralized and decentralized choice systems, and list the advantages and disadvantages of each system.

30.5 PROPERTY RIGHTS: Explain what property rights are and discuss the difference between private property rights and public or communal property rights.

30.6 INCENTIVES: PRIVATE VS. PUBLIC PROPERTY RIGHTS: Explain why there is greater incentive to invest and produce under a system of private property rights than under a system of public property rights.

30.7 FOUR ECONOMIC SYSTEMS: List the four main economic systems discussed in this chapter, and explain how they differ regarding decision-making, centralized versus decentralized, and property rights, private versus public.

30.8 CAPITALISM DEFINED: Define capitalism; list the advantages and disadvantages of capitalism as an economic system; and give an example of a capitalist nation.

30.9 PLANNED SOCIALISM DEFINED: Define planned socialism; list its advantages and disadvantages; and give an example of a planned socialist economy.

30.10 MARKET SOCIALISM DEFINED: Define market socialism; list its advantages and disadvantages; and give an example of a market socialist economy.

30.11 FASCISM DEFINED: Define fascism; list its advantages and disadvantages and give an example of a fascist economy.

30.12 MIXED ECONOMY: Explain what is meant by the term mixed economy, and explain why all modern countries are really mixed economies.

30.13 ECONOMY OF THE SOVIET UNION: Explain how production is organized in the Soviet Union, and discuss the role of private enterprise in the Soviet plan.

30.14 GOSPLAN: Describe Gosplan; list the successes and problems of central planning in the Soviet Union; and explain why the lack of true markets leads to distribution problems in the Soviet Union.

30.15 ECONOMY OF YUGOSLAVIA: Explain how firms are organized in Yugoslavia, and discuss the role of the state versus that of the workers in making production decisions.

30.16 YUGOSLAVIAN WORKER-MANAGEMENT: Explain why worker-management, Yugoslavia-style, leads to low levels of investment, and explain why Yugoslavian firms tend to expand using more capital rather than increased labor inputs.

30.17 CONVERGENCE HYPOTHESIS: Explain what is meant by the convergence hypothesis and give evidence that socialist and capitalist economies are growing more alike.

30.1 ECONOMIC SYSTEM

Anyone who even briefly studies the world economy is quickly aware of two characteristics of the international scene: interdependence and diversity.

You learned about international economic interdependence in Chapters 28 and 29. Nations depend on each other for many things, such as goods, credit, markets, and more. This interdependence is a knife that cuts both ways. Trading partners that buy a nation's goods are also competitors, selling things that domestic firms would otherwise produce. International trade, where nations depend on one another for goods and services, whittles down the problem of scarcity by making more things available from the same supply of world resources. Specialization and trade along comparative advantage lines makes this possible. Interdependence, however, carves out new problems such as the balance of payments deficits and exchange rate troubles discussed in Chapter 29.

In this chapter we focus on the diversity of economic systems within the world economy. All nations face roughly the same basic economic problems, but they try to solve these problems in many different ways. We first look at the fundamental economic problems that all nations face regardless of size, culture, or political philosophy. We next discuss centralized versus decentralized decision making and private versus public ownership, two basic issues that shape the economic system. We see how various combinations of these ideas lead to different economic systems. Finally, we briefly examine the economic systems of the Soviet Union and Yugoslavia to see how they have dealt with these problems and issues in searching for the key to scarcity's puzzle.

BUILDING AN ECONOMIC SYSTEM

An **economic system** is a set of institutions that society uses to solve the economic problem of scarcity and choice. Scarcity, finite resource limits combined with the reality of unlimited wants, means that society must choose which goods and services to have and which to forego. An economic system is the human process that makes these choices.

The economic system of the United States includes the laws, ideas, and traditions that shape economic actions, the system of markets where goods and services are exchanged, and the political system that makes public choices and regulates private ones. An economic system is that complex set of relationships that ends up deciding what is produced and who gets it.

There are as many different economic systems as there are nations in the world. Capitalist systems primarily depend on free markets; little government help is required. Socialist systems count on central planners to solve economic problems. Mixed economies use planning and central decision making sometimes, but let free markets rule elsewhere.

THREE CHOICES AN ECONOMIC SYSTEM MUST MAKE

> **30.2 ECONOMIC SYSTEM CHOICES**

Solving the scarcity problem is not easy. It means finding answers to three important questions.

1. *The allocation choice: How should scarce resources be allocated among competing uses?* Which goods should be produced in what amounts? There is a world of desirable items that might be produced, but resource scarcity means they cannot all be attained at once. Hard trade-offs are required in allocating resources.

2. *The production choice: How should these goods be produced?* With many workers and few machines? In long, computerized production lines that limit human input? What techniques and processes should be used? Should government planners or individual entrepreneurs decide the best way to produce?

3. *The distribution choice: How should goods and services be distributed?* Who gets the ripe fruit of the economic tree and who gets the pits? Should goods and services be distributed according to the economic power of dollars and cents, political power, or some ideal of economic justice?

Figure 30-1 shows how these three choices are related. An economy with scarce resources must avoid inefficient methods of production — such as those used at point A in the figure — that waste resources. All combinations on the production possibilities frontier are efficient in a technical sense in that they are not wasteful. Only one combination (*B* in the figure) results in the combination of goods that society prefers over all others available. The allocation problem is to achieve this combination. This allocation goal is impossible if inefficient production techniques are used. Finally, this combination of goods and services must be distributed among individuals in an acceptable way.

Consider who makes these decisions in the United States. The U.S. is an example of a **mixed economy** where economic choices are made by both individuals and government agents. Individuals make allocation decisions, for example, when they buy and sell goods and services. Markets take the actions of millions of buyers and sellers and convert them into the key price signals that tell producers which items are desired and which are not, which resources have high opportunity cost and which have low alternative value. Not all allocation decisions are made by markets, however. Government controls many resources directly, as through government purchases of goods and services, and indirectly through laws and subsidy and tax programs that affect individual choices.

Production decisions are both a private and public choice in the United States. Most production decisions are made by individual managers who choose profit-maximizing techniques, but government influences these decisions in many ways. Direct regulation, as with pollution control restrictions and child labor laws, alter some private production decisions. Wage legislation, interest rate controls, and differential tax treatment of capital and labor also alter producer decisions.

The distribution decision is the hardest of all and the one where government is most involved in the United States. Most goods and services are

Mixed Economy
An economy that uses both free markets and government controls to make economic decisions.

FIGURE 30-1

The Job of an Economic System. An economic system makes production choices, avoiding wasteful methods that result in points like *A* that lie inside the production possibilities frontier. The allocation problem is to choose the combination of goods (*B*) that society most prefers. Finally, an economic system distributes these goods in some way, as between the rich, who get the goods in the shaded area of this figure, and the poor who get what is left.

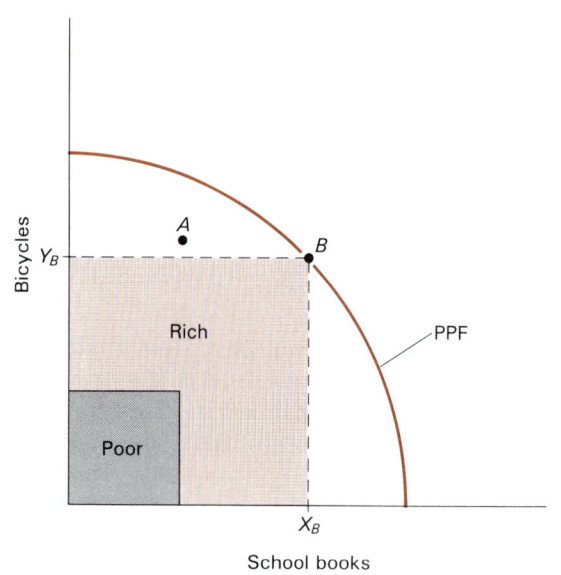

distributed through free markets, but government policies alter who gets what through today's broad system of transfer payments, such as unemployment insurance and social security benefits, wage and price regulations, and trade restrictions.

EVALUATING ALTERNATIVE ECONOMIC SYSTEMS

Political, moral, and economic criteria must all be considered in attempting to determine how effective the U.S. economic system is and how it compares with other systems. Any economic system, however, should make efficient use of resources both now and for the future, and should distribute the economy's bounty in a socially desirable way. Following is a brief discussion of three important criteria for an effective economic system.

> **30.3 ECONOMIC SYSTEM CRITERIA**

Static Efficiency
Allocation of existing resources to produce the combination of goods society prefers above all others; also called economic efficiency.

Static Efficiency An economic system should make the best use of today's scarce resources. **Static efficiency** requires that resources be used to produce the bundle of goods and services that society most prefers. Resources should not be wasted in production, nor should they be used to make one good, ballet shoes, for example, if it means giving up another good, such as chocolate bars, that society prefers.

Dynamic Efficiency
Optimal allocation of resources over time; resource use that takes into account future needs, not just current desires.

Dynamic Efficiency An economic system should also make efficient decisions over time. Allocation and distribution choices today should lead to desirable long-run consequences. Production decisions today should not ignore investments, such as new factories and machines, research and development expenditures, and training and education, that improve and expand the goods and services available to future consumers. Dynamic efficiency requires that scarce resources be used to produce the most preferred stream of benefits over time.

Desirable Distribution of Income An economic system should also distribute income and wealth in some socially desirable pattern. What is the ideal distribution of income? The answer depends on who you ask. For some it is a completely level distribution, where everyone benefits equally from economic activity. Others might consider a distribution pattern desirable if it prevents anyone from being very poor or limits income inequality to a prescribed range. Finally, some think that any distribution that results from a voluntary exchange is a fair one.

Centralized Decision Making
An economic system where important choices are made by central planners.

CENTRALIZED OR DECENTRALIZED CHOICE?

> **30.4 CENTRALIZED AND DECENTRALIZED CHOICE**

All economic systems face the same problems: allocation, production, and distribution of goods, and all economic systems try to attain the same goals: static efficiency, dynamic efficiency, and desirable income distribution. Economic systems are different, however, in the way they organize consumers, producers, and government controls to solve these problems and achieve these goals.

Decentralized Decision Making
An economic system where most important choices are made by individuals through market actions.

One important way that economic systems differ is in whether they depend on **centralized** or **decentralized decision making.** A centralized system gives the power of allocation, production, and distribution decisions to central planners who make choices for all society. These planners try to coordinate all sectors of the economy to achieve specific allocation and distribution goals.

A decentralized system lets individuals make important allocation, production, and distribution choices. No individual or group devises a master plan in a decentralized system. An overall pattern emerges from the interdependent actions of millions of buyers and sellers.

A decentralized system has the advantage of choice. Individuals choose the work they do, the goods and services they consume, and the way they use their time. This freedom of economic choice is one reason decentralized systems are favored by many economists. There is no guarantee, however, in our imperfect world, that private choices yield public benefits, no assurance that resources are used efficiently or distributed equitably. This is the reason economists examine centrally planned economies as well as decentralized systems. There is no guarantee, however, that central planners always know best, either.

PROPERTY RIGHTS: PRIVATE VERSUS PUBLIC OWNERSHIP

> **30.5 PROPERTY RIGHTS**

A second important difference among economic systems concerns the ownership of resources; differences in the laws and traditions that economists call property rights.

Property rights are the basic building blocks of an economic system. Property rights are the rights to ownership, use, and profit from some resource. Property rights can be defined in different ways, and the difference is important. Changes in the way property rights are defined affect allocation, production, and distribution outcomes. We will discuss two property rights systems: public and private.

> **30.6 INCENTIVES: PRIVATE VS. PUBLIC PROPERTY RIGHTS**

Private Property Rights
A system where individuals own the rights to goods and services; individuals control the use of and have a right to the value of resources.

Private Property Rights Individuals have unrestricted ownership claims over resources. No one else can use or gain from a resource without the agreement of its owner. An inventor, for example, has the right to all profits that stem from his innovation under a system of purely private property rights. Anyone who wants to use an invention must buy the rights from its owner. If a family owns a house, they have the right to use, rent or sell it. If an entrepreneur owns a factory, he has the right to any gains from operating it.

Public Property Rights
Public or communal property rights is a system where resources are owned in common. No individual has the right to exclude others from their use and no individual has exclusive right to any increase in resource value.

Public Property Rights Individuals share goods and services with all others under a system of communal or public property rights. A new invention, for example, becomes property of the people. Anyone can use it without restriction. The innovation resource is owned by all collectively and by no one individually. Housing and factories are not owned by any individual, but belong to the population collectively.

No economic system is made up of purely private or completely public property rights. Some goods such as national parks, are collectively owned even in private economies like the United States. Some areas of private property rights, such as the right to one's labor or personal possessions, exist even in collective economies, such as China and the Soviet Union. Laws, religion, and tradition all contribute to a country's system of property rights.

Property rights are important because they determine incentives and incentives help determine whether scarce resources are efficiently used.

Property rights, however, also help determine the distribution of income and resources. The dual role of efficiency and distribution forces hard trade-offs in property rights choices. Two examples make this trade-off clear.

Society benefits, for example, if innovations are quickly put into widespread use. This argues for a system of public property rights to new inventions where no individual or group can restrict access to a new production process or innovation. Someone, however, must make a discovery before it can be used. Who is most likely to risk time and money on innovation—the inventor who has the right to the full value of his or her work in a system of private property rights, or the one who must share the work with all in a system of public property rights?

The private property rights system that most likely produces innovations also limits their use. The solution, in the United States and many other countries, is patent and copyright law that allows inventors, authors, artists, and others private rights to their work for fixed periods of time before the property enters public domain.

Here is another trade-off. If housing is privately owned, then the best housing goes to those with the most resources, while the poor may live in squalor. If housing is communally owned, however, almost no one would invest individual effort to improve it knowing that others have claim to the improvement. A private property rights system might result in an undesirable distribution of housing, but communal property rights might bring inefficiently low quality or quantity.

KEY CONCEPT 30.6

Property rights systems are a trade-off among economic goals. Public rights may improve unequal distribution of resources, but private rights contain incentives that promote efficient use of those resources. An advantage of capitalism is that it provides incentives for efficient production. Individuals invest and innovate because they can claim the benefits of their efforts.

THE RANGE OF ECONOMIC SYSTEMS

30.7 FOUR ECONOMIC SYSTEMS

You can get a feel for the range of possible economic systems by analyzing different combinations of centralized versus decentralized decision making and private versus public property rights. Each of the four systems described below and classified in Table 30-1 has important advantages in the way it attacks the scarcity problem, but faces significant problems as well.

30.8 CAPITALISM DEFINED

Capitalism Private property rights with decentralized choice. **Capitalism** is a system where individual resources are owned by individuals, not the state, and social choices are made through buyers and sellers, not by central planners. Production, allocation, and distribution decisions are made through mutually advantageous transactions in free markets. Government's role in this economy is relatively small.

Capitalism has two important advantages. First, its system of private property rights provides an incentive for individuals to produce efficiently because such effort benefits them by increasing the value of their property rights. An entrepreneur who risks capital and succeeds keeps all the gain. A worker who puts in extra effort is suitably rewarded. None of the gain, in

Capitalism
An economic system of private property rights where markets are used to make decentralized allocation, production, and distribution decisions.

TABLE 30-1

Four Economic Systems. Combinations of different decision-making schemes and property rights systems lead to the four basic economic systems shown here.

	Decision Making	
Property Rights	**Decentralized (Markets)**	**Centralized (Planned)**
Private	Capitalism *Example:* United States	Fascism *Example:* Nazi Germany
Communal or Public	Market Socialism *Example:* Yugoslavia	Planned Socialism *Example:* Soviet Union

either case, is shared with "free riders" who took no risk and made no effort. Productive efficiency is likely under such a system.

The second advantage is that this system allocates resources and makes production and distribution decisions at low cost. No costly central planning staff is needed. No expensive computer data banks are required to keep track of where resources are going and how much they produce. No unwieldy set of plans, goals, and quotas is required. All choices are made by individuals acting on their own. Markets costlessly sum individual choices into societal allocation and distribution decisions. Managers, acting on their own, and with complete knowledge of their own firms, determine the best way to produce. Once market prices are known, individuals have all the information they need to maximize utility or profit.

Capitalism is guided only by the invisible hand of self-interest. This is also its principal advantage and disadvantage. The problem is that, in real world economies with externalities, public goods, monopolies, and other market imperfections, there is no guarantee that resources are efficiently allocated or equitably distributed. Monopolies might produce too few of some valuable goods, while external costs result in too many of others. The rich might get fat while the poor starve. Capitalism produces, allocates, and distributes efficiently, but the results are not always perfect and are sometimes far from good.

30.9 PLANNED SOCIALISM DEFINED

Planned Socialism
An economic system where resources are owned by the state for the people and most production, allocation, and distribution decisions are made by central planners.

Planned Socialism Public property rights with centralized choice. At the opposite end of the spectrum is a system that might be called **planned socialism**. Economic resources are owned by the people and production, allocation, and distribution choices are made by central planners.

One advantage of planned socialism as an economic system is its ability to achieve any desired distributional goal. Central planners, by moving goods from one sector to another, can level incomes and smooth out inequality. Distributional ideals are a common thread among socialist systems. Communal ownership of resources, in theory, leads to a uniform income distribution. Socialism, with its plans and work orders, avoids the problems of market failures that distort resource allocation simply because markets play no major role in the economy.

Input-Output Table
A table showing the amount of inputs of different goods necessary to produce a unit of output.

The advantages of planned socialism must be weighed against two important disadvantages that have plagued socialist systems. The first is the problem of incentives. Almost no one would be willing to put in extra effort if economic rewards were uniformly distributed to everyone and not allocated according to performance. Would you study as hard for an exam if everyone got a *C* regardless of how much they knew? Distorted incentives in a system of public property rights, and the resultant waste of resources, keeps the economy from reaching the production possibilities frontier. Goods are evenly distributed, but fewer of them are produced.

A second problem is technical. How can central planners decide where resources should go, how they should be used, what they should produce, and where that production should go? Planning a modern industrial economy is like "solving" a 10,000-sided Rubik's Cube. Here's an example that shows how hard a "simple" planning problem can be.

Table 30-2 is an example of a simple **input-output table**, a kind of table that any planner must use. This table describes a simple economy that produces just three goods: steel, fuel, and food. Even this simple economy is complex, however, since production of any of these items requires inputs from them all. The table shows, for example, that the output of a unit of steel requires the input of one-half unit of steel (foundry and mining equipment), one-half unit of fuel (to fire-up the furnace) and one-third unit of food (to feed the workers). Producing a unit of fuel, according to this table, means using up ⅓ unit of steel, ¼ unit of fuel, and ¼ unit of food. Read the table to see how many inputs are used to make a unit of food.

Let's ignore the problem of production decisions. Assume there is just one way to make each output. Let's also ignore allocation and distribution problems, and try to do just one thing: plan an economy so that each output is produced in sufficient quantity to satisfy input demand, with nothing left over and no shortages. That is, let's plan a three-market equilibrium. We must decide how much steel, fuel, and food should be produced.

Suppose that the central planners order one unit each of steel, fuel, and food produced. This plan clearly does not work. A quick look at the table shows the plan's problems. One unit of steel is produced, but how much is needed to fulfill the plan's goals? The steel industry itself uses ½ steel. The fuel industry needs ⅓, and the food sector requires ¼. The result is that a total of more than one unit of steel is needed, but only one unit is produced. Someone will run short of steel before this plan is through. Food, however, will be left over. This plan orders one unit of food produced, but uses just ⅓ unit (to produce steel) + ¼ (to produce fuel) + ⅓ (to produce food) = ¹¹⁄₁₂

| TABLE 30-2 | A Simple Input-Output Table |

Inputs Used Per Unit of Output	Outputs		
	Steel	Fuel	Food
Steel	$\frac{1}{2}$	$\frac{1}{3}$	$\frac{1}{4}$
Fuel	$\frac{1}{2}$	$\frac{1}{4}$	$\frac{1}{4}$
Food	$\frac{1}{2}$	$\frac{1}{4}$	$\frac{1}{3}$

of it. Some adjustment is required if shortages and surpluses are to be avoided. A new plan, with more steel and less food is required.

Finding an input-output equilibrium in this small system is a relatively simple matter. It requires solving a system of three equations with three unknowns. Imagine the problem of balancing a complex economy with hundreds of sectors, thousands of products, and perhaps millions of producers.

Central planners would need much information to solve the simple market equilibrium problem posed here. Think of the extra data about different production processes, distribution routes, and opportunity costs needed to make a detailed economy-wide plan and you get a sense of how unwieldy centralized decision making can be. Complete plans take years to construct and may be outdated even before they appear.

Errors in central plans are not just possible, they are inevitable. Allocation, production, and distribution decisions may be no better in the aggregate, and can be much worse in specific cases, than the unplanned "chaos" of decentralized markets.

30.10 MARKET SOCIALISM DEFINED

Market Socialism
An economic system where capital is owned by the state, but most production and allocation decisions are made through decentralized markets.

Market Socialism Public property rights with decentralized choice. **Market socialism** combines public ownership of important resources, capital and natural resources in particular, with allocation and distribution decisions made through decentralized market structures.

At first glance, market socialism seems to combine all the advantages of capitalism and planned socialism with few of the disadvantages. Public ownership of the means of production tends to equalize the distribution of income within the economy. Everyone is a worker or an employee, because factories and farms are owned by the public.

Allocation and distribution choices are made through decentralized markets that accomplish these tasks efficiently and at low cost. Production decisions are made by firm managers, who know their business, not computers and economists thousands of miles away.

One problem with market socialism is that public ownership of resources removes the incentive for individuals to invest, innovate, or carefully use scarce public goods. Since everyone owns communal resources, such as capital and land, no individual has a vested interest in seeing that they are wisely used and preserved. The tendency is to over-use goods that you share with others, and to take better care of goods that are yours alone. Some central planning is needed to prevent deterioration of common resources in such a system. You will read more about the problems of common ownership when Yugoslavia's economic system is discussed later in the chapter.

In the 1930's, Polish-American economist Oskar Lange proposed an interesting system of market socialism where central planners did not set input and output targets for each sector, industry and firm, in hopelessly complicated 5-year plans. Lange's planners did just one thing — they set prices. Once the "right" prices were announced, following a trial and error period, according to Lange, planners could let decentralized markets alone, as they would swiftly make production, allocation, and distribution decisions that, given the right set of price signals, would achieve equity and efficiency goals. Lange's utopia, combining the magic of the market with the assumed wisdom of efficient price controls, was influential and illustrated the variety of economic systems that are possible. However, Lange abandoned his system in favor of central planning, when he became Polish economic minister following the Second World War.

30.11 FASCISM DEFINED

Fascism
An economic system where resources are owned by individuals, but most important economic decisions are made by the government.

Fascism Private property rights with centralized choice. **Fascism** is an economic system that combines private property rights with centralized control. Individuals still own resources, but central authorities take an active role in allocating and distributing them. Planners may exercise control by setting prices or otherwise regulating markets. Individuals may grow rich, but they have little choice and little economic freedom. Germany under Hitler and Italy under Mussolini are examples of fascist systems.

One problem with a fascist economy lies in the difficulty of combining private ownership with the loss of economic freedom over the use of goods. More important, however, is the seemingly inevitable deterioration in political freedom and personal liberty that accompanied fascist regimes in the past. Economic freedom and personal freedom have historically followed hand-in-hand. When one is lost, the other also soon disappears.

Modern Mixed Economy

30.12 MIXED ECONOMY

No economy today falls neatly into any of the four categories of Table 30-1. Every modern economy is a compromise, a combination of private property rights in some spheres and communal rights in others. Some choices are made by individuals acting alone, but others are the result of centralized activity. All economies today are mixed; that is, they combine aspects of all four systems discussed here. Some, like the Soviet Union, come closest to the planned socialism definition, while still retaining some private markets. Others, like Yugoslavia, come closest to the market socialism mark.

The major issues we are concerned with in mixed economies are (1) how they work; and (2) what are the consequences of different levels of command, of centralized vs. decentralized decision making, and of property rights systems. One way to better understand different systems is to briefly examine the economies of the Soviet Union and Yugoslavia.

THE ECONOMY OF THE SOVIET UNION

30.13 ECONOMY OF THE SOVIET UNION

Command Economy
An economy characterized by detailed central planning and little free enterprise.

The United States and the Soviet Union are economic and political competitors who approach fundamental economic problems in far different ways. While the U.S. economy relies primarily on decentralized markets, with government controls applied where needed, the Soviets employ a system of detailed plans, making theirs a **command economy,** where decentralized decision making is used only where planning fails entirely. Let's look at three aspects of the Soviet economy that differ dramatically from western norms.

Private Property Rights Private property rights are restricted in the Soviet Union. Individuals are allowed to own only personal effects such as household items, clothes and books, and perhaps an automobile, if one can be obtained. All other goods are owned by the state on behalf of the people.

The state is the only employer. State-run enterprises employ workers at fixed wages. Individuals are allowed to engage in trade, but they cannot employ others and cannot resell goods. This limits private firms to individuals selling items they have produced themselves. These stern rules cannot be enforced everywhere, so black markets are common. Scarce goods are bought and resold at illegal prices, earning profiteers substantial incomes.

Agriculture is the one sector of the Soviet economy where private production is important. Farmers are allowed to work part-time on small private plots on the giant state-owned farms. These private plots account for less that two percent of land under cultivation in the Soviet Union, but produce about one-fourth of all agricultural output. Russian workers treat the "people's" land and their "own" plots differently. The incentive to work for personal gain motivates them to cultivate tiny private plots much more intensively than the big, mechanized farms. One must wonder how much Soviet farms could produce if they were freed from the state and run as private, profit-making firms.

30.14 GOSPLAN

Gosplan, The State Planning Agency Allocation, production, and distribution decisions in the Soviet public sector are made by Gosplan, the government planning agency. Gosplan, through national and regional offices, issues detailed annual and five-year plans that set output quotas for the economy's sectors, industries, and individual enterprises. These complex plans, together with government-set prices, determine industrial production for the nation.

Planning has been both a success and a failure in the Soviet Union. The success is that planning agencies have been able to divert resources from the production of consumer goods to projects to build factories, expand transportation networks, and develop natural resources. Low levels of consumer goods production made possible tremendous economic growth and also high levels of defense spending. Chances are that no decentralized system would have generated as much investment spending as the planned forced saving system did. The Soviet system earns good marks for dynamic efficiency.

Gosplan gets a poor grade in static efficiency, however. The Soviet system is best characterized by bottlenecks, waste, and mismanagement. Detailed plans depend on all agents meeting their goals. If one industry, such as steel, comes up short of its quota, it distorts and delays production in other factories, such as those for tractors and machine tools, that need steel for their inputs. The result is a widening ring of shortages, bottlenecks, and missed quotas.

One of the major problems under the Soviet system is how to motivate managers to use resources efficiently when there is no profit incentive. Managers who fail to meet quota amounts must bear the wrath of their superiors, while those who exceed them are rewarded. Given the high goals planners set however, this system sometimes leads to less than efficient production choices.

Many stories are told of managers who resort to inefficient schemes in an effort to meet planning quotas. For example, a paper plant whose quota was set in tons is supposed to have produced tons and tons of heavy poster board, but no toilet or writing paper, to achieve its production goal. This happened because poster board weighs more than toilet or writing paper and was therefore easier for the factory to produce and easier for the factory to meet its quota. A nail factory is said to have produced heavy spikes, but no smaller nails suitable for construction, for the same reason. Its quota was set in weight instead of specific types of output. Inefficient decisions in these factories resulted, as you might imagine, in headaches for enterprises that used paper or nails in production.

There are two morals to this story. The first is that it is difficult for planners to motivate managers as well as markets do. In the market,

PROMINENT ECONOMIST

Karl Marx (1818–1883)

Karl Marx, probably the most well-known social economist, was born in Trier, Germany, the son of a successful Jewish lawyer. Because of their active participation in the European revolutionary socialist movement, Marx and his best friend, Friedrich Engels, were commissioned to prepare a statement of principles for the Communist League. It was published as *The Communist Manifesto* in 1848 and became the most celebrated pamphlet of the international communist movement. A complete statement of Marx's view is formed in his work *Das Kapital*. Marx's strongest argument was for collective ownership of the nation's capital assets. He was unlike many socialists in his support of violent revolution as the means of ushering in the new socialist order. In Marx's opinion, a revolution overthrowing the capitalist system was inevitable.

The ideas of Marx attracted attention throughout Europe. Vladimir Lenin was a follower of Marx's writings. With Marx's influence, Lenin developed the strategy for and served as a leader in the Russian revolution.

During his studies at the University of Berlin, Marx developed a strong interest in Hegelian philosophy which influenced his own ideological views. After completing his doctorate in philosophy at the University of Jena, Marx traveled throughout Europe promoting revolutionary worker causes. His revolutionary ideas and his outspoken ways led to his exile from Germany and France. He spent the remaining 34 years of his life in London struggling to survive with the help of his friend Engels. His energy during exile was focused on writing his best-known text, *Das Kapital*.

Marx viewed history as a dynamic process of class struggle. He predicted that the ruling class would become outmoded and, after a violent struggle, be replaced by a new ruling class. The new ruling class would be representative of the economically productive forces of society. Marx anticipated that this new class would "centralize all instruments of production in the hands of the state," and consequently increase all productive forces. Once the bourgeoisie (capitalists) were removed from power, the dynamic process would initiate the formation of the classless society. As the classless society established itself, the former instrument of oppression (the state) would dissolve since it would be no longer necessary. Marx envisioned a communist society in which each individual would contribute on a volunteer basis "according to his ability" in exchange for rewards "according to his needs."

History demonstrates that much of Marx's analysis was wrong. The current communist societies developed differently from Marx's plan, which called for the revolution to take place first in the most highly developed industrial societies, then much later in the agricultural societies. Marx's followers have had difficulty decreasing the role of the state. In the Soviet Union, a highly developed Communist society, the powerful bureaucratic state is most imposing.

Marx vehemently disagreed with the ideas of Adam Smith, who had no faith in institutions or other means to change man's nature. At the heart of Marxism lies the concept of changing the nature of man. Marx viewed history as a dynamic process perpetuated by class struggle and conflict; Smith felt that market coordination brought individual self-interest and economic progress into harmony. Marx believed that individuals could be freed from the oppression of capitalist economic activity through social intervention; Smith felt that market exchange would be the key to release people from government oppression.

One third of the world's population now lives under a communist-socialist economic system where Marx is revered. While this communist-socialist form of government may be quite different from what Marx envisioned as ideal communism, many of his ideas have certainly shaped the history of the world in which we live.

---

inefficient choices are punished with low profits. There are few corresponding incentives for efficiency under a planning system. The second moral is that it is easier to plan quantity than quality, but both are necessary for economic success.

The Problem of Distribution Income in the Soviet Union is not distributed according to Marx's "From each according to ability, to each according to need" prescription, but there is evidence that income is more evenly distributed than in the United States and other western nations. A bigger problem, perhaps, is in the distribution of the actual goods and services that individuals want to buy with their income.

Shortages are common. The Russian rule of thumb is that if you see a line, get in it. Chances are that the goods being sold, whatever they might be, are scarce, and will not be available tomorrow, so buy them up. If you cannot use them, chances are that someone else you know can.

Plans that fail to predict demand accurately lead to shortages of vital goods in some cities and large surpluses of them elsewhere. Individuals are forbidden from balancing these markets by reselling surplus goods in shortage markets. Since the plan is assumed to work, no state enterprise has this function, either. Prices, also set by plan, cannot adjust as they do in western markets, making scarce items more expensive and abundant ones cheaper. Planning errors remain until the plan changes, demand adjusts, or black marketeers correct Gosplan mistakes.

CHANGES IN THE SOVIET SYSTEM?

There were several indications in 1983 that the Soviet Union would change its planning system to decentralize decision making and improve productivity. The first step, according to some observers, is a plan to give individual plant managers greater authority to make production decisions. Under the current system, each plant manager reports through a multi-level chain-of-command, with each level's decisions subject to review at a higher level. Such a system discourages individual initiative. It takes weeks, months, or years to make necessary changes in inputs or outputs. The new system would cut bureaucracy and let at least some managers make their own decisions.

Other efficiency reforms, such as pay based on productivity and increased private ownership, may also be in the offing. These reforms would give workers and managers greater incentive to efficiently use scarce resources.

Some economists think the changes pending in the Soviet system are based on the trade-off between consumer goods and military needs. Figure 30-2 illustrates this trade-off using a production possibilities frontier. If Soviet consumers made production decisions through markets, they might pick a combination like A in the figure, with many consumer goods and few resources allocated to military production. Soviet leaders have put a high priority on military spending, however, and used the planning system to move the economy to a point like B. This point is inefficient. It is inside the production possibilities frontier. Because planners often make poor decisions, planning is unresponsive to change, and workers and managers have little individual incentive to use resources effectively. The Soviet leaders were willing to give up efficiency to gain the many military goods they desire.

Today's Soviet leaders are apparently putting greater emphasis on satisfying consumer desires, but they still want to keep military spending high. The figure shows the route the Soviets may be taking to achieve this goal. A planning system with fewer controls and more production incentives might move the economy from B to C, with the same amount of military goods, but a more efficient use of resources. Increased efficiency allows

FIGURE 30-2   **Changes in the Soviet Economy.** Soviet consumers would choose point *A* if markets made allocation decisions. Soviet leaders want more military goods and are willing to tolerate inefficient planning systems to get them. They "command" the economy to point *B*. Rumored planning reforms might move the economy from *B* to *C*, with greater efficiency allowing higher output of consumer goods with no reduction in military production.

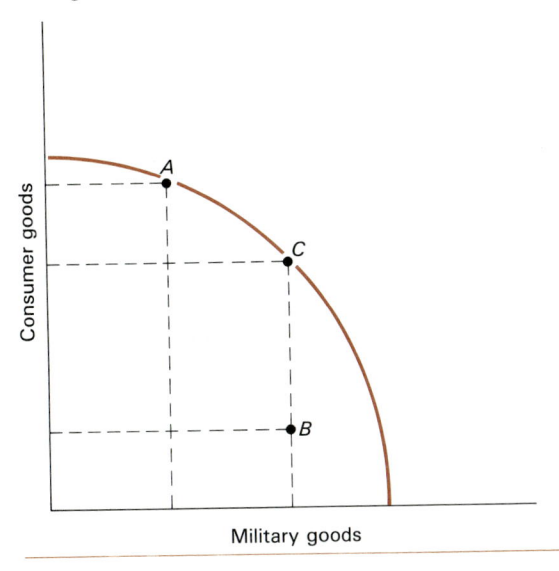

higher output of consumer goods at the same time. However, it is too early to tell if this is really the Soviet aim, or if decentralization will continue.

YUGOSLAVIA: THE WORKER-MANAGED FIRM

30.15 ECONOMY OF YUGOSLAVIA

Yugoslavia briefly dabbled with Soviet-style central planning after the Second World War, but finally settled into a unique system of market socialism featuring employee-managed firms. The state owns the means of production, the capital used to build factories and machines. Scarce capital is allocated to factories that produce goods and compete in markets. The employees of the firms are, in effect, the capitalists and they receive the capitalist's share of the profits. They split the profits among themselves and manage the firm according to a one-man one-vote rule.

30.16 YUGOSLAVIAN WORKER-MANAGEMENT

The major issue we want to examine is how well the Yugoslav system works. In theory, Yugoslavian firms should be as profit-seeking and efficient as those in capitalist countries. The firm seeks profits for its stockholder-workers, just as capitalist corporations do. Worker-managed firms have no central plan to follow, so they produce goods to satisfy market demand. Firms that produce more efficiently, or that better read consumer demand, succeed and increase profits. Inefficient firms incur losses and change their ways or go out of business. Yugoslavia's system looks like efficient capitalism, but with the profits spread more evenly than in the United States. However, this picture of theoretical efficiency breaks down in the real world.

The Yugoslav system results in low investment, inefficient capital use, and little innovation. Workers have little reason to vote for their firm to retain profits and plow them back into expansion because this vote means

ECONOMIC ISSUES

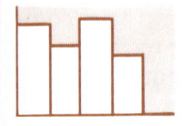

China Rejects Marx for the Market

When George Orwell wrote his famous novel *1984*, he foresaw a time of increased government control over private activities. It is ironic, therefore, that 1984 was the year that the Peoples' Republic of China moved to radically reduce government restrictions on many of its citizens' private economic affairs. In October of 1984, the Central Committee of the Communist Party of China adopted a five-year plan designed to make the Chinese economy more efficient through greater use of private enterprise-type incentives, even if that meant that the distribution of economic rewards would become less equal.

The focus of the Chinese plan is on changing the system of incentives that producers and consumers face, with greater emphasis on markets and market prices. The plan is designed to change China from a Soviet-style centrally-planned economy to a system of market socialism along the lines of the economic systems of Yugoslavia and Hungary. Hungary has the highest standard of living of all the iron curtain socialist nations.

From 1949 to 1978, China's economy was dominated by central planning much like the system found in the Soviet Union. Individual managers had little discretionary authority concerning who they employed, the pay their workers received, what their enterprises produced, how they produced it, and what price they could charge. Prices, fixed by government edict, frequently failed to reflect actual market conditions. The prices of food and basic necessities were set artificially low, for example, with ration coupons used to assure even or "equitable" distribution of scarce goods.

Otto Sieber, visiting his family in China in 1980, found that the price of rice had not changed since 1950. Using ration coupons, Sieber's Chinese relatives were able to purchase the ingredients for a six-course dinner for seven people for the equivalent of $1.64. Prices were low, but ration coupons were needed because of persistent shortages, particularly of agricultural goods.

Economic reforms introduced in 1978 allowed limited private incentives for greater production. Workers on agricultural communes, for example, were allowed greater freedom to grow produce on private plots, which could then be sold in private markets. This system gave farmers an incentive to work harder for individual gain. These incentives quickly increased agricultural production, reducing shortages in urban areas. Similar reforms, which gave individuals greater economic freedom and provided market-like incentives for greater production, were introduced in other sectors of the economy on a limited scale between 1978 and 1984.

giving up sure income now with no guarantee of return later. The result is factories that grow old and inefficient while each generation of workers takes its profit without investing for the future.

Capital is scarce in Yugoslavia, yet factories use many machines and few workers. This happens because when a firm expands production by adding extra machines, the additional profit is split among those already employed. However, if output is increased by adding workers, it just means more people with whom to divide the profit. Self-interested worker-managers face strong incentives not to increase the size of the workforce — even though total production and profits may rise — if it means sharing their profits with others.

Finally, Yugoslavian workers have little incentive to behave like capitalist entrepreneurs and branch out into new firms or invent new products. New firms must compete with established ones for scarce government-controlled capital. New firms in any country typically lose money for a few years while they establish a market and become efficient producers. This is an impossible choice for Yugoslav workers, who must live on their share of firm profits.

The reforms introduced in 1984 aim to thoroughly restructure the Chinese economy. They represent a basic change in philosophy concerning efficiency and equality. The traditional Marxian slogan is "From each according to his ability, to each according to his needs." This philosophy emphasizes equality of distribution. The new Chinese system, according to statements released by the Central Committee, is "More pay for more work; less pay for less work." Efficiency and production incentives are now seen as more important than perfect equality, which the Chinese now hold to be "utterly incompatible" with their view of socialism. (All quotations in the remainder of this section are taken from the October 20, 1984, statement of the Chinese Central Committee.*

The 1984 Chinese economic reforms do not attempt to convert China to a complete free-market economy. Government controls will still remain in vital industries. Greater emphasis on individual incentives and market prices will prevail throughout much of the Chinese economy, however. Among the policies that China will adopt are:

- Greater independence of decision making for the managers of individual economic units. Enterprises will continue to be owned by the state ("the whole people"), but government ownership will no longer imply government control of all economic decisions.
- Greater emphasis on markets. "Our enterprises are put to the test of direct judgement by consumers in the marketplace so that only the best survive."
- Greater use of market prices. "The prices of many commodities reflect neither their value nor the relation of supply to demand." This does not mean that market prices will always be used. Instead, planners will allow markets to set prices in some sectors, and adjust prices in other markets up or down, within limits, based on the existence of shortages and surpluses.
- Greater emphasis on incentives. "The policy of encouraging some people to get better off earlier accords with the law of socialist development and is the only road to prosperity for the whole of society." A closer link between productivity and pay will be established. For example, workers and staff members will receive pay bonuses based on the success (profits) of their enterprise.

Overall, the 1984 economic reforms will make the Chinese economy less rigid and allow more individual economic freedom. Some Chinese workers will become much richer than others, but the Chinese anticipate that their overall standard of living will improve because of greater economic efficiency and better production incentives.

Additional References

Bennet, Amanda, "China Plans a Transformation of Economy to Unpeg Prices, Reduce State Planning Role," *Wall Street Journal,* October 11, 1984.

"China Reaches Decision on Widespread Reform of Economic Structure," *IMF Survey,* November 12, 1984.

*"Excerpts from Chinese Plan for the Economy," *New York Times,* October 21, 1984.

Kifner, John, "New Ingredient Spices 'Goulash Communism,'" *New York Times,* November 10, 1983.

Sieber, Otto, "People's Capitalism Flourishes in China's Markets," *Seattle Times,* May 5, 1980.

Wren, Christopher S., "China's Courtship of Capitalism," *New York Times,* December 25, 1983.

Wren, Christopher S., "Chinese Announce Sweeping Changes in Their Economy," *New York Times,* October 21, 1984.

The Yugoslav system seemingly combines the best aspects of socialism and capitalism. It uses decentralized capitalist decision making with a more even social-income distribution. The result, however, has been inefficiency and slower growth.

THE CONVERGENCE HYPOTHESIS

30.17 CONVERGENCE HYPOTHESIS

Are the world's economic systems growing more alike or more different? Many experts think the convergence hypothesis is valid. They see capitalism and socialism converging upon similar solutions to fundamental economic problems.

Casual empiricism supports the convergence hypothesis. Socialist countries are coming to rely more heavily on markets and decentralized decision making to solve some problems. Private markets have been expanded in the Soviet Union to encourage greater production and more efficient distribution. Even China, probably the most heavily controlled economy of all, has introduced reforms in recent years to provide managers with profit-linked incentives. Official announcements suggest that market experiments will be expanded in the future.

At the same time socialism adopts markets, capitalist countries consider more central controls. One theme of the 1984 elections in the United States was the need for a national industrial policy, some plan for the whole economy to promote investment and development of competitive industries. U.S. firms are increasingly becoming owned by employees, as worker pension funds become big owners of corporate stock.

The problems of scarcity and choice, of using scarce resources efficiently, then distributing the gains equitably, are the same in all nations. Perhaps it is not surprising to see different economic systems converging on common solutions to these common problems.

SUMMARY

30.1
1. The world economy is characterized by two facts. The first is interdependence. Nations depend on one another for markets, natural resources, and credit. Second, interdependence is both a benefit and a risk to a nation. Trading partners are both markets for domestic goods and competition for domestic firms. Nations are diverse in their different solutions to the common problems of scarcity and choice.

30.2
2. An economic system is the set of institutions that society uses to solve economic problems. All economic systems must find answers to three important questions: (a) The allocation choice: how should scarce resources be allocated among competing uses? (b) The production choice: how should these goods be produced? (c) The distribution choice: how should scarce resources be distributed?

30.3
3. Evaluating an economic system involves weighing economic, political, and social factors. Three economic criteria used in this evaluation are static efficiency, dynamic efficiency, and income distribution. Static efficiency is one criteria for economic performance. Static efficiency requires that today's resources be used to produce the combination of goods society prefers above all others. Dynamic efficiency requires that resources be used to maximize their value over time. Economic systems should look to the future, not narrowly focus on the present. The third goal is a desirable distribution of income or resources generally. This criteria is difficult to achieve in part because individuals disagree about which distribution of income is best.

30.4
4. Economic systems differ in whether key choices are made by planners (centralized choice) or by individuals acting through markets (decentralized choice). There is no guarantee that markets perfectly solve economic problems in our imperfect world, but no assurance, either, that planners can do any better.

30.5, 30.6
5. Private and communal or public property rights are two different systems of ownership and control. Private property rights allow individuals to control resources. Owners have a right to any gain that results from efforts that increase the value of their rights.

30.6 ▶ 6. Public or communal property rights exist when ownership of resources is shared by all. These rights are often held by the state for the people. Property rights systems are a trade-off among economic goals. Public rights may improve unequal distribution of resources, but private rights contain incentives that promote efficient use of those resources.

30.7, 30.8 ▶ 7. Capitalism combines private property rights with decentralized choice through markets. An advantage of capitalism is that it provides incentives for efficient production. Individuals invest and innovate because they can claim the benefits of their efforts. Decentralized markets make allocation, production, and distribution choices at low cost. The inexpensive invisible hand is the only planner required. Capitalism's disadvantages are that the market failures such as externalities and monopolies reduce efficiency, and that there is no guarantee of a desirable income distribution.

30.7, 30.9 ▶ 8. Planned socialism combines communal property rights with centralized decision making. The advantages of planned socialism are its ability to achieve a more equal income distribution and to avoid the pitfalls caused by market failures. The disadvantages of planned socialism are that planning is expensive and necessarily imperfect. Planners must be able to balance supply and demand without the help of markets and market prices. Errors in central plans are not just possible, they are inevitable. The input-output table shows how sectors of the economy are interrelated. The output of one sector is the input of others, and vice versa.

30.7, 30.10 ▶ 9. Market socialism combines public property rights with a decentralized choice system. The state owns the means of production under market socialism systems, but allocation and distribution choices are made through market institutions, not by central planners. Incentives are a problem under this system. Individuals have little incentive to wisely use communal resources. Oskar Lange proposed a different system of market socialism, where planners set prices, but otherwise left allocation, production, and distribution choices to markets.

30.7, 30.11 ▶ 10. A fascist system combines private property rights with collective decision making. Fascist systems in the past have been noted for their lack of political and economic freedom. Nazi Germany is an example of a fascist economic system. The United States is a capitalist system. The Soviet Union displays the characteristics of planned socialism, while Yugoslavia is an example of market socialism.

30.12 ▶ 11. No economic system really fits perfectly into any of the four categories described above. All economic systems combine aspects of central and decentralized choice with those of both private and communal property rights.

30.13 ▶ 12. Private property rights are strictly limited in the Soviet Union. Individuals can own only personal possessions. Private enterprise is limited in the Soviet Union. Despite limits, however, private farm plots, which account for less than two percent of total farmland, supply about 25 percent of total Soviet agricultural output.

13. Gosplan is the Soviet state planning agency. Gosplan provides detailed annual and five-year economic plans. Central planning has been successful in diverting resources from production of consumer goods to defense and investment projects. Planning has failed to achieve economic efficiency. Production bottlenecks, failed managerial incentives, distribution problems, and quality problems all exist in the Soviet Union. Persistent shortages and surpluses prevail due to the absence of market adjustments.

14. Market socialism in Yugoslavia takes place through worker-managed firms. The state owns capital that firms use to generate profits. Firms are managed by vote of employees who split the profits.

15. On first glance, worker-managed firms appear to be efficient. Firms have a profit motive to produce efficiently, and workers take the place of capitalist stockholders. Yugoslavian firms are inefficient in several respects, however. Profit-conscious workers vote to pay most profits to themselves, retaining little for investment and growth. Worker-run firms use many machines, but few workers. Worker-owners have little incentive to expand through a bigger workforce, since new workers reduce the share of the profit that current workers receive.

16. The convergence hypothesis holds that economic systems as divergent as capitalism and socialism slowly become more alike in the way they solve economic problems. Two trends that support that convergence hypothesis are that socialist countries are introducing more market-like methods while capitalist countries consider industrial policies that look like the modest beginnings of central planning.

DISCUSSION QUESTIONS

1. Explain how allocation, production, and distribution systems differ in capitalist and socialist economic systems. Which system solves economic problems better? Defend your answer.

2. "Capitalist economies are efficient, but socialist economies are more equitable." Agree or disagree with this statement, and defend your choice.

3. What are property rights? Why is there a link between production incentives and property rights? Which system gives the greater incentive to produce: private or public property rights? Explain.

4. Socialist systems are characterized by public ownership of capital. Capital is privately owned in the United States. Why is this difference important? What are the consequences of public versus private ownership of capital? Explain.

5. Fascist systems are characterized by little economic choice and limited political freedom. How are political and economic freedom related? Does a society need economic freedom to have political freedom? Explain.

30.13, 30.14, 30.15 → 6. Compare and contrast the economies of the United States, the Soviet Union, and Yugoslavia. Make a list of similarities and differences among these nations.

30.17 → 7. Do you agree with the convergence hypothesis? Give evidence to support your view.

SELECTED READINGS

Burns, John F., "Soviet Study Urges Relaxing of Controls to Revive Economy," *New York Times*, August 5, 1983, p. 1.

Friedman, Milton, *Capitalism and Freedom*, Chicago: University of Chicago Press, 1972.

Gregory, Paul R., and Stuart, Robert C., *Soviet Economic Structure and Performance*, New York: Harper & Row, 1974.

Knight, Frank H. "Social Economic Organization," reprinted in *Readings in Microeconomics*, 2nd ed., William Breit and Harold M. Hochman (eds.), New York: Holt, Rinehart, and Winston, 1971.

Lange, Oskar and Taylor, Fred M., *On the Economic Theory of Socialism*, New York: McGraw Hill, 1964.

Marx, Karl, "Capital," reprinted in Charles W. Needy (ed.), *Classics of Economics*, Oak Park, IL: Moore Publishing Company, Inc., 1980.

Smith, Hedrick, *The Russians*, New York: The New York Times Book Company, 1976.

Glossary

Ability-to-pay Taxation The concept that taxes should be based on a person's ability to pay, as measured by income, wealth, or some other factor.

Absolute Advantage The ability to produce a good or service with fewer resources than other nations.

Absolute Poverty Poverty defined as a physical standard of living.

Accounting Profit Profit equal to the total revenue minus the sum of all explicit costs.

Adaptive Expectations Hypothesis The economic theory that contends that the primary determinants of future expectations are the actual recent past experiences of decision makers.

Administered Prices Prices that are set by management and not completely determined by demand and cost factors.

Administrative Cost Premium The portion of the interest rate that compensates lenders for costs of administering the loan.

Agenda The order in which issues are considered and votes taken.

Aggregate Demand (AD) The desired total spending in the economy (measured in real GNP).

Aggregate Demand Curve A graphic device showing the relationship between desired real purchases (for some time period) and the price level, all else held constant.

Aggregate Supply (AS) The total intended production of goods and services in the economy (measured in real GNP).

Aggregate Supply Curve A graphic device showing the relationship between desired real output (for some time period) and the price level, all else held constant.

Aggregates Measures of economic activity involving one or more sectors of the economy.

Aggregation The principle whereby coincidence of wants is more easily attained when surplus and deficit units are brought together in large, organized groups.

Announcement Effects Changes in economic behavior that occur due to the Fed's announcement of plans to expand or contract the money supply.

Annually Balanced Budget The idea that the federal government's budget must be balanced, with tax revenues equal to total outlays, each and every year.

Antitrust Laws Laws designed to prevent businesses from engaging in activities that reduce competition, set price, or in other ways restrain trade.

Antitrust Legislation Laws developed to regulate competition. They prohibit activities in restraint of trade.

Appreciate To increase in the relative value of a currency.

Arbitrage Riskless speculation; buying currencies on one foreign exchange market to sell at a profit elsewhere.

Atomistic Competition Competitive markets in which individual buyers and sellers are too small to affect prices.

Automatic Stabilizers A system of institutional structures whose purpose is to moderate the effects of changes in the equilibrium levels of income and employment.

Autonomous Consumption The part of total consumption that does not depend on level of income.

Average Fixed Cost (AFC) Fixed cost divided by the level of output.

Average Propensity to Consume (APC) The ratio of consumption to income. This ratio represents the portion of total income that consumers are consuming.

Average Propensity to Save (APS) The ratio of saving to total income. This ratio represents the portion of total income that consumers save.

Average Revenue (AR) Total revenue divided by the units sold; the per-unit revenue received by the firm.

Average Tax Rate The percentage of total income that is paid to taxes.

Average Total Cost (ATC) The total cost of producing goods or services divided by the quantity that is produced — a measure of the cost per unit of production.

Average Variable Cost (AVC) Variable cost divided by the level of output.

Balance of Payments The record of a nation's international payments; total money inflows minus total money outflows.

Balance of Payments Deficit A condition where total money outflows exceed total money inflows for a nation.

Balance of Payments Surplus A condition where total money inflows exceed total money outflows for a nation.

Balance of Trade The value of exports minus the value of imports.

Balance of Trade Deficit The condition in which the value of a nation's exports is less than the value of imported goods.

Balance of Trade Equilibrium The condition in which the value of a nation's exports equals the value of imported goods.

Balance of Trade Surplus The condition in which the value of a nation's exports is greater than the value of imported goods.

Balanced Budget Multiplier An economic principle that states that equal increases or decreases in government spending and taxation will increase or decrease equilibrium income by the amount of the original change in government spending.

Bank Assets Those items that the bank itself owns. Claims the bank has upon others are the bank's assets. Banks primarily hold their assets in the form of loans, reserves, securities, buildings, and equipment.

Bank Liabilities Those items on the bank's balance sheet that are owed to someone else by the bank. Claims upon the bank, such as demand deposits, are the bank's liabilities.

Bank Reserves Funds held by banks to meet the withdrawal demands of depositors. Reserves are held in the form of vault cash or deposits held at the Federal Reserve.

Barter Economy A system with no money, where goods are exchanged for other goods.

Base Year A reference year used to construct a price index. The price index market basket is constructed for the base year.

Benefits-Received Taxation The concept that taxes should be based on the value of the benefits that a person receives from the public sector.

Black Market The buying and selling of illegal goods or the buying and selling of goods for illegal prices.

Blacklist Lists of "undesirable" workers, frequently those with pro-union sympathies. Blacklisted workers are often unable to find work.

Board of Governors Seven federal government employees appointed by the president of the United States and confirmed by the Senate who serve as the overall policymaking and controlling body of the Federal Reserve System.

Bonds Promises-to-pay issued by firms and governments.

Bottleneck Economy Aggregate supply in an economy with rising marginal costs and production bottlenecks.

Boycotts Organized attempts to influence labor negotiations by refusing to purchase a firm's products.

Break-even Point The production level at which the firm earns zero economic profit; the level of output at which price equals ATC.

Budget Deficit A government budget whose tax revenues are less than spending and transfer payment totals. The government must borrow the amount of the deficit.

Budget Line A graph showing the combinations of two goods that can be purchased by spending a given amount of money.

Budget Surplus A government budget whose total revenues are greater than its total outlays.

Business Cycles Periods of national economic expansion that are followed by periods of declining output and income.

Business Sector The part of the economy that purchases resources, organizes production, and sells goods and services.

Capacity The ability of a borrower to generate sufficient revenue (through labor or investment) to repay a loan. It is also the physical ability of the economy to produce, limited by the stock of factories, machines, tools, and so on.

Capacity Utilization Rate Current production as a percentage of the production at the economy's maximum use of factories and equipment.

Capital Formation The sacrificing of present consumption in order to increase the present production of machinery, human skills, and other capital goods, which will in turn increase the ability to produce output in the future.

Capital Goods Those goods used to increase society's ability to produce goods and services in the future, such as factories and equipment.

Capital-Intensive Production A production process that uses relatively more capital than labor to produce goods.

Capitalism An economic system of private property rights where markets are used to make decentralized allocation, production, and distribution decisions.

Cardinal Measure A measure that allows qualitative and quantitative comparisons. Length measures (such as feet, inches, and yards) are cardinal, for example, since two yards is twice as long as one yard.

Cartel An organization of producers that attempts to increase profits by restricting supply in a market.

Causation Causation exists when it can be shown that a change in one variable actually brings about a change in another. Correlation is often taken as evidence of causation, but it is not proof of causation.

Central Bank The organization in a nation that determines monetary policy, regulates the banking system, and engages in international economic relations. The Federal Reserve is the U.S. central bank.

Centralized Control Control which is concentrated in the hands of a single authority.

Centralized Decision Making An economic system where important choices are made by central planners.

Change in Demand A shift of the entire demand curve and an actual change in the demand relationship caused by a change in a determinant of demand other than the price of the item itself.

Change in Quantity Demanded A movement along the original demand curve caused by a change in price.

Change in Quantity Supplied A movement along a given supply curve caused by a change in price.

Change in Supply An actual change in the supply relationship caused by a change in one of the five major determinants of supply, which results in a shift of the supply curve.

Character The tendency of a borrower to honor liabilities.

Choice The process of selecting among limited alternatives. Through choice, human beings deal with the economic problem of scarcity.

Circular Flow of Spending and Income A model of the relationship between spending and income for the entire economy.

Classical Economists Economists of the nineteenth and early twentieth century who did not believe that sustained recession was possible in a market economy.

Classical Medicine Policies that attempt to reduce trade deficits by causing recessions that reduce domestic income.

Clayton Antitrust Act The 1914 federal law outlawing such monopoly pricing practices as price discrimination.

Closed Economy An economy with no interaction with other countries.

Coefficient of Elasticity A measure of price elasticity; a ratio that compares the percentage change in quantity demanded with the percentage change in price.

Coincidence of Wants The necessary condition for a barter exchange to occur, where each party to the exchange must want to acquire what the other party has to offer in exchange for what they are willing to give up. For example, a butcher who wants to acquire bread in return for meat must find and trade with a baker who wants to acquire meat in return for bread.

Collateral Assets that are pledged against an obligation. Collateral becomes the property of the lender if a loan is not repaid.

Collusion A secret agreement to engage in illegal activity. The joining together of producers to restrict supply (limit output), thereby forcing prices to increase, or consumer action to limit demand, thereby forcing prices to decrease.

Command Economy An economic system that answers the questions of what, how, and for whom to produce primarily through social choices made by a central planning agency. It is characterized by detailed central planning and little free enterprise.

Commerical Banks Financial institutions

with the primary purpose of collecting funds from depositors and loaning them out at a profit.

Communal Goods Goods where exclusion does not exist but rivalry does; for example, highways and fisheries.

Comparative Advantage The ability to produce a good or service at a lower opportunity cost.

Complementary Goods Goods or services that are used together, thereby enhancing each other's value; for example, a tape player and cassettes.

Comptroller of the Currency A federal office established to control and supervise the activities of national banks.

Concentration Ratio The proportion of total sales in a given market accounted for by the activity of a particular number of firms. High concentration ratios indicate markets dominated by a few firms.

Constant Growth Rate Rule Milton Friedman's proposal that the Federal Reserve should expand the money supply at a constant rate and not attempt to fine tune the economy through discretionary monetary policies.

Constant Returns to Scale Constant long-run *ATC* over the relevant output range.

Consumer Burden The part of a tariff paid by consumers as higher price.

Consumer Price Index (CPI) A measure of inflation based on a market basket of goods and services that an average urban family would purchase.

Consumption Function A description of the way that consumption spending varies with disposable income.

Consumption Spending The value of the final goods and services that households purchase. Consumption spending includes everyday items such as expenditures for food, clothing, legal services, and haircuts.

Contractionary Fiscal Policy The use of decreased government spending or increased taxes in an attempt to reduce aggregate demand.

Corporation A business firm owned by many individuals collectively. Each individual owner has a right to a share of the corporation's profits, but the individual's liability is limited to the amount of his or her initial investment.

Correlation Two things are correlated when there is a systematic relationship between changes in one variable and changes in the other.

Cost of Living Adjustments (COLAs) Contractual agreements that link changes in wages and salaries to changes in a price index. COLAs are misnamed because price indexes measure inflation; they do not measure the cost of living.

Cost-Push Inflation Inflation caused by rising production costs and accompanied by falling real GNP caused by falling aggregate supply.

Countercyclical Fiscal Policy Government spending or taxation policies that will tend to move output, employment, and income in the opposite direction than it is currently heading. These policies are used in an attempt to stabilize the economy.

Credit Controls Government regulations that attempt to regulate the availability of credit in order to stabilize the economy.

Credit Unions Nonprofit organizations that provide bank-like services to members of a particular social or occupational group. Many labor unions have formed credit unions to provide financial services to their members, for example.

Crowding Out The tendency of government deficits to raise interest rates and reduce borrowing for private investment spending.

Crowding-Out Effect A situation where investments in growth for the future are curtailed or crowded out because of current high energy costs.

Customs Union Groups of nations having free trade among themselves and unified tariff barriers with other countries.

Cyclical Deficit That part of the deficit that results from the interaction of automatic stabilizer programs and the business cycle.

Cyclical Unemployment Unemployment due to changes in the demand for the goods and services that workers produce.

Cyclically Balanced Budget The idea that the federal government's budget must be balanced, with tax revenues equal to total outlays, over the course of the business cycle, with surpluses during years of rising income being used to make up for deficits during years of falling income.

Deadweight Loss Scarce resources that are used to prevent loss or harm rather than being used to produce goods and services.

Decentralized Decision Making An economic system where most important choices are made by individuals through market actions.

Decentralized Markets Markets which are not controlled by a centralized regulatory authority.

Decreasing Returns to Scale Rising long-run *ATC* over the relevant output range.

Deduction The part of the scientific method concerned with developing theories or hypotheses, then testing them against real-world facts and data.

Deficit The amount of government borrowing; the amount by which spending exceeds tax revenues.

Deficit Units Households, businesses, and governments that desire to consume more resources in the present time period than are currently available to them.

Deflation A decrease in the general level of prices.

Demand The relationship between the price of a good and the amount of it that consumers are willing and able to purchase in a given period of time. The demand curve shows the quantity demanded per unit of time at each possible price, with all factors except price assumed constant.

Demand Curve The graphic representation of the relationship between price and quantity demanded. The curve slopes downward and to the right, illustrating the law of demand.

Demand Deposits Checking accounts traditionally held only in commercial banks; today they are held at most financial institutions.

Demand-Pull Inflation Inflation accompanied by rising real GNP caused by increases in aggregate demands.

Demand-Side Fiscal Policies Government policies designed to influence aggregate demand.

Deposit Expansion Multiplier The principle that states that an increase in reserves in the banking system causes a greater increase in total bank deposits and therefore the money supply. The deposit expansion multiplier is the reciprocal of the reserve requirement. For example, a required reserve ratio of 25 percent would yield a deposit expansion multiplier of 1/.25, or 4.

Depository Institutions Deregulation Act of 1980 A federal law that altered the regulation of depository institutions by allowing interest payments on checkable deposits, reduced the scope of interest rate ceilings, and changed the nature of bank regulation to expand the allowable activities of savings and loans, mutual savings banks, and credit unions. In addition, the legislation gives the Federal Reserve greater control over the money supply. The Fed can now set reserve requirements for savings and loan associations, credit unions, and all other non-members of the Federal Reserve System. In addition to other stipulations, the act plans to have all interest rate ceilings removed from banks by 1986.

Depreciate To decrease in the relative value of a currency.

Depreciation The decline in the value of productive assets, such as equipment and structures, due to their wearing out. Depreciation can be thought of as the investment necessary to offset the wearing out of capital goods. Depreciation is sometimes listed as capital consumption allowance in the GNP accounts.

Depression Economy Aggregate supply in an economy with many unemployed resources.

Deregulation The policy of reducing or eliminating government regulations that affect private individuals and firms.

Derived Demand Demand for one product or resource that depends and is based on the demand for another product or resource.

Devaluation Lowering a currency's fixed exchange rate.

Diminishing Marginal Returns The property that, as more and more resources are allocated to the production of a particular item, all else held constant, the additional output from each extra resource declines.

Diminishing Marginal Utility The property that marginal utility declines as the quantity consumed per unit of time increases.

Direct Relationship The relationship between two variables such that an increase (or decrease) in one implies a corresponding increase (or decrease) in the other. A direct relationship implies that the variables tend to move together in the same direction.

Direct Subsidies Direct cash payments to producers of certain goods to encourage the production of those goods.

Dirty Float Limited intervention by the central bank or government to prevent exchange rates from floating freely with supply and demand.

Discount Rate The interest rate that commercial banks are charged when they borrow short-term funds from their Federal Reserve district bank.

Discount Window The "window" or office through which the Federal Reserve lends reserves to member banks. Loans are technically made through a process by which the FRS purchases loan assets from the bank at a discount.

Discouraged Workers People who have been unemployed so long that they have stopped looking for work and are, therefore, no longer included in the unemployment statistics.

Discretionary Fiscal Policy The deliberate use of government's powers to spend, lay, and collect taxes in an effort to bring about desired changes in economic conditions in an attempt to attain an optimum level of employment and income within the economy.

Diseconomies of Scale Factors that increase average cost as production expands in the long run.

Disinflation A falling inflation rate; the general level of prices is rising, but the rate of increase is slowing.

Disposable Personal Income The income available for households to spend or save.

Dissaving The amount by which personal spending exceeds personal income.

Dry Wells The injection of steam into oil wells to force heavy residual oils to the surface.

Durable Goods Goods that have a service life of greater than one year. Automobiles and boats are examples of durable goods.

Dynamic Efficiency Optimal allocation of resources over time; resource use that takes into account future needs, not just current desires; the use of resources that leads to high rates of economic growth in the future.

Economic Boycott A consumer action in which consumers agree to restrict market demand and gain advantages for themselves (for example, lower prices) at a cost to producers.

Economic Efficiency The optimal allocation of scarce resources in an economy to produce those goods and services that society most prefers. Under certain conditions, free markets automatically achieve economic efficiency.

Economic Goods Goods that are scarce, for which our desires exceed the amount freely supplied to us by nature.

Economic Growth An increase in the economy's overall ability to produce goods and services.

Economic Profit Profit in which both explicit and implicit costs are considered; economic profit is different from accounting profit.

Economic Rent Payment to a resource above that required to induce its supply.

Economic System The set of economic, political, and social institutions the society uses to solve the economic problem of scarcity.

Economic Tax Incidence The distribution of the tax burden, after all economic effects have been accounted for.

Economics The social science that studies how society chooses to allocate scarce resources among its unlimited wants and desires.

Economies of Scale Factors that reduce average cost as production expands in the long run.

Economist One who observes the human choice process with the goal of analyzing, understanding, and predicting human economic behavior.

Effluent Taxes Taxes based on the amount of pollution a firm produces.

Elastic Demand Demand in which the quantity demanded changes proportionately more than price (the elasticity coefficient is greater than one).

Elasticity of Supply A measure of supply response to changing prices; the percentage change in quantity supplied divided by the percentage change in price.

Employment Act of 1946 An act of Congress that created the President's Council of Economic Advisors and set the macroeconomic goals of price stability, full employment, and economic growth.

Energy Substitution Effects The move away from items or processes that use large amounts of energy to those that use smaller amounts of energy.

Engine of Competition The existence of many consumers and producers in the market for a certain good or service.

Entrepreneurs Individuals who organize resources for production, form new enterprises, or make innovations in production. Entrepreneurs accept the risk of failure in exchange for the potential of financial gain.

Entry New firms come into the industry, generally because they are attracted by economic profits.

Equation of Exchange Defined as money supply times velocity equals average price times real quantity:
$$M \times V = P \times Q.$$
Total spending on goods and services is equal to the money supply times the number of times that the money supply turns over.

Equilibrium Any point at which conflicting forces are in balance. In economics market equilibrium occurs at the price at which quantity supplied is equal to quantity demanded.

Equilibrium of the Firm The output level at which the firm maximizes profit; the point where marginal revenue equals marginal cost.

Equitable Distribution of Income A distribution of income in the economy that is considered fair or just.

Eurodollar Deposits Dollar denominated deposits held in banks outside of the United States.

European Economic Community (EEC) A customs union including major European nations; also called Common Market.

Excess Reserves The amount of reserves that a bank has above and beyond its legally required reserves.

Exchange The process whereby individuals trade goods or services to make themselves better off. The existence of exchange makes specialization possible.

Exchange Rate The value of one currency in terms of foreign currencies.

Excise Taxes Taxes based on the value of goods purchased.

Exclusion The condition where individuals can exclude others from benefiting from a good or service.

Exit Old firms leave the industry, generally because they are in pursuit of economic profits in other industries.

Exogenous Policy Variable A part of an economic system that can be controlled by forces outside of that specific economic system.

Expansionary Fiscal Policy The use of increased government spending or reduced taxation in an attempt to increase aggregate demand.

Expansions Periods of rising total output as measured by rising real GNP.

Expenditure Method A method of calculating GNP by summing the dollar value of all types of expenditures. The expenditure method calculates GNP as the sum of consumption, investment, net export, and government spending.

Explicit Costs Out-of-pocket costs paid by a firm (accounting costs).

Exports Sales of goods and services to purchasers located in other countries.

External Benefit A benefit that an individual receives for which no market payment was made.

External Cost A cost borne by an individual as the result of another's choice.

Externalities Costs or benefits that decision makers impose on others not party to their decisions. For example, pollution generated by industrial production passes on a reduction in quality of life to those living in the area. This is obviously a cost to these people that is incurred outside the marketplace. Externalities are also sometimes referred to as spill-over effects or neighborhood effects.

Factors of Production Inputs that are used to make outputs. Land, labor, capital, and knowledge, or "know-how," are frequently cited as the most important factors of production because they are the most important inputs used in production.

Fallacy of Composition The incorrect belief that what is true for the individual is also true for the entire group.

Fascism An economic system where resources are owned by individuals, but most important economic decisions are made by the government.

Federal Advisory Council (FAC) A Federal Reserve group consisting of private bankers from the FRS districts, which meets to provide advice and exchange data regarding monetary policy and economic conditions.

Federal Funds Market The system through which some commercial banks who hold excess reserves indirectly make very short-term loans to other commercial banks in need of reserves.

Federal Funds Rate The interest rate charged on loans made in the federal funds market.

Federal Open Market Committee (FOMC) Committee charged with the responsibility of setting Federal Reserve policy regarding open market buying and selling of U.S. securities. The members of this committee include the seven members of the Board of Governors, the president of the New York Federal Reserve District Bank, and four presidents of the remaining Federal Reserve district banks.

Federal Reserve Bank A reference to one of the 12 district banks that make up the Federal Reserve System.

Federal Savings and Loan Insurance Corporation An agency similar to the FDIC that provides insurance for deposits in savings and loan banks.

Final Goods and Services Those goods and services that are purchased by their ultimate users in a given period of time.

Financial Intermediaries Institutions that act as middlemen, completing credit transactions between savers and borrowers.

Financial Sector The part of the economy that receives savings from households and businesses, and finances investment spending. Banks, credit unions, and insurance companies are included in the financial sector.

Finite Resources Resources for which there is a limited supply and which are virtually impossible to reproduce in the future.

Fiscal Federalism The division of government tax and spending responsibilities into federal, state, and local levels of government.

Fiscal Policy The practice of managing government spending and taxes as a means of arriving at stable prices or other economic goals, such as growth or high levels of employment.

Fiscal Year The government's accounting year. The federal fiscal year runs from October 1 to the following September 30.

Fixed Cost The cost of fixed inputs; cost that does not vary with the level of output in the short run.

Fixed Exchange Rates Exchange rates that are set by central banks.

Fixed Input Input whose use does not change with the level of output in the short run.

Fixed Investment Business purchases of new equipment or structures that add to the stock of capital.

Flexible Exchange Rates Exchange rates that are set by supply and demand.

Float An asset that is temporarily owned by two individuals, as would sometimes occur in financial transactions that take place over a period of time.

Flow Concept A concept relating to the amount of an economic activity within a given period of time. Investment (a flow concept) adds to the economy's total amount of capital (a stock concept).

Foreign Exchange Foreign currencies; people purchase foreign exchange because they want to purchase foreign goods.

Foreign Sector The sector of the economy that engages in trade with the residents of other countries.

Fractional Reserve Banking The banking system that requires banks to keep only a portion of their total deposits in the form of cash reserves to meet the needs of their customers withdrawals. Remaining reserves may be utilized for profit-making purposes such as extending loans or purchasing securities.

Free Rider An individual who receives a benefit without making payment for it. Free riders exist when public goods or external benefits are present.

Frictional Unemployment Unemployment due to the inability of the labor market to match jobless workers with unfilled jobs; caused by poor information, lack of mobility, barriers to occupational entry, and discrimination.

Full Employment The level of unemployment that would occur in a growing, healthy economy.

Full-Capacity Economy Aggregate supply in an economy that has reached production limits determined by finite capacity.

Functional Finance The philosophy that states government should take whatever fiscal actions are necessary to promote a noninflationary full-employment equilibrium without substantial concern for the size of deficits or surpluses.

Garn–St. Germain Depository Institutions Act of 1982 A federal law that widened the sources of funds for depository institutions, contributed toward the removal of interest rate ceilings, and gave regulators expanded emergency powers to deal with financially unstable depository institutions.

Government Sector The part of the economy owned by the public as a whole. The government sector includes federal, state, and local governments.

Government Spending Purchase of final goods and services by federal, state, and local governments.

Gross Investment New investment, not including any adjustment for wear and tear to existing capital.

Gross National Product (GNP) The market value in current prices of all final goods and services produced in an economy in a specified period of time (usually a year).

Gross National Product Implicit Price Deflator Index A price index used to adjust GNP for inflation. All final goods and services form the market basket for the GNP Index.

Guest Workers Foreign workers who are allowed to participate in a nation's labor market in order to relieve a labor shortage.

Horizontal Equity Tax fairness that is achieved when people in similar circumstances pay similar taxes.

Horizontal Merger A merger between two previously competing firms.

Household Sector The part of the economy that provides resources to businesses in return for income, which is used for consumption spending, saving, and to pay taxes.

Human Capital The available stock of knowledge, learning, and skills.

Hypothesis A supposition or conjecture advanced as an explanation for certain facts or events.

Implicit Costs The opportunity costs of business operation.

Imports Purchases of goods and services from producers located in other countries.

Incentives The forces that influence or encourage an action or choice. Economic incentives exert a strong effect on the choice behavior of members of our society.

Income Effect The change in buying behavior that results from a change in purchasing power, relative prices held constant.

Income Elastic Demand Demand in which the quantity demanded changes proportionately more than income.

Income Elasticity A measure of the responsiveness of demand to changing income.

Income Inelastic Demand Demand in which the quantity demanded changes proportionately less than income.

Income Method A method of calculating GNP by summing the value of the payments to the owners of the resources that are used in production.

Increasing Returns to Scale Falling long-run *ATC* over the relevant output range.

Indexation A system in which wages or other payments are automatically adjusted to reflect inflation according to changes in a price index.

Indifference Curve A graph showing all the combinations of two goods that yield the same total utility.

Indirect Business Taxes Social security contributions and other taxes that are imposed on households but collected from them indirectly through the business sector.

Individual Retirement Accounts (IRAs) Special accounts at financial institutions that allow individuals to defer taxes on funds that are saved for retirement.

Induced Consumption The portion of total consumption that does depend on level of income. Induced consumption increases as income increases and decreases as income decreases.

Induction The part of the scientific method concerned with observing human beings and using these observations to derive hypotheses or general behavior rules.

Industrial Development Policy A set of government policies designed to encourage growth, investment, and technological change in specific industries.

Inelastic Demand Demand in which the quantity demanded changes proportionately less than price (the elasticity coefficient is less than one).

Inferior Good A good for which demand varies inversely with income.

Inflation Premium The portion of the interest rate that compensates lenders for expected inflation, which reduces the purchasing power of repaid funds.

Inflation Rate A measure of the rate of increase in the general level of prices in a given period of time.

Inflation A substantial, sustained increase in the general level of prices.

Inflationary Gap The difference between equilibrium income and the full-employment level of income (assuming that equilibrium income is above the full-employment level).

Injections Economic activities that stimulate the circular flow of spending and income; investment, government, and export spending are injections.

In-Kind Benefits Benefits supplied as goods or services (such as medical care) instead of cash.

Input Resources used in production.

Input-Output Table A table showing the amount of inputs of different goods necessary to produce a unit of output.

Insurance Companies Firms that accept current payments (insurance premiums) from clients in return for contingent claims to the future payment of specified sums (insurance claims).

Intergovernmental Grants Transfer payments made from one level of government to another (e.g., from the federal government to a state government).

Intermediate Goods and Services Those goods and services that businesses purchase to aid in the production of some other (final) good. Intermediate goods are not included in GNP in order to avoid double counting production.

International Monetary Fund (IMF) The central bankers' central bank; international organization that makes loans to nations to finance balance of payments deficits.

Intervention Government or central bank foreign-exchange transactions intended to alter the exchange rate.

Inventory Investment The change in the value of the stock of resources that businesses have on hand for future resale or future productive use.

Inverse Relationship The relationship between two variables such that an increase (or decrease) in one implies a decrease (or increase) in the other. An inverse relationship implies that the variables tend to move in opposite directions.

Investment in Human Capital Investment in training and education aimed at increasing worker productivity.

Investment Rule The rule that investments are made if and only if their expected rate of return is greater than or equal to the interest rate on securities of similar risk and period.

Investment Spending The purchase of goods that increase the capacity to produce in the future. Purchases of factories, equipment, inventories, or new technology are examples of investment spending.

Investment Tax Credit A tax program that allows firms to deduct a percentage of the cost of a current investment from their current federal tax liabilities.

Invisible Hand Adam Smith's name for the beneficial forces of competitive markets.

Iron Law of Wages Theory held by Malthus and Marx, among others, that wages fall to subsistence levels in the long run.

Kinked Demand Curve The demand curve in which competitors will match a price decrease but will not match a price increase. The curve is therefore elastic above the market price and inelastic below the market price.

Labor Force The number of people with jobs plus the number of unemployed workers.

Labor-Intensive Production A production process that uses relatively more labor than capital to produce goods.

Laissez Faire Policies Government policies that seek a minimal level of interference with market actions.

Landrum-Griffin Act Labor legislation that primarily required regularly scheduled elections of union officers and prohibited certain persons from holding office. It also made certain illegal acts involving unions federal crimes.

Law of Comparative Advantage Theory that international trade and production specialization is based on differences in opportunity cost.

Law of Demand The principle of economics that states that the quantity demanded per unit of time varies inversely with price, all else being equal.

Law of Increasing Costs The opportunity cost of producing an item tends to rise as more and more of it is produced, assuming that other factors such as resource availability and technology do not change.

Law of Supply The economic principle that describes the direct relationship between price and quantity supplied.

Leading Indicator An economic statistic that tends to foretell future changes in the economy.

Leakages Economic activities that reduce the circular flow of spending and income; savings, taxes, and imports are leakages.

Leaky-Bucket Problem The problem that government transfer payment programs use up resources as they transfer them among income groups, thereby reducing the size of the net transfer.

Legal Tax Incidence The distribution of the legal responsibility for tax payment.

Liquidity The characteristic of an asset that enables it to be quickly and easily converted into cash without loss of value.

Lockouts An antistrike tactic; employers close their doors rather than paying higher wages or negotiating with unions.

Long Run (in production) A time frame sufficiently long to make all inputs and costs variable.

Long Run A length of time sufficiently long so that individual producers are able to alter production capacity to suit market conditions.

Long-Run *ATC* The curve connecting segments of the short-run *ATC* curve that illustrates different plant sizes.

Long-Run Phillips Curve A graphic device that illustrates the relationship between the inflation rate and the unemployment rate in the long run.

Long-Term Capital Gains Profits made from the sale of an asset that was owned for more than six months.

Lorenz Curve A graphic technique used to illustrate the degree of equality or inequality of income distribution.

Macroeconomic Equilibrium In the Keynesian model, a condition in which total spending equals total income, or stated differently, total leakages equal total injections.

Macroeconomics The study of the national economy, focusing on such social problems as inflation, unemployment, and economic growth.

Marginal The effects of one additional unit that is produced or consumed.

Marginal Benefit (Utility) The amount of satisfaction received from the production or consumption of one additional unit of a good or service.

Marginal Cost (*MC*) The change in total cost (or variable cost) that occurs when output changes by one unit; in other words, the extra cost of producing one more item.

Marginal Efficiency of Investment (*MEI*) The return on an additional dollar of investment spending. This is a measure of the profitability of additional investment spending.

Marginal Physical Product (*MPP*) The change in total production that occurs when the amount of a single input is changed by one unit, holding all else fixed.

Marginal Product The change in total product when one input is added, all other inputs held constant.

Marginal Productivity Theory The theory that resources are paid according to their marginal products.

Marginal Propensity to Consume (*MPC*) The ratio of the change in consumption to the change in income. This ratio represents the percentage of each additional dollar earned as income that is spent on consumption. The fraction of a change in income that becomes a change in consumption spending.

Marginal Propensity to Save (*MPS*) The ratio between the change in saving and the change in income. This ratio represents the percentage of each additional dollar in income that is saved.

Marginal Rate of Substitution The ratio at which two goods substitute for each other to yield a constant level of utility to the consumer; the slope of the indifference curve.

Marginal Resource Cost (*MRC*) The increase in total resource cost when one more input is employed.

Marginal Revenue (*MR*) The change in total revenue or receipts when the quantity sold changes by one unit.

Marginal Revenue Product (*MRP*) The extra revenue an additional input produces for a monopoly, other inputs held fixed (*MPP* multiplied by *MR*).

Marginal Tax Rate The tax rate that would apply to any increase in income, not taking into account the tax burden on income already earned.

Marginal Utility The change in utility that accompanies a one-unit change in the amount of a good or service consumed, with preferences and the quantities of other goods held constant.

Market Basket A list of types and quantities of goods and services that is used to calculate a price index in order to measure inflation.

Market Economy An economic system that answers the questions of what, how, and for whom to produce primarily through choices in the marketplace.

Market Socialism An economic system where capital is owned by the state, but most production and allocation decisions are made through decentralized markets.

Markets The general term for the institutions through which the exchange of goods and services takes place. Institutions that coordinate individual choices and provide the basis for the exchange of goods and services.

Mark-up Pricing A pricing rule that sets price by adding a fixed percentage to cost.

Median Household Income The median of any series is the figure at the center of the distribution when all the elements of the series are ordered from lowest to highest. For example, $200 is the median number in the series $100, $200, $500. Median household income is therefore the income of the household at the center of the income distribution when household incomes are ordered from lowest to highest.

Medium of Exchange A mutually acceptable third commodity among the two parties in an exchange. Money, as a medium of exchange, serves as a common denominator for all goods and services.

Mercantilists 18th century merchants and economists who favored trade restrictions to protect gold accumulations.

Merger An action in which one firm acquires ownership of another or several firms join under single management.

Microeconomics The study of economic choices made by individual consumers and producers, and the markets where consumers and producers exchange goods and services.

Middlemen Individuals who specialize in bringing buyers and sellers together for mutually advantageous exchange.

Minimum Wage Law A federal law that sets wage floors in many labor markets.

Mixed Economy An economic system that combines the characteristics of both market and command economies. Some choices are made by individuals, while other choices are made by government.

Models Simplified descriptions of real-world processes that help us better understand the more complex real events and relationships.

Monetarism An economic theory that stresses the importance of changes in the money supply on economic activities and policies.

Monetary Policy Using various controls on the money supply of an economy to strive for a relatively stable price level and desired economic growth.

Monetary Transmission Mechanism The link between the credit market and aggregate demand. The relationship between interest rates and investment spending provides the monetary transmission mechanism. Monetary policy affects aggregate demand through its impact on interest rates and investment spending.

Money Anything that is generally accepted in exchange for goods and services and in payment of debt.

Money Market Deposit Accounts (MMDA) A type of bank account that pays interest rates that correspond to those offered by money market mutual funds.

Money Market Mutual Fund (MMMF) A system in which the funds of many individuals are pooled and used to purchase corporate and government bonds.

Money Supply A measure of the total amount of money available in an economy in a given time period.

Monopolistic Competition Competitive markets characterized by product differentiation; each firm has a limited monopoly over its particular good.

Monopoly A market with only one supplier.

Monopsony A market with a single buyer; a monopoly purchaser of a resource.

Multiplier Principle The economic principle that states that an initial independent increase or decrease in net exports, government spending, consumption, or investment will, through the responding multiplier effect, cause a larger increase or decrease in equilibrium income.

Mutual Funds Organizations that sell individual household shares in a diversified portfolio of assets.

$M1$ The money supply in its narrowest form, defined as the sum of coin and currency in circulation, demand deposits in commercial banks, other checkable accounts in depository institutions, and travelers checks.

$M2$ A broader definition of the money supply, which includes $M1$ plus savings and small time deposits (under $100,000), money market mutual funds, overnight loans from customers to commercial banks, and overnight Eurodollar deposits held by residents of the United States.

$M3$ This more broadly defined category of the money supply includes $M2$ plus large-denomination (over $100,000) time deposits and long-term loans by customers to financial institutions.

National Banks Banks that are chartered by the federal Comptroller of the Currency. National banks must be members of the Federal Reserve System.

National Credit Union Administration An agency similar to the FDIC that provides insurance for credit union deposits.

National Debt The total amount of debt accumulated by the federal government.

National Income The total of all wages, interest, profits, and rents paid in the economy in a given period of time. The sum of all payments to the owners of productive resources.

Natural Monopoly A market in which a single supplier has lower costs than do many smaller, competitive firms.

Natural Unemployment Rate The unemployment rate that results when labor markets have found their long-run equilibrium.

Negative Income Tax A proposal to substitute a system that pays cash transfers (through the income tax system) for the current transfer payment system.

Net Exports The total value of exports minus the total value of imports for a given period of time; the net addition to total spending resulting from the foreign sector of the economy.

Net Foreign Spending The component of gross national product that results from international transactions.

Net Investment Gross investment minus depreciation.

Net National Product (NNP) Gross national product adjusted for the existence of depreciation.

Nominal Interest Rate The interest rate, as it is commonly stated, unadjusted for inflation. Also, the interest rate stated in ordinary terms, as a fraction of the amount of the loan.

Nondurable Goods Goods with a useful service life of less than one year. Food and shampoo are examples of nondurable goods.

Nonneutral Taxes Taxes that alter the incentives faced by the private sector.

Normal Profit The profit available in the best alternative use of the firm's resources; normal profit takes into account the implicit costs of production.

Normative Economics The type of economic analysis that describes how the economy should be, through the use of value judgments.

Norris–Laguardia Act Labor legislation that, among other things, outlawed the yellow dog contract.

NOW Accounts (Negotiable Orders of Withdrawal) Bank accounts upon which we can quickly and easily write checks.

Oil Shocks Large increases in the price of oil which greatly affect the oil-using economies of the world because of the short term inelastic demand for the product.

Oligopoly A market with relatively few interdependent producers; in such a market, actions taken by one firm affect output decisions by the others.

Open Economy An economy that trades with other countries.

Open Market Operations The most frequently utilized instrument of monetary policy. It consists of the Fed's buying or selling existing U.S. securities to expand or contract the money supply.

Open Market Purchase Purchase of securities by the Federal Reserve to increase the money supply and make credit more available.

Open Market Sale Sale of securities by the Federal Reserve to decrease the money supply and make credit less available.

Opportunity Cost The highest-valued alternative that must be forgone when another alternative is selected. With every choice, there is an opportunity cost.

Ordinal Measure A measure that alllows qualitative comparison only. Temperature is an ordinal measurement, since 32 degrees is warmer than 16 degrees but not twice as warm.

Output The goods and services that result from production.

Over-valued An exchange rate below market equilibrium.

Paradox of Thrift The idea that, while it may benefit individuals to save more, the economy may suffer if everyone saves more, assuming that the decrease in consumption is not matched by an increase in investment spending.

Partnership A business firm that is owned by several individuals collectively. Each individual owner shares both the profits from the partnership and the risk of loss.

Pension Funds Organizations that use funds that workers and employers save for retirement to invest in stocks, bonds, and real assets. Pension fund assets are used to provide retirement income for participating workers.

Per Capita Real GNP A measure of economic growth that takes into consideration both changes in output and population growth.

Perfect Competition The model of an ideal market; a market characterized by many buyers and sellers trading identical products under conditions of perfect information, free entry and exit, and zero transactions costs.

Permanent Income Hypothesis A concept developed by Milton Friedman that states that consumers make their consumption decisions based more upon what they believe their permanent income to be than their actual income at the time consumption expenditures occur.

Personal Income The income received by the household sector.

Personal Saving Saving by households. These resources are made available for investment spending and other uses. Total saving for the economy includes both personal saving and business retained earnings.

Phillips Curve A graphic device that illustrates an inverse relationship or trade-off between the inflation rate and the unemployment rate.

Planned Socialism An economic system where resources are owned by the state for the people and most production, allocation, and distribution decisions are made by central planners.

Political Economy The study of the economic causes and effects of political actions.

Portfolio A collection of assets. A stock portfolio, for example, is a collection of different quantities and types of corporate stock shares.

Positive Economics Scientific, factual economics that deals with what actually exists and can be verified, without the use of value judgment or opinions.

Post Hoc Reasoning The principle that states that the chronological order in which events occur is related to the cause and effect of those events. It incorrectly assumes that correlation implies causation.

Poverty The condition of inadequate earnings; lacking earnings that are sufficient to purchase some minimum living standard.

Predatory Pricing The act of one firm cutting price to drive competing firms from the market.

Present Value The current value of a payment due at some future date.

Price Ceiling A maximum legal price in a particular market.

Price Discrimination The practice of selling identical goods to different buyers for different prices.

Price Elasticity of Demand A measure of the responsiveness of demand to changing price.

Price Floor A minimum legal price in a particular market.

Price Index A standardized measure of the prices of certain types of goods and services.

Price Leadership A situation in which one firm sets prices that are adopted by competing producers.

Price Stability A constant general level of prices.

Price Takers Individual buyers and sellers who behave as if they cannot alter market price through buying or selling.

Prime Interest Rate The interest rate that large banks charge their best customers; the interest rate on short-term low risk loans.

Private Benefits The benefits received by the individual making an economic choice.

Private Costs The costs borne by the individual making an economic choice.

Private Property Rights A system where individuals own the rights to goods and services; individuals control the use of and have a right to the value of resources.

Private Sector That part of the economy that is owned by individuals and operated for their exclusive benefit.

Producer Burden The part of a tariff paid by sellers in lower net price.

Producer Price Index (PPI) A measure of inflation based on a market basket of goods and services that business firms purchase.

Product Markets Markets where households purchase goods and services from businesses.

Production Function The relationship between the various inputs to a production process and the maximum output that can be produced per unit of time.

Production Possibilities Frontier (PPF) A model that analyzes the various maximum combinations of total output of two goods. A PPF curve is a graphic representation of this model. At any point on the frontier (curve) all resources are used efficiently and are fully employed. A constant level of time, resources, and technology is assumed.

Productivity The amount of output per unit of labor input or more generally, the ability to produce efficiently. The change in productivity is an important determinant of economic growth.

Profit The difference between total revenue and total cost (see Economic Profit).

Progressive tax A situation in which the burden of a tax increases with the taxpayer's income.

Property Rights The rights to own, occupy, or benefit from property within the economy. They define the acceptable and unacceptable limits of behavior regarding property.

Proportional Tax A situation in which the burden of a tax is the same for taxpayers of all income levels.

Proprietors' Income As proprietors supply all four factors of production (land, labor, capital, and management skills), their income is in part a combination of wages, profits, rents, and interest.

Proprietorship A business firm that is owned by a single individual.

Public Choice Choices made by society through government.

Public Good An item from which nonowners cannot be excluded from benefiting but whose use by nonowners does not reduce the benefits available to the owner. A lighthouse is an example of a public good.

Public Property Rights Public or communal property rights is a system where resources are owned in common. No individual has the right to exclude others from their use and no individual has exclusive right to any increase in resource value.

Public Sector The part of the economy that is owned by and for the public, not by any individual. Economists frequently use the term public sector and government interchangeably.

Purchasing Power The quantity of real goods and services that can be obtained for a given quantity of money.

Quota A physical limitation on the quantity of imports.

Rational Expectations Hypothesis The economic theory that contends that people will consider all the relevant information available to them in formulating their future economic expectations including past trends and current actions.

Rational Expectations Theory An economic theory that stresses the importance of expectations on economic activities and policies.

Real Gross National Product (Real GNP) Gross national product adjusted for changes in the price level. Real GNP is the best measure of the economy's total output over time.

Real Interest Rate The nominal interest rate adjusted for inflation. The real interest rate is calculated by subtracting the expected inflation rate from the nominal interest rate.

Recessionary Gap The difference between equilibrium income and the full-employment level of income (assuming that equilibrium income is less than the full-employment level).

Recessions Periods of declining total output as measured by falling real GNP. Unemployment rates generally increase during recessions.

Regressive Tax A situation in which the burden of a tax increases as the taxpayer's income falls.

Relative Poverty Poverty defined as the gap between income groups.

Relative Prices The price of one good compared to the prices of other goods.

Required Reserves The minimum amount of total reserves that a bank is required by law to hold. The reserve requirement sets the legal minimum percentage of deposits that banks must maintain as reserves.

Resource Markets Markets where businesses purchase labor, capital, land, and entrepreneurial skills from households.

Resources Those goods and services used to satisfy wants and needs. Nearly all resources are limited in quantity.

Retained Earnings Profits from business operations that are not distributed to the owners of business. Retained earnings are used to finance future investments or other purchases.

Right of Exclusion That right afforded to individuals, corporations, or institutions in the private sector that allows them to prohibit the public from using or benefiting from private property.

Risk Premium The portion of the interest rate that compensates lenders for the risk that they will not be repaid.

Rivalry The condition where use of a good by one person reduces the amount available for consumption by others.

Saving Income that is not spent on goods or paid in taxes in the current time period.

Savings The total accumulation of resources through past and current saving.

Say's Law of Markets The concept, attributed to Jean Baptiste Say, that supply creates its own demand.

Scarcity The problem that exists when the resources available to the economy are insufficient to satisfy the unlimited human desires.

Scientific Method The process of induction, deduction, and the verification of hypotheses used by economists (and all scientists) to analyze problems.

Secondary Effects Results of an initial action that are realized over time, often having the opposite effect of that action and frequently being of much greater importance.

Securities Assets that represent payment obligations that one party owes to another. Securities pay interest and therefore produce income for their holder.

Services Labor, expertise, counsel, advice, or representation provided for a fee.

Sherman Antitrust Act The 1890 federal law making most monopoly practices illegal.

Short Run (in production) A time frame sufficiently brief that firms must treat some costs as fixed.

Short Run A length of time short enough so that individual producers are not able to vary production capacity.

Shortage A situation in which the quantity demanded exceeds the quantity supplied at the market price.

Shut-down Point The production level at which total revenues just equal variable costs, below this point the most profitable output level is zero in the short run; the level of output at which price equal AVC.

Slope Mathematical measure of the relative steepness of lines or relationships. The slope is calculated as the change in the Y-axis variable divided by the change in the X-axis variable, or more simply, "the rise over the run."

Social Benefits The benefits of a choice to society; the sum of private and external benefits.

Social Costs The costs of a choice to society; the sum of private and external costs.

Sole Proprietorship A business firm that is owned by a single individual who receives all the firm's profits and is liable for all the firm's debts.

Special Drawing Rights (SDRs) International central bank reserve; sometimes called paper gold because SDRs can be used like gold for central bank transactions.

Special-Interest Groups Organizations that have joined together in a common special interest. Special-interest groups attempt to influence the voting behavior of legislators to the specific benefit of the group.

Special-Interest Issue An issue that, if voted into law, provides a small cost to individual voters and a large benefit to the special-interest groups lobbying for the issue.

Specialization The process whereby an individual or group devotes more resources to the production of a single good or service, as opposed to producing many goods, then exchanges that particular item for other items that are desired.

Stabilization Policies Government policies designed to dampen swings in economic activity, reduce the impact of recessions, and moderate inflation.

Stagflation High or rising inflation rates accompanied by high or rising unemployment rates.

Static Efficiency Allocation of existing resources to produce the combination of goods society prefers above all others; also called economic efficiency.

Sticky Prices Prices that do not fully respond to market forces, such as wages that do not fall in response to a surplus of labor.

Stock Concept A concept relating to the accumulated amount of an economic activity over time; a measure of total amount. The total accumulation of capital in the economy is a stock concept.

Store of Value As a store of value, money enables its holder to convert goods and services into stored-up purchasing power for the future.

Strike A situation in which organized labor withholds its services in order to gain concessions from an employer.

Structural Deficit That part of the deficit that results from discretionary fiscal policy actions.

Structural Unemployment Unemployment that occurs when workers do not have the skills that are required for current job openings.

Subsidy A government payment to an individual or a group designed to increase their welfare or encourage certain private activities.

Substitute Goods Goods or services that can be used in place of each other; for example, butter and margarine.

Substitution Effect The change in buying behavior that results from a change in relative price, purchasing power held constant. Also, changes in spending behavior due to nonneutral taxation.

Supply The relationship between the price of a good and the quantity of it that producers are willing and able to sell. The supply curve shows the quantity supplied at each price, all factors except price assumed constant.

Supply Interdependence A change in the

price of an energy source which creates a change in the price of some other energy source.

Supply-Side Economics An economic theory that stresses the importance of policies that try to increase aggregate supply by cutting tax rates, increasing investment, or reducing regulation. Focuses on capital formation, production incentives, and regulatory costs.

Supply-Side Fiscal Policies Government policies designed to influence aggregate supply.

Surplus A situation in which the quantity supplied exceeds the quantity demanded at the market price.

Surplus Units Households, businesses, and governments that desire to consume fewer resources in the present time period than are currently available to them.

Taft–Hartley Act Labor legislation that, among other things, gave the president of the United States the power to force unions back to work for a 90-day period when the nation's safety or welfare was endangered by a strike.

Tariff A tax on imported goods.

Tax Burden The proportion of income that is used to pay a tax.

Technical Efficiency Uses of scarce resources that produce maximum combinations of goods and services. All points on the PPF display technical efficiency. All points within the PPF are inefficient in this sense.

Technology Know-how. The application of scientific knowledge to some useful purpose. It frequently enables us to reduce production costs per unit of output.

Terms of Trade The ratio of two goods in international trade.

The Federal Deposit Insurance Corporation (FDIC) The FDIC insures each deposit account in commercial banks up to $100,000. This organization was created by the federal government to generate faith and stability in commercial banks.

Time Deposits Savings account balances.

Total Physical Product (TPP) Total production, measured in the number of items produced in a given time period.

Total Product The total quantity of goods produced.

Total Utility The total satisfaction (total utils) derived from consuming a combination of goods.

Trade Possibilities Curve A graph showing combinations a nation can trade for with given terms of trade.

Trade Secrets Processes or products kept hidden by a firm to prevent competition and assure a return on its research and development investment.

Traditional Economy An economic system that makes decisions based on established beliefs, customs, and traditions.

Transfer Payments Payments made from government to private individuals for which no good or service is expected in return. Social security benefits and unemployment payments are examples of transfer payments.

Underemployed Workers Part-time workers who desire full-time jobs and workers who have jobs that do not make full use of their skills and training.

Underground Economy A term used to describe the "economy" in which unreported employment and unreported production and exchange of goods and services exist.

Under-valued An exchange rate above market equilibrium.

Unemployed Workers People who are willing and able to work and who are actively seeking employment but are unable to find work in their occupational area at the going wage rate.

Unemployment Rate A measure of the unemployment problem. The unemployment rate is equal to the number of unemployed workers as a percentage of the labor force.

Uniform Unit of Accounting Money, as a uniform unit of accounting, provides a common basis of comparison for the monetary value of goods and services.

Union Shop A firm where all employees must belong to a union.

Unitary Income Elasticity Demand in which there is an equal proportionate change in income and quantity demanded.

Unitary Price Elasticity Demand in which there is an equal proportionate change in price and quantity demanded (the elasticity coefficient is equal to one).

Usury Laws State laws that limit legal interest rates.

Utility A measure of the satisfaction or value that an individual derives from a good or service.

Value Added The increase in the value or selling price of resources that results from the production process.

Value Marginal Product (VMP) The extra revenue an additional input produces for a competitive firm, other inputs held fixed (MPP multiplied by selling price).

Variable Cost The cost of variable inputs; cost that depends on and changes with the level of output in the short run.

Variable Input Inputs whose use varies with output in the short run.

Variable Lag The period of time, of uncertain length, between the implementation of monetary policy and when its force is felt by the economy.

Velocity of Money The term used to describe the number of times that the average dollar in the money supply is used over and over again in a year.

Verification The part of scientific method concerned with comparing theories with measurements taken from the real world to determine if the theories are valid.

Vertical Equity Tax fairness that is achieved when people in different circumstances pay different taxes, and the difference in tax is appropriate to the difference in circumstances.

Vertical Merger A merger in which one firm produces inputs used by another (e.g., beer maker merges with a bottle producer).

Very Short Run A time period so short that firms are unable to change output.

Voluntary Export Agreements Quota agreements that are negotiated between exporting and importing countries. These agreements are substitutes for trade restrictions imposed without negotiation by importing countries.

Wage and Price Controls Laws that freeze or control most wages and prices in an economy.

Wage-Lag Theory A hypothesis concerning the cause of the Phillips curve that holds that inflation can temporarily reduce unemployment if wages lag behind the rise in prices.

Wages Compensation to households for use of their individual labor. Wages are the largest source of household income.

Wagner Act Labor legislation that, among other things, officially recognized labor's right to organize and bargain collectively.

World Bank International organization that makes loans to less developed countries to encourage economic development (also known as the International Bank for Reconstruction and Development).

Yellow-Dog Contracts Contracts in which workers pledge not to join or support a union. Some employers once made workers sign these agreements as a condition of employment.

Photo Credits

p. 36, Kenneth E. Boulding, University of Colorado; p. 203, Simon Kuznets, AP/Wide World; p. 266, John Maynard Keynes, Brown Brothers; p. 350, Paul Samuelson, AP/Wide World; p. 456, Milton Friedman, Courtesy of Milton Friedman; p. 477, John Kenneth Galbraith, AP/Wide World; p. 531, Freidrich A. VonHayek, AP/Wide World; p. 581, Joan Robinson, Nicholas Lee of Ramsey & Muspratt; p. 586, George Stigler, AP/Wide World; p. 650, Joseph Schumpter, The Bettmann Archive; p. 670, Lester Thurow, AP/Wide World; p. 699, Kenneth Arrow, AP/Wide World; p. 706, James Buchanan, Courtesy of James Buchanan; p. 813, Karl Marx, Brown Brothers.

INDEX

Ability-to-pay taxation, 164
Absolute advantage, 740
Accounting profit, 506
　economic profit and, 645–46
Adaptive expectations hypothesis, 458–60
Administered prices, 580
Administration cost premium, interest rate and, 654–55
Agenda, voting, 707
Affluent Society, The (Galbraith), 477
Aggregate demand, 306
　determinants
　　consumption spending, 306–307
　　investment spending, 307
　　net exports, 308–309
　　exchange rates and, 783
　　shifts in, 309–310
Aggregate demand curve, 306, 309
　shifts in, 309–310
Aggregate demand–aggregate supply model, 305–306
　equilibrium, 316–18
Aggregate supply
　determinants, 310–13
　exchange rates and, 783
　increasing, 325–26
　shifts in, 315–16
Aggregate supply curve, 306
　bottleneck economy, 314–15
　depression economy, 313–14
　full-capacity economy, 314
Aggregates, 186
Aggregation, 380
Allocation function of government, 150–51
Announcement effects, 414
Annually balanced budget, 359–60
Antipoverty policies
　cash vs. in-kind transfers, 680
　federal transfer payment programs, 680–81
　governmental tools, 676–77
　redistributional, 677–79
Antipoverty programs
　criticisms, 681–82

limits to, 684
Antitrust laws, 557–58
Antitrust legislation, 110
Antitrust policies
　Clayton Antitrust Act, 558
　government regulations and, 561–62
　importance of, 561–62
　limits to legislation, 559–60
　monopoly price regulations, 558–59
　Sherman Antitrust Act, 558
APC. *See* Average propensity to consume
Appreciation, currency, 764
APS. *See* Average propensity to save
Arbitrage, 768
Arrow, Kenneth, 699
Assets
　of banks, 384
　float, 381
ATC. *See* Average total cost
Automatic stabilizers, 342–44
　government spending and, 308
Autonomous consumption, 268
AVC. *See* Average variable cost
Average analysis, marginal variables and, 38–39
Average fixed cost, 512
Average propensity to consume, 37, 271
Average propensity to save, 271
Average revenue, 528
Average tax rate, 167
Average total cost, 40–41, 509–11
　long-run, 518
Average variable cost, 511
Average variables, graphing relationships, 39–40
Balance of payments
　deficit, 758–59
　definition, 758
　exchange rates and, 772–73
　surplus, 758
Balance of trade, 758–61
Balanced budget amendment, 360–61
Balanced budget multiplier, 341–42
Balanced budget philosophies

　annually balanced budget, 359–60
　cyclically balanced budget, 360–61
　functional finance, 361–62
Banker's bank, Federal Reserve System as, 407
Banks
　assets of, 384
　banker's, 407
　central, 385
　commercial, 384–85
　federal reserve, 385
　fractional reserve, 382–84
　liabilities of, 384
　money creation by, 387–90
　reserves of, 384
Barriers to entry
　monopoly markets, 550
　oligopolies, 580–81
Barriers to trade. *See* Trade barriers
Barro, Robert, 356, 464–65
Barter economy, 373
Base year, 248
Behavior
　economic, 29–30
　rent-seeking, 661–62
　scientific method and, 30–31
　unions, economic model of, 631–33
Benefits
　external, 105, 693–94
　in-kind, 670
　marginal, 28
Benefits-received taxation, 164
Black market, 537
Blacklists, 628
Board of Governors, Federal Reserve System, 404
Bonds, interest rates and, 657–58
Borrower
　inflation effects on, 246–47
　"three Cs" of, 379
Borrowing deficit, interest rates and, 422–24
Bottleneck economy, 314–15
Boulding, Kenneth, 36, 685
Boycotts, 628

economic, 108–109
Bradley, Bill, 346
Break-even point, 510–11
Buchanan, James, 587, 706
Budget
  balanced. *See* Balanced budget philosophies
  share, elasticity and, 487–88
  surplus, 352
Budget deficit
  crowding-out effect, 354–55
  cyclical and structural deficits, 353
  Gramm–Rudman–Hollings Act, 358–59
  and interest rates, 355–56
  reduction, 357
  supply-side view of, 355
Budget lines, 489
  definition, 490
  mechanics, 490–91
Business cycles, 334
Business sector, 187
  corporations, 137–38
  household sector and, 129–30
  industrial development policy and, 141–42
  organization, 136
  partnerships, 139
  proprietorships, 136–37
Buyers, as price takers, 527

Capacity
  aggregate supply determinant, 310–11
  of borrower, 379
Capacity utilization rates, 275
Capital
  formation, 12
  goods, 274
  human, 12, 627
  resources, 5
  wage differentials and, 624
Capital and Rates of Return in Manufacturing Industries (Stigler), 587
Capital formation, 12
  personal saving and, 135
Capital gains, long-term, 167
Capitalism, 807–808
Capitalism, Socialism and Democracy (Schumpeter), 650
Cardinal measure, of utils, 478
Career planning, future labor market conditions and, 638–39
Cartels
  impact of, 794
  oligopoly firms and, 583
  OPEC, 230–31, 722–24
  starting, 584–85
  successful, 585
Carter, Jimmy, 232, 279, 326, 445
Cash transfers, in-kind transfers and, 680
Causation, correlation and, 19
Central bank, 385
Centralized control, energy policy and, 730
Centralized decision making, 805–806

Character, of borrower, 379
Cheating, detection and punishment by cartels, 585
Check-clearing services, Federal Reserve banks and, 407
Choice(s)
  centralized and decentralized, 805–806
  consumer. *See* Consumer choice
  informed, career planning and, 638
  private vs. public, 705–710
  public, 693
  scarcity and, 5
  voting. *See* Voting
Circular flow of spending and income, 129–30, 186–88, 260
  complete model of, 191
Classical economists, 261
Classical medicine, balance of trade deficit and, 795
Clayton Antitrust Act, 558
Closed economy, 738
Coincidence of wants, 372
Collateral
  of borrower, 379
  interest rate and, 653–54
Collusion, 110
  in oligopolies, 583, 585–87
Command economy, 58, 811
Commercial banks, 384
Communal goods, 703–704
Communication, price and, 94
Comparative advantage, law of, 739–42
Competition
  atomistic, 527
  corporate, concentration and, 140–41
  among demanders, 108–109
  engine of, 95
  government policies to promote, 110–11
  perfect. *See* Perfect competition
  process of, 526–29
  profits to encourage, 648–49
  scarcity and, 6
  among suppliers, 107–108
  tariffs and, 749
Competitive markets
  economic rent in, 661
  minimum wages and, 634–36
  resource supply and, 614
Complementary goods, 72
Complexity, antipoverty programs, 682
Comptroller of the Currency, 403
Concentration ratio
  corporations, 140
  oligopolies, 579–80
Constant returns to scale, 519
Consumer choice
  indifference curves and, 493–94
  problem of, 472–73
  process of, 475–76
Consumer Price Index, 248, 251
  calculation formula, 249
Consumers
  expectations of price and income, 72–73

  tastes and preferences, 73
Consumption
  autonomous, 268
  function, 268
  functions, graphing, 269–71
  induced, 268
  Keynesian, 268–69
  long-run, 272–74
  mandatory, external benefits and, 702
  personal, 134
  spending, 266–67, 306–307
Consumption spending method for GNP calculation, 194
Contractionary fiscal policy, 334–35
Contractionary monetary policy, 430–31
Convergence hypothesis, 817–18
Coordination, price and, 94
Corporate income tax, 170–72
Corporations, 137–38, 503
  competition and concentration, 140–41
  concentration ratio, 140
Correlation, causation and, 19
Cost-of-living adjustments, 324–25
Cost-push inflation, 232, 319–20
Cost(s)
  antipoverty programs, 681
  average
    fixed, 512
    total, 509–11
    variable, 511
  changing, economic profits and, 647
  energy. *See* Energy costs
  external. *See* External cost
  fixed
    as barriers to entry in monopolistic markets, 550
    changes in, 515–16
  high transaction, externalities and, 702–703
  increasing, law of, 9–10
  information, 28–29
  marginal, 28
  opportunity. *See* Opportunity costs
  production, resource supply and, 612–13
  private, 694–95
  production
    explicit and implicit, 506
    fixed and variable, 506–507
  resource, supply and, 78
  social, 694–95
  variable, changes in, 514–15
  zero transaction, 527
Countercyclical fiscal policy, 334
CPI. *See* Consumer Price Index
Credit
  cost and availability, consumption spending and, 307
  demand for, 416–17
  rationing, 658
  supply, determinants, 418–19
Credit markets, 657–58
  equilibrium, 419–21
  exchange rates and, 784–85

Credit unions, as financial intermediaries, 382
Crowding out, 176
Crowding-out effect, 354–55
  energy costs and, 727
Currency
  devaluation, 774
  foreign. *See* Foreign currency
  issuance by Federal Reserve banks, 406
  value, 767
Currency Act of 1863, 403
Customs
  social, labor supply and, 623
  unions, 752
Cycles, voting, 707–708
Cyclical unemployment, 241
Cyclically balanced budget, 360–61

Deadweight loss, 247–48
Decentralized decision making, 805–806
Decentralized markets, energy policy and, 730
Decision making
  centralized and decentralized, 805–806
  group, government inefficiencies and, 119–20
Decreasing returns to scale, 519–20
Deduction, in scientific method, 30
Deficit borrowing, interest rates and, 422–24
Deficit(s)
  balance of payments, 758–59
  budget. *See* Budget deficit
  crowding out by government, 176
  cyclical, 353
  national debt and, 174–76
  structural, 353
  units, 378
Deflation, 244–45
Demand
  adjustments between market and firm, 604
  changes, 73–75
    economic profits and, 647
    long-run market adjustments, 533–34
    short-run market adjustments, 532–33
    and supply curve shifts, 517
  concept of, 67–69
  for credit, determinants, 417–18
  curves, 68
    deriving, 478–79
    downward slope of, 480
    tastes and preferences and, 480
  derived. *See* Derived demand
  determinants
    consumers' expectations, 72–73
    consumers' money income, 70
    consumers' tastes and preferences, 73
    market size, 71
    price of related goods, 71–72
  for the dollar, 764–65
  elasticity, taxes and, 160–62
  energy
    short-run, 719–20
    and supply, 720
  income elastic and inelastic, 489
  law of, 68
  loanable funds, interest rate and, 656–57
  money
    factors affecting, 448–51
    and money velocity, 451
  monopoly, 551–52
  for output, wage differentials and, 625
  price elasticity of
    calculation, 482–83
    definition, 482
    demand curve and, 484–86
    determinants, 486–88
    total revenue and, 484
  resource. *See* Resource demand
  utility and, 67
Demand curves
  definition, 68
  elastic and inelastic, 483
  indifference curves and, 494–95
  kinked, 587–89
  in monopolistic competition, 570–72
Demand deposits, 375
Demanders, competition among, 108–109
Demand-pull inflation, 232, 318–19
Demand-side fiscal policy, 333–35
  automatic stabilizers, 342–44
  balanced budget multiplier and, 341–42
  government spending, 335–36
  spending multiplier, 336–38
  taxation, 338–39
  transfer payments, 339–40
Deposit expansion multiplier, 390–92
Depository institutions, Federal Reserve banks and, 407
Depository Institutions Deregulation Act of 1980, 393
Depository Institutions Deregulation and Monetary Control Act of 1980, 407
Deposits
  Eurodollar, 376
  money market accounts, 376
  safety of, 385–87
  time, 376
Depreciation, 207
  currency, 763
Depression economy, 313–14
Deregulation
  financial sector (U.S.), 392–94
  monopolies, 563
  perils of, 393–94
Derived demand
  for the dollar, 766
  for foreign currency, 764–65
  foreign exchange rate and, 762–63
  in resource markets, 599–600
Devaluation, 774
Differentiation, desirability of, 577–78
Diminishing marginal returns, principle of, 9

Diminishing returns, production possibilities frontier and, 538
Direct relationship, in graphs, 18–19
Dirty float, 771–72
Discount rate, Federal Reserve System, 413–14
Discretionary fiscal policy, 334
Discrimination
  poverty and, 675–76
  price. *See* Price discrimination
  wage differentials and, 626–27
Disinflation, 245
Disposable personal income, 218
Dissaving, 135
Distribution
  costs and benefits, voting and, 708–09
  gains and losses from tariffs, 750–51
  of income. *See* Income distribution
  of tax burden, 165
Distribution function of government, 151–52
District lines, and voting, 709
Durant, Will, 54
Dynamic efficiency, of monopolies, 561

Earnings, retained, 218
Ease of substitution
  elasticity and, 486–87
  elasticity of resource demand and, 605–606
Economic Analysis (Boulding), 36
Economic behavior, examples of, 29–30
Economic efficiency, 54–56
  market and, 103–105
  technical efficiency and, 55–56
Economic forces
  against OPEC, 723–24
  government, 109–110
Economic goals, 52–57
  domestic and international, 791–93
  efficiency, 54–56
  environmental quality, 56–57
  equitable income distribution, 56
  for growth, 54, 795–97
  macroeconomic. *See* Macroeconomic goals
  resource employment, 52–54
  stable prices, 54
Economic goods, 4
Economic growth, 11
  capital formation and, 12
  economic goals and, 54
  energy costs and, 726–27
  energy crisis and, 720–21
  foreign exchange rates and, 769–70
  government regulation and, 349–52
  human capital and, 12
  in Japan, 212–15
  measurement of, 204–207
  poverty and, 678
  taxes and incentives for, 346–48
  technology and, 11
  vested interests and, 207–11
Economic policies. *See also* Fiscal policy; Monetary policy

classical medicine, 795
exchange rate intervention, 794–95
tariff and quota trade restrictions, 793–94
voluntary export agreements, 794
Economic profit
accounting profit and, 645–46
definition, 506
functions of, 648–49
good and bad, 649–50
sources of, 646–48
Economic questions
categories and, 59
economic organization and, 59
how to produce, 48–50
what to produce, 46–48
for whom to produce, 50–51
Economic rent, 658
as a surplus, 659–60
land and, 659
in monopolies and competitive markets, 661
Economic systems, 802–803
capitalism, 807–808
centralized and decentralized choice, 805–806
choices of, 803–805
command economy, 58
convergence hypothesis, 817–18
criteria for evaluating, 805
fascism, 811
market economy, 58
market socialism, 810
mixed economy, 58–60
modern mixed economy, 811
planned socialism, 808–810
property rights, 806–807
Soviet Union. *See* Soviet Union
traditional economy, 60
Economic tax incidence, 159–60
Economic theory, post-Keynesian evolution, 304–306
Economic way of thinking, 26–30
Economies
open and closed, 738
of scale
as barriers to entry in monopolistic markets, 550
oligopolies and, 581–82
Economist
in academe, 35–36
in government, 36–37
in private sector, 35
Education
external benefits and, 700
income distribution among households and, 132
poverty and, 675
EEC. *See* European Economic Community
Efficiency
dynamic, of monopolies, 561
economic, 54–56, 538–40
market. *See* Market efficiency
production possibilities frontier and, 538–40

profits as rewards for, 648
static, of monopolies, 561
Effluent taxes, external costs and, 698–99
Elasticity of income
definition, 488
unitary, 488
uses of, 489
Elasticity of demand
calculation, 482–83
definition, 482
demand curve and, 484–86
determinants
budget share, 487–88
ease of substitution, 486–87
time frame, 488
product, 607
tariff burden and, 746–47
total revenue and, 484
Elasticity of supply, 534–35
Ely, Richard T., 394
Employers, Japan's growth policy and, 213
Employers' association monopsony, 631–32
Employment, goal of full, 241–42
Employment Act of 1946, 224–25
Energy
conservation policy, 730
demand
short-run, 719–20
and supply interdependence, 720
uses, 719
environmental quality and, 730–31
finite resources, 717–19
sources, new, 727–28
supply, 717
Energy costs
economic growth and, 726–27
output effects, 726
price effects, 726
redistribution of income and, 727
substitution effects, 725
Energy crisis
economic growth and, 720–21
energy price controls and, 721–22
environmental regulations and, 722
future of, 725
oil shocks and, 722
solutions
higher prices, 728–29
laws and regulations, 729
new energy sources, 727–28
new technology, 728
rationing, 729–30
subsidies, 729
subsidized production, 728
Entrepreneurs, exchange and, 16
Entrepreneurship
economic profits and, 648
as resource, 5
Entry
free, 527
into industry, 511
Entry barriers
monopolies, 549
oligopolies, 580–81

types of, 550
Environmental quality
economic goals and, 56–57
energy and, 730–31
Environmental regulations, energy crisis and, 722
Equality and Efficiency: The Big Trade-off? (Okun), 668
Equation of exchange, 394–96, 446–47
Equilibrium
aggregate demand–aggregate supply model, 316–18
firm, 529
Keynesian model of, 280, 283, 284
long-run, in monopolistic competition, 575–77
macroeconomic, 264–65
market, 81–83
changes in, 84–89
foreign exchange, 766–68
short- and long-run, 84
surplus and shortage, 83
profit and, 529–31
Equilibrium income, 280–86
consumption spending and, 280–82
government spending added to total spending, 284–86
inflationary gap and, 286
injections equal leakages, 282
inventories and, 282–83
investment and, 282–83
Keynesian model, 280, 282–84
net exports added to total spending, 283–84
recessionary gap and, 286
total spending equals total income, 280–82
Equilibrium interest rate, 419
Equity (tax), 163–64
ability-to-pay and benefits-received, 164
horizontal and vertical, 163–64
Eurodollar deposits, 376
European Economic Community, 752
Evans, Paul, 355–56
Exchange
entrepreneurs and, 16
foreign market. *See* Foreign exchange market
incentives and, 15–16
markets, 14–15
middlemen and, 16–17
production possibilities frontier and, 12–14
profits and, 15
Exchange rates, 762
aggregate demand and, 783
aggregate supply and, 783
balance of payments and, 772–73
credit market conditions and, 784–85
differences in, 771
economic growth and, 769
effect on prices, 782
fixed, 773–75
fiscal policy with, 789–91
monetary policy with, 788–89

flexible, 773–75
    fiscal policy with, 787–88
    monetary policy with, 785–87
  income distribution and, 782
  inflation and, 770, 783–84
  intervention and, 794–95
  net export spending and, 278–79
  net exports and, 308
  unemployment and, 783–84
Excise taxes, 158
Exclusion, of private goods, 703
Exit, free, 527
Exogenous policy variable, 279
Expansionary fiscal policy, 334
Expansionary monetary policy, 429–30
Expectations
  adaptive, 458–60
  aggregate supply determinant, 312–13
  consumption spending and, 307
  income, credit demand and, 417–18
  inflation
    credit demand and, 417
    credit supply and, 418
    interest rates 425–26
  investment spending and, 275–76, 307
  monetary policy and, 432–33
  problem of, 326–27
  role in macro policy, 456–65
Expenditure method for GNP calculation, 193–94
Explicit costs, 506
External benefits, 693–94
  education and, 700
  government policy and, 700–702
External costs, 693–94
  government actions to control
    direct regulation, 696–98
    effluent taxes, 698–99
    marketable pollution rights, 699–700
    output taxes, 698
  pollution and, 694–95
Externalities, 541–42, 693–94
  high transaction costs and, 702–703
  market efficiency and, 105–107

FAC. *See* Federal Advisory Council
Fallacies
  of composition, 33
  post hoc reasoning, 33–34
  secondary effects, 34
Fascism, 811
FDIC. *See* Federal Deposit Insurance Corporation
Federal Advisory Council, 404–405
Federal Aviation Administration, 326
Federal Deposit Insurance Corporation, 385–86
Federal funds market, 413
Federal funds rate, 413
Federal income tax, 166–168
Federal Open Market Committee, 404–405
Federal Reserve Act of 1913, 403
Federal Reserve bank, 385

Federal Reserve System
  banking system and, 408–409
  Board of Governors, 404
  discount rate, 413–14
  Federal Advisory Council, 404
  Federal Open Market Committee, 404
  functions, 406–408
  open market operations, 409–13
  origins, 403–404
  policies
    credit supply and, 418–19
    interest rates and, 424–25
  reserve requirement, 414–16
  structure, 404–405
  the Treasury and, 409
Federal Savings and Loan Insurance Corporation, 386
Federalism, fiscal, 149–50
Feldstein, Martin, 450
Final goods and services, 187
  gross national product and, 188
Finance, functional, 361–62
Financial intermediaries, 378–82
Financial intermediation, 380–82
  principles of, 379
Financial sector, 189
  in circular flow model, 371
  deregulation (U.S.), 392–94
Finite resources, energy and, 717–19
Firm(s)
  equilibrium, 529
  goals of, 504
  in perfectly competitive market, 527–29
  supply cycles, 513–14
  types of, 503–504
  worker-managed, in Yugoslavia, 815–17
Fiscal federalism, 149–50
Fiscal policy, 54, 265, 333
  contractionary, 334–35
  countercyclical, 334
  demand-side. *See* Demand-side fiscal policy
  discretionary, 334
  expansionary, 334
  with fixed exchange rates, 789–91
  with flexible exchange rates, 787–88
  importance of, Keynesian and monetarist views, 452–53
  supply-side. *See* Supply-side fiscal policy
Fiscal year, 151
Fisher, Irving, 246
Fixed costs, 506–507
  as barriers to entry in monopolistic markets, 550
  changes in, 515–16
Fixed investment, 195
Float, 381
Flow concept, 189
FOMC. *See* Federal Open Market Committee
Ford, Gerald, 232, 267, 325
Foreign currency, appreciation and depreciation, 763–65
Foreign exchange market, 762–63

economic growth and, 769–70
  effect of tariffs on currency values, 768–69
  equilibrium, 766–68
  inflation and, 770
  official intervention in, 771–72
Foreign sector, 190–92
Fractional reserve banks, 382–84
Fraud, in antipoverty programs, 682
Free provision of external benefits, 702
Frictional unemployment, 241
Friedman, Milton, 272, 441, 454–56
Full Employment and Balanced Growth Act of 1978. *See* Humphrey–Hawkins Bill
Full-capacity economy, 314
Functional finance, 361–62
Future value, 651–52

Galbraith, John Kenneth, 477
Garn–St. Germain Depository Institutions Act of 1982, 393
General sales tax, 172
General Theory of Employment, Interest, and Money, The (Keynes), 261–62
George, Henry, 660–61
GNP. *See* Gross national product
Goals. *See* Economic goals; Macroeconomic goals
Goods
  communal, 703–704
  complementary, 72
  durable and nondurable, 134
  public, 115, 542, 693, 704–705
  substitute, 71–72
Gosplan, 812–13
Government
  borrowing, 174–76
  definition and enforcement of property rights, 111–14
  as economic force, 109–110
  economic functions
    allocation, 150–51
    conflicts among, 153–54
    distribution, 151–52
    public choice, 152–53
    stabilization, 152
  Federal Reserve banks as fiscal agents for, 407
  inefficiencies
    costs and benefits of programs, 122–23
    group decision making, 119–20
    growth incentives, 121–22
    shortsightedness effect, 123
    special interest groups, 120–21
  provision for public goods, 115
  redistribution of income, 115–19
  resources
    sources of, 158–59
    uses of, 155–57
Government policies
  aggregate supply determinant, 313
  competitive markets and, 542
  credit demand and, 418
  external benefits and, 700–702

external costs
  direct regulation, 696–98
  effluent taxes, 698–99
  marketable pollution rights, 699–700
  output taxes, 698
 investment spending and, 307
 labor supply and, 623
 to promote competition, 110–111
 tools of
  laws and regulations, 155
  spending, 154
  subsidies, 154–55
  taxation, 154
Government regulations
 as barriers to entry in monopolistic markets, 550
 economic profits and, 647
 supply-side cuts in, 345
Government sector, 190
Government spending, 335–38
 added to total spending, 284–86
 as aggregate demand determinant, 308
 as antipoverty tool, 677
 GNP calculation with, 195
 spending multiplier, 336–37
Gramm–Rudman–Hollings Act, 358–59
Grants, intergovernmental, 156
Graphs, 17–21
 correlation and causation, 19
 direct relationship, 18–19
 inverse relationship, 19
Great Depression, 208–209, 260–61, 274–75, 293, 301
Gross domestic product, 193
Gross investment, 195
Gross national product
 accounts for 1984, 215–19
 calculation methods
  consumption spending, 194
  expenditure, 193–94
  income method, 196–97
  investment spending, 194–95
  net foreign spending, 195
  value-added method, 197
 intermediate goods and services and, 192
 national income and, 188–89
 NNP calculation, 215
 quality of life and, 200–202
 real. See Real gross national product
 stabilization policies and, 202
Gross National Product Implicit Price Deflator Index, 251
Growth, recession, 204
Guest workers, 623
Guilder, George, 542

Harberger, Arnold, 561
Horizontal equity, of taxes, 163–64
Horizontal merger, 582
Household sector, 187
 income distribution, 132–33
  median household income, 131–32

  private resource ownership and, 130
  relationship with business sector, 129–30
  sources and uses of income, 130–31
  uses of income by, 133–35
Humphrey–Hawkins Bill, 224–25
Hypotheses, in scientific method, 30–31

Implicit costs, 506
Incentives, 27
 exchange and, 15–16
 market economy, 50–51
 negative work, antipoverty programs and, 681–82
 role of, 53
Incidence, tax. See Tax incidence
Income
 consumer, demand and, 70
 credit demand and, 417–18
 demand for money and, 448–49
 disposable, consumption spending and, 306–307
 elastic and inelastic demand, 489
 elasticity. See Income elasticity
 equilibrium. See Equilibrium income
 fixed, inflation effects, 245
 household
  factors affecting distribution, 131–33
  sources, 131
  uses of, 133–35
 national, 217
 permanent income hypothesis, 272–74
 personal, 217–28
 redistribution
  energy costs and, 727
  government, 115–19
 and spending, circular flow of, 129–30
 United States, trends in, 671–76
Income distribution. See Distribution of income
 exchange rates and, 782
 resource markets and, 598
 Soviet Union, 814
 United States, 668–71
Income effect, 480
 indifference curve analysis, 495–96
 on labor supply, 621–22
 of taxes, 162–63
Income elasticity
 definition, 488
 unitary, 488
 uses of, 489
Income method for GNP calculation, 196–97
Income tax, federal, 166–68
Increasing returns to scale, 519
Indexation, 324–25
Indifference curves, 489, 491–94
 definition, 491
 families of, 492–93
 individual choice and, 493–94
 marginal rate of substitution, 491
Indirect business taxes, 217

Individual retirement accounts, 345
Induced consumption, 268
Induction, in scientific method, 30
Industrial development policy, 211–12
 for private-sector firms, 141–42
Industry
 entry into, 511
 infant, tariffs and, 748
 supply cycles, 513–14
Inflation
 in the 1960s and 1970s, 302–304
 cost-push, 232, 319–20
 credit demand and, 417
 credit supply and, 418
 definition, 244
 demand-pull, 232, 318–19
 economic effects
  on borrowers and lenders, 246–47
  deadweight loss, 247–48
  on fixed incomes, 245
  on interest rates, 245–46
  on relative prices, 245
  on savings, 247
 exchange rates and, 770, 783–84
 interest rates and, 425–26
 measurement, 248–53
 price indices for, 251
 as self-fulfilling prophesy, 248
Inflation premium, interest rate and, 655–56
Inflation rate
 definition, 244
 expected, demand for money and, 449–50
 between two years, calculation, 250
Inflationary gap, 286
Information
 cost of, 28–29
 imperfections, wage differentials and, 626
 income distribution among households and, 132–33
Injections, equilibrium income and, 282
In-kind benefits, 670
In-kind transfers, vs. cash transfers, 680
Innovation, profits and, 649
Input-output table, 809
Input(s)
 control of substitutes by unions, 630–31
 fixed, 504
 production, 504
 variable, 505
Inquiry into the Nature and Causes of the Wealth of Nations, An (Smith), 13, 94–95, 163
Institutional forces, labor supply and, 623
Insurance companies, as financial intermediaries, 382
Interdependence, oligopolies, 580
Interest, 650–51
Interest rates
 credit demand and, 417
 credit markets, 657–58
 credit supply and, 418
 determinants, 653–57
 exchange rates and, 784–85

factors affecting, 421–27
  deficit borrowing, 422–24
  Federal Reserve policies, 424–25
  inflation and inflation expectations, 425–26
  profitability of business investment, 426–27
inflation effects, 245–46
investment spending and, 276, 307
nominal, 417
payment values and, 651–52
as price signal, 652–53
rationing loanable funds with, 658
real, 246, 417
Intergovernmental grants, 156
Intermediate goods and services, 192
Intermediates, financial, 378–82
Intermediation
  mechanics of, 380–82
  principles of, 379
International credit movements, exchange rates and, 784–85
International Monetary Fund, 761
International trade, winners and losers in, 743–44
Intervention, in foreign exchange market, 771–72
Inventories, equilibrium income and, 282–83
Inventory investment, 195
Inverse relationship, in graphs, 19
Investment
  aggregate supply determinant, 310–11
  equilibrium income and, 282–83
  fixed, 195
  as governmental antipoverty tool, 677
  gross, 195
  in human capital, 627
  inventory, 195
  Japan's growth policy and, 214
  marginal tax rates and, 347–48
  net, 207
  profitability and interest rates, 426–27
  return, investment spending and, 276–77
  supply-side incentives, 345–46
Investment rule, 427–28
Investment spending, 274–75
  as aggregate demand determinant, 307
  determinants, 275–77
  GNP calculation with, 194–95
Invisible hand, 537

Japan
  growth policy, 212–15
  technology in, 214–15
Johnson, Lyndon, 227–28, 267, 322
Johnson's tax surcharge, 322

Kahn, Alfred, 326
Kemp, Jack, 346, 355, 357

Kennedy, John F., 227, 320–21
Kennedy tax cut, 227, 320–21
Keynes, John Maynard, 185, 261–62, 264–67, 279, 326, 346, 402, 427–33, 439–40
  circular flow of spending and income, 260
Keynesian economics, 185, 261–93
  circular flow diagram, 263
  consumption and saving, 268–71
  exports, 262
  imports, 264
  injections, 262
  leakages, 264
  macroeconomic equilibrium and economic policy, 264–65
  model of equilibrium, 280–86
  monetarism and, 301
  monetary policy, 429–33, 453–56
  monetary theory, 427–33, 439–40, 451–53
  net exports, 264
  rational expectations theory and, 302
  supply-side economics and, 302
Keynesian theory of money, 427–33
Kinked demand curves, 587–89
Kuznets, Simon, 202–203, 272

Labor
  demand, unions and, 630
  force, unemployment measurement and, 235
  market, future, 638–39
  quality, wage differentials and, 625
  resources, 5
Labor supply
  determinants, 622–23
  substitution and income effects, 621–22
  unions and, 630
Laffer, Arthur, 348–49, 357
Laffer curve, 348–49
Laissez-faire policies, 265
Land
  economic rent and, 659
  resources, 5
Landrum–Griffin Act, 628
Law of comparative advantage, 739–42
Law of demand, 478–79
Law of increasing costs, 9–10
Laws
  energy demand and, 729
  government, private sector and, 155
  as governmental antipoverty tools, 677
Leakages, equilibrium income and, 282
Leaky-bucket problem, 678–79
Legal tax incidence, 159–60
Lenders, inflation effects on, 246–47
Liabilities, of banks, 384
Life of Greece, The (Durant), 54
Line, slope calculation, 20–21
Lock-outs, 628
Logrolling, 709–710
Long run, in production, 504
Long-term capital gains, 167
Lorenz curve, 668–71

Macroeconomic equilibrium, 264–65
Macroeconomic goals
  1960s, 227–28
  1970s, 230–32
  1980s, 235–37
  Employment Act of 1946, 224–25
  Humphrey–Hawkins Bill, 224–25
  Phillips curve in the 1960s, 228–30
Macroeconomics, 4
  Keynesian. *See* Keynesian economics
Malthus, Thomas, 620–21
Marginal
  definition, 27–28
  benefit, 28
  cost, 28
  efficiency of investment, 276–77
  product, 505
  rate of substitution, of indifference curves, 491
  returns, diminishing, 9
  revenue, 512–13
  revenue product, 608
  tax rate, 166–67
Marginal analysis, vs. average analysis, 37–38
Marginal physical product, 600–602
  curve, elasticity of resource demand and, 605
Marginal propensity to consume, 38, 271
Marginal propensity to save, 271–72
Marginal resource cost, 610
Marginal utility, 71, 473–74
  diminishing, 474–75
Marginal variables
  average variables and, 38–39
  graphing relationships, 39–40
Market basket, 248
Market economy, 58
  incentives, 50–51
Markets
  adjustments to changing demand, 532–34
  black, 537
  competition, resource supply and, 614
  competitive, efficiency in, 537–42
  conditions, income distribution among households and, 133
  economic efficiency and, 103–105
  efficiency, 105–109
  failures, 540–42
  federal funds, 413
  forces in, 66–67
  markets forces and, 66–67
  product, 187
  resource. *See* Resource markets
  role of price and, 14–15
  Say's law of, 261
  size, demand and, 71
Mark-up pricing, 573
Marx, Karl, 621, 813
Maximization rule of utility, 477
Medium of exchange, 372
MEI. *See* Marginal efficiency of investment
Mercantilists, 761

Mergers
  horizontal, 582
  interfirm, in oligopolies, 582–83
  vertical, 582
Microeconomics, 4, 472–73
Middlemen, exchange and, 16–17
Minimum wage
  competitive markets and, 634–36
  in monopsony markets, 636–37
  right to, 637
Minimum wage law, 633, 636
Mixed economy, 58–60, 102–103, 811
MMMF. *See* Money market mutual fund
MMP. See Marginal physical product
Mobility
  career planning and, 638–39
  income distribution among households and, 132–33
  lack of, wage differentials and, 625–26
Monetarism, 301, 440–41
  equation of exchange, 446–47
  expected inflation rate, 449–50
  income, 448–49
  institutional factors, 450–51
  Keynesian theories and, 451–53
  opportunity cost, 450
  policies, 453–56
  price level, 449
  theory development, 446–51
Monetary control, monetary policy and, 432
Monetary policy, 54
  contractionary, 430–31
  expansionary, 429–30
  with fixed exchange rates, 788–89
  with flexible exchange rates, 785–87
  importance of, Keynesian and monetarist views, 453
  Keynesian, 429–33
  problems with, 431–33
  recent, 442–46
Monetary policy (Federal Reserve System)
  discount rate, 413–14
  open market operations, 409–13
  reserve requirement, 414–16
Monetary theories. *See* Keynesian monetary theory; Monetarism; Rational expectations theory
Monetary transmission mechanism
  Keynesian, 427–28
  Keynesian vs. monetarist models, 451–52
Money
  creation by banks, 387–90
  definition, 370–71
  functions
    as medium of exchange, 373
    as store of value, 374
    as uniform unit of accounting, 373–74
  Keynesian theory of, 427–33
  supply, 375–78
  velocity of, 395
Money market deposit accounts, 376
Money market mutual fund balances, 376
Money supply

definition and measures of, 374–75
  $M1$, $M2$, and $M3$, 375–78
Monopolies, 110, 540–41
  antitrust policies, 557–60
  assumptions, 549
  competition. *See* Monopolistic competition
  demand and revenue, 551–52
  deregulation, 563
  economic profits and, 647
  economic rent in, 661
  perfect competition and, 556–57
  price and quantity decisions, 553–54
  price regulations, 558–59
  profits as promoting, 649
  regulation
    political economy of, 562–63
    special interests and, 562
  resource demand, 607–609
  static vs. dynamic efficiency of, 561
  union, 631
Monopolistic competition
  characteristics, 569–70
  definition, 569
  demand curves in, 570–72
  desirability of differentiation and, 577–78
  long-run equilibrium, 575–77
  price and output decisions, 572–77
  short-run profits, 573–75
Monopsony, 541, 609–12
  employers' association, 631–32
Monopsony markets, minimum wages in, 636–37
Mordecai, Kurz, 681
Motivation, price and, 94–95
MPC. *See* Marginal propensity to consume
MPS. *See* Marginal propensity to save
MRC. *See* Marginal resource cost
Multiplier principle, 288–89
Mundell, Robert, 355, 357
Mutual funds, as financial intermediaries, 382

National Bank Act of 1864, 403
National banks, 403
National Credit Union Administration, 386
National debt
  crowding out and, 176
  deficits and, 174–76
National defense, tariffs and, 749–50
National emergencies, government spending and, 308
National income, 188–89, 217
National Income: A Summary of Findings (Kuznets), 202–203
National Income and Its Composition: 1919–1938 (Kuznets), 203
Natural unemployment rate, 233–35
Negative income tax, antipoverty programs and, 682–84
Negative work incentives, in antipoverty programs, 681–82
Negotiable orders of withdrawal, 375

Net exports
  added to total spending, 283–84
  as aggregate demand determinant, 308–309
  spending, 278–79
Net foreign spending, GNP calculation with, 195
Net investment, 207
Net national product, calculation, 215–16
Nixon, Richard, 230, 322–23
NNP. *See* Net national product
Nominal interest rate, 245, 417
Normative economics, 32
Norris–LaGuardia Act, 628
NOW accounts. *See* Negotiable orders of withdrawal

Oil import quotas, OPEC and, 723
Oil shocks, 722
Okun, Arthur, 668, 678–79
Oligopolies, 541
  behavior, 583–85
  cartels. *See* Cartels
  causes, 581–83
  characteristics, 578–81
  collusion, 583, 585–87
  definition, 578
  kinked demand curves, 587–89
  regulation of, 589–90
Olson, Mancur, 207–11, 213
OPEC. *See* Organization of Petroleum Exporting Countries
Open economy, 738
Open market operations, 404
  Federal Reserve System, 409–13
Open market purchase, 410
Open market sale, 412
Opportunity cost(s), 5–6
  consumer choice and, 472–73
  demand for money and, 450
  and supply, 78–79
Optimal resource use rule, 614–15
Ordinal measure, of utils, 478
Organization of Petroleum Exporting Countries, 230–31
  history of, 723–24
  oil shocks and, 722
Outlines of Economics (Ely), 394
Output
  demand, wage differentials and, 625
  energy costs and, 726
  price, resource demand and, 603–604
  production, 504
  profit-maximizing, 512–13
  taxes, external costs and, 698

Paper gold, 774
Paradox of thrift, 291–93
Partnerships, 139, 503
Payment values, interest rate and, 651–52
Payoffs, nonpecuniary, 639
Pechman, Joseph A., 173

Pension funds, as funancial intermediaries, 382
Per capita real gross national product, 204
Perfect competition, 526
  assumption of, 526–27
  market, firms in, 527–29
  market failures, 540–42
  monopoly and, 556–57
  profit maximization rule, 529
Perfect information, perfect competition and, 527
Permanent income hypothesis, 272–74
Personal income, 217–18
  disposable, 218
Personal saving, 218
Phillips curve, 457–58
  in the 1960s, 228–30
  disappearance of, 232–35
  long-run, 233
  shifts, adaptive expectations hypothesis and, 459–60
Pigou, A. C., 701
Policy, industrial development for private sector, 141–42
Political economy, 150
Political philosophy, government spending and, 308
Politics, net exports and, 308–309
Pollution rights, marketable, 699–700
Population, labor supply and, 623
Positive economics, 31–32
Posner, Richard, 561–62
Post hoc reasoning, 33–34
Poverty
  absolute, 678
  antipoverty policies. See Antipoverty policies
  causes, 674–76
  definition and characterization, 667–68
  groups, 672–74
  relative, 678
  and scarcity, 46
PPI. See Producer Price Index
Preferences
  demand curves and, 480
  time, interest rate and, 653
  voters, 706–707
Present value, 651–52
Price discrimination, 481
  monopolies, 554–56
  successful, necessary conditions, 556–57
Price index, 248
  adjustments, 252–53
  consumer, 251
  Gross National Product Implicit Price Deflator Index, 251
  producer, 251
Price takers, 527
Price(s)
  administered, 580
  ceilings, 90–92, 535–37
  controls, energy, 721–22
  decisions by monopolies, 553–54

discrimination. See Price discrimination
elasticity of demand. See Elasticity of demand
energy, 726, 728–29
exchange rate and, 762
exchange rate effect, 782
floors, 89–90
inflation effects, 245
leadership, in oligopolies, 585–86
level, demand for money and, 449
markets and, 14–15
output and resource demand, 603–604
power of, 92–95
relative, 245, 480
signal, interest rate as, 652–53
stability, 245
stable, economic goals and, 54
sticky, 262
Pricing, predatory, 586–87
Prime interest rate, 656–57
Private benefits, 700
Private costs, 694–95
Private markets, public goods and, 705
Private sector
  business. See Business sector
  government and
    laws and regulation, 155
    spending, 154
    subsidies, 154–55
    taxation, 154
  household. See Household sector
  public sector and, 148–49
  right of exclusion, 128–29
Producer Price Index, 251
Producers
  number of, and supply, 77–78
  price expectations and supply, 79–80
Product markets, 187
Production
  capital, 599
  costs, resource supply and, 612–13
  incentives, marginal tax rate and, 347
  labor-intensive, 599
  quotas, assignment by cartels, 584
  subsidized, for increasing energy supply, 728
Production function, 504–12
  cost curves, 507–12
  types of costs, 506
Production possibilities frontier, 6–7
  curve analysis, 7–10
  diminishing returns and, 536
  economic efficiency and, 538–40
  for entire economy, 10–12
  exchange and, 12–14
  specialization and, 12–14
  technology and, 7
  trade and, 741
Productive capacity, investment spending and, 275
Productivity
  aggregate supply determinant, 312
  changes, resource demand and, 604

as measure of economic growth, 205
Product(s)
  identical, perfect competition and, 527
  marginal, 505
  single, in monopoly market, 549
  total, 505
Profit maximization rule
  for perfect competitors, 529
  for monopolists, 554
Profit(s)
  accounting, 506
  business. See Accounting profit
  economic. See Economic profit
  equilibrium and, 529–31
  exchange and, 15
  functions of, 531
  as goal of firm, 504
  normal, 511
  short-run, in monopolistic competition, 573–75
Progress and Poverty (George), 660–61
Progressive taxes, 165
Property rights, 95, 806–807
  government and, 109
  government definition and enforcement of, 111–14
  private, in the Soviet Union, 811–12
Property taxes, 172–73
Proportional taxes, 165
Proprietorships, 136–37
Protection, tariffs and, 747–48
Protectionism, voluntary export agreements and, 751–52
Public choices, 693
Public goods, 542, 693, 704–705
  government provision for, 115
  private markets and, 705
Public sector
  divisions, 149–50
  growth incentives and, 121–22
  policies, costs and benefits of, 122–23
  and private sector, 148–49
Public services, 51–52
Public-choice function of government, 152–53
Purchase, open market, 410

Quality
  of labor, wage differentials and, 625
  of life, GNP and, 200–202
Quantity decisions, by monopolies, 553–54
Quotas, 744–45
  impact of, 793–94

Rational expectations theory, 302, 441–42, 460–65
Rationing, energy, 729–30
Reagan, Ronald, 235, 326, 345–46, 445, 464–65
Real gross national product, 198–200
  expansions and, 199

per capita, 204
recessions and, 198
Real interest rate, 417
Reasoning (economic), logical fallacies and, 32–34
Recession, growth, 204
Recessionary gap, 286
Redistribution
 of income
  energy costs and, 727
  government, 115–19
 and poverty
  direct, 678–79
  indirect, 679
Regressive taxes, 165
Regulation(s)
 direct, external costs and, 696–98
 energy demand and, 729
 government, private sector and, 155
 oligopolies, 589–90
Relative price, 480
Rent, economic. *See* Economic rent
Rent-seeking behavior, 661–62
Reserve requirement, Federal Reserve System, 414–16
Reserves, of banks, 384–85
Resource demand
 changes in productivity and, 604
 elasticity of, 604–607
 monopoly, 607–609
 price of output and, 603–604
 value marginal product, 602–603
Resource markets, 187, 597–99
 demand adjustments between market and firm, 604
 derived demand and, 599–600
 income distribution and, 598
 optimal resource use rule, 614–15
 production and, 599
 resource allocation and, 598–99
Resources
 allocation, resource markets and, 598–99
 availability and cost, as aggregate supply determinant, 312
 costs, supply and, 78
 control of, monopolistic markets and, 551
 distribution, 670
 employment, economic goals and, 52–54
 energy, finite, 717–19
 government
  sources of, 158–59
  uses of, 155–57
 limits, 613
 optimal resource use rule, 614–15
 supply, 612–14
 technical efficiency and, 55
 types of, 5
Restrictions, wage differentials and, 626
Retained earnings, 218
Returns to scale, 518–20
Revenue
 marginal, 512–13
 monopoly, 551–52
 total, elasticity and, 484

Right of exclusion, 128–29
Rise and Decline of Nations (Olson), 207–11
Risk
 economic profits and, 648
 profits as compensations for, 648
 wage differentials and, 625
Risk premium, interest rate and, 653
Rivalry, of private goods, 703
Roberts, Paul Craig, 357
Robinson, Joan, 581
Russians, The (Smith), 96–97

Sale(s)
 current, investment spending and, 275
 open market, 412
Samuelson, Paul, 350
Saving
 credit supply and, 418
 dissaving and, 135
 functions, graphing, 269–71
 inflation effects on, 247
 Japan's growth policy and, 214
 Keynesian, 268–69
 marginal tax rates and, 347–48
 personal, 135, 218
 supply-side incentives, 345–46
 total, 218–19
Say, Jean Baptiste, 261
Say's law of markets, 261
Scale
 economies and diseconomies of, 518–20
 returns to, 519–20
Scarcity, 4
 and choice, 5
 competition and, 6
 problem of, 46
Schumpeter, Joseph, 561, 650
Schwartz, Anna Jacobsen, 455
Scientific method, 30–31
SDRs. *See* Special drawing rights
Secondary effects, 34
Securities, as bank assets, 385
Self-fulfilling prophesy, inflation as, 248
Sellers
 atomistic competition, 527
 single, in true monopoly, 549
Services, household income and, 134
Sherman Antitrust Act, 558
Short run, in production, 504
Shortage, market equilibrium and, 83
Shortsightedness effect, 123
Shut-down point, 511
Single-tax movement, 660–61
Skills, income distribution among households and, 132
Slope, calculation, 20–21
Smith, Adam, 13, 94–95, 163, 537, 761
Smith, Hedrick, 96–97
Social benefits, 700
Social costs, 694–95
Social security tax, 169–70
Socialism
 market, 810

 planned, 808–810
Sole proprietorship, 503
Soviet Union
 changes in planning system, 814–15
 Gosplan, 812–13
 income distribution, 814
 private property rights, 811–12
Special drawing rights, 774
Special interest groups, government inefficiencies and, 120–21
Special interests, monopolies and, 562
Specialization, production possibilities frontier and, 12–14
Spending
 consumption, 266–67
 government
  determinants, 279–80
  private sector and, 154
Suppliers, competition among, 107–108
Supply
 change, vs. change in quantity supplied, 80–81
 concept of, 75–77
 determinants
  level of technology, 78–79
  number of producers, 77–78
  opportunity costs, 79
  producers' price expectations, 79–80
  resource costs, 77
 elasticity, 534–35
 energy, 717
 labor. *See* Labor supply
 law of, 76–77
 loanable funds, interest rate and, 656–57
 resource, 612–14
Supply curves, shifting, 514–18
Supply interdependence, 720
Supply-side economics, 235, 302
Supply-side fiscal policies, 333
 cuts in government regulations, 345
 saving and investment incentives, 345–46
 tax cuts, 345
Surplus
 balance of payments, 758
 budget. *See* Budget surplus
 economic rent as, 659–60
 market equilibrium and, 83
 units, 378

Taft–Hartley Act, 628
Tariff burden, 746–47
Tariff(s), 744–45
 arguments for and against, 747–50
 consumer burden of, 746
 distribution of gains and losses from, 750–51
 effect on currency values, 768–69
 impact of, 793–94
 restrictions, 793–94
 voluntary export agreements and, 751–52
Tastes, demand curves and, 480
Tax burden
 distribution of, 165

Index

total, 173–74
Tax cuts
  supply-side, 345
  President Kennedy's, 330–31
Tax incidence, legal and economic, 159–60
Tax rates
  average, 167
  marginal, 166–67
    and incentives to save and invest, 347–48
    and production incentive, 347
    and tax avoidance, 347
    and work incentives, 346–47
Tax shifting, 159–62
Tax surcharge, President Johnson's, 322
Taxation
  ability-to-pay, 164
  benefits-received, 164
  classification of, 165
  as fiscal policy tool, 338–39
  government, private sector and, 154
Taxation multiplier, 338
Tax(es)
  as antipoverty tool, 676
  avoidance, marginal tax rate and, 347
  corporate income, 170–72
  demand elasticity and, 160–62
  economic effects, 162–63
  effluent, external costs and, 698–99
  equity
    ability-to-pay and benefits-received, 164
    horizontal and vertical, 163–64
  excise, 158
  federal income, 166–68
  general sales, 172
  horizontal and vertical equity, 163–64
  incentives
    to produce, 347
    to save and invest, 347–48
    tax avoidance and the underground economy, 347
    to work, 346–47
  indirect business, 217
  Japan's growth policy and, 213–14
  negative income, 682–84
  output, external costs and, 698
  personal, 135
  progressive, 165
  property, 172–73
  proportional, 165
  rebates, President Ford's, 325
  regressive, 165
  social security, 169–70
Technical efficiency, 55
Technology
  aggregate supply determinant, 311–12
  economic growth and, 11
  economic profits and, 647
  for increasing energy supply, 728
  Japan's growth policy and, 214–15
  level of, and supply, 78–79
  production possibilities frontier and, 7
  resource supply and, 613
  wage differentials and, 624

Theory of Price, The (Stigler), 587
"Three Cs" of potential borrower, 379
Thrift, paradox of, 291–93
Thurow, Lester Carl, 670
Time deposits, 376
Time frame
  elasticity and, 488, 534–35
  elasticity of resource demand and, 606
Time preference, interest rate and, 653
Tobin, James, 453
Total cost, elasticity of resource demand and, 607
Total physical product, 600–601
Total product, 505
Total revenue, elasticity and, 484
Total saving, 218–19
Total tax burden, 173–74
Total utility, 473
Tract on Monetary Reform (Keynes), 266
Trade
  balance of, 759–61
  direction of, 740
  economic effects, 743–44
  international, 743–44
  law of comparative advantage, 739–41, 742
  possibilities curve, 741
  production possibilities frontier and, 741
  reasons for, 739
  tariff and quota restrictions, 793–94
  terms of, 741
  United States, future of, 752
Trade barriers, 748–49
  net exports and, 308
Trade deficit, economic policy options, 793–95
Trade secrets, 649
  as barriers to entry in monopolistic markets, 550–51
Traditional economy, 60
Traditions, labor supply and, 623
Transaction costs, externalities and, 702–703
Transfer payment programs, federal government, 680–81
Transfer payments
  fiscal policy and, 339–40
  government, private sector and, 155
  as governmental antipoverty tool, 677
  intergovernmental grants, 156
Transfer payments multiplier, 339–40
Treasury, U.S., 409
TTP. *See* Total physical product
Tullock, Gordon, 587
Twain, Mark, 667

Uncertainty, economic profits and, 648
Underemployment, 239
Underground economy, 240
  marginal tax rate and, 347
Unemployment
  in the 1960s and 1970s, 302–304
  cyclical, 240–41
  exchange rates and, 783–84

frictional, 241
measurement, 237–39
poverty and, 674
problem, seriousness of, 242–44
structural, 241
unemployment rate and, 239–41
voluntary, 239–40
Unemployment rate
  natural, 233–35
  unemployment and, 239–41
  unemployment measurement with, 237–39
Uniform unit of accounting, 373
Union shop, 630
Unions
  anti-union era, 627–28
  customs, 752
  economic models of, 631–32
  pro-union era, 628
  regulated-union era, 628–29
  strong, characteristics, 632–33
  wages and, 629–31
Unitary income elasticity, 488
Unitary price elasticity, 485–86
United States
  balance of payments, 759
  balance of trade, 759–61
  economic goals, 791–93
  federal government transfer payment programs, 680–81
  history of unions in, 627–29
  income, trends in, 671–76
  income distribution in, 668–71
  major taxes in, 166–73
  models of union behavior in, 631–32
  trade, future of, 752
Usury laws, 651
Utility
  cardinal and ordinal measures of, 477–78
  definition, 27
  marginal, 28, 71, 473–75
  maximization rule, 477
  maximizing, 476–77
  total, 473

Value, currency, 767
Value marginal product, 602–603
Value-added method, for GNP calculation, 197–98
Variable costs, 506–507
  changes in, 514–15
Variable lag, monetary policy and, 431–32
Velocity of money, 395
  and money demand, 451
Verification, in scientific method, 31
Vertical equity, of taxes, 163–64
Vertical merger, 582
Vested interests, economic growth and, 207–11
VMP. See Value marginal product
Volcker, Paul, 444–45
Voluntary export agreements
  impact of, 794
  protectionism and, 751–52

Voluntary unemployment, 239–40
Vote trading, 709–710
Voters, preferences, 706–707
Voting
  cycles, 707–708
  direct, 706–707
  distribution of costs and benefits, 708–709
  district lines and, 709
  representative, problems with, 709–710

Wage and price controls
  economics of, 323–24
  President Nixon's, 322–23
Wage differentials, 623–25
  market imperfections and, 625–27
Wage-lag theory, 230

Wage-Price Guidelines, 321–22
Wages
  minimum. *See* Minimum wage
  unions and, 629–31
  wage differentials, 623–25
Wagner Act, 628
Walter, Alan, 454
Wealth, income distribution among households and, 133
Wealth and Poverty (Guilder), 542
Wealth of Nations (Smith), 761
Whip Inflation Now, 232
Who Paid the Taxes (Pechman), 173
WIN. *See* Whip Inflation Now
Work
  incentives, marginal tax rate and, 346–47

  negative incentives in antipoverty programs, 681–82
Workers
  discouraged, 239
  firm management in Yugoslavia, 815–17
  Japan's growth policy and, 213
  preferences, wage differentials and, 625
  underemployed, 239
  unemployed, 235
World Bank, 761–62

Yellow-dog contracts, 628
Yugoslavia, economy of, 815–17

Zero transaction costs, perfect competition and, 527